Also by Robert M. Parker, Jr.

BORDEAUX
The Definitive Guide for the Wines Produced Since 1961

THE WINES OF THE RHÔNE VALLEY AND PROVENCE

PARKER'S WINE BUYER'S GUIDE

PARKER'S WINE BUYER'S GUIDE
Second Edition

BURGUNDY
A Comprehensive Guide to the Producers, Appellations, and Wines

BORDEAUX
A Comprehensive Guide to the Wines Produced from 1961–1990

PARKER'S WINE BUYER'S GUIDE
Third Edition

PARKER'S WINE BUYER'S GUIDE
Fourth Edition

THE WINES OF THE RHÔNE VALLEY
Revised and Expanded Edition

BORDEAUX
A Comprehensive Guide to the Wines Produced from 1961–1997

PARKER'S WINE BUYER'S GUIDE
Fifth Edition

PARKER'S WINE BUYER'S GUIDE
Sixth Edition

BORDEAUX

REVISED FOURTH EDITION

A CONSUMER'S GUIDE TO THE WORLD'S FINEST WINES

ROBERT M. PARKER, JR.

Drawings by
CHRISTOPHER WORMELL

Maps by
JEANYEE WONG

SIMON & SCHUSTER
New York   London   Toronto   Sydney   Singapore

SIMON & SCHUSTER
Rockefeller Center
1230 Avenue of the Americas
New York, NY 10020

Copyright © 1985, 1991, 1998, 2003 by Robert M. Parker, Jr.
All rights reserved,
including the right of reproduction
in whole or in part in any form.

Simon & Schuster and colophon are
registered trademarks of Simon & Schuster, Inc.

For information regarding special discounts for bulk purchases,
please contact Simon & Schuster Special Sales at
1–800–456–6798 or business@simonandschuster.com

Manufactured in the United States of America

3   5   7   9   10   8   6   4   2

Library of Congress Cataloging-in-Publication Data
Parker, Robert M.
Bordeaux : a consumer's guide to the world's finest wines /
Robert M. Parker, Jr. ; drawings by Christopher Wormell ;
maps by Jeanyee Wong.—Rev. 4th ed.
p.   cm.
1. Wine and wine making—France—Bordelais.   I. Title.
TP553.P36   2003
614.2'2'09447144—dc21   2003045722
ISBN 0-7432-2946-0

To my precious Pat and Maia

ACKNOWLEDGMENTS

To the following people . . . thanks for your support: Jim Arseneault; Anthony Barton; Ruth and the late Bruce Bassin; Hervé Berland; Bill Blatch; Thomas B. Böhrer; Daniel Boulud; Christopher Cannan; Dick Carretta; Jean-Michel Cazes; Corinne Cesano; Jean-Marie Chadronnier; M. and Mme. Jean-Louis Charmolue; Charles Chevalier; Bob Cline; Jeffrey Davies; Hubert de Bouard; Jean and Annie Delmas; Jean-Hubert Delon and the late Michel Delon; Jean-Luc Le Dû; Dr. Albert H. Dudley III; Barbara Edelman; Fédéric Engérer; Michael Etzel; Paul Evans; Terry Faughey; Joel Fleischman; Han Cheng Fong; Maryse Fragnaud; Mme. Capbern Gasqueton; Laurence and Bernard Godec; Dan Green; Josué Harari; Alexandra Harding; Ken-ichi Hori; Dr. David Hutcheon; Barbara G. and Steve R. R. Jacoby; Jean-Paul Jauffret; Daniel Johnnes, Nathaniel, Archie, and Denis Johnston; Ed Jonna; Elaine and Manfred Krankl; Allen Krasner; Françoise Laboute; Patrick Leon; Susan and Bob Lescher; Pierre Lurton; Bernard Magrez; Patrick Maroteaux; Christian, Jean-François, and Jean-Pierre Moueix; Jerry Murphy; Bernard Nicolas; Jill Norman; Les Oenarchs (Bordeaux); Les Oenarchs (Baltimore); François Pinault; Frank Polk; Paul Pontallier; Bruno Prats; Jean-Guillaume Prats; Dr. Alain Raynaud; Martha Reddington; Dominique Renard; Michel Richard; Alan Richman; Huey Robertson; Dany and Michel Rolland; Pierre-Antoine Rovani; Yves Rovani; Robert Roy; Carlo Russo; Ed Sands; Erik Samazeuilh; Bob Schindler; Ernie Singer; Park B. Smith; Betsy Sobolewski; Elliott Staren; Daniel Tastet-Lawton; Lettie Teague; Alain Vauthier; Steven Verlin; Peter Vezan; Robert Vifian; Sona Vogel; Jeanyee Wong; and Gérard Yvernault.

A very special thanks is in order for several people who have done a splendid job in bringing this mass of information to book form. At Simon & Schuster, my editor Amanda Murray; her assistant, Christina Richardson; and the production team of Scott Gray, Jeanette Olender, and John Wahler. Thanks also to Joan Passman, my assistant state-side; Annette Piatek, who did much of the typing for this book; Elisabeth Jaubert, the wizard responsible for the procurement of the labels that so attractively adorn its pages; and my former *Wine Advocate* proofreader, editor, and lifelong drinking, eating, and tasting friend, Dr. Jay Miller.

CONTENTS

PREFACE TO THE 2003 EDITION

WHY BORDEAUX IS SIGNIFICANTLY BETTER TODAY THAN IT WAS 25 AND 50 YEARS AGO

The oldest courtier firm in Bordeaux, Tastet and Lawton, has provided Bordeaux vintage assessments since 1795. In order to make the following argument I have used their evaluations of vintages in which the highest are rated exceptional, then good to very good, followed by mediocre or poor. For the period from 1900–1939 (40 vintages) only three vintages were rated exceptional, 10 good to very good, and 27 mediocre or poor. In contrast, during the last 21 years, 1980–2000, four vintages were rated exceptional by Tastet and Lawton, 13 were good to very good, but only three were mediocre or poor (1992, 1991, and 1984). I do not believe that global warming can be held accountable for this extraordinary change in the quality of Bordeaux vintages.

Looking back over my tasting notes of the last quarter of a century, it is interesting to note how many truly legendary wines were produced in some of the most noteworthy vintages. Being as generous as possible, the 1945 Bordeaux vintage, considered to be one of the mythical vintages of the last 100 years, actually produced only 25–30 profoundly great red wines. Even in 1982, which established my reputation as a serious wine critic, the number of monumental reds is less than three dozen. In 2000, according to my tastings, approximately 150–160 great wines—about 28–30% of what I tasted—were produced. Obviously I cannot go back in time, but my instincts suggest the raw materials available in 1945 as well as 1982 were not dissimilar from those that were harvested in 2000.

Why is modern-day Bordeaux so much better than it was a mere 20, 30, 40, or 50 years ago? I have listed the reasons in five categories: 1. progressive changes in the vineyard, 2. techniques and modern methods that take place in the wine cellars, 3. changes in the wine's upbringing and bottling, 4. the competition that exists in the modern world and the role of the informed consumer, as well as the influence of wine critics, and 5. miscellaneous changes such as improved methods for weather forecasting.

PROGRESSIVE CHANGES IN THE VINEYARD

In the 1960s and 1970s, octogenarian professor Dr. Emile Peynaud and famed professor of oenology Dr. Pascal Ribeau-Gayon, departmental head of oenology at the University of Bordeaux between 1977 and 1995, began advocating significant changes in viticultural management. Later harvest dates were encouraged in order to pick riper fruit with lower acid levels as well as sweeter tannin and greater fruit characteristics.

Later harvesting automatically produces wines lower in acidity and slightly higher in alcohol. Moreover, if the harvest is not undone by rain, exceptional fruit and ripeness can be achieved. This advice is 30–40 years old.

Along with these changes, modern-day sprays and treatments aimed at preventing rot in the vineyard were begun in the 1970s and accelerated in the 1980s. Recent good vintages such as 1999, 1994, 1983, 1979, and 1978 would undoubtedly have been destroyed by mildew in the 1950s and 1960s. At the same time, there was a growth in the philosophy of going back to the vineyard (where most serious wine producers believe 90% of the quality emerges) to promote more organic techniques to encourage the health of the vines. There was also a movement toward developing a better understanding of viticulture. New techniques (called "extreme" or "radical" viticulture) became standard practice in the late 1980s and 1990s. This included the curtailing of yields by aggressive pruning in the winter and spring and crop thinning (cutting off bunches of grapes) in summer to encourage lower yields. With extremely healthy vines, yields would be expected to rise, but the opposite is actually the case as yields have dropped significantly for the top estates, from highs of 60–100 hectoliters per hectare in the mid-1980s, to 25–50 hectoliters per hectare in recent vintages. At the same time, other more radical viticulture techniques have been implemented. These include leaf pulling (to encourage air flow as well as allowing more contact with the sun), shoot positioning (to enhance sun exposure), and the ongoing research with clones and root stocks designed to eliminate those root stocks and clones that produce overly prolific crops of large-size berries. The movement of harvested grapes is also done with much more care and, in smaller containers, is designed to prevent bruising and skin breakage.

In 2003, the Bordeaux vineyards are healthier, have lower vigor, and are producing smaller and smaller berries and crops of higher and higher quality fruit. All of this is designed to produce the essence of the *terroir*, enhance the character of the vintage, and reveal the personality of the varietal or blend.

TECHNIQUES AND MODERN METHODS THAT TAKE PLACE IN THE WINE CELLARS

The famed first-growths Haut-Brion and Latour were two of the earliest estates to invest in temperature-controlled stainless-steel fermenters: Haut-Brion in the early 1960s and Latour in 1964. The advantage of temperature-controlled fermenters, which are now being replaced by some avant garde producers with open-top temperature-controlled wood fermenters (a new wrinkle on the old wooden vats used prior to the advent of temperature-controlled steel), is that it allows a producer to harvest as late as possible, picking grapes at full phenolic maturity and with high sugars. In the old days, this often happened by accident. In fact, it was often both feared and discouraged, as fully ripe grapes were tricky to vinify without temperature control. Many of the Médoc 1947s, not to mention some of the 1929s, were ruined by excessive volatile acidity because producers did not have the ability to control fermentation temperatures. If temperatures soar to dangerously high levels, the yeasts that convert the sugar into alcohol are killed, setting off a chain reaction that results in spoiled wines with excessive levels of volatile acidity. This was frequently a problem when harvests occurred during hot weather. Stories of producers throwing in blocks of ice to cool down their fermentations is not just another vineyard legend. It actually happened in 1959, 1949, and 1947. Certainly the advent of temperature-controlled fermenters, whether steel or wood, has been a remarkable technological step for the advancement of wine quality. It allows producers to harvest (assuming weather permits) at their leisure and bring in fully mature grapes knowing that at the push of a button they can control the temperature of each of their fermentation vats. This has resulted in significantly better wines with fewer defects, sweeter fruit, as well as riper tannin in addition to lower acidity.

Moreover, all of the top properties do an extraordinary selection (or culling out damaged or vegetal material) on what they call the *table de tri*. This is essentially a labor force that inspects the grapes as they come in to the cellars, discarding any that appear rotten, unripe, unhealthy, or blemished. The degree of this inspection varies from property to property, but it is safe to assume that those properties producing the finest wines practice the most severe selection. Some perfectionist estates have a second *table de tri* after the grapes are destemmed. This means another sorting team searches through the destemmed grape bunches to further pull out any vegetal material, stems, leaves, or questionable looking berries.

Cold soaks, or pre-fermentation macerations, have become increasingly à la mode. They have been used in the past in some of the colder northern viticulture areas (Burgundy and the northern Rhone) because fermentations often did not kick off for four or five days simply because the cellars were so cold. In Bordeaux, cold soaks have been gathering support, with some avant garde producers utilizing 4–8 day cold soaks hoping to extract more phenolic material, greater aromatics, and darker colors.

Fermentations, which used to be 10–15 days, are now often extended, the theory being that the molecular chain that forms the tannin structure will become sweeter and riper with prolonged fermentations of 21–30 or more days.

The bottom line is that every top Bordeaux property has invested in state-of-the-art temperature-controlled fermenters, whether they be stainless-steel or the smaller open-top wood type (which have become the rage in St.-Emilion over the last decade). All the top properties do a severe triage before and sometimes after destemming. More and more properties use cold soaks and some use extended macerations, but overall, the vinification of modern-day Bordeaux is done under strictly supervised, temperature-controlled conditions in a far more sanitary, healthy environment than 30–50 years ago. It is a far cry from the seat-of-your-pants fermentations of the past that could become stuck or troubled, thus causing the development of unwanted organisms and/or volatile acidity.

Lastly, the most controversial technique in the wine cellar today is the use of reverse osmosis and entrophy (the removal of water under a vacuum system to concentrate the grape must). In the past, the technique generally employed was called *saignée,* which consisted of siphoning off a portion of the juice in the fermentation tank to increase the percentage of skins to grape must. That worked reasonably well, but in the early 1980s some top châteaux (Léoville-Las Cases was one of the first) discreetly began using reverse osmosis. This technique involved pushing the grape must through an apparatus to remove the water. The practice called entrophy was also developed. These concen-

tration techniques have now been in use for 20 years, and while I was initially skeptical, the fact is Léoville-Las Cases has been producing wines of first-growth quality. In
years where there is good ripeness but dilution from harvest rains, these machines,
when used with discretion, can increase the quality of the wine with apparently no
damage. Twenty years after Las Cases first used reverse osmosis, the results are impressive. At many top châteaux, reverse osmosis is now standard operating procedure
in years where there is some dilution from harvest rain. It is not without some risks. The
danger is that you not only concentrate the wine, you concentrate the defects as well.
That is why such practices must still be approached with caution. However, in the
hands of talented, capable operators who use them prudently as well as selectively, it is
hard to argue that they are actually changing the character of the wine other than to improve the quality of the final wine by removing water that would dilute the wine's character. After being skeptical, even critical of these machines, I have come to believe
they work well when used properly.

CHANGES IN THE WINE'S UPBRINGING AND BOTTLING

Perhaps the primary reason for improved quality as well as uniformity of Bordeaux
wines has been the movement, encouraged by Dr. Emile Peynaud and Dr. Pascal
Ribeau-Gayon (and their protégés), to bottle wines over a much shorter period of time
(1–2 weeks) as opposed to bottling on demand, or over a 6–9 month period (often the
case 30–50 years ago). Prior to 1970, many châteaux sold barrels of their wines to brokers, even shipping them to merchants in England or Belgium who then bottled the
wines at their leisure. Thankfully, that practice came to a halt nearly 30 years ago.
Today, the shorter time in barrel has resulted in wines that are more primary, richer in
fruit, and have far greater potential to develop in the bottle.

In addition, sanitation in the cellars has changed dramatically in the past 25 years.
Many critics claim the percentage of new oak has jumped significantly, and there is no
doubting that far more new oak is seen in Bordeaux than 20–30 years ago. One Burgundian (actually a Belgian) put the issue of new oak in perspective saying, "Never has
a wine been over-oaked . . . it's been under-wined." While new oak is an ingredient
that works well with Bordeaux's Cabernet Sauvignon, Merlot, Cabernet Franc, and
Petit Verdot, it should be utilized prudently, as a great chef approaches the use of salt,
pepper, or garlic. New oak can improve Bordeaux, but excessive use will destroy the
flavors and obliterate varietal character, vintage personality, and terroir characteristics. A great advantage in working with new oak is that it is sanitary. Part of the problem when working with old oak is that it is a fertile home for unwanted bacteria,
resulting in off flavors and potential spoilage problems. New oak does not have that
problem. However, if the wine does not have sufficient concentration and depth to
stand up to new oak, the producer would be wiser to use a neutral vessel for aging.

A controversial (actually it's not, but it is perceived as such by uninformed observers) practice initiated by some of Bordeaux's smaller estates is malolactic fermentation in barrel, a technique employed for decades in Burgundy. Every red Bordeaux
goes through malolactic fermentation, which, in short, is the conversion of the sharp,
tart malic acids in the grape must into softer, creamier, lower lactic acids. For the most

part, the largest estates continue to do malolactic in tank, and then move the wine into barrels for 16–20 months of aging. Small estates prefer to do malolactic in barrel because they believe it integrates the wood better and gives the wine a more forward sweetness early in life, making the young, grapy wine more appealing to that predatory, freeloading, insufferably arrogant species known as wine journalists/critics that descend on Bordeaux every spring to taste the newest vintage. Malolactic in barrel is not new. To reiterate, it has been practiced in Burgundy for decades and was often utilized in Bordeaux a century ago. It fell out of favor when large fermentation vats were developed. Malolactic in barrel gives a wine a certain seductiveness/sexiness early in its life, but at the end of a 12-month period, there is virtually no difference between a red Bordeaux given malolactic in barrel and one where malolactic occurs in tank and is subsequently moved to barrel. The latter wines often start life more slowly, but at the end of a year they have absorbed their wood just as well as those that have had malolactic in barrel.

Significant changes in the selection process for the grand vin have resulted in tremendous improvements in many Bordeaux wines. The development of second wines is also not new. Léoville-Las Cases instituted a second wine more than 100 years ago, and Château Margaux has been producing one nearly as long. However, in the 1980s and 1990s the selection process for top estates became increasingly draconian. It is not unusual for a high-quality estate to declassify 35% to as much as 70% of their production in order to put only the finest essence of their vineyard into the top wine. Such selections, although less brutal, also exist in the right bank appellations of St.-Emilion and Pomerol, where 30–50% of the crop is often eliminated from the final blend. Much of it goes into the second wine, but the most serious properties also produce a third wine or sell it in bulk. Keep in mind that in a great vintage like 1961 or 1982, there was little selection made by most great Bordeaux estates. Contrast that to 2000, when nearly every estate produced a second wine and sometimes a third. To reiterate, this has resulted in significantly better quality at the top echelon.

Other changes in the *élevage* include less racking and brutal movement of the wines. Today, many wines are moved under gas, and the racking process (often done 3–4 times during the first year) has been modified as many progressive wine-makers believe it bruises the wine and causes accelerated development as well as fruit desiccation. This has also encouraged a small group of producers to begin aging their wines on the lees. Lees are sedimentary materials consisting of yeasts and solid particles that often separate after fermentation and after the wine has been pressed into tank and barrel. These progressives feel that aging on the lees, assuming they are healthy lees, adds more texture, richness, vineyard character, and varietal personality. I tend to agree with them. However, there is no doubting that many a great Bordeaux has been produced that was never aged on any significant lees. Lees aging, which is done routinely in Burgundy, remains controversial in Bordeaux, where it is regarded as an avant garde technique.

Another new development has been micro-bullage, which originated in France's appellation of Madiran (to sweeten and soften the notoriously hard tannin of those wines) and quickly caught on in Cahors and, to a certain extent, St.-Emilion. This technique involves the diffusion of tiny amounts of oxygen through a tube into fermentation vats post fermentation, or into the actual barrels during the upbringing of the wines. In St.-Emilion, the talented Stéphane Dérénoncourt has made this a popular technique for the wines he oversees. The philosophy behind micro-bullage (or micro-oxygenation) is sound. The idea is to avoid labor-intensive and sometimes brutal/traumatic racking, and feed the wine oxygen in a reductive state while it is aging in the barrel. It is believed that this measured, oxidative process preserves more of the *terroir* and fruit character than a harsher racking process. A variation of this technique is called *clicage*. It is essentially the same thing, but the term is only applied to those who use micro-oxygenation in barrel, not tank. Early results from those producers who practice this technique have been positive. The wines have not fallen apart (as their critics charged) and in truth, there is no reason they should since the technique itself, if not abused, is far more gentle than traditional racking.

The addition of tannic, highly pigmented press wine to the higher-quality "free-run juice," was often applied in ancient times without any regard for balance or harmony. Today, it is done judiciously or not at all depending on whether or not the wine needs it. Small, measured dosages are frequently added incrementally to be sure the wine does not end up with an excess of tannin.

Lastly, perhaps the single most important factor after the selection process is the decision of whether to fine and/or filter, and the degree to which this is done. Both procedures can eviscerate a wine, destroying texture as well as removing aromatics, fruit, and mid-palate flesh. In the old days, a wine was rarely filtered, but egg white fining was often done in order to soften the harsh tannin. Moreover, years ago, grapes were often unripe and not destemmed, so the tannin was extremely aggressive, even vegetal. Fining helped soften this astringency. Today, with later harvests and for the other reasons already expressed, the tannin is sweeter, and unless the wine has a bacterial problem (suspended proteins or other matter that make the wine unattractive aesthetically), there is no need to fine.

In summary, less fining and filtering are practiced today, resulting in wines with more intense flavors, textures, aromatics, and *terroir* characters. Most of the finest estates tend to look at fining and filtering not in black and white terms, but on a vintage-by-vintage basis. The good news, and one of the reasons why Bordeaux is so much better today, is that wineries actually make a conscious decision whether they really need to fine or filter as opposed to doing it automatically (which was the situation during the 1960s, 1970s, and early 1980s). Presently, producers who are trying to capture the essence of their vineyards do not fine or filter unless mandatory. This has significantly raised the overall quality of Bordeaux.

THE COMPETITION THAT EXISTS IN THE MODERN WORLD AND THE ROLE OF THE INFORMED CONSUMER, AS WELL AS THE INFLUENCE OF WINE CRITICS

Unquestionably, there has been a revolution in terms of the amount of information available to wine consumers. The old role, dominated by the British, of never writing a negative thing about wine, has long been replaced, largely by America's pro-consumer standards of wine writing. The quality of wine writing has never been better.

Add to that the proliferation of wine information in newspapers, wine magazines, and on the Internet. There can be no doubt that consumers, as well as the wine trade, are better informed, more selective, and more knowledgeable when it comes to buying fine wine.

Bordeaux's wine trade and producers are well aware of the impact this has on their products. The idea of making mediocre wine from a great *terroir* and selling it at a high price has not been an intelligent option for more than 20 years. This has helped increase the competitive nature of the Bordeaux estates and resulted in better and better quality wines. The negative aspect of influential wine critics is that when they give a wine a complimentary review, it results in high demand and thus higher prices. That seems to be a small (pardon the pun) price to pay for increasingly high-quality wines at all levels.

MISCELLANEOUS CHANGES SUCH AS IMPROVED METHODS FOR WEATHER FORECASTING

Believe it or not, 20 years ago it was impossible to receive weather forecasts longer than 24–48 hours in advance. Today, because of satellites and climate specialists, in most years the weather forecast for a viticultural area can be predicted with 90–100% accuracy 5–7 days in advance. This has been an immense help for producers in developing their harvest strategies based on a seven-day forecast that in most cases will be highly accurate. This advantage was not available 20 or 30 years ago. Additionally, there are multiple services available today from experts designed to help vignerons plant and manage vineyards, adding to the extraordinary amount of expertise available to a grape grower/wine-maker.

CONCLUSION

In conclusion, I would strongly argue that the finest wines of Bordeaux today are far superior to the great Bordeaux wines of 50–100 years ago. Today, one sees more of the *terroir* essence and vintage character in a bottle of great Bordeaux than they did 20, 30, 40, or 50 years ago. Not only are the wines more accessible young, but the aging curve of top Bordeaux wines has been both broadened and expanded. Contrary to the doom and gloom kindergarten critics, most Bordeaux vintages of today will live longer and drink better during the entire course of their lives than their predecessors. However, there are some negatives to consider. For example, some of the prodigious 1947 Bordeaux (Pétrus, Cheval Blanc, Latour à Pomerol, L'Evangile, Lafleur, and most notably Cheval Blanc), had residual sugar, elevated volatile acidity, extremely high alcohol, and pH levels that would cause most modern-day oenologists to faint. Sadly, despite all the improvements that have been made, few modern-day oenologists would permit a wine such as the 1947 Cheval Blanc to get into the bottle under the name Cheval Blanc. Anyone who has tasted a pristine bottle of this wine recognizes why most competent observers feel this is one of the most legendary wines ever produced in Bordeaux. All of its defects are outweighed by its extraordinary positive attributes. It is also these defects that often give the wine its singular individuality and character. So, a word of warning . . . despite all the techniques designed to make higher-quality wine, there is still a place for wines with a handful of defects that give a wine its undeniable character as well as greatness. Somehow, all these new techniques need to make an allowance for wines such as these 1947s.

That being said, there is no question that 1. the increased knowledge of viticulture, vinification, and weather that exists today has resulted in greater wines, 2. the improved health of the vineyards has resulted in higher-quality grapes, 3. the movement toward more natural winemaking has led to less traumatic bruising of the fruit and wine, 4. the preservation of the fruit, vintage, and *terroir* characteristics has reached a pinnacle because of these soft handling techniques, and 5. the bottling process today is aimed at putting the essence of the vineyard into the bottle in a less oxidized and evolved condition. Logically, it makes sense that these wines will have the ability to age better and longer than their predecessors.

It cannot be underscored strongly enough: The ignorant belief that the Bordeaux wines of today are more forward, and therefore shorter lived, is a myth. Wines today are produced from healthier, riper fruit, and thus they possess lower acidity as well as sweeter tannin. Analytically, great modern-day vintages have indices of tannin and dry extract as high or higher than the legendary vintages of the past. However, because their tannin is sweeter and the acidity lower, they can be enjoyed at an earlier age. This does not compromise their aging potential. An example would be 1959, which was considered entirely too low in acidity to age (most of the great 1959s are still in pristine condition), and 1982, which many uninformed observers claimed would have to be drunk by 1990 for fear the wine would turn into vinegar. The finest 1982s are still evolving, with the best wines possessing another 20–30 years of life.

Think it over: Does anyone want to return to the Bordeaux of 30–40 years ago when 1. less than one-fourth of the most renowned estates made wines proportional to their official pedigree, 2. dirty, unclean aromas were justified as part of the *terroir* character, 3. disappointingly emaciated, austere, excessively tannic wines from classified growths were labeled "classic" by a subservient wine press that existed at the largesse of the wine industry, and 4. wines were made from underripe grapes that were too high in acidity and tannin to ever fully become harmonious?

Anyone who has taken a history class has heard the famous expression: *Those who do not learn the lessons of history are condemned to repeat it.* The Bordelais know their history well and have worked enthusiastically and progressively to increase the quality of their wines. Consequently, in 2003, Bordeaux quality has never been better.

1: USING
THIS BOOK

There can be no question that the romance, if not mysticism, of opening a bottle of Bordeaux from a famous château has a grip and allure that are hard to resist. For years, writers have written glowing accounts of Bordeaux wines, sometimes giving them more respect and exalted status than they have deserved. How often has that fine bottle of Bordeaux from what was allegedly an excellent vintage turned out to be diluted, barely palatable, or even repugnant? How often has a wine from a famous château let you and your friends down when tasted? On the other hand, how often has a vintage written off by the critics provided some of your most enjoyable bottles of Bordeaux? And how often have you tasted a great Bordeaux wine, only to learn that the name of the château is uncelebrated?

This book is about just such matters. This is a book for those who drink Bordeaux; it is a wine consumer's guide to Bordeaux. Who is making Bordeaux's best and worst wines? What has a specific château's track record been over the last 20–30 years?

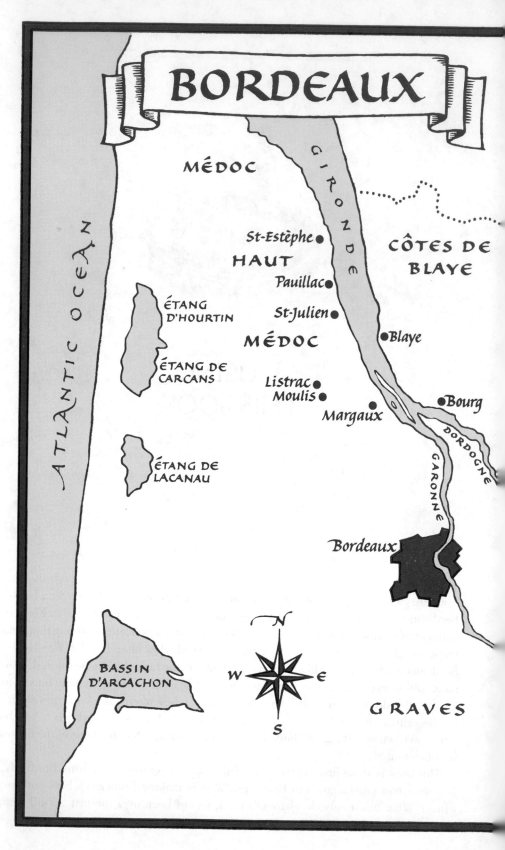

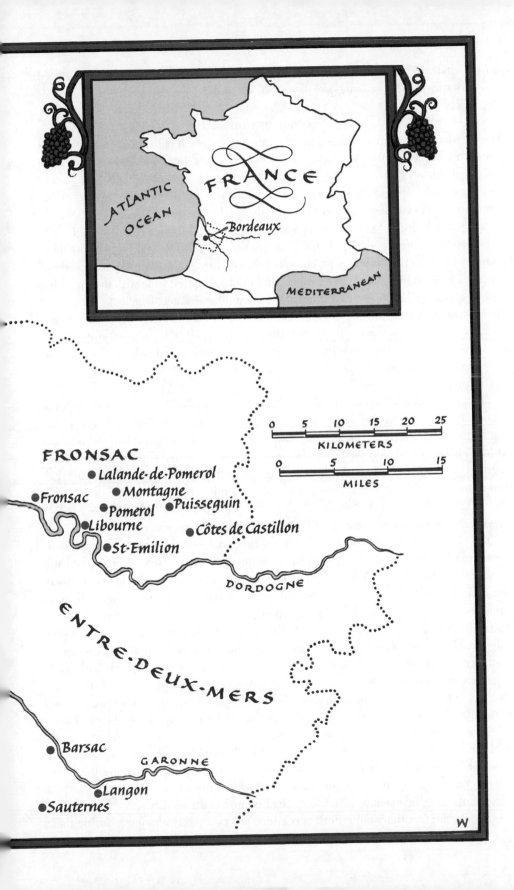

FRANCE

ATLANTIC OCEAN

Bordeaux

MEDITERRANEAN

KILOMETERS
0   5   10   15   20   25

MILES
0   5   10   15

FRONSAC

● Lalande-de-Pomerol
   ● Montagne
● Fronsac   ● Puisseguin
   ● Pomerol
● Libourne   ● Côtes de Castillon
   ● St-Emilion

DORDOGNE

ENTRE-DEUX-MERS

● Barsac
        GARONNE
   ● Langon
● Sauternes

W

Which châteaux are overrated and overpriced and, of course, which are underrated and underpriced? These issues are discussed in detail.

TASTING METHODS

The evaluations that are contained in this work are the result of extensive tastings conducted in Bordeaux and America. I have been visiting Bordeaux every year since 1970, and since 1978 I have gone to Bordeaux as a professional at least twice a year to conduct barrel tastings of the young wines, as well as to do comparative tastings of different wines and vintages that have been bottled and released for sale.

It is patently unfair to an estate to issue a final judgment about a wine after only tasting it one time. Consequently, when I do tastings of young Bordeaux, I try to taste them as many times as possible to get a clear, concise picture of the wine's quality and potential. I have often equated the tasting of an infant, unbottled wine with that of taking a photograph of a long-distance runner at the beginning of a race. One look or tasting of such a wine is only a split-second glimpse of an object that is constantly changing and moving. To evaluate effectively the performance and quality in a given vintage, one must look at the wine time after time during its 16–24-month prebottling evolution and then evaluate it numerous times after bottling to see if the quality or expected potential is still present.

Obviously, some wines as well as general vintages are much easier to assess than others. For certain, tasting young wine requires total concentration and an extreme dedication to tasting the wine as many times as possible in its youth, both at the individual châteaux and in comparative tastings against its peers. This is the only valid method by which to obtain an accurate look at the quality and potential of the wine. For this reason, I visit Bordeaux at least twice a year, spending more than a month in the region visiting all the major châteaux in all of the principal appellations of the Médoc, Graves, Sauternes, St.-Emilion, and Pomerol.

The châteaux visits and interviews with the wine-makers are extremely important in accumulating the critical data about the growing season, the harvest dates, and the vinification of the château's wines. Most of the wine-makers at the Bordeaux châteaux are remarkably straightforward and honest in their answers, whereas owners will go to great lengths to glorify the wine they have produced.

In addition to doing extensive visits to the specific Bordeaux châteaux in all appellations of Bordeaux in poor, good, and great vintages, I insist on comparative tastings of cask samples of these new vintages. For these tastings I call many of Bordeaux's leading *négociants* to set up what most consumers would call massive comparative day-long tastings of 60–100 wines. In groups of 10–15 wines at a time, an entire vintage, from major classified growths to minor Crus Bourgeois, can be reviewed several times over a course of two weeks of extensive tastings. Such tastings corroborate or refute the quality I have found to exist when I have visited the specific château. Because I do these types of broad, all-inclusive tastings at least three times before the young Bordeaux wine is bottled, I am able to obtain numerous looks at the infant wine at 6, 9, and 18 months of age, which usually give a very clear picture of the quality.

Despite the fact that young Bordeaux wines are constantly changing during their evolution and aging process in the barrel, the great wines of a given vintage are usually apparent. It has also been my experience that some wines that ultimately turn out to be good or very good may be unimpressive or just dumb when tasted in their youth from the cask. But the true superstars of a great vintage are sensational, whether they are 6 months or 20 months old.

When I taste young Bordeaux from cask, I prefer to judge the wine after the final blend or assemblage has been completed. At this stage, the new wine has had only negligible aging in oak casks. For me, it is essential to look at a wine in this infant stage (normally in late March and early April following the vintage) because then most wines can be judged with only minimal influence of oak, which can mask fruit and impart additional tannin and aromas to the wine. What one sees at this stage is a naked wine that can be evaluated on the basis of its richness and ripeness of fruit, depth, concentration, body, acidity, and natural tannin content, unobscured by evidence of oak aging.

The most important components I look for in a young Bordeaux are fruit and balance. Great vintages, characterized by ample amounts of sunshine and warmth, result in grapes that are fully mature and that produce rich, ripe, deeply fruity wines with significant but velvety tannin. If the fruit is missing or unripe and green, the wine can never be great. In contrast, grapes that are allowed to stay on the vine too long in hot, humid weather become overripe and taste pruny and sometimes raisiny, and are also deficient in acidity. They too have little future. This is rarely a problem in Bordeaux. Throughout all appellations of Bordeaux, recent vintages that, in their youth, have been marked by the greatest ripeness, richness, and purity of fruit have been 2000, 1998, (for Graves, St.-Emilion, and Pomerol), 1996 (for the Médoc), 1995, 1990, 1989, 1986 (for the Médoc), 1985, and 1982—all high-quality vintages. Vintages that exhibited the least fruit and an annoying vegetal character have been 1984, 1977, and 1974, poor to mediocre vintages.

Later in the year, I return to Bordeaux to get another extensive look at the wines. By this time the wines have settled down completely, but are also marked by the scent of new oak barrels. The intense grapy character of their youth has begun to peel away, as the wines have now had at least 10–12 months of cask aging. If extensive tastings in March or April give a clear overall view of the vintage's level of quality, comprehensive tastings 9–10 months later are always conclusive evidence of where the vintage stands in relation to other Bordeaux vintages and how specific wines relate in quality to one another.

With regard to vintages of Bordeaux in bottle, I prefer to taste these wines in what is called a "blind tasting." A blind tasting can be either "single blind" or "double blind." This does not mean one is actually blindfolded and served the wines, but rather that in a single-blind tasting, the taster knows the wines are from Bordeaux, but does not know the identities of the châteaux or the vintages. In a double-blind tasting, the taster knows nothing other than that several wines from anywhere in the world, in any order, from any vintage, are about to be served.

For bottled Bordeaux, I purchase the wines at retail, and usually conduct all my tastings under single-blind conditions—I do not know the identity of the wine, but since I prefer to taste in peer groups, I always taste wines from the same vintage. Additionally, I never mix Bordeaux with non-Bordeaux wines, simply because whether it be California or Australia Cabernet Sauvignons, the wines are distinctly different, and while comparative tastings of Bordeaux versus California may be fun and make interesting reading, the results are never very reliable or especially meaningful to the wine consumer who desires the most accurate information. Remember that whether one employs a 100-point rating system or a 20-point rating system, the objectives and aims of professional wine evaluations are the same—to assess the quality of the wine vis-à-vis its peers and to determine its relative value and importance in the international commercial world of wine.

When evaluating wines professionally, it goes without saying that proper glasses and the correct serving temperature of the wine must be prerequisites to any objective and meaningful tasting. The best glasses for critical tasting are made by Riedel and its rival, Spiegelau. Both companies offer a plethora of sizes and shapes, but I prefer a tulip-shaped glass no larger than 10–12 ounces. As for the temperature, 60–62°F is best for evaluating both red and white wines. Too warm a temperature and the bouquet becomes diffuse and the taste flat. Too cold a temperature and there is no discernible bouquet and the flavors are completely locked in by the overly chilling effect on the wine. Moreover, cold temperatures exaggerate a wine's acidity and oak.

When I examine a wine critically, there is both a visual and physical examination. Against a white background, the wine is first given a visual exam for brilliance, richness, and intensity of color. A young Bordeaux wine that is light in color, hazy, or cloudy (or all three) has serious problems. For Bordeaux red wines, color is extremely important. Virtually all the great Bordeaux vintages have shared a very deep, rich, saturated purple color when young, whereas the poorer vintages often have weaker, less rich-looking colors because of poor weather and rain. Certainly, in 2000, 1996, 1995, 1990, 1989, 1986, 1985, and 1982 the general color of the red wines of Bordeaux has been very dark. In 1978 and 1975, it was dark but generally not so deep in color as the aforementioned vintages. In 1984, 1980, 1974, and 1973 the color was rather light.

In looking at an older wine, the rim of the wine next to the glass should be examined for amber, orange, rust, and brown colors. These are signs of maturity and are normal. When they appear in a good vintage of a wine less than 6–7 years old, something is awry. For example, young wines that have been sloppily made and exposed to unclean barrels or air will mature at an accelerated rate and take on the look of old wines when in fact they are still relatively young by Bordeaux standards.

In addition to looking at the color of the wines, I examine the "legs" of the wines. The legs are the tears or residue of the wine that run down the inside of the glass. Rich Bordeaux vintages tend to have "good legs" because the grapes are rich in glycerol and alcohol, giving the wine a viscosity that causes this "tearing" effect. Examples of Bordeaux vintages that produced wines with good to excellent legs would be 2000, 1998, 1996, 1995, 1990, 1989, 1986, 1985, and 1982.

After the visual examination is completed, the actual physical examination of the wine takes place. The physical exam is composed of two parts: the wine's smell, which depends on the olfactory sense, and the wine's taste, the gustatory sense, which is tested on the palate. After swirling a wine, one's nose is placed into the glass (not the wine) to smell the aromas that issue from the wine. This is an extremely critical step because the aroma and odor of the wine will tell the examiner the ripeness and richness of the underlying fruit, the state of maturity, and whether there is anything unclean or suspicious about the wine. The smell of a wine, young or old, will tell a great deal about the wine's quality and no responsible professional taster understates the significance of a wine's odors and aromas, often called the "nose" or "bouquet." Emile Peynaud, in his classic book on wine tasting, *Le Goût du Vin* (Bordas, 1983), states that there are nine principal categories of wine aromas.

1. Animal odors: smells of game, beef, venison
2. Balsamic odors: smells of pine trees, resin, vanilla
3. Woody odors: smells of the new wood of oak barrels
4. Chemical odors: smells of acetone, mercaptan, yeasts, hydrogen sulfide, acidity, and fermentation
5. Spicy odors: smells of pepper, cloves, cinnamon, nutmeg, ginger, truffles, anise, mint
6. Empyreumatic odors: smells of crème brûlée, smoke, toast, leather, coffee
7. Floral odors: smells of violets, roses, lilacs, jasmine
8. Fruity odors: smells of black currants, raspberries, cherries, plums, apricots, peaches, figs
9. Vegetal odors: smells of herbs, tea, mushrooms, vegetables

The presence or absence of some or all of these aromas, their intensity, their complexity, and their persistence all serve to create the bouquet or nose of a wine that can be said to be distinguished, complete, and interesting—or flawed and simple.

Once the wine's aroma or bouquet has been examined thoroughly, the wine is tasted, sloshed, or chewed around on the palate while also inhaled, which releases the wine's aromas. The weight, richness, depth, balance, and length of a wine are apparent from the tactile impression the wine leaves on the palate. Sweetness is experienced on the tip of the tongue, saltiness just behind the tongue's tip, acidity on the sides, and bitterness at the back. Most professional tasters will spit the wine out, although some wine is swallowed in the process.

The finish or length of a wine, its ability to give off aromas and flavors even though it is no longer on the palate, is the major difference between a good young wine and a great young wine. When the flavor and the aroma of the wine seem to last and last on the palate, it is usually a great, rich wine. The great wines and great vintages are always characterized by a purity, opulence, richness, depth, and ripeness of the fruit from which the wines are made. When the wines have both sufficient tannin and acidity, the balance is struck. It is these qualities that separate a profound Bordeaux from a good one.

TASTING NOTES AND RATINGS

All of my tastings were done in peer-group conditions when possible (meaning that the same type of wines were tasted against one another), in my tasting room, in the cellars of the producers, or in the offices of major Bordeaux *négociants*. The ratings reflect an independent, critical look at the wines. Neither price nor the reputation of the producer/grower affects the rating in any manner. I spend a minimum of three months of every year tasting in vineyards. During the other nine months of the year, six- and sometimes seven-day work weeks are devoted solely to tasting and writing. I do not participate in wine judgings or trade tastings for many reasons, but principal among these are the following: 1. I prefer to taste from an entire bottle of wine. 2. I find it essential to have properly sized and cleaned professional tasting glasses. 3. The temperature of the wine must be correct. 4. I alone will determine the time allocated to the number of wines to be critiqued.

THE RATING SYSTEM

96–100	Extraordinary
90–95	Outstanding
80–89	Above average to very good
70–79	Average
50–69	Below average to poor

The numerical rating given is a guide to what I think of the wine vis-à-vis its peer group. Certainly, wines rated above 85 are good to excellent, and any wine rated 90 or above will be outstanding for its particular type. While some have suggested that scoring is not well suited to a beverage that has been romantically extolled for centuries, wine is similar to other consumer products. There are specific standards of quality that full-time wine professionals recognize, and there are benchmark wines against which all others can be judged. I know of no one with three or four different glasses of wine in front of him or her, regardless of how good or bad the wines might be, who cannot say "I prefer this one to that one." Scoring wines is simply taking a professional's opinion and applying some sort of numerical system to it on a consistent basis. Scoring permits rapid communication of information to expert and novice alike. In essence, I strongly believe in a scoring system backed up by intelligent tasting notes. Scoring wine makes the critic accountable to both the wine consumer and winery. Each knows precisely where the critic stands vis-à-vis the wine, and they can calibrate their palate and judgment with that of the critic. I further believe scoring promotes higher- and higher-quality wine, as no winery is able to hide behind obtuse and meaningless 19th-century prose such as "fine; very fine; very, very fine; and very, very, very fine."

The rating system I employ in my wine journal, *The Wine Advocate*, is the one I have utilized in this book. It is a 50–100-point scale: the most repugnant of all wines meriting 50 since that is the starting point of the scale, and the most glorious gustatory experience commanding 100. I prefer my system to the once widely quoted 20-point scale called the Davis Scale—of the University of California at Davis—because it permits much more flexibility in scoring. It is also easier to understand because the numbers correspond to the American grading system, and it avoids the compression of scores from which the Davis Scale suffers. It is not without problems, however, because readers will often wonder what the difference is between an 86 and 87, both very good wines. The only answer I can give is a simple one: When tasted side by side, I thought the 87-point wine slightly better than the 86-point wine.

The score given for a specific wine reflects the quality of the wine at its best. As I mentioned earlier, I often tell people that evaluating a wine and assigning a score to a beverage that will change and evolve in many cases for up to 10 or more years is analogous to taking a photograph of a marathon runner. Much can be ascertained but, like a picture of a moving object, the wine will also evolve and change. I retry wines from obviously badly corked or defective bottles, since a wine from such a single bad bottle does not indicate an entirely spoiled batch. Many of the wines reviewed here I have tasted many times, and the score represents a cumulative average of the wine's performance in tastings to date. Scores do not tell the entire story of a wine. The written commentary that accompanies the ratings is often a better source of information regarding the wine's style and personality, the relative quality level vis-à-vis its peers, the relative value, and its aging potential than any score could ever indicate.

Here then is a general guide to interpreting the numerical ratings:

A score of 90–100 is equivalent to an A and is given only for an outstanding or special effort. Wines in this category are the very best produced for their type and, like a three-star Michelin restaurant, merit the trouble to find and try. There is a big difference between a 90 and a 99, but both are top marks. As you will note throughout the text, there are few wines that actually make it into this top category simply because there are just not many truly great wines.

A score of 80–89 is equivalent to a B in school and such a wine, particularly in the 85–89 range, is very, very good; many of the wines that fall into this range are often great values as well. I would not hesitate to have any of these wines in my own personal collection.

A score of 70–79 represents a C, or an average mark, but obviously 79 is a much more desirable score than 70. Wines that receive scores between 75 and 79 are generally pleasant, straightforward wines that simply lack complexity, character, or depth. If inexpensive, they may be ideal for uncritical quaffing.

Below 70 is a D or an F, depending on where you went to school; for wine, too, it is a sign of an unbalanced, flawed, or terribly dull or diluted wine that will be of little interest to the knowledgeable wine consumer.

In terms of awarding points, my scoring system gives every wine a base of 50 points. The wine's general color and appearance merit up to 5 points. Since most wines today are well made, thanks to modern technology and the increased use of professional oenologists, they tend to receive at least 4, often 5 points. The aroma and bouquet merit up to 15 points, depending on the intensity level and extract of the aroma and bouquet as well as the cleanliness of the wine. The flavor and finish merit up to 20 points, and again, intensity of flavor, balance, cleanliness, and depth and length on the palate are all important considerations when giving out points. Finally, the overall quality level or potential for further evolution and improvement—aging—merits up to 10 points.

Scores are important to let the reader gauge a professional critic's overall qualitative placement of a wine vis-à-vis its peers. Anyone who scores a wine is accountable to the reader. Accountable for the score that is bestowed, but also accountable for justifying that score with an intelligent tasting note that analyzes the wine and lets the reader realize why it is scored the way it is. However, it is also vital to consider the description of the wine's style, personality, and potential. No scoring system is perfectly objective, but a system that provides for flexibility in scores, if applied without prejudice, can quantify different levels of wine quality and provide the reader with a professional's judgment. However, there can never be any substitute for your own palate, nor any better education than tasting the wine yourself.

ANTICIPATED MATURITY— WHAT IS IT?

Because of the number of inquiries I receive regarding when a given Bordeaux wine has reached the point in its evolution that it is said to be ready to drink, I have provided an estimated range of years over which the châteaux's wines should be consumed for the specific vintage. I call this time frame the "anticipated maturity." Before one takes my suggestions too literally, let me share with you the following points.

1. If you like the way a wine tastes when young, do not hesitate to enjoy it in spite of what the guidelines may say. There can never be any substitute for your own palate.
2. I have had to make several assumptions, the primary ones being that the wine was purchased in a healthy state and you are cellaring the wine in a cool, humid, odor- and vibration-free environment that does not exceed 65°F, especially in the summer.
3. The estimates are an educated guess based on how the wine normally ages, its quality, its balance, and the general depth of the vintage in question.
4. The estimates are conservative. I have assumed a maturity based on my own palate, which tends to prefer a wine that is fresher and more exuberant (younger) over one that has begun to fade, but one that may still be quite delicious and complex.

Consequently, if you have cool, ideal cellars, the beginning year in the estimated range of maturity may err in favor of drinking the wine on the young side. I presume most readers would prefer, given a choice, to open a bottle too early rather than too late.

This philosophy has governed my projected maturity period for each wine. One of Bordeaux's greatest virtues is its extraordinary longevity. The finest Bordeaux wines, if purchased in pristine condition and stored properly, are nearly immortal in terms of aging capacity. Given the sweeter, more velvety tannin that modern-day producers attain, these wines can be drunk young, but in top vintages they have 15–30+ years of positive evolution ahead of them.

EXAMPLES

Now. Totally mature; immediate drinking is suggested within several years of the "last tasted" date.

Now–may be in decline. Based on the age of the wine and knowledge of the château and the specific vintage, this designation is utilized where a fully mature wine discussed in the first edition (1985) has not been recently retasted and is believed to have passed its apogee and begun its decline.

Now–probably in serious decline. Based on the age of the wine and knowledge of the château and the specific vintage, this designation is utilized when a wine discussed in the first edition (1985) was at the end of its plateau of maturity and, while not recently retasted, is believed to be well past its plateau of maturity.

Now–2020. The wine has entered its plateau of maturity where it should be expected to remain until 2020, at which time it may begin to slowly decline. The "now" dates from the time of the last tasted note.

2005–2015. This is the estimated range of years during which I believe the wine will be in its plateau period—the years over which it will be at its best for drinking. Please keep in mind that Bordeaux wines from top vintages tend to decline slowly (just the opposite of Burgundy) and that a wine from an excellent vintage may take another 10–15 years to lose its fruit and freshness after the last year in the stated plateau period.

ABOUT THE BOOK'S ORGANIZATION

This book has been divided into the major geographical regions of Bordeaux. Within each region, the famous châteaux and many minor châteaux deserving recognition are reviewed. The emphasis, for obvious reasons, is on the major Bordeaux estates that are widely available and well known in this country. The quality of these wines over the last quarter-century has been examined closely. For lesser known châteaux, the selection process has been based on two factors, quality and recognition. High-quality, lesser known estates are reviewed, as well as those estates that have gotten distribution into the export markets, regardless of quality. I have made every effort during the last 25 years to discover and learn about the underpublicized châteaux in Bordeaux. Because older vintages of these wines are virtually impossible to find, plus the fact that the majority of the Crus Bourgeois wines must be drunk within 5–7 years of the vintage, the focus for most of these lesser known Crus Bourgeois wines is on what they have accomplished recently. I feel the châteaux that are reviewed are the best of these lesser known estates, but to err is human, and it would be foolish for both you and me to believe that there is not some little estate making exquisite wine that I have omitted altogether.

At the beginning of each chapter on the Bordeaux appellations is my classification of the wines from that appellation. This analysis is based on their overall quality vis-à-vis one another. This is not a book that will shroud quality differences behind skillfully worded euphemisms. Within each appellation the châteaux are reviewed in alphabetical order. For those who love lists, my overall classification of the top 182 wine-producing estates of Bordeaux may be found beginning on page 24.

With respect to the specific vintages covered, tasting emphasis has generally been given to only the most renowned vintages. Vintages such as 1993, 1992, 1991, 1977, 1972, 1968, 1965, and 1963 are generally not reviewed because they were very poor years, and few Bordeaux châteaux made acceptable quality wine in those years. Furthermore, such vintages are not commercially available. As for the actual tasting notes, the "anticipated maturity" refers to the time period at which I believe the wine will be at its apogee. This is the time period during which the wine will be fully mature and should ideally be drunk. These estimates as to anticipated maturity are conservative and are based upon the assumption that the wine has been purchased in a sound, healthy condition and has been kept in a vibration-free, dark, odor-free, relatively cool (below 65°F) storage area. For the wine-tasting terms I employ and for the proper methods of cellaring Bordeaux wines, see Chapter 6, "A User's Guide to Bordeaux" and Chapter 8, "A Glossary of Wine Terms."

ONE FURTHER CAVEAT

When a book such as this is revised, difficult decisions must be made regarding the retention of tasting notes on wines that have not been reevaluated in the years that have lapsed since I wrote the previous edition. As readers will discover, many of the finest wines in top vintages have been retasted since the last edition and the changes in text and ratings, where warranted, have been made. Because a serious tasting note is the professional's photograph of a wine during its life, and, moreover, since all the tasting notes in this book are dated, I have opted to leave some of the original tasting critiques in the book as part of the history of that property's record of wine quality, especially when the note relates to a famous vintage.

IN VINO VERITAS?

I have no doubt that the overwhelming majority of rare and fine wine that is sold today, either at retail or through one of the numerous wine auctions, involves legitimate bottles. Yet I have accumulated enough evidence to suggest that some warning flags need to be raised before this insidious disease becomes a vinous ebola. Shrewd buyers, reputable merchants, and auction companies that specialize in top vintages take considerable measures to authenticate bottles of wine that may cost thousands of dollars. In fact, the top auction houses, aware of the growing evidence of phony bottles, are actually going to great lengths to authenticate the legitimacy of each wine they sell. Nevertheless, a con artist can easily reproduce a bottle (the finest Bordeaux châteaux choose to use glass bottles that are among the cheapest and easiest to obtain in the world), a label, a cork, and a capsule, deceiving even the most astute purchaser. Think it over: high quality, limited production—rare wine may be the only luxury-priced commodity in the world that does not come with a guarantee of authenticity, save for the label and cork, and the former can be easily duplicated, particularly with one of today's high-tech scanners.

The wine marketplace has witnessed obscene speculation for such modern-day vintages as 1990, certain 1989s, and, of course, 1982. The appearance of dishonest segments of society with only one objective, to take full advantage of the enormous opportunity that exists to make a quick buck by selling bogus wines, is not that shocking. This has always been a problem, but based on the number of letters and telephone calls I have received from victims who have been the recipients of suspiciously labeled wines, with even more unusual contents, it is a subject that needs to be addressed.

It was nearly 25 years ago that I saw my first fraudulent bottles of fine wine. Cases of 1975 Mouton Rothschild were being sold in New York for below their market value. Furthermore, the wine was packed in shabby cardboard cases with washed-out labels. In addition to those warning signs, the bottles had the words "made in Canada" on the bottom and the capsules had no embossed printing, a characteristic of Mouton. Blatant recklessness and slipshod work of the criminal made the fraud easy to detect.

Many producers of these limited production, rare wines are aware of the frauds perpetuated with their products, but they have largely chosen to maintain a low profile for fear that widespread dissemination of potentially inflammatory information will unsettle (to put it mildly) the fine-wine marketplace. No doubt the news that a hundred or so phony cases of Château ABC floating around in the world marketplace would suppress the value of the wine. Lamentably, those estates that make the world's most cherished wines (and we all know who they are) need to develop a better system for guaranteeing the authenticity of their product, but to date few have been so inclined. Four of the elite Bordeaux châteaux do make it more difficult for counterfeiting pirates. Pétrus has, since the 1988 vintage, utilized a special label that when viewed under a specific type of light, reveals a code not apparent under normal lighting conditions. In 1996, Pétrus went further, instituting an engraved bottle with the word "Pétrus" etched in the glass. Château d'Yquem incorporates a watermark in their label to discourage bogus imitators. Haut-Brion was among the first to utilize a custom embossed bottle in 1957. In 1996, Lafite Rothschild also launched an anti-fraud engraved bottle. More recently, Château Margaux and Château Latour have inserted special codes in the print of each bottle or in the glass itself. Whether creating more sophisticated labels that are not as easy to reproduce (with serial numbers, watermarks, etc.), engraved bottles, or employing a fraud squad devoted to tracking down the provenance of these phony bottles—something must be done.

Consider the following instances of fraudulent bottles, all of which I have carefully documented.

A longtime friend of mine, fearing the worst (he is also extremely knowledgeable about fine wine), asked if I could come to his house and take a look at some wines he had purchased, including the 1992 Domaine Leflaive Montrachet. After examining the bottle, it was clear the wine was a fraud. Domaine Leflaive brands each cork with the vintage and vineyard, but in this case the only words on the cork were "Domaine Leflaive." No vintage or vineyard designation was shown. Someone had easily affixed the Domaine Leflaive label and the 1992 neck label. My friend had spent $600 (this wine usually sells for $750–950) for what was probably a generic white burgundy worth no more than $15. The retailer was shocked and was totally cooperative in refunding my friend's money.

In another shipment, this same person had acquired a case of one of my favorite wines, the 1990 Rayas. When I saw the suspicious bottle of Leflaive, I carefully scrutinized the Rayas. It appeared to have a legitimate label. Until the late nineties, the Rayas cork never indicated the estate's name or vintage. However, when I held the bottle in front of an incandescent light, the color appeared disturbingly light. Furthermore, I noticed that there was no sediment. Coincidentally, I had drunk the 1990 Rayas several days earlier while vacationing in Colorado. That bottle had considerable sediment and a dense ruby/purple color. I asked if I could take the bottle home to compare it to the 1990 Rayas in my cellar. The wine was another fraud. Further comparison with bottles from my cellar revealed two other glaring discrepancies. First and foremost, all Château Rayas wines have a red capsule with the words "Château Rayas" and a coat of arms embossed on the top of the capsule. The phony bottle had a red capsule that was identical in color, but nothing embossed on the top. Secondly, in the lower left hand corner of the label on authentic bottles of 1990 Rayas are the words "Proprietaire J. Reynaud." In 1992 Reynaud became the French equivalent of a corporation, and all vintages from 1992 carry the words "S.C.E.A. Château Rayas." These corporate words appeared on the label of the phony bottle of 1990.

Another well-informed wine buyer called to tell me that he was worried about his magnums of Domaine Leflaive 1992 Bâtard- and Chevalier-Montrachet, purchased through the "gray market" (wines purchased by American retailers outside the authorized distribution system, from independent brokers in Europe). An expansive definition of the gray market includes all those who purchase wine directly from producers, private consumers, restaurants, and even retailers (all in Europe) for resale to America, Central America, and Asia. The gray market vendors I know are honest and respected professionals, but this nebulous group obviously has some dishonest interlopers.

The European economic community now requires that virtually all beverages show an "L" followed by a serial number, a result of the Perrier fiasco several years ago when some tainted Perrier was released into the marketplace. This friend's questionable 1992 Domaine Leflaive displayed a lot number ending with the numbers "91." All legitimate 1992 Domaine Leflaive wines have a lot number that ends with the numbers "92." Other bottles had no lot numbers. Moreover, a number of these magnums had no vineyard name or vintage stamped on the cork, further confirming that these wines were not the 1992 Chevalier or 1992 Bâtard-Montrachets, as Domaine Leflaive brands all of its premiers and grands crus with the vineyard name and vintage.

I should point out that in the case of Domaine Leflaive, none of the questionable bottles came through the authorized American importer, Frederick Wildman and Sons.

As for the Château Rayas, someone had printed Rayas's principal American importer, Martine's Wines of Novato, California, on the label. A call to Martine Saunier established that her last sale of 1990 Rayas had occurred in the fall of 1993. This was supported by the owner of Rayas, the late Jacques Reynaud, who, along with Martine Saunier, was adamant about this story being made public. Reynaud informed me that 100 cases of his 1993 Côtes du Rhône-La Pialade had been stolen from the winery in 1995, and that in all likelihood these wines had been relabeled with a bogus 1990 Rayas label. In tasting the phony 1990 Rayas, the wine did seem like a product of Reynaud given its ripe, jammy, cherry fruit, but it lacked intensity, concentration, and body, suggesting it was from a rain-plagued harvest (1993 or 1992 for example). As a result of this, in 1995, Rayas began stamping the vintage on the corks of all Château Rayas Châteauneuf-du-Pape.

If these had been the only instances of fraud I ran across, I would have hesitated about discussing them. However, another merchant called me about a suspicious case of magnums of 1947 Cheval Blanc purchased in Europe by an American merchant. Incredulous, I asked if he would send me a bottle by overnight delivery, which I would inspect and return. The bottle had a label that looked as if it had been produced by a copier or scanner. The capsule had been meticulously slit with a razor blade. Under the capsule was a brand new cork with the words "Cheval Blanc—Rébouché 1988." Where the vintage date would normally appear, someone had taken an instrument and scratched it out. The wine had a fill in the upper neck (not surprising if in fact this was a legitimately recorked 1947, done at the château), but the light ruby color and small quantity of sediment (this wine possesses heavy sediment and is extremely dense in color) made me suspicious. At more than $20,000 a magnum, I was not going to taste it, but I am 90% sure this wine was anything but 1947 Cheval Blanc.

Two further instances of fraud require mentioning. Another source, concerned about the authenticity of his 1945 Vieux Château Certan and 1989 Le Pin, shipped me a bottle of each to inspect and taste. The 1945 Vieux Château Certan's label was unusually wrinkled, as if it had been removed from another bottle and reset on this bottle.

The pink capsule was sitting loosely on the neck. Although the château's name was on the cork, the cork was too new for a 51-year-old wine, and where the vintage should have been, there were only scratch marks. What did the wine taste like? Surprisingly, it was fully mature, delicious, and I believe, a legitimate VCC, but not from the 1945 vintage. It was much lighter, so perhaps it was a 1971, 1967, or 1962, but who will ever know? With respect to the 1989 Le Pin, I pulled a bottle from my cellar with which to compare the questionable bottle. The label for the latter bottle was scanner reproduced as the distinctive copper print of Le Pin's label was closer to a blue. The corks were identical except that the suspicious bottle's cork had a slightly different print size. When tasted, I was sure the suspicious bottle was Le Pin, but probably from the 1987 vintage. It was not nearly rich enough to be a 1989.

Other reports of phony bottles have come in with surprising frequency. These reports have been confirmed in conversations with retailers, both in this country and in England. They have told me of fraudulent cases of 1989 and 1982 Le Pin, 1982 Pétrus, 1982 Lafleur, 1975 Lafleur, 1947 Cheval Blanc, 1928 Latour, and 1900 Margaux, with non-branded blank corks and photocopied labels! With respect to the 1928 Latour, the merchant, suspecting he had been duped, opened it and told me he was sure it was a young California Pinot Noir.

A wine buyer from one of this country's most prominent restaurants recently told me about some of the problems he had encountered when opening expensive bottles for his clients. All of these wines had been purchased from a reputable merchant who had bought the wine from a gray marketeer selling private cellars in Europe. Corks of 1961 Haut-Brion and 1970 Latour were either illegible or the vintage was intentionally scratched off. Since this buyer had vast tasting experience with these wines, detection of the fraud was relatively easy. He was convinced that the 1961 Haut-Brion was fraudulent, as it tasted like a much lighter vintage of Haut-Brion (he suspected it to be the 1967). In the case of the 1970 Latour, the cork had been badly altered to resemble the 1970, but closer inspection revealed it to be the 1978 Latour. In these cases, only a person who knows the wine well would suspect that the contents were bogus. One major American merchant, outraged at being sold phony wine, attempted to contact the European seller, only to find out he had moved, with no forwarding address from his office in Paris. The seller hasn't been found to this day.

What is so surprising is that most fraudulent efforts to date appear to be the work of kindergarten criminals, as indicated by the washed-out, photocopied labels that were attached to many of the 1982s. However, with the technology available today, authentic-looking bottles, capsules, corks, and labels can be easily duplicated. In these cases, only a person who knows the taste of the wine could tell if the contents were bogus.

SAFETY GUIDELINES

DEALING WITH THE GRAY MARKET

To date, almost all the fraudulent bottles have come from wines purchased in the so-called "gray market." This means the wines have not gone through the normal distribution channel, where a contractual relationship exists between the producer and the vendor. Bottles of French wines with the green French tax stamps on the top of the capsule have obviously been purchased in France and then resold to gray market operators. I do not want to denigrate the best of the gray market operators, because those that I know (I am a frequent purchaser from these sources) are legitimate, serious, and professional about what they buy. Nevertheless, it is an irrefutable fact that most of the suspicious wines showing up in these quarters are from rogue gray market operators.

LABEL AWARENESS

Wine bottles that have easily removable neck labels that indicate the vintage are especially prone to tampering. It is easy to replace a neck label from a poor vintage with one from a great vintage. Sadly, almost all Burgundies fall into this category, as well as some Rhône Valley wines. Many of the top Burgundy producers have begun to brand the cork with the appropriate vintage and vineyard, particularly if it is a premier or grand cru. However, this is a relatively recent practice, largely implemented in the late 1980s by top estates and *négociants*. The only way a buyer can make sure the cork matches the neck and bottle labels is to remove the capsule. Any purchaser who is the least bit uneasy about the provenance of a wine should not hesitate to pull off the capsule. Irregular, asymmetrical labels with tears and smears of glue are a sign that someone may have tampered with the bottle. Perhaps the trend (now widely employed by California wineries such as Robert Mondavi and Kendall-Jackson) to discontinue the use of capsules should be considered by top estates in France, Italy, and Spain. An alternative would be to design a capsule with a window slot, permitting the purchaser a view of the cork's vintage and vineyard name. A more practical as well as inexpensive alternative would be to print the name of the vineyard and vintage on the capsule, in addition to the cork.

Badly faded, washed-out labels (or a photocopied label) should be viewed with sheer horror! However, readers should realize that moldy or deteriorated labels that are the result of storage in a damp, cold cellar are not signs of fraudulent wines, but rather, superb cellaring conditions. I have had great success at auctions buying old vintages that have moldy, tattered labels. Most speculators shy away from such wines because their priority is investing, not consumption.

KNOW THE MARKET VALUE

Most purchasers of expensive rare wines are extremely knowledgeable about the market value of these wines. If the wine is being offered at a significantly lower price than fair market value, it would seem incumbent for the purchaser to ask why he or she is the beneficiary of such a great deal. Remember, if it sounds too good to be true, it probably is.

ORIGIN VERIFICATION

For both rare, old vintages and young wines, demanding a guarantee as to the provenance of the wine that is being purchased is a prudent step to take. As a corollary, it is imperative that readers deal with reputable merchants who will stand behind the products they sell. If a merchant refuses to provide details of the origin of where the wine was purchased, take your business elsewhere, even if it means laying out more money for the same wine.

LOT NUMBERS

Because of the tainted Perrier water a few years ago, the European community now requires most potable beverages to carry a lot number (but only for beverages sold to member nations, thus excluding the United States). This is usually a tiny number located somewhere on the label that begins with the letter "L" followed by a serial number that can range from several digits to as many as eight or more. Most producers use the vintage as part of the lot number. In the case of Domaine Leflaive, the vintage year is indicated by the last two digits of the lot number. However, in some instances (i.e., Comte Lafon), the first two numbers provide the vintage year. And for Lynch-Bages or Pichon-Longueville-Baron, the vintage appears in the middle of the lot number. But be advised, many tiny growers do not use lot numbers on those wines sold to non-ECC countries (the United States, for example). Virtually all the Bordeaux châteaux have used lot numbers since the 1989 vintage.

NO SEDIMENT IN OLDER WINES

In wines more than 10–15 years old, lack of sediment and fill levels that reach the bottom of the cork should always be viewed with suspicion. Several Burgundian *négociants* sell "reconditioned" bottles of ancient vintages that have fills to the cork and lack sediment. I have always been skeptical of this practice, but those *négociants* claim they have a special process for siphoning off the sediment. Certainly no Bordeaux château utilizes such an unusual and debatable method. Wines that have been recorked at a Bordeaux château will indicate that either on the cork or on both the label and the cork. The year in which the wine was recorked will usually be indicated. Among the most illustrious estates of Bordeaux, only Pétrus refuses to recork bottles because so many suspicious bottles have been brought to them for recorking. Both Cheval Blanc and Latour indicate on both the cork and the label the date and year of recorking. In these cases, the authentic bottles will have very good fills as the wine has been topped off, but older vintages still display considerable sediment.

UNMARKED CARDBOARD CASES

Wines that have been packaged in unlabeled cardboard boxes are always suspicious, particularly since every domaine uses its own customized cardboard box with the name of the estate as well as the importer's name printed on the box. Almost all the prominent Bordeaux châteaux use wooden boxes with the name of the château as well as the vintage branded into the wood. To complicate matters, readers should realize that wines from private cellars consigned to auction houses must usually be repackaged in unmarked cardboard boxes since they had been stored in bins in the private cellar.

RARE, MATURE VINTAGES IN LARGE FORMATS

Great wines from ancient rare vintages such as 1950, 1949, 1947, 1945, 1929, 1928, 1926, 1921, and 1900 (especially the Pomerols) that are offered in large formats, particularly double-magnums, jeroboams, Imperials, and the extremely rare Marie-Jeanne (a three-bottle size) should be scrutinized with the utmost care. Christian Moueix told me that a European vendor had offered rare vintages of Pétrus in Marie-Jeanne formats. To the best of Moueix's knowledge, Pétrus never used Marie-Jeanne bottles! Large formats of rare, old vintages were used very sparingly at most top châteaux, so if anyone is contemplating purchasing an Imperial of 1900 Margaux, be sure to verify the wine's authenticity.

COMMON SENSE

The need to develop a relationship with experienced and reputable merchants is obvious, but too often consumers are seduced by the lowest price. If it is an $8 Corbières, that's fine, but a prized vintage of a first-growth Bordeaux is not likely to be sold cheaply . . . think about it.

I hope the industry will address these issues in a more forthright manner and begin to take more action to protect its members and consumers. Additionally, I urge those renowned estates that benefit from glowing reviews to recognize that it is only in their long-term interest to relentlessly seek a solution to this problem and combine their efforts and resources to track down those who are responsible for fabricating fraudulent bottles of expensive wine. Surely the time has come for the use of more sophisticated labels (with serial numbers and watermarks), designer bottles that are less easy to replicate, and capsules with vintages and vineyard names. An open avenue of communication with the wine buyer, where these frauds can be identified, confirmed, and the commercial and consumer marketplace fully apprised of the problem, is essential to preserving the authenticity of the world's finest wines, as well as the integrity and security of purchasing fine wine.

WHAT CONSTITUTES A GREAT WINE?

What is a great wine? One of the most controversial subjects of the vinous world, isn't greatness in wine much like a profound expression of art or music, something very personal and subjective? As much as I agree that the appreciation and enjoyment of art, music, or wine is indeed personal, high quality in wine, as in art and music, does tend to be subject to widespread agreement. Except for the occasional contrarian, greatness in art, music, or wine, if difficult to precisely define, enjoys a broad consensus. I would even argue that the appreciation of fine art and music is even more subjective than the enjoyment of fine wine. However, few art aficionados would disagree with the fact that Picasso, Rembrandt, Bacon, Matisse, Van Gogh, or Michelangelo were extraordinary artists. The same is true with music. Certainly some dissenters can be found regarding the merits of composers such as Chopin, Mozart, Beethoven, or Brahms or, in the modern era, such musicians/song writers as Bob Dylan, the Beatles, or the Rolling Stones, but the majority opinion is that exceptional music emanated from them.

It is no different with wine. Many of the most legendary wines of our time—1945 Mouton Rothschild, 1945 Haut-Brion, 1947 Cheval Blanc, 1947 Pétrus, 1961 Latour, 1982 Mouton Rothschild, 1982 Lafleur, 1982 Le Pin, 1986 Léoville-Las Cases, 1989 Haut-Brion, 1990 Margaux, 1990 Pétrus, 1998 Pétrus, 2000 Pavie, 2000 Margaux,

2000 Lafite Rothschild, 2000 Cheval Blanc, 2000 Lafleur, and 2000 Pétrus, to name some of the most renowned red Bordeaux, are profoundly riveting wines, even though an occasional discordant view about them may surface. Tasting is indeed subjective, but like most of the finest things in life, there is considerable agreement as to what represents high quality, yet no one should feel forced to feign fondness for a work from Picasso or Beethoven, much less a bottle of 1961 Latour.

One issue about the world's finest wines that is subject to little controversy relates to how such wines originate. Frankly, there are no secrets to the origin and production of the world's finest wines. Great wines emanate from well-placed vineyards with microclimates favorable to the specific types of grapes grown. Profound wines, whether they are from France, Italy, Spain, California, or Australia, are also the product of conservative viticultural practices that emphasize low yields and physiologically rather than analytically ripe fruit. After 25 years spent tasting more than 250,000 wines, I have never tasted a superb wine that was made from underripe fruit. Does anyone enjoy the flavors present when biting into an underripe orange, peach, apricot, or cherry? Low yields and ripe fruit are essential for the production of extraordinary wines, yet it is amazing how many wineries never seem to understand this fundamental principle.

In addition to the common sense approach of harvesting mature (ripe) fruit and discouraging, in a viticultural sense, the vine from overproducing, the philosophy employed by a winery in making wine is of paramount importance. Exceptional wines (whether they be red, white, or sparkling) emerge from a similar philosophy, which includes the following: 1. permit the vineyard's *terroir* (soil, microclimate, distinctiveness) to express itself, 2. allow the purity and characteristics of the grape varietal or blend of varietals to be faithfully represented in the wine, 3. produce a wine without distorting the personality and character of a particular vintage by excessive manipulation, 4. follow an uncompromising, non-interventionalistic winemaking philosophy that eschews the food-processing, industrial mindset of high-tech winemaking—in short, to give the wine a chance to make itself naturally without the human element attempting to sculpture or alter the wine's intrinsic character, and 5. follow a policy of minimal handling, clarification, and treatment of the wine so that what is placed in the bottle represents as natural an expression of the vineyard, varietal, and vintage as is possible. In keeping with this overall philosophy, wine-makers who attempt to reduce such traumatic clarification procedures as fining and filtration, while also lowering sulphur levels (which can dry out a wine's fruit, bleach color from a wine, and exacerbate the tannin's sharpness), produce wines with far more aromatics and flavors, as well as more enthralling textures. In short, these are wines that offer consumers their most compelling and rewarding drinking experiences.

Assuming there is a relatively broad consensus as to how the world's finest wines originate, what follows is my working definition of an exceptional wine. In short—what are the characteristics of a great wine?

THE ABILITY TO PLEASE BOTH THE PALATE AND THE INTELLECT

Great wines offer satisfaction on both a hedonistic level of enjoyment as well as the intellectual level. The world offers many delicious wines that are purely hedonistic, but

not complex. The ability to satisfy the intellect is a more subjective iss
experts call "complex" are those that offer multiple dimensions in both
and flavor profiles and have more going for them than simply ripe fruit an
pleasurable, yet one-dimensional quality.

CLASSIC EXAMPLES

1982 Latour *(Pauillac)*	1989 La Conseillante *(Pomerol)*
1990 Montrose *(St.-Estèphe)*	2000 Cheval Blanc *(St.-Emilion)*
1990 Troplong Mondot *(St.-Emilion)*	2000 Pavie *(St.-Emilion)*

THE ABILITY TO HOLD THE TASTER'S INTEREST

I have often remarked that the greatest wines I have ever tasted could be easily recognized by bouquet alone. They are wines that could never be called monochromatic or simple. Profound wines hold the taster's interest, not only providing the initial tantalizing tease, but possessing a magnetic attraction because of their aromatic intensity and nuance-filled layers of flavors.

CLASSIC EXAMPLES

1989 Haut-Brion *(Graves)*	1982 Le Pin *(Pomerol)*
1998 L'Evangile *(Pomerol)*	1998 Clos l'Église *(Pomerol)*
1982 Pichon-Lalande *(Pauillac)*	2000 Haut-Bergey *(Graves)*

THE ABILITY OF A WINE TO OFFER INTENSE AROMAS AND FLAVORS WITHOUT HEAVINESS

An analogy can be made to eating in the finest restaurants. Extraordinary cooking is characterized by its purity, intensity, balance, texture, and compelling aromas and flavors. What separates exceptional cuisine from merely good cooking, as well as great wines from good wines, is their ability to offer extraordinary intensity of flavor without heaviness. It has been easy in the New World (especially in Australia and California) to produce wines that are oversized, bold, big, and rich—but heavy. Europe's finest wineries, with many centuries more experience, have mastered the ability to obtain intense flavors without heaviness. However, New World viticultural areas (particularly in California) are quickly catching up, as evidenced by the succession of remarkable wines produced during the decade of the 1990s in Napa, Sonoma, and elsewhere in the Golden State. Many of California's greatest wines of the 1990s have sacrificed none of their power and richness, but no longer possess the rustic tannin and oafish feel on the palate that characterized so many of their predecessors of 10 and 20 years ago. Yet for the world's most elegant yet authoritatively flavored wines, Bordeaux has no equal.

CLASSIC EXAMPLES

1961 Haut-Brion *(Graves)*	1990 Cheval Blanc *(St.-Emilion)*
1966 Palmer *(Margaux)*	1986 Léoville-Las Cases *(St.-Julien)*

THE ABILITY OF A WINE TO TASTE BETTER WITH EACH SIP

Most of the finest wines I have ever drunk were better with the last sip than the first, revealing more nuances and more complex aromas and flavors as the wine unfolded in the glass. Do readers ever wonder why the most interesting and satisfying glass of wine is often the one that finishes the bottle?

CLASSIC EXAMPLES

2000 Lafleur *(Pomerol)* 1998 Château L'Eglise-Clinet *(Pomerol)*

1996 Mouton Rothschild *(Pauillac)* 1990 Haut-Brion *(Graves)*

1996 Château Léoville-Las Cases 1990 Troplong Mondot (St.-Emilion)
(St.-Julien)

THE ABILITY OF A WINE TO IMPROVE WITH AGE

This is, for better or worse, an indisputable characteristic of great wines. One of the unhealthy legacies of the British wine writers (who dominated wine writing until the last decade) is the belief that in order for a wine to be exceptional when mature, it had to be nasty when young. My experience has revealed just the opposite—wines that are acidic, astringent, and generally fruitless and charmless when young become even nastier and less drinkable when old. With that being said, new vintages of top wines are often unformed and in need of 10 or 12 years of cellaring (in the case of top California Cabernets, Bordeaux, and Rhône wines), but those wines should always possess a certain accessibility so that even inexperienced wine tasters can tell that the wine is—at the minimum—made from very ripe fruit. If a wine does not exhibit ripeness and richness of fruit when young, it will not develop nuances with aging. Great wines unquestionably improve with age. I define "improvement" as the ability of a wine to become significantly more enjoyable and interesting in the bottle, offering more pleasure old than when it was young. Many wineries (especially in the New World) produce wines they claim "will age," but this is nothing more than a public relations ploy. What they should really say is "will survive." They can endure 10–20 years of bottle age, but they were actually more enjoyable in their exuberant youthfulness.

CLASSIC EXAMPLES

1982 Château Latour *(Pauillac)* 1994 Laville Haut-Brion *(Graves)*

1959 Haut-Brion *(Graves)* 1961 Pétrus *(Pomerol)*

1990 Château Climens *(Barsac/* 1975 La Mission Haut-Brion *(Graves)*
Sauternes) 1959 Mouton Rothschild *(Pauillac)*

THE ABILITY OF A WINE TO OFFER A SINGULAR PERSONALITY

When one considers the greatest wines produced, it is their singular personalities that set them apart. It is the same with the greatest vintages. The abused usage of a description such as "classic vintage" has become nothing more than a reference to what a viticultural region does in a typical (normal) year. Exceptional wines from exceptional vintages stand far above the norm, and they can always be defined by their singular qualities—both aromatically and in their flavors and textures. The opulent, sumptuous qualities of the 1990 and 1982 red Bordeaux; the rugged tannin and immense ageability of the 1986 red Bordeaux; the seamless, perfectly balanced 1994 Napa and Sonoma Cabernet Sauvignons and proprietary blends; and the plush, sweet fruit, high alcohol, and glycerin of the 1990 Barolos and Barbarescos are all examples of vintage individuality.

CLASSIC EXAMPLES

1990 Château Le Tertre-Roteboeuf *(St.-Emilion)*

1990 Yquem *(Sauternes)*

1989 Château Clinet *(Pomerol)*

1982 Le Pin *(Pomerol)*

1982 Mouton Rothschild *(Pauillac)*

1986 Château Margaux *(Margaux)*

1996 Lafite Rothschild *(Pauillac)*

2000 Magrez-Fombrauge *(St.-Emilion)*

2000 Ausone *(St.-Emilion)*

2: A SUMMARY OF BORDEAUX VINTAGES

1945–2001

This chapter is a general assessment and profile of the Bordeaux vintages 2001–1945. While the top wines for each acceptable vintage are itemized, the perception of a vintage is a general view of that particular viticultural region. In mediocre and poor vintages, good wines can often be made by skillful vintners willing to make a careful selection of only the best grapes and *cuvées* of finished wine. In good, even great years, thin, diluted, characterless wines can be made by incompetent and greedy producers. For wine consumers, a vintage summary is important as a general guide to the level of potential excellence that could have been attained in a particular year by a conscientious grower or producer of wine.

2001—A Quick Study
(9-27-2001)

St.-Estèphe***　　　　　　　　　　　　Graves Red***

Pauillac****　　　　　　　　　　　　　Graves White*****

St.-Julien****　　　　　　　　　　　　Pomerol****

Margaux****　　　　　　　　　　　　　St.-Emilion****

Médoc/Haut-Médoc Crus Bourgeois***　　Barsac/Sauternes*****

Size: Another large crop, but after the selections, less grands vins, than in 2000 was produced in the top estates.

Important information: An extremely cold (but also dry) month of September has given the wines fresh acidity and a more tangy, elegant, medium-bodied style than some of the bigger vintages. It is still a little too early to see how these wines will evolve, but they are consistently excellent, although overshadowed by 2000. It is a great vintage in Sauternes.

Maturity status: This vintage will probably be relatively slow to evolve given the good acid levels and tannins most wines possess. None of them have the size of the 2000s or the best 1998s, but they are certainly not wimpish wines.

Price: The Bordelais, recognizing a market saturated with not only their wine but wine from throughout the world, dropped prices significantly in an effort to move these wines through the marketplace. Even that was not enough to sell them as wine futures, but these wines look relatively attractively priced vis-à-vis their counterparts in 2000, and intelligent buyers should be seeking them out in 2003/2004.

Statistically, the winter of 2001 was wet and warm. The following spring was largely uneventful save for some frost alerts in an unusually cool, overcast April. By the end of May 2001, temperatures were high. In fact, according to Bill Blatch at Vintex, in his annual weather report, it was an "unusually violent heat wave." High temperatures occurred again in late June and early July, but then summer disappeared, as anyone who vacationed in Europe realized. Cloudy skies, cold temperatures, and a freakish succession of drizzly days made for an unusually cool, uncomfortable July, creating concerns about when the 2001 harvest might take place. August was irregular, experiencing periods of both high heat and below-normal temperatures. When September arrived, it appeared that the harvest would occur during the last week of the month for Merlot, and the beginning of October for the Cabernets.

I was in the Rhône Valley during the first two weeks of September 2001, and even there it was cold, with 14 straight days of intense Mistral winds howling through the Valley from the north. In Bordeaux, temperatures were 5 degrees below normal, a significant trend that lasted the entire month. However, Bordeaux was also extremely dry during this period. According to the statistics, rainfall in September was off by 66%, always a positive sign. The only rain was on September 22 and 23.

Pomerol's and St.-Emilion's Merlot harvest did not begin in earnest until the end of

September. It continued through the first week of October. In the Médoc, the Merlot harvest lasted from October 1–10. Cabernet Franc throughout Bordeaux was harvested during the same period. The Cabernet Sauvignon was picked unusually late, most coming in between October 7–12. A handful of estates waited even later. Rainfall in October was more problematic, with showers occurring on October 2, 3, 6, 7, and 8, but no inundations.

Production was enormous, although slightly below 2000. Vinifications were tricky, with malolactics far slower than in previous years.

To no one's surprise, most claim this vintage is qualitatively superior to 1999, but in a classic style with fresh acidity, a cooler-climate taste, and more noticeable tannin. Comparisons along the lines of so-called "classic" vintages, such as 1988, 1981, 1979, and 1955, are commonly heard. Yet much has changed in terms of lower crop yields, different vinification techniques, and more severe selections in both the vineyard and the cellars. For those reasons, older vintages are generally useless for comparison purposes. That being said, no appellation stands out as having succeeded more than another, at least for red wines. The Médoc appears to be more uneven than expected, particularly one of my favorite appellations, St.-Julien. With the later than normal malolactics and the vintage's more austere tannin, producers hope that cask aging will flesh out many of the wines that appear hollow with deficient mid-palates. My gut instincts suggest Merlot, overall, has done better than Cabernet Sauvignon, and both have eclipsed Cabernet Franc. Pomerol has come through with consistently excellent wines, and St.-Emilion and its satellite appellations (especially Côtes de Castillon) continue to provide many high class wines, often from little known estates and terroirs.

My tastings suggest that 2001 has produced wines that are denser than the 1999s (more concentrated), but also with higher levels of tannin. What I admire about the finest 1999s is their exceptional equilibrium, undeniable charm and finesse, and a balance that gives them immediate accessibility yet suggests greater longevity than many might guess. Most 2001s have added flesh and fat after looking attenuated and skinny in 2002. They also possess structure and tannin, with increasing amounts of charm of succulence evident. Undeniably, the style of the vintage is lighter, less impressive, and less concentrated than 2000 . . . with some notable exceptions to this general observation. For the red wines, one can safely say it is a very good, at times exceptional, but irregular vintage. In spite of the strong, tannic presence displayed by many 2001s.

With respect to Bordeaux's sweet white wines, the onset of botrytis was ideal and the higher than normal acidity (because of the cool temperatures) resulted in a sensational vintage for many Sauternes and Barsac producers. Clearly, 2001 is the finest year for this region since the outstanding trio of 1990, 1989, and 1988. Tasting these sweet wines early is always difficult, but there is no question 2001 is a vintage of great complexity, ripeness, richness, freshness, and delineation.

THE BEST WINES

St.-Estèphe: Calon-Ségur, Cos d'Estournel, Montrose

Pauillac: Clerc Milon, Grand-Puy-Lacoste, Lafite Rothschild, Latour, Lynch-Bages, Mouton Rothschild, Pichon Longueville Comtesse de Lalande, Pichon-Longueville Baron

St.-Julien: Branaire Ducru, Ducru-Beaucaillou, Gruand-Larose, Léoville Barton, Léoville Las Cases, Léoville Poyferré

Margaux: Brane Cantenac, Clos du Jaugueyron, d'Issan, Lascombes, Château Margaux, Marojallia, Palmer, Prieuré-Lichine

Pessac-Léognan/ Graves Red: Branon, Haut-Bergey, Haut-Brion, Larrivet-Haut-Brion, La Mission-Haut-Brion, Pape-Clément, Smith Haut Lafitte

Pessac-Léognan/ Graves White: Carbonnieux, de Fieuzal, Haut-Brion Blanc, Laville Haut-Brion, La Louvière, Malartic-Lagravière, Pape-Clément Blanc

Pomerol: Le Bon Pasteur, Clos l'Église, La Croix St.-Georges, L'Eglise-Clinet, L'Evangile, La Fleur de Gay, Gazin, Hosanna, Lafleur, Pétrus, Le Pin, Vieux Château Certan

St.-Emilion: Angelus, L'Arrosée, Ausone, Beau Séjour Bécot, Beauséjour, Bellevue-Mondotte, Canon-la-Gaffelière, Cheval Blanc, Clos de Sarpe, Clos St.-Martin, La Clusière, La Couspaude, Ferrand Lartigue, La Fleur Morange, Fombrauge, Gracia, Grand-Pontet, Les Grandes Murailles, L'Hermitage, Magrez Fombrauge, Monbousquet, La Mondotte, Pavie, Pavie Decesse, Péby Faugères, Quinault l'Enclos, Rol Valentin, Troplong Mondot, Valandraud

Barsac/Sauternes: Climens, Clos Haut-Peyraguey, Coutet, Doisy-Daëne l'Extravagance, Doisy-Védrines, Guiraud, Lafaurie-Péyraguey, de Malle, Raymond-Lafon, Rieussec, Sigalas-Rabaud, Suduiraut, La Tour-Blanche

2000—A Quick Study
(9-12-2000)

St.-Estèphe*****	Graves Red*****
Pauillac*****	Graves White***
St.-Julien*****	Pomerol*****
Margaux*****	St.-Emilion*****
Médoc/Haut-Médoc Crus Bourgeois****	Barsac/Sauternes***

Size: Another very large crop.

Important information: The millennium vintage produced great quality and historically high prices that, in a worldwide recession (2003), may not be matched for many years to come.

Maturity status: These very powerful, very concentrated, muscular wines will, in many cases, take years to evolve. They are loaded but, at the same time, quite tannic and dense. Masochists might get a kick out of them much earlier, but don't underestimate the tannins in this vintage. I even predict revisionists will be questioning the vintage's quality in 10 years, given how slowly I think these wines will evolve.

Price: They came out at preposterously high prices; soared higher until the terrorism
attack of September 2001, followed by the corporate scandals of 2002, and then sta-
bilized. This vintage will always represent liquid gold to those who have bought
them. Prices for this vintage will only get higher and higher, given its greatness and
extraordinary potential for longevity—and the fact that it's a millennium year.

What is an undoubtedly fabled millennium vintage for the history books certainly did
not begin that way. Since I am in Bordeaux in January and March each year, my diaries
suggest that while January seemed reasonably cold for mid-winter, March was mild
and warm. As *négociant* Bill Blatch of Vintex points out in his meticulously thorough
summary of the weather conditions leading to the 2000 harvest, the major problem in
spring 2000 was one of the worst outbreaks of mildew Bordeaux had experienced in
many decades. Vignerons expended considerable effort to control it. It also dampened
their early enthusiasm for what was shaping up as a very difficult beginning to the 2000
growing season. Flowering came later than in 1999, but despite concerns about the
schizophrenic weather of alternating heat and cold in June, the result was a relatively
large, uniform crop of Cabernet Sauvignon, Merlot, and Cabernet Franc. Despite fraz-
zled nerves, there were only small outbreaks of the dreaded *coulure* and *millerandange,* surprising in view of the patchy weather throughout May, June, and July. In
short, no one expected the flowering or the vintage to turn out so well.

As anyone who spent time in Western Europe during the summer of 2000 knows,
June was an unusually damp, overcast, and cool month. However, Bordeaux's actual
rainfall came in two large storms in early June, with the remainder of the month being
dry. The threat of rain, always apparent, remained more of a menace than a reality. July
was an even more difficult month of cool, overcast conditions and rain. The average
temperatures for the month, however, fell within the normal range for Bordeaux. Moreover, despite the general impression from vignerons that it was a deficient month in
terms of sunshine, final statistics proved otherwise. The break in what seemed an uninspiring weather pattern beginning in March finally broke on July 29 when a huge high
pressure area stalled over France. This dry and hot stationary system remained over
Bordeaux (and much of southern France) for most of the next two months. Despite what
had appeared to have been sufficient rainfall in early summer, drought-like conditions
began to emerge. As the grapes began to size up, they also developed thick skins from
a lack of moisture, particularly in August. As is always the case, those vineyards
planted on the most gravelly, thin soils were far more affected from hydric stress than
those with moisture retentive, clay-based soils.

To quote Bill Blatch, "For the first time in 10 years, it did not rain—or almost didn't,
during the harvest." Bordeaux's average amount of rainfall in September is 75 millimeters (about 3 inches). In 2000, it was a meager 43 mm (less than 2 inches), with
most of that coming in a September 19 thunderstorm. September also experienced
some exceptional heat waves, particularly early in the month, which helped to thicken
what were already dense skins. This only served to further concentrate the wines. The
harvest began on September 14 for the precocious *terroirs* of Merlot in Pomerol and St.-
Emilion. It continued for the next 2–3 weeks, with virtually all of the right bank Merlot

fermenting in the vat by September 28. The earlier harvesters began the Cabernet Sauvignon harvest in late September. Essentially, the entire harvest was finished by October 10. The weekend of September 29–October 1 was rainy, but it did not cause any concerns given the fact that the Merlot harvest was finished and the thick-skinned Cabernet Sauvignon had no problem withstanding the rain. Nor was the Cabernet Franc affected, with most producers picking "exceptional" Cabernet Franc during the end of September and the first few days of October.

In summary, what began as a mixed, uninspiring, unusual early growing season from March through July turned around completely in August and September. French wine producers often say that June makes the quantity, August makes the style, and September makes the quality. That was never more true than in 2000, when August left its stylistic imprint on the wines' enormous tannic content and richness, and the nearly flawless month of September (the finest since 1990) produced many wines of exhilarating quality . . . at all levels of the Bordeaux hierarchy.

The Wines

At the top level, yields of 35–55 hectoliters per hectare were modest by modern-day standards. Most producers experienced textbook vinifications (because of decent acidities), with very few difficulties despite grapes with high sugars. Many Merlots hit 14% and Cabernets pushed 13%. However, for reasons that are not totally clear, many wines possess good acidity levels in addition to robust but ripe tannin as well as a surprising textural fatness. While technical measurements of tannin and dry extract can be misleading, especially when compared to the taste performances, there is no doubt that many wines possess record levels of tannin as well as extract.

My tastings from bottle confirm that the 2000 vintage has produced some of the most immense, black colored, concentrated, powerful, and tannic wines of the last 30 years. For that reason, the vintage is difficult to compare with any of its predecessors that qualify as superstar years. The wines are generally less accessible than the 1990s, 1989s, and 1982s, but are possibly more concentrated, blacker-colored, heavier, and thicker than the 1996s, 1995s, or 1986s were at a similar age. Moreover, the finest 2000s possess the most impressive length, structure, concentration, and delineation that I have experienced in 25 years of tasting new Bordeaux vintages. Additionally, the vintage appears to be remarkably consistent throughout all appellations, although the sweetest spots in 2000 are St.-Julien, Pauillac, and the sector straddling the Pomerol/St.-Emilion border (precisely where Cheval Blanc faces L'Evangile and La Conseillante). But don't get obsessed by this simplistic analysis, as there are superb wines in all appellations!

In 1998, Merlot was the undeniably favored varietal, with Pomerol, St.-Emilion, and Graves turning in more consistent as well as higher-level qualitative performances than the Médoc. In 1999, it was difficult to pick a favorite varietal, as it came down to yields, selection, and overall winemaking. In 2000, there are fabulous Merlots and profound Cabernet Sauvignons, as well as compelling wines made with high percentages of Cabernet Franc, a varietal that excelled. While some feel this vintage is a modern-day clone of 1955 or 1970, it seems to me that the 2000s are vastly superior. Why? Better winemaking (look at the renaissance occurring in Margaux and Graves as well as the explosion of sumptuous wines in St.-Emilion), improved viticulture, fully equipped cellars, riper fruit, and a more rigorous selection process in putting only the finest vats under the grand vin label are the easy answers. Worldwide competition, educated consumers, and relentless critical scrutiny from the wine press are more complicated reasons. In short, it is a phenomenal year that appears to be one of the greatest vintages Bordeaux has ever produced, particularly in view of the number of outstanding (90 points or higher) wines.

For the first time since 1990, the smaller wineries of Bordeaux, from the Cru Bourgeois to the Petit Châteaux, have often produced wines well above their modest pedigrees. Readers will notice the wines' saturated black/purple colors (which have more in common with a young Napa Cabernet or New World Syrah than Bordeaux). At the same time, the wines are extraordinarily powerful, concentrated, and dense, with dazzling levels of extract, high tannin, good acidity levels, and formidable concentration as well as length. The finest 2000s appear to possess a staggering 30–40 years of longevity. Are they a hypothetical blend of 1990 and 1996?

THE BEST WINES

St.-Estèphe: Calon-Ségur, Lafon-Rochet, Montrose

Pauillac: d'Armailhac, Clerc Milon, Les Forts de Latour, Grand-Puy-Lacoste, Lafite Rothschild, Latour, Lynch-Bages, Mouton Rothschild, Pichon-Longueville Baron, Pichon-Longueville–Comtesse de Lalande, Pontet-Canet

St.-Julien: Beychevelle, Branaire Ducru, Clos du Marquis, Ducru-Beaucaillou, Gruaud Larose, Lagrange, Léoville Barton, Léoville Las Cases, Léoville Poyferré, Talbot

Margaux: Brane Cantenac, Cantenac Brown, Clos du Jaugueyron, Giscours, d'Issan, Kirwan, Lascombes, Maléscot St.-Exupèry, Marojallia, Château Margaux, Palmer, Pavillon Rouge du Château Margaux

Pessac-Léognan/ Branon, Les Carmes Haut-Brion, de Fieuzal, Haut-Bailly, Haut-
Graves Red: Bergey, Haut-Brion, Larrivet-Haut-Brion, La Louvière, Malartic-Lagravière, La Mission Haut-Brion, Pape-Clément, Smith Haut Lafitte, La Tour Haut-Brion

Pomerol: Le Bon Pasteur, Certan de May, Clinet, Clos l'Église, La Conseillante, La Croix St.-Georges, L'Eglise-Clinet, L'Evangile, La Fleur de Gay, Hosanna, Lafleur, Le Moulin, Nenin, Les Pensées de Lafleur, Petit Village, Pétrus, Le Pin, Rouget, Trotanoy, Vieux Château Certan

Fronsac, Canon-
Fronsac: Fontenil, Haut Carles, La Vieille Cure

St.-Emilion: Angelus, Ausone, Barde-Haut, Beau Séjour Bécot, Beauséjour, Berliquet, Canon-la-Gaffelière, Chapelle d'Ausone, Chauvin, Cheval Blanc, Clos Dubreuil, Clos Fourtet, Clos de l'Oratoire, Clos St.-Martin, Clos de Sarpe, La Clusière, La Couspaude, Croix de Labrie, La Dominique, Faugères, Figeac, La Fleur de Jaugue, La Gaffelière, La Gomerie, Gracia, Grand Mayne, Grand-Pontet, Les Grandes Murailles, L'Hermitage, Lusseau, Magdelaine, Magrez Fombrauge, Monbousquet, La Mondotte, Pavie, Pavie Decesse, Pavie Macquin, Péby Faugères, Quinault l'Enclos, Rol Valentin, Le Tertre-Rôteboeuf, Troplong Mondot, Valandraud, Yon-Figeac

Barsac/Sauternes: Climens, Guiraud, Lafaurie-Péyraguey, Rieussec, Suduiraut

1999—A Quick Study
(9-12-1999)

St.-Estèphe***	Graves Red***
Pauillac***	Graves White***
St.-Julien***	Pomerol***
Margaux****	St.-Emilion****
Médoc/Haut-Médoc Crus Bourgeois**	Barsac/Sauternes***

Size: A humongous crop.

Important information: Another user-friendly, seductive, low-acid, but generally ripe vintage where the wines seem like better, more concentrated clones of the 1997 vintage.

Maturity status: Another vintage that should mature quickly, but will certainly last significantly longer than 1997. Most of these wines will be drinkable by age seven or eight and last for 15–20 years. The best examples will be reminiscent of modern-day versions of the underrated 1962s.

Price: Realistic and fair . . . some of the best values in Bordeaux today.

It is hard to believe, but in the decade of the 1990s, only 1990 and 1997 have given Bordeaux relatively dry Septembers. As much as it rained in September 1999 (more than 150 millimeters or 6 inches), this year will be remembered for several other weather extremes. The tempest (in reality a hurricane) that slashed across the Bordeaux region the night of December 27 was the singular weather event of the year. The violence of this storm devastated huge forests and destroyed 100–200-year-old trees with the undiscriminating fury of a barbarian army razing the countryside. Anyone who visited the Médoc or the forest of Les Landes to the south of the city in early 2000 could attest to the unprecedented damage caused by this hurricane, which hit wind speeds of more than 120 miles an hour. Heightening the tragedy of Bordeaux's furious storm was that two days before, an equally powerful storm of hurricane force winds ripped apart northern France, causing major destruction in Paris's beautiful Bois de Boulogne and the nearby Palace of Versailles.

The other extreme weather event that had a more direct effect on the harvest was the freak hailstorm that punched its way through a small zone of St.-Emilion's most famous vineyards on September 5. All the vineyards that were touched, which included such premiers grand crus as Canon, Angelus, Beau Séjour Bécot, Beauséjour (Duffau-Lagarrosse), and Clos Fourtet, as well as the grand crus Côte de Baleau, Patris, Laniote, Grand-Pontet, Franc-Mayne, Grand Mayne, Les Grandes Murailles, Clos St.-Martin, Dassault, Larmande, Berliquet, and La Gomerie, were forced to harvest immediately to save whatever they could. Surprisingly, many of these wines are much better than early forecasters predicted.

Aside from these extreme and unusual weather events, 1999 can be summed up as an excessively wet and abnormally hot year that has produced few compelling wines.

The climatic circumstances and grape maturation in the summer of 1999 was not unusual. The flowering occurred quickly as well as under fine conditions in late May and early June. On average, June and July were dry and hot, but August was extremely hot as well as stormy. In early August, major storms dumped more than 2–3 inches of water across the region on August 3, 6, and 7. With the lunar eclipse on August 11, the storms stopped and Bordeaux was virtually rain/storm free until the heavens reopened prior to the harvest on September 12. The one exception was the aforementioned hailstorm on September 5. Virtually everyone in Bordeaux harvested between September 12 and October 5. The success of such châteaux as Lafleur in Pomerol and Haut-Brion in Graves can be attributed to the fact that much of their harvest was finished before the *grosses pluies* (large rains) fell on September 20. There was only one totally dry day after September 20 and by the time the Médoc châteaux had brought in their last Cabernet Sauvignon, a beautiful high pressure system settled over Bordeaux on October 5 and continued uninterrupted for nearly two weeks, a pattern that had occurred in 1998 as well, but seemed doubly cruel in 1999.

The heavy rainfall, which would have devastated Bordeaux harvests in the early 1980s, 1970s, and before, are now handled with greater care. Lower crop yields, meticulous leaf pulling, as well as anti-rot spraying are effective up to a point, but many of the most renowned châteaux have invested significantly in the concentration machines that eliminate water from the grape must, either through osmosis or entropy. In the mid-1980s, there were only a few of these machines in operation (Léoville Las Cases was one of the first to use reverse osmosis to try to concentrate diluted grape must). Now, just about every wealthy estate has such a machine, save for a handful of traditionalists (Haut-Brion, Pétrus, Château Margaux) who still believe concentration is best achieved in the vineyard, not by high technology in the cellar. However, though there is no doubt that these machines work, only 10–20 years of bottle aging will reveal whether or not they alter or mute important *terroir* nuances at the expense of concentration.

The 1999 crop size was large, about 5% bigger than 1998. There is no shortage of wine, but once again, virtually all of the châteaux that received high scores made severe selections, declassifying 25–70% of their production in order to put the finest wine possible into the bottle. Contrast this to the situation 10–15 years ago where an extreme declassification represented no more than 10–15% of the crop.

The Style of the Wines

In many vintages it is easy to say that this or that grape, or this or that particular appellation appeared to have fared better than another. With the exception of St.-Estèphe, a disappointment, every other appellation has its share of excellent, good, mediocre, and diluted wines. If one appellation appears more consistent in quality, it is Margaux. For decades the region's most notable underachiever, the resurrection of this once moribund appellation is a reality. It is good to see so many Margaux châteaux getting their act together. Many very good 1999s were produced in Margaux.

Because of the extremely warm August and September, there is a hot year character to the wines—low acidity, generally sweet, silky tannin, and an absence of herbaceousness and austerity. However, even with concentration machines, the effect of more than 6 inches of rain cannot be totally eliminated. In my tasting notes, I frequently used the words "not much middle," meaning that the wine smelled and tasted good initially, but had a huge hole in the middle as well as a tannic, alcoholic finish. I wrote these words so often that I began abbreviating them as "nmm." In many ways, that abbreviation symbolizes the problem many châteaux experienced when trying to harvest under the drenching rain while extracting as much flavor as possible from ripe but diluted grapes. The wines have good color, aromas, and tannin, but there is an absence of fat, succulence, charm, and pleasure in their middle. Nevertheless, there are some excellent wines. In particular, the first growths appear to have risen above the trials and tribulations of this frustrating harvest to produce wines that are significantly better than the super-seconds and other classified growths. In that sense, it is a year where the first growths shine and justify their prestigious pedigrees as well as their dot.com-like prices.

In addition to the proliferation of reverse osmosis and entropy concentration machines, increasing numbers of "garage" wines are being produced, particularly in St.-Emilion. There is no stopping this new phenomenon in spite of the hostility it has received from *négociants,* the Médoc's aristocracy, and those reactionaries in favor of preserving Bordeaux's status quo. These wines are not the destabilizing influence many old-timers would have consumers believe. What's wrong with an energetic person taking a small piece of property and trying to turn out something sensational? Admittedly, the prices for many of these wines are ridiculous and no one knows how they will evolve or taste 10 years from now, but the present level of quality can be thrilling. If they are overpriced, it is because too many consumers can't say no, and they continue to drive up prices for these limited quantity gems. Nevertheless, they are here to stay, and there now appears to be movement to produce garage wines in the Médoc, an extremely unsettling idea for many of the big, landed estates who, frankly, are jealous of the high prices these wines fetch.

THE BEST WINES

St.-Estèphe: Montrose

Pauillac: d'Armailhac, Lafite Rothschild, Latour, Lynch-Bages, Mouton Rothschild, Pichon-Longueville Baron

St.-Julien: Ducru-Beaucaillou, Léoville Las Cases

Margaux: Brane Cantenac, Clos du Jaugueyron, d'Issan, Kirwan, Château Margaux, Marojallia, Château Palmer

Pessac-Léognan/ Graves Red: Haut-Brion

Pessac-Léognan/ Graves White: Haut-Brion Blanc, Laville Haut-Brion, Pape-Clément, Plantiers Haut-Brion

Pomerol: Le Bon Pasteur, L'Eglise-Clinet, La Fleur de Gay, Gazin, Hosanna, Lafleur, Pétrus

St.-Emilion: Angelus, Ausone, Barde-Haut, Canon-la-Gaffelière, Cheval Blanc, Clos Dubreuil, Clos de l'Oratoire, La Clusière, Croix de Labrie, Figeac, La Gomerie, Gracia, Grand Mayne, Pierre de Lune, Monbousquet, La Mondotte, Pavie, Pavie Decesse, Pavie Macquin, Péby Faugères, Quinault l'Enclos, Le Tertre-Rôtebocuf, Valandraud

Barsac/Sauternes: Climens, Lafaurie-Péyraguey, Raymond-Lafon, Rieussec, Suduiraut, La Tour-Blanche

1998—A Quick Study
(9-15-1998)

St.-Estèphe***	Graves Red*****
Pauillac***	Graves White*****
St.-Julien****	Pomerol*****
Margaux***	St.-Emilion*****
Médoc/Haut-Médoc Crus Bourgeois**	Barsac/Sauternes***

Size: An abundant vintage.

Important information: This is at once a vintage of great diversity in quality, with stunning wines produced in St.-Emilion, Pomerol, and Graves, and less complete but still relatively successful wines in the Médoc. The Cabernet Sauvignon certainly had more problems ripening than the Merlot and Cabernet Franc. When all the dust settles 20 years after the vintage, the Right Bank and Graves wines of 1998 will certainly compete with the greatest wines of these areas of the last 30 years.

Maturity status: This vintage has a lot of tannin, but most of the Merlot tannins are sweet. The Cabernet tannins can border on being vegetal.

Price: Like most vintages, the best wines tend to be expensive, but prices have not escalated to the extent one might think, given the overall quality of Pomerol, St.-Emilion, and Graves. By and large, the prices are far lower than comparable wines in 2000.

In 20 years of tasting young Bordeaux, there have always been vintages where one appellation or a certain sector produces more complete and interesting wines. Never before have I tasted a vintage where the differences between regions have been so extreme. There may be some historical references among ancient vintages, but so much has changed today that I question the legitimacy of such analogies. Certainly 1975 turned out a bevy of exceptionally powerful, tannic Pomerols and a handful of stunning wines from Graves, but elsewhere, relatively hard, charmless wines were produced. In Bordeaux, it is not uncommon to hear 1964 being compared to 1998, especially by successful producers. The former French Minister of Agriculture declared 1964 "the vintage of the century" before any grapes were picked. Early harvesters, particularly those in the precocious *terroirs* of Pomerol and to a lesser extent St.-Emilion and Graves, turned in very good to superlative performances (i.e., Cheval Blanc, Pétrus, Lafleur, La Mission Haut-Brion, Trotanoy, Figeac), but the Médoc's Cabernet Sauvignon had not been harvested by the time the deluge arrived. The result was a dreadful vintage for the Médoc, with only a handful of surprising exceptions (i.e., Latour and Montrose).

The 1998 is different. Viticulture is better, vineyards are healthier, the serious châteaux practice strict selections for their grand vin, and modern-day technology offers temperature-controlled fermentation tanks; the wealthiest have concentration machines that incorporate reverse osmosis and the removal of water by vacuum. For those reasons alone, 1998 is superior to both 1975 and 1964.

March 1998 was an exceptionally hot month in Bordeaux, which propelled the vineyards off to a roaring and precocious start. However, April was generally cold and wet. May also began unseasonably cold and damp, but by the second week a high pressure system settled over much of southwestern France and the remainder of the month was warm and dry. The number crunchers predicted the harvest would begin in mid-September if the summer turned out to be normal. In spite of erratic weather in June, the flowering in most regions took place with none of the dreaded problems such as *coulure.* The end of June was spectacularly warm and sunny, causing optimism to rise throughout Bordeaux.

Is any weather normal today? July was a bizarre month by Bordeaux standards. High temperatures with occasional thunderstorms serving to irrigate the vineyards traditionally defines this month in the Aquitaine. Yet July 1998 was unseasonably cool, overcast, and, as Bill Blatch said in his Vintage Report, "drab." The hours of sunshine during the month were particularly deficient, even though the average temperatures fell within the normal parameters. In short, there had been only three days of extremely hot weather. One weather phenomena that might explain some of the super-concentrated, massive Pomerols was a hailstorm that damaged some of the vineyards in Pomerol's tenderloin district—the so-called plateau, which forced the vignerons to do an early *vendange verte* (green harvest and/or crop thinning). Unquestionably, this accounts for the fact that yields in Pomerol were extremely low by modern-day standards (30–35 hectoliters per hectare on average).

August was destined to put its imprint on the 1998 Bordeaux. The boring, overcast conditions of July were replaced by an intense high pressure system that produced one of the most torrid heat waves Bordeaux has ever had to suffer. For more than half the month, temperatures were in excess of 95°F, and from August 7–11, the mercury soared over 100°F (not unusual in northern Napa Valley, but rare in Bordeaux). Because of qualitative advances in viticulture such as leaf pulling and culling out excess bunches, this intense heat wave had the effect of roasting/sunburning many grapes, a common problem in hotter climates such as southern France and California, but rarely encountered in Bordeaux. In addition to the punishing heat, August brought on drought conditions. By the end of the month, the vines had begun to exhibit extraordinary stress. Leaves turned yellow and the malnourished vines began to curtail photosynthesis (blockage of maturity). As many producers have said, this huge heat wave, accompanied by the excessive drought, largely determined the style of many 1998s. The grapes shriveled up with their skins becoming extremely thick, resulting in the powerful, tannic constitution of the 1998s.

By the beginning of September, growers were hoping for rain to reignite the maturity process. Their wishes came true. On September 2, 3, and 4, the area received a series of light showers, which were beneficial for the rain-starved vineyards. The weather cleared on September 5, and ideal conditions ensued through September 11. During this period, much of the white wine crop, not only in the high-rent district of Pessac-Léognan but also in the generic Bordeaux appellations as well as Entre-Deux-Mers, was harvested under textbook conditions. Beginning on September 11, much of Bordeaux experienced three days of relatively heavy rainfall. If August had been wet, this would have undoubtedly been deleterious, but the water-depleted soil and vines thrived with the additional rainfall. To the surprise of most observers, the analyses of the vineyards after these rains showed little difference in sugars, acids, and dry extract. In short, the heavy rains of early September and lighter showers of the following days had no serious effect on quality. September 15–27 was a period of exceptional weather. It was during this period that most of the Merlot in Pomerol, the Médoc, and St.-Emilion was harvested—under superb conditions. By the time the weather began to disintegrate, during the weekend of September 26–27, Pomerol had virtually finished the harvest, and much of the Merlot in St.-Emilion and the Médoc had been picked. It takes no genius to realize that this beneficial period of weather undoubtedly explains why Pomerol is 1998's most favored appellation.

Between September 26 and October 1, a whopping 70 millimeters of rain (nearly 3 inches) fell throughout Bordeaux. The late Jean-Eugène Borie, the proprietor of Ducru-Beaucaillou, was buried on October 1, and more than a dozen people told me that driving to his funeral was nearly impossible because the Médoc's Route du Vin was inundated by the soaking rains. The Médoc's Cabernet Sauvignon was not yet ripe, but how much water could it take? By the end of September, the amount of rainfall in the Médoc was virtually the same as had fallen in 1994, an interesting statistic to remember as readers peruse my tasting notes. The Cabernet Franc harvest was completed after the heavy rainfall of late September and early October. In the Médoc, the Cabernet Sauvignon harvest continued until mid-October. Another important statistic to remember is that except for October 3, 6, and 7, rain, sometimes heavy, fell every day from October 1–12. By the time the weather cleared on October 13, there was little unharvested Cabernet Sauvignon left in the Médoc.

Yields in Pomerol were relatively small (between 25–40 hectoliters per hectare), and in the Médoc, around 50 hectoliters per hectare. All things considered, this would appear to be a year in which the top appellations have produced less wine than 1997, 1996, 1995, or, for that matter, 1994.

The northern Médoc (St.-Julien, Pauillac, and St.-Estèphe) has so many superstar estates it is usually the source for a bevy of terrific wines, even in difficult vintages. Certainly there are good Médocs in 1998, but these areas represent the most uninspiring appellations of the vintage. If readers were to buy on color alone, they would invest huge sums in the 1998 northern Médocs since they are all well-colored wines (the influence of modern technology and the grapes' thick skins). However, the wines lack fat, charm, and are often exceedingly tannic with pinched/compressed personalities. They possess plenty of grip and a boatload of tannin, but are irrefutably inferior to the Médocs of 1996 and 1995. Moreover, most of them lack the charm of the finest 1997s. This is not to say that some fine wines won't emerge, but the Médoc is the least impressive region of 1998. However, several qualitative titans did emerge, i.e., Lafite Rothschild and Mouton Rothschild.

In the southern Médoc, particularly the appellation of Margaux (usually the most disappointing area for high-quality wines), the wines are more complete with sweeter tannin and riper fruit. There are few great wines, but there are many good ones. Many châteaux that have been beaten up by my critical prose over recent years have turned in competent performances. Overall, it appears that the area's finer drainage served these vineyards well.

South of Bordeaux, in Pessac-Léognan, 1998 is a superb year. Some of the most elegant, complete wines of the vintage were produced in Pessac-Léognan, and the appellation's most precocious *terroirs* (Haut-Brion, La Mission Haut-Brion, Pape-Clément) were favored by the early ripening Merlot and the excellent weather during the first three weeks of September. The dry white wines of Graves and Pessac-Léognan are also very good, but, paradoxically, only a handful have proven to be exceptional.

There is plenty of excitement in St.-Emilion and Pomerol for this vintage. It does not take a great palate to recognize wines that are often black in color, extremely ripe, thick and rich, yet also tannic. In St.-Emilion, Bordeaux's most exciting appellation given the extraordinary number of sexy wines being produced, there are few disappointments and many superb wines, although a shortage of true superstars.

THE BEST WINES

St.-Estèphe:　Montrose

Pauillac:　Clerc Milon, Grand-Puy-Lacoste, Lafite Rothschild, Latour, Mouton Rothschild, Pichon-Longueville Baron

St.-Julien: Ducru-Beaucaillou, Léoville Barton, Léoville Las Cases

Margaux: Kirwan, Malescot St.-Exupéry, Château Margaux, Palmer

Pessac-Léognan/ Les Carmes Haut-Brion, Haut-Brion, Larrivet-Haut-Brion, La
Graves Red: Mission-Haut-Brion, Pape-Clément, Smith Haut Lafitte

Pessac-Léognan/ Carbonnieux, Haut-Brion Blanc, Laville Haut-Brion,
Graves White: La Louvière, Pape-Clément, Plantiers Haut-Brion, Smith Haut
Lafitte

Pomerol: Le Bon Pasteur, Clinet, Clos l'Église, La Conseillante, La Croix
du Casse, L'Eglise-Clinet, L'Evangile, La Fleur de Gay, La Fleur-
Pétrus, Gazin, La Grave à Pomerol, Lafleur, Latour à Pomerol,
Le Moulin, Nenin, Pétrus, Trotanoy, Vieux Château Certan

St.-Emilion: Angelus, Ausone, Barde-Haut, Beau Séjour Bécot, Canon-la-
Gaffelière, Cheval Blanc, Clos Dubreuil, Clos de l'Oratoire, Clos
St.-Martin, Clos de Sarpe, La Clusière, La Couspaude, Croix de
Labrie, La Dominique, Faugères, Ferrand Lartigue, Figeac, La
Fleur de Jaugue, La Gomerie, Gracia, Grand Mayne, Les Grandes
Murailles, Magdelaine, Monbousquet, La Mondotte, Pavie, Pavie
Decesse, Pavie Macquin, Péby Faugères, Quinault l'Enclos, Rol
Valentin, Le Tertre-Rôteboeuf, Troplong Mondot, Valandraud,
Vieux-Château Chauvin

Barsac/Sauternes: Climens, Lafaurie-Péyraguey, Raymond-Lafon, Rieussec,
Suduiraut, La Tour-Blanche

1997—A Quick Study
(9-5-1998)

St.-Estèphe**	Graves Red***
Pauillac***	Graves White**
St.-Julien***	Pomerol***
Margaux***	St.-Emilion***
Médoc/Haut-Médoc Crus Bourgeois**	Barsac/Sauternes***

Size: An exceptionally abundant vintage, but slightly less than in 1996 and 1995.

Important information: A seductive, user-friendly, soft (low acidity/high pH) vintage
that will have broad appeal because of the wines' precociousness and evolved personalities. Most wines will have to be drunk during their first decade of life, by
2007–2010.

Maturity status: A quickly evolving vintage that, except for the most concentrated
wines, will be over the hill by 2012.

Price: Prices for 1997 Bordeaux wine futures were preposterously high when released.
Despite the talk of dropping prices in view of the fact that the vintage was less successful than the very high-priced vintages of 1996 and 1995, most producers in-

creased prices, justified, they said, because of the unprecedented ruthless selections they made in order to put good wine in the bottle. Consumers throughout the world failed to be impressed. The 1997s continue to be found in the discount bins.

There can be no doubt that this is a good vintage. Stylistically, the wines, whether Merlot or Cabernet Sauvignon–based, are characterized by good ripeness (often an element of overripeness is present), extremely low acidity, high pHs, and juicy personalities with sweet tannin and an easily appreciated, friendly style. While exceptions exist, some concentrated, long-lived wines were produced; this is a vintage that will require consumption at a relatively early age. Almost all the best Petits Châteaux, Crus Bourgeois, and lesser cru classé wines already offer delicious drinking and should be consumed by 2005. The top classified growths, particularly those estates that produced bigger, more dense wines, will last until 2010–2012.

In contrast to 1996, where the Cabernet Sauvignon–dominated wines were clearly superior to the Merlot-based wines, no appellation stands out in 1997 as being superior to any other. The Pomerols are often as good as their 1996 counterparts and there is a bevy of tasty 1997 St.-Emilions, but soft, open-knit, supple-textured, somewhat diffuse wines are commonplace in every appellation. After considerable reflection over which vintage 1997 could be compared to, I found it impossible to find a similar vintage in my 25 years of tasting Bordeaux. Most 1997s are not "big," muscular wines, but rather graceful, seductive wines full of charm and elegance, yet somewhat fragile. I believe this vintage will be ideal for restaurants and consumers looking for immediate gratification.

In conclusion, I think everyone who enjoys a good glass of wine will find the 1997s attractive. Readers are unlikely to be knocked out by their depth or flavor intensity, but they are well-made, soft, user-friendly wines that are highly complementary to such vintages as 2001, 2000, 1996, 1995, and 1994, all tannic years that require significant bottle age. If there is a problem with 1997, it is the 1999s, a similarly styled vintage that produced a number of more complete wines.

The 1997 vintage began auspiciously. Temperatures in late March were in the mid-80s and even hit 90°F on occasion, making many think it was late June rather than March. This hot weather jump-started the vineyards, causing a roaring vegetative cycle. The flowering occurred at the earliest dates on record, leading many châteaux to conclude that the harvest would be well under way by mid-August.

The flowering hit a few glitches and tended to drag on for nearly a month, always a bad sign. The irregular flowering and thus a subsequent uneven ripening of the grapes were problems that became increasingly exacerbated by the unusual pattern of summer weather. The weather was hot at the beginning of June, but it cooled off and became very wet later in the month. July was abnormal. Usually a torridly hot month in Bordeaux, in 1997 it was cool yet humid. By the end of July, high pressure had settled in and the weather became sultry. July was followed by unusual tropical-like weather in August, with record-breaking levels of humidity as well as high temperatures. Despite extensive crop thinning and leaf pulling by well-run châteaux, the prolonged flowering, unusual end of June, and tropical August (growers said it felt more like

Bangkok than Bordeaux) created severe uneven ripening within each grape bunch. The most-heard complaint was that within each bunch of grapes there were red grapes, green grapes, and rosé colored grapes—a nightmare scenario for growers.

The incredibly early spring, bud break, and flowering did result in some Pessac-Léognan properties harvesting (in full view of the nation's television cameras) their white wine grapes as early as August 18. This made 1997 an "earlier" vintage than the legendary year of 1893. Just after the beginning of the harvest for the whites, the hot tropical weather deteriorated and a succession of weather depressions buffeted Bordeaux. From August 25 through September 1, sizable quantities of rain fell throughout the region. Many 1997s are soft with low acidity, but without the great concentration and density. One need not be a nuclear physicist to understand the taste of wines made from bloated grapes. Producers who panicked and began picking in early September, fearing the onset of rot and further weather deterioration, made the vintage's least successful wines. However, those who had the intestinal fortitude/discipline to wait were rewarded with a fabulous finish to the month of September. Aside from a few scattered rain showers on the 12 and 13, it was one of the driest, sunniest Septembers last century. The later a producer was able to wait, the more the vines and, subsequently, the wine benefitted.

Virtually all of the Merlot was picked from September 2–23. The Cabernet Franc was harvested between mid-September and early October. The Cabernet Sauvignon harvest began slowly in mid-September but lasted even longer, with some producers waiting until mid-October to harvest their last Cabernet Sauvignon parcels.

One of the more intriguing statistics about this unusual weather pattern is the extraordinary hang-time the grapes enjoyed between the date of flowering and the harvest date. In Bordeaux, the general rule is that if the producer can get 110 days between flowering and harvest, they will harvest mature grapes. In 1997, it was not bizarre for the Merlot vineyards to be harvested 115–125 days after flowering. For the Cabernet Sauvignon, a whopping 140 days was not an unusual hang-time. Normally this would be a sign of extraordinary flavor concentration, but the weather at the end of August precluded the possibility of this vintage being great.

THE BEST WINES

St.-Estèphe: Cos d'Estournel, Montrose

Pauillac: Lafite Rothschild, Latour, Lynch-Bages, Mouton Rothschild, Pichon-Longueville Baron

St.-Julien: Branaire Ducru, Gloria, Gruaud Larose, Lagrange, Léoville Barton, Léoville Las Cases, Léoville Poyferré, Talbot

Margaux: d'Angludet, Château Margaux

Médoc/Haut-Médoc
Crus Bourgeois: Sociando-Mallet

Graves Red: Les Carmes Haut-Brion, Domaine de Chevalier, Haut-Brion, Pape-Clément, Smith Haut Lafitte

Graves White: Domaine de Chevalier, de Fieuzal, Haut-Brion, Laville Haut-Brion, Smith Haut Lafitte

Pomerol: Clinet, Clos l'Église, L'Eglise-Clinet, L'Evangile, La Fleur-Pétrus, Lafleur, Pétrus, Le Pin, Trotanoy

St.-Emilion: Angelus, Ausone, Cheval Blanc, Clos de l'Oratoire, Faugères, Gracia, Les Grandes Murailles, L'Hermitage, Monbousquet, La Mondotte, Moulin St. Georges, Pavie Decesse, Pavie Macquin, Troplong Mondot, Valandraud

Barsac/Sauternes: Climens, Coutet, Guiraud, Lafaurie-Péyraguey, Raymond-Lafon, Rieussec, Suduiraut, La Tour-Blanche, Château d'Yquem

1996—A Quick Study
(9-16-1996)

St.-Estèphe*****	Graves Red****
Pauillac*****	Graves White***
St.-Julien*****	Pomerol***
Margaux****	St.-Emilion***
Médoc/Haut-Médoc Crus Bourgeois***	Barsac/Sauternes****

Size: An exceptionally large crop.

Important information: The most expensive young Bordeaux vintage until 2000 broke all records, with opening prices 50–100% above the opening future prices of the 1995s. This is a great vintage for the Médoc and Cabernet Sauvignon–based wines. Elsewhere caution is the operative word, although there are many fine Graves.

Maturity status: The powerful Cabernet Sauvignon–based wines of the Médoc will be more accessible than 1986, the vintage 1996 most closely resembles, but in general, the wines require 10–15 years of cellaring following bottling. The wines from Graves and the right bank will be more accessible at a younger age and should be drinkable by 7–10 years of age.

Price: As indicated, this is a very expensive vintage offered in 1997 at record-breaking prices, yet nearly a decade after the vintage, prices have not moved. The finest Médocs actually look like bargains compared to 2000 prices.

Most of Bordeaux's greatest years have been the product of exceptionally hot, dry summers, with below-average rainfall and above-average temperatures. While a number of last century's celebrated vintages have had moderate amounts of rain in September, unless a significant quantity falls, the affect on quality has usually been minor.

Given the number of high-quality Cabernet Sauvignon–based wines produced in 1996, Bordeaux's weather from March through mid-October was decidedly unusual. The winter of 1996 was wet and mild. When I arrived on March 19, 1996, I thought it was mid-June rather than March given the blast of heat the region was experiencing.

This heat wave lasted the entire 12 days I was there. Many growers predicted an early flowering and, consequently, an early harvest. The heat wave broke in early April with a cold period followed by another burst of surprisingly high temperatures in mid-April. Atypically, the month of May was relatively cool.

When I returned to France for 17 days in mid-June, the country was experiencing blazingly torrid temperatures in the 90°+ range. This made for a quick and generally uniform flowering. In Bordeaux, most estates were thrilled with the flowering that took only 3–4 days, rather than the usual 7–10. The cold spell that hit during the end of May and the beginning of June caused severe *millerandange* (the failure of a vine to fully set its entire bunch, thus reducing yields) for the warmer *terroirs* on the plateau of Pomerol. By the end of June, a large, precocious crop was anticipated. Except for the reduced crop size in Pomerol, viticulturally speaking, things could not have looked better. But then the weather turned unusually bizarre.

While the period between July 11 and August 19 was relatively normal (statistically it was slightly cooler and wetter than usual), the first 11 days of July and the period between August 25 and 30 received abnormally huge quantities of rainfall, in addition to below-normal temperatures. Statistics can be misleading, as evidenced by the fact that while the normal amount of rainfall for Bordeaux during the month of August is just more than 2 inches (53 millimeters), in 1996 the quantity of rainfall that fell was a whopping 6 inches (150 millimeters). Yet the heaviest rainfall was localized, with more than 4 inches falling on Entre-deux-Mers and St.-Emilion, 2 inches on Margaux, 1.75 inches on St.-Julien, 1.5 inches on Pauillac, and less than an inch in St.-Estèphe and the northern Médoc. I remember telephoning several friends in Bordeaux around Labor Day weekend in America and receiving conflicting viewpoints about the prospects for the 1996 vintage. Those in the southern Graves and on the right bank were obviously distressed, expressing concern that the vintage was going to be a disaster along the lines of 1974. They hoped that a miraculous September would turn it into a 1988 or 1978. In contrast, those in the Médoc, especially from St.-Julien north, were optimistic, sensing that a good month of September would result in a terrific vintage. The large quantities of rain that had bloated the grapes to the south and east had largely missed the Médoc. The below-average quantity of rain the Médoc did receive kept the vines flourishing, as opposed to shutting down photosynthesis as a result of excessive heat and drought, as had occurred in 1995 and 1989.

Large quantities of early September rain had been a pernicious problem in 1991, 1992, 1993, 1994, and, to a lesser extent, 1995, but this climatic pattern would not repeat itself in 1996. Between August 31 and September 18 there was a remarkable string of 18 sunny days, followed by light showers throughout the region on September 18 and 19. There were several days of clear weather, then drizzle on September 21, and finally, the arrival of heavy rains the evening of September 24 that lasted through September 25.

Another important characteristic of this period between August 31 and September 24 was the omnipresent gusty, dry, easterly and northeasterly winds that played a paramount role in drying the vineyards after the late-August rains. Moreover, these winds were consistently cited by producers as being responsible for the sugar accumulating at rates that seemed impossible at the end of August. Another beneficial aspect to this windy period was that any potential for rot was minimalized by Mother Nature's anti-biotic.

The Merlot harvest took place during the last two weeks of September. The Caber-net Franc was harvested during late September and the first 4–5 days of October. The later-ripening, thicker-skinned Cabernet Sauvignon grapes were harvested between the end of September and October 12. Except for a good-sized rainfall throughout the region on October 4, the weather in October was sunny and dry, offering textbook con-ditions for harvesting Cabernet Sauvignon. In fact, most Médoc producers saw a dis-tinct parallel between the Cabernet Sauvignon harvest in 1996 and that of 1986. While rain had marred the 1986 harvest for the early ripening varietals (i.e., Merlot and Cabernet Franc), it stopped, to be followed by a nearly perfect four weeks of dry, windy, sunny weather during which the Cabernet Sauvignon harvest took place under ideal conditions.

Given this weather pattern, it is not surprising that most of 1996's finest wines emerged from the Médoc, which harvested Cabernet 10–18 days later than vineyards having high proportions of Merlot.

As was expected from the highly successful flowering during the torrid month of June, the 1996 Bordeaux harvest produced an abundant crop (6.5 million hectoliters), which is marginally below the 1995 crop size (6.89 million hectoliters). However, read-ers should recognize that the production of some of the top Pomerol estates, especially those on the plateau, was off by 30–50%. In St.-Emilion, many estates produced 10–15% less wine than normal. Most of the top Médoc estates produced from 45–55 hectoliters per hectare, about 20–30% less than their 1986 yields.

THE BEST WINES

St.-Estèphe: Calon-Ségur, Cos d'Estournel, Haut-Marbuzet, Lafon-Rochet, Montrose

Pauillac: d'Armailhac, Batailley, Clerc Milon, Duhart-Milon, Grand-Puy-Lacoste, Haut-Batailley, Lafite Rothschild, Latour, Lynch-Bages, Mouton Rothschild, Pichon-Longueville Baron, Pichon Longueville Comtesse de Lalande, Pontet-Canet

St.-Julien: Branaire Ducru, Ducru-Beaucaillou, Gloria, Gruaud Larose, Lagrange, Léoville Barton, Léoville Las Cases, Léoville Poyferré, Talbot

Margaux: d'Angludet, d'Issan, Kirwan, Maléscot-St Exupèry, Château Margaux, Palmer, Rauzan-Ségla , du Tertre

Médoc/Haut-Médoc Crus Bourgeois: Cantemerle, Charmail, La Lagune, Lanessan, Sociando-Mallet

Graves Red: Les Carmes Haut-Brion, Haut-Bailly, Haut-Brion, La Mission Haut-Brion, Pape-Clément, Smith Haut Lafitte, La Tour Haut-Brion

Graves White: de Fieuzal, Haut-Brion, Laville Haut-Brion, Pape-Clément, Smith Haut Lafitte

Pomerol: Beau Soleil, Le Bon Pasteur, Clinet, La Conseillante, La Croix du Casse, L'Eglise-Clinet, L'Evangile, La Fleur de Gay, La Fleur-Pétrus, Gazin, Lafleur, Latour à Pomerol, Pétrus, Le Pin, Trotanoy, Vieux Château Certan

St.-Emilion: Angelus, L'Arrosée, Ausone, Beau Séjour Bécot, Beauséjour, Canon-la-Gaffelière, Cheval Blanc, Clos Fourtet, Clos de l'Oratoire, La Couspaude, La Dominique, Ferrand Lartigue, La Gaffelière, La Gomerie, Grand Mayne, Grand-Pontet, Larmande, Monbousquet, La Mondotte, Moulin St. Georges, Pavie Macquin, Rol Valentin, Le Tertre-Rôteboeuf, Troplong Mondot, Trotte Vieille, Valandraud

Barsac/Sauternes: Climens, Coutet, Guiraud, Lafaurie-Péyraguey, Rieussec, Suduiraut, La Tour-Blanche, Château d'Yquem

1995—A Quick Study
(9-20-1996)

St.-Estèphe****	Graves Red****
Pauillac****	Graves White***
St.-Julien****	Pomerol*****
Margaux****	St.-Emilion****
Médoc/Haut-Médoc Crus Bourgeois***	Barsac/Sauternes**

Size: Another huge harvest, just short of the record-setting crop of 1986. However, most major châteaux crop-thinned, and yields were more modest. In addition to crop-thinning, the selection process of the top first growths, super-seconds, and quality-oriented châteaux was severe, resulting in far less wine being produced under the grand vin label.

Important information: The most consistent vintage between 1990 and 2000. Almost all the major appellations turned in dense, tannic wines of uniform quality.

Maturity status: While it has been reported that the highly successful 1995 Merlot crop resulted in precocious wines meant to be consumed immediately, all of my tastings have revealed that while the Merlot is undoubtedly successful, the Cabernet Sauvignon and Cabernet Franc produced wines with considerable weight, tannin, and structure. Although there are obvious exceptions, most of the finest 1995 Bordeaux are classic *vin de garde* wines with considerable tannin and require bottle age. The big wines are not close to full maturity, and won't be prior to 2008–2012. These will be very long-lived wines and slow to reveal their character . . . a modern-day 1995?

Price: A very expensive Bordeaux vintage, both as futures and in the bottle. But in 2003, prices have not moved since the futures offerings of 1996.

June, July, and August made the 1995 vintage as they were among the driest and hottest months in the last 40 years. However, like its four predecessors, 1994, 1993, 1992, and 1991, the Bordelais could not get past the first week of September without the deterioration of weather conditions. Unlike 1993 and 1994, the showery weather lasted only from September 7–19, rather than the entire month as it had in 1994, 1993, and 1992 and, to a lesser extent, 1991. Unlike the record rainfall of 275 millimeters in September 1992, and 175 millimeters in September 1994, only 145 millimeters fell in September 1995. In the northern Médoc communes of St.-Julien, Pauillac, and Pomerol, the amount of rain ranged from 91–134 millimeters.

While it was a huge harvest, the key to the most successful 1995s appears to have been a severe selection once the wines had finished alcoholic and malolactic fermentations. The Merlot was certainly ripe, but this was the first vintage since 1990 where the Cabernet Sauvignon (at least the late-harvested Cabernet) enjoyed phenolic maturity. Most of the châteaux that delayed their harvest until late September were rewarded with physiologically mature Cabernet Sauvignon.

THE BEST WINES

St.-Estèphe: Calon-Ségur, Cos d'Estournel, Cos Labory, Lafon-Rochet, Montrose

Pauillac: d'Armailhac, Clerc Milon, Grand-Puy-Lacoste, Haut-Batailley, Lafite Rothschild, Latour, Lynch-Bages, Mouton Rothschild, Pichon-Longueville Baron, Pichon Longueville Comtesse de Lalande, Pontet-Canet

St.-Julien: Branaire Ducru, Ducru-Beaucaillou, Gloria, Gruaud Larose, Lagrange, Léoville Barton, Léoville Las Cases, Léoville Poyferré, Talbot

Margaux: d'Angludet, Malescot St.-Exupéry, Château Margaux, Palmer, Rauzan-Ségla

Médoc/Haut-Médoc
Crus Bourgeois: Charmail, La Lagune, Sociando-Mallet

Graves Red: de Fieuzal, Haut-Bailly, Haut-Brion, La Mission Haut-Brion, Pape-Clément, Smith Haut Lafitte, La Tour Haut-Brion

Graves White: de Fieuzal, Haut-Brion, Laville Haut-Brion, Pape-Clément, Smith Haut Lafitte

Pomerol: Le Bon Pasteur, Bourgueneuf, Certan de May, Clinet, La Conseillante, La Croix du Casse, L'Eglise-Clinet, L'Evangile, La Fleur de Gay, La Fleur-Pétrus, Gazin, Grand-Puy-Lacoste, La Grave à Pomerol, Lafleur, Latour à Pomerol, Pétrus, Le Pin, Trotanoy, Vieux Château Certan

St.-Emilion: Angelus, L'Arrosée, Ausone, Beau Séjour Bécot, Canon-la-Gaffelière, Cheval Blanc, Clos Fourtet, Clos de l'Oratoire,

Corbin Michotte, La Couspaude, La Dominique, Ferrand Lartigue, Figeac, La Fleur de Jaugue, La Gomerie, Grand Mayne, Grand-Pontet, Larmande, Magdelaine, Monbousquet, Moulin St. Georges, Pavie Macquin, Le Tertre-Rôteboeuf, Troplong Mondot, Valandraud

Barsac/Sauternes: Climens, Château d'Yquem

1994—A Quick Study
(9-24-1994)

St.-Estèphe***	Graves Red****
Pauillac***	Graves White*****
St.-Julien***	Pomerol****
Margaux***	St.-Emilion***
Médoc/Haut-Médoc Crus Bourgeois**	Barsac/Sauternes*

Size: Another exceptionally large Bordeaux crop, however, the top properties had to be exceptionally severe in their selection process in order to bottle only the finest *cuvées* under the grand vin label. Consequently, production of the top estates is relatively modest.

Important information: A hot, dry summer provided the potential for a great vintage, but the weather deteriorated in September and a massive 175 millimeters (7 inches) of rain fell from September 7–29. Producers who were unwilling to declassify 30–50% of their harvest were incapable of making quality wines. Those who did enjoyed success. Merlot was the most successful grape in this inconsistent vintage. Even the Médoc châteaux employed a higher percentage of Merlot in their final blend to counterbalance the Cabernet Sauvignon, which had a tendency to be austere and herbaceous, with very high tannin. Another key to understanding 1994 is that the best drained vineyards (those laying next to the Gironde in the Médoc and Graves) tended to produce very good wines, assuming they made a strict selection.

Maturity status: Most 1994s have been slow to evolve given their relatively high tannin levels. This is a classic *vin de garde* vintage with the top wines being well colored and quite structured and powerful. They require additional bottle age. The worry is that many of them, especially in the Médoc, will always remain too astringent à la 1975.

Price: Prices appear to be high for the vintage's potential, but increasing consumer skepticism has resulted in the finest wines being relative bargains in 2003.

At the top level, 1994 has produced some excellent wines, with far higher peaks of quality than 1993. However, some wines have not fared well since bottling, with the fragile fruit stripped out by excessive fining and filtration. As a result, the more negative characteristics, a hollowness and high level of harsh tannin, are well displayed. The 1994 could have been an exceptional vintage had it not rained, at times heavily, for 13 days between September 7 and September 29. As is so often the case with a vintage that enjoyed three months of superb weather during the summer only to be negatively impacted by excessive rain before and during the harvest, the willingness of the producer to declassify 30–50% of the harvest was often the difference between producing a high-quality wine and one that is out of balance.

The overall characteristic of the 1994s is a backwardness, caused in large part by the high tannin levels. Yet the vintage's successes possess the fruit and extract necessary to balance out the tannin. Those who failed to make a strict selection or had too little Merlot to flesh out and counterbalance the more austere Cabernet Sauvignon have turned out dry, hard, lean, and attenuated wines. 1994 is unquestionably an irregular vintage and is often frustrating to taste. Shrewd buyers will find a number of excellent wines, but this is a vintage where cautious selection is mandatory.

In 1994, much like 1993, the most favored appellations were those that either had a high percentage of Merlot planted or had exceptionally well-drained soils. As in 1993, Pomerol appears once again to have been the most favored region. However, that is not a blanket endorsement of all Pomerols, as there are disappointments. The Graves and Médoc estates close to the Gironde, with gravelly, deep, stony, exceptionally well-drained soils, also had the potential to produce well-balanced wines. However, it was essential in 1994, particularly in the Médoc, to eliminate a considerable quantity of the crop (the top estates eliminated 30–50% or more) and to utilize a higher percentage of Merlot in the final blend. Moreover, the wines had to be bottled "softly," without excessive fining and filtering, which will eviscerate flavors and body.

THE BEST WINES

St.-Estèphe: Cos d'Estournel, Lafon-Rochet, Montrose

Pauillac: Clerc Milon, Grand-Puy-Lacoste, Lafite Rothschild, Latour, Lynch-Bages, Mouton Rothschild, Pichon-Longueville Baron, Pichon Longueville Comtesse de Lalande, Pontet-Canet

St.-Julien: Branaire Ducru, Ducru-Beaucaillou, Lagrange, Léoville Barton, Léoville Las Cases, Léoville Poyferré

Margaux: Maléscot-St Exupèry, Château Margaux

Médoc/Haut-Médoc
Cru Bourgeois: Sociando-Mallet

Graves Red: Bahans Haut-Brion, Haut-Bailly, Haut-Brion, La Mission Haut-Brion, Pape-Clément, Smith Haut Lafitte

Graves White: Domaine de Chevalier, de Fieuzal, Haut-Brion, Laville Haut-Brion, Pape-Clément, Smith Haut Lafitte, La Tour-Martillac

Pomerol: Beauregard, Le Bon Pasteur, Clinet, La Conseillante, La Croix du Casse, La Croix de Gay, L'Eglise-Clinet, L'Evangile, La Fleur de Gay, Gazin, Lafleur, Pétrus, Le Pin

St.-Emillion: Angelus, L'Arrosée, Beau Séjour Bécot, Beauséjour, Canon-la-Gaffelière, Cheval Blanc, Clos Fourtet,

La Dominique, Ferrand Lartigue, Grand-Pontet, Monbousquet, Pavie Macquin, Le Tertre-Rôteboeuf, Troplong Mondot, Valandraud

Barsac/Sauternes: none

1993—A Quick Study
(9-26-1993)

St.-Estèphe**	Graves Red***
Pauillac**	Graves White***
St.-Julien**	Pomerol***
Margaux*	St.-Emilion**
Médoc/Haut-Médoc Crus Bourgeois*	Barsac/Sauternes*

Size: A very large crop.

Important information: Another vintage conceived under deplorable weather conditions. However, the vintage offers a number of pleasant surprises: It has produced more attractive Clarets than either 1992 or 1991.

Maturity status: The finest wines should continue to drink well through the next 5–8 years (2008–2011).

Price: The last reasonably priced vintage of the 1990s still available in the marketplace, the 1993s came out at low prices and have remained essentially reasonably priced.

In some quarters, 1993 has been written off as a terrible vintage due to the enormous amount of September rainfall. The amount of rainfall in 1991 and 1992 was frightfully high, but what fell in and around Bordeaux in September 1993, broke a 30-year average rainfall record by an astonishing 303%! For this reason it was easy to conclude that no one could have possibly made good wine. Moreover, the spring weather was equally atrocious, with significant rainfall in both April and June.

However, July was warmer than normal and August was exceptionally hot and sunny. In fact, before the weather deteriorated on September 6, the proprietors were beginning to think that an exceptional vintage was attainable. The September rain destroyed this optimism, but because of exceptionally cold, dry weather between the deluges, the rot that growers feared the most did not occur. Most châteaux harvested when they could, finishing around mid-October.

The better wines of 1993 suggest it is a deeply colored, richer, potentially better vintage than either 1992 or 1991. The wines can be characterized as deeply colored, with an unripe, weedy Cabernet Sauvignon character, good structure, more depth and length than expected, and some evidence of dilution.

THE BEST WINES

St.-Estèphe:　Cos d'Estournel, Montrose

Pauillac:　Clerc Milon, Latour, Mouton Rothschild

St.-Julien:　Lagrange, Léoville Barton, Léoville Las Cases, Léoville Poyferré

Margaux:　Château Margaux

Médoc/Haut-Médoc
Cru Bourgeois:　Sociando-Mallet

Graves Red:　de Fieuzal, Haut-Bailly, Haut-Brion, La Mission Haut-Brion, Smith Haut Lafitte, La Tour Haut-Brion

Graves White:　Haut-Brion, Laville Haut-Brion, Smith Haut Lafitte

Pomerol:　Beaurégard, Le Bon Pasteur, Clinet, La Conseillante, L'Eglise-Clinet, L'Evangile, La Fleur de Gay, Gazin, Lafleur, Latour à Pomerol, Pétrus, Le Pin, Trotanoy

St.-Emilion:　Angelus, L'Arrosée, Beau Séjour Bécot, Beauséjour, Canon-la-Gaffelière, Cheval Blanc, La Dominique, Grand-Pontet, Pavie Macquin, Le Tertre-Rôteboeuf, Troplong Mondot, Valandraud

Barsac/Sauternes:　none

1992—A Quick Study
(9-29-1992)

St.-Estèphe**	Graves Red**
Pauillac**	Graves White***
St.-Julien**	Pomerol***
Margaux*	St.-Emilion**
Médoc/Haut-Médoc Crus Bourgeois*	Barsac/Sauternes*

Size: A large crop was harvested, but the top properties implemented a ruthless selection. Consequently, quantities of the top wines were modest.

Important information: At the top level, the 1992s are pleasantly soft, yet even the finest wines had trouble avoiding the taste of dilution and herbaceousness from the excessive amounts of rain that fell before and during the harvest.

Maturity status: Most 1992s should be drunk by 2005.

Price: Because of the vintage's poor to mediocre reputation, prices are very low. The real value of this vintage is that many of the first growths could be purchased for $35–40, and the second through fifth growths for $15–25 . . . remarkably low prices in the overheated Bordeaux wine market.

The 1992 vintage was not marked by a tragic frost as in 1991, but, rather, by excessive rainfall at the worst possible time. Following a precocious spring, with an abundance of humidity and warm weather, the flowering of the vines occurred eight days earlier than the 30-year average, raising hopes of an early harvest. The summer was exceptionally hot, with June wet and warm, July slightly above normal in temperature, and August well-above normal. However, unlike such classic hot, dry years as 1990, 1989, and 1982, there was significant rainfall (more than three times the normal amount) in August. For example, 193 millimeters of rain were reported in the Bordeaux area in August 1992 (most of it falling during several violent storms the last two days of the month), compared to 22 millimeters in 1990 and 63 millimeters in 1989.

By mid-August, it was evident that the harvest would be enormous. For the serious estates, it was imperative that crop thinning be employed to reduce the crop size. Properties that crop-thinned produced wines with more richness than the light, diluted offerings of those that did not.

The first two weeks of September were dry, although abnormally cool. During this period the Sauvignon and Sémillon were harvested under ideal conditions, which explains the excellent and sometimes outstanding success (despite high yields) of the 1992 white Graves.

From September 20 through most of October the weather was unfavorable, with considerable rain interspersed with short periods of clear weather. The harvest for the majority of estates took place over a long period of time, although most of the Merlot crop from both sides of the Gironde was harvested during three days of clear, dry weather on September 29, 30, and October 1. Between October 2 and October 6, more violent rain storms lashed the region, and the châteaux, realizing nothing could be gained from waiting, harvested under miserable weather conditions. To make good wine it was essential to hand-pick the grapes, leaving the damaged, diseased fruit on the vine. An even stricter selection was necessary in the cellars.

Overall, 1992 is a more successful vintage than 1991 because no appellation produced a high percentage of poor wines, such as happened in Pomerol and St.-Emilion in 1991. The 1992s are the modern-day equivalents of the 1973s. But with better vinification techniques, stricter selection, better equipment, and more attention to yields, the top properties produced 1992s that are more concentrated, richer, and overall better wines than the best 1973s, or, for that matter, the 1987s. All the 1992s tend to be soft, fruity, and low in acidity, with light to moderate tannin levels and moderate to good concentration.

The appellation that appears to have fared best is Pomerol. Certainly the top properties of the firm of Jean-Pierre Moueix crop-thinned severely. In the case of their two flagship estates, Trotanoy and Pétrus, Christian Moueix boldly employed an innovative technique, covering these two vineyards with black plastic at the beginning of September. The heavy rains that subsequently fell accumulated on the plastic and ran off instead of saturating the soil. I have seen photographs of this elaborate, costly endeavor and, after tasting the wines, I can say that Moueix's daring and brilliance paid off. Trotanoy and Pétrus are two of the three most concentrated wines of the vintage, confirming that the incredible amount of labor required to cover the 21-acre Trotanoy vineyard and 28-acre Pétrus vineyard with the black plastic was well worth the effort. The irony of their endeavor is that this technique was declared illegal by the INAO eight years later.

Elsewhere there are successes and failures in every appellation, with no real consistency to be found. Those properties that were attentive to the enormous crop size and crop-thinned, who were lucky enough to complete part of their harvest before the deluge of October 2–6, and discarded any questionable grapes, have turned out fruity, soft, charming wines that will have to be drunk in large part prior to 2005.

THE BEST WINES

St.-Estèphe: Haut-Marbuzet, Montrose

Pauillac: Lafite Rothschild, Latour, Pichon-Longueville Baron

St.-Julien: Ducru-Beaucaillou, Gruaud Larose, Léoville Barton, Léoville Las Cases

Margaux: Giscours, Château Margaux, Palmer, Rauzan-Ségla

Médoc/Haut-Médoc
Crus Bourgeois: none

Graves Red: Carbonnieux, Haut-Bailly, Haut-Brion, La Louvière, La Mission Haut-Brion, Smith Haut Lafitte

Graves White: Domaine de Chevalier, de Fieuzal, Haut-Brion, Laville Haut-Brion, Smith Haut Lafitte

Pomerol: Le Bon Pasteur, Certan de May, Clinet, La Conseillante, L'Eglise-Clinet, L'Evangile, La Fleur de Gay, La Fleur-Pétrus, Gazin, Lafleur, Pétrus

St.-Emilion: Angelus, L'Arrosée, Beauséjour, Canon, Fonroque, Magdelaine, Troplong Mondot, Valandraud

Barsac/Sauternes: none

1991—A Quick Study
(9-30-1991)

St.-Estèphe**	Graves White 0
Pauillac**	Pomerol 0
St.-Julien**	St.-Emilion 0
Margaux*	Barsac/Sauternes**
Graves Red**	

Size: A very small crop, largely because the killer freeze during the weekend of April 20–21 destroyed most of the crop in Pomerol and St.-Emilion.

Important information: A disaster in the right bank appellations of Pomerol and St.-Emilion, but the quality improves as one proceeds north in the Médoc. Some surprisingly pleasant, even good wines were produced in Pauillac, St.-Estèphe, and occasionally in the Graves.

Maturity status: The wines have matured quickly and should be drunk by 2004.

Price: Because of the vintage's terrible reputation, this has always been an easily affordable, low-priced vintage.

This was the year of the big freeze. During the weekend of April 20–21, temperatures dropped as low as –9°C destroying most vineyard's first generation buds. The worst destruction occurred in Pomerol and St.-Emilion, east of the Gironde. Less damage occurred in the northern Médoc, especially in the northeastern sector of Pauillac and the southern half of St.-Estèphe. The spring that followed the devastating freeze did see the development of new buds, called second generation fruit by viticulturists.

Because the crop size was expected to be small, optimists began to suggest that 1991 could resemble 1961 (a great year shaped by a spring killer frost that reduced the crop size). Of course, all of this hope was based on the assumption that the weather remain sunny and dry during the growing season. By the time September arrived, most estates realized that the Merlot harvest could not begin until late September and the Cabernet Sauvignon harvest in mid-October. The second generation fruit had retarded most vineyards' harvest schedules, yet sunny skies in late September gave hope for another 1978-ish "miracle year." Then, on September 25, an Atlantic storm dumped 116 millimeters of rain, precisely twice the average rainfall for the entire month!

Between September 30 and October 12 the weather was generally dry. Most of the Merlot vineyards on the right bank (Pomerol and St.-Emilion) were harvested during this period as quickly as possible. In Pomerol and St.-Emilion there was significant dilution, some rot, and unripe grapes. In the Médoc much of the Cabernet Sauvignon was not yet fully ripe, but many estates recognized that it was too risky to wait any longer. Those estates that harvested between October 13 and 19, before the outbreak of six consecutive days of heavy rain (another 120 millimeters), picked unripe but surprisingly healthy and low-acid Cabernet Sauvignon. Those properties that had not harvested by the time the second deluge arrived were unable to make quality wine.

The 1991 vintage is a poor, frequently disastrous year for most estates in Pomerol and St.-Emilion. I find it inferior to 1984, making it the worst vintage for these two appellations since the appalling 1969s. Many well-known estates in Pomerol and St.-Emilion completely declassified their wines, including such renowned St.-Emilion estates as L'Arrosée, Ausone, Canon, Cheval Blanc, La Dominique, and Magdelaine. In Pomerol, several good wines were somehow made, but overall it was a catastrophe for this tiny appellation. The following Pomerol châteaux are among the better-known properties that declassified their entire crop: Beauregard, Le Bon Pasteur, L'Evangile, Le Gay, La Grave à Pomerol, Lafleur, Latour à Pomerol, Pétrus, Trotanoy, and Vieux Château Certan.

Despite all this bad news, some soft, pleasant, light- to medium-bodied wines did emerge from Graves and those Médoc vineyards adjacent to the Gironde. Consumers will be surprised by the quality of many of these wines, particularly from St.-Julien, Pauillac, and St.-Estèphe. In these northern Médoc appellations, especially those vineyards adjacent to the Gironde, much of the first generation fruit was not destroyed by the frost, resulting in diluted but physiologically riper fruit than second generation fruit produced. However the good wines must be priced low or no consumer interest will be justified.

Because the intelligent properties in the Médoc utilized more Merlot in the blend rather than the unripe Cabernet Sauvignon, the 1991s are soft, forward wines that will need to be drunk in their first decade of life.

THE BEST WINES

St.-Estèphe: Cos d'Estournel, Lafon-Rochet, Montrose

Pauillac: Les Forts de Latour, Grand-Puy-Lacoste, Lafite Rothschild, Latour, Lynch-Bages, Mouton Rothschild, Pichon-Longueville Baron, Pichon Longueville Comtesse de Lalande

St.-Julien: Beychevelle, Branaire Ducru, Clos du Marquis, Ducru-Beaucaillou, Langoa Barton, Léoville Barton, Léoville Las Cases

Margaux: Giscours, Château Margaux, Palmer, Rauzan-Ségla

Graves Red: Carbonnieux, Domaine de Chevalier, Haut-Brion, La Mission Haut-Brion

Graves White: none

Pomerol: Clinet

St.-Emilion: Angelus, Troplong Mondot

Barsac/Sauternes: none

1990—A Quick Study
(9-12-1990)

St.-Estèphe*****   Graves Red****

Pauillac*****   Graves White***

St.-Julien*****   Pomerol*****

Margaux****   St.-Emilion*****

Médoc/Haut-Médoc Crus Bourgeois**** Barsac/Sauternes*****

Size: Enormous; one of the largest crops ever harvested in Bordeaux.

Important information: The hottest year since 1947 and the sunniest year since 1949 caused extraordinary stress in some of the best vineyards in the Graves and Médoc. Consequently, the heavier soils from such appellations as St.-Estèphe, the limestone hillsides and plateau areas of St.-Emilion as well as the Fronsacs excelled, as did those top châteaux that made a severe selection.

Maturity status: Exceptionally low-acid wines, but high yet sweet tannins have consistently suggested early accessibility. The most complete wines have another 20–25

years of longevity, but there is not a wine from this vintage that cannot be drunk with pleasure in 2003.

Price: Opening future prices were down 15–20% below 1989, but no modern-day Bordeaux vintage, with the exception of 1982, has appreciated as much in price as 1990.

Most of the great Bordeaux vintages of the last one hundred years are the result of relatively hot, dry years. For that reason alone, 1990 should elicit considerable attention. The most revealing fact about the 1990 vintage is that it is the second-hottest vintage of the century, barely surpassed by 1947. It is also the second-sunniest vintage, eclipsed only by 1949 in the post–World War II era. The amount of sunshine and the extraordinarily hot summers Bordeaux enjoyed during the 1980s are frequently attributed to the so-called "greenhouse effect" and consequent global warming about which such ominous warnings have been issued by the scientific community. Yet consider the Bordeaux weather for the period from 1945–1949. Amazingly, that era was even more torrid than 1989–1990. (One wonders if there was concern then about the glaciers of the north and south poles melting.)

The weather of 1990 was auspicious because of its potential to produce great wines, but weather is only one part of the equation. The summer months of July and August were the driest since 1961, and August was the hottest since 1928, the year records were first kept. September (the month that most producers claim "makes the quality") was not, weather-wise, a particularly exceptional month. The year 1990 was the second wettest year among the great hot-year vintages, surpassed only by 1989. As in 1989, the rain fell at periods that were cause for concern. For example, on September 15 a particularly violent series of thunderstorms swept across Bordeaux, inundating much of the Graves region. From September 22–23 there was modest rainfall over the entire region. On October 7 and October 15, light showers were reported throughout the region. Most producers claimed the rain in September was beneficial. They argue that the Cabernet Sauvignon grapes were still too small and their skins too thick. Many Cabernet vines had shut down and the grapes refused to mature because of the excessive heat and drought. The rain, the producers suggest, promoted further ripening and alleviated the blocked state of maturity. This is an appealing argument that has merit. While some panicked and harvested too soon after these rain storms, the majority of the top estates got the harvest dates they wanted covered.

When tasting the wines from 1990, the most striking characteristics are their opulence, layered texture, and roasted quality, the latter attribute the result of the extremely hot summer. The September rains may have partially alleviated the stress from which those vineyards planted with Cabernet in the lighter, better-drained soils were suffering, but they also swelled many of the grape bunches and no doubt contributed to another prolifically abundant crop size.

There is no doubt that the great vintages have all been relatively hot, dry years. One of the keys to understanding this vintage is that the finest wines of 1990 have emerged from (1) those vineyards planted on the heavier, less well-drained, less desirable vineyard soil, and (2) those top châteaux that employed a particularly ruthless selection process. For example, in my tasting notes, heavier soils from such appellations as St.-Estèphe, Fronsac, and the hillside and plateau vineyards of St.-Emilion produced richer, more concentrated, and more complete wines than many of the top vineyards planted on the fine, well-drained, gravel-based soils of Margaux and the Graves.

The crop size was enormous in 1990, approximately equivalent to the quantity of wine produced in 1989. In reality, more wine was actually made, but because the French authorities intervened and required significant declassifications, the actual declared limit matches 1989, which means that for both vintages the production is 30% more than in 1982, another superb, hot-year vintage. Officially, however, many châteaux (especially the first growths and super-seconds) made even stricter selections in 1990 than in 1989 and the actual quantity of wine declared by many producers under the grand vin label is less than in 1989.

Across almost every appellation, the overall impression one gets of the dry red wines is that of extremely low acidity (as low and in some cases even lower than in 1989) and high tannins (in most cases higher than in 1989), but an overall impression of full-bodied softness and forward, precocious, extremely ripe, generous yet sometimes roasted flavors. Because the tannins are so soft (as in 1989, 1985, and 1982), these wines provide considerable enjoyment even when young, yet they possess decades of longevity.

The strengths in this vintage include most of the Médoc first growths (Mouton-Rothschild being the exception). Astoundingly, it can be said that they have made richer, fuller, more complete wines in 1990 than in 1989. Elsewhere in the Médoc, particularly in St.-Julien and Pauillac, a bevy of full-bodied, generous, opulent, relatively soft, round, forward, fruity wines with high alcohol, high, soft tannin, and extremely low acidity have been made. For me, the most intriguing aspect of the 1990 vintage is that as the wines aged in cask and continued their evolution in bottle, the vintage took on additional weight and structure, much like 1982 (but not 1989). I clearly underestimated some of the St.-Juliens and Pauillacs early on, as it was apparent at the time of bottling that these appellations had generally produced many profoundly rich, concentrated wines that were to be the greatest young Bordeaux between 1982 and 2000.

The fly in the ointment remains the performance of two of Bordeaux's superstars, Mouton Rothschild and Pichon-Lalande. They produced wines that were far less complete than their 1989s. Their wines were somewhat disappointing for the vintage and well below the quality of their peers. The puzzling performances of these two châteaux continues to be confirmed by my tastings. However, the other top wines in the Médoc have gained considerable stature and richness. They are the most exciting wines produced in Bordeaux between 1982 and 2000.

On the right bank, it first appeared that Pomerol enjoyed a less successful vintage than 1989, with the exception of those estates situated on the St.-Emilion border—L'Evangile, La Conseillante, and Le Bon Pasteur—which from the beginning had obviously produced wines that were richer than their 1989 counterparts. However, as the Pomerols have evolved in cask, they have strengthened, with the wines gaining weight, definition, and complexity. 1990 is a vintage that produced some profoundly great Pomerols, but overall, the vintage is less harmonious than 1989.

St.-Emilion, never a consistent appellation, has produced perhaps its most homogeneous and greatest vintage (until 1998 and 2000), for all three sectors of the appellation—the plateau, the vineyards at the foot of the hillsides, and the vineyards on sandy, gravelly soil. It is interesting to note that Cheval Blanc, Figeac, Pavie, L'Arrosée, Ausone, and Beauséjour produced far greater 1990s than 1989s. In particular, both Cheval Blanc and Beauséjour look to be wines of legendary quality. Figeac is not far behind, with the 1990 being the finest wine made at this estate since its 1982 and 1964.

The dry white wines of Graves, as well as generic white Bordeaux, have enjoyed a very good vintage that is largely superior to 1989, with two principal exceptions, Haut-Brion Blanc and Laville Haut-Brion. There is no doubt that the 1989 Haut-Brion Blanc and 1989 Laville Haut-Brion are two of the greatest white Graves ever produced. Both are far richer and more complete than their 1990s. Poor judgment in picking the 1989s too soon was not repeated with the 1990s, which have more richness and depth than most 1989s.

As for the sweet white wines of the Barsac/Sauternes region, this vintage was historic in the sense that most of the sweet white wine producers finished their harvest before the red wine producers, something that had not happened since 1949. These are powerful and sweet and have slowly begun to take on more complexity and focus. It really comes down to personal preference as to whether readers prefer 1990, 1989, or 1988 Barsacs and Sauternes, but there is no question this is the third and last vintage of a glorious trilogy, with the most powerful and concentrated Barsacs and Sauternes produced in many years. The wines, which boast some of the most impressive statistical credentials I have ever seen, are monster-sized in their richness and intensity. They possess 30–50 years of longevity. Will they turn out to be more complex and elegant than the 1988s? My instincts suggest they will not, but they are immensely impressive, blockbuster wines.

THE BEST WINES

St.-Estèphe: Calon-Ségur, Cos d'Estournel, Cos Labory, Haut-Marbuzet, Montrose, Phélan Ségur

Pauillac: Les Forts de Latour, Grand-Puy-Lacoste, Lafite Rothschild, Latour, Lynch-Bages, Pichon-Longueville Baron

St.-Julien: Branaire Ducru, Cloria, Gruaud Larose, Lagrange, Léoville Barton, Léoville Las Cases, Léoville Poyferré

Margaux: Maléscot St.-Exupèry, Château Margaux, Palmer, Rauzan-Ségla

Graves Red: Haut-Bailly, Haut-Brion, La Louvière, La Mission Haut-Brion, Pape-Clément

Graves White: Domaine de Chevalier, de Fieuzal, La Tour-Martillac

Pomerol: Le Bon Pasteur, Certan de May, Clinet, La Conseillante, L'Eglise-Clinet, L'Evangile, La Fleur de Gay, Gazin, Lafleur, Petit Village, Pétrus, Le Pin, Trotanoy, Vieux Château Certan

Fronsac/Canon　Canon-de-Brem, de Carles, Cassagne Haut-Canon La Truffière,
　　　Fronsac:　Fontenil, Pey-Labrie, La Vieille Cure

　St.-Emilion:　Angelus, L'Arrosée, Ausone, Beauséjour, Canon,
　　　　　　　Canon-la-Gaffelière, Cheval Blanc, La Dominique, Figeac, Grand
　　　　　　　Mayne, Pavie, Pavie Macquin, Le Tertre-Rôteboeuf, Troplong
　　　　　　　Mondot

Barsac/Sauternes:　Climens, Coutet, Coutet Cuvée Madame, Doisy-Daëne, Guiraud,
　　　　　　　Lafaurie-Péyraguey, Rabaud-Promis, Raymond-Lafon, Rieussec,
　　　　　　　Sigalas-Rabaud, Suduiraut, La Tour-Blanche, Château d'Yquem

1989—A Quick Study
(8-31-1989)

St.-Estèphe****	Graves Red***
Pauillac*****	Graves White**
St.-Julien****	Pomerol*****
Margaux***	St.-Emilion****
Médoc/Haut-Médoc Crus Bourgeois****	Barsac/Sauternes*****

Size: Mammoth; along with 1990 and 1986, one of the largest declared crops in the history of Bordeaux.

Important information: Excessively hyped vintage by virtually everyone but the Bordeaux proprietors. American, French, even English writers were all set to declare it the vintage of the century until serious tasters began to question the extract levels, phenomenally low-acid levels, and the puzzling quality of some wines. However, plenty of rich, dramatic, fleshy wines have been produced that should age reasonably well.

Maturity status: High tannins and extremely low acidity, much like 1990, suggest early drinkability, with only the most concentrated wines capable of lasting 20–30 or more years.

Price: The most expensive opening prices of any vintage, until 1995 and 1996, and of course 2000.

The general news media, primarily ABC television and *The New York Times,* first carried the news that several châteaux began their harvest during the last days of August, making 1989 the earliest vintage since 1893. An early harvest generally signifies a torrid growing season and below-average rainfall—almost always evidence that a top-notch vintage is achievable. In his annual Vintage and Market Report, the late Peter Sichel reported that between 1893 and 1989 only 1982, 1970, 1949, and 1947 were years with a similar weather pattern, but none of these years was as hot as 1989. Of course, he didn't know, but 1990 would be even more torrid.

Perhaps the most revealing and critical decision (at least from a qualitative perspective) was the choice of picking dates. Never has Bordeaux enjoyed such a vast span of time (August 28–October 15) over which to complete the harvest. Some châteaux, most notably Haut-Brion and the Christian Moueix–managed properties in Pomerol and St.-Emilion, harvested during the first week of September. Other estates waited and did not finish their harvesting until mid-October. During the second week of September, one major problem developed. Much of the Cabernet Sauvignon, while analytically mature and having enough sugar to potentially produce wines with 13% alcohol, was actually not ripe physiologically. Many châteaux, never having experienced such growing conditions, became indecisive. Far too many deferred to their oenologists, who saw technically mature grapes that were quickly losing acidity. The oenologists, never ones to take risks, advised immediate picking. As more than one proprietor and *négociant* said, by harvesting the Cabernet too early, a number of châteaux lost their chance to produce one of the greatest wines of a lifetime. This, plus the enormously large crop size, probably explains the good yet uninspired performance of so many wines from the Graves and Margaux appellations.

There was clearly no problem with the early picked Merlot as much of it came between 13.5% and a whopping 15% alcohol level—unprecedented in Bordeaux. Those properties that crop-thinned—Pétrus and Haut-Brion—had yields of 45–55 hectoliters per hectare and super concentration. Those who did not crop-thin had yields as preposterously high as 80 hectoliters per hectare.

Contrary to the reports of a totally "dry harvest," there were rain showers on September 10, 13, 18, and 22 that did little damage unless the property panicked and harvested the day after the rain. Some of the lighter-styled wines may very well be the result of jittery châteaux owners who unwisely picked after the showers.

The overall production was, once again, staggeringly high.

Acidities are extremely low and tannin levels surprisingly high. Consequently, in looking at the structural profile of the 1989s, one sees wines 1–2% higher in alcohol than the 1982s or 1961s; with much lower acidity levels than the 1982s, 1961s, and 1959s, yet high tannin levels. Fortunately, the tannins are generally ripe and soft, à la 1982, rather than dry and astringent as in 1988. This gives the wines a big, rich fleshy feel in the mouth similar to the 1982s. The top 1989s have very high glycerin levels, but are they as concentrated as the finest 2000s, 1990s, and 1982s? In Margaux the answer is a resounding "no," as this is clearly the least-favored appellation, much as it was in 1982. In Graves, except for Haut-Brion, La Mission Haut-Brion, Haut-Bailly, and de Fieuzal, the wines are relatively light and undistinguished. In St.-Emilion, the 2000s, 1998s, 1990s, and 1982s are more consistent as well as more deeply concentrated. Some marvelously rich, enormously fruity, fat wines were made in St.-Emilion in 1989, but there is wide irregularity in quality. However, in the northern Médoc, primarily St.-Julien, Pauillac, and St.-Estèphe, as well as in Pomerol, many exciting, full-bodied, very alcoholic, and tannic wines have been made. The best of these seem to combine the splendidly rich, opulent, fleshy texture of the finest 1982s with the power and tannin of the 1990s, yet curiously taste less concentrated than these two vintages and certainly far less concentrated than either 2000 or 1996.

As with the 1982s, this vintage is an enjoyable year to drink over a broad span of years. Despite the high tannin levels, the low acidities combined with the high glycerin and alcohol levels give the wines a fascinatingly fleshy, full-bodied texture. While there is considerable variation in quality, the finest 1989s from Pomerol, St.-Julien, Pauillac, and St.-Estèphe will, in specific cases, rival some of the greatest wines of the last twenty years.

THE BEST WINES

St.-Estèphe: Cos d'Estournel, Haut-Marbuzet, Meyney, Montrose, Phélan Ségur

Pauillac: Clerc Milon, Grand-Puy-Lacoste, Lafite Rothschild, Lynch-Bages, Mouton Rothschild, Pichon-Longueville Baron, Pichon Longueville Comtesse de Lalande

St.-Julien: Beychevelle, Branaire Ducru, Gruaud Larose, Lagrange, Léoville Barton, Léoville Las Cases, Talbot

Margaux: Cantemerle, Margaux, Palmer, Rauzan-Ségla

Graves Red: Bahans Haut-Brion, Haut-Bailly, Haut-Brion, La Louvière, La Mission Haut-Brion

Graves White: Clos Floridene, Haut-Brion, Laville Haut-Brion

Pomerol: Le Bon Pasteur, Clinet, La Conseillante, Domaine de L'Eglise, L'Eglise-Clinet, L'Evangile, Lafleur, La Fleur de Gay, La Fleur-Pétrus, Le Gay, Les Pensées de Lafleur, Pétrus, Le Pin, Trotanoy, Vieux Château Certan

St.-Emilion: Angelus, Ausone, Cheval Blanc, La Dominique, La Gaffelière, Grand Mayne, Magdelaine, Pavie, Pavie Macquin, Soutard, Le Tertre-Rôteboeuf, Troplong Mondot, Trotte Vieille

Barsac/Sauternes: Climens, Coutet, Coutet Cuvée Madame, Doisy-Védrines, Guiraud, Lafaurie-Péyraguey, Rabaud-Promis, Raymond-Lafon, Rieussec, Suduiraut, Suduiraut Cuvée Madame, La Tour-Blanche, Château d'Yquem

1988—A Quick Study
(9-20-1988)

St.-Estèphe***	Graves Red*****
Pauillac****	Graves White***
St.-Julien****	Pomerol****
Margaux***	St.-Emilion***
Médoc/Haut-Médoc Crus Bourgeois**	Barsac/Sauternes*****

Size: A large crop equivalent in size to 1982, meaning 30% less wine than was produced in 1990 and 1989.

Important information: Fearing a repeat of the rains that destroyed the potential for a great year in 1987, many producers once again pulled the trigger on their harvesting teams too soon. Unfortunately, as a result, copious quantities of Médoc Cabernet Sauvignon were picked too early.

Maturity status: Because of good acid levels and relatively high, more astringent tannins, there is no denying the potential of the 1988s to last for 20–30 years. How many of these wines will retain enough fruit to stand up to the tannin remains to be seen.

Price: Prices range 20–50% below more glamorous vintages, so the best wines offer considerable value.

The year 1988 is a good but rarely thrilling vintage of red wines, and it is one of the greatest vintages of the last century for the sweet wines of Barsac and Sauternes.

The problem with the red wines is that there is a lack of superstar performances on the part of the top châteaux. This will no doubt ensure that 1988 will always be regarded as a very good rather than excellent year. While the 1988 crop size was large, it was exceeded in size by the two vintages that followed it, 1989 and 1990. The average yield in 1988 was between 45–50 hectoliters per hectare, which was approximately equivalent to the quantity of wine produced in 1982. The wines tend to be well colored, tannic, and firmly structured. The less successful wines exhibit a slight lack of depth and finish short, with noticeably green, astringent tannins. Yet Graves and the northern Médoc enjoyed a fine, rather deliciously styled vintage.

These characteristics are especially evident in the Médoc where it was all too apparent that many châteaux, apprehensive about the onset of rot and further rain (as in 1987) panicked and harvested their Cabernet Sauvignon too early. Consequently, they brought in Cabernet that often achieved only 8–9% sugar readings. Those properties that waited or made a severe selection produced the best wines.

In Pomerol and St.-Emilion the Merlot was harvested under ripe conditions, but because of the severe drought in 1988 the skins of the grapes were thicker and the resulting wines were surprisingly tannic and hard.

In St.-Emilion many properties reported bringing in Cabernet Franc at full maturity and obtaining sugar levels that were reportedly higher than ever before. However, despite such optimistic reports much of the Cabernet Franc tasted fluid and diluted in quality. Therefore, St.-Emilion, despite reports of a very successful harvest, exhibits great irregularity in quality.

The appellation of Graves probably produced the best red wines of Bordeaux in 1988.

While there is no doubt that the richer, more dramatic, fleshier 1989s have taken much of the public's attention away from the 1988s, an objective look at the 1988 vintage will reveal some surprisingly strong performances in appellations such as Margaux, Pomerol, and Graves, and in properties in the northern Médoc that eliminated their early-picked Cabernet Sauvignon, or harvested much later. The year 1988 is not a particularly good one for the Crus Bourgeois because many harvested too soon. The lower prices they receive for their wines do not permit the Crus Bourgeois producers to make the strict selection that is necessary in years such as 1988.

The one appellation that did have a superstar vintage was Barsac and Sauternes. With a harvest that lasted until the end of November and textbook weather conditions for the formation of the noble rot, *Botrytis cinerea,* 1988 is considered by some authorities to be one of the finest vintages since 1937. Almost across the board, including the smaller estates, the wines have an intense smell of honey, coconut, oranges, and other tropical fruits. It is a remarkably rich vintage with wines of extraordinary levels of botrytis and great concentration of flavor; yet the rich, unctuous, opulent textures are balanced beautifully by zesty, crisp acidity. It is this latter component that makes these wines so special.

THE BEST WINES

St.-Estèphe: Calon-Ségur, Haut-Marbuzet, Meyney, Phélan Ségur

Pauillac: Clerc Milon, Lafite Rothschild, Latour, Lynch-Bages, Mouton Rothschild, Pichon-Longueville Baron, Pichon-Longueville– Comtesse de Lalande

St.-Julien: Gruaud Larose, Léoville Barton, Léoville Las Cases, Talbot

Margaux: Monbrison, Rauzan-Ségla

Graves Red: Les Carmes Haut-Brion, Domaine de Chevalier, Haut-Bailly, Haut-Brion, La Louvière, La Mission Haut-Brion, Pape-Clément

Graves White: Domaine de Chevalier, Clos Floridene, Couhins-Lurton, de Fieuzal, Laville Haut-Brion, La Louvière, La Tour-Martillac

Pomerol: Le Bon Pasteur, Certan de May, Clinet, L'Eglise-Clinet, La Fleur-de-Gay, Gombaude Guillot Cuvée Speciale, Lafleur, Petit Village, Pétrus, Le Pin, Vieux Château Certan

St.-Emilion: Angelus, Ausone, La Gaffelière, Clos des Jacobins, Larmande, Le Tertre-Rôteboeuf, Troplong Mondot

Barsac/Sauternes: d'Arche, Broustet, Climens, Coutet, Coutet Cuvée Madame, Doisy-Daëne, Doisy Dubroca, Guiraud, Lafaurie-Péyraguey, Lamothe-Guignard, Rabaud-Promis, Rayne-Vigneau, Rieussec, Sigalas-Rabaud, Suduiraut, La Tour-Blanche, Château d'Yquem

1987—A Quick Study
(10-3-1987)

St.-Estèphe**	Graves Red***
Pauillac**	Graves White****
St.-Julien**	Pomerol***
Margaux**	St.-Emilion**
Médoc/Haut-Médoc Crus Bourgeois*	Barsac/Sauternes*

Size: A moderately sized crop that looks almost tiny in the scheme of the gigantic yields during the decades of the 1980s and 1990s.

Important information: The most underrated vintage of the decade of the 1980s, producing a surprising number of ripe, round, tasty wines, particularly from Pomerol, Graves, and the most seriously run estates in the northern Médoc.

Maturity status: The best examples are deliciously drinkable and need to be consumed in 2003.

Price: Low prices are the rule rather than the exception for this sometimes attractive, low-priced vintage.

More than one Bordelais has said that if the rain had not arrived during the first two weeks of October 1987, ravaging the quality of the unharvested Cabernet Sauvignon and Petit Verdot, then 1987—not 1989 or 1982—would be the most extraordinary vintage of the decade of the 1980s. Wasn't it true that August and September had been the hottest two months in Bordeaux since 1976? But, the rain did fall, plenty of it, and it dashed the hopes for a top vintage. Yet much of the Merlot was primarily harvested before the rain. The early-picked Cabernet Sauvignon was adequate, but that picked after the rains began was in very poor condition. Thanks in part to the two gigantic-sized crops of 1985 and 1986, both record years at the time, most Bordeaux châteaux had full cellars and were mentally prepared to eliminate the vats of watery Cabernet Sauvignon harvested in the rains that fell for 14 straight days in October. The results for the top estates are wines that are light to medium bodied, ripe, fruity, round, even fat, with low tannins, low acidity, and lush, captivating, charming personalities.

While there is a tendency to look at 1987 as a poor year and to compare it with such other recent uninspiring vintages as 1984, 1980, and 1977, the truth is that the wines could not be more different. In the 1984, 1980, and 1977 vintages, the problem was immaturity because of cold, wet weather leading up to the harvest. In 1987, the problem was not a lack of maturity, as the Merlot and Cabernet were ripe. In 1987, the rains diluted fully mature, ripe grapes.

The year 1987 is the most underrated vintage of the decade for those estates where a strict selection was made and/or the Merlot was harvested in sound condition. The wines have tasted deliciously fruity, forward, clean, fat, and soft, without any degree of rot. Prices remain a bargain even though the quantities produced were relatively small. However, most 1987s need drinking up.

THE BEST WINES

*Only pristinely stored bottles of these wines will be vibrant.

St.-Estèphe:	Cos d'Estournel
Pauillac:	Lafite Rothschild, Latour, Mouton Rothschild*, Pichon-Longueville Baron, Pichon Longueville Comtesse de Lalande
St.-Julien:	Gruaud Larose, Léoville Barton*, Léoville Las Cases*, Talbot
Margaux:	d'Angludet, Margaux*, Palmer

Médoc/Haut-Médoc/
Moulis/Listrac/
Crus Bourgeois: none

Graves Red: Bahans Haut-Brion, Domaine de Chevalier, Haut-Brion,
La Mission Haut-Brion*, Pape-Clément

Graves White: Domaine de Chevalier, Couhins-Lurton, de Fieuzal, Laville
Haut-Brion, La Tour-Martillac

Pomerol: Certan de May, Clinet*, La Conseillante*, L'Evangile*,
La Fleur de Gay*, Petit Village, Pétrus*, Le Pin

St.-Emilion: Ausone*, Cheval Blanc, Clos des Jacobins, Clos St.-Martin,
Grand Mayne, Magdelaine, Le Tertre-Rôteboeuf,
Trotte Vieille

Barsac/Sauternes: Coutet, Lafaurie-Péyraguey

1986—A Quick Study
(9-23-1986)

St.-Estèphe****	Graves Red***
Pauillac*****	Graves White**
St.-Julien*****	Pomerol***
Margaux****	St.-Emilion***
Médoc/Haut-Médoc/Crus Bourgeois***	Barsac/Sauternes*****

Size: Colossal; one of the largest crops ever produced in Bordeaux.

Important information: An irrefutably great year for the Cabernet Sauvignon grape in
the northern Médoc, St.-Julien, Pauillac, and St.-Estèphe. The top 1986s beg for
more cellaring, and one wonders how many purchasers of these wines will lose their
patience before the wines ever reach full maturity?

Maturity status: The wines from the Crus Bourgeois, Graves, and right bank can be
drunk now, but the impeccably structured Médocs need until 2005 or later to become accessible.

Price: Still realistic except for a handful of the superstar wines.

The year 1986 is without doubt a great vintage for the northern Médoc, particularly for
St.-Julien and Pauillac, where many châteaux produced wines that are their deepest
and most concentrated since 1982, with 20–30 plus years of longevity. Yet it should be
made very clear to readers that unlike the great vintage of 1982 or very good vintages
of 1983 and 1985, the 1986s are not flattering wines to drink. If readers are not prepared to wait for the 1986s to mature, this is not a vintage that makes sense to buy. If
consumers can defer their gratification, then many will prove to be exhilarating Bordeaux wines dominated by their pure, very fruity Cabernet content.

Why did 1986 turn out to be such an exceptional year for many Médoc wines, as well as Graves, and produce Cabernet Sauvignon grapes of uncommon richness and power? The weather during the summer of 1986 was very dry and hot. In fact, by the beginning of September, Bordeaux was in the midst of a severe drought that began to threaten the final maturity process of the grapes. Rain did come, first on September 14–15, which enhanced the maturity process and mitigated the drought conditions. This rain was welcome, but on September 23, a ferocious, quick-moving storm thrashed the city of Bordeaux, the Graves region, and the major right bank appellations of Pomerol and St.-Emilion.

The curious aspect of this major storm, which caused widespread flooding in Bordeaux, was that it barely sideswiped the northern Médoc appellations of St.-Julien, Pauillac, and St.-Estèphe. Those pickers who started their harvest around the end of September found bloated Merlot grapes and unripe Cabernets. Consequently, the top wines of 1986 came from those châteaux that (1) did most of their harvesting after October 5, or (2) eliminated from their final blend the early picked Merlot, as well as the Cabernet Franc and Cabernet Sauvignon harvested between September 23 and October 4. After September 23 there was an extraordinary 23 days of hot, windy, sunny weather that turned the vintage into an exceptional one for those who delayed picking. It is, therefore, no surprise that the late-harvested Cabernet Sauvignon in the northern Médoc picked after October 6, but primarily October 9–16, produced wines of extraordinary intensity and depth. To no one's surprise, Château Margaux and Château Mouton Rothschild, which produced the vintage's two greatest wines, took in the great majority of their Cabernet Sauvignon between October 11 and 16.

In Pomerol and St.-Emilion, those châteaux that harvested soon after the September 23 deluge got predictably much less intense wines. Those that waited (i.e., Vieux Château Certan, Lafleur, Le Pin) made much more concentrated, complete wines. As in most vintages, the harvest date in 1986 was critical, and without question the late pickers made the finest wines. Perhaps the most perplexing paradox to emerge from the 1986 vintage is the generally high quality of the Graves wines, particularly in spite of the fact that this area was ravaged by the September 23 rainstorm. The answer in part may be that the top Graves châteaux eliminated more Merlot from the final blend than usual, therefore producing wines with a much higher percentage of Cabernet Sauvignon.

Lastly, the size of the 1986 crop established another record, as the harvest exceeded the bumper crop of 1985 by 15%, and was 30% larger than the 1982 harvest. This overall production figure, equaled in both 1990 and 1989 and surpassed numerous times since, is somewhat deceiving, as most of the classified Médoc châteaux made significantly less wine in 1986 than in 1985. It is for that reason, as well as the super maturity and tannin levels of the Cabernet Sauvignon grape, that most Médocs are noticeably more concentrated, more powerful, and more tannic in 1986 than they were in 1985.

All things considered, 1986 offers numerous exciting as well as exhilarating Médocs of profound depth and exceptional potential for longevity. Yet I continue to ask, how many consumers are willing to defer their gratification until 2010 or later, when the biggest wines might be ready to drink?

THE BEST WINES

St.-Estèphe: Cos d'Estournel, Montrose

Pauillac: Clerc Milon, Grand-Puy-Lacoste, Haut-Bages Libéral, Lafite Rothschild, Latour, Lynch-Bages, Mouton Rothschild, Pichon-Longueville Baron, Pichon Longueville Comtesse de Lalande

St.-Julien: Beychevelle, Ducru-Beaucaillou, Gruaud Larose, Lagrange, Léoville Barton, Léoville Las Cases, Talbot

Margaux: Margaux, Palmer, Rauzan-Ségla

Médoc/Haut Médoc/ Chasse-Spleen, Fourcas Loubaney, Gressier-Grand-
Moulis/Listrac/ Poujeaux, Lanessan, Maucaillou, Poujeaux, Sociando-
Crus Bourgeois: Mallet

Graves Red: Domaine de Chevalier, Haut-Brion, La Mission Haut-Brion, Pape-Clément

Graves White: none

Pomerol: Certan de May, Clinet, L'Eglise-Clinet, La Fleur de Gay, Lafleur, Pétrus, Le Pin, Vieux Château Certan

St.-Emilion: L'Arrosée, Canon, Cheval Blanc, Figeac, Pavie, Le Tertre-Rôteboeuf

Barsac/Sauternes: Climens, Coutet Cuvée Madame, de Fargues, Guiraud, Lafaurie-Péyraguey, Raymond-Lafon, Rieussec, Château d'Yquem

1985—A Quick Study
(9-29-1985)

St.-Estèphe***	Graves Red****
Pauillac****	Graves White****
St.-Julien****	Pomerol****
Margaux***	St.-Emilion***
Médoc/Haut-Médoc Crus Bourgeois***	Barsac/Sauternes**

Size: A very large crop (a record at the time) that was subsequently surpassed by harvest sizes in 1986, 1989, and most of the harvest of the 1990s.

Important information: The top Médocs may turn out to represent clones of the gorgeously seductive, charming 1953 vintage. Most of the top wines are surprisingly well developed, displaying fine richness, a round, feminine character, and exceptional aromatic purity and complexity. It is one of the most delicious vintages to drink in 2003 and over the next decade.

Maturity status: Seemingly drinkable from their release, the 1985s developed quickly, are fully mature in 2003, yet should last for another 10–15 years. The top Crus Bourgeois are past their prime.

Price: Released at outrageously high prices, the 1985s have not appreciated in value to the extent of other top vintages.

Any vintage, whether in Bordeaux or elsewhere, is shaped by the weather pattern. The 1985 Bordeaux vintage was conceived in a period of apprehension. January 1985 was the coldest since 1956. (I was there on January 16 when the temperature hit a record low of −14.5°C.) However, fear of damage to the vineyard was greatly exaggerated by the Bordelais. One wonders about the sincerity of such fears and whether they were designed to push up prices for the 1983s and create some demand for the overpriced 1984s. In any event, the spring and early summer were normal, if somewhat more rainy and cooler than usual in April, May, and June. July was slightly hotter and wetter than normal; August was colder than normal, but extremely dry. The September weather set a meteorological record—it was the sunniest, hottest, and driest September ever measured. The three most recent top vintages—1989, 1982, and 1961—could not claim such phenomenal weather conditions in September.

The harvest commenced at the end of September and three things became very apparent in that period between September 23 and 30. First, the Merlot was fully mature and excellent in quality. Second, the Cabernet Sauvignon grapes were not as ripe as expected and barely reached 11% natural alcohol. Third, the enormous size of the crop caught everyone off guard. The drought of August and September had overly stressed the many Cabernet vineyards planted in gravelly soil and actually retarded the ripening process. The smart growers stopped picking Cabernet, risking foul weather but hoping for higher sugar levels. The less adventurous settled for good rather than very good Cabernet Sauvignon. The pickers who waited and picked their Cabernet Sauvignon in mid-October clearly made the best wines as the weather held up. Because of the drought, there was little botrytis in the Barsac and Sauternes regions. Those wines have turned out to be monolithic, straightforward, and fruity, but, in general, lacking complexity and depth.

In general, 1985 is an immensely seductive and attractive vintage that has produced numerous well-balanced, rich, very perfumed yet tender wines. The 1985s should be consumed over the next 5–10 years while waiting for the tannins of the 1986s to melt away and for richer, fuller, more massive wines from vintages such as 2000, 1996, 1995, 1990, 1989, and 1982 to reach full maturity.

In the Médoc, 1985 produced an enormous crop. Where the châteaux made a strict selection, the results are undeniably charming, round, precocious, opulent wines with low acidity and an overall elegant, almost feminine quality. The tannins are soft and mellow. Interestingly, in the Médoc it is one of those years where the so-called super-seconds, such as Cos d'Estournel, Lynch-Bages, Léoville Las Cases, Ducru-Beaucaillou, Pichon Longueville Comtesse de Lalande, and Léoville Barton, made wines that rival and in some cases surpass the more illustrious first growths. In many vintages (1986 for example) the first growths soar qualitatively above the rest. That is not the case in 1985, with the exception of Châteaux Margaux.

Most of the Médoc growers, who were glowing in their opinion of the 1985s, called the vintage a blend in style between 1982 and 1983. Others compared the 1985s to the

1976s. Both of these positions seem far off the mark. The 1985s are certainly lighter, without nearly the texture, weight, or concentration of the finest 2000s, 1998s, 1996s, 1995s, 1990s, 1989s, 1986s, or 1982s.

On Bordeaux's right bank, in Pomerol and St.-Emilion, the Merlot was brought in at excellent maturity levels, although many châteaux had a tendency to pick too soon (i.e., Pétrus and Trotanoy). It is less consistent in St.-Emilion because too many producers harvested their Cabernet before it was physiologically fully mature. Interestingly, many of the Libourneais producers compared 1985 stylistically to 1971.

The vintage, which is one of seductive appeal, was priced almost too high when first released. The wines have not appreciated to the extent that many deserve and now look more reasonably priced than at any time in the past. But be careful, most of these wines are fully mature.

THE BEST WINES

St.-Estèphe: Cos d'Estournel, Haut-Marbuzet

Pauillac: Lafite Rothschild, Lynch-Bages, Mouton Rothschild, Pichon Longueville Comtesse de Lalande

St.-Julien: Ducru-Beaucaillou, Gruaud Larose, Léoville Barton, Léoville Las Cases, Talbot

Margaux: d'Angludet, Margaux, Palmer, Rauzan-Ségla

Graves Red: Haut-Brion, La Mission Haut-Brion

Graves White: Domaine de Chevalier, Haut-Brion, Laville Haut-Brion

Pomerol: Certan de May, La Conseillante, L'Eglise-Clinet, L'Evangile, Lafleur, Le Pin

St.-Emilion: Canon, Cheval Blanc, Ferrand, Soutard, Le Tertre-Rôteboeuf

Barsac/Sauternes: Château d'Yquem

1984—A Quick Study
(10-5-1984)

St.-Estèphe*	Graves Red**
Pauillac*	Graves White*
St.-Julien*	Pomerol*
Margaux*	St.-Emilion**
Médoc/Haut-Médoc Crus Bourgeois*	Barsac/Sauternes*

Size: A small- to medium-sized crop of primarily Cabernet-based wine.

Important information: The least attractive current vintage for drinking today, the 1984s, because of the failure of the Merlot crop, are essentially Cabernet-based wines that remain well colored but compact, stern, and forbiddingly backward and tannic.

Maturity status: Mature, yet the wines remain hard, stingy, and still alive because of painfully high acid and tannin levels.

Price: Virtually any 1984 can be had for a song as most retailers who bought this vintage are stuck with the wines.

After three abundant vintages, 1983, 1982, and 1981, the climatic conditions during the summer and autumn of 1984 hardly caused euphoria among the Bordelais. The vegetative cycle began rapidly, thanks to a magnificently hot, sunny April. However, that was followed by a relatively cool and wet May, which created havoc in the flowering of the quick-to-bud Merlot grape. The result was that much of the 1984 Merlot crop was destroyed long before the summer weather actually arrived. The terrible late spring and early summer conditions made headlines in much of the world's press, which began to paint the vintage as an impending disaster. However, July was dry and hot, and by the end of August, some overly enthusiastic producers were talking about the potential for superripe, tiny quantities of Cabernet Sauvignon. There were even several reporters who were calling 1984 similar to the 1961 vintage. Their intentions could only be considered sinister as 1984 could never be compared to 1961.

Following the relatively decent beginning in September, the period between September 21 and October 4 was one of unexpected weather difficulties, climaxed by the first cyclone (named Hortense) ever to hit the area, tearing roofs off buildings and giving nervous jitters to wine-makers. However, after October 4 the weather cleared up and producers began to harvest their Cabernet Sauvignon. Those who waited picked relatively ripe Cabernet, although the Cabernet's skin was somewhat thick and the acid levels extremely high, particularly by the standards of more recent vintages.

The problem that existed early on with the 1984s and that continues to present difficulties today is that the wines lack an important percentage of Merlot to counterbalance their narrow, compact, high-acid, austere, and tannic character. Consequently, there is a lack of fat and charm, but these herbaceous wines are deep in color, as they were made from Cabernet Sauvignon.

In St.-Emilion and Pomerol, the vintage, if not quite an unqualified disaster, is disappointing. Many top properties—Ausone, Canon, Magdelaine, Belair, La Dominique, Couvent des Jacobins, and Tertre Daugay—declassified their entire crop. It was the first vintage since 1968 or 1972 where many of these estates made no wine under their label. Even at Pétrus, only 800 cases were made, as opposed to the 4,500 cases produced in both 1985 and 1986.

In 2003, the better 1984s remain relatively narrowly constructed, tightly knit wines still displaying a healthy color, but lacking fat, ampleness, and charm. It is unlikely they will ever develop any charm, but there is no doubt that the better-endowed examples will keep for another decade.

THE BEST WINES

St.-Estèphe: Cos d'Estournel

Pauillac: Latour, Lynch-Bages, Mouton Rothschild, Pichon-Longueville–
Comtesse de Lalande

St.-Julien:　Gruaud Larose, Léoville Las Cases

Margaux:　Margaux

Graves Red:　Domaine de Chevalier, Haut-Brion, La Mission Haut-Brion

Graves White:　none

Pomerol:　none

St.-Emilion:　none

Barsac/Sauternes:　Château d'Yquem

1983—A Quick Study
(9-26-1983)

St.-Estèphe**	Graves Red****
Pauillac***	Graves White****
St.-Julien***	Pomerol***
Margaux*****	St.-Emilion****
Médoc/Haut-Médoc Crus Bourgeois**	Barsac/Sauternes****

Size: A large crop, with overall production slightly inferior to 1982, but in the Médoc, most properties produced more wine than they did in 1982.

Important information: Bordeaux, as well as all of France, suffered from atypically tropical heat and humidity during the month of August. This caused considerable overripening, as well as the advent of rot in certain *terroirs,* particularly in St.-Estèphe, Pauillac, Pomerol, and the sandier plateau sections of St.-Emilion.

Maturity status: At first the vintage was called more classic (or typical) than 1982, with greater aging potential. Twenty years later, the 1983s are far more evolved and, in most cases, fully mature—unlike the finest 1982s. In fact, this is a vintage that attained full maturity at an accelerated pace, and needs to be drunk by 2010–2015.

Price: Prices for the best 1983s remain fair.

The year 1983 was one of the most bizarre growing seasons in recent years. The flowering in June went well for the third straight year, ensuring a large crop. The weather in July was so torrid that it turned out to be the hottest July on record. August was extremely hot, rainy, and humid, and as a result, many vineyards began to have significant problems with mildew and rot. It was essential to spray almost weekly in August 1983 to protect the vineyards. Those properties that did not spray diligently had serious problems with mildew-infected grapes. By the end of August, a dreadful month climatically, many pessimistic producers were apprehensively talking about a disastrous vintage like 1968 or 1965. September brought dry weather, plenty of heat, and no excessive rain. October provided exceptional weather as well, so the grapes harvested late were able to attain maximum ripeness under sunny, dry skies. Not since 1961 had the entire Bordeaux crop, white grapes and red grapes, been harvested in completely dry, fair weather.

The successes that have emerged from 1983 are first and foremost from the appellation of Margaux, which enjoyed its finest vintage of the decade. In fact, this perennial underachieving appellation produced many top wines, with magnificent efforts from Margaux, Palmer, and Rauzan-Ségla (the vintage of resurrection for this famous name), as well as d'Issan and Brane Cantenac. These wines remain some of the best-kept secrets of this era.

The other appellations had numerous difficulties, and the wines have not matured as evenly or as gracefully as some prognosticators had suggested. The northern Médoc, particularly the St.-Estèphes, are disappointing. The Pauillacs range from relatively light, overly oaky, roasted wines that are hollow in the middle, to some successes, most notably from Pichon Longueville Comtesse de Lalande, Mouton Rothschild, and Lafite Rothschild.

The St.-Juliens will not be remembered for their greatness, with the exception of a superb Léoville Poyferré. In 1983 Léoville Poyferré is amazingly as good as the other two Léovilles, Léoville Las Cases and Léoville Barton. During the 1980s, there was not another vintage where such a statement could be made. Both Gruaud Larose and Talbot made good wines, but overall, 1983 is not a memorable year for St.-Julien.

In Graves, the irregularity continues, with wonderful wines from those Graves châteaux in the Pessac-Léognan area (Haut-Brion, La Mission Haut-Brion, Haut-Bailly, Domaine de Chevalier, and de Fieuzal), but with disappointments elsewhere.

On the right bank, in Pomerol and St.-Emilion, inconsistency is again the rule of thumb. Most of the hillside vineyards in St.-Emilion performed well, but the vintage was mixed on the plateau and in the sandier soils, although Cheval Blanc made one of its greatest wines of the decade. In Pomerol, it is hard to say who made the best wine, but the house of Jean-Pierre Moueix did not fare well in this vintage. Other top properties, such as La Conseillante, L'Evangile, Lafleur, Certan de May, and Le Pin, all made good wines.

THE BEST WINES

St.-Estèphe: none

Pauillac: Lafite Rothschild, Mouton Rothschild, Pichon-Longueville–Comtesse de Lalande

St.-Julien: Gruaud Larose, Léoville Las Cases, Léoville Poyferré, Talbot

Margaux: d'Angludet, Brane Cantenac, Cantemerle (southern Médoc), d'Issan, Margaux, Palmer, Prieuré-Lichine, Rauzan-Ségla

Graves Red: Domaine de Chevalier, Haut-Bailly, Haut-Brion, La Louvière, La Mission Haut-Brion

Graves White: Domaine de Chevalier, Laville Haut-Brion

Pomerol: Certan de May, La Conseillante, L'Evangile, Lafleur, Le Pin

St.-Emilion: L'Arrosée, Ausone, Belair, Canon, Cheval Blanc, Figeac, Larmande

Barsac/Sauternes: Climens, Doisy-Daëne, de Fargues, Guiraud, Lafaurie-
                    Péyraguey, Raymond-Lafon, Rieussec, Château d'Yquem

1982—A Quick Study
(9-13-1982)

St.-Estèphe*****	Graves Red***
Pauillac*****	Graves White**
St.-Julien*****	Pomerol*****
Margaux***	St.-Emilion*****
Médoc/Haut-Médoc Crus Bourgeois****	Barsac/Sauternes***

Size: An extremely abundant crop, which at the time was a record year, but has since been equaled in size and surpassed in volume by virtually every vintage of the late 1980s and the decade of the 1990s.

Important information: The most concentrated and potentially complex and profound wines between 1961 and 1990 were produced in virtually every appellation.

Maturity status: Most Crus Bourgeois should have been drunk by 1995, and the lesser wines in St.-Emilion, Pomerol, Graves, and Margaux have been fully mature since the mid-1990s. For the bigger-styled Pomerols, St.-Emilions, and northern Médocs—St.-Julien, Pauillac, and St.-Estèphe—the wines are evolving at a glacial pace. They have lost much of their baby fat and have gone into a much more tightly knit, massive yet structured tannic state. As of 2003, the Médoc first growths will benefit from another 5–10 years of cellaring. Most of the other classified growths have entered their plateau of maturity. In short, the top two dozen or so wines will earn "immortal" status.

Price: With the exception of 1990, no modern-day Bordeaux vintage since 1961 has accelerated as much in price and yet continues to appreciate in value. Prices are now so frightfully high that consumers who did not purchase these wines as futures can only look back with envy at those who bought the 1982s when they were first offered at what now appear to be bargain-basement prices. Who can remember a great vintage being sold at opening prices of Pichon-Lalande ($110), Léoville Las Cases ($160), Ducru-Beaucaillou ($150), Pétrus ($600), Cheval Blanc ($550), Margaux ($550), Certan de May ($180), La Lagune ($75), Grand-Puy-Lacoste ($85), Cos d'Estournel ($145), and Canon ($105)? And these were the prices for 12-bottle cases! These are the average prices for which the 1982s were sold during the spring, summer, and fall of 1983. Yet, potential buyers should be careful as many fraudulent 1982s have shown up in the marketplace, particularly Pétrus, Lafleur, Le Pin, Cheval Blanc, and the Médoc first growths. Another concern regarding provenance is the storage of 1982s. These wines have been heavily traded at the various auctions, and badly stored, heat damaged bottles are commonly encountered, so purchasers of 1982 today need to be very diligent and selective.

When I issued my report on the 1982 vintage in the April 1983 *Wine Advocate,* I remember feeling that I had never tasted richer, more concentrated, more promising wines than the 1982s. Twenty-one years later, despite some wonderfully successful years such as 2000, 1998, 1996, 1995, 1990, 1989, 1986, and 1985, the 1982 remains the modern-day reference for many of the greatest wines in Bordeaux, yet not every property was committed to producing top-quality wine. Because of that, 2000 and 1990 are much more consistent vintages, with higher numbers of wines meriting outstanding scores.

The finest wines of the vintage have emerged from the northern Médoc appellations of St.-Julien, Pauillac, and St.-Estèphe, as well as Pomerol and St.-Emilion. They have aged much more slowly (where well cellared) than I initially predicted. They continue to display a degree of richness, opulence, and intensity equaled only by some 2000s, 1998s, 1990s, and 1989s. As they approach their 21st birthday, the vintage's first growths remain relatively unevolved and backward.

The wines from other appellations have matured much more quickly, particularly those from Graves, Margaux, and the lighter, lesser wines from Pomerol, St.-Emilion, and the Crus Bourgeois. Most of these wines have been delicious since the mid-1990s and should be drunk by 2010.

Today, no one could intelligently deny the greatness of the 1982 vintage. However, in 1983 this vintage was received among America's wine press with a great deal of skepticism. There was no shortage of outcries about these wines' lack of acidity and "California" style after the vintage's conception. It was suggested by some writers that 1981 and 1979 were "finer vintages," and that the 1982s, "fully mature," should have been "consumed by 1990." Of course, wine tasting is subjective, but such statements have been proven time after time to be nonsense. It remains impossible to justify such criticism of this vintage, particularly in view of how well the top 1982s taste in 2003, and how rich as well as slowly the first growths, super-seconds, and big wines of the northern Médoc, Pomerol, and St.-Emilion have evolved. Even in Bordeaux the 1982s are now placed on a pedestal and spoken of in the same terms as 1961, 1949, 1945, and 1929. Moreover, the marketplace and auction rooms, perhaps the only true measure of a vintage's value, continue to push prices for the top 1982s to stratospheric levels. Yet lamentably, controversy continues to surround the vintage, in large part because it was the year that established my reputation as a serious wine critic. Sadly, too many of the vintage evaluations by a few of my colleagues have always sounded more like reviews of the author rather than of the actual wines.

The reason why so many 1982s were so remarkable was because of the outstanding weather conditions. The flowering occurred in hot, sunny, dry, ideal June weather that served to ensure a large crop. July was extremely hot and August slightly cooler than normal. By the beginning of September the Bordeaux producers were expecting a large crop of excellent quality. However, a September burst of intense heat that lasted for nearly three weeks sent the grape sugars soaring, and what was considered originally to be a very good to excellent vintage was transformed into a great vintage for every appellation except Margaux and the Graves, whose very thin, light, gravelly soils suffered during the torrid September heat. For the first time many producers had to vinify their wines under unusually hot conditions. Many lessons were learned that were employed again in subsequent hot vinification years such as 1990, 1989, and 1985. Rumors of disasters from overheated or stuck fermentations proved to be without validity, as were reports that rain showers near the end of the harvest caught some properties with Cabernet Sauvignon still on the vine.

When analyzed, the 1982s are the most concentrated, high-extract wines since 1961, with acid levels that while low, are no lower than in years of exceptional ripeness such as 1961, 1959, 1953, 1949, and 1947. Though some skeptics pointed to the low acidity, many of those same skeptics fell in love with the 1990s, 1989s, and 1985s—all Bordeaux vintages that produced wines with significantly lower acids and higher pH's than the 1982s. Tannin levels were extremely high, but subsequent vintages, particularly 2000, 1996, 1995, 1990, 1989, 1988, and 1986 produced wines with even higher tannin levels than the 1982s.

Multiple tastings of the 1982s as they celebrated their 20th birthday continue to suggest that the top wines of the northern Médoc need another 5–10 years of cellaring. Most of the best wines seem largely unevolved since their early days in cask. They have fully recovered from the bottling and display the extraordinary expansive, rich, glycerin- and extract-laden palates that should serve these wines well over the next 10–20 years. If the 1982 vintage remains sensational for the majority of St.-Emilions, Pomerols, St.-Juliens, Pauillacs, and St.-Estèphes, the weakness of the vintage becomes increasingly more apparent with the Margaux and Graves wines. Only Château Margaux seems to have survived the problems of overproduction, loosely knit, flabby Cabernet Sauvignon wines from which so many other Margaux properties suffered. The same can be said for the Graves, which are light and disjointed when compared to the lovely 1983s Graves produced. Only La Mission Haut-Brion, La Tour Haut-Brion, and Haut-Brion produced better 1982s than 1983s.

On the negative side are the prices one must now pay for a top wine from the 1982 vintage. Is this also a reason why the vintage still receives cheap shots from a handful of American writers? Those who bought them as futures made the wine buys of the century. For today's generation of wine enthusiasts, 1982 is what 1961, 1959, 1949, 1947, and 1945 were for earlier generations of wine lovers.

Lastly, the sweet wines of Barsac and Sauternes in 1982, while maligned originally for their lack of botrytis and richness, are not that bad. In fact, Château d'Yquem and the Cuvée Madame of Château Suduiraut are two remarkably powerful, rich wines that can stand up to the best of the 1988s, 1986s, and 1983s.

THE BEST WINES

St.-Estèphe: Calon-Ségur, Cos d'Estournel, Haut-Marbuzet, Meyney, Montrose

Pauillac: Les Forts de Latour, Grand-Puy-Lacoste, Haut-Batailley, Lafite Rothschild, Latour, Lynch-Bages, Mouton Rothschild, Pichon-Longueville Baron, Pichon Longueville Comtesse de Lalande

St.-Julien: Beychevelle, Branaire Ducru, Ducru-Beaucaillou, Gruaud Larose, Léoville Barton, Léoville Las Cases, Léoville Poyferré, Talbot

Margaux: Margaux, La Lagune (southern Médoc)

Graves Red: Haut-Brion, La Mission Haut-Brion, La Tour Haut-Brion

Graves White: none

Pomerol: Le Bon Pasteur, Certan de May, La Conseillante, L'Evangile, Le Gay, Lafleur, Latour à Pomerol, Petit Village, Pétrus, Le Pin, Trotanoy, Vieux Château Certan

St.-Emilion: L'Arrosée, Ausone, Canon, Cheval Blanc, La Dominique, Figeac, Pavie

Barsac/Sauternes: Raymond-Lafon, Suduiraut Cuvée Madame, Château d'Yquem

1981—A Quick Study
(9-28-1981)

St.-Estèphe**	Graves Red**
Pauillac****	Graves White****
St.-Julien***	Pomerol***
Margaux**	St.-Emilion**
Médoc/Haut-Médoc Crus Bourgeois*	Barsac/Sauternes*

Size: A moderately large crop that in retrospect now looks small.

Important information: The first vintage in a succession of hot, dry years that would continue nearly uninterrupted through 1990. The year 1981 would have been a top vintage had the rain not fallen immediately prior to the harvest.

Maturity status: Most 1981s are close to full maturity, yet the best examples are capable of lasting for another 5–10 years.

Price: A largely ignored and overlooked vintage, 1981 remains a reasonably good value.

Initially, this vintage was labeled more "classic" than either 1983 or 1982. What classic means to the woefully misinformed who call 1981 a classic vintage is that this year is a typically good Bordeaux vintage of medium-weight, well-balanced, graceful wines. Despite a dozen or so excellent wines, 1981 is in reality only a good vintage, surpassed in quality by most recent vintages.

The year 1981 could have been an outstanding vintage had it not been for the heavy rains that fell just as the harvest was about to start. There was a dilution of the intensity of flavor in the grapes as heavy rains drenched the vineyards between October 1 and 5, and again between October 9 and 15. Until then, the summer had been perfect. The flowering occurred under excellent conditions; July was cool, but August and September hot and dry. One can only speculate that had it not rained, 1981 might well have also turned out to be one of the greatest vintages in the post–World War II era.

The year 1981 did produce a large crop of generally well-colored wines of medium weight and moderate tannin. The dry white wines have turned out well, but should have been consumed by now. Both Barsacs and Sauternes suffered as a result of the rains and no truly compelling wines have emerged from these appellations.

There are a number of successful wines in 1981, particularly from such appellations as Pomerol, St.-Julien, and Pauillac. The wines' shortcomings are their lack of the richness, flesh, and intensity that more recent vintages have possessed. Most red wine producers had to chaptalize significantly because the Cabernets were harvested under 11% natural alcohol and the Merlot under 12%, no doubt because of the rain.

THE BEST WINES

St.-Estèphe: none

Pauillac: Lafite Rothschild, Latour, Pichon Longueville Comtesse de Lalande

St.-Julien: Ducru-Beaucaillou, Gruaud Larose, Léoville Las Cases, St.-Pierre

Margaux: Giscours, Margaux

Graves Red: La Mission Haut-Brion

Graves White: none

Pomerol: Certan de May, La Conseillante, Pétrus, Le Pin, Vieux Château Certan

St.-Emilion: Cheval Blanc

Barsac/Sauternes: Climens, de Fargues, Château d'Yquem

1980—A Quick Study
(10-14-1980)

St.-Estèphe*	Graves Red**
Pauillac**	Graves White*
St.-Julien**	Pomerol**
Margaux**	St.-Emilion*
Médoc/Haut-Médoc Crus Bourgeois*	Barsac/Sauternes****

Size: A moderately sized crop was harvested.

Important information: Nothing very noteworthy can be said about this mediocre vintage.

Maturity status: With the exception of Château Margaux and Pétrus, virtually every 1980 should have been consumed.

Price: Low.

For a decade that became known as the golden age of Bordeaux, or the decade of the century, the 1980s certainly did not begin in an auspicious fashion. The summer of 1980 was cool and wet, the flowering was unexciting because of a disappointing June, and by early September the producers were looking at a return of the two most dreadful vintages of the last 30 years, 1968 and 1963. However, modern-day antirot sprays did a great deal to protect the grapes from the dreaded *pourriture*. For that reason, the growers were able to delay their harvest until the weather began to improve at the end of September. The weather in early October was favorable until rains began in the middle of the month, just as many producers began to harvest. The results have been light, diluted, frequently disappointing wines that have an unmistakable vegetal and herbaceous taste and are often marred by excessive acidity as well as tannin. Those producers who made a strict selection and who picked exceptionally late, such as the Mentzelopoulos family at Château Margaux (the wine of the vintage), made softer, rounder, more interesting wines that began to drink well in the late 1980s, but need immediate consumption. The number of properties that could be said to have made wines of good quality are few.

As always in wet, cool years, those vineyards planted on lighter, gravelly, well-drained soils, such as some of the Margaux and Graves properties, tend to get better maturity and ripeness. Not surprisingly, the top successes generally come from these areas, although several Pauillacs, because of a very strict selection, also have turned out well.

As disappointing as the 1980 vintage was for the red wine producers, it was an excellent year for the producers of Barsac and Sauternes. The ripening and harvesting continued into late November, generally under ideal conditions. This permitted some rich, intense, high-class Barsac and Sauternes to be produced. Unfortunately, their commercial viability suffered from the reputation of the red wine vintage. Anyone who comes across a bottle of 1980 Climens, Château d'Yquem, or Raymond-Lafon will immediately realize that this is an astonishingly good year.

THE BEST WINES

St.-Estèphe:	none
Pauillac:	Latour, Pichon Longueville Comtesse de Lalande
St.-Julien:	Talbot
Margaux:	Margaux
Médoc/Haut-Médoc/ Moulis/Listrac/ Crus Bourgeois:	none
Graves Red:	Domaine de Chevalier, La Mission Haut-Brion
Graves White:	none
Pomerol:	Certan de May, Pétrus
St.-Emilion:	Cheval Blanc
Barsac/Sauternes:	Climens, de Fargues, Raymond-Lafon, Château d'Yquem

1979—A Quick Study
(10-3-1979)

St.-Estèphe**	Graves Red****
Pauillac***	Graves White**
St.-Julien***	Pomerol***
Margaux****	St.-Emilion**
Médoc/Haut-Médoc Crus Bourgeois**	Barsac/Sauternes*

Size: A huge crop that established a record at that time.

Important information: In the last two decades, this is one of the only cool years that turned out to be a reasonably good vintage.

Maturity status: Contrary to earlier reports, the 1979s have matured very slowly, largely because the wines have relatively hard tannins and good acidity, two characteristics that most of the top vintages during the decade of the 1980s have not possessed.

Price: Because of the lack of demand and the vintage's average-to-good reputation, prices remain low except for a handful of the limited production, glamour wines of Pomerol.

The year 1979 has become the forgotten vintage in Bordeaux. A record-setting crop that produced relatively healthy, medium-bodied wines that displayed firm tannins and good acidity closed out the decade of the 1970s. Over the next decade this vintage was rarely mentioned in the wine press. No doubt most of the wines were consumed long before they reached their respective apogees. Considered inferior to 1978 when conceived, the 1979 vintage will prove superior—at least in terms of aging potential. Yet aging potential alone is hardly sufficient to evaluate a vintage, and many 1979s remain relatively skinny, malnourished, lean, compact wines that naïve commentators have called classic rather than thin.

Despite the inconsistency from appellation to appellation, a number of strikingly good, surprisingly flavorful, rich wines have emerged from appellations such as Margaux, Graves, and Pomerol.

With few exceptions, there is no hurry to drink the top 1979s since their relatively high acid levels (compared to more recent hot-year vintages), good tannin levels, and sturdy framework should ensure that the top 1979s age well for at least another 10–15 years.

This was not a good vintage for the dry white wines or sweet white wines of Barsac and Sauternes. The dry whites did not achieve full maturity and there was never enough botrytis for the Barsac and Sauternes to give the wines that honeyed complexity that is fundamental to their success.

Prices for 1979s, where they can still be found, are the lowest of any good recent Bordeaux vintage, reflecting the general lack of excitement for most 1979s.

THE BEST WINES

St.-Estèphe: Cos d'Estournel

Pauillac: Lafite Rothschild, Latour, Pichon Longueville Comtesse de Lalande

St.-Julien: Gruaud Larose, Léoville Las Cases

Margaux: Giscours, Margaux, Palmer, Du Tertre

Graves Red: Les Carmes Haut-Brion, Domaine de Chevalier, Haut-Bailly, Haut-Brion, La Mission Haut-Brion

Pomerol: Certan de May, L'Enclos, L'Evangile, Lafleur, Pétrus

St.-Emilion: Ausone

Barsac/Sauternes: none

1978—A Quick Study
(10-7-1978)

St.-Estèphe**	Graves Red****
Pauillac***	Graves White****
St.-Julien***	Pomerol**
Margaux***	St.-Emilion***
Médoc/Haut-Médoc Crus Bourgeois**	Barsac/Sauternes**

Size: A moderately sized crop was harvested.

Important information: The late Harry Waugh, England's gentlemanly wine commentator, dubbed this "the miracle year."

Maturity status: Most wines are either fully mature or in decline.

Price: Overpriced for years, 25 years after the vintage the 1978s are fairly-priced.

The year 1978 turned out to be an outstanding vintage for the red wines of Graves and a good vintage for the red wines from the Médoc, Pomerol, and St.-Emilion. There was a lack of botrytis for the sweet white wines of Barsac and Sauternes and the results were monolithic, straightforward wines of no great character. The dry white Graves, much like the red wines of that appellation, turned out exceedingly well.

The weather profile for 1978 was hardly encouraging. The spring was cold and wet, and poor weather continued to plague the region through June, July, and early August, causing many growers to begin thinking of such dreadful years as 1977, 1968, 1965, and 1963. However, in mid-August a huge anticyclone, high pressure system settled over southwestern France and northern Spain and for the next nine weeks the weather was sunny, hot, and dry, except for an occasional light rain shower that had negligible effects.

Because the grapes were so behind in their maturation (contrast that scenario with the more recent advanced maturity years such as 1990 and 1989), the harvest began extremely late, on October 7. It continued under excellent weather conditions, which seemed, as Harry Waugh put it, miraculous, in view of the miserable weather throughout much of the spring and summer.

The general view of this vintage is that it is a very good to excellent year. The two best appellations are Graves and Margaux, which have the lighter, better drained soils that support cooler weather years. In fact, Graves (except for the disappointing Pape-Clément) probably enjoyed its greatest vintage after 1961 and before 1982. The wines, which at first appeared intensely fruity, deeply colored, moderately tannic, and medium bodied, have aged much faster than the higher acid, more firmly tannic 1979s, the product of an even cooler, drier year. Most 1978s had reached full maturity a decade after the vintage and some commentators were expressing their disappointment that the wines were not better than they had believed.

The problem is that, much like in 1988, 1981, and 1979, there is a shortage of truly superstar wines. There are a number of good wines, but the lack of excitement in the majority of wines has tempered the post-vintage enthusiasm. Moreover, the lesser wines in 1978 have an annoyingly vegetal, herbaceous taste because those vineyards not planted on the best soils never fully ripened despite the impressively hot, dry *fin de saison*. Another important consideration is that the selection process, so much a fundamental principle in the decade of the 1980s; was employed less during the 1970s as many properties simply bottled everything under the grand vin label. In talking with proprietors today, many feel that 1978 could have lived up to its early promise had a stricter selection been in effect when the wines were made.

This was a very difficult vintage for properties in the Barsac/Sauternes region because very little botrytis formed due to the hot, dry autumn. The wines, much like the 1979s, are chunky, full of glycerin and sugar, but lack grip, focus, and complexity.

THE BEST WINES

St.-Estèphe: none

Pauillac: Les Forts de Latour, Grand-Puy-Lacoste, Latour, Pichon Longueville Comtesse de Lalande

St.-Julien: Ducru-Beaucaillou, Gruaud Larose, Léoville Las Cases, Talbot

Margaux: Giscours, La Lagune (southern Médoc), Margaux, Palmer, Prieuré-Lichine, Du Tertre

Médoc/Haut-Médoc/ Moulis/Listrac/ Crus Bourgeois: none

Graves Red: Les Carmes Haut-Brion, Domaine de Chevalier, Haut-Bailly, Haut-Brion, La Mission Haut-Brion, La Tour Haut-Brion

Graves White: Domaine de Chevalier, Haut-Brion, Laville Haut-Brion

Pomerol: Lafleur

St.-Emilion: L'Arrosée, Cheval Blanc

Barsac/Sauternes: none

1977—A Quick Study
(10-3-1977)

St.-Estèphe 0	Graves Red*
Pauillac 0	Graves White*
St.-Julien 0	Pomerol 0
Margaux 0	St.-Emilion 0
Médoc/Haut-Médoc Crus Bourgeois 0	Barsac/Sauternes*

Size: A small crop was produced.

Important information: A dreadful vintage, clearly the worst of the decade; it remains, in a pejorative sense, unequaled since.

Maturity status: The wines, even the handful that were drinkable, should have been consumed by the mid-1980s.

Price: Despite distress sale prices, there are no values to be found.

This is the worst vintage for Bordeaux during the decade of the 1970s. Even the two mediocre years of the 1980s, 1984 and 1980, are far superior to 1977. Much of the Merlot crop was devastated by a late spring frost. The summer was cold and wet. When warm, dry weather finally arrived just prior to the harvest, there was just too little time left to save the vintage. The harvest resulted in grapes that were both analytically and physiologically immature and far from ripe.

The wines, which were relatively acidic and overtly herbaceous to the point of being vegetal, should have been consumed years ago. Some of the more successful wines included a decent Figeac, Giscours, Gruaud Larose, Pichon-Lalande, Latour, and three Graves estates of Haut-Brion, La Mission Haut-Brion, and Domaine de Chevalier. However, I have never been able to recommend any of these wines. They have no value from either a monetary or pleasure standpoint. Life is too short to drink 1977 Bordeaux.

1976—A Quick Study
(9-13-1976)

St.-Estèphe***	Graves Red*
Pauillac***	Graves White***
St.-Julien***	Pomerol***
Margaux**	St.-Emilion***
Médoc/Haut-Médoc Crus Bourgeois*	Barsac/Sauternes****

Size: A huge crop, the second largest of the decade, was harvested.

Important information: This hot, droughtlike vintage could have proved to be the vintage of the decade had it not been for preharvest rains.

Maturity status: The 1976s tasted fully mature and delicious when released in 1979. Yet the best examples continue to offer delightful, sometimes delicious drinking. It is one of a handful of vintages where the wines have never closed up or been unappealing. Yet, virtually every 1976 (with the exception of Ausone and large-format bottles of Lafite Rothschild) should have been consumed prior to 2000.

Price: The 1976s have always been reasonably priced because they have never received accolades from the wine pundits.

A very highly publicized vintage, 1976 has never quite lived up to its reputation. All the ingredients were present for a superb vintage. The harvest date of September 13 was the earliest harvest since 1945. The weather during the summer had been torridly hot, with the average temperatures for the months of June through September only exceeded by the hot summers of 1949 and 1947. However, with many vignerons predicting a "vintage of the century," very heavy rains fell between September 11 and 15, bloating the grapes.

The crop that was harvested was large, the grapes were ripe, and while the wines had good tannin levels, the acidity levels were low and their pH's dangerously high. The top wines of 1976 have offered wonderfully soft, supple, deliciously fruity drinking since they were released. I had fully expected that these wines would have to be consumed before the end of the decade of the 1980s. Until the early nineties, the top 1976s stayed at their peak of maturity without fading or losing their fruit. But for most 1976s, their time has passed. They have not made "old bones," and one must be very careful with the weaker 1976s, which have lacked intensity and depth from the beginning. These wines were extremely fragile and have increasingly taken on a brown cast to their color as well as losing their fruit. Nevertheless, the top wines continue to offer delicious drinking and persuasive evidence even in a relatively diluted, extremely soft-styled vintage, with dangerously low acid levels.

The 1976 vintage was at its strongest in the northern Médoc appellations of St.-Julien, Pauillac, and St.-Estèphe, weakest in Graves and Margaux, and mixed in the Libournais appellations of Pomerol and St.-Emilion. The wine of the vintage is Ausone.

For those who admire decadently rich, honeyed, sweet wines, this is one of the two best vintages of the 1970s, given the abundant quantities of botrytis that formed in the vineyards and the lavish richness and opulent style of the wines of Barsac/Sauternes. These wines, unlike their red siblings, can last another 20–30 years.

THE BEST WINES

St.-Estèphe: Cos d'Estournel, Montrose

Pauillac: Haut-Bages Libéral, Lafite Rothschild, Pichon-Longueville–Comtesse de Lalande

St.-Julien: Beychevelle, Branaire Ducru, Ducru-Beaucaillou, Léoville Las Cases, Talbot

Margaux: Giscours, La Lagune (southern Médoc)

Médoc/Haut-Médoc/
Moulis/Listrac/
Crus Bourgeois: Sociando-Mallet

Graves Red: Haut-Brion

Graves White: Domaine de Chevalier, Laville Haut-Brion

Pomerol: Pétrus

St.-Emilion: Ausone, Cheval Blanc, Figeac

Barsac/Sauternes: Climens, Coutet, de Fargues, Guiraud, Rieussec, Suduiraut, Château d'Yquem

1975—A Quick Study
(9-22-1975)

St.-Estèphe**	Graves Red**
Pauillac***	Graves White***
St.-Julien***	Pomerol*****
Margaux**	St.-Emilion***
Médoc/Haut-Médoc Crus Bourgeois***	Barsac/Sauternes****

Size: After the abundant vintages of 1974 and 1973, 1975 was a moderately sized crop.

Important information: After three consecutive poor-to-mediocre years, the Bordelais were ready to praise the 1975 vintage to the heavens.

Maturity status: The slowest-evolving vintage in the last 30 years.

Price: Trade and consumer uneasiness concerning the falling reputation of this vintage, as well as the style of even the top wines that remain hard, closed, and nearly impenetrable, make this an attractively priced year for those with the knowledge to select the gems and the patience to wait for them to mature.

Is this the year of the great deception, or the year where some irrefutably classic wines were produced? Along with 1983 and 1964, this is perhaps the most tricky vintage with which to come to grips. There are some undeniably great wines in the 1975 vintage, but the overall quality level is distressingly uneven and the number of failures is too numerous to ignore.

Because of the three previous large crops and the international financial crisis brought on by high oil prices, the producers, knowing that their 1974, 1973, and 1972 vintages were already backed up in the marketplace, pruned their vineyards to guard against a large crop. The weather cooperated; July, August, and September were all hot months. However, in August and September several large thunderstorms dumped enormous quantities of rain on the area. It was localized, and most of it did little damage except to frazzle the nerves of wine-makers. However, several hailstorms did ravage the central Médoc communes, particularly Moulis, Lamarque, and Arcins, and some isolated hailstorms damaged southern Pessac-Léognan.

The harvest began during the third week of September and continued under generally good weather conditions through mid-October. Immediately after the harvest, producers were talking of a top-notch vintage, perhaps the best since 1961. So what happened?

Looking back after having had numerous opportunities to taste and discuss the style of this vintage with many proprietors and wine-makers, it is apparent that the majority of growers should have harvested their Cabernet Sauvignon later. Many feel it was picked too soon, and the fact that at that time many were not totally destemming only served to exacerbate the relatively hard, astringent tannins in the 1975s.

This is one of the first vintages I tasted (although on a much more limited basis) from cask, visiting Bordeaux as a tourist rather than a professional. In 1975, many of the young wines exhibited great color, intensely ripe, fragrant noses, and immense potential. Other wines appeared to have an excess of tannin. The wines immediately closed up 2–3 years after bottling, and in most cases still remain stubbornly hard and backward. There are a number of badly made, excessively tannic wines where the fruit has already dried out and the color has become brown. Many of them were aged in old oak barrels (new oak was not nearly as prevalent as it is now) and the sanitary conditions in many cellars were less than ideal. However, even allowing for these variations, I have always been struck by the tremendous difference in the quality of wines in this vintage. To this day the wide swings in quality remain far greater than in any other recent year. For example, how could Haut-Brion, La Mission Haut-Brion, La Tour Haut-Brion, Pétrus, L'Evangile, Trotanoy, and Lafleur produce such profoundly great wines, yet many of their neighbors fail completely? This remains one of the vintage's mysteries.

This is a vintage for true Bordeaux connoisseurs who have the patience to wait the wines out. The top examples, which usually come from Pomerol, St.-Julien, and Pauillac (the extraordinary success of La Mission Haut-Brion, La Tour Haut-Brion, and Haut-Brion is an exception to the sad level of quality in Graves), are wines that are just reaching their apogees. Could these great 1975s turn out to resemble wines from a vintage such as 1928 that took 30+ years to reach full maturity? The successes of this vintage are capable of lasting and lasting because they have the richness and concentration of ripe fruit to balance out their tannins. However, there are many wines that are too dry, too astringent, or too tannic to develop gracefully.

I purchased this vintage as futures, and I remember thinking I secured great deals on the first growths at $350 a case. But I have invested in 28 years of patience with very mixed results. This is the vintage for delayed gratification.

THE BEST WINES

St.-Estèphe: Meyney

Pauillac: Lafite Rothschild, Latour, Mouton Rothschild

St.-Julien: Branaire Ducru, Gloria, Gruaud Larose, Léoville Barton, Léoville Las Cases

Margaux: Giscours, Palmer

Graves Red: Haut-Brion, La Mission Haut-Brion, Pape-Clément, La Tour Haut-Brion

Pomerol: L'Eglise-Clinet, L'Enclos, L'Evangile, La Fleur-Pétrus, Le Gay, Lafleur, Nenin, Pétrus, Trotanoy, Vieux Château Certan

St.-Emilion: Cheval Blanc, Figeac, Magdelaine, Soutard

Barsac/Sauternes: Climens, Coutet, de Fargues, Raymond-Lafon, Rieussec, Château d'Yquem

1974—A Quick Study
(9-20-1974)

St.-Estèphe*	Graves Red**
Pauillac*	Graves White*
St.-Julien*	Pomerol*
Margaux*	St.-Emilion*
Médoc/Haut-Médoc Crus Bourgeois*	Barsac/Sauternes*

Size: An enormous crop was harvested.

Important information: Should readers still have stocks of the 1974s, my sincere condolences.

Maturity status: A handful of the top wines of the vintage are still "alive," but aging them any further will prove fruitless . . . literally.

Price: These wines were always inexpensive and I could not imagine them fetching a decent price unless you find someone in need of this year to celebrate a birthday.

As a result of a good flowering and a dry, sunny May and June, the crop size was large in 1974. The weather from mid-August through October was cold, windy, and rainy. Despite the persistent soggy conditions, the appellation of choice in 1974 turned out to be Graves. While most 1974s remain hard, tannic, hollow wines lacking ripeness, flesh, and character, a number of the Graves estates did produce surprisingly spicy, interesting wines, although they are compact and attenuated. The two stars are La Mission-Haut-Brion and Domaine de Chevalier, followed by Latour in Pauillac and Trotanoy in Pomerol. Should you have remaining stocks of these wines in your cellar, it would be foolish to push your luck.

The vintage was equally bad in the Barsac/Sauternes region. I have never seen a bottle to taste.

It is debatable as to which was the worst vintage during the decade of the 1970s—1977, 1974, or 1972.

1973—A Quick Study
(9-20-1973)

St.-Estèphe**	Graves Red*
Pauillac*	Graves White**
St.-Julien**	Pomerol**
Margaux*	St.-Emilion*
Médoc/Haut-Médoc Crus Bourgeois*	Barsac/Sauternes*

Size: Enormous; one of the largest crops of the 1970s.

Important information: A sadly rain-bloated, swollen crop of grapes in poor-to-mediocre condition was harvested.

Maturity status: The odds are stacked against finding a 1973 that is still in good condition, at least from a regular-size bottle.

Price: Distressed sale prices still don't make these wines attractive.

In the mid-1970s, the best 1973s had some value as agreeably light, round, soft, somewhat diluted yet pleasant Bordeaux wines. With the exception of Domaine de Chevalier, Pétrus, and the great sweet classic, Château d'Yquem, all of the 1973s have faded into oblivion.

So often the Bordelais are on the verge of a top-notch vintage when the rains arrive. The rains that came during the harvest bloated what would have been a healthy, enormous grape crop. Modern-day sprays and techniques such as *saigner* were inadequately utilized in the early 1970s, and the result in 1973 was a group of wines that lacked color, extract, acidity, and backbone. The wines were totally drinkable when released in 1976. By the beginning of the 1980s, they were in complete decline, save Pétrus.

THE BEST WINES

St.-Estèphe:	none
Pauillac:	Latour
St.-Julien:	Ducru-Beaucaillou
Margaux:	none
Médoc/Haut-Médoc/ Moulis/Listrac/ Crus Bourgeois:	none
Graves Red:	Domaine de Chevalier, La Tour Haut-Brion
Graves White:	none
Pomerol:	Pétrus
St.-Emilion:	none
Barsac/Sauternes:	Château d'Yquem

1972—A Quick Study
(10-7-1972)

St.-Estèphe 0	Graves Red*
Pauillac 0	Graves White 0
St.-Julien 0	Pomerol 0
Margaux*	St.-Emilion*
Médoc/Haut-Médoc Crus Bourgeois 0	Barsac/Sauternes 0

Size: A moderately sized crop was harvested.

Important information: The worst vintage of the decade.

Maturity status: Most wines have long since been over the hill.

Price: Extremely low.

The weather pattern of 1972 was one of unusually cool, cloudy summer months with an abnormally rainy month of August. While September brought dry, warm weather, it was too late to save the crop. The 1972 wines turned out to be the worst of the decade—acidic, green, raw, and vegetal tasting. The high acidity did manage to keep many of them alive for 10–15 years, but their deficiencies in fruit, charm, and flavor concentration were far too great for even age to overcome. As in any poor vintage, some châteaux managed to produce decent wines, with the well-drained soils of Margaux and Graves turning out slightly better wines than elsewhere.

There are no longer any wines from 1972 that would be of any interest to consumers.

THE BEST WINES*

*This list is for informational purposes only as I suspect all of the above wines, with the possible exception of Pétrus, are in serious decline unless found in larger-format bottlings that have been perfectly stored.

St.-Estèphe:	none
Pauillac:	Latour
St.-Julien:	Branaire Ducru, Léoville Las Cases
Margaux:	Giscours, Rauzan-Ségla
Médoc/Haut-Médoc/ Moulis/Listrac/ Crus Bourgeois:	none
Graves Red:	La Mission Haut-Brion, La Tour Haut-Brion
Graves White:	none
Pomerol:	Trotanoy
St.-Emilion:	Cheval Blanc, Figeac
Barsac/Sauternes:	Climens

1971—A Quick Study
(9-25-1971)

St.-Estèphe**	Graves Red***
Pauillac***	Graves White**
St.-Julien***	Pomerol****
Margaux***	St.-Emilion***
Médoc/Haut-Médoc Crus Bourgeois**	Barsac/Sauternes****

Size: Small to moderate crop size.

Important information: A good to very good, stylish vintage with the strongest efforts emerging from Pomerol and the sweet wines of Barsac/Sauternes.

Maturity status: Every 1971 has been fully mature for nearly a decade, with only the best *cuvées* capable of lasting another decade.

Price: The small crop size kept prices high, but most 1971s, compared to other good vintages of the last 30 years, are slightly undervalued.

Unlike 1970, 1971 was a small vintage because of a poor flowering in June that caused a significant reduction in the Merlot crop. By the end of the harvest, the crop size was a good 40% less than the huge crop of 1970.

Early reports of the vintage have proven to be overly enthusiastic. Some experts (particularly Bordeaux's late Peter Sichel), relying on the small production yields when compared to 1970, even claimed that the vintage was better than 1970. This has proved to be largely in error. Certainly the 1971s were forward and delicious, as were the 1970s when first released. But unlike the 1970s, the 1971s lacked the depth of color, concentration, and tannic backbone. The vintage was mixed in the Médoc, but it was a fine year for Pomerol, St.-Emilion, and Graves.

The cardinal rule of purchasing any wine is to be sure it is in pristine condition. Buying 1971s now could prove dangerous unless the wines have been exceptionally well stored. Twenty years after the vintage, there are a handful of wines that will continue to drink well—Pétrus, Latour, Trotanoy, La Mission Haut-Brion. Well-stored examples of these wines may last, not improve, for another 3–10 years. Elsewhere, storage is everything. This could be a vintage at which to take a serious look, provided one can find reasonably priced, well-preserved bottles.

The sweet wines of Barsac and Sauternes were successful and are in full maturity. The best of them have at least 1–2 decades of aging potential and will certainly outlive all of the red wines produced in 1971.

THE BEST WINES

St.-Estèphe:	Montrose
Pauillac:	Latour, Mouton Rothschild
St.-Julien:	Beychevelle, Gloria, Gruaud Larose, Talbot
Margaux:	Palmer
Médoc/Haut-Médoc/ Moulis/Listrac/ Crus Bourgeois:	none
Graves Red:	Haut-Brion, La Mission Haut-Brion, La Tour Haut-Brion
Graves White:	none
Pomerol:	La Fleur-Pétrus, Petit Village, Pétrus, Trotanoy
St.-Emilion:	Cheval Blanc, La Dominique, Magdelaine
Barsac/Sauternes:	Climens, Coutet, de Fargues, Château d'Yquem

1970—A Quick Study
(9-27-1970)

St.-Estèphe***	Graves Red****
Pauillac***	Graves White***
St.-Julien***	Pomerol****
Margaux***	St.-Emilion***
Médoc/Haut-Médoc Crus Bourgeois***	Barsac/Sauternes***

Size: An enormous crop that was a record setter at the time.

Important information: The first modern-day abundant crop that combined high quality with large quantity.

Maturity status: Initially, the 1970s were called precocious and early maturing. Most of the big 1970s have aged very slowly and are now in full maturity, with only a handful of exceptions. The smaller wines, Crus Bourgeois, and lighter-weight Pomerols and St.-Emilions should have been drunk by 1980.

Price: Expensive, no doubt because this is the most popular vintage between 1961 and 1982.

Between the two great vintages 1961 and 1982, 1970 has proved to be the best year, producing wines that were attractively rich and full of charm and complexity. They have aged more gracefully than many of the austere 1966s and seem fuller, richer, more evenly balanced and consistent than the hard, tannic, large-framed but often hollow and tough 1975s. The year 1970 proved to be the first modern-day vintage that combined high production with good quality. Moreover, it was a uniform and consistent vintage throughout Bordeaux, with every appellation able to claim its share of top-quality wines.

The weather conditions during the summer and early fall were perfect. There was no hail, no weeks of drenching downpours, no frost, and no spirit-crushing inundation at harvest time. It was one of those rare vintages where everything went well and the Bordelais harvested one of the largest and healthiest crops they had ever seen.

The year 1970 was the first vintage that I tasted out of cask, visiting with my wife as tourists a number of châteaux on my way to the cheap beaches of Spain and North Africa during summer vacations in 1971 and 1972. Even from their early days I remember the wines exhibiting dark color, an intense richness of fruit, fragrant, ripe perfume, full body, and high tannin. Yet when compared to the finest vintages of the 1980s and 1990s, 1970 seems to suffer. Undoubtedly, the number of top wines from vintages such as 2000, 1999, 1996, 1995, 1990, 1989, 1988, 1986, 1985, and 1982 easily exceed those produced in 1970.

As for the sweet wines, they have had to take a back seat to the 1971s because there was less botrytis. Although the wines are impressively big and full, they lack the complexity, delicacy, and finesse of the best 1971s.

THE BEST WINES

St.-Estèphe: Cos d'Estournel, Lafon-Rochet, Montrose, Les Ormes de Pez, de Pez

Pauillac: Grand-Puy-Lacoste, Latour, Lynch-Bages, Mouton Rothschild, Pichon Longueville Comtesse de Lalande

St.-Julien: Ducru-Beaucaillou, Gloria, Gruaud Larose, Léoville Barton, St.-Pierre

Margaux: Giscours, Lascombes, Palmer

Médoc/Haut-Médoc/
Moulis/Listrac/
Crus Bourgeois: Sociando-Mallet

Graves Red: Domaine de Chevalier, de Fieuzal, Haut-Bailly, La Mission Haut-Brion, La Tour Haut-Brion

Graves White: Domaine de Chevalier, Laville Haut-Brion

Pomerol: La Conseillante, La Fleur-Pétrus, Lafleur, Latour à Pomerol, Pétrus, Trotanoy

St.-Emilion: L'Arrosée, Cheval Blanc, La Dominique, Figeac, Magdelaine

Barsac/Sauternes: Château d'Yquem

1969—A Quick Study
(10-6-1969)

St.-Estèphe 0	Graves Red*
Pauillac 0	Graves White 0
St.-Julien 0	Pomerol*
Margaux 0	St.-Emilion 0
Médoc/Haut-Médoc Crus Bourgeois 0	Barsac/Sauternes*

Size: Small.

Important information: My candidate for the most undesirable wines produced in Bordeaux in the last 30 years.

Maturity status: I never tasted a 1969, except for Pétrus, that could have been said to have had any richness or fruit. I have not seen any of these wines except for Pétrus for a number of years, but they must be unpalatable.

Price: Amazingly, the vintage was offered at a relatively high price, but almost all the wines, except for a handful of the big names, are totally worthless.

Whenever Bordeaux has suffered through a disastrous vintage (like that of 1968) there has always been a tendency to lavish false praise on the following year. No doubt Bordeaux, after their horrible experience in 1968, badly wanted a fine vintage in 1969, but despite some overly optimistic proclamations by some leading Bordeaux experts at the time of the vintage, 1969 has turned out to be one of the least attractive vintages for Bordeaux wines in the last two decades.

The crop was small and while the summer was sufficiently hot and dry to ensure a decent maturity, torrential September rains dashed everyone's hopes for a good vintage, except for some investors who irrationally moved in to buy these insipid, nasty, acidic, sharp wines. Consequently, the 1969s, along with being extremely unattractive wines, were quite expensive when they first appeared on the market.

I can honestly say I have never tasted a red wine in 1969 I did not dislike. The only exception would be a relatively decent bottle of Pétrus (rated in the upper 70s) that I had 20 years after the vintage. Most wines are harsh and hollow with no flesh, fruit, or charm, and it is hard to imagine that any of these wines are today any more palatable than they were during the 1970s.

In the Barsac and Sauternes region, a few proprietors managed to produce acceptable wines, particularly d'Arche.

1968—A Quick Study
(9-20-1968)

St.-Estèphe 0	Graves Red*
Pauillac 0	Graves White 0
St.-Julien 0	Pomerol 0
Margaux 0	St.-Emilion 0
Médoc/Haut-Médoc Crus Bourgeois 0	Barsac/Sauternes 0

Size: A small, disastrous crop in terms of both quality and quantity.

Important information: A great year for California Cabernet Sauvignon, but not for Bordeaux.

Maturity status: All of these wines must be passé.

Price: Another worthless vintage.

The year 1968 was another of the very poor vintages the Bordelais had to suffer through in the 1960s. The culprit, as usual, was heavy rain (it was the wettest year since 1951) that bloated the grapes. However, there have been some 1968s that I found much better than anything produced in 1969, a vintage with a "better" (I am not sure that is the right word to use) reputation.

At one time wines such as Figeac, Gruaud Larose, Cantemerle, La Mission Haut-Brion, Haut-Brion, and Latour were palatable. Should anyone run across these wines today, the rule of caveat emptor would seemingly be applicable, as I doubt that any of them would have much left to enjoy.

1967—A Quick Study
(9-25-1967)

St.-Estèphe**	Graves Red***
Pauillac**	Graves White**
St.-Julien**	Pomerol***
Margaux**	St.-Emilion***
Médoc/Haut-Médoc Crus Bourgeois*	Barsac/Sauternes****

Size: An abundant crop was harvested.

Important information: A Graves, Pomerol, St.-Emilion year that favored the early harvested Merlot.

Maturity status: Most 1967s were drinkable when released in 1970 and should have been consumed by 1980. Only a handful of wines (Pétrus and Latour, for example), where well stored, will keep for another few years but are unlikely to improve.

Price: Moderate.

The year 1967 was a large, useful vintage in the sense that it produced an abundant quantity of round, quick-maturing wines. Most should have been drunk before 1980, but a handful of wines continue to display remarkable staying power and are still in the full bloom of their maturity. This is a vintage that clearly favored Pomerol and, to a lesser extent, Graves. Holding on to these wines any longer seems foolish, but some of the biggest wines, such as Latour, Pétrus, Trotanoy, and Palmer, were still drinking well in 2000. Should one find any of the top wines listed below in a large-format bottle (magnums, double magnums, etc.) at a reasonable price, my advice would be to take the gamble.

As unexciting as most red wines turned out in 1967, the sweet wines of Barsac and Sauternes were rich and honeyed, with gobs of botrytis present. However, readers must remember that only a handful of estates were truly up to the challenge of making great wines during this very depressed period for the wine production of Barsac/Sauternes.

THE BEST WINES

St.-Estèphe:	Calon-Ségur, Montrose
Pauillac:	Latour
St.-Julien:	none
Margaux:	Giscours, La Lagune (southern Médoc), Palmer
Médoc/Haut-Médoc/ Moulis/Listrac/ Crus Bourgeois:	none
Graves Red:	Haut-Brion, La Mission Haut-Brion
Graves White:	none
Pomerol:	Pétrus, Trotanoy, La Violette

St.-Emilion: Cheval Blanc, Magdelaine, Pavie

Barsac/Sauternes: Suduiraut, Château d'Yquem

1966—A Quick Study
(9-26-1966)

St.-Estèphe***	Graves Red****
Pauillac***	Graves White***
St.-Julien***	Pomerol***
Margaux***	St.-Emilion**
Médoc/Haut-Médoc Crus Bourgeois**	Barsac/Sauternes**

Size: An abundant crop was harvested.

Important information. The most overrated "top" vintage of the last 25 years.

Maturity status: The best wines are in their prime, but most wines are losing their fruit before their tannins.

Price: Expensive and overpriced.

The majority opinion is that 1966 is the best vintage of the decade after 1961. For Graves, Pomerol, and St.-Emilion, 1964 is clearly the second-best vintage of the decade. But I think that even 1962, that grossly underrated vintage, is, on overall merit, a better year than 1966. Conceived in somewhat the same spirit as 1975 (overhyped after several unexciting years, particularly in the Médoc), 1966 never developed as well as many of its proponents would have liked. The wines, now 37 years of age, for the most part have remained austere, lean, unyielding, tannic wines that lost their fruit before their tannin. Some notable exceptions do exist. Who could deny the exceptional wine made at Latour (the wine of the vintage) or the great Palmer or Lafleur?

All the disappointments that emerged from this vintage were unexpected in view of the early reports that the wines were relatively precocious, charming, and early maturing. If the vintage is not as consistent as first believed, there is an adequate number of medium-weight, classically styled wines. However, they are all overpriced as this vintage has always been fashionable and it has had no shortage of supporters, particularly from the English wine-writing community.

The sweet wines of Barsac and Sauternes are also mediocre. Favorable conditions for the development of the noble rot, *Botrytis cinerea,* never occurred.

The climatic conditions that shaped this vintage started with a slow flowering in June, intermittently hot and cold weather in July and August, and a dry and sunny September. The crop size was large and the vintage was harvested under sound weather conditions.

I would be skeptical about buying most 1966s except for one of the unqualified successes of the vintage.

THE BEST WINES

St.-Estèphe: none

Pauillac: Grand-Puy-Lacoste, Latour, Mouton Rothschild, Pichon Longueville Comtesse de Lalande

St.-Julien: Branaire Ducru, Ducru-Beaucaillou, Gruaud Larose, Léoville Las Cases

Margaux: Lascombes, Palmer

Médoc/Haut-Médoc/ Moulis/Listrac/ Crus Bourgeois: none

Graves Red: Haut-Brion, La Mission Haut-Brion, Pape-Clément

Pomerol: Lafleur, Trotanoy

St.-Emilion: Canon

Barsac/Sauternes: none

1965—A Quick Study
(10-2-1965)

St.-Estèphe 0	Graves Red 0
Pauillac 0	Graves White 0
St.-Julien 0	Pomerol 0
Margaux 0	St.-Emilion 0
Médoc/Haut-Médoc Crus Bourgeois 0	Barsac/Sauternes 0

Size: A tiny vintage.

Important information: The quintessential vintage of rot and rain.

Maturity status: The wines tasted terrible from the start and must be totally reprehensible today.

Price: Worthless.

The vintage of rot and rain. I have had little experience tasting the 1965s. It is considered by most experts to be one of the worst vintages in the post–World War II era. A wet summer was bad enough, but the undoing of this vintage was an incredibly wet and humid September that caused rot to voraciously devour the vineyards. Antirot sprays had not yet been developed. It should be obvious that these wines are to be avoided.

1964—A Quick Study
(9-22-1964)

St.-Estèphe***   Graves Red*****

Pauillac*   Graves White***

St.-Julien*   Pomerol*****

Margaux**   St.-Emilion****

Médoc/Haut-Médoc Crus Bourgeois*   Barsac/Sauternes*

Size: A large crop was harvested.

Important information: The classic examples of a vintage where the early picked Merlot and Cabernet Franc produced great wine, and the late-harvested Cabernet Sauvignon, particularly in the Médoc, was inundated. The results included numerous big name failures in the Médoc.

Maturity status: The Médocs are past their prime, but the larger-scaled wines of Graves, Pomerol, and St.-Emilion can last for another 5–10 years.

Price: Smart Bordeaux enthusiasts have always recognized the greatness of this vintage in Graves, Pomerol, and St. Emilion, and consequently prices have remained high. Nevertheless, compared to such glamour years as 1961 and 1959, the top right bank and Graves 1964s are not only underrated, but in some cases underpriced as well.

One of the most intriguing vintages of Bordeaux, 1964 produced a number of splendid, generally underrated and underpriced wines in Pomerol, St.-Emilion, and Graves where many proprietors had the good fortune to have harvested their crops before the rainy deluge began on October 8. Because of this downpour, which caught many Médoc châteaux with unharvested vineyards, 1964 has never been regarded as a top Bordeaux vintage. While the vintage can be notoriously bad for some of the properties of the Médoc and the late-harvesting Barsac and Sauternes estates, it is excellent to outstanding for the three appellations of Pomerol, St.-Emilion, and Graves.

The summer had been so hot and dry that the French Minister of Agriculture announced at the beginning of September that the "vintage of the century was about to commence." Since the Merlot grape ripens first, the harvest begins in the areas where it is planted in abundance. St.-Emilion and Pomerol harvested at the end of September and finished their picking before the inundation began on October 8. Most of the Graves properties had also finished harvesting. When the rains came, most of the Médoc estates had just begun to harvest their Cabernet Sauvignon and were unable to successfully complete the harvest because of torrential rainfall. It was a Médoc vintage noted for some extraordinary and famous failures. Pity the buyer who purchased Lafite Rothschild, Mouton Rothschild, Lynch-Bages, Calon-Ségur, or Margaux! Yet not everyone made disappointing wine. Montrose in St.-Estèphe and Latour in Pauillac made the two finest wines of the Médoc.

Because of the very damaging reports about the rainfall, many wine enthusiasts approached the 1964 vintage with a great deal of apprehension.

The top wines from Graves, St.-Emilion, and Pomerol are exceptionally rich, full-bodied, opulent, and concentrated wines with high alcohol, an opaque color, super length, and unbridled power. Amazingly, they are far richer, more interesting and complete wines than the 1966s, and in many cases, compete with the finest wines of the 1961 vintage. Because of low acidity, all of the wines reached full maturity by the mid-1980s. The best examples have been fully mature for more than a decade. Only Pétrus, Cheval Blanc, Lafleur, Trotanoy, Montrose, and Latour will last another 5–10 years.

THE BEST WINES

St.-Estèphe:	Montrose
Pauillac:	Latour
St.-Julien:	Gruaud Larose
Margaux:	none
Médoc/Haut-Médoc/ Moulis/Listrac/ Crus Bourgeois:	none
Graves Red:	Domaine de Chevalier, Haut-Bailly, Haut-Brion, La Mission Haut-Brion
Pomerol:	La Conseillante, La Fleur-Pétrus, Lafleur, Pétrus, Rouget, Trotanoy, Vieux Château Certan
St.-Emilion:	L'Arrosée, Cheval Blanc, Figeac, Soutard
Barsac/Sauternes:	none

1963—A Quick Study
(10-7-1963)

St.-Estèphe 0	Graves Red 0
Pauillac 0	Graves White 0
St.-Julien 0	Pomerol 0
Margaux 0	St.-Emilion 0
Médoc/Haut-Médoc Crus Bourgeois 0	Barsac/Sauternes 0

Size: A small to moderate-sized crop was harvested.

Important information: A dreadfully poor year that rivals 1965 for the feebleness of its wines.

Maturity status: The wines must now be awful.

Price: Worthless.

The Bordelais have never been able to decide whether 1965 or 1963 was the worst vintage of the 1960s. Rain and rot, as in 1965, were the ruination of this vintage. I have not seen a bottle of 1963 for more than 20 years.

1962—A Quick Study
(10-1-1962)

St.-Estèphe****	Graves Red***
Pauillac****	Graves White****
St.-Julien****	Pomerol***
Margaux***	St.-Emilion***
Médoc/Haut-Médoc Crus Bourgeois***	Barsac/Sauternes****

Size: An abundant crop size, in fact, one of the largest of the decade of the 1960s.

Important information: A terribly underrated vintage that had the misfortune of following one of the greatest vintages of the century.

Maturity status: The Bordeaux old-timers claim the 1962s drank beautifully by the late 1960s and continued to fill out and display considerable character, fruit, and charm in the 1970s. As the new millennium begins, the top 1962s are still lovely, rich, round wines full of finesse and elegance, but provenance and storage are everything.

Price: Undervalued, particularly when one considers the prices of its predecessor, 1961, and the overpriced 1966s.

Coming after the great vintage of 1961, it was not totally unexpected that 1962 would be underestimated. This vintage appears to be the most undervalued year for Bordeaux in the post–World War II era. Elegant, supple, very fruity, round, and charming wines that were neither too tannic nor too massive were produced in virtually every appellation. Because of their precociousness, many assumed the wines would not last, but they have kept longer than anyone would have ever imagined. Most 1962s do require consumption, but they continue to surprise, and well-preserved examples of the vintage can still be kept.

The weather was acceptable but not stunning. There was a good flowering because of a sunny, dry May, a relatively hot summer with some impressive thunderstorms, and a good, as the French say, *fin de saison,* with a hot, sunny September. The harvest was not rain free, but the inundations that could have created serious problems never occurred.

Not only was the vintage very successful in most appellations, but it was a top year for the dry white wines of Graves as well as the sweet nectars from Barsac/Sauternes.

THE BEST WINES

St.-Estèphe: Cos d'Estournel, Montrose

Pauillac: Batailley, Lafite Rothschild, Latour, Lynch-Bages, Mouton Rothschild, Pichon Longueville Comtesse de Lalande

St.-Julien: Ducru-Beaucaillou, Gruaud Larose, Talbot

Margaux: Margaux, Palmer

Médoc/Haut-Médoc/
    Moulis/Listrac/
    Crus Bourgeois: none

      Graves Red: Haut-Brion, Pape-Clément, La Mission Haut-Brion

   Graves White: Domaine de Chevalier, Laville Haut-Brion

       Pomerol: Lafleur, Pétrus, Trotanoy, La Violette

    St.-Emilion: Magdelaine

Barsac/Sauternes: Château d'Yquem

1961—A Quick Study
(9-22-1961)

St.-Estèphe*****	Graves Red*****
Pauillac*****	Graves White***
St.-Julien*****	Pomerol*****
Margaux*****	St.-Emilion***
Médoc/Haut-Médoc Crus Bourgeois***	Barsac/Sauterness**

Size: An exceptionally tiny crop was produced: In fact, this is the last vintage where a minuscule crop resulted in high quality.

Important information: One of the legendary vintages of the century.

Maturity status: The wines, drinkable young, have, with only a handful of exceptions, reached maturity and were all at their apogee by 1990. In 2003, most of the prestigious examples will keep for another 5–10 years, but most 1961s have begun to fade.

Price: The tiny quantities plus exceptional quality have made the 1961s the most dearly priced, mature vintage of great Bordeaux in the marketplace. Moreover, prices continue to increase, given the microscopic amounts of top wine that remain—an auctioneer's dream vintage. But buyers beware—many 1961s have been poorly stored or traded frequently. Moreover, some fraudulent 1961s show up in the marketplace.

The year 1961 is one of eight great vintages produced in the post–World War II era. The others—2000, 1990, 1989, 1982, 1959, 1953, 1949, 1947, 1945—all have their proponents, but none is as revered as 1961. The wines have always been prized for their sensational concentration and magnificent penetrating bouquets of superripe fruit and rich, deep, sumptuous flavors. Delicious when young, these wines, which have all reached full maturity except for a handful of the most intensely concentrated examples, are marvelous to drink. However, I see no problem in holding the best-stored bottles for at least another 10 years.

    The weather pattern was nearly perfect in 1961, with spring frosts reducing the crop size, and then sunny, hot weather throughout the summer and the harvest, resulting in splendid maturity levels. The small harvest guaranteed high prices for these wines, and today's prices for 1961s make them the equivalent of liquid gold.

The vintage was excellent throughout all appellations of Bordeaux except for the Barsac/Sauternes. This region benefitted greatly from the vintage's reputation, but a tasting of the 1961 sweet wines will reveal that even Château d'Yquem is mediocre. The incredibly dry weather conditions resulted in very little botrytis, and the results are large-scaled but essentially monolithic sweet wines that have never merited the interest they have enjoyed. The only other appellation that did not appear to be up to the overall level of quality was St.-Emilion, where many vineyards had still not fully recovered from the killer freeze of 1956.

In tasting the 1961s, the only two vintages that are somewhat similar in richness and style are 1982 and 1959. The 1959s tend to be lower in acidity, but have actually aged more slowly than the 1961s, whereas the 1982s would appear to have the same physical profile of the 1961s, but less tannin.

THE BEST WINES

St.-Estèphe: Cos d'Estournel, Haut-Marbuzet, Montrose

Pauillac: Grand-Puy-Lacoste, Latour, Lynch-Bages, Mouton Rothschild, Pichon Longueville Comtesse de Lalande, Pontet-Canet

St.-Julien: Beychevelle, Ducru-Beaucaillou, Gruaud Larose, Léoville Barton

Margaux: Maléscot St.-Expuéry, Margaux, Palmer

Médoc/Haut-Médoc/
Moulis/Listrac/
Crus Bourgeois: none

Graves Red: Haut-Bailly, Haut-Brion, La Mission Haut-Brion, La Tour Haut-Brion, Pape-Clément

Graves White: Domaine de Chevalier, Laville Haut-Brion

Pomerol: L'Eglise-Clinet, L'Evangile, Lafleur, Latour à Pomerol, Pétrus, Trotanoy

St.-Emilion: L'Arrosée, Canon, Cheval Blanc, Figeac, Magdelaine

Barsac/Sauternes: none

1960—A Quick Study
(9-9-1960)

St.-Estèphe**	Graves Red**
Pauillac**	Graves White*
St.-Julien**	Pomerol*
Margaux*	St.-Emilion*
Médoc/Haut-Médoc Crus Bourgeois 0	Barsac/Sauternes*

Size: A copious crop was harvested.

Important information: The two rainy months of August and September were this vintage's undoing.

Maturity status: Most 1960s should have been consumed within their first 10–15 years of life.

Price: Low.

I remember drinking several delicious magnums of 1960 Latour, as well as having found good examples of 1960 Montrose, La Mission Haut-Brion, and Gruaud Larose in Bordeaux. However, the last 1960 I consumed, a magnum of Latour, was drunk more than 15 years ago. I would guess that even that wine, which was the most concentrated wine of the vintage according to the Bordeaux cognoscenti, is now in decline.

1959—A Quick Study
(9-20-1959)

St.-Estèphe*****	Graves Red*****
Pauillac*****	Graves White****
St.-Julien****	Pomerol***
Margaux****	St.-Emilion**
Médoc/Haut-Médoc Crus Bourgeois***	Barsac/Sauternes*****

Size: Average.

Important information: The first of the modern-day years to be designated "vintage of the century."

Maturity status: The wines, maligned in their early years for having low acidity and lacking backbone (reminiscent of criticism by the uninformed regarding the 1982s), have aged more slowly than the more highly touted 1961s. In fact, comparisons between the top wines of the two vintages often reveal the 1959s to be less evolved with deeper color and more richness and aging potential.

Price: Never inexpensive, the 1959s have become increasingly more expensive as serious connoisseurs have begun to realize that this vintage not only rivals 1961 but, in specific cases, surpasses it.

This is an irrefutably great vintage that inexplicably was criticized at its inception, no doubt because of all the hype and praise it received from its conception. The wines, especially strong in the northern Médoc and Graves while less so on the right bank (Pomerol and St.-Emilion were still recovering from the devastating deep freeze of 1956), are among the most massive and richest ever made in Bordeaux. In fact, the two modern-day vintages that are frequently compared to 1959 are the 1989 and 1982. Those comparisons may have merit.

The 1959s have evolved at a glacial pace and are often in better condition (especially the first-growths Lafite Rothschild and Mouton Rothschild) than their 1961 counterparts, which are even more highly touted. The wines do display the effects of having been made in a classic, hot, dry year, with just enough rain to keep the vineyards from being stressed. They are full bodied, extremely alcoholic, and opulent, with high degrees of tannin and extract. Their colors have remained impressively opaque and dark, and the display less brown and orange than the 1961s.

THE BEST WINES

St.-Estèphe: Cos d'Estournel, Montrose, Les Ormes de Pez

Pauillac: Lafite Rothschild, Latour, Lynch-Bages, Mouton Rothschild, Pichon-Longueville Baron

St.-Julien: Ducru-Beaucaillou, Langoa Barton, Léoville Barton, Léoville Las Cases

Margaux: Lascombes, Maléscot St.-Expuèry, Margaux, Palmer

Graves Red: Haut-Brion, La Mission Haut-Brion, Pape-Clément, La Tour Haut-Brion

Pomerol: L'Evangile, Lafleur, Latour à Pomerol, Pétrus, Trotanoy, Vieux Château Certan

St.-Emilion: Cheval Blanc, Figeac

Barsac/Sauternes: Climens, Suduiraut, Château d'Yquem

1958—A Quick Study
(10-7-1958)

St.-Estèphe*	Graves Red***
Pauillac*	Graves White**
St.-Julien*	Pomerol*
Margaux*	St.-Emilion**
Médoc/Haut-Médoc Crus Bourgeois*	Barsac/Sauternes*

Size: A small crop was harvested.

Important information: An unfairly maligned vintage.

Maturity status: The wines are now fading badly. The best examples almost always emerge from the Graves appellation.

Price: Inexpensive.

I have less than two dozen tasting notes for 1958s, but several that do stand out are all from the Graves appellation. Haut-Brion, La Mission Haut-Brion, and Pape-Clément all made very good wines. They probably would have provided excellent drinking if consumed during the 1960s or early 1970s. I most recently had the 1958 Haut-Brion in January 1996. It was still a relatively tasty, round, soft, fleshy, tobacco- and mineral-scented and flavored wine, but one could see that it would have been much better if it had been consumed 10–15 years before. Even richer was the 1958 La Mission Haut-Brion, which should still be excellent if well-preserved bottles can be found.

1957—A Quick Study
(10-4-1957)

St.-Estèphe**	Graves Red***
Pauillac***	Graves White**
St.-Julien**	Pomerol*
Margaux*	St.-Emilion*
Médoc/Haut-Médoc Crus Bourgeois*	Barsac/Sauternes***

Size: A small crop.

Important information: A brutally cold, wet summer.

Maturity status: Because the summer was so cool, the red wines were extremely high in acidity, which has helped them stand the test of time. Where well-kept examples of 1957 can be found, this could be a vintage to purchase, provided the price is low . . . real low!

Price: The wines should be realistically and inexpensively priced given the fact that 1957 does not enjoy a good reputation.

For a vintage that has never been received very favorably, I have been surprised by how many respectable and enjoyable wines I have tasted, particularly from Pauillac and Graves. In fact, I would be pleased to serve my most finicky friends the 1957 La Mission Haut-Brion or 1957 Haut-Brion. And I would certainly be pleased to drink the 1957 Lafite Rothschild. I had two excellent bottles of Lafite in the early 1980s, but have not seen the wine since.

It was an extremely difficult year weather-wise, with very wet periods from April through August that delayed the harvest until early October. The wines had good acidity, and in the better-drained soils there was surprising ripeness given the lack of sunshine and excessive moisture. The 1957 Bordeaux, much like their Burgundy counterparts, have held up relatively well given the high acid and green tannins these wines have always possessed.

1956—A Quick Study
(10-14-1956)

St.-Estèphe 0	Graves Red 0
Pauillac 0	Graves White 0
St.-Julien 0	Pomerol 0
Margaux 0	St.-Emilion 0
Médoc/Haut-Médoc Crus Bourgeois 0	Barsac/Sauternes 0

Size: Minuscule quantities of pathetically weak wine were produced.

Important information: The coldest winter in Bordeaux since 1709 did unprecedented damage to the vineyards, particularly those in Pomerol and St.-Emilion.

Maturity status: I have not seen a 1956 in more than 15 years, and I only have a total of five notes on wines from this vintage.

Price: A worthless vintage produced worthless wines.

The year 1956 stands out as the worst vintage in modern-day Bordeaux, even surpassing such unspeakably bad years as 1972, 1969, 1968, 1965, and 1963. The winter and unbelievably cold months of February and March killed many of the vines in Pomerol and St.-Emilion and retarded the budding of those in the Médoc. The harvest was late, the crop was small, and the wines were virtually undrinkable.

1955—A Quick Study
(9-21-1955)

St.-Estèphe****	Graves Red****
Pauillac****	Graves White***
St.-Julien****	Pomerol***
Margaux***	St.-Emilion****
Médoc/Haut-Médoc Crus Bourgeois**	Barsac/Sauternes****

Size: A large, healthy crop was harvested.

Important information: For a vintage that is nearly 50 years old, this tends to be an underrated, undervalued year, although it is not comparable to 1959 or 1953. Yet the wines have generally held up and are firmer and more solidly made than the once-glorious 1953s.

Maturity status: After a long period of sleep, the top wines appear to finally be fully mature. They exhibit no signs of decline, but obviously provenance is everything when drinking a wine of this age.

Price: Undervalued, except for La Mission Haut-Brion and Mouton Rothschild, the two wines of the vintage.

For the most part, the 1955s have always come across as relatively stern and slightly tough-textured, yet impressively deep, full wines with fine color and excellent aging potential. What they lack, as a general rule, is fat, charm, and opulence.

The weather conditions were generally ideal, with hot, sunny days in June, July, and August. Although some rain fell in September, its effect was positive rather than negative.

For whatever reason, the relatively large 1955 crop has never generated the excitement that other vintages in the 1950s such as 1959 and 1953, elicited. Perhaps it was the lack of many superstar wines that kept enthusiasm muted. Among more recent years, could 1995 or 1988 be a rerun of 1955?

THE BEST WINES

St.-Estèphe: Calon-Ségur, Cos d'Estournel, Montrose, Les Ormes de Pez

Pauillac: Latour, Lynch-Bages, Mouton Rothschild

St.-Julien: Léoville Las Cases, Talbot

Margaux: Palmer

Graves Red: Haut-Brion, La Mission Haut-Brion, Pape-Clément

Pomerol: L'Evangile, Lafleur, Latour à Pomerol, Pétrus, Vieux Château Certan

St.-Emilion: Cheval Blanc, La Dominique, Soutard

Barsac/Sauternes: Château d'Yquem

1954—A Quick Study
(10-10-1954)

St.-Estèphe 0	Graves Red*
Pauillac*	Graves White 0
St.-Julien*	Pomerol 0
Margaux 0	St.-Emilion 0
Médoc/Haut-Médoc Crus Bourgeois 0	Barsac/Sauternes 0

Size: A small crop was harvested.

Important information: A terrible late-harvest vintage conducted under appalling weather conditions.

Maturity status: It is hard to believe anything from this vintage would still be worth drinking.

Price: The wines have no value.

The year 1954 was a miserable vintage throughout France, but especially in Bordeaux where the producers continued to wait for full maturity after an exceptionally cool, wet August. While the weather did improve in September, the skies opened toward the end of the month and for nearly four weeks, one low pressure system after another passed through the area, dumping enormous quantities of water that served to destroy any chance for a moderately successful vintage.

1953—A Quick Study
(9-28-1953)

St.-Estèphe*****	Graves Red****
Pauillac*****	Graves White***
St.-Julien*****	Pomerol***
Margaux****	St.-Emilion***
Médoc/Haut-Médoc Crus Bourgeois***	Barsac/Sauternes***

Size: An average-sized crop was harvested.

Important information: One of the most seductive and hedonistic Bordeaux vintages ever produced.

Maturity status: According to Bordeaux old-timers, the wines were absolutely delicious during the 1950s, even more glorious in the 1960s, and sublime during the 1970s. Charm, roundness, fragrance, and a velvety texture were the hallmarks of this vintage, which now must be approached with some degree of caution unless the wines have been impeccably stored and/or the wines are available in larger-format bottlings.

Price: No vintage with such appeal will ever sell at a reasonable price. Consequently, the 1953s remain luxury-priced wines.

The year 1953 must be the only Bordeaux vintage where it is impossible to find a dissenting voice about the quality of the wines. Bordeaux old-timers and some of our senior wine commentators (particularly the late Edmund Penning-Rowsell, David Peppercorn, and Michael Broadbent) talk of 1953 with adulation. Apparently the vintage never went through an unflattering stage. They were delicious from cask, and even more so from bottle. For that reason, much of the vintage was consumed before its 10th birthday. Those who waited saw the wines develop even greater character during the 1960s and 1970s. Many wines, especially on this side of the Atlantic, began displaying signs of age (brown color, dried-out fruit flavors) during the 1980s. In Bordeaux, when a château pulls out a 1953 they are usually in mint condition and they are some of the most beautifully sumptuous, rich, charming Clarets anyone could ever desire. A more modern-day reference point for 1953 may be the very best 1985s, perhaps some of the lighter 1982s, or even some 1999s.

If you have the discretionary income necessary to buy this highly prized vintage, prudence should dictate that the wines be from cold cellars, and/or in larger-format bottles.

THE BEST WINES

St.-Estèphe:	Calon-Ségur, Cos d'Estournel, Montrose
Pauillac:	Grand-Puy-Lacoste, Lafite Rothschild, Lynch-Bages, Mouton Rothschild
St.-Julien:	Beychevelle, Ducru-Beaucaillou, Gruaud Larose, Langoa Barton, Léoville Barton, Léoville Las Cases, Talbot
Margaux:	Cantemerle (southern Médoc), Margaux, Palmer
Graves Red:	Haut-Brion, La Mission Haut-Brion
Pomerol:	La Conseillante
St.-Emilion:	Cheval Blanc, Figeac, Magdelaine, Pavie
Barsac/Sauternes:	Climens, Château d'Yquem

1952—A Quick Study
(9-17-1952)

St.-Estèphe**	Graves Red***
Pauillac***	Graves White***
St.-Julien***	Pomerol****
Margaux**	St.-Emilion***
Médoc/Haut-Médoc Crus Bourgeois**	Barsac/Sauternes**

Size: A small crop was harvested.

Important information: The 1952 vintage was at its best in Pomerol, which largely completed its harvest prior to the rains.

Maturity status: Most wines have always tasted hard, too astringent, and lacking fat, charm, and ripeness. The best bottles could provide surprises.

Price: Expensive, but well-chosen Pomerols may represent relative values.

An excellent spring and summer of relatively hot, dry weather with just enough rain was spoiled by stormy, unstable, cold weather before and during the harvest. Much of the Merlot and some of the Cabernet Franc in Pomerol and St.-Emilion was harvested before the weather turned foul and, consequently, the best wines tended to come from these appellations. The Graves can also be successful because of the superb drainage of the soil in that appellation, particularly in the Pessac-Léognan area. The Médocs have always tended to be relatively hard and disappointing, even the first growths.

THE BEST WINES

St.-Estèphe:	Calon-Ségur, Montrose
Pauillac:	Latour, Lynch-Bages
St.-Julien:	none
Margaux:	Margaux, Palmer
Graves Red:	Haut-Brion, La Mission Haut-Brion, Pape-Clément
Pomerol:	La Fleur-Pétrus, Lafleur, Pétrus, Trotanoy
St.-Emilion:	Cheval Blanc, Magdelaine
Barsac/Sauternes:	none

1951—A Quick Study
(10-9-1951)

St.-Estèphe 0	Graves Red 0
Pauillac 0	Graves White 0
St.-Julien 0	Pomerol 0
Margaux 0	St.-Emilion 0
Médoc/Haut-Médoc Crus Bourgeois 0	Barsac/Sauternes 0

Size: A tiny crop was harvested.

Important information: Even today, 1951 is considered one of the all-time worst vintages for dry white, dry red, and sweet wines from Bordeaux. If you were born in this year, think positively . . . it was a great year for Napa Valley Cabernet Sauvignon!

Maturity status: Undrinkable young, undrinkable old.

Price: Another worthless vintage.

Frightfully bad weather in the spring, summer, and before and during the harvest (rain and unseasonably cold temperatures) was the complete undoing of this vintage, which has the ignominious pleasure of having one of the worst reputations of any vintage in the post–World War II era.

1950—A Quick Study
(9-17-1950)

St.-Estèphe**	Graves Red***
Pauillac***	Graves White***
St.-Julien***	Pomerol*****
Margaux***	St.-Emilion****
Médoc/Haut-Médoc Crus Bourgeois*	Barsac/Sauternes****

Size: An abundant crop was harvested.

Important information: Many Pomerols are prodigious, yet they have been totally ignored by the chroniclers of the Bordeaux region.

Maturity status: Most Médocs and Graves are now in decline. The top heavyweight Pomerols can be splendid with years of life still left.

Price: The quality of the Pomerols is no longer a secret.

The year 1950 is another example where the Médoc formed the general impression of the Bordeaux vintage. This relatively abundant year was the result of good flowering, a hot, dry summer, and a difficult early September complicated by large amounts of rain.

The Médocs, all of which are in decline, were soft, forward, medium-bodied wines that probably had a kinship to more recent vintages such as 1999, 1981, or 1971. The Graves were slightly better, but even they are probably passé. The two best appellations were St.-Emilion, which produced a number of rich, full, intense wines that aged quickly, and Pomerol, which had its fourth superb vintage in succession—unprecedented in the history of that area. The wines are unbelievably rich, unctuous, and concentrated and, in many cases, are capable of rivaling the greatest Pomerols of more highly renowned vintages such as 1949 and 1947.

The other appellation that prospered in 1950 was Barsac/Sauternes. Fanciers of these wines still claim 1950 is one of the greatest post–World War II vintages for sweet wines.

THE BEST WINES

St.-Estèphe: none

Pauillac: Latour

St.-Julien: none

Margaux: Margaux

Médoc/Haut-Médoc/
Moulis/Listrac/
Crus Bourgeois: none

Graves Red: Haut-Brion, La Mission Haut-Brion

Pomerol: L'Eglise-Clinet, L'Evangile, La Fleur-Pétrus, Le Gay, Lafleur, Latour à Pomerol, Pétrus, Vieux Château Certan

St.-Emilion: Cheval Blanc, Figeac, Soutard

Barsac/Sauternes: Climens, Coutet, Suduiraut, Château d'Yquem

1949—A Quick Study
(9-27-1949)

St.-Estèphe*****   Graves Red*****

Pauillac*****   Graves White***

St.-Julien*****   Pomerol****

Margaux****   St.-Emilion****

Médoc/Haut-Médoc Crus Bourgeois***   Barsac/Sauternes*****

Size: A small crop was harvested.

Important information: The driest and sunniest vintage since 1893, and rivaled in more recent years only by 1990.

Maturity status: The finest wines are still in full blossom, displaying remarkable richness and concentration, but their provenance and history of storage are critical factors when contemplating a purchase.

Price: Frightfully expensive.

Among the four extraordinary vintages of the late 1940s—1949, 1948, 1947, and 1945—this has always been my favorite. The wines, slightly less massive and alcoholic than the 1947s, also appear to possess greater balance, harmony, and fruit than the 1945s and more complexity than the 1948s. In short, the top wines are magnificent. The year 1949 is certainly one of the most exceptional vintages of the last 100 years. Only the right bank wines (except for Cheval Blanc) appear inferior to the quality of their 1947s. In the Médoc and Graves it is a terrific vintage, with nearly everyone making wines of astounding ripeness, richness, opulence, power, and length.

The vintage was marked by the extraordinary heat and sunny conditions that Bordeaux enjoyed throughout the summer. Those consumers who have been worried that

1990 and 1989 were too hot to make great wine only need to look at the weather statistics for 1949. It was one of the two hottest vintages (the other being 1947) since 1893, as well as the sunniest vintage since 1893. It was not a totally dry harvest, but the amount of rainfall was virtually identical to that in a year such as 1982. Some of the rain fell before the harvest, which, given the dry, parched condition of the soil, was actually beneficial.

Even the sweet wines of Barsac and Sauternes were exciting. Buying 1949s today will cost an arm and a leg as these are among the most expensive and sought-after wines of the 20th century.

THE BEST WINES

St.-Estèphe: Calon-Ségur, Cos d'Estournel, Montrose

Pauillac: Grand-Puy-Lacoste, Latour, Mouton Rothschild

St.-Julien: Gruaud Larose, Léoville Barton, Talbot

Margaux: Palmer

Graves Red: Haut-Brion, La Mission Haut-Brion, Pape-Clément

Pomerol: La Conseillante, L'Eglise-Clinet, L'Evangile, Lafleur, Latour à Pomerol, Pétrus, Trotanoy, Vieux Château Certan

St.-Emilion: Cheval Blanc

Barsac/Sauternes: Climens, Coutet, Château d'Yquem

1948—A Quick Study
(9-22-1948)

St.-Estèphe***	Graves Red****
Pauillac****	Graves White***
St.-Julien****	Pomerol***
Margaux****	St.-Emilion***
Médoc/Haut-Médoc Crus Bourgeois***	Barsac/Sauternes**

Size: An average to below-average crop size was harvested.

Important information: A largely ignored but good-to-excellent vintage overshadowed by both its predecessor and successor.

Maturity status: The hard and backward characteristics of these wines have served them well during their evolution. Most of the larger, more concentrated 1948s are still attractive wines.

Price: Undervalued given their age and quality.

When Bordeaux has three top vintages in a row it is often the case that one is totally forgotten, and that has certainly proven correct with respect to 1948. It was a very good year that had the misfortune to fall between two legendary vintages.

Because of a difficult flowering due to wet, windy, cool weather in June, the crop size was smaller than in 1949 and 1947. However, July and August were fine months weather-wise, with September exceptionally warm and dry.

Despite the high quality of the wines, they never caught on with Claret enthusiasts. And who can fault the wine buyers? The 1947s were more flashy, opulent, alcoholic, and fuller bodied, and the 1949s more precocious and richer than the harder, tougher, more tannic, and unforthcoming 1948s.

This is a vintage that in many cases has matured more gracefully than the massive 1947s. The top wines tend to still be in excellent condition. Prices remain reasonable, if only in comparison to what one has to pay for 1949 and 1947.

THE BEST WINES

St.-Estèphe:	Cos d'Estournel
Pauillac:	Grand-Puy-Lacoste, Latour, Lynch-Bages, Mouton Rothschild
St.-Julien:	Langoa Barton, Léoville Barton (the wine of the Médoc)
Margaux:	Cantemerle (southern Médoc), Margaux, Palmer
Graves Red:	La Mission Haut-Brion, Pape-Clément
Pomerol:	L'Eglise-Clinet, Lafleur, Latour à Pomerol, Petit Village, Pétrus, Vieux Château Certan
St.-Emilion:	Cheval Blanc
Barsac/Sauternes:	none

1947—A Quick Study
(9-15-1947)

St.-Estèphe***	Graves Red****
Pauillac***	Graves White***
St.-Julien***	Pomerol*****
Margaux**	St.-Emilion*****
Médoc/Haut-Médoc Crus Bourgeois*	Barsac/Sauternes***

Size: An abundant crop was harvested.

Important information: A year of extraordinary extremes in quality with some of the most Port-like, concentrated wines ever produced in Bordeaux, but such wines only emanated from Pomerol and St.-Emilion. This is also a vintage of unexpected failures (i.e., Lafite Rothschild).

Maturity status: Except for the most concentrated and powerful Pomerols and St.-Emilions, this is a vintage that requires immediate consumption as many wines have gone over the top and are now exhibiting excessive volatile acidity and dried-out fruit.

Price: Preposterously high given the fact that this was another "vintage of the century." Beware of many fraudulent bottles of Pétrus and Cheval Blanc.

This quintessentially hot-year vintage produced many wines that are among the most enormously concentrated, Port-like, intense wines I have ever tasted. Most of the real heavyweights in this vintage have emerged from Pomerol and St.-Emilion. In the Médoc, it was a vintage of remarkable irregularity. Properties such as Calon-Ségur and Mouton Rothschild made great wines, but certain top-growths, such as Lafite Rothschild and Latour, as well as super-seconds, such as Léoville Barton, produced wines with excessive acidity.

The top wines are something to behold if only because of their excessively rich, sweet style that comes closest, in modern-day terms, to 1982. Yet I know of no 1982 that has the level of extract and intensity of the greatest 1947s.

The reasons for such intensity were the exceptionally hot months of July and August, which were followed (much like in 1982) by a torridly hot, almost tropical heat wave in mid-September just as the harvest began. Those properties that were unable to control the temperatures of hot grapes had stuck fermentations, residual sugar in the wines, and, in many cases, levels of volatile acidity that would horrify modern-day oenologists. Those who were able to master the tricky vinification made the richest, most opulent red wines Bordeaux has produced during the 20th century.

THE BEST WINES

St.-Estèphe:	Calon-Ségur
Pauillac:	Grand-Puy-Lacoste, Mouton Rothschild
St.-Julien:	Ducru-Beaucaillou, Léoville Las Cases
Margaux:	Margaux
Graves Red:	Haut-Brion, La Mission Haut-Brion, La Tour Haut-Brion
Pomerol:	Clinet, La Conseillante, L'Eglise-Clinet, L'Enclos, L'Evangile, La Fleur-Pétrus, Le Gay, Lafleur, Latour à Pomerol, Nenin, Pétrus, Rouget, Vieux Château Certan
St.-Emilion:	Canon, Cheval Blanc, Figeac, La Gaffelière Naudes
Barsac/Sauternes:	Climens, Suduiraut

1946—A Quick Study
(9-30-1946)

St.-Estèphe**	Graves Red*
Pauillac**	Graves White 0
St.-Julien**	Pomerol 0
Margaux*	St.-Emilion 0
Médoc/Haut-Médoc Crus Bourgeois 0	Barsac/Sauternes 0

Size: A small crop was harvested.

Important information: The only year in the post–World War II era where the Bordeaux vineyards were invaded by locusts.

Maturity status: The wines must certainly be over the hill.

Price: Except for the rare bottle of Mouton Rothschild (needed by billionaires to complete their collections), most of these wines have little value.

A fine, hot summer, particularly in July and August, was spoiled by an unusually wet, windy, cold September that delayed the harvest and caused rampant rot in the vineyards. The 1946s are rarely seen in the marketplace. I have only 11 tasting notes for the entire vintage. I do not know of any top wines, although Edmund Penning-Rowsell, the late British dean on the wines of Bordeaux, claimed the 1946 Latour was excellent. I have never seen a bottle.

1945—A Quick Study
(9-13-1945)

St.-Estèphe****	Graves Red*****
Pauillac*****	Graves White*****
St.-Julien*****	Pomerol*****
Margaux****	St.-Emilion*****
Médoc/Haut-Médoc Crus Bourgeois****	Barsac/Sauternes*****

Size: A tiny crop was harvested.

Important information: The most acclaimed vintage of the century.

Maturity status: Certain wines from this vintage (only those that have been stored impeccably) are still not fully mature.

Price: The most expensive and overpriced Clarets of the century.

No vintage in the post–World War II era, not 2000, 1990, 1989, 1982, 1961, 1959, or 1953, enjoys the reputation that the 1945 vintage does. The celebration of the end of an appallingly destructive war, combined with the fact that the weather was remarkable, produced one of the smallest, most concentrated crops of grapes ever seen. In the late 1980s I had the first growths on two separate occasions, and there seems to be no doubt that this is indeed a remarkable vintage that has taken almost 45 years to reach its peak. The great wines, probably about a dozen, could well last for another 20–30 years, making a mockery of most of the more recent great vintages that must be consumed within 25–30 years of the vintage.

The vintage is not without critics, some of whom have said that the wines are excessively tannic and many are drying out. There are many wines that match these descriptions, but if one judges a vintage on the performance of the top properties, such as the first growths, super-seconds, and leading domaines in Pomerol and St.-Emilion, 1945 remains a formidable vintage.

The reason for the tiny crop was the notoriously frigid spell during the month of May (*la gelée noire*) that was followed by a summer of exceptional heat and drought. An early harvest began on September 13, the same day that the harvest began in both 1982 and 1976.

THE BEST WINES

St.-Estèphe: Calon-Ségur, Montrose, Les Ormes de Pez

Pauillac: Latour, Mouton Rothschild, Pichon Longueville Comtesse de Lalande, Pontet-Canet

St.-Julien: Gruaud Larose, Léoville Barton, Talbot

Margaux: Margaux, Palmer

Graves Red: Haut-Brion, La Mission Haut-Brion, La Tour Haut-Brion

Graves White: Laville Haut-Brion

Pomerol: L'Eglise-Clinet, La Fleur-Pétrus, Gazin, Lafleur, Latour à Pomerol, Pétrus, Rouget, Trotanoy, Vieux Château Certan

St.-Emilion: Canon, Cheval Blanc, Figeac, La Gaffelière-Naudes, Larcis Ducasse, Magdelaine

Barsac/Sauternes: Suduiraut, Château d'Yquem

3: EVALUATING
THE WINES
OF BORDEAUX

ST.-ESTÈPHE

Of all the wines produced in the Haut-Médoc, those of St.-Estèphe have the reputation of being the slowest to mature and the toughest, most tannic wines. While this generalization may have been true 30 or 40 years ago, the wines now being made in St.-Estèphe reveal an increasing reliance on the softer, fleshier Merlot grape, as well as a vinification aimed at producing more supple, earlier-maturing wines.

St.-Estèphe, which has 3,404 acres under vine, is the least prestigious of the four well-known Haut-Médoc appellations, including Margaux, Pauillac, and St.-Julien. In the 1855 classification, only five wines were considered outstanding enough to be ranked. However, from a consumer's perspective, the commune of St.-Estèphe has numerous Cru Bourgeois châteaux that are currently making wine as good as several clas-

ST·ESTÈPHE

● CHÂTEAU   ═══ ROAD

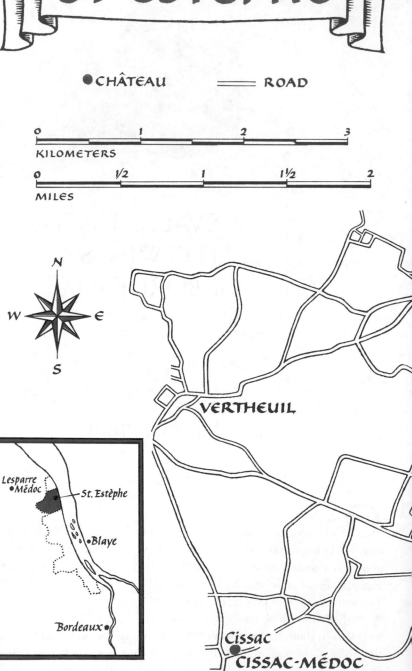

VERTHEUIL

Lesparre
● Médoc — St. Estèphe

● Blaye

Bordeaux ●

Cissac
CISSAC-MÉDOC

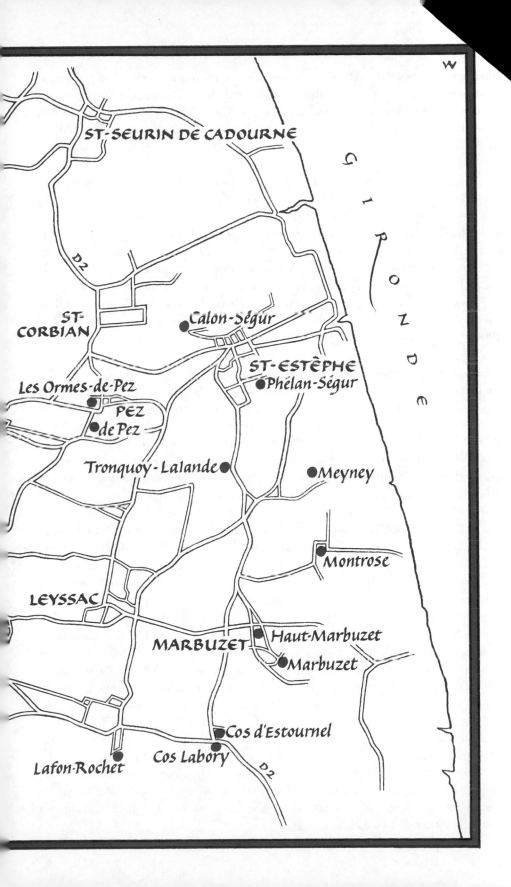

s. Several of these Cru Bourgeois estates are producing better wine, at
esting as one of the five classified growths in St.-Estèphe. Disappointing
, Cos Labory's recent vintages have been more promising. Top-notch,
n estates making very good wine, such as Haut-Marbuzet, Meyney, and Les
Ormes de Pez, would certainly merit serious consideration for elevation into the ranks
of the classified growths.

Even though the growers of St.-Estèphe are consciously trying to make a more supple style of wine, the wines of this region generally remain among the most backward
and unyielding produced in Bordeaux. Part of the explanation is the soil. There is less
gravel in St.-Estèphe, and there is a higher clay content. Consequently the drainage is
slower. The resulting wines are relatively higher in acidity and lower in pH, and their
textures are chunkier and more burly than, for example, wines made from vineyards
planted in the light, gravelly soil of Margaux and Graves. However, this clay is beneficial in extremely hot drought years, such as was 1970. Moisture retention is better than
the gravel beds farther south, and St.-Estèphe can soar in quality in such vintages as
1990.

At present, virtually everyone agrees that Cos d'Estournel is making this commune's most popular wine, particularly since the early 1980s. Coincidentally, it is also
the first châteaux one sees when crossing the Pauillac boundary into St.-Estèphe. The
eccentric pagoda-styled château sits on a ridge overlooking the gardens and château of
Pauillac's famous Lafite Rothschild. Several recent vintages, particularly the 2001,
1996, 1995, 1990, 1986, 1985, and 1982, would even suggest that Cos d'Estournel has
first-growth aspirations. Cos d'Estournel's wine represents a brilliant combination of
modern technology and respect for tradition. It is a wine supple enough to drink by age
five or six, but made to age and improve for as many as 10–25 years.

The chief rivals to Cos d'Estournel are Montrose and Calon-Ségur. Montrose is hidden on one of St.-Estèphe's tiny back roads, closer to the Gironde River. Until the mid-
1970s, Montrose made one of Bordeaux's biggest, deepest, and slowest-maturing wines.
Many Bordelais compared it to Latour because of its weight and richness, in addition to
its close geographical proximity to the river. During the mid-1980s, Montrose curiously
lightened its style, but fortunately this flirtation with a more commercial style was short-
lived. Vintages of Montrose still need a good 15–20 years to shed their cloak of tannin.
The profound 1990 and 1989 Montrose represent a return to the style that made Montrose among the most heralded wines of the Médoc during much of this century. These
reassuringly profound wines were followed by great classics in 1996 and 2000.

Potentially as complex and complete as any St.-Estèphe, as well as just about any
Médoc, is Calon-Ségur, the white-walled château just outside the village of St.-
Estèphe. When Calon-Ségur does everything right, as it did in 2000, 1996, 1995,
1982, 1953, 1947, 1929, 1926, and 1921, one cannot find a better Bordeaux. But
Calon-Ségur has always been unpredictable, and when looking at its wines from the
1980s and 1990s, Calon's propensity for inconsistency remains as troublesome as ever.
Since Madame Capbern Gasqueton assumed full control over the estate following the
death of her husband, Calon-Ségur has become more consistent in quality, while also
representing excellent value.

Lafon-Rochet continues to improve, moving toward a more accessible, friendlier wine than the solid, tannic, backward style of wine that fanciers of hard, tough St.-Estèphe wines found so authentic in the 1970s and 1980s. The fifth-growth Cos Labory, once this commune's most overrated wine, has rebounded nicely, with recent vintages showing improvement in quality.

One of the great attractions of St.-Estèphe is the glorious number of expertly made Cru Bourgeois wines, some of which merit elevation to classified growths.

Haut-Marbuzet, for openers, makes a splendid wine, flamboyantly spicy and oaky, and filled with the flavors and aromas of black currants. If one were to mistake it for a classified growth, I would not be surprised. Phelan Ségur is enjoying a renaissance and is a wine that lasts nearly as long as any wine of St.-Estèphe. Shrewd collectors are now beating a path to this property's wines, but the quality in the late 1990s was surprisingly inconsistent. Meyney is another of St.-Estèphe's reliable Cru Bourgeois properties. Superbly located north of Montrose near the river, Meyney is a large producer, and its reliability for big, rich, deep, fine wines makes this St.-Estèphe a wine to seek out, although vintages in the late 1990s were largely indifferent.

Perhaps the two Crus Bourgeois that bear watching the closest are de Pez and its neighbor, Les Ormes de Pez. De Pez is now owned by the Roederer champagne firm, and significant investments were made in the late 1990s. This is an ancient property (once part of the estate of the 17th-century Pontacs, who also owned Haut-Brion) that has considerable potential, although in 2003, much of it still remains unrealized.

Les Ormes de Pez is owned by the Cazes family of Lynch-Bages. This has always been an extremely reliable wine, juicy, fat, succulent, and fairly priced. Shrewd consumers have been stockpiling it away for decades.

St.-Estèphes are not wines to look for and buy in mediocre or poor Bordeaux vintages. The best performers in off-vintages are Cos d'Estournel, Montrose, and Haut-Marbuzet. However, the great vintages for this region are ones in which there are plenty of sunshine and heat, and all the grapes, particularly the Merlot, become fully mature. For these reasons, vintages such as 2000, 1996, 1995, 1990, 1989, 1986, 1982, 1970, 1961, and 1959 are superlative years for St.-Estèphe. Excessively hot and dry years, which can stress the vineyards planted on light, gravelly soil, are frequently outstanding vintages in the heavier soils of St.-Estèphe. Both 1990 and 1989, two of the hottest and driest vintages this century, are convincing case studies. Remember, the soils of this region are less porous, and so drainage is not as good as in other Médoc appellations. Vintages where there was abundant rainfall are frequently less successful in St.-Estèphe than in nearby St.-Julien or Margaux. For example, 1999, 1997, 1987, 1983, and 1980 were more successful in other Médoc appellations. An important factor for the success of the vintage in St.-Estèphe is a healthy, very ripe Merlot crop, which helps cut the normally higher than average acidity and tannins of St.-Estèphe's wines. The years 2000, 1998, 1995, 1990, 1989, 1982, 1976, and 1970 all favored the Merlot grape, and as a consequence, St.-Estèphe produced numerous outstanding wines.

St.-Estèphe wines, as the least glamorous wines of the famous Médoc, offer excellent wine values. This applies not only to the famous classified growths, but also to the appellation's excellent array of Cru Bourgeois wines.

ST.-ESTÈPHE
(An Insider's View)

Overall Appellation Potential: Average to superb

The Most Potential for Aging: Calon-Ségur, Cos d'Estournel, Montrose

The Most Elegant: Cos d'Estournel

The Most Concentrated: Calon-Ségur, Cos d'Estournel, Montrose

The Best Value: Lafon-Rochet, Meyney, Les Ormes de Pez, Petit Bocq

The Most Exotic: Haut-Marbuzet

The Most Difficult to Understand (when young): Calon-Ségur

The Most Underrated: Calon-Ségur, Lafon-Rochet

The Easiest to Appreciate Young: Haut-Marbuzet, Les Ormes de Pez, Petit Bocq

Up-and-Coming Estates: Lafon-Rochet, Cos Labory

Greatest Recent Vintages: 2000, 1996, 1995, 1990, 1989, 1986, 1982, 1961, 1959

ST.-ESTÈPHE—AN OVERVIEW

Location: The most northern of the four principal Médoc appellations, St.-Estèphe is on the left bank of the Gironde River, approximately 28 miles north of the city of Bordeaux

Acres Under Vine: 3,404

Communes: St.-Estèphe

Average Annual Production: 765,000 cases

Classified Growths: Total of 5:2 second-growths, 1 third-growth, 1 fourth-growth, and 1 fifth-growth; there are 43 Crus Bourgeois

Principal Grape Varieties: Cabernet Sauvignon and Merlot dominate, with Cabernet Franc and Petit Verdot used in small proportions

Principal Soil Type: Diverse soils; the finest vineyards are on gravel ridges, but sandy and clay soils with some limestone are commonplace

A CONSUMER'S CLASSIFICATION
OF THE CHÂTEAUX OF ST.-ESTÈPHE

OUTSTANDING
Calon-Ségur, Cos d'Estournel, Montrose

EXCELLENT
None

VERY GOOD
Haut-Marbuzet, Lafon-Rochet, Les Ormes de Pez

GOOD
Chambert-Marbuzet, Cos Labory, Coutelin-Merville, Lavillotte, Meyney, Petit Bocq, de Pez, Phelan Ségur, Tronquoy-Lalande

OTHER NOTABLE ST.-ESTÈPHE PRODUCERS

Andron Blanquet, Beau-Site, Bel Air, Le Boscq, Capbern Gasqueton, Cave Coopérative Marquis de St.-Estèphe, La Commanderie, Le Crock, Haut-Beauséjour, Haut-Coteau, Château La Haye, Houissant, Marbuzet, Pomys, Ségur de Cabanac, Tour de Marbuzet, Tour de Pez, Tour des Termes, Valrose, Vieux Coutelin

ANDRON BLANQUET

Classification: Cru Bourgeois

Owner: SCE Domaines Audoy

Address: 33180 St.-Estèphe

Telephone: 05 56 59 30 22; Telefax: 05 56 59 73 52

E-mail: cos-labory@wanadoo.fr

No visits

VINEYARDS

Surface area: 39.5 acres

Grape varietals: 50% Cabernet Sauvignon, 30% Merlot, 20% Cabernet Franc

Average age of vines: 30 years

Density of plantation: 8,700 vines per hectare

Average yields: 50 hectoliters per hectare

Elevage: Fermentation at 30°C in temperature-controlled epoxy-lined concrete tanks with frequent but short pumping-overs. Maceration of 25 days. Aging in barrels for 14 months with 25% new oak. Fining, no filtration.

WINES PRODUCED

Château Andron Blanquet: 70,000 bottles

Château Saint-Roc: 36,000 bottles

Plateau of maturity: Within 3–8 years of the vintage

GENERAL APPRECIATION

Despite its enviable location near Lafite Rothschild and Cos d'Estournel, this estate produces wines that are mediocre at their worst and so-so at their best, regardless of vintage conditions. One can find many Crus Bourgeois of a higher level than Andron Blanquet, and at fairer prices.

Andron Blanquet should produce better wine. The vineyard, which is close to those of Lafite Rothschild in neighboring Pauillac and the famous Cos d'Estournel in St.-Estèphe, is located on a plateau of gravelly soil that is considered to be slightly warmer than other microclimates in St.-Estèphe. The wine is vinified properly, with a relatively long maceration period, yet Andron Blanquet consistently lacks concentration, character, and charm. The institution of a second wine at the request of the oenologist and proprietor, Bernard Audoy, may lead to better quality.

BEAU-SITE

Classification: Cru Bourgeois Exceptionnel

Owner: Castéja family

Address: 33180 St.-Estèphe

Mailing Address: c/o Domaines Borie Manoux, 86, cours Balguerie-Stuttenberg, 33000 Bordeaux

Telephone: 05 56 00 00 70; Telefax: 05 57 87 48 61

E-mail: borie-manoux@dial.oleane.com

Visits: By appointment only

Contact: Domaines Borie-Manoux

VINEYARDS

Surface area: 93.9 acres

Grape varietals: 60% Cabernet Sauvignon, 35% Merlot, 3% Cabernet Franc, 2% Petit Verdot

Average age of vines: 35 years

Density of plantation: 8,300 vines per hectare

Average yields: 54 hectoliters per hectare

Elevage: Three-week fermentation and maceration in temperature-controlled stainless-steel vats. Eighteen months aging with 40% new oak (the same proportion of the yield undergoes malolactics in barrel). Fining, no filtration.

WINES PRODUCED

Château Beau-Site: 200,000 bottles

Château Haut Vignoble Seguin: 40,000 bottles

Plateau of maturity: Within 3–10 years of the vintage

GENERAL APPRECIATION

This estate, which merits its Cru Bourgeois status, has improved over recent years, but its wines remain rather austere. However, the quality/price ratio is interesting.

The lovely, well-situated Château Beau-Site was acquired by the well-known Bordelais family of Emile Castéja in 1955. The main part of the vineyard is situated on a plateau overlooking the Gironde River near the village of St.-Corbian. Beau-Site should be an excellent wine, but its performance in the 1960s and 1970s was spotty. Did the high percentage of Cabernet Sauvignon result in a wine that was too often tannic and tough? Whatever the reason, the decisions to harvest later and to utilize 40% new oak casks (with some malolactic in barrel) have all produced increasingly more supple and popular wines in the 1980s and 1990s. Nevertheless, this is still a fickle St.-Estèphe, with an abundance of tannin, although now the tannins are riper and smoother.

The wines of Beau-Site are distributed exclusively through the *négociant* firm of Borie-Manoux.

CALON-SÉGUR

Classification: Third growth in 1855

Owner: GFA Calon-Ségur

Address: 33180 St.-Estèphe

Telephone: 05 56 59 30 08; Telefax: 05 56 59 71 51

Visits: By appointment only

Contact: Denise Capbern Gasqueton

VINEYARDS

Surface area: 130.9 acres

Grape varietals: 65% Cabernet Sauvignon, 20% Merlot, 15% Cabernet Franc

Average age of vines: 35 years

Average yields: 40 hectoliters per hectare

Elevage: Prolonged fermentation (3 weeks) in temperature-controlled stainless-steel vats. Part of the yield undergoes malolactics in barrel. Aging in barrels for 18 months with 50% new oak. Fining, no filtration. Most of the Merlot is given malolactic fermentation in barrel.

WINES PRODUCED

Calon-Ségur: 240,000 bottles

Marquis de Calon: 40,000 bottles

Plateau of maturity: Within 8–30 years of the vintage

GENERAL APPRECIATION

Calon-Ségur has produced wines of first-growth quality from the 1920s to the beginning of the 1960s. After a period of slump, it came back on track in the 1990s, with profound wines in 1995, 1996, and 2000. Prices are reasonable, so much so that Calon is often considered as one of the best buys of the Médoc. However, quality is not always regular and it is advisable to be cautious when picking a vintage.

Situated on a bed of sandy gravel and iron-enriched limestone in the northernmost reaches of the commune of St.-Estèphe is Calon-Ségur, the most northerly classified growth. Like its nearby neighbor, Château Montrose, there is a live-in owner, the no-nonsense, suffer-no-fools Madame Capbern Gasqueton. The white château of Calon-Ségur dominates the landscape, with its two towers that have unusually rounded roofs. Surrounding the château is a stone wall, or *clos*, which, while common in Burgundy, is unusual for Bordeaux.

The history of Calon-Ségur dates back to Roman times, when the commune of St.-Estèphe was known as "Calones." Notoriety as a wine-producing estate is no doubt enhanced by the famous 18th-century quotation attributed to the Marquis de Ségur, who surprised friends with his statement, "I make my wine at Lafite and Latour, but my heart is in Calon." His emotional attachment to Calon has been immortalized with a heart on Calon's label (the perfect gift for Valentine's Day).

For much of the 20th century, Calon-Ségur did everything right, often producing wines that were every bit as compelling as the first-growths. There were extraordinary efforts in 1929, 1928, and 1926, and in the dismal decade of the 1930s a fine 1934 was produced. In the late 1940s and early 1950s, few properties in Bordeaux could match the stunning successes that Calon-Ségur enjoyed in 1953, 1949, 1948, 1947, and 1945. Following 1953, there was not another truly profound wine produced at Calon-Ségur until 1982. They were not bad, but even the top years during the 1960s and 1970s tended to turn out wines that were slightly oxidized, with tired fruit and some-times musty, old-wood flavor, as well as excessive, astringent tannins. The feeling by knowledgeable insiders in Bordeaux was that bringing up the wine in the cellars—the so-called *élevage*—was suspect, the wines were bottled too late, and the rack-ing and cleanliness of the old barrels was often handled in a casual, if not indifferent, manner.

Since 1982 Calon-Ségur has regained its form, turning out fine wines in 1990, 1989, and 1988, and prodigious wines in 2000, 1996, and 1995. This great historic estate, seemingly directionless in the 1970s, has come back strongly and, while totally differ-ent in style, the wines are capable of challenging Cos d'Estournel and Montrose. Madame Gasqueton (and before his death, her husband) would argue that of all the St.-Estèphes, Calon-Ségur remains the most faithful to the traditional style of long-lived wines that are slow to evolve and blossom. In that sense, she is correct, and traditional-ists would be well advised to consider the recent efforts of this beautifully situated, his-torically significant estate that is the last (geographically speaking) of the classified growths in the famed 1855 classification.

IMPORTANT VINTAGES

2001　Approximately 65% of the crop made it into the 2001 Calon-Ségur, which is a
89–91　standard blend of 60% Cabernet Sauvignon, 30% Merlot, and 10% Cabernet Franc. Half the crop enjoyed malolactic in barrel and half in tank. Although this is a richer effort than the 1999 and the 1998, it falls short of the profound 2000 Calon-Ségur. The deep ruby/purple-colored 2001 exhibits a sweet nose of mulber-ries, cherries, dried herbs, earth, and licorice, a sweet attack, ripe tannin, good definition, and a medium-bodied, long finish with impressive purity. If this St.-Estèphe fleshes out, it will merit an outstanding score. Anticipated maturity: 2006–2018. Last tasted, 1/03.

2000　Unquestionably the greatest Calon-Ségur since the 1982, this blend of 60%
95+　Cabernet Sauvignon, 30% Merlot, and 10% Cabernet Franc exhibits an opaque plum/purple color along with gorgeous aromas of creosote intermixed with black cherries, cassis, licorice, and stony, liquid minerals. An amazing effort, full-bodied and opulent, it possesses abundant tannin that is well concealed by the wealth of fruit, glycerin, and intensity. This large-scaled wine may be tremendous right from release, but I suspect it will require patience. Given this estate's history of closing down for considerable time after bottling, despite how precocious the wine shows, look for it to be at its best between 2010–2040. Last tasted, 1/03.

1999　An elegant, lighter-styled Calon-Ségur, particularly when compared to the 2000,
87　this supple 1999 exhibits an evolved color, sweet cherry and dusty berry fruit, and hints of dried herbs. It is a spicy, cherry-flavored effort with a style reminiscent of a Beaune premier cru. The blend of 60% Cabernet Sauvignon, 30% Merlot, and

10% Cabernet Franc has resulted in a wine of elegance and finesse rather than one with a lot of stuffing and power. Drink it during its first 7–10 years of life. Last tasted, 12/02.

1998
89+
Although austere tannin may keep this wine from obtaining an outstanding score, it exhibits plenty of complexity in its earthy, truffle, black cherry, currant, plum, and herb-scented bouquet and flavors. Moderately tannic with good weight, it is a classically styled 1998. Despite the fact that Calon-Ségur tends to utilize about 35% Merlot in the final blend, it is not one of the more precocious efforts of the vintage. Anticipated maturity: 2008–2030. Last tasted, 12/02.

1997
77
A soft, weedy Calon-Ségur, with a washed-out ruby color, herb, pepper, and earthy aromas, light to medium body, and low tannin, this 1997 should be consumed over the next 3–4 years. Last tasted, 11/02.

1996
92
Prior to bottling, I thought the 1996 Calon-Ségur would be a match for the spectacular 1995, but the two vintages, tasted blind, side by side, and on two occasions, convinced me that the 1995 has the edge because of its element of *sur-maturité* and more accessible, richer mid-palate. The 1996 may not be as profound as I had predicted from cask, but it is an exceptional wine. Dark ruby–colored with a complex nose of dried herbs, Asian spices, and black cherry jam intermixed with cassis, it possesses outstanding purity and considerable tannin in the finish. This classic, medium to full-bodied, traditionally made wine improves dramatically with airing, suggesting it will have a very long life. Anticipated maturity: 2009–2028. Last tasted, 12/02.

1995
92+
The 1995 Calon-Ségur is one of the great sleepers of the vintage. It has closed down completely since bottling, but it is a sensational effort. The wine is opaque purple-colored. With coaxing, the tight aromatics reveal some weedy cassis intertwined with truffles, chocolate, and beef blood–like aromas. On the palate, there is an element of *sur-maturité* (1995 was an extremely late harvest at Calon-Ségur), fabulous density and purity, and a boatload of tannin. This deep, broodingly backward, classic Bordeaux will require cellaring. Anticipated maturity: 2007–2035. Last tasted, 12/02.

1994
84?
Attenuated and compressed, this dark ruby–colored wine has a closed, truffle-like aroma with earthy soil scents. It is a concentrated, stern, tannic wine that has weight, medium body, but abundant astringent tannin. Anticipated maturity: now–2012. Last tasted, 3/00.

1990
88
The dark ruby–colored 1990 is exhibiting an evolved color with considerable amber. It offers a fragrant bouquet of spicy, oaky, ripe cherry, and herb-like fruit. This is an admirably concentrated, well-balanced wine with excellent depth and purity of fruit to its medium-bodied personality. Surprisingly, it is fully mature. Anticipated maturity: now–2010. Last tasted, 11/01.

1989
89
This property has turned in an excellent effort in 1989 that is slightly deeper and richer than the 1990. It possesses a deep ruby/garnet color, a sweet, chewy, dense texture, full body, high alcohol, and moderately high tannin. Quite precocious, it will have a life span of at least 15 years. A downsized version of the 1982, but more rustic and evolved, the wine is in full maturity. Anticipated maturity: now–2012. Last tasted, 11/01.

1988
91
The 1988 Calon-Ségur outshines both wines from the more heralded vintages of 1989 and 1990. Deeply colored, superbly balanced, rich and full-bodied, it appears to be a worthy candidate for another 15 years of longevity. It is a classic example of this château's wine—cedary, very fragrant, with plenty of earthly, sweet red and black currant fruit. I should also note that it is a surprisingly powerful wine for the vintage. It gets my nod as the finest Calon-Ségur between 1982 and 1995. Anticipated maturity: now–2020. Last tasted, 9/02.

1986 The 1986 possesses a deep ruby/garnet color, with a tight, yet ripe, black currant
88   bouquet backed up with subtle scents of herb, cedar, and sweet oak. On the palate,
       the wine is muscular, rich, and medium- to full-bodied, with a pronounced smoky,
       mineral, and currant character. It has fine length, with some rustic tannin still no-
       ticeable. Curiously, in this vintage Calon-Ségur used an inordinately high per-
       centage of Cabernet Sauvignon (90% Cabernet Sauvignon, 10% Merlot). Normally
       the percentage of Merlot in the blend is significantly higher. Anticipated maturity:
       now–2015. Last tasted, 11/01.

1985 The 1985 was bottled very late (January 1988), which has tended to dry out the
84   wine. Medium ruby/garnet–colored with considerable amber, it has a sweet,
       earthly, berry, spicy, somewhat herbaceous nose. This medium-bodied wine is
       pleasant, but it lacks depth and fat. In addition, it is fully mature. Anticipated ma-
       turity: now–2005. Last tasted, 11/01.

1983 When I first tasted this wine in spring 1984, it was surprisingly soft, with grapy
79   flavors, a hot, alcoholic finish, a rather fragile framework. Later in the year, it was
       ripe and flavorful, but low in acidity, and again, alcoholic. In style, color, and tex-
       ture, it reminded me of a 1976. Revealing considerable amber and rust to its color,
       this fully mature, loosely structured, weedy wine should be drunk up, as it is fad-
       ing badly. Anticipated maturity: now. Last tasted, 6/98.

1982 This wine, which was brilliant from cask, went into a frightfully backward, hard,
94   austere period for nearly two decades. Finally, the 1982 Calon-Ségur is revealing
       its true personality. The wine had an opulent, unctuous texture and thickness from
       cask that reminded me of the estate's legendary 1947. Those characteristics are
       beginning to emerge as the wine has begun to develop more complexity and shed
       some of its formidable tannin. This is a large-scaled, super-concentrated, dark
       plum/garnet–colored wine that needs at least an hour of decanting. The intense
       nose of roasted coffee, sweet, jammy, fruity, leather and spice is followed by a full-
       bodied, tannic wine that is thick and opulent. Still young and backward and made
       in a traditional "no holds barred" style, this classic Calon-Ségur is just reaching
       its plateau of maturity. Anticipated maturity: now–2030. Last tasted, 9/02.

ANCIENT VINTAGES

Between 1960 and 1981, most vintages were largely disappointing except for the 1966
and 1975. Largely forgotten today, Calon-Ségur has one of the greatest *terroirs* in Bordeaux. This property made extraordinary wines in the 1920s, 1940s, and early 1950s.
The 1953, 1949, 1947, 1945, 1929, 1928, 1926, and 1924 can be exquisite wines. I
have heard that the 1953 (96 points; last tasted 10/94) was sumptuous even before it
reached 10 years of age. When drunk from magnum, the wine was a classic example of
the glorious fragrance and velvety richness this vintage achieved. While most Calon-
Ségurs possess a hefty degree of tannin, this wine offers a glorious concoction of cedar,
sweet jammy fruit, full body, and remarkable intensity without the husky roughness
Calon-Ségur can display. Although the color exhibits noticeable amber at the edge,
this wine remains in magnificent condition.

    The 1945 Calon-Ségur (90 points; last tasted 12/95) is a powerful, dense, dark
garnet–colored wine with plenty of earth, mineral, and black fruits in its nose. Although tannin is still present, this is a formidably concentrated, thick, hugely extracted, amazingly youthful wine. It can be drunk now or cellared for another 25–30
years. The most opulent, generous, and decadent Calon-Ségur I have ever tasted is the

1947 (96 points; last tasted 7/97). It revealed considerable amber and rust in its color, but the sweet, jammy nose of fruitcake, cedar, and colossal quantities of unctuously textured black fruits is the stuff of legend. Thick and rich, with more glycerin, fruit, and alcohol than tannin, this is a juicy, fat wine that has been fully mature for 20+ years. It exhibited no signs of decline or fruit loss. I have experienced bottle variation with the 1949 Calon-Ségur (94 points; last tasted 12/95), ranging from bottles that were slightly austere and undernourished, to those that were superb. This bottle was an outstanding example. It did not possess the weight, unctuosity, and thickness of the 1947, or the power, youthfulness, and muscle of the 1945. It revealed considerable amber at the edge of its dark garnet color. The nose displayed a Médoc-like, cedar, spice, currant, mineral, and damp forest scent. Medium- to full-bodied, with high tannin, excellent concentration, and an element of overripe fruit, this was an impressive, fully mature Calon-Ségur that can be drunk now or cellared for another 10–20 years.

The decade of the 1920s was a legendary one for Calon-Ségur. The 1928 (96 points; last tasted 12/95) revealed an opaque garnet color with a coffee-like look at the edge. Late-harvest-like in the nose, with a plummy, Asian spice, leather, and molasses-like aromas and flavors, this thick, extremely sweet, rich, full-bodied wine is astonishingly intense. It is all glycerin, richness, and intensity, with no hard edges, making one a true believer of the extraordinary longevity of Bordeaux's greatest wines. This may be the greatest ancient vintage of Calon-Ségur, although the 1926 is a close rival.

The 1926 (94 points; last tasted 12/95) is not a wine for modern-day oenologists. The color is mainly orange/rust with some ruby remaining. Noticeable volatile acidity blows off within several minutes. The sweet, plummy, cedary, roasted nut, and clove nose is followed by a surprisingly sweet wine, with fine ripeness and chewy glycerin. The well-balanced finish is long, authoritative, and generous. Although the feeble color suggests a degree of decrepitude, such is not the case.

CHAMBERT-MARBUZET

Classification: Cru Bourgeois

Owner: GFA des Vignobles H. Duboscq et fils

Address: 33180 St.-Estèphe

Telephone: 05 56 59 30 54; Telefax: 05 56 59 70 87

E-mail: henriduboscq@hotmail.com

Visits: By appointment only

Contact: Alfred Teixeira

VINEYARDS

Surface area: 17.3 acres

Grape varietals: 70% Cabernet Sauvignon, 30% Merlot

Average age of vines: 25 years

Density of plantation: 8,300 vines per hectare

Average yields: 50 hectoliters per hectare

Elevage: Three-week fermentation and 28-day maceration in temperature-controlled concrete tanks with micro-oxygenation of the lees. Aging in oak barrels that are renewed by a third each year. No fining, no filtration.

WINES PRODUCED

Château Chambert-Marbuzet: 48,000 bottles

No second wine is produced.

Plateau of maturity: Within 2–8 years of the vintage

GENERAL APPRECIATION

This Cru Bourgeois is worth its status, producing wines that are generally of good quality. However, do not expect Chambert-Marbuzet to be a great or long-lived wine.

The talented and flamboyant Henri Duboscq, proprietor of the better-known Château Haut-Marbuzet in St.-Estèphe, is also the owner of this small estate located near the village of Marbuzet. It was acquired by the Duboscq family in 1962. Like Haut-Marbuzet, the vinification consists of a relatively high fermentation temperature, a long *cuvaison*, the bringing up of the wine in at least 50% new oak casks, and the avoidance of any type of filtration at the time of bottling. The wines of Chambert-Marbuzet have exhibited rich fruit, married with abundant, sometimes excessive quantities of toasty new oak. They are easy to understand and drink. If Chambert-Marbuzet is to be criticized at all, it would be because at times the wine can be entirely too obvious, and their potential to age beyond a decade is suspect. Nevertheless, the quality is reasonably high, and the wine enjoys increasing popularity.

IMPORTANT VINTAGES

The best recent vintages have been the fully mature 1989 and 1990.

COS D'ESTOURNEL

Classification: Second-growth in 1855

Owner: Domaines Reybier

Address: 33180 St.-Estèphe

Telephone: 05 56 73 15 50; Telefax: 05 56 59 72 59

E-mail: estournel@estournel.com

Website: www.estournel.com

Visits: By appointment only

Contact: Jean-Guillaume Prats

VINEYARDS

Surface area: 158 acres

Grape varietals: 60% Cabernet Sauvignon, 38% Merlot and 2% Cabernet Franc

Average age of vines: 35 years

Density of plantation: 8,000 to 10,000 vines per hectare

Average yields: 50 hectoliters per hectare

Elevage: Three-week maceration in double-lined temperature-controlled stainless-steel tanks. Eighteen months aging in casks with 80% new oak. Fining, no filtration.

WINES PRODUCED

Château Cos d'Estournel: 250,000 bottles

Pagodes de Cos: 120,000 bottles

Plateau of maturity: Within 10–30 years of the vintage

GENERAL APPRECIATION

A famed estate indeed, Cos d'Estournel has unquestionably produced some excellent wines during the 1980s and until the mid-1990s, when it was well worth a first growth. Today, though Cos is still good, it is not as consistent as one would expect a growth of its pedigree to be, and vintages from 1997 onward have been inferior to their predecessors, exhibiting slightly green and vegetal characteristics. Prices are high in view of the quality. The other St.-Estèphe crus classés represent better value/price ratios. The 2001 vintage should represent a return to the glory years.

Until it was sold in the mid-1990s to the group BernardTaillan SA, who resold it to Swiss magnate Michel Reybier, Cos d'Estournel (pronounced, surprisingly, with a sounded "oss" in *Cos*) had risen to the top of its class in St.-Estèphe under the inspired direction of Bruno Prats. Between 1982 and 1996, the wines had gone from one strength to another, and in most vintages Cos d'Estournel could be expected to produce one of the Médoc's finest wines. This château, which resembles an Asian pagoda, sits on a ridge immediately north of the Pauillac border, looking down on its famous neighbor, Lafite Rothschild. Atypically for a Médoc, Cos is distinguished by the high percentage of Merlot used in the blend—40%—and the elevated use of new oak casks—60–100%. This proportion of Merlot is among the highest used in the Haut-Médoc and also accounts for the fleshy, richly textured character so noticeable in recent vintages of Cos d'Estournel. Bruno Prats, the manager and owner until the late 1990s, belonged to the avant-garde of new wine technology. This is one of the few major Bordeaux estates that was adamantly in favor of filtration of wine, both before cask aging and bottling. However, Prats had second thoughts, as he decided to eliminate the second filtration prior to the bottling of the 1989. In 2002, his son, the estate manager Jean-Guillaume Prats, eschews any filtration. The results speak for themselves—Cos d'Estournel, after having to play runner-up to Montrose in the 1950s and 1960s, emerged in the 1980s as one of the most popular wines in Bordeaux. Readers should also note that Cos d'Estournel has been particularly successful in difficult vintages, for example, 1993, 1992, and 1991. In spite of the changes in ownership in the late 1990s, this estate remains impeccably managed.

IMPORTANT VINTAGES

2001   Jean-Guillaume Prats compares the 2001 Cos to the 1988 and 1979, classic ef-
91–94   forts with good acidity, definition, and tannin. One of the vintage's greatest successes, this 2001 is one of the dozen or so wines that appear to be superior to their

2000 counterparts. A blend of 55% Cabernet Sauvignon and 45% Merlot representing 40% of the total production, it boasts an opaque ruby/purple color as well as a sweet nose of cassis, spice, licorice, and vanilla. What makes it stand out in the company of other 2001s are its terrific multilayered texture and tremendous length. Anticipated maturity: 2008–2025. Last tasted, 1/03.

2000

90+

This wine has put on weight and fleshed out its mid-palate during its *élevage*, and has thrown off the subtle herbaceous notes detectable at my first tasting in March 2001. A blend of 65% Cabernet Sauvignon, 33% Merlot, and 2% Cabernet Franc, it exhibits an inky ruby/purple color, a luscious perfume of blackberries, cassis, licorice, spice, and toasty oak, medium to full body, a beautiful texture, a concentrated mid-palate, sweet tannin, and a long, elegant, refined finish. Anticipated maturity: 2006–2025. Last tasted, 1/03.

1999

88

A supremely elegant effort, the dark ruby–colored 1999 Cos offers notes of dried Provençal herbs, smoke, licorice, black cherries, and cassis. This medium- to full-bodied St.-Estèphe is cerebral; intellectual, and refined, but lacking soul and hedonism. Anticipated maturity: 2004–2018. Last tasted, 12/02.

1998

88

This elegant, stylish, graceful wine is an attractive, dark ruby/purple–colored effort with subtle notes of sweet oak, licorice, herbs, and black fruits. While not massive, it is medium bodied and ripe, with sweet tannin. Forty-eight percent of the production was utilized in this blend of 60% Cabernet Sauvignon and 40% Merlot. Anticipated maturity: 2004–2018. Last tasted, 12/02.

1997

87

Forty percent of the harvest made it into this flattering, delicious wine with abundant charm and herb-tinged blackberry and cherry fruit. A dark ruby color is accompanied by a medium-bodied, appealing St.-Estèphe. A blend of 55% Cabernet Sauvignon and 45% Merlot, it should drink well for 4–5 years. Last tasted, 12/02.

1996

93+

Made from 65% Cabernet Sauvignon and 35% Merlot, this is a huge, backward wine reminiscent of the 1986 Cos d'Estournel. The 1996 possesses an opaque purple color as well as pure aromatics consisting of cassis, grilled herbs, coffee, and toasty new oak. Massive in the mouth and one of the most structured and concentrated young Cos d'Estournels I have ever tasted, this thick, structured, tannic wine has closed down significantly since bottling. It requires 2–3 years of cellaring, and it should last for 30–35 years. It is a fabulous Cos, but patience is required. Anticipated maturity: 2006–2030. Last tasted, 12/02.

1995

95

A wine of extraordinary intensity and accessibility, the 1995 Cos d'Estournel is a sexier, more hedonistic offering than the muscular, backward 1996. Opulent, with forward aromatics (gobs of black fruits intermixed with toasty scents and a boatload of spice), this terrific Cos possesses remarkable intensity, full body, and layers of jammy fruit nicely framed by the wine's new oak. Because of low acidity and sweet tannin, the 1995 will be difficult to resist young, although it will age for 2–3 decades. Anticipated maturity: now–2025. Last tasted, 12/02.

1994

88

Cos d'Estournel's dark ruby 1994 is one of the better wines of the vintage. It boasts an opaque color, as well as a sweet nose of cedar, black fruits, licorice, toast, and Asian spices. Medium bodied, with sweet, herb-tinged fruit that reveals a touch of the vintage's tough tannin, this rich, well-balanced, classic wine will prove to be long-lived. Anticipated maturity: 2005–2020. Last tasted, 4/01.

1990

95

The 1990 has consistently charmed tasters with its flashy display of opulent Merlot (about 40% of the blend) mixed with jammy Cabernet Sauvignon. This super-concentrated wine possesses a roasted herb, sweet, jammy black fruit–scented nose, infused with opulent and succulent licorice, spice box, and cedar. Pure and full-bodied, this concentrated wine has entered its plateau of maturity. The wine is open, flattering, and impossible to resist. Anticipated maturity: now–2015. Last tasted, 12/01.

1989   The 1989, although good, does not live up to expectations given the *terroir* and the
88   vintage. Its deep ruby color shows some amber. A spicy vanilla, curranty nose,
       medium body, and excellent depth is followed by a monolithic personality. It pos-
       sesses neither the concentration nor dimension of the exceptional 1990. The 1989
       possesses some astringent tannin in the finish, but it is well integrated with the
       wine's ripe fruit. An excellent yet somewhat uninspiring wine. Anticipated matu-
       rity: now–2014. Last tasted, 12/02.

1988   The 1988 has an intriguing bouquet of exotic Asian spices, cedar, black tea, and
87   black fruits. Tannic in its youth, the wine has softened and developed more charm
       and appeal. Still deep ruby/purple in color with pink/amber at the rim, this
       medium-bodied, slightly austere wine possesses good cassis fruit, excellent pu-
       rity, and an elegant, classic style. Anticipated maturity: now–2012. Last tasted,
       3/00.

1986   The 1986 is a highly extracted wine, with a black/ruby color (some pink is show-
93+   ing at the rim) and plenty of toasty, smoky notes in its bouquet that suggest ripe
       plums, licorice, and black currants. Evolving at a glacial pace, it exhibits massive,
       huge, ripe, extremely concentrated flavors with impressive depth and richness. It
       possesses power, weight, and tannin, and it is a wine for long-term aging. Antici-
       pated maturity: 2004–2020. Last tasted, 2/00.

1985   Forward, with a fabulously scented toasty bouquet toast and concentrated red and
92   black fruits (especially black cherries), the 1985 is rich, lush, long, and medium-
       to full-bodied. Very fragrant, with gobs of sweet black fruits, minerals, and spice in
       both its flavors and aromatics, this wine is fully mature and not likely to improve.
       Anticipated maturity: now–2010. Last tasted, 3/01.

1983   This wine matured quickly. Weedy, attenuated, with herb-dominated red currant
78   fruit, this effort from Cos has become more compressed and charmless over time.
       A disappointment. Anticipated maturity: now. Last tasted, 2/01.

1982   Like many 1982s, Cos d'Estournel was flattering, opulent, and easy to drink in its
96   youth. The 1982 is atypically thick, super-concentrated, rich, and powerful. The
       wine reveals no signs of age in its opaque dark ruby/purple color. The tannin is
       present, yet the wine reveals that fabulous inner-core of sweet, jammy, black cur-
       rant and black cherry fruit. There is considerable glycerin and body in this youth-
       ful but immensely promising example of Cos d'Estournel that has entered its
       plateau of maturity. It has at least 15 years of life remaining. Anticipated maturity:
       now–2018. Last tasted, 9/02.

ANCIENT VINTAGES

Cos d'Estournel was largely a disappointment between 1964 and 1981. The best vintage was 1970, now tiring. The 1953 (93 points; last tasted 10/94), most recently drunk
from magnums, is a classic example of the vintage, displaying a huge, fragrant, flowery,
berry-scented nose. The 1928 (rated 95) can be outrageously sweet and delicious, but
readers would have to drink it from a pristinely kept bottle.

COS LABORY

Classification: Fifth Growth in 1855

Owner: SCE Domaines Audoy

Address: 33180 St.-Estèphe

Telephone: 05 56 59 30 22; Telefax: 05 56 59 73 52

E-mail: cos-labory@wanadoo.fr

Visits: By appointment Monday to Friday, 9 A.M.–to noon and 2–5 P.M.

Contact: Bernard or Martial Audoy

VINEYARDS

Surface area: 44.5 acres

Grape varietals: 55% Cabernet Sauvignon, 35% Merlot, 10% Cabernet Franc

Average age of vines: 35 years

Density of plantation: 8,700 vines per hectare

Average yields: 55 hectoliters per hectare

Elevage: Fermentations at 29–30°C in temperature-controlled stainless-steel tanks of 150-hectoliter capacity with frequent pumping-overs. Maceration lasts 20–30 days. Twelve to fifteen months aging in barrels with 40% new oak. Fining, no filtration.

WINES PRODUCED

Château Cos Labory: 65,000 bottles

Le Charme Labory: 45,000 bottles

Plateau of maturity: Within 5–12 years of the vintage

GENERAL APPRECIATION

Since the beginning of the 1990s, Cos Labory has improved. No longer producing mediocre wines, Cos Labory's recent efforts are compatible with its fifth-growth status. Reasonable prices rank them amongst some of the most interesting values of the Médoc.

For decades one of the most disappointing of all the classified growths, Cos Labory has emerged over the last 10 years as a property well worth tasting as well as visiting. The resurrection of quality began with excellent wines in 1989 and 1990 and has continued through the 2000 vintage, although many of the vintages of the 1990s have provided raw materials that were far less promising than those Mother Nature provided in 1989 and 1990. The wine is now a well-made, deeply colored, rich, muscular, and tannic St.-Estèphe. A stricter selection by proprietor Bernard Audoy, malolactic fermentation in barrel, and bottling the wine without filtration have all helped to significantly elevate the quality of Cos Labory.

IMPORTANT VINTAGES

2000 A saturated opaque ruby/purple color offers up scents of jammy red and black
88   fruits, smoke, and new oak. Low acidity, moderately high tannin, excellent density, and medium to full body add up to a strong effort from this château. A

possible sleeper of the vintage? Anticipated maturity: 2006–2016. Last tasted, 1/03.

1999   A medium to dark ruby color is followed by aromas of sweet currants and new oak
87   in this moderately intense, soft, low-acid, charming St.-Estèphe. With sweet tannin and an up-front personality, it will provide plenty of pleasure over the next 8 years. Last tasted, 12/02.

1998   This medium-bodied, peppery, herbaceous offering lacks depth. The color is a
86   dark ruby, and the wine reveals nice berry and cassis fruit, but little else. Drink it over the next 4–5 years. Last tasted, 11/02.

1997   The 1997 Cos Labory is far better from bottle than it was from cask. A medium
86   plum/ruby color is followed by a charming raspberry/cherry, Burgundian-like fruitiness, excellent ripeness, and a superficial attack and finish. This is a tasty, accessible, user-friendly wine to drink over the next 3–6 years. Last tasted, 3/00.

1996   My concerns about the 1996's tannic ferocity were alleviated by its performance
88   out of bottle. It has turned out to be a classic, dark ruby/purple-colored St.-Estèphe with earthy black currant fruit, medium to full body, moderate tannin, and excellent purity. As the wine sits in the glass, blackberry jam and mineral notes emerge. This well-made, reasonably priced wine should drink well between 2005–2018. Last tasted, 3/00.

1995   Although this dark ruby/purple-colored Cos Labory is more charming since bot-
88+?   tling, aromatically it is closed, with red and black fruits just beginning to emerge. In the mouth, dusty tannin appears elevated, giving the wine a hard, dry, rough-textured finish. However, there is medium to full body, plenty of sweet, ripe fruit on the attack, and my instincts suggest there is good extract behind the wall of tannin. Anticipated maturity: now–2015. Last tasted, 3/00.

1994   This tannic, medium-bodied 1994 possesses a deep ruby/purple color and plenty
86   of ripe black currant and licorice-flavored fruit. Cos Labory's 1994 is a solid 85/86-point effort. Anticipated maturity: 2004–2012. Last tasted, 1/97.

1993   The 1993 Cos Labory exhibits a dark ruby color and a spicy, low-key, pleasant but
85   undistinguished nose of red fruits, earth, and wood. The wine is hard, but there is good depth, and perhaps the fruit will ultimately balance out the wine's structure. Anticipated maturity: now–2008. Last tasted, 1/97.

1992   This soft 1992 is well made, with moderate depth, medium body, fine ripeness,
82?   and adequate length. The high tannin in the finish is worrisome. Will the modest level of fruit extraction dry out before the tannin melts away? Last tasted, 11/94.

1991   The 1991 exhibits a surprisingly saturated color and a tight but promising nose of
86   pepper, black currant, and smoky new oak scents. Medium bodied and tannic with good depth, this wine should be drunk over the next 2–6 years. Last tasted, 1/94.

1990   The 1990 is nearly black in color with a reticent, spicy, licorice, mineral, and
89   cassis-scented nose. In the mouth there is great extraction, rich, full-bodied, chewy texture, and a splendidly long, moderately tannic finish. Anticipated maturity: now–2010. Last tasted, 3/99.

1989   The 1989 is undeniably the finest example of Cos Labory I have ever tasted.
89   Black/ruby in color with a huge bouquet of cassis, this formidable 1989 has layers of extract, a very high tannin level, and a hefty level of alcohol. This vintage signals the beginning of a renaissance of Cos Labory. Anticipated maturity: now–2015. Last tasted, 3/99.

1988   The 1988 Cos Labory is a pleasant, well-colored, tannic, medium-bodied wine,
84   with fine overall balance and good length. It should provide decent rather than inspired drinking. Anticipated maturity: now. Last tasted, 3/90.

1986 The 1986 Cos Labory is light, but it does exhibit a pleasant, as well as charming
79   berry fruitiness married with an attractive subtle oakiness. It seems to reveal some
      of the vast size of the 1986 crop, particularly the lightness of the Merlot that was
      apparent in some vineyards in that vintage. Anticipated maturity: now. Last
      tasted, 11/89.

ANCIENT VINTAGES

My experience with the better vintages in the 1970s and 1980s has been disappointing.

LE CROCK

Classification: Cru Bourgeois

Owner: Domaines Cuvelier

Address: Marbuzet, 33180 St.-Estèphe

Telephone: 05 57 77 11 50; Telefax: 05 56 86 57 16

E-mail: cuvelier.bordeaux@wanadoo.fr

Website: cuvelier-bordeaux.com

Visits: By appointment only

Contact: Isabelle Davin

VINEYARDS

Surface area: 79 acres

Grape varietals: 55.7% Cabernet Sauvignon, 26.6% Merlot, 12.9% Cabernet Franc

Average age of vines: 38 years

Density of plantation: 7,900 vines per hectare

Average yields: 54 hectoliters per hectare

Elevage: Three-week fermentation and maceration in concrete and stainless-steel
temperature-controlled tanks. Eighteen to twenty months aging in oak barrels that are
renewed by a third at each vintage. Fining, no filtration.

WINES PRODUCED

Château Le Crock: 130,000 bottles

Château La Croix St.-Estèphe: 70,000 bottles

Plateau of maturity: Within 5–12 years of the vintage

GENERAL APPRECIATION

Le Crock is worth its Cru Bourgeois status, but no more. The wines are generally tannic
and hard, quite austere, and priced much in the same way as many better Crus Bourgeois.

This attractive, two-story château, located south of the village of St.-Estèphe, has been
owned by the Cuvelier family since 1903. While the superbly situated château—
which sits on a hill overlooking a lake usually inhabited by numerous swans—is a site
even the most jaded photographer could hardly ignore, the wines have rarely been ex-

citing. The high percentage of Merlot used would seemingly insure plenty of flesh and suppleness, but my experience with the wines of Le Crock indicates they are entirely too tannic and tough textured and often give the impression of being severe and excessively austere.

There is nothing to criticize about the attention given by the Cuvelier family to the vineyard and the modern vinification. Nevertheless, the wines of Le Crock generally seem to lack fruit, although they are certainly full-bodied, dense wines capable of lasting 10–12 years.

IMPORTANT VINTAGES

Since 1982, the only vintage to merit a score above 86 was the rich, fully mature 1990.

HAUT-MARBUZET

Classification: Cru Bourgeois

Owner: GFA des Vignobles H. Duboscq et fils

Address: 33180 St.-Estèphe

Telephone: 05 56 59 30 54; Telefax: 05 56 59 70 87

E-mail: henriduboscq@hotmail.com

Visits: By appointment only

Contact: Alfred Teixeira

VINEYARDS

Surface area: 143.3 acres

Grape varietals: 50% Cabernet Sauvignon, 40% Merlot, 10% Cabernet Franc

Average age of vines: 30 years

Density of plantation: 8,300 vines per hectare

Average yields: 45 hectoliters per hectare

Elevage: Three-week fermentation and maceration in temperature-controlled concrete and wooden tanks with bleeding of about 10% and daily pumping-overs. Aging in 100% new oak barrels. No fining, no filtration.

WINES PRODUCED

Château Haut-Marbuzet: 360,000 bottles

Mac Carthy: 60,000 bottles

Plateau of maturity: Within 3–15 years of the vintage

GENERAL APPRECIATION

Two decades ago, Haut-Marbuzet, a pioneer in terms of new oak aging, ranked amongst the most exotic Bordeaux. Today, most wines are treated in this manner and have greatly improved, so Haut-Marbuzet is no longer considered an exception. However, this wine has its followers. Personally, I consider it as being of fourth- or third-growth level, even if the more recent vintages tend to show some aggressive woody characteristics. It also represents a good value in today's marketplace.

Haut-Marbuzet is one of the oldest estates in St.-Estèphe, but fame can be traced only to 1952, when it was purchased by the father of the current proprietor, Henri Duboscq. The vineyard is beautifully situated facing the Gironde River, on a gradual slope of gravelly soil intermixed with calcareous clay. Duboscq, a flamboyant personality who tends to describe his wines by making analogies to the body parts of prominent female movie stars, has created one of the most immensely popular wines of Bordeaux, particularly in France, Belgium, Holland, and England, where the great majority of Haut-Marbuzet is sold. He believes in late harvesting, thereby bringing in grapes that are nearly bursting with ripeness, macerating them for at least three weeks and then aging the entire crop for 18 months in 100% new oak barrels. Indeed, his methods result in an intense, opulent, and lavish fruitiness, with a rich, spicy, exotic bouquet. To the wine enthusiast, Haut-Marbuzet produces one of the most obvious yet sexiest wines of the entire Bordeaux region.

Some Duboscq critics have charged that his winemaking style borders on vulgarity, but he would argue that the new oak simply adds a charm and unctuous quality to the traditional muscular, tough texture that emerges from so many wines made in St.-Estèphe. Other critics have suggested that Haut-Marbuzet fails to age gracefully. While the wine is usually delicious when released, my tastings of old vintages back through 1961 have generally indicated that Haut-Marbuzet is best when drunk within the first 10–15 years of life.

Despite the criticisms, no one argues with the success proprietor Duboscq has enjoyed. He produces a Bordeaux that behaves more like a decadent Burgundy or Rhône.

IMPORTANT VINTAGES

2001
87–88
The 2001 Haut-Marbuzet reveals copious quantities of sweet black fruits intermixed with lavish quantities of toasty oak and earth. Spicy and savory, with more vibrancy to its fruit than usual and a medium-bodied, moderately long finish, it should drink well for 7–8 years. Last tasted, 1/03.

2000
87
My first tasting of the 2000 Haut-Marbuzet revealed a brutally tannic, out of balance, and disjointed wine. When retasted two months later, the 2000 Haut-Marbuzet was performing at essentially the same level as the 2001. It was just more textured and fatter, but qualitatively no better. Last tasted, 1/03.

1999
88
Opaque purple with better integrated wood than many young Haut-Marbuzets exhibit, this supple-textured, medium- to full-bodied 1999 is loaded with jammy black fruits, spicy wood, herbs, and cedar. Attractive and seductive, it will drink well for a decade. Last tasted, 3/02.

1998
87
Medium weight, with a noticeable overlay of spicy new oak, this wine has rounded out in the bottle. Relatively soft, with notes of charcoal, strawberry/cherry fruit, and cedar, it is evolving quickly and requires consumption over the next decade. Last tasted, 3/01.

1997
85
While good, the 1997 Haut-Marbuzet is not up to the château's usual standards. This aggressively woody wine reveals a hollow mid-section, but it does offer soft, ripe, coffee, earthy, black cherry fruit presented in a pleasant, medium-bodied format. A bit more concentration, extract, and length would have been preferable. Drink now. Last tasted, 3/02.

1996 Telltale, lavish, toasty new oak aromas jump from the glass of the dark ruby/
87 purple–colored 1996. Well made, attractive, and boldly wooded, the wine's rich
fruit easily compensates for all the oak. This medium-bodied, spicy, lush, open-
knit 1996 will keep for another 5–6 years. Last tasted, 3/01.

1995 The 1995 reveals gobs of kirsch and coffee in its nose, along with smoky, toasty,
87 oaky notes. Medium bodied, with smoky, black currant fruit, low acidity, good
lushness, and a layered palate, this is a hedonistic, accessible Haut-Marbuzet to
consume over the next 3–4 years. Last tasted, 3/02.

1990 The fully mature 1990 is a classic, concentrated example of Haut-Marbuzet that
91 needs to be drunk up. The wine displays a dark garnet color followed by a lavishly
oaked, vanilla, roasted nut, herb, and sweet, jammy black currant, and olive-
scented nose. Rich and opulent, with a thick, chewy texture, low acidity, and gobs
of fruit, this hedonistic, decadently oaky, fruity wine will not improve, so why
tempt the ill-effects of Father Time? It is the finest Haut-Marbuzet since the fabulous 1982. Anticipated maturity: now–2007. Last tasted, 3/01.

1989 Haut-Marbuzet's 1989 revealed considerable amber to its color, as well as a pro-
86 nounced nose of cedar, jammy cherry fruit, seaweed, and spice. The wine tasted
fully mature, is low in acidity, round, and sweet, and is just beginning to tire. Anticipated maturity: now. Last tasted, 3/01.

1988 The 1988 was another flashy, seductive, full-bodied, amply endowed, generously
87 oaked wine. The tannins have melted away and the fruit is beginning to fade. The
wine still exhibits plenty of extract and size, but requires consumption. Anticipated maturity: now. Last tasted, 3/99.

1982 This wine was one of the most decadent and seductive wines of the vintage
89 between 1984 and 1995. It continues to offer copious quantities of vanilla-tinged,
sweet, opulent, black cherry and currant fruit with intriguing aromas of coffee and
cedar. Thick, juicy, and succulent, this plush, fat wine is beginning to tire ever
so slightly. Intense, with no hard edges, this once-glorious example of Haut-
Marbuzet, one of the most consistent and crowd-pleasing wines of the vintage, has
finally lost its flamboyant, over-the-top personality. Still delicious, it demands immediate consumption. Anticipated maturity: now. Last tasted, 11/01.

LAFON-ROCHET

Classification: Fourth Growth in 1855

Owner: Tesseron family

Address: 33180 St.-Estèphe

Telephone: 05 56 59 32 06; Telefax: 05 56 59 72 43

E-mail: lafon@lafon-rochet.com

Website: www.lafon-rochet.com

Visits: By appointment Monday to Friday, 9 A.M.–noon and
2–4 P.M.

Contact: Isabelle Noizee

VINEYARDS

Surface area: 103.7 acres

Grape varietals: 55% Cabernet Sauvignon, 40% Merlot, 5% Cabernet Franc

Average age of vines: 30 years

Density of plantation: 9,000 vines per hectare

Average yields: 54 hectoliters per hectare

Elevage: Twenty-one day fermentation in stainless-steel vats. Malolactics and 20 months aging in barrels, with 50% new oak. Fining and filtration.

WINES PRODUCED

Château Lafon-Rochet: 120,000 bottles

Les Pélerins de Lafon-Rochet: 120,000 bottles

Plateau of maturity: Within 8–20 years of the vintage

GENERAL APPRECIATION

After a major slump in the 1970s, Lafon-Rochet has improved, especially from 1994 on, the 2000, 1996 and 1995 representing its finest successes to date. The estate now produces wines well worth their fourth-growth status, and sometimes better. Prices remain reasonable.

While this vineyard was ranked fourth growth in the 1855 classification, most observers today argue that the superbly situated Lafon-Rochet (adjacent to both Lafite Rothschild and Cos d'Estournel) should routinely produce wine with more character and flavor than it habitually does. The current owners, the Tesserons, purchased the property in 1959 and began a gradual but significant program to restore the vineyards and the run-down château. Today the estate has been totally renovated, and the new cellars are housed in a bright, almost vulgar, yellow-colored one-story château. Over the last decade, a combination of intelligent, quality-oriented decisions, such as (1) to harvest slightly later, (2) to increase the percentage of new oak, (3) to increase the percentage of Merlot in both the vineyard and the blend, and (4) to make a second wine from weaker vats, has resulted in more impressive first wines.

While Lafon-Rochet produced numerous disappointing wines (given the château's pedigree) during the 1970s, the efforts made in the 1990s clearly support its position in the 1855 classification.

IMPORTANT VINTAGES

2001 If it were not for a pinched, compressed finish, I would have rated this 2001
86–88 higher. It offers a dark ruby/purple color, good acidity, medium body, moderate tannin, and a tangy, vivacious personality. Anticipated maturity: 2005–2015. Last tasted, 1/03.

2000 This is a low-acid, black/purple-colored effort displaying a perfumed bouquet of
90 smoke, herbs, leather, incense, and black fruits. Full-bodied, opulent, and viscous, it exhibits plenty of power as well as moderate tannin. A sleeper of the vintage. Anticipated maturity: now–2016. Last tasted, 1/03.

1999 Scents of dried Provençal herbs, spicy new oak, red currants, and a hint of cassis
87 jump from the glass of this dark ruby/plum–colored 1999. Soft and seductive, with cherry and licorice characteristics discernable in the flavors, it can be drunk now and over the next 6–10 years. Last tasted, 3/02.

1998
88
A dense purple color is accompanied by a tannic, smoky, concentrated, earthy wine with abundant blackberry and cassis fruit, underbrush, minerals, and a steely character, as well as a powerful, tannic finish. Anticipated maturity: now–2016. Last tasted, 3/02.

1997
86
This dark plum–colored, sexy, soft, medium-bodied, low-acid Lafon-Rochet reveals chewy black fruits intermixed with new wood and minerals. Exhibiting good density and ripeness, it is a very good effort in this accessible, drinker-friendly vintage. Anticipated maturity: now–2008. Last tasted, 3/02.

1996
90
One of the sleepers of the 1996 vintage, Lafon-Rochet has turned out an atypically powerful, rich, and concentrated wine bursting with black currant fruit. The opaque purple color gives way to a medium- to full-bodied, tannic, backward wine with terrific purity, a sweet, concentrated mid-palate, and a long, blockbuster finish. This wine remains one of the finest values from the luxury-priced 1996 vintage and is well worth purchasing by readers who are willing to invest a few years of patience; it should keep for 12–15 years. Anticipated maturity: 2005–2020. Last tasted, 3/02.

1995
89
Although it has closed down since bottling, this wine is an impressively endowed, rich, sweet, cassis-smelling and -tasting Lafon-Rochet. The wine's impressively saturated deep ruby/purple color is accompanied by vanilla, earth, and spicy scents, medium to full body, excellent to outstanding richness, and moderate tannin in the powerful, well-delineated finish. Anticipated maturity: now–2018. Last tasted, 4/02.

1994
88+
A breakthrough vintage for this estate, the outstanding 1994 exhibits an opaque purple color, followed by a sweet, pure nose of cassis, new oak, and beef blood. Muscular and massive, with huge body and a boatload of tannin, this wine is crammed with extract and power. It will last for 20–25 years. Anticipated maturity: now–2025. Last tasted, 4/02.

1993
86
A spicy, green pepper, vegetal component detracted from this dark, opaque-colored wine. While it possesses hard tannin, there is also plenty of fruit (especially for a 1993). The wine is likely to dry out quickly, but those who like a rough-and-tumble style of Bordeaux with plenty of guts and muscle are advised that this wine represents a good value. It will provide a beefy mouthful of claret to consume over the next five years. Last tasted, 1/97.

1990
89
The 1990, a stunning effort for this property, offers further proof of just how successful 1990 turned out in St.-Estèphe. Very dark ruby with no lightening at the rim and a tightly knit nose of damp earth, olives, and black fruits, this well-endowed wine is a powerful and concentrated Lafon-Rochet. Just beginning to shed its cloak of tannin, this 1990 has force, volume, and increasing suppleness. Anticipated maturity: now–2020. Last tasted, 7/99.

1989
88
Dark ruby with an intense bouquet of overripe cassis, this chewy, full-bodied wine has some dusty tannin, excellent concentration, and a slightly compressed finish. Anticipated maturity: now–2015. Last tasted, 7/99.

1988
86
The herbaceous, austere 1988 has medium body, good ripe fruit, and decent harmony. Concentrated for the vintage, this dark ruby–colored wine has some rustic tannin that remains unintegrated. Anticipated maturity: now–2010. Last tasted, 10/00.

1986
88
On numerous occasions this wine seemed forbiddingly tannic from cask and virtually impossible to evaluate, but it has turned out to be one of the estate's best wines made during the 1980s. Deep ruby/purple, with a full-intensity, smoky, spicy, rich, curranty bouquet, this full-bodied, powerful, tannic wine lacks finesse, but readers who like big, monolithic, tannic behemoths will appreciate the style. Anticipated maturity: now–2015. Last tasted, 3/98.

1982
87
This 1982 is plump, rich, and concentrated, but essentially one-dimensional and simple. It offers thick, jammy fruit, but little complexity. There is some tannin in the finish. My instincts suggest this wine needs to be drunk up over the next 5–10 years. Last tasted, 3/99.

LILIAN LADOUYS

Classification: Cru Bourgeois

Owner: Natexis Banque

Address: Blanquet, 33180 St.-Estèphe

Telephone: 05 56 59 71 96; Telefax: 05 56 59 35 97

E-mail: lilian-ladouys@château-lilian-ladouys.com

Website: www.château-lilian-ladouys.com

Visits: By appointment only

Contact: François Peyran (telephone 06 80 01 88 35; telefax 05 56 59 35 97)

VINEYARDS

Surface area: 113.6 acres

Grape varietals: 58% Cabernet Sauvignon, 38% Merlot, 4% Cabernet Franc

Average age of vines: 40 years

Density of plantation: 8,300 vines per hectare

Average yields: 55 hectoliters per hectare

Elevage: Twenty-one to thirty-five day long fermentation and maceration boosted with indigenous yeasts at a maximum of 31–33°C in temperature-controlled stainless-steel tanks. One to 18 months aging in barrels that are renewed by a third at each vintage. Racking every three months. Fining with egg whites, light filtration.

WINES PRODUCED

Château Lilian Ladouys: 277,000 bottles

La Devise de Lilian: 69,000 bottles

Plateau of maturity: Within 5–15 years of the vintage

GENERAL APPRECIATION

Despite its enviable location (its vineyards are close to those of Cos d'Estournel and Lafite Rothschild), this estate only produces so-so wines that are generally hard, tannic, and lacking in fruit. It can surely do much better, judging by the quality of the 1990s and 1989s. Adventurous readers are advised to be cautious and to drink the better vintages sooner rather than later. Better Crus Bourgeois are available at the same price level.

IMPORTANT VINTAGES

Recent vintages 2001, 2000, 1999, and 1998 cannot be recommended. Readers lucky enough to find any pristine bottles of 1990 and 1989 are advised that these are the only two wines that have excited me.

MEYNEY

Classification: Cru Bourgeois Exceptionnel

Owner: Prieur de Meyney SAS

Address: 33180 St.-Estèphe

Mailing Address: Prieur de Meyney SAS, 109, rue Achard, BP 154, 33042 Bordeaux Cedex

Telephone: 05 56 95 53 00; Telefax: 05 56 95 53 01

E-mail: contact@cordier-wines.com

Visits: By appointment and for professionals of the wine trade only

VINEYARDS

Surface area: 126 acres

Grape varietals: 70% Cabernet Sauvignon, 24% Merlot, 4% Cabernet Franc, 2% Petit Verdot

Average age of vines: 35–40 years

Density of plantation: 9,000 vines per hectare

Average yields: 55 hectoliters per hectare

Elevage: Twenty to twenty-five day fermentation and maceration at 30–32°C with frequent pumping-overs. Fifteen percent of yield undergoes malolactics in new oak barrels. Twenty months aging. Fining and light filtration.

WINES PRODUCED

Château Meyney: 293,000 bottles

Prieur du Château Meyney: 73,000 bottles

Plateau of maturity: Within 8–25 years of the vintage

GENERAL APPRECIATION

In the 1980s, Meyney was easily a fifth-growth in quality, producing superb wines. Since the mid-1990s, the estate appears to be going through a difficult period. Though still worth its Cru Bourgeois status, it does not seem to be as reliable as it was 10–15 years ago.

Meyney, the large vineyard of 126 acres immediately north of Montrose, with a splendid view of the Gironde River, has made notably flavorful, robust wines that offer considerable value to the shrewd consumer looking for quality rather than prestige. The wines have been consistent with some vintages rivaling the Médoc's classified growths.

The quality during the 1990s declined. At best, Meyney is fairly big styled, with good fruit and excellent aging potential of 20–25 years. Some observers have even commented that Meyney's distinctive perfume of licorice, prunes, and truffles is caused by a geological aberration; much of the Meyney vineyard sits on an outcropping of iron-enriched blue clay that has never been found elsewhere in the Médoc. Ironically, such soils also exist in Pomerol, particularly underlying the famed vineyard of

Château Pétrus. For visitors to St.-Estèphe, Meyney also merits attention, because this is one of the few old ecclesiastical buildings in the Médoc and has been well preserved by its owner, the Cordier firm.

Fortunately for consumers, the wines of Meyney continue to be underpriced. Vinification and upbringing are controlled by one of Bordeaux's most respected oenologists, Georges Pauli.

IMPORTANT VINTAGES

Note: The late vintages of the 1990s (1996–1999) were not kind to Meyney.

1996
85
A soft, easygoing, ripe, dried herb and red current–scented wine, this 1996 is surprisingly open and evolved. It is made in a mainstream, consumer-friendly style that will have wide appeal, although it is neither concentrated nor complex. Drink it over the next 6–7 years. Last tasted, 3/99.

1995
89
The 1995 exhibits an opaque purple color and a super nose of jammy black cherries and cassis intertwined with scents of earth, licorice, and toasty oak. Sweet, ripe, low-acid flavors cascade over the palate, creating an unctuous texture and an impressive mouth-feel. This ripe, medium-to full-bodied, concentrated Meyney should drink well for another eight years. Last tasted, 3/96.

1994
88
The attractive 1994 has a dark purple color, a sweet plummy, herb, mineral, and spice-scented nose, and powerful, medium- to full-bodied, concentrated flavors with adequate acidity and moderate tannin. This wine has a certain precociousness, as well as fruit and good balance. It should keep eight more years. Last tasted, 3/96.

1990
88
Though not as rich as the 1989, the 1990 is still a fine effort from Meyney. It offers deep ruby/purple color, a fine nose of black fruits, herbs, and oak, ripe, generous, tannin-dominated flavors, good concentration, and a moderately long, tough finish. Anticipated maturity: now–2010. Last tasted, 7/97.

1989
90
The opaque, black/ruby colored 1989 has a bouquet of minerals, damson plums, damp earth, and tar. The alcoholic, massive flavors and the mouthcoating tannins all combine to create a sensory overload. A large-scaled, fat, intense Meyney, it is now approaching full maturity. Anticipated maturity: now–2025. Last tasted, 3/00.

1988
88
If you lack patience, you will want no part of the 1988. More brutally tannic than the 1989 yet packed with fruit, the 1988 has softened but remains rigid and somewhat austere. It recalls the wonderful 1975 Meyney that is just now beginning to drink well. Anticipated maturity: now–2015. Last tasted, 4/91.

1986
90
More mature than many northern Médoc 1986s, the Meyney 1986 is a deep, dark garnet/purple–colored wine with a moderately intense fragrance of minerals, licorice, smoke, roasted herbs, and sweet black currant fruit. On the palate, the wine still has some tannin to shed, but its expansive, savory style suggests full maturity. With admirable extract and layers of fruit, this wine is a candidate for another 5–10 years of cellaring. Anticipated maturity: now–2015. Last tasted, 4/00.

1985
87
Totally mature, the 1985 Meyney exhibits a deep ruby color with some amber at the edge. The wine possesses a seductive nose of weedy black fruits intertwined with aromas of plums, tea, earth, and licorice. Sweet on the attack, this medium-bodied, deliciously fruity, round, silky-textured wine should continue to drink well. Anticipated maturity: now–2006. Last tasted, 9/97.

1982
90
One of the overachievers of the vintage, Meyney's 1982 has taken on an opaque garnet color with some amber. It offers a flamboyant nose of licorice, Asian spices, smoked meats, leather, and jammy black cherries. Full-bodied, with sweet, ex-

pansive fruit and a chewy texture, this wine has always been delicious. It is a juicy, well-delineated, fully mature Meyney for drinking now and over the next 5–10 years. Last tasted, 11/00.

ANCIENT VINTAGES

In 1978, the superb oenologist, Georges Pauli, began to exercise his talents with the making of Meyney. Previously, the wine had a tendency to turn out overly tannic and astringent. Vintages of the 1960s, particularly 1966, 1962, and 1961, are good wines, but not comparable to the super Meyneys of the 1980s. The finest old Meyney I have tasted is the 1959 (rated 86 and drunk most recently in 1987). In the 1970s, only the 1975 (rated 91 in 10/99) proved to be an exceptional wine and a welcome surprise from this irregular vintage.

MONTROSE

Classification: Second Growth in 1855

Owner: Jean-Louis Charmolüe

Address: 33180 St.-Estèphe

Telephone: 05 56 59 30 12; Telefax: 05 56 59 38 48

Visits: By appointment only

Contact: Philippe de Laguarigue

VINEYARDS

Surface area: 169.2 acres

Grape varietals: 65% Cabernet Sauvignon, 25% Merlot, 8% Cabernet Franc, 2% Petit Verdot

Average age of vines: 43 years

Density of plantation: 9,000 vines per hectare

Average yields: 42 hectoliters per hectare

Elevage: Twenty-one to twenty-five day long fermentation and maceration in temperature-controlled stainless-steel tanks with frequent pumping-overs. Malolactics in tanks. Eighteen months aging in barrels with 50–70% new oak with six rackings. Fining with egg whites. No filtration.

WINES PRODUCED

Château Montrose: 200,000 bottles

La Dame de Montrose: 150,000 bottles

Plateau of maturity: Within 3–25 years of the vintage post-1970; 15–25 years pre-1970

GENERAL APPRECIATION

Since 1989, Montrose has been the most reliable St.-Estèphe cru classé. Over recent vintages, it has regularly surpassed Cos d'Estournel, its closest rival, and Calon-Ségur, despite the improved quality of the latter wine. A revised classification might even rank it amongst the Médoc first growths. Shrewd buyers would also be well advised to seek its second wine (vintages from 1990 onward).

One of the Médoc's best-situated vineyards and one of the commune's most impeccably clean and well-kept cellars, Montrose was for years associated with huge, dense, powerful wines that needed several decades of cellaring to be soothing enough to drink. For example, Jean Paul Jauffret, the former head of Bordeaux's CIVB, served me the 1908 Montrose in 1982, blind, to see if I could guess its age. The wine had plenty left in it and tasted like it was at least 30 years younger.

The owner, the affable Jean-Louis Charmolüe, has obviously lightened the style of Montrose in response to his perception that dense, excruciatingly tannic wines are no longer popular with consumers. The change in style is particularly noticeable with the vintages of the late 1970s and early 1980s, as more Merlot has been introduced into the blend at the expense of Cabernet Sauvignon and Petit Verdot. Montrose fans were not amused by the "nouveau" style. Since 1986 Montrose has returned to a more forceful, muscular style, reminiscent of pre-1975 vintages. Certainly the 2000, 1996, 1990, and 1989 vintages for Montrose produced true blockbuster wines not seen from this property since 1961. Anyone who has had the pleasure of drinking some of Montrose's greatest vintages—1970, 1964, 1961, 1959, 1955 and 1953—can no doubt attest to the fact that Montrose produced a bevy of massive wines that deserve to be called the Latour of St.-Estèphe. The wines of Montrose have been especially strong in the periods 1953–1971 and 1989–present, when they were usually among the finest wines produced in the northern Médoc.

Visitors to St.-Estèphe will find the modest château of Montrose situated on high ground with a magnificent view of the Gironde River. The property, owned by the Charmolüe family since 1896, does make a worthy visit, given the splendid *cuverie*, with its old, huge, open oak vats and striking new barrel and fermentation cellar. Like many of its neighbors, Château Montrose has a new state-of-the-art tasting room and reception area.

IMPORTANT VINTAGES

2001
90–91+
Montrose is justifiably proud of having fashioned one of the vintage's most powerful and concentrated wines. Yields were a mere 32 hectoliters per hectare, and the 2001 Montrose (which represents 64% of the total production) is a blend of 62% Cabernet Sauvignon, 34% Merlot, 3% Petit Verdot, and 1% Cabernet Franc. A classic effort in the style, according to the château, "of the highly successful 1955," it is backward, tannic, and impressively concentrated. It possesses good freshness, full body, high tannin, low acidity, admirable extract, and loads of crème de cassis fruit intermixed with chocolate, liquid minerals, and earth. There is more noticeable tannin than in the blockbuster 2000. The 2001 will require a decade of cellaring to shed its tannic clout. Anticipated maturity: 2012–2030. Last tasted, 1/03.

2000
97
The 2000 Montrose is the finest effort produced since the compelling 1990 and 1989. Gigantically sized, its saturated inky purple color is followed by a huge nose of crushed blackberries, crème de cassis, vanilla, hickory smoke, and minerals. Extremely full-bodied, powerful, dense, and chewy, this unreal Montrose should last for 30+ years. Anticipated maturity: 2008–2040. Last tasted, 1/03.

2000
89
La Dame de Montrose: A great second wine, 39% of the production made it into the 2000 La Dame de Montrose. It offers wonderful sweetness, abundant quantities of fat, juicy, chocolaty, black cherry, and curranty-flavored Merlot, and a he-

donistic personality. It will drink well for 8–10 years. Don't miss it! Last tasted, 1/03.

1999
90 The black/purple-colored 1999 Montrose offers up notes of pure black fruits intermixed with minerals, smoke, and earth. Extremely concentrated, surprisingly powerful and dense, with moderate tannin, its size, strength, and medium- to full-bodied power are atypical for the vintage. Anticipated maturity: 2006–2025. Last tasted, 11/02.

1999
87 La Dame de Montrose: The 1999 La Dame de Montrose includes 40% Merlot in the blend, which provides a soft character in its elegant, medium-bodied personality. Consume this attractive effort over the next 5–7 years. Last tasted, 11/02.

1998
90+ A classic effort, the 1998 Montrose exhibits a dense purple color in addition to a sweet nose of jammy cassis, licorice, earth, and smoke. It is a powerful and full-bodied wine with well-integrated tannin. Given Montrose's tendency to shut down, it is performing better out of bottle than I expected. Anticipated maturity: 2005–2030. Last tasted, 3/02.

1997
87 The 1997 Montrose has turned out even better than expected. Although lighter and less concentrated than usual, fragrant aromas of plum liqueur, soil, cedar, and leather are attractive. Round and tasty, with good fruit, low acidity, and fine ripeness, it will drink well for 2–3 years. Last tasted, 3/02.

1996
91+ The 1996 Montrose reveals outstanding potential. It boasts a saturated dark ruby/purple color and aromas of new oak, jammy black currants, smoke, minerals, and new saddle leather. This multilayered wine is rich and medium- to full-bodied, with sweet tannin, a nicely textured, concentrated mid-palate, and an impressively long finish. Anticipated maturity: 2009–2025. Last tasted, 11/02.

1995
93 An explosively rich, exotic, fruity Montrose, the 1995 displays even more fat and extract than the 1996. There is less Cabernet Sauvignon in the 1995 blend, resulting in a fuller-bodied, more accessible and friendlier style. The wine exhibits an opaque black/ruby/purple color, as well as a ripe nose of black fruits, vanilla, and licorice. Powerful yet surprisingly accessible (the tannin is velvety and the acidity low), this terrific example of Montrose should be at its peak until 2028. Last tasted, 11/02.

1994
90 An opaque purple color suggests a wine of considerable intensity. One of the most successful 1994s of the northern Médoc, the wine presents closed aromatics of jammy black fruits, plums, spice, and earth. On the palate, there is impressive extract, purity, and copious amounts of sweet black currant fruit nicely balanced by moderate yet ripe tannin. Medium bodied, with excellent to outstanding concentration, this impressive Montrose is approachable now and will hold until 2020. Last tasted, 3/99.

1990
100 This majestic wine is remarkably rich, with a distinctive nose of sweet, jammy fruit, liquefied minerals, new saddle leather, and grilled steak. In the mouth, the enormous concentration, extract, high glycerin, and sweet tannin slide across the palate with considerable ease. It is a huge, corpulent, awesomely endowed wine that is relatively approachable, as it has not yet begun to shut down and lose its baby fat. Because of its enormous sweetness, dense concentration, high extract, and very low acidity, the 1990 Montrose can be appreciated today, yet this is a legend for the future. Anticipated maturity: now–2030. Last tasted, 2/03.

1989
97 An outstanding Montrose, the 1989 is one of the vintage's superstars. It possesses an opaque dark ruby/purple color, a sweet nose of minerals, black fruits, acacia flower, cedar, and wood. A full-bodied, highly extracted wine with low acidity and moderate tannin in the long finish, it has developed even more richness and layers of flavors than I originally thought. It has layers of sweet fruit as well as an elevated

level of glycerin. A brilliant effort, the 1989 Montrose is very close in quality to the perfect 1990. Anticipated maturity: now–2025. Last tasted, 2/03.

1988
83
Consistently unimpressive, the 1988 Montrose is light, too tannic, and lacking in richness and depth as well as finish. High yields and a too early harvest date have left their emaciated, austere mark on the 1988. Anticipated maturity: now–2008. Last tasted, 4/99.

1986
91
Made during a period when Montrose was flirting with a lighter style, the 1986 is one of the beefier efforts from that short-lived, stylistic detour. The wine reveals a dense ruby/purple color with only a hint of lightening at the edge. Fleshy, muscular, and powerful, with aromas of red and black fruits, mineral, and spice, this medium- to full-bodied, tannic, brawny Montrose is still youthful, yet accessible. It possesses a layered, chewy character, along with plenty of sweet tannin in the finish. Anticipated maturity: now–2025. Last tasted, 4/99.

1985
85
A surprisingly light, innocuous style of Montrose, the 1985 exhibits a medium ruby color with a pink rim, followed by pleasant but washed-out aromas of sweet red currants, earth, and herbs. This medium-bodied wine displays some charm and sweet fruit on the attack, but it narrows out in the mid-palate and finish. There is also tannin and herbaceousness in the aftertaste. A disappointment for the *terroir* and vintage. Anticipated maturity: now–2008. Last tasted, 4/99.

1983
83
Not nearly as big or as tannic as one might expect, the ruby-colored, lightweight 1983 Montrose has adequate tannin, a decent ruby color, a spicy, plummy nose, medium body, and an astringent finish. Anticipated maturity: now. Last tasted, 4/99.

1982
91
The 1982 Montrose has developed rapidly, yet it remains a candidate for another 15 years of cellaring. The wine reveals a healthy dark ruby/garnet color, followed by a fragrant, sweet nose of black fruits intermingled with new oak, licorice, and floral scents. Full-bodied and opulent, with dusty tannin in the finish, this gorgeously proportioned, rich, concentrated wine can be drunk now. A very impressive example of Montrose that has consistently been atypically evolved and forward. Anticipated maturity: now–2015. Last tasted, 9/02.

ANCIENT VINTAGES

The 1970 (92 points), 1964 (92 points), and 1961 (95 points) are classic, full-throttle, massive wines. The 1959 (95 points; last tasted 10/94) is a surprising clone of the 1961, with sweeter fruit, a more rustic, tannic personality, and the same enormous weight, richness, and distinctively old style found in both the 1961 and 1959. The 1959 is just reaching full maturity.

Both the 1955 (91 points; last tasted 12/01) and 1953 (90 points; last tasted 12/01) are superb wines if drunk from well-stored bottles.

The 1921 Montrose (74–90 points; tasted four times in 1995 and 1996) is variable. In one tasting, the wine started off with a promising nose of cedar, smoked meats, and a peppery, Rhône-like character, but high acidity and ferocious tannin dominated the meager flavors. Other tastings have revealed a rich, sweet, opulently textured wine that was alive and still endowed.

LES ORMES DE PEZ

Classification: Cru Bourgeois

Owner: Jean-Michel Cazes

Address: 33180 St.-Estèphe

Telephone: 05 56 73 24 00; Telefax: 05 56 59 26 42

E-mail: infochato@ormesdepez.com

Website: www.ormesdepez.com

No visits

VINEYARDS

Surface area: 86.5 acres

Grape varietals: 70% Cabernet Sauvignon, 20% Merlot, 10% Cabernet Franc

Average age of vines: 30 years

Density of plantation: 9,000 vines per hectare

Average yields: 50 hectoliters per hectare

Elevage: Fifteen to seventeen day fermentation and maceration in temperature-controlled stainless-steel tanks. Fifteen months aging in oak barrels. Fining. Filtration only if necessary.

WINES PRODUCED

Les Ormes de Pez: 204,000 bottles

No second wine is produced.

Plateau of maturity: Within 5–12 years of the vintage

GENERAL APPRECIATION

In the best vintages, this reliable Cru Bourgeois is worth a fifth growth. Modest prices rank this wine among some of the finest values in the Médoc.

Les Ormes de Pez is a popular wine, due in large part to the wine's generously flavored, plump, sometimes sweet and fat personality. Don't discount the extensive promotional efforts of the owner, Jean-Michel Cazes, either. The wine rarely disappoints. The color of Les Ormes de Pez tends to be quite dark, and since 1975, the flavors are increasingly supple and designed for easy comprehension by the masses. However, the wine can age for 5–12 years. Older vintages from the 1940s and 1950s made in a more massive, dense style, can often represent outstanding values because the wine has been impeccably made for decades. Les Ormes de Pez is a wine that consumers, looking for high quality at modest prices, should always give serious consideration.

IMPORTANT VINTAGES

2000 A sleeper of the vintage, this is the finest Les Ormes de Pez since 1982 and 1970.
89   Its dense purple color and aromas of licorice and black fruits are followed by a stuffed, muscular wine with a layered texture, low acidity, and ripe tannin. It will

be accessible early on, yet prove to be long-lived. Anticipated maturity: now–2015. Last tasted, 1/03.

1999
86
A lovely, forward offering, the dark ruby–colored 1999 Les Ormes de Pez offers aromas of black currant and cherry fruit, medium body, soft tannin, and an up-front style that requires consumption over the next 4–5 years. Last tasted, 3/02.

1998
87
A successful effort, as well as reasonably good value, this dark ruby/purple–colored 1998 exhibits copious quantities of cassis fruit along with earthy, underbrush notes. Medium- to full-bodied, with fine concentration, excellent texture, and a soft, spicy, peppery finish, it will drink well for eight years. Last tasted, 3/02.

1996
86
A sleeper of the vintage, this wine exhibits a saturated dark ruby color and an excellent blackberry- and cassis-scented nose with smoky oak in the background. It is sweet, opulently textured, surprisingly accessible and round, with an excellent finish. This is one of the finest wines from Les Ormes de Pez, along with the 2000 and 1998. Anticipated maturity: now–2014. Last tasted, 3/01.

1995
86
I am tempted to say this wine is too obviously commercial, but it is still an attractive, soft, round, medium to dark ruby–colored claret with herb, black cherry, and currant fruit notes. Lush, with some elegance, medium body, soft tannin, and an easygoing finish, this wine should be drunk within the next 1–2 years. Last tasted, 3/98.

ANCIENT VINTAGES

The best of this estate include the splendid 1990 (89 points), 1982 (87 points), and the remarkable, still glorious 1970 (93 points), the latter wine drunk in September 2001.

During the mid-1980s, I had the opportunity to drink the 1961, 1959, 1955, 1953, and 1947, all plucked off the wine lists of several Bordeaux restaurants. All of them were still in fine condition—massive, robust, nearly coarse wines that represented the old style of Bordeaux winemaking. I have no doubt that well-stored examples of this château's wines from the 1960s, 1950s, and 1940s could represent fine values today.

DE PEZ

Classification: Cru Bourgeois

Owner: Jean-Claude Rouzaud; Champagne Louis Roederer

Address: lieu-dit Pez, 33180 St.-Estèphe

Telephone: 05 56 59 30 26; Telefax: 05 56 59 39 25

Visits: By appointment Monday to Friday, 9 A.M.–noon and 2 P.M.–5 P.M.

Contact: Philippe Moureau

VINEYARDS

Surface area: 59.3 acres

Grape varietals: 45% Cabernet Sauvignon, 44% Merlot, 8% Cabernet Franc, 3% Petit Verdot

Average age of vines: 33 years

Density of plantation: 6,500 vines per hectare

Average yields: 50 hectoliters per hectare

Elevage: Twenty to thirty-day long fermentation and maceration in wooden vats. Forty percent of total volume undergoes malolactics in new oak barrels. Fifteen to eighteen months aging in oak barrels with 40% new oak. Racking every three months. Fining with egg whites, no filtration.

WINES PRODUCED:

Château de Pez: 130,000 bottles

No second wine produced.

Plateau of maturity: Within 8–10 years of the vintage

GENERAL APPRECIATION

Considerable investments have been made by the Roederer firm. Though quality has improved since 1995, the wines still remain rather hard and tannic and do not show the opulence that characterizes some peers like Les Ormes de Pez or Haut-Marbuzet. Nevertheless, this is an estate most observers expect to soar in quality.

It is difficult to miss Château de Pez and the twin towers as one passes through the one-horse village of Pez. For decades this estate has made a muscular yet excellent, sometimes tough-textured wine that is capable of lasting for up to two decades. If the wine of de Pez is to be criticized at all, it is for rarely attaining an exceptional rating. Reliable and solid as it may be, de Pez seems incapable of hitting the heights of the appellation's most notable Crus Bourgeois. I have often wondered whether an increased percentage of Merlot in the blend might not give the unduly restrained, frequently lean de Pez more flesh and character.

It will be interesting to follow de Pez given the fact that the property was acquired by the Champagne house of Louis Roederer several years ago. The former proprietor, Robert Dousson, has spent much of his life at de Pez, having been born there in 1929. A hands-on proprietor, always at the property, he believed strongly in unmanipulated wines. Additionally, the longevity of his wines and their popularity in England and northern Europe never went to his head.

IMPORTANT VINTAGES

2000   2000 is the first impressive effort under the Roederer administration. A blend of
87   equal parts of Merlot and Cabernet Sauvignon, with 7% Cabernet Franc, this wine exhibits the vintage's deep ruby/purple color, high tannin levels, a muscular structure, and medium- to-full-bodied, dense cassis flavors with a hint of mineral/wet stones. Anticipated maturity: 2007–2020. Last tasted, 1/03.

PHÉLAN SÉGUR

Classification: Cru Bourgeois

Owner: Xavier Gardinier

Address: 33180 St.-Estèphe

Telephone: 05 56 59 74 00; Telefax: 05 56 59 74 10

E-mail: phelan.segur@wanadoo.fr

Visits: By appointment Monday to Friday

Contact: Thierry Gardinier

VINEYARDS

Surface area: 158 acres

Grape varietals: 60% Cabernet Sauvignon, 35% Merlot, 5% Cabernet Franc

Average age of vines: 35 years

Density of plantation: 8,300 vines per hectare

Average yields: 41 hectoliters per hectare

Elevage: Twenty-day fermentation and maceration in temperature-controlled stainless-steel tanks. Eighteen months aging with 50–60% new oak. Fining and filtration.

WINES PRODUCED

Château Phélan Ségur: 160,000 bottles

Frank Phélan: 120,000 bottles

Plateau of maturity: Within 5–14 years of the vintage

GENERAL APPRECIATION

Given its fine location between Montrose and Calon-Ségur, one could expect better from Phélan Ségur. While quality soared from the mid-1980s to the mid-1990s, recent vintages have been indifferent.

This beautiful estate, recently cleaned and refurbished by the new owners, has always had the potential to produce one of the finest wines of St.-Estèphe because the vineyard borders both those of Montrose and Calon-Ségur. The progress made by the new owners was especially evident with excellent wines produced in the late 1980s, but the quality during the 1990s was inconsistent.

IMPORTANT VINTAGES

The only high-quality vintages on my radar screen are the 2000 (87 points), 1996 (86 points), 1990 (89 points), and 1988 (87 points).

OTHER ST.-ESTÈPHE ESTATES

BEL AIR

Classification: Cru Bourgeois

Owner: SCEA du Château Bel Air

Address: 4, chemin de Fontaugé, 33180 St.-Estèphe

Mailing Address: 15, route de Castelnau, 33480 Avensan

Telephone: 05 56 58 21 03; Telefax: 05 56 58 17 20

E-mail: jfbraq@aol.com

Visits: By appointment only

Contact: Jean-François Braquessac

VINEYARDS

Surface area: 12.4 acres

Grape varietals: 75% Cabernet Sauvignon, 20% Merlot, 5% Cabernet Franc

Average age of vines: 40 years

Density of plantation: 8,000 vines per hectare

Average yields: 50 hectoliters per hectare

Elevage: Cold pre-fermentation followed by fermentation and maceration in temperature-controlled stainless-steel tanks with cap immersed. Fourteen months aging in barrels with 30% new oak. No fining, no filtration.

WINES PRODUCED

Château Bel Air: 24,000 bottles

Château Bel Air Coutelin: 12,000 bottles

Plateau of maturity: Within 4–12 years of the vintage

Note: Grapes are hand-picked and there is a first sorting right in the vineyards, which are located in front of Cos d'Estournel, Marbuzet, and Montrose. Green pruning is carried out on the younger vines if necessary.

LE BOSCQ

Classification: Cru Bourgeois

Owner: SC du Château Le Boscq

Farmed by: Dourthe (CVBG)

Address: 33180 St.-Estèphe

Mailing Address: Dourthe, 35, rue de Bordeaux, 33290 Parempuyre

Telephone: 05 56 35 53 00; Telefax: 05 56 35 53 29

E-mail: contact@cvbg.com

Visits: By appointment Monday to Friday; No visits at harvest time

Contact: Marie-Hélène Inquimbert

VINEYARDS

Surface area: 41 acres

Grape varietals: 51% Merlot, 42% Cabernet Sauvignon, 7% Petit Verdot

Average age of vines: 30 years

Density of plantation: 8,000 vines per hectare

Average yields: 45–47 hectoliters per hectare

Elevage: Fermentation in small temperature-controlled stainless-steel vats. Duration of maceration depends upon the quality of grapes. Part of yield undergoes malolactics in barrels and micro-oxygenation of lees. Eighteen months aging with 50% new oak. Fining if necessary (with egg whites). No filtration.

WINES PRODUCED

Château Le Boscq: 70,000–73,000 bottles

Héritage de Le Boscq: 35,000–36,000 bottles

Plateau of maturity: Within 3–10 years of the vintage

GENERAL APPRECIATION

Wines of Le Boscq have greatly improved over recent vintages and are now worth their Cru Bourgeois status. Prices remain modest in view of the quality.

The vineyard of Le Boscq is located at the very northern end of the appellation of St.-Estèphe, with a good view of the Gironde River. It has extremely gravelly, clay soil, and the wine is vinified in stainless-steel vats and aged in small oak casks for 18 months. Given the high percentage of Merlot, it is not surprising that the wine is soft and fruity. In years where there is a tendency toward overripeness, Le Boscq can be disjointed and flabby. Nevertheless, in good vintages, this wine provides reasonably priced, fine drinking in its first decade of life.

CAPBERN GASQUETON

Classification: Cru Bourgeois

Owner: GFA Capbern Gasqueton

Address: 33180 St.-Estèphe

Telephone: 05 56 59 30 08; Telefax: 05 56 59 71 51

Visits: By appointment only

Contact: Denise Capbern Gasqueton

VINEYARDS

Surface area: 91.4 acres

Grape varietals: 65% Cabernet Sauvignon, 15% Cabernet Franc, 20% Merlot

Average age of vines: 30 years

Density of plantation: 9,000 vines per hectare

Average yields: 35 hectoliters per hectare

Elevage: Twenty-one day fermentation and maceration. Eighteen months aging in barrels, with 30% new oak. Fining, no filtration.

WINES PRODUCED

Capbern Gasqueton: 135,000 bottles

No second wine is produced.

Plateau of maturity: Within 5–10 years of the vintage

CAVE COOPERATIVE MARQUIS DE ST.-ESTÈPHE

Reputed to be the finest and most modernly equipped cooperative in the Médoc, this conglomerate of 85 producers (controlling 300 acres of vineyards) turns out an enormous quantity of wine that is sold not only under the name of the cooperative, Marquis de St.-Estèphe, but also under the name of the estate. Some of the small but reputable estates that have their wines produced and bottled at the cooperative include Château Léo des Prades (37.3 acres; 115,000 bottles), Château Ladouys (23 acres; 72,000 bottles), and Château Mignot (6.5 acres; 20,000 bottles). All of these wines are vinified and bottled separately.

The standard *cuvée* is Marquis de St.-Estèphe, representing 270,000 bottles. It is aged 12 months in concrete tanks. The cooperative also produces a special *cuvée*, Prestige du Marquis (75,000 bottles), that undergoes a three-week fermentation and maceration followed by 12 months aging in barrels with 70% new oak. The rest of the production is sold in bulk to *négociants*.

The cellars are equipped with concrete and stainless-steel tanks, and there is an aging cellar for the *élevage* of the special *cuvée* and the three estate labeled wines.

LA COMMANDERIE

Classification: Cru Bourgeois

Owner: GFA des Château Canteloup et La Commanderie

Address: 33180 St.-Estèphe

Mailing Address: Kressmann, 35, rue de Bordeaux, 33280 Parempuyre

Telephone: 05 56 35 53 00; Telefax: 05 56 35 53 29

E-mail: contact@cvbg.com

Visits: By appointment only

Contact: Marie-Hélène Inquimbert

VINEYARDS

Surface area: 39.5 acres

Grape varietals: 55% Cabernet Sauvignon, 40% Merlot, 5% Cabernet Franc

Average age of vines: 27 years

Density of plantation: 6,600 vines per hectare

Average yields: 57 hectoliters per hectare

Elevage: Duration of fermentation of maceration depends on the quality of the grapes and the vintage. Twelve months aging in barrels with 35% new oak. Fining with egg whites. Filtration at bottling.

WINES PRODUCED

Château La Commanderie: 78,000 bottles

No second wine is produced

Plateau of maturity: Within 4–8 years of the vintage

GENERAL APPRECIATION

Pleasant, commercially styled, and fairly priced wines.

This wine is made in a modern, commercial style, emphasizing supple, easygoing fruit and smooth, light tannins, and it is already to drink when bottled. It could be more complex, but it is certainly clean and understandable to the masses.

COUTELIN-MERVILLE

Classification: Cru Bourgeois

Owners: Bernard and François Estager

Address: c/o G. Estager et Fils, Blanquet, 33180 St.-Estèphe

Telephone and Telefax: 05 56 59 32 10

Visits: Every day of the week; by appointment only on weekends

VINEYARDS

Surface area: 61.7 acres

Grape varietals: 50% Merlot, 25% Cabernet Sauvignon 23% Cabernet Franc 2% Petit Verdot

Average age of vines: 30 years

Density of plantation: 55 vines per hectare

Average yields: 55 hectoliters per hectare

Elevage: Eighteen to twenty-one day fermentation and maceration. Twelve months aging in barrels with 25% new oak. Fining, filtration upon bottling.

WINES PRODUCED

Château Coutelin-Merville: 120,000 bottles

Château Merville: 60,000 bottles

Plateau of maturity: Within 8–15 years of the vintage

GENERAL APPRECIATION

Firm, tannic, earthy, often rustic wines are produced at this estate.

NOTE: This château is situated on the highest point in St.-Estèphe.

I wish I were more familiar with the wines of this moderately sized estate. Those vintages I have tasted—1996, 1995, 1986, 1982, 1975, and 1970—all represented intensely concentrated, powerful, highly tannic, yet interesting old-style, well-made wines. The proprietors Bernard and François Estager, from France's Corrèze region (like many Bordeaux families, including the family of Jean-Pierre Moueix in Libourne the Bories of Ducru-Beaucaillou, and the Theils of Poujeaux), march to the beat of a different drummer in St.-Estèphe, as the blend of grapes suggests they are a great proponent of Cabernet Franc. Perhaps this explains why their wines have a compelling fragrance, but it does not explain their aging potential, power, and muscle. All things considered, this is a wine that the Estagers claim needs at least 15–20 years in the top vintages to reach maturity! They would appear to be right. This could well be a property to look at more seriously.

DOMEYNE

Classification: Cru Bourgeois

Owner: GFA du Château Domeyne

Address: 3, espace Guy Guyonnaud, 33180 St.-Estèphe

Telephone: 05 56 59 72 29; Telefax: 05 56 59 75 55

Visits: By appointment only

VINEYARDS

Surface area: 17.8 acres

Grape varietals: 65% Cabernet Franc, 35% Merlot

Average age of vines: 30–35 years

Density of plantation: 7,600 vines per hectare

Average yields: 55 hectoliters per hectare

Elevage: Twenty-one day fermentation and maceration. Twelve months aging in barrels with 40% new oak. Fining and filtration.

WINES PRODUCED

Château Domeyne: 51,000 bottles

No second wine is produced.

Plateau of maturity: Within 4–10 years of the vintage

HAUT-BARADIEU

Classification: Cru Bourgeois

Owner: SCEA Vignobles Jean Anney

Address: 33180 St.-Estèphe

Mailing Address: Château Tour des Termes, Saint-Corbian, 33180 St.-Estèphe

Telephone: 05 56 59 32 89; Telefax: 05 56 59 73 74

Visits: Monday to Friday, 8:30 A.M.–12:30 P.M. and 2:00–4:30 P.M.

Contact: Christophe Anney

VINEYARDS

Surface area: 27.2 acres

Grape varietals: 50% Merlot, 50% Cabernet Sauvignon

Average age of vines: 15–20 years

Density of plantation: 6,666 vines per hectare

Average yields: 57 hectoliters per hectare

Elevage: Three to four week long fermentation and maceration in temperature-controlled stainless-steel tanks with two daily pumping-overs. Twelve months aging in one- and two-year-old oak barrels. Fining, no filtration.

WINES PRODUCED

Château Haut-Baradieu: 80,000 bottles

No second wine is produced.

Plateau of maturity: Within 4 to 12 years of the vintage

HAUT-BEAUSÉJOUR

Classification: Cru Bourgeois

Owner: Jean-Claude Rouzaud; Champagne Louis Roederer

Address: rue de la Mairie, 33180 St.-Estèphe

Mailing Address: Château de Pez, lieu-dit Pez, 33180 St.-Estèphe

Telephone: 05 56 59 30 26; Telefax: 05 56 59 39 25

Visits: By appointment only

Contact: Philippe Moureau

VINEYARDS

Surface area: 49.4 acres

Grape varietals: 52% Merlot, 40% Cabernet Sauvignon, 8% Petit Verdot and Cot

Average age of vines: 15 years

Density of plantation: 8,500 vines per hectare

Average yields: 50 hectoliters per hectare

Elevage: Twenty to thirty day long fermentation (29–30°C) and maceration in temperature-controlled tanks. Malolactics in barrel for 3% of total volume. Twelve to fifteen months aging in oak barrels that are renewed by a third at each vintage. Fining with egg whites, no filtration.

WINES PRODUCED

Château Haut-Beauséjour: 100,000 bottles

No second wine is produced.

Plateau of maturity: Within 4–12 years of the vintage

HAUT COTEAU

Classification: Cru Bourgeois

Owners: Bernard and Bernadette Brousseau

Address: Saint-Corbian, 33180 St.-Estèphe

Telephone: 05 56 59 39 84; Telefax: 05 56 59 39 09

E-mail: château.haut-coteau@wanadoo.fr

Visits: Monday to Friday, 8 A.M.–noon and 2–6 P.M.

Contact: Bernadette Brousseau

VINEYARDS

Surface area: 47 acres

Grape varietals: Equal parts of Merlot, Cabernet Sauvignon, and Cabernet Franc

Average age of vines: 30 years

Density of plantation: 8,500 vines per hectare

Average yields: 55–60 hectoliters per hectare

Elevage: Five to eight-day alcoholic fermentation and 3–4 week maceration in temperature-controlled stainless-steel vats. Twelve to fifteen months aging in barrels with 33% new oak. Fining, no filtration.

WINES PRODUCED

Château Haut Coteau: 40,000 bottles

Château Brousseau Haut-Vignobles: 30,000 bottles

Plateau of maturity: Within 4–12 years of the vintage

LA HAYE

Classification: Cru Bourgeois

Owner: Georges Lécailler

Address: Leyssac, 33180 St.-Estèphe

Mailing Address: 28, rue d'Armenonville, 98200 Neuilly-sur-Seine

Telephone: 001 47 38 24 42; Telefax: 01 47 38 14 41

E-mail: château.lahaye@free.fr

Website: www.vigneron-independant.com//membres//lahaye

Visits: June 15 to September 15: Monday to Friday, 10 A.M.–6P.M. At other times, by appointment only.

Contact: Sylvie Jaffre

VINEYARDS

Surface area: 24.7 acres

Grape varietals: 59% Merlot, 36% Cabernet Sauvignon, 4.5% Merlot, 0.5% Cabernet Franc

Average age of vines: 35 years

Density of plantation: 8,600 vines per hectare

Average yields: 45 hectoliters per hectare

Elevage: Twenty to thirty day long fermentation (28–30°C) and maceration in temperature-controlled stainless-steel tanks with two daily pumping-overs. Eighteen months aging in barrels with 30% new oak. Fining and filtration.

WINES PRODUCED

Château La Haye: 45,000 bottles

Fief de La Haye: 45,000 bottles

Plateau of maturity: Within 4–12 years of the vintage

HOUISSANT

Classification: Cru Grand Bourgeois Exceptionnel

Owner: Jean Ardouin

Address: 33180 St.-Estèphe

Telephone: 05 56 59 32 21; Telefax: 05 56 59 73 41

Visits: Monday to Thursday, 8 A.M.–noon and 2–6 P.M. Friday, 8 A.M.–noon and 2–5 P.M.

VINEYARDS

Surface area: 52 acres

Grape varietals: 60% Merlot, 30% Cabernet Sauvignon, 10% Petit Verdot

Average age of vines: 30 years

Density of plantation: 6,000 vines per hectare

Average yields: 55 hectolitres per hectare

Elevage: Twenty-eight to thirty day fermentation and maceration in vats, 12 months aging with half the yield in vats and half in barrels (no new oak).

WINES PRODUCED

Château Houissant: 120,000 bottles

Château Tour Pomys: 72,000 bottles

Plateau of maturity: Within 3–8 years of the vintage

GENERAL APPRECIATION

Should be downgraded to a Cru Bourgeois. The half-dozen or so vintages of Houissant I have tasted have never made a favorable impression. The wine tends to be disjointed, austere, and very tannic.

LAFFITTE-CARCASSET

Classification: Cru Bourgeois

Owner: SCI Château Laffitte-Carcasset, de Padirac family

Address: 33180 St.-Estèphe

Telephone: 05 56 59 34 52; Telefax: 05 56 59 35 75

Visits: By appointment only

Contact: Constance de Padirac (telephone 06 14 70 45 08)

VINEYARDS

Surface area: 71.6 acres

Grape varietals: 55% Cabernet Sauvignon, 35% Merlot, 10% other Cépages

Average age of vines: 30–40 years

Density of plantation: 9,000 vines per hectare

Average yields: 50 hectoliters per hectare

Elevage: Fermentation in temperature-controlled stainless-steel vats. Twelve to fourteen months aging with 30% of total volume in vats and 70% in barrel, and 30% new oak. Fining and filtration.

WINES PRODUCED

Château Laffitte-Carcasset: 150,000 bottles

Château La Vicomtesse: 50,000 bottles

Plateau of maturity: Within 5–8 years of the vintage

GENERAL APPRECIATION

This is not a wine that I know well, but those vintages I have tasted—1988, 1986, 1985, and 1982—seem to belong to the elegant, finesse school of winemaking. Somewhat light but still tasty and harmonious, with none of the tough-textured, often excessive tannin that many St.-Estèphes reveal, the wines from Laffitte-Carcasset seem to be at their best within 7–8 years of the vintage. The vineyard is well located on high ground in the very northern part of the St.-Estèphe appellation.

LAVILLOTTE

Classification: Cru Bourgeois

Owner: SCEA des Domaines Pedro

Address: 33180 St.-Estèphe

Mailing Address: SCEA des Domaines Pedro, 33180 Vertheuil

Telephone: 05 56 73 32 10; Telafax: 05 56 41 98 89

E-mail: dompedro@aol.com

Visits: Monday to Friday, 9 A.M.–noon and 2–5 P.M. Groups must please secure an appointment.

Contact: Jacques Pedro or Frank Maroszak

VINEYARDS

Surface area: 29.6 acres

Grape varietals: 72% Cabernet Sauvignon, 25% Merlot, 3% Petit Verdot

Average age of vines: 37 years

Density of plantation: 7,500 vines per hectare

Average yields: 50 hectoliters per hectare

Elevage: Prolonged fermentation and maceration in temperature-controlled stainless-steel tanks with frequent pumping-overs. Twenty months aging with 30–40% new oak. Fining with egg whites, no filtration.

WINES PRODUCED

Château Lavillotte: 50,000–60,000 bottles

Château Aillan: 20,000–30,000 bottles

Plateau of maturity: Within 8–15 years of the vintage

GENERAL APPRECIATION

At the time proprietor Jacques Pedro purchased Lavillotte in 1962, it was in deplorable condition. Pedro comes from a family of French viticulturists who had lived in Algeria until it was granted independence from France. His philosophy combines a mixture of modern technology and healthy respect for tradition. This contrast is evident: His vineyards are harvested by machine, but the *cuvaison* is at least three weeks long. The results, based on vintages such as 1989, 1986, 1985, and 1982—the only vintages I have tasted—are surprisingly concentrated, full-bodied wines, with fragrance, complexity, and richness. Each of the aforementioned vintages will easily mature gracefully for more than a decade. This would appear to be one of the best yet least known sources for fine wine from St.-Estèphe.

MARBUZET

Classification: Cru Bourgeois Exceptionnel
Owner: Domaines Reybier
Address: 33180 St.-Estèphe
Telephone: 05 56 73 15 50; Telefax: 05 56 59 72 59
No visits

VINEYARDS
Surface area: 17.3 acres
Grape varietals: 62% Merlot, 27% Cabernet Sauvignon, 11% Petit Verdot
Average age of vines: 35 years
Density of plantation: 7,900–9,500 vines per hectare
Average yields: 50 hectoliters per hectare
Elevage: Three-week fermentation and maceration in temperature-controlled stainless-steel vats. Twelve months aging in barrels with 50% new oak. Fining, no filtration.

WINES PRODUCED
Château Marbuzet: 60,000 bottles
No second wine is produced.
Plateau of maturity: Within 2–12 years of the vintage

GENERAL APPRECIATION
A sound, reliable wine that is well made, very refined, and accessible. Most vintages need to be drunk within 8–12 years of the vintage.

If I had to pick one of the most beautiful and romantically situated properties in the Médoc, it would be this gloriously situated château with its superb terrace and wonderful gardens. In fact, the château (still owned by the Prats family even though the vineyards were sold), which faces the Gironde River, bears a remarkable resemblance to the White House in Washington, D.C.

PETIT BOCQ

Classification: Cru Bourgeois
Owner: SCEA Lagneaux-Blaton
Address: 3, rue de la Croix de Pez, 33180 St.-Estèphe
Mailing Address: BP 33, 33180 St.-Estèphe
Telephone: 05 56 59 35 69; Telefax: 05 56 59 32 11
E-mail: petitbocq@hotmail.com
Website: www.chateau-petit-bocq
Visits: By appointment only
Contact: Gaëtan Lagneaux

VINEYARDS

Surface area: 36.3 acres

Grape varietals: 55% Merlot, 43% Cabernet Sauvignon, 2% Cabernet Franc

Average age of vines: 35 years

Density of plantation: 8,500–10,000 vines per hectare

Average yields: 55 hectoliters per hectare

Elevage: Twenty-one day fermentation and maceration in temperature-controlled stainless-steel vats of 25–100 hectoliter capacity. The Merlot lots undergo malolactics in barrel. Twelve months aging in barrels with 50% new oak. Fining, no filtration.

WINES PRODUCED

Château Petit Bocq: 85,000–90,000 bottles

Plateau of maturity: Within 3–12 years of the vintage

GENERAL APPRECIATION

Recent vintages of Petit Bocq are well worth a fifth growth. Prices remain modest since the estate is not yet well-known to consumers. Shrewd buyers should take note as this wine is really worthy of interest.

Unfortunately, this distinctive wine, with the highest percentage of Merlot on any property in St.-Estèphe, has never, to my knowledge, been seen in the export markets. The proprietor fashions one of St.-Estèphe's most hedonistic wines. The 2000, 1996, 1990, 1989, 1985, and 1982 were bursting with black fruits, were explosively rich and full and possessed a juicy, thick texture, causing me to wonder why this property has not gained more recognition from Bordeaux wine enthusiasts. While the high percentage of Merlot suggests that Petit Bocq will not age well, the 1982, last tasted in 1994, was fresh and lively. This is clearly a property worth representation in the world's export markets, although the quantities of wine available will no doubt be minuscule.

POMYS

Classification: Cru Bourgeois

Owner: Arnaud family

Address: Leyssac, 33180 St.-Estèphe

Telephone: 05 56 59 32 26; Telefax: 05 56 59 35 24

Website: chateaupomys.com

Visits: By appointment only

Contact: Geneviève Rechaudiat

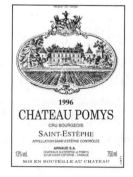

VINEYARDS

Surface area: 32.1 acres

Grape varietals: 60% Cabernet Sauvignon, 30% Merlot, 10% Cabernet Franc

Average age of vines: 25 years

Density of plantation: 7,500 vines per hectare

Average yields: 50 hectoliters per hectare

Elevage: Prolonged fermentation and maceration in temperature-controlled stainless-steel vats. Twelve to eighteen months aging in barrels with 35% new oak. Fining, no filtration.

WINES PRODUCED

Château Pomys: 70,000 bottles

Château Saint-Louis: 10,000 bottles

Plateau of maturity: Within 4–12 years of the vintage

ST.-ESTÈPHE

Classification: Cru Bourgeois

Owner: Arnaud family

Address: Leyssac, 33180 St.-Estèphe

Telephone: 05 56 59 32 26; Telefax: 05 56 59 35 24

Website: chateaupomys.com

Visits: By appointment only

Contact: Laure Marcou

VINEYARDS

Surface area: 27.2 acres

Grape varietals: 55% Cabernet Sauvignon, 35% Merlot, 5% Cabernet Franc, 5% Petit Verdot

Average age of vines: 25 years

Density of plantation: 7,500 vines per hectare

Average yields: 50 hectoliters per hectare

Elevage: Prolonged fermentation and maceration in temperature-controlled concrete tanks. Twelve to eighteen months aging in barrels with 30% new oak. Fining, no filtration.

WINES PRODUCED

Château St.-Estèphe: 50,000 bottles

Château Tour Coutelin: 12,000 bottles

Plateau of maturity: Within 4–12 years of the vintage

SÉGUR DE CABANAC

Classification: Cru Bourgeois

Owner: GFA des Domaines Guy Delon

Address: 33180 St.-Estèphe

Mailing Address: SCEA Guy Delon & fils, 33180 St.-Estèphe

Telephone: 05 56 59 70 10; Telefax: 05 56 59 73 94

Visits: By appointment only

Contact: Guy Delon

VINEYARDS

Surface area: 17.5 acres

Grape varietals: 60% Cabernet Sauvignon, 30% Merlot, 5% Cabernet Franc, 5% Petit Verdot

Average age of vines: 25 years

Density of plantation: 8,500 vines per hectare

Average yields: 50 hectoliters per hectare

Elevage: Three-week fermentation and maceration in temperature-controlled stainless-steel vats with frequent pumpings-over. Twenty months aging in oak barrels that are renewed by a third at each vintage, with seven rackings and one fining with egg whites. No filtration.

WINES PRODUCED

Château Ségur de Cabanac: 40,000 bottles

No second wine is produced.

Plateau of maturity: Within 4–12 years of the vintage

TRONQUOY-LALANDE

Classification: Cru Bourgeois

Owner: Arlette Castéja-Texier

Address: 33180 St.-Estèphe

Mailing Address: c/o Dourthe, 35, route de Bordeaux, BP 49, 33290 Parempuyre

Telephone: 05 56 35 53 00; Telefax: 05 56 35 53 29

E-mail: contact@cvbg.com

Visits: By appointment only

Contact: Marie-Hélène Inquimbert

VINEYARDS

Surface area: 42 acres

Grape varietals: 48% Cabernet Sauvignon, 48% Merlot, 4% Petit Verdot

Average age of vines: 26 years

Density of plantation: 9,000 vines per hectare

Average yields: 55 hectoliters per hectare

Elevage: Three-week fermentation in temperature-controlled stainless-steel tanks. Fifteen to eighteen months aging in barrels with 25% new oak. Fining and filtration.

WINES PRODUCED

Château Tronquoy-Lalande: 90,000 bottles

Tronquoy de Sainte-Anne: 40,000 bottles

Plateau of maturity: Within 5–14 years of the vintage

GENERAL APPRECIATION

Burly, dense colored, very concentrated wines are produced. The problem is that too many of the wines are excessively tannic and rustic.

Tronquoy-Lalande is a historic property with a fine twin-towered château on the premises. The wine was highly regarded a century ago but has lost popularity. I have followed every wine since the late 1970s, and Tronquoy-Lalande wines lack consistency from vintage to vintage. At best, it is a very dark, huge, clumsy sort of wine, with an earthy, distinctive character. The wine is distributed exclusively by the Bordeaux firm of Dourthe. The finest recent vintage is the black-colored, dense, superripe 1989, and somewhat promising 2000.

TOUR DE MARBUZET

Classification: Cru Bourgeois

Owner: GFA des Vignobles H. Duboscq et fils

Address: 33180 St.-Estèphe

Telephone: 05 56 59 30 54; Telefax: 05 56 59 70 87

E-mail: henriduboscq@hotmail.com

Visits: By appointment Monday to Saturday, 9 A.M.–noon and 2–6 P.M.

Contact: Alfred Teixeira

VINEYARDS

Surface area: 12.4 acres

Grape varietals: 40% Cabernet Sauvignon, 40% Merlot, 20% Cabernet Franc

Average age of vines: 30 years

Density of plantation: 8,300 vines per hectare

Average yields: 54 hectoliters per hectare

Elevage: Three week fermentation and maceration in temperature-controlled concrete tanks with micro-oxygenation and one daily pumping-over. Eighteen months aging in oak barrels that are renewed by a quarter every year. Racking every three months. No fining, no filtration.

WINES PRODUCED

Château Tour de Marbuzet: 36,000 bottles

No second wine is produced.

Plateau of maturity: Within 4–12 years of the vintage

TOUR DE PEZ

Classification: Cru Bourgeois

Owner: Philippe Bouchara

Address: lieu-dit l'Hereteyre, 33180 St.-Estèphe

Telephone: 05 56 59 31 60; Telefax: 05 56 59 71 12

E-mail: chtrpez@terre-net.fr

Visits: Monday to Friday, 9:30 A.M.–noon and 2–5:30 P.M.

Contact: Valérie Duprat

VINEYARDS

Surface area: 40.5 acres

Grape varietals: 52% Merlot, 44% Cabernet Sauvignon, 4% Petit Verdot

Average age of vines: 35 years

Density of plantation: 8,000 vines per hectare

Average yields: 52 hectoliters per hectare

Elevage: Cold maceration followed by three- to four-week fermentation (29–30°C) and maceration in temperature-controlled stainless-steel tanks with frequent pumpings-over. Fifteen months aging with 40% new oak and 60% one-year-old barrels. Fining. Filtration depending upon the vintage.

WINES PRODUCED

Château Tour de Pez: 80,000 bottles

Tour de Pez: 35,000 bottles

Plateau of maturity: Within 4–12 years of the vintage

TOUR DES TERMES

Classification: Cru Bourgeois

Owner: SCEA Vignobles Jean Anney

Address: Saint-Corbian, 33180 St.-Estèphe

Telephone: 05 56 59 32 89; Telefax: 05 56 59 73 74

Visits: Monday to Friday, 8:30 A.M.–12:30 P.M. and 2–4:30 P.M.

Contact: Christophe Anney

VINEYARDS

Surface area: 39.5 acres

Grape varietals: 50% Cabernet Sauvignon, 50% Merlot

Average age of vines: 30 years

Density of plantation: 6,666 vines per hectare

Average yields: 55 hectoliters per hectare

Elevage: Three- to four-week fermentation and maceration in temperature-controlled stainless-steel tanks with two daily pumping-overs. Malolactics in barrels for 45% of total volume. Twelve months aging in barrels with 45% new oak. Fining, no filtration.

WINES PRODUCED

Château Tour des Termes: 100,000 bottles

Les Aubarèdes du Château Tour des Termes: 25,000 bottles

Plateau of maturity: Within 4–12 years of the vintage

NOTE: This estate also produces 4,000 bottles of a special *cuvée* called Château Tour des Termes Collection Prestige. This wine is produced from a special plot of old vines (40 years), essentially from Merlot (70%) located on a gravelly subsoil. Vinification is traditional, but malolactics occur in barrels and the wines spend 15 months in new oak.

VALROSE

Classification: Cru Bourgeois

Owner: Gérard Néraudau

Address: 5, rue Michel Audoy, 33180 St.-Estèphe

Mailing Address: Château Jonqueyres, 33750 Saint-Germain du Puch

Telephone: 05 57 34 51 66; Telefax: 05 56 30 11 45

VINEYARDS

Surface area: 13.25 acres

Grape varietals: 55% Merlot, 25% Cabernet Sauvignon, 20% Cabernet Franc

Average age of vines: 40 years

Density of plantation: 8,000 vines per hectare

Average yields: 50 hectoliters per hectare

Elevage: Cold maceration; 30-day fermentation and maceration with frequent pumpings-over and micro-oxygenation of lees. Malolactics in barrel with stirring of lees twice a week. Twelve months aging with 70% new oak. Fining, no filtration.

WINES PRODUCED

Cuvée Aliénor du Château Valrose: 24,000 bottles

Château Valrose: 9,000 bottles

Plateau of maturity: Within 2–8 years of the vintage

VIEUX COUTELIN

Classification: None

Owner: Vignobles Rocher Cap de Rive SA

Address: 33180 St.-Estèphe

Mailing Address: BP 89, 33350 Saint-Magne-de-Castillon

Telephone: 05 57 40 08 88; Telefax: 05 57 40 19 93

Visits: By appointment only

VINEYARDS

Surface area: 14.8 acres

Grape varietals: 70% Cabernet Sauvignon, 25% Merlot, 5% Petit Verdot

Average age of vines: 20 years

Density of plantation: 7,500 vines per hectare

Average yields: 59 hectoliters per hectare

Elevage: 18 months aging in vats and barrels with 20% new oak. Fining and filtration.

WINES PRODUCED

Château Vieux Coutelin: 36,000 bottles

Chevalier Coutelin: 14 000 bottles

Plateau of maturity: Within 4–12 years of the vintage

PAUILLAC

There isn't a more famous appellation of the Haut-Médoc and Bordeaux than Pauillac. While the commune of Margaux has a more lyrical and romantic name, as well as a famous first-growth château of the same title, it is Pauillac's vineyards that lay claim to three of the Médoc's four first growths. The fabled, fabulously expensive Pauillac trio of Lafite Rothschild, Mouton Rothschild, and Latour are the most revered residents, but they are formidably backed up by a bevy of wines, some brilliant, some overrated, and a few mysteriously overlooked or forgotten. Eighteen wines from Pauillac were included in the original 1855 classification, and today only two or three estates would have trouble holding on to their position should an independent study of quality be done.

The textbook Pauillac would tend to have a rich, full-bodied texture, a distinctive bouquet of black currants, licorice, and cedary scents, and excellent aging potential.

Since virtually all of the permitted vineyard space (2,965 acres) is controlled by the 18 classified growths, there are fewer Cru Bourgeois wines in Pauillac than in a commune such as St.-Estèphe. However, a wide diversity in the Pauillac styles is apparent. Among the three famous first growths, for example, the wines could not be more different. Granted, their soils all share the gravelly composition that reflects the sun's heat and affords excellent drainage. However, Lafite Rothschild's vineyard—tucked in a northern part of Pauillac right on the St.-Estèphe border—has a limestone base, resulting in wines that are Pauillac's most aromatically complex and subtly flavored. Lafite's bouquet has, of course, the telltale Pauillac "cedarwood" aroma in addition to a compelling scent of lead pencil shavings. Lafite rarely matches Mouton Rothschild in sheer opulence and power or Latour in consistency. Until the early 1980s, Lafite was a poster child for inconsistency, with few truly monumental wines actually produced (the 1959 and 1953 tower over the others). Of the other, non-first-growth Pauillacs, the lighter, aromatic Lafite style, albeit on a lower level, is best exemplified by the silky, medium-bodied Haut-Batailley.

Mouton Rothschild sits on a gravel ridge above the Médoc's largest town, Pauillac. In the 25-plus years that I have been visiting Bordeaux two or three times a year, I have seen the transformation of this sleepy, somewhat bland town into a noteworthy tourist attraction with the Médoc's only prestigious restaurant, Cordeillan-Bages. In addition to the gravelly soil, Mouton has more sandstone in the soil base and uses an abnormally high percentage of Cabernet Sauvignon in making the wine. When everything works right, these factors can produce the most decadently rich, fleshy, and exotic wine of not only Pauillac, but of the entire Médoc. In many ways, the wine of Mouton was personified by the flamboyant, bold, former owner, the Baron Philippe de Rothschild, who died in 1988. His daughter, Philippine, no shy flower, admirably continues to manage this estate with considerable flair. Mouton, of course, is not the only Pauillac made in a big, rich, opulent style. Several kilometers south, on another slightly elevated ridge called the Bages plateau, Lynch-Bages makes a dense, corpulent wine that can be splendidly deep and concentrated, clearly earning its reputation as the "poor man's Mouton."

Latour is Pauillac's other first growth, and this grand old estate has few if any peers when it comes to consistency from one vintage to the next. For most of the last century, Latour, along with Montrose in St.-Estèphe and Ausone in St.-Emilion, has been the slowest maturing and the longest-lived wine made in Bordeaux. The vineyard's location in southern Pauillac—next to St.-Julien—would seemingly suggest a more supple style of wine, but except for a brief hiccup in the 1980s (1983–1989), when a softer, less formidable style of Latour surprisingly emerged, Latour's wine has been as backward and as tannic as any. The soil at Latour is almost pure fine gravel that affords superb drainage, better than that enjoyed by Lafite Rothschild or Mouton Rothschild. That in itself may help explain why in rainy vintages such as 1999, 1994, 1993, 1992, 1974, 1972, 1969, 1968, and 1960, Latour easily outdistanced many other Médocs. Latour is simply Latour, and in Pauillac, there are no "look-alikes" in style or character.

There are several other Pauillacs that have distinctive styles, making generalizations about the wine of this commune difficult. Perhaps the most interesting wine of this group is Pichon Longueville Comtesse de Lalande (called Pichon-Lalande by

PAUILLAC

● CHÂTEAU

═══ ROAD

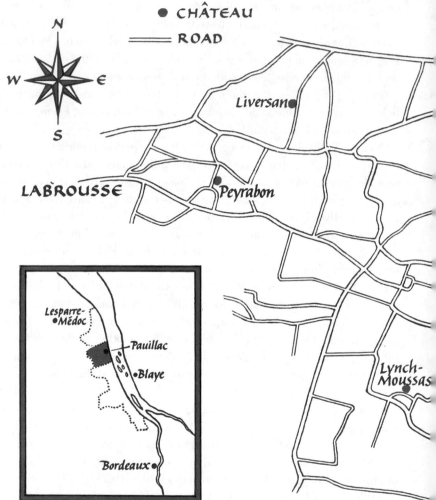

Liversan●

LABROUSSE

Peyrabon●

Lesparre-
●Médoc

Pauillac

●Blaye

Bordeaux●

Lynch-
Moussas●

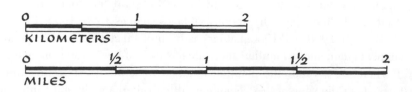

```
0            1            2
├──────────┼──────────┤
KILOMETERS

0        ½        1        1½        2
├──────┼──────┼──────┼──────┤
MILES
```

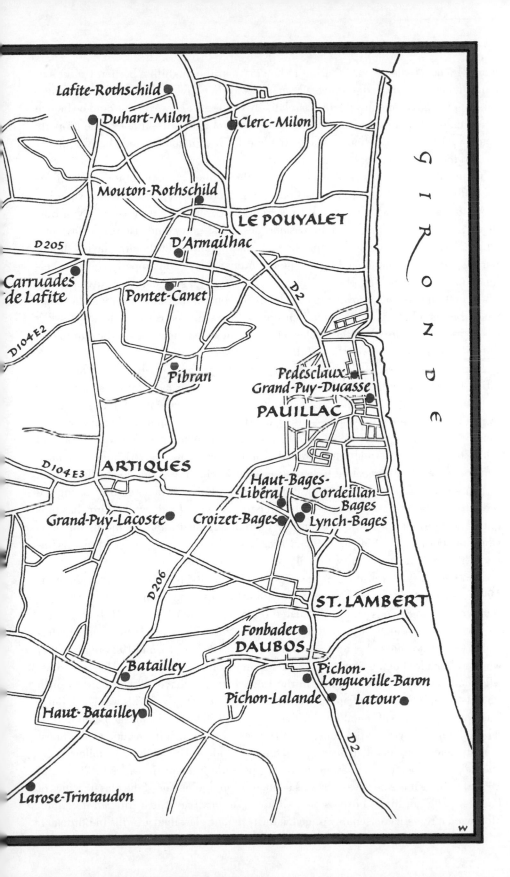

most). Pichon-Lalande sits adjacent to Latour, near the St.-Julien border. Unlike Latour, Pichon does indeed produce a Pomerol/St.-Julien-styled Pauillac—silky, graceful, supple, suave, and drinkable at a relatively young age. However, it would be foolish
to assume that this precocious-tasting wine does not age well—it does. The property
has always made great wine, but since the late 1970s, Pichon-Lalande has frequently
rivaled the finest wines of Pauillac.

Grand-Puy-Lacoste never seems to receive the publicity that the other top Pauillacs
do, but shrewd Bordeaux enthusiasts have long been squirreling away this wine. For
years this property, which sits well back from the Gironde River, was the joy of Bordeaux's leading gourmet (and from some accounts, gourmand as well), Raymond
Dupin. Nearly 30 years after Dupin's death, his reputation for holding lavish dinner
parties remains unchallenged by anyone in Bordeaux. Now the property, the wine cellars, and the winemaking philosophy are in the capable, sure hands of Xavier Borie.
Their first vintage was a lovely 1978. This is a property to follow, with a style somewhere between Latour and Mouton Rothschild—powerful and rich with layers of sweet
cassis fruit. It is a true Pauillac—cleaner, more consistent now than in the Dupin era,
but still robust, layered, very flavorful, and long-lived.

Several other classified Pauillacs merit their rating today, largely because of the exciting progress they have made since the late 1980s. The most impressive rags-to-
riches story is that of Pichon-Longueville Baron, the turreted château that sits across
from Pichon Longueville Comtesse de Lalande as well as Château Latour. Pichon-
Longueville Baron was Pauillac's most prominent underachiever between 1960 and
1985, but since 1986 quality has soared. The property's owners, the huge insurance
conglomerate AXA, benefitted from putting Jean-Michel Cazes and his brilliant team
in charge of this estate, in addition to pumping millions of francs into restoring the
property and building a new state-of-the-art cellar. Pichon-Longueville Baron has produced some exceptional wines under the current administration, including fabulous
wines in 2000, 1996, 1990, and 1989. Cazes has retired, but this property remains impeccably managed under the watchful eyes of Christian Seely.

Another château whose wines have jumped in quality, particularly since the mid-
1990s, is Pontet-Canet. This property, owned by the Tesseron family, possesses a huge,
relatively homogeneous vineyard situated opposite Mouton Rothschild. Both estates
occupy Pauillac's highest ground (about 100 feet above sea level). Anyone who has
tasted the extraordinary Pontet-Canets produced in 1961, 1945, and 1929 realizes that
when well made, Pontet-Canet is far better than its fifth-growth status. The Tesserons,
who made their fame and fortune in the Cognac region, have worked hard to push
Pontet-Canet into the elite Pauillac châteaux. The quality in the 1980s was good, but it
was apparently not sufficient for the Tesserons. In 1994 a decision was made to brutally eliminate any wine not considered perfect, and the result was one of the finest
Pontet-Canets produced in more than three decades. The 1994 was followed by
another terrific wine in 1995 and powerful, potentially majestic wines in 2000 and
1996. I believe it is safe to say that this château is producing one of the classic wines of
Pauillac. The antithesis of the softer, silkier style of wine, it is a true *vin de garde*.
Moreover, it remains reasonably priced, a rarity among classified growths in Bordeaux.

A wine I find to be the most difficult Pauillac to understand is Batailley. The estate has been well run by the Castéja family, but it produces stern, austere, broodingly tannic wines that take a decade or more to shed their tannic cloaks and exhibit charm. I consistently underrate this muscular, backward Pauillac, but I have noted that the wine appears to possess sweeter, riper fruit in recent vintages. It is another classic, old-style Pauillac that is underpriced for its ultimate potential, but patience is most certainly required.

Batailley's sister château, at least in name, Haut-Batailley, is owned by the Borie family, who also owns the famed Ducru-Beaucaillou in St.-Julien and Grand-Puy-Lacoste in Pauillac. The latter two properties tend to overshadow Haut-Batailley. In contrast to Batailley, Haut-Batailley is a silky, soft, richly fruity, seductive style of wine that may never hit the highest level of quality but is both consistent and delicious. A Pauillac in pedigree, it often tastes more like a St.-Julien.

Readers looking for a wine made in the style of Haut-Batailley, but more lavishly oaked, exotic, and plump, are advised to check out the two efforts of the Baronness Philippine de Rothschild—Clerc Milon and d'Armailhac. Both are forward, richly fruity wines that critics claim are aggressively oaked, but they have many admirers. The wines are, unquestionably, interesting, flavorful, and seductive. Moreover, quality at both châteaux soared in the mid- to late 1990s while pricing remained largely unaffected.

An estate on which to keep an eye, given its extraordinary financial underpinning and its well-placed vineyards, is Duhart-Milon. Made by the winemaking staff at Lafite Rothschild, Duhart-Milon appears poised to consistently offer a classic Pauillac made in an elegant yet ageworthy style. The Rothschilds have invested significantly in Duhart-Milon, and the wine has improved immensely, but in 2003 this wine still trails its rivals, Clerc Milon and Grand-Puy-Lacoste.

A relatively unknown Pauillac château is Haut-Bages Libéral. One of my more reliable buying choices in the 1980s, I thought it was reminiscent of the "poor person's Lynch-Bages," as it was always a fairly priced wine that offered plenty of cedar, black currant, and other jammy fruit in a chunky, fat style. However, the wine has become distressingly irregular in the 1990s and it is difficult to forecast which direction it will move.

Lastly, such Pauillac châteaux as Lynch-Moussas, Grand Puy Ducasse, Croizet-Bages, and Pédesclaux remain the forgotten quartet of Pauillac. For the first three, quality inched forward in the 1990s, but purchasers of these wines tend to be those who are wholly ignorant of what is going on in Bordeaux.

More than any other Médoc appellation, Pauillac, because of the dominance of the three first growths and some prominent super seconds, tends to establish the overall reputation for a particular vintage in the Médoc. Some would even argue that how goes Pauillac, so goes the public's image of a Bordeaux vintage. Although nothing so complex and nuanced can be viewed in black-and-white terms, there is no doubt that the quality of winemaking in Pauillac has improved significantly since the first edition of this book in 1985, and if Pauillac has a great vintage, as it did in 2000, 1996, 1995, 1990, 1986, and 1982, most other appellations seem to benefit.

Pauillac, with its well-drained soils, still seems to excel in the relatively hot, dry years. The 1980s were a golden age for all of Bordeaux, but no appellation profited more than Pauillac. After a good vintage in 1981, 1982 was spectacular—the greatest overall vintage for the appellation since 1961; 1983 was a good if uneven year, largely because of high yields; and 1984, as for most of Bordeaux, proved poor. The 1985 was overrated, and 1986 was an excellent if true *vin de garde* vintage, in which many profoundly rich, tannic wines were being produced that, at age 17, are still youthful wines. The vintage of 1988 was very good, while 1989 was uneven and extremely overrated. The 1990s have been less kind to Pauillac, as they have been to all Bordeaux—1990 was an extraordinary year for both Latour and Lafite Rothschild but was surprisingly disappointing for Mouton Rothschild. Among the other top estates, Pichon Longueville Comtesse de Lalande produced a herbaceous, uninspiring 1990, but Pichon-Longueville Baron, Lynch-Bages, and Grand-Puy-Lacoste all produced fabulous 1990s. In Pauillac more than in any other region except for Margaux, it is essential to have a healthy crop of Cabernet Sauvignon for a top vintage. Most estates have at least two-thirds of their vineyards planted with Cabernet, so that if this grape fails to achieve phenolic maturity, the entire appellation will have problems. In the 1990s, both 1996 and 1995 have turned out to be consistently excellent years. If the 1995s are impressive, tannic, and long-lived, the 1996s are even more prodigious wines, undeniably powerful, immense in structure, and destined to have very long lives. They are the 1990's version of 1986, but possibly better. 1996 was a great year for Cabernet Sauvignon as was the millennium vintage . . . 2000.

PAUILLAC
(An Insider's View)

Overall Appellation Potential: Excellent to superb

The Most Potential for Aging: Batailley, Grand-Puy-Lacoste, Lafite Rothschild, Latour, Lynch-Bages, Mouton Rothschild, Pichon-Longueville Baron, Pontet-Canet

The Most Elegant: Duhart-Milon-Rothschild, Grand Puy Ducasse, Haut-Batailley, Lafite Rothschild, Pichon Longueville Comtesse de Lalande

The Most Concentrated: Grand-Puy-Lacoste, Lafite Rothschild, Latour, Lynch-Bages, Mouton Rothschild, Pichon-Longueville Baron, Pichon Longueville Comtesse de Lalande, Pontet-Canet (since 1994)

The Best Value: d'Armailhac, Clerc Milon, Grand-Puy-Lacoste, Pontet-Canet

The Most Exotic: Clerc Milon, Mouton Rothschild, Pichon Longueville Comtesse de Lalande

The Most Difficult to Understand (when young): Batailley, Lafite Rothschild

The Most Underrated: Grand-Puy-Lacoste, Pontet-Canet (since 1994)

The Easiest to Appreciate Young: d'Armailhac, Clerc Milon, Grand Puy Ducasse, Haut-Batailley, Pichon Longueville Comtesse de Lalande

Up-and-Coming Estates: Clerc Milon, Pontet-Canet

Greatest Recent Vintages: 2000, 1996, 1995, 1990, 1986, 1982, 1970, 1961, 1959

PAUILLAC—AN OVERVIEW

Location: On the left bank of the Gironde River, Pauillac is sandwiched between St.-Estèphe to the north and St.-Julien to the south. It is approximately 23 miles from the center of Bordeaux.

Acres under vine: 2,965

Communes: Pauillac

Average Annual Production: 640,000 cases

Classified Growths: Total of 18: 3 first-growths, 2 second-growths, 1 fourth-growth, and 12 fifth-growths; there are 16 Crus Bourgeois

Principal Grape Varieties: Cabernet Sauvignon, followed by Merlot. There is very little Cabernet Franc and Petit Verdot found in Pauillac.

Principal Soil Type: Sandy gravel with significant iron and marl deposits.

A CONSUMER'S CLASSIFICATION OF THE CHATEAUX OF PAUILLAC

OUTSTANDING

Lafite Rothschild, Latour, Lynch-Bages, Mouton Rothschild, Pichon-Longueville Pichon Longueville Comtesse de Lalande

EXCELLENT

Clerc Milon, Grand-Puy-Lacoste, Pontet Canet (since 1994)

VERY GOOD

Duhart-Milon, Les Forts de Latour, Haut-Batailley

GOOD

d' Armailhac (known as Mouton-Baronne-Philippe from 1956–1989), Batailley, Carruades de Lafite, Grand Puy Ducasse

OTHER NOTABLE PAUILLAC PROPERTIES

La Bécasse, Bellegrave, La Bernadotte, Colombier-Monpelou, La Couronne, Croizet-Bages, La Fleur Milon, Fonbadet, Gaudin, Haut-Bages Libéral, Haut-Bages Monpelou, Lynch-Moussas, Pédesclaux, Pibran, Plantey, La Rose Pauillac

D'ARMAILHAC

(Formerly Mouton-Baronne-Philippe)

Classification: Fifth Growth in 1855

Owner: GFA Baronne Philippine de Rothschild

Address: 33250 Pauillac

Mailing Address: B.P. 117, 33250 Pauillac

Telephone: 05 56 59 22 22; Telefax: 05 56 73 20 44

E-mail: webmaster@bpdr.com

No visits

VINEYARDS

Surface area: 123.5 acres

Grape varietals: 56% Cabernet Sauvignon, 22% Merlot, 20% Cabernet Franc, 2% Petit Verdot

Average age of vines: 47 years

Density of plantation: 8,500 vines per hectare

Average yields: 45 hectoliters per hectare

Elevage: Fifteen to twenty-day fermentation in temperature-controlled stainless-steel vats at 25°C. Fifteen to sixteen months aging in oak barrels with approximately 35% new oak. No details regarding fining and filtration.

WINES PRODUCED

Château d'Armailhac: 220,000 bottles

No second wine is produced.

Plateau of maturity: Within 5–14 years of the vintage

GENERAL APPRECIATION

This estate has greatly improved over recent years, producing wines that show better concentration and density than in the past. Vintages prior to 1989 are generally sound but not exciting, while those after 1995 have consistently been very good to excellent. Because it is overshadowed by its two stable mates Mouton Rothschild and Clerc Milon, d'Armailhac is still available at reasonable prices. This is a wine shrewd buyers should seek, especially in good vintages. Be careful, though—it is better drunk sooner than later. d'Armailhac could be upgraded to fourth-growth status.

This remains the least known and, to the consuming public, the most obscure property of the late Baron Philippe de Rothschild's trio of Pauillac estates. The Baron acquired Mouton-Baronne-Philippe in 1933 when it was known as Mouton d'Armailhac. In 1956 the name was changed to Mouton-Baron-Philippe and in 1975 to Mouton-Baronne-Philippe in tribute to the Baron's wife, who died the following year. The name, beginning with the 1989 vintage, was changed once again to d'Armailhac. The cellars are adjacent to Mouton Rothschild, and the winemaking team led by Patrick Léon and Hervé Berlaud, who oversees the renowned Mouton Rothschild and Clerc Milon, also attends to the winemaking at d'Armailhac.

Despite the impressive age of the vineyard, the wine has tended to be relatively light, quick to mature, and easily outdistanced in complexity, character, and longevity by the two siblings. However, there has been a noticeable trend to upgrade the quality of the wines. While the quality of the 1982 is no doubt due to the vintage itself, the higher quality of d'Armailhac began in earnest with the fine 1985 and has been continued since. Since the mid-1990s, this estate has produced a succession of excellent wines at realistic prices.

IMPORTANT VINTAGES

2001   This blend of 60% Cabernet Sauvignon and 40% Merlot was produced from mod-
88–90   est yields of 36 hectoliters per hectare. According to administrator Patrick Léon,
        no Cabernet Franc was utilized because its quality was not satisfactory. A dark

ruby color is followed by a tight, firm, medium-bodied Pauillac with noticeable tannin and an aggressive palate impression. As with many estates, this 2001 is blown away by the 2000. Anticipated maturity: 2005–2014. Last tasted, 1/03.

2000   One of the most seductive and luscious d'Armailhacs I have ever tasted, the 2000
91   is a blend of 58% Cabernet Sauvignon and 42% Merlot. It boasts a saturated purple color along with smoky, licorice-infused, cedary, black currant–scented aromas with plenty of toasty oak. Dense, opulent, seamless, and medium- to full-bodied with sweet tannin, it has more volume, depth, and power than either the 2001 or the 1999. Anticipated maturity: now–2016. Last tasted, 1/03.

1999   The dense ruby/purple-colored 1999 d'Armailhac displays a gorgeous perfume of
89   spice box, coffee, cedar, licorice, and leather scents. Sexy, with loads of fruit, medium body, and sweet tannin in the smoky, flamboyant finish, it will drink well for 12–15 years. Last tasted, 3/02.

1998   This is another Médoc 1998 that is revealing more mid-palate, flesh, concentra-
89   tion, and sweeter tannin after bottling than it did during its *élevage*. A blend of 42% Cabernet Sauvignon, 20% Cabernet Franc, and 38% Merlot, this black/purple colored claret exhibits sweet aromas of licorice, incense, Asian spices, cedar, plums, and black currants. Full-bodied and sweet on the entry, with good acidity, definition, and ripe tannin, it will be drinkable young, yet last for 12–15 years. Last tasted, 3/02.

1997   Dark plum/garnet–colored, with an evolved, mature, cedary, spice box, fruit cake,
87   coffee, smoky, fruit-scented bouquet, this seductive, medium-bodied, fruit-driven 1997 offers plenty of appeal. Drink this spicy Pauillac over the next 5–6 years. Last tasted, 3/01.

1996   Nearly as seductive as the 1995, the 1996 exhibits a saturated ruby color that is
87   followed by sweet, roasted herb and black currant aromas with lush toasty oak notes. A blend of 45% Cabernet Sauvignon, 30% Merlot, and 25% Cabernet Franc, this medium-weight, elegant yet richly fruity wine possesses enough tannin to last two decades, but it will be one 1996 Médoc that will be drinkable at an early age. Anticipated maturity: 2004–2018. Last tasted, 3/01.

1995   One of the best d'Armailhacs ever produced (along with the 2000, 1999 and
89   1998), the 1995 blend is 50% Cabernet Sauvignon, 18% Cabernet Franc, and 32% Merlot. This deep ruby/purple–colored wine possesses low acidity, plenty of sweet tannin, and, in both its aromatics and flavors, gobs of ripe cassis fruit are nicely framed by the judicious use of toasty oak. Flavorful, round, generous, and hedonistic, this is a crowd-pleaser! Anticipated maturity: now–2012. Last tasted, 3/01.

1994   Made in an attractive, more muscular style, the 1994 displays a dark ruby/purple
86?   color, spicy, meaty, curranty aromas with a touch of cedar and earth, moderate tannin, and good flesh and structure. It may develop into an upper-80-point wine if the tannin melts away without a loss of fruit. Anticipated maturity: now–2010. Last tasted, 3/99.

1993   This soft, peppery, herb-tinged, dark ruby–colored wine possesses excellent fruit,
84   a supple texture, and round, agreeable, easy to understand and consume flavors. It should be drunk over the next 6–8 years. It is a good, reasonably priced Pauillac for restaurants and consumers looking for immediate gratification. Last tasted, 4/99.

1992   D'Armailhac's fully mature 1992 is a charming, straightforward, fruity wine
81   with moderate to dark garnet color and a spicy nose of roasted nuts and jammy black currants. The attack offers lush, velvety-textured fruit that fades quickly. Nevertheless, this is a pure, attractive, elegant wine for drinking now. Last tasted, 4/99.

1991 The 1991 exhibits superficial appeal in its oaky, sweet, herb-tinged nose, but once
74 past the makeup, the wine is thin and angular, with little depth and a short, tannic, tough finish. It will get more attenuated with age. Anticipated maturity: now. Last tasted, 4/99.

1990 The 1990 d'Armailhac is dark ruby/purple, with an expressive nose of smoked
85 nuts, cassis, smoke, and chocolate. This velvety-textured, round, agreeable wine lacks structure and length on the palate. It is charming but less concentrated than the 1989. Anticipated maturity: now. Last tasted, 11/96.

BATAILLEY

Classification: Fifth Growth in 1855

Owner: Castéja family

Address: Domaines Borie-Manoux, 86 cours
Balquerie-Stuttenberg 33082 Bordeaux

Telephone: 05 56 00 00 70; Telefax: 05 57 87 48 61

E-mail: borie-manoux@dial.oleane.com

Visits: By appointment Monday to Friday,
9 A.M.–noon and 2–5 P.M.

Contact: Domaines Borie-Manoux (specify Château Batailley)

VINEYARDS

Surface area: 138.3 acres

Grape varietals: 70% Cabernet Sauvignon, 26% Merlot, 3% Cabernet Franc, 1% Petit Verdot

Average age of vines: 35 years

Density of plantation: 10,000 and 8,500 vines per hectare

Average yields: 50–54 hectoliters per hectare

Elevage: Fermentation and maceration in temperature-controlled stainless-steel tanks. Eighteen months aging with 60% new oak. Fining, no filtration.

WINES PRODUCED

Château Batailley: 300,000 bottles

No second wine is produced.

Plateau of maturity: Within 10–25 years of the vintage

GENERAL APPRECIATION

A traditionally made Pauillac, Batailley is generally austere and tannic and more accessible after a decade of aging than in its youth. Recent vintages show considerable improvement. However, while the wines are sound and worth their fifth-growth status, they are never truly exciting and lack the opulence and generosity of some of their peers (like Grand-Puy-Lacoste or Lynch-Bages).

Batailley, an attractive château sitting in a small clearing surrounded by large trees, is located well inland from the Gironde River. The vineyards, which were all part of the

1855 classification, are situated between those of Haut-Batailley to the south and Grand-Puy-Lacoste to the north. England's David Peppercorn has frequently made the point (and I would agree) that because the *négociant* firm of Borie-Manoux controls the distribution of Batailley and because the wines are not freely traded or available for tasting in the normal commercial circles of Bordeaux, there has been a tendency to ignore this estate. This has resulted in a wine that is undervalued in some vintages.

The property has long been run by the Castéja family, who continue to turn out relatively old-style, solid, well-colored, somewhat rustic Pauillac that can be difficult to assess at a young age. I have frequently commented that while the wine can handle significant cellaring, it rarely excites or inspires, but is essentially reliable and fairly priced. Although I stand by those comments, I have begun to believe that I have underrated several of the vintages. Wine enthusiasts who have patience no doubt admire Batailley's reputation for longevity, as well as its reasonable prices. Given the increased efforts to improve the quality that began in the late 1980s, it is unlikely that Batailley can remain the lowest-priced classified-growth Pauillac.

IMPORTANT VINTAGES

2001 Spicy, cedar, evolved aromatics are accompanied by an opaque ruby/purple–
87–88 colored, medium-bodied Pauillac revealing moderate tannin as well as good purity, but not much excitement. Anticipated maturity: 2006–2016. Last tasted, 1/03.

2000 Always a tight-fisted, traditionally styled Pauillac that performs better at 10 years
87 of age than during its youth, the 2000 Batailley reveals a dark ruby color along with sweet black currant fruit presented in an uncomplicated, medium-bodied, firmly tannic, well-delineated style. Anticipated maturity: 2008–2020. Last tasted, 1/03.

1999 Dark ruby–colored with medium body and notes of weedy black currants inter-
86 mixed with earth and saddle leather, this ripe wine has moderate tannin and a firm finish. Anticipated maturity: 2004–2012. Last tasted, 3/02.

1998 An excellent dark plum color is followed by scents of tobacco, cedar, black cur-
87 rants, and earth. There is good ripeness, medium to full body, smoky, herb-tinged flavors, and fine length. The tannin is firm, but not excessive. This 1998 is tasting significantly better from bottle than it did during its *élevage*. Anticipated maturity: 2004–2017. Last tasted, 3/02.

1997 Notes of herbs, tobacco, and currant fruit mixed with damp soil aromas can be
84 found in this traditionally made Pauillac. With medium body, grip, and tannin, it is more evolved and softer than expected for this generally ageworthy wine. Consume it over the next eight years. Last tasted, 3/01.

1996 Batailley's 1996 is a well-structured, old-style Pauillac with a dense ruby/purple
87 color, earthy, cedar-tinged, black currant fruit in the aromatics and flavors, medium body, an excellent mid-palate, good depth, and a moderately tannic, and firm but pure finish. This very good to excellent Batailley will keep for two decades. Anticipated maturity: now–2020. Last tasted, 3/01.

1995 The 1995 has turned out well, displaying a dark ruby/purple color and aromas of
87 minerals, black currants, and smoky new oak. In the mouth, it is a medium-weight, backward, well-delineated Pauillac with plenty of tannin and a true *vin de garde* style. Anticipated maturity: now–2015. Last tasted, 3/01.

1994   An attractive black/ruby/purple color is followed by aromas of sweet curranty fruit
85   and new oak. Medium bodied with good ripeness, this sound, straightforward,
        well-made wine lacks depth and complexity, but it will provide pleasant, four-
        square drinking for another 10 years. Last tasted, 1/97.

1990   The 1990 offers a medium, dark ruby color, as well as an open-knit, fragrant,
86   spicy, sweet nose. In the mouth, the wine is decidedly less structured and tannic
        when compared with the 1989, but more soft, elegant, and, at least for now, flatter-
        ing. A clone of Batailley's 1962? Anticipated maturity: now–2010. Last tasted,
        1/93.

1989   The 1989 has gone into a hard, tannic, tough stage that suggests considerable pa-
87   tience will be necessary. The ruby/purple color is sound, and the bouquet of toasty,
        smoky oak, chocolate, and superripe cassis is followed by a medium-bodied, rich,
        extracted wine with ferocious tannins and good acidity. This is a large-scale, tra-
        ditionally styled wine requiring patience. Anticipated maturity: 2005–2020. Last
        tasted, 10/02.

1988   Typically stern, tough, closed, and difficult to penetrate, the 1988 displays a dark
85   ruby color, a reticent bouquet of minerals, black currants, and oak, medium body,
        and an elevated tannin level. Anticipated maturity: now–2008. Last tasted, 4/90.

1986   Made from 70% Cabernet Sauvignon, 20% Merlot, and the balance Petit Verdot
87   and Cabernet Franc, the dark garnet–colored 1986 is full-bodied but extremely
        hard and tannic. However, it appears to have the depth and concentration of
        fruit necessary to outlast the firm tannins. Anticipated maturity: now. Last tasted,
        3/97.

1985   Not surprisingly, the garnet-colored 1985 Batailley has the ripeness of the vintage
86   well displayed in the sweet currant/cherry aromas and flavors, but also carries the
        Batailley firmness and tannic austerity. Approaching full maturity, it is well made,
        reserved, and elegant. Anticipated maturity: now–2007. Last tasted, 3/97.

1982   Soft, relatively fat, fruity flavors lack the profound concentration of the best 1982s,
88   but nevertheless offer juicy black currants nicely mixed with a pleasing spicy oak-
        iness. Medium- to full-bodied, moderately tannic, with notes of minerals, earth,
        and herbs, this wine is just reaching full maturity. Anticipated maturity: now–
        2012. Last tasted, 3/01.

ANCIENT VINTAGES

Among the relics of the past, only the very good 1964 (88 points; last tasted 3/92) and
1962 (87 points; last tasted 1/00) stand out with merit.

CLERC MILON

Classification: Fifth Growth in 1855

Owner: GFA Baronne Philippine de Rothschild

Address: 33250 Pauillac

Mailing Address: BP 117, 33250 Pauillac

Telephone: 05 56 59 22 22; Telefax: 05 56 73 20 44

E-mail: webmaster@bpdr.com

No visits

VINEYARDS

Surface area: 74 acres

Grape varietals: 46% Cabernet Sauvignon, 35% Merlot, 15% Cabernet Franc, 3% Petit Verdot, 1% Carmenère

Average age of vines: 51 years

Density of plantation: 8,450 vines per hectare

Average yields: 55 hectoliters per hectare

Elevage: Fifteen to twenty-two day long fermentation in temperature-controlled stainless-steel tanks at 21°C. Sixteen to eighteen months aging in oak barrels with approximately 30% new oak. No details regarding fining and filtration.

WINES PRODUCED

Château Clerc Milon: 170,000 bottles

No second wine is produced.

Plateau of maturity: Within 5–14 years of the vintage

GENERAL APPRECIATION

This estate benefits from a fine location between Mouton Rothschild and Lafite Rothschild. Its wines have improved considerably after 1985 and vintages from 1995 onward have consistently been excellent. One of the most fruity and savory Pauillacs, Clerc Milon is generally forward and requires fairly early consumption. Judging by the level of quality exhibited over recent years, it could be upgraded to fourth-growth, if not third-growth status, especially in the best vintages. A must buy.

Another of the Baronness Philippine Rothschild estates, Clerc Milon was acquired in 1970. While there is no château, the vineyard is brilliantly placed next to both Mouton Rothschild and Lafite Rothschild, immediately adjacent to the defunct oil re-finery that dominates the tranquil town of Pauillac. Until 1985, the wine produced was frequently light and undistinguished. Recent vintages have displayed a lush fruity quality, lavish quantities of toasty new oak, as well as greater depth and flavor dimension. In comparison with the baronness's other estate-bottled wines, Clerc Milon is the most forward and easiest to appreciate when young. Given the quality of recent vintages, the wine is undervalued.

IMPORTANT VINTAGES

2001   The 2001 is another strong effort from Clerc Milon. A blend of 64% Cabernet
89–92   Sauvignon and the rest primarily Merlot with some Cabernet Franc, it exhibits notes of roasted espresso, crème de cassis, licorice, and fudge. Concentrated for a 2001, with moderately high tannin and impressive intensity as well as grip, this medium-bodied Pauillac will be at its finest between 2007–2016. It may rival and/or surpass the 2000. Last tasted, 1/03.

2000   The full-bodied, concentrated, dense 2000 has muscle and fat to burn. Opaque
91   ruby/purple–colored, with an unctuous texture and notes of black cherry liqueur, cassis, smoke, leather, and licorice, this blend of 67% Cabernet Sauvignon and 33% Merlot displays noticeable tannin in the finish, and thus early on will not be as charming as the 1999. Anticipated maturity: 2005–2020. Last tasted, 1/03.

1999
90
A blend of 55% Cabernet Sauvignon, 27% Merlot, and 18% Cabernet Franc, this saturated purple-colored 1999 displays a dense, flamboyant bouquet of roasted herbs, cedar, cassis, new saddle leather, and espresso. Soft, seductive, velvety-textured, and endearing in a concentrated, lush style, it will provide enjoyment for 15 years. It is a top effort for the vintage. Last tasted, 3/02.

1998
91
A superb effort, the 1998 is, along with the 2000, the finest Clerc Milon I have tasted. A blend of 50% Cabernet Sauvignon, 33% Merlot, 14% Cabernet Franc, and 3% Petit Verdot, this is a blockbuster, over-sized offering for this estate. Full-bodied and super-extracted, with power to burn, this rich, concentrated wine demands 4–5 years of cellaring. It is not dissimilar from the enormously constituted, majestic yet backward 1998 Mouton Rothschild. Anticipated maturity: 2008–2025. Last tasted, 3/02.

1997
87
Because of its low acidity and evolved style, the 1997 Clerc Milon deserves consumers' attention. Readers will enjoy its lush, concentrated, cassis/blackberry notes intertwined with coffee, smoke, spice, and chocolate. Drink this lush, hedonistic offering over the next 6–7 years. Last tasted, 3/01.

1996
90
Lavishly oaked, with gobs of toast and rich fruit, the 1996 is more massive and concentrated than previous vintages. The color is dense ruby/purple. The bouquet offers notes of roasted coffee, tobacco, and jammy cassis. Although surprisingly soft and opulent on the attack, the mid-section and finish reveal the wine's full body, high flavor extraction, and moderate tannin. This complete, large-scaled Clerc Milon will be at its finest between 2005–2018. Last tasted, 3/01.

1995
89
The 1995 Clerc Milon, a 56% Cabernet Sauvignon, 30% Merlot, 14% Cabernet Franc blend, reveals more tannin and grip than the 1996 (ironically, the 1995 has more of a 1996 vintage character, and vice versa for the 1996). This attractive dark ruby/purple–colored wine has impressive credentials. It offers a gorgeous nose of roasted herbs, meats, cedar, cassis, spice, and vanilla. This dense, medium- to full-bodied wine possesses outstanding levels of extract, plenty of glycerin, and a plush, layered, hedonistic finish. A luscious, complex effort, it reveals enough tannin and depth to warrant 10 or more years of cellaring. A sleeper. Anticipated maturity: now–2015. Last tasted, 3/00.

1990
86
Not as concentrated, opulent, and velvety as the 1989, the 1990 is still a sexy and smooth wine, with a fragrant nose of cassis, smoke, vanilla, roasted nuts, and exotic scents. This luscious wine, with a creamy texture and excellent color, falls off on the palate, much like its siblings, d'Armailhac and Mouton Rothschild. It is now fully mature. Last tasted, 12/00.

1989
90
The 1989 Clerc Milon is a hedonistic wine. Deep ruby, with an intense, roasted, smoky bouquet of plums, leather, herbs, and currants, this full-bodied wine is packed with fruit, chewy and opulent, soft and alcoholic. In spite of the precocious impression, the tannin levels are high—similar, in fact, to the 1986. This wine is significantly better than the 1990, as are the Mouton Rothschild and d'Armailhac. A great value. Anticipated maturity: now–2010. Last tasted, 12/00.

1988
89
The 1988 is deep in color with a moderately intense bouquet of herbs, smoke, and black currants. The hardness it revealed when it was young has melted away and, at present, a rich, creamy texture offers up considerable roasted fruit flavors complemented by lavish amounts of oak. Anticipated maturity: now. Last tasted, 3/95.

1986
90
Dark ruby/purple with some pink at the rim, this wine has a super bouquet of sweet, toasty new oak, plums, black currants, licorice, and cedar. The wine is concentrated on the palate, rich and powerful, yet atypically soft and fleshy for a 1986. While this wine should age well for another decade it has matured faster than many of the 1986 Pauillacs. Anticipated maturity: now–2010. Last tasted, 3/00.

1985   The plum/garnet 1985 is fully mature. It offers a complex bouquet of black cur-
89   rants, minerals, herbs, and smoke. On the palate, this wine is rich, medium bod-
       ied, soft, and round, having shed all of its tannin. Anticipated maturity: now. Last
       tasted, 3/00.

ANCIENT VINTAGES

Quality prior to 1985 was irregular, with few vintages of high quality.

COLOMBIER-MONPELOU

Classification: Cru Bourgeois

Owner: Bernard Jugla

Address: 33250 Pauillac

Telephone: 05 56 59 01 48; Telefax: 05 56 59 12 01

Visits: By appointment only

Contact: Bernard Jugla

VINEYARDS

Surface area: 37 acres

Grape varietals: 65% Cabernet Sauvignon, 25% Merlot, 5% Cabernet Franc, 5% Petit
Verdot

Average age of vines: 35 years

Density of plantation: 8,500 vines per hectare

Average yields: 55 hectoliters per hectare

Elevage: Three to four-week fermentation and maceration in temperature-controlled
stainless-steel tanks. Eighteen months aging in barrels that are renewed by a third at each
vintage. Fining, no filtration.

WINES PRODUCED

Château Colombier-Monpelou: 100,000 bottles

Château Puy La Rose: 50,000 bottles

Plateau of maturity: Within 3–5 years of the vintage

GENERAL APPRECIATION

The wines of this estate are generally lacking in concentration, density, and substance.
Rather light and tannic, they must be drunk within a decade of the vintage. Given the fine
location of the vineyard (near Mouton Rothschild) and the age of the vines, one could
expect better from Colombier-Monpelou. Crus Bourgeois of higher quality may be
purchased within the same price range.

This property, purchased by proprietor Bernard Jugla in 1970, consists of one contiguous vineyard well situated on the high plateau above the village of Pauillac. Given the
high percentage of Cabernet Sauvignon and the fact that the average age of the vines is
an impressive 34 years, one would expect a great deal more concentration and inten-

sity. Certainly, the vinification and *élevage* are completely traditional, as the wine is kept in oak casks for 15–18 months. The problem is that most of the wines I have tasted from Colombier-Monpelou are light, lacking concentration and distinction. Nevertheless, there is a considerable market for these wines in France.

CROIZET-BAGES

Classification: Fifth Growth in 1855

Owner: Jean-Michel Quié

Address: rue du Port de la Verrerie, Bages, 33250 Pauillac

Telephone: 05 56 59 01 62; Telefax: 05 56 59 23 39

Visits: Monday to Saturday, 9 A.M.–12:30 P.M. and 1:30–5:30 P.M.

Contact: Martine Dausson (Telephone 05 56 59 66 69; Telefax 05 56 59 29 80)

VINEYARDS

Surface area: 74 acres

Grape varietals: 54% Cabernet Sauvignon, 38% Merlot, 8% Cabernet Franc

Average age of vines: 28 years

Density of plantation: 6,500 and 8,000 vines per hectare

Average yields: 55 hectoliters per hectare

Elevage: Three-week fermentation and maceration in temperature-controlled stainless-steel tanks, with part of the yield undergoing malolactics in new oak. Eighteen months aging, with fourteen months in barrels and 25% new oak. Fining with egg whites. Filtration upon bottling.

WINES PRODUCED

Château Croizet-Bages: 150,000 bottles

La Tourelle de Croizet-Bages: 30,000 bottles

Plateau of maturity: Within 5–10 years of the vintage

GENERAL APPRECIATION

Until 1994, Croizet-Bages's track record ranked it as the most mediocre classified growth in Bordeaux, on par with Pédesclaux. Vintages from 1995 have improved, but are still unworthy of their classification. At their best, the wines of this estate are equivalent to a good Cru Bourgeois. It must be stressed, however, that prices are extremely affordable. In vintages like 2000, Croizet-Bages merits consumers' interest as it is a good wine for better than casual drinking. Do not cellar for more than 8–10 years.

Croizet-Bages is owned and managed by the Quié family, who also own the well-known Margaux estate, Rauzan-Gassies, and the reliable Cru Bourgeois, Bel Orme Tronquoy de Lalande. I have always found Croizet-Bages to be one of the lightest and quickest-maturing Pauillacs. The wine has been a consistent underachiever. The vineyard is ideally located on the Bages plateau, the vines are of a reasonable age (20 years), and the vinification is traditional. High crop yields may in part explain the disappointing results. Never terribly deep or spectacular, Croizet-Bages is a sound, gentle, soft, fruity wine, which is generally fully mature within 4–5 years. The positive showing of several vintages in the mid-1990s is an encouraging trend.

IMPORTANT VINTAGES

2000 A charming, mid-weight Pauillac, the 2000 Croizet-Bages reveals sweet fruit and
86 good depth, but a short finish. It is best consumed during its first decade of life. Last tasted, 1/03.

1999 Readers desiring light-bodied, pleasant wines may find the 1999 Croizet-Bages
78 more appealing than I did. However, this medium ruby–colored, soft effort is not up to the standards of a classified growth Pauillac. It will drink well for 5–10 years. Last tasted, 3/02.

1998 Soft, herbal, superficial characteristics as well as notes of cedar, licorice, and red
81 currants describe this medium-bodied, straightforward effort. Drink it over the next 5–6 years. Last tasted, 3/02.

1997 This soft, round, elegant wine is not concentrated, but it does possess moderately
81 sweet jammy cassis and red currant fruit intermixed with spicy, smoky oak. Already soft, it is ideal for consuming during its first decade of life. Anticipated maturity: now–2010. Last tasted, 3/01.

1996 This wine has turned out even better than I had expected. The dark ruby color is
87 followed by sweet, elegant notes of black currants, cherries, spicy oak, and cedar. The wine is medium bodied with sweet tannin and a moderately long finish. Purely made with good depth, it represents one of the more forward Pauillacs of the vintage. Anticipated maturity: now–2014. Last tasted, 3/00.

1995 The medium ruby color of the 1995 is followed by straightforward, soft, berry, and
85 black currant aromatics. In the mouth, the wine reveals an attractive, spicy, fleshy feel, not much weight or depth, but a superficial charm and fruitiness. This effort should last for 5–6 more years. Anticipated maturity: now–2009. Last tasted, 3/02.

DUHART-MILON

Classification: Fourth Growth in 1855

Owner: Barons de Rothschild (Lafite)

Address: 33250 Pauillac

Mailing Address: Les Domaines Barons de Rothschild, 33, rue de la Baume, 75008 Paris

Telephone: 01 53 89 78 01; Telefax: 01 53 89 78 00

E-mail: clesure@lafite.com

Website: www.lafite.com

Visits: By appointment Monday to Friday, 2 P.M. and 3:30 P.M. (one-hour visit). Estate closed on weekends, public holidays, in August, and at harvest time.

Contact: Christophe Salin

VINEYARDS

Surface area: 185.2 acres

Grape varietals: 70% Cabernet Sauvignon, 28% Merlot, 2% Cabernet Franc

Average age of vines: 30 years

Density of plantation: 7,500 vines per hectare

Average yields: 52 hectoliters per hectare

Elevage: Eighteen to twenty-four day fermentation and maceration in temperature-controlled stainless-steel tanks. Fourteen to sixteen months aging in barrels with 50% new oak after malolactics. Racking every three months. Fining with egg whites, no filtration.

WINES PRODUCED

Château Duhart-Milon: 280,000 bottles

Moulin de Duhart: 130,000 bottles

Plateau of maturity: Within 8–25 years of the vintage

GENERAL APPRECIATION

Since 1982, the wines of this estate have been very good to excellent. Close in style to their stablemates of Lafite, they represent fairly good values in today's marketplace. After a so-so track record in the 1960s and 1970s, Duhart-Milon clearly merits its classification and could be upgraded to third-growth status.

The "other" Pauillac château owned by the Rothschilds of Lafite Rothschild fame, Duhart-Milon was purchased in 1962. The poorly maintained vineyards were totally replanted during the mid- and late 1960s. Because the vineyard is young, particularly for a classified growth, the wines of the late 1960s and 1970s have not lived up to the expectations of wine enthusiasts who assume the Rothschild name is synonymous with excellence. The quality began to improve in 1978, and since 1982, Duhart's wines have been generally very good and occasionally outstanding. The style veers toward the balanced elegance and finesse school of winemaking exemplified by this estate's bigger sister, Lafite Rothschild.

IMPORTANT VINTAGES

2001　A blend of 86.7% Cabernet Sauvignon and 13.3% Merlot representing 54% of the
88–90　crop, the 2001 Duhart-Milon exhibits excellent sweet, juicy black currant and cherry fruit intermixed with a hint of herbs, earth, and new saddle leather. Medium bodied and moderately tannic with a vivacious, vibrant personality, it is not yet complex, but that should change with several years of aging. Anticipated maturity: 2006–2018. Last tasted, 1/03.

2000　One of the finest Duharts produced since 1996, the dense purple–colored 2000
90　offers an exquisite combination of black currant fruit, minerals, tobacco, smoke, and earth. It possesses excellent definition, a sweet attack, and a medium- to full-bodied, layered finish with moderate tannin. Anticipated maturity: 2006–2018. Last tasted, 1/03.

1999　This attractive, dark ruby–colored, well-balanced, medium-bodied 1999 exhibits
88　notes of underbrush, cassis, and dried herbs. Possessing finesse, harmony, and copious fruit, it can be consumed now and over the next 12 years. Last tasted, 3/02.

1998 This dense ruby/purple–colored blend of 77% Cabernet Sauvignon and 23%
89+ Merlot has filled out nicely during its upbringing in wood. It exhibits a fruitcake,
cedar, spice box, plum, black raspberry, and currant-scented bouquet, excellent
richness, moderate levels of sweet tannin, fine purity, and a complex style. Anticipated maturity: 2005–2020. Last tasted, 3/02.

1997 This impressively saturated dark ruby/purple–colored wine offers up copious
87 quantities of sweet black currant fruit, vanilla, and minerals. Suave, with sweet
fruit on the attack, medium body, ripe tannin, and a lush finish, it will drink well
for eight years. Last tasted, 3/00.

1996 A strong case can be made that this is the finest Duhart produced since the 1982.
91 The color is a saturated dark ruby/purple. The bouquet offers aromas of blackberry fruit intermixed with licorice, minerals, and dried herbs. Rich and intense
with considerable finesse and medium to full body, it also displays outstanding
concentration and purity. Anticipated maturity: 2005–2020. Last tasted, 3/00.

1995 Made from a blend of 80% Cabernet Sauvignon and 20% Merlot, the 1995 is
87 slightly sweeter and more supple and slender than the broader-shouldered 1996.
The wine's bouquet offers aromas of ripe berry fruit intermixed with minerals,
toasty oak, and spice. Medium-bodied with fine extract, it is a finesse-styled Pauillac (in the best sense of the word). Anticipated maturity: now–2014. Last tasted,
3/99.

1990 Dark plum/garnet, this vintage exhibits a sweet perfume of lead pencil and cassis.
89 While the tannins remain firm, the wine is expansive on the palate and the finish
is long. There is a strong tobacco, cassis, Cabernet character to the wine, as well as
a sense of elegance, balance, rich extract, and tannin. Impressive. Anticipated
maturity: 2004–2015. Last tasted, 3/01.

1989 The dark ruby 1989 has developed a bouquet of creamy black currant fruit, Asian
88 spices, and tobacco. There is even a touch of the famous Pauillac lead-pencil
smell. Medium bodied, rich, and expansive, this has always been a voluptuous-
styled wine. Fully mature, it should evolve for at least another decade. Anticipated
maturity: now–2012. Last tasted, 3/01.

1988 The 1988 Duhart-Milon exhibits a bouquet of ripe fruit, spices, cedar, and herbs.
88 The wine is rich, full-bodied, admirably concentrated, and long, with plenty of
tannin, yet fully mature aromas. Anticipated maturity: now–2010. Last tasted,
3/01.

1986 Still youthful yet evolving at a glacial pace, the plum/ruby–colored 1986 has ex-
87 cellent depth, plenty of richness, some spicy wood, as well as a classy bouquet of
herbaceous black currants and cedar. The wine is still revealing tannin, but it is
not intrusive. Anticipated maturity: now–2012. Last tasted, 3/01.

1985 The fully mature 1985 Duhart is a fine, medium-bodied wine that needs to be
86 drunk over the next 4–5 years. Medium deep garnet with an open-knit, spicy oak,
tobacco-tinged, currany bouquet, elegant and stylish, the 1985 lacks depth, but
requires drinking. Anticipated maturity: now. Last tasted, 3/01.

1982 This wine continues to be the finest example of Duhart that I have tasted. It has
92 surprised me in one blind tasting after another with its power, complexity, and
concentration. The wine's taste suggests full maturity, but there is plenty of grip,
extract, and tannin still in evidence. Additionally, the color displays only slight
lightening at the edge. The wine is a classic Pauillac, offering large quantities of
cedar and black currants in a full-bodied, fleshy, chewy style. It should continue to
drink well for another decade. Last tasted, 3/01.

FONBADET

Classification: Cru Bourgeois

Owner: SCEA Domaines Peyronie

Address: 33250 Pauillac

Telephone: 05 56 59 02 11; Telefax: 05 56 59 22 61

E-mail: pascale@château fonbadet.com

Website: www.château fonbadet.com

Visits: By appointment only

Contact: Pascale Peyronie

VINEYARDS

Surface area: 49.4 acres

Grape varietals: 60% Cabernet Sauvignon, 20% Merlot, 15% Cabernet Franc, 5% Petit Verdot and Malbec

Average age of vines: 50+ years

Density of plantation: 10,000 vines per hectare

Average yields: 50 hectoliters per hectare

Elevage: Twenty-one to twenty-eight day fermentation and maceration in concrete vats. Twenty-four months aging after malolactics, partly in vats and partly in barrels with 25% new oak. Fining, no filtration.

WINES PRODUCED

Château Fonbadet: 80,000 bottles

No second wine is produced.

Plateau of maturity: Within 5–15 years of the vintage

GENERAL APPRECIATION

At its best, this is one of the finest Pauillac Cru Bourgeois. Yet quality in the last decade has been irregular.

Fonbadet is a well-vinified wine that can, in vintages such as 1990, 1986, 1982, and 1978, surpass several of the classified growths of Pauillac. Vintages in the mid- to late 1990s were disappointing and behind the quality exhibited in the 1980s. In style it is always darkly colored, with a very rich, black currant bouquet, an intense concentration of flavor, and full body.

GRAND-PUY DUCASSE

Classification: Fifth Growth in 1855

Owner: SC du Château Grand-Puy Ducasse

Address: quai Antoine Ferchaud, 33250 Pauillac

Mailing Address: SC du Château, 109, rue Achard, BP 154, 33042 Bordeaux Cedex

Telephone: 05 56 01 30 10; Telefax: 05 56 79 23 57

E-mail: contact@cordier-wines.com

Visits: By appointment Monday to Friday, 9 A.M.–noon and 2–5 P.M. (for professionals of the wine trade only)

VINEYARDS

Surface area: 98.8 acres

Grape varietals: 60% Cabernet Sauvignon, 40% Merlot

Average age of vines: 25 years

Density of plantation: 8,000–10,000 vines per hectare

Average yields: 40 hectoliters per hectare

Elevage: Eighteen to twenty-one day fermentation and maceration in temperature-controlled stainless-steel tanks. Eighteen months aging in barrels with 50% new oak. Fining and filtration.

WINES PRODUCED

Château Grand-Puy Ducasse: 120,000–140,000 bottles

Prélude à Grand-Puy Ducasse: 18,000–30,000 bottles

Plateau of maturity: Within 5–12 years of the vintage

GENERAL APPRECIATION

The wines of Grand-Puy Ducasse generally merit their fifth-growth status. Well made but uninspiring, they should not be kept more than 10–12 years after the vintage. Though they are still proposed at reasonable prices, some of their peers, like Grand-Puy-Lacoste, represent better value for the money.

This fifth-growth Pauillac has been largely ignored by consumers and the wine press. Unquestionably, the current prices for vintages of Grand-Puy Ducasse are below those of most other Pauillacs, making it a notable value given the fine quality that now routinely emerges from the modern cellars located not in the middle of a beautiful vineyard, but in downtown Pauillac.

Extensive renovations as well as replanting began in 1971, culminating in 1986 with the installation of a new *cuverie* equipped with computerized stainless-steel tanks. The percentage of new oak casks has been increased to 50%. As a consequence, the future looks encouraging for Grand-Puy Ducasse. With the well-placed vineyard, one parcel adjacent to Mouton Rothschild and Lafite Rothschild, another on the gravelly plateau near Batailley, Grand-Puy Ducasse is a château to which value-conscious consumers should be giving more consideration.

The style of wines here is fruity and supple rather than tannic, hard, and backward. Most vintages of Grand-Puy Ducasse are drinkable within five years of the vintage, yet exhibit the potential to last for 10–15 years.

IMPORTANT VINTAGES

2001
86–87 A fruit-driven, elegant, light- to medium-bodied Pauillac with adequate acidity, light tannin, and notes of cedar as well as black currants, this charming, straightforward, moderately weighty 2001 will drink well during its first decade of life. Last tasted, 1/03.

2000
88 A saturated dark ruby/purple color is accompanied by aromas of sweet black currants, medium body, fine elegance, and nicely textured finish displaying well-integrated oak, tannin, and acidity. Anticipated maturity: 2004–2012. Last tasted, 1/03.

1999
86 Aromas of red currants, dried herbs, tobacco, and wood emerge from this medium-bodied 1999. Plum, currant, and cherry fruit, soft acidity, and light tannin suggest consumption is warranted over the next 5–6 years. Last tasted, 1/02.

1998
87 Black fruits dominate the moderately intense nose of this saturated ruby/purple–colored 1998. Medium bodied, savory, and user-friendly, it suffers only from a lack of complexity. Drink it over the next eight years. Last tasted, 1/02.

1997
85 The 1997 Grand-Puy Ducasse is dark ruby–colored with a sweet, black fruit–scented nose intermixed with weedy scents, vanilla, and earth. The mid-palate is plump and round, but the wine displays an abrupt finish with a certain austerity and angularity. Anticipated maturity: now–2007. Last tasted, 3/00.

1996
87 The color of the 1996 is a healthy dark ruby with purple nuances. The nose offers up aromas of cassis, dusty, earthy notes, tobacco leaf, cedar, and spice. Medium bodied with excellent depth and ripeness and the Cabernet Sauvignon component dominating its personality, this is a fine Grand-Puy Ducasse. Anticipated maturity: now–2015. Last tasted, 3/02.

1995
87 Dark ruby–colored with purple nuances, this supple, lush, fruity Pauillac possesses medium body, light intensity, new oak, soft tannin, and low acidity. Made in a clean, medium-bodied, user-friendly, accessible style, this wine will have many fans. Anticipated maturity: now–2010. Last tasted, 3/02.

GRAND-PUY-LACOSTE

Classification: Fifth Growth in 1855

Owner: Borie family

Address: 33250 Pauillac

Telephone: 05 56 73 16 73; Telefax: 05 56 59 27 37

Visits: By appointment Monday to Friday, 9 A.M.–noon and 2–5 P.M. (except in August and at harvest time)

Contact: François-Xavier Borie

VINEYARDS

Surface area: 128.4 acres

Grape varietals: 70% Cabernet Sauvignon, 25% Merlot, 5% Cabernet Franc

Average age of vines: 35 years

Density of plantation: 10,000 vines per hectare

Average yields: 50 hectoliters per hectare

Elevage: Seventeen to twenty-day fermentation and maceration in temperature-controlled stainless-steel tanks. Eighteen to twenty months aging in barrels with 45–55% new oak. Fining, light filtration upon bottling.

WINES PRODUCED

Château Grand-Puy-Lacoste: 195,000 bottles

Lacoste-Borie: 120,000 bottles

Plateau of maturity: Within 7–20 years of the vintage

GENERAL APPRECIATION

Grand-Puy-Lacoste is a longtime favorite of Bordeaux insiders. This wine, which has been remarkably regular post–World War II, usually performs much better than its pedigree and could be upgraded to third-growth status. It is generally rich, ripe, fruity, and intense—in a word, it delivers the goods, often more than that, and at extremely reasonable prices. Grand-Puy-Lacoste is one of the best values not only of Pauillac, but in Bordeaux.

I never had the pleasure of meeting Raymond Dupin, the late owner of Grand-Puy-Lacoste. Dupin had a monumental reputation as one of Bordeaux's all-time great gourmets. According to some of his acquaintances, he was a gourmand as well. Prior to his death in 1980, in 1978 he sold Grand-Puy-Lacoste to the highly talented and respected late Jean-Eugène Borie, who then installed his son, Xavier, at the château. An extensive remodeling program for Grand-Puy's ancient and dilapidated cellars was completed by 1982, just in time to produce one of the finest wines made to date by Xavier Borie. Borie continues to live at the modernized château with his wife and family. As expected by the cognoscenti of Bordeaux, Grand-Puy-Lacoste has surged to the forefront of leading Pauillacs.

Grand-Puy-Lacoste, which sits far back from the Gironde River on the Bages plateau, has enjoyed a solid reputation for big, durable, full-bodied Pauillacs, not unlike its neighbor a kilometer away, Lynch-Bages. However, the wines of the 1960s and 1970s, like those of Lynch-Bages, showed an unevenness in quality that in retrospect may have been due to the declining health of the owner. For example, vintages such as 1975 and 1966 were less successful at Grand-Puy than its reputation would lead one to expect. Other vintages during this period, particularly the 1976, 1971, 1969, and 1967, were close to complete failures for some unexplained reason, but probably inattentiveness to detail.

However, since 1978 Grand-Puy-Lacoste has been making excellent wines. In the case of the 2000, 1996, 1995, 1990, and 1982, great wines were produced that will be remembered as some of the finest examples in this château's long history. In comparison to the Dupin style, the Borie style of Grand-Puy-Lacoste has been to harvest later and thereby produce wines with an intense cassis fruitiness and considerable glycerin, power, and body. Until the mid-1990s, the price of Grand-Puy-Lacoste had not kept pace with the quality, remaining modest, even somewhat undervalued.

IMPORTANT VINTAGES

2001
88–90
Soft crème de cassis, aromas dominate the aromatics of this medium-bodied, elegant effort. Consistently a sleeper of the vintage, this blend of 70% Cabernet Sauvignon, 28% Merlot, and 2% Cabernet Franc offers a soft, fleshy, glycerin-imbued attack, medium body, very good to excellent concentration, and light to moderate tannin. It should drink well between 2004–2015. Last tasted, 1/03.

2000
92
The large-scaled 2000 Grand-Puy-Lacoste rivals the stunning 1996, 1995, 1990, and 1982. The saturated purple color is accompanied by a perfume redolent with aromas of cassis, tobacco, and licorice. Deep, rich, muscular, and full-bodied, it is a prototype Pauillac emphasizing ripe cassis fruit and purity. There is plenty of tannin, but it is not out of balance. Anticipated maturity: 2008–2025. Last tasted, 1/03.

1999
89
This deep ruby/purple–colored 1999 has some tannin to resolve, but it is an elegant, medium-bodied, delicious effort that will reward readers who have the patience to cellar it for several years. Not a blockbuster in the style of the 2000 or 1996, the 1999 offers charming roundness, sweet cassis fruit, excellent purity, and fine overall balance. It should last for 15+ years. Last tasted, 8/02.

1998
90
The 1998 reveals a classic crème de cassis–scented nose along with powerful, tight, firmly structured flavors. While moderate tannin is present, there is more than enough extract and depth behind the tannin to support the enthusiastic rating. However, this wine needs 2–3 more years of cellaring and should keep for 12 years. No, it's not the 1990 or 1982, but it is a topflight claret. Anticipated maturity: 2006–2016. Last tasted, 3/02.

1997
87
The telltale blackberry/cassis character is well displayed in this dark ruby/purple–colored wine. There is excellent ripe fruit, soft tannin, low acidity, and a delicious, easygoing personality. Although it will not make "old bones," it is a ripe, soft, attractive, evolved Bordeaux for consuming over the next 4–5 years. Last tasted, 3/02.

1996
93+
This is unquestionably a profound Grand-Puy-Lacoste, but it is excruciatingly backward. It reveals an essence of crème de cassis character that sets it apart from other Pauillacs. The wine is displaying plenty of tannin, huge body, and sweet black currant fruit intermixed with minerals and subtle oak. Massive, extremely structured, with 20–25 or more years of longevity, this immensely styled Grand-Puy-Lacoste will require another 3–4 years of patience, perhaps longer. A superb, classic Pauillac. Anticipated maturity: 2007–2030. Last tasted, 1/02.

1995
95
Another unbelievably rich, multidimensional, broad-shouldered wine, with slightly more elegance and less weight than the powerhouse 1996, this gorgeously proportioned, medium- to full-bodied, fabulously ripe, rich, cassis scented and flavored Grand-Puy-Lacoste is another beauty. Although it will age for 20–25 years, this classic Pauillac still remains stubbornly backward. Anticipated maturity: 2010–2025. Last tasted, 1/02.

1994
90
The 1994 has turned out to be an outstanding effort for this estate. The wine reveals even more flesh than it did prior to bottling, as well as the high tannin that marks many of this vintage's wines. The color is ruby/purple and the nose offers up a pure blast of sweet cassis fruit. Medium bodied, with impressive layers of extract, this classic, rich, powerful Pauillac will be at its best before 2020. Anticipated maturity: 2005–2020. Last tasted, 3/01.

1990
95
The stunning 1990, which continues to evolve at a glacial pace, possesses an opaque ruby/purple–color, as well as a stunning nose of jammy black currants, cedar, spice, and smoke. Full-bodied with magnificent extract, excellent delineation, outstanding purity, and layers of intensity, this massive, dense, well-

balanced Pauillac is the finest Grand-Puy-Lacoste since the 1982. Sumptuous! Anticipated maturity: now–2018. Last tasted, 5/02.

1989   When I first tasted the dark garnet–colored 1989 Grand-Puy-Lacoste, I thought it
  89   possessed a Graves-like tobacco/mineral character. In contrast with the block-
        buster, full-blown, massive wines produced by this estate in 2000, 1996, 1995,
        1990, and 1982, the medium-weight 1989 is elegant, spicy, evolved, and already
        revealing plenty of cedar and tobacco-tinged cassis fruit. A delicious, generously
        endowed, low-acid wine, it lacks the depth and expansiveness of this estate's
        finest vintages. Anticipated maturity: now–2014. Last tasted, 5/02.

1988   This vintage has turned out better than initially expected. Still somewhat austere,
  87   the 1988 has reached full maturity. Deep garnet/ruby with a cedary bouquet inter-
        mixed with currants, earth, and compost, this medium-bodied wine has noticeable
        richness and depth, as well as some firm tannins. Anticipated maturity: now–
        2009. Last tasted, 6/02.

1986   This wine is the finest Grand-Puy-Lacoste produced after 1990 or 1982 and before
  90   1995. The 1986 still possesses an impressive deep ruby/purple color, as well as a
        classic nose of cedar, black currants, smoke, and vanilla. It is full-bodied, power-
        ful, authoritatively rich, and loaded with fruit, with a solid lashing of tannin not
        likely to ever totally melt away. This wine can be drunk now, although it is back-
        ward and unyielding. Certainly, it is one of the better northern Médocs of the vin-
        tage. Anticipated maturity: 2004–2018. Last tasted, 12/01.

1985   The 1985 has reached full maturity quickly. It is an excellent, nearly outstanding
  88   example of a juicy, succulent Pauillac oozing with sweet cedar, herb-tinged, black
        currant fruit. Medium- to full-bodied with low acidity and a supple, nearly opulent
        texture, this dark garnet–colored wine is intensely charming and delicious. The
        only negative is its short finish, which suggests it needs to be consumed over the
        next decade. Anticipated maturity: now–2009. Last tasted, 12/01.

1983   Medium garnet with considerable amber, this fully mature, uninspiring wine is
  86   open-knit and ripe with a rich, weedy, black currant aroma. A rapidly evolving
        wine, it exhibits good concentration, a round, gentle texture, and a decent finish
        with some dry tannin. Anticipated maturity: now. Last tasted, 3/99.

1982   Absolutely spectacular, the 1982 Grand-Puy-Lacoste must be one of the most un-
  95   derrated wines of the vintage. The color remains an opaque ruby/purple, and there
        is no doubting the level of quality after one sniff and sip. The wine reveals the clas-
        sic black currant, cedary profile of a Pauillac. Mature yet tasting young, this mas-
        sive, sensationally concentrated, full-bodied wine offers layers of pure cassis-like
        fruit that comes across as grapy because of its intensity and youthfulness. It is a
        thrill to drink even though the wine is still extremely young and only hints at the
        possibilities that exist with another 5–10 years of cellaring. The finish lasts for 40
        seconds or more. Potentially, this is the greatest Grand-Puy-Lacoste of the last
        three decades. A tour de force in winemaking! Anticipated maturity: now–2020.
        Last tasted, 9/02.

ANCIENT VINTAGES

Bottle variation has been a problem with the two finest vintages of Grand-Puy-Lacoste: 1970 and 1961. Both wines, when "on," are 90–92 point performers. Nearly as good is the 1978 (90 points; last tasted 12/02). This was the first vintage made under the current administration of Xavier Borie.

The 1959 Grand-Puy-Lacoste (92 points) exhibited plenty of power and muscle as well as outstanding concentration in a chunky, husky, Pauillac manner. The 1959 truly could have been called the "non-wealthy person's Latour."

The 1949 (96 points; last tasted 10/94) exhibits a fragrant nose of cedar, black currants, and woodsy, truffle-like aromas. Gorgeously opulent and full-bodied, it is a super-concentrated, velvety-textured, fully mature wine.

At a dinner party in Bordeaux in 1989, I was astonished by the superb 1947 (I rated it 94). From a private cellar in that city, it was remarkably concentrated, rich, and expansively flavored, and it admirably demonstrated why Grand-Puy-Lacoste was so highly regarded in the post–World War II vintages.

HAUT-BAGES LIBÉRAL

Classification: Fifth Growth in 1855

Owner: Claire Villars-Lurton

Address: 33250 Pauillac

Mailing Address: c/o Château Ferrière, 3, rue de Trémoille, 33460 Margaux

Telephone: 05 57 88 76 65; Telefax: 05 57 88 98 33

Website: www.hautbagesliberal.com

Visits: By appointment Monday to Friday, 9 A.M.–5 P.M.

Contact: Nathalie Lemire

VINEYARDS

Surface area: 69 acres

Grape varietals: 75% Cabernet Sauvignon, 25% Merlot

Average age of vines: 30 years

Density of plantation: 10,000 vines per hectare

Average yields: 55 hectoliters per hectare

Elevage: Fermentation and maceration in temperature-controlled stainless-steel and concrete vats. Forty percent of yield undergoes malolactics in barrels. Fourteen to sixteen months aging in barrels with 40% new oak. Fining, no filtration.

WINES PRODUCED

Château Haut-Bages Libéral: 120,000 bottles

Chapelle de Bages: 50,000 bottles

Plateau of maturity: Within 5–12 years of the vintage

GENERAL APPRECIATION

Even though the level of quality at the estate has dropped slightly in the 1990s, the wines of Haut-Bages Libéral are soundly made and worth their fifth-growth status. Still underestimated by consumers and the specialized press, they are never great but always worthy of interest—especially in the best vintages, in view of their reasonable pricing.

This modest-size château sitting just off Bordeaux's main road of wine, D2, has been making consistently fine undervalued wine since the mid-1970s. The vineyard, consisting of three parcels, is superbly situated. The major portion (just more than 50%) is adjacent to the main Latour vineyard. Another parcel is next to Pichon-Lalande, and a third is farther inland near Grand-Puy-Lacoste.

The famous Cruse family of Bordeaux had thoroughly modernized Haut-Bages Libéral in the 1970s, but in 1983 they decided to sell the property to the syndicate run by the Villars family, who owns and manages two other well-known châteaux, Chasse-Spleen in Moulis and La Gurgue in Margaux. The vineyard, replanted in the early 1960s, is now coming into maturity. No doubt the young vines accounted for the mediocre quality of the wine in the 1960s and early 1970s. However, in 1975 an excellent wine was produced, and this success has been followed by several recent vintages that have also exhibited high quality, particularly 1995, 1990, 1986, and 1985.

Haut-Bages Libéral produces a strong, ripe, rich, very black currany wine, no doubt as a result of the high percentage of Cabernet Sauvignon.

IMPORTANT VINTAGES

1998
86
In spite of dry, hard tannin in the finish, this wine has turned out well. The color is a dark ruby/purple. The bouquet offers aromas of cassis, earth, dried herbs, and licorice. Medium bodied, with good ripeness and moderately hard tannin, this wine needs 2–4 years to shed some astringency. Anticipated maturity: now–2014. Last tasted, 3/02.

1997
79
The light-bodied, soft, fruity 1997 is essentially one-dimensional, even though it is pleasant and charming. It requires consumption during its first 8–10 years of life. Last tasted, 1/02.

1996
87+
This very good 1996 reveals an element of jammy black currant fruit intermixed with dried roasted herbs, sweet earthy smells, and new oak. It offers excellent definition, moderate tannin, medium to full body, and a long finish. As the wine sits in the glass, elements of the Cabernet Sauvignon's *sur-maturité* become noticeable. It is a potential sleeper of the vintage. Anticipated maturity: 2004–2017. Last tasted, 3/02.

1995
85?
The 1995 possesses a bit more depth and intensity than its younger sibling, but it is also lean and austere. The attractive saturated ruby/purple color suggests plenty of intensity, which is evident on the attack, but the mid-palate is deficient in fruit, glycerin, and concentration, and the finish is dry, with a high level of tannin. Anticipated maturity: now–2012. Last tasted, 1/01.

1994
86?
This dark ruby–colored 1994 displays no hard tannin or herbaceous/greenness to its aromatics or flavors. The wine is admirably rich with dense, black cherry, chocolaty, cassis fruit, firm but sweet tannin, and a medium-bodied, spicy finish. Anticipated maturity: now–2010. Last tasted, 1/01.

1990
87
Deeply colored, with a sweet, plummy, oaky nose, the 1990 represents a major improvement over the indifferent 1989. Opulent and rich, this low-acid, fleshy wine lacks grip, but it does offer a big, meaty mouthful of juicy Pauillac. Anticipated maturity: now–2010. Last tasted, 1/93.

1989
84
The 1989 Haut-Bages Libéral tastes surprisingly light. It has a brilliant ruby/purple color, decent acidity, and moderate tannin, but it finishes short. It is a good effort, but is atypically restrained and subdued. Anticipated maturity: now. Last tasted, 1/93.

1986 The percentage of new oak casks used at Haut-Bages Libéral was increased
90 and the selection process tightened, and the result in 1986 is their finest wine
since the 1975 and certainly one of the best wines made at the property during the
last two decades. Still dark ruby/purple, with an expansive bouquet of plums,
sweet toasty oak, and black currants, this dense, full-bodied, chewy wine has a
sweet suppleness on the mid-palate and has resolved much of its tannin. The balance, richness, and tannin content suggest drinking it over the next decade. Anticipated maturity: now–2013. Last tasted, 3/02.

1985 The dense, chunky 1985 now exhibits some ruby at the rim. It remains a rich, full-
88 bodied wine with impressive extract and a powerful, long, ripe finish. What it
lacks in elegance/finesse, it makes up for in power and body. Anticipated maturity: now–2008. Last tasted, 3/02.

1982 Surprise, surprise! One of the least acclaimed 1982s, the Haut-Bages Libéral has
91 developed beautifully. It is crammed with thick, juicy, licorice/olive/smoky,
roasted, ripe black currant fruit. Full-bodied, thick, and juicy and with just
enough complexity to merit an outstanding rating, this mouth-filling, savory,
super-concentrated, jammy Pauillac is already delicious, yet it reveals no signs of
age. The color is a healthy opaque garnet/purple. This wine should drink well for
another 15+ years. Anticipated maturity: now–2016. Last tasted, 11/01.

HAUT-BATAILLEY

Classification: Fifth Growth in 1855

Owner: Françoise des Brest-Borie

Address: 33250 Pauillac

Mailing Address: c/o X. Borie SA, 33250 St.-Julien
Beychevelle

Telephone: 05 56 73 16 73; Telefax: 05 56 59 27 37

No visits

Contact: François-Xavier Borie

VINEYARDS

Surface area: 54.3 acres

Grape varietals: 65% Cabernet Sauvignon, 25% Merlot, 10% Cabernet Franc

Average age of vines: 28 years

Density of plantation: 10,000 vines per hectare

Average yields: 50 hectoliters per hectare

Elevage: Sixteen to twenty-day fermentation and maceration in temperature-controlled
stainless-steel vats. Sixteen to twenty months aging in barrels with 30–50% new oak.
Fining, light filtration upon bottling.

WINES PRODUCED

Château Haut-Batailley: 110,000 bottles

Château La Tour l'Aspic: 35,000 bottles

Plateau of maturity: Within 4–20 years of the vintage

GENERAL APPRECIATION

The wines of Haut-Batailley are still somewhat of an insider's secret. Well worth their fifth-growth status, they are generally very good to excellent and represent sound values (they are surpassed, though, by the likes of Grand-Puy-Lacoste).

Haut-Batailley is not one of the better-known estates in Pauillac. The vineyard is managed by the reputable and well-known Xavier Borie, who lives at Grand-Puy-Lacoste. Perhaps the reasons for obscurity within the Pauillac firmament are the modest production, the lack of a château on the estate, and secluded location on the edge of a woods, far away from the Gironde River and the Médoc's famed Route du Vin.

Recent vintages of Haut-Batailley have demonstrated the full potential of the property under the expert winemaking team of Xavier Borie. However, the wines of this estate have not always been the model of consistency one would expect. In general, the weakness tends toward lightness and excessive softness in style. Most wines of Haut-Batailley are fully mature long before their first decade ends, an anomaly for a Pauillac. Nevertheless, recent vintages, particularly the 2000, 1996, and 1995, have shown greater concentration and grip than before. I tend to think of Haut-Batailley as having more of a St.-Julien personality than that of a true Pauillac. That is ironic given the fact that this estate was created in 1942, when it was severed from the original vineyard of Batailley—irrefutably a classic Pauillac in both taste and character.

IMPORTANT VINTAGES

2001
87–89
Displaying a deep color but light body, this low-acid, soft, pleasant, charming Pauillac is a blend of 68% Cabernet Sauvignon, 30% Merlot, and 2% Cabernet Franc. There is not much follow-through on the palate, suggesting it is a wine to consume during its first 10–12 years of life. Last tasted, 1/03.

2000
90+
This 2000 has turned out to be one of the finest Haut-Batailleys ever made (rivaling the 1996). The deep ruby/purple–colored 2000 offers sweet aromas of cassis, cedar, tobacco, and spice box. Dense, fat, chewy, and seductive, with low acidity, ripe tannin, and abundant fruit, this sexy effort will drink well for 12–15 years. Last tasted, 1/03.

1999
87
Although this 1999 is pinched and compressed in the finish, it offers elegant, sweet/spicy black currant fruit intermixed with notions of toast, cedar, and dried herbs. This medium-bodied Pauillac is best consumed during its first decade of life. Last tasted, 3/02.

1998
86
A touch of austerity recalls some of the less desirable characteristics of this vintage in the Médoc. The 1998 exhibits firmness along with good, sweet, berry fruit intermixed with mineral, cassis, and spice notes. Medium bodied and elegant, this effort is best drunk earlier rather than later. Anticipated maturity: now–2014. Last tasted, 3/02.

1997
85
Made in a lighter, finesse style, this fluid, charming, ripe, medium-bodied 1997 exhibits smoky, black currant fruit, pleasing ripeness, and attractive levels of fruit. It should be drunk over the next 2–3 years for its undeniable easygoing personality. Last tasted, 3/01.

1996
90
This wine exhibits a dense purple color, as well as a wonderfully sweet, classic Pauillac nose of black currants and cigar box notes. Powerful for Haut-Batailley (normally a light, elegant, supple Pauillac), the 1996 possesses intense fruit, medium to full body, ripe tannin, and a surprisingly long, layered finish. This ap-

pears to be a classic and may ultimately merit an outstanding score. Anticipated maturity: now–2015. Last tasted, 3/01.

1995
89
Silky, sexy, supple, and altogether a gorgeous effort from Haut-Batailley, the 1995 is a medium-bodied, seamless, beautifully pure Pauillac with gobs of black currant fruit intermixed with smoke, vanilla, and lead pencil. Already approachable, it promises to become even better over the next 7–8 years. A very hedonistic wine. Anticipated maturity: now–2010. Last tasted, 3/01.

1994
86
Following some mediocre performances from cask, the 1994 has turned out to be better in bottle. A dark ruby color is followed by a spicy, moderately tannic, well-concentrated, elegant wine that reveals some tannin, but also copious quantities of fruit. It should be drunk before 2008. Last tasted, 1/00.

1990
88
Fully mature, the garnet-colored 1990 offers a forward, smoky, sweet oaky nose intertwined with aromas of black currants, compost, and weedy tobacco. Medium bodied with low acidity, light tannins, and layers of ripe fruit, this finesse-styled wine should continue to provide superlative drinking for 5–10 years. Last tasted, 11/01.

1989
87
Fully mature, the 1989 Haut-Batailley has up-front, satiny fruit. (Considerable pink and amber appear at the rim.) It is lush, ripe, and medium bodied. The finish exhibits sweet, jammy fruit and some dry tannin. Anticipated maturity: now. Last tasted, 3/00.

1988
83?
The 1988 Haut-Batailley is a lightweight, lean, closed, hard-edged wine that lacks charm and finesse. The tannin level appears excessive for the fruit component. Anticipated maturity: now. Last tasted, 1/93.

1986
80
Atypically supple and silky for a 1986 with a pleasing currant fruitiness married nicely to toasty oak, this medium-bodied wine falls off on the palate, revealing a diffuse character. Anticipated maturity: now. Last tasted, 11/02.

ANCIENT VINTAGES

Pristinely kept bottles of 1982 (rated 89 in 9/95) might still be intact, but the other top vintages, 1970, 1966, and 1961, were falling apart years ago.

LAFITE ROTHSCHILD

Classification: First Growth in 1855 and 1973

Owner: Barons de Rothschild (Lafite)

Address: 33250 Pauillac

Mailing Address: Domaines Barons de Rothschild (Lafite)

Telephone: 01 53 89 78 01; Telefax: 01 53 89 78 00

E-mail: clesure@lafite.com

Website: www.lafite.com

Visits: By appointment, Monday to Friday, 2 P.M. and 3:30 P.M. (one-hour visit). Estate closed on weekends, public holidays, in August, and at harvest time.

Contact: Christophe Salin

VINEYARDS

Surface area: 247 acres

Grape varietals: 70% Cabernet Sauvignon, 25% Merlot, 3% Cabernet Franc, 2% Petit Verdot

Average age of vines: 45 years

Density of plantation: 7,500 vines per hectare

Average yields: 48 hectoliters per hectare

Elevage: Eighteen to twenty-four day fermentation and maceration in stainless-steel and wooden tanks. Sixteen to twenty months aging in new oak barrels. Fining. No filtration.

WINES PRODUCED

Château Lafite Rothschild: 210,000 bottles

Carruades de Lafite: 280,000 bottles

Plateau of maturity: Within 10–50 years of the vintage

GENERAL APPRECIATION

The wines of Lafite, which were generally mediocre prior to 1974, have improved greatly between 1975 and the beginning of the 1990s. From 1994 onward, they rank amongst the finest Bordeaux. In fact, Lafite is now considered to be among Bordeaux's greatest wines. It wonderfully marries finesse and power. While critics including myself have been laudatory about this positive trend, it must be kept in mind that this estate is simply living up to its mythical status . . . and to the prices its wines fetch on the market. In buying Lafite, especially the more recent vintages, consumers are sure to latch on to superb bottles and can look forward to one of the finest possible tasting experiences. However, prices make this wine accessible only to the richest. Value seekers would do better to turn their attention elsewhere. Note that the estate's second wine, Carruades de Lafite, is worthy of interest, particularly since the mid-1990s.

Bordeaux's most famous property and wine, with its elegant, undersized, and understated label, has become a name synonymous with wealth, prestige, history, respect, and wines of remarkable longevity.

While the vintages since 1975 have witnessed the production of a succession of superlative Lafites, the record of Lafite between 1961 and 1974 was one of surprising mediocrity for a first-growth. It has always remained a mystery to me why more wine critics did not cry foul after tasting some of the Lafite wines made during this period. The official line from the château has always been that the wines were made in such a light, elegant style that they were overmatched in blind tastings by bigger, more robust wines. Certainly such things do happen, but the mediocrity of Lafite was particularly evidenced by wines from very fine vintages—1971, 1970, 1966, 1961, 1949, 1945—that were surprisingly deficient in color, excessively dry, overly oaked, and abnormally high in acidity. Several vintages—1974, 1971, 1969—were complete failures yet released for high prices under the Lafite name.

The reasons for such occurrences are not likely to ever be revealed by the Rothschild family, but given the record of successes since 1975, the problems in the 1960s and early 1970s seem related to the following: First, the absentee owners lived in Paris and only casually supervised the goings-on at Lafite. Certainly the management of Lafite since 1975 has been diligent by a concerned and committed Eric de Rothschild. Second, the wine at Lafite was kept too long in oak barrels. In the past, the wine often aged a minimum of 32–36 months in oak barrels, whereas now 20–30 months is maximum. This change has undoubtedly caused Lafite to taste fruitier and fresher. Third, the current winemaking staff at Lafite consciously pick the grapes later to obtain greater ripeness and lower acidity in their wines. The selection process is undoubtedly more severe than in the past. In the abundant vintages of the late 1980s, Lafite routinely eliminated half of their crop. Since 1990, it has not been unusual for Lafite to eliminate at least a whopping 60% of the harvest, which is either sold off in bulk or relegated to the second wine. Finally, Lafite Rothschild is being bottled over a shorter period of time. There have been unsubstantiated reports that Lafite often dragged out the bottling operation over as many as 8–12 months. If true, then more than acceptable levels of bottle variation would exist. Today the entire crop is bottled within 2–3 weeks.

Regardless of the record of the immediate past, Lafite Rothschild is now producing compelling wines, and the turnabout in quality clearly occurred with the 1975 and accelerated even further in the mid-1990s when Charles Chevalier was asked to manage the estate. One could successfully argue that since 1981, Lafite Rothschild has produced one of the Médoc's best wines in years such as 2001, 2000, 1999, 1998, 1997, 1996, 1995, 1990, 1988, 1987, 1986, 1983, 1982, and 1981.

IMPORTANT VINTAGES

2001 A classic Lafite Rothschild, the 2001 is a wine of concentrated elegance, finesse,
92–94+ and delicacy. This blend of 86.5% Cabernet Sauvignon and 13.5% Merlot (only 43% of the crop was acceptable) is reminiscent of the 1999, but it reveals additional tannin as well as a more austere finish. An impressive deep ruby/purple color is followed by sweet aromas of cedar, black currants, lead-pencil shavings, and subtle toasty oak. It is medium bodied with a nicely layered mid-palate (something many 2001s are not yet revealing), admirable delicacy and precision, and a long finish. It will be drinkable at an early age, yet will last two decades. Anticipated maturity: 2008–2022. Last tasted, 1/03.

2001 Carruades de Lafite: Once again, Lafite's second wine, the 2001 Carruades de
88–90 Lafite, is an impeccably made effort. A blend of 50.4% Cabernet Sauvignon, 22.2% Merlot, 6% Cabernet Franc, and the rest Petit Verdot, it represents 42.5% of Lafite's harvest. Revealing excellent red and black currant characteristics intermixed with hints of new saddle leather, wood, and spice box, it possesses a sweeter, more developed personality than its bigger sibling, and fine length. Anticipated maturity: 2004–2015. Last tasted, 1/03.

2000 The opaque purple–colored 2000 Lafite Rothschild has put on weight during its
100 *élevage*. Despite the fact that it is 93% Cabernet Sauvignon and only 7% Merlot, it is the essence of Lafite, a fuller, riper, more concentrated, and muscular version of the 1999 and 1998. While the 2000 does not yet reveal the aromatic complexity of the 1999, it boasts layers of concentration as well as phenomenal purity and personality. The finish lasts more than a minute. It is a compelling effort (only 36% of the crop made it into Lafite) from what is undoubtedly the greatest vintage Bordeaux has enjoyed from a perspective of the number of prodigious wines produced. Anticipated maturity: 2010–2050. Last tasted, 1/03.

2000 Carruades de Lafite: A candidate for the finest Carruades de Lafite ever made,
91 the 2000 (a blend of 55% Cabernet Sauvignon, 40% Merlot, and 5% Cabernet
Franc) is head and shoulders above such vintages of Lafite as 1979, 1978, 1973,
1971, and 1970, all reasonably good years. The Carruades is deep, fat, plush, and
layered with concentration, and has more depth than any other second wine I
tasted. Anticipated maturity: 2004–2020. Last tasted, 1/03.

1999 The 1999 Lafite Rothschild sports an engraved "1999" on the bottle along with an
95 eclipse to mark that significant historical event of August 1999. A quintessential
offering from Lafite Rothschild, this prodigious wine is both elegant and intensely
flavored and almost diaphanous in its layers that unfold with no heaviness. An
opaque ruby/purple color is accompanied by a complex bouquet of lead pencil,
graphite, cedar, crème de cassis, toast, and vanilla. Medium bodied with extravagant layers of richness yet little weight and a finish that is all sweetness, ripeness,
and harmony, this extraordinary Lafite increasingly appears to be a modern day
clone of the majestic 1953. A mere one-third of the crop made it into the grand vin!
Anticipated maturity: 2007–2030. Last tasted, 9/02.

1999 Carruades de Lafite: Made in the style of its bigger sibling, the 1999 Carruades
89 de Lafite reveals graphite, lead pencil, black currant, and cedary aromas, medium
body, sweet glycerin, and a gorgeously expansive texture and palate. Long and
Lafite-like, it is unbelievably impressive. Anticipated maturity: now–2015. Last
tasted, 9/02.

1998 A blend of 81% Cabernet Sauvignon and 19% Merlot, this wine represents only
98 34% of Lafite's total harvest. In a less than perfect Médoc vintage, it has been
spectacular since birth, putting on more weight and flesh during its *élevage*. This
opaque purple–colored 1998 is close to perfection. The spectacular nose of lead
pencil, smoky, mineral, and black currant fruit soars majestically from the glass.
The wine is elegant yet profoundly rich, revealing the essence of Lafite's character.
The tannin is sweet, and the wine is spectacularly layered yet never heavy. The
finish is sweet, superrich, yet impeccably balanced and long (50+ seconds). Anticipated maturity: 2007–2035. Last tasted, 9/02.

1998 Carruades de Lafite: The 1998 Carruades de Lafite (a blend of 61% Cabernet
90 Sauvignon, 33% Merlot, 4.5% Cabernet Franc, and 1.5% Petit Verdot) is an outstanding effort. While very Lafite-like, although more supple and forward, it exhibits a dense ruby/purple color in addition to an excellent bouquet of black fruits,
smoke, earth, and minerals, supple tannin, an excellent texture, and a long, fine
finish. Anticipated maturity: now–2015. Last tasted, 9/02.

1997 Only 26% of the crop made it into the final blend, resulting in only 15,000 cases of
92 the 1997 Lafite Rothschild. Readers should not ignore this wine because of the
negative press surrounding the 1997 vintage. It boasts an opaque dense purple
color in addition to a gorgeously sweet, expansive perfume of cedar wood, black
currants, lead pencil, and minerals, a fat mid-palate, medium body, explosive fruit
and richness, soft tannin, and a velvety texture. It is a beautiful, compelling Lafite
Rothschild that can be drunk young, yet promises to evolve for 15+ years. Although one of the most forward Lafites ever tasted, it is all the more captivating because of this characteristic. Don't miss it! Anticipated maturity: now–2017. Last
tasted, 1/02.

1997 Carruades de Lafite: The 1997 Carruades de Lafite includes 40% Merlot, result-
88 ing in a floral, opulent, rich, round effort. This offering is meant to be drunk young,
but will last for another 10 years. Last tasted, 1/02.

1996 Tasted six times since bottling, the 1996 Lafite Rothschild is unquestionably this
100 renowned estate's greatest wine since the 1986 and 1982. Will the 2000 be this
profound? Only 38% of the crop was deemed grand enough to be put into the final

blend, which is atypically high in Cabernet Sauvignon (83% Cabernet Sauvignon, 7% Cabernet Franc, 7% Merlot, and 3% Petit Verdot). This massive wine may be the biggest, largest-scaled Lafite I have ever tasted. It will require many years to come around, so I suspect all of us past the age of fifty might want to give serious consideration as to whether we should be laying away multiple cases of this wine. It is also the first Lafite Rothschild to be put into a new engraved bottle, designed to prevent fraudulent imitations. The wine exhibits a thick-looking, ruby/purple color and a knockout nose of lead pencil, minerals, flowers, and black currant scents. Extremely powerful and full-bodied, with remarkable complexity for such a young wine, this huge Lafite is oozing with extract and richness, yet has managed to preserve its quintessentially elegant personality. This wine is even richer than it was prior to bottling. It should unquestionably last for 40–50 years. Anticipated maturity: 2012–2050. Last tasted, 9/02.

1996
88
Carruades de Lafite: The 1996 Carruades de Lafite is a blend of 63% Cabernet Sauvignon and 37% Merlot. It possesses fine power, ripeness, and fleshy fruit (because of the high percentage of Merlot). While it does not quite have the characteristics of Lafite, being fleshier and more accessible, it is a beautifully made wine with a subtle dosage of toasty new oak, appealing texture, and excellent length. Given its power, this second wine should keep for 12+ years (though I would not be surprised to see it last for 15–18 years). Last tasted, 9/02.

1995
95
The 1995 Lafite Rothschild (only one-third of the harvest made it into the final blend) is 75% Cabernet Sauvignon, 17% Merlot, and 8% Cabernet Franc. It exhibits a dark ruby purple color and a sweet, powdered mineral, smoky, weedy, cassis-scented nose. Beautiful sweetness of fruit is present in this medium-bodied, tightly knit, but gloriously pure, well-delineated Lafite. The 1995 is not as powerful or as massive as the 1996, but it is beautifully made with outstanding credentials, in addition to remarkable promise. Anticipated maturity: 2008–2028. Last tasted, 9/02.

1995
87
Carruades de Lafite: The 1995 Carruades de Lafite is a 60% Cabernet Sauvignon/40% Merlot blend. It exhibits more of the trademark characteristics of its bigger sibling. Elegant, with spicy new oak, lead pencil, and creamy black currant fruit, this is a medium-bodied, finesse-styled wine with excellent purity and overall equilibrium. It is much more accessible than the 1996, and it should drink well between now and 2010. Last tasted, 1/02.

1994
90+?
Made from nearly 100% Cabernet Sauvignon, this dark ruby/purple–colored wine is stubbornly backward, unappealing, and severe and astringent on the palate. There is plenty of weight, and the wine possesses admirable purity, with no suggestion of herbaceousness or underripe fruit, but the wine's personality refuses to be coaxed from the glass. The 1994 Lafite may turn out to be austere and disappointing flavor-wise, but possesses a fabulous set of aromatics (does that sound reminiscent of the 1961, another Lafite that was primarily Cabernet Sauvignon?). I am not giving up on this wine, but purchasers should be willing to wait another 7–8 years before pulling a cork. Anticipated maturity: 2010–2030. Last tasted, 1/02.

1993
88
A successful wine for Lafite, this dark ruby/purple–colored 1993 is tightly wound and medium bodied, with a closed set of aromatics that reluctantly reveal hints of sweet black currant fruit, weedy tobacco, and lead-pencil scents. Polished and elegant, with Lafite's noble restraint, this is an excellent, classy, slightly austere wine. Anticipated maturity: 2004–2020. Last tasted, 1/97.

1992
87
In 1992, only 36% of the harvest was utilized, resulting in a deeply colored wine with an enticing cedary, chocolaty, cassis character, medium body, surprisingly concentrated flavors, as well as the classic Lafite aromatic profile. Readers should

take the opportunity to experience Lafite's finesse in a softer, more precocious vintage. The dark ruby 1992 Lafite already tastes mature, but will last for 10–12 more years. Last tasted, 11/01.

1990 The 1990 is a ripe, rich, well-textured, yet elegant, mouth-filling style of Lafite.
92   The wine possesses excellent richness, a hint of the unmistakable Lafite perfume of minerals, cedar, graphite, and red fruits, medium to full body, moderate weight, admirable richness, and overall balance. Tannin is very noticeable in the finish. It should be a 40- to 50-year Lafite. As outstanding as I believe it will ultimately turn out to be, I do not think the 1990 Lafite matches the sheer class, quality, and complexity of the 2000, 1998, 1996, 1988, 1986, and 1982. Anticipated maturity: 2008–2040. Last tasted, 8/02.

1989 A medium-weight, classic Lafite, the 1989 is just coming out of a period of
90   dormancy. This dark ruby–colored, medium-bodied wine reveals new oak in the nose and a spicy finish. It is a quintessentially elegant, restrained, understated style of Lafite. In the final analysis, this wine lacks the profound depth and midsection of the estate's greatest efforts. Anticipated maturity: 2006–2025. Last tasted, 12/01.

1988 The 1988 is a classic expression of Lafite. This deeply colored wine (deep
94   plum/ruby) exhibits the telltale Lafite bouquet of cedar, subtle herbs, dried pit fruits, minerals, asphalt, lead pencil, and cassis. Extremely concentrated, with brilliantly focused flavors and huge tannins, this backward, yet impressively endowed Lafite Rothschild increasingly looks like the wine of the vintage! Anticipated maturity: now–2035. Last tasted, 8/02.

1986 At 15 years of age, the 1986 Lafite is accessible yet still has the personality of a
100 young, adolescent wine. The prodigious 1986 possesses outstanding richness, a deep color, medium body, a graceful, harmonious texture, and superb length. The penetrating fragrance of cedar, chestnuts, minerals, and rich fruit is a hallmark of this wine. Powerful, dense, rich, and tannic, as well as medium- to full-bodied with awesome extraction of fruit, this Lafite has immense potential. Patience is still required. Anticipated maturity: 2005–2040. Last tasted, 12/01.

1985 The charming 1985 Lafite should be better, but for followers of fashion, its star-
87   studded price will fetch you a moderately intense, cedary, woody, herb-and-leather-scented bouquet, and attractive, forward, developed flavors displayed in a medium-bodied format. The finish is soft and, after a pensive sip, one is likely to ask, "Is this all there is?" Elegance, lightness, and charm characterize this fully mature wine. Anticipated maturity: now–2010. Last tasted, 12/01.

1983 The wine exhibits a deep ruby/garnet color with only a slight amber at the edge.
92   The perfumed nose of lead pencil, toast, red and black fruits, minerals, and roasted herbs is provocative. In the mouth, this wine displays considerable body for a Lafite, plenty of power, and a fleshy, rich, sweet mid-palate. Long, elegant, plump, and surprisingly fleshy, this outstanding example of Lafite seems largely forgotten given the number of high-quality vintages during the golden decade of the 1980s. Anticipated maturity: now–2019. Last tasted, 1/02.

1982 Still extraordinarily youthful, this large-scaled (massive by Lafite's standards)
100 wine should prove to be the greatest Lafite made after the 1959. It continues to offer an exceptionally intense, compelling bouquet of herbs, black currants, vanilla, lead pencil, and cedar. The wine reveals considerable tannin as well as amazing, atypical power and concentration for Lafite. The hallmark elegance of this wine has not been compromised because of the vintage's tendency to turn out powerful and unctuously textured, thick, juicy wines. Rich, full, and still youthful, this has turned out to be a fabulous Lafite Rothschild, and a modern-day clone of the 1959. Anticipated maturity: 2004–2040. Last tasted, 8/02.

1981   This wine is fully mature but showing no signs of decline in spite of its rather light
91   style. It reveals the classic Lafite bouquet of red and black fruits, cedar, fruitcake, and tobacco-like aromas. In the mouth, this medium ruby/garnet–colored wine displays a delicacy of fruit and sweet attack, but has subtle, well-defined flavors ranging from tobacco, cigar box, cedar, and fruitcake. This is a savory, soft Lafite Rothschild that is pleasing to both the intellect and the palate. Anticipated maturity: now–2015. Last tasted, 3/02.

1979   I overrated this wine when it was young and have not been as pleased with its evo-
87   lution in the bottle. The wine has retained a cool-climate high acidity, giving it a more compressed personality than I had envisioned. The color remains a ruby/garnet with considerable amber at the edge. The nose has taken on a more vegetal, earthy note to go along with the oak and sweet red currants. The wine's crisp acidity keeps its tannic edge aggressive and the palate relatively compressed. This looks to becoming increasingly attenuated. Anticipated maturity: now–2012. Last tasted, 12/01.

1978   This garnet-colored wine is distinctively herbaceous, tarry as well as cedary, with
87   surprisingly high acidity and aggressive tannin. Its medium garnet color and smoky, roasted herb–scented nose are followed by a wine with good fruit on the attack, but an angular, sharp finish. Fully mature, the 1978 is showing signs of cracking up—drying fruit and pronounced acids and tannin. Anticipated maturity: now–2007. Last tasted, 12/01.

1976   A beautiful bouquet of seductive cedarwood, spices, and ripe fruit precedes a con-
90   centrated, dark colored wine, with excellent length and texture. Some amber is just beginning to appear at the edge. The 1976 has turned out to be the finest Lafite of the 1970s, but it has been fully mature for 5–6 years and is on a quick evolutionary track. Still intact and impressive, but the wine requires consumption. Anticipated maturity: now–2005. Last tasted, 12/01.

1975   Why is it that Lafite Rothschild is often so distressingly irregular from bottle to
90?   bottle? Much of the inconsistency during the 1960s and mid-1970s can be explained by the relaxed bottling schedule, which saw the wines blended and bottled over an unusually long period (12+ months, compared to the estate's modern-day bottling operation, which never takes longer than 2–4 weeks). I have had some great bottles of the 1975 Lafite, most of them in the wine's first 15 years of life. Since then, I have seen wines that appeared cooked and stewed with a Barolo tar-like aroma, as well as others with the classic Pauillac, lead pencil, cedar, cassis, and tobacco aromatic dimension. The 1975 is a powerful Lafite, and troublesome bottles tend to reveal more tannin and funkiness than others, which have a roasted character, combined with a gravelly, mineral underpinning. As this wine has aged, it appears to be less of a sure bet. In most cases it has been an outstanding wine. The aromatics indicate the wine is fully mature, but the tough tannin level clearly underscores the dark side of the 1975 vintage. This wine will undoubtedly last for another 25+ years, but I am not sure the fruit will hold. It is a perplexing wine that may still turn out to be an exceptional Lafite. In contrast, the 1976 has always been much more forward and consistent. However, I would still take the 1975 over the overrated, mediocre 1970, 1966, and 1961. Last tasted, 12/01.

1970   Lafite's 1970 has consistently left me disappointed. The wine reveals some of the
85   classic Lafite nose of cedar, lead pencil, dried red and black fruits, and spice. The wine's bouquet would merit an outstanding rating, but the palate is mediocre. Annoyingly high acidity continues to be problematic, largely because the wine does not possess the flesh, fat, and extract to cover its angular structure. It is drying out, with rustic tannins taking over. This is a wine that has far greater value on the auction block than on the dinner table. Anticipated maturity: now–2005. Last tasted, 12/01.

1966 With a light to medium ruby/garnet color, this wine exhibited a classy, weedy,
84 herbal, Cabernet-dominated nose, soft, washed-out flavors, and little body and
    length. It is also beginning to dry out. I suppose if one were to taste a 30-year-old
    Cabernet from Monterey County, California, it might reveal similar characteris-
    tics. The 1966 Lafite Rothschild has consistently been a major disappointment
    from what is an irregular, but very good vintage. Last tasted, 12/95.

1962 The 1962 Lafite Rothschild exhibits the château's telltale cedary, cigar box–like,
88 understated bouquet, and light-bodied, delicate flavors. Although it is soft, round,
    and delicious, like so many Lafites of this epoch, its stiff price always makes me
    think that the quality of Lafite is rarely proportional to the wine's cost. Last tasted,
    12/95.

1961 This wine has a phenomenal reputation. However, I have now tasted the wine on
84 nine separate occasions where I found it to be shockingly light, too acidic, dis-
    turbingly austere, and surprisingly ungenerous for a 1961. Moreover, recent tast-
    ings have suggested that the wine was clearly drying out. The color is light ruby
    with a brownish cast. The wine does have the penetrating "cigar box" Lafite bou-
    quet, yet even it seems shy, given the legendary status of this wine. Lacking the
    weight, concentration, and majesty of the great 1961s, this is a wine that far too
    many writers have euphemistically said "needed time" or was "elegant" or "not
    properly understood," when they should have used the words "overrated" and
    "disappointing." In the context of the vintage and the estate of Lafite Rothschild,
    it represents an indifferent winemaking effort. Caveat emptor. Anticipated matu-
    rity: now. Last tasted, 12/01.

ANCIENT VINTAGES

The 1959 (100 points; last tasted 3/02) is unquestionably the greatest Lafite Rothschild that has approached full maturity. It remains to be seen whether vintages such
as 2000, 1996, 1986, and 1982 will reach a similar height. The super-aromatic bouquet of flowers, black truffles, cedar, lead pencil, and red fruits is followed by one of the
most powerful and concentrated Lafites I have tasted. Medium to full-bodied, velvety
textured, rich, and pure, it is a testament to what this great estate can achieve when it
hits the mark. This youthful wine will last for another 30 or more years. On two occasions I gave the 1953 a rating of 100 and on another occasion, a nearly perfect 99. According to some old-timers, the wine has been fully mature for almost 30 years. It
possesses that extraordinary Lafite fragrance of minerals, lead pencil, cedar, and spice.
It is velvety textured, wonderfully round, and sweet, but so well delineated and balanced. It is best purchased today in magnum and larger formats unless you can be assured the wine came from a cold cellar and has not been traded frequently.

Other famous vintages for Bordeaux have produced uninspiring duds at Lafite Rothschild, above all the 1952, 1949, 1947, and 1945.

Vintages of the 19th century have tended to be quite exhilarating, in contrast with
most Lafites of the 20th century. Consider the following: The 1832 Lafite Rothschild
(76 points; last tasted 9/95) offered a cigar box, ice tea, herbal-scented nose, fragile,
light-bodied, round, diluted flavors, and a quick, hard finish. The fact that this wine
still retained some fruit was remarkable.

Michael Broadbent has long claimed that the 1848 Lafite Rothschild was one of the
great wines of the last century. In his last tasting in 1988, he awarded it five stars.

Seven years later it was again extraordinary! (I rated it 96 points in December 1995.) The color was light ruby/garnet, but the exceptionally penetrating bouquet of sweet cedar, ripe, jammy fruit, earth, fruitcake, and lead pencil was followed by a remarkably dense yet elegant wine with exceptional expansion and a velvety texture. It was wonderfully concentrated, sweet, and ripe, with neither acidity nor tannin showing through the wine's quantity of fruit. It could easily pass for a 45–50-year-old wine. Quite stunning, this is truly a legendary wine with an unmistakable Lafite character!

The amber/ruby–colored 1864 Lafite Rothschild (92 points; last tasted 9/95) possessed a Mouton-like nose of cedar and cassis, accompanied by surprising intensity and ripeness. In the mouth, the wine revealed remarkable freshness, sweet fruit, surprisingly high alcohol, and wonderful, exotic, Asian spice, tobacco, and Graves-like flavors. There was surprising power and intensity in the finish of this totally delicious, compelling wine!

The 1865 Lafite Rothschild (98 points; last tasted 9/95) was otherworldly. The first word I wrote after smelling it was "Wow!" The color is a medium garnet with considerable rust and orange at the edge. The wine possessed an extraordinary fragrance, great density, and fabulous intensity of chocolate, herb, and cedar-like flavors with a wonderful sweet, inner core of opulent fruit. The finish is long and velvety, with no hard edges. It is hard to imagine a 130-year-old wine (made when American Civil War adversaries Robert E. Lee and Ulysses S. Grant were alive) tasting so extraordinary, but I was there—I saw it, I smelled it, I tasted it, and I drank it! Unreal!

After two disappointing tastings of the immortal 1870 Lafite Rothschild (96 points; last tasted 9/95), the Hardy Rodenstock tasting in Munich in September 1995 finally provided me a provocative, compelling, profound bottle of this legendary wine. The color is a healthy dark garnet, and the huge nose of freshly sliced celery, mint, cedar, and cassis unfolded quickly but held in the glass during the 30–40 minutes it remained there before it became just a mere component of my bodily fluids. The wine exhibited sweet fruit, surprising glycerin and opulence for a Lafite, and a sweet, jammy, powerful finish. It is an extraordinary wine!

For all of these superlative wines, my Lafite scorecard is dotted with far more disappointments than successes. The 1955, 1952, and 1950 are uninspiring. The 1957, while not great, is nevertheless surprisingly good (twice I have rated it in the 86–88 range). In the 1940s, the 1949 is good but far from profound, the 1947 is disappointing, and the 1945 excessively astringent and out of balance. Among the ancient vintages, I have very good notes only for one vintage in the 1930s (not a good decade for Bordeaux). The 1934 (rated 90), drunk from magnum in 1986, was wonderful.

In April 1991, I had the opportunity to taste (from a friend's cellar in Bordeaux) the 1929, 1928, 1926, and 1924. The wines had been purchased in the 1930s and kept in a cold Bordeaux cellar until this tasting. All of them were disappointing with scores of 59 for the 1929 (faded and sickly), 68 for the 1928 (some elegance but attenuated and short as well as the only Lafite ever pasteurized), 67 for the 1926 (hard, dried out), and 69 for the 1924 (slightly more freshness than the 1926). Yet I was stunned by the 1921 (93 points; last tasted 9/95). The 1921's garnet color, with considerable amber on the edge and sweet, overripe nose of red and black fruits, cedar, herbs, and spices was followed by a medium-bodied, remarkably well-preserved wine with a roasted character. Some acidity began to appear in the finish as the wine sat in the glass, but this is a sweet, fragrant, delicious Lafite that has probably been fully mature for 40–50 years.

LATOUR

Classification: First Growth in 1855 and 1973

Owner: François Pinault

Address: Saint-Lambert, 33250 Pauillac

Telephone: 05 56 73 19 80; Telefax: 05 56 73 19 81

E-mail: info@château-latour.com

Website: www.château-latour.com

Visits: By appointment Monday to Friday, 9–11 A.M. and 2–4 P.M.

Contact: Julie Lagarde (j.lagarde@château-latour.com)

VINEYARDS

Surface area: 160.5 acres

Grape varietals: 75% Cabernet Sauvignon, 20% Merlot, 4% Cabernet Franc, 1% Petit Verdot

Average age of vines: 40 years

Density of plantation: 10,000 vines per hectare

Average yields: 45 hectoliters per hectare

Elevage: Twenty-one day fermentation and maceration in temperature-controlled stainless-steel vats. Seventeen months aging in barrels with 85–100% new oak depending upon the vintage. Fining with egg whites. No filtration.

WINES PRODUCED

Grand Vin de Château Latour: 175,000 bottles

Les Forts de Latour: 140,000 bottles

Plateau of maturity: Within 15–50 years of the vintage

GENERAL APPRECIATION

Even allowing for a difficult period throughout the 1980s, Latour is unquestionably the most consistent of Bordeaux's first growths (though equaled by Lafite and Haut-Brion over recent years). True to its reputation, this wine is as remarkable in the finest vintages as in the lesser ones. Generally powerful, tannic, rich, dense, and intense, the wines of Latour are always topflight and extremely long-lived. Unfortunately (and the same goes for the finest Bordeaux), prices reflect the quality, name, reputation, and insatiable worldwide demand. Consumers looking for values should search elsewhere or seek the estate's second wine, Les Forts de Latour, equivalent to a fourth classified growth.

Impressively situated on the Pauillac/St.-Julien border, immediately north of the walled vineyard of Léoville Las Cases, Latour's vineyard can be easily spotted from the road because of the creamy-colored, fortress-like tower. Notably depicted on the wine's label, this formidable tower overlooking the vineyards and the Gironde River remains from the 17th century, when it was built on the site of a 15th-century fortress used by the English to fend off attacks by pirates.

Latour was one of a handful of major Bordeaux châteaux to have been controlled by foreign interests. Between 1963 and 1994, Latour was under English ownership, but in 1994 French business tycoon François Pinault purchased this estate, returning it to French ownership.

The wine produced here has been an impeccable and classic model of consistent excellence, in great, mediocre, and poor vintages. For that reason, many have long considered Latour to be the Médoc's finest wine. Latour's reputation for making Bordeaux's best wine in mediocre or poor vintages—such as 1974, 1972, and 1960—has been totally justified, although in the recent poor Bordeaux vintages—1984, 1980, and 1977—Latour's wines were surprisingly light and eclipsed in quality by a number of other châteaux. The wine of Latour also has a remarkable record of being a stubbornly slow-developing wine, requiring a good 20–25 years of bottle age to shed its considerable tannic clout and reveal its stunning power, depth, and richness. This style, often referred to by commentators as virile, masculine, and tough, may have undergone a subtle yet very perceptible softening up between 1983 and 1989. This was adamantly denied by the staff at Latour, but my tastings suggest a more gentle and accessible style. Fortunately, this ignoble trend was quickly abandoned, as Latour has once again been producing blockbuster wines since 1990.

While the 1982 and to a lesser extent the 1986 are undeniably great Latours, on the whole the estate did not have a distinguished decade. It was no secret that the *cuverie* was too small to handle the gigantic crop sizes of 1986, 1985, and 1983. As a consequence, the fermentation tanks had to be emptied too soon in order to make room for the arriving grapes. The underground cellars and *cuverie* were subsequently enlarged—just in time to handle 1989, the largest vintage ever harvested in Bordeaux. In 2000, a massive renovation project costing millions has given Latour a state-of-the-art winemaking and storage facility. However, an objective tasting analysis of the 1989, 1988, 1985, and 1983 Latours leaves one with the impression that in these years, Latour is a significantly lighter, less powerful, and less concentrated wine than it was in any decade earlier in the last century. However, the decade of the 1990s witnessed a return to form, and under the impeccable administration of proprietor François Pinault and his man on the spot, Frédéric Engerer, nothing less than perfection will be permitted.

Latour remains one of the most concentrated, rich, tannic, and full-bodied wines in the world. When mature, it has a compelling bouquet of fresh walnuts and leather, black currants, and gravelly, mineral scents. On the palate, it can be a wine of extraordinary richness, yet it is never heavy.

IMPORTANT VINTAGES

2001　The grand vin's final blend of 79% Cabernet Sauvignon, 18% Merlot, 2% Petit 92–94+ Verdot, and 1% Cabernet Franc constitutes 53% of the total production. The saturated ruby/purple–colored 2001 Latour boasts sweet black currant fruit aromas, plenty of extract, density, and volume, and a tangy, vibrant fruit character. It does not possess the size of the 2000 or 1996, but it may turn out more aromatic and evolved than those two vintages. One of the finest efforts of the vintage, it is the first wine made in Latour's new state-of-the-art cellar. Anticipated maturity: 2008–2025. Last tasted, 1/03.

2000   Only 48% of the crop made it into the prodigious 2000 Latour. A synthesis in style
98+   between the 1996, 1990, and 1982, it has the structure of the 1996, but the suc-
       culence, ripeness, and rich, concentrated fruit of both the 1990 and 1982. The
       2000's saturated ruby/purple color is accompanied by sumptuous aromas of
       jammy black fruits intermixed with earth, vanilla, grilled nuts, and minerals. It is
       remarkably seamless for a young Latour, but as the wine sits in the glass, its acid
       and unevolved high tannin level begin to make an impact. This is an unctuously
       styled effort where tasters may not discern the tannin until the finish. A fascinat-
       ing offering, it will flirt with perfection when fully mature. Anticipated maturity:
       2012–2050. Last tasted, 1/03.

1999   Readers looking for a modern day version of Latour's magnificent 1971 or 1962
93   should check out the sensational 1999 Latour. A big, concentrated offering, it ex-
       hibits a dense ruby/purple color and a classic nose of minerals, black currants,
       leather, and vanilla. Long, ripe, and medium bodied, with high levels of sweet tan-
       nin, this surprisingly full, concentrated 1999 should be drinkable in five years; it
       will last for three decades. Last tasted, 8/02.

1998   Not a blockbuster, super-concentrated classic such as the 1996, 1995, 1990, or
90   1982, the 1998 possesses a dark garnet/purple color in addition to a complex bou-
       quet of underbrush, cedar, walnuts, and licorice-tinged black currants. Although
       medium to full-bodied and moderately tannic, it lacks the expansiveness in the
       mid-palate necessary to be truly great. Moreover, the tannin is slightly aggressive,
       although that is hardly unusual in such a young Latour. Anticipated maturity:
       2009–2030. Last tasted, 8/02.

1997   A flavorful, savory Latour, without a great deal of density or power, the 1997 ex-
86   hibits sweet, walnut-tinged, black currant fruit intertwined with minerals and sub-
       tle wood. Nicely textured with adequate acidity, ripe tannin, and a medium-bodied
       finish, this smooth effort should drink well for 10 years. Last tasted, 8/02.

1996   A spectacular Latour, the 1996 may be the modern day clone of the 1966, only
99   riper. This vintage, which is so variable in Pomerol, St.-Emilion, and Graves, was
       fabulous for the late-harvested Cabernet Sauvignon of the northern Médoc be-
       cause of splendid weather in late September and early October. An opaque purple
       color is followed by phenomenally sweet, pure aromas of cassis infused with
       subtle minerals. This massive offering possesses unreal levels of extract, full body,
       intensely ripe but abundant tannin, and a finish that lasts for nearly a minute.
       More classic and denser than the 1995, it displays the potential for 50–75 years of
       longevity. Although still an infant, it would be educational to taste a bottle. Antic-
       ipated maturity: 2015–2050. Last tasted, 3/02.

1995   A beauty, the opaque, dense purple–colored 1995 exhibits jammy cassis, vanilla,
96+   and minerals in its fragrant but still youthful aromatics. Medium to full-bodied
       with exceptional purity, superb concentration, and a long, intense, ripe, 40-
       second finish, this is a magnificent example of Latour. As the wine sat in the glass,
       scents of roasted espresso and toasty new oak emerged. This classic will require
       considerable cellaring. Anticipated maturity: 2012–2050. Last tasted, 6/00.

1990   This is not the awesome blockbuster I thought it would be. A dark ruby/purple
96   color does not possess the saturation found in vintages such as 2000, 1996, and
       1995. There is a roasted, earthy, hot year character with extremely low acidity,
       fleshy, seductive, opulently textured flavors, and a full-bodied finish with consid-

erable amounts of glycerin and tannin. The wine was sweet, accessible, and seductive on the attack, but it closed down in the mouth. It needs at least 6–10 years
of further cellaring. It will last 25–30 years, but is it the immortal classic many observers, including myself, thought it was? Anticipated maturity: 2009–2036. Last
tasted, 8/02.

1989
89

The 1989 Latour possesses many characteristics that make great vintages of Bordeaux so alluring—softness, overripeness, and sweet fruit. The problem is that
there are insufficient quantities of these components. An evolved dark ruby color
reveals amber at the edge. The nose offers aromas of caramel, coffee, ripe black
cherry and currant fruit, cedar, and spice box. Although medium bodied with low
acidity, the wine lacks richness in the mid-palate and is surprisingly abrupt in the
finish. It is a very fine, delicious Latour, but it is hard to believe it will attain the
weight and flavor dimensions its producers suggest. Anticipated maturity: now–
2020. Last tasted, 6/00.

1988
91

The best showing yet for a wine from this underrated vintage, the dark garnet-
colored 1988 Latour reveals slight amber at the edge. A bouquet of melted tar,
plums, black currants, cedar, and underbrush is followed by a sweet entry with
medium to full body, excellent ripeness, and mature tannin. It is a classic, elegant
Latour with more meaty, vegetable-like flavors than are found in a riper year, such
as 1990 and 1989. The 1988 has just begun to enter its plateau of maturity, where
it should remain for 25 years. Anticipated maturity: now–2025. Last tasted, 6/00.

1986
90+

The 1986 has consistently been outstanding, falling short of being sublime. The
spicy, peppery bouquet reveals aromas of dried herbs and red currant fruit.
Medium bodied, austere, but youthful, vigorous, and concentrated, this wine still
requires 4–5 years of cellaring. It is surpassed in this vintage (which favored the
northern Médoc and Cabernet Sauvignon) by its rivals, Lafite Rothschild and
Mouton Rothschild. Anticipated maturity: 2005–2020. Last tasted, 6/00.

1985
88

The 1985 Latour is a soft, open-knit example, without much structure, delineation, and depth. The dark ruby color displays amber at the edge. The bouquet of
tobacco, black fruits, herbs, earth, and new oak is pleasant, but neither intense nor
persistent. The wine is medium bodied, with sweet fruit on the attack, but it narrows out to reveal dry tannin and herbaceous notes. Anticipated maturity:
now–2012. Last tasted, 6/00.

1983
88

This wine is fully mature, not terribly concentrated, and slightly herbaceous, exhibiting aromas of sweaty saddle leather, melted asphalt, tobacco, and red as well
as black fruits. Notions of caramel and roasted nuts also emerge. A medium-
bodied effort with soft tannin but little persistence and length, it requires consumption over the next decade. Last tasted, 6/00.

1982
100

This is an unusual Latour in the fact that it has always been precocious. It has
been jammy, forward, and delicious no matter when the cork was pulled, in total
contrast to its two Pauillac first-growth siblings, Mouton Rothschild and Lafite
Rothschild. The dense, opaque garnet-colored 1982 Latour reveals slight amber
at the edge. Sweet, smoky, roasted aromas in the nose combine with jammy levels
of black currant, cherry, and prune-like fruit. It possesses extraordinary concentration and unctuosity, with a thick, fat texture oozing notes of cedar wood, tobacco, coffee, and overripe fruit. Low acidity as well as high alcohol (for Bordeaux)
give the wine even more glycerin and textural chewiness. The finish lasts forever.
The only Latour that remotely resembles the 1982 is the 1961, which has a similar
texture and succulence. Anticipated maturity: now–2040. Last tasted, 8/02.

1978
90

Medium garnet colored with moderate amber at the edge, the 1978 Latour offers a
spicy, saddle leather, tobacco, dried herb, earthy nose with sweet fruit trying to
poke through. Interestingly, new oak also makes an appearance in the flavors.

Medium bodied, elegant, and fragrant, but possibly beginning to dry out, this fully mature wine requires consumption over the next decade. Anticipated maturity: now–2010. Last tasted, 6/00.

1975 With bottle age, most 1975 Médocs have become leaner, more austere, and in-
90?   creasingly problematic. In contrast, some Graves (particularly Haut-Brion and La Mission Haut-Brion) and most Pomerols have deepened in flavor and are the stars of this overrated vintage. The dark ruby/garnet–colored 1975 Latour offers up a dry, mineral, tobacco, stony-scented nose with red and black currants competing with cedar, spice box, and balsam wood aromas. Hard and dense in the mouth with tough, astringent tannin, a steely constitution, plenty of concentration, but an un-flattering, backward style, this youthful 1975 is capable of lasting two more de-cades. Will it become increasingly attenuated and hard? Anticipated maturity: now–2020. Last tasted, 6/00.

1971 The 1971 Latour is undoubtedly the wine of the Médoc and possibly the wine of
94   the vintage (Pétrus and Trotanoy are also splendid efforts). Drinkable young, it has continued to evolve, offering extraordinary aromatic complexity as well as surpris-ingly deep, concentrated flavors atypical for the vintage. A dark opaque garnet color with amber at the edge is followed by a spectacular bouquet of dried herbs, cedar, smoky black fruit, and coffee. Rich but structured, with moderate tannin, this medium-bodied, elegant yet complex wine possesses a sweet mid-palate in addition to a long, concentrated finish with abundant tannin. This underrated 1971 has been fully mature for more than a decade, but it reveals no signs of cracking up or becoming attenuated. Anticipated maturity: now–2012. Last tasted, 6/00.

1970 I have consumed more than a case of this wine, and consistently rated it in the
97   mid- to upper 90s. The three bottles I tasted from the Château's cellars in June 2000, were variable, but seemed surprisingly herbal, with notes of soy, cedar, roasted vegetables, leather, and earth dominating the wine's fruit. These bottles suggested a wine that was tasty, elegant, medium bodied, and fully mature. The 1970 is excellent, but not inspirational. A bottle from my cellar drunk in late Au-gust 2002, was rated 97. It appeared to have at least two decades of life remaining, in contrast to the Château's bottles, which require immediate consumption. Read-ers who purchase old vintages of great wines, regardless of whether they are Bor-deaux, Burgundy, or California Cabernet, need to remember the expression, "There are no great wines, just great bottles," particularly after a wine reaches 30 years of age. Last tasted, 8/02.

1966 The wine of the vintage, the 1966 Latour is a classic, old-style Bordeaux that has
96   required decades to become drinkable. A dark, opaque garnet color is followed by a fabulous nose of cedar, sweet leather, black fruits, prunes, and roasted walnuts, refreshing underlying acidity, sweet but noticeable tannin, and a spicy finish. This powerful, vigorous, immensely impressive, concentrated Latour has reached its plateau of maturity, where it will remain for another 10–20 years. Last tasted, 6/00.

1962 Another vintage that was overlooked because of the publicity surrounding 1961
95   and 1959, the 1962 Latour continues to be one of the great vintages for this château. A dense opaque garnet color reveals amber at the edge, as well as an in-credible perfume of cedar wood, balsam, coffee, black fruits, leather, and cigar smoke. The wine is supple and full-bodied with sweet tannin, glorious levels of fruit and extract, abundant glycerin, and a seductive, truffle-flavored finish. While it has been drinkable for two decades, it is capable of lasting another 20 years. It is a perfectly balanced, exciting Latour that remains undervalued as well as un-derrated. Last tasted, 6/00.

1961
100
Port-like, with an unctuous texture and a dark garnet color with considerable amber at the edge, the 1961 Latour possesses a viscosity and thickness approached only by vintages such as 1982 and 1959. One of the three bottles served at the Château's tasting in 2000 revealed a surprisingly aggressive, minty, herbaceous nose, but the other two bottles were liquid perfection, exhibiting fragrant, cedary, truffle, leather, mineral, and sweet, jammy aromatics, full-bodied, voluptuous textures, exquisite purity and concentration, and a layered, highly nuanced finish that represents the essence of compellingly great wine. The 1961 has been fully mature for more than 15 years, but, much like the 1982, it seems to get richer, holding on to its succulence and fat and developing more aromatic nuances without losing any sweetness or concentration. An extraordinary wine, it is unquestionably one of the Bordeaux legends of the century! Anticipated maturity: now–2025. Last tasted, 6/00.

1959
96
Dark garnet with an amber edge, the 1959 Latour reveals a touch of volatile acidity in the nose, along with aromas of melted caramel, tobacco, and jammy red and black fruits. As the wine sat in the glass, notes of minerals, coffee, spice, and underbrush emerged. Given its thick, full-bodied unctuosity, texturally, the 1959 resembles the 1982 and 1961. There is still copious tannin in the finish (I am not sure it will ever be fully resolved), but this sumptuous, complex, fragrant, super-rich Latour cuts a broad swath across the palate. Fully mature, it is best consumed over the next decade. Last tasted, 6/00.

1955
94
A spectacular Latour, from a vintage that has provided many superb surprises (especially in the Médoc and Graves), the deep garnet-colored 1955 reveals some amber at the edge. It remains tannic, but its extraordinary perfume of smoked meats, dried herbs, cedar, black fruits, underbrush, and leather is seductive. Reminiscent of such vintages as 1970 and 1966, it is full-bodied with a sweet, intense mid-palate, plenty of power, and decades of life remaining. This is an underrated, stunning Latour that may even improve. Anticipated maturity: now–2020. Last tasted, 6/00.

1949
98
On each of the previous occasions I have had this wine it has flirted with perfection. This bottle was again a riveting, opulently textured drinking experience. Its spectacularly perfumed bouquet consists of truffles, black tea, soy, minerals, and copious sweet prune, coffee-infused, black currant fruit. Sweet on the attack, with a rare opulence, a voluptuous texture, full body, terrific freshness, and a chewy, fleshy, succulent finish, this has always been great stuff. This bottle was no exception. It has been fully mature for 25–30 years, but well stored or larger format bottlings will last another two decades. Last tasted, 6/00.

1947
92?
I never had much luck with this wine (from my birth year), but a bottle tasted in late March 2000, was the finest I have ever had. Although fragile, with considerable amber to its color, it offers a nose of smoked herbs, caramel, and sweet roasted fruit. The palate impression of sweet fruit and abundant glycerin make it a delicious, alluring Latour. The wine dried out in the glass, becoming more marked by acidity and tannin after 10–15 minutes. While still impressive, it needs to be drunk up. Last tasted, 3/00.

1945
90?
This has always been an irregular vintage. I purchased a mixed case of the 1945 Latour, some of which had been reconditioned at the Château and others with the original corks. Those with the original corks always seemed to be the best, with a handful of them meriting ratings in the 95–98 range. This particular bottle revealed the austerity and mouth-searing tannin levels that afflict so many 1945s. However, the aromatics were topflight, revealing scents of dried fruit, tobacco, smoke, earth, and soy. In the mouth, the wine is medium bodied, attenuated, and

just beginning to lose its fruit, exhibiting austerity and astringent tannin. Nevertheless, this is another example where each bottle may be considerably different.

1934
91
From what is considered to be the finest vintage of a disappointing decade, Latour's 1934 possesses a deep garnet color in addition to a smoky, mineral, sweet, cedary-scented nose with hints of tobacco, iron, asphalt, and a Provençal *garrigue* note. Ripe and long with moderate tannin and admirable sweetness, the 1934 was showing exceptionally well. It appears capable of lasting for another decade. Last tasted, 6/00.

1929
60
All three bottles of the 1929 Latour were dead on arrival. I have had some interesting bottles of this vintage in the past, where the wine was always fragile with some volatile acidity, but considerable character. This bottle exhibited notes of sweet cedar, but its light amber color suggested a tired wine. As it sat in the glass, aromas of stale tea, musty wood, and decaying mushrooms made an appearance. Obviously this was a rich, opulent Latour in its youth, but it has totally declined based on these bottles from the Château. It would be interesting to compare it to a 1929 that had been kept in a very cold cellar. Last tasted, 6/00.

1928
76
I had looked forward to tasting this wine with great anticipation as I had given the 1928 a perfect score on two occasions, most recently in September 1994. There was no such score for any of the three bottles served at the Christie's tasting. The wine revealed substantial amber in its garnet color in addition to spicy, cedar, roasted tobacco, dried herb, and mineral aromas. Medium bodied, but attenuated and losing its fruit, this Latour fell off the palate, leaving only acidity and tannin in the finish. What a disappointment. However, readers should recognize that pristine bottles and those in larger formats might taste perfect. Last tasted, 6/00.

1924
90
Medium amber/ruby–colored, this aromatic (cinnamon, ginger, leather, dried herbs, and iron) Latour possesses fine ripeness, sweetness, and medium body. Some tannin and acidity are present in the finish, but the wine remains in remarkable condition. It is capable of lasting another 10–20 years. Last tasted, 6/00.

1918
64
Light ruby–colored with significant amber, this diluted, lean, austere Latour exhibits mushroom-like aromas, an absence of fruit, and a thin, tannic finish. Although still alive, it is devoid of pleasure. Drink up. Last tasted, 6/00.

1909
92
A remarkable wine, Latour's 1909 exhibited a deep amber color with ruby/garnet nuances. A sweet nose of caramel, jammy red and black fruits, mushrooms, cedar, and spice box aromas jumps from the glass. In the mouth, the wine displays vigorous, ripe flavors, medium body, sweet tannin, and a long finish. What a nice surprise! Anticipated maturity: now–2010. Last tasted, 6/00.

1900
87
Surprisingly alive but firm, foursquare, and monolithic, this dark amber/ruby–colored Latour is reticent but vigorous and concentrated. There is noticeable acidity as well as smoky, mineral, tobacco, and herb aromas, good depth, but not much charm or sweetness. It will continue to age for 15–20 years. Last tasted, 6/00.

1899
98
Served side by side, the 1899 Latour blew away the 1900. Dark garnet with considerable amber, the nearly perfect 1899 exhibited a stunningly sweet nose of roasted herbs, smoked meats, underbrush, cedar, and sweet fruit with noticeable overripeness, as evidenced by marmalade notes. In the mouth, the wine was full-bodied, plush, and opulent, with roasted coffee flavors competing with sweet glycerin. The finish was all velvet, glycerin, and alcohol with no intrusive acidity or tannin. This splendid wine proves the extraordinary aging potential of great Bordeaux. Anticipated maturity: now–2020. Last tasted, 6/00.

1893
62
Amber colored with diluted soy, old saddle leather, and sweaty locker-room smells, this dry, hard, tannic, astringent wine had more volatile acidity than fruit. Anticipated maturity: Drink up! Last tasted, 6/00.

1881   A spicy, cinnamon, gingery bouquet emerges from this amber-colored wine with a
68   few ruby tints. On the palate, it was tough, astringent, and unpleasant. Anticipated
     maturity: now. Last tasted, 6/00.

1863   A revelation at the very least, the 1863 Latour possesses a dark garnet color as
90   well as a terrific nose of ginger, allspice, smoke, mint, cedar, and briny fruit. As
     this medium-bodied wine sat in the glass, acidity began to push its way through
     the fragile aromatics and fruit flavors, revealing elements of singed leather. The
     wine is alive with an impressive bouquet and a surprising amount of fruit and
     depth—a testament to the extraordinary longevity of some Bordeaux vintages.
     Amazingly, after a half-hour of airing, the wine seemed to stabilize in the glass!
     Anticipated maturity: now. Last tasted, 6/00.

SECOND WINE
LES FORTS DE LATOUR* *(unclassified)*

Evaluation: The quality equivalent of a fourth growth

The staff at Latour have always maintained that the "second" wine of Latour was equivalent in quality terms to a "second growth" in the 1855 classification. In fact, they claim that blind tastings of Forts de Latour are held at Latour against the wines produced by the second growths. If Forts de Latour does not do extremely well, then a decision must be made whether to declassify it as a Pauillac. In specific vintages, for example, 2000, 1996, and 1982, I would agree with their assessment, but in more objective terms, the wine is comparable to a fourth growth in quality, which still establishes this wine as the finest "second wine" produced in Bordeaux.

The wine, which is vinified exactly the same way as Latour, comes from three vineyards called Petit Batailley, Comtesse de Lalande, and Les Forts de Latour. Additionally, selected lots of Latour (often from young vines) not considered quite "grand" enough are also blended with the wine from the aforementioned vineyards. The character of Forts de Latour is astonishingly similar to Latour itself, only lighter and quicker to mature. Les Forts de Latour is certainly the finest of the second labels, or *marques*, produced by the well-known châteaux in Bordeaux.

IMPORTANT VINTAGES

2001   The 2001 Forts de Latour is a blend of 79% Cabernet Sauvignon and 21% Merlot
88–90   and represents 35% of the production. It exhibits abundant quantities of sweet
     tannin, medium body, admirable fruit extraction as well as ripeness, and plenty of
     cedar, black currant, and earthy fruit. It should drink well for 14 years. Last
     tasted, 1/03.

2000   The 2000 Forts de Latour (a blend of 60% Cabernet Sauvignon and 40% Merlot)
90   elicited a big "wow" from me. Potentially one of the finest Forts de Latour ever
     made (clearly on a qualitative par with the 1982), it is extremely concentrated,
     powerful, dense, and not dissimilar from its big brother. This sensational second
     wine should be at its best in 8 years and drink well for 25. Last tasted, 1/03.

* Because Les Forts de Latour is widely regarded as the finest of all the "second wines" and in tastings, frequently rated above more famous Pauillacs, its stature is such that it merits separate coverage.

1999 Latour has long produced one of Bordeaux's greatest second wines. The beautiful,
 90   pure, deep purple–colored 1999 Forts de Latour reveals sweet, cedary, cassis
      scents, medium to full body, ripe tannin, and a long finish. It should drink well for
      12+ years. Last tasted, 8/02.

1998 The 1998 Forts de Latour exhibits a dark ruby/purple color as well as a nose of
 88   black fruits, ketchup, earth, and minerals. Moderately tannic and closed, it is rem-
      iniscent of its bigger brother. Give it 1–2 years of cellaring and enjoy it over the
      next two decades. Last tasted, 8/02.

1997 The 1997 Les Forts de Latour is an elegant, ripe, supple-textured, easy to drink ef-
 87   fort. Anticipated maturity: now. Last tasted, 3/01.

1996 The dense ruby/purple–colored 1996 Les Forts de Latour is exceedingly tannic
 90   with cassis and mushroom-like notes in the aromatics. This full-bodied wine is im-
      pressively constituted and one of the finest Forts de Latours of the last two de-
      cades. Anticipated maturity: 2005–2018. Last tasted, 3/01.

1995 The terrific, dark ruby/purple–colored 1995 Forts de Latour possesses a sweet,
 89+ jammy black fruit scented nose intertwined with smoky minerals, earth, and spicy
      oak. The wine is surprisingly thick and rich in the mouth, with its glycerin and
      concentration of fruit largely concealing the moderate tannin. This excellent,
      sweet wine is less powerful, but more accessible than the 1996. Anticipated matu-
      rity: now–2015. Last tasted, 6/02.

ANCIENT VINTAGES

The fully mature 1990 (90 points; last tasted 3/01) and 1982 (91 points; last tasted
8/02) are both exceptional wines that will last respectively another 15 and 10 years.

LYNCH-BAGES

Classification: Fifth Growth in 1855

Owner: Jean-Michel Cazes

Address: 33250 Pauillac

Mailing Address: BP 120, 33250 Pauillac

Telephone: 05 56 73 24 00; Telefax: 05 56 59 26 42

E-mail: infochato@lynchbages.com;
she@lynchbages.com

Website: www.lynchbages.com

Visits: By appointment only Monday to Friday, 9 A.M.–noon and 2–5 P.M.

Contact: Stéphanie Heinz

VINEYARDS

Surface area: 222 acres

Grape varietals: 73% Cabernet Sauvignon, 15% Merlot, 10% Cabernet Franc,
2% Petit Verdot

Average age of vines: 30 years

Density of plantation: 9,000 vines per hectare

Average yields: 50 hectoliters per hectare

Elevage: Fifteen to seventeen-day fermentation and maceration in temperature-controlled stainless-steel vats. Fifteen months aging in oak barrels with 60% new oak. Racking every three months. Fining with egg whites. Filtration only if necessary.

WINES PRODUCED

Château Lynch-Bages: 420,000 bottles

Château Haut-Bages Averous: 120,000 bottles

Plateau of maturity: Within 6–25 years of the vintage

GENERAL APPRECIATION

Since the mid-1980s, Lynch-Bages has been performing well above its fifth-growth status, producing wines equivalent to a second growth. Often referred to as the "poor man's Mouton Rothschild," it is a sure bet in most vintages and represents extremely good value for the money. In fact, this wine is, along with Grand-Puy-Lacoste, one of the best buys not only among Pauillacs, but among Bordeaux in general. Value seekers take note.

This château is located just west of Bordeaux's Route du Vin (D2) as one approaches the dull, commercial town of Pauillac from the south. It is situated on a small ridge that rises above the town and the adjacent Gironde River called, not surprisingly, the Bages plateau. The luxury hotel/restaurant, Château Cordeillan-Bages, sits directly in front of Lynch-Bages. Until recently the kindest thing that could be said about the buildings was that they were utilitarian. However, Lynch-Bages has benefited enormously from a major face-lift and renovation. The château now sports a new façade, new cellars exhibiting large stainless-steel tanks, and a state-of-the-art tasting room.

Except for these recent changes, this large estate has remained essentially intact since the 16th century. Half the name is taken from the plateau upon which the château and cellars are located and the rest results from 75 years of ownership (during the 17th and 18th centuries) by Thomas Lynch, the son of an Irish immigrant whose family ran the property. After Thomas Lynch sold Lynch-Bages it passed through the hands of several wine merchants before being purchased in 1937 by Jean Charles Cazes, the grandfather of the current-day proprietor, Jean-Michel Cazes. In his time, Jean Charles Cazes was already a renowned proprietor and wine-maker, having directed the fortunes of one of the leading Cru Bourgeois of St.-Estèphe, Château Les Ormes de Pez. He continued to handle both châteaux until 1966 when his son André, a prominent politician who had been the mayor of Pauillac for nearly two decades, took control. André's reign lasted until 1973, when Jean-Michel Cazes assumed control of both Lynch-Bages and Les Ormes de Pez. Jean-Michel, who spent several years in America, had developed an international perspective of wine as well as of business. He made perhaps the smartest decision of his business career in 1976 when he hired the brilliant Daniel Llose as director of Château Lynch-Bages and Les Ormes de Pez.

After the great success Lynch-Bages enjoyed under Jean-Michel's father, André, in the 1950s (1959, 1957, 1955, 1953, and 1952 were all among the top wines of that decade) and in the 1960s (1966, 1962, and 1961), Jean-Michel's inheritance consisted of a disappointing 1972 still in cask. Even his first vintage, 1973, was largely a washout.

This was followed by another disappointing year in 1974 and, for Lynch-Bages, less than exhilarating wine from the sometimes troublesome vintage of 1975. Jean-Michel Cazes recognized that the old wooden vats created sanitation problems and also made it difficult to control the proper fermentation temperature in both cold and hot years. At the same time (the late 1970s), Cazes flirted with a newer style, producing several vintages of Lynch-Bages that were lighter and more elegant. Longtime fans and supporters of Lynch-Bages were dismayed. Fortunately, after Jean-Michel Cazes installed 25 large stainless-steel vats in 1980, the slump in quality between 1971 and 1979 came to an abrupt end. Lynch-Bages produced a competent 1981 and continued to build on that success with highly successful wines in nearly every vintage since.

The vineyard itself is located midway between Mouton Rothschild and Lafite Rothschild to the north, and Latour, Pichon Longueville Comtesse de Lalande, and Pichon-Longueville Baron to the south. Despite the enormous amount of modernization and rebuilding that has taken place at Lynch-Bages, the general philosophy of making wine remains traditional, but in an enlightened sense. Since 1980, as I have mentioned, the vinification has taken place in new steel tanks. After that, the wine is put directly into small French oak casks. The percentage of new casks has increased from 25% in the 1982 vintage to 60% in more recent vintages. Lynch-Bages spends an average of 12–15 months in these oak casks, is fined with egg whites, and occasionally filtered prior to bottling. Now that the vineyards are fully planted, production has soared from an average of 20,000–25,000 cases in the 1970s to nearly 35,000 cases in abundant years. In addition, a minimum of 20–30% of the harvest is relegated to the second wine of Lynch-Bages, Haut-Bages Averous.

In 1990 Cazes began making a dry, rich white Bordeaux from a vineyard in the northern Médoc. The wine, a blend of 40% Sémillon, 40% Sauvignon Blanc, and 20% Muscadelle, was fermented in new oak and aged in cask for nearly 12 months prior to bottling. The debut vintage was impressive, with a level of quality reminiscent of a top white Graves. In the famous 1855 Classification of the Wines of Gironde, Lynch-Bages was positioned in the last tier as a fifth growth. I know of no professional in the field today who would not argue that its present-day quality is more akin to a second growth. Englishman Oz Clarke lightheartedly argues that those responsible for the 1855 classification must have been essentially Puritans because they "couldn't bear to admit that a wine as openheartedly lovely as Lynch-Bages could really be as important as other less-generous growths."

Just as it is difficult not to enjoy a bottle of Lynch-Bages, so is it difficult not to appreciate the affable, seemingly always open and gregarious Jean-Michel Cazes, the architect behind Lynch-Bages's stratospheric rise to international prominence. The confident Cazes, who, having attended school in America, speaks English like a native, has a global vision, and anyone who talks with him knows he wants his wines to be lusty, open, and direct yet also reflect the class and character of a top Pauillac. For that reason he always prefers vintages such as 1985 and 1982 to more tannic and severe years such as 1988 and 1986. He is also an untiring ambassador not only for his own wines, but for the wines of the entire Bordeaux region. There rarely seems to be a conference, symposium, or international tasting of Bordeaux where one does not encounter

Monsieur Cazes. There is no other producer in Pauillac (with the possible exception of Madame Lencquesaing of Pichon-Lalande) who travels so extensively and who pleads his case so eloquently for both his beloved Lynch-Bages and also all the wines of Bordeaux. President Chirac finally recognized this man's enormous contributions to French prestige and culture in 2001, bestowing on him that country's highest decoration, knighthood in the Legion of Honor.

IMPORTANT VINTAGES

2001 Showing far better after 13–14 months in cask than it did early in its life, this wine
89–91 has fleshed out, put on weight, and shows the typical full-bodied, corpulent, earthy, leathery, black currant style that has made Lynch-Bages so popular with consumers. The wine is lush, pure, and just a lot of fun to drink. Anticipated maturity: 2005–2017. P.S. Think of it as a slightly beefier version of the charming, elegant yet flavorful 1999. Last tasted, 1/03.

2000 A great—make that profound—Lynch-Bages, the 2000 represents a hypothetical
95+ blend of the 1990 and 1989. It is a huge, massive, concentrated effort that coats the palate with an unctuous display of black currant fruit bolstered by considerable levels of glycerin and extract. There are no hard edges, but there is considerable tannin in this beefy, full-bodied, muscular, incredibly well-balanced, pure wine. It should drink well young, yet last for 25 years. A tour de force for Lynch-Bages. Anticipated maturity: 2008–2025. Last tasted, 1/03.

1999 A modern-day clone of this estate's wonderful 1962, the dense ruby/purple–
90 colored 1999 reveals forward, open-knit notes of crème de cassis and earth. Fleshy, medium to full-bodied, and succulent, with supple tannin, excellent balance, as well as a long, pure, ripe finish, this seductive effort will drink well for 12–15 years, possibly longer. Last tasted, 8/02.

1998 Made somewhat in the style of the 1988, this austere, medium-weight Lynch-
89 Bages reveals notes of new saddle leather, tobacco, olives, and black fruits. Although not a big, concentrated Pauillac, it is graceful, elegant, with character and style. Anticipated maturity: now–2016. Last tasted, 8/02.

1997 The good news is that this tastes like Lynch-Bages, with jammy black currant fruit
86 intermixed with cedar wood, herbs, spice, and pepper. However, it is a lighter-styled yet friendly Lynch-Bages with creamy new oak, low acidity, and a medium-bodied, attractive albeit superficial appeal. Drink it over the next 3–4 years. Last tasted, 8/02.

1996 Lynch-Bages has turned out an outstanding 1996 that is less forward than the
91+ 1995 or 1990 and built along the lines of the tannic, blockbuster 1989. It offers an opaque purple color and outstanding aromatics consisting of dried herbs, tobacco, cassis, and smoky oak. Full-bodied and classic in its proportions, this dense, chewy, pure Lynch-Bages will have considerable longevity. Anticipated maturity: 2005–2025. Last tasted, 8/02.

1995 While most 1995 Médocs remain stubbornly closed, Lynch-Bages is attractive
90 and soft, yet reveals obvious tannin in the background. The 1995 is not made in the blockbuster style of the 1996, 1990, 1989, or 1986. Deep ruby–colored, with an evolved nose of sweet, smoky, earthy, black currant fruit, this fleshy, round, seductive, fat, and fruity Lynch-Bages should drink well young, yet age for 12+ years. Anticipated maturity: now–2015. Last tasted, 8/02.

1994 Deep ruby–colored with a purple center, this wine displays ripe black currant
88 fruit, with only a hint of vegetal and weedy notes. Medium bodied and ripe, with surprising softness, fatness, and precociousness for a wine from this vintage,

Lynch-Bages' 1994 possesses well-integrated toasty oak, as well as an attractive, hedonistic style that should please the followers of this corpulent Pauillac. It should drink well now and over the next 5–7 years. Last tasted, 8/02.

1990
95
A sumptuous, even flamboyant wine, the 1990 is a forward, flattering, and delicious to drink wine, in contrast to the more massive, backward, tannic 1989. Lynch-Bages' 1990 offers sweet, beefy, leathery, black currant aromas intermingled with smoky, toasty oak and roasted herbs. The wine offers a hedonistic turn-on of fruit, extract, and high levels of glycerin, all crammed into a full-bodied, supple-textured, rich, powerful, low-acid Lynch-Bages with no hard edges. Anticipated maturity: now–2020. Last tasted, 1/02.

1989
95
The opaque purple–colored 1989 is less evolved and showy than the 1990. However, it looks to be a phenomenal example of Lynch-Bages, perhaps the finest vintage in the last 30 years. Oozing with extract, this backward, muscular, dense wine possesses great purity, huge body, and a bulldozer-like power that charges across the palate. It is an enormous wine with unbridled quantities of power and richness. Anticipated maturity: 2005–2020. Last tasted, 1/02.

1988
90
Undoubtedly, the 1988 Lynch-Bages is among the biggest wines produced in the northern Médoc in this vintage. The saturated ruby/purple color suggests excellent ripeness and plenty of concentration. The oaky bouquet exhibits roasted black raspberries, currants, and licorice as well as an earthy, robust character. The wine is full-bodied, rich, with an attractive cedary, herbaceous, black fruit character. This fleshy, broad-shouldered wine characterizes the style of the château. Anticipated maturity: now–2010. Last tasted, 1/02.

1986
90
The 1986 is dark purple in color and extremely rich and tannic. But are the tannins too prominent and astringent? I doubt that anyone will be capable of answering that question for at least a decade. As for now, this wine is more admirable for its remarkable size and weight than for charm and enjoyability. Impressively built and approaching maturity, this is still a very youthful wine. Anticipated maturity: 2005–2020. Last tasted, 11/99.

1985
90
This has been a deliciously charming, seductive wine since its birth. Fully mature, this plum/garnet–colored wine offers a fragrant bouquet of sweet black currant fruit intermixed with smoky toasty oak and roasted herbs. Medium bodied (with far less girth, weight, and richness than the 1990, 1989, 1986, and 1982), the 1985 Lynch-Bages is a gorgeously fleshy, well-proportioned wine that should continue to drink well for another 4–5 years. Its low acidity, corpulent fleshiness, sweet tannin, and amber edge suggest full maturity. Anticipated maturity: now–2006. Last tasted, 12/01.

1983
86
A success for this very good, yet surprisingly inconsistent vintage, the Lynch-Bages 1983 is a full-blown, ripe, gutsy Pauillac, with an intense bouquet of ground beef and black currant fruit and deep, rich, briery flavors. Full-bodied, alcoholic, and long, this substantial wine has a heady, alcoholic finish with some rustic tannins beginning to dominate the finish. Anticipated maturity: now–2005. Last tasted, 11/01.

1982
94
The 1982 Lynch-Bages continues to develop well. Delicious since age 5–6, it remains a husky, forceful, grapy, exuberant wine with gobs of cassis fruit presented in an unctuously textured, thick, succulent style. The wine has not developed much complexity aromatically, but it is a weighty, textbook example of a wine from this popular estate. Stylistically, the 1990 is similar. Full-bodied, soft, and supple, it will continue to drink well for 10–12 more years. Last tasted, 8/02.

ANCIENT VINTAGES

Lynch-Bages had an undistinguished record during the 1970s and 1960s, save for the exceptional 1970 (93 points; last tasted 11/01), 1962 (90 points; last tasted 4/98), and 1961 (95 points; last tasted 2/00). A tasting in December 1995 revealed a relatively strong showing for the 1945 Lynch-Bages (92 points). This wine exhibited a minty, cassis-scented nose that did indeed seem reminiscent of the "poor man's Mouton Rothschild." A dense, opaque ruby/garnet color was followed by a full-bodied, powerful, but tough-textured, hard, astringently tannic wine that may lose its fruit before the tannin fully melts away. Although impressive for its overall size and intensity, this wine will never win any awards for grace and harmony. It will keep for another 15–20 years.

Lynch-Bages also enjoyed a glorious decade in the 1950s, producing superlative wines in 1959 (94 points), 1957 (88 points), 1955 (92 points), 1953 (90 points), and 1952 (91 points). Such consistent brilliance was not again evident until the succession of super performances that began in 1982.

LYNCH-MOUSSAS

Classification: Fifth Growth in 1855

Owner: Castéja family

Address: 33250 Pauillac

Mailing Address: Domaines Borie-Manoux, 86, cours Balguerie Stuttenberg, 33082 Bordeaux Cedex

Telephone: 05 56 00 00 70; Telefax: 05 57 87 48 61

E-mail: borie-manoux@dial.orleane.com

Visits: By appointment only Monday to Friday, 9 A.M.–noon and 2–5 P.M.

Contact: Domaines Borie-Manoux

VINEYARDS

Surface area: 143.3 acres

Grape varietals: 70% Cabernet Sauvignon, 30% Merlot

Average age of vines: 25 years

Density of plantation: 8,300 vines per hectare

Average yields: 55 hectoliters per hectare

Elevage: Twenty-one day fermentation and maceration in temperature-controlled stainless-steel tanks. Twelve to sixteen months aging with 60% new oak and 40% one-year-old barrels. Fining, no filtration.

WINES PRODUCED

Château Lynch-Moussas: 248,000 bottles

No second wine is produced.

Plateau of maturity: Within 4–10 years of the vintage

GENERAL APPRECIATION

Despite the fine location of its vineyards and some noticeable improvement in quality since 1994, this estate seems to be content producing so-so wines that compensate for their lack of substance and fat with noticeable tannins. This fifth growth is performing at a similar level to a Cru Bourgeois. Better wines are available within the same price range. Moreover, it is not advisable to keep Lynch-Moussas for too long, its fruit tending to fade before its tannins are fully melted.

Lynch-Moussas is owned and controlled by the Castéja family, who also operate the well-known Bordeaux *négociant* business Borie-Manoux. The wines of the firm of Borie-Manoux have demonstrated considerable improvement in vintages since the early 1980s, particularly their famous estates in Pauillac (Château Batailley), St.-Emilion (Château Trotte Vieille), and in Pomerol (Domaine de L'Eglise). However, this estate continued to turn out light, often diluted, simple wines that lacked character and stature. In 1994 a modest improvement in quality began.

IMPORTANT VINTAGES

2001   An evolved, pleasant but uninspiring wine, this medium dark ruby-colored effort
85–82   offers up notes of plums, cherries, damp earth, and hints of mushrooms and wood. Straightforward and medium-bodied, it is best drunk over the next decade. Last tasted, 1/03.

2000   Probably the best effort I have tasted from Lynch-Moussas . . . in my career! Deep
88   ruby/purple, with a sweet nose of *crème de cassis* intermixed with licorice, dried herbs, and vanilla, the wine is rich in fruit, has good glycerin, silky tannin, and a nice, spicy, layered finish. This will certainly have broad appeal, and it is good to see this property turn out something this interesting. Anticipated maturity: 2005–2015. Last tasted, 1/03.

1999   This light to medium ruby-colored, cassis-scented Pauillac exhibits medium
85   body, good balance, and sweet fruit. Drink this straightforward, picnic-styled Claret over the next 5–6 years. Last tasted, 3/02.

1998   One of the finest Lynch-Moussas yet produced (along with the 2000), the 1998 ex-
87   hibits a deep ruby/purple color in addition to a sweet nose of cassis (not dissimilar from its nearby neighbor, Grand-Puy-Lacoste), medium body, fine purity, and admirable harmony. Not a blockbuster, it will provide delicious drinking and last for 12 years. Last tasted, 3/02.

1996   A very good example of this underachieving estate, the 1996's saturated dark
86   ruby/plum color is accompanied by textbook aromas of black currants, smoky new oak, minerals, and tobacco. Well made with moderate tannin, excellent purity, and a medium-bodied, ripe, melted asphalt–flavored finish, this seductive Lynch-Moussas should drink well at a young age. Anticipated maturity: 2004–2012. Last tasted, 3/01.

1995   The 1995 Lynch-Moussas is a very good wine, with a dark ruby color, spicy,
86   cedary, cassis fruit in its moderately endowed nose, good ripeness and flesh on the attack, and a dry, clean, moderately tannic finish with grip and delineation. Anticipated maturity: now–2016. Last tasted, 11/97.

1994   A palatable effort, this deep ruby–colored wine exhibits a sweet bouquet with
82   scents of ripe red currant, cedar, herbs, and spice. Medium bodied, soft, and fruity, this is a cleanly made, straightforward Pauillac to drink over the next three years. Last tasted, 1/97.

MOUTON ROTHSCHILD

Classification: First Growth in 1973

Owner: GFA Baronne Philippine de Rothschild

Address: 33250 Pauillac

Mailing Address: BP 117, 33250 Pauillac

Telephone: 05 56 59 22 22; Telefax: 05 56 73 20 44

E-mail: webmaster@bpdr.com

Website: www.mouton-rothschild.com

Visits: By appointment only

Contact: Telephone: 05 56 73 21 29;
Telefax: 05 56 73 21 28

VINEYARDS

Surface area: 192.7 acres

Grape varietals: 77% Cabernet Sauvignon, 11% Merlot, 10% Cabernet Franc, 2% Petit Verdot

Average age of vines: 45 years

Density of plantation: 8,500 vines per hectare

Average yields: 40–50 hectoliters per hectare

Elevage: Fifteen to twenty-five day fermentation and maceration in wooden vats. Nineteen to twenty-two months aging in new oak barrels. Fining, no filtration.

WINES PRODUCED

Château Mouton Rothschild: 300,000 bottles

Le Petit Mouton de Mouton Rothschild: variable

Aile d'Argent (white Bordeaux): 18,000–24,000 bottles

Plateau of maturity: Within 12–15 years of the vintage

GENERAL APPRECIATION

This estate was once difficult to understand, producing superb wines as well as numerous disappointingly mediocre vintages, particularly for a first growth. However, it has performed more consistently since the mid-1990s, asserting itself with the rich, dense, and opulent style that characterizes the mythical Moutons such as 1982, 1959, 1947, and 1945. While quality and regularity are unquestionably better than in the past, the estate is not on par with its two peers of Pauillac—it has not improved as much as Lafite and still needs to catch up with Latour. While topflight, the wines of Mouton sometimes seem slightly out of balance because of their abundant tannins. Again, as with the other finest Bordeaux, prices have skyrocketed during recent vintages. Also, though very good, Mouton's second wine, Le Petit Mouton, is less consistent than Les Forts de Latour and Carruades de Lafite.

Mouton Rothschild is the place and wine that the late Baron Philippe de Rothschild singularly created. No doubt his aspirations for Mouton, beginning at the age of 21 when he acquired the estate, were high. However, through the production of an opulently rich and remarkably deep and exotic style of Pauillac, he has been the only person able to effectuate a change in the 1855 classification of the wines of the Médoc. The Baron died in January 1988, and his daughter, the equally charismatic Philippine, is now the spiritual head of this winemaking empire. She continues to receive extraordinary assistance from the talented Mouton team led by Patrick Léon and Hervé Berlaud.

In 1973, Mouton Rothschild was officially classified a "first-growth," which permitted the flamboyant baron to change his defiant wine labels from *"Premier ne puis, second ne daigne Mouton suis"* ("First I cannot be, second I will not call myself, Mouton I am") to *"Premier je suis, second je fus, Mouton ne change"* ("First I am, second I was, Mouton does not change").

There is no question that some of the greatest bottles of Bordeaux I have ever drunk have been Moutons. The 1996, 1995, 1986, 1982, 1959, 1955, 1953, 1947, 1945, and 1929 are stunning examples of Mouton at its best. However, I have also experienced too many mediocre vintages of Mouton that are embarrassing for a first growth to produce and obviously irritating for a consumer to purchase and taste. The 1990, 1980, 1979, 1978, 1977, 1976, 1974, 1973, 1967, and 1964, however, fell well below first-growth standards. Even the 1990 and 1989, two renowned vintages, produced wines that were surprisingly austere and lacking the concentration expected from a first-growth in a superb vintage.

The reasons for the commercial success of this wine are numerous. To begin with, the labels of Mouton are collector's items. Since 1945, the Baron Philippe de Rothschild has commissioned an artist to do an annual painting, which is depicted on the top of the label. There has been no shortage of masters to appear on the Mouton Rothschild labels, from such Europeans as Miro, Picasso, Chagall, and Cocteau, to the Americans Warhol, Motherwell, and, in 1982, John Huston. Second, the opulence of Mouton in the great vintages differs significantly in style from the austere elegance of Lafite Rothschild and the powerful, tannic, dense, and muscular Latour. Third, the impeccably kept château itself, with its superb wine museum, is the Médoc's (and possibly the entire Bordeaux region's) top tourist attraction. Last, there was the baron himself, who did so much to promote not only his wines, but all the wines of Bordeaux. His daughter, Philippine, appears more than capable of continuing her father's legacy.

IMPORTANT VINTAGES

2001 A blend of 86% Cabernet Sauvignon, 12% Merlot, and 2% Cabernet Franc pro-
91–93+ duced from small yields of 28 hectoliters per hectare, 66% of the production made it into the 2001 Mouton. The entire Cabernet Sauvignon crop was harvested October 8–10. While the 2001 does not possess the charm or finesse of the 1999, or the massive power and body of the virtually perfect 2000, it possesses forward,

evolved aromatics consisting of espresso, crème de cassis, Asian spice, licorice, and toasty oak. Low-acid and high tannin result in an austere finish. It will need to flesh out to justify a 93 or better score, but for now, it is dominated by its Cabernet Sauvignon. Additional fat should emerge as the wine evolves in the barrel. Anticipated maturity: 2010–2025. Last tasted, 1/03.

2000
97+
A behemoth, the gigantic 2000 Mouton Rothschild (86% Cabernet Sauvignon and 14% Merlot) boasts a saturated purple color as well as aromas of ink, cassis, licorice, damp earth, and sweet oak. It reveals a cassis-like flavor profile with a hint of truffles. Unquestionably the greatest Mouton since the 1986 and 1982, this majestic effort will undoubtedly close down, but enjoy an exceptionally long life. Anticipated maturity: 2012–2050+. Last tasted, 1/03.

2000
89
Le Petit Mouton: The 2000 Le Petit Mouton is somewhat monolithic, but reveals impressive concentration, power, depth, and fat. An atypical blend of 70% Cabernet Franc, 25% Cabernet Sauvignon, and 5% Merlot, it has 15 years of aging potential. Last tasted, 1/03.

1999
93
Mouton's 1999 (78% Cabernet Sauvignon, 18% Merlot, and 4% Cabernet Franc) represents 60% of the total production. The beautiful 1999 Mouton Rothschild may be a modern-day clone of their 1985 or 1962. Its saturated ruby/purple color is followed by sumptuous aromas of cedar wood, crème de cassis, wood smoke, coffee, and dried herbs. Forward, lush, and full-bodied, it is already complex as well as succulent, fleshy, and long. Tannin in the finish suggests more nuances will emerge in 1–2 years. It is a complex, classic Mouton. Anticipated maturity: 2005–2030. Last tasted, 3/02.

1999
88
Le Petit Mouton: Made in limited quantities (30,000 bottles), the 1999 Le Petit Mouton is a ripe, seductive, low-acid, plump effort. A blend of 90% Cabernet Sauvignon and 10% Cabernet Franc, this fleshy second wine offers notes of mocha, spice box, cassis, and oak. It will drink well for 10–12 years. Last tasted, 3/02.

1998
96
The 1998 Mouton has emerged as the greatest wine produced at this estate since the perfect 1986, of which the 1998 is somewhat reminiscent. Like many of its 1998 peers, it has filled out spectacularly. Now in the bottle, this opaque black/purple–colored offering has increased in stature, richness, and size. A blend of 86% Cabernet Sauvignon, 12% Merlot, and 2% Cabernet Franc (57% of the production was utilized), it is an extremely powerful, super-concentrated wine offering notes of roasted espresso, crème de cassis, smoke, new saddle leather, graphite, and licorice. It is massive in the mouth, with awesome concentration, mouth-searing tannin levels, and a saturated flavor profile that grips the mouth with considerable intensity. This is another 50-year Mouton, but patience will be required as it will not be close to drinkability for at least a decade. However, this wine rivals the 1995, 1990, and 1986! Anticipated maturity: 2012–2050. Last tasted, 8/02.

1998
88
Le Petit Mouton: The 1998 Le Petit Mouton, a blend of 61% Merlot, 25% Cabernet Sauvignon, and 14% Cabernet Franc, exhibits more of a Clerc Milon–like character than Mouton. It offers good color, medium to full body, plenty of smoky cassis and licorice, and a soft, expansive, drinkable style. Anticipated maturity: now–2012. Last tasted, 3/02.

1997
90
Only 55% of the harvest was utilized for the 1997 Mouton Rothschild. One of the most forward and developed Moutons over recent years, it possesses all the charm and fleshiness this vintage can provide. A blend of 82% Cabernet Sauvignon, 13% Merlot, 3% Cabernet Franc, and 2% Petit Verdot, the wine exhibits a dense ruby/purple color and an open-knit nose of cedar wood, blackberry liqueur, cassis, and coffee. Fleshy, ripe, and mouth-filling, with low acidity, soft tannin, and ad-

mirable concentration and length, this delicious Pauillac should age for 15+ years. It is an impressive effort for this vintage. Last tasted, 3/02.

1996 This estate's staff believes that the 1996 Mouton Rothschild is far more complex
94+   than the 1995, but less massive. I agree that among the first growths, this wine is showing surprising forwardness and complexity in its aromatics. It possesses an exuberant, flamboyant bouquet of roasted coffee, cassis, smoky oak, and soy sauce. The 1996 Mouton Rothschild offers impressive aromas of black currants, framboise, coffee, and new saddle leather. This full-bodied, ripe, rich, concentrated, superbly balanced wine is paradoxical in the sense that the aromatics suggest a far more evolved wine than the flavors reveal. Anticipated maturity: 2007–2030. Last tasted, 3/02.

1995 This profound Mouton is more accessible than the more muscular 1996. A blend
95+   of 72% Cabernet Sauvignon, 19% Merlot, and 9% Cabernet Franc, it reveals an opaque purple color and reluctant aromas of cassis, truffles, coffee, licorice, and spice. In the mouth, the wine is "great stuff," with superb density, a full-bodied personality, rich mid-palate, and a layered, profound finish that lasts for 40+ seconds. There is outstanding purity and high tannin, but my instincts suggest this wine is lower in acidity and slightly fleshier than the brawnier, bigger 1996. Anticipated maturity: 2010–2030. Last tasted, 11/97.

1994 The 1994 Mouton exhibits a dense, saturated purple color, followed by a classic
90   Mouton nose of sweet black fruits intermingled with smoke, toast, spice, and cedar. Medium to full-bodied, with outstanding concentration, a layered feel, plenty of tannin, and rich, concentrated fruit, this wine is similar to the fine 1988. Anticipated maturity: 2005–2025. Last tasted, 3/02.

1990 The 1990 is a hard, lean, austere, tannic style of Mouton that will never shed
87   enough tannin to attain complete harmony and balance. The wine exhibits a deep ruby color, subtle sweet oak, hints of ripe black currant fruit, and an attenuated, angular, tough style that is uncharacteristic of this château's winemaking or the character of the vintage. This wine needs another 10 years of cellaring, but don't expect a balanced Mouton when the tannin fades away—the wine lacks concentration. In the context of a great vintage, Mouton's 1990 is a disappointment, something the baroness agreed with when we shared it over dinner in Bordeaux. Anticipated maturity: 2006–2020. Last tasted, 8/02.

1989 The 1989 Mouton Rothschild is the superior wine, but in no sense is this a com-
90   pelling wine if compared with the Moutons produced in 2000, 1998, 1996, 1995, 1986, and 1982. The 1989 displays a dark ruby color that is already beginning to reveal pink and amber at the rim. The bouquet is surprisingly evolved, offering up scents of cedar, sweet black fruits, lead pencil, and high levels of toasty oak. An elegant, medium-bodied, restrained wine, it is beautifully made, stylish, and not dissimilar to the 1985, but ultimately lacking the profound depth one anticipates in the greatest vintages. It is an excellent to outstanding Mouton that is close to full maturity. It will drink well for 15–20 years. Anticipated maturity: 2005–2020. Last tasted, 3/01.

1988 One of the biggest Médocs of the vintage, the dense garnet/plum–colored 1988
92   Mouton has an attractive aroma of Asian spices, dried herbs, minerals, coffee, black currants, and sweet oak. Much like the 1989, the bouquet is alluring. The flavors continue to add bulk and the wine is better than I initially thought. In the mouth, it is a much firmer, tougher, more obviously tannic wine than the 1989, with full body and admirable ripeness. This is a muscular, large-scaled 1988 that will last another 15–20 years. I clearly underestimated this wine in its infancy. If the truth be known, it is superior to the more renowned vintages of 1990 and 1989! Anticipated maturity: 2008–2030. Last tasted, 3/02.

1987
89
This would appear to be a sure bet for the wine of the vintage. Certainly it is the most complete and backward 1987, with at least another 10 years of aging potential. The touching dedication from the late Baron Philippe de Rothschild's daughter on the label is nearly worth the price of one bottle. Additionally, 1987 was the last vintage of the Baron and thus will probably fetch a small fortune in 40–50 years. One of the deepest and most opaque wines of the vintage, with a tight yet promising bouquet of cedar and black currants, this wine exhibits surprising depth, medium to full body, and sweet tannin in the finish. A revelation for the vintage, the 1987 Mouton can stand toe-to-toe with more highly acclaimed years such as 1990 and 1989. Anticipated maturity: now–2015. Last tasted, 3/01.

1986
100
An enormously concentrated, massive Mouton Rothschild, comparable in quality, but not style, to the 1982, 1959, and 1945, this impeccably made wine is still in its infancy. Interestingly, in 1998 I had this wine served to me blind from a magnum that had been opened and decanted 48 hours previously. Even then, it still tasted like a barrel sample! I suspect the 1986 Mouton Rothschild requires a minimum of 15–20 more years of cellaring; it has the potential to last for 50–100 years! Given the outrageously high prices being fetched by recent vintages, it appears this wine might still be one of the "relative bargains" in the fine wine marketplace. I wonder how many readers will be in shape to drink it when it does finally reach full maturity? The telltale characteristics of this wine are pure Moutonian—crème de cassis in abundance, exhilarating purity, and awesome layers of finish. It still tastes like a wine of 5–6 years old! A tour de force! Anticipated maturity: 2008–2060. Last tasted, 8/02.

1985
90+
While the estate compares their 1985 to their 1959, it is more akin to their 1989, 1962, or 1953. The rich, complex, well-developed bouquet of Asian spices, toasty oak, herbs, and ripe fruit is wonderful. On the palate, the wine is also rich, forward, long, and sexy. It ranks behind both Haut-Brion and Château Margaux in 1985. Readers looking for a savory, boldly scented Mouton should search out other vintages, as this is a tame, forward, medium-weight, elegant wine that is fully mature. It is capable of lasting another 15+ years. Anticipated maturity: now–2015. Last tasted, 12/01.

1983
90
The classic Mouton lead-pencil, cedary nose has begun to emerge. Medium dark ruby, this elegant, medium-bodied wine will never be a legendary Mouton. The flavors are ripe and moderately rich. With good depth and some firm tannins to resolve, this offering from Mouton is bigger and richer than the 1981, 1979, or 1978. Austere by the standards of Mouton and the vintage, the 1983 resembles the château's fine 1966. Anticipated maturity: now–2015. Last tasted, 12/01.

1982
100
The saturated purple-colored Mouton Rothschild remains the most backward and unevolved wine of 1982. It flaunted a knockout, fabulously rich and ostentatious personality during its first 5–6 years after bottling. Since the late 1980s it has gradually closed down, and it is hard to estimate when this wine might reemerge. I routinely decant this wine 12–24 hours prior to service. The thick, unctuously textured, jammy fruit and enormous flavor concentration remain the hallmarks of the vintage, but the wine is extremely unevolved and behaves like a wine that is less than a decade old. This massive, powerful example of Mouton exhibits huge tannin and immense body. Significantly richer than the 1970 or 1961, it is not far-fetched to suggest that it is comparable to either the 1959 or 1945! Owners who do not want to commit infanticide should cellar it for another 5–10 years. Like Latour, the 1982 Mouton Rothschild is a potential 50–60-year wine, but far less accessible than the 1982 Latour. To those masochists who lack discipline, be sure to decant this wine at least 8–12 hours in advance. The wine will reveal its extraor-

dinary potential with approximately 30 hours of breathing in a closed decanter. A legend! Anticipated maturity: 2007–2065. Last tasted, 8/02.

1975   This wine has finally begun to reveal some potential after being closed and fright-
88   fully tannic for the last decade. The wine exhibits a good dark ruby/garnet color, a sweet nose of cedar, chocolate, cassis, and spices, good ripe fruit and extraction, and a weighty, large-scaled, tannic finish. Although still unevolved, it is beginning to throw off its cloak of tannin and exhibit more complexity and balance. I remain concerned about how well the fruit will hold, but this wine will undoubtedly hit its plateau around the turn of the century. Putting it in the context of what is a largely disappointing range of Mouton Rothschilds in the 1970s great bottles of the 1970 are superior to the 1975, but this is clearly the second-best Mouton of an uninspiring decade for this estate. Last tasted, 11/01.

1970   I have had a remarkable number of opportunities to taste this wine. One of the
90   most frustratingly irregular wines I have ever encountered, the 1970 Mouton can range from pure nectar to a wine that is angular, austere, and frightfully hard and tannic. This bottle (one of the Reserve du Château bottlings that was mistakenly released by the estate and labeled with the letters "R.C." rather than a number) was impossible to assess when decanted, owing to its hard, tough, impenetrable style. Nearly eight hours later the wine had opened magnificently to reveal a classic bouquet of sweet cassis, tobacco, minerals, and exotic spice aromas. Opulent, full-bodied, thick, and juicy, this particular wine would make a persuasive argument for long-term decanting given such an extraordinary evolution. After being perplexed throughout much of this wine's evolution, I was reassured by this bottle. No doubt Mouton's high Cabernet Sauvignon content causes this wine to go through a tight, hard, ungenerous stage. The 1970 has entered its plateau of maturity, but retains a level of rustic tannin common in many wines from this era. Last tasted, 8/02.

1961   I have found the 1961 Mouton Rothschild to be distressingly variable in quality,
98   much like the consistently inconsistent 1970. At its best the wine is a great Mouton. Huge cedary, cassis, lead pencil, menthol-like aromas soar from the glass. The dark purple color is just beginning to reveal some amber at the edge. Full-bodied, rich, and super-intense, this is a profound bottle of 1961 Mouton that is more evolved than the compelling 1959. Anticipated maturity: now–2020. Last tasted, 3/98.

ANCIENT VINTAGES

The 1960s and 1970s were not kind to Mouton Rothschild. Only 1975, 1970, 1966, 1962, and 1961 merit serious interest. On the other hand, the decade of the 1950s produced three legendary wines. The 1959 Mouton (100 points; last tasted 1/02) is one of the greatest Moutons ever made. Every time I have this wine it is undeniable that Mouton made a richer, more persuasive wine in 1959 than in 1961. Astonishingly young and unevolved, with a black/purple color, the wine exhibits a youthful nose of cassis, mint, minerals, and new oak. Exceptionally powerful and super-extracted with the fruit supported by high levels of tannin and some lusty quantities of alcohol, this mammoth, full-bodied Mouton Rothschild should continue to evolve for another 20–30 years. It may well be a 100-year wine and a preview of what the 1982 may taste like. The 1955 (97 points; last tasted 3/98) should be a vintage to buy at auction, as I suspect the price is more reasonable than what such acclaimed vintages as 1961 and 1959 fetch. The color reveals no amber or rust, only a slight lightening of intensity at the edge. The nose offers up that explosive Mouton perfume of mint, leather, cassis, black olives, and lead pencil. In the mouth, there is stunning concentration, magnificent extraction of fruit, and plenty of tannin in the long finish. The wine still tastes remarkably young and could easily last another 20–30 years. Amazing! I remember a friend of mine decanting a magnum of the 1953 (95 points; last tasted 3/99) and sticking it under my nose to share the incredible bouquet. In addition to the exotic aromas of soy sauce, new saddle leather, cassis, herbs, and spices, the 1953 offers a deep ruby color with some amber at the edge. Sweet and fat with voluptuously textured fruit, this low-acid wine has no noticeable tannin. While it may be living dangerously, it is a decadent treat if it is drunk immediately after decanting.

The 1949 (94 points; last tasted 10/94) was always considered to be the late baron's favorite vintage. While I find it a formidable Mouton, I have a preference for the 2000, 1998, 1996, 1995, 1986, 1982, 1959, 1947, and 1945. The bouquet offers copious amounts of sweet, ripe cassis fruit, herbs, spicy oak, and a touch of coffee and cinnamon. Medium bodied with moderate tannin still noticeable, this compact, dark garnet, opaquely colored wine possesses superb concentration and a remarkably long finish. It appears to be fully mature, yet the balance, length, and tannin level suggest this wine could last for another 20 years. A sleeper vintage is the 1948 (92 points; last tasted 3/00). Fully mature, aromatically profound, the 1948 is one of the great Médocs in the vintage.

I have never had anything but extraordinary, decadent, fabulously rich, concentrated bottles of the 1947 Mouton Rothschild (98 points; last tasted 3/98). The exotic, ostentatious bouquet of ginger, mint, coffee, cedar, and gobs of cassis fruit is followed by a syrupy, viscously textured, thick, juicy Mouton that is bursting with fruit. Although drinkable since I first tasted it more than a decade ago, it exhibits no signs of fruit loss or color deterioration. It is one of the most exotic and opulent Mouton Rothschilds I have ever tasted, but it needs to be consumed.

A consistent 100-point wine (only because my point scale stops at that number), the 1945 Mouton Rothschild (last tasted 8/97) is truly one of the immortal wines of the century. This wine is easily identifiable because of its remarkably exotic, overripe, sweet nose of black fruits, coffee, tobacco, mocha, and Asian spices. An extraordinarily dense, opulent, and rich wine, with layers of creamy fruit, it behaves more like a 1947 Pomerol than a structured, powerful, and tannic 1945. The wine finishes with more than a 60-second display of ripe fruit, extract, and sweet tannin. This remarkably youthful wine (only light amber at the edge) is mind-boggling! Will it last another 50 years?

I know of no great Moutons from the 1930s but the 1929 (rated 86 in April 1991) is still drinkable, though only a shadow of what it was. The 1928, 1926, and 1924, all tasted in April 1991, were fading badly. None of them merited a score above the mid-70s. The 1921 Mouton Rothschild (72 points) offered a ruby/garnet color and an old, musty nose with hints of cedar, ginger, and jammy fruit. In the mouth, the wine was acidic, sinewy, compact, and angular, with no charm, fat, or fruit. Moreover, there was excessive tannin in the finish. Interestingly, the minty side of Mouton was still noticeable in the wine's aromatics.

PIBRAN

Classification: Cru Bourgeois

Owner: Axa Millésimes

Address: 33250 Pauillac

Mailing Address: BP 46, 33250 Pauillac

Telephone: 05 56 73 17 17; Telefax: 05 56 73 17 28

No visits

Administrator: Christian Seely

VINEYARDS

Surface area: 42 acres

Grape varietals: 60% Cabernet Sauvignon, 30% Merlot, 5% Cabernet Franc, 5% Petit Verdot

Average age of vines: 30 years

Density of plantation: 9,000 vines per hectare

Average yields: 50 hectoliters per hectare

Elevage: Fifteen to seventeen day fermentation in temperature-controlled stainless-steel tanks. No malolactics in barrel. Twelve to fifteen months aging with 50% new oak and 50% one-year-old barrels. Fining and filtration.

WINES PRODUCED

Château Pibran: 54,000 bottles

Château Tour Pibran: 65,000 bottles

Plateau of maturity: Within 4–12 years of the vintage

GENERAL APPRECIATION

The wines of Pibran are worth their Cru Bourgeois status. Prices remain reasonable.

Pibran, which is usually well colored, is aged in oak casks and has a dense, concentrated, moderately tannic style. If it lacks complexity and finesse, it more than compensates for that with its power and muscular personality. Given its moderate price, it provides one with a good introduction to the wines of Pauillac. Since Jean-Michel Cazes and his wine-maker, Daniel Llose, took over responsibility for the making of Pibran, the wine has become more noticeably fruity, plump, and tasty.

IMPORTANT VINTAGES

2000
87   Readers looking for a generous, full-flavored, uncomplicated, supple-textured, reasonably priced 2000 Pauillac should check out this wine. A deep ruby/purple color is accompanied by copious quantities of black currant fruit, low acidity, and some viscosity. This is a hedonistic, full-throttle Pauillac that should drink well for 10–12 years. If it develops more complexity, it will merit an even higher score. Anticipated maturity: 2005–2017. Last tasted, 1/03.

1999   The 1999 Pibran exhibits a dense ruby color in addition to a classic Pauillac nose
86   of cedarwood, black currants, underbrush, and new oak. A dense, plush, forward, precocious offering, it is meant to be drunk upon release, and it should age nicely for a decade or more. Anticipated maturity: now–2015. Last tasted, 3/02.

1998   A fine effort from Pibran, the 1998 exhibits austere tannin as well as copious
87   quantities of ripe cassis fruit, a straightforward, medium- to full-bodied style, plenty of spice, and a user-friendly personality. Anticipated maturity: now–2015. Last tasted, 3/02.

1996   The 1996 Pibran has turned out to be a sleeper of the vintage. A big, muscular
89   wine, it boasts a saturated purple color and sweet cassis fruit intermeshed with cedar and spice. In the mouth, it is medium to full-bodied with ripe, well-integrated tannin, adequate acidity, and a long, well-delineated finish. It is a blend of 70% Cabernet Sauvignon and the balance mostly Merlot with a small dollop of Cabernet Franc. This large-scale Pauillac should drink well from 2004–2016. Last tasted, 3/00.

PICHON-LONGUEVILLE BARON

Classification: Second Growth in 1855

Owner: Axa Millésimes

Address: Saint-Lambert, 33250 Pauillac

Mailing Address: BP 112, 33250 Pauillac

Telephone: 05 56 73 17 17; Telefax: 05 56 73 17 28

E-mail: infochato@pichonlongueville.com

Website: www.chateaupichonlongueville.com

Visits: By appointment only

Contact: Céline Nicomme

Administrator: Christian Seely

VINEYARDS

Surface area: 180.3 acres

Grape varietals: 60% Cabernet Sauvignon, 35% Merlot, 4% Cabernet Franc, 1% Petit Verdot

Average age of vines: 30 years

Density of plantation: 9,000 vines per hectare

Average yields: 45 hectoliters per hectare

Elevage: Fifteen to seventeen day fermentation and maceration in temperature-controlled stainless-steel tanks. Part of the yield undergoes malolactics in barrel. Fifteen to eighteen months aging with 70% new oak and 30% one-year-old barrels. Fining, no filtration.

WINES PRODUCED

Château Pichon-Longueville Baron: 240,000 bottles

Les Tourelles de Longueville: 180,000 bottles

Plateau of maturity: Within 8–25 years of the vintage

GENERAL APPRECIATION

After a slump in the 1950s and 1960s, Pichon-Longueville Baron has rebounded marvelously and has consistently produced topflight wines, especially from 1986 onward. Though its present quality level will not allow it to be upgraded to first-growth status, this estate is often referred to as a "super-second," performing above its official pedigree. Considering the difference in pricing with the first growths, Pichon-Longueville Baron represents a good buy among the top Bordeaux classified growths.

This noble-looking château opposite Pichon Longueville Comtesse de Lalande and Latour, which made a modest comeback in wine quality in the early 1980s, was sold in the late 1980s by its owners—the Bouteiller family—to the insurance conglomerate known as AXA. To the company's credit, they hired Jean-Michel Cazes of Château Lynch-Bages to oversee the vineyard and winemaking. The Cazes touch, which included later picking dates, a stricter selection, the introduction of a second wine, and the utilization of a higher percentage of new oak casks, made for a dramatic turnaround in quality. As a consequence, Pichon-Longueville Baron frequently called Pichon-Baron, now merits its prestigious second-growth status. With Cazes taking a well-deserved retirement in 2000, highly respected Christian Seely is now the administrator.

The vineyard is superbly situated on gravelly soil with a full southerly exposure. Much of the vineyard is adjacent to that of Château Latour. It has been speculated that the lack of brilliance in many of Pichon-Baron's wines in the 1960s and 1970s was a result of both casual viticultural practices and poor cellar management. I remember passing by the cellars on a torridly hot afternoon in July, only to see the newly bottled vintage stacked up outside the cellars, roasting in the relentless sunshine. Such recklessness has no doubt stopped.

Rhetoric and public relations efforts aside, the best evidence that Pauillac once again has two great Pichons are the wines that have been produced at Pichon-Baron since 1986. This château has proven to be one of the great superstars of the 1990s. This is routinely one of the Médoc's most majestic wines.

IMPORTANT VINTAGES

2001   Medium to full-bodied, with notes of tobacco intermixed with espresso roast,
89–91 chocolate, black cherry, and cassis fruit, this medium to full-bodied wine shows excellent density, good concentration, and a relatively soft finish. It is hardly a profound Pichon Baron, but it looks to have the potential to turn out to be outstanding. Anticipated maturity: 2006–2016. Last tasted, 1/03.

2000   A spectacular effort, this is a profound Pichon Baron and clearly my favorite vin-
96   tage of this wine since the 1989 and 1990. An inky purple color offers up notes of barbecue spices intermixed with new saddle leather, *crème de cassis*, melted licorice, creosote, and a hint of vanilla. The wine is full-bodied, tremendously concentrated, with sweet tannin and a seamless finish that goes on for close to one minute. This wine has great purity, tremendous texture, and fabulous upside potential. This is a prodigious 2000! Anticipated maturity: 2008–2028. Last tasted, 1/03.

1999
89
The dark ruby/purple–colored Pichon-Longueville Baron reveals aromas of charcoal, black currants, and sweet toasty oak. This low-acid, medium-bodied, charming, lush 1999 possesses good stuffing, ripe tannin, and a moderately long finish. Enjoy it now as well as over the next 10–12 years. Last tasted, 3/02.

1998
90
A definitive Pauillac, the dense purple–colored 1998 Pichon-Baron offers up a sweet bouquet of licorice, smoke, asphalt, blackberries, and crème de cassis. In the mouth, the wine is elegant rather than full-blown, with medium body, sweet fruit, nice texture on the attack and mid-palate, and moderate tannin in the long finish. No, this is not as profound as the 1996, 1990, or 1989, but it is an outstanding effort. Anticipated maturity: 2006–2020. Last tasted, 3/02.

1997
86
Complex, evolved, mature cedar, spice box, and black currant aromas emerge from this ruby/garnet–colored offering. Soft, with sweet tannin, spicy oak, and ripe fruit, but no significant depth, this is an open-knit, attractive Pauillac to enjoy now and over the next 3–4 years. Last tasted, 3/02.

1996
91
Pichon-Longueville Baron's 1996's high percentage of Cabernet Sauvignon (about 80%) has resulted in a wine that has put on weight. An opaque purple color is accompanied by beautiful aromas of tobacco, new saddle leather, roasted coffee, and cassis. It is dense, medium to full-bodied, and backward, with moderately high tannin, but plenty of sweet fruit, glycerin, and extract to balance out the wine's structure. This well-endowed, classic Pauillac should be at its finest from 2007–2028. Last tasted, 3/01.

1995
90
A stylish, elegant, more restrained style of Pichon-Baron with less obvious new oak than usual, this deep ruby/purple–colored wine offers a pure black currant–scented nose with subtle aromas of coffee and smoky toasty oak. In the mouth, the wine displays less weight and muscle than the 1996, but it offers suave, elegant, rich fruit presented in a medium- to full-bodied, surprisingly lush style. Anticipated maturity: now–2016. Last tasted, 3/01.

1994
88
Dark ruby/purple colored, with a crushed, pure cassis aroma, this excellent, medium-bodied wine reveals sweet fruit on the attack and plenty of tannin, but not the inner core of richness and density exhibited by such other 1994 Pauillacs as Pichon-Lalande and Pontet-Canet. To its credit, the 1994 Pichon-Baron does not reveal any vegetal notes. It should evolve nicely over the next 10 years, representing an attractive, well-made, medium-bodied, classically rendered Bordeaux. Anticipated maturity: now–2014. Last tasted, 3/00.

1990
96
A fabulous effort, the dense purple–colored 1990 Pichon-Longueville Baron exhibits the roasted overripeness of this vintage, but it manages to keep everything in perspective. The wine is opulent and flamboyant, with lower acidity and noticeably less tannin than the 1989. It is equally concentrated, with a more evolved nose of cedar, black fruits, earth, minerals, and spices. On the palate, the wine offers sensational quantities of jammy fruit, glycerin, wood, and sweet tannin. It is far more fun to taste and drink (more hedonistic) than the more structured, backward, yet exceptional 1989. Ideally, readers should have both vintages in their cellars. The 1990 can be drunk now as well as over the next 25+ years. Last tasted, 8/02.

1989
95+
Evolving at a glacial pace, the 1989 Pichon-Longueville Baron exhibits an opaque, dense purple color that suggests a massive wine of considerable extraction and richness. The dense, full-bodied 1989 is brilliantly made, with huge, smoky, chocolaty, cassis aromas intermingled with scents of toasty oak. Well layered with a sweet inner core of fruit, this awesomely endowed, backward, tannic, prodigious 1989 needs additional cellaring; it should last for three decades or more. It is unquestionably a great Pichon-Longueville Baron. Anticipated maturity: 2006–2030. Last tasted, 4/02.

1988 The 1988 Pichon-Longueville Baron is one of the most successful wines of this
90   vintage. Surprisingly large-scale for a 1988, with a bouquet of oak, cassis, and
      licorice, it is deep in color (some pink and amber are emerging), rich, softly tannic,
      as well as medium to full-bodied. It has thrown off its cloak of tannin and inched
      into full maturity. Anticipated maturity: now–2010. Last tasted, 4/02.

1986 Deep opaque ruby in color, with a fragrant, expansive bouquet of oak, cedar,
89   tobacco, and black currants, this brawny, full-bodied, rich wine still possesses
      plenty of tannin, yet its pleasing suppleness suggests it has attained its apogee.
      Anticipated maturity: now–2010. Last tasted, 4/02.

1985 The 1985 Pichon-Longueville Baron is fruity and agreeable, but diffuse, slightly
83   flabby, and unstructured. It is a tasty but essentially one-dimensional wine. Antic-
      ipated maturity: now. Last tasted, 10/90.

1983 The 1983 is certainly a better-structured wine than the 1982, but as it has aged, it
85   has, curiously, become less interesting. Dark ruby, with a spicy, cassis-and-herb-
      scented bouquet, this medium-bodied wine still has plenty of tannin but appears
      to be maturing rapidly. Anticipated maturity: now–2005. Last tasted, 3/89.

1982 I certainly bungled the early reviews of this wine! In barrel and early in bottle, it
92   was a big, ripe, fruit bowl of a wine with virtually no acidity or structure in evi-
      dence. However, it is safe to say the one component Bordeaux never lacks, even in
      the ripest, fattest vintages, is tannin. As this wine has evolved it has become much
      more delineated as well as classically proportioned. In fact, it is an exceptional ex-
      ample of Pichon-Longueville Baron produced during a period when this estate
      was best known for the mediocrity of its wines. Fully mature, the 1982 reveals a
      dense, opaque ruby/purple/garnet color, and a huge nose of cedar, sweet cassis,
      and spice. The wine's full body, marvelous concentration, a 1982-like opulence
      and unctuosity, and a thick, jammy, moderately sweet finish, all combine to offer a
      splendid drinking experience. Given its ripe, creamy personality, this wine should
      be drunk over the next 10–15 years. Last tasted, 8/02.

ANCIENT VINTAGES

Between 1961 and 1981, finding a topflight wine was impossible. The finest old vintages of Pichon-Longueville Baron I have tasted included the 1959 (better as well as
less evolved than the 1961, and a wine I have rated between 87 and 90), a fine, dense
1955 (rated 87), and a robust, fragrant, fully mature 1953 (rated 89). I have only tasted
the following vintages once, but I was disappointed with the 1949, 1947, and 1945.

PICHON LONGUEVILLE COMTESSE DE LALANDE

Classification: Second Growth in 1855

Owner: May-Eliane de Lencquesaing

Address: 33250 Pauillac

Telephone: 05 56 59 19 40; Telefax: 05 56 59 26 56

E-mail: pichon@pichon-lalande.com

Website: www.pichon-lalande.com

Visits: By appointment only

Contact: accueil@pichon-lalande.com and above
telephone and fax numbers

VINEYARDS

Surface area: 185.3 acres

Grape varietals: 45% Cabernet Sauvignon, 35% Merlot, 12% Cabernet Franc, 8% Petit Verdot

Average age of vines: 30 years

Density of plantation: 9,000 vines per hectare

Average yields: 45 hectoliters per hectare

Elevage: Eighteen to twenty-four day fermentation and maceration in temperature-controlled stainless-steel tanks. Eighteen to twenty months aging in barrels that are renewed by half every year. Racking every three months. Fining. No filtration.

WINES PRODUCED

Château Pichon Longueville Comtesse de Lalande: 180,000 bottles

Réserve de la Comtesse: 160,000 bottles

Plateau of maturity: Within 5–25 years of the vintage

GENERAL APPRECIATION

Under the inspired leadership of the talented May-Eliane de Lencquesaing, this estate has greatly improved as from the beginning of the 1980s, so much so that its wines are now consistently excellent and in some vintages of first-growth quality. Since they are priced well below the latter, they unquestionably represent good values. Moreover, Pichon-Lalande is generally long-lived and remarkably consistent, irrespective of vintage conditions.

At present, Pichon Longueville Comtesse de Lalande (Pichon-Lalande) is unquestionably the most popular and, since 1978, one of Pauillac's most consistently brilliant wines. It can rival the three famous first growths of this commune. The wines of Pichon-Lalande have been very successful since 1961, but there is no question that in the late 1970s and early 1980s, under the energetic helm of Madame de Lencquesaing (who is affectionately called *La Générale* by her peers), the quality rose dramatically.

The wine is made in an intelligent manner and is darkly colored, supple, fruity, and smooth enough to be drunk young. It has the distinction, along with Château Palmer in Margaux, of being one of the most famous Médoc estates that utilizes a significant quantity of Merlot in the blend. Yet Pichon-Lalande has the requisite tannin, depth, and richness to age gracefully for 10–20 years. The high proportion of Merlot (35%) no doubt accounts for part of the wine's soft, fleshy characteristic.

The property was once part of a single estate called Pichon-Longueville, which was divided in 1850. Madame de Lencquesaing's father, Édouard Miailhe, purchased it in 1924, but it is his daughter who has been responsible for the current fame. Significant investments were made during the 1980s. A new *cuvier* was built in 1980 and a new barrel-aging cellar and tasting room (with a spectacular vista of neighboring Château Latour) in 1988; in 1990, the renovations of the château were completed. A fine museum now sits atop the barrel room. Madame Lencquesaing resides at the château, which sits across the road from Pichon-Longueville Baron. Its vineyards lay both in

Pauillac and St.-Julien, the latter characteristic often given as the reason for Pichon-Lalande's supple style.

IMPORTANT VINTAGES

2001
89–91+ Proprietor Madame de Lencquesaing is justifiably proud of her 2001 Pichon-Lalande. Only 37% of the production made it into the grand vin (a blend of 50% Cabernet Sauvignon, 36% Merlot, and a whopping 14% Petit Verdot—a historic high for this varietal). Yields were 45 hectoliters per hectare. The normally late to mature Petit Verdot was actually harvested before the Cabernet Sauvignon, which was picked between October 3–14. The dense purple/blue/black-colored Pichon-Lalande exhibits a spicy perfume offering scents of cedar, incense, earth, black currant, and berry fruit. Firm, pure, and surprisingly more Pauillac in style than usual (many Pichon-Lalandes reveal a silky, St.-Julien-like character), the 2001 does not have the power, volume, or size of the 2000. A strong effort for the vintage, it possesses high acidity as well as more noticeable tannin. Anticipated maturity: 2007–2018. Last tasted, 1/03.

2000
97 A dramatic effort, the 2000 is a blend of 50% Cabernet Sauvignon, 34% Merlot, 6% Cabernet Franc, and a whopping 10% Petit Verdot. Only 40% of the harvest made it into the grand vin. Its dense purple color is followed by fabulous aromas of crème de cassis intermixed with roasted espresso, violets, and toast. It has a superb entry on the palate, full body, an opulent texture, silky tannin, and a finish that lasts for nearly a minute. This stunning wine will provide unreal drinking early on, but age for three decades. Bravo! Anticipated maturity: 2005–2025. Last tasted, 1/03.

1999
87 The 1999 Pichon-Lalande performed inconsistently, showing better at the château than at several competitive tastings. A blend of 47% Merlot, 37% Cabernet Sauvignon, 9% Cabernet Franc, and 7% Petit Verdot, it offers a complex, evolved bouquet of cedar, underbrush, red currants, and spice box. The dark ruby color is not as saturated as many 1999s, and the wine possesses the weight and style of the 1981 and 1979 (both of which are superior to the 1999). There is medium body, excellent ripeness, and an angular finish, without the persistence typically found at this château. Anticipated maturity: now–2012. Last tasted, 3/02.

1998
87 Aromas of tobacco smoke, cedar, cherries, and black currants emerge from the moderately intense, complex bouquet. This wine has evolved nicely, revealing less austerity as it has evolved in bottle. Nevertheless, this is a medium-weight, delicate wine lacking the dimensions of aroma and flavor found in the top years. Drink it over the next 12 years. Last tasted, 3/02.

1997
89 One of the vintage's stars in the Médoc, this hedonistic, luscious, sexy, opulently textured Pichon-Lalande is a blend of 55% Cabernet Sauvignon, 30% Merlot, 10% Petit Verdot, and 5% Cabernet Franc. Exhibiting a dark ruby color with purple nuances, it is open-knit with plentiful quantities of roasted herbs, smoky oak, vanilla, and creamy black currant fruit. A lush texture, low acidity, and an accessible, velvety-textured style will have many admirers. Consume it over the next 5–6 years. Last tasted, 3/02.

1996
96 The 1996 Pichon-Lalande is awesome. For Pichon-Lalande, the percentage of Cabernet Sauvignon utilized in the final blend is atypically high. This wine normally contains 35–50% Merlot in the blend, but the 1996 is a blend of 75% Cabernet Sauvignon, 15% Merlot, 5% Cabernet Franc, and 5% Petit Verdot. Only 50% of the estate's production made it into the grand vin. The color is a saturated ruby/purple. The nose suggests sweet, nearly overripe Cabernet Sauvignon, with its blueberry/blackberry/cassis scents intermixed with high quality, subtle, toasty

new oak. Deep and full-bodied, with fabulous concentration and a sweet, opulent texture, this wine was singing in full harmony when I tasted it in January. Given the wine's abnormally high percentage of Cabernet Sauvignon, I would suspect it will close down. It possesses plenty of tannin, but the wine's overwhelming fruit richness dominates its personality. Could the 1996 turn out to be as extraordinary as the 1982? Anticipated maturity: 2007–2025. Last tasted, 8/02.

1995 The 1995 is an exquisite example of Pichon-Lalande with the Merlot component
95 giving the wine a coffee/chocolaty/cherry component to go along with the Cabernet Sauvignon's and Cabernet Franc's complex blackberry/cassis fruit. The wine possesses an opaque black/ruby/purple color, and sexy, flamboyant aromatics of toast, black fruits, and cedar. Exquisite on the palate, this full-bodied, layered, multidimensional wine should prove to be one of the vintage's most extraordinary success stories. Anticipated maturity: now–2020. Last tasted, 8/02.

1994 One of the stars of the vintage, this opaque purple-colored wine possesses a gor-
91 geously perfumed, exotic, smoky, black currant, Asian spice, and sweet vanilla bouquet. It is followed by thick, rich, moderately tannic flavors that exhibit medium to full body, good structure, outstanding purity, and a classically layered, long, pure finish. This terrific Pichon-Lalande should evolve effortlessly for 15–18 years. Anticipated maturity: now–2020. Last tasted, 9/02.

1990 I have been consistently disappointed by my tastings of the 1990 Pichon-Lalande.
79 The wine is unmistakably vegetal, austere, and lacking the seductive, sweet, ripe fruit this estate produces in top years. Something clearly went awry for Pichon-Lalande to miss so badly in an exceptional vintage. In this tasting, the wine tasted lean, diluted, intensely herbaceous, and lacking sweetness, depth, ripeness, and charm. Apologists who have badly overrated this wine will no doubt insist that its owners give it additional cellaring, but aging will only exaggerate this wine's lack of balance. Like its northern neighbor in Pauillac, Mouton Rothschild, this wine is a major disappointment. Last tasted, 3/02.

1989 Approaching full maturity, Pichon-Lalande's 1989 has a deep ruby/plum color
93 with some lightening at the edge. The nose offers sweet plums and crème de cassis intermixed with vanilla and graphite. The wine is lush, medium to full-bodied, and layered with texture, low acidity, sweet tannin, and the hallmark purity and elegance this estate routinely produces. Some tannins remain, but this wine has reached its plateau of maturity, where it should remain for another 10–15 years. Anticipated maturity: now–2017. Last tasted, 5/02.

1988 Somewhat austere but very successful for the vintage, Pichon-Lalande's 1988 has
90 a dark garnet color and an intriguing nose of compost, earth, black currants, licorice, and weedy tobacco. The wine is medium bodied with a sweet, relatively expansive mid-palate and slightly rugged tannins in the increasingly attenuated finish. This wine has reached full maturity and should be drunk over the next 5–10 years. Anticipated maturity: now–2008. Last tasted, 5/02.

1986 Just now emerging from a very clumsy dormant period, Pichon-Lalande's dense
94 ruby/purple–colored 1986 still has the color of a 4–5-year-old wine. This is the most tannic and backward Pichon-Lalande after 1975 and before 1996. The wine was completely closed down until just recently. The wine shows notes of cedar, black currants, earth, spice box, and licorice, followed by a medium- to full-bodied, very concentrated, intense palate with a still noticeable tannic structure, a relatively big, muscular style for Pichon-Lalande. Anticipated maturity: now–2015. Last tasted, 5/02.

1985 Fully mature, this wine shows some pink at the edge, a sweet nose of herb-tinged
90 cherries and black currants intermixed with dusty notes and new oak. The wine is medium bodied, elegant, very flattering, and perfumed. It does not have the

weight, depth, or dimensions of the top vintages, but it is quite seductive. Anticipated maturity: now–2005. Last tasted, 5/02.

1983

90

This wine seems to be just beginning to turn the corner and was excellent in its most recent tasting. For much of its life it has been a stunning wine, not far off the mark from the prodigious 1982. The color is still a healthy dark garnet with some amber creeping in at the edge. The wine shows a very distinctive nose of asphalt, tobacco, and cigar box, intermixed with some sweet cherries and black currants. In the mouth it is medium to full-bodied, but the fruit seems to be ever-so-slightly fading. In the finish, the tannins and acidity are beginning to poke through. Nevertheless, this is still underrated and always a sleeper vintage for Pichon-Lalande, but it requires consumption. Anticipated maturity: now. Last tasted, 9/02.

1982

100

Tasted at least a half dozen times in 2002, I keep waiting for this wine to fall off. It has been prodigious from its early days, and in bottle continues to be one of the most satisfying wines of this great vintage, both intellectually and hedonistically. The color is still a dense, dark garnet/plum/purple. The nose offers spectacularly sweet crème de cassis intermixed with plums, cherries, vanilla, and smoke. The wine is full bodied, opulently textured, very plush, with a viscous texture and extravagant quantities of fruit, glycerin, and alcohol. It has always been incredibly low in acidity, very decadent, and about as hedonistic as a Pichon-Lalande—or any Bordeaux, for that matter—can be. It has surprised me with its longevity and should still continue to show no amber at its rim nor any evidence of breaking up. However, I wouldn't push my luck, as this wine is already 20 years old. Anticipated maturity: now–2012. Last tasted, 4/03.

ANCIENT VINTAGES

Pichon-Lalande produced a very fine 1981 (89 points; last tasted 5/02) and top-notch efforts that are now both fully mature in 1979 and 1978 (both 90 points; last tasted 5/02). All three need to be drunk over the next 3–4 years. The 1975 can be very good, but can also be attenuated, tough, and tannic. 1971, 1970, 1966, and 1961 were once very impressive vintages but are now in decline. Among the very ancient vintages, I have not seen any of these wines since the last edition of the book was printed. However, pristinely stored, large-format bottles (magnums or bigger) of 1953 and 1952 could be special. As I have indicated in the past, the 1959, 1955, 1949, 1947, and 1945 have never impressed me.

PONTET-CANET ————————————————

Classification: Fifth Growth in 1855

Owner: Tesseron family

Address: 33250 Pauillac

Telephone: 05 56 59 04 04; Telefax: 05 56 59 26 63

E-mail: pontet@pontet-canet.com *or*
pontet-canet@wanadoo.fr

Website: www.pontet-canet.com

Visits: By appointment only

Contact: Alfred Tesseron

VINEYARDS

Surface area: 195 acres

Grape varietals: 60% Cabernet Sauvignon, 33% Merlot, 5% Cabernet Franc, 2% Petit Verdot

Average age of vines: 30 years

Density of plantation: 8,500 vines per hectare

Average yields: 50 hectoliters per hectare

Elevage: Three to four week fermentation and maceration boosted with natural yeasts in wooden (50%), concrete (40%), and stainless steel (10%) tanks. Sixteen months aging in barrels with 60% new oak. Light fining and filtration.

WINES PRODUCED

Château Pontet-Canet: 250,000 bottles

Les Hauts de Pontet: 230,000 bottles

Plateau of maturity: Within 8–30 years of the vintage

GENERAL APPRECIATION

Soundly made but lacking in charm and interest until the mid-1980s, the wines of Pontet-Canet have noticeably improved since the mid-1990s. While the trend of the pricing has followed the quality curve over recent vintages, Pontet-Canet still represents a good quality/price ratio.

With the largest production of any classified-growth wine of the Médoc and with the enviable vineyard position of directly across from Mouton Rothschild, one would expect the quality and stature of the wines of Pontet-Canet to be exceptionally high. Yet take a close look at the track record of Pontet-Canet over the period of 1962–1985. While the wines were sound and competent, they have lacked that special ingredient called excitement. Since 1994, a renewed vigor and commitment, as evidenced by the ownership, has commenced. A totally new vinification cellar was constructed, a secondary label for weaker vats was launched, and a higher percentage of new oak was inaugurated. Mechanical harvesting has been discontinued.

Until 1975, the ubiquitous Cruse firm owned Pontet-Canet and tended to treat the wines as a brand name to be used for promotional purposes, rather than as a distinctive, individual, estate-bottled wine from Pauillac. The wine was not château-bottled until 1972, and for years batches of the wine were sold to the French railways without a vintage date, yet always marketed as Pontet-Canet. In 1975, the Cruse firm was forced to sell Pontet-Canet as a result of a trial that had found the firm negligent in blending and labeling practices. Guy Tesseron, a well-known Cognac merchant, purchased Pontet-Canet and has delegated responsibility for the management of this estate to his son, Alfred. I believe everyone in Bordeaux agrees that Pontet-Canet possesses a vineyard with enormous potential, provided it is carefully managed and exploited. Alfred Tesseron has responded to the challenge, investing heavily in the vineyards and cellars in addition to implementing a very strict selection process. Since 1994, Pontet-Canet has been one of the emerging stars of the Médoc.

IMPORTANT VINTAGES

2001
88–89+ Less evolved than usual at the time of my tasting (many estates had slow malolactics in 2001), Pontet-Canet's 2001 reveals hard, angular characteristics along with sweet cassis fruit, medium body, and excellent purity. At present, it is austere and lacking the fat and texture obvious in Pontet-Canet's superb 2000. It should flesh out with additional barrel aging, but I do not expect it to achieve the heights of the 2000, 1996, 1995, or 1994. Time will tell. Anticipated maturity: 2008–2020. Last tasted, 1/03.

2000
92+ A stunning offering that rivals the 1996 and 1995, the 2000 may turn out to be a modern-day clone of the 1961. An opaque purple color is accompanied by an impressive aromatic display of pure crème de cassis, high-quality oak, sweet earth, and smoke. It is a steely, extremely long classic with noticeable tannin as well as fine concentration and power, and a 45-second finish. This broodingly backward, hulking Pontet-Canet will require patience. Anticipated maturity: 2010–2030+. Last tasted, 1/03.

1999
88+ Licorice, crème de cassis, and toasty oak are typical of this classic Pauillac. Full bodied, with excellent sweetness, grip, structure, and more tannin than many 1999s possess, this structured, muscular effort will require patience. Anticipated maturity: 2005–2016. Last tasted, 3/02.

1998
86 A pleasant, dark ruby–colored, elegant Pauillac, the 1998 displays hollowness on the mid-palate along with notes of red and black currants, tobacco, dried herbs, and earth. Although solidly made, there is not much depth. Anticipated maturity: 2004–2012. Last tasted, 3/02.

1997
85? This wine, which had performed well from cask (particularly for the vintage), was severe, tannic, gritty, and attenuated on two of the three occasions I had it from bottle. I have lowered the score and added a question mark because the wine lacks the color saturation of the barrel samples, exhibits more herbaceousness, and the tannin is astringent. Perhaps it is going through an awkward stage of development, but right now I am less enthusiastic. Anticipated maturity: now–2010. Last tasted, 3/01.

1996
92+ I remain shocked by how backward the 1996 Pontet-Canet has tasted. This wine possesses superb potential, but it appears 7–8 years' worth of patience will be necessary. The color is a saturated dark purple. With coaxing, the wine offers aromas of black currant jam intertwined with minerals, sweet oak, and spice. A full-bodied wine, it possesses layered, concentrated, sweet fruit, with an elevated level of ripe tannin. Anticipated maturity: 2010–2035. Last tasted, 3/02.

1995
92 An old-style Pauillac, yet made with far more purity and richness than the estate's ancient vintages, this broad-shouldered, muscular, classic wine exhibits a saturated purple color and sensationally dense, rich, concentrated, cassis flavors that roll over the palate with impressive purity and depth. The wine is tannic and closed, but powerful and rich. It appears to possess length and intensity similar to the 1996. This is a great Pauillac. Anticipated maturity: 2005–2025. Last tasted, 3/02.

1994
91+ One of the finest as well as longest-lived wines of the vintage, this opaque purple-colored 1994 needs 2–3 more years of cellaring. A rich, impressive, full-bodied wine, it represents the finest Pontet-Canet produced since the 1961. Obviously, recent vintages such as 2000, 1996, and 1995 have surpassed the 1994. This purely made wine is crammed with black currant fruit and is forbiddingly tannic and backward. Impressive! Anticipated maturity: 2005–2025. Last tasted, 3/02.

1990
89 This wine has quickly reached full maturity. Still a deep garnet/purple color with a classic nose of cassis intermixed with licorice and earth, this robust, medium- to full-bodied wine still has some tannin, but the bouquet is complex, the tan-

nin sweet, and the wine very tasty. Anticipated maturity: now–2015. Last tasted, 9/02.

1989
88

A somewhat disjointed wine with impressive component parts but still somewhat ruggedly thrown together, and with tannins that are dry and all too noticeable. Nevertheless, the color remains a healthy ruby/garnet and the smoky nose of melted licorice intermixed with crème de cassis, earth, and dried herbs is alluring. In the mouth it is medium bodied, moderately tannic, but somewhat dry in the finish. Anticipated maturity: 2004–2015. Last tasted, 9/02.

1988
85

This wine has put on some weight and, although fully mature and somewhat herbaceous, I like the complex cedar, spice box, Provençal herb sort of nose intermixed with some red and black currants. In the mouth, it is medium bodied and slightly austere but well made and it represents a traditional taste of old-style Bordeaux. Anticipated maturity: now–2007. Last tasted, 9/02.

1986
89+

This wine still remains relatively young with a dark plum/garnet color and an intriguing nose of black currants intermixed with compost, earth, and a hint of mushroom. The wine is dense, muscular, tannic, and very masculine. The tannins seemed slightly elevated for the concentration, but there is a lot going on here. This wine certainly saturates the palate, but will it ever come into complete harmony? Anticipated maturity: 2004–2015. Last tasted, 9/02.

1985
85

Considerable pink and amber at the edge suggests full maturity. The nose shows notes of old wood intermixed with red currants, mushrooms, and cedar. The wine is medium bodied, elegant, but relatively short. Anticipated maturity: now. Last tasted, 9/02.

1982
87

Always a husky, robust style of wine that has never quite escaped its characterization as a monolithic Pauillac, this wine still has a deep ruby/purple color and notes of earth, spice, smoke, sweet cherries, and black currants. The wine shows medium to full body, relatively high tannins, and a slightly rustic finish. The wine is capable of lasting at least another 10–15 years, but I am not sure it will ameliorate. Anticipated maturity: now–2015. Last tasted, 9/02.

ANCIENT VINTAGES

Pontet-Canet has a dreadful track record throughout the 1970s and most of the 1960s. I have had fabulous bottles of the 1961 (rated as high as 94 when last tasted in March 1996). The 1959 has always been dull and the 1955 charmless, but on two occasions, the 1945 and 1929 were rated in the low 90s, but that comes from tastings of well over a decade ago. Buying vintages of Pontet-Canet older than 1982 is akin to the proverbial pig in a poke.

OTHER PAUILLAC ESTATES

LA BÉCASSE

Classification: None

Owner: Georges and Roland Fonteneau

Address: Bages, 33250 Pauillac

Mailing Address: 21, rue Édouard de Pontet, 33250 Pauillac

Telephone: 05 56 59 07 14; Telefax: 05 56 59 18 44

Visits: By appointment only

Contact: Roland Fonteneau

VINEYARDS

Surface area: 9.9 acres

Grape varietals: 55% Cabernet Sauvignon, 36% Merlot, 9% Cabernet Franc

Average age of vines: 35 years

Density of plantation: 8,000 vines per hectare

Average yields: 57 hectoliters per hectare

Elevage: Three-week fermentation and maceration. Eighteen months aging in barrels with 40–60% new oak. Fining, no filtration.

WINES PRODUCED

Château La Bécasse: 30,000 bottles

No second wine is produced.

Plateau of maturity: Within 5–15 years of the vintage

GENERAL APPRECIATION

Worth a Cru Bourgeois.

I owe a great deal of thanks to the late Bernard Ginestet, who first told me about this Pauillac that has previously been known only to a fiercely loyal group of insiders who buy the production. In the handful of vintages I have tasted, the wine possessed good concentration and aging potential.

BELLEGRAVE

Classification: Cru Bourgeois Supérieur

Owner: SCI Château Bellegrave

Address: 22, route des Châteaux, Saint-Lambert, 33250 Pauillac

Telephone: 05 56 59 06 47; Telefax: 05 56 59 06 47

Website: www.château.bellegrave.fr

Visits: By appointment Monday to Friday, 8 A.M.–noon and 2–6 P.M.

Contact: Ludovic Meffre (ludovicmeffre@yahoo.fr)

VINEYARDS

Surface area: 17.3 acres

Grape varietals: 62% Cabernet Sauvignon, 31% Merlot, 7% Cabernet Franc

Average age of vines: 20 years

Density of plantation: 8,333 vines per hectare

Average yields: 56 hectoliters per hectare

Elevage: Cold maceration. Three-week fermentation and maceration in temperature-controlled stainless-steel tanks. Twelve months aging in barrels with 50% new oak. Fining and filtration.

WINES PRODUCED

Château Bellegrave: 30,000 bottles

Les Sieurs de Bellegrave: 15,000 bottles

Plateau of maturity: Within 3–10 years of the vintage

GENERAL APPRECIATION

Worth a Cru Bourgeois.

LA COURONNE

Classification: Cru Bourgeois Exceptionnel

Owner: Françoise des Brest-Borie

Address: 33250 Pauillac

Mailing Address: c/o J. E. Borie SA, 33250 Pauillac

Telephone: 05 56 76 13 73; Telefax: 05 56 59 27 37

No visits

VINEYARDS

Surface area: 9.9 acres

Grape varietals: 70% Cabernet Sauvignon, 30% Merlot

Average age of vines: 25 years

Density of plantation: 10,000 vines per hectare

Average yields: 46 hectoliters per hectare

Elevage: Fifteen to eighteen day fermentation and maceration in stainless-steel vats. Twelve to fourteen months aging in barrels with 20% new oak. Fining, light filtration upon bottling.

WINES PRODUCED

Château La Couronne: 20,000 bottles

No second wine is produced.

Plateau of maturity: Within 5–10 years of the vintage.

LA FLEUR MILON

Classification: Cru Bourgeois

Owner: Gimenez family

Address: 14, rue de l'horte, Le Pouyalet, 33250 Pauillac

Telephone: 05 56 59 29 01; Telefax: 05 56 59 23 22

E-mail: contact@lafleurmilon.com

Website: www.lafleurmilon.com

Visits: Monday to Friday, 8:30 A.M.–noon and 2–5 P.M.

Contact: Claude Mirande

VINEYARDS

Surface area: 30.9 acres

Grape varietals: 65% Cabernet Sauvignon, 25% Merlot, 10% Cabernet Franc and Petit Verdot

Average age of vines: 45 years

Density of plantation: 8,000 vines per hectare

Average yields: 55 hectoliters per hectare

Elevage: Twenty-one to twenty-eight day fermentation and maceration in concrete tanks. Fourteen months aging in barrels that are renewed by a third at each vintage. Fining, no filtration.

WINES PRODUCED

Château La Fleur Milon: 66,000 bottles

Château Chantecler Milon: 24,000 bottles

Plateau of maturity: Within 5–12 years of the vintage

GENERAL APPRECIATION

Classification should be maintained.

I rarely see the wines from this producer, but the vineyard, which consists of a number of small parcels, is located on the high plateau north of the town of Pauillac, near both Mouton Rothschild and Lafite Rothschild.

GAUDIN

Owner: Linette Capdevielle

Address: 2, route des Châteaux, 33250 Pauillac

Mailing Address: BP 12, 33250 Pauillac

Telephone: 05 56 59 24 39; Telefax: 05 56 59 25 26

Visits: By appointment every day from 10 A.M.–6 P.M.

Contact: Linette Capdevielle

VINEYARDS

Surface area: 24.7 acres

Grape varietals: 85% Cabernet Sauvignon, 10% Merlot, 5% Petit Verdot

Average age of vines: 45 years

Density of plantation: 8,500 vines per hectare

Average yields: 50 hectoliters per hectare

Elevage: Thirty-day fermentation and maceration. Eighteen months aging in concrete vats and two-year-old barrels, with racking every three months. Fining, no filtration.

WINES PRODUCED

Château Gaudin: 75,000 bottles

No second wine is produced.

Plateau of maturity: Within 5–12 years of the vintage

GENERAL APPRECIATION

Worth a Cru Bourgeois Exceptionnel.

HAUT-BAGES MONPELOU

Classification: Cru Bourgeois

Owner: Castéja family

Address: 33250 Pauillac

Mailing Address: c/o Borie Manoux, 86, cours Balguerie Stuttenberg, 33082 Bordeaux Cedex

Telephone: 05 56 00 00 70; Telefax: 05 57 87 48 61

E-mail: domainesboriemanoux@dial.oléane.com

No visits

VINEYARDS

Surface area: 29.6 acres

Grape varietals: 70% Cabernet Sauvignon, 30% Merlot

Average age of vines: 35 years

Density of plantation: 8,500 vines per hectare

Average yields: 55 hectoliters per hectare

Elevage: Twenty-one day fermentation and maceration in stainless-steel vats. Aging with 20% new oak and 80% one-year-old barrels. Fining, no filtration.

WINES PRODUCED

Château Haut-Bages Monpelou: 80,000 bottles

No second wine is produced.

Plateau of maturity: Within 2–8 years of the vintage

GENERAL APPRECIATION

Classification should be maintained.

This vineyard, located inland near that of Grand-Puy-Lacoste, has been owned by the Castéja family since 1947. The wines, light, fruity, and generally undistinguished, are commercialized exclusively by Mr. Castéja's *négociant* firm, Borie-Manoux.

PÉDESCLAUX

Classification: Fifth Growth in 1855

Owner: GFA du Château Pédesclaux - Jugla family

Address: 33250 Pauillac

Telephone: 05 56 59 22 59; Telefax: 05 56 59 63 19

E-mail: contact@château-pedesclaux.com

Visits: By appointment only, on weekdays (except Wednesdays) 9 A.M.–noon

Contact: Denis Jugla

VINEYARDS

Surface area: 30.9 acres

Grape varietals: 50% Cabernet Sauvignon, 45% Merlot, 5% Cabernet Franc

Average age of vines: 35 years

Density of plantation: 8,333 vines per hectare

Average yields: 48 hectoliters per hectare

Elevage: Eighteen to twenty-two day fermentation and maceration in temperature-controlled stainless-steel tanks. Fifteen months aging in barrels with 60% new oak. Fining, no filtration.

WINES PRODUCED

Château Pédesclaux: 75,000 bottles

Lucien de Pédesclaux: 7,000 bottles

Plateau of maturity: Within 3–10 years of the vintage

GENERAL APPRECIATION

The least-known and probably the most mediocre of all the 1855 classified growths. Should be downgraded to Cru Bourgeois level.

Pédesclaux gets my nod as the most obscure classified growth in the 1855 Classification of the Wines of Gironde. Much of the wine is sold in Europe, particularly Belgium. I have never been impressed, finding it robust but straightforward, lacking depth and, to my taste, having an excess of tannin. In short, life is too short to drink Pédesclaux.

PLANTEY

Classification: Cru Bourgeois

Owner: Vignobles Meffre

Address: Artigues, 33250 Pauillac

Mailing Address: c/o Vignobles Meffre, 84810 Aubignan

Telephone: 04 90 62 61 37; Telefax: 04 90 65 03 73

Visits: By appointment Monday to Friday, 8 A.M.–noon and 2–6 P.M.

Contact: Claude Meffre (Telephone: 05 56 59 32 30)

VINEYARDS

Surface area: 64.2 acres

Grape varietals: 50% Cabernet Sauvignon, 45% Merlot, 5% Cabernet Franc

Average age of vines: 28 years

Density of plantation: 6,600 vines per hectare

Average yields: 57 hectoliters per hectare

Elevage: Twenty-one day fermentation and maceration in concrete tanks. Twelve months aging in barrels with 50% new oak. Fining and filtration.

WINES PRODUCED

Château Plantey: 160,000 bottles

Château Artigues: 70,000 bottles

Plateau of maturity: Within 3–8 years of the vintage

LA ROSE PAUILLAC

This cooperative, consisting of 125 vineyard owners who control 272 acres of vineyards in Pauillac, was created in 1932. At present, it is the most successful cooperative in Bordeaux, with 6,000 private clients as well as significant sales to many of Bordeaux's most prestigious *négociants*. The cooperative produces three *cuvées*, the majority of which is labeled La Rose Pauillac. In addition, two domains that vinify their wines at the cooperative Château Haut-Milon and Château Haut-St.-Lambert, sell their wines under their own label, but it is entirely made and bottled at the cooperative. The cooperative has been using increasing percentages of small oak barrels, with a tiny percentage of them new. The wines exhibit a soft, agreeable, clean, but not particularly distinguished style. These wines should be drunk in their first 5–7 years of life.

SAINT MAMBERT

Classification: None

Owner: Domingo Reyes

Address: Bellevue, St.-Lambert, 33250 Pauillac

Telephone: 05 56 59 22 72; Telefax: 05 56 59 22 72

Website: www.château-saint-mambert.fr.st

Visits: By appointment

Contact: Mrs. Reyes

VINEYARDS

Surface area: 1.63 acres

Grape varietals: 65% Cabernet Sauvignon, 25% Cabernet Franc, 10% Merlot

Average age of vines: 45 years

Density of plantation: 10,000 vines per hectare

Average yields: 58 hectoliters per hectare

Elevage: Three week fermentation and maceration in stainless-steel tanks. Eighteen months aging in barrels, with 30% new oak. Fining, no filtration.

WINES PRODUCED

Château Saint Mambert: 4,200 bottles

No second wine is produced.

Plateau of maturity: Within 3–8 years of the vintage

ST.-JULIEN

If Pauillac is famous for having the Médoc's largest number of first growths and Margaux for being the most widely known appellation, St.-Julien is the Médoc's most underrated commune. The winemaking in St.-Julien—from the lesser-known Cru Bourgeois châteaux such as Gloria, Terrey-Gros-Cailloux, and Lalande-Borie, to the five flagship estates of this commune, Léoville Las Cases, Ducru-Beaucaillou, Léoville Poyferré, Léoville Barton, and Gruaud Larose—is consistently both distinctive and brilliant. The first four of these estates all have riverside vineyards with superb drainage. The last estate, Gruaud Larose, is inland. St.-Julien starts where the commune of Pauillac stops, and this is no better demonstrated than where Léoville Las Cases and Latour meet at the border. Heading south from Pauillac, Léoville Las Cases and Léoville Poyferré straddle both sides of D2 (the Médoc's Route du Vin), Langoa Barton and Léoville Barton follow on the right, Ducru-Beaucaillou on the left, Branaire Ducru on the right, and Beychevelle on the left. At normal driving speeds, the time necessary to pass all of these illustrious properties is no more than five minutes. Farther inland and lacking a view of the Gironde are the large estates of Gruaud Larose, Talbot, Lagrange, and Saint-Pierre.

While St.-Emilion and the Côtes de Castillon lead Bordeaux's avant garde winemaking/experimentation revolution and the creation of new micro-estates, there is no commune in the Médoc or, for that matter, in Bordeaux where the art of winemaking is practiced as highly as in St.-Julien. Consequently, the wine consumer has the odds stacked in his or her favor when purchasing a St.-Julien. In addition to a bevy of fine wines from the Cru Bourgeois châteaux of St.-Julien, in particular Gloria, the eleven classified growths are all turning out impeccably crafted wines, yet all vary greatly in style.

Léoville Las Cases is the most Pauillac-like of the St.-Juliens for two main reasons. The vineyards sit next to those of Pauillac's famous first growth, Latour, and the owner, the late Michel Delon, and his son Jean-Hubert make a prodigiously concentrated and pure, tannic wine marked by the scent of subtle vanilla oakiness allied to majestic levels of cassis and sweet cherry fruit. In most vintages, this wine needs a minimum of a decade to shed its cloak of tannin. With the possible exceptions of Gruaud Larose and Léoville Barton, no other St.-Julien is this stubbornly backward at the outset; most other top properties seem to make wines that do not require as much patience from the consumer.

Léoville Las Cases is one of a trio of St.-Julien estates with the name Léoville. At present, all of them produce superb wines, but Las-Cases is the best of the three, largely because the proprietors, the Delons, have been perfectionists. Of the other two,

Léoville Poyferré has immense potential and, fortunately, has begun to exploit it. Like Léoville Las Cases, the office and wine *chai* sit in the tiny, sleepy town of St.-Julien-Beychevelle. Poyferré's record was less than brilliant in the 1960s and 1970s, irregular in the 1980s (the 1983 and 1982 were superb), yet highly promising in the 1990s (2000, 1996, and 1990 are triumphant). Today, the wines display much greater strength and richness and a noticeably darker color.

The other Léoville is Léoville Barton. It is an outstanding wine and increasingly consistent, particularly in the vintages that produce lighter, more elegant wines. Since the mid-1980s, the handsome Anthony Barton, one of Bordeaux's impeccable gentlemen and most charming wine advocates, has been in full command, and consistency has been the rule. Léoville Barton reeks of cedarwood when mature and is a classic, traditionally made St.-Julien that is the most masculine of the St.-Juliens. It is also among the most fairly priced wines in the Médoc.

Anthony Barton also has another St.-Julien property, Langoa Barton. This impressive château sits right on top of the heavily traveled Route du Vin (D2) and houses the winemaking facilities for both Léoville Barton and Langoa Barton. Not surprisingly, Langoa is very similar in style to Léoville Barton— cedary, rich, and flavorful, yet rarely as concentrated as its bigger sister.

The Italianate mansion dominates the St.-Julien estate of Ducru-Beaucaillou. This estate can challenge Léoville Las Cases and the Médoc first growths in quality each year. I vividly remember my first visit to Ducru-Beaucaillou in 1970 when I asked the old cellar master, M. Prévost, what the secret to Ducru's remarkable consistency was. He simply stated, "Selection, selection, selection." This is an expertly run property where the owners, the genteel Borie family, oversee every step of the winemaking procedure. The château has a gorgeous location overlooking the Gironde, and the style of wine made here, while less massive and tannic than Léoville Las Cases or Léoville Barton and less overtly powerful and heady than Gruaud Larose, is a classic St.-Julien that needs 8–10 years to reveal the rich, fruity, elegant, suave flavors. If Léoville Las Cases is the Latour of St.-Julien, Ducru-Beaucaillou is St.-Julien's Lafite Rothschild. The estate went through an unexpected slump in the late 1980s, but quickly regained form, producing spectacular wines in 2000, 1996, and 1995.

Within shouting distance of Ducru-Beaucaillou are Branaire Ducru and Beychevelle, the two most southern St.-Juliens. Beychevelle is widely known, perhaps because tourists love the gardens (among the Médoc's most photogenic), and the wine is supple, fruity, light, and quick to mature. While good, even outstanding as in 1989, 1986, and 1982, Beychevelle has always had a better reputation than its performance record would lead one to believe. Call it Château Inconsistency on my scoring sheet.

Just the opposite is the case with Branaire, the rather drab, sullen-looking château across the road from Beychevelle. Despite a slump in quality after 1982, Branaire rebounded strongly with a fine effort in 1989, followed by very good offerings in 1995 and 1994 and exceptional wines in 1996 as well as 2000. Furthermore, the price for Branaire remains one of the lowest for a wine of such quality. Branaire is a slightly bigger wine than its neighbor, Beychevelle, but it clearly emerges from the school of winemaking that favors finesse over massive power and extract. It possesses an unmis-

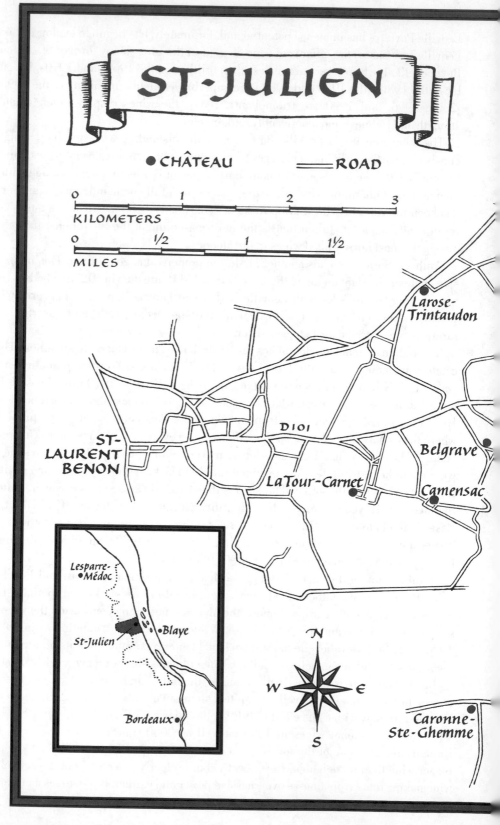

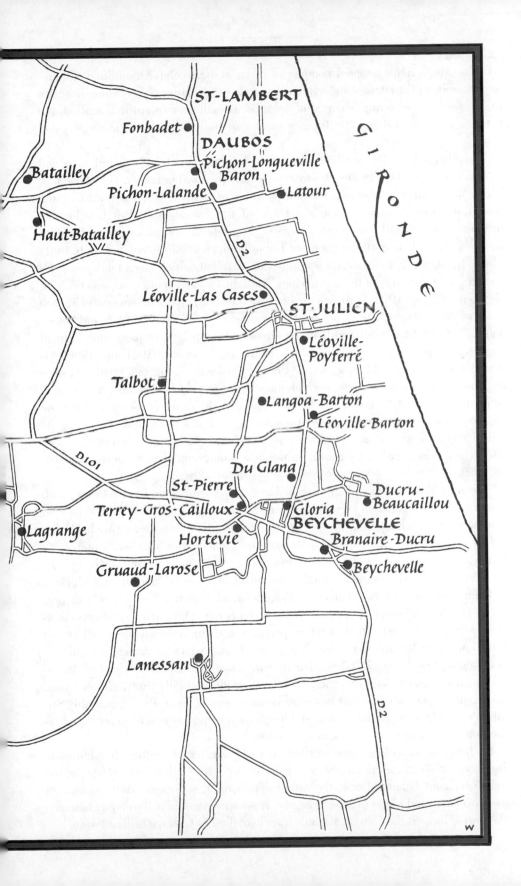

takable exotic, richly scented bouquet of cedar and chocolate in addition to blueberry/raspberry fruit flavors and a liquid minerality. A singular style of wine, Branaire will never have the aging potential of the three Léovilles or Ducru-Beaucaillou, but between the ages of 8 and 20, Branaire can be an opulently rich, distinctive style of wine.

Two other potentially excellent wines of St.-Julien are made at Gruaud Larose and Talbot. For years, these two estates were owned by the Cordier family. They have now been sold, and that is reflected in somewhat different styles of wine emerging from the new proprietors. Gruaud Larose sits back off the river behind Beychevelle and Branaire Ducru. Until the recent change in proprietors, Gruaud Larose and stablemate and immediate northern neighbor Talbot produced densely colored, rich, fruity wines. In most vintages, Gruaud was superior to Talbot, which has a tendency to be austere, but the quality of these two wines, while historically quite good, was brilliant between 1978 and 1990. Furthermore, because they both produce in excess of 35,000 cases of wine, fetching a price per bottle that always appeared modest, Gruaud Larose and Talbot immensely satisfied both the purse and the palate. In particular, Gruaud Larose often performed at a first-growth quality level between 1961 and 1990. Although critics of Gruaud Larose suggest that it can lack the great complexity and staying power of a true first growth, such charges have proved baseless when the wine is compared in blind tastings against the first growths. Under the new owners, the wine appears to be made in a supple, more fruity and accessible style, without sacrificing its full-blooded, meaty, robust style. Talbot, still under partial Cordier ownership, looks also to be producing a more forward, fruitier, less tannic wine than the older pre-1990 offerings.

The remaining two St.-Julien classified growths, Lagrange and Saint-Pierre, both have undergone significant personality changes. Lagrange, lowly for decades, took on new owners from Japan, and with some expert start-up advice from the late Michel Delon of Léoville Las Cases, the improvements have been remarkable. This is now one of St.-Julien's great wines—powerful, full-bodied, very concentrated, and obviously ageworthy. Moreover, its price is still reasonable, making it an insider's choice from St.-Julien.

Saint-Pierre has always been a terribly underrated property. The style of wine produced is rich in color and extract, full-bodied, sometimes a bit rustic, but always satisfyingly fat, robust, and fruity. Now the property and the wine are under the watchful eye of the late Henri Martin's son-in-law, Jean-Louis Triaud, who also manages St.-Julien's most famous Cru Bourgeois, Gloria. The transition to a "Martinized" style of St.-Julien was readily apparent with their first vintage, the 1983, a richly fruity, almost sweet, easy to drink, supple wine that has huge popular appeal. Saint-Pierre, probably St.-Julien's most lavishly oaked, exotic, and flamboyant wine, has also been on a qualitative hot streak and merits considerable interest.

St.-Julien is not without some meritorious Cru Bourgeois properties. In addition to the excellent Gloria, there are the very good Terrey-Gros-Cailloux and Hortevie; the stylish, elegant Lalande-Borie; the rather commercial, sometimes dull, sometimes good du Glana; and a bevy of good *deuxième,* or second wines, from the major châteaux. The best of these is the Clos du Marquis from Léoville Las Cases, a brilliant wine.

St.-Julien is a good commune for treasure hunting when Bordeaux has a poor or mediocre vintage. In fact, St.-Julien's soil is similar to the light, gravel-based earth of Margaux, except that it is richer in clay. This affords the wines more body and viscosity. Since most of the major vineyards are close to the Gironde, they tend to have excellent, well-drained, deep beds of gravel soil. In 1992, 1987, 1984, and 1980, all rain-plagued years, St.-Julien produced more acceptable wines than elsewhere in Bordeaux.

In the excellent-to-great vintages, St.-Juliens are quintessential Médocs. The 2000, 1996, 1995, 1990, 1989, 1986, 1985, 1982, 1970, 1961, and 1959 are the truly great vintages for this appellation, followed by 2001, 1988, 1983, 1966, and 1962.

ST.-JULIEN
(An Insider's View)

Overall Appellation Potential: Excellent to Superb (from top to bottom the most consistent appellation of Bordeaux)

The Most Potential for Aging: Ducru-Beaucaillou, Gruaud Larose, Lagrange, Léoville Barton, Léoville Las Cases, Léoville Poyferré

The Most Elegant: Branaire Ducru, Ducru-Beaucaillou, Léoville Las Cases

The Most Concentrated: Ducru-Beaucaillou, Gruaud Larose, Lagrange, Léoville Barton, Léoville Las Cases, Léoville Poyferré

The Best Value: Branaire Ducru, Gloria, Hortevie, Saint-Pierre, Talbot

The Most Exotic: Branaire Ducru, Saint-Pierre

The Most Difficult to Understand (when young): Ducru-Beaucaillou

The Most Underrated: Lagrange, Saint-Pierre, Talbot

The Easiest to Appreciate Young: Gloria, Talbot

Up-and-Coming Estates: Lagrange, Saint-Pierre

Greatest Recent Vintages: 2000, 1996, 1995, 1990, 1989, 1986, 1985, 1982, 1961

ST.-JULIEN—AN OVERVIEW

Location: In many ways the center point of the Médoc, laying to the north of Margaux, bordered on the south by the village of Cussac-Fort-Médoc and on the north by Pauillac; it is approximately 22 miles north of the city of Bordeaux.

Acres Under Vine: 2,175

Communes: St.-Julien is the major commune, along with small parcels of Cussac and St.-Laurent; some of the St.-Julien commune actually sits within Pauillac

Average Annual Production: 490,000 cases

Classified Growths: Total of 11: 5 second-growths, 2 third-growths, and 4 fourth-growths; there are 8 Crus Bourgeois

Principal Grape Varieties: Cabernet Sauvignon followed by Merlot and small quantities of Cabernet Franc. Varietal composition in St.-Julien tends to mirror Pauillac

Principal Soil Type: St.-Julien's soil consists of extremely fine gravel, especially for the great vineyards adjacent to the river. Farther inland, there is considerable gravel but more clay

A CONSUMER'S CLASSIFICATION OF THE CHÂTEAUX OF ST.-JULIEN

OUTSTANDING
Ducru-Beaucaillou, Gruaud Larose, Léoville Barton, Léoville Las Cases, Léoville Poyferré

EXCELLENT
Branaire Ducru, Lagrange, Saint-Pierre, Talbot

VERY GOOD
Beychevelle, Gloria, Hortevie, Langoa Barton

GOOD
Lalande Borie, Terrey-Gros-Cailloux

OTHER NOTABLE ST.-JULIEN PROPERTIES
La Bridane, Domaine Castaing, du Glana, Lalande, Moulin de la Rose, Teynac

BEYCHEVELLE

Classification: Fourth Growth in 1855

Owner: Grands Millésimes de France (GMF and Suntory)

Address: 33250 St.-Julien-Beychevelle

Telephone: 05 56 73 20 70; Telefax: 05 56 73 20 71

E-mail: beychevelle@beychevelle.com

Website: www.beychevelle.com

Visits: By appointment Monday to Friday, 10 A.M.–noon and 1:30–5 P.M.

VINEYARDS

Surface area: 222.3 acres

Grape varietals: 62% Cabernet Sauvignon, 31% Merlot, 5% Cabernet Franc, 2% Petit Verdot

Average age of vines: 28 years

Density of plantation: 8,300 and 10,000 vines per hectare

Average yields: 55 hectoliters per hectare

Elevage: Eight- to ten-day alcoholic fermentation, eighteen-day maceration in temperature-controlled stainless-steel and concrete vats at 28°C. Eighteen months aging in barrels with 57% new oak. Fining with egg whites. Regarding filtration, the estate decides on a per vintage basis.

WINES PRODUCED

Château Beychevelle: 265,000 bottles

Amiral de Beychevelle: 198,000 bottles

Plateau of maturity: Within 7–15 years of the vintage

GENERAL APPRECIATION

The wines of this estate have improved considerably since 1982. They are rarely profound yet are soundly made, charming, elegant, and finesse-styled. Some vintages lack that additional depth, structure, complexity, and substance that characterize the best St.-Juliens. Because of Beychevelle's irregular performance, readers should be cautious. While it does not rank amongst the best St.-Julien, this wine is interesting because of its reasonable pricing. The superb 2000, 1989, 1986, and 1982 clearly demonstrate the estate's potential. In the best years, Beychevelle can rival a third growth; in lesser ones, it does not surpass a fifth growth or even a top-quality Cru Bourgeois.

Tourists visiting Bordeaux are unlikely to miss Château Beychevelle because it is the first major château passed on the D2 road leading north into the commune of St.-Julien. The beautiful flowering gardens that face the road have caused many speeding drivers to stop and take photographs.

Although consistently inconsistent, the wines of Beychevelle can also be beautifully produced. During the decades of the 1960s and 1970s, quality from vintage to vintage was a problem. Moreover, the wine has been disappointing in mediocre years, such as 1993, 1992, 1987, and 1974, and sometimes uninspiring in great years (1990). Even in top years, Beychevelle tastes uncommonly smooth, supple, and drinkable at a young age. This seems to give purists and traditionalists cause for unnecessary concern. Most recent top vintages of Beychevelle, while fully mature by the time they are 10 years old, have the requisite stuffing to age well for 15 or more years. However, this is generally not a property whose wines require laying away for decades.

In the early 1980s the owners began to realize that the ultra-smooth style of Beychevelle was, as the English say, "not making old bones." Since 1982 there has been an increasing reliance on the firmer, more muscular Cabernet Sauvignon in the blend, a lengthening of the all-important *cuvaison* period, the increased usage of new oak, and the introduction of a second label for lighter vats of wine. These techniques have significantly improved the quality of Beychevelle, with fine efforts in 2000, 1989, 1986, and 1982. The light, supple, elegant, quick-maturing style of wine made in the 1960s and 1970s has, since 1982, moved to a firmer constructed, more concentrated type of St.-Julien without, however, sacrificing any of the wine's flattering up-front style, charm, and finesse.

Beychevelle is not one of St.-Julien's most expensive wines, selling at a price level well below that of Léoville Las Cases and Ducru-Beaucaillou.

IMPORTANT VINTAGES

2001 A stylish, restrained, light to medium-bodied effort, the 2001 possesses undeniable
86–88 elegance, light to moderate tannin, and sweet red and black currant fruit notes intermixed with some loamy soil, cherry, licorice, and cedar. Anticipated maturity: 2006–2015. Last tasted, 1/03.

2000
91+
Deep ruby/purple in color, with a sweet nose of black currants, earth, licorice, and mineral, the 2000 is relatively powerful and dense for the normally restrained and elegant Beychevelle. Medium to full-bodied, dense, and chewy, it is showing even better out of bottle than it was from cask. While it appears to be the finest example made at Beychevelle since the 1989 and 1982, patience will be required. Anticipated maturity: 2007–2020. Last tasted, 1/03.

1999
86
This is a pleasant, medium-bodied 1999 displaying notes of herbs and damp earth in its austere, undernourished personality. Notions of strawberry, cherry, and currant fruit also emerge, but there is not a lot to get excited about in this uninspiring 1999. It will last for a decade. Last tasted, 3/02.

1998
87
This elegant, stylish, well-delineated Beychevelle offers finesse and beauty in a medium-bodied, firmly structured, flavorful format. Red and black currants, licorice, minerals, spice, and tar notes are subtle but persuasive. While it does not cut an enormous swath across the palate, the wine's acidity, alcohol, and tannin are well balanced. Anticipated maturity: now–2016. Last tasted, 3/02.

1996
86
Beychevelle's 1996 reveals an evolved, dark plum color. The nose offers toasty new oak in an open, charming style with berry fruit intermixed with spice. It is an uninspiring example, particularly for such a top-notch *terroir*, but the wine is medium bodied and cleanly made, with moderate longevity. Anticipated maturity: now–2012. Last tasted, 1/01.

1995
85
Out of bottle, this wine displays a medium ruby color and a distinctive nose of underbrush, damp earth, and loamy-tinged black currant fruit. Moderately tannic, with medium body and some angularity, the 1995 possesses good extract but not much soul or character. Anticipated maturity: now–2012. Last tasted, 1/01.

1994
83?
This light- to medium-weight wine exhibits a dark ruby color and a straightforward, red currant–scented nose with toast, compost, herbs, and earth in the background. Low acidity, high tannin, and sweet fruit result in a good but uninspiring, somewhat disjointed effort. The 1994 Beychevelle should drink well for another five years. Last tasted, 1/01.

1990
79
An uninspiring effort, the dark garnet–colored 1990 continues to reveal a greenness to its tannin, a hollowness in the mid-palate, and coarse tannin in the finish. A significant flop. Last tasted, 1/01.

1989
89
The dark garnet, very perfumed 1989 is an elegant, medium-bodied wine with soft tannin, copious quantities of ripe, herb-tinged, black currant fruit, some evidence of toasty oak, and a generous, velvety-textured finish. It has evolved quickly and is fully mature. Anticipated maturity: now–2012. Last tasted, 1/01.

1986
92
This remains one of the best Beychevelles in the last 30 years. With its saturated garnet color and bouquet of roasted fruit, licorice, plums, and currant, this full-bodied, concentrated, rich wine is close enough to full maturity. Anticipated maturity: now–2015. Last tasted, 1/01.

1985
87
Fully mature, the medium garnet–colored 1985 (considerable orange/pink at the rim) reflects the character of this charming vintage. Low in acidity, ripe, round, fruity, and precocious, this medium-bodied, supple wine needs to be drunk up over the next 4–6 years. Anticipated maturity: now. Last tasted, 1/01.

1983
77
Now falling apart, this earthy, herbaceous, medium garnet–colored wine is revealing less and less fruit and more and more acidity as well as tannin. The 1983's aggressive tannins will only make this wine taste more attenuated. Drink up! Anticipated maturity: now. Last tasted, 1/01.

1982
95
A profound Beychevelle, the slowly developing 1982 is a powerful, full-bodied, intensely concentrated wine that has revealed far greater potential for extended cellaring than I expected. It has lost all of its baby fat, and those unctuously thick, forward flavors have settled down to reveal a more classic bouquet of cedar, herb,

tobacco, licorice, and black currant scents, along with aromas of new saddle leather and truffles. Powerful, rich, and broad-shouldered, this brawny Beychevelle may not develop the finesse of the 1989, but it will always be a richer, more powerful wine. Anticipated maturity: now–2025. Last tasted, 11/02.

ANCIENT VINTAGES

The 1960s and 1970s were filled with poor efforts. Only the 1975, 1966, and 1961 managed to be successful wines, but all three of these vintages are probably in decline.

For unexplainable reasons, Beychevelle does not frequently appear in my tasting notes of historic vintages. The 1959 and 1952, each tasted only once, were solid but hardly inspiring. A 1953 (rated 92 in 1987) was terrific, the best Beychevelle I have ever tasted, along with the 1982. The finest mature Beychevelle I have tasted was the 1928, drunk in October 2002 (rated 92).

BRANAIRE DUCRU

Classification: Fourth Growth in 1855

Owner: Marotteaux family

Administrator: Patrick Maroteaux

Address: 33250 St.-Julien-Beychevelle

Telephone: 05 56 59 25 86; Telefax: 05 56 59 16 26

E-mail: branaire@branaire.com

Website: www.branaire.com

Visits: Preferably by appointment, Monday to Friday, 9 A.M.–noon and 2–5 P.M.

Contact: Philippe Dhalluin

VINEYARDS

Surface area: 123.5 acres

Grape varietals: 70% Cabernet Sauvignon, 22% Merlot, 4% Cabernet Franc, 4% Petit Verdot

Average age of vines: 35 years

Density of plantation: 10,000 vines per hectare

Average yields: 48 hectoliters per hectare

Elevage: Three-week fermentation and maceration in temperature-controlled stainless-steel vats. Part of the yield undergoes malolactics in barrels. Eighteen to twenty-two months aging in barrels with 50% new oak. Fining with egg whites. Light filtration.

WINES PRODUCED

Château Branaire Ducru: 150,000–180,000 bottles

Château Duluc: 150,000 bottles

Plateau of maturity: Within 5–20 years of the vintage

GENERAL APPRECIATION

During recent years, Branaire Ducru has improved discreetly but surely. Vintages from 1991 onward have been extremely consistent in quality, the wines exhibiting more depth, concentration, and stuffing while retaining the characteristic elegance and chocolaty spiciness of Branaire. A wine largely ignored by speculators, Branaire is favored by wine drinkers, which explains why it is rarely seen in auction sales. Because of this, prices remain reasonable. In the best vintages, Branaire Ducru can rival a third growth.

Note: Since 1991, the estate has benefitted from a state-of-the-art cellar where everything is operated by gravity. It was the first cellar in Bordeaux to be designed this way.

I have always found Branaire Ducru to be curiously underrated, undervalued, and somewhat forgotten whenever Bordeaux enthusiasts discuss their favorite wines. Travelers passing through St.-Julien have no doubt noted the indifferent beige building directly opposite Beychevelle on the Médoc's main wine road. The finest vintages are magnificently scented, deep, rich wines that are as good as the other top wines of St.-Julien. Until the mid- to late 1990s, Branaire Ducru was no model of consistency, with a dubious series of indifferent wines produced in the 1980s. This may have reflected an overly abundant crop size and less than strict selections. The construction of a new cellar and the introduction of a new winemaking team, as well as a second label, appear to have been the necessary cures to get Branaire Ducru back on track, as evidenced by very strong efforts since the mid-1990s. One cannot underestimate Patrick Marotteaux, the energetic administrator, who is also the president of Bordeaux's Union des Grands Crus.

The vineyards of Branaire Ducru, like those of many Bordeaux châteaux, are spread out in a morseled fashion throughout the commune of St.-Julien.

The wines of Branaire Ducru have a distinctive character. For a St.-Julien they are particularly spicy, with an almost exotic aroma of spice, oak, and vanilla. On the palate, the wine often has a pronounced, distinctive, chocolaty component that makes Branaire Ducru relatively easy to spot in blind tastings. This personality trait is especially noticeable in the great vintages of 2000, 1996, 1995, 1989, 1982, 1976, and 1975.

IMPORTANT VINTAGES

2001 Complex, sweet, blueberry, mineral, and floral aromas set this St.-Julien apart
89–91 from its peers. Elegant and medium bodied, with good underlying acidity, sweet fruit on the attack, ripe tannin, and abundant freshness as well as delineation, it will be at its finest from 2005–2016. Last tasted, 1/03.

2000 This effort has put on richness, depth, and power during its *élevage*. From bottle,
93+ it is a stunning wine. The opaque purple–colored 2000 Branaire offers a terrific perfume of wet gravel, sweet jammy black raspberries, cassis, violets, and subtle new oak. A wine of opulence, strength, richness, structure, purity, and depth, this is unquestionably the finest Branaire since the 1996 and 1982. Anticipated maturity: 2007–2025. Last tasted, 1/03.

1999 The 1999 Branaire is a beautifully perfumed effort revealing scents of graphite,
89 lead pencil shavings, blueberries, raspberries, and black currants. Rich, layered, medium bodied, pure, and elegant, it is a complex St.-Julien with good flavor

depth, soft tannin, and unobtrusive acidity. Drink it now and over the next 12–15+ years. Last tasted, 3/02.

1998 A dense ruby/purple color is accompanied by an attractive bouquet of lead pencil,
89 graphite, black currants, raspberries, and spice. Medium bodied, with beautifully knit flavors revealing excellent definition, this subtle, restrained yet persuasive 1998 displays a distinctive style. Anticipated maturity: now–2016. Last tasted, 3/02.

1997 This is a delicious, attractive, dark ruby/plum–colored offering with complex
86 notes of lead pencil, minerals, black raspberries, currants, and new oak. Medium bodied with light tannin, this elegant wine is on a fast evolutionary track. Drink this delicious Claret over the next 2–3 years. Last tasted, 1/02.

1996 A textbook Branaire, the opaque ruby/purple–colored 1996 has a telltale floral,
91 raspberry, and black currant–scented nose intermixed with minerals and floral nuances. Elegant and pure, with surprising lushness, layers of flavor, and sweet, well-integrated tannin, this medium-bodied, finesse-styled wine should be at its finest between 2005–2020. Last tasted, 8/02.

1995 A beauty in the elegant, restrained, finesse school of winemaking, the dark
90 ruby/purple–colored 1995 Branaire exhibits a floral, cranberry, cherry, and black currant–scented nose intermixed with high-quality toasty new oak. Medium bodied, with excellent definition, supple tannin, and an attractive, alluring personality, this pleasant, measured yet complex wine should drink well young and keep for 15 years. Last tasted, 1/02.

1994 One of the most stylish, complex, and remarkably delicious wines of the vintage,
88 this charmer possesses a dark ruby/purple color, as well as an excellent, sweet nose of cassis, spice, and an intriguing floral component. Soft and savory, with pure, toasty, black fruit flavors, this luscious, low-acid wine has managed to avoid the vintage's tough tannin. I'm not sure this wine has the potential to be outstanding, but it is very close. It is one of the vintages's more attractive values for a top-classified growth. It should drink well for 10 years. Last tasted, 3/01.

1990 Dark garnet with a pink rim, this is a somewhat loosely structured wine with low
88 acidity, some spicy wood, and sweet jammy fruit, but on the palate a diffuseness and disjointedness are present. Totally seductive and richly fruity, the 1990 is medium bodied, shows good purity and some excellent fruit up-front, but where is the structure and delineation? Anticipated maturity: now–2010. Last tasted, 3/02.

1989 Approaching full maturity, the sumptuous, fleshy, dark garnet–colored 1989 is a
90 top success for Branaire. This flashy wine exhibits sweet raspberry and black currant fruit intermixed with some lead pencil, cedar, chocolate, and new oak. The wine is medium bodied, supple textured, and luscious. A very sexy effort, this wine should be drunk over the next 10–12 years. Last tasted, 3/02.

1986 Tannins are likely to always dominate this vintage for Branaire. Dark garnet with
88 an attractive bouquet of earth, minerals, cedar, spice, and currants, this wine remains firm and structured. Cedar, graphite, red currants, and mineral flavors are present in its medium-bodied presentation on the palate. Drink it over the next 6–8 years. Last tasted, 3/02.

1985 Beginning to decline, this surprisingly light, uninspiring effort reveals consider-
84 able pink and amber at the edge. A nose of sweet red fruits intermixed with herb, cedar, earth, and wood is followed by a light- to medium-bodied wine that is pleasant but undistinguished. Drink it up. Last tasted, 3/02.

1982 A consistently elegant wine with Branaire's telltale smoky, raspberry, blueberry,
91 currant, and mineral perfume, this medium-bodied Branaire has always exhibited considerable suppleness, a dense ruby color that has begun to show some lightening at the rim, excellent balance, sweet chocolaty, currant-infused flavors, and a

long finish with more fat than any vintage of Branaire I have tasted. Anticipated maturity: now–2012. Last tasted, 9/02.

ANCIENT VINTAGES

One of the wines to search out is the 1975 (93 points; last tasted 9/02). This is one of the glorious successes of the vintage and easily has 10–15 more years of life to it. Other prominent successes include 1966, a wine that is probably now tiring.

DUCRU-BEAUCAILLOU

Classification: Second Growth in 1855

Owner: Borie family

Administrator: Bruno Borie

Address: 33250 St.-Julien-Beychevelle

Telephone: 05 56 73 16 73; Telefax: 05 56 59 27 37

Visits: By appointment only Monday to Friday, 9 A.M.–noon and 2–5 P.M. Closed in August and at harvest time.

Contact: François-Xavier Borie

VINEYARDS

Surface area: 128.4 acres

Grape varietals: 70% Cabernet Sauvignon, 25% Merlot, 5% Cabernet Franc

Average age of vines: 38 years

Density of plantation: 10,000 vines per hectare

Average yields: 49 hectoliters per hectare

Elevage: Seventeen to twenty-one-day fermentation and maceration in temperature-controlled stainless-steel and concrete tanks. Eighteen to twenty months aging in barrels with 50–65% new oak. Fining, light filtration upon bottling.

WINES PRODUCED

Château Ducru-Beaucaillou: 220,000 bottles

La Croix de Beaucaillou: 85,000 bottles

Plateau of maturity: Within 10–30 years of the vintage

GENERAL APPRECIATION

Ducru-Beaucaillou returned to form after a slump at the end of the 1980s and the beginning of the 1990s, when some of its wines were marred by aromas of wet cardboard, probably attributable to a TCA contamination in one of the aging cellars. Vintages from 1994 onward are on par with the best wines ever produced at the estate. Much like Branaire (to which it is superior) and Léoville Las Cases (which generally surpasses it), Ducru-Beaucaillou is rarely seen at auction. More a connoisseur's buy than a speculator's target, it is one of the most interesting Bordeaux super-seconds in terms of quality/price ratio.

Ducru-Beaucaillou, sitting among an outcropping of trees with a splendid view of the Gironde River, enjoys a picture-postcard setting. The property belongs to the Borie family. The late Jean-Eugène Borie was one of the Médoc's few resident proprietors as well as one of the region's great gentlemen. In the last three decades, he brought the quality of Ducru-Beaucaillou up to a level where vintages such as 2000, 1996, 1995, 1985, 1982, 1981, 1978, 1976, 1973, 1970, 1966, and 1961 could challenge any of the Médoc first growths. Passion for his wine, an obsessive commitment to quality, remarkable modesty, and numerous trips abroad as ambassador for Bordeaux made him one of this region's most respected wine personalities. With his death several years ago, his son Xavier, who lives at Grand-Puy-Lacoste, assumed full control of Ducru until 2003 when his brother Bruno took over.

The wine of Ducru-Beaucaillou is the essence of elegance, symmetry, balance, breed, class, and distinction. It is never one of the most robust, richest, or fruitiest wines of St.-Julien and by its nature is a stubbornly slow developer. Most of the finest vintages of Ducru-Beaucaillou usually take at least 10 years to reveal their stunning harmony of fruit and power. Ducru-Beaucaillou is a great wine for a number of reasons. The meticulous attention to detail, the brutal selection process—whereby only the finest grapes and finest barrels of wine are permitted to go into the bottle—and the conservative viticultural practices followed, all play major roles in the success of this wine.

That being said, Ducru-Beaucaillou had a problem with the vintages between 1987 and 1990. All of my tasting notes reflect the fact that many bottles from these vintages had a musty component in the aromatics, probably attributable to some noxious aromas given off by the insulation in the old *chai* at Ducru. This *chai* was completely rebuilt and the source for the off smells eliminated. This problem, which does not affect all bottles of these vintages (1990, 1989, and 1988), has been eradicated. Because of these defects, I have not included these vintages in the tasting notes.

Ducru-Beaucaillou is one of Bordeaux's most expensive second growths, reflecting the international demand for the wine and the consistently high quality.

IMPORTANT VINTAGES

2001
90–92   A late harvest (October 1–12) produced a surprisingly fruit-driven, pure, up-front 2001 Ducru. Xavier Borie thinks this blend of 68% Cabernet Sauvignon, 30% Merlot, and 2% Cabernet Franc is "better than the 1999, riper, denser, and fuller." When tasted next to the 1999, the only difference is a firmer style of tannin in the 2001, whereas the 1999 is pure charm and elegance. The 2001 is a medium-bodied, pure example displaying notes of red and black currants intermixed with minerals, spice box, and hints of cedar as well as toast. Anticipated maturity: 2005–2016. Last tasted, 1/03.

2000
94+   An ethereal effort, the 2000 Ducru-Beaucaillou offers a combination of the 1982 or 1990's ripe fruit and the 1975's style of tannin. It is a reserved, backward yet authoritative Ducru with a firm structure, plenty of grip, significant concentration, and floral, black raspberry, and currant notes intermixed with telltale mineral characteristics. This gorgeous offering will require 8–10 years of cellaring. Anticipated maturity: 2010–2035. Last tasted, 1/03.

1999
91   A beauty, the deep purple–colored 1999 Ducru-Beaucaillou, which represents 60% of the crop, offers aromas of crushed stones, raspberry liqueur, and black currants. Sweet, pure, and harmonious, it is a wine of elegance, finesse, and mul-

tiple nuances rather than power, concentration, and structure. This is Bordeaux at its finest. Anticipated maturity: 2004–2018. Last tasted, 3/02.

1998
91+
A supremely elegant, dense purple–colored effort, the 1998 reveals aromas of cassis, black raspberries, minerals, and currants. Precise, well delineated, and medium to full-bodied, with magnificent purity and understated elegance, this noble, restrained wine reveals a tannic finish, suggesting 1–2 more years of cellaring is warranted. Anticipated maturity: 2005–2025. Last tasted, 3/02.

1997
87
A classy, complex bouquet of lead pencil, mineral, earth, cassis, and flowers jumps from the glass of this dark ruby/purple–colored 1997. Evolved and elegant with noticeable tannin, it exhibits both breed and class as well as moderate weight, excellent depth, purity, and symmetry. Enjoy it now and over the next 10 years . . . at the minimum. Last tasted, 1/02.

1996
96
The 1996 Ducru-Beaucaillou was tasted on numerous occasions blind against the fabulous 1995. Which vintage is superior? It is a marginal call, but the 1996 appears slightly longer, with a deeper mid-palate. It also reveals more tannin in the finish. The 1996 is more muscular, concentrated, and classic. This wine exhibits a saturated ruby/purple color, as well as a knockout nose of minerals, licorice, cassis, and an unmistakable lead pencil smell that I often associate with top vintages of Lafite Rothschild. It is sweet and full-bodied yet unbelievably rich with no sense of heaviness or flabbiness. The wine possesses high tannin, but it is extremely ripe and the sweetness of the black currant, spice-tinged Cabernet Sauvignon fruit is pronounced. This profound, backward Ducru-Beaucaillou is a must purchase. It will be fascinating for readers who own both the 1996 and 1995 to follow the evolution of these two exceptional vintages. Anticipated maturity: 2008–2035. Last tasted, 8/02.

1995
94
More open-knit and accessible than the 1996, Ducru's 1995 exhibits a saturated ruby/purple color, followed by a knockout nose of blueberry and black raspberry/cassis fruit intertwined with minerals, flowers, and subtle toasty new oak. Like its younger sibling, the wine possesses a sweet, rich mid-palate (from extract and ripeness, not sugar), layers of flavor, good delineation and grip, but generally unobtrusive tannin and acidity. It is a classic, compelling example of Ducru-Beaucaillou that should not be missed. Anticipated maturity: 2005–2025. Last tasted, 8/02.

1994
89
A top-notch effort in this vintage, Ducru-Beaucaillou's 1994 displays a dark purple color, a textbook cassis, mineral, licorice, and floral-scented nose, medium body, outstanding extract and purity, moderate tannin, and a persuasively rich, sweet, spicy finish. Everything is well integrated (including the tannin). This should prove to be a classic St.-Julien. Anticipated maturity: 2004–2022. Last tasted, 8/02.

1986
90+
At 16 years of age, this wine continues to taste more like a 5–7-year-old Bordeaux. The color is a handsome dark ruby with just a bit of pink at the edge. The wine exhibits sweet red and black currant fruit intermixed with wet stones, spice, and flowers. Medium bodied and still moderately tannic but very concentrated, this firmly structured, slightly austere wine has tremendous upside to it. By the way, this was the first vintage where I began to notice on some bottles the wet cement/damp cardboard aromas that were far more increasingly evident in the subsequent vintages, 1990, 1989, 1988, and 1987. Interestingly, the last five times I have tasted the 1986 Ducru-Beaucaillou, they were totally pristine bottles. Anticipated maturity: 2006–2030. Last tasted, 5/02.

1985
92
A wine of extraordinary charm and elegance, the dark garnet–colored 1985 Ducru-Beaucaillou has a floral, cedary nose intermixed with red and black currants as well as flowers. The wine is fully mature and soft, with beautiful concentration and

purity. It is not a blockbuster and certainly not nearly as powerful and massive as the 1986, but it is certainly much more seductive. This wine should continue to drink well for at least another 10–15 years. Anticipated maturity: now–2012. Last tasted, 5/02.

1983
86
In decline, the 1983 Ducru-Beaucaillou is showing notes of asphalt, earth, compost, and peppery, herb-tinged black fruits. The aromas in the attack exhibit good complexity, but then the wine becomes attenuated, even desiccated in the finish. The wine is medium bodied and needs to be drunk up. Anticipated maturity: now–2006. Last tasted, 5/02.

1982
95
One of the few top Médocs that seems to be close to full maturity, the 1982 Ducru-Beaucaillou shows a dense, almost inky, plum/garnet color, a striking nose of minerals intermixed with cedar, black currant, autumnal leaves, and spice box. The wine is chewy and opulent, particularly for a Ducru-Beaucaillou, with a lot of flesh and concentration. The tannins are still there but are sweet, and the velvety finish is suggestive of a wine that has entered its plateau of maturity. A gorgeous effort and certainly the best Ducru-Beaucaillou until the mid- to late 1990s. Anticipated maturity: now–2016. Last tasted, 1/03.

1981
88
Consistently one of the most successful wines of this vintage, this mid-weight Ducru-Beaucaillou is showing some pink and amber at the edge. The wine has an attractive nose of wet stones, sweet currant, and mulberry fruit intermixed with a hint of spice and earth. The wine has medium body, light tannin, and an easygoing finish. Anticipated maturity: now–2007. Last tasted, 5/02.

ANCIENT VINTAGES

In the 1970s, the 1978 was one of the stars of the vintage and was still in great shape when last tasted (rated 90 in 5/02). Another terrific wine is the 1970, now beginning its decline. This wine (which I have rated as high as 92–93 when last drunk in 3/99) is a classic Ducru-Beaucaillou with great finesse, complexity, and elegance that is textbook St.-Julien. However, the wine requires consumption now.

In the 1960s, Ducru-Beaucaillou turned in competent efforts in 1966 and 1962, but probably the greatest Ducru-Beaucaillou I ever tasted was the 1961, last tasted in 1999 and in serious decline. At one time, this was among the highest rated Ducrus in my experience, rated 96 in 5/91. I am sure it is just a shadow of itself now, unless of course readers have access to pristinely stored magnums or even larger format bottles.

GLORIA

Classification: Cru Bourgeois

Owner: Françoise Triaud

Address: c/o Domaines Martin, 33250
St.-Julien-Beychevelle

Telephone: 05 56 59 08 18; Telefax: 05 56 59 16 18

Visits: By appointment only, Monday to Friday, 8 A.M.–noon and 2–6 P.M.

Contact: Corine Favereau

VINEYARDS

Surface area: 118.6 acres

Grape varietals: 65% Cabernet Sauvignon, 25% Merlot, 5% Cabernet Franc, 5% Petit Verdot

Average age of vines: 42 years

Density of plantation: 10,000 vines per hectare

Average yields: 50 hectoliters per hectare

Elevage: Prolonged fermentation and maceration in temperature-controlled tanks with pumpings over and *pigéages*. Fourteen months aging in barrels that are renewed by a third each year. Concentration by evaporation. Fining and filtration.

WINES PRODUCED

Château Gloria: 200,000 bottles

Château Peymartin: 50,000 bottles

Plateau of maturity: Within 5–10 years of the vintage

GENERAL APPRECIATION

Gloria's wines are fruit-driven and supple, always soundly made and consistently reliable. Because Gloria is not classified (it was created in the 1940s, after the 1855 and 1932 classifications), its prices remain reasonable, but in terms of quality, it can rival a fourth or fifth growth in some vintages. This wine, which is much less expensive than most St.-Juliens, represents one of the best buys of the appellation, if not of the Médoc.

Gloria has always been used as an example of why the 1855 classification of the Médoc wines is so outdated. Not included in the original classification are wines Gloria has made (from vineyards purchased from neighboring classified châteaux) during the last 25 years that in vintages such as 2000, 1996, 1995, 1994, 1989, 1986, 1985, 1982, 1976, 1975, 1971, 1970, 1966, and 1961 are certainly as good as many of the wines produced by many of the classified growths. Shrewd merchants and consumers have long known Gloria's quality, and the wine has been widely merchandised in America and abroad.

The late Henri Martin, Gloria's owner, died in February 1991. He was one of the Médoc's legendary figures. His wines were no doubt made for sheer crowd appeal. They were round, generous, and very ripe, with wonderful cedary, spicy, almost exaggerated bouquets. Nothing appears to have changed under the management of his son-in-law, Jean-Louis Triaud. The wines perform surprisingly well young but can age for up to 12–15 years. The Gloria style of the 1960s and early 1970s changed after the mid-1970s. Gloria vintages from 1978–1993 definitely appear to be wines that are lighter, more obviously fruity, and less tannic than those wines that were made previously. However, the 2000, 1996, and 1995 were clearly beefier, richer wines, perhaps foreshadowing a return to the pre-1978 style. Gloria remains, in either style, a gloriously exuberant, delicious St.-Julien that continues to sell at a price well below its actual quality level. On a cautionary note, several vintages of the late 1990s had an alarmingly high percentage of "corked" bottles.

IMPORTANT VINTAGES

2000 Dense ruby/purple, the 2000 Gloria is a very fat, ripe, seductive effort. An excel-
89 lent, complex, evolved, and deliciously fruity effort, this medium-bodied 2000
exhibits sweet, herb-tinged, cassis fruit, cedar, and spice box notes along with
abundant glycerin and flesh. This well-endowed Gloria should drink well between
2004–2015. Last tasted, 1/03.

1998 This is an attractively fat, commercially styled, surprisingly soft 1998. It displays
85 herb-tinged berry fruit, notes of saddle leather, and a medium-bodied, round finish. It should drink well for 5–6 years. Last tasted, 3/02.

1996 One of the finest Glorias produced in recent vintages, the 1996 is uncommonly he-
88 donistic, plump, and precociously styled. Low in acidity, rich in cedary, black currant fruit, medium bodied, and lush, it will provide delicious drinking young, yet
will age for 10 years. Last tasted, 3/02.

1995 The 1995 is lower in acidity and may not possess quite the density and power of
88 the 1996, but readers looking for high-class Claret with immediate appeal would
be foolish to pass it by. It, too, should be consumed within the next 10 years. Last
tasted, 3/02.

ANCIENT VINTAGES

For whatever reason, the 1990 and 1989 never lived up to be as good as those vintages'
reputations. Among my favorite Glorias of the past is the 1982 (89 points; last tasted
8/02). This wine has consistently been one of the most pleasant surprises of the vintage. Drinkable on release, drinkable in its youth, and drinkable in its full maturity,
this wine exhibits gorgeous weedy, black currant fruits, full body, and a very luscious,
fleshy mouth-feel. I would not push the wine much further, but certainly from pristine
cellars, this wine is probably capable of lasting until at least 2005–2006. Although I
have not tasted the wine in more than a decade, the 1970 was also a gorgeous wine, but
I am sure it is now in decline.

GRUAUD LAROSE

Classification: Second Growth in 1855

Owner: Bernard Taillan Vins (Merlaut family)

Address: 33250 St.-Julien-Beychevelle

Mailing Address: BP 6, 33250 St.-Julien-Beychevelle

Telephone: 05 56 73 15 20, Telefax: 05 56 59 64 72

E-mail: contact@chateau-gruaud-larose.com

Visits: By appointment only

Contact: Régine Peyrille

VINEYARDS

Surface area: 202.5 acres

Grape varietals: 57% Cabernet Sauvignon, 31% Merlot, 7.5% Cabernet Franc, 3% Petit
Verdot, 1.5% Malbec

Average age of vines: 40 years

Density of plantation: 8,500–10,000 vines per hectare

Average yields: 50–60 hectoliters per hectare

Elevage: Fermentation at 31–33°C with indigenous yeasts and 21–35 day maceration in temperature-controlled concrete and wooden vats, with two daily pumpings-over. Half the yield undergoes malolactics in oak. Sixteen to eighteen months aging in barrels that are renewed by a third each year. No details regarding fining and filtration are forthcoming from the château.

WINES PRODUCED

Château Gruaud Larose: 300,000 bottles

Sarget de Gruaud Larose: 200,000 bottles

Plateau of maturity: Within 10–35 years of the vintage

GENERAL APPRECIATION

This can be one of the most massive and backward St.-Juliens. Since the mid-1990s, a more supple and elegant style has emerged. Unfortunately, some vintages still reveal excessive tannins in view of the fruit and stuffing of the wines. As a matter of fact, Gruaud's recent track record is irregular—when the estate does well, it is consistent with its pedigree and often better, but a great effort is sometimes followed by one that is overly tannic and structured (i.e., 1998 and 1997; 1994 and 1993). Readers seeking Gruaud Larose for long-term aging (i.e., wines whose fruit will not fade before the tannins are fully melted) should be careful when picking a vintage. Prices are equivalent to those of most Bordeaux second growths.

For decades, Gruaud Larose produced St.-Julien's most massive and backward wine. Under the new proprietor, Jacques Merlaut, there has been an obvious trend to produce a more refined, less rustic and tannic style of Gruaud. Merlaut has invested significantly in this estate, establishing a computerization of all data from the estate's 66 different parcels. In addition, an expensive drainage system was installed. I expect this recent winemaking direction to continue. The production is large and the quality consistently high. Gruaud Larose produced wines of first-growth quality in vintages such as 2000, 1990, 1986, 1985, 1983, 1982, and 1961. The beautiful château, which sits on the plateau of St.-Julien rather than riverside, is not likely to be seen unless the visitor to the Médoc turns off the main Route du Vin (D2) at the town of St.-Julien-Beychevelle and takes route D101 in a westerly direction.

Those critics of Gruaud Larose who found the wine too chunky, solid, and massive may want to revisit this wine now that it is taking on more finesse and elegance.

IMPORTANT VINTAGES

2001 Gruaud Larose's, astringent tannin gives the 2001 a certain austerity. Does it pos-
88–90 sess sufficient substance and fat to cover the massive structure? A deep ruby/purple color is followed by aromas of underbrush, tar, mint, and black currants. The big framework is there, and the charm, flesh, and richness have begun to emerge. A medium to full-bodied wine. The 2001 is a deeper, richer wine than the charming 1999. I cannot see it ever performing up to the quality of the spectacular 2000. Anticipated maturity: 2008–2020. Last tasted, 1/03.

2000 This immense, opaque black/purple–colored, structured offering possesses high
94+   tannin, full body, and a broodingly backward personality (similar to the 2000
      Léoville Barton) with immense extract, concentration, and power. This long-lived
      behemoth will require patience as it is the densest, most powerful and tannic wine
      made since the estate's sumptuous 1990. Anticipated maturity: 2015–2030+. Last
      tasted, 1/03.

1999 An exotic perfume of tapenade, new saddle leather, damp earth, black currants,
89   cherries, and smoke jumps from the glass of this impressive, powerful 1999.
      Medium bodied with moderate tannin, this dark plum/ruby-colored St.-Julien re-
      quires another 1–2 years of cellaring. Anticipated maturity: 2005–2015. Last
      tasted, 3/02.

1998 Gruaud Larose has fashioned an elegant, less rustic wine than previous vintages.
88   The color is a healthy dark ruby/purple. The bouquet offers aromas of plums,
      black raspberries, and cassis. Stylish, with medium to full body, sweet tannin, and
      excellent purity as well as overall symmetry, it will drink well between 2004–
      2016. Last tasted, 3/02.

1997 The 1997 Gruaud Larose is a soft, fleshy effort loaded with olive and licorice-
86   tinged, black cherry and cassis fruit. Smoky, new saddle leather notes also emerge
      as the wine sits in the glass. Offering excellent richness, medium body, moderate
      weight, low acidity, and soft tannin, it will provide delicious as well as surprisingly
      complex, savory drinking for 5–6 years. Last tasted, 1/02.

1996 This is a stylish, surprisingly civilized, medium-bodied wine that, however, does
89   not possess the muscle and power expected from both this *terroir* and vintage. It
      still possesses excellent density, as well as roasted herb, licorice, and black cur-
      rant flavors intermixed with incense-like smells. The wine is medium to full-
      bodied, pure, rich, and forward, especially for a 1996. Anticipated maturity:
      2004–2018. Last tasted, 3/02.

1995 Revealing good grip and tannin, the 1995 Gruaud Larose exhibits a dark ruby
89   color and a nose of sweet black cherries, licorice, earth, and spice. Rich,
      with medium to full body, high tannin, and subtle oak in the background, the
      1995 is nearly as structured and tannic as the 1996. The two vintages are
      more similar than dissimilar. Anticipated maturity: 2007–2020. Last tasted,
      3/02.

1994 The 1994 has dropped much of its mid-palate sweetness and fatness, tastes herba-
82?   ceous, and possesses a mouth-searing harsh, bitter tannin. Perhaps it remains dor-
      mant, but does it possess sufficient ripeness, fruit, and texture to balance out the
      tannins? I don't think so. Anticipated maturity: 2006–2015. Last tasted, 3/02.

1990 This wine continues to get better and better and is certainly one of the great suc-
96   cesses in what is a profound vintage for Bordeaux. While the wine still tastes
      young, it is already complex, with so much sweet tannin and lavish fruit that it is
      impossible to resist, even though it probably will not hit its plateau of maturity for
      another 5–6 years. A stunning nose of licorice, earth, cedar, Provençal herbs,
      black currants, asphalt, and cherries soars from the glass. Full-bodied, opulent,
      with fabulous concentration, a seamless texture, and remarkable stuffing and
      power, this low-acid, thick, almost viscous wine can be drunk now or cellared for
      at least another two decades.
         For trivia buffs, this was the wine President Chirac served former President
      Clinton when he hosted Clinton in Paris at the famous Parisian bistro L'Ami Louis
      in June 1999. I know, because several days later President Chirac gave me the Le-
      gion of Honor. In his speech, he acknowledged the fact that President Clinton only
      wanted to "drink a wine rated highly by Robert Parker." Anticipated maturity:
      now–2020. Last tasted, 9/02.

1989 Somewhat of a letdown when tasted side by side with the 1990, the dark garnet–
89 colored 1989 Gruaud Larose offers up notes of cedar, tobacco leaf, red and black currants, and some hints of compost. The nose smells mature, on the palate it is relatively ripe and sweet, but then the wine seems to have plenty of tannin and toughness without that incredible, chewy mid-palate the 1990 possesses. The wine still seems somewhat disjointed, but there are plenty of good things to be found. Perhaps the real problem is that it just suffers in comparison to the profound 1990. Anticipated maturity: 2005–2018. Last tasted, 5/02.

1988 Dark plum/garnet, with a powerful nose of licorice, roasted meats, smoke, and
89 sweet berry and black currant flavors, this medium-bodied, relatively austere but robust and concentrated Gruaud Larose still seems like a young wine, and possibly will be longer-lived than its more renowned sibling, the 1989. There is an earthiness and underlying streak of herbaceousness, but there is plenty of depth, concentration, and power to this somewhat burly Gruaud Larose. Anticipated maturity: now–2025. Last tasted, 9/02.

1986 Still tasting as if it were only 7–8 years of age, the dense, garnet/purple-colored
96 1986 Gruaud Larose is evolving at a glacial pace. The wine still has mammoth structure, tremendous reserves of fruit and concentration, and a finish that lasts close to a minute. The wine is massive, very impressively constituted, with still some mouth-searing tannin to shed. Decanting of one to two hours in advance seems to soften it a bit, but this is a wine that seems to be almost immortal in terms of its longevity. It is a great Médoc classic and certainly one of the most magnificent Gruaud Larose ever made. Anticipated maturity: 2006–2035. Last tasted, 10/02.

1985 Fully mature, the dark garnet–colored 1985 exhibits notes of tapenade, earth,
91 sweet berry, and black currant fruit, and possibly a hint of black truffles. The wine is lush, medium to full-bodied, and fleshy, with no hard edges. Sweet fruit, plenty of glycerin, and a very seductive style make for a very sumptuous, complex, fully mature Gruaud Larose. Anticipated maturity: now–2008. Last tasted, 8/02.

1983 Beginning to show a few cracks around the edges, this once outstanding wine still
89 has a very complex nose of roasted meats, cigar smoke, asphalt, licorice, and black, juicy cherries and currants. The wine's succulence and fat, once one of its hallmarks, are beginning to dry out ever so slightly. The tannins and acids seem a bit more noticeable in the finish than I remember during its first 10–15 years of life. I would suspect this wine is still at its peak of perfection from magnum or bigger formats, but from regular bottle, even from my very cold cellar, this wine is starting to show some of the telltale signs of wear and tear. Anticipated maturity: now–2008. Last tasted, 8/02.

1982 Along with the 1961, the 1982 is one of the two greatest Gruaud Laroses I have
98 ever tasted. It needs decanting of a good one to two hours in advance not only for aeration purposes, but also to get it off of its very heavy sediment. The color remains a murky, opaque purple/garnet. The phenomenal nose smells like a Spanish tapas bar with notes of new saddle leather, licorice, tar, crème de cassis, olives, and grilled meats. Extremely full-bodied with a viscous texture, remarkable levels of glycerin, and fabulous concentration, the 1982 Gruaud Larose is still an adolescent in terms of its development. The finish is filled with extract and tannin in a large, massively scaled style. I misidentified this wine as a first growth when tasted blind . . . it is that compelling. Anticipated maturity: 2004–2025. Last tasted, 11/02.

ANCIENT VINTAGES

This property has an enviable track record, with excellent wines made in 1981 (88 points; last tasted 3/00), 1979 (88 points; last tasted 12/00), and even a successful 1975 (90? points; last tasted 2/02). The latter wine still has an excess of tannin, but the sheer concentration and power of the wine remains unchanged. This is the kind of wine that most people will probably give up on, but we will not really know if it is ever going to achieve greatness until about 2020. Nevertheless, I am still an optimist, and I hope I am alive to see it hit its plateau of maturity. It is probably available for a song since most people have given up on it, but this wine still tastes relatively young, just very tannic. The 1970 was somewhat of a disappointment, but Gruaud Larose made excellent wines in 1966, 1964, 1962, and, of course one of their all-time greats, the 1961 (that wine was last tasted on New Year's Day 2001, and was still a fabulous wine that I would rate 96). Except for the 1949, I have not tasted any of the historic vintages since the last edition of this book, but pristine bottles, preferably in magnums or bigger, of the 1955 (90, last tasted 3/98), 1953 (93, last tasted 3/98), 1949 (90?, last tasted 1/02), 1945 (96+, last tasted 10/94), and 1928 (97, last tasted 10/94) might well be worth their high cost of admission, given how stunning they were when I last had them.

HORTEVIE

Classification: Cru Bourgeois

Owner: Henri Pradère

Address: 33250 St.-Julien-Beychevelle

Telephone: 05 56 59 06 27; Telefax: 05 56 59 29 32

No visits

VINEYARDS

Surface area: 8.6 acres

Grape varietals: 70% Cabernet Sauvignon, 25% Merlot, 5% Petit Verdot

Average age of vines: 40 years

Density of plantation: 10,000 vines per hectare

Average yields: 50 hectoliters per hectare

Elevage: Three week fermentation and maceration in temperature-controlled stainless-steel vats. Twenty months aging in oak barrels that are renewed by 25% each year. Fining, no filtration.

WINES PRODUCED

Château Hortevie: 18,000 bottles

No second wine is produced.

Plateau of maturity: Within 3–10 years of the vintage

GENERAL APPRECIATION

This well-made wine, worth a Cru Bourgeois Exceptionnel, remains reasonably priced and represents a good value among St.-Juliens. Unfortunately, the production is very small.

The tiny production of Hortevie comes from a vineyard of Henri Pradère, who also owns Terrey-Gros-Cailloux. Although both these wines are made by identical methods from the same vineyard, Hortevie is said to be produced from older vines and is treated as somewhat of *a tête de cuvée* of Terrey-Gros-Cailloux. Pradère's tendency to pick late has always resulted in rich, concentrated, low-acid wines that begged for some structure from new oak casks. These were finally introduced at Hortevie in the late 1980s, although much of the production of both Hortevie and Terrey-Gros-Cailloux is still aged in tank until the proprietor deems it ready for bottling. Hortevie is a consistently good St.-Julien and has long represented a fine value. While not long-lived, the top vintages, such as 1996, 1995, 1989, 1986, and 1982, are capable of aging well for 10–15 years.

LAGRANGE

Classification: Third Growth in 1855

Owner: Château Lagrange SA (Suntory)

Address: 33250 St.-Julien-Beychevelle

Telephone: 05 56 73 38 38; Telefax: 05 56 59 28 09

E-mail: chateau-lagrange@chateau-lagrange.com

Website: www.chateau-lagrange.com

Visits: By appointment Monday to Thursday, 9–11 A.M. and 2–4 P.M.

Contact: Marcel Ducasse

VINEYARDS

Surface area: 269.2 acres

Grape varietals: 66% Cabernet Sauvignon, 27% Merlot, 7% Petit Verdot

Average age of vines: 25 years

Density of plantation: 8,500 vines per hectare

Average yields: 58 hectoliters per hectare

Elevage: Fermentation at 28°C and three-week maceration in temperature-controlled stainless-steel tanks. Twenty months aging in barrels with 60% new oak. Fining and filtration.

WINES PRODUCED

Château Lagrange: 300,000 bottles

Les Fiefs de Lagrange: 450,000 bottles

Plateau of maturity: Within 7–15 years of the vintage

GENERAL APPRECIATION

After producing mediocre wines in the 1960s and 1970s, Lagrange had improved spectacularly after its acquisition by Japan's Suntory. Lagrange merits its present classification and represents a reasonably good value, given the fact that it remains less renowned than its more famous siblings of St.-Julien.

Prior to 1983, Lagrange (a third growth) had suffered numerous blows to its reputation as a result of a pathetic track record of quality in the 1960s and 1970s. The well-situated vineyards represent a rare unmorseled property adjacent to Gruaud Larose so there was no reason why good wine should not have been produced.

In 1983 the huge Japanese company Suntory purchased Lagrange and began an extraordinary renovation of not only the château and the *chais,* but also the vineyards. No expense has been spared, and such talented people as administrator Marcel Ducasse and the property's young, enthusiastic oenologist, Kenji Suzuta, have begun to make stunning wines in an amazingly short period of time.

Not only has the quality of the wines been upgraded, but Lagrange is now a beautiful château with tranquil gardens and a lake teeming with swans and ducks.

If vintages from 1985 on reveal any particular style, it is one that favors an impressive depth of flavor welded to plenty of tannin, toasty new oak, and an underlying succulence and fatness that is no doubt due to a strict selection and the harvesting of very ripe fruit with an element of *sur-maturité.* Clearly the new proprietors seem intent on producing a wine that can age for 20 or more years, yet have appeal when young.

While the world press has applauded the extraordinary turnaround made at Château Margaux by the Mentzelopoulos family, less has been written about the turn of events at Château Lagrange, although in 1990 *The Wall Street Journal,* amazingly, ran a front-page story about this showpiece property. Nevertheless, this wine currently remains considerably underpriced given the quality level of the wines that have emerged.

IMPORTANT VINTAGES

2001
88–90?   This is among the most extracted, concentrated St.-Juliens of the vintage. An ambitious effort, it possesses a dense, thick purple color in addition to an aggressive overlay of heavy new oak and sweet black currants, cherries, licorice, smoke, and coffee notes. The oak is out of sync and the finish is angular as well as austere. If the tannin melts away and the oak becomes less evident, this 2001 may merit an outstanding rating. It is a big, muscular, structured style of Lagrange. Anticipated maturity: 2007–2018. Last tasted, 1/03.

2000
93   The most impressive Lagrange produced in more than a decade, the 2000 exhibits an opaque purple color along with a big, smoky nose of new oak intermixed with crème de cassis, cherries, saddle leather, and spice. With medium to full body, high tannin, and impressive richness as well as length, it will be at its finest between 2008–2025. A brilliant wine! Last tasted, 1/03.

1999
86   This 1999's aggressive new oak seems excessive for the amount of depth and fruit it possesses. There is excellent purity as well as texture, but the oak dominates at present, causing the tannin to taste dry and astringent. Nevertheless, it has the potential to become an elegant, midsized St.-Julien to drink during its first decade of life. Last tasted, 3/02.

1998
88
This dark ruby–colored, elegant, attractive effort offers spicy new oak, medium body, excellent concentration as well as depth, surprising softness, and early appeal. As with many Médocs, Lagrange's tannins have become much friendlier after bottling. Anticipated maturity: now–2015. Last tasted, 3/02.

1997
85
Light to medium bodied with spicy oak, red currant, and cherry fruit, this well-made, lightly tannic effort will provide uncritical drinking over the next 3–4 years. Last tasted, 3/01.

1996
92
The superb 1996 is opaque purple-colored with a backward yet promising nose of classically pure cassis intermixed with toast and spice. This medium to full-bodied, powerful yet stylish wine possesses superb purity, a nicely layered feel in the mouth, and plenty of structure. It will not be an early drinking St.-Julien, but one to lay away for 2–3 more years and enjoy over the next two decades. Anticipated maturity: 2006–2022. Last tasted, 3/03.

1995
90
The 1995 Lagrange is similar to the 1996, but the fruit is sweeter, the acidity lower, and the wine less marked by Cabernet Sauvignon. The color is a deep ruby/purple. The wine boasts a roasted herb, charcoal, black currant, mineral, and new oak–scented nose. Medium to full-bodied and ripe, with copious quantities of jammy black cherry and cassis flavors presented in a low-acid, moderately tannic style, this is a well-endowed, purely made wine. Anticipated maturity: 2007–2020. Last tasted, 1/00.

1994
87
The 1994 is a backward, tannic wine that needs cellaring. It is a wine that recalls the style of the more tannic vintages of the 1960s and 1970s. The healthy dark ruby/purple color is followed by copious quantities of smoky, toasty new oak. There is an impression of ripe fruit, but for now the wine's personality remains dominated by excruciatingly strong tannin. Give this wine several more years of cellaring; it should last for 12–15 years. Anticipated maturity: 2006–2014. Last tasted, 1/00.

1990
94
The 1990 is a massive, highly extracted, boldly wooded, spicy, dark purple–colored wine with high tannin, low acidity, and layers of jammy fruit. The huge glycerin and massive mouth-feel in this unctuously textured wine are difficult to ignore. I suspect this wine will become more defined after it loses its baby fat. Although fun to taste at present, it does need 3–4 more years of cellaring; it should last for 20–25 years. Last tasted, 3/03.

1989
90
The 1989 is a smoky, tar, cassis, roasted herb, jammy style of wine, with a dense purple color, sweet tannin, and low acidity. It is easy to drink, although the bouquet has not changed since I tasted it several years ago. The wine is soft and fat, but not flabby. It should drink well for 15+ years, probably developing more focus as well as a more classical profile. The 1989 Lagrange is a big, rich, boldly flavored wine made in a California-like style. Last tasted, 1/97.

1988
86
The 1988 exhibits a dark ruby/purple color and a closed but spicy, reticent bouquet vaguely suggestive of cedar, plums, and green olives. This medium-bodied, surprisingly hard and tannic wine will need 4–6 years of bottle age to soften. Last tasted, 1/97.

1986
92
Here is a classic example of a wine that is showing significantly more complexity and richness from the bottle than out of cask, although it was certainly a potentially outstanding wine when tasted from the barrel. In a vintage that produced a number of enormously structured, rich, concentrated wines. Lagrange is another of the blockbuster wines that seems capable of lasting 30–35 years. Black/ruby in color with a closed but burgeoning bouquet of spicy new oak, black fruits, and flowers, this muscular, full-bodied, tannic wine is packed with fruit and is clearly one of the great long-distance runners from this vintage. I admire how the significant investment made by the Japanese owners in this property has paid off with a

thrilling, albeit amazingly backward wine. The finest Lagrange to date! Anticipated maturity: now–2025. Last tasted, 1/97.

1985   Lagrange's recent vintages are powerfully constructed wines made to survive sev-
89   eral decades of aging with grace and complexity. The dark ruby–colored 1985 is deep, rich, long, and, for a 1985, surprisingly backward and tannic. Medium bodied, elegant, and packed with fruit, it is a long-distance runner. Anticipated maturity: now–2010. Last tasted, 1/97.

1983   The 1983 Lagrange is deep in color, spicy, and rich, with full-bodied, briery, cas-
86   sis flavors, good firm tannins, and a long finish. If the wine resembles the style of Léoville Las Cases, it's not surprising because Michel Delon, the gifted wine-maker at Las-Cases, oversaw the vinification of Lagrange in 1983. Anticipated maturity: now. Last tasted, 3/89.

1982   This dark garnet wine has a well-developed bouquet of ripe berry fruit, herbs, as-
85   phalt, and vanilla. The wine is fully mature and medium bodied with nicely concentrated flavors. The finish is somewhat flat. Anticipated maturity: now. Last tasted, 8/02.

LANGOA BARTON

Classification: Third Growth in 1855

Owner: Barton family

Address: 33250 St.-Julien-Beychevelle

Telephone: 05 56 59 06 05; Telefax: 05 56 59 14 29

Visits: By appointment Monday to Thursday, 9–11 A.M. and 2–4 P.M.

Contact: Maud Pinto

VINEYARDS

Surface area: 42 acres

Grape varietals: 70% Cabernet Sauvignon, 20% Merlot, 10% Cabernet Franc

Average age of vines: 30 years

Density of plantation: 9,000 vines per hectare

Average yields: 50 hectoliters per hectare

Elevage: Fifteen to twenty-one-day fermentation and maceration in temperature-controlled wooden vats of 200 hectoliter capacity. Twenty months aging in barrels with 50% new oak. Fining and filtration.

WINES PRODUCED

Château Langoa Barton: 90,000 bottles

Lady Langoa: 30,000 bottles

Plateau of maturity: Within 8–22 years of the vintage

GENERAL APPRECIATION

One of the least known of Bordeaux classified growths, Langoa is overshadowed by its more prestigious stablemate Léoville Barton. Often overly tannic and backward, it is less charming than most St.-Juliens. All in all, Langoa is a good buy, but only for patient consumers . . . or gamblers.

Langoa Barton is an impressively large château that sits directly on the well-traveled D2, or Médoc Route du Vin. The wine of the well-known second-growth Léoville Barton is also made in the château's cellars. Both Langoa and Léoville Barton are the properties of Anthony Barton, an Irishman whose family has had an interest in the Bordeaux area since 1821.

The late Ronald Barton and now his handsome nephew Anthony have produced top-class wine that critics have called uncompromisingly traditional and classic. Both are St.-Juliens with a distinctive Pauillac character and personality. Since the wines are made in the same wine cellar, by the same staff, the first question someone always asks is how they differ. In most years, Léoville Barton surpasses the quality of Langoa. Both are big, ripe, concentrated, spicy wines that frequently lack the youthful suppleness and commercial up-front charm of some of their neighbors. Nevertheless, they age extremely well and when mature combine the savory, complex, graceful fruitiness of St.-Julien with the cedary toughness and virility of Pauillac.

Rarely has Léoville nor Langoa Barton enjoyed the reputation of Léoville Las Cases and Ducru-Beaucaillou. That has changed since Anthony Barton has had full responsibility for the property, taking over when his uncle Ronald died in 1986. A stricter selection and the increased usage of new oak were immediately noticeable. These moves, plus a hard-headed, refreshingly realistic view that wine is not really sold until the consumer buys a bottle and drinks it, have all combined to make Langoa Barton and Léoville Barton grossly underpriced, particularly now that the quality level is close to the "super-second" level.

My only criticism of Langoa Barton and Léoville Barton is that in some of the lighter Bordeaux vintages such as 1979, 1974, 1973, and 1971 the wines of these two châteaux taste less successful than many of their peers.

IMPORTANT VINTAGES

2001
89–91
A promising effort, the 2001 has a deep ruby/purple color, with a sweet nose of creosote, licorice, cedar, and cassis. Medium to full-bodied deep, very tannic, Langoa's 2001 is not far off the quality of the even bigger 2000. Anticipated maturity: 2009–2021. Last tasted 1/03.

2000
91+
This impressive, big, muscular, broodingly backward, strong, masculine 2000 is not yet revealing much complexity, but it does display tremendous depth, full-bodied, concentrated flavors, a boatload of tannin, and exciting length as well as potential. This is a wine for patient connoisseurs. As the French say, it is a *vin de garde*. Anticipated maturity: 2010–2035. Last tasted, 1/03.

1999
87?
A big, tannic, muscular effort for the vintage, Langoa Barton's 1999 is atypically backward and stubborn. However, there is attractive cassis/currant fruit under all the tannin. The question is, will the tannin subside sufficiently for the fruit to fully emerge? Anticipated maturity: 2006–2015. Last tasted, 1/03.

1998
89+
A dense ruby/purple color as well as a muscular, ageworthy personality are found in this "no BS" sort of wine. It possesses loads of body, impressive concentration, and firm tannin in the finish. However, it is a wine for those who are able to defer

their gratification, as it requires another 2–3 years of cellaring. Anticipated maturity: 2006–2025. Last tasted, 3/02.

1997
84
Not a top-notch effort, Langoa Barton's medium ruby–colored 1997 exhibits sweet, herb-tinged, berry, and currant aromas, spicy, cedary, medium-bodied flavors, low acidity, and a pleasant but undistinguished finish. Drink it over the next 3–4 years. Last tasted, 3/01.

1996
86+?
I consistently found this 1996 to be a hard wine. Despite its deep ruby/purple color, it is monolithic, with notes of earth and black currant fruit submerged beneath a tannic structure. Although medium bodied with some weight and extract, the wine is ferociously hard and backward. Give it 3–4 years of cellaring, and hope for the best. Anticipated maturity: 2008–2020. Last tasted, 3/01.

1995
86+?
The 1995 Langoa Barton has been perplexing to evaluate. It is woody, monolithic, and exceptionally tannic without the fruit and flesh necessary to provide equilibrium. There are some positive components—a saturated dark ruby/purple color, hints of ripe fruit, and pure, clean flavors—but the wine's angularity/austerity is troublesome. It will probably be a good but old-style Claret that will never resolve all of its tannic bite. Anticipated maturity: now–2016. Last tasted, 11/00.

1994
86+?
Dark ruby colored with an unexpressive nose, this wine may turn out too austere and severe. It exhibits good power and fruit extraction, but the astringent tannin may cause the fruit to dry out before the wine has shed its bitterness. Don't touch a bottle for 2–3 years . . . and keep your fingers crossed. Last tasted, 1/97.

1990
88
Always an elegant wine but at the same time possessing rustic tannins, this dark garnet–colored wine seems to still be a few years away from full maturity, yet it does not have the opulence, flesh, and overall expansiveness and volume of its bigger sibling, Léoville Barton. The wine shows notes of tar, black currant, spice box, and cedar, and it has excellent density and flavors, but a somewhat rugged finish that I am not sure is ever going to age out. Anticipated maturity: now–2012. Last tasted, 9/01.

1989
87
The 1989 Langoa Barton is a perplexing wine to evaluate, as the aromas and flavors seem to suggest full maturity, but there is still plenty of tannin in the finish. My instincts suggest the tannins will never be totally resolved. It is a medium-bodied, elegant wine that has complex notes of camphor, cedar, spice, herbs, and sweet red as well as black currants. The wine shows low acidity, moderately high tannin, and very good concentration, but the tannins still dominate. Anticipated maturity: now–2009. Last tasted, 9/01.

1988
85
Increasingly austere, firmly structured, and unyielding, the 1988 Langoa Barton shows a dark garnet color, some spice, licorice, asphalt, and weedy currants on the nose, and firm, tannic, moderately endowed flavors in a rather harsh finish. I do not think it is going to get any better, but will become increasingly attenuated. The wine is certainly capable of lasting 5–8 more years. Anticipated maturity: now–2012. Last tasted, 9/01.

1986
88?
Readers who have a touch of masochism in them may find this wine to be even better than I did. Every time I have tasted it, it has been burly and muscular with monster tannins and impressive concentration, but absurdly backward and unyielding. The color is still a dense garnet with only a bit of lightening at the edge. The nose offers up aromas of truffle, licorice, dried herbs, mushrooms, and sweet currant fruit. In the mouth, the wine remains closed, tannic, and austere. It is probably fashionable to give up on wines such as this, but there is a lot underneath the tannin. Anticipated maturity: 2006–2025. Last tasted, 9/01.

1985
88
If its younger sibling, the 1986, is all sinew, muscle, and tannin, the 1985 is its charming counterpart. Open-knit, fully mature, with sweet cherry and black currant, earthy notes, this ripe, graceful, very flavorful St.-Julien is at its peak, where

it should last for another 7–10 years. Anticipated maturity: now–2012. Last tasted, 9/01.

1982 This wine has turned out even better than I predicted. The wine still shows some
90 rustic tannin in the finish, but the gorgeous nose of caramel, cedar, spice box, black currant, and earth is followed by a dense, full-bodied, muscular, expansively flavored wine that still possesses considerable tannin. The wine is gorgeous to drink with several hours of decanting, but is still not at its peak of maturity. Anticipated maturity: now–2018. Last tasted, 9/01.

ANCIENT VINTAGES

Langoa Barton rarely appears at the auction market, but some of the vintages that I have had good experience with have been the 1970, 1961, 1959, 1953, 1952, and 1948. The greatest Langoa Barton I have ever tasted in my life was the 1948, which was rated 93 in March 1995.

LÉOVILLE BARTON

Classification: Second Growth in 1855

Owner: Barton family

Address: 33250 St.-Julien-Beychevelle

Telephone: 05 56 59 06 05; Telefax: 05 56 59 14 29

E-mail: chateau@leoville.barton.com

Visits: By appointment only

Contact: Maud Pinto

VINEYARDS

Surface area: 118.6 acres

Grape varietals: 72% Cabernet Sauvignon, 20% Merlot, 8% Cabernet Franc

Average age of vines: 30 years

Density of plantation: 9,000 vines per hectare

Average yields: 50 hectoliters per hectare

Elevage: Fifteen to twenty-one-day fermentation and maceration in temperature-controlled wooden vats of 200 hectoliter capacity. Twenty months aging in barrels with 50% new oak. Fining and filtration.

WINES PRODUCED

Château Léoville Barton: 264,000 bottles

La Réserve de Léoville Barton: 70,000 bottles

Plateau of maturity: Within 10–30 years of the vintage

GENERAL APPRECIATION

Since 1985, Léoville Barton has unquestionably improved and its pricing (except for the 2000) has not yet followed the quality curve, which is good news. One of the best buys among the super-seconds, this wine is, however, tannic and needs considerable time to fully express itself. While Léoville Barton rarely attains the level of Léoville Las Cases, the unrivaled St.-Julien, it is much less expensive.

Léoville Barton is generally acknowledged to have a huge qualitative edge on its sibling, Langoa Barton. Both properties are owned by Anthony Barton. Unlike other proprietors, Barton uses only a small amount of the supple, fleshy Merlot in the blend (although it has been increased to 20% with plantings in the mid-1980s), whereas the proportion of Cabernet Sauvignon is high not only for the commune of St.-Julien, but for the Médoc in general.

Léoville Barton is made at Langoa Barton because there is no château at Léoville. The main vineyard for Léoville Barton sits immediately behind the town of St.-Julien-Beychevelle and runs in a westerly direction, where it intersects with the large vineyard of Château Talbot.

The inconsistencies of the 1970s have been replaced by a consecutive string of brilliantly successful wines in the 1980s and 1990s. Since 1985 Anthony Barton has refined rather than changed the traditional style of this wine. Among all the top wines of St.-Julien, it represents the finest value.

IMPORTANT VINTAGES

2001
89–92
Following their profound 2000, Léoville Barton's 2001 appears to be an excellent effort from this perennial overachiever. The color is a handsome dense ruby/purple. The nose offers up hints of black fruits, licorice, earth, and cedar. High tannin gives this full-bodied wine an astringent bite, but its time in cask has been beneficial. Sufficient fat and stuffing to achieve total harmony has emerged, in addition to a layered texture. This has turned out much better than I initially expected. Anticipated maturity: 2008–2018? Last tasted, 1/03.

2000
96+
Undoubtedly one of the most majestic wines ever made at Léoville Barton, this behemoth displays massive power and structure. A prodigious, saturated purple–colored effort, it boasts layers of concentrated fruit along with notes of graphite, camphor, damp earth, and jammy cassis. Immense, even monstrous in the mouth, it possesses awesome extraction and richness, but the boatload of tannin will keep it from being fully appreciated for at least a decade, possibly longer. A modern day classic; it is an authentic *vin de garde* for patient wine connoisseurs. Amazing vino! Anticipated maturity: 2015–2040. Last tasted, 1/03.

1999
88+?
Dry tannin and a backward, austere, muscular, brooding personality characterize Léoville Barton's 1999. However, it is packed with grip, body, and depth. Give it 4–5 years of cellaring and hope the tannin melts away sufficiently for the fruit to come forward. It should last for two decades, but will it ever be balanced? Last tasted, 3/02.

1998
91
This opaque purple–colored, muscular, full-bodied, classically made St.-Julien displays impressive concentration, chewy, highly extracted flavors of black fruits, iron, earth, and spicy wood, a powerful mouth-feel, and three decades of longevity. A pure, uncompromising, traditionally styled wine, it is to be admired for its authenticity, class, and quality. Anticipated maturity: 2007–2035. Last tasted, 3/02.

1997
86
The elegant, spice box, cedary, oaky, red and black currant–scented and flavored 1997 Léoville Barton reveals surprising softness, medium body, low acidity, and ripe tannin. Drink it over the next 5–6 years. Last tasted, 1/02.

1996 The impressive 1996 is a classic. Although backward, it exhibits a dense ruby/
92+   purple color in addition to abundant black currant fruit intertwined with spicy oak
      and truffle-like scents. The wine is brilliantly made, full-bodied, and tightly struc-
      tured with plenty of muscle and outstanding concentration and purity. It should
      turn out to be a long-lived Léoville Barton (almost all this estate's recent top vin-
      tages have shared that characteristic) and somewhat of a sleeper of the vintage.
      However, patience is required. Anticipated maturity: 2007–2030. Last tasted,
      9/01.

1995 Somewhat closed and reticent after bottling but still impressive, this 1995 pos-
91   sesses a dark ruby/purple color, as well as an oaky nose with classic scents of cas-
      sis, vanilla, cedar, and spice. Dense and medium to full-bodied, with softer tannin
      and more accessibility than the 1996, but not quite the packed and stacked effect
      on the palate, the 1995 is an outstanding textbook St.-Julien. Anticipated matu-
      rity: 2004–2025. Last tasted, 9/01.

1994 An impressive, serious, classic Bordeaux for collectors who are willing to forget
89?   about it for at least a decade, this well-endowed offering is a 30-year wine. The
      dense, murky, purple color, closed aromatics, massive flavor richness, and high
      tannin recall the old, non-compromised, beefy, blockbuster Médocs produced 30
      years ago. However, this wine possesses relatively sweeter tannin. It is a classic,
      but patience is definitely required. Anticipated maturity: 2010–2025. Last tasted,
      9/01.

1990 Still backward, tannic, and formidably endowed, but beginning to budge from its
94   infancy, this opaque garnet/purple–colored wine offers up notes of licorice, damp
      earth, sweet black currants, wood, and some underbrush. Very full-bodied with
      huge amounts of glycerin and concentration backed up by some impressive levels
      of tannin, this wine is one of the more backward 1990s, but is just beginning to
      move out of infancy into adolescence. It is an exceptional wine that seems to have
      gotten even better than I predicted it would be from the cask and from its life early
      in the bottle. Anticipated maturity: 2004–2030. Last tasted, 9/01.

1989 This wine continues to lose out to its younger sibling, the 1990. Aromatically, the
89   dark garnet (some amber is beginning to creep in at the edge) 1989 seems fully
      mature until it hits the palate. There is big, spicy, cedary, sweet cherry and black
      currant fruit, along with some tobacco notes in the impressive aromatics. On the
      palate, the wine is more narrowly constructed and medium bodied, with excellent
      richness on the attack but then some relatively dry, dusty tannins in the finish.
      This kind of performance tends to suggest the wine needs to be drunk sooner
      rather than later. Anticipated maturity: now–2016. Last tasted, 9/01.

1988 Like several other 1988s, this wine's rather hard, unyielding style has given way to
89+   a classically structured Bordeaux with a very youthful color (younger than the
      1989), deep, earthy, cassis fruit intermixed with wood, smoke, mineral, and a hint
      of roasted herbs. The wine has excellent depth, medium to full body, moderate tan-
      nin, and a very youthful, vigorous feel. It is approachable, but seems destined to
      outlive the more renowned and expensive 1989. Somewhat of a sleeper of the vin-
      tage. Anticipated maturity: 2004–2018. Last tasted, 9/01.

1986 Still backward (frustratingly so), this wine shows a very dark ruby color with a hint
91+   of pink at the rim. The aromatics are beginning to emerge from just pure fruit-
      driven notes to secondary characteristics. Sweet earth, truffle, black currant, un-
      derbrush, and licorice emerge with coaxing. In the mouth, the wine is powerful,
      dense, with high tannin, impressive concentration, and a formidable, sort of old-
      style personality. The best 1986 Médocs are terrific wines, but have never been
      wines that show a lot of charm. Like so many of its siblings from the Médoc,
      one admires the wines more than actually enjoys them. I still have high hopes

that everything will come together. Anticipated maturity: 2006–2030. Last tasted, 5/02.

1985 The 1985 is a gorgeous example that may well represent a more modern-day clone
92 of the splendid 1953. Dark ruby/garnet with an open-knit, complex, ripe nose of sweet red as well as black currants, vanilla, fruitcake, tobacco, cedar, and earth, the wine is medium bodied with exceptional sweetness, soft tannin, and a supple, very nicely layered finish. A classic mid-weight Bordeaux, it will drink now and over the next decade. Anticipated maturity: now–2010. Last tasted, 1/02.

1983 Like many 1983s, this wine shows an evolved garnet color with some amber. Aro-
84? matically, the wine exhibits full maturity with notes of tree bark, sweet black cherry and currant fruit, mushrooms, and earth. In the mouth, the wine shows signs of cracking up, with the tannins and acidity dominating increasingly meager amounts of fruit. The finish was a bit desiccated. Anticipated maturity: now. Last tasted, 9/02.

1982 Still one of the most backward wines of the vintage, Léoville Barton's 1982 is a
94 wine of huge extract, high tannin, and a somewhat ancient style that recalls some of the Bordeaux of the late 1940s. The color is still a dense, even murky, opaque ruby/garnet. The wine offers up notes of licorice, cedar, black truffles, and sweet currant fruit. I had the wine twice in 2002, and my tasting notes were almost identical to the last time I had it in 1997, showing just how slowly this wine is evolving. The wine is enormous in the mouth, but still has some rather gritty, high tannins. It is a classic St.-Julien, with meat and black currants, great structure, and an amazingly youthful, vigorous feel. I would not touch a bottle for another 5–6 years. Proprietor Anthony Barton thinks it is more "rustic" than younger vintages. No new oak was used in 1982. Anticipated maturity: 2009–2035. Last tasted, 9/02.

ANCIENT VINTAGES

There is no question that, under Anthony Barton, this estate has been far more consistent than in the past. Nevertheless, there are some great wines to keep an eye out for, including a fabulous 1975 (now fully mature, but one of the most successful wines in the Médoc; rated 90 when last tasted 12/00). The 1970 can often hit the peak, but seems very irregular from bottle to bottle. Among the vintages of the 1960s, the fabulous 1961 stands out (92 points; last tasted 9/97). Even better than the 1961, but hard to know how good it would be today unless it was tasted out of pristinely stored magnums or larger formats, was the 1959 (94 points; last tasted 10/94). The 1953 is also glorious (95 points; last tasted 10/94), and of course in the late 1940s, Léoville Barton made some magnificent wines, including 1949 (95 points; last tasted 10/94), 1948 (one of the highest rated with 96 points; last tasted 10/94), and of course, probably the greatest Léoville Barton I have ever tasted, the 1945 (98 points; last tasted 10/94). I am sure these wines are still profound if they have been stored properly, as the great vintages of Léoville Barton seem capable of lasting 25–50 years or more.

LÉOVILLE LAS CASES

Classification: Second Growth in 1855

Owner: SC du Château Léoville Las Cases (Delon family)

Address: 33250 St.-Julien-Beychevelle

Telephone: 05 56 73 25 26; Telefax: 05 56 59 18 33

E-mail: leoville-las-cases@wanadoo.fr

Website: (under construction)

Visits: By appointment only

Contact: Jacqueline Marange

VINEYARDS

Surface area: 240 acres

Grape varietals: 65% Cabernet Sauvignon, 19% Merlot, 13% Cabernet Franc, 3% Petit Verdot

Average age of vines: 30 years

Density of plantation: 8,000 vines per hectare

Average yields: 42–50 hectoliters per hectare

Elevage: Twelve to twenty-day fermentation and maceration in temperature-controlled wooden, concrete, and stainless-steel vats. Twelve to twenty-four-months aging in barrels with 50–100% new oak depending upon the vintage. Fining, no filtration.

WINES PRODUCED

Château Léoville Las Cases: 216,000 bottles

Clos du Marquis: 240,000 bottles

Plateau of maturity: Within 8–30 years of the vintage

GENERAL APPRECIATION

Léoville Las Cases, the undisputed King of the St.-Julien, is one of the few Bordeaux classified growths that may be bought blindly year after year. Consistently of first-growth quality, this wine's track record has been remarkable in the 1980s and 1990s. Over recent years, it has turned toward a more elegant style while retaining its characteristic richness, depth, structure, and close-to-perfect equilibrium. Despite the fact that it is the most expensive St.-Julien, Las-Cases' pricing remains within acceptable limits. It is not a speculator's wine and is rarely seen at auctions. At consumer level, it is less expensive than the first growths but often equal in quality. The second wine of the estate, Clos du Marquis, is very good and in the best vintages competes favorably with third and fourth growths.

Léoville Las Cases is unquestionably one of the great names and wines of Bordeaux. Situated next to Latour, Léoville Las Cases' main vineyard of more than 100 acres is the picturesque, enclosed vineyard depicted on the wine's label. The estate is one of Bordeaux's largest, and while the meticulous and passionate commitment to quality may be equaled by several others, it is surpassed by no one. The man responsible was the late Michel Delon, and more recently, his son Jean-Hubert. Michel Delon was a proud man who was as admired as he was scorned. A perfectionist, his critics, and there were many, claimed he played games when selling his wines, doling out tiny quantities in great vintages to artificially drive up the price. Yet no one can argue about the splendid quality of his wines, the product of an almost maniacal obsession to be the finest, not just in St.-Julien, but in the entire Médoc! Who else would declassify more than 50% of their crop in an abundant vintage such as 1986 or an astonishing 67% in 1990? Who else would introduce not only a second wine, but a third wine (Bignarnon) as well? Who else would lavishly install marble floors in the air-conditioned *chais*? Like him or not, Michel Delon, ably assisted by Michel Rolland (not the Libourne oenologist) and Jacques Depoizier, consistently made one of the greatest wines in the Médoc during the 1980s and 1990s. His son seems more than capable of continuing in the path of his father.

The wines of Léoville Las Cases were erratic in the post–World War II era, yet the period from 1975 onward has witnessed the production of a string of successes that have come close to perfection in vintages such as 2000, 1996, 1995, 1994, 1990, 1986, 1985, 1982, 1978, and 1975. In fact, these wines are as profound as most of the Médoc's first growths in those vintages.

In comparison to Ducru-Beaucaillou, its chief rival in St.-Julien, the wines of Léoville Las Cases tend to be a shade darker in color, more tannic, larger scaled, more concentrated, and of course, built for extended cellaring. They are traditional wines, designed for connoisseurs who must have the patience to wait the 10–15 years necessary for them to mature properly. Should a reclassification of Bordeaux's 1855 classification take place, Léoville Las Cases, like Ducru-Beaucaillou and possibly Léoville Barton and Gruaud Larose, would merit and receive serious support for first-growth status.

IMPORTANT VINTAGES

2001　One of the classics of the vintage, this is a model of concentrated power and ele-
92–94+　gance. Only 40% of the production made it into the grand vin, which was produced from low yields of 32 hectoliters per hectare (compared to 43 hectoliters per hectare in 2000). A blend of 69% Cabernet Sauvignon, 19.5% Merlot, and 11.5% Cabernet Franc, it boasts a saturated, thick purple color as well as sweet black cherry, black currant, graphite, licorice, and subtle new oak aromas. Extremely rich, closed, backward, and brutally concentrated, this 2001 is more substantial than many of its peers. It will require patience given the high tannin in the finish. Anticipated maturity: 2012–2030. Last tasted, 1/03.

2000　Great purity of cassis and black cherry fruit dominates the aromatics of the
100　medium to full-bodied, austere, tannic, concentrated, voluminous 2000 Léoville Las Cases. Opaque purple with sweet, very pure flavors redolent with cherries, vanilla, mineral, and black currant, this textured, multilayered, full-bodied wine has prodigious density and depth; it will require significant patience. Will the 2000 rival the virtually perfect Las-Cases' efforts of 1996, 1990, 1986, and 1982? Probably, but the tannin still overlays it, giving it a youthful, backward, unevolved personality. Anticipated maturity: 2015–2040. Last tasted, 1/03.

1999　The 1999 Léoville Las Cases possesses a dense purple color as well as classic
93　aromas of vanilla, black cherries, and currants mixed with subtle toasty oak. While medium bodied with sweet tannin, it remains young, backward, and un-

evolved (unusual for a 1999). Its extraordinary purity and overall harmony give it a character all its own. This excellent Las-Cases will be at its finest between 2006–2022. This is one of the wines of the vintage! Last tasted, 1/03.

1998 The 1998 has turned out to be one of the vintage's superb Médocs. It boasts an
93   opaque black/purple color as well as a classic Léoville Las Cases display of lead pencil, gorgeously pure black raspberries and cherries, smoke, and graphite. A classic entry on the palate reveals firm tannin, medium to full body, superb concentration and purity, as well as a totally symmetrical mouth-feel. This wine is a worthy successor to such classic Las-Cases vintages as 1996, 1995, and 1988. Anticipated maturity: 2006–2025. Last tasted, 3/02.

1997 A star of the vintage, this classy, cedary, black currant, and sweet cherry–scented,
89   dense ruby–colored Las-Cases exhibits a beautiful dosage of new oak, medium body, expansive, sweet, concentrated flavors, plenty of glycerin, and exceptional purity. For a Léoville Las Cases, it is low in acidity and already delicious. Anticipated maturity: now–2016. Last tasted, 3/02.

1996 A profound Léoville Las Cases, this is one of the great modern-day wines of Bor-
98+   deaux, rivaling what the estate has done in vintages such as 2000, 1990, 1986, and 1982. The 1996's hallmark remains a sur-maturité (overripeness) of the Cabernet Sauvignon grape. Yet the wine has retained its intrinsic classicism, symmetry, and profound potential for complexity and elegance. The black/purple color is followed by a spectacular nose of cassis, cherry liqueur, toast, and minerals. It is powerful and rich on the attack, with beautifully integrated tannin, massive concentration, yet no hint of heaviness or disjointedness. As this wine sits in the glass it grows in stature and richness. It is a remarkable, seamless, palate-staining, and extraordinarily elegant wine—the quintessential St.-Julien made in the shadow of its next door neighbor, Latour. Despite the sweetness of the tannin, I would recommend cellaring this wine for another 4–5 years. Anticipated maturity: 2010–2040. Last tasted, 9/02.

1995 If it were not for the prodigious 1996, everyone would be concentrating on getting
95   their hands on a few bottles of the fabulous 1995 Léoville Las Cases, which is one of the vintage's great success stories. The wine boasts an opaque ruby/purple color and exceptionally pure, beautifully knit aromas of black fruits, minerals, vanilla, and spice. On the attack, it is staggeringly rich yet displays more noticeable tannin than its younger sibling. Exceptionally ripe cassis fruit, the judicious use of toasty new oak, and a thrilling mineral character intertwined with the high quality of fruit routinely obtained by Las-Cases make this a compelling effort. There is probably nearly as much tannin as in the 1996, but it is not as perfectly sweet as in the 1996. The finish is incredibly long in this classic. Only 35% of the harvest was of sufficient quality for the 1995 Léoville Las Cases. Anticipated maturity: 2008–2025. Last tasted, 9/02.

1994 One of the more massive Médocs of the vintage, this opaque purple–colored wine
91   exhibits fabulous richness and volume in the mouth. Layers of pure black cherry and cassis fruit are intermixed with stony, mineral-like scents, earth, and high-quality toasty oak. Medium to full-bodied with a sweet, rich entry, this wine possesses plenty of tannin, yet impressive extract and length. Léoville Las Cases is one of the half dozen great wines of the Médoc in 1994. Anticipated maturity: now–2025. Last tasted, 3/00.

1990 I underestimated this wine young, as it continues to put on weight and character.
97   In fact, of the great vintages of Léoville Las Cases, this is one of the more forward wines, largely because of the seamlessness of the 1990 and its exceptionally sweet tannin, combined with relatively low acidity. The color remains a healthy opaque dark plum/purple. The classic Las-Cases nose of sweet black currants, cherries,

minerals, lead pencil, and vanilla soars from the glass. Very full-bodied, expansive, and super-concentrated, yet so symmetrical and perfectly balanced (always a hallmark of Léoville Las Cases), this wine seems youthful yet very approachable. Anticipated maturity: now–2035. Last tasted, 12/01.

1989
90
Dark ruby (a far less saturated color than the 1990, for example), this wine offers up a somewhat internationally styled nose of new oak and ripe black currant fruit, with a hint of mineral and graphite. The wine is a medium weight, relatively elegant style of wine without nearly the power, density, and layers of concentration that the 1990 possesses. Like so many 1989s, there is a feeling that the selection was not as strict as it could have been, or that the harvest occurred perhaps a few days earlier than it should have to achieve full phenolic ripeness. This wine will continue to improve for at least another 15 or more years, and while it is an outstanding wine, it is hardly a profound example of Léoville Las Cases. Anticipated maturity: now–2016. Last tasted, 12/01.

1988
92
This wine continues to show brilliantly and is certainly a more successful effort than the more renowned and expensive 1989. The color is a dark, murky garnet/purple. The wine shows notes of underbrush, fruitcake, cedar, black cherries, and currants. The wine still shows some moderate tannins in the mouth, but the fruit is sweet, the wine is expansive, and the overall impression is a very symmetrical, medium- to full-bodied, rather classic Médoc. Anticipated maturity: now–2020. Last tasted, 12/01.

1986
100
The late Michel Delon always thought that this was the greatest vintage he had produced. We often tasted it side by side with the 1982, because I always preferred the latter vintage. Of course, the two vintages are quite different in style: The 1986 is a monument to classicism, with great tannin, extraordinary delineation, and a huge, full-bodied nose of sweet, ripe cassis fruit intermixed with vanilla, melon, fruitcake, and a multitude of spices. The wine has always been phenomenally concentrated yet wonderfully fresh and vigorous. The wine still seems young, yet it is hard to believe it is not close to full maturity. It is a great example of Léoville Las Cases and another compelling reason to take a serious look at the top Cabernet Sauvignon–based Médocs of 1986. Anticipated maturity: 2005–2035. Last tasted, 9/02.

1985
94
The 1985 is a gorgeously open-knit Las-Cases with a sweet nose of lead pencil, sweet black cherries and currants, and a hint of underbrush and new oak. Medium to full-bodied with expansiveness, supple tannins, and outstanding concentration, this is a beautifully made wine that still tastes like it is an adolescent and may even have an even greater upside as it continues to age. The low acidity and sweet tannin, however, suggest it has entered its plateau of maturity. Anticipated maturity: now–2018. Last tasted, 8/02.

1983
89
Like so many 1983s, this wine entered full maturity 6–7 years ago and now seems to be suggesting that it needs to be drunk up quickly, as the tannins and acidity continue to take hold and the fruit fades. The wine has a dark plum/garnet color with some amber at the edge. The wine is medium-bodied with a bit of sharpness in the finish. The aromas and attack of the wine are still intact, but consumption definitely seems warranted. Anticipated maturity: now–2010. Last tasted, 3/02.

1982
100
Still stubbornly backward, yet beginning to budge from its pre-adolescent stage, this dense, murky ruby/purple–colored wine offers up notes of graphite, sweet caramel, black cherry jam, cassis, and minerals. The nose takes some coaxing and the decanting of 2–4 hours prior to service is highly recommended. For such a low-acid wine, it is huge, well delineated, extremely concentrated, and surprisingly fresh. Perhaps because I lean more toward the hedonistic view of wine than the late Michel Delon, I have always preferred this to the 1986, but the truth is that

any lover of classic Médoc should have both vintages in their cellar as they represent perfection in the glass. This wine has monstrous levels of glycerin, extract, and density, but still seems very youthful and tastes more like a 7- to 8-year-old Bordeaux than one that is past its 20th birthday. A monumental effort. Anticipated maturity: 2005–2035. Last tasted, 9/02.

ANCIENT VINTAGES

Léoville Las Cases' record between 1975 and 1981 is very impressive, often with some of the best wines of the vintage, such as 1981 (89 points; last tasted 7/00), 1978 (90 points; last tasted 2/02), and of course, the 1975, a blockbuster that still has an excess of tannin but has a tremendous wealth of fruit and concentration (92? points; last tasted 3/02). The early 1970s were largely disappointing, including the 1970. In the 1960s, the 1966 (89 points; last tasted 5/95) and 1962 (88 points; last tasted 5/95) are the two top vintages. I tasted the 1961 several times (87 points; last tasted 3/99) with Michel Delon and simply thought it was not nearly the wine it should have been for the vintage. I actually preferred the 1959 (88 points; last tasted 3/99).

CLOS DU MARQUIS

The Clos du Marquis, the second label of Léoville Las Cases, was created at the end of the 19th century. This name, which has been used on a regular basis since the beginning of the last century, originates from the small "clos" (walled parcel) situated near the Château de Léoville (the residence of the late marquis de Las-Cases).

Clos du Marquis could be considered the precursor of the Bordeaux second wines, a movement that generally took hold in the mid- to late 1980s. It has always been made from the younger vines, or *cuvées* deemed of insufficient quality for the grand vin.

However, with time, the Clos du Marquis has acquired an identity of its own. Today the wine emerges from well-defined *terroirs* situated outside the Grand Clos de Las Cases and within the Petit Clos. These selected vineyards are surrounded by those of Pichon-Lalande, Léoville Poyferré, Léoville Barton, Lagrange, and Talbot.

Since 1989, Clos du Marquis has been close to the quality of a third or fourth growth.

IMPORTANT VINTAGES (CLOS DU MARQUIS)

2001
88–90 The powerful, concentrated 2001 Clos du Marquis is not dissimilar from its bigger sibling. This dense purple–colored offering exhibits admirable purity, medium body, abundant quantities of sweet fruit, and ripe tannin. It should drink well between 2004–2015. Last tasted, 1/03.

2000
92 The compelling 2000 Clos du Marquis exhibits a deep ruby/purple color along with aromas and flavors of cherries and cassis. Its textbook style reveals elegance, purity, and overall harmony. Rich, medium bodied, and moderately tannic, it will be at its peak between 2004–2020. It is the greatest Clos du Marquis ever made! Last tasted, 1/03.

1999
86 The 1999 Clos du Marquis reveals sweet black currant fruit on the attack, but the finish is tannic and compressed. Drink it over the next decade. Last tasted, 3/02.

1998 A superb effort, the 1998 exhibits abundant quantities of black currant and cherry
90   fruit subtly dosed with toasty oak. A medium to full-bodied, nicely textured, pure
      effort, with a moderately tannic finish, it resembles Léoville Las Cases but with-
      out the weight, overall length, and power. Anticipated maturity: now–2014. Last
      tasted, 3/02.

1996 A terrific Clos du Marquis and clearly of second- or third-growth quality, this dark
90   purple–colored wine reveals much of its bigger sibling's structure, brooding back-
      wardness, and rich, expansive character. The wine is less massive than Léoville
      Las Cases, but exhibits plenty of sweet kirsch black currant fruit intermixed with
      high quality, subtle new oak, and steely, mineral characteristics. Rich and
      medium to full-bodied with ripe tannin, this is a dazzling Clos du Marquis. Antic-
      ipated maturity: now–2018. Last tasted, 1/01.

1995 The outstanding 1995 Clos du Marquis is the quintessentially elegant style of Las-
90   Cases, with copious quantities of sweet fruit, outstanding depth, ripeness, and
      overall equilibrium, but no sense of heaviness. Like so many of this estate's great
      wines, everything is in proper proportion, with the acidity, alcohol, and tannin well
      integrated. The 1995 is slightly more up-front and precocious than the 1996; It
      can be drunk now as well as over the next 10 years. Last tasted, 1/01.

LÉOVILLE POYFERRÉ

Classification: Second Growth in 1855

Owner: GFA Domaine St.-Julien

Address: 33250 St.-Julien-Beychevelle

Telephone: 05 56 59 08 30; Telefax: 05 56 59 60 09

E-mail: lp@leoville-poyferre.fr

Website: www.leoville-poyferre.fr

Visits: By appointment Monday to Friday,
9 A.M.–noon and 2–5:30 P.M.

Contact: Didier Cuvelier

VINEYARDS

Surface area: 197.6 acres

Grape varietals: 65% Cabernet Sauvignon, 25% Merlot, 8% Petit Verdot,
2% Cabernet Franc

Average age of vines: 25 years

Density of plantation: 8,000 vines per hectare

Average yields: 45–50 hectoliters per hectare

Elevage: Seven-day fermentation and 15–30 day maceration in temperature-controlled
tanks. Twenty-two months aging in barrels with 75% new oak. Fining with egg whites,
no filtration.

WINES PRODUCED

Château Léoville Poyferré: 250,000 bottles

Moulin Riche: 130,000 bottles

Plateau of maturity: Within 8–20 years of the vintage

GENERAL APPRECIATION

The least well-known of the three Léovilles, Poyferré had an irregular track record until the end of the 1980s, but has slowly begun to achieve parity with its two more prestigious siblings. Improvements have been noticeable since the beginning of the 1990s.

Talk to just about any knowledgeable Bordelais about the potential of the vineyard of Léoville Poyferré, and they will unanimously agree that Poyferré has the soil and capacity to produce one of the Médoc's most profound red wines. In fact, some will argue that Léoville Poyferré has better soil than any of the other second-growth St.-Juliens. But the story of Léoville Poyferré since 1961, while largely one of disappointments, has the makings of a happy ending. Modernizations to the cellars, the introduction of a second wine, the elevated use of new oak, the increasingly watchful eyes of Didier Cuvelier, and the genius of the Libourne oenologist, Michel Rolland, have finally pushed Léoville Poyferré into the elite of St.-Julien. The two finest vintages of the 1980s remain the gloriously fruity 1983 and the prodigious 1982. Both years exhibit the depth and richness that this property is capable of attaining. In the 1990s, a top 1990 followed by strong efforts in 2000, 1996, and 1995 suggest this estate has begun to finally exploit its considerable potential.

IMPORTANT VINTAGES

2001
89–92
A fine effort for the vintage, this St.-Julien exhibits a deep ruby/purple color as well as sweet black currant fruit that has not yet taken on additional nuances, medium body, excellent purity, or an elegant, moderately weighty style. The tannin is ripe in this well-delineated, pure, finesse-styled Léoville Poyferré. Anticipated maturity: 2005–2013. Last tasted, 1/03.

2000
95
This extraordinary effort builds incrementally in the mouth with a cunning display of power that is not initially evident. At first, the wine seems subtle and elegant, but then, wow! The length, impressive purity, and layers of concentrated fruit build upward like a skyscraper. There is sweet tannin as well as copious quantities of glycerin, concentrated crème de cassis fruit intermixed with minerals, smoke, and earth. This 2000 may even improve further given the manner in which it is developing. Undoubtedly it is the finest Léoville Poyferré since the great 1990 and 1996; it is also more accessible than the other big St. Juliens such as Léoville Las Cases and Léoville Barton. Anticipated maturity: 2007–2025. Last tasted, 1/03.

1999
89
A perfumed bouquet of flowers, jammy cassis, sweet oak, and truffles jumps from the glass of this ripe, classic, mid-weight claret. Elegant rather than powerful, it possesses intense fruit and admirable ripeness as well as balance and a long finish. Enjoy this beautiful, sexy Poyferré over the next 12–14 years. Last tasted, 1/03.

1998
88
The dark ruby–colored, medium-bodied 1998 offers aromas of underbrush, black currants, cherries, minerals, and vanilla. While sweet, rich, and stylish, it lacks the depth necessary to merit an outstanding score. Drink it over the next 10–12 years. Last tasted, 3/02.

1996
93
This fabulous 1996 was tasted three times from bottle, and it is unquestionably, along with the 2000, the finest wine produced by this estate since their blockbuster 1990. Medium to full-bodied with a saturated black/purple color, the nose offers notes of cedar, jammy black fruits, smoke, truffles, and subtle new oak. In the mouth, there is impressive fruit extraction, a tannic, full-bodied structure, and a classic display of power and finesse. The longer it sat in the glass, the more im-

pressive the wine became. Backward and massive in terms of its extract and richness, this should prove to be a sensational Léoville Poyferré for drinking over the next three decades. Anticipated maturity: 2007–2028. Last tasted, 9/02.

1995
90+

While not as backward as the 1996, the opaque purple–colored 1995 is a tannic, unevolved, dense, concentrated wine that will require another 2–3 years of cellaring. The 1995 exhibits toast, black currant, mineral, and subtle tobacco in its complex yet youthful aromatics. Powerful, dense, concentrated cassis and blueberry flavors might be marginally softer than in the 1996, but there is still plenty of grip and structure to this big wine. Anticipated maturity: 2005–2030. Last tasted, 9/02.

1994
87

The dark ruby/purple–colored 1994 offers up scents of toasty vanilla and sweet black currant fruit. This medium-bodied Claret possesses good fat, moderate tannin, and a traditional, backward feel. Although still youthful, there is enough fruit to balance out the tannin. This should develop into an excellent wine with 2–3 more years of cellaring. Anticipated maturity: now–2015. Last tasted, 3/00.

1990
96

One of the profound Léoville Poyferrés of the last 25 years, this wine, so open in its youth, seems to be shutting down ever so slightly. The color still remains a saturated, dense, opaque ruby/purple. The nose has great purity of jammy, sweet cassis fruit intermixed with hints of espresso, vanilla, white flowers, and minerals. Very full-bodied with low acidity, extremely high tannin, yet fabulous extract and a layered personality, this is a prodigious Léoville Poyferré that may be just shutting down, based on three tastings in 2002. Anticipated maturity: 2008–2030. Last tasted, 9/02.

1989
88

This wine has a dark ruby color, sweet notes of cola, black currants, earth, herbs, and vanilla. The wine is medium bodied with some noticeable tough tannin and a lean, angular finish. The wine's aromatics show far more evolution than the flavors. Nevertheless, this wine pales in comparison to the sensational 1990 and the other vintages of Poyferré from the mid-1990s onward. Anticipated maturity: 2007–2018. Last tasted, 10/02.

1986
87

One of the more developed of the Médoc's 1986s, this dark plum/ruby–colored wine is already showing some pink at its rim. The wine shows medium body, some dusty, gritty tannins, yet a sweet, spicy, plummy nose with black currants, minerals, and underbrush. The wine has reached its plateau of maturity, where it should stay for at least 10–15 years. A very good but unexciting effort from Léoville Poyferré. Anticipated maturity: now–2010. Last tasted, 3/02.

1985
86

A very flaccid, diffuse style of Léoville Poyferré with an evolved medium ruby color already exhibiting amber, the nose offers up notes of herbs intermixed with currants, licorice, and vanilla. The mouth is round and medium bodied with good concentration. The finish shows some sweet tannin. This wine is fully mature. Anticipated maturity: now–2006. Last tasted, 3/02.

1983
91

One of the superstar 1983s that is not beginning to crack up and decline, Léoville-Poyferré's effort exhibits a dark garnet color, a sweet nose of plum liqueur intermixed with licorice, black currants, weedy tobacco, and *herbes de Provence*. The wine is round and seductive with a certain degree of opulence, low acidity, gorgeous fruit, and a nice layered palate impression. Drink it over the next 7–8 years. Last tasted, 3/02.

1982
94

A great Léoville Poyferré, not nearly as majestic as the 1990, but chunkier, more muscular, with high levels of tannins equaled by equally prodigious levels of extract and density, this wine still exhibits a youthful deep purple color. The tannins seem less polished than in more recent vintages, but the wine is so concentrated and massive that clearly it looks set to overcome the brutality of its tannin structure. The wine is very full-bodied, very concentrated, and somewhat of a sleeper in this vintage. It still needs time in the cellar. Anticipated maturity: 2006–2025. Last tasted, 9/02.

ANCIENT VINTAGES

Léoville Poyferré had a dreadful record in the 1970s, with most vintages meriting scores between the mid-60s and the low 80s. The record in the 1960s was even more pathetic, except for a very good 1961 (87 points; last tasted 9/99 in a horizontal tasting). Of the museum pieces considered great, none of the highly rated vintages in Bordeaux have ever produced a Léoville Poyferré that I would rate higher than the mid-80s, and that includes 1959, 1955, 1953, and 1945.

SAINT-PIERRE

Classification: Fourth Growth in 1855

Owner: Françoise Triaud

Address: c/o Domaines Martin, 33250 St.-Julien-Beychevelle

Telephone: 05 56 59 08 18; Telefax: 05 56 59 16 18

Visits: By appointment only Monday to Friday, 8 A.M.–noon and 2–6 P.M.

Contact: Corinne Favereau

VINEYARDS

Surface area: 42 acres

Grape varietals: 75% Cabernet Sauvignon, 15% Merlot, 10% Cabernet Franc

Average age of vines: 42 years

Density of plantation: 10,000 vines per hectare

Average yields: 50 hectoliters per hectare

Elevage: Prolonged fermentation and maceration in temperature-controlled stainless-steel vats with four daily pumpings-over and *pigéages*. Concentration by evaporation. Fourteen months aging in barrels that are renewed by half at each vintage. Fining and filtration.

WINES PRODUCED

Château Saint-Pierre: 60,000 bottles

Plateau of maturity: Within 7–20 years of the vintage

GENERAL APPRECIATION

One of the most underestimated classified growths of Bordeaux, Saint-Pierre is of good quality, though some of the recent vintages too frequently exhibit aromas of cardboard/wet concrete.

Saint-Pierre is the least known of the classified-growth St.-Julien châteaux. Much of the production of Saint-Pierre has traditionally been sold to wine enthusiasts in Belgium, no doubt because the former owners, Monsieur Castelein and Madame Castelein-Van den Bussche, were Belgian. In 1982 one of the Médoc's great personalities, the late Henri Martin, purchased the property.

The vineyards of Saint-Pierre are well located right behind the town of St.-Julien-Beychevelle, and a drive past them will reveal a high percentage of old and gnarled vines, always a sign of quality. The style of wine of Saint-Pierre has tended to be rich, corpulent, chunky, and full-bodied, even thick and coarse in some vintages. Always deeply colored, sometimes opaque, Saint-Pierre is a big, rustic, dusty-textured wine. While it can lack the finesse and charm of many St.-Juliens, such as Ducru-Beaucaillou and Léoville-Las Cases, it compensates for that deficiency with its obvious (some would say vulgar) display of power and muscle.

Assuming the corky bottles so evident in the late 1990s are not symptomatic of a more serious problem in the cellars, the wines of Saint-Pierre, when compared with those of the top châteaux of St.-Julien, are vastly underrated. This estate continues to languish in the shadows cast by the glamorous superstars of the St.-Julien appellation. Given the usually realistic price, consumers should put this lack of recognition to good use.

IMPORTANT VINTAGES

2001
88–90 A strong effort from Saint-Pierre, this excellent 2001 exhibits a saturated ruby/purple color and sweet aromas of black currants and damp foresty notes. Medium bodied with great fruit on the attack and a dry, moderately tannic finish displaying impressive purity, it will be at its finest between 2007–2017. Last tasted, 1/03.

2000
89+ Smoky and earthy with copious jammy cassis fruit and sweet tannin, this is an excellent, full-bodied Saint-Pierre. The saturated deep purple color is followed by a persistent, concentrated wine with copious sweet tannin. Three bottles tasted revealed no traces of wet cardboard. Anticipated maturity: 2007–2020. Last tasted, 1/03.

1999
87 Soft, briery, berry fruit intermixed with herbs, earth, and spice box are moderately intense. Low in acidity with sweet tannin and fleshy fruit, this medium-bodied, tasty, flavorful St.-Julien should be drunk during its first 10–12 years of life. Last tasted, 3/02.

1998
? Sixty percent, or three out of five bottles that I have tasted of this wine have been marred by a corked character. This has me spooked with respect to what this wine might be. Certainly the healthy examples of 1998 Saint-Pierre have exhibited a deep ruby/purple color and notes of dried herbs intermixed with underbrush, black currant, and compost. The wine is tannic, somewhat austere, and angular, but classic, if that means a typical, rather leanly styled Bordeaux. Anticipated maturity: 2006–2016. Last tasted, 3/02.

1996
88+ Just emerging from a relatively disjointed, awkward stage, this dark ruby/purple–colored wine offers up notes of new saddle leather, a hint of chocolate, black currants, and earth. The wine is medium bodied, relatively tannic, yet has good underlying sweetness. It still seems a bit disjointed and potentially too austere, but time will tell. Anticipated maturity: 2007–2020. Last tasted, 3/02.

1995
87 Dark ruby with some sweet, herbaceous, cherry, and black currant notes intermixed with licorice and herb, this ripe, medium-bodied wine seems to finish a bit quickly on the palate. Anticipated maturity: 2004–2014. Last tasted, 3/02.

1994
86 From barrel this wine showed relatively good opulence and almost too much new oak, but from bottle the wine showed some hard tannins, medium body, some spicy, herb-tinged black currant fruit, and an angular finish. Anticipated maturity: 2005–2012. Last tasted, 3/02.

1990
90 One of the best Saint-Pierres I have ever tasted, this dense ruby/purple–colored wine seems to be approaching full maturity. With a big, sweet nose of vanilla, smoke, black cherry, and currant jam intermixed with some tobacco and licorice, this opulent, full-bodied wine is fleshy, low in acidity, and a treat to drink. Anticipated maturity: now–2012. Last tasted, 3/02.

1989
88 Showing some amber at its rim, this dark garnet–colored wine is another low-acid, chewy, lush mouthful of wine with notes of licorice, fruitcake, spice box, and sweet currant fruit. The wine has relatively high alcohol, low acidity, and some moderate tannins still lingering in the finish. Nevertheless, I would drink it over the next decade. Last tasted, 3/02.

1988
88 This wine has evolved nicely, showing a classic Bordeaux nose of fruitcake, cedar, licorice, tobacco, and black currants. Medium bodied with moderate tannin yet excellent concentration, this wine should continue to develop and last where well stored. Anticipated maturity: now–2008. Last tasted, 3/02.

1986
89 Still powerful, backward, muscular, and concentrated, with high tannin and some earthy, leathery, cherry, and black currant fruit notes, this brawny, relatively muscular, corpulent wine is a bit rustic but still impressive. Anticipated maturity: now–2015. Last tasted, 3/02.

1985
87 Fully mature, this relatively spicy wine has a medium ruby color with some considerable pink at the edge. The wine exhibits licorice, weedy black currants, and a spiciness to its open-knit, moderately endowed flavors. Drink it over the next 5–6 years. Last tasted, 11/00.

1982
89 Fully mature, the 1982 has a dark garnet color with some amber creeping in at the edge. The wine offers up a big, smoky nose with licorice, cigar box, cedar, and sweet cherry and black currant fruit. The wine is lush, medium to full-bodied, low in acidity, and very expansive and user-friendly. Anticipated maturity: now–2007. Last tasted, 9/02.

ANCIENT VINTAGES

Saint-Pierre has a relatively consistent record, with very strong efforts in 1970 (88 points; last tasted 1/02) and 1961 (87 points; last tasted 7/85).

TALBOT

Classification: Fourth Growth in 1855

Owner: Lorraine Rustmann Cordier and Nancy Bignon Cordier

Address: 33250 St.-Julien-Beychevelle

Telephone: 05 56 73 21 50; Telefax: 05 56 73 21 51

E-mail: chateau-talbot@chateau-talbot.com

Website: www.chateau-talbot.com

Visits: By appointment Monday to Friday, 9–11 A.M. and 2–4:30 p.m. (Friday afternoons, until 3 P.M.)

Contact: Marisol Compadre

VINEYARDS

Surface area: 252 acres

Grape varietals: 66% Cabernet Sauvignon, 26% Merlot, 5% Petit Verdot, 3% Cabernet Franc

Average age of vines: 35 years

Density of plantation: 7,700 vines per hectare

Average yields: 52 hectoliters per hectare

Elevage: Three-week fermentation and maceration in temperature-controlled stainless-steel and wooden vats. Fifteen months aging in barrels with 40% new oak. Fining, light filtration.

WINES PRODUCED

Château Talbot: 300,000 bottles

Connétable de Talbot: 300,000 bottles

Plateau of maturity: Within 7–25 years of the vintage

GENERAL APPRECIATION

Talbot is consistently of high quality and represents one of the best buys of the Médoc. Vintages such as 1986 and 1982 remain the reference point for how great this wine can be.

The huge single vineyard of Talbot is situated inland from the Gironde River, well behind the tiny hamlet of St.-Julien-Beychevelle and just north of Gruaud Larose.

Talbot is named after the English commander John Talbot, Earl of Shrewsbury, who was defeated in battle at Castillon in 1453. The château made consistently fine, robust, yet fruity, full-bodied wines under the Cordier administration and deserved promotion should any new reclassification of the wines of the Médoc be done. The new administration appears to be moving in the direction of a softer, more elegant style, with more consistency from vintage to vintage.

A modest amount of delicious, dry white wine is made at Talbot. Called Caillou Blanc du Château Talbot, it is a fresh, fragrant white—one of the finest produced in the Médoc. It must, however, be drunk within 2–4 years of the vintage.

IMPORTANT VINTAGES

2001 A well-balanced St.-Julien, an appellation that produced numerous hard wines in
87–89 this vintage, the dark ruby/purple–colored 2001 Talbot offers sweet, earthy, black currant, and cherry fruit, medium body, light tannin, a supple texture, and more charm than most 2001s. It appears the wine-maker knew what could be achieved in this vintage, and went for charm and delicacy as opposed to power. The result is a wine that should drink well for 10–12 years without drying out or becoming attenuated. Last tasted, 1/03.

2000 Although not a blockbuster, this outstanding St.-Julien reveals admirable rich-
90 ness, a layered texture, sweet tannin, and abundant quantities of smoky cassis, licorice, herb, earth, and leather characteristics. With complex aromatics and splendid richness, it admirably blends power with elegance. Some tannin suggests

2–3 years of cellaring is warranted. Anticipated maturity: 2006–2020. Last tasted, 1/03.

1999
88
Scents of dried herbs, underbrush, cassis, and currants emerge from this attractively perfumed, supple, spicy, medium-bodied St.-Julien. It possesses a succulent texture, low acidity, and soft tannin. Enjoy it over the next decade. Last tasted, 3/02.

1998
88
This wine is performing better out of bottle than it did from cask. With age, the mid-section has filled out and the wine has put on weight. A deep plum/garnet color is accompanied by an up-front, seductive nose of melted licorice, cedar, plums, black cherries, and cassis. This attractive Talbot is nicely textured and medium to full-bodied, with sweet tannin. It is pleasing to see how this wine has matured. Anticipated maturity: now–2016. Last tasted, 3/02.

1996
89
This wine is close to being outstanding, exhibiting a saturated dark ruby color and excellent aromatics, consisting of black fruits intermixed with licorice, dried herbs, and roasted meat smells. It is full with impressive extract, a fleshy texture, low acidity, excellent purity, and a long, deep, chewy finish. Anticipated maturity: now–2017. Last tasted, 3/01.

1995
88
This charming, intensely scented, dark plum/garnet–colored wine has a telltale olive, earth, grilled beef, and black currant–scented bouquet that soars from the glass. Medium to full-bodied, with low acidity and round, luscious, rich fruity flavors, this is a meaty, fleshy, delicious Talbot that can be drunk now. Anticipated maturity: now–2012. Last tasted, 3/01.

1990
87
A somewhat understated, less powerful wine than normal, the 1990 Talbot exhibits a dark ruby color with some pink at the edge. The wine has an attractive, very evolved perfume of earth, sweet cherries, and smoky herbal notes. The wine is medium bodied, low in acidity, with ripe tannin, but it lacks the concentration one expects in this great vintage and from Talbot. Anticipated maturity: now–2008. Last tasted, 10/01.

1989
87
Dark ruby with moderately endowed notes of sweet black currants intermixed with licorice, compost, and some weedy tobacco, this medium-bodied wine has low acidity and attractively ripe fruit, but a somewhat short finish. Anticipated maturity: now–2012. Last tasted, 10/02.

1988
88
Dark plum/garnet/ruby, with more color saturation than the 1990 or 1989, this wine has notes of new saddle leather intermixed with smoked beef, tapenade, vanilla, and an almost chocolaty mocha character. Some moderate tannins still need to be integrated, but this medium-bodied wine has excellent grip, depth, and overall character. As it has aged, it seems to have developed more personality, depth, and style than the more highly renowned 1989. Anticipated maturity: now–2012. Last tasted, 10/01.

1986
96
A fabulous wine, and one of the two greatest Talbots of the last 50 years, this wine still has a very murky garnet/plum/purple color and a spectacular nose of sweet crème de cassis, intermixed with freshly ground pepper, melted road tar, *herbes de Provence*, and beef blood. It is followed by an enormously concentrated wine of full body, layers of concentration, and sweet tannin. The wine seems to be just hitting its plateau of maturity, where it should last for at least 10–15 more years. A prodigious Talbot. Anticipated maturity: now–2020. Last tasted, 6/02.

1985
90
Extremely fragrant, supple, expansive, and elegant, this fully mature 1985 has a dark garnet color with plenty of pink and amber at the edge. Fleshy, medium bodied, and smooth as silk, this wine has excellent balance, loads of fruit, and a low-acid, lush finish. Anticipated maturity: now–2005. Last tasted, 6/02.

1983
90
Still one of the best wines from this vintage, particularly in the Médoc, this wine shows notes of licorice, compost, saddle leather, and black fruits. Medium to full-

bodied, fleshy and lush, with low acidity, ripe fruit, and an intriguing underlying smoky, herbaceous note, this concentrated, fully mature Talbot should be drunk over the next 5–7 years. Anticipated maturity: now–2010. Last tasted, 6/02.

1982   A magnificent wine that is just reaching full maturity, the huge nose of black
95   truffles, anise, steak tartar, new saddle leather, and copious quantities of black cherries and currants jumps from the glass of this dense, opaque garnet/purple–colored wine. The wine is full-bodied with enormous quantities of glycerin, low acidity, and a very corpulent, heady, chewy style. This is a treat for both the intellectual and hedonistic senses. Anticipated maturity: now–2012. Last tasted, 6/02.

ANCIENT VINTAGES

Talbot has a relatively distinguished record for producing very good wines in just about every reasonably good vintage Bordeaux had in the 1970s. The 1978 (87 points; last tasted 6/99), 1975 (87? points; last tasted 11/01), and 1971 (87 points; last tasted 3/00) are all fine efforts. In the 1960s, Talbot had to take a backseat to its sister château, Gruaud Larose. Gruaud Larose consistently produced a far better wine than Talbot in the top vintages of 1966, 1962, and 1961. Recently, I have not tasted any of the Talbots from those vintages. Perhaps the greatest two ancient vintages of Talbot I have tasted, although I have not had them in many years, is the 1953 Talbot (90 points; last tasted 12/95) and 1945 (94 points; last tasted 3/88).

OTHER ST.-JULIEN ESTATES

LA BRIDANE

Classification: Cru Bourgeois

Owner: Bruno Saintout

Address: 33250 St.-Julien-Beychevelle

Mailing Address: c/o SCEA de Cartujac, 33112 Saint-Laurent de Médoc

Telephone: 05 56 59 91 70; Telefax: 05 56 59 46 13

Website: www.vignobles.saintout.com

Visits: July and August: Monday to Saturday,
10 A.M.–12:30 P.M. and 2–7 P.M.

Contact: Bruno Saintout

VINEYARDS

Surface area: 37 acres

Grape varietals: 47% Cabernet Sauvignon, 36% Merlot, 13% Cabernet Franc, 4% Petit Verdot

Average age of vines: 35 years

Density of plantation: 6,500 vines per hectare

Average yields: 50 hectoliters per hectare

Elevage: Twenty-day fermentation and maceration in temperature-controlled stainless-steel vats. Nine to sixteen months aging in barrels with 33% new oak. Fining, no filtration.

WINES PRODUCED

Château La Bridane: 50,000 bottles

No second wine is produced.

Plateau of maturity: Within 5–14 years of the vintage

GENERAL APPRECIATION

A reasonably priced and fun-to-drink wine.

This solidly made wine usually has considerable power, weight, and a chunky fruiti-ness. What it frequently lacks are those elusive qualities called charm and finesse. Nevertheless, the wine keeps well and is usually reasonably priced.

DOMAINE CASTAING

Classification: Cru Bourgeois

Owner: Jean-Jacques Cazeau

Address: 54, grand rue, 33250 St.-Julien-Beychevelle

Telephone: 05 56 59 25 60; Telefax:—Not available

Visits: By appointment Monday–Thursday

Contact: Jean-Jacques Cazeau

VINEYARDS

Surface area: 3 acres

Grape varietals: 50% Cabernet Sauvignon, 40% Merlot, 10% Cabernet Franc

Average age of vines: 50 years

Density of plantation: 10,000 vines per hectare

Average yields: 58 hectoliters per hectare

Elevage: Twenty-day fermentation and maceration. Twenty months aging in barrels that are renewed by a third at each vintage. Fining, no filtration.

WINES PRODUCED

Domaine Castaing: 9,000 bottles

No second wine is produced.

Plateau of maturity: Within 3–10 years of the vintage

DU GLANA

Classification: Cru Bourgeois Exceptionnel

Owner: GFA Vignobles Meffre

Address: 5, Le Glana, 33250 St.-Julien-Beychevelle

Mailing Address: c/o Vignobles Meffre, Les Applanats, 84190 Beaumes-de-Venise

Telephone: 05 56 59 06 47; Telefax: 05 56 59 06 47

E-mail: ludovicmeffre@yahoo.fr

Visits: By appointment Monday to Friday, 8 A.M.–noon and 2–6 P.M.

Contact: Ludovic Meffre

VINEYARDS

Surface area: 106.2 acres

Grape varietals: 65% Cabernet Sauvignon, 30% Merlot, 5% Cabernet Franc

Average age of vines: 20 years

Density of plantation: 6,666 vines per hectare

Average yields: 250,000 hectoliters per hectare

Elevage: Cold maceration. Three-week fermentation and maceration in temperature-controlled vats. Twelve months aging in barrels with 25% new oak. Fining and filtration.

WINES PRODUCED

Château du Glana: 150,000 bottles

Pavillon du Glana or Château Sirène: 100,000 bottles

Plateau of maturity: Within 2–8 years of the vintage

GENERAL APPRECIATION

This St.-Julien merits its Cru Bourgeois status. Usually reliable, Du Glana does represent an interesting quality/price ratio.

It has been said that Du Glana produces a blatantly commercial wine—soft, overtly fruity, and too easy to drink. Yet the prices are reasonable and the wine is ripe, cleanly made, and ideal for newcomers to Bordeaux. Some vintages tend to be jammy—2000, 1996, 1990, 1989, 1985, and 1982, for example—but in tastings people always seem to enjoy this plump St.-Julien. It must be drunk within its first decade of life, preferably before it turns eight years old.

DOMAINE DU JAUGARET

Classification: None

Owner: Fillastre family

Address: 33250 St.-Julien-Beychevelle

Telephone: 05 56 59 09 71

Visits: By appointment only

Contact: Jean-François Fillastre

VINEYARDS

Surface area: 3.3 acres

Grape varietals: 75% Cabernet Sauvignon; 20% Merlot; 5% Malbec, Petit Verdot, and Cabernet Franc

Average age of vines: 50+ years

Density of plantation: 10,000 vines per hectare

Average yields: 40 hectoliters per hectare

Elevage: Ten-day fermentation and 20-day maceration. Thirty to thirty-six months aging in barrels (no new oak). Fining, no filtration.

WINES PRODUCED

Domaine du Jaugaret: 5,000–6,000 bottles

No second wine is produced.

LALANDE

Classification: None

Owner: Jean-Paul Meffre

Address: 2, Grand Rue, 33250 St.-Julien-Beychevelle

Mailing Address: c/o Vignobles Meffre, Les Applanats, 84190 Beaumes-de-Venise

Telephone: 05 56 59 06 47; Telefax: 05 56 59 06 47

Visits: By appointment Monday to Friday, 8 A.M.–noon and 2–6 P.M.

Contact: Jean-Paul Meffre

VINEYARDS

Surface area: 79 acres

Grape varietals: 55% Cabernet Sauvignon, 40% Merlot, 5% Cabernet Franc

Average age of vines: 22 years

Density of plantation: 6,666 vines per hectare

Average yields: 58 hectoliters per hectare

Elevage: Cold maceration. Three-week fermentation and maceration. Twelve months aging in barrels with 25% new oak for 80% of the yield. Fining and filtration.

WINES PRODUCED

Château Lalande: 150,00 bottles

Château Marquis de Lalande: 30,000 bottles

LALANDE-BORIE

Classification: Cru Bourgeois

Owner: Borie family

Address: 33250 St.-Julien-Beychevelle

Telephone: 05 56 73 16 73; Telefax: 05 56 59 27 37

No visits

VINEYARDS

Surface area: 44.5 acres

Grape varietals: 65% Cabernet Sauvignon, 25% Merlot, 10% Cabernet Franc

Average age of vines: 25 years

Density of plantation: 10,000 vines per hectare

Average yields: 45 hectoliters per hectare

Elevage: Fifteen to eighteen-day fermentation in stainless-steel vats. Fourteen to sixteen months aging in barrels with 25–35% new oak. Fining, light filtration upon bottling.

WINES PRODUCED

Château Lalande-Borie: 90,000 bottles

No second wine is produced.

Plateau of maturity: Within 5–10 years of the vintage

MOULIN DE LA ROSE

Classification: Cru Bourgeois in 1932

Owner: GFA des Domaines Guy Delon

Address: 33250 St.-Julien-Beychevelle

Telephone: 05 56 59 08 45; Telefax: 05 56 59 73 94

Visits: By appointment only

Contact: Guy Delon

VINEYARDS

Surface area: 11.9 acres

Grape varietals: 62% Cabernet Sauvignon, 28% Merlot, 5% Cabernet Franc, 5% Petit Verdot

Average age of vines: 30 years

Density of plantation: 8,500 vines per hectare

Average yields: 50 hectoliters per hectare

Elevage: Three-week fermentation and maceration in temperature-controlled stainless-steel tanks with frequent pumpings-over. Twenty months aging in barrels with 33% new oak. Seven rackings. Fining with egg whites. No filtration.

WINES PRODUCED

Château Moulin de la Rose: 30,000 bottles

No second wine is produced.

TERREY-GROS-CAILLOUX

Classification: Cru Bourgeois

Owner: SCEA du Château Terrey-Gros-Cailloux

Address: 33250 St.-Julien-Beychevelle

Telephone: 05 56 59 06 27; Telefax: 05 56 59 29 32

Visits: Monday to Thursday, 9 A.M.–noon and 2–7 P.M.; Fridays, 9 A.M.–noon

Contact: Henri Pradère

VINEYARDS

Surface area: 34.5 acres

Grape varietals: 70% Cabernet Sauvignon, 25% Merlot, 5% Petit Verdot

Average age of vines: 35 years

Density of plantation: 10,000 vines per hectare

Average yields: 55 hectoliters per hectare

Elevage: Three-week fermentation in stainless-steel temperature-controlled vats. Twenty months aging in oak barrels that are renewed by 25% each year. Fining, no filtration.

WINES PRODUCED

Château Terrey-Gros-Cailloux: 100,000 bottles

No second wine is produced.

Plateau of maturity: Within 5–8 years of the vintage

The cellars of this well-run Cru Bourgeois are located just off the famous D2 in the direction of Gruaud Larose and Talbot. They house not only Terrey-Gros-Cailloux, but also the wine of Hortevie. Terrey-Gros-Cailloux tends to be a richly fruity, round, occasionally full-bodied wine that offers delicious drinking if consumed within the first 7–8 years. It is not long-lived, but the decision by the proprietors in the late 1980s to begin to use some new oak casks to give the wine more definition and structure should prove beneficial to the wine's longevity.

TEYNAC

Classification: None

Owner: Fabienne et Philille Pairault

Address: Grand Rue, Beychevelle, 33250 St.-Julien-Beychevelle

Telephone: 05 56 59 12 91; Telefax: 05 56 59 46 12

E-mail: philetfab3@wanadoo.fr

Visits: By appointment only

Contact: Patrick Bussier

Telephone: 05 56 59 93 04; Telefax: 05 56 59 46 12

VINEYARDS

Surface area: 30.1 acres

Grape varietals: 78% Cabernet Sauvignon, 20% Merlot, 2% Petit Verdot

Average age of vines: 45 years

Density of plantation: 7,500 vines per hectare

Average yields: 50 hectoliters per hectare

Elevage: Three-week fermentation and maceration in temperature-controlled stainless-steel vats. Fourteen months aging in barrels with 40% new oak. Fining and filtration.

WINES PRODUCED

Château Teynac: 53,000 bottles

Château Les Ormes: 10,000 bottles

MARGAUX AND THE SOUTHERN MÉDOC

Margaux is certainly the largest and most sprawling of all the Médoc's principal wine-producing communes. The 3,350 acres under vine exceed those of St.-Estèphe. A first-time tourist to Margaux immediately realizes just how spread out the châteaux of Margaux are. Only a few sit directly on Bordeaux's Route du Vin (D2), and these are

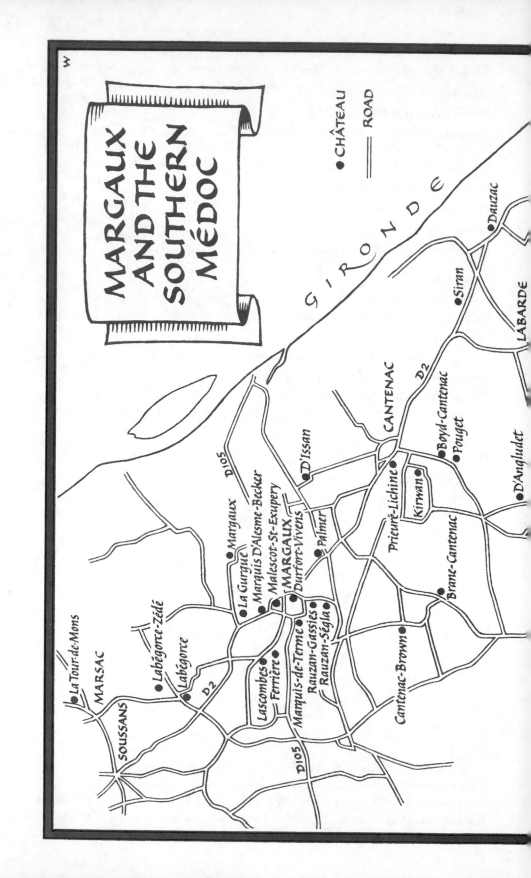

MARGAUX AND THE SOUTHERN MÉDOC

• CHÂTEAU
— ROAD

GIRONDE

D105

Margaux
Marquis D'Alesme-Becker
Malescot-St-Exupery
MARGAUX
Durfort-Vivens
Palmer

D'Issan

CANTENAC

D2

Prieuré-Lichine

Kirwan

Boyd-Cantenac
Pouget

Siran

LABARDE

Dauzac

D'Angludet

Brane-Cantenac

Cantenac-Brown

La Gurgue

La Tour-de-Mons
MARSAC

Labégorce-Zédé

SOUSSANS

Labégorce

D2

D105

Lascombes
Ferrière

Marquis-de-Terme
Rauzan-Gassies
Rauzan-Ségla

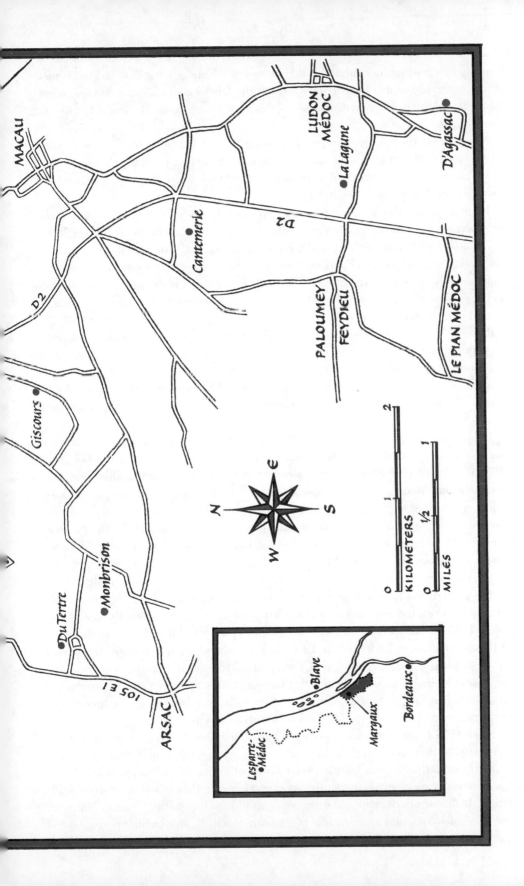

Dauzac, Prieuré-Lichine, Palmer, and Malescot St.-Exupéry. Château Margaux is just off the main road in the town of Margaux, but the other major châteaux are sprinkled throughout the five principal communes of this appellation: Arsac, Labarde, Cantenac, Margaux, and Soussans.

Margaux has the greatest number of classified-growth châteaux (crus classé) in the 1855 classification. A total of 21 Margaux châteaux made the grade, which is four more than Pauillac's 17 châteaux that were included, 10 more than St.-Julien's 11, and 16 more than St.-Estèphe's five châteaux.

From an outsider's view, Margaux thus appears to have the highest number of quality wine producers; however, nothing was further from the truth for much of the 1960s, 1970s, and 1980s. During this era, there were at least a half dozen estates in Margaux that had a dreadful record of performance, and at least another four or five properties that should have been downgraded if a revised classification of the wines of the Médoc had been accomplished. Since the late 1990s, most of these estates have turned things around and improved the quality of their wines. Yet compared to the other major appellations, Margaux still remains Bordeaux's leading appellation of underachievers. Even the regal first-growth queen herself, Château Margaux, went through a period of mediocrity that was dramatically reversed when the Mentzelopoulos family purchased Château Margaux in 1977 from the Ginestets, who had inadvertently permitted this *grande dame* to slip considerably in quality, but not price, below first-growth standards.

Despite the irregularity and lackluster track record of many Margaux châteaux for much of the last three decades, the fragrant bouquet and seductive charm of a few great Margaux wines are what set these wines apart from a St.-Julien or Pauillac. The bouquet of a fine Margaux is unquestionably more intense and compelling than those found in the wines of St.-Julien, Pauillac, and St.-Estèphe. This has been well chronicled in virtually all the writings on Bordeaux wine, but what is not said is that the great wines of Margaux are in real terms limited to Château Margaux and Palmer. More recently, Rauzan-Ségla, Malescot St.-Exupéry, Lascombes, Brane-Cantenac, Kirwan, du Tertre, Giscours, and d'Issan have joined the ranks of quality-conscious producers.

The great diversity of soils and quality level of wines produced in Margaux is challenging for even the most devoted Bordeaux wine enthusiast. Generally, the white-colored soils in Margaux are the lightest and most gravelly of the Médoc. To the south of the appellation, in Ludon where La Lagune is located, sand dominates the *terroir*. In these soils, a high percentage of Cabernet Sauvignon is planted. For example, much less Merlot is grown in Margaux (Château Palmer being the exception) than in St.-Julien, Pauillac, or St.-Estèphe. These thin soils work in favor of the finesse and aromatic complexity that a top Margaux enjoys in a fine vintage.

Since 1977 Château Margaux has made unquestionably the greatest and most powerful wine of this appellation. It is a virile, very concentrated, and densely colored wine. Historically, Château Margaux's chief competitor has been Palmer. In 2003, that historic rivalry remains as competitive as ever. However, Palmer's style of wine is different. It shares a dark color and deep concentration of flavor with Château Margaux, but it is a more supple, rounder, less tannic wine resulting from a high percentage of

Merlot used in the blend. Palmer does have a fabulously complex bouquet that in certain vintages—2000, 1999, 1998, 1996, 1989, 1983, 1970, 1966, and 1961 come to mind immediately—is hauntingly perfect. The newest pretender to the Margaux throne is Rauzan-Ségla, a superb vineyard that until 1983 could claim to be this appellation's most notorious underachiever of the 20th century. Today Rauzan-Ségla produces powerful Cabernet Sauvignon–based wines of striking flavor, depth, and complexity, with a purity that is breathtaking. However, the one weakness of Rauzan-Ségla remains a certain tannic ferocity that is difficult to tame.

Another recognizable style of Margaux wine would be typified by those with an intense fragrance, but lighter weight, less concentration, and less tannin. Certainly Prieuré-Lichine, Lascombes, d'Issan, and Malescot St.-Exupéry all produce wines in this manner.

Prieuré-Lichine, the home of the late Alexis Lichine, tends to produce stylish, elegant, fragrant wines. The property has generally been much more consistent than many of its more famous neighbors. Lascombes is a wine that I adore when it is made well. In the 1970s, 1980s, and 1990s, it declined dramatically in quality. The reports from its new corporate owners of a renewed vigor and commitment to higher quality were immediately evident in the quality of the 2000 and 2001, the finest wines made at Lascombes in nearly 35 years.

Malescot St.-Exupéry enjoys a fine reputation, and I have tasted a few superb older vintages from this property, yet many of the vintages of the 1960s, 1970s, and 1980s were uninspiring. That being said, vintages since 1990 have been immensely impressive, giving reason for renewed interest in this estate. Today, Malescot St.-Exupéry is not far behind the two titans of Margaux, Château Margaux and Palmer.

Despite the number of mediocre wines produced by such noteworthy Margaux estates as d'Issan, Brane-Cantenac, Durfort-Vivens, Dauzac, and Kirwan in the 1960s, 1970s, and 1980s, the encouraging thing is that all of these properties have halted their nosedives and, in the late 1980s and mid-1990s, turned in some of their best winemaking efforts in more than a generation. Of this group, Durfort-Vivens might be the only estate that should be demoted in any new classification.

Both Brane-Cantenac and Durfort-Vivens have provided far too many unexciting, often flawed wines. Throughout the 1960s and 1970s, the wines from these two estates were terribly inconsistent. Because of a more careful selection process, the 1980s and 1990s have been kinder to Brane-Cantenac. Brane-Cantenac's performances in 2000, 1999, and 1998 were the strongest efforts from this estate in nearly 30 years. Durfort-Vivens is an enigma.

Dauzac's wines have also made significant progress since the late 1980s, as have those of Kirwan. Yet both of these properties, even allowing for their improvements, rarely produce wines that provide compelling drinking. Hopefully, the encouraging efforts of both properties in the mid-1990s will reverse their fortunes.

There are a handful of other classified-growth Margaux estates. The most promising estate is du Tertre, which since 1978 has produced excellent wine under the capable hand of Madame Denise Capbern Gasqueton. Eric Albada Jelgersma, the new owner, has continued the upward spiral in quality. Cantenac Brown, the producer of rustic, tannic, hard wines that appeal to those with 19th-century tastes, has finally moved into the new century in terms of its wine style now that AXA oversees the winemaking. To date, the results have been mixed, yet overall, somewhat encouraging. Rauzan-Gassies can be good, but leans toward a chunky, full-bodied St.-Estèphe style of wine rather than a true Margaux. Furthermore, the property is terribly inconsistent. Marquis d'Alesme Becker, hardly known and rarely seen, produces a light wine.

Two other classified châteaux, Giscours and Marquis de Terme, can make some of the richest and longest-lived wines of the appellation. Giscours was a proven performer during the 1960s and 1970s, but seriously declined in the 1980s. Recent vintages of Giscours suggest this property has convincingly rebounded. The 2000 Giscours is the finest wine in a quarter century from this large estate. In contrast, Marquis de Terme, off form during the 1960s and 1970s, began to make more interesting wine, among the richest of the appellation, starting with the 1983 vintage.

Among the Crus Bourgeois in Margaux, most observers would say that three properties consistently make the finest wine. D'Angludet, Labégorce Zédé, and Siran are very good estates making typically elegant, perfumed, aromatic wine. Labégorce Zédé's wine tends to be the most robust and richest, Siran the most masculine and tannic, and d'Angludet the most supple and charming.

Lastly, two major properties and classified growths to the south of Margaux's appellation borders can both make excellent wine. For much of my professional career, La Lagune has been one of my favorite wines. Brilliantly made, the wine can resemble both a Pomerol and a Burgundy, but it tends to be deliciously rich, round, fruity, and complex. Until a succession of disappointments in the late 1990s, La Lagune's quality was consistent and the price friendly to consumers. Cantemerle is the other treasure of the southern Médoc, and after an uneven period in the late 1970s, Cantemerle made excellent wine in both 1989 and 1983, but has been an irregular performer since. Both La Lagune and Cantemerle, no doubt because they are not in the famous Margaux appellation, are undervalued in the scheme of Bordeaux wine pricing. Their inconsistency of late may also work against these estates fetching higher prices.

Vintages for Margaux and southern Margaux can often be vastly different from those for the communes of St.-Julien, Pauillac, and St.-Estèphe, which sit a good distance to the north. This is not a region in which to look for good wines in off-vintages. The light soils seem to produce thin wines in rainy years, although there are exceptions. Also, extremely torrid, drought-like summers without adequate rainfall tend to stress those vineyards with high plantations of Cabernet Sauvignon in well-drained gravelly beds, retarding the ripening process while at the same time roasting the grapes. This explains why 1982 and 1990, both great vintages, were less consistent in Margaux than in the northern Médoc. The finest vintages for Margaux wines have been 2000, 1998, 1996, 1995, 1986, 1983, 1979, 1978, 1970, 1966, and 1961.

MARGAUX AND THE SOUTHERN MEDOC
(An Insider's View)

Overall Appellation Potential: Average to Outstanding

The Most Potential for Aging: Château Margaux, Palmer, Rauzan-Ségla

The Most Elegant: Cantemerle, Brane-Cantenac, Malescot St.-Exupéry, Château Margaux, Palmer

The Most Concentrated: Château Margaux, Kirwan, Lascombes (since 2000), Palmer, Rauzan-Ségla

The Best Value: d'Angludet, Cantemerle, Dauzac, La Lagune, du Tertre

The Most Exotic: Palmer, Lascombes

The Most Difficult to Understand (when young): Rauzan-Ségla

The Most Underrated: La Lagune, Malescot St.-Exupéry, du Tertre

The Easiest to Appreciate Young: La Lagune, Palmer

Up-and-Coming Estates: Brane-Cantenac, Dauzac, Giscours, Kirwan, Lascombes, Malescot St.-Exupéry, du Tertre

Greatest Recent Vintages: 2000, 1999, 1998, 1996, 1990, 1983, 1961

MARGAUX—AN OVERVIEW

Location: Margaux is the southernmost of the four principal Médoc appellations, lying on the left bank of the Gironde, 13 miles north of the city of Bordeaux

Acres under Vine: 3,350

Communes: Arsac, Cantenac, Labarde, Margaux, Soussans

Average Annual Production: 640,000 cases

Classified Growths: Total of 21: 10 in the commune of Margaux, 8 in the commune of Cantenac, 2 in the commune of Labarde, and 1 in the commune of Arsac; the appellation has 1 first growth, 5 second growths, 10 third growths, 4 fourth growths, and 2 fifth growths; 25 Crus Bourgeois

Principal Grape Varieties: Cabernet Sauvignon dominates, followed by Merlot, Petit Verdot, and minuscule quantities of Cabernet Franc

Principal Soil Type: As a general rule, this large and diverse commune has thin top soil, and the top vineyards, situated close to the river, have fine, gravelly soils not much different than those found in Pessac-Léognan. Farther inland, more clay and sand are found.

A CONSUMER'S CLASSIFICATION OF THE CHÂTEAUX OF MARGAUX AND THE SOUTHERN MÉDOC

OUTSTANDING
Margaux

Palmer

EXCELLENT

Brane-Cantenac (since 1998)
d'Issan
Kirwan
Lascombes (since 2000)
Malescot St.-Exupéry (since 1990)
Rauzan-Ségla (since 1983)

VERY GOOD

d'Angludet, Cantemerle, Giscours, La Lagune, Marquis de Terme,
Prieuré-Lichine, du Tertre

GOOD

Boyd-Cantenac, Cantenac Brown, Charmant, Dauzac, La Gurgue, Labégorce Zédé,
Marsac Ségineau, Monbrison, Siran

OTHER NOTABLE MARGAUX AND SOUTHERN MÉDOC PROPERTIES

Château d'Arsac, Bel Air-Marquis d'Aligre, Desmirail, Deyrem Valentin, Durfort-
Vivens, Ferrière, Haut Breton Larigaudière, Labégorce, Marquis d'Alesme Becker,
Martinens, Mongravey, Paveil-de-Luze, Pontac Lynch, Pouget, Rauzan-Gassies,
Tayac, La Tour de Bessan, La Tour de Mons, Trois Chardons

D'ANGLUDET

Classification: Cru Bourgeois Exceptionnel

Owner: Sichel family

Address: 33460 Cantenac

Telephone: 05 57 88 71 41; Telefax: 05 57 88 72 52

E-mail: contact@chateau-angludet.fr

Website: www.chateau-angludet.fr

Visits: By appointment Monday to Friday,
9 A.M.–noon and 2–5 P.M.

VINEYARDS

Surface area: 84 acres

Grape varietals: 55% Cabernet Sauvignon, 35% Merlot, 10% Petit Verdot

Average age of vines: 25 years

Density of plantation: 6,666 vines per hectare

Average yields: 48 hectoliters per hectare

Elevage: Eight day fermentation in temperature-controlled stainless-steel vats
(temperatures going from 25°C at the beginning of the process to 28°C at the end)
followed by 25–30 day maceration. Twelve months aging in barrels with 30–35%, new oak
followed by 5–6 months aging in vats. Fining, no filtration.

WINES PRODUCED

Château d'Angludet: 140,000 bottles

La Ferme d'Angludet: 30,000–40,000 bottles

Plateau of maturity: Within 6–15 years of the vintage

GENERAL APPRECIATION

D'Angludet has much improved, but its wines, though sound, are rarely great. However, they are frequently superior to their Cru Bourgeois status. Generally equivalent to a fifth growth, they represent very good values, especially in the context of their appellation.

The late Peter A. Sichel (he died in early 1998), was a multifaceted individual. He was not only a highly respected Bordeaux wine broker, but he was the past president of the promotional arm of the Bordeaux wine industry, the Union des Grands Crus. He was also a part owner of the famous Margaux estate of Palmer, as well as proprietor of his own château and residence, d'Angludet.

Sichel purchased this property in 1961 when it was in deplorable condition, and was solely responsible for taking the property, which sits in the southwestern corner of Margaux on what is called the plateau Le Grand Poujeau (shared by three Margaux estates, Giscours, du Tertre, and d'Angludet), from virtual post–World War II obscurity to international prominence. It is irrefutable that the wine made at d'Angludet frequently surpasses some of its more illustrious siblings in the Margaux appellation.

The history of the estate is old, even by Bordeaux standards, and can be traced back to the early 14th century. The estate's wines had a good reputation, and appear numerous times in wine references from the 16th through the 18th centuries, but by the time of the famous classification of 1855, the property was in bad condition—a reason often offered as to why it was excluded from that classification.

This coincides with the fact that so much of the vineyard was replanted in the early 1960s. Today, the wine is clearly of classified-growth quality, yet the price has remained extremely modest. Vintages prior to 1978 are generally undistinguished, but since that time there have been some marvelous to excellent wines, including a superb 1983, and excellent wines in 2000, 1999, 1996, 1995, 1989, and 1986.

IMPORTANT VINTAGES

2000 A smooth, silky offering (there is some tannin lurking below the surface), the 2000
88   d'Angludet possesses admirable density, body, and concentration as well as velvety tannin and pure black currant fruit. Well made, with low acidity, excellent ripeness, and a lovely textured mouth-feel, this strong effort will drink well until 2016. Last tasted, 1/03.

1999 Seductive, elegant, sweet red and black currants intertwined with floral notes
87   characterize the stylish, restrained, fruity, medium-bodied, classic, dark ruby–colored 1999 d'Angludet. With good acidity and soft tannin, it is ideal for drinking over the next decade. Last tasted, 1/03.

1998 Dark ruby–colored, with a peppery, cassis, mineral, anise, plum, and subtle herb-
86   scented bouquet, the 1998 d'Angludet is round, straightforward, and monolithic. Consume it over the next 5–6 years. Last tasted, 3/02.

1996   The 1996 d'Angludet is deeply colored, with a ripe, cassis- and blackberry-scented
88   nose, and subtle notions of licorice and melted road tar. There is excellent rich-
      ness, medium body, and moderate tannin in the jammy, rich finish. This effort
      should age nicely. Anticipated maturity: now–2015. Last tasted, 1/02.

1995   In contrast to the powerful, tannic 1996, the 1995 is a silky, supple, charming,
88   forthcoming wine that is well above its Cru Bourgeois classification. The color is a
      healthy, saturated, deep ruby/purple, and the wine offers up gobs of jammy black
      fruits intermixed with subtle herbs, spice, and toast. In the mouth, the wine dis-
      plays excellent richness, a layered, medium-bodied personality, well-disguised
      tannin and acidity, and a hedonistic mouth-feel. A sleeper of the vintage. Antici-
      pated maturity: now–2010. Last tasted, 1/01.

1990   The somewhat diffuse 1990 has an evolved garnet color, hints of the vintage's
85   sweet fruit and opulence, but tastes somewhat flat as well as fully mature. It ex-
      hibits deep color, rich, herbaceous fruit, medium body, and light tannin in its fin-
      ish. Anticipated maturity: now. Last tasted, 10/01.

1989   Fully mature, the dark garnet–colored 1989 d'Angludet is one of this property's
87   best wines since their excellent 1983. It is a fat, plump, intensely fruity wine with
      a supple texture, lusty alcohol, and silky tannins. Drink it over the next 4–5 years.
      Anticipated maturity: now. Last tasted, 10/01.

ANCIENT VINTAGES

A wine that is still holding beautifully (88 points; last tasted 12/00) is the 1983. This
was a beautiful vintage for the Margaux appellation, and d'Angludet has come through
with flying colors. The wine is fully mature, so holders of it should not push their luck.

BOYD-CANTENAC

Classification: Third Growth in 1855

Owner: GFA du Château Boyd-Cantenac

Address: 33460 Cantenac

Telephone: 05 57 88 90 82 *or* 05 57 88 30 58;
Telefax: 05 57 88 33 27

Visits: By appointment only

Contact: Lucien Guillemet

VINEYARDS

Surface area: 42 acres

Grape varietals: 60% Cabernet Sauvignon, 25% Merlot, 8% Cabernet Franc, 7% Petit
Verdot

Average age of vines: 35 years

Density of plantation: 10,000 vines per hectare

Average yields: 42 hectoliters per hectare

Elevage: Grape picking is done both by hand and machine. Fermentations and
macerations are rather long and take place in epoxy-coated cement vats. Wines are
afterward aged 12–18 months in oak barrels, 50% of which are new. Fining, but no
filtration since 1997.

WINES PRODUCED

Château Boyd-Cantenac: 60,000–70,000 bottles

Jacques Boyd: 12,000–30,000 bottles

Plateau of maturity: Within 8–20 years of the vintage

Located in the heart of the commune of Cantenac, south of Brane-Cantenac and Kirwan, this is a distressingly inconsistent estate that, unfortunately, no longer merits its rank as a third growth. It, and the nearby Château Pouget, have been owned by the well-known Guillemet family since the early 1930s. Since there is no official château at Boyd-Cantenac, the wines are vinified and cellared in a warehouse adjoining Château Pouget. It has always been a mystery why these wines are not better. For every good vintage of Boyd-Cantenac, there seem to be several where the wine falls well short of expectations. Perhaps a stricter selection, utilization of more wine for the second label, and a higher percentage of new oak might result in more consistency in the cellars. I have often found the wine impressive prior to bottling, but a bit coarse and attenuated in tastings afterward. As a consequence, this wine is never on my purchasing list, and I suspect many strangers to Bordeaux often confuse it with the two better-known, and now better-made, wines with the word Cantenac as part of their name, Brane-Cantenac and Cantenac Brown.

IMPORTANT VINTAGES

2001 An underachiever that has finally strung together several consecutive noteworthy
87–88 efforts, Boyd-Cantenac's dense ruby/purple–colored 2001 offers good grapy, berry fruit intertwined with earth and licorice characteristics. Medium bodied, with crisp, tangy, underlying acidity, and moderate tannin in the finish, its anticipated maturity is 2007–2015. Last tasted, 1/03.

2000 A sleeper of the vintage as well as one of the finest Boyd-Cantenacs I have ever
88+ tasted, this opaque purple-colored Margaux offers a sweet perfume of acacia flowers, smoke, black currants, and foresty notes. Medium to full-bodied, concentrated, and pure, with outstanding equilibrium as well as noticeable, but well-integrated, sweet tannin, it will drink well between 2006 and 2018. Last tasted, 1/03.

1999 Elegant, sweet, leather, currant, and foresty characteristics emerge from this
86 medium-bodied, dark ruby–colored Margaux. Well made, with ripe tannin, elegance, and palate presence, it will drink well for eight years. Last tasted, 3/02.

1998 Elegant and sweet, but relatively light, this medium-bodied, attenuated Margaux
86 reveals dusty, earthy, black currant, and cedary notes as well as moderate length and depth. It is meant to be drunk over the next 6–7 years. Last tasted, 1/02.

1996 A very strong effort for Boyd-Cantenac, a harvest that dragged on until October 15
88 produced wines that are dense, ruby/purple, with a sweet nose of weedy black currants, earth, mineral, and a hint of licorice. The wine is medium bodied, very concentrated, and chewy, with high levels of tannin. This is certainly a classic *vin de garde* that will require patience from its buyers. Anticipated maturity: 2010–2020. Last tasted, 3/01.

1995 The product of a very hot, dry summer, but with rain during the critical month of
87 September, this structured, concentrated wine seems to be very closed down and dense, with a healthy garnet/purple color and a big nose of mineral, underbrush, compost, and black fruits. Relatively powerful, but at the same time coarse and

still a bit rude, this wine needs plenty of time in the cellar. Anticipated maturity: 2008–2018. Last tasted, 3/00.

1990   A successful wine, the 1990 exhibits an impressive deep black/ruby color, a spicy,
86   rich, jammy nose, ripe, rich flavors, medium to full body, and plenty of tannin in the low-acid finish. Anticipated maturity: now–2008. Last tasted, 1/93.

1989   The 1989 is a thick, unctuous, heavyweight wine, low in acidity, but enormously
86   rich, fruity, and full. It has high alcohol and plenty of tannin, so it should age well, yet be drinkable early. Anticipated maturity: now. Last tasted, 4/91.

ANCIENT VINTAGES

The only vintage, looking through all my past tasting notes, that performed relatively well was the 1983 (87 points; last tasted 3/94).

BRANE-CANTENAC

Classification: Second Growth in 1855

Owner: Henri Lurton

Address: 33460 Margaux

Telephone: 05 57 88 83 33; Telefax: 05 57 88 72 51

E-mail: hlurton@chateaubranecantenac.fr *or* slafeuillade@chateaucantenac.fr

Website: Under construction

Visits: By appointment only

Contact: Sylvie Lafeuillade or Isabelle Mastoumecq (Telephone: 05 57 88 83 32)

VINEYARDS

Surface area: 222.3 acres

Grape varietals: 65% Cabernet Sauvignon, 30% Merlot, 5% Cabernet Franc

Average age of vines: 25 years

Density of plantation: 6,600–8,800 vines per hectare

Average yields: 42 hectoliters per hectare

Elevage: Three to four week fermentation at 31°C and maceration at 28°C in temperature-controlled wooden vats. Malolactics in barrel for the Merlot and in wooden vats for the Cabernet. Eighteen months aging in barrels with 60% new oak. Racking every three months. Fining with egg whites, filtration if necessary.

WINES PRODUCED

Château Brane-Cantenac: 140,000 bottles

Le Baron de Brane: 160,000 bottles

Plateau of maturity: Within 8–20 years of the vintage (for post-1995 vintages)

GENERAL APPRECIATION:

This once perennial underperformer is enjoying a renaissance. Since the late 1990s, Brane-Cantenac has justified its second-growth status, with its vintages from 1995 going from strength to strength. Fortunately, young Henri Lurton is fully committed to making wines in the most uncompromising manner. Though this trend is relatively recent, Brane-Cantenac is one of the rising stars of Margaux, if not of Bordeaux. Prices have not yet caught up to the quality curve, so consumers should take note! In 2003, this is one of the best bargain-priced Bordeaux classified growths.

Brane-Cantenac is owned by one of the most famous winemaking families in Bordeaux. The Lurtons live in the modest château, the viticultural history of which traces back to the early part of the 18th century. This property enjoyed an outstanding reputation in the early 19th century when the wines were made by the owner who named it, the Baron de Branne. Once the owner of the famous Pauillac estate now called Mouton Rothschild, Baron de Branne was a highly respected viticulturist whose political connections were so formidable that Brane-Cantenac was rated a second-growth in the 1855 classification despite some skeptics who felt that the vineyards did not produce wines that merited such a high standing. Today, the huge Lurton family, who have considerable holdings in the Graves and Entre-Deux-Mers, qualify as the largest winemaking family of the region.

One of the Médoc's largest properties, Brane-Cantenac's extensive vineyards lie west of the village of Cantenac and well inland from the Gironde River. Because of the property's large production, the wines of Brane-Cantenac have enjoyed a large measure of commercial success throughout the world. This has occurred notwithstanding a record of mediocrity that was particularly acute throughout the period 1967–1981. Curiously, most wine writers turned their heads in the other direction rather than point out what were obvious flaws in the makeup of Brane-Cantenac's wines during this era. The most prominent problems with Brane-Cantenac during this slump were the wines' excessive lightness and frequent distressing barnyard aromas. One can only speculate, but such flaws must have been caused by a lack of selection and sloppy, as well as unsanitary, management of the cellars.

However, Brane-Cantenac's inconsistent track record has dramatically improved. Even with this renewed level of quality, the wines of Brane-Cantenac are made in a forward, fruity, soft style that makes the wine easily appreciated when young, yet capable of 15–20 years of life.

IMPORTANT VINTAGES

2001 Brane-Cantenac continues its strong rebound from the throes of mediocrity with
88–90 its third consecutive impressive effort. The 2001 exhibits a dark purple color along with a sweet nose of charcoal-infused black currant and cherry fruit mixed with damp foresty notes. Pure, ripe, medium bodied, deep, subtle, and introspective, it will be drinkable between 2005–2017. Last tasted, 1/03.

2000 The 2000 is undoubtedly the greatest Brane-Cantenac in the post–World War II
92 era. Its dense ruby/purple color is accompanied by spectacular aromas of graphite, black currants, tobacco, earth, and an intriguing floral note. The stunning aromatic display is followed by a rich, opulent, seamless, medium-bodied wine with great concentration as well as fabulous purity. It is a sensational effort! Anticipated maturity: 2006–2020+. Last tasted, 1/03.

1999
89+
A beautifully complex perfume of fresh tobacco as well as cigar smoke, sweet licorice, and black currants is followed by an elegant, pure, harmonious Margaux. While not a big wine, it is medium bodied, intense, and moderately structured. It should improve in the bottle and merit an outstanding score in 2–3 years. Anticipated maturity: 2004–2016. Last tasted, 3/02.

1998
88
This dark ruby–colored, elegant, savory effort offers abundant quantities of herb-tinged, smoky, earthy, black currant fruit intermixed with licorice and toast. Fleshy, medium bodied, and ripe, with moderate tannin, this is a well-made, classic Margaux that should be at its best between 2005–2017. Last tasted, 3/02.

1996
88
A reasonably strong effort from Brane-Cantenac, this wine exhibits a bit of lightening to its dark garnet/ruby color and very fragrant aromas of cedar, tobacco leaf, black currants, and some licorice. Medium bodied with some sweet tannin, excellent purity, and a nicely textured, mid-weight finish, this wine is already approachable. Anticipated maturity: 2005–2016. Last tasted, 9/02.

1995
86
Close to full maturity, this wine is already showing some lightening at the edge, with notes of compost, mushrooms, and earthy red and black fruits. In the mouth, the wine is medium bodied with some firm tannin, but has a short, somewhat attenuated finish. It is a competent but unexciting effort for the vintage. Anticipated maturity: now–2012. Last tasted, 1/02.

1990
87
Seemingly fully mature, this wine has evolved quickly. The color shows some amber at the edge. A sweet nose of smoked herbs, jammy cherries, and black currants is intermixed with spice box, cedar, and a weediness. The wine is lush, medium bodied, and very soft. Anticipated maturity: now–2010. Last tasted, 3/01.

1989
87
This excellent wine shows a dark garnet color and a nose of damp earth, mushrooms, black fruits, cedar, and spice box. In the mouth it is medium to full-bodied, with excellent fruit in the attack but some rather dry tannins in the finish. The aromatics and attack suggest the wine is close to full maturity, but the finish suggests more to come. I am not sure I would risk extended aging of this vintage of Brane-Cantenac. Anticipated maturity: now–2007. Last tasted, 5/02.

1986
88
A very strong effort during a period when Brane-Cantenac was somewhat of a hit-or-miss proposition, the dark garnet–colored 1986 has notes of fennel, black fruits, earth, and underbrush. The wine is medium bodied, still shows some good, vibrant, vigorous fruit, medium to full body, and moderate tannin in the finish. It still tastes relatively youthful, and it is a lot younger than its more renowned siblings, the 1989 and 1990. Anticipated maturity: now–2012. Last tasted, 5/02.

1985
85?
Fully mature, this wine seems to be just beginning to dry out and drop its fruit. The color shows considerable amber and pink at the edge. The wine is medium bodied, with some dry, hard tannins in the finish. The finish has dried out considerably since the last time I tasted it, so I suspect this wine is now beginning to decline. Anticipated maturity: now. Last tasted, 5/02.

1983
88
This wine has been fully mature for a number of years but is still a very sensual, seductive, fragrant style of Brane-Cantenac, with notes of melted asphalt intermixed with damp earth, plum, cherry, and currant. The wine is heady, medium to full-bodied, very supple, with light tannins in the finish. Anticipated maturity: now–2005. Last tasted, 5/02.

1982
82?
In a blind tasting of the 1982s in the fall of 2002, this wine put on its best performance ever. Some of the objectionable, dirty aromas that had been such a flaw earlier seem to have taken a backseat to the herbaceous-scented sweet cherry and plum-like fruit. The wine is medium bodied, shows considerable amber at the edge, and still has a somewhat earthy, mushroomy, even manure-like aroma, but it is not nearly as intense as it once was. In any event, this is a controversial wine to drink up, as it is not going to get any better. Last tasted, 9/02.

ANCIENT VINTAGES

Brane-Cantenac's track record in the 1970s and 1960s was dreadful. At a vertical tasting done at the château in the late 1980s, there was not one wine I could find with merit.

CANTEMERLE

Classification: Fifth Growth in 1855

Owner: SMABTP (a mutual insurance company)

Address: 1, chemin Guittot, 33460 Macau

Telephone: 05 57 97 02 82; Telefax: 05 57 97 02 84

E-mail: cantemerle@cantemerle.com

Website: www.chateau-cantemerle.com

Visits: By appointment only

Contact: Laurence Dufau

VINEYARDS

Surface area: 214.9 acres

Grape varietals: 52% Cabernet Sauvignon, 40% Merlot, 5% Petit Verdot, 3% Cabernet Franc

Average age of vines: 25 years

Density of plantation: 10,000 vines per hectare

Average yields: 55 hectoliters per hectare

Elevage: Fermentation in wooden and concrete vats for grapes from the best lots and in stainless-steel vats for the rest of the yield. Fermentation temperatures vary between 26–28°C for the Merlot, 28–30°C for the Cabernet, and between 30–32°C for the Petit Verdot. Thirty day maceration at minimum temperature of 22°C. Twenty percent of yield (Merlot only) undergoes malolactics in new oak. Twelve months aging in barrels with 40% new oak and three rackings at 12°C. Light fining if necessary, no filtration.

WINES PRODUCED

Château Cantemerle: 350,000 bottles (Haut-Médoc)

Les Allées de Cantemerle: 130,000 bottles (Haut-Médoc)

Plateau of maturity: Within 5–15 years of the vintage

GENERAL APPRECIATION

When will Château Cantemerle repeat its magical performances of 1989, 1983, or 1961? For some reason, this estate has never fully recovered after the slump it went through in the 1970s and 1980s. Though well made, its wines are never extraordinary, but they generally live up to their status. However, readers are advised to watch out for the (all too rare) great successes, which are definitely worthy of attention since they stand on par with a third growth. All things considered, the quality/price ratio can be interesting.

Just south of the one-horse village of Macau is the lovely château of Cantemerle. It sits amidst a heavily wooded park just adjacent to the famous D2 (the major route leading from Bordeaux to the Médoc). Cantemerle has a winemaking history that goes back to the late 16th century. For most of the last century the property was owned by the Dubos family, who established this property's reputation for gloriously fragrant, elegantly rendered wines. However, financial problems, along with family quarrels, led to the sale of Cantemerle in 1980. In the 1970s the property was allowed to deteriorate and the wine suffered in vintages after 1975. Cantemerle's cellars, *chai*, and château have been completely renovated with new cellars, a new winemaking facility, a state-of-the-art tasting room, and, most important, a greater commitment to quality.

Prior to 1980 there was also considerable bottle variation, and in a number of vintages the wines suffered from old barrel smells and a lack of fruit. To date, the 1989 and 1983 are the two best wines made under the new management. Quality should only increase, as the vineyard, which has been significantly replanted, comes of age. The style of Cantemerle is a rich, supple fruitiness and intensely fragrant bouquet. Given the lighter soils of their vineyards and the high percentage of Merlot, this will never be a blockbuster wine. Cantemerle at its best always possesses a degree of fragrance and precociousness that give undeniable early appeal. Yet in spite of the high expectations, Cantemerle has not produced a wine in the last decade as superb as the 1989 and 1983.

IMPORTANT VINTAGES

2000
88 A dark ruby/purple color is followed by sweet cranberry, mulberry, and cherry fruit aromas. The wine reveals excellent ripeness on the attack, a lush, low-acid, medium-bodied personality, and moderate tannin. The 2000 will not make anyone forget the glorious 1989 Cantemerle, but it is very good. Anticipated maturity: 2006–2014. Last tasted, 1/03.

1999
79 A disappointment, this herbaceous, light- to medium-bodied wine is cleanly made but has no substance or depth. In addition, the finish is attenuated. Drink it over the first decade of life. Last tasted, 1/02.

1998
84 Dark ruby–colored with a purple edge, this slightly herbaceous, medium-bodied, lighter-styled 1998 offers attractive aromas and flavors, but it lacks depth and length. Drink it over the next 6–7 years. Last tasted, 3/02.

1996
87 I had hoped this wine would turn out closer to outstanding, but it is an excellent Cantemerle, if not quite as stunning as I had expected. The wine offers a dark ruby color and a sweet nose of black raspberries, subtle new oak, and acacia smells. There is fine sweetness and solid tannin in this elegant, symmetrical wine. It is more forward and lighter than it was from cask, but it is a stylish example of Cantemerle. Anticipated maturity: now–2015. Last tasted, 3/01.

1995
86 The 1995 does not possess the depth of the 1996, and it reveals a more evolved medium ruby color that is already lightening at the edge. Peppery, herb-tinged red currant fruit aromas are pleasant, but uninspiring. This medium-bodied, straightforward wine lacks the depth, dimension, and power of a topflight classified growth. It will be at its best until 2010. Last tasted, 1/02.

1990
87 This wine has matured nicely and is now fully mature. Dark ruby with some pink at the edge, this elegant textbook Cantemerle has medium body and a very floral, sweet nose of plums, currants, white flowers, cedar, and mineral. Low in acidity, with light and supple tannin, this is a classic lighter weight Bordeaux that is all charm and finesses. Anticipated maturity: now–2006. Last tasted, 12/01.

1989
92

A perfect success for Cantemerle and one of the most monumental wines of the last 40 years, the 1989 Cantemerle remains a dense ruby color with plenty of purple in its mid-section. The wine has the classic Cantemerle nose of flowers intermixed with black currants, blackberries, and mineral. Surprisingly opulent, lush, and very fragrant, this wine has supple texture and a gorgeous finish. Not a blockbuster by any means, but it is silky and beautifully pure. Anticipated maturity: now–2010. Last tasted, 9/02.

1988
86

This wine shows a dark plum/garnet color and a moderately intense nose of tobacco and weedy red as well as black currants. This medium-bodied wine shows some sharp tannins in the finish and seems to be close to full maturity. A straightforward, pleasant, but generally undistinguished effort. Anticipated maturity: now–2006. Last tasted, 11/00.

1986
84

This wine is close to full maturity, but remains relatively austere, compact, and lean. With high tannins and some sweet currant and cherry fruit as well as leather, compost, and earth overtones, the wine is medium bodied but not likely to improve. Anticipated maturity: now. Last tasted, 11/00.

1985
86

Fully mature and beginning to dry out ever so much, this medium ruby–colored wine is already showing considerable amber at the edge. The floral, spicy nose offers up notes of cherries, red currants, leather, and a hint of fennel. The wine is medium bodied, soft, and relatively undistinguished, but quite pleasant. Anticipated maturity: now. Last tasted, 11/00.

1983
90

Fully mature, this gorgeous wine has consistently offered a saturated dark ruby/ garnet color, a gorgeous nose of melted licorice, lilacs, ripe black currants and plums, and a hint of blackberry. Always generous and supple, with sweet tannin, low acidity, and loads of fruit, this is a beauty and one of the most successful Cantemerles of the last 30 years. Anticipated maturity: now–2006. Last tasted, 9/02.

1982
87

This wine has continued to surprise me, although it is hardly a profound effort for the vintage. The color shows considerable amber at the edge, but the wine shows nice, sweet cedar, ground pepper, and herbaceous notes intermixed with strawberry and black cherry jam. The wine is medium bodied and supple, with some attractive levels of glycerin still present. It does not have the complexity of the 1983, but there is a fleshiness and lush texture that is very disarming. Anticipated maturity: now. Last tasted, 11/00.

ANCIENT VINTAGES

Most of the vintages of the 1970s were extremely disappointing. It has been well over a decade since I last tasted the great 1961 (92 points; last tasted 1/88). I suspect that wine could still be holding together where properly stored. Of the historic vintages, the 1959 (89 points) was not far off the pace of the 1961, and of course the 1953 (94 points; last tasted 11/96) is legendary, and probably the finest Cantemerle ever made, at least in the last 60 years.

CANTENAC BROWN

Classification: Third Growth in 1855

Owner: AXA Millésimes

Administrator: Christian Seely

Address: 33460 Cantenac

Telephone: 05 57 88 81 81; Telefax: 05 57 88 81 90

E-mail: infochato@cantenacbrown.com

Website: www.chateaucantenacbrown.com

Visits: By appointment only

Contact: Jennifer Hornor

VINEYARDS

Surface area: 104 acres

Grape varietals: 65% Cabernet Sauvignon, 30% Merlot, 5% Cabernet Franc

Average age of vines: 32 years

Density of plantation: 8,500 vines per hectare

Average yields: 55 hectoliters per hectare

Elevage: Fifteen to eighteen months aging in barrels with 50% new oak. Fining, no filtration.

WINES PRODUCED

Château Cantenac Brown: 144,000 bottles

Château Canuet: 120,000 bottles

Plateau of maturity: Within 5–10 years of the vintage for post-1980 vintages and within 10–20 years for pre-1980 vintages

GENERAL APPRECIATION

One of the least known classified growths, Cantenac Brown has, to my knowledge, never lived up to its status, producing tannic, dry, rather astringent wines that lack charm and suppleness. Despite some improvements during the 1980s and 1990s, this estate rarely merits its lofty classification.

Cantenac Brown has had a checkered recent history. Sold in 1968 by the famous Bordelais Jean Lawton to the Du Vivier family, the property was sold again in 1980 to the huge Cognac house Rémy-Martin. The property was sold once again to the huge insurance conglomerate AXA. They had the intelligence to put Jean-Michel Cazes and his brilliant team of wine-makers, led by Daniel Llose, in charge. Since the retirement of Cazes, Christian Seely has assumed full responsibility for Cantenac Brown.

The vineyard is not among the best situated in the commune of Cantenac and has traditionally produced relatively hard, tannic wines that were often too burly and muscular. Under the recent owners, the direction has tried to move toward wines that are softer and less robust. The results have been mixed. This is a positive development, yet far too many recent vintages of Cantenac Brown still possess an excess of tannin as well as a dry, charmless character. The sad truth is that many of the estate's new vintages will lose their fruit long before their tannins. More skeptical observers claim the vineyard, which sits on deep, gravelly soil, will never produce wines of great elegance.

Visitors to the region are well advised, if for photogenic reasons only, to follow the well-marked road (right before the village of Issan) that passes in front of this exceptional Victorian château with its striking red brick and Tudor decor. It is one of the more impressive edifices in the Médoc, yet it stands out as atypically un-French in appearance, resembling an oversize English manor house more than a French château.

IMPORTANT VINTAGES

2000
90 — The saturated purple-colored 2000 is a sleeper of the vintage. Deep, medium to full-bodied, and crammed with concentrated black fruits, it reveals an underlying sweet earthiness, terrific purity, a layered, multitextured mid-palate, and a large, dense finish with moderate tannin. Anticipated maturity: 2005–2018. Last tasted, 1/03.

1999
89 — The dense ruby/purple–colored, charming, finesse-styled 1999 Cantenac Brown offers excellent sweetness, medium body, and abundant black currant fruit intermixed with truffle, toasty oak, and subtle dried herb notes. With good tannin, lively fruit, and excellent purity as well as balance, it should drink well for 12–15 years. Last tasted, 3/02.

1998
88 — Elegant, sweet, floral-infused, black currant and blackberry fruit, along with licorice, earth, and even a note of truffles are present in this medium-bodied wine's aromas and flavors. Moreover, there is excellent concentration, good purity, and sweet tannin. Not a blockbuster, it is a well-made, symmetrical 1998 to drink before 2006. Last tasted, 3/02.

1996
86+ — I generally find Cantenac Brown too tough-textured, tannic, and dry. Therefore, I am happy to say the 1996, while tannic, looks to be one of the better balanced efforts to emerge from this estate. The color is a deep ruby/purple. The wine offers simple but pleasing aromas of black currants, licorice, and vanilla. In the mouth, it is medium to full-bodied, powerful, muscular, somewhat foursquare, but mouthfilling and rich. Anticipated maturity: 2004–2015. Last tasted, 3/02.

1995
78 — Although the 1995 reveals a good color, it has been consistently angular, austere, and too tannic. This is a lean, spartan style of Claret that is likely to dry out before enough tannin melts away to reach a balance with the wine's fruit. Anticipated maturity: now–2010. Last tasted, 3/02.

1990
88 — Dark plum/garnet, this dusty, somewhat earthy, rustic wine does not lack for concentration and full body, but readers looking for finesse and elegance would be best advised to search elsewhere. The wine has plenty of smoky cassis intermixed with weedy tobacco and a distinct, loamy soil note. The wine seems to be close to full maturity, but I do not ever expect the tannins to become completely integrated. Anticipated maturity: now–2010. Last tasted, 6/00.

1989
85 — Soft, straightforward, monolithic, and medium bodied, with some sweet plum and currant fruit, this wine does not follow through on the palate and has an attenuated finish. It has reached full maturity and is a very unexciting wine characteristic of most of the Cantenac Browns of the 1980s, 1970s, and 1960s. Anticipated maturity: now. Last tasted, 6/00.

ANCIENT VINTAGES

A very dismal level of performance in both the 1960s and 1970s produced no interesting wines that I would rate in the mid- or upper 80s. Old timers in Bordeaux speak fondly of the 1928 and 1926, but I have never tasted them.

DAUZAC

Classification: Fifth Growth in 1855

Owner: MAIF (an insurance company)

Administrator: André Lurton

Address: Labarde, 33460 Margaux

Telephone: 05 57 88 32 10; Telefax: 05 57 88 96 00

E-mail: andrelurton@andrelurton.com

Website: www.andrelurton.com

Visits: Monday to Friday, 10 A.M.–5 P.M.

Contact: Danielle Sicard

VINEYARDS

Surface area: 98.8 acres

Grape varietals: 60% Cabernet Sauvignon, 37% Merlot, 3% Cabernet Franc

Average age of vines: 30 years

Density of plantation: 10,000 vines per hectare

Average yields: 57 hectoliters per hectare

Elevage: Prolonged and slow fermentation in temperature-controlled stainless-steel vats (lots separate) with frequent breakings of the cap. Fourteen months aging with 50% new oak and 50% one-year-old barrels. Fining, no filtration.

WINES PRODUCED

Château Dauzac: 125,000 bottles

Château La Bastide Dauzac: 140,000 bottles

Plateau of maturity: Within 5–15 years of the vintage

GENERAL APPRECIATION

André Lurton's magic touch, which usually works marvels, has undoubtedly improved the wines at Dauzac, but is this estate capable of making an outstanding (90-point or better) Margaux?

Dauzac's impressive new winery is one of the first major classified growths the visitor to the Médoc encounters after passing through Macau on the famous D2 heading north. Significant improvements have been made since 1978, including the installation of stainless-steel fermentation tanks, an extensive program of new vineyard plantings, and the increased usage of new oak barrels. A noteworthy improvement of the wine has also occurred, particularly since the mid-1990s. With André Lurton, the well-known proprietor of numerous Bordeaux châteaux particularly in Pessac-Léognan, in full administrative control of Dauzac, the future should be more promising than the dismal past.

IMPORTANT VINTAGES

2001 An impressive deep ruby/purple color is followed by a muscular, pumped-up of-
87–88 fering with plenty of oak, depth, extract, and richness. Ultimately, it may fall short on charm and finesse, but there is no doubting the size, strength, and aging potential. Anticipated maturity: 2006–2015. Last tasted, 1/03.

2000 This is a corpulent, chunky, foursquare but undeniably endearing, mouth-filling,
89 fleshy offering. Tannin is present, but it is well hidden by the wine's substantial meatiness. Anticipated maturity: 2005–2016. Last tasted, 1/03.

1999 One of the finest Dauzacs to date, the 1999's opaque purple color is followed by
88 aromas and flavors of black currant and blueberry fruit, Asian spices, minerals, smoke, and toasty new oak. Powerful and extracted, with low acidity, it will be at its best before 2016. Last tasted, 3/02.

1998 A saturated dark ruby/purple color is followed by elegant, floral, red and black
87 currant aromas. The wine is well structured, medium bodied, and ripe, with fine length as well as a deep mid-palate. It can be drunk early, but promises to last for nearly two decades. Anticipated maturity: now–2017. Last tasted, 1/02.

1996 This dark ruby/purple colored wine offers sweet black currant fruit intertwined
86 with smoke, herbs, and new oak. Medium bodied, with good extract, moderate depth and tannin, and a ripe finish, it will drink well until 2015. It is a good, middle-weight, yet monolithic Margaux. Last tasted, 3/00.

1995 A broodingly backward, tannic, dark ruby–colored wine, Dauzac's 1995 borders
86? on being too austere, but there is enough sweet black currant fruit, as well as medium body and a fleshy mid-palate to encourage die-hard optimists. While this will never be a great Claret, it is a well-made, competent Margaux that will age nicely. Anticipated maturity: 2005–2015. Last tasted, 3/00.

ANCIENT VINTAGES

Surprisingly, the difficult, rain-plagued years of 1993 and 1994 produced competent efforts from Dauzac, largely because of the efforts of André Lurton. The other vintages of the 1990s as well as those of the 1980s were mediocre at best, usually meriting scores from me from the low to upper 70s.

DURFORT-VIVENS

Classification: Second Growth in 1855

Proprietor: Gonzague Lurton

Address: 33460 Margaux

Telephone: 05 57 88 83 33; Telefax: 05 57 88 72 51

Visits: By appointment only

Contact: Gonzague Lurton

VINEYARDS

Surface area: 49.4 acres

Grape varietals: 82% Cabernet Sauvignon, 10% Cabernet Franc, 8% Petit Verdot

Average age of vines: 25 years

Density of plantation: 6,600 vines per hectare

Average yields: 50 to 55 hectoliters per hectare

Elevage: Aging for 12–18 months in barrels (30–50% new oak). Fining and filtration.

WINES PRODUCED

Château Durfort-Vivens: 70,000–75,000 bottles

Domaine de Cure-Bourse: Variable

Plateau of maturity: Within 6–18 years of the vintage

A forgotten château (it sits at the entrance to the village of Margaux), this second growth is run by Gonzague Lurton. The vineyards of Durfort-Vivens should produce better wine than they do. It is unfair to blame the current Lurton for the miserable track record of Durfort-Vivens between 1961 and 1981. The vineyards are now a respectable age and are certainly well placed within the appellation. One wonders if the high percentage of Cabernet Sauvignon (the highest of any southern Médoc) gives the wine less charm and more toughness than is ideal.

Vintages since 1982 have exhibited improvement, but this still looks to be a château where the owner, who is the current president of the Margaux appellation, needs to realize that this is the 21st century, and the global wine market is based on quality, not pedigree. To his credit, Gonzague Lurton, who is in his early 30s and the son of Lucien Lurton, has proposed standards about tasting young Bordeaux. Much of this probably has to do with the fact that his wines often do not do as well as many of his peers' in the early *en primeur* tastings. He has tended to falsely assume that his peers fix or adulterate their samples and present journalists with wines that are far better than what ultimately comes on the marketplace. For 20 years I have been buying all of the highly rated wines out of bottle to make sure that what I taste in barrel, which is tasted probably 8–12 times prior to bottling, does correlate with what is served. Rarely have I seen any kind of discrepancy. In most cases, the bottled Bordeaux tastes better and is superior to the barrel sample, and this is the way it should be. I totally agree that there should be standardized rules for all châteaux submitting barrel samples, but I also think the young Lurton needs to sit down and taste his wine in bottle against other wines in Bordeaux. If he still does not realize that he is behind the quality curve, then so be it. In any event, this is a property that has made improvements, but Lurton's youthful arrogance and unrealistic observation that everyone is cheating except him seems misplaced. The track record of Durfort-Vivens in recent vintages is certainly better than the mediocrities produced by his predecessors, but this is hardly an inspiring wine . . . at least for my palate.

IMPORTANT VINTAGES

2000 Dark ruby, with a nose of loamy soil and mineral intermixed with black cherry,
88+? currant, and herbs, this medium-bodied wine shows very good depth, as well as moderately high tannins and plenty of structure and good acidity. This wine

should be cellared for at least 5–6 years. Anticipated maturity: 2008–2020. Last tasted, 1/03.

1999
86
Notes of tapenade, red currant, earth, and underbrush jump from the glass of this moderately dark ruby–colored wine. Elegant, medium bodied, restrained, with good acidity, this wine should develop quickly and drink well for 10–15 years. Anticipated maturity: 2005–2014. Last tasted, 3/02.

1998
86
Somewhat chunky with robust tannins, this dark garnet–colored wine has hints of licorice, black currants, compost, and sweet mushrooms. The wine is moderately tannic and medium bodied in a restrained, rather elegant style. Anticipated maturity: 2006–2014. Last tasted, 3/02.

1996
84?
High tannins and only moderate levels of fruit and ripeness suggest a troubled future for this wine. The color is a healthy dark ruby with some purple tints. The wine is austere and very lean, with a hint of underripe fruit, and the finish is dry, even attenuated. Unless more flesh and fruit emerge, this will prove to be even more disappointing than my score. Anticipated maturity: 2006–2015. Last tasted, 11/01.

1995
83
Herbal notes continue to dominate this meagerly endowed wine. Tannins have taken hold, and the fruit seems to have gone into hiding. The wine shows some earthy old wood, mushroom notes, and a desiccated finish in a lightweight style. It was more pleasant right after bottling than it is today, raising legitimate fears about its future. Anticipated maturity: now–2010. Last tasted, 12/00.

ANCIENT VINTAGES

No interesting wines emerged from Durfort-Vivens in the 1980s. The best two vintages were the 1983 and 1982, both of which I have not tasted since the early 1990s. Other than that, my experience with vintages of Durfort-Vivens in the 1970s and 1960s is painful: one mediocre, washed-out, dirty wine after another. Obviously that period of insipid performances has been put to rest under the relatively young Gonzague Lurton, but more should be expected of this classified growth.

GISCOURS

Classification: Third Growth in 1855

Owner: Eric Albada Jelgersma

Address: 10, route de Giscours, Labarde, 33460 Margaux

Telephone: 05 57 97 09 09; Telefax: 05 57 97 09 00

E-mail: giscours@chateau-giscours.fr

Website: www.chateau-giscours.fr

Visits: By appointment only

Contact: Vincent Rey

VINEYARDS

Surface area: 197.6 acres

Grape varietals: 55% Cabernet Sauvignon, 40% Merlot, 5% Cabernet Franc

Average age of vines: 30 years

Density of plantation: 8,300 vines per hectare

Average yields: 45 hectoliters per hectare

Elevage: Six to eight day fermentation and 15–18 day maceration in temperature-controlled stainless-steel tanks. Eighteen months aging in barrels that are renewed by a third each year. Fining with egg whites, no filtration.

WINES PRODUCED

Château Giscours: 300,000–350,000 bottles

La Sirène de Giscours: 50,000–80,000 bottles

Plateau of maturity: Within 6–20 years of the vintage

GENERAL APPRECIATION

Potentially a top performer (1975 and 1978, for example), Giscours has had an irregular track record over the last 20–30 years. Things seem to be changing for the better under the recent administration of Eric Albada Jelgersma, with the 2001, 2000, and 1999 being the finest Giscours trilogy to date. Despite these improvements, Giscours currently performs at fourth-growth level, and has a realistic pricing policy.

Giscours is a vast estate of more than 600 acres (less than a third are under vine) in the most southern portion of the Margaux commune known as Labarde. The estate, once in deplorable condition, was rescued in 1952 by the Tari family and has experienced a resurgence in quality and prestige. Pierre Tari began to assume more control in 1970 and has become one of the leading spokespersons for Bordeaux. Until the late 1980s he was president of Bordeaux's Union des Grands Crus, an association of châteaux banded together for one common cause: to promote the virtues of Bordeaux.

The imposing château of Giscours is one of the largest of the Médoc, and well worth a visit. It is set in a beautiful park with many ancient trees. Except for the slump in quality during much of the 1980s and early 1990s (the wine tasted too overtly commercial, flabby, and soft), Giscours has been characterized by a deep, often opaque color, gobs of concentration, and a muscular and rich construction with plenty of tannin. Furthermore, in the 1970s, Giscours' record in "off" vintages was far superior to most other renowned Bordeaux châteaux.

In 1995, the Tari family sold Giscours to Dutch businessman Eric Albada Jelgersma. His investments as well as passion for Giscours resulted in an impressive trilogy of vintages at the end of the millennium.

IMPORTANT VINTAGES

2001
88–89   With a dark ruby/purple color, aromas of sweet black fruits, lively acidity, and medium body, this pure, elegant Giscours should develop more mid-palate, texture, and flesh with cask aging. It is an aromatic, pure, sexy 2001 to enjoy between 2006–2014. Last tasted, 1/03.

2000
92   The black/purple-colored 2000 offers up terrific notes of blackberry and currant jam intermixed with high-quality toast. Smoky, rich, sexy, and sumptuously built, with a full-bodied, low-acid, super-concentrated personality, this sleeper of the vintage is one of the most attractively priced offerings of 2000. Anticipated maturity: 2006–2020. Last tasted, 1/03.

1999 A dense ruby/purple color is followed by seductive aromas of smoky dried herbs,
89 jammy currants, and a rich, dense, layered, velvety-textured wine. The sumptuous
attack narrows slightly in the mid-palate and finish, but this is a totally charming,
well-balanced, pure beauty to consume over the next 12–14 years. Last tasted,
1/03.

1998 The 1998 Giscours is a supple, consumer-friendly, commercially styled offering
87 with considerable appeal. Jammy black fruits intermingle with spicy oak in this
medium-bodied, straightforward, yet plump, cedary, tasty, savory effort. Enjoy it
over the next 10 years. Last tasted, 1/03.

1996 A disappointment for the Médoc in this vintage, the 1996 Giscours has an evolved
83 plum color with some pink at the rim. The wine is soft, shows some herbaceously
tinged berry fruit, hints of licorice and black currants, but not much depth or texture. Obviously, little selection was employed at Giscours when putting together
the final blend for 1996. Anticipated maturity: now–2008. Last tasted, 3/02.

1995 A supple, picnic-style Claret with considerable appeal but no depth or intensity to
85 its flavors, this soft, fully mature wine exhibits a plum/ruby color and has an
herbaceous, cedary nose of sweet cherries and currants. The wine is medium bodied, spicy, and pleasant, but undistinguished. Drink it over the next 5–7 years.
Last tasted, 3/02.

ANCIENT VINTAGES

Giscours declined significantly in quality during the 1980s and early 1990s. Both the
1989 and 1990 are fully mature and far below the expectations from these two
renowned vintages. The 1988 was a disappointment for this underrated vintage. Ditto
for the thin, herbal 1986 and 1985. Both the 1983 and 1982 were better, but one has to
return, surprisingly, to the 1979, 1978, and 1975 to find Giscours that reflect its classification in the 1855 hierarchy of Bordeaux wine quality. The 1979 continues to evolve
beautifully, and the last time I tasted it (11/01) I rated it 88. The 1978 (90 points; last
tasted 11/01) and 1975 (92 points; last tasted 11/01) are two gorgeous Giscours wines
that are rich, concentrated, and reflect what is possible at this property. Certainly
under the new management, quality such as this should be routinely encountered, as
opposed to the string of disappointments in the mid-1980s through the mid-1990s.

The museum vintages of Giscours are probably over the hill. Certainly the 1970
seems to be cracking up after a long, 30-year run as a very tasty, delicious wine. The
1961 is now fading, as is the 1959.

D'ISSAN

Classification: Third Growth in 1855

Owner: Emmanuel Cruse family

Address: 33460 Cantenac

Telephone: 05 57 88 35 91; Telefax: 05 57 88 74 24

E-mail: issan@chateau-issan.com

Website: www.chateau-issan.com

Visits: By appointment in winter. Monday to Friday,
9 A.M.–noon and 2–5 P.M. in the summer.

Contact: Emmanuel Cruse

VINEYARDS

Surface area: 123.5 acres (only 74 under Margaux appellation)

Grape varietals: 70% Cabernet Sauvignon, 30% Merlot

Average age of vines: 35 years

Density of plantation: 8,500 vines per hectare

Average yields: 48 hectoliters per hectare

Elevage: Twenty-one day fermentation and maceration in temperature-controlled stainless-steel vats. Sixteen to eighteen months aging in barrels with 50% new oak. Fining, light filtration upon bottling.

WINES PRODUCED

Château d'Issan: 110,000 bottles

Blason d'Issan: 60,000 bottles

Plateau of maturity: Within 8–20 years of the vintage for post-1996 vintages and within 5–15 years of the vintage for pre-1996 vintages

GENERAL APPRECIATION

Under the talented management of young Emmanuel Cruse, this estate has clearly come around since 1995 with the 2001, 2000, and 1999 being its finest successive vintages to date. As cautious as one may be with pre-1995 bottles, consumers are advised to latch on to post-1996 d'Issans, which represent great values. This classified growth is well worth its status, producing wines of great finesse and elegance.

The 17th-century Château d'Issan is one of the most strikingly beautiful estates in the Médoc. It is surrounded by a moat and has a Sleeping Beauty castle ambience. Since 1945 d'Issan has been owned by the famous Cruse family of Bordeaux, who for many years exclusively controlled the marketing of this wine through their *négociant* business. Now the wine is freely sold to all *négociants* in Bordeaux. Undoubtedly the quality has improved, especially in the late 1990s but I have had too many indifferent experiences with other vintages.

When good (the 1900 is considered one of the greatest wines ever made in Bordeaux), d'Issan is prized for its soft yet delicate character and provocative perfume. Until the mid-1990s, finding an d'Issan with such characteristics was no easy task.

Most vintages of d'Issan can be drunk at an extremely early age, yet have the ability to last.

IMPORTANT VINTAGES

2001 — A successful effort, d'Issan's dark ruby/purple–colored 2001 reveals a floral-
88–90 scented bouquet with notes of pure black currants and cherries. It builds incrementally in the mouth, becoming medium bodied and stylish, with sweet tannin, unobtrusive acidity, and subtle wood. A beautifully knit, elegant, classic Margaux, it should drink well between 2005–2016. Last tasted, 1/03.

2000 — The 2000 is a large-scaled yet delicate, finesse-styled offering. Its opaque ruby/
93 purple color is accompanied by sweet aromas of flowers, black fruits, licorice, and subtle new oak. Extremely graceful, symmetrical, and refined, with flavors that build incrementally, this stylish yet savory Margaux should prove to be the finest

d'Issan produced in more than four decades. Anticipated maturity: 2006–2020. Last tasted, 1/03.

1999
89+
A gorgeously elegant style of wine, with notes of violets, black currants, and sweet oak, this delicate yet authoritatively flavored 1999 is the quintessential example of the finesse and nuance of a classified-growth Margaux. Pure, graceful, with delicacy rather than weight and lovely balance, it can be drunk now and over the next 12–14 years. Last tasted, 11/01.

1998
87
The dark ruby–colored, elegant, finesse-filled 1998 d'Issan reveals a floral, licorice, herb, and blackberry/currant-scented bouquet. Medium bodied, with sweet tannin, a soft entry on the palate, fine concentration, a pure finish, and moderate tannin, it will be at its best before 2014. Last tasted, 11/01.

1996
88
The 1996 d'Issan exhibits a dark ruby/purple color as well as an elegant, floral, blackberry, and smoky-scented nose. The wine is medium bodied and complex in the mouth, with subtle new oak, gorgeously ripe, sweet black currant fruit, and well-integrated tannin and acidity. This quintessential Margaux-styled wine is elegant and rich. Anticipated maturity: 2004–2020. Last tasted, 11/01.

1995
87
An excellent d'Issan, with more noticeable tannin than the 1996, the dark plum/ruby–colored 1995 possesses an excellent spicy, weedy, licorice, and black currant–scented nose, sweet fruit on the attack, and very good purity, ripeness, and overall balance. A medium-bodied wine, it is well made and still relatively closed. Anticipated maturity: 2005–2014. Last tasted, 11/01.

ANCIENT VINTAGES

This is another property that had an uninspiring record of performance for most of the 1970s, 1980s, and 1990s. The only highlight, and it is not terribly significant, was the relatively lightweight but perfumed, rather classic 1983, which I consistently rated 87 (last tasted 11/01). This wine is fully mature and not likely to get any better. Certainly some of the top Bordeaux vintages, such as 1990, 1989, 1986 (in the Médoc), and 1985, turned out very lightweight, uninteresting wines at d'Issan. Going back into the pre-1970 vintages, nothing has ever come across my radar screen as being particularly interesting. Obviously, it is safe to say that the vintages young Emmanuel Cruse has produced since 1995 will certainly surpass anything d'Issan made in the previous 50 or so years.

KIRWAN

Classification: Third Growth in 1855

Owner: Schyler family

Address: Cantenac, 33460 Margaux

Telephone: 05 57 88 71 00; Telefax: 05 57 88 77 62

E-mail: mail@chateau-kirwan.com

Website: www.chateau-kirwan.com

Visits: Monday to Friday, 9:30 A.M.–12:30 P.M. and 2–5:30 P.M. By appointment on Saturdays.

Contact: Astrid Weissenborn

VINEYARDS

Surface area: 86.5 acres

Grape varietals: 40% Cabernet Sauvignon, 30% Merlot, 20% Cabernet Franc, 10% Petit Verdot

Average age of vines: 27 years

Density of plantation: 8,000 vines per hectare

Average yields: 48 hectoliters per hectare

Elevage: Six to seven day fermentation and three week maceration in temperature-controlled stainless-steel tanks. Eighteen months aging in barrels with 30–50% new oak. Fining with egg whites. Light filtration.

WINES PRODUCED

Château Kirwan: 80,000–120,000 bottles

Les Charmes de Kirwan: 90,000–100,000 bottles

Plateau of maturity: Within 5–14 years of the vintage

GENERAL APPRECIATION

Kirwan has improved considerably since the mid-1990s. This longtime underperformer is now back on track, year in and year out producing wines that at least are worth their status and at best are equal to a third growth. Prices have remained reasonable. The style of wine produced is one of power and extraction. Time will tell if the "Margaux finesse" develops.

Until 1995, Kirwan was another Margaux estate that would have had a hard time holding its position in Bordeaux's 1855 classification. Like many Margaux classified growths, Kirwan had an undistinguished track record. While I have been a longtime critic of Kirwan's wines, consistently finding them too light, dull, and bland to justify the lofty classification and price tag, quality rebounded in the mid-1990s, and dramatically.

While Kirwan used to be a light-bodied, compact, acidic Bordeaux, the impressive performances during the 1990s, often in difficult vintages, suggest a wine with more color, flesh, body, and intensity. Prices have not yet caught up with Kirwan's new level of quality, so readers who complain about the extravagant prices fetched by many classified-growth Bordeaux châteaux should take another look at Kirwan.

IMPORTANT VINTAGES

2001 An impressively saturated dense ruby/purple color is followed by obvious toasty
87– new oak, black fruit, earth, and Asian spice scents. High tannin results in a cer-
88+? tain angularity, but it cuts a large swath across the palate. If the oak and tannin become better integrated, this Margaux will merit a score in the upper 80s. If not, it will be an austere wine with the potential to dry out. Anticipated maturity: 2007–2015. Last tasted, 1/03.

2000 This is another Margaux estate enjoying a renaissance with full-flavored, muscu-
90+ lar wines being produced. Probably the finest Kirwan I have ever tasted, the 2000 is a full-bodied, multidimensional, rich powerhouse exhibiting a black/purple color and a sweet, chewy, concentrated style with superb intensity, ripeness, and

length. It should last for decades. Anticipated maturity: 2010–2030. Last tasted, 1/03.

1999 The aromatic, oaky, modern-styled 1999 Kirwan boasts a deep ruby/purple color
89+ as well as considerable size, depth, and muscle (atypical for the vintage), abundant texture, and loads of flavor (primarily licorice, cassis, and earth). Anticipated maturity: 2004–2015. Last tasted, 3/02.

1998 A sleeper of the vintage, the opaque purple–colored 1998 boasts a smoky, licorice,
90 cassis, and mineral-scented bouquet. Full-bodied, powerful, yet elegant, it successfully balances complexity with an unbridled richness and power. Very impressive, particularly in view of its exceptional concentration, it will handsomely repay cellaring of two decades or more. Anticipated maturity: 2006–2025. Last tasted, 3/02.

1997 An attractive, dark ruby/purple colored effort, the 1997 Kirwan offers sweet cas-
87 sis fruit, copious new oak, a fleshy, succulent texture, and an attractive, well-balanced finish with nicely integrated acidity and tannin. Consume this sexy Margaux over the next 6–7 years. Last tasted, 3/01.

1996 The first of the new breed of Kirwans, the 1996 is a highly extracted, rich,
88 medium-bodied wine with a deep ruby/purple color and ripe cassis fruit intermixed with a touch of new oak, prunes, and spice. The wine has come together nicely. It appears to be an excellent, nearly outstanding effort. There is moderate tannin in the finish, so give this beefy, rich, muscular wine at least another 2–3 years of cellaring. Anticipated maturity: 2006–2025. Last tasted, 3/02.

1995 Aggressive new oak and vanilla continue to dominate this wine's personality. The
85 dark ruby/purple–colored wine displays sweet cranberry and jammy black currant fruit on the attack, but it narrows in the mouth with a compressed personality. Nevertheless, there is fine purity, medium body, and copious tannin. Anticipated maturity: 2006–2018. Last tasted, 3/02.

ANCIENT VINTAGES

Aside from a very competent, actually quite good 1983 (87 points; last tasted 9/97), this has been a property that has turned out one mediocrity after another in the 1960s, 1970s, 1980s, and early 1990s.

LA LAGUNE

Classification: Third Growth in 1855

Owner: SCA Château La Lagune

Address: 81, avenue de l'Europe, 33290 Ludon-Médoc

Telephone: 05 57 88 82 77; Telefax: 05 57 88 82 70

E-mail: lalagune@club-internet.fr

Visits: By appointment Monday to Thursday, 9–11:30 A.M. and 2–4:30 P.M.

Contact: Patrick Moulin or Béatrice Gaillot

VINEYARDS

Surface area: 185.3 acres

Grape varietals: 50% Cabernet Sauvignon, 20% Merlot, 20% Cabernet Franc, 10% Petit Verdot

Average age of vines: 35 years

Density of plantation: 6,666 vines per hectare

Average yields: 50 hectoliters per hectare

Elevage: Twenty-one day fermentation and maceration in epoxy-lined temperature-controlled vats. Eighteen to twenty-four months aging in barrels with 50–90% new oak, depending upon the vintage. Fining, no filtration.

WINES PRODUCED

Château La Lagune: 250,000 bottles

Moulin de La Lagune: 230,000 bottles

Plateau of maturity: Within 5–15 years of the vintage for post-1990 vintages and within 5–20 years of the vintage for vintages of the 1980s.

GENERAL APPRECIATION

As a wine producing estate, La Lagune has a great potential, as evidenced by such fine successes as 1990, 1989, and 1982. Unfortunately, vintages after 1990 have been unimpressive. While this estate was once one of Bordeaux's blue chip overachievers, it seems to have lost its direction and now performs below its official status.

La Lagune was one of Bordeaux's shining success stories. In the 1950s the property was so run down that numerous potential buyers, including the late Alexis Lichine, scoffed at the herculean task of replanting the vineyards and rebuilding the winery to reestablish La Lagune as a truly representative member of Bordeaux's elite group of 1855 cru classé châteaux. In 1958 George Brunet, an entrepreneur, acquired the property and totally replanted the vineyard and constructed what today remains one of the more sophisticated wineries in the Médoc. Brunet did not stay long enough to reap the accolades from his massive investment in the property; he moved to Provence, where he built, and again sold, one of that area's best wineries, Château Vignelaure. He sold La Lagune in 1962 to the Ayala Champagne firm, which has continued to renovate and manage La Lagune with the same fervor and passion. Their most revolutionary concept (which has remained uncopied) was the construction of a series of pipelines from the vats to the barrel aging cellars for transporting the wine without any exposure to air.

La Lagune is the very first classified growth encountered on the famous D2 road to the Médoc from Bordeaux. It is less than 10 miles from the city. The vineyard is set on very light, gravel-like, sandy soils not unlike those of the Graves appellation south of Bordeaux. In 1964 La Lagune was also the first château to position a woman, the late Jeanne Boyrie, as manager of the estate. In the chauvinist world of Bordeaux, this was a revolutionary development. While she was never able to penetrate the inner circle of the male-dominated, conservative Bordeaux wine society, no one took lightly her stern, formidable, meticulous personality, as she was undoubtedly one of the most conscientious and competent managers in Bordeaux. Following her mother's death in November 1986, Jeanne Boyrie's daughter, Caroline Desvergnes, assumed the responsibilities for running this property. Today the estate is administered by Thierry Budin.

At its best, the style of wine produced at La Lagune has been described as both

Pomerol-like and Graves-like. One notable connoisseur (this author) has called it "very Burgundian." All three of these descriptions have merit. It can be a rich, fleshy, solid wine, with sometimes an overpowering bouquet of vanilla oak and black cherries. The wine of La Lagune is usually fully mature by the 10th year of life, but will certainly keep 15–20 years. The quality and strength of La Lagune improved significantly between 1966 and 1990. As the vineyard has gotten older, La Lagune continued to emerge as one of the great—and surprisingly reasonably priced—wines of the Médoc. Between 1976 and 1990, a bevy of fine wines emerged, yet sadly, since 1990 La Lagune's track record has been uninspiring.

IMPORTANT VINTAGES

2000
86
The 2000 vintage was not up to my expectations for this property. The diluted, medium-bodied 2000 is a pleasant but undistinguished effort, particularly in such a great vintage. While the color is a dark ruby, the wine lacks substance, depth, and intensity. It has nowhere to go. Anticipated maturity: now–2014. Last tasted, 3/01.

1999
85
Medium/dark ruby with a nose of toasty oak, dried herbs, sweet cherries, and spice, this elegant, medium-bodied wine finishes quickly. Drink it over the next 7–8 years. Last tasted, 3/02.

1998
82
The good news is that this is an elegant, friendly wine. The bad news is that there is not much to it, and the finish is short and compressed. The wine reveals toasty new oak, moderately ripe cherry fruit, and sweet tannin, but there is little concentration or mid-palate in this good, mid-weight Bordeaux. Consume it over the next 4–5 years. Last tasted, 3/02.

1996
86
This is another tannic, austere 1996, but it is well endowed. Copious aromas of spicy new oak are present in the moderately intense bouquet, as well as cherry notes intertwined with dried herbs. The wine is medium bodied and well made, with good spice, a slight austerity, and moderate tannin in the long finish. In many vintages La Lagune can be drunk at an early age, but this effort will require another 2–3 years of patience. Anticipated maturity: 2006–2018. Last tasted, 3/01.

1995
88
La Lagune's seductively styled 1995 displays a dark ruby color, as well as copious amounts of black cherry, kirsch, and plum-like fruit nicely dosed with high-quality smoky, toasty oak. This medium-bodied, elegant, round, generous, charming wine can be drunk young or cellared for a decade or more. Anticipated maturity: now–2015. Last tasted, 3/02.

1990
90
Like so many 1990s, this wine appears to have put on more weight and added a dimension or two to its personality. The color is dense ruby, with no lightening at the edge. The sweet nose of grilled nuts, smoked herbs, sweet, lavishly ripe black currant fruit, and chocolate is followed by a gutsy, medium-bodied wine that is about as fleshy as La Lagune can be. While the wine does not have the intensity, fat, and power of the 1982 (the greatest La Lagune I have ever tasted), it is a gorgeously proportioned, velvety-textured, sweet, and expansive wine that is already drinking well. Anticipated maturity: now–2010. Last tasted, 9/97.

1989
90
I have always enjoyed the 1989 La Lagune. At first I thought it was marginally superior to the 1990, but they are essentially equivalent in quality, although the 1989 possesses less fat and a more ruggedly tannic structure. The color is a healthy dark ruby, and the wine offers up a smoky, sweet vanilla, jammy berry–scented nose with aromas of weedy tobacco. The wine is medium bodied with excellent purity and richness and gobs of red and black currant fruit nicely dosed with new oak. The wine's grip is more noticeable than in the 1990, and the finish

more attenuated but still impressively long. Interestingly, the 1990 seems more evolved (or at least more drinkable) than the more obviously tannic 1989. Anticipated maturity: now–2012. Last tasted, 9/97.

1988
85　　La Lagune's 1988 has a streak of herbaceousness and tart, aggressive tannins that appear to have the upper hand in the wine's balance. Medium bodied, spicy, and straightforward, it lacks the flesh and chewy opulence of top vintages of La Lagune, but it should prove to be long-lived. The question remains: Is there enough fruit? Anticipated maturity: now. Last tasted, 1/93.

1986
90　　This wine continues to get better and better, yet is still not close to full maturity, despite what I would have thought 16 years ago. The wine has a dense, dark plum/ruby color with just a bit of lightening at the edge. A sweet nose of black cherries intermixed with balsam wood, vanilla, and Provençal herbs has an almost Rhône-like character to it. The wine is medium to full-bodied, rich, with a lot of flesh, light to moderate tannin, and great balance and purity. This wine has approached its plateau of drinking. It should hold for at least another 10–15 years. Very impressive! Anticipated maturity: now–2015. Last tasted, 12/02.

1985
87　　Fully mature, the 1985 La Lagune has a dark plum color and a sweet nose of plums, cherries, and licorice intermixed with some toasty new oak. Always open-knit, somewhat too obvious, but tasty, in a medium-bodied, moderately weighty style, this soft, supple-textured wine is best drunk over the next 3–5 years. Last tasted, 12/02.

1983
86　　Beginning to crack up at the seams, the dark garnet–colored 1983 shows some amber at the edge. The nose shows notes of ashtray and asphalt intermixed with some earth, compost, and dark fruits. A certain mushroomy quality has entered the formula, and the once-sweet fruit seems to be ever-so-slightly becoming drier and the character of the wine more desiccated/attenuated. Drink up. Anticipated maturity: now. Last tasted, 12/02.

1982
93　　This is a sumptuous La Lagune that has hit full maturity but shows no signs of decline. The color is a dense, opaque dark garnet. The wine offers up smoky notes intermixed with jammy black cherries, currants, licorice, and earth. The wine is thick, unctuously textured, with still some moderate tannin to shed. The wine is loaded, very rich, thick, and juicy, with very complex aromatics and surprising weight and power in the mouth. To my thinking, there has never been a more powerful, concentrated La Lagune ever produced. Anticipated maturity: now–2010. Last tasted, 11/02.

ANCIENT VINTAGES

There are some surprises, particularly if the wines have been stored properly, in some of the vintages of the 1970s—1978, consistently a top-notch vintage (88 points; last tasted 2/98), 1976 (88 points; last tasted 12/89), 1975 (87 points; last tasted 1/01), and 1970 (87 points; last tasted from magnum 1/01). These wines were all solidly made, classic Bordeaux that probably still have considerable pleasure left in them if they have been taken care of. The vintages in the 1960s were largely disappointments.

LASCOMBES

Classification: Second Growth in 1855

Owner: Colony Capital Europe

Administrator: Sébastien Bazin

Address: Cours de Verdun, 33460 Margaux

Mailing address: BP 4, 33460 Margaux

Telephone: 05 57 88 70 66; Telefax: 05 57 88 72 17

E-mail: chateau-lascombes@chateau-lascombes.fr

Website: www.chateau-lascombes.com

Visits: Monday to Friday, 9:30–11:30 A.M. and 2–4:30 P.M.

Contact: Géraldine Platon

VINEYARDS

Surface area: 207.5 acres

Grape varietals: 50% Cabernet Sauvignon, 45% Merlot, 5% Petit Verdot

Average age of vines: 40 years

Density of plantation: 8,000–10,000 vines per hectare

Average yields: 29 hectoliters per hectare

Elevage: Ten day cold maceration. Thirty day fermentation and maceration in temperature-controlled wooden and stainless-steel vats. Malolactics in barrels. Twenty months aging (including four months lees aging) with 80–100% new oak depending upon the vintage. Fining, no filtration.

WINES PRODUCED

Château Lascombes: 250,000 bottles

Chevalier de Lascombes: 50,000 bottles

Plateau of maturity: Within 8–20 years of the vintage for post-1999 vintages and within 5–10 years of the vintage for pre-1999 vintages.

GENERAL APPRECIATION

Once one of the better known châteaux of Margaux, Lascombes declined in quality in the 1980s and 1990s. Under the new ownership of Colony Capital, it has been resurrected. Drastic measures, including important reduction of yields and stricter selections, have made this possible for the estate, which performed at Cru Bourgeois level for most of the 1980s and 1990s. It may be too soon to predict Lascombes' future, but judging by the commitment to quality of the consultants behind its turnaround (Yves Vatelot of Reignac Alain Raynaud of Quinault), one can bet it will be impressive. Despite a dramatic increase in pricing, Lascombes remains realistically priced . . . for now.

Lascombes is one of the largest estates in the Médoc. The vineyards are not contiguous, but they consist of nearly four dozen parcels of vines spread throughout the Margaux appellation. Because of this, the harvest at Lascombes can be one of the most difficult to manage and may, in part, help explain why the wines can be inconsistent.

Lascombes' onetime popularity was no doubt a result of the herculean efforts made by the late Alexis Lichine, who owned the property between 1951 and 1971. He oversaw a thorough renovation of the wine cellars, as well as an aggressive plan of vineyard acquisition from surrounding properties. Because of Lichine's commitment to high-quality wines, a succession of very good vintages of wine from Lascombes resulted.

In 1971, Lichine sold Lascombes to the English firm of Bass Charrington, and the quality and consistency of Lascombes dropped noticeably. Many vintages bordered on undrinkable, an embarrassment to Bordeaux.

The revelation of the Médoc, Lascombes was a moribund property until it was sold in 2000. The new owner brought in such hot-shot gurus as Yves Vatelot (Reignac), Bruno Lemoine (Montrose), Alain Raynaud (Quinault l'Enclos and La Fleur de Gay), and Michel Rolland (of worldwide renown). They were given carte blanche authority to make all the necessary changes in the vineyard and cellars to produce the finest wine possible. Yields are now one-third of what they were pre-2000. For example, only a meager 27 hectoliters per hectare was produced in 2001!

IMPORTANT VINTAGES

2001 This beauty is undoubtedly the finest Lascombes produced in more than 30 years.
90–93 Lascombes' 2001 reveals the appellation's savory elegance and lightness, but more fruit purity, texture, and intensity than any Lascombes I have ever tasted. Beautifully balanced with a dense ruby/purple/plum color and a gorgeous nose of smoky black currants, minerals, flowers, and blackberries, it is sweet, ripe, light on its feet, and textured, with an extraordinary seamlessness. It is undoubtedly better than the 2000, no small achievement. Bravo! Anticipated maturity: 2007–2018. Last tasted, 1/03.

2000 A tribute to an incredibly severe selection as well as the consulting skills of Alain
90 Raynaud and Yves Vatelot, this 2000 continues to develop beautifully. Its deep purple color is accompanied by a sweet perfume of smoke, licorice, minerals, and black fruits. With excellent texture, low acidity, a long, concentrated mid-palate, and an impressive finish, this medium-bodied Margaux should be drinkable early, but evolve nicely for 15–18 years. Last tasted, 1/03.

ANCIENT VINTAGES

The 1999, 1997, 1995, 1994, 1993, and 1992 were undrinkable and diluted, or herbaceous and dirty. The last palatable wines Lascombes produced were the 1990 (85 points; last tasted 11/01) and 1989 (84 points; last tasted 11/01). Other than those, it has been six years since I tasted both the 1982 and 1983 (both rated 87 points), probably the two best Lascombes vintages before the new ownership took over in 2000. The other vintages of the early 1980s and late 1970s, the 1981, 1980, 1979, and 1978, were appallingly vegetal, thin, acidic wines with no redeeming characteristics. The 1975 (88 points; last tasted 12/02) stands out as a somewhat atypically powerful, tannic, but dense and full Lascombes that still has the potential to last another 10–15 years.

For readers lucky enough to have access to vintages of Lascombes made under the administration of the late Alexis Lichine, there were some glorious wines made in the 1960s, including a superb 1966, 1962, and of course, 1961. However, I suspect most of those wines, unless they emerge from a very cold, damp cellar, are largely over the hill.

MALESCOT ST.-EXUPÉRY

Classification: Third Growth in 1855

Owner: Roger Zuger

Address: 33460 Margaux

Telephone: 05 57 88 97 20; Telefax: 05 57 88 97 21

E-mail: Jeanluczuger@malescot.com

Visits: By appointment Monday to Friday,
10 A.M.–noon and 2–5 P.M.

Contact: Jean-Luc Zuger

VINEYARDS

Surface area: 58 acres

Grape varietals: 50% Cabernet Sauvignon, 35% Merlot, 10% Cabernet Franc, 5% Petit
Verdot

Average age of vines: 35 years

Density of plantation: 10,000 vines per hectare

Average yields: 52 hectoliters per hectare

Elevage: Eight to ten day alcoholic fermentation in temperature-controlled vats at
30–32°C. Twelve to sixteen months aging in barrels with 80% new oak. No fining, no
filtration.

WINES PRODUCED

Château Malescot St.-Exupéry: 120,000 bottles

La Dame de Malescot: 60,000 bottles

Plateau of maturity: Within 8–20 years of the vintage for post-1990 vintages

GENERAL APPRECIATION

Another Margaux estate that has turned around over the past years, Malescot St.-Exupéry
has changed dramatically. While it performed at Cru Bourgeois level in many vintages, it
is now a legitimate third growth, with prices that remain realistic. This wine represents
one of Margaux's best buys, and at its finest, is the quintessential expression of finesse,
power, and *terroir*.

Malescot St.-Exupéry sits right in the town of Margaux, a few blocks north of Château
Palmer on Bordeaux's main Route du Vin (D2). Malescot has long enjoyed a very favorable reputation, particularly for long-lived, traditionally made, firmly styled wines.

The Zuger family, the proprietors since 1955, claims that the style of Malescot will
not be changed so as to be more supple and drinkable when released. However, it
seems to me that recent vintages, particularly those since the late 1980s are not nearly
as tannic or as hard as the wines of the 1960s. The well-placed vineyards (some of them
adjacent to those of Château Margaux) now tend to produce a medium-weight wine that
can be compelling because of its combination of elegance and authoritative flavors.
Since 1990, the undernourished, austere style of Malescot has taken on a great deal

more richness and intensity. This is another property that has returned to form after a largely disappointing period during the 1960s, 1970s, and 1980s.

IMPORTANT VINTAGES

2001
87–89 An undeniably successful effort, this 2001's appealing aromatics consist of floral, leafy, berry notes with a hint of damp forest. There is sweet tannin, good texture, and a pure, elegant, Margaux-like style. A medium-bodied wine of delicacy, nuance, and subtleness, it is a candidate for drinking during its first 10–12 years of life. Anticipated maturity: 2004–2014. Last tasted, 1/03.

2000
92+ This property is fashioning beautiful wines that are quintessential examples of elegance, finesse, and lightness allied to considerable flavor richness . . . something only Bordeaux can do. The greatest Malescot since 1961, the 2000 boasts a saturated purple color in addition to superripe fruit in the nose suggesting black currants infused with floral, anise, and subtle wood characteristics. With great purity, flavor concentration, and depth, this is a tour de force in elegant winemaking, where the word "elegant" is not used as a euphemism for dilution. This wine is loaded, yet is remarkably delicate and nuanced. It is a brilliant achievement. Anticipated maturity: 2005–2020. Last tasted, 1/03.

1999
90 One of the finest efforts of the vintage, this 1999 offers up complex aromatics consisting of herbs, red and black fruits, minerals, acacia flowers, and licorice. The dark plum color does not possess the saturation of a vintage such as 2000, but this is pure seduction in a medium-bodied, beautifully balanced, nicely textured effort. It is virtually impossible to duplicate such a wine anywhere else in the world. Anticipated maturity: now–2012. Last tasted, 3/02.

1998
90 A classic, this 1998 combines elegance with lovely textured, rich flavors of black cherries and currants, resulting in a quintessential Bordeaux that is unlike any other wine produced in the world. The wine possesses an ethereal lightness, layers of fruit, and a diaphanous framework. More nuances appear with each sip. Tasters will find notes of blackberries, plums, currants, tar, spice box, and minerals. A beautifully etched wine, it will be at its finest before 2017. Last tasted, 3/02.

1996
91 This impressively constructed wine offers a saturated deep ruby/purple color, followed by elegant aromas of berry fruit intermixed with tobacco, flowers, and vanilla scents. It is layered and medium to full-bodied, with outstanding purity and fruit extraction. Although deep, rich, and powerful for a wine from this estate, it has not lost any of its elegance or potential complexity. Anticipated maturity: 2006–2025. Last tasted, 1/02.

1995
90 Dark garnet/purple, the 1995 offers a classic Margaux combination of elegance and richness. Medium bodied, with delicate, beautifully ripe, black currant and floral aromas that compete with subtle new oak, the 1995 Malescot hits the palate with a lovely concoction of fruit, nicely integrated tannin and acidity, and a stylish, graceful feel. This quintessentially elegant Bordeaux should continue to improve in the bottle. A beauty! Anticipated maturity: now–2018. Last tasted, 1/02.

1994
87+ A dark ruby color and a herbaceous, curranty, vanilla-scented nose are attractive, but what I find especially appealing about the 1994 Malescot St.-Exupéry is its layered, richly fruity, beautifully pure style. It is not a big wine, but it possesses good intensity, a sense of grace and balance, and the impressive ability to open and expand after 5–10 minutes of airing. This should turn out to be a stylish effort that may merit a higher score if the herbaceousness turns into a cedary component. Anticipated maturity: now–2016. Last tasted, 1/97.

1990 This wine continues to develop impressively. While not one of the vintage's block-
90 busters, it possesses all the classic elegance, fragrance, and harmony one expects of a high-quality Margaux. The color remains a healthy dark ruby with a purple hue. The nose offers up lush, sweet, jammy black currant fruit intermixed with aromas of white flowers, spice, and a touch of smoky oak. Medium bodied, with a savory, expansive mouth-feel, this low-acid, rich, multilayered wine is approachable, yet capable of evolving gracefully. Anticipated maturity: now–2010. Last tasted, 3/97.

1989 Historically, I believe 1989 will be the vintage that marks the turnaround in qual-
87 ity for Malescot St.-Exupéry. The 1989 is overshadowed by the 1990, as well as by subsequent vintages, but it is a very good example and far superior to much of what was produced during the 1980s, 1970s, and 1960s. The color is a dark ruby/garnet. The bouquet reveals scents of roasted herbs, sweet blackberry and red currant fruit, earth, and spice. The wine possesses moderately high tannin and some austerity, but a sweetness in the mid-palate that comes from ripe fruit and attractive levels of glycerin. This is an elegant, soft Malescot St.-Exupéry that can already be drunk. Anticipated maturity: now–2010. Last tasted, 4/90.

ANCIENT VINTAGES

Unlike many Bordeaux properties, Malescot St.-Exupéry failed to show up for 1982 as well as 1983 (a particularly strong vintage in the appellation of Margaux). The 1970s were equally disappointing. In the 1960s, the 1961 stands out as a singular effort of great quality and intensity. The wine, when last tasted December 1998, still merited the very high score of 92. A great Margaux that is a prototype for the appellation—feminine with delicate yet fragrant perfume, luscious flavors, but nothing out of balance. Other terrific wines produced were the 1959 (93 points; last tasted from an Imperial 12/95) and 1953 (given widely variable scores, but as high as 90 when last tasted 12/99). This estate is capable of hitting the high marks, and certainly recent vintages prove that Malescot St.-Exupéry can produce a wine with the seductive and elegant characteristics that one associates with a topflight Margaux.

MARGAUX

Classification: First Growth in 1855

Owner: The Mentzelopoulos Family

Address: 33460 Margaux

Mailing address: BP 31, 33460 Margaux

Telephone: 05 57 88 83 83; Telefax: 05 57 88 31 32

E-mail: chateau-margaux@chateau-margaux.com

Website: www.chateau-margaux.com

Visits: By appointment Monday to Friday, 10 A.M.–noon and 2–4 P.M.

Contact: Tina Bizard

Telephone: 05 57 88 83 93

VINEYARDS

Surface area: 192.7 acres (under vine)

Grape varietals: 75% Cabernet Sauvignon, 20% Merlot, 5% Cabernet Franc and Petit Verdot

Average age of vines: 35 years

Density of plantation: 10,000 vines per hectare

Average yields: 45 hectoliters per hectare

Elevage: Three week fermentation and maceration in temperature-controlled wooden vats. Eighteen to twenty-four months aging in new oak barrels. Fining, no filtration.

WINES PRODUCED

Château Margaux: 200,000 bottles

Pavillon Rouge du Château Margaux: 200,000 bottles

Best recent vintages: 2001, 2000, 1999, 1998, 1996, 1995, 1994

Best older vintages: 1990, 1986, 1985, 1983, 1982, 1981, 1979, 1978, 1961, 1953, 1949, 1928, 1900

Plateau of maturity: Within 9–35 years of the vintage

GENERAL APPRECIATION

After dismal performances in the 1960s and 1970s, Château Margaux was literally resurrected in the 1980s and since then has produced a string of close to perfect wines. Qualitywise, this estate has been on par with its status for the last 20 years, and its second wine, Pavillon Rouge du Château Margaux, merits consumer attention.

After a distressing period of mediocrity in the 1960s and 1970s, when far too many wines lacking richness, concentration, and character were produced under the inadequately financed administration of Pierre and Bernard Ginestet (the international oil crisis and wine market crash of 1973 and 1974 proved their undoing), Margaux was sold in 1977 to André and Laura Mentzelopoulos. Lavish amounts of money were immediately spent on the vineyards and the winemaking facilities. Emile Peynaud was retained as a consultant to oversee the vinification of the wine. Apprehensive observers expected the passing of many harvests before the new financial and spiritual commitments to excellence would be exhibited in the wines of Margaux. It took just one vintage, 1978, for the world to see just how great Margaux could be.

Unfortunately, André Mentzelopoulos died before he could see the full transformation of a struggling first-growth into a brilliantly consistent wine of stunning grace, richness, and complexity. His elegant wife, Laura, and more recently his savvy, street-smart daughter Corinne run the show. They are surrounded by considerable talent—most notably, Paul Pontallier. The immediate acclaim for the 1978 Margaux has been followed by a succession of other brilliantly executed wines that are so stunning, rich, and balanced that it is not unfair to suggest that during the 1980s there was no better wine made in all of Bordeaux than that of Margaux.

The style of the rejuvenated wine at Margaux is one of opulent richness, a deep, multidimensional bouquet with a fragrance of ripe black currants, spicy vanilla oakiness, and violets. The wine is now considerably fuller in color, richness, body, and tannin than the wines made under the pre-1977 Ginestet regime.

Margaux also makes a dry white wine. Pavillon Blanc du Château Margaux is produced entirely from a 29.6-acre vineyard planted exclusively with Sauvignon Blanc. It is fermented in oak barrels and bottled after 10 months aging in cask. Trivia buffs will want to know that it is made at the small building, called Château Abel-Laurent, several hundred yards up the road from the magnificent château of Margaux. It is the Médoc's finest white wine, crisp, fruity, subtly herbaceous, and oaky.

IMPORTANT VINTAGES

2001
91–93
A Cabernet Sauvignon–based offering (82% Cabernet Sauvignon, 7% Merlot, 7% Petit Verdot, 4% Cabernet Franc), the 2001 Margaux is the result of a severe selection (35% of the crop made it into the grand vin). A deep ruby color is followed by aromas of sweet cassis fruit intermixed with licorice and subtle toasty oak. Elegant, medium weight, and stylish, it is similar to the 1999 with seemingly more concentration and tannin. With beautiful balance as well as low acidity, it will be drinkable young. Anticipated maturity: 2005–2018. Last tasted, 1/03.

2000
100
Only 40% of the crop made it into the 2000 Château Margaux, a blend of 90% Cabernet Sauvignon and 10% Merlot. Picked by many of my colleagues as the "wine of the vintage," it now merits an even higher score than the lofty ratings I gave it following my *en primeur* tastings. It is moving in the direction of the 1990, but there is a freshness and delineation to it that sets it apart from the riper 1990. The color is a saturated purple. The exquisite nose reveals blackberries, crème de cassis, and subtle new oak and graphite aromas. The tannin has become more supple, the texture is sensational, and the wine is like a towering skyscraper in the mouth without being heavy or disjointed. The finish is splendid. Anticipated maturity: 2010–2050. Last tasted, 1/03.

2000
89
Pavillon Rouge du Château Margaux: The excellent 2000 Pavillon Rouge du Château Margaux is a fat, dense purple-colored offering with more obvious intensity and muscle. It will evolve nicely for 15 years. Last tasted, 1/03.

1999
94
The sexy, dark plum/purple–colored 1999 Margaux is already revealing complex aromatics. Surprisingly charming and round, it is reminiscent of a vintage such as 1985. Although neither a blockbuster nor a heavyweight, it grows in the mouth revealing tremendous length as well as purity. Administrator Paul Pontallier prefers it to the more austere 1998, as do I. An archetypical Château Margaux of richness, finesse, balance, and symmetry, it can be drunk young, but promises to age nicely for two decades. Extrapolating backward, it would probably have something in common with the underrated 1962 Médocs. Anticipated Maturity: 2004–2017. Last tasted, 10/02.

1999
87
Pavillon Rouge du Château Margaux: The 1999 Pavillon Rouge de Château Margaux exhibits notes of herbs in its elegant, medium-bodied, forward, complex personality. It possesses the character of its big sister, but not the weight, concentration, or length. Enjoy it over the next decade. Last tasted, 10/02.

1998
91+
The 1998 Margaux is taking on a character reminiscent of the 1988 vintage. The color is a dense ruby/purple. The wine is tannic and austere, but elegant, with notes of asphalt, blackberries, acacia flowers, and sweet, toasty oak. Subtle, rich, nicely textured, and medium bodied, it is built for the long haul. Anticipated maturity: 2008–2030. Last tasted, 10/02.

1997   Undoubtedly a brilliant success for the vintage, this immensely charming, dark
90   ruby/purple–colored wine exhibits floral, black currant, and smoky, toasty oak
         aromas. There is admirable richness and excellent ripeness, not a great deal of
         density or the superb concentration found in such renowned vintages as 1996,
         1995, and 1990, but plenty of finesse, suppleness, and character. It can be drunk
         young or cellared for 10–15 years. Last tasted, 9/02.

1996   The 1996 Château Margaux is undoubtedly one of the great classics produced
99   under the Mentzelopoulos regime. In many respects, it is the quintessential
         Château Margaux, as well as the paradigm for this estate, combining measured
         power, extraordinary elegance, and admirable complexity. In short, it's a beauty!
         The color is opaque purple. The wine offers extraordinarily pure notes of black-
         berries, cassis, toast and flowers, gorgeous sweetness, a seamless personality, and
         full body, with nothing out of place. The final blend (85% Cabernet Sauvignon,
         10% Merlot, and the rest Petit Verdot and Cabernet Franc) contains the highest
         percentage of Cabernet Sauvignon since the 1986. This wine has shut down, yet
         the fruit remains exceptionally sweet and pure. Moreover, there are layers of flavor
         in the mouth and a surreal lightness/elegance in spite of the wine's obvious power
         and density. Is it capable of surpassing the quality of the 2000, 1995, 1990, 1986,
         1983, and 1982? Time will tell. Personally, I prefer the opulence and viscosity of
         the 1990 from a purely hedonistic standpoint, but I do believe this wine will de-
         velop an extraordinary perfume and possess the same level of richness as the most
         concentrated vintages Margaux has produced. It is one of the strongest candidates
         for the wine of the vintage. Anticipated maturity: 2010–2045. Last tasted, 3/02.

1995   The 1995 has continued to flesh out, developing into one of the great classics
95   made under the Mentzelopoulos regime. The color is opaque ruby/purple. The
         nose offers aromas of licorice and sweet smoky new oak intermixed with jammy
         black fruits, licorice, and minerals. The wine is medium to full-bodied, with ex-
         traordinary richness, fabulous equilibrium, and hefty tannin in the finish. In spite
         of its large size and youthfulness, this wine is user-friendly and accessible. This is
         a thrilling Margaux that will always be softer and more evolved than its broader-
         shouldered sibling, the 1996. How fascinating it will be to follow the evolution of
         both of these vintages over the next half century. Anticipated maturity: 2010–
         2040. Last tasted, 3/02.

1994   This largely forgotten vintage seems to have turned the corner in the last year or
91+   two. Because of strict selections made at the top châteaux, the wines always had
         density, but the level of tannin was frequently too high and the type of tannin was
         more green and astringent. Château Margaux's 1994 has always been one of the
         candidates for the "wine of the vintage." The wine still has a dense plum/purple
         color and a big, sweet nose of black fruits intermixed with licorice, camphor,
         vanilla, and a hint of flowers. The wine is dense and powerful, but the tannins have
         softened and do not seem as hard and intrusive as they did in the late 1990s. This
         wine will last for decades and hopefully become even more seamless, although it
         is hard to believe all the tannin will gradually dissipate. Anticipated maturity:
         2008–2025. Last tasted, 10/02.

1993   In a difficult vintage, Château Margaux produced a relatively mid-weight, soft,
88   richly fruity wine with some hints of weedy tobacco in the aromas and flavors of
         this dark plum–colored wine. The wine is medium bodied, reaching full maturity,
         and has surprising depth, ripeness, and sweetness for a wine from such a horrific
         year. Anticipated maturity: now–2010. Last tasted, 10/02.

1992   Deep ruby with some purple nuances, this wine offers up relatively light, some
87   what muted notes of cassis, licorice, and new oak. In the mouth, the wine is
         medium bodied, soft, and fully mature, with surprising elegance and purity. The

finish is a bit short, but nevertheless, this is another very impressive wine from a vintage that requires consumption over the next 4–5 years. Anticipated maturity: now–2009. Last tasted, 10/02.

1990
100
A prototype Château Margaux that combines power and elegance, this wine, which seemed to be sound asleep for nearly a decade, has begun to open over the last several years. Dense ruby/purple with a developing yet compellingly ethereal bouquet of sweet black fruits, violets, smoke, camphor, and licorice, this medium-to full-bodied, silky-textured wine still tastes like a four- or five-year-old barrel sample, but the aromatics are emerging and the wine has thrown off that somewhat monolithic, sleepy stage it was in for nearly a decade. Despite the fact that, analytically, the acidity is low, this wine reveals plenty of delineation, very high levels of tannin, and tremendous concentration of ripe fruit, glycerin, and extract. The color shows very few signs of development. The fabulous bouquet is just emerging, and the wine is full-bodied, opulent, and very rich. It is a great achievement in this vintage and should be drinkable in another 4–5 years and last for at least 3–4 decades. Anticipated maturity: 2005–2040. Last tasted, 10/02.

1989
90
Dwarfed by its younger sibling, the 1990, the 1989 Château Margaux has a dark plum/garnet color and a big, sweet nose of new saddle leather, toasty oak, and weedy black cherry and cassis fruit. The wine is medium bodied, with relatively elevated tannins, outstanding concentration and purity, but a somewhat clipped as well as compressed finish. This certainly outstanding wine has put on a bit of weight in its evolution in the bottle, but it is hardly one of the most profound efforts from Château Margaux. Anticipated maturity: 2006–2025. Last tasted, 10/02.

1988
89
In a somewhat chunky, full-bodied, rather muscular style, with a dark, almost opaque garnet color, a big, smoky, earthy nose, and hints of compost, melted asphalt, black fruits, mushrooms, and new oak, this wine lacks the elegance one expects from Château Margaux, but it does have plenty of tough-textured tannin and an almost rustic, corpulent style to it. The wine is mouth-staining as well as mouth-filling, but in a relatively chunky style. Anticipated maturity: now–2018. Last tasted, 3/02.

1986
98
A magnificent example of Château Margaux and one of the most tannic, backward Margaux of the last 50 years, the 1986 continues to evolve at a glacial pace. The color is still a dense ruby/purple with just a hint of lightening at the rim. With several hours of aeration, the aromatics become striking, with notes of smoke, toast, crème de cassis, mineral, and white flowers. Very full-bodied, with high but sweet tannin, great purity, and a very masculine, full-bodied style, this wine should prove nearly immortal in terms of its aging potential. It is beginning to budge from its infantile stage and approach adolescence. Anticipated maturity: 2008–2050. Last tasted, 12/02.

1985
95
Approaching full maturity, this beautifully sweet Château Margaux has a dense plum/purple color and a huge, sweet nose of black currants intermixed with licorice, toast, underbrush, and flowers. Medium to full-bodied with supple tannin and a fleshy, juicy, very succulent and multilayered mid-palate, this expansive, velvety wine has entered its plateau of maturity, where it should remain (assuming good storage) for at least another 10–15 years. A very delicious, seductive, and opulent Château Margaux to drink over the next two decades. Anticipated maturity: now–2015. Last tasted, 10/02.

1983
96?
As I have noted consistently, this can be a breathtaking wine, but having tasted it close to a dozen times since the last edition of this book, more than half the bottles were marred by tainted corks. In fact, one would almost wonder if there was a TCA problem in part of the wine storage area. The percentage of corked half bottles is even higher than in the regular format. However, when clean this 1983, which has

seemingly reached full maturity far faster than I would have guessed a mere four years ago, has a dense, murky plum/purple color and a gorgeous nose of smoked herbs, damp earth, mushrooms, and sweet crème de cassis intermixed with vanilla and violets. The wine is medium to full-bodied, deep, rich, and powerful, with sweet tannins and loads of fruit concentration. Anticipated maturity: now–2020. Last tasted, 11/02.

1982   At one time I thought the 1983 was the more classic and better effort from Château
98+ Margaux, but I am human: The 1982 has overtaken the 1983 and is obviously the superior effort. It started off life as a somewhat ruggedly constructed, powerful, masculine, even coarse style of Château Margaux with high levels of tannin, huge extract, and richness. Increasingly civilized, with the tannin becoming seamlessly integrated, this opaque purple/garnet–colored wine offers up hints of incense, sweet truffles, smoke, black currants, flowers, and damp earth. Very full-bodied, with remarkable levels of glycerin, extract, and tannin, this is probably the largest scaled, most concentrated Château Margaux under the Mentzelopoulos administration. It is doubtful it will ever rival the 2000, 1996, or 1990 for pure finesse or elegance. In spite of its high levels of tannin, it does not seem to have the classicism of these vintages, but this wine goes from strength to strength and is quickly becoming one of the all-time compelling efforts of Château Margaux. Anticipated maturity: now–2035. Last tasted, 12/02.

ANCIENT VINTAGES

The 1981 is a surprisingly elegant, beautiful example that is certainly one of the strongest candidates for "wine of the vintage." When I last tasted it in October 2002, I rated it 91, but the 1979 and 1978 are also outstanding wines that have consistently scored between 90 and 93 points, with the 1979 slightly fresher and more delineated than the 1978, which is chunkier and burlier. Both wines are fully mature yet capable of lasting at least another 10–15 years.

Of course, 1978 was the first vintage produced under the Mentzelopoulos regime. Prior to that is a succession of failures under the Ginestet ownership. Vintages such as 1975 (now rated 73), 1970 (now rated 67), 1966 (now rated 86), and 1964 (now rated 69) are curiosities because they are first-growth Bordeaux, but they are washed out, mediocre shells of what they could have been. Of course, there is the superb 1961 (last tasted 12/01 and still a classic 94-pointer). Among the other vintages, 1959 can hit 90 points, but it is not nearly as good as the 1961. The 1953 is legendary (98 points; last tasted from magnum 1/01). This is a spectacular Château Margaux. Perhaps the 1990 may ultimately prove to be similar in style. Assuming readers can find pristinely stored bottles, the 1928 (98 points; last tasted 10/94) was a hauntingly near-perfect wine and far better than the 1949, 1947, and 1945, which have proven disappointing. Of course, one of the most famous wines ever made in Bordeaux is the 1900 Margaux (100 points when tasted 12/96). Tasted five times since, three of the bottles were clearly fraudulent and the other two tired but authentic. I wouldn't dare touch this wine today, because the number of fraudulent imitations far exceed those that are legitimate. Nevertheless, those who have a chance to taste this wine from a pristinely stored, real bottle will instantly recognize its immortality.

MAROJALLIA

Classification: It is too soon to make a judgment, but of the few vintages produced, this wine has second-growth quality written all over it.

Owner: Philippe Porcheron

Address: route de Bordeaux, 33460 Margaux

Mailing address: 287, avenue de la Libération, 33110 Le Bouscat

Telephone: 05 56 49 69 50; Telefax: 05 56 42 62 88

Visits: By appointment only

Contact: Philippe Porcheron

VINEYARDS

Surface area: 8.2 acres

Grape varietals: 55% Cabernet Sauvignon, 45% Merlot

Average age of vines: 15 years

Density of plantation: 10,000 vines per hectare

Average yields: 25 hectoliters per hectare

Elevage: Three week fermentation and maceration in temperature-controlled stainless-steel vats. Malolactics in barrel. Eighteen to twenty-four months aging in 100% new oak. No fining, no filtration.

WINES PRODUCED

Marojallia: 6,000 bottles

Clos Margalaine: 12,000 bottles

Plateau of maturity: Within 8–20 years of the vintage

GENERAL APPRECIATION

This newly created estate has caused an uproar on the Bordeaux left bank. The first garage wine made in the Médoc, its first three vintages were unquestionably of top quality. Though it is too soon to predict the future of Marojallia, one can expect this micro-estate trend to continue. At present, this wine is on par with a second growth. Prices are expensive, yet seemingly justifiable in view of the wine's quality, but alarmingly arrogant in view of the wine's short history. The second wine is Clos Margalaine.

This new 18.2-acre vineyard (1999 was the debut vintage), owned by Philippe Porcheron, produces 420 cases of its grand vin. St.-Emilion's *bête-noir*, Jean-Luc Thunevin and his wife, Muriel, are responsible for the production.

IMPORTANT VINTAGES

2001   In 2001, this new garage operation from Margaux has produced a worthy rival to
90–93   their stunning 2000. A saturated purple color is accompanied by aromas of paper white narcissus, crème de cassis, and roasted espresso. Medium to full-bodied, with admirable purity, underlying freshness, and delineation, this long, concentrated, impressive 2001 is a tour de force. It admirably demonstrates what can be

accomplished by extraordinarily talented and passionate people with a heretofore unknown *terroir*. Anticipated maturity: 2005–2018. Last tasted, 1/03.

2000

93+

A blend of equal parts Merlot and Cabernet Sauvignon, the 2000 Marojallia has added considerable weight during its *élevage*. An opaque purple color is followed by scents of licorice, violets, graphite, black raspberries, and cassis. Noble, elegant, full-bodied; exceptionally flavorful as well as delicate, it achieves that rare combination of finesse and power. Anticipated maturity: 2005–2020. Last tasted, 1/03.

1999

91

This exceptional wine exhibits notes of violets, charcoal, vanilla, and pure crème de cassis. A dense ruby purple color is followed by a medium- to full-bodied, textured beauty with extraordinary elegance and savory sweetness. The finish lasts more than 30 seconds. This brilliant debut wine from a heretofore unknown vineyard merits serious attention. Anticipated maturity: 2005–2018. Last tasted, 1/03.

MARQUIS DE TERME

Classification: Fourth Growth in 1855

Owner: SCA du Château Marquis de Terme Sénéclauze

Address: 3, route de Rauzan, 33460 Margaux

Mailing address: BP 11, 33460 Margaux

Telephone: 05 57 88 30 01; Telefax: 05 57 88 32 51

E-mail: marquisterme@terrenet.fr

Website: www.chateau-marquis-de-terme.com

Visits: Monday to Thursday, 9 A.M.–noon and 2–5 P.M. Friday, 9 A.M.–noon.

Contact: Nathalie Serani

VINEYARDS

Surface area: 93.9 acres

Grape varietals: 55% Cabernet Sauvignon, 35% Merlot, 7% Petit Verdot, 3% Cabernet Franc

Average age of vines: 35 years

Density of plantation: 10,000 vines per hectare

Average yields: 50 hectoliters per hectare

Elevage: Two to three week fermentation and maceration in temperature-controlled concrete tanks. After malolactics, 18 months aging in barrels with 30–35% new oak. Fining with egg whites, no filtration.

WINES PRODUCED

Château Marquis de Terme: 160,000 bottles

Terme des Gondats: 30,000 bottles

Plateau of maturity: Within 5–18 years of the vintage

GENERAL APPRECIATION

This estate has improved after a long slump.

One of the least known and most disappointing classified growths of Margaux, Marquis de Terme has had an infusion of much-needed money to modernize the cellars and purchase at least 30–33% new oak casks for each vintage. The owners have also instituted a stricter selection policy with the introduction of a secondary wine. Like most of the top *terroirs* of the Margaux appellation, Marquis de Terme's two primary vineyards are located in Cantenac and Margaux and are composed of 10–20% clay, 3–12% loamy soils, 30–50% sand, and 20–45% gravel.

IMPORTANT VINTAGES

2000
87
The only vintage after 1996 that merits attention from serious wine lovers, the 2000 Marquis de Terme has a dense, murky ruby/purple color and a sweet nose of berry fruit intermixed with some earth, licorice, and new oak. The wine is medium weight and much more developed than most 2000s, with very good concentration and purity. Anticipated maturity: 2006–2015. Last tasted, 1/03.

1996
89+?
A very tannic, structured wine with an opaque purple color and a sweet crème de cassis nose intermixed with damp earth, vanilla, and licorice, this relatively massive wine has mouth-searing levels of tannin, medium body, and a very backward style that will require considerable patience from its buyers. Anticipated maturity: 2009–2025. Last tasted, 3/02.

1995
87
This wine has completely shut down after being in bottle for several years. It still has an impressively saturated ruby/purple color and a nose of sweet berry fruit intermixed with licorice, tapenade, mineral, and herbs. The wine is deep, medium bodied, with excellent purity and some relatively elevated and rustic tannin in the finish that may not become fully integrated. In any event, this wine needs extended cellaring. Anticipated maturity: 2007–2018. Last tasted, 3/02.

ANCIENT VINTAGES

Looking back at my tasting notes over the last quarter century for Marquis de Terme, this property was remarkably consistent between 1983 and 1990, with nearly outstanding wines produced in 1990 (87 points; last tasted 3/97), 1989 (89 points; last tasted 3/97), 1988 (86 points; last tasted 1/93), 1986 (89 points; last tasted 3/97), 1985 (88 points; last tasted 3/89), and 1983 (88 points; last tasted 3/97). Other than that, the period of the 1970s was largely one of undeniable disappointments, with many mediocre wines produced. All in all, this is a very difficult property to handicap. The potential is there—the property's two main vineyards are well located in Cantenac and along the plateau of Margaux—but quality, which seemed to be coming back strongly in the mid-1990s, seems to have fallen off once again.

MONBRISON

Classification: Cru Bourgeois in 1932

Owner: Elisabeth Davis and sons

Address: 1, allée de Monbrison, 33460 Arsac

Telephone: 05 56 58 80 04; Telefax: 05 56 58 85 33

Visits: By appointment only

Contact: Laurent Vonderheyden

VINEYARDS

Surface area: 32.6 acres

Grape varietals: 50% Cabernet Sauvignon, 30% Merlot, 15% Cabernet Franc, 5% Petit Verdot

Average age of vines: 38 years

Density of plantation: 6,500–10,000 vines per hectare

Average yields: 45 hectoliters per hectare

Elevage: Three week fermentation and maceration in temperature-controlled stainless-steel tanks with two daily pumpings-over and considerable airing. Fourteen to eighteen months aging in barrels with 40–60% new oak depending upon the vintage. Fining, no filtration.

WINES PRODUCED

Château Monbrison: 48,000 bottles

Bouquet de Monbrison: 30,000 bottles

Plateau of maturity: Within 5–15 years of the vintage

GENERAL APPRECIATION

Monbrison was at the top of its game between 1986 and 1990, then went through a difficult period (consumers should be cautious when picking vintages between 1991 and 1997), and seems to have rebounded nicely since 1998. It has not, however, attained its level of the 1980s. The estate seems to have adopted a lighter and more subtle style of wine, which is undoubtedly appealing. Monbrison's quality and reasonable pricing policy ranks it among the very good values of Bordeaux.

At the time of the first edition of this book 18 years ago, Monbrison was one of the up-and-coming stars of the Médoc's Cru Bourgeois estates. Lamentably much has changed, although the wine remains a good example of the Margaux appellation. The architect behind the extraordinary resurrection of Monbrison was the late Jean-Luc Vonderheyden. His extraordinary discipline in keeping production low and doing everything he could to produce a high-quality wine won praise from everybody—from France's esteemed wine critic Michel Bettane to this author. However, Vonderheyden's life was tragically cut short by cancer, and his brother, Laurent, is now in control of Monbrison.

Laurent Vonderheyden's style appears to have moved toward a lighter, more delicate wine, with more than a few hiccups in the early 1990s. Such recent vintages as 1995 and 1996 have been more impressive. Monbrison is certainly a wine worth tasting, and should readers come across any of the splendid wines made between 1986 and 1990 by the late Jean-Luc, they should undoubtedly give them a taste.

IMPORTANT VINTAGES

2000
88 The finest Monbrison produced in many years, the ruby/purple-colored, medium-bodied 2000 exhibits sweet floral, mineral, and currant notes, subtle toasty oak, ripe tannin, and a long, persistent finish. Anticipated maturity: 2004–2014. Last tasted, 1/03.

1999 The medium plum–colored 1999 Monbrison displays elegant, light- to medium-
 85 bodied, attractive flavors that finish abruptly on the palate. Nevertheless, it is
   cleanly made, pleasant, and enjoyable. Drink it over the next 4–5 years. Last
   tasted, 3/02.

1998 An excellent ripe black currant, cherry, and spicy new oak–scented bouquet is fol-
 87 lowed by a medium-bodied, soft yet structured wine with plenty of ripe fruit as
   well as an earthy, dusty finish. This complex, pure offering is best drunk during its
   first decade of life. Last tasted, 12/00.

ANCIENT VINTAGES

The fully mature 1990 (87 points; last tasted 11/98), 1989 (89 points; last tasted 4/91),
1988 (90 points; last tasted 4/91), and 1986 (87 points; last tasted 3/98) were the stars
of a bygone era for Monbrison.

PALMER

Classification: Third Growth in 1855

Owner: SCI du Château Palmer

Address: Cantenac, 33460 Margaux

Telephone: 05 57 88 72 72; Telefax: 05 57 88 37 16

E-mail: chateau-palmer@chateau-palmer.com

Website: www.chateau-palmer.com

Visits: By appointment only. April to November: Every day, 9 A.M.–noon and 2–6:30 P.M.
November to March: Monday to Friday, 9 A.M.–noon and 4–5:30 P.M.

Contact: Claire Thepenier

VINEYARDS

Surface area: 128.4 acres

Grape varietals: 47% Cabernet Sauvignon, 47% Merlot, 6% Petit Verdot

Average age of vines: 35 years

Density of plantation: 10,000 vines per hectare

Average yields: 46 hectoliters per hectare

Elevage: Twenty-eight to thirty day fermentation and maceration in temperature-
controlled stainless-steel cone-shaped vats. Twenty to twenty-one months aging in oak
barrels, with 45% new oak. Fining, no filtration.

WINES PRODUCED

Château Palmer: 120,000–150,000 bottles

Alter Ego de Palmer: 100,000–110,000 bottles

Plateau of maturity: Within 5–25 years of the vintage

GENERAL APPRECIATION

Palmer unquestionably produces one of the most compelling wines of Margaux. When
Palmer has a great vintage, no other left bank growth is as aromatically seductive to the

nose and palate. Prices have increased significantly, reflecting the insatiable worldwide demand for this wine.

The impressive turreted château of Palmer is majestically situated adjacent to Bordeaux's Route du Vin (D2), in the middle of the tiny village of Issan. It is a worthy spot to stop for a photograph. More important to wine enthusiasts is the fact that the château also produces one of Bordeaux's greatest wines.

The château takes its name from an English general who served under Wellington and arrived in Bordeaux with his army in 1814. He subsequently purchased the property, which was then called Château de Gascq, and began an extensive program of land acquisition and vineyard planting. In less than 20 years the property became known as Château Palmer. Sadly, Charles Palmer, who did so much to create this estate, saw his fortune dissipate, became bankrupt, and had been forced out of Château Palmer by a bank foreclosure at the time of his death in 1836. The property has, since 1939, been owned by a syndicate involving the family of the late Peter A. Sichel, the Mahler-Besse family, and four other participants, the most notable of whom is Bertrand Bouteiller, who manages the day to day affairs of Palmer.

Palmer can be as profound as any of the first growths. In vintages such as 2001, 2000, 1999, 1998, 1996, 1995, 1989, 1983, 1975, 1970, 1967, 1966, and 1961, it can be better than many of them. While Palmer is officially a third growth, the wine sells at a price level between the first and second growths, no doubt reflecting the high respect Bordeaux merchants, foreign importers, and consumers throughout the world have for this wine.

Palmer is still a traditionally made wine, and the enviable track record of success is no doubt attributable to a number of factors. The assemblage (blend of grapes) at Palmer is unique in that a very high percentage of Merlot (47%) is used to make the wine. This high proportion of Merlot no doubt accounts for Palmer's Pomerol-like richness, suppleness, and generous, fleshy character. However, its compelling fragrance is quintessentially Margaux. Palmer also has one of the longest maceration periods (20–28 days), wherein the grape skins stay in contact with the grape juice. This explains the richness of color, excellent extract, and abundant tannins that are found in most vintages of Palmer. Finally, this is an estate whose proprietors remain adamantly against the filtration of their wine.

Palmer consistently made the best wine of the Margaux appellation between 1961 and 1977, but the resurgence of Château Margaux in 1978, which has now taken the place at the top of the Margaux hierarchy, has—for the moment—left Palmer in the runner-up spot, although Palmer's most recent performances suggest first-growth aspirations. The significant cellar renovations of the late 1990s and the introduction of a second wine have all resulted in even greater wines at Palmer.

The style of Palmer's wine is one characterized by a sensational fragrance and bouquet. I have always felt that Palmer's great vintages can often be identified in blind tastings by smell alone. The bouquet has the forward fruity richness of a great Pomerol but the complexity and character of a Margaux. The wine's texture is rich, often supple, and lush, but always deeply fruity and concentrated.

IMPORTANT VINTAGES

2001
90–92
An elegant rendition of Palmer, the 2001 reveals less power and muscle than the 2000 and possibly less charm than the 1999. This blend of 51% Cabernet Sauvignon, 44% Merlot, and 5% Petit Verdot exhibits a dense ruby/purple color as well as a stylish nose of flowers, black fruits, and new oak. It offers a sweet attack, medium body, moderate tannin, and a crisp finish. Surprisingly, the acidity is lower in the 2001 than in the 2000. Fifty percent of the crop made it into the final blend. Yields were 44 hectoliters per hectare. Anticipated maturity: 2006–2015. Last tasted, 1/03.

2000
95+
The 2000 Palmer may ultimately be as good as the 1999, but it is altogether a different animal. If the 1999 is pure Palmer elegance and femininity, the 2000 is more masculine, powerful, muscular, and tannic. Only 50% of the production made it into the grand vin, a blend of 53% Cabernet Sauvignon and 47% Merlot. While it is still revealing plenty of tannin, the tannin has sweetened. A dense inky/purple color is accompanied by a wine with abundant extract as well as a brawny, expansive mouth feel. It will require more patience than the seductive 1999. Anticipated maturity: 2010–2035. Last tasted, 1/03.

1999
95
One of the superstars of the vintage, 1999 is the greatest Palmer made since 1961 and 1966. A blend of 48% Cabernet Sauvignon, 46% Merlot, and 6% Petit Verdot, it boasts a staggering bouquet of violets and other spring flowers intermixed with licorice, black currants, and subtle wood. Only 50% of the production made it into the grand vin. A multidimensional, compelling effort with both power and elegance, it offers sweet tannin along with flavors that caress the palate and a 45-second finish. This is terrific stuff! Anticipated maturity: 2004–2025. Last tasted, 10/02.

1998
91
A classic Margaux, the 1998 Palmer put on weight and fleshed out during its *élevage* in barrel. It displays a dense purple color as well as a sumptuous bouquet of black fruits, licorice, melted asphalt, toast, and a touch of acacia flowers. Full-bodied with brilliant definition, this blend of equal parts Merlot and Cabernet Sauvignon, with a dollop of Petit Verdot, will age well for 20–25 years. It is one of the Médoc's, as well as the Margaux appellation's, finest wines of the vintage. Anticipated maturity: 2005–2028. Last tasted, 10/02.

1997
87
A seductive style of Palmer, the 1997 will have many admirers. It boasts a dark ruby/plum/purple color in addition to a seductive bouquet of sweet berry fruit and an elegant, medium-bodied, fruit-driven, easygoing, fleshy personality. While there is little weight and density, the wine's harmony is excellent. Drink it over the next 4–5 years. Last tasted, 3/01.

1996
91+
This wine, a blend of 55% Cabernet Sauvignon, 40% Merlot, and 5% Petit Verdot, is performing well in bottle. It boasts an impressively saturated purple color in addition to a backward yet intense nose of black plums, currants, licorice, and smoke. Following terrific fruit on the attack, the wine's structure and tannin take over. This impressively endowed, surprisingly backward Palmer may develop into a modern-day version of the 1966. There is plenty of sweet fruit. The tannin is well integrated, but the wine requires 3–4 years of cellaring. Anticipated maturity: 2007–2028. Last tasted, 3/01.

1995
90
This wine includes an extremely high percentage of Merlot (about 43%). It is a gloriously opulent, low-acid, fleshy Palmer that will be attractive early and keep well. Dark ruby/purple–colored, with smoky, toasty new oak intertwined with gobs of jammy cherry fruit and floral and chocolate nuances, this medium- to full-bodied, plump yet elegant wine is impressive. Anticipated maturity: now–2020. Last tasted, 3/01.

1994   I had hoped this wine would be better, but it has turned out to be a good yet unin-
86   spiring Palmer. The medium dark ruby color is followed by a straightforward,
sweet, berry-scented nose. In the mouth, the wine is medium bodied, with decent
concentration, some noticeable tannin, and a spicy, short finish. It is a good wine,
but disappointing for a Palmer. Anticipated maturity: now–2010. Last tasted, 1/01.

1990   This wine has become more delineated after a period where it seemed diffuse and
90   disjointed. Dark plum/garnet with a sweet nose of baked fruit, spice box, incense,
and sweet licorice intermixed with some chocolate, plum, and black cherries, this
lush, low-acid, velvety-textured wine has reached full maturity, yet promises to
last at this level for at least 5–10 years when properly stored. The wine shows real
up-front, luscious depth in a very sexy, open-knit style. Anticipated maturity:
now–2012. Last tasted, 5/02.

1989   One of the superstars of the vintage, Palmer's 1989 retains a dark plum/purple
95   color with some pink and a hint of amber creeping in at the rim. A big nose of charcoal, white flowers (acacia?), licorice, plums, and black currants comes from the
glass of this elegant, medium- to full-bodied, very concentrated, seamlessly made
wine. Gorgeous, seemingly fully mature, yet brilliantly balanced, this wine may
well turn out to be a modern-day clone of the glorious 1953. Anticipated maturity:
now–2020. Last tasted, 5/02.

1988   This wine, like a number of 1988s, has matured well and is just beginning to show
88   maturity. It has a dense, somewhat rugged constitution, with plenty of density and
some earthy black fruits intermixed with licorice, compost, camphor, and roasted
herbs. The wine is dense, medium to full-bodied, with some coarse tannins in the
finish. I do not expect the tannins to ever melt away, but there is plenty of depth to
this mouth-filling Palmer. Anticipated maturity: now–2010. Last tasted, 5/02.

1986   The great 1986 Médocs have turned the corner and, while they are still young
89+   wines, they are approaching their adolescence. This wine still has a dense ruby/
purple color with a bit of lightening at the edge. The nose offers up hints of minerals, sweet black cherry and black currant fruit, medium to full body, moderately
high tannin, and outstanding purity in a very stern yet impressively concentrated
style. The wine still tastes young, but it is budging from its very closed, dormant
period, where it had rested for nearly 15 years. Anticipated maturity: 2006–2022.
Last tasted, 5/02.

1985   A somewhat diffuse, open-knit, easygoing Palmer, with plenty of amber to its dark
88   garnet color, the 1985 Palmer has reached full maturity. Low acidity, sweet cherry,
plum and currant fruit intermixed with some licorice, mushroom, and damp earth
jumps from the glass of this medium-weight, very fragrant, fruity wine. It lacks the
concentration as well as length to be great, but it is a very seductive wine, as are so
many 1985s. Anticipated maturity: now–2008. Last tasted, 5/02.

1983   This wine goes from strength to strength and is certainly a candidate for "wine of
98   the vintage." It has surpassed even Château Margaux in recent tastings. The color
is an opaque plum/purple. The wine has a fabulously complex nose of smoked
duck, white flowers, cedar, Asian spice, crème de cassis, melted licorice, and
espresso. Super-concentrated, very powerful, full-bodied, and huge, this is undeniably one of the biggest, most concentrated, and powerful Palmers made in the
last 40 years. The wine has thrown off the rugged tannins that were so prominent
during its first 10–15 years of life and has become increasingly seamless and compelling. Potentially this wine remains the most extraordinary Palmer after the
1961. Anticipated maturity: now–2020. Last tasted, 10/02.

1982   A somewhat older version of the 1990, the 1982 Palmer is a soft, easygoing, gen-
87   erous, and fleshy style of wine with plenty of amber to its color and an open-knit,
fragrant bouquet of plums, cherries, and jammy black fruits. The wine is soft, al-

most flat in the mouth with a lack of acidity, and very sweet tannin. The wine has sometimes hit the magical 90-point score in tastings, but seems to consistently lack the definition and depth to merit a score above the upper 80s. Nevertheless, this is pure charm and seduction. Anticipated maturity: now–2008. Last tasted, 5/02.

ANCIENT VINTAGES

Palmer made a stunning 1979 (90 points; last tasted 5/02), a brilliant 1978 (89 points; last tasted 5/02), and one of the better 1975s (90 points; last tasted 5/02), an irregular year in the Médoc. The 1970 is a monumental example and one of the vintage's top dozen or so wines. It is still going strong and is a fabulous example of a classic Palmer (96 points; last tasted 5/02). I have not had the 1967 since December 1996 (87 points), though I suspect it is probably in decline. Certainly the 1966 continues to be another great Palmer, and it is still a vivid, vigorous example and one of the three or four best wines of the vintage (96 points; last tasted 5/02). The 1962 was a brilliant wine (91 points; last tasted 12/06), and of course the sometimes perfect 1961 (99 points; last tasted 5/02).

The museum pieces among Palmer's impressive portfolio include the 1945 (97 points; last tasted 10/94), the 1928 (96 points; last tasted 10/94), and the 1900 Palmer (96 points; last tasted 12/95). While not officially a first growth in name, Palmer often can produce a wine of first-growth quality.

PRIEURÉ-LICHINE

Classification: Fourth Growth in 1855

Owner: Ballande family

Address: 34, avenue de la 5ᵉ République, 33460 Cantenac

Telephone: 05 57 88 36 28; Telefax: 05 57 88 78 93

E-mail: prieure-lichine@wanadoo.fr

Visits: Monday to Saturday, 9 A.M.–noon and 2–6 P.M.

Contact: Régine Darqué

VINEYARDS

Surface area: 173 acres

Grape varietals: 56% Cabernet Sauvignon, 34% Merlot, 10% Petit Verdot

Average age of vines: 30 years

Density of plantation: 8,000 vines per hectare

Average yields: 45 hectoliters per hectare

Elevage: Twenty-five to thirty day fermentation (with three daily pumpings-over) and maceration in temperature-controlled stainless-steel and concrete vats. Malolactics in barrel. Eighteen months aging (on lees, without racking) with 60% new oak and 40% one-year-old barrels. Fining with egg whites. Filtration if necessary.

WINES PRODUCED

Château Prieuré-Lichine: 240,000 bottles

Château de Clairefont: 120,000 bottles

Plateau of maturity: Within 5–12 years of the vintage

GENERAL APPRECIATION

Prieuré-Lichine's fame probably owes more to the personality of its former owner Alexis Lichine than to the intrinsic quality of its wines. The estate has just begun to benefit from considerable investments and from the commitment of the new owners. A reliable wine, Prieuré-Lichine still has much to do to catch up with other up-and-coming estates like Kirwan, d'Issan, or Malescot St.-Exupéry.

One of the few major châteaux in the Médoc open to tourists seven days a week, every week of the year, Prieuré-Lichine was the beloved home of Alexis Lichine, the world-famous wine writer, merchant, wine authority, and promoter of France's wines, who died in June 1989. Lichine purchased Prieuré in 1951 and began an extensive program of improvements that included tripling the vineyard area. I have always thought that harvest time must be an incredibly complex operation because Prieuré-Lichine's vineyard is among the most morcellated in the Médoc, with in excess of several dozen parcels spread throughout the vast appellation of Margaux.

The wine of Prieuré tends to be made in a modern yet intelligent style. It is supple and quick to mature but has enough tannin and, in good vintages, substance to age well for 8–12 years. The price has always been reasonable.

Following the death of his father, Sacha Lichine took over running this lovely ivy-covered, onetime Benedictine priory. Lichine sold the estate in 1999 to the Ballande family. Their goal has been to produce a wine with more concentration, body, and potential longevity. This change is probably in response to a number of critics who have argued that many vintages of Prieuré-Lichine were somewhat light for the reputation of this classified growth. Right bank winemaking guru Stéphane Derénoncourt has been installed at Prieuré-Lichine to oversee this attempt to improve wine quality. His philosophy of minimal intervention as well as his belief in extended lees contact will undoubtedly weave more fruit, texture, and character into this wine.

IMPORTANT VINTAGES

2001 Produced from yields of 40 hectoliters per hectare, the 2001 Prieuré-Lichine is a
87–89 delicious, medium-weight, elegant, smoky, earthy, black currant–scented Margaux with moderate concentration as well as balance, attractive elegance and symmetry. This 2001 has avoided the austerity and astringent tannin some of the more overly extracted offerings possess. Anticipated maturity: 2005–2014. Last tasted, 1/03.

2000 A significant improvement over the 1999, the 2000 exhibits a dense ruby/purple
88 color along with a full, rich style with abundant fruit, glycerin, extract, and silky tannin. Made in Prieuré-Lichine's elegant, finesse-filled style, it will be at its best between 2005–2012. Last tasted, 1/03.

1999 A light, soft, pretty but unsubstantial effort, the 1999 Prieuré-Lichine reveals
85 notes of red currants, earth, dried herbs, and oak in a medium-bodied format. It is best consumed over the next 5–6 years. Last tasted, 3/02.

1998
87
Finesse, elegance, as well as admirable flavors are characteristics of this dark ruby–colored, lighter-styled 1998. Offering abundant quantities of berry fruit, cassis, and spice box aromas and flavors and an excellent texture, this evolved, delicious Margaux is best consumed during its first decade of life. Last tasted, 3/02.

1996
86
Very weedy, leafy, dried herb notes compete with sweet strawberries and red currants in this fragrant, light- to medium-bodied wine, which exhibits good ripeness but not a lot of depth or intensity. It is atypical for the vintage and therefore best drunk over the next 4–6 years. Last tasted, 3/01.

1995
84
An underwhelming effort for sure, this medium-bodied wine exhibits a moderately garnet color and a sweet nose of dusty red fruits intermixed with some balsam wood, Provençal herbs, and damp earth—perhaps even mushrooms. The wine is pleasing on the attack, but then becomes increasingly compressed and attenuated. Anticipated maturity: now–2006. Last tasted, 3/01.

1990
88
By far the best fully mature Prieuré-Lichine over the last 20 years, the dark garnet–colored 1990 has a very fragrant nose of spice box, Christmas fruitcake, cedar, tobacco, smoke, and jammy red as well as black currant flavors. The wine is medium bodied and quite ripe, with low acidity, a lush expansiveness, and fine purity in its lusty, heady finish. Anticipated maturity: now–2008. Last tasted, 3/01.

1989
88
Another very successful vintage, the 1989 Prieuré-Lichine has a dark garnet color with some amber at the edge. The wine shows full body, soft tannins, and a sweet black currant nose intermixed with notes of licorice, smoked herbs, and tobacco. The wine is very lush with some heady alcohol and plenty of glycerin. It is quite a seductive, mouth-filling effort from Prieuré-Lichine. Anticipated maturity: now–2007. Last tasted, 3/01.

1988
85
This wine is beginning to crack up and decline. Considerable amber at the edge of its garnet color is followed by a wine with an attractive bouquet of underbrush, compost, licorice, and sweet currant fruit. In the mouth, the wine shows dry, astringent tannin and a lack of sweetness and depth. Aromatically it is impressive, but on the palate the wine is beginning to lose its fruit. Anticipated maturity: now. Last tasted, 3/01.

1986
88
A vintage that celebrated the 35th harvest for the late Alexis Lichine, this wine has turned out very impressively. The wine still has a dark garnet color with only a bit of lightening at the edge. The wine exhibits notes of mineral, smoked herbs, and sweet red and black currant fruits in addition to a hint of licorice. The wine is medium bodied, very concentrated for a Prieuré-Lichine, with surprising muscle and tannic power. The wine is just reaching its plateau of maturity, where it should last for at least 5–10 years. Anticipated maturity: now–2010. Last tasted, 3/01.

ANCIENT VINTAGES

As disappointing as the 1982 from Prieuré-Lichine turned out to be, the 1983, which is now fully mature (87 points; last tasted 11/00), was an undeniable success. Prior to that, there were not a whole lot of encouraging results, with very disappointing wines in the 1970s.

RAUZAN-GASSIES

Classification: Second Growth in 1855

Owner: SCI Château Rauzan-Gassies (Jean-Michel Quié)

Address: 33460 Margaux

Telephone: 05 57 88 71 88; Telefax: 05 57 88 37 49

Visits: By appointment Monday to Friday

Contact: Jean-Marc Espagnet

VINEYARDS

Surface area: 74 acres

Grape varietals: 62% Cabernet Sauvignon, 30% Merlot, 5% Cabernet Franc, 3% Petit Verdot

Average age of vines: 28 years

Density of plantation: 10,000 vines per hectare

Average yields: 50 hectoliters per hectare

Elevage: Three week fermentation and maceration in temperature-controlled stainless-steel tanks with frequent pumpings-over. Part of yield undergoes malolactics in barrel. Twelve to eighteen months aging with 30% new oak. Fining with egg whites. Light filtration upon bottling.

WINES PRODUCED

Château Rauzan-Gassies: 150,000 bottles

Chevalier de Rauzan-Gassies: 30,000 bottles

Plateau of maturity: Within 5–12 years of the vintage

GENERAL APPRECIATION

Once one of the most notorious underachievers among Bordeaux's classified growths, Rauzan-Gassies has made better wines since 1995.

The vineyards of Rauzan-Gassies are situated on alluvial terraces. Sixty percent of them are situated just around the château itself, and the remaining vineyards (gravelly soils) border Château Margaux, Palmer, and Lascombes. In short, the *terroir* has unlimited potential, but the will to excel is absent.

Historically, Rauzan-Gassies was part of Rauzan-Ségla until the French Revolution of 1789. Since 1943 it has belonged to the Quié family. In style, Rauzan-Gassies tends toward heaviness and corpulence for a Margaux, without the fragrance or finesse normally associated with the better wines of this commune. However, it can make fairly concentrated, powerful wines. In most vintages, the wines of Rauzan-Gassies have reached maturity surprisingly fast for a classified growth, usually within 7–8 years of the vintage.

IMPORTANT VINTAGES

2001
87–88

An excellent effort from this property (which has been producing better wines over the last 3–4 years), the 2001 exhibits an earthy, melted licorice, and black currant–scented bouquet with underlying notes of foresty underbrush. Although monolithic, it is ripe and sweet, with good density, depth, and weight, as well as some tannin to be resolved. Anticipated maturity: 2006–2015. Last tasted, 1/03.

2000
90

The finest wine I have tasted from this estate in over four decades, this dense purple-colored 2000 offers up a sweet perfume of black cherry liqueur intermixed with cassis, graphite, licorice, and incense. Full-bodied and concentrated, with high tannin and loads of extract, this is a serious, broodingly backward, high-class offering for patient connoisseurs. Anticipated maturity: 2008–2022. Last tasted, 1/03.

1999
87

Licorice, black fruit, herb, earth, and wood aromas emerge from this moderately perfumed, medium-bodied Margaux. Displaying fruit and ripeness as well as some tannin, the 1999 is a good effort from this underperformer, which finally appears to be getting its act together. Drink it over the next decade. Last tasted, 3/02.

1998
85

This elegant, soft, fresh, light- to medium-bodied, pleasant wine lacks substance as well as depth. It will provide superficial charm over the next 3–4 years. Last tasted, 3/01.

ANCIENT VINTAGES

Having tasted virtually every vintage produced from 1961–1997, my score card for Rauzan-Gassies reveals a level of mediocrity that is simply intolerable for a château rated as a second growth in the 1855 classification. Of course, things have now improved, but anyone buying a pre-1998 Rauzan-Gassies is purchasing the proverbial "pig in a poke." Too many of the wines lack color, are deficient in concentration, or have rustic tannins and a very disturbing herbaceousness in addition to a sometimes mushroom-like fruitiness. All in all, this property has one of the most undistinguished records between 1961 and 1997 of any major property in Bordeaux.

RAUZAN-SÉGLA

Classification: Second Growth in 1855

Owner: Château Rauzan-Ségla SA, Wertheimer family

Administrator: John Kolasa

Address: route de Rauzan, 33460 Margaux

Mailing address: route de Rauzan, BP 56, 33460 Margaux

Telephone: 05 57 88 82 10; Telefax: 05 57 88 34 54

E-mail: elise-gourdet@rauzan-segla.com

Visits: By appointment only

Contact: Elise Gourdet

Telephone: 05 57 88 82 14

VINEYARDS

Surface area: 126 acres

Grape varietals: 54% Cabernet Sauvignon, 41% Merlot, 4% Petit Verdot, 1% Cabernet Franc

Average age of vines: 25 years

Density of plantation: 6,500–10,000 vines per hectare

Average yields: 40–45 hectoliters per hectare

Elevage: Six to eight day fermentation and 10–14 day maceration in temperature-controlled stainless-steel vats with twice daily pumpings-over. Eighteen to twenty months aging in barrels with 65% new oak. Racking every three months. Fining with egg whites. No filtration.

WINES PRODUCED

Château Rauzan-Ségla: 100,000 bottles

Ségla: 100,000 bottles

Plateau of maturity: Within 7–25 years of the vintage

GENERAL APPRECIATION

Despite its dismal performance during the 1960s, 1970s, and early 1980s, Rauzan-Ségla has always enjoyed a reputation for potential brilliance. At the beginning of the 1980s, the estate made a complete turnaround, as evidenced by the string of superb wines produced in that decade.

Rauzan-Ségla can trace its history back to 1661, when the vineyard was created by Pierre des Mesures de Rauzan, who at the time was also the owner of the vineyards that now make up Pichon-Longueville—Comtesse de Lalande and Pichon-Longueville Baron. In 1855, Rauzan-Ségla was considered Bordeaux's best wine after the quartet of premiers grands crus Lafite Rothschild, Latour, Margaux, Haut-Brion, and the top-ranked second-growth, Mouton Rothschild. In 1973 Mouton Rothschild was elevated, and now Rauzan-Ségla sits at the head of the class of the remaining fourteen second growths. This position hardly seemed justified by the wines produced during the decades of the 1960s and 1970s, but the indifferent quality changed dramatically with the 1983 vintage.

Looking back, there appear to be a number of valid reasons for the disappointing wines prior to 1983. First, many of the vintages were marred by a musty, damp, almost barnyard-like aroma that is believed to have come from a bacterial infection in the old wooden vats used to ferment the wine. These were replaced in the 1980s with stainless steel. Secondly, there was major replanting after the killer frost of 1956 by then owner, Monsieur de Meslon. The replanting was largely of prolific clones of Merlot. Many of the wines made in the 1960s and 1970s no doubt reflected not only the young vines, but also a badly chosen clone. These plantings have been grubbed up in favor of more Cabernet Sauvignon and higher-quality Merlot. Lastly, the fact that Rauzan-Ségla was sold exclusively through Eschenauer—one of Bordeaux's famous *négociants*—resulted in the wine's exclusion from the comparative tastings that are common for wines sold on the open market. Obviously the incentive to improve quality is far greater when the wine is sold on the open market rather than through exclusive arrangements. Since 1983 the improvements have been remarkable. In that year, Jacques Théo, formerly the head of Alexis Lichine & Company, took over the running of Rauzan-Ségla. Additionally, Monsieur Pruzeau replaced the ailing Monsieur Joyeaux as *maître de chai*. The construction of a new *chai* and improvements to the winemaking facility—including the addition of the stainless-steel vats—an increased percentage of new oak, and Théo's severe selections ensuring that only the best of the crop appears in the wine have resulted in a succession of brilliant wines from Rauzan-Ségla. The quality of the recent wines puts this estate clearly in the elite group of Bordeaux super-seconds. Since 1983 Rauzan-Ségla has done only one thing wrong. Jacques Théo irritated many of his Bordeaux peers by declaring the 1987 Bordeaux vintage disappointing. Rauzan-Ségla became the first significant Médoc classified growth in decades to not produce a wine for a specific vintage—the 1987. In 1994 the *haute couture* house of Chanel, owned by the Wertheimer family, purchased Rauzan-Ségla.

This is a splendid wine worth laying in, as prices have not yet caught up with the new level of quality at this famous old estate. The recent change in ownership should only reinforce the generally held view that Rauzan-Ségla will continue to produce splendid wines, but wines that require significant patience/discipline in view of their high tannin content.

IMPORTANT VINTAGES

2001 The 2001 reveals the telltale herbaceousness and distinctive earthy, smoky, black
87–   cherry, and cassis characteristics found in recent vintages. The color is dark, but
88+? there is a lack of texture, at least at this stage in the wine's evolution. Only 39% of the harvest was utilized, and yields were a modest 45.6 hectoliters per hectare. My instincts suggest there is a lot more to this wine than it is revealing, but, as always, it is one of the more difficult and backward to assess at such an early age. Anticipated maturity: 2008–2020. Last tasted, 1/03.

2000 This wine has evolved nicely. The tannin has sweetened (a positive sign), although
90+   this Margaux has not yet put on the weight expected given how its peers have developed. An impressive opaque purple color is followed by an elegant, fragrant bouquet of black fruits, minerals, dried Provençal herbs, and vanilla. Medium bodied, with high but sweet tannin, a nice texture, and a moderately long finish, this classically elegant as well as authoritatively flavored effort will be at its finest between 2006–2020. Last tasted, 1/03.

1999 A substantial effort for the vintage, the dark ruby/purple–colored 1999 Rauzan-
88   Ségla possesses medium to full body, impressive structure, moderate tannin, and excellent plum, black currant, and cherry fruit infused with camphor, earth, and iron characteristics. This is a 1999 that will benefit from 1–2 years of cellaring, and keep for 15+. Last tasted, 3/02.

1998 A blend of 65% Cabernet Sauvignon and 35% Merlot, this classic, austerely
89   styled Margaux exhibits medium to full body, true breed as well as class, and excellent aromas of subtle herbs, cedar, cassis, and new wood. Rich, medium to full-bodied, sweet on the attack, and moderately tannic, it will benefit from 2–3 more years of cellaring. Anticipated maturity: 2006–2018. Last tasted, 3/02.

1996 The dense, ruby/purple-colored, unfriendly styled 1996 is tannic, backward, and
88   in need of 7–8 years of cellaring. The wine does seem to possess the requisite fruit and extract, however, to stand up to its powerful structure. Although pure and rich,

this wine should not be touched for at least a decade. The sweet cassis aromas of this Cabernet Sauvignon–dominated wine are combined with floral and mineral notes. Anticipated maturity: 2010–2025. Last tasted, 3/01.

1995
90
A classic *vin de garde* with a saturated ruby/purple color and a tight but promising nose of sweet plum and cassis fruit intertwined with underbrush, vanilla, and licorice scents, the 1995 is ripe, medium to full-bodied, and rich, as well as un-yielding, ferociously tannic, pure, and layered. The finish is extremely dry (*sec*, as the French would say), with a brooding angularity and toughness. In spite of this, my instincts suggest the requisite depth is present to balance out the structure. This effort will also require a decade of cellaring. Anticipated maturity: 2010–2025. Last tasted, 3/01.

1994
87?
A saturated dark purple color is accompanied by sweet, earthy, herb, and black currant aromas. The wine is dominated by its tannin and structure. There is good weight, medium body, and an impression of ripeness and sweet fruit, but patience will most definitely be required. This muscular, virile style of Rauzan may always be too tannic, but it should be at its peak of maturity between 2006–2020. Last tasted, 1/97.

1990
93
A fabulous effort from Rauzan-Ségla, this full-bodied, opulently textured, "pedal to the metal" wine still reveals an opaque purple color with only a bit of lightening at the edge. The wine still has plenty of tannin, but there is more than adequate sweet, concentrated, tobacco-tinged black currant fruit to compensate for the tannic clout this wine still possesses. The wine has immense flavor extraction and mouth-searing levels of tannin in a full-bodied, very concentrated, massive style. This wine is approachable now, but promises to have a significant upside and a very long life. Anticipated maturity: 2006–2035. Last tasted, 10/02.

1989
90
At first disjointed and a bit diffuse, the 1989 Rauzan-Ségla has turned itself around in bottle and is now an outstanding effort. The very forward nose of black fruits intermixed with Provençal herbs, underbrush, licorice, and new oak is followed by a medium- to full-bodied wine with a roasted ripeness, silky tannin, and a long, lusty finish. The wine is showing exceptionally well and seems destined to drink, at least at this level of quality, for another decade. Anticipated maturity: now–2012. Last tasted, 3/02.

1988
91
A very strong, powerful wine with an opaque ruby/purple color and a tight but promising bouquet of black currants intermixed with iron, smoke, licorice, and dried herbs, this muscular, very masculine, brawny wine seems built for the long haul. Will it ever shed all of its tannin? Anticipated maturity: 2004–2018. Last tasted, 3/02.

1986
96
A great effort from Rauzan-Ségla and one of the finest wines made at the estate in many a decade, this youthful, exhilarating effort still reveals a dense ruby/purple color with no signs of lightening. Tasting more like a 5–8 year old wine than one that is already 16 years of age, this wine reluctantly offers up a nose of liquid minerals intermixed with tobacco, smoke, black currants, melted licorice, and hints of blueberry and compost. Very full-bodied but still exceptionally tannic in an intense, concentrated, very delineated style, this wine remains an infant in terms of its development. Anticipated maturity: 2007–2040. Last tasted, 3/02.

1985
87
Fully mature and beginning to dry out in the finish, the 1985 Rauzan-Ségla shows a very weedy nose of red cherries, black currants, and licorice. The wine is medium bodied, very elegant, stylish, and certainly a classic Bordeaux in a moderately weighty style. Anticipated maturity: now–2007. Last tasted, 3/02.

1983
91
Fully mature, this has always been one of the best wines of the vintage. The stunning aromatics soar out of the glass, offering up notes of acacia flower intermixed with black currants, smoke, tobacco, and incense. A luscious texture in a beauti-

fully concentrated but very pure, medium- to full-bodied style displays layers of flavor as well as a seamlessness that is endearing if not compelling. The wine is a beauty and is the first vintage to signal the return of Rauzan-Ségla to the ranks of quality Bordeaux château. Anticipated maturity: now–2009. Last tasted, 3/02.

1982   This wine is beginning to fall apart. It was never one of the vintage's stronger ef-
84?   forts, and now is becoming increasingly disjointed, with rather astringent, attenu-
ated tannins poking through the finish of this medium-bodied, herbaceous wine. It is lightweight for a 1982 and fully mature. Drink up. Last tasted 3/02.

ANCIENT VINTAGES

Rauzan-Ségla's performance in the 1970s and 1960s was appalling. Ironically, one of their better efforts was from the disastrous vintage of 1972, where Rauzan-Ségla actually produced a powerful wine—a better wine than many of the vintages that produced far greater raw materials. The 1970 is still alive and well, but austere and tannic. The 1961 is a failure, as is the 1959.

Oddly enough, several of the most amazing Rauzan-Séglas I have tasted were museum pieces. The 1900 Rauzan-Ségla (88 points; last tasted 12/95) has an enticing, seductive, licorice, herb, old cedar-scented nose, with hints of ripe fruit. The 1858 (92 points; last tasted 9/95) displayed an orange/amber color, followed by a fragrant nose of orange marmalade, melted caramels, and curranty fruit. It was sweet, with amazing ripeness and medium body. Another great museum piece was the 1868 Rauzan-Ségla (96 points; last tasted 9/95). Its huge nose of cedar, chocolate, roasted coffee, and smoked herbs was followed by a surprisingly full-bodied wine with relatively high alcohol. Another Rauzan-Ségla that was hard to believe when tasted was the 1865 (99+ points; last tasted 12/95). This wine had a deep garnet color, a fabulous bouquet of cedar and cassis, and a remarkably youthful intensity to its full-bodied, exceptionally unctuous flavors. It could have been a 40- to 50-year-old wine just from the way it performed.

SIRAN

Classification: Cru Bourgeois in 1832

Owner: William-Alain Miailhe

Address: Labarde, 33460 Margaux

Telephone: 05 57 88 34 04; Telefax: 05 57 88 70 05

E-mail: chateau-siran@wanadoo.fr

Website: www.chateau-siran.com

Visits: All year around except for Christmas and New Year's, 10 A.M.–6 P.M.

Contact: Denise Bourgine

VINEYARDS

Surface area: 59.3 acres (in Margaux)

Grape varietals: 43% Merlot, 38% Cabernet Sauvignon, 12% Petit Verdot, 7% Cabernet Franc

Average age of vines: 30 years

Density of plantation: 10,000 vines per hectare

Average yields: 51 hectoliters per hectare

Elevage: Twenty-five day fermentation and maceration in temperature-controlled stainless-steel tanks. Twelve to fourteen months aging in barrels with 60% new oak and 40% one-year-old barrels. Fining, filtration upon bottling.

WINES PRODUCED

Château Siran: 90,000–100,000 bottles

Château Bellegarde: 32,000 bottles

Plateau of maturity: Within 5–15 years of the vintage

GENERAL APPRECIATION

A consistently reliable Cru Bourgeois, Siran is the equivalent of a fifth growth in its finest vintages.

This property in Labarde in the southern part of the Margaux appellation is making consistently delicious, fragrant, deeply colored wines that are frequently on a quality level with a Médoc fifth growth.

The estate is owned and managed by William Alain B. Miailhe, a meticulous grower, who produces in an average year 12,000 cases of rich, flavorful, polished wine that admirably reflects the Margaux appellation. The wine is also distinguished by a Mouton Rothschild-like label that boasts a different artist's painting each year.

Siran's wine usually needs 5–6 years of bottle age to mature properly, and recent vintages have all been successful. Above all, this is a wine that repays the patient consumer because of its ability to support extended cellaring. The long maceration period (25 days) and elevated percentage of the tannic Petit Verdot in the blend give the wine at least 15 years of aging potential in top vintages.

If a new classification of the wines of the Médoc was ever done, Siran would surely be given significant consideration for inclusion as a fifth growth.

IMPORTANT VINTAGES

2001   This Cru Bourgeois has turned out a 2001 of classified-growth quality. A dark
87–88 ruby/purple color is followed by a smoky nose with notions of melted licorice, tar, black currants, and incense, sweet tannin, medium body, and a moderately long finish. With good balance, purity, and definition, this attractive Margaux should drink well between 2005–2014. Last tasted, 1/03.

2000   Highly extracted, powerful, chewy, ripe black currant flavors mixed with fennel,
88+   leather, iron, and new oak jump from the glass of this opaque ruby/purple–colored 2000. Full, dense, moderately tannic, and potentially long-lived, it may turn out to be even better than the score indicates. Anticipated maturity: 2005–2020. Last tasted, 1/03.

1999   This is a seductive, charming, fruity offering with plenty of dark fruits, medium
87   body, soft tannin, and considerable elegance. Enjoy it over the next 5–6 years. Last tasted, 3/02.

1998   A powerful, structured, dark ruby/purple–colored effort, the muscular, dense,
87   ageworthy 1998 is one of the finest Médoc Cru Bourgeois (black currants, earth,
       and oak dominate). Made in a closed but classic style, it will be at its finest be-
       tween 2005–2020. Last tasted, 3/02.

ANCIENT VINTAGES

I have strong tasting notes on the 1990 (87 points; last tasted 3/98), the 1986 (88
points; last tasted 11/90), and 1983 (88 points; last tasted 1/98).

DU TERTRE

Classification: Fifth Growth in 1855

Owner: Eric Albada Jelgersma

Address: Chemin de Ligondras, 33460 Arsac

Mailing address: c/ SAE Château Giscours,
33460 Labarde

Telephone: 05 56 58 82 27; Telefax: 05 56 58 86 29

Visits: By appointment only

Contact: Céline Dupuy

Telephone: 05 57 88 52 52; Telefax: 05 57 88 52 51

VINEYARDS

Surface area: 128.4 acres

Grape varietals: 40% Cabernet Sauvignon, 35% Merlot, 20% Cabernet Franc, 5% Petit
Verdot

Average age of vines: 30 years

Density of plantation: 7,500 vines per hectare

Average yields: 45 hectoliters per hectare

Elevage: Five to seven day fermentation and 15–18 day maceration. Eighteen months
aging in oak barrels, 60% of which are renewed each year. Fining with egg whites. No
filtration.

WINES PRODUCED

Château du Tertre: 200,000–250,000 bottles

Les Hauts du Tertre: 50,000–80,000 bottles

Plateau of maturity: Within 6–15 years of the vintage

GENERAL APPRECIATION

One of the finest values amongst the Bordeaux classified growths, du Tertre has been
consistent since 1978. Under the recent ownership of Eric Albada Jelgersma, it has
improved dramatically, as evidenced by the string of superb vintages produced during the
last 4–5 years. This is an estate consumers should keep a close watch on as prices remain
fair.

Du Tertre, located on one of the highest plateaus in the Margaux appellation, was acquired in 1961 by the late Philippe Capbern Gasqueton, the proprietor of the famous St.-Estèphe estate Calon-Ségur. The property was in deplorable condition, and Gasqueton and his investors began an extensive plan to rebuild the château and replant the vineyard. Until 12 years ago, it was extremely easy to forget the wines of this property. The sandy-colored, plain yet elegant, two-story château is located in one of the most obscure areas of the Médoc (less than a kilometer from Arsac, near Monbrison). In 1998, the estate was sold by Madame Gasqueton to Eric Albada Jelgersma, who had also acquired the nearby estate of Giscours.

The vineyard is unusual because it is one contiguous parcel and not morcellated as so many Bordeaux château vineyards are. At first glance it is visually reminiscent of Domaine de Chevalier. Since 1978, the wine has been characterized by relatively deep color and a good bit of power and richness in the top vintages, but perhaps a lack of finesse and that extra-special fragrance that can make a Margaux so enthralling. Nevertheless, the wine continues to sell at a modest price, making it one of the most undervalued of the classified growths of Bordeaux.

IMPORTANT VINTAGES

2001
87–88 Fresh acidity underlies attractive berry, cherry, and licorice-infused cassis fruit. Elegant, medium bodied, pure, well balanced, and impeccably made, the 2001 du Tertre is not a blockbuster, massive-styled effort in the style of the 2000, but will provide abundant enjoyment between 2006–2015. Last tasted, 1/03.

2000
90 A dense purple color is accompanied by layers of concentrated blackberry and fruit intertwined with damp earth, mushroom, and sweet, toasty *barrique* smells. With ripe tannin, medium to full body, a layered texture, and a concentrated, impressively endowed finish, this is the finest du Tertre since their 1979. Anticipated maturity: 2004–2018. Last tasted, 1/03.

1999
87 An excellent du Tertre, the deep dark ruby–colored 1999 exhibits aromas of herbs, leather, licorice, red and black currants, sweet fruit on the attack, medium body, and a round, charming, pretty finish. Enjoy it now and over the next 10 years. Last tasted, 3/02.

1998
88+ A potential sleeper of the vintage, du Tertre's 1998 exhibits a dense ruby/purple color in addition to a sweet black cherry and cassis-scented nose, soft, velvety-textured tannin, medium body, and a surprisingly succulent, fat mid-palate. The wine reveals good length and a charming, up-front, expansive appeal. This is another estate that did not overextract, thus producing a wine of charm, ripe fruit, and harmony. Anticipated maturity: now–2012. Last tasted, 3/02.

1996
90 A sleeper, du Tertre's 1996 exhibits a black ruby/purple color, a sweet black fruit–scented nose, medium to full body, well-integrated tannin, and fine purity and depth. This wine should age nicely, yet have a degree of accessibility young. Anticipated maturity: now–2018. Last tasted, 3/01.

1995
86 A chocolaty, berry-scented nose with weedy cassis, licorice, and earth aromas is followed by a medium-bodied wine with fine concentration. Although monolithic, the 1995 is well made, mouth-filling, and moderately tannic. Anticipated maturity: now–2015. Last tasted, 11/97.

1990
87 The 1990 represents a strong effort for this property. It is surprisingly dark in color, with medium body, fine structure, plenty of depth and richness, and an interesting bouquet of olives, smoky oak, and overripe black fruits. This wine re-

minds me somewhat of a lighter version of the 1979. Anticipated maturity: now–2008. Last tasted, 1/93.

1989
86
The 1989 du Tertre is a charming, soft, medium-bodied wine that lacks concentration and structure. It is evolved, very perfumed (with jammy black currants), low in acidity, and ideal for drinking during its first 6–8 years. Anticipated maturity: now. Last tasted, 4/91.

1988
86
The 1988 du Tertre is a good example for the vintage. Medium deep ruby with a curranty, smoky, oak-dominated nose, this wine continues to bear a resemblance to the château's excellent 1979. Anticipated maturity: now. Last tasted, 1/93.

1986
86
The spicy, ripe, mineral, and curranty bouquet is followed by a wine with medium body and good grip. Approachable now and evolving more rapidly than I would have thought possible several years ago, this elegantly wrought wine remains bargain priced for the vintage. Anticipated maturity: now–2005. Last tasted, 3/90.

1985
87
I have tasted the 1985 du Tertre nine times—five times from cask and four times from the bottle. While I have never seen a wine behave so differently, the two most recent tastings have revealed positive results. The last two examples (both tasted in France) exhibited a nice deep ruby/purple color with no signs of age and a forward, earthy (truffles?), curranty bouquet that was enticing. In the mouth, the wine possessed plenty of fat, ripe, supple blackberry and curranty flavors, with just enough soft tannin and acidity to give the wine grip and focus. This is a luscious, very forward style of du Tertre. Anticipated maturity: now. Last tasted, 11/90.

1983
86
Medium to deep ruby, with an intensely spicy, slightly herbaceous nose, du Tertre's 1983 is rich and ripe, with medium-bodied flavors that exhibit good concentration and moderate tannins that are beginning to melt away. This is a very good, rather than exceptional, wine from the 1983 vintage. Anticipated maturity: now. Last tasted, 11/90.

1982
87
A wonderful, fragrant bouquet of violets, damp earth, cedar wood, black currants, and white chocolate jumps from the glass. On the palate, the wine is lush, medium-bodied, and concentrated, with ripe fruity flavors. Like most Margaux of this vintage, it has reached its plateau of maturity. Anticipated maturity: now. Last tasted, 1/90.

ANCIENT VINTAGES

A vintage to search out has always been the 1979, actually one of the top eight or ten wines of that harvest. I bought several cases of it for a song and continue to drink through my remaining stock. When last tasted in October 2002 (rated 90), it still had a dense ruby/purple color and a sweet nose of melted licorice intermixed with crème de cassis and white flowers. The wine is medium to full-bodied, with outstanding definition, great purity, a surprising texture, and a long finish. It is one of the top sleepers from any vintage in Bordeaux, and probably still can be picked up for a low price. It should continue to drink well for another 10–15 years. Other than the 1979, most of du Tertre's wines from the 1970s and 1960s were largely disappointing.

OTHER MARGAUX ESTATES

ARSAC

Classification: Cru Bourgeois

Owner: Philippe Raoux

Address: 33460 Arsac

Mailing address: 80, rue Emile Counord, 33300 Bordeaux

Telephone: 05 56 58 83 90; Telefax: 05 56 58 83 08

E-mail: philippe.a.raoux@wanadoo.fr

Website: www.chateau-arsac.net

Visits: By appointment only

Contact: Hélène Schönbuck

VINEYARDS

Surface area: 276.6 acres (103.7 acres under Margaux appellation)

Grape varietals: 60% Cabernet Sauvignon, 40% Merlot

Average age of vines: 15 years

Density of plantation: 6,600 vines per hectare

Average yields: 55 hectoliters per hectare

Elevage: Three to four week fermentation and maceration in temperature-controlled stainless-steel vats. Twelve months aging in oak barrels that are renewed by a third each year. Fining and filtration.

WINES PRODUCED

Château d'Arsac: 280,000 bottles

Ruban Bleu du Château d'Arsac: 470,000 bottles

Plateau of maturity: Within 5–10 years of the vintage

BEL AIR-MARQUIS D'ALIGRE

Classification: Cru Grand Bourgeois Exceptionnel

Owner: Jean-Pierre Boyer

Address: 33460 Soussans

Telephone: 05 57 88 70 70

No visits

VINEYARDS

Surface area: 29.6 acres

Grape varietals: 35% Merlot, 30% Cabernet Sauvignon, 20% Cabernet Franc, 10% Petit Verdot, 5% Malbec

Average age of vines: 35 years

Density of plantation: 10,000 vines per hectare

Average yields: 26 hectoliters per hectare

Elevage: Three to four week fermentation and maceration. Two to three year aging in barrels and in vats, no new oak. Fining with egg whites. No filtration.

WINES PRODUCED

Château Bel Air-Marquis d'Aligre: 30,000 bottles

No second wine is produced.

CLOS DU JAUGUEYRON

Classification: None

Owner: Farmed by Michel Théron

Address: 4, rue de la Haille, 33460 Arsac

Telephone: 05 56 58 89 43

Visits: By appointment only

Contact: Michel Théron or Stéphanie Destruhaut

VINEYARDS

Surface area: 1 acre

Grape varietals: 60% Cabernet Sauvignon, 25% Merlot, 10% Petit Verdot, 5% Cabernet Franc

Average age of vines: More than 50 years

Density of plantation: 6,500 vines per hectare

Average yields: 45 hectoliters per hectare

Elevage: Fermentations and macerations last between 3–6 weeks. Wines undergo maololactics in barrels and are aged in 25–30% new oak for 20 months. They are fined and filtered.

WINE PRODUCED

Clos du Jaugueyron: 2,500 bottles

Best recent vintages: 2001, 2000, 1999

Plateau of maturity: Within 4–16 years of the vintage

There are just more than 100 cases of this brilliant wine emerging from an old vineyard situated next to Palmer. A quintessential garage wine, it is produced from a tiny plot of vines believed to be largely pre-phylloxera, and is aged 18 months on its lees prior to being bottled with a light filtration.

IMPORTANT VINTAGES

2001 Composed of 50% Cabernet Sauvignon, 35% Merlot, and 15% Cabernet Franc,
90–91+ the 2001 Clos du Jaugueyron boasts a black/ruby color as well as a sweet perfume of cassis, creosote, and violets with subtle wood in the background. Medium bod-

ied as well as pure, it possesses a stunning texture and a lightness typical of many of the finest Margaux offerings. The tannin, acidity, and wood are impressively integrated. Anticipated maturity: 2008–2018. Last tasted, 1/03.

2000 This blend of 60% Cabernet Sauvignon, 30% Merlot, 5% Cabernet Franc, and 5%
92   Petit Verdot reveals a saturated color along with a lot of muscle, mineral, and tannin in the amazingly long finish. It would be interesting to see how this serious Margaux would fare in a blind tasting against some of the appellation's classified growths. Anticipated maturity: 2006–2022. Last tasted, 1/03.

1999 The stunning 1999 Clos du Jaugueyron boasts a dense ruby/purple color as well as
91   a sensational aromatic profile of spring flowers, black and red fruits, minerals, and subtle wood. It offers great complexity, medium body, beautifully integrated acidity, tannin, wood, and a long finish with no hard edges. Anticipated maturity: now–2015. Last tasted, 1/02.

1998 A dense dark ruby/purple color is accompanied by an elegant, seductive, fleshy
88   mid-palate, copious glycerin, and gorgeous floral-infused black currant fruit with a touch of licorice and toast. This outstanding 1998 should be consumed over the next seven years. Last tasted, 3/02.

CHARMANT

Classification: None

Owner: Christiane Renon

Address: 20, cours Pey-Berland, 33460 Margaux

Telephone: 05 57 88 35 27; Telefax: 05 57 88 70 59

Visits: By appointment Monday to Friday, 9–11:30 A.M. and 3–5:30 P.M.

Contact: Christiane Renon

VINEYARDS

Surface area: 11.6 acres

Grape varietals: 50% Merlot, 25% Cabernet Sauvignon, 20% Cabernet Franc, 5% Petit Verdot

Average age of vines: 60 years

Density of plantation: 9,000 vines per hectare

Average yields: 50 hectoliters per hectare

Elevage: Three week fermentation and maceration in stainless-steel and concrete vats. Twelve months aging in barrels with 20% new oak. Fining, no filtration.

WINES PRODUCED

Château Charmant: 32,000 bottles

Plateau of maturity: Within 2–10 years of the vintage

DESMIRAIL

Classification: Third Growth in 1855

Proprietor: Lucien Lurton

Address: 33460 Margaux

Telephone: 05 57 88 83 33; Telefax: 05 57 88 72 51

Visits: By appointment only

VINEYARDS

Surface area: 44.5 acres

Grape varietals: 80% Cabernet Sauvignon, 10% Merlot, 5% Cabernet Franc, 5% Petit Verdot

Average age of vines: 20 years

Density of plantation: 6,666 vines per hectare

Average yields: 60 hectoliters per hectare

Elevage: 16–18 months in small oak casks

WINES PRODUCED

Château Desmirail: 55,000 bottles

Château Baudry: Variable

Plateau of maturity: Within 3–12 years of the vintage

DEYREM VALENTIN

Classification: Cru Bourgeois

Owner: Jean Sorge

Address: 1, rue Valentin Deyrem, 33460 Soussans

Telephone: 05 57 88 35 70; Telefax: 05 57 88 36 84

Visits: By appointment only

Contact: Jean Sorge

VINEYARDS

Surface area: 34.6 acres

Grape varietals: 55% Cabernet Sauvignon, 45% Merlot

Average age of vines: 30 years

Density of plantation: 9,000 vines per hectare

Average yields: 56 hectoliters per hectare

Elevage: Three week fermentation and maceration. Eighteen months aging in barrels with 50% new oak. Fining, no filtration

WINES PRODUCED

Château Deyrem Valentin: 60,000 bottles

Château Soussans: 30,000 bottles

Plateau of maturity: Within 4–10 years of the vintage

FERRIÈRE

Classification: Third Growth in 1855 Classification

Owner: Claire Villars-Lurton

Address: 33 bis, rue de la Trémoille, 33460 Margaux

Telephone: 05 57 88 76 65; Telefax: 05 57 88 98 33

E-mail: n.lemire@ferriere.com

Website: www.ferriere.com

Visits: By appointment only (closed during holiday periods)

Contact: Nathalie Lemire

VINEYARDS

Surface area: 19.8 acres

Grape varietals: 80% Cabernet Sauvignon, 15% Merlot, 5% Petit Verdot

Average age of vines: 35 years

Density of plantation: 10,000 vines per hectare

Average yields: 55 hectoliters per hectare

Elevage: Fermentation and maceration in temperature-controlled stainless-steel tanks. Malolactics in new oak. Sixteen to eighteen months aging with 60% new oak barrels. Fining.

WINES PRODUCED

Château Ferrière: 35,000 bottles

Les Remparts de Ferrière: 10,000 bottles

Plateau of maturity: Within 5–10 years of the vintage

LA GALIANE

Classification: None

Owner: Christiane Renon

Address: 33460 Soussans

Telephone: 05 57 88 35 27; Telefax: 05 57 88 70 59

Visits: Monday to Friday, 9–11:30 A.M. and 3–5:30 P.M.

Contact: Christiane Renon

VINEYARDS

Surface area: 14.1 acres

Grape varietals: 50% Merlot, 30% Cabernet Sauvignon, 15% Cabernet Franc, 5% Petit Verdot

Average age of vines: 55 years

Density of plantation: 9,000 vines per hectare

Average yields: 56 hectoliters per hectare

Elevage: Three week fermentation and maceration in temperature-controlled concrete vats. Twelve months aging in barrels with 18% new oak. Fining, no filtration.

WINES PRODUCED

Château La Galiane: 38,000 bottles

No second wine is produced.

LA GURGUE

Classification: Cru Bourgeois

Owner: Claire Villars Lurton

Address: 33 bis, rue de la Trémoille, 33460 Margaux

Telephone: 05 57 88 76 65; Telefax: 05 57 88 98 33

E-mail: n.lemire@ferriere.com

Visits: By appointment (no visits weekends and holiday periods)

Contact: Nathalie Lemire

VINEYARDS

Surface area: 24.7 acres

Grape varietals: 70% Cabernet Sauvignon, 30% Merlot

Average age of vines: 25 years

Density of plantation: 10,000 vines per hectare

Average yields: 46 hectoliters per hectare

Elevage: Seventeen to twenty-three day fermentation and maceration in temperature-controlled stainless-steel tanks. After malolactics, 12 months aging in barrels that are renewed by 25% each year. Fining.

WINES PRODUCED

Château La Gurgue: 60,000 bottles

No second wine is produced.

Best recent vintages: 1996

Best older vintages: 1989, 1988, 1986

Plateau of maturity: Within 5–12 years of the vintage

HAUT BRETON LARIGAUDIÈRE

Classification: Cru Bourgeois in 1932

Owner: M. de Schepper

Address: 3, rue des Anciens Combattants, 33460 Soussans

Telephone: 05 57 88 94 17; Telefax: 05 57 88 39 14

E-mail: ch.larigaudiere@aol.com

Visits: By appointment Monday to Friday, 8 A.M.–noon and 2–6 P.M.

Contact: M. Garcion

VINEYARDS

Surface area: 37 acres

Grape varietals: 63% Cabernet Sauvignon, 31% Merlot, 4% Petit Verdot, 2% Cabernet Franc

Average age of vines: 22 years

Density of plantation: 10,000 vines per hectare

Average yields: 58 hectoliters per hectare

Elevage: Three to five week fermentation and maceration in temperature-controlled vats (trickle-cooling system). Twelve to fifteen months aging in barrels that are renewed by 50–70% each year. Fining and filtration.

WINES PRODUCED

Château Haut Breton Larigaudière: 60,000 bottles

Château du Courneau: 15,000 bottles

LABÉGORCE

Classification: Cru Bourgeois

Owner: Hubert Perrodo

Address: 33460 Margaux

Telephone: 05 57 88 71 32; Telefax: 05 57 88 35 01

Visits: Every day of the week, 8:30 A.M.–6 P.M.

Contact: Maïté Augerot

VINEYARDS

Surface area: 94 acres

Grape varietals: 60% Cabernet Sauvignon, 35% Merlot, 5% Cabernet Franc

Average age of vines: 25 years

Density of plantation: 8,000 vines per hectare

Average yields: 45 hectoliters per hectare

Elevage: Grapes are hand-picked. Fermentations last about 3–4 weeks in temperature-controlled vats. Forty percent of the grand vin completes malolactics in new oak barrels. All wines are aged in oak casks, of which 30% are new. Fined but not filtered.

WINES PRODUCED

Château Labégorce: 150,000 bottles

La Mouline de Labégorce: 25,000 bottles

Plateau of maturity: Within 3–8 years of the vintage

LABÉGORCE ZÉDÉ

Classification: Cru Bourgeois in 1932

Owner: SCEA Labégorce Zédé

Administrator: Luc Thienpont

Address: 33460 Margaux

Telephone: 05 57 88 71 31; Telefax: 05 57 88 72 54

Visits: Monday to Sunday, 8 A.M.–1 P.M. and 2–5 P.M.

Contact: Luc Thienpont

VINEYARDS

Surface area: 69.2 acres

Grape varietals: 50% Cabernet Sauvignon, 35% Merlot, 10% Cabernet Franc, 5% Petit Verdot

Average age of vines: 45 years

Density of plantation: 10,000 vines per hectare

Average yields: 50 hectoliters per hectare

Elevage: Two to three week fermentation (at 30°C) and maceration in temperature-controlled concrete vats. Eighteen months aging in barrels with 50% new oak. Fining with egg whites, no filtration.

WINES PRODUCED

Château Labégorce Zédé: 70,000 bottles

Domaine Zédé: 100,000 bottles

Plateau of maturity: Within 5–10 years of the vintage

GENERAL APPRECIATION

Post-1995 vintages of Labégorce Zédé are hardly inspirational, but soundly made and well worth their status. In today's marketplace, they represent good values.

The Belgian Thienpont family owns and manages Labégorce Zédé, and like the wine of their famous Pomerol estate of Vieux Château Certan, this is traditionally made. Since 1979, when young Luc Thienpont took over, the quality increased. Labégorce Zédé, with a plain, drab farmhouse and vineyards in both the communes of Soussans and Margaux, usually requires 5–6 years to reach maturity but can retain fruit and harmony for 5–10 more years in top vintages. I personally prefer the wines of Labégorce Zédé to Labégorce, given the extra measure of perfume and richness often found in the former.

LARRUAU

Classification: Cru Bourgeois in 1980

Owner: Bernard Chateau

Address: 4, rue de la Trémoille, 33460 Margaux

Telephone: 05 57 88 35 50; Telefax: 05 57 88 76 69

Visits: By appointment

Contact: Bernard Chateau

VINEYARDS

Surface area: 29.6 acres

Grape varietals: 50% Cabernet Sauvignon, 50% Merlot

Average age of vines: 20 years

Density of plantation: 10,000 vines per hectare

Average yields: 55 hectoliters per hectare

Elevage: Fermentation and maceration in temperature-controlled tanks. After malolactics, 18 months aging in barrels that are renewed by a third each year. Racking every three months. Fining, no filtration.

WINES PRODUCED

Château Larruau: 76,000 bottles

No second wine is produced.

MARQUIS D'ALESME BECKER

Classification: Third Growth in 1855

Owner: Jean-Claude Zuger

Address: 33460 Margaux

Telephone: 05 57 88 70 27; Telefax: 05 57 88 73 28

Visits: Monday to Friday, 10 A.M.–noon and 2–5 P.M.

Contact: Jean-Claude Zuger

VINEYARDS

Surface area: 39.5 acres

Grape varietals: 45% Merlot, 30% Cabernet Sauvignon, 15% Cabernet Franc, 10% Petit Verdot

Average age of vines: 35 years

Density of plantation: 7,500 vines per hectare

Average yields: 57 hectoliters per hectare

Elevage: Three week fermentation and maceration in temperature-controlled stainless-steel vats. Twelve months aging in barrels that are renewed by a third each year. Fining, no filtration.

WINES PRODUCED

Château Marquis d'Alesme Becker: 100,000 bottles

Marquis d'Alesme: 20,000 bottles

GENERAL APPRECIATION

Like neighbors d'Issan, Kirwan, Palmer, and Malescot St.-Exupéry, Marquis d'Alesme Becker is a third growth but, unlike its peers, this estate hardly justifies its place in the 1855 classification. Its lean and hard wines lack the fruit and elegance characteristic of the appellation.

This small vineyard produces one of the most obscure wines in the famous classification of 1855. The château itself is a beautiful Victorian mansion sitting opposite the mayor's office in the village of Margaux. It has, since 1979, been run by Jean-Claude Zuger, the brother of Roger Zuger, the proprietor of the better-known nearby Margaux château of Malescot St.-Exupéry. So little is known about this wine in the export markets because virtually all the production is sold directly to private customers in France, Switzerland, and Belgium. On the occasions I have had to taste the wine, I have been surprised, given the high percentage of Merlot employed at this property, that the wine is not fuller and more plump. In fact, looking at the actual winemaking process, the maceration period is relatively long, and Zuger claims that the wine is rarely filtered prior to bottling. Why it does not have more extract and flavor remains a mystery. Nevertheless, Marquis d'Alesme Becker does have admirers.

IMPORTANT VINTAGES

While I have tasted the 2001, 2000, 1990, 1988, 1986, 1985, 1983, 1982, 1981, 1979, 1978, 1976, and 1975, there is not a vintage of these wines that I have ever rated higher than 85. Though I realize everyone has their own personal taste, this wine lacks concentration, depth, and seems shockingly one-dimensional and simple for a classified growth. Hopefully, improvements will be forthcoming in the 21st century.

MARSAC SÉGUINEAU

Classification: Cru Bourgeois

Owner: SC du Château Marsac Séguineau

Address: 33460 Soussans

Mailing address: 17, cours de la Martinique, 33027 Bordeaux

Telephone: 05 56 01 30 10; Telefax: 05 56 79 23 57

Visits: Exclusively by appointment and for professionals of the wine trade only

Contact: Brigitte Cruse

VINEYARDS

Surface area: 25.3 acres

Grape varietals: 60% Merlot, 28% Cabernet Sauvignon, 12% Cabernet Franc

Average age of vines: 29 years

Density of plantation: 10,000 vines per hectare

Average yields: 56 hectoliters per hectare

Elevage: Harvest is done by both hand and machine. Fermentations last 21 days. Wines are transferred to oak casks for aging for 18–21 months. The percentage of new oak is usually 30%. Wines àre fined and filtered (for safety) at the time of bottling.

WINES PRODUCED

Château Marsac Séguineau: 50,000 bottles

Château Gravières de Marsac: 21,000 bottles

Plateau of maturity: Within 5–15 years of the vintage

MARTINENS

Classification: Cru Bourgeois

Owner: Jean-Pierre Seynat-Dulos and Simone Dulos

Address: 33460 Cantenac

Telephone: 05 57 88 71 37; Telefax: 05 57 88 38 35

Visits: By appointment

Contact: Jean-Pierre Seynat-Dulos

VINEYARDS

Surface area: 61.8 acres

Grape varietals: 63% Merlot, 22% Cabernet Sauvignon, 10% Petit Verdot, 5% Cabernet Franc

Average age of vines: 25 years

Density of plantation: 6,666 and 8,333 vines per hectare

Average yields: 54 hectoliters per hectare

Elevage: Three week fermentation and maceration in temperature-controlled tanks. Sixteen to eighteen months aging in barrels with 45% of yield in new oak, the rest being in vats. Fining and filtration.

WINES PRODUCED

Château Martinens: 180,000 bottles

Château Bois de Monteil: 38,000 bottles

Plateau of maturity: Within 3–10 years of the vintage

MONGRAVEY

Classification: Cru Bourgeois

Owner: Regis Bernaleau

Address: 8, avenue Jean-Luc Vonderheyden, 33460 Arsac

Telephone: 05 56 58 84 51; Telefax: 05 56 58 83 39

E-mail: chateau.mongravey@wanadoo.fr

Visits: By appointment only

Contact: Karine Bernaleau

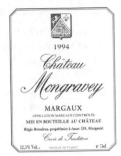

VINEYARDS

Surface area: 24.7 acres

Grape varietals: 55% Cabernet Sauvignon, 45% Merlot

Average age of vines: 25 years

Density of plantation: 6,600–10,000 vines per hectare

Average yields: 50 hectoliters per hectare

Elevage: Six to ten day alcoholic fermentation and 3–4 week maceration in temperature-controlled stainless-steel vats. Twenty-four months aging in new oak. Fining, no filtration.

WINES PRODUCED

Château Mongravey: 54,000 bottles

Château Cazauviel: 12,000 bottles

Plateau of maturity: Within 2–8 years of the vintage

Note: This estate also produces two other *cuvées:*

Mongravey Prestige: Aged 14–18 months in barrels with 60% new oak

Mongravey Tradition: Aged 14–18 months in oak barrels with 35% new oak

PONTAC LYNCH

Classification: Cru Bourgeois

Owner: Marie-Christine Bondon

Address: Issan-Cantenac, 33460 Margaux

Mailing address: Issan-Cantenac, BP 7, 33460 Margaux

Telephone: 05 57 88 30 04; Telefax: 05 57 88 32 63

Visits: By appointment Monday to Friday, 9 A.M.–5 P.M.

Contact: Marie-Christine Bondon

VINEYARDS

Surface area: 24.7 acres (including 4.9 acres under the Haut-Médoc appellation)

Grape varietals: 40% Merlot, 35% Cabernet Sauvignon, 20% Cabernet Franc, 5% Petit Verdot

Average age of vines: 30 years

Density of plantation: 10,000 vines per hectare

Average yields: 52 hectoliters per hectare

Elevage: Two to four week fermentation and maceration in temperature-controlled concrete tanks. Eighteen months aging in barrels with 35–50% new oak depending upon the vintage. Fining, no filtration.

WINES PRODUCED

Château Pontac Lynch: 50,000 bottles

Château Pontac-Phénix: 12,000 bottles (Haut-Médoc)

PONTET-CHAPPAZ

Classification: Cru Bourgeois

Owner: Vignobles Rocher Cap de Rive SA

Address: 33460 Margaux

Mailing address: c/o Château Rocher Bellevue, BP 89, 33350 Saint-Magne de Castillon

Telephone: 06 80 73 44 23; Telefax: 05 56 58 84 83

No visits

VINEYARDS

Surface area: 19.2 acres

Grape varietals: 55% Merlot, 45% Cabernet Sauvignon

Average age of vines: 35 years

Density of plantation: 7,800 vines per hectare

Average yields: 60 hectoliters per hectare

Elevage: Three week fermentation and maceration in temperature-controlled stainless-steel tanks. Twelve months aging with 80% of yield in barrels that are renewed by a third each year and 20% of yield in vats. Fining, no filtration.

WINES PRODUCED

Château Pontet-Chappaz: 60,000 bottles

No second wine is produced.

POUGET

Classification: Fourth Growth in 1855

Owner: GFA des Châteaux Boyd-Cantenac et Pouget

Address: 33460 Cantenac

Telephone: 05 57 88 90 82; Telefax: 05 57 88 33 27

Visits: By appointment only

Contact: Lucien Guillemet

VINEYARDS

Surface area: 24.7 acres

Grape varietals: 60% Cabernet Sauvignon, 32% Merlot, 8% Cabernet Franc

Average age of vines: 30 years

Density of plantation: 10,000 vines per hectare

Average yields: 38 hectoliters per hectare

Elevage: Fermentations last approximately three weeks in stainless-steel vats. Wines are then transferred into oak casks (50% of which are new) for 12–18 months. They are fined and lightly filtered (for additional safety) at the time of bottling.

WINES PRODUCED

Château Pouget: 36,000 bottles

La Tour Massac: 12,000–30,000 bottles

Plateau of maturity: Within 5–15 years of the vintage

TAYAC

Classification: Cru Bourgeois

Owner: GFA Château Tayac

Address: Lieu-dit Tayac, 33460 Soussans

Mailing address: BP 10, 33460 Soussans

Telephone: 05 57 88 33 06; Telefax: 05 57 88 38 06

Visits: Monday to Friday, 10 A.M.–12:30 P.M. and from 2–6 P.M.

Contact: Nadine Portet

VINEYARDS

Surface area: 89 acres

Grape varietals: 65% Cabernet Sauvignon, 33% Merlot, 2% Petit Verdot

Average age of vines: 30 years

Density of plantation: 8,500 vines per hectare

Average yields: 58 hectoliters per hectare

Elevage: Eight to twelve day fermentation and 30–45 day maceration. Ten to twelve months aging in barrels with 38% new oak. Fining. No precision regarding filtration.

WINES PRODUCED

Château Tayac: 130,000 bottles

Château du Grand Soussans: 13,000 bottles

LA TOUR DE BESSAN

Classification: None

Owner: Marie-Laure Lurton-Roux

Address: Route d'Arsac, 33460 Margaux

Mailing address: SC Les Grands Crus Réunis, 2036 Chalet, 33480 Moulis-en-Médoc

Telephone: 05 56 58 22 01; Telefax: 05 56 58 15 10

E-mail: lgcr@wanadoo.fr

Visits: By appointment only

Contact: Viviane Grouffier

VINEYARDS

Surface area: 44.5 acres

Grape varietals: 43.5% Cabernet Sauvignon, 33.3% Merlot, 23.2% Cabernet Franc

Average age of vines: 24 years

Density of plantation: 6,667 and 7,692 vines per hectare

Average yields: 46.5 hectoliters per hectare

Elevage: Twelve to twenty-eight day fermentation and maceration, lots separate, depending upon the age of the vines. Eighteen months aging by rotation in vats and barrels (including six months in barrels with 50% new oak). Fining and filtration.

WINES PRODUCED

Château La Tour de Bessan: 84,700 bottles

No second wine is produced.

LA TOUR DE MONS

Classification: Cru Bourgeois Supérieur

Owner: Grand Cru Investissements

Address: 33460 Soussans

Telephone: 05 57 88 33 03; Telefax: 05 57 88 32 46

Visits: By appointment only

Contact: Dominique Laux

VINEYARDS

Surface area: 106.2 acres

Grape varietals: 49% Merlot, 37% Cabernet Sauvignon, 8% Petit Verdot, 6% Cabernet Franc

Average age of vines: 32 years

Density of plantation: 8,333 vines per hectare

Average yields: 58 hectoliters per hectare

Elevage: Four to five week fermentation (at 27–31°C, with two daily pumpings-over) and maceration in temperature-controlled stainless-steel tanks of small capacity (ranging from 30 hectoliters to 150 hectoliters). Twelve months aging in barrels with 30% new oak. Fining, no filtration.

WINES PRODUCED

Château La Tour de Mons: 150,000 bottles

Château Marquis de Mons: 100,000 bottles

Plateau of maturity: Within 5–14 years of the vintage

TROIS CHARDONS

Classification: Cru Artisan in 1939

Owner: Yves and Claude Chardon

Address: Issan, 33460 Cantenac

Telephone: 05 57 88 39 13 *or* 05 57 88 33 94; Telefax: 05 57 88 39 13

Visits: By appointment only

Contact: Yves or Claude Chardon

VINEYARDS

Surface area: 7 acres

Grape varietals: 50% Cabernet Sauvignon, 45% Merlot, 5% Petit Verdot

Average age of vines: 30 years

Density of plantation: 10,000 vines per hectare

Average yields: 51 hectoliters per hectare

Elevage: Twenty-five day fermentation and maceration in stainless-steel tanks. Twenty months aging in barrels with 15% new oak. Fining. No precision regarding filtration.

WINES PRODUCED
Château des Trois Chardons: 14,000 bottles

LES VIMIÈRES LE TRONQUÉRA

Classification: Cru Artisan

Owner: Jacques Boissenot

Address: 47, rue Principale, 33460 Lamarque

Telephone: 05 56 58 91 74; Telefax: 05 56 58 98 36

Visits: By appointment every day, 8 A.M.–noon and 3–6 P.M.

Contact: Jacques Boissenot

VINEYARDS

Surface area: 1.1 acres

Grape varietals: 100% Merlot

Average age of vines: 60 years

Density of plantation: 10,000 vines per hectare

Average yields: 46 hectoliters per hectare

Elevage: Three week fermentation (at 27–28°C) and maceration. Twenty months aging in new oak barrels. Fining, no filtration.

WINES PRODUCED

Château Les Vimières Le Tronquéra: 3,000 bottles

THE LESSER-KNOWN APPELLATIONS: MÉDOC, HAUT-MÉDOC, LISTRAC, AND MOULIS

There are hundreds of châteaux in the vast Médoc that produce notable wines of quality, character, and interest. They frequently offer fine value in good vintages and superb value in excellent vintages. A few of these estates make wine as good as (and in a few instances better than) some of the famous classified growths. However, most of these properties make solid, reliable wines, which, if never spectacularly exciting, are nevertheless sound and satisfying. In recent top Médoc vintages—1996 and 2000, for example—the wines from the best of these properties especially deserve seeking out. To enjoy Bordeaux on a regular basis, knowledge of these appellations' most serious estates is essential.

The Médoc appellation refers to a vast area that now encompasses more than 11,610 acres of vineyards. The appellation name has caused some confusion because the entire region north of the city of Bordeaux, bordered on the west by the Atlantic Ocean and to the east by the Gironde River, is geographically called "the Médoc." However, in terms of the Médoc appellation, the area corresponds to the very northern part of the Bordeaux viticultural area that has long been called the Bas-Médoc. Most of the wines entitled to the Médoc appellation come from the seven communes of Bégadan, St.-Yzans, Prignac, Ordonnac, St.-Christoly, Blaignan, and St.-Germain d'Esteuil.

Making any generalization about the wines of the Médoc appellation is impossible because of the huge variation in quality. However, in this remote, backwater region of Bordeaux, there has been a noticeable trend in the last several decades to plant more Merlot in the region's heavier, thicker, less porous soils. This has meant the wines possess more up-front charm and more fruit, as well as popular appeal. There also have been several classifications of the wines themselves, but for the purpose of this chapter, I have called everything "Cru Bourgeois" because the classifications—observed objectively—appear to be political creations rather than any valid attempt to classify the châteaux by their commitment to quality. For informational purposes, a new classification of the Crus Bourgeois was scheduled to be announced in June 2003.

The Haut-Médoc appellation also comprises just more than 10,375 acres of vineyards. It is a massive area, stretching from the industrial suburb north of Bordeaux called Blanquefort, north to where the Bas-Médoc begins. This region, which skirts around the Médoc appellation, produces wines from 15 communes, the most famous of which are St.-Seurin, St.-Laurent, Cussac, St.-Sauveur, Cissac, and Vertheuil. Many of the most notable estates are sandwiched in the eight mile corridor that separates the appellation of Margaux from that of St.-Julien. A few producers in the Haut-Médoc make wines that rival some of the classified growths, and as in the Médoc, the quality of many of the Crus Bourgeois has improved immensely during the last two decades.

Listrac is another obscure appellation of Bordeaux. It, like neighboring Moulis, sits well inland and covers just more than 1,730 acres of vines. The wines justifiably have a reputation for being tough textured, dry, and astringent, with little charm and fruit. These characteristics have undermined the success of Listrac wines in export markets. Today the wines are less rugged and tough than in the past, but they are still relatively tannic efforts that could use more charm. They appeal mostly to consumers with 19th-century tastes.

Moulis is, for me, the best of the lesser-known Bordeaux appellations. Perhaps this is because a handful of talented proprietors extract the highest quality possible from this small appellation of just more than 1,420 acres. The wines from Moulis are reasonably long-lived and, in top vintages, are strikingly rich, full-bodied, and powerful. There is a bevy of châteaux in Moulis, including the likes of Chasse-Spleen, Gressier Grand-Poujeaux, Maucaillou, and Poujeaux.

I have organized this chapter by listing the properties in alphabetical order.

LISTRAC—AN OVERVIEW

Location: This backwater appellation, southwest of St.-Julien, is 19 miles from Bordeaux's city center

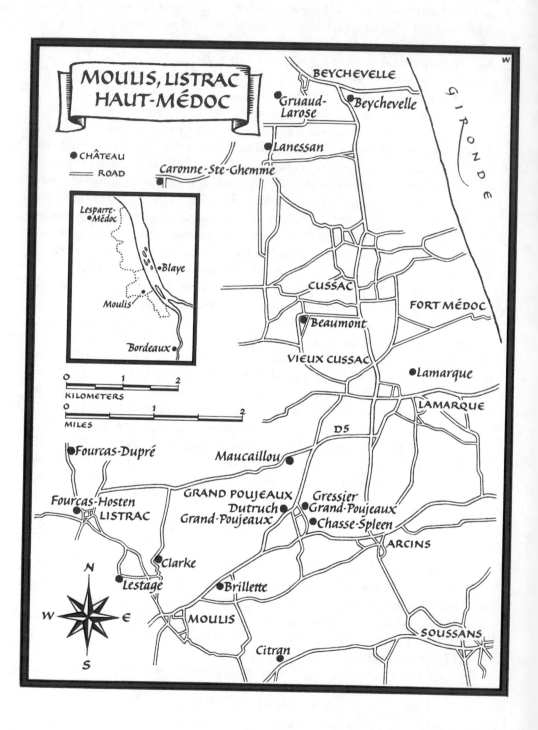

MOULIS, LISTRAC HAUT-MÉDOC

● CHÂTEAU
═══ ROAD

Lesparre-Médoc
Blaye
Moulis
Bordeaux

KILOMETERS
0   1   2

MILES
0   1   2

BEYCHEVELLE
Gruaud-Larose
Beychevelle
Lanessan
Caronne-Ste-Ghemme

GIRONDE

CUSSAC

Beaumont

VIEUX CUSSAC

FORT MÉDOC

Lamarque

LAMARQUE

D5

Fourcas-Dupré
Maucaillou

GRAND POUJEAUX
Fourcas-Hosten
LISTRAC
Dutruch
Grand-Poujeaux
Gressier
Grand-Poujeaux
Chasse-Spleen

ARCINS

Clarke
Lestage
Brillette

MOULIS

Citran

SOUSSANS

N
W   E
S

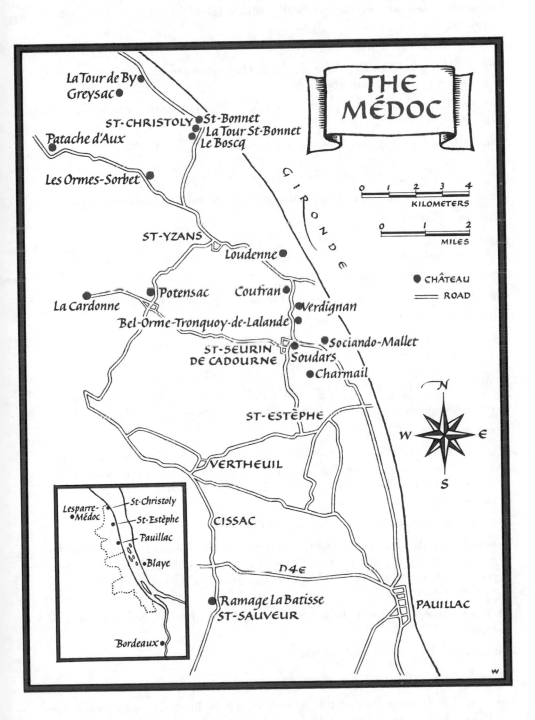

THE MÉDOC

La Tour de By ●
Greysac ●

ST-CHRISTOLY ● ● St-Bonnet
● La Tour St-Bonnet
Patache d'Aux ● ● Le Boscq

Les Ormes-Sorbet ●

GIRONDE

0 1 2 3 4
KILOMETERS

0 1 2
MILES

● CHÂTEAU
─── ROAD

ST-YZANS

● Loudenne

● Potensac ● Coufran
La Cardonne ●
Bel-Orme-Tronquoy-de-Lalande ● ● Verdignan

ST-SEURIN ● Sociando-Mallet
DE CADOURNE Soudars
● Charmail

N

ST-ESTÈPHE

W ⊕ E

VERTHEUIL

S

Lesparre- : ─ St-Christoly
● Médoc ─ St-Estèphe
─ Pauillac

● Blaye

CISSAC

D4E

● Ramage La Batisse
ST-SAUVEUR

Bordeaux ●

PAUILLAC

W

Acres under Vine: 1,729

Communes: There are several specifically defined parcels, but Listrac is the principal one

Average Annual Production: 300,000 cases

Classified Growths: None, but there are 29 Crus Bourgeois and 12 other estates, as well
as one cooperative boasting 60 members

Principal Grape Varieties: Cabernet Sauvignon, followed by Merlot, with lesser quantities of Cabernet Franc and Petit Verdot

Principal Soil Type: Clay, limestone, and gravel

MOULIS—AN OVERVIEW

Location: 18 miles northwest of Bordeaux, northwest of the Margaux appellation

Acres under Vine: 1,420

Communes: Moulis-en-Médoc and a handful of estates located in specific areas of
Arcins, Castelnau, Lamarque, and Listrac-Médoc

Average Annual Production: 285,000 cases

Classified Growths: None, but there are 31 Crus Bourgeois and 13 other estates

Principal Grape Varieties: Cabernet Sauvignon, followed by Merlot

Principal Soil Type: Limestone and sandy, gravelly, clay-like soils

HAUT-MÉDOC—AN OVERVIEW

Location: Just north of the city of Bordeaux, the lower two-thirds of the entire Médoc
peninsula encompasses what is known as the Haut-Médoc appellation

Acres under Vine: 10,375

Communes: From north to south, the communes include St.-Seurin-de-Cadourne, Vertheuil, Cissac, St.-Sauveur, St.-Laurent, Cussac-Fort-Médoc, Lamarque, Arcins,
Avensan, Castelnau-de-Médoc, Arsac, Macau, Le Pian-Médoc, Ludon, Parempuyre, Le Taillan, Blanquefort

Average Annual Production: In excess of 2 million cases

Classified Growths: Total of five, including third-growth Château La Lagune, fourth-
growth Château La Tour Carnet, and three fifth-growths, Château Belgrave, Camensac, and Cantemerle. There are 140 Crus Bourgeois and 116 other estates, as well
as five cooperatives.

Principal Grape Varieties: Cabernet Sauvignon, followed by Merlot and Cabernet
Franc

Principal Soil Type: Sandy, gravelly soil

MÉDOC—AN OVERVIEW

Location: The northern third of the peninsula north of Bordeaux is entitled to the
Médoc appellation; its southern boundary begins approximately 30 miles north of
the city of Bordeaux

Acres under Vine: 11,610

Communes: From north to south, they are Ste.-Vivien-de-Médoc, Jau-Dignac-et-
Loirac, Vensac, Valeyrac, Queyrac, Bégadan, St.-Christoly-Médoc, Civrac-en-
Médoc, Couquèques, Prignac, Gaillanen, Lesparre, Blaignan, St.-Yzans-de-Médoc,
Ordonnac, St.-Germain-d'Esteuil

Average Annual Production: 2,550,000 cases

Classified Growths: None, but there are 127 Crus Bourgeois and 113 other estates in
addition to five cooperatives boasting more than 400 members

Principal Grape Varieties: Cabernet Sauvignon dominates, followed by Merlot and, to
a lesser extent, Cabernet Franc, Malbec, and Petit Verdot

Principal Soil Type: There is far more diversity in the Médoc appellation than in Haut-
Médoc, with considerable gravel, limestone, and sandy soils

A CONSUMER'S CLASSIFICATION OF THE CHÂTEAUX
OF THE MÉDOC, HAUT-MÉDOC, LISTRAC, AND MOULIS

OUTSTANDING
Sociando-Mallet

EXCELLENT
Belle-Vue, Bernadotte Cambon La Pelouse, Charmail, Chasse-Spleen, Citran,
d'Escurac, Haut-Condissas, Karolus, Lanessan, Maucaillou, Potensac, Poujeaux,
La Tour Carnet, Tour Haut-Caussan, Tour du Haut-Moulin

VERY GOOD
Ducluzeau, Les Grands Chênes, Larose-Trintaudon, du Moulin Rouge,
Les Ormes Sorbet, Peyredon Lagravette, Larose-Trintaudon, Rollan de By,
La Tour St.-Bonnet

GOOD
Anthonic, Arnauld, Beaumont, Belgrave, Le Boscq, Branas Grand Poujeaux,
Brillette, Camensac, La Cardonne, Caronne-Ste.-Gemme, Cissac, Clarke,
Clément-Pichon, Coufran, Dutruch Grand Poujeaux, Fonréaud, Fourcas Dupré,
Fourcas Hosten, Fourcas Loubaney, Gressier Grand Poujeaux, Greysac, Lamarque,
Lestage, Liversan, Magnol, Malescasse, Mayne Lalande, Moulin à Vent,
Patache d'Aux, Plagnac, Sansarot Dupré, Ségur, Sémeillan-Mazeau, Sénéjac,
Soudars, La Tour de By, Verdignan, Vieux Robin

OTHER NOTABLE PROPERTIES
d'Agassac, Bel Orme Tronquoy de Lalande, Clos des Demoiselles,
Duplessis, Duplessis Fabré, Hanteillan, Loudenne, Moulis, Peyrabon,
Ramage La Bâtisse, Villegeorge

D'AGASSAC (HAUT-MÉDOC)

Classification: Cru Bourgeois

Location of vineyards: Ludon-Médoc

Owner: Groupama Assurances

Address: 15, rue du Château d'Agassac, 33290 Ludon-Médoc

Telephone: 05 57 88 15 47; Telefax: 05 57 88 17 61

E-mail: contact@agassac.com

Website: www.agassac.com

Visits: By appointment only Monday to Friday, 9 A.M.–noon and 2–5 P.M.

Contact: Emmanuelle Plougouln or Jean-Luc Zell

VINEYARDS

Surface area: 93.3 acres

Grape varietals: 50% Merlot, 47% Cabernet Sauvignon, 3% Cabernet Franc

Average age of vines: 25 years

Density of plantation: 6,650 vines per hectare

Average yields: 41 hectoliters per hectare

Elevage: Fermentation and three week maceration in temperature-controlled vats. Malolactics in barrel for part of the yield. Fifteen months aging on lees with regular stirring in barrels that are renewed by a third at each vintage. Fining, light filtration upon bottling.

WINES PRODUCED

Château d'Agassac: 165,000 bottles

Château Pomiès d'Agassac: 55,000 bottles

Plateau of maturity: Within 4–10 years of the vintage

This property, one of only two (the other is La Lagune) to be located on the sandy soils of Ludon, is in the southermost part of the Médoc.

The wines of d'Agassac have had a track record of inconsistency despite relatively low yields and a conservative and traditional vinification. Robust, frequently lacking charm and fruit, it is a wine to drink within the first decade of life. The best recent vintages have been 1990, 1989, and 1982, which is now beginning to tire. I found the 1988, 1986, and 1983 indifferent winemaking efforts.

Visitors to the region are well advised to make a detour and go inland from the famous D2 to visit d'Agassac, as it represents a superb example of a medieval fortified castle. The edifice, accessible via multiple tours, is one of the most impressive in the Bordeaux region.

ANTHONIC (MOULIS)

Classification: Cru Bourgeois

Owner: Jean-Baptiste Cordonnier

Address: 33480 Moulis

Telephone: 05 56 58 34 60; Telefax: 05 56 58 72 76

E-mail: chateau.anthonic@terre-net.fr

Visits: By appointment only

Contact: Jean-Baptiste Cordonnier

VINEYARDS

Surface area: 71.6 acres

Grape varietals: 50.1% Merlot, 47.8% Cabernet Sauvignon, 2.1% Petit Verdot

Average age of vines: 20 years

Density of plantation: 6,700–10,000 vines per hectare

Average yields: 56 hectoliters per hectare

Elevage: Fermentation with three daily pumpings-over and 21–25 day maceration in temperature-controlled stainless-steel vats. Eighteen months aging with 12 months in barrels that are renewed by a third at each vintage. Fining, filtration depending upon the vintage.

WINES PRODUCED

Château Anthonic: 150,000 bottles

Les Aigles d'Anthonic: 12,000 bottles

Plateau of maturity: Within 3–10 years of the vintage

I have had the occasion to taste numerous vintages of Anthonic, and I have been duly impressed by the stylish, elegant character of these wines. The vineyard is still young, but it is well placed near the more famous Château Clarke. Proprietor Cordonnier utilizes stainless-steel tanks and 30% new oak each year.

ARNAULD (HAUT-MÉDOC)

Classification: Cru Bourgeois

Location of vineyards: Arcins

Owner: SCEA Theil-Roggy

Address: 33460 Margaux

Telephone: 05 57 88 89 10; Telefax: 05 57 88 50 35

Visits: Monday to Saturday, 9 A.M.–noon and 2–6 P.M.

Contact: François Theil

VINEYARDS

Surface area: 59.3 acres

Grape varietals: 50% Cabernet Sauvignon, 50% Merlot

Average age of vines: 25 years

Density of plantation: 6,600 vines per hectare

Average yields: 56 hectoliters per hectare

Elevage: Fermentations and macerations last approximately four weeks in concrete and stainless-steel tanks. After malolactics in vats, wines are aged 12 months in oak barrels (40% new oak). They are fined and filtered.

WINES PRODUCED

Château Arnauld: 120,000 bottles

Le Comte d'Arnauld: 60,000 bottles

Plateau of maturity: Within 3–8 years of the vintage

North on the famous D2, just past the village of Arcins, is Château Arnauld. This property is owned by the Theil-Roggy family, who long ago established the reputation of Château Poujeaux in nearby Moulis for one of the most distinctive wines of the Médoc.

The wine produced at Arnauld is less structured, no doubt reflecting the elevated percentage of Merlot (50%) used in the blend. Consequently, Arnauld, for all the attractive, rich fruit, is a wine to be drunk in its first 7–8 years of life. It has been well made since the early 1980s, with the better Bordeaux vintages offering wines that are supple, exceptionally fruity, and with good color, yet limited long-term aging potential. Prices, however, remain reasonable for this tasty wine.

BEL ORME TRONQUOY DE LALANDE (HAUT-MÉDOC) ──

Classification: Cru Bourgeois

Location of vineyards: St.-Seurin-de-Cadourne

Owner: Jean-Michel Quié

Address: Chemin de la Hontête, 33180 St.-Seurin-de-Cadourne

Telephone: 05 56 59 38 29; Telefax: 05 56 59 72 83

Visits: By appointment only every day, 9 A.M.–noon and 1:30–6 P.M. at Château Croizet-Bages (Pauillac).

Contact: Martine Dausson (Telephone: 05 56 59 66 69)

VINEYARDS

Surface area: 74.1 acres

Grape varietals: 60% Merlot, 30% Cabernet Sauvignon, 10% Cabernet Franc

Average age of vines: 35 years

Density of plantation: 6,500 and 10,000 vines per hectare

Average yields: 55 hectoliters per hectare

Elevage: Three to four week fermentation and maceration in temperature-controlled stainless-steel vats. Six months aging in vats followed by 12 months aging in barrels (renewed by a fifth at each vintage) after assemblage. Fining, filtration upon bottling.

WINES PRODUCED

Château Bel Orme Tronquoy de Lalande: 160,000 bottles

No second wine is produced.

Plateau of maturity: Within 5–15 years of the vintage

I remember a profound 1945 Bel Orme Tronquoy de Lalande drunk on New Year's Day 1985. I also have good notes on the 1982 and, more recently, an opulent, chewy, full-bodied 1989 and 1990. But generally, my experience with this property, located in the very northern part of the Médoc near the village of St.-Seurin-de-Cadourne, has been uninspiring.

In the 1980s and 1990s the ancient style of winemaking, which combined immense power and excruciatingly painful tannin levels, gave way to a more supple style that often resulted in wines lacking concentration and character.

BELGRAVE (HAUT-MÉDOC)

Classification: Fifth growth in 1855

Location of vineyards: St.-Laurent du Médoc

Owner: SC du Château Belgrave

Farmed by: Dourthe Frères

Address: 33112 St.-Laurent du Médoc

Mailing address: c/o Dourthe, 35, rue de Bordeaux, 33290 Parempuyre

Telephone: 05 56 35 53 00; Telefax: 05 56 35 53 29

E-mail: contact@cvbg.com

Visits: By appointment only. No visits on weekends or at harvest time.

Contact: Marie-Hélène Inquimbert

VINEYARDS

Surface area: 135.9 acres

Grape varietals: 55% Cabernet Sauvignon, 32% Merlot, 12% Cabernet Franc, 1% Petit Verdot

Average age of vines: 25 years

Density of plantation: 6,500 and 9,000 vines per hectare

Average yields: 46 hectoliters per hectare

Elevage: Cold maceration. Fermentation with 3–5 daily pumpings-over and maceration in temperature-controlled vats. Part of yield undergoes malolactics in barrels. Fifteen to eighteen months aging in barrels (part of yield ages on lees) with 40–60% new oak. Fining if necessary, no filtration.

WINES PRODUCED

Château Belgrave: 230,000 bottles

Diane de Belgrave: 135,000 bottles

Plateau of maturity: Within 5–12 years of the vintage

When the huge firm of Dourthe (or C.V.B.G., as it is known in Bordeaux) acquired this property in 1980, it was one of the Médoc's most-neglected estates. The owners made significant investments, and the property is now a showpiece château that also provides lodging for Dourthe's best clients. Michel Rolland is the consulting oenologist, and there have been major replantings of the vineyard to lower the exceptionally high percentage of Merlot and increase the percentage of Cabernet Sauvignon.

There was little noticeable improvement in the wines, however, until Michel Rolland, the famed Libourne oenologist, was hired to provide counseling for the winemaking, too. Since that time, Belgrave has taken on more color, depth, and ripeness.

I still wonder whether or not Belgrave will improve to the point where it again can be considered the qualitative equivalent of a fifth growth. That said, the 2000 is the finest Belgrave I have ever tasted.

LE BOSCQ (MÉDOC)

Classification: Cru Bourgeois

Location of vineyards: St.-Christoly

Owner: Jean-Michel Lapalu

Address: 33340 St.-Christoly de Médoc

Mailing address: Domaines Lapalu, 1, rue du 19 mars, 33340 Bégadan

Telephone: 05 56 41 50 18; Telefax: 05 56 41 54 65

E-mail: info@domaines-lapalu.com

Website: www.domaines-lapalu.com

No visits

VINEYARDS

Surface area: 66.7 acres

Grape varietals: 70% Cabernet Sauvignon, 20% Merlot, 10% Cabernet Franc,

Average age of vines: 25 years

Density of plantation: 7,000 vines per hectare

Average yields: 57 hectoliters per hectare

Elevage: Four to five week fermentation and maceration in temperature-controlled stainless-steel and wooden vats. Twelve months aging in barrels that are renewed by 15–20% each year. Fining, light filtration.

WINES PRODUCED

Château Le Boscq Vieilles Vignes: 50,000 bottles

Château Le Boscq: 120,000 bottles

Plateau of maturity: Within 3–7 years of the vintage

This is a reliable Cru Bourgeois made from a vineyard sandwiched between the two excellent Cru Bourgeois vineyards of La Tour de By and La Tour St.-Bonnet near the village of St.-Christoly. The estate is managed by Jean-Michel Lapalu, who also owns the more-famous Patache d'Aux. The style sought at Le Boscq is one of unbridled, up-front, in-your-face fruit and suppleness. Consequently, this is a wine to drink in its first 3–7 years. The vineyard is harvested by mechanical machines, and the vinification and upbringing of the wine are designed to put a wine in the bottle that is drinkable immediately.

BRANAS GRAND POUJEAUX (MOULIS)

Classification: Cru Bourgeois

Owner: Justin Onclin

Address: Grand Poujeaux, 33480 Moulis en Médoc

Telephone: 05 56 58 08 62; Telefax: 05 56 58 08 62

Visits: By appointment only

Contact: Luc Pasqueron de Fommervault
(Telephone: 06 13 32 11 56)

VINEYARDS

Surface area: 13.6 acres

Grape varietals: 50% Merlot, 40% Cabernet Sauvignon, 10% Petit Verdot

Average age of vines: 28 years

Density of plantation: 7,000 vines per hectare

Average yields: 60 hectoliters per hectare

Elevage: Fermentation and maceration in temperature-controlled wooden vats. Malolactics and 15–18 months aging in barrels with 80% new oak. No fining, no filtration.

WINES PRODUCED

Château Branas Grand Poujeaux: 10,000 bottles

No second wine is produced.

Plateau of maturity: Within 6–15 years of the vintage

Note: This estate was recently sold to Justin Onclin (manager of Prieuré-Lichine) and Michel Rolland has been brought in as consulting oenologist.

This is one of the smallest and least known of the Moulis properties. However, in the vintages I have tasted, the wines have exhibited a great deal of full-bodied flavor concentration and the potential for 10–15 years of longevity.

BRILLETTE (MOULIS)

Classification: Cru Bourgeois

Location of vineyards: Moulis

Owner: Jean-Louis Flageul

Address: 33480 Moulis-en-Médoc

Telephone: 05 56 58 22 09; Telefax: 05 56 58 12 26

E-mail: secretariat@chateau-brillette.fr

Visits: Monday to Friday, 9 A.M.–noon and 2–5 P.M.

Contact: Yann Olivier

VINEYARDS

Surface area: 98.8 acres

Grape varietals: 48% Merlot, 40% Cabernet Sauvignon, 9% Cabernet Franc, 3% Petit Verdot

Average age of vines: 45 years

Density of plantation: 7,142 vines per hectare

Average yields: 45 hectoliters per hectare

Elevage: Fermentation and 3–4 week maceration in temperature-controlled stainless-steel vats. Twelve months aging in barrels that are renewed by a third each year. No fining, filtration.

WINES PRODUCED

Château Brillette: 150,000 bottles

Château Berthault Brillette: 50,000 bottles

Plateau of maturity: Within 7–10 years of the vintage

Just about one kilometer north of the town of Moulis-en-Médoc is the vast, 374-acre estate of Brillette, which has only 98.8 acres under vine. The wines of Brillette are not yet well known, but the quality of winemaking is high and the wines are made in a spicy, oaky, rich, fruity style that appeals to many tasters.

Brillette's vineyard, which remains relatively young—with the great majority of it planted in the 1960s and 1970s—is one entire parcel located on gravelly, sandy soil. Since the early 1980s the grapes have been harvested by machine. One-third new oak is used each year, which no doubt gives the wine a telltale smoky, toasty character.

This is a wine for those who admire a hefty dose of oak in their wines. It is best drunk within a decade of the vintage.

CAMENSAC (HAUT-MÉDOC)

Classification: Fifth Growth in 1855

Location of vineyards: St.-Laurent du Médoc

Owner: GFA du Château Camensac

Address: Route de St.-Julien, 33112 St.-Laurent du Médoc

Mailing address: BP 9, 33112 St.-Laurent du Médoc

Telephone: 05 56 59 41 69; Telefax: 05 56 59 41 73

E-mail: chateaucamensac@wanadoo.fr

Website: www.chateaucamensac.com

Visits: By appointment only

VINEYARDS

Surface area: 185.2 acres

Grape varietals: 60% Cabernet Sauvignon, 40% Merlot

Average age of vines: 35 years

Density of plantation: 10,000 vines per hectare

Average yields: 45 hectoliters per hectare

Elevage: Fermentation and 18–21 day maceration. Eighteen months aging in barrels with 35% new oak. Fining and filtration.

WINES PRODUCED

Château Camensac: 280,000 bottles

La Closerie de Camensac: 80,000 bottles

Plateau of maturity: Within 5–14 years of the vintage

Camensac is among the least known of the 1855 classified growths. No doubt its location, well inland and west of St.-Julien in the commune of St.-Laurent, explains in part the relative obscurity. In addition, the record of mediocrity, unchanged until the 1970s certainly added to a general lack of interest. However, things have changed for the better at Camensac.

The individuals responsible for the revival of Camensac are the Forner brothers, who purchased this estate in 1965 and set about the expensive task of replanting the vineyards and renovating the *chai* and winemaking facilities. The Forners are best known for the modern-style wines made at their winery called Marqués de Cacères located in the Rioja region of Spain.

Camensac's wines have lightened up in style and emphasize more suppleness and fruit. Even though Camensac is now making better wines, they are not representative of fifth-growth quality. They do have a certain St.-Julien-like personality, with good fruit, medium body, and enough tannin to warrant a decade of cellaring in good vintages. In my tastings during the late 1980s many bottles had a damp cardboard-like smell, but that problem was rectified in the 1990s. The wines possess good concentration and a straightforward, foursquare style.

LA CARDONNE (MÉDOC)

Classification: Cru Bourgeois

Location of vineyards: Blaignan and Ordonnac

Owner: Domaines CGR

Address: 33340 Blaignan

Mailing address: Les Domaines CGR, 40, rue Notre-Dame des Victoires, 75002 Paris

Telephone: 05 56 73 31 51 *or* 01 42 21 11 80;
Telefax: 05 56 73 31 52 *or* 01 42 21 11 85

E-mail: gcharloux@domaines-cgr.com

Website: www.chateau-griviere.com

Visits: Monday to Friday, 8:30 A.M.–12:30 P.M. and 1:30–5 P.M.

Contact: Annelis Bosq (Telephone: 05 56 73 31 51; Telefax: 05 56 73 31 52)

VINEYARDS

Surface area: 197.6 acres

Grape varietals: 50% Merlot, 45% Cabernet Sauvignon, 5% Cabernet Franc

Average age of vines: 20 years

Density of plantation: 7,500 vines per hectare

Average yields: 59 hectoliters per hectare

Elevage: Fermentation and maceration in temperature-controlled stainless-steel tanks. Twelve months aging in barrels that are renewed by half each year. Fining, filtration not systematic.

WINES PRODUCED

Château La Cardonne: 400,000 bottles

Cardus: Variable

Plateau of maturity: Within 3–6 years of the vintage

Immense optimism sprang forth in 1973 when the Rothschild family (owners of such famed Pauillacs as Lafite Rothschild and Duhart-Milon) acquired this property in Blaignan. It is a huge enterprise, and the wine is made in a relatively light, indifferent, yet commercially correct style. I have always maintained that the enormous yields and heavy reliance on filtration rob this wine of much concentration and character. It is a wine that must be drunk within 5–6 years of the vintage. Given the level of quality, it is overpriced, but I did think the fine 1990 was the best wine I have yet tasted from this estate. The Rothschilds sold the estate in 1990 to Gaëton Charloux, who has made significant improvements. In particular, the 2000 and 2001 were both noteworthy efforts.

CARONNE STE.-GEMME (HAUT-MÉDOC)

Classification: Cru Bourgeois

Location of vineyards: St.-Laurent du Médoc

Owner: Jean and François Nony

Address: 33112 St.-Laurent du Médoc

Mailing address: SCE des Vignobles Nony-Borie, 73, quai des Chartrons, 33000 Bordeaux

Telephone: 05 67 87 56 81; Telefax: 05 56 51 71 51

Visits: By appointment only

Contact: François Nony

VINEYARDS

Surface area: 111.2 acres

Grape varietals: 55% Cabernet Sauvignon, 43% Merlot, 2% Petit Verdot

Average age of vines: 30 years

Density of plantation: 10,000 vines per hectare

Average yields: 59 hectoliters per hectare

Elevage: Fermentation and 25–30 day maceration in stainless-steel and concrete vats. Twelve months aging in barrels with 25% new oak. Fining and filtration.

WINES PRODUCED

Château Caronne Ste.-Gemme: 266,000 bottles

Parc Rouge de Caronne: 64,000 bottles

Plateau of maturity: Within 4–8 years of the vintage

This estate in St.-Laurent receives little publicity. For both tourists and writers who desire to visit, the property is virtually impossible to find on the back roads of the Médoc. Moreover, the wine is hardly an inspiring gustatory pleasure. In my limited experience with this label, I have found the wine to be generally dark in color, with a good bouquet and a solid, rather rustic taste with no shortage of tannin.

CHARMAIL (HAUT-MÉDOC)

Classification: Cru Bourgeois

Location of vineyards: St.-Seurin-de-Cadourne

Owner: Olivier Sèze

Address: Charmail 33180 St.-Seurin-de-Cadourne

Telephone: 05 56 59 70 63; Telefax: 05 56 59 39 20

Visits: By appointment only Monday to Friday, 9 A.M.–noon and 1–5 P.M.

Contact: Olivier Sèze

VINEYARDS

Surface area: 55.6 acres

Grape varietals: 50% Merlot, 30% Cabernet Sauvignon, 20% Cabernet Franc

Average age of vines: 25 years

Density of plantation: 6,700–8,300 vines per hectare

Average yields: 50 hectoliters per hectare

Elevage: Fifteen day cold maceration at 5°C. Fermentation and three-week maceration in temperature-controlled vats. Twelve months aging in barrels with 35% new oak. No fining, no filtration.

WINES PRODUCED

Château Charmail: 105,000 bottles

Tours de Charmail: 40,000 bottles

Plateau of maturity: Within 5–15 years of the vintage

These singular wines, fermented under cold nitrogen (at 5°C for 15 days), are revolutionary in their fruit intensity and richness for Haut-Médoc. Made from a blend of 50% Merlot, 30% Cabernet Sauvignon, and 20% Cabernet Franc, from a property that does not possess one of the finest *terroirs*, these wines continue to amaze me with their inky intensity, purity, and richness. Given the high quality of recent efforts, this property is well on its way to meriting a position alongside the likes of Sociando-Mallet. The 2001, 2000, 1999, 1996, and 1995 are all brilliant wines.

CHASSE-SPLEEN (MOULIS)

Classification: Cru Bourgeois

Location of vineyards: Moulis

Owner: SA du Château Chasse-Spleen

Address: 33480 Moulis

Telephone: 05 56 58 02 37; Telefax: 05 56 58 05 70

Visits: By appointment only

Contact: Claire Villars

VINEYARDS

Surface area: 197.6 acres

Grape varietals: 70% Cabernet Sauvignon, 25% Merlot, 5% Petit Verdot

Average age of vines: 30 years

Density of plantation: 10,000 vines per hectare

Average yields: 50 hectoliters per hectare

Elevage: Fermentations and macerations last 3–4 weeks in temperature-controlled stainless-steel and concrete (epoxy-lined) tanks. Wines are aged 14–18 months in oak barrels that are renewed by 40% at each vintage. They are fined but remain unfiltered.

WINES PRODUCED

Château Chasse-Spleen: 280,000 bottles

L'Ermitage de Chasse-Spleen: 150,000 bottles

L'Oratoire de Chasse-Spleen: 150,000 bottles

Plateau of maturity: Within 5–18 years of the vintage

An outstanding property, Chasse-Spleen has consistently produced fine wine that for the last three decades has often been as good as a third growth. Even in poor and mediocre vintages, the wine is characterized by a very pronounced, deep ruby color, a bouquet of plummy ripeness, and rich, round, substantial flavors.

The great vintages for Chasse-Spleen, in which the wine can compare favorably with top Médoc classified growths, are 2000, 1990, 1989, 1986, 1985, 1978, 1975, 1970, and 1966.

Chasse-Spleen was owned by the Lahary family until 1976, when it was purchased by a syndicate whose controlling interest was the Société Bernard Taillan. The director of the firm, Jacques Merlaut, has made many intelligent decisions with respect to the administration of this château. The results have been increasingly inspired wines, with absolutely top-class wines in the late 1980s. The vineyard, consisting of four parcels, sits on primarily deep, gravelly soil and boasts many old vines; their average age is an impressive 35 years. This is a property that still adheres to very traditional practices. It is one of only a handful in the Médoc that does not filter after either the malolactic fermentation or before bottling. In fact, the only compromise toward modern-day technology is that part of the crop gets harvested by machine. Improvements under Claire Villars are obvious with the introduction of a second wine, the increased usage of 50% new oak casks for aging, and the impeccable attention to every detail. Prices have jumped as the world has begun to discover that Chasse-Spleen was undervalued.

CISSAC (HAUT-MÉDOC)

Classification: Cru Bourgeois

Location of vineyards: Cissac Médoc

Owner: Vialard family

Address: 33250 Cissac Médoc

Telephone: 05 56 59 58 13; Telefax: 05 56 59 55 67

E-mail: marie.vialard@chateau-cissac.com

Website: www.chateau-cissac.com

Visits: Monday to Friday, 9 A.M.–noon and 2–5 P.M.

Contact: Marie Vialard

VINEYARDS

Surface area: 123.5 acres

Grape varietals: 75% Cabernet Sauvignon, 20% Merlot, 5% Petit Verdot

Average age of vines: 30 years

Density of plantation: 7,200 vines per hectare

Average yields: 50 hectoliters per hectare

Elevage: Three to four week fermentation and maceration in temperature-controlled stainless-steel and wooden vats. Eighteen to twenty-four months aging in barrels with 30–40% new oak. Fining and filtration.

WINES PRODUCED

Château Cissac: 160,000 bottles

Reflets du Château Cissac: 120,000 bottles

Plateau of maturity: Within 7–15 years of the vintage

The proprietor of Cissac, the Vialard family, is one of Bordeaux's most dedicated. Consequently, their beloved Château Cissac produces one of the best Bourgeois wines of the central Médoc.

Located just north of the town of Cissac, this property produces approximately 18,000 cases of very traditional, full-bodied, tannic, interesting, darkly colored wine. Normally unyielding and reserved when young, Cissac begins to show its true character at around age six and can easily age and improve in the bottle for 10–15 years.

The wine of Cissac is especially popular in England and seems to have a growing following among American connoisseurs who have the patience to wait for its slow (for a Cru Bourgeois) but sure evolution.

CITRAN (HAUT-MÉDOC)

Classification: Cru Bourgeois

Location of vineyards: Avensan

Owner: SA Château Citran, Merlaut family

Address: Chemin de Citran, 33480 Avensan

Telephone: 05 56 58 21 01; Telefax: 05 57 88 84 60

E-mail: info@citran.com

Website: www.citran.com

Visits: By appointment only Monday to Friday, 9 A.M.–noon and 2–5 P.M.

Contact: Pascale Thiel

VINEYARDS

Surface area: 222.3 acres

Grape varietals: 58% Cabernet Sauvignon, 42% Merlot

Average age of vines: 28 years

Density of plantation: 6,600 vines per hectare

Average yields: 43 hectoliters per hectare

Elevage: Twenty-four day fermentation and maceration in temperature-controlled stainless-steel vats. Twelve to fourteen months aging in barrels with 40% new oak. Fining and filtration.

WINES PRODUCED

Château Citran: 300,000 bottles

Moulins de Citran: 200,000 bottles

Plateau of maturity: Within 6–14 years of the vintage

In the ten years (1987–1997) following the acquisition of Citran by a Japanese syndicate, the quality of this estate's wines soared. In spite of their success, Citran was sold to the Société Bernard Taillan, run by the dynamic Jacques Merlaut. The renovation of the cellars, the commitment of the new owners, an increased percentage of new oak, a stricter selection process (and subsequent second wine), and excellent overall administration have resulted in glorious wines over recent years. If there is any criticism, it would be that the elevated use of new oak gives the wine such a dramatic, smoky, even charred character that those who admire Claret for delicacy and subtlety might be put off by its flamboyant boldness.

Nevertheless, the new vintages should age well for up to a decade and are considerably more interesting and pleasurable than anything Citran previously produced. It should also be noted that prices have edged up to take into account the new designer bottle with its striking label that has replaced the old, traditional, somber Château Citran package. This is one of the finest Cru Bourgeois estate, often making wines of classified growth quality. Vintages such as 2000, 1996, 1990, and 1989 are topflight.

CLARKE (LISTRAC)

Classification: Cru Bourgeois

Location of vineyards: Listrac

Owner: Baron Benjamin de Rothschild

Address: 33480 Listrac-Médoc

Telephone: 05 56 58 38 00; Telefax: 05 56 58 26 46

Visits: By appointment and for professionals of the wine trade only

Contact: Hélène Combabessouse

VINEYARDS

Surface area: 133.4 acres

Grape varietals: 70% Merlot, 30% Cabernet Sauvignon

Average age of vines: 22–25 years

Density of plantation: 6,600 vines per hectare

Average yields: 49 hectoliters per hectare

Elevage: Cold maceration. Fermentation and 25–30 day maceration in temperature-controlled stainless-steel vats with pumpings-over, *pigéages,* and micro-oxygenation. Malolactics and 16 months aging in barrels with 60–80% new oak. Fining and filtration depend upon the vintage.

WINES PRODUCED

Château Clarke: 250,000 bottles

Les Grandes des Domaines Edmond de Rothschild: Variable (Haut-Médoc)

Plateau of maturity: Within 3–7 years of the vintage

One of the most remarkable developments in the Médoc has been the complete restoration and rejuvenation of the old vineyard of Château Clarke. The property boasts a history dating to 1750, and it took the considerable resources of a wealthy member of the famous Rothschild family—the late Baron Edmond de Rothschild—to accomplish the resurrection. In 1973 work began, and in the following five years the area under vine increased dramatically to 136 acres, large enough to have the potential to produce more than 20,000 cases of wine. The first wines released, a 1978 and 1979, were given a great deal of hoopla from the wine press, but in actuality they were light, medium-bodied examples that clearly tasted like the product of a young vineyard. However, the commitment to high quality, the financial resources, and the management are all present, so as the vineyard matures, Château Clarke should become one of the more reliable wines made in Listrac.

Château Clarke also produces a delicious dry rosé and a kosher *cuvée* (made according to strict Jewish requirement) of its red wine.

CLÉMENT-PICHON (HAUT-MÉDOC)

Classification: Cru Bourgeois

Location of vineyards: Parempuyre

Owner: Clément Fayat

Address: 33290 Parempuyre

Telephone: 05 56 35 23 79; Telefax: 05 56 35 85 23

E-mail: info@vignobles.fayat-group.com

Visits: By appointment Monday to Friday, 9 A.M.–noon and 2–6 P.M.

Contact: Sandrine Aucher

VINEYARDS

Surface area: 61.8 acres

Grape varietals: 50% Merlot, 40% Cabernet Sauvignon, 10% Cabernet Franc

Average age of vines: 20 years

Density of plantation: 6,500 vines per hectare

Average yields: 45 hectoliters per hectare

Elevage: Cold maceration. Fermentation with 3–4 daily pumpings-over and 25–30 day maceration in temperature-controlled stainless-steel vats. Part of yield undergoes malolactics in barrels. Eighteen months aging in barrels with 50–70% new oak. Fining and filtration.

WINES PRODUCED

Château Clément-Pichon: 110,000 bottles

La Motte de Clément-Pichon: 20,000 bottles

Plateau of maturity: Within 3–8 years of the vintage

This beautiful château, located just to the north of Bordeaux near the sprawling industrial suburb of Parempuyre, is owned by one of the most driven proprietors of the region, Clément Fayat, an industrialist who also has been responsible for the renaissance of the famed St.-Emilion vineyard La Dominique. Fayat totally renovated the château, which formerly was known as Château de Parempuyre, and originally renamed it Château Pichon. However, that caused legal problems with Madame de Lencquesaing, who felt the name could be confused with her Château Pichon Longueville Comtesse de Lalande. The name was then changed to Château Clément-Pichon.

The huge baroque and gothic château was constructed at the end of the 19th century and is now inhabited by the Fayat family, who purchased this domaine in 1976. They totally replanted the vineyards, which, consequently, are extremely young. The Fayats were shrewd enough to ask their oenologist at La Dominique, the famed Libournais Michel Rolland, to look after the winemaking at Clément-Pichon. He has performed miracles with a vineyard this young. No doubt Rolland realized the limitations of making a true *vin de garde* and to date has emphasized wines with an up-front, exceptionally fruity, supple style that are meant to be consumed young.

COUFRAN (HAUT-MÉDOC)

Classification: Cru Bourgeois

Location of vineyards: St.-Seurin-de-Cadourne

Owner: Jean Miailhe group

Address: 33180 St.-Seurin-de-Cadourne

Telephone: 05 56 59 31 02; Telefax: 05 56 59 32 35

E-mail: contact@chateau-coufran.com

Visits: By appointment only. No visits in August or at harvest time.

Contact: Eric Miailhe (Telephone: 05 56 59 72 39)

VINEYARDS

Surface area: 187.7 acres

Grape varietals: 85% Merlot, 15% Cabernet Sauvignon

Average age of vines: 35–40 years

Density of plantation: 8,000 vines per hectare

Average yields: 54 hectoliters per hectare

Elevage: Fermentation and 30 day maceration in temperature-controlled stainless-steel vats. Eight to ten months aging in barrels that are renewed by a quarter at each vintage. Fining and filtration.

WINES PRODUCED

Château Coufran: 500,000 bottles

Château La Rose Maréchale: 50,000 bottles

Plateau of maturity: Within 3–12 years of the vintage

The large vineyard of Coufran is situated three miles north of the boundary of St.-Estèphe, contiguous to Route D2 after passing through the village of St.-Seurin-de-Cadourne. Since 1924 the property has been in the Miailhe family, a prominent name in the promotion of quality among Crus Bourgeois of Bordeaux, and is now run by them.

The most distinctive aspect of Coufran is the high percentage of Merlot used in the blend, which the proprietors have decided succeeds well in the heavier, thicker soils common to this part of the Médoc. This has led some people to rashly conclude that the wine is drinkable upon release. I have not found that to be the case. In top vintages, Coufran is often supple and fruity in cask but can go into a dumb, tannic stage in the bottle. The wine is a good Médoc, but the yields are extremely high, and again, one wonders whether the property's use of machine harvesters has any effect on the ultimate quality.

Over the last few years, 2000, 1996, 1995, and 1990 stand out for quality.

DUCLUZEAU (LISTRAC)

Classification: Cru Bourgeois

Location of vineyards: Listrac

Owner: GFA du Château Ducluzeau

Mailing address: c/o J.E. Borie S.A. 33480 Listrac

Telephone: 05 56 73 16 73; Telefax: 05 56 59 27 37

E-mail: je-borie@je-borie-sa.com

No visits

VINEYARDS

Surface area: 12.8 acres

Grape varietals: 90% Merlot, 10% Cabernet Sauvignon

Average age of vines: 35 years

Density of plantation: 10,000 vines per hectare

Average yields: 50 hectoliters per hectare

Elevage: Three to four week fermentation and maceration in temperature-controlled vats. Twelve months aging in barrels with 25% new oak. Fining, filtration depends upon the vintage.

WINES PRODUCED

Château Ducluzeau: 35,000 bottles

No second wine is produced.

Plateau of maturity: Within 3–10 years of the vintage

This property, owned by Monique Borie, the wife of the deceased proprietor of Ducru-Beaucaillou, Haut-Batailley, and Grand-Puy-Lacoste, has, to my knowledge, the highest percentage of Merlot of any wine of the Médoc. The result is an extremely supple yet deliciously round, seductive wine with a great deal of charm and elegance. This wine has been estate bottled since 1976.

DUPLESSIS (MOULIS)

Classification: Cru Bourgeois

Location of vineyards: Moulis

Owner: Marie-Laure Lurton-Roux

Address: 2036 Chalet, 33480 Moulis-en-Médoc

Telephone: 05 56 58 22 01; Telefax: 05 56 58 15 10

E-mail: lgcr@wanadoo.fr

Visits: By appointment only

Contact: Viviane Grouffier

VINEYARDS

Surface area: 47.6 acres

Grape varietals: 60% Merlot, 26% Cabernet Sauvignon, 12% Cabernet Franc, 2% Petit Verdot

Average age of vines: 25 years

Density of plantation: 6,667 and 10,000 vines per hectare

Average yields: 52 hectoliters per hectare

Elevage: Fermentation and 15–28 day maceration in temperature-controlled vats. Eighteen months aging, with six months in vats and eight to twelve months in barrel with 20–25% new oak. Fining and filtration.

WINES PRODUCED

Château Duplessis: 74,800 bottles

Château La Licorne de Duplessis: 32,700 bottles

Plateau of maturity: Within 4–10 years of the vintage

This property, sometimes called Duplessis-Hauchecorne (after one of the former owners), now belongs to the ubiquitous family of Lucien Lurton. The wine is typical of an older-styled Moulis—coarse, robust, and lacking charm and fruit.

DUPLESSIS FABRÉ (MOULIS)

Classification: Cru Bourgeois

Location of vineyards: Moulis

Owner: Philippe Dourthe

Address: 33480 Moulis-en-Médoc

Mailing address: c/o SARL Maucaillou,
33480 Moulis-en-Médoc

Telephone: 05 56 58 01 23; Telefax: 05 56 58 00 88

Visits: Every day, 10 A.M.–noon and 2–6 P.M.

Contact: Philippe Dourthe

VINEYARDS

Surface area: 6.2 acres

Grape varietals: 55% Merlot, 45% Cabernet Sauvignon

Average age of vines: 20 years

Density of plantation: 8,300 vines per hectare

Average yields: 57 hectoliters per hectare

Elevage: Cold maceration. Fermentation at low temperatures and 20 day maceration in
temperature-controlled stainless-steel tanks. Fifteen to eighteen months aging in barrels
with 30% new oak. Fining and filtration.

WINES PRODUCED

Château Duplessis Fabré: 18,000 bottles

No second wine is produced.

Plateau of maturity: Within 5–10 years of the vintage

In 1989 this property was sold by the Pagès family to Philippe Dourthe of Château
Maucaillou. There is plenty of potential for a more interesting wine to be produced,
which should happen given the quality of this estate's bigger sibling, Maucaillou.

DUTRUCH GRAND POUJEAUX (MOULIS)

Classification: Cru Bourgeois

Location of vineyards: Moulis

Owner: François and Jean-Baptiste Cordonnier

Address: 33480 Moulis-en-Médoc

Telephone: 05 56 58 02 55; Telefax: 05 56 58 06 22

E-mail: chateau-dutruch@aquinet.net

Visits: Monday to Friday, 9:30 A.M.–noon and 2–5 P.M.

Contact: François and Jean-Baptiste Cordonnier

VINEYARDS

Surface area: 69.2 acres

Grape varietals: 50% Merlot, 45% Cabernet Sauvignon, 5% Petit Verdot

Average age of vines: 29 years

Density of plantation: 8,500 and 10,000 vines per hectare

Average yields: 52 hectoliters per hectare

Elevage: Fermentation (21–25°C) and 21–25 day maceration in temperature-controlled vats. Twelve months aging in barrels that are renewed by a third at each vintage. Fining, no filtration.

WINES PRODUCED

Château Dutruch Grand Poujeaux: 129,000 bottles

Château La Bernède Grand Poujeaux: 40,000 bottles

Plateau of maturity: Within 6–12 years of the vintage

Dutruch Grand Poujeaux, like so many wines of Moulis, often lack a great deal of charm when young. Unlike some neighbors, this is one wine that can have the requisite concentration and depth to stand up to the tannin. After 5–7 years, I have often been pleased by just how well this wine turns out. Part of the reason for the excellent concentration is not only the respectable age of the vines, but the fact that much of this vineyard is planted by the ancient system of 10,000 vines per hectare, as opposed to the more conventional 6,600 vines per hectare. This, of course, is believed to create more stress, resulting in more concentrated grapes.

This is an underrated, impressively run property that merits more attention.

FONRÉAUD (LISTRAC)

Classification: Cru Bourgeois

Location of vineyards: Listrac-Médoc and Moulis

Owner: Chanfreau family

Address: 33480 Listrac-Médoc

Telephone: 05 56 58 02 43; Telefax: 05 56 58 04 33

E-mail: vignobles.chanfreau@wanadoo.fr

Website: www.chateau-fonreaud.com

Visits: Monday to Friday, 9 A.M.–noon and 2–5 P.M.

Contact: Jean Chanfreau

VINEYARDS

Surface area: 79 acres

Grape varietals: 52% Cabernet Sauvignon, 45% Merlot, 3% Petit Verdot

Average age of vines: 30 years

Density of plantation: 6,666 vines per hectare

Average yields: 45 hectoliters per hectare

Elevage: Two to three day cold maceration at 12°C. Fermentation and 25–30 day maceration in temperature-controlled concrete vats. Twelve months aging on fine lees in barrels that are renewed by a third at each vintage. Fining depends upon the vintage, no filtration.

WINES PRODUCED

Château Fonréaud: 140,000 bottles

Les Tourelles de Château Fonréaud: 60,000 bottles

Plateau of maturity: Within 5–7 years of the vintage

This impressively symmetrical white château, with a dominating center turret and spire, sits on the left-hand side of Route D1 as one leaves the tiny village of Bouqueyran in the direction of Lesparre. Since 1982 the property has been owned by the Chanfreau family, who also control the nearby Château Lestage.

The style emphasized is one of soft, fruity, immediately drinkable wines that are limited to 6–7 years of aging ability. The high percentage of Merlot, as well as the owner's decision to age the wine for six months in oak casks and six months in *cuvées*, results in a soft, round wine with immediate appeal. The best recent vintages have been 2000, 1996, and 1995.

FOURCAS DUPRÉ (LISTRAC)

Classification: Cru Bourgeois

Location of vineyards: Listrac-Médoc

Owner: SC du Château Fourcas Dupré

Address: Le Fourcas, 33480 Listrac-Médoc

Telephone: 05 56 58 01 07; Telefax: 05 56 58 02 27

E-mail: chateau-fourcas-dupre@wanadoo.fr

Website: www.chateaufourcasdupre.com

Visits: Monday to Friday, 8 A.M.–noon and 2–5 P.M.

Contact: Patrice Pagès (director) or Gilles Bererot (cellar master)

VINEYARDS

Surface area: 113.6 acres

Grape varietals: 44% Cabernet Sauvignon, 44% Merlot, 10% Cabernet Franc, 2% Petit Verdot

Average age of vines: 25+ years

Density of plantation: 8,500 vines per hectare

Average yields: 54 hectoliters per hectare

Elevage: Fermentation with daily pumpings-over and 2–4 week maceration in temperature-controlled vats. Twelve months aging in barrels that are renewed by a third each year. Fining, no filtration.

WINES PRODUCED

Château Fourcas Dupré: 240,000–250,000 bottles

Château Bellevue Laffont: 50,000–60,000 bottles

Plateau of maturity: Within 5–10 years of the vintage

FOURCAS HOSTEN (LISTRAC)

Classification: Cru Bourgeois

Location of vineyards: Listrac

Owner: SC du Château Fourcas Hosten

Address: 33480 Listrac-Médoc

Telephone: 05 56 58 01 15; Telefax: 05 56 58 06 73

E-mail: fourcas@club.inter.net

Website: www.chateaufourcashosten.com

Visits: Preferably by appointment Monday to Friday, 9 A.M.–noon and 2–5 P.M.

Contact: Annette Monge

VINEYARDS

Surface area: 115.3 acres

Grape varietals: 45% Cabernet Sauvignon, 45% Merlot, 10% Cabernet Franc

Average age of vines: 25 years

Density of plantation: 8,500 vines per hectare

Average yields: 54 hectoliters per hectare

Elevage: Three to five week fermentation and maceration in temperature-controlled vats with regular pumpings-over. Twelve months aging in barrels that are renewed by a third at each vintage. Fining, no filtration.

WINES PRODUCED

Château Fourcas Hosten: 260,000 bottles

Les Cèdres d'Hosten: 60,000 bottles

Plateau of maturity: Within 5–10 years of the vintage

The style of Fourcas Hosten still tends toward hard, tannic, robust, coarse wines, with impressive color and body but often excessive tannins. It is a serious but charmless style.

FOURCAS LOUBANEY (LISTRAC)

Classification: Cru Bourgeois

Location of vineyards: Listrac

Owner: François Marret

Address: Moulin de Laborde, 33480 Listrac

Telephone: 05 56 58 03 83; Telefax: 05 56 58 06 30

Visits: Every day, 2–6 P.M.

Contact: Yann Ollivier

VINEYARDS

Surface area: 30.9 acres

Grape varietals: 55% Cabernet Sauvignon, 35% Merlot, 10% Petit Verdot

Average age of vines: 35 years

Density of plantation: 6,700 and 10,000 vines per hectare

Average yields: 45 hectoliters per hectare

Elevage: Fermentations and macerations last four weeks in stainless-steel tanks equipped with a cooling system. Pumpings-over are done twice a day. Wines are aged 15–18 months after malolactics in oak barrels that are renewed by a third at each vintage. They are fined but not filtered.

WINES PRODUCED

Château Fourcas Loubaney: 80,000 bottles

No second wine is produced.

Plateau of maturity: Within 5–12 years of the vintage

This is one of the best wines of the Listrac appellation. Unfortunately, the modest production is rarely seen except by a small group of avid Bordeaux aficionados. Although I have not tasted a fully mature vintage of Fourcas Loubaney, the vintages I have tasted have been impressive.

GRESSIER GRAND POUJEAUX (MOULIS)

Classification: Cru Bourgeois

Location of vineyards: Moulis

Owner: Bertrand de Marcellus

Address: 33480 Moulis

Telephone: 05 56 58 02 51

Visits: By appointment only

Contact: Bertrand de Marcellus

VINEYARDS

Surface area: 54.3 acres

Grape varietals: 60% Cabernet Sauvignon, 25% Merlot, 10% Cabernet Franc, 5% Petit Verdot

Average age of vines: 27 years

Density of plantation: 8,500 vines per hectare

Average yields: 50 hectoliters per hectare

Elevage: Manual harvest; 25 day fermentations and macerations in stainless-steel vats; aging for 15 months in barrel (of which nine months are spent in small new oak barrels). Fining and filtration.

WINES PRODUCED

Château Gressier Grand Poujeaux: 150,000 bottles

No second wine is produced.

Plateau of maturity: Within 7–20 years of the vintage

GREYSAC (MÉDOC)

Classification: Cru Bourgeois

Location of vineyards: Bégadan

Owner: Groupe EXOR

Address: By, 33340 Bégadan

Telephone: 05 56 73 26 56; Telefax: 05 56 73 26 58

Visits: By appointment only

Contact: Philippe Dambrine

VINEYARDS

Surface area: 54.3 acres

Grape varietals: 45% Merlot, 40% Cabernet Sauvignon, 10% Cabernet Franc, 5% Petit Verdot

Average age of vines: 25 years

Density of plantation: 7,600 vines per hectare

Average yields: 55 hectoliters per hectare

Elevage: Fermentations (27–32°C) last 4–5 days in temperature-controlled stainless-steel vats. Wines undergo malolactics in tanks and are transferred to oak barrels (20% of which are new) for 12 months aging. They are fined but not filtered.

WINES PRODUCED

Château Greysac: 360,000 bottles

Domaine de By: 120,000 bottles

Plateau of maturity: Within 5–12 years of the vintage

Greysac has become one of the most popular Cru Bourgeois wines in the United States. High quality and the dynamic personality and marketing ability of the now-deceased, gregarious proprietor—Baron François de Gunzburg—were totally responsible for this wine's acceptance by Americans (who are normally so classification conscious when it comes to Bordeaux wines).

The style of wine at Greysac is one that I have always found very elegant, smooth, and medium bodied, with a complex bouquet filled with currant fruit and a true, mineral, soil-like aroma. Never an aggressive or overly tannic wine, Greysac is usually fully mature by its sixth or seventh year and keeps well for up to 12 years.

HANTEILLAN (HAUT-MÉDOC)

Classification: Cru Bourgeois

Location of vineyards: Cissac

Owner: Catherine Blasco

Address: 12, route d'Hanteillan, 33250 Cissac Médoc

Telephone: 05 56 59 35 31; Telefax: 05 56 59 31 51

E-mail: chateau-hanteillan@wanadoo.fr

Website: www.chateau-hanteillan.com

Visits: Monday to Thursday, 9 A.M.–noon and 2–5:30 P.M.; Fridays, 9 A.M.–noon.

Contact: Marylène Brossard

VINEYARDS

Surface area: 202.5 acres

Grape varietals: 50% Merlot, 40% Cabernet Sauvignon, 6% Cabernet Franc, 4% Petit Verdot

Average age of vines: 15 years

Density of plantation: 6,500 and 8,300 vines per hectare

Average yields: 55 hectoliters per hectare

Elevage: Fermentation and 2–4 week maceration in temperature-controlled stainless-steel vats with micro-oxygenation. Eighteen months aging with half the yield in vats and half the yield in barrels that are renewed by half at each vintage. No fining, filtration.

WINES PRODUCED

Château Hanteillan: 300,000–350,000 bottles

Château Laborde: 200,000 bottles

Plateau of maturity: Within 4–8 years of the vintage

This is a highly promoted Cru Bourgeois that I have always found to be lacking in fruit and charm. It is classically made with a high-tech *cuverie* designed to produce wines of quality. Nevertheless, the wine comes across as relatively tannic, austere, and compact.

LAMARQUE (HAUT-MÉDOC)

Classification: Cru Bourgeois

Location of vineyards: Lamarque

Owner: Gromand d'Evry family

Address: 33460 Lamarque

Telephone: 05 56 58 90 03; Telefax: 05 56 58 93 43

E-mail: chdelamarq@aol.com

Visits: Preferably by appointment Monday to Friday,
9 A.M.–noon and 2–5 P.M.

Contact: Francine Prévot

VINEYARDS

Surface area: 86.5 acres

Grape varietals: 41% Merlot, 37% Cabernet Sauvignon, 18% Cabernet Franc, 4% Petit
Verdot

Average age of vines: 30 years

Density of plantation: 6,500 vines per hectare

Average yields: 40–50 hectoliters per hectare

Elevage: Twenty-eight day fermentation and maceration in temperature-controlled
concrete tanks. Malolactics in vats for drip wines and in barrels for press wines. Sixteen to
eighteen months aging in barrels with 35–50% new oak. Fining, no filtration.

WINES PRODUCED

Château de Lamarque: 145,000–170,000 bottles

D de Lamarque: 30,000–50,000 bottles

Plateau of maturity: Within 4–7 years of the vintage

One of the outstanding medieval fortress castles in the Bordeaux region, Lamarque,
named after the town of the same name, sits just off the main Route du Vin (D2) of the
Médoc directly on the road to the ferry boat that traverses the Gironde to Blaye.

Lamarque is a typically good, middle-weight, central Médoc wine. It seems to have
a touch of the St.-Julien elegance mixed with round, supple, soft, ripe fruity flavors.
The owners, the Gromand family, make the wine with great care. Lamarque should be
consumed within 7–8 years of the vintage. Prices remain among the more reasonable
for a Cru Bourgeois.

LANESSAN (HAUT-MÉDOC)

Classification: Cru Bourgeois

Location of vineyards: Cussac-Fort-Médoc

Owner: GFA des Domaines Bouteiller

Address: 33460 Cussac-Fort-Médoc

Telephone: 05 56 58 94 80; Telefax: 05 56 58 93 10

Visits: Every day, 9 A.M.–noon and 2–6 P.M.

Contact: Hubert Bouteiller

VINEYARDS

Surface area: 98.8 acres

Grape varietals: 75% Cabernet Sauvignon, 20% Merlot, 5% Cabernet Franc and Petit Verdot

Average age of vines: 25 years

Density of plantation: 10,000 vines per hectare

Average yields: 55 hectoliters per hectare

Elevage: Fermentations and macerations last 12–18 days in temperature-controlled concrete tanks. After malolactics in vats, wines are transferred to oak barrels, 5% of which are new, for 18–30 months aging, depending upon the vintage. They are fined and filtered.

WINES PRODUCED

Château Lanessan: 250,000–300,000 bottles

No second wine is produced.

Plateau of maturity: Within 7–18 years of the vintage

Lanessan can be one of the outstanding wines of the Haut-Médoc appellation. The wine could probably be given serious consideration for fifth-growth status should any reclassification of the wines of the Médoc take place.

Lanessan, which is located in Cussac immediately south of the commune of St.-Julien, opposite the big vineyard of Gruaud Larose, makes intensely flavored wines, with deep color, a robust, large-scaled frame, and chewy texture. If they can be criticized for lacking finesse, they more than compensate for that weakness with rich, gutsy, black currant flavors.

The nearly 99 acres, which are being augmented each year with new plantings, produce in excess of 20,000 cases of wine. The property is owned and managed by the Bouteiller family. Lanessan ages extremely well, as attested by a delightful but tired 1920 I shared with a friend in 1983. Of more recent vintages, the top successes include the 2001, 2000, 1996, 1995, 1990, 1989, 1988, 1986, 1982, 1978, 1975, and 1970. The wines are powerful and individualized, somewhat similar in style and character to the fifth-growth Pauillac Lynch-Bages.

I have noted above that Lanessan can be inconsistent. Part of the spottiness of

Lanessan's performance (the only criticism one could possibly make) is probably due to the château's insistence on using primarily old barrels for aging the wine. Perhaps a small percentage of new barrels each year might prove beneficial for such a robust wine. For visitors to the region, this lovely château, which has been owned by the same family since 1890, is now a museum displaying numerous carriages and an assortment of harnesses. It is open to the public.

LAROSE-TRINTAUDON (HAUT-MÉDOC)

Classification: Cru Bourgeois

Location of vineyards: St.-Laurent du Médoc and Pauillac

Owner: AGF Allianz Group

Address: Route de Pauillac, 33112 St.-Laurent du Médoc

Telephone: 05 56 59 41 72; Telefax: 05 56 59 93 22

E-mail: info@trintaudon.com

Website: www.trintaudon.com

Visits: By appointment only Monday to Friday, 9:30 A.M.–5 P.M.

Contact: Matthias von Campe

VINEYARDS

Surface area: 424.8 acres

Grape varietals: 65% Cabernet Sauvignon, 35% Merlot

Average age of vines: 32 years

Density of plantation: 6,600 vines per hectare

Average yields: 55 hectoliters per hectare

Elevage: Prolonged fermentation and maceration (21–28 days) in temperature-controlled stainless-steel vats. Twelve months aging in barrels with 25% new oak. Fining and filtration.

WINES PRODUCED

Château Larose-Trintaudon: 900,000 bottles

La Rose St.-Laurent/Les Hauts de Trintaudon: 50,000–100,000 bottles

Plateau of maturity: Within 4–7 years of the vintage

For years, the largest vineyard in the Médoc produced a straightforward, supple, correct wine of no great distinction, but since the late 1990s the wines have become richer and more interesting. Excellent efforts were produced in 2001, 2000, and 1999.

LESTAGE (LISTRAC)

Classification: Cru Bourgeois

Location of vineyards: Listrac-Médoc and Moulis

Owner: Chanfreau family

Address: 33480 Listrac-Médoc

Telephone: 05 56 58 02 43; Telefax: 05 56 58 04 33

E-mail: vignobles.chanfreau@wanadoo.fr

Website: www.chateau-fonreaud.com

Visits: Monday to Friday, 9 A.M.–noon and 2–5 P.M.

Contact: Jean Chanfreau

VINEYARDS

Surface area: 103.7 acres

Grape varietals: 52% Merlot, 44% Cabernet Sauvignon, 2% Cabernet Franc, 2% Petit Verdot

Average age of vines: 30 years

Density of plantation: 6,666 vines per hectare

Average yields: 55 hectoliters per hectare

Elevage: Two to three day cold maceration at 12°C. Fermentation and 25–30 day maceration in temperature-controlled concrete vats. Twelve months aging on fine lees in barrels that are renewed by a third at each vintage. Fining depends upon the vintage, no filtration.

WINES PRODUCED

Château Lestage: 190,000 bottles

La Dame de Coeur du Château Lestage: 50,000 bottles

Plateau of maturity: Within 3–8 years of the vintage

I have fond memories of many vintages of Lestage. They are supple, straightforward, richly fruity efforts, cleanly made and tasty. The entire production was aged in large vats until 1985, when the proprietor began employing small oak barrels. That decision has resulted in wines with more structure and character. This is never a profound wine and there is a tendency to produce too much wine per hectare, but this large vineyard in Listrac, with a charming three-story, 19th-century château, easily fulfills the needs of consumers looking for wines that offer immediate drinkability at a fair price.

LIVERSAN (HAUT-MÉDOC)

Classification: Cru Bourgeois

Location of vineyards: St.-Sauveur

Owner: Jean-Michel Lapalu

Address: 1, route de Farpiqueyre,
33250 St.-Sauveur de Médoc

Mailing address: 1, rue du 19 mars, 33340 Bégadan

Telephone: 05 56 41 50 18; Telefax: 05 56 41 54 65

E-mail: info@domaines-lapalu.com

Website: www.domaines-lapalu.com

Visits: By appointment Monday to Friday, 9 A.M.–noon and 2–4 P.M.

Contact: Domaines Lapalu

VINEYARDS

Surface area: 96.3 acres

Grape varietals: 50% Merlot, 49% Cabernet Sauvignon, 1% Cabernet Franc

Average age of vines: 25 years

Density of plantation: 7,000 vines per hectare

Average yields: 56 hectoliters per hectare

Elevage: Four to five week fermentation and maceration in temperature-controlled stainless-steel and wooden vats. Twelve to fifteen months aging in barrels that are renewed by 25–30% each year. Fining, light filtration.

WINES PRODUCED

Château Liversan: 250,000 bottles

Les Charmes de Liversan: 40,000 bottles

Plateau of maturity: Within 4–10 years of the vintage

Many Bordeaux observers have long considered the excellently placed vineyard of Liversan, which sits between the city of Pauillac and the hamlet of St.-Sauveur, to have the potential to produce wines of classified-growth quality. The construction of a new winery, increased use of new oak barrels, and conservative yields have resulted in a series of good to very good wines.

The style produced at Liversan aims for wines with a deep color, fine extract, soft tannins and grip, concentration, and length.

LOUDENNE (MÉDOC)

Classification: Cru Bourgeois

Location of vineyards: St.-Yzans-de-Médoc

Owner: Marie-Claude and Jean-Paul Lafragette

Address: 33340 St.-Yzans-de-Médoc

Telephone: 05 56 73 17 80; Telefax: 05 56 09 02 87

E-mail: chateau-loudenne@wanadoo.fr

Visits: By appointment only

Contact: Florence Lafragette

VINEYARDS

Surface area: 86.5 acres

Grape varietals: 55% Merlot, 40% Cabernet Sauvignon, 4% Cabernet Franc, 1% Petit Verdot

Average age of vines: 27 years

Density of plantation: 5,000–6,500 vines per hectare

Average yields: 55 hectoliters per hectare

Elevage: Fermentation and three week maceration in temperature-controlled stainless-steel and concrete tanks. Part of yield undergoes malolactics in barrel. Twelve months aging with 25–30% new oak. Fining and filtration.

WINES PRODUCED

Château Loudenne: Variable

Pavillon de Loudenne: Variable

Plateau of maturity: Within 3–6 years of the vintage

Note: From 35 acres of vineyards, Loudenne also produces 45,000 bottles of a 62% Sauvignon Blanc/38% Sémillon dry white Bordeaux. This wine is aged 6–8 months on lees in barrels with 25–30% new oak. It is fined and filtered before bottling. The château also commercializes a rosé called Rosé de Loudenne.

The lovely pink Château Loudenne's vineyard, planted on sandy, stony soils, is located at the very northern end of the Médoc, near St.-Yzans. While I have enjoyed the fruity, straightforward white wine, made from a blend of 50% Sauvignon and 50% Sémillon, I find the red wine extremely light. Although it is correctly made, it lacks complexity, richness, and staying power.

Given the attention to detail exhibited at Loudenne, I have often wondered whether or not this area of the Médoc is capable of producing wines of staying power. Improvements in quality in the mid-1990s augur well for more complete and interesting red wines.

MAGNOL (HAUT-MÉDOC)

Classification: Cru Bourgeois

Location of vineyards: Blanquefort

Owner: Barton & Guestier

Address: 87, rue du Dehez, 33290 Blanquefort

Mailing address: BP 30, 33292 Blanquefort Cedex

Telephone: 05 56 95 48 00; Telefax: 05 56 95 48 01

E-mail: barton-guestier@diageo.com

Website: www.barton-guestier.com

No visits

VINEYARDS

Surface area: 42 acres

Grape varietals: 50% Cabernet Sauvignon, 50% Merlot

Average age of vines: 18 years

Density of plantation: 8,500 vines per hectare

Average yields: 56 hectoliters per hectare

Elevage: Fermentation and three week maceration in temperature-controlled stainless-steel vats with micro-oxygenation of lees. Twelve months aging in barrels with 25% new oak. Fining and filtration.

WINES PRODUCED

Château Magnol: 100,000 bottles

No second wine is produced.

Plateau of maturity: Within 3–5 years of the vintage

I have been impressed with the soft, fruity, easy to like, and easy to drink wines of Château Magnol, a property owned by the huge firm of Barton & Guestier. The vineyard is located just north of the city of Bordeaux, east of the sprawling suburb of Blanquefort. The wine is extremely well made in a modern, commercial style, and there is no doubting its seductive, forward charms. Magnol is not a wine to lay away in your cellar; it should be drunk early.

MALESCASSE (HAUT-MÉDOC)

Classification: Cru Bourgeois

Location of vineyards: Lamarque

Owner: Alcatel-Alsthom

Address: 6, route du Moulin Rose, 33460 Lamarque

Mailing address: 6, route du Moulin Rose, BP 16, 33460 Lamarque

Telephone: 05 56 73 15 20; Telefax: 05 56 59 64 72

E-mail: malescasse@free.fr

Website: www.chateau-malescasse.com

Visits: By appointment Monday to Friday,
10 A.M.–noon and 2–4 P.M.

Contact: François Peyran

VINEYARDS

Surface area: 91.4 acres

Grape varietals: 55% Cabernet Sauvignon, 35% Merlot, 10% Cabernet Franc

Average age of vines: 23 years

Density of plantation: 6,500 vines per hectare

Average yields: 55 hectoliters per hectare

Elevage: Fermentation (31–33°C) and 3–4 week maceration in temperature-controlled vats. Malolactics and 18 months aging in barrels with 35% new oak. Fining and light filtration.

WINES PRODUCED

Château Malescasse: 160,000 bottles

La Closerie de Malescasse: 70,000 bottles

Plateau of maturity: Within 4–7 years of the vintage

Malescasse is a well-situated vineyard located just to the north of the village of Arcins and south of Lamarque. The vineyard was extensively replanted in the early 1970s, and the vines are now reaching maturity.

This is a seriously run Cru Bourgeois, and since the early 1980s the wines have been richly fruity, medium bodied, and ideal for drinking between the ages of 4 and 8.

MAUCAILLOU (MOULIS)

Classification: Cru Bourgeois

Location of vineyards: Moulis and Listrac

Owner: Philippe Dourthe

Address: Quartier de la Game, 33480 Moulis-en-Médoc

Telephone: 05 56 58 01 23; Telefax: 05 56 58 00 88

E-mail: chateau@maucaillou.com

Website: www.chateau-maucaillou.com

Visits: Every day, 11 A.M.–noon and 2–6 P.M.

Contact: Michelins Larrue or Cécile Verger

VINEYARDS

Surface area: 148.2 acres

Grape varietals: 56% Cabernet Sauvignon, 35% Merlot, 7% Petit Verdot, 2% Cabernet Franc

Average age of vines: 25 years

Density of plantation: 8,800 vines per hectare

Average yields: 55 hectoliters per hectare

Elevage: Cold maceration. Fermentation at low temperature, 20 day maceration in temperature-controlled stainless-steel vats. Fifteen to eighteen months aging in barrels with 50% new oak. Fining and filtration.

WINES PRODUCED

Château Maucaillou: 400,000 bottles

Cap de Haut de Maucaillou: 100,000 bottles

Plateau of maturity: Within 4–12 years of the vintage

Maucaillou has consistently represented one of the best wine values in the Médoc. The wine is impeccably made by the robust and exuberant Philippe Dourthe. There is little to criticize at this estate. Maucaillou is a deeply colored wine with a splendid ripe concentration of fruit, good body, soft tannins, and enough grip and extract to mature gracefully over a 10–12 year period. Since the early 1980s the wines have been aged in as much as 50% new oak casks, with the remainder in two-year-old casks purchased from prominent classified-growth châteaux.

It is not easy to make wines so rich and fat that they can be drunk young while maintaining their ability to age for up to a decade. Maucaillou has clearly succeeded in taming the soil of Moulis, which can render hard, tannic wine. They have produced exceptionally elegant, highly satisfying wines that are among only a handful of underpriced Bordeauxs. For the adventurous travelers who enjoy the back roads of the Médoc, I highly recommend a visit to Château Maucaillou, where there is an attractive winemaking museum. In addition, visitors have the opportunity to taste the new wine.

MAYNE LALANDE (LISTRAC)

Classification: Cru Bourgeois

Location of vineyards: Listrac

Owner: Bernard Lartigue

Address: 33480 Listrac-Médoc

Telephone: 05 56 58 27 63; Telefax: 05 56 58 22 41

E-mail: blartigue@terre-net.fr

Website: www.isasite.net/mayne.lalande

Visits: Monday to Friday, 8 A.M.–noon and 2–6 P.M.

Contact: Bernard Lartigue

VINEYARDS

Surface area: 49.4 acres

Grape varietals: 45% Cabernet Sauvignon, 45% Merlot, 5% Cabernet Franc, 5% Petit Verdot

Average age of vines: 25 years

Density of plantation: 7,000–9,000 vines per hectare

Average yields: 40–50 hectoliters per hectare

Elevage: Four to five week fermentation and maceration. Twelve to sixteen months aging in barrels with 30–50% new oak. No fining, no filtration.

WINES PRODUCED

Château Mayne Lalande: 50,000 bottles

Château Malbec Lartigue: 50,000 bottles

Plateau of maturity: Within 5–15 years of the vintage

This little-known Listrac property produces one of the better wines of the appellation. The key to their success is low yields and the dedication of proprietor Bernard Lartigue. For now, this wine remains known only to insiders and some of Bordeaux's most innovative restaurateurs, such as Jean-Pierre Xiradakis, who sells this wine at his well-known restaurant, La Tupina. The price has yet to take off, and therefore Mayne Lalande appears to be undervalued.

DU MOULIN ROUGE (HAUT-MÉDOC)

Classification: Cru Bourgeois

Location of vineyards: Cussac-Fort-Médoc

Owner: Pelon and Ribeiro families

Address: 18, rue de Costes, 33460 Cussac-Fort-Médoc

Telephone: 05 56 58 91 13; Telefax: 05 56 58 93 68

E-mail: laurence.ribeiro@free.fr

Visits: Every day, 9 A.M.–noon and 1:30–6 P.M.;
Sundays by appointment.

Contact: Laurence Ribeiro

VINEYARDS

Surface area: 44.5 acres

Grape varietals: 50% Merlot, 40% Cabernet Sauvignon, 10% Cabernet Franc

Average age of vines: 35–40 years

Density of plantation: 6,000–7,000 vines per hectare

Average yields: 50 hectoliters per hectare

Elevage: Cold maceration. Twenty-one to twenty-eight day fermentation and maceration in temperature-controlled stainless-steel tanks. Twelve months aging in barrels that are renewed by a third at each vintage. Fining and filtration.

WINES PRODUCED

Château du Moulin Rouge: 100,000 bottles

L'Ecuyer du Moulin Rouge: 20,000 bottles

Plateau of maturity: Within 5–10 years of the vintage

Du Moulin Rouge is one of my favorite Crus Bourgeois. The highly morcellated vineyard (there must be at least six separate parcels) is located north of the village of Cussac-Fort-Médoc, just south of the appellation of St.-Julien. Not surprisingly, the wine often has the character of a good St.-Julien. It is always deep in color and since the 1980s has been rich, fleshy, full-bodied, and somewhat reminiscent of such wines as Hortevie and Terrey-Gros-Cailloux. Of course, du Moulin Rouge is significantly less expensive, since it is entitled to only the Haut-Médoc appellation.

This is one of the more solid, chunky, fleshy Crus Bourgeois, and while it may not have great finesse, it does offer considerable richness, muscle, and character.

MOULIN À VENT (MOULIS)

Classification: Cru Bourgeois

Location of vineyards: Moulis and Listrac

Owner: Dominique and Marie-Hélène Hessel

Address: Bouqueyran, 33480 Moulis-en-Médoc

Telephone: 05 56 58 15 79; Telefax: 05 56 58 39 89

E-mail: hessel@moulin-a-vent.com

Website: www.moulin-a-vent.com

Visits: Monday to Friday, 9 A.M.–noon and 2–6 P.M. By appointment on weekends.

Contact: Dominique Hessel

VINEYARDS

Surface area: 61.8 acres

Grape varietals: 55% Merlot, 43% Cabernet Sauvignon, 2% Cabernet Franc

Average age of vines: 25 years

Density of plantation: 6,666 vines per hectare

Average yields: 47 hectoliters per hectare

Elevage: Four week fermentation and maceration in temperature-controlled stainless-steel vats with daily pumpings-over the first week. Twenty-two months aging in barrels and vats (by rotation) with 12 months in barrels (25% new oak). No fining, light filtration upon bottling.

WINES PRODUCED

Château Moulin à Vent: 140,000 bottles

Château Moulin de St.-Vincent: 20,000 bottles

Plateau of maturity: Within 5–10 years of the vintage

This property continues to produce an older style of Moulis—dense, tannic, and requiring several years in the bottle to soften and evolve. The property uses a significant amount of press wine, resulting in a dark-colored, forceful, powerful style of Moulis that seems to be best when the grapes are fully ripe.

Overall, this is a property that has made considerable improvement in the quality of its wines since Dominique Hessel began to manage the estate's winemaking.

MOULIS (MOULIS)

Classification: Cru Bourgeois

Location of vineyards: Moulis

Owner: Alain Daricarrère

Address: 33480 Moulis

Telephone: 05 57 68 40 66

Visits: By appointment only

Contact: Alain Daricarrère

VINEYARDS

Surface area: 61.8 acres

Grape varietals: 50% Cabernet Sauvignon, 50% Merlot

Average age of vines: 25 years

Density of plantation: 6,700 vines per hectare

Average yields: 50 hectoliters per hectare

Elevage: Fermentations and macerations last three weeks in stainless-steel tanks. Temperature control is manual. The wines undergo malolactics in vats. They are then aged 12 months, by rotation, in vats (75% of the yield) and oak barrels (25% of the yield). Very little new oak is utilized. The wines are fined and filtered.

WINES PRODUCED

Château Moulis: 120,000 bottles

No second wine is produced.

Plateau of maturity: Within 4–7 years of the vintage

Most vintages from Moulis have been deep in color, but compact, relatively austere, straightforward wines without the complexity and charm one expects. Nevertheless, this is a well-situated vineyard, and the approach to the wine's vinification is traditional.

LES ORMES SORBET (MÉDOC)

Classification: Cru Bourgeois

Location of vineyards: Couquèques

Owner: Jean Boivert

Address: 33340 Couquèques

Telephone: 05 56 73 30 30; Telefax: 05 57 73 30 31

E-mail: ormes-sorbet@wanadoo.fr

Website: www.ormes-sorbet.com

Visits: Monday to Friday, 9 A.M.–noon and 2–6 P.M.

Contact: Jean Boivert

VINEYARDS

Surface area: 51.9 acres

Grape varietals: 60% Cabernet Sauvignon, 35% Merlot, 5% Carmenère and Petit Verdot

Average age of vines: 25 years

Density of plantation: 8,333 vines per hectare

Average yields: 55 hectoliters per hectare

Elevage: Three to four week fermentation and maceration in stainless-steel and epoxy-lined vats. Eighteen months aging in barrels with 50% new oak. Fining, no filtration.

WINES PRODUCED

Château Les Ormes Sorbet: 100,000 bottles

Château de Conques: 20,000 bottles

Plateau of maturity: Within 6–12 years of the vintage

The current proprietor, Jean Boivert (who took over this estate in 1970), has produced one of the best wines in the northern Médoc since the mid-1980s. Boivert is the eighth generation of his family (since 1730) to run this vineyard near the sleepy village of Couquèques. The dense planting and Jean Boivert's decision in the 1970s to increase the percentage of Cabernet Sauvignon have paid off with an excellent string of good vintages since 1982. The style that has emerged at Les Ormes Sorbet is one of deep color and a pronounced toasty vanilla oakiness from excellent Troncalais barrels. They are wines that have the potential for a decade of longevity.

Recently, the 2000, 1996, 1995, and 1990 were all well-made wines. This is an up-and-coming domaine in the northern Médoc.

PATACHE D'AUX (MÉDOC)

Classification: Cru Bourgeois

Location of vineyards: Bégadan

Owner: Jean-Michel Lapalu

Address: 1, rue du 19 mars, 33340 Bégadan

Telephone: 05 56 41 50 18; Telefax: 05 56 41 54 65

E-mail: info@domaines-lapalu.com

Website: www.domaines-lapalu.com

Visits: Weekdays, 9 A.M.–noon and 2–5 P.M. (until 4 P.M. on Fridays).

Contact: Aline Buiatti

VINEYARDS

Surface area: 106.2 acres

Grape varietals: 60% Cabernet Sauvignon, 30% Merlot, 7% Cabernet Franc, 3% Petit Verdot

Average age of vines: 35 years

Density of plantation: 8,500 vines per hectare

Average yields: 53 hectoliters per hectare

Elevage: Four to five week fermentation and maceration in temperature-controlled stainless-steel and wooden vats. Twelve to fifteen months aging in barrels that are renewed by a quarter each year. Fining, light filtration.

WINES PRODUCED

Château Patache d'Aux: 260,000 bottles

Le Relais de Patache d'Aux: 40,000 bottles

Plateau of maturity: Within 5–8 years of the vintage

Patache d'Aux produces wines that have an almost California-like herbaceous, juicy, black currant fruitiness, supple texture, and easy drinkability. In years where the Cabernet does not attain full ripeness, the wine has a tendency to be too vegetal. However, in ripe vintages, such as 2000, 1996, 1995, 1990, 1989, 1986, and 1982, this can be an immensely impressive Cru Bourgeois for drinking in the first 5–8 years of its life. It is often jammy and opulent, and rarely elegant, but for those consumers looking for a well-made, reasonably priced Cru Bourgeois that does not require deferred gratification, this is a worthy choice.

PEYREDON LAGRAVETTE (LISTRAC)

Classification: Cru Bourgeois

Location of vineyards: Listrac and Moulis

Owner: Paul Hostein

Address: 2062 Médrac-Est, 33480 Listrac-Médoc

Telephone: 05 56 58 05 55; Telefax: 05 56 58 05 50

Website: www.peyredon.lagravette.com

Visits: October 10th to February 28: Monday to Saturday, 9 A.M.–6 P.M. March 1 to September 20: Monday to Saturday, 9 A.M.–12:30 P.M. and 2–7 P.M. Closed between September 20 and October 10.

Contact: Paul Hostein

VINEYARDS

Surface area: 17.3 acres

Grape varietals: 65% Cabernet Sauvignon, 30% Merlot, 5% Petit Verdot

Average age of vines: 25 years

Density of plantation: 9,090 vines per hectare

Average yields: 48 hectoliters per hectare

Elevage: Fermentation and 21–25 day maceration in temperature-controlled vats with regular pumpings-over. Eighteen months aging in barrels with 30% new oak. Fining, no filtration.

WINES PRODUCED

Château Peyredon Lagravette: 44,000 bottles

No second wine is produced.

Plateau of maturity: Within 6–15 years of the vintage

This excellent Listrac is not well-known, but if vintages such as 1995, 1990, 1989, 1986, 1983, and 1982 are any indication, this may be one of the best-kept secrets of Listrac. The tiny vineyard sits to the east of most of the other Listrac properties, adjacent to the appellation of Moulis. Two of the best Moulis vineyards, Chasse-Spleen and Maucaillou, are closer to Peyredon Lagravette than most of the other Listrac vineyards. The wine is very traditionally made with an extremely long *cuvaison*. The result is an intensely concentrated, full-bodied, ripe, impressively built wine for drinking over 10–15 years.

The property itself is quite old, tracing its origin to 1546. The current proprietor, Paul Hostein, eschews the mechanical harvesters so frequently employed in this part of the Médoc, as well as all of the antibotrytis treatments that have become in vogue among the properties to fight mold and rot. Hostein prefers an organic method of winemaking. Additionally, his dense vineyard plantations of more than 9,000 vines per hectare represent many more vines per hectare than most Bordeaux vineyards.

I have yet to taste a wine from Peyredon Lagravette that has been fully mature, so this would appear to be one of the longer-lived Listracs, with a character more closely associated with Moulis than Listrac. More attention needs to be paid to Château Peyredon Lagravette.

PLAGNAC (MÉDOC)

Classification: Cru Bourgeois

Location of vineyards: Bégadan

Owner: Domaines Cordier

Address: Bégadan, 33340 Lesparre

Mailing address: SAS Château Plagnac, 109, rue Achard, BP 154, 33042 Bordeaux Cedex

Telephone: 05 56 11 29 00; Telefax: 05 56 11 29 01

E-mail: contact@cordier-wines.com

Visits: By appointment and for professionals of the wine trade only

Contact: Domaines Cordier (Telephone: 05 56 41 54 34; Telefax: 05 56 41 59 02)

VINEYARDS

Surface area: 74.1 acres

Grape varietals: 65% Cabernet Sauvignon, 35% Merlot

Average age of vines: 25 years

Density of plantation: 5,000 vines per hectare

Average yields: 60 hectoliters per hectare

Elevage: Fermentation and 21 day maceration in temperature-controlled stainless-steel tanks. Twelve months aging in barrels with 25% new oak. Fining and filtration.

WINES PRODUCED

Château Plagnac: 230,000 bottles

Les Tours de Plagnac: Variable

Plateau of maturity: Within 2–6 years of the vintage

Looking for a reasonably priced, soft, fruity, easy to drink, straightforward Bordeaux? This wine, managed and looked after by the exceptionally talented Cordier team, is the type of Bordeaux that pleases the crowd and satisfies both the palate and purse. It is meant to provide charm and immediate drinkability. Drink this wine within its first 5–6 years of life.

POTENSAC (MÉDOC)

Classification: Cru Bourgeois

Location of vineyards: Ordonnac

Owner: Delon family

Address: 33340 Ordonnac

Mailing address: c/o Château Léoville Las Cases, 33250 St. Julien Beychevelle

Telephone: 05 56 73 25 26; Telefax: 05 56 59 18 33

Visits: By appointment only

Contact: Château Léoville Las Cases

VINEYARDS

Surface area: 140.8 acres

Grape varietals: 60% Cabernet Sauvignon, 25% Merlot, 15% Cabernet Franc

Average age of vines: 30 years

Density of plantation: 8,000 vines per hectare

Average yields: 55 hectoliters per hectare

Elevage: Fifteen to eighteen day fermentation and maceration in temperature-controlled stainless-steel and concrete tanks. Twelve to sixteen months aging in barrels with 10–15% new oak. Fining, no filtration.

WINES PRODUCED

Château Potensac: Production not disclosed

Goudy La Cardonne, Gallais Bellevue, Lassalle: Production not disclosed

Plateau of maturity: Within 4–12 years of the vintage

Since the mid-1970s, Potensac, under the inspired and strong leadership of the late Michel Delon and (since 2000) his son, Jean-Hubert (the proprietor of the famed Léoville Las Cases in St.-Julien and Nenin in Pomerol), has been making wines that are clearly of classified-growth quality. This large vineyard, situated near St.-Yzans, produces wines so far above the level of quality found in this region of the Médoc that they are a tribute to the efforts of the Delons and the *maître de chai*, Michel Rolland.

The wine has a rich, cassis and berry-like character, excellent structure, a wonderful purity and balance characteristic of the Delons' wines, and surprising aging potential. This area of the northern Médoc is rarely capable of producing wines of this quality, but the Delons consistently manage to do that at Potensac.

Delon also owns another group of vineyards that make up the secondary labels for Potensac. A few years ago Potensac was somewhat of an insiders' wine, but that is no longer the case. Nevertheless, this is such a high-quality wine that any serious Bordeaux enthusiast would be making a mistake if he or she did not try it. Vintages to search out include 2001, 2000, 1998, 1996, and 1995.

POUJEAUX (MOULIS)

Classification: Cru Bourgeois

Location of vineyards: Grand-Poujeaux in Moulis

Owner: Theil family

Address: 33480 Moulis-en-Médoc

Telephone: 05 56 58 02 96: Telefax: 05 56 58 01 25

E-mail: chateau-poujeaux@wanadoo.fr

Website: www.chateau-poujeaux.com

Visits: Preferably by appointment. October 1 to May 31: Monday to Friday, 9 A.M.–noon and 2–5 P.M. June 1 to September 31: Monday to Saturday, 9 A.M.–noon and 2–6 P.M.

Contact: Christophe Labenne

VINEYARDS

Surface area: 135.9 acres

Grape varietals: 50% Cabernet Sauvignon, 40% Merlot, 5% Cabernet Franc, 5% Petit Verdot

Average age of vines: 35 years

Density of plantation: 10,000 vines per hectare

Average yields: 50 hectoliters per hectare

Elevage: Four week fermentation and maceration in temperature-controlled stainless-steel, wooden, and concrete tanks. Twelve months aging in barrels that are renewed by half at each vintage. Fining, no filtration.

WINES PRODUCED

Château Poujeaux: 350,000 bottles

Château La Salle de Poujeaux: 50,000 bottles

Plateau of maturity: Within 6–20 years of the vintage

While there is a considerable rivalry between Poujeaux, Chasse-Spleen, and Maucaillou, most observers agree that year in and year out, these are the three best wines of

Moulis. Poujeaux is one of the oldest estates, dating back to 1544, when the vineyards and surrounding area were called La Salle de Poujeaux. The property is now run by the Theil brothers, whose family acquired Poujeaux in 1920.

Poujeaux's style is typical of the wines of Moulis. It is dark ruby in color, tannic, sometimes astringent and hard when young, and therefore usually needs a minimum of 6–8 years to soften and mature. It is a slower-developing wine than neighbor Chasse-Spleen, yet it has the potential to be one of the longest lived. A splendid bottle of 1928 served to me in 1985 and again in 1988 proved just how magnificent, as well as age-worthy, Poujeaux can be. Poujeaux is clearly a wine that deserves to be ranked as a fifth growth in any new classification of the Bordeaux hierarchy. Recently, Poujeaux has produced superb wines in 2001, 2000, and one of the best wines of the vintage in 1997.

RAMAGE LA BATISSE (HAUT-MÉDOC)

Classification: Cru Bourgeois

Location of vineyards: St.-Sauveur

Owner: SCI Ch. Ramage La Batisse

Address: 33250 St.-Sauveur

Mailing address: c/o Gironde et Gascogne, Belcier, 33350 les Salles de Castillon

Telephone: 05 57 56 40 40; Telefax: 05 57 40 64 25

E-mail: gironde-et-gascogne@wanadoo.fr

Visits: By appointment Monday to Friday

Contact: Jean-Paul Thilbaut (Telephone: 05 56 59 57 24; Telefax: 05 56 59 54 14)

VINEYARDS

Surface area: 210 acres (165.5 in production)

Grape varietals: 50% Cabernet Sauvignon, 50% Merlot

Average age of vines: 30 years

Density of plantation: 8,350 vines per hectare

Average yields: 55 hectoliters per hectare

Elevage: Fermentation and 18 day maceration (28–30°C) in temperature-controlled concrete tanks. Malolactics in oak for 30% of the yield. Fifteen months aging in barrels that are renewed by a third at each vintage.

WINES PRODUCED

Château Ramage La Batisse: 380,000 bottles

Clos de Ramage: 130,000 bottles

Plateau of maturity: Within 5–8 years of the vintage

The vineyards of Ramage La Batisse are located in St.-Sauveur, a small wine-producing region situated inland and west from the small town of Pauillac. The vineyard has been completely replanted since 1961. The wines from the late 1970s, particularly the 1979 and 1978, were quite impressive—supple, oaky, richly fruity wines of style and character. Performances since have been surprisingly irregular.

This property is well placed, and it has the potential to turn out top wines, as it did in the 1970s. Most vintages of Ramage La Batisse are best drunk between 5–10 years of age.

SARANSOT-DUPRÉ (LISTRAC)

Classification: Cru Bourgeois

Location of vineyards: Listrac

Owner: Yves Raymond

Address: 33480 Listrac-Médoc

Telephone: 05 56 58 03 02; Telefax: 05 56 58 07 64

E-mail: yraymond@wanadoo.fr

Visits: By appointment only

Contact: Yves Raymond

VINEYARDS (RED)

Surface area: 37 acres

Grape varietals: 56% Merlot, 24% Cabernet Sauvignon, 15% Cabernet Franc, 5% Petit Verdot

Average age of vines: 23 years

Density of plantation: 6,700 vines per hectare

Average yields: 50 hectoliters per hectare

Elevage: Three to four week fermentation and maceration in temperature-controlled stainless-steel vats. Twelve months aging in barrels that are renewed by a third at each vintage. No fining, filtration if necessary.

RED WINES PRODUCED

Château Saransot-Dupré: 60,000 bottles

Roc de Saransot: 20,000 bottles

Plateau of maturity: Within 4–12 years of the vintage

Note: This château also produces a 60% Sémillon, 30% Sauvignon, and 10% Muscadelle dry Bordeaux white from a 40-year-old, two-hectoliter plot of vines.

The high percentage of Merlot ensures that in ripe vintages, this wine has a degree of opulence and fullness not often found in Listrac wines. The wine is usually dark ruby in color, with a bouquet redolent of black fruits, such as plums as well as licorice and flowers.

Given the high extraction, ripeness, and intensity of the wines made at Saransot-Dupré, an elevated use of new oak could be beneficial. This is a wine that needs 4–5 years to reach its plateau of maturity, but can last for 12–15 years. To date, this château remains largely undiscovered in the export markets.

A delicious, dry white wine, made from 4.3 acres of Sémillon, Sauvignon, and Muscadelle, is produced at Saransot-Dupré. I have never seen a bottle outside of France, but it is a delicious Bordeaux Blanc.

SÉGUR (HAUT-MÉDOC)

Classification: Cru Bourgeois

Location of vineyards: Parempuyre

Owner: SCA Château Ségur

Address: 33290 Parempuyre

Telephone: 05 56 35 28 25: Telefax: 05 56 35 82 32

Visits: Monday to Friday, 8 A.M.–noon and 1:30–5 P.M.
Saturday by appointment only.

Contact: Jean-Pierre Grazioli

VINEYARDS

Surface area: 93.9 acres

Grape varietals: 42% Merlot, 35% Cabernet Sauvignon, 17% Cabernet Franc, 6% Petit Verdot

Average age of vines: 26 years

Density of plantation: 6,700 vines per hectare

Average yields: 52 hectoliters per hectare

Elevage: Manual harvest. Fermentations and macerations take place in temperature-controlled stainless-steel vats. Wines remain in vats for six months and are afterward transferred to oak barrels, one third of which are new, for 12 months aging. They are fined with albumin and filtered.

WINES PRODUCED

Château Ségur: 95,000 bottles

Château Ségur Fillon: 145,000 bottles

Plateau of maturity: Within 4–7 years of the vintage

SÉMEILLAN-MAZEAU (LISTRAC)

Classification: Cru Bourgeois

Location of vineyards: Listrac

Owner: Vignoble Jander

Address: 33480 Listrac

Telephone: 05 56 58 01 12; Telefax: 05 56 58 01 57

Visits: Monday to Friday, 8 A.M.–noon and 2–6 P.M.

Contact: Alain Bistodeau

VINEYARDS

Surface area: 46.4 acres

Grape varietals: 50% Cabernet Sauvignon, 50% Merlot

Average age of vines: 20 years

Density of plantation: 10,000 and 6,700 vines per hectare

Average yields: 53 hectoliters per hectare

Elevage: Fermentations last 3–4 weeks in stainless-steel tanks equipped with a temperature control system. Wines are then aged 18 months in oak barrels, 50% of which are new. They are fined and filtered.

WINES PRODUCED

Château Sémeillan-Mazeau: 60,000 bottles

Château Decorde: 60,000 bottles

Plateau of maturity: Within 5–15 years of the vintage

I have had limited experience with the wines of Sémeillan-Mazeau, but those vintages I have tasted exhibited a rich, highly extracted, old style of wine with admirable power and tannin. My guess is that most of the wines from top vintages can last for 10–15 years.

SÉNÉJAC (HAUT-MÉDOC)

Classification: Cru Bourgeois

Location of vineyards: Le Pian-Médoc

Owner: Charles de Guigne

Address: 33290 Le Pian-Médoc

Telephone: 05 56 70 20 11; Telefax: 05 56 70 23 91

Visits: By appointment only

Contact: Bruno Vonderheyden

VINEYARDS

Surface area: 61.8 acres

Grape varietals: 60% Cabernet Sauvignon, 25% Merlot, 14% Cabernet Franc, 1% Petit Verdot

Average age of vines: 18 years

Density of plantation: 6,600 vines per hectare

Average yields: 48–52 hectoliters per hectare

Elevage: Fermentations and macerations last approximately 20 days. Fifteen percent of the yield undergoes malolactics in barrels, the rest in vats. Wines are aged in oak barrels, 30% of which are new. They are fined but not systematically filtered.

WINES PRODUCED

Château Sénéjac: 135,000 bottles

Artigue de Sénéjac/La Bergerie de Sénéjac: 65,000 bottles

Plateau of maturity: Within 4–6 years of the vintage

A marvelously photogenic estate (poplar-lined roads and ponds), Sénéjac is located in the southern part of the Médoc, west of the town of Parempuyre and just south of the village of Arsac. The vineyard sits on very light, sandy, gravelly soil and produces a soft, fruity red wine that is meant to be drunk young. Recent vintages, particularly 2001 and 2000, have shown much more stuffing and character. In addition, the producers have introduced an excellent, 800-case prestige *cuvée* called Karolus. This wine is made from a 7.5 acre parcel of 50% Merlot, 33% Cabernet Sauvignon, and 17% Cabernet Franc planted in gravelly soil. The blend has varied significantly. In 2000, it was 85% Cabernet Sauvignon and 15% Merlot; in 2001, it was 48% Cabernet Sauvignon, 26% Merlot, and 26% Cabernet Franc.

SOCIANDO-MALLET (HAUT-MÉDOC)

Classification: Cru Bourgeois

Location of vineyards: St.-Seurin-de-Cadourne

Owner: Jean Gautreau

Address: 33180 St.-Seurin-de-Cadourne

Telephone: 05 56 73 38 80; Telefax: 05 56 73 38 88

E-mail: scea.jean.gautreau@wanadoo.fr

Visits: By appointment only on weekdays, 9 A.M.–noon and 2–5 P.M. Fridays, closed in the morning.

Contact: Jean Gautreau

VINEYARDS

Surface area: 163 acres

Grape varietals: 54% Cabernet Sauvignon, 45% Merlot, 1% Cabernet Franc and Petit Verdot

Average age of vines: 25–30 years

Density of plantation: 8,800 vines per hectare

Average yields: 50–55 hectoliters per hectare

Elevage: Fermentation and 20 day maceration in temperature-controlled vats. Eleven months aging in 100% new oak barrels. No fining, no filtration.

WINES PRODUCED

Château Sociando-Mallet: 300,000 bottles

La Demoiselle de Sociando-Mallet: 100,000 bottles

Plateau of maturity: Within 8–25 years of the vintage

Located in St.-Seurin-de-Cadourne, Sociando-Mallet is making uncompromising wines of extremely high quality that are meant to age gracefully for 10–25 years. The vineyards are superbly situated overlooking the Gironde, and the style of wine produced by the meticulous owner—Jean Gautreau, who purchased this run-down property in 1969—is inky black ruby in color, extremely concentrated, full-bodied, and loaded with mouth-puckering tannin. Some observers have even claimed that Sociando-Mallet has the greatest potential for longevity of any wine in the Médoc. The keys to the quality of Sociando-Mallet are numerous. First there is the superb vineyard, with excellent exposure and well-drained, gravelly soil, a high density of vines per hectare (8,800), as well as manual-harvesting techniques. A fermentation temperature of 32–33°C, a three-week or longer maceration period, the use of 100% new oak, and no fining and filtration are further evidence of the château's high standards.

The result of all this is irrefutable. Sociando-Mallet is easily the equal of many of the classified growths, and its surging reputation among France's wine connoisseurs has already assured that much of it is purchased within that country.

IMPORTANT VINTAGES

2001
89–91 A complete effort, this dense blue/purple–colored 2001 reveals classic, pure notes of crème de cassis, minerals, and subtle new oak. Layered, voluminous, and expansive, with enough acidity to provide vibrancy, and high but sweet tannin, it is another long-lived classic from the superb, northern Médoc estate of Sociando-Mallet. Anticipated maturity: 2009–2022. Last tasted, 1/03.

2000
92+ A superb, thick purple color accompanies a bouquet of licorice, intensely ripe, black currant fruit, wet stones, and cedar wood. Extremely unevolved, impressively concentrated, massive, powerful, tannic, and unquestionably of classified growth quality, this large-scaled Sociando will require a decade of cellaring. Anticipated maturity: 2012–2030+ Last tasted, 1/03.

1999
89+ Sociando-Mallet's opaque ruby/purple–colored 1999 reveals notes of wet steel, liquified minerals, black cherries/black currants, and subtle wood. Aromatically, there is not much difference between this wine and a renowned classified growth such as Léoville Las Cases. In the mouth, it is medium bodied with high tannin for a 1999, a long, persistent finish, and very good to excellent concentration and purity. This is a surprisingly backward wine, but then this is Sociando-Mallet, the perennial overachiever making wines of exceptional longevity. Anticipated maturity: 2007–2018. Last tasted, 1/02.

1997
90 The 1997 is one of the most forward, up-front wines produced at this estate in the last decade. The color is a saturated opaque purple, and the wine extremely low in acidity, but oh, so captivating. There are gorgeous layers of sweet cassis-like fruit intermixed with vanilla, lead pencil, and mineral aromas. Medium bodied with outstanding concentration, and as smooth a texture as will ever be found in such a young Sociando-Mallet, this wine will drink beautifully young and will last for 12–15 years. Very impressive. Anticipated maturity: now–2014. Last tasted, 3/98.

1996
90 An impressive Cru Bourgeois, Sociando-Mallet's opaque purple–colored 1996 displays a tight but nicely scented nose of minerals, licorice, cassis, and high-quality vanilla from new oak barrels. In the mouth, the wine is dense and full-bodied, with a boatload of tannin, as well as gobs of extract, glycerin, and depth. This example will age at a glacial pace. However, it is unquestionably of high quality, and the requisite fruit and depth are present to balance out the wine's structural components. Anticipated maturity: 2009–2025. Last tasted, 10/02.

1995 This accessible yet tannic example of Sociando-Mallet possesses a deep ruby/pur-
90   ple color and excellent aromatics consisting of jammy black cherries, blackber-
      ries, and cassis, as well as subtle notes of minerals, earth, and new oak. This is a
      deep, long, muscular, tannic wine that is structurally similar to the 1996. Patience
      will be required from purchasers of this high-class wine. Anticipated maturity:
      2008–2025. Last tasted, 10/02.

1994 The 1994 is reminiscent of the 1985, with more structure and tannic ferocity. The
89   wine reveals a deep purple color and a tight but emerging nose of black fruits, lead
      pencil, and well-integrated oak. Substantial on the palate, with moderate tannin,
      this medium-bodied, classically built Bordeaux should be at its peak from 2000–
      2010. Last tasted, 1/97.

1993 A more than competent effort was turned in by Sociando-Mallet in 1993. The wine
87   possesses a dense ruby/purple color, a surprisingly evolved, forward, cedary,
      black cherry, currant, and mineral nose, spicy, fleshy flavors that exhibit excellent
      texture, and, for this château, a beguiling suppleness for its youthfulness. Jean
      Gaudreau obviously handled the potential difficulties of the 1993 vintage in a suc-
      cessful manner. This wine should drink well for 5–10 years. Last tasted, 1/97.

1990 The 1990 is a plump, fat, and atypically fleshy, lush Sociando. It appears to be the
93   finest Sociando-Mallet since the sensational 1982. The wine possesses an opaque
      purple color and a tight but promising nose of thick, cassis, black currant fruit, sub-
      tle roasted herbs, smoke, licorice, and minerals. Powerful, super-concentrated,
      and backward, with layers of flavor and high tannin, this striking wine should
      evolve for 2–3 decades. Anticipated maturity: now–2022. Last tasted, 10/02.

1989 The 1989 reveals a garnet/purple color, followed by a sweet nose of black fruits,
90   minerals, earth, compost, and vanilla. The wine remains youthful (much more so
      than most 1989s), with medium to full body, good tannin, and little of the vintage's
      soft, evolved personality in evidence. Dense, rich, and concentrated, this wine
      needs another 4–5 years of cellaring; it should keep for 20+ years. Last tasted,
      10/02.

1988 The 1988 is medium bodied, somewhat lighter than one might expect from this
87   property, but still concentrated and spicy, with a true sense of balance and a long
      finish. It lacks the strength and highly extracted flavors seen in the top vintages,
      but it should last for 12–15 years. Last tasted, 1/93.

1986 Jean Gautreau's 1986 is a blockbuster of a wine. Enormously rich and full-bodied,
90   with awesome power, it is a classic Médoc with its extraordinary depth and well-
      focused bouquet of minerals, black currants, violets, and spicy oak. It is an exqui-
      site wine, but not for everybody. Anticipated maturity: 2005–2040. Last tasted,
      1/91.

1985 The 1985 Sociando-Mallet is typically dense ruby/purple and has a rich, black
90   currant, classically Médoc bouquet, full body, and sensational concentration and
      balance. Anticipated maturity: now–2015. Last tasted, 4/91.

1983 At one time I had high hopes for this wine, but the fruit does not seem nearly as
85   ripe or as concentrated as it once was. Still medium to dark ruby, with a spicy,
      mineral-like bouquet that lacks intensity and ripeness, on the palate the wine is
      medium to full-bodied, exhibits good rather than great concentration, and has a
      somewhat sinewy, muscular texture and a good, long finish with moderate tannins.
      Anticipated maturity: now. Last tasted, 1/90.

1982 This amazing Cru Bourgeois estate produced a 1982 that remains young and vi-
92   brant, with little sign of evolution. Even from half bottles, the wine exhibits a sat-
      urated dark purple color tending toward garnet, with no lightening at the edge. The
      nose could be that of a 1990, revealing exuberant, pure, ripe black currant aromas
      intermixed with scents of minerals and spices. Full-bodied, with high extraction,

copious quantities of glycerin, and huge tannin, this is a young, backward, impressively endowed Sociando-Mallet that may prove to be one of the slowest agers of the vintage. A classic, this wine has just entered its peak period of drinkability where it should remain for 10–15 years. Anticipated maturity: now–2018. Last tasted, 10/02.

SOUDARS (HAUT-MÉDOC)

Classification: Cru Bourgeois

Location of vineyards: St.-Seurin-de-Cadourne

Owner: Vignobles E.F. Miailhe SAS

Address: 33180 St.-Seurin-de-Cadourne

Telephone: 05 56 59 36 09; Telefax: 05 56 59 72 39

Visits: By appointment only. No visits in August or at harvest time.

Contact: Eric Miailhe

VINEYARDS

Surface area: 56.8 acres

Grape varietals: 55% Merlot, 44% Cabernet Sauvignon, 1% Cabernet Franc

Average age of vines: 20–25 years

Density of plantation: 6,500 vines per hectare

Average yields: 35 hectoliters per hectare

Elevage: Fermentation and 30 day maceration in temperature-controlled vats. Twelve to fourteen months aging in barrels that are renewed by a third at each vintage. Fining and filtration.

WINES PRODUCED

Château Soudars: 160,000 bottles

Château Marquis de Cadourne: Variable (not produced each year)

Plateau of maturity: Within 3–6 years of the vintage

The high percentage of Merlot used at Soudars results in a wine that is relatively fat, round, fruity, and easy to drink. Vintages since the early 1980s have been impeccably made by young Eric Miailhe. This is not a wine to lay away for more than 5–6 years, but to drink in its youth. Soudars has a great deal to offer at a reasonable price.

LA TOUR DE BY (MÉDOC)

Classification: Cru Bourgeois

Location of vineyards: Bégadan and St.-Christoly

Owner: Marc Pagès family

Address: 33340 Bégadan

Telephone: 05 56 41 50 03; Telefax: 05 56 41 36 10

E-mail: la.tour.de.by@wanadoo.fr

Visits: Monday to Thursday, 8 A.M.–noon and 1:30–5:30 P.M. Friday, 8 A.M.–noon and 1:30–4:30 P.M. By appointment for groups. Open on weekends in July and August.

VINEYARDS

Surface area: 182.8 acres

Grape varietals: 55% Cabernet Sauvignon, 42% Merlot, 3% Cabernet Franc

Average age of vines: 40 years

Density of plantation: 5,500–10,000 vines per hectare

Average yields: 55 hectoliters per hectare

Elevage: Three to four week fermentation and maceration in temperature-controlled stainless-steel and wooden vats. Fourteen months aging in barrels with 25% new oak. Fining and filtration.

WINES PRODUCED

Château La Tour de By: 450,000 bottles

La Roque de By: 50,000 bottles

Plateau of maturity: Within 5–10 years of the vintage

This is one of the best-known Crus Bourgeois for a number of reasons. One is that the vast estate of 182.8 acres produces nearly 40,000 cases of wine. The property was purchased in 1965 by well-known Médoc vineyard owners, Messieurs Cailloux, Lapalu, and Pagès, and they have built new cellars that hold nearly 1,400 aging barrels. Given the huge production and yields of 55–70 hectoliters per hectare, one might think this wine would lack stuffing, but there is always a relatively severe selection process, as well as two secondary labels where weaker vats and wine from younger vines are relegated.

La Tour de By produces well-colored, richly fruity, solid wines that only lack complexity and intensity in the bouquet. The high percentage of Cabernet Sauvignon gives the wines their deep color and firm tannic background. I do not remember tasting a badly made La Tour de By from any good vintage.

LA TOUR CARNET (HAUT-MÉDOC)

Classification: Fourth growth in 1855

Location of vineyards: St.-Laurent du Médoc

Owner: Bernard Magrez

Address: Route de Beychevelle,
33112 St.-Laurent du Médoc

Telephone: 05 56 73 30 90; Telefax: 05 56 59 48 54

Website: www.la-tour-carnet.com

Visits: Monday to Friday, 8 A.M.–noon and 1:30–5:30 P.M.

Contact: Mr. Despeaux

VINEYARDS

Surface area: 113.6 acres

Grape varietals: 52% Cabernet Sauvignon, 42% Merlot, 4% Cabernet Franc, 2% Petit Verdot

Average age of vines: 30 years

Density of plantation: 8,000 vines per hectare

Average yields: 45 hectoliters per hectare

Elevage: Cold maceration. Fermentation (28–30°C) with four daily *pigéages* and three week maceration in temperature-controlled vats. Malolactics and 16–18 months aging on lees with weekly stirrings in new oak barrels. Fining, no filtration.

WINES PRODUCED

Château La Tour Carnet: 180,000 bottles

Les Douves de Carnet: 90,000 bottles

Plateau of maturity: Within 5–15 years of the vintage

La Tour Carnet is located in St.-Laurent, and despite its inclusion in the 1855 classification, it has remained largely anonymous. This beautiful property has been restored completely and boasts a medieval castle and moat. The wine has suffered considerably from, I suspect, extensive replanting in the 1960s. More recent vintages, particularly 2001 and 2000, are very promising. Because of the commitment of Bernard Magrez, with considerable expertise provided by the incomparable oenologist, Michel Rolland, this property will be one to watch carefully.

TOUR HAUT-CAUSSAN (MÉDOC)

Classification: Cru Bourgeois

Location of vineyards: Blaignan

Owner: Philippe Courrian

Address: 33340 Blaignan

Telephone: 05 56 09 00 77; Telefax: 05 56 09 06 24

Visits: By appointment only

Contact: Véronique Courrian

VINEYARDS

Surface area: 39.5 acres

Grape varietals: 50% Cabernet Sauvignon, 50% Merlot

Average age of vines: 30 years

Density of plantation: 7,000 vines per hectare

Average yields: 60 hectoliters per hectare

Elevage: Fermentation and prolonged maceration in temperature-controlled concrete tanks of small capacity (at different temperatures depending upon the grape varietals). Fourteen months aging in barrels that are renewed by a third at each vintage. Fining, no filtration.

WINES PRODUCED

Château Tour Haut-Caussan: 90,000 bottles

Château La Landotte: 6,000 bottles

Plateau of maturity: Within 6–15 years of the vintage

Philippe Courrian is the most recent proprietor from this family, which has run this excellent Cru Bourgeois since 1877. Not surprisingly, the property takes its name not only from a beautiful windmill situated in the midst of the vineyards, but also from the nearest village, Caussan. The vineyard is located near the more famous properties of Potensac and La Cardonne. Everything about the winemaking is extremely traditional. The extremely low yields of 40–60 hectoliters per hectare, the manual harvesting in an area where most vineyards are picked by machine, the declassifying of inferior lots to a second wine, and the policy against filtration all typify an estate dedicated to high quality. As Mr. Courrian has said many times, "Why filter? My wine does not contain anything bad."

TOUR DU HAUT-MOULIN (HAUT-MÉDOC)

Classification: Cru Bourgeois

Location of vineyards: Cussac Fort-Médoc

Owner: Béatrice and Lionel Poitou

Address: 22, avenue du Fort-Médoc,
33460 Cussac-Fort-Médoc

Telephone: 05 56 58 91 10; Telefax: 05 57 88 83 13

E-mail: contact@tour-du-haut-moulin.com

Website: www.tour-du-haut-moulin.com

Visits: Monday to Friday, 9 A.M.–noon and 1–5:30 P.M.
Open on Saturdays from May to October.

Contact: Lionel Poitou

VINEYARDS

Surface area: 79 acres

Grape varietals: 50% Cabernet Sauvignon, 45% Merlot, 5% Petit Verdot

Average age of vines: 25 years

Density of plantation: 10,000 vines per hectare

Average yields: 48–50 hectoliters per hectare

Elevage: Ten to twelve day fermentation with two daily pumpings over, 4–5 week maceration in temperature-controlled vats. Malolactics and 15 months aging in barrels that are renewed by a third each year. No fining, no filtration.

WINES PRODUCED

Château Tour du Haut-Moulin: 160,000 bottles

Florilège du Tour du Haut-Moulin: 15,000–20,000 bottles

Plateau of maturity: Within 5–14 years of the vintage

The vineyards of this excellent Cru Bourgeois, located near Cussac, are situated just to the north of Château Lamarque. There is no doubt that proprietor Laurent Poitou produces one of the most concentrated and intensely flavored wines among the Crus Bourgeois. He is not averse to letting the fermentation temperature reach a dangerously high 34–35°C and he favors a long *cuvaison* of nearly one month. Additionally, the conservative yields from a densely planted vineyard of 10,000 vines per hectare no doubt account for the impressively dark ruby/purple color of these wines in top years, as well as their admirable depth and concentration. This is clearly one of the top Crus Bourgeois. In fact, in a blind tasting, it would embarrass some classified growths.

LA TOUR ST.-BONNET (MÉDOC)

Classification: Cru Bourgeois

Location of vineyards: St.-Christoly

Owner: GFA La Tour St.-Bonnet

Address: 33340 St.-Christoly

Telephone and telefax: 05 56 41 53 03

Visits: By appointment only

Contact: Nicole Merlet

VINEYARDS

Surface area: 98.8 acres

Grape varietals: 45% Cabernet Sauvignon, 45% Merlot, 5% Malbec, 5% Petit Verdot

Average age of vines: 30–35 years

Density of plantation: 9,000 vines per hectare

Average yields: 40–50 hectoliters per hectare

Elevage: Fermentations and macerations last approximately three weeks, and wines are aged in wooden vats for 18 months. They are fined but not systematically filtered.

WINES PRODUCED

Château La Tour St.-Bonnet: 200,000 bottles

La Fuie St.-Bonnet: 20,000 bottles

Plateau of maturity: Within 6–14 years of the vintage

La Tour St.-Bonnet has always been one of my favorite Crus Bourgeois. The first vintage I tasted, and subsequently purchased, was the 1975. The vineyard of nearly 100 acres is well situated on a gravelly ridge adjacent to the Gironde River, near the village of St.-Christoly.

This is not a commercially made, supple, ready to drink Cru Bourgeois, but, rather, a deeply colored, firm, tannic, full-bodied wine with surprising concentration. Most vintages need at least 3–4 years to shed their tannins, and in top years, such as 2000, 1996, 1995, and 1990 they need 10 years or longer. The vineyard is machine harvested, and yields of 40–50 hectoliters per hectare are conservative by today's standards. Interestingly, the wine is not aged in small oak casks, but in larger oak *foudres*. The proprietor, the Lafon family, feels this preserves the wine's intensity and rich, concentrated fruit extract.

VERDIGNAN (HAUT-MÉDOC)

Classification: Cru Bourgeois

Location of vineyards: St.-Seurin-de-Cadourne

Owner: Jean Miailhe group

Address: 33180 St.-Seurin-de-Cadourne

Telephone: 05 56 59 31 02; Telefax: 05 56 59 32 35

E-mail: contact@chateau-coufran.com

Visits: By appointment only. No visits in August or at harvest time.

Contact: Eric Miailhe

VINEYARDS

Surface area: 148.2 acres

Grape varietals: 50% Cabernet Sauvignon, 45% Merlot, 5% Cabernet Franc

Average age of vines: 25–30 years

Density of plantation: 8,000 vines per hectare

Average yields: 54 hectoliters per hectare

Elevage: Fermentation and 30 day maceration in temperature-controlled stainless-steel vats. Twelve to fourteen months aging in barrels that are renewed by a third at each vintage. Fining and filtration.

WINES PRODUCED

Château Verdignan: 400,000 bottles

Château Plantey de Lacroix: 50,000 bottles

Plateau of maturity: Within 4–8 years of the vintage

Another one of the Miailhe family's solidly run Cru Bourgeois properties, Verdignan's château and vineyards are located near the northern Médoc village of St.-Seurin-de-Cadourne. A wine I have consistently enjoyed, it is ripe, supple, richly fruity, and possesses a straightforward yet powerful black currant aroma. Made in a style designed for early drinking, it is best drunk between 4–8 years of age. Since the early 1980s the wine has taken on more concentration and character. The vineyard is machine harvested and averages 50–65 hectoliters per hectare. The price for Verdignan has remained reasonable, no doubt due to the significant production.

VILLEGEORGE (HAUT-MÉDOC)

Classification: Cru Bourgeois

Location of vineyards: Avensan and Soussan

Owner: Marie-Laure Lurton Roux

Address: Lieu-dit La Tuilerie, 33460 Avensan

Mailing address: SC Les Gránds Crus Réunis, 2036 Chalet, 33480 Moulis-en-Médoc

Telephone: 05 56 58 22 01; Telefax: 05 56 58 15 10

E-mail: lgcr@wanadoo.fr

Visits: By appointment only

Contact: Viviane Grouffier

VINEYARDS

Surface area: 49.4 acres

Grape varietals: 55% Cabernet Sauvignon, 45% Merlot

Average age of vines: 16 years

Density of plantation: 6,667 vines per hectare

Average yields: 49 hectoliters per hectare

Elevage: Fermentation and 15–28 day maceration in temperature-controlled vats. Eighteen months aging, with six months in vats and 6–12 months in barrel with 20–30% new oak. Fining and filtration.

WINES PRODUCED

Château Villegeorge: 47,600 bottles

Refrain du Château Villegeorge: 20 600 bottles

Plateau of maturity: Within 3–6 years of the vintage

In 1973 the Lurton family added this small property to their collection of Bordeaux châteaux. The wine is loosely knit, soft, pleasantly fruity, straightforward, and uninspiring. Perhaps the high yields and significant percentage of Merlot, which is planted in very gravelly soil, are the reasons this wine is relatively light and one-dimensional.

OTHER CRU BOURGEOIS ESTATES

D'ARCHE (HAUT-MÉDOC)

Classification: Cru Bourgeois

Location of vineyards: Ludon-Médoc

Owner: Grands Vignobles de Gironde, Mahler-Besse SA

Address: 33290 Ludon-Médoc

Mailing address: 49, rue Camille Godard, 33000 Bordeaux

Telephone: 05 56 56 04 30; Telefax: 05 56 56 04 59

E-mail: contact@malher-besse.com

Website: www.mahler-besse.com

Visits: By appointment only

Contact: Export department, Mahler-Besse SA

VINEYARDS

Surface area: 22.2 acres

Grape varietals: 45% Cabernet Sauvignon, 40% Merlot, 15% Cabernet Franc (a dollop of Petit Verdot and Carmenère)

Average age of vines: 30 years

Density of plantation: 9,000 vines per hectare

Average yields: 50 hectoliters per hectare

Elevage: Prolonged fermentation and maceration in temperature-controlled stainless-steel vats. Sixteen months aging in barrels with 30% new oak. Fining, no filtration.

WINES PRODUCED

Château d'Arche: 60,000 bottles

No second wine is produced.

Plateau of maturity: 2–6 years

BEAUMONT (HAUT-MÉDOC)

Classification: Cru Bourgeois

Location of vineyards: Cussac-Fort-Médoc

Owner: Grands Millésimes de France

Address: 33460 Cussac-Fort-Médoc

Telephone: 05 56 58 92 29; Telefax: 05 56 58 90 94

E-mail: beaumont@chateau-beaumont.com

Website: www.chateau-beaumont.com

Visits: Monday to Friday, 9 A.M.–noon and 2–5 P.M.

Contact: Etienne Priou

VINEYARDS

Surface area: 279.1 acres

Grape varietals: 60% Cabernet Sauvignon, 35% Merlot, 3% Cabernet Franc, 2% Petit Verdot

Average age of vines: 22 years

Density of plantation: 6,666 vines per hectare

Average yields: 50–55 hectoliters per hectare

Elevage: Fermentation (28–30°C) and three week maceration in temperature-controlled stainless-steel vats. Twelve to fourteen months aging in barrels that are renewed by a third at each vintage. Fining and filtration.

WINES PRODUCED

Château Beaumont: 400,000–500,000 bottles

Château d'Arvigny: 200,000–300,000 bottles

Plateau of maturity: Within 4–8 years of the vintage

This large estate had a checkered history until it was acquired by two insurance companies in 1986. The progression in quality since then has been significant, and this is now one of the more interesting, best made, and reasonably priced Crus Bourgeois in the Médoc. The goal has been to produce a supple and amply endowed wine with a great deal of up-front fruit intelligently married with toasty vanilla aromas from a small percentage of new oak barrels. Recent vintages taste as if the percentage of Merlot is considerably higher than the 36% the property claims. This is a wine to seek out for the cunningly made, yet extremely attractive, crowd-pleasing style. The château itself is also noteworthy and worth visiting. An old fortified tower as well as an impressive twin-turreted façade dominate the landscape around the village of Cussac-Fort-Médoc.

BELLE-VUE (HAUT-MÉDOC)

Classification: Cru Bourgeois

Location of vineyards: Macau

Owner: SC de la Gironville

Address: 69, route de Louens, 33460 Macau

Telephone: 05 57 88 19 79; Telefax: 05 57 88 41 79

E-mail: contact@scgironville.com

Website: www.scgironville.com

Visits: By appointment only

Contact: Rémy Fouin (Telephone: 06 08 51 70 22)

VINEYARDS

Surface area: 24 acres

Grape varietals: 42% Cabernet Sauvignon, 38% Merlot, 20% Petit Verdot

Average age of vines: 23 years

Density of plantation: 6,700 vines per hectare

Average yields: 37 hectoliters per hectare

Elevage: Fermentation and 5–8 week maceration in temperature-controlled stainless-steel vats of small capacity. Malolactics and 14–20 months aging in barrels with 80–90% new oak. Light fining, no filtration.

WINES PRODUCED

Château Belle-Vue: 48,000 bottles

No second wine is produced.

Plateau of maturity: Within 3–10 years of the vintage

BERNADOTTE (HAUT-MÉDOC)

Classification: Cru Bourgeois Supérieur

Location of vineyards: St.-Sauveur

Owner: SCI du Château Pichon Longueville Comtesse de Lalande

Address: Le Fournas Nord, 33250 St.-Sauveur

Telephone: 05 56 59 57 04; Telefax: 05 56 59 54 84

E-mail: bernadotte@chateau-bernadotte.com

Website: www.chateau-bernadotte.com

Visits: By appointment only

Contact: Visits desk (Telephone: 05 56 59 19 40; Telefax: 05 56 59 26 56)

VINEYARDS

Surface area: 86.5 acres

Grape varietals: 62% Cabernet Sauvignon, 36% Merlot, 2% Cabernet Franc and Petit Verdot

Average age of vines: 25 years

Density of plantation: 6,500 vines per hectare

Average yields: 50 hectoliters per hectare

Elevage: Three to four week fermentation and maceration in temperature-controlled stainless-steel vats. Twelve to eighteen months aging in barrels that are renewed by a third at each vintage. Fining, filtration not systematic.

WINES PRODUCED

Château Bernadotte: 120,000 bottles

Château Fournas Bernadotte: 110,000 bottles

Plateau of maturity: Within 5–12 years of the vintage

BOUQUEYRAN (MOULIS)

Classification: Cru Bourgeois

Location of vineyards: Moulis-en-Médoc

Owner: Philippe Porcheron

Address: route d'Avensan, 33480 Moulis-en-Médoc

Mailing address: 287, avenue de la Libération, 33110 Le Bouscat

Telephone: 05 56 42 69 50; Telefax: 05 56 42 69 88

E-mail: philippe.porcheron@wanadoo.fr

Visits: By appointment only

Contact: Philippe Porcheron

VINEYARDS

Surface area: 30.9 acres

Grape varietals: 58% Merlot, 41% Cabernet Sauvignon, 1% Petit Verdot

Average age of vines: 25 years

Density of plantation: 6,600 vines per hectare

Average yields: 42 hectoliters per hectare

Elevage: Prolonged fermentation and 3–4 week maceration in temperature-controlled stainless-steel vats. Twelve months aging in barrels with 30% new oak. Fining, no filtration.

WINES PRODUCED

Château Bouqueyran: 50,000 bottles

No second wine is produced.

Plateau of maturity: Within 5–15 years of the vintage

BOURNAC (MÉDOC)

Classification: Cru Bourgeois

Location of vineyards: Civrac-en-Médoc

Owner: Bruno Secret

Address: 11, route des Petites Granges, 33180 Civrac-en-Médoc

Telephone: 05 56 73 59 24; Telefax: 05 56 73 59 23

E-mail: bournac@terre-net.fr

Visits: By appointment only

Contact: Bruno Secret

VINEYARDS

Surface area: 35.1 acres

Grape varietals: 60% Cabernet Sauvignon, 40% Merlot

Average age of vines: 23 years

Density of plantation: 5,100 vines per hectare

Average yields: 54 hectoliters per hectare

Elevage: Fermentation and 5–6 week maceration in temperature-controlled vats with frequent pumpings-over. Twelve months aging in vats for 10% of the yield and in barrels for the rest, with 33% new oak. No fining, no filtration.

WINES PRODUCED

Château Bournac: 60,000 bottles

Le Branna: 30,000 bottles

Plateau of maturity: Within 2–8 years of the vintage

DE BRAUDE (HAUT-MÉDOC)

Classification: Cru Bourgeois

Location of vineyards: Arsac

Owner: Régis Bernaleau

Address: 33460 Arsac

Mailing address: c/o Château Mongravey,
8 rue Jean-Luc Vonderheyden, 33460 Arsac

Telephone: 05 56 58 84 51; Telefax: 05 56 58 83 39

E-mail: chateau.mongravey@wanadoo.fr

Visits: By appointment only

Contact: Karin Bernaleau

VINEYARDS

Surface area: 14.8 acres

Grape varietals: 55% Cabernet Sauvignon, 45% Merlot

Average age of vines: 20 years

Density of plantation: 6,600 vines per hectare

Average yields: 52 hectoliters per hectare

Elevage: Six to ten day fermentation and 3–4 week maceration in temperature-controlled stainless-steel vats. Fourteen to eighteen months aging in barrels with 33% new oak. Fining and filtration.

WINES PRODUCED

Château de Braude: 40,000 bottles

No second wine is produced.

Plateau of maturity: Within 3–9 years of the vintage

DU BREUIL (HAUT-MÉDOC)

Classification: Cru Bourgeois

Location of vineyards: Cissac Médoc

Owner: Vialard family

Address: 33250 Cissac Médoc

Telephone: 05 56 59 58 13; Telefax: 05 56 59 55 67

E-mail: marie.vialard@chateau-cissac.com

Website: www.chateau-cissac.com

Visits: By appointment only

Contact: Marie Vialard

VINEYARDS

Surface area: 61.8 acres

Grape varietals: 34% Merlot, 28% Cabernet Sauvignon, 23% Cabernet Franc, 11% Petit Verdot, 4% Malbec

Average age of vines: 20 years

Density of plantation: 7,000 vines per hectare

Average yields: 45 hectoliters per hectare

Elevage: Three to four week fermentation and maceration in temperature-controlled epoxy-lined concrete vats. Eighteen to twenty-four months aging in barrels with 25% new oak. Fining and filtration.

WINES PRODUCED

Château du Breuil: 60,000 bottles

Haut-Médoc: 80,000 bottles

Plateau of maturity: Within 7–15 years of the vintage

CAMBON LA PELOUSE (HAUT-MÉDOC)

Classification: Cru Bourgeois

Location of vineyards: Macau

Owner: Annick and Jean-Pierre Marie

Address: 5, chemin de Canteloup, 33460 Macau

Telephone: 05 57 88 40 32; Telefax: 05 57 88 19 12

E-mail: contact@cambon-la-pelouse.com

Website: www.cambon-la-pelouse.com

Visits: By appointment only Monday to Friday,
9 A.M.–noon and 2–6 P.M.

VINEYARDS

Surface area: 143.3 acres

Grape varietals: 50% Merlot, 50% Cabernet Sauvignon

Average age of vines: 25 years

Density of plantation: 5,000–7,000 vines per hectare

Average yields: 48 hectoliters per hectare

Elevage: Cold fermentation at 5–7°C. Fermentation and 20–25 day maceration in temperature-controlled stainless-steel vats. Eighteen months aging in barrels that are renewed by half at each vintage. Fining, no filtration.

WINES PRODUCED

Château Cambon La Pelouse: 200,000 bottles

Château Trois Moulins: 160,000 bottles

Plateau of maturity: Within 3–12 years of the vintage

CAP DE HAUT (HAUT-MÉDOC)

Classification: Cru Bourgeois

Location of vineyards: Lamarque

Owner: Gromand d'Evry family

Address: 33460 Lamarque

Telephone: 05 56 58 90 03; Telefax: 05 56 58 93 43

E-mail: chdelamarq@aol.com

Visits: Preferably by appointment Monday to Friday, 9 A.M.–noon and 2–5 P.M.

Contact: Francine Prévot

VINEYARDS

Surface area: 2.5 acres

Grape varietals: 45% Cabernet Sauvignon, 39% Merlot, 16% Cabernet Franc

Average age of vines: 25 years

Density of plantation: 6,500 vines per hectare

Average yields: 40–50 hectoliters per hectare

Elevage: Three week fermentation and maceration in temperature-controlled stainless-steel tanks. Malolactics in vats for drip wines and in barrels for press wines. Twelve months aging in barrels with 30% new oak. Fining, no filtration.

WINES PRODUCED

Château Cap de Haut: 50,000 bottles

No second wine is produced.

Plateau of maturity: Within 4–7 years of the vintage

CHANTELYS (MÉDOC)

Classification: Cru Bourgeois

Owner: Christine Courrian

Address: Lafon, Prignac, 33340 Lesparre

Telephone: 05 56 09 02 78 *and* 06 10 02 12 92;
Telefax: 05 56 09 09 07

E-mail: jfbraq@aol.com

Visits: By appointment only

Contact: Christine Courrian

VINEYARDS

Surface area: 39.5 acres

Grape varietals: 60% Merlot, 30% Cabernet Sauvignon, 10% Petit Verdot

Average age of vines: 35 years

Density of plantation: 8,000 vines per hectare

Average yields: 50 hectoliters per hectare

Elevage: Cold maceration. Prolonged fermentation and maceration in epoxy-lined concrete tanks. Thirteen to eighteen months aging in barrels (with little new oak). No fining, no filtration.

WINES PRODUCED

Château Chantelys: 40,000 bottles

Les Iris de Chantelys: 40,000 bottles

Plateau of maturity: Within 3–9 years of the vintage

CLOS DU JAUGUEYRON (HAUT-MÉDOC)

Classification: None

Location of vineyards: Cantenac

Owner: Michel Théron

Address: 4, rue de la Halle, 33460 Arsac

Telephone and telefax: 05 56 58 89 43

Visits: By appointment only

Contact: Michel Théron

VINEYARDS

Surface area: 5.1 acres

Grape varietals: 60% Cabernet Sauvignon, 36% Merlot, 2% Petit Verdot, 2% other varietals

Average age of vines: 35 years

Density of plantation: 6,666 vines per hectare

Average yields: 48 hectoliters per hectare

Elevage: Prolonged fermentation and maceration in temperature-controlled concrete tanks. Part of yield undergoes malolactics in barrels. Fifteen months aging in barrels that are renewed by a third at each vintage. Fining and filtration.

WINES PRODUCED

Clos du Jaugueyron: 9,000 bottles

No second wine is produced.

Plateau of maturity: Within 5–15 years of the vintage

COMTESSE DU PARC (HAUT-MÉDOC)

Classification: Cru Bourgeois

Location of vineyards: Vertheuil

Owner: SCEA Vignobles Anney

Address: 33180 Vertheuil

Mailing address: c/o Château Tour des Termes, 33180 St.-Estèphe

Telephone: 05 56 59 32 89; Telefax: 05 56 59 73 74

Visits: Monday to Friday, 8:30 A.M.–12:30 P.M. and 2–4:30 P.M.

Contact: Christophe Anney

VINEYARDS

Surface area: 14.8 acres

Grape varietals: 50% Cabernet Sauvignon, Merlot 50%

Average age of vines: 15 years

Density of plantation: 6,666 vines per hectare

Average yields: 57 hectoliters per hectare

Elevage: Fermentation and 3–4 week maceration in temperature-controlled stainless-steel vats. Twelve months aging in one- and two-year-old barrels. Fining, no filtration.

WINES PRODUCED

Château Comtesse du Parc: 40,000 bottles

No second wine is produced.

Plateau of maturity: Within 2–6 years of the vintage

D'ESCURAC (MÉDOC)

Classification: Cru Bourgeois

Location of vineyards: Civrac-en-Médoc

Owner: Jean-Marc Landureau

Address: Route d'Escurac, 33340 Civrac-en-Médoc

Telephone: 05 56 41 50 81; Telefax: 05 56 41 56 48

E-mail: chateau.d'escurac@wanadoo.fr

Visits: By appointment Monday to Friday, 9 A.M.–5 P.M.

Contact: Jean-Marc Landureau

VINEYARDS

Surface area: 49.4 acres

Grape varietals: 50% Cabernet Sauvignon, 50% Merlot

Average age of vines: 18 years

Density of plantation: 5,000 vines per hectare

Average yields: 55 hectoliters per hectare

Elevage: Fermentation at low temperatures with twice daily pumpings-over and *pigéages* and four week maceration in temperature-controlled vats with the cap immersed. Twelve months aging in barrels with 30–45% new oak. Fining, no filtration.

WINES PRODUCED

Château d'Escurac: 60,000–80,000 bottles

La Chapelle d'Escurac: 60,000–80,000 bottles

Plateau of maturity: Within 4–10 years of the vintage

FONTIS (MÉDOC)

(Formerly Hontemieux)

Classification: Cru Bourgeois

Location of vineyards: Ordonnac and Blaignan

Owner: Vincent Boivert

Address: 33340 Ordonnac

Telephone: 05 56 73 30 30; Telefax: 05 56 73 30 31

Visits: By appointment only

Contact: Hélène Boivert

VINEYARDS

Surface area: 24.7 acres

Grape varietals: 50% Cabernet Sauvignon, 50% Merlot

Average age of vines: 20 years

Density of plantation: 8,333 vines per hectare

Average yields: 56 hectoliters per hectare

Elevage: Three week fermentation and maceration in temperature-controlled stainless-steel vats. Twelve months aging in vats for half the yield and in barrels (with 50% new oak) for the rest. Fining, no filtration.

WINES PRODUCED

Château Fontis: 35,000 bottles

Château Montoya: 35,000 bottles

Plateau of maturity: Within 2–6 years of the vintage

LES GRANDS CHÊNES (MÉDOC)

Classification: Cru Bourgeois

Location of vineyards: St.-Christoly-de-Médoc

Owner: Bernard Magrez

Address: 13, route de Lesparre,
33340 Saint-Christoly-de-Médoc

Telephone: 05 56 41 53 12; Telefax: 05 56 41 39 06

Visits: By appointment only

Contact: Patrick Nevoux (Telephone: 06 07 55 14 75)

VINEYARDS

Surface area: 34.6 acres

Grape varietals: 45% Cabernet Sauvignon, 45% Merlot, 10% Cabernet Franc

Average age of vines: 30 years

Density of plantation: 8,000 vines per hectare

Average yields: 45 hectoliters per hectare

Elevage: Four day cold maceration. Fermentation and 22 day maceration in temperature-controlled vats. Malolactics and 18 months aging on lees with stirring in barrels that are renewed by half at each vintage.

WINES PRODUCED

Château Les Grands Chênes Cuvée Prestige: 60,000 bottles

Château Les Grands Chênes: 22,000 bottles

Plateau of maturity: Within 3–12 years of the vintage

GRAVAT (MÉDOC)

Classification: Cru Bourgeois

Location of vineyards: Valeyrac

Owner: Claude Ganelon

Address: Villeneuve, 33340 Valeyrac

Mailing address: BP no. 5, 33460 Arcins

Telephone: 05 56 58 95 74; Telefax: 05 57 88 50 65

Visits: By appointment only

Contact: Claude Ganelon

VINEYARDS

Surface area: 37 acres

Grape varietals: 60% Merlot, 40% Cabernet Sauvignon

Average age of vines: 30 years

Density of plantation: 8,000 vines per hectare

Average yields: 60 hectoliters per hectare

Elevage: Fermentation and maceration in concrete vats. Aging depends upon requirements of buyers.

WINES PRODUCED

Château Gravat or Château Haute Rivière: 100,000 bottles

Plateau of maturity: Within 2–6 years of the vintage

GRIVIÈRE (MÉDOC)

Classification: Cru Bourgeois

Location of vineyards: Prignac

Owner: Domaines CGR

Address: 33340 Blaignan

Mailing address: Les Domaines CGR, 40, rue Notre-Dame des Victoires, 75002 Paris

Telephone: 05 56 73 31 51 *or* 01 42 21 11 80; Telefax: 05 56 73 31 52 *or* 01 42 21 11 85

E-mail: gcharloux@domaines-cgr.com

Website: www.chateau-griviere.com

Visits: Monday to Friday, 8:30 A.M.–5 P.M.

Contact: Annelis Bosq (Telephone: 05 56 73 31 51; Telefax: 05 56 73 31 52)

VINEYARDS

Surface area: 42 acres

Grape varietals: 59% Merlot, 32% Cabernet Sauvignon, 9% Cabernet Franc

Average age of vines: 23 years

Density of plantation: 7,500 vines per hectare

Average yields: 59 hectoliters per hectare

Elevage: Fermentation and maceration in temperature-controlled stainless-steel tanks. Twelve months aging in barrels that are renewed by half each year. Fining, filtration not systematic.

WINES PRODUCED

Château Grivière: 60,000 bottles

Château Ribeiron: Variable

Plateau of maturity: Within 2–10 years of the vintage

HAUT-CONDISSAS (MÉDOC)

Classification: Cru Bourgeois

Location of vineyards: Bégadan

Owner: Jean Guyon

Address: 7, route Rollan de By, 33340 Bégadan

Telephone: 05 56 41 58 59; Telefax: 05 56 41 37 82

E-mail: rollan-de-by@wanadoo.fr

Website: www.rollandeby.com

Visits: By appointment only Monday to Friday, 9 A.M.–noon and 2–5 P.M.

VINEYARDS

Surface area: 9.9 acres

Grape varietals: 80% Merlot, 10% Cabernet Sauvignon, 10% Petit Verdot

Average age of vines: 30 years

Density of plantation: 8,500 vines per hectare

Average yields: 35 hectoliters per hectare

Elevage: Fermentation, maceration, malolactics, and aging on fine lees in new oak barrels. No fining, no filtration.

WINES PRODUCED

Château Haut-Condissas: 16,000 bottles

No second wine is produced.

Plateau of maturity: Within 4–15 years of the vintage

JANDER (LISTRAC)

Classification: Cru Bourgeois

Location of vineyards: Listrac

Owner: Jander family

Address: 41, avenue de Soulac, 33480 Listrac-Médoc

Telephone: 05 56 58 01 12; Telefax: 05 56 58 01 57

E-mail: vignobles.jander@wanadoo.fr

Website: www.vignobles-jander.com

Visits: By appointment

Contact: Alain Bistodeau

VINEYARDS

Surface area: 35.8 acres

Grape varietals: 50% Cabernet Sauvignon, 50% Merlot

Average age of vines: 30 years

Density of plantation: 10,000 vines per hectare

Average yields: 32 hectoliters per hectare

Elevage: Eighteen months aging in barrels with 50% new oak. Fining and filtration.

WINES PRODUCED

Château Jander: 15,000–20,000 bottles

Château Sémeillan Mazeau: 70,000–75,000 bottles

Plateau of maturity: Within 2–12 years of the vintage

LACHESNAYE (HAUT-MÉDOC)

Classification: Cru Bourgeois

Location of vineyards: Cussac-Fort-Médoc

Owner: GFA des Domaines Bouteiller

Address: 33460 Cussac-Fort-Médoc

Telephone: 05 56 58 94 80; Telefax: 05 56 58 93 10

Visits: By appointment only

Contact: Hubert Bouteiller

VINEYARDS

Surface area: 49.4 acres

Grape varietals: 50% Cabernet Sauvignon, 50% Merlot

Average age of vines: 20 years

Density of plantation: 7,500 vines per hectare

Average yields: 57 hectoliters per hectare

Elevage: Fermentations and macerations last 12 days in temperature-controlled concrete tanks. After malolactics in vats, wines are transferred to oak barrels (no new oak) for 12 months aging.

WINES PRODUCED

Château Lachesnaye: 150,000 bottles

No second wine is produced.

Plateau of maturity: Within 2–10 years of the vintage

LACOMBE NOAILLAC (MÉDOC)

Classification: Cru Bourgeois

Location of vineyards: Bégadan

Owner: Jean-Michel Lapalu

Address: Le Broustera, 1, rue du 19 mars, 33340 Bégadan

Mailing address: SC du Château Lacombe Noaillac, Le Broustera, 33590 Jau Dignac et Loirac

Telephone: 05 56 41 50 18; Telefax: 05 56 41 51 65

E-mail: info@domaines-lapalu.com

Website: www.domaines-lapalu.com

No visits

VINEYARDS

Surface area: 98.8 acres

Grape varietals: 47% Cabernet Sauvignon, 45% Merlot, 5% Cabernet Franc, 3% Petit Verdot

Average age of vines: 20 years

Density of plantation: 5,500 vines per hectare

Average yields: 57 hectoliters per hectare

Elevage: Fermentation and maceration in temperature-controlled vats. Twelve months aging in vats and in barrels that are renewed by 15–20% each year. Fining and filtration.

WINES PRODUCED

Château Lacombe Noaillac: 200,000 bottles

Château Les Rives de Gravelongue: 100,000 bottles

Plateau of maturity: Within 4–15 years of the vintage

LALAUDEY (MOULIS)

Classification: Cru Bourgeois

Location of vineyards: Moulis-en-Médoc

Owner: Régis Bernaleau

Address: 33480 Moulis-en-Médoc

Mailing address: c/o Château Mongravey,
8 rue Jean-Luc Vonderheyden, 33460 Arsac

Telephone: 05 56 58 84 51; Telefax: 05 56 58 83 39

E-mail: chateau.mongravey@wanadoo.fr

Visits: By appointment only

Contact: Karin Bernaleau

VINEYARDS

Surface area: 16.1 acres

Grape varietals: 55% Cabernet Sauvignon, 45% Merlot

Average age of vines: 20 years

Density of plantation: 6,600 vines per hectare

Average yields: 50 hectoliters per hectare

Elevage: Six to ten day fermentation and 3–4 week maceration in temperature-controlled stainless-steel vats. Fourteen to eighteen months aging in barrels with 50% new oak. Fining and filtration.

WINES PRODUCED

Château Lalaudey: 40,000 bottles

No second wine is produced.

Plateau of maturity: Within 3–9 years of the vintage

LAMOTHE BERGERON (HAUT-MÉDOC)

Classification: Cru Bourgeois

Location of vineyards: Cussac-Fort-Médoc

Owner: Domaines Cordier

Address: Bégadan, 33460 Cussac-Fort-Médoc

Mailing address: SCC GPD, 109 rue Achard,
BP 154, 33042 Bordeaux Cedex

Telephone: 05 56 11 29 00; Telefax: 05 56 11 29 01

E-mail: contact@cordier-wines.com

Visits: By appointment and for professionals of the wine trade only. Monday to Friday, 9 A.M.–noon and 2–5 P.M.

Contact: Domaines Cordier (Telephone: 05 56 58 94 77; Telefax: 05 56 58 98 18)

VINEYARDS

Surface area: 165.5 acres

Grape varietals: 49% Merlot, 44% Cabernet Sauvignon, 7% Cabernet Franc

Average age of vines: 25 years

Density of plantation: 6,000 vines per hectare

Average yields: 45 hectoliters per hectare

Elevage: Fermentation and 18–21 day maceration in temperature-controlled stainless-steel tanks. Sixteen to twenty months aging in barrels with 25% new oak. Fining and filtration.

WINES PRODUCED

Château Lamothe Bergeron: 200,000 bottles

Château Romefort: 150,000 bottles

Plateau of maturity: Within 3–12 years of the vintage

LAROSE PERGANSON (HAUT-MÉDOC)

Classification: Cru Bourgeois

Location of vineyards: St.-Laurent du Médoc

Owner: AGF.Allianz Group

Address: Route de Pauillac, 33112 St.-Laurent du Médoc

Telephone: 05 56 59 41 72; Telefax: 05 56 59 93 22

E-mail: info@trintaudon.com

Website: www.trintaudon.com

Visits: By appointment only Monday to Friday, 9:30 A.M.–5 P.M.

Contact: Matthias von Campe

VINEYARDS

Surface area: 81.5 acres

Grape varietals: 60% Cabernet Sauvignon, 40% Merlot

Average age of vines: 35 years

Density of plantation: 6,600 vines per hectare

Average yields: 55 hectoliters per hectare

Elevage: Prolonged fermentation and maceration (21–28 days) in temperature-controlled stainless-steel vats. Twelve months aging in barrels with 40% new oak. Fining and filtration.

WINES PRODUCED

Château Larose Perganson: 150,000 bottles

Château La Tourette: 50,000 bottles

Plateau of maturity: Within 4–7 years of the vintage

LA LAUZETTE-DECLERCQ (LISTRAC)

Classification: Cru Bourgeois

Location of vineyards: Couhenne, north of Listrac

Owner: Vignobles Declercq

Address: Hameau de Couhenne, 33480 Listrac-Médoc

Mailing address: Gravenstafel, 32 Sneppestraat, B-8860 Lendelede (Belgium)

Telephone: 05 56 58 02 40 *or* 32 51 30 40 81; Telefax: 32 51 31 90 54

E-mail: vignobles.declercq@belgacom.net

Website: www.medoc.wines.com

Visits: By appointment only

Contact: Jean-Louis Declercq

VINEYARDS

Surface area: 37 acres

Grape varietals: 47% Cabernet Sauvignon, 46% Merlot, 5% Petit Verdot, 2% Cabernet Franc

Average age of vines: 28 years

Density of plantation: 6,666 and 10,000 vines per hectare

Average yields: 50 hectoliters per hectare

Elevage: Fermentation and 21 day maceration in temperature-controlled stainless-steel vats. Twelve months aging in barrels that are renewed by a third at each vintage. Fining, no filtration.

WINES PRODUCED

Château La Lauzette: 60,000 bottles

Galets de La Lauzette: 25,000 bottles

Plateau of maturity: Within 3–12 years of the vintage

LIEUJEAN (HAUT-MÉDOC)

Classification: Cru Bourgeois

Location of vineyards: Saint-Sauveur de Médoc

Administrators: Jean-Michel Lapalu and Patrice Ricard

Address: 16, route de la Chatole, 33250 St.-Sauveur de Médoc

Mailing address: 1, rue du 19 mars, 33340 Bégadan

Telephone: 05 56 41 50 18; Telefax: 05 56 41 54 65

E-mail: info@domaines-lapalu.com

Website: www.domaines-lapalu.com

Visits: By appointment only

Contact: Domaines Lapalu

VINEYARDS

Surface area: 123.5 acres (93.9 in production)

Grape varietals: 69% Cabernet Sauvignon, 31% Merlot

Average age of vines: 25 years

Density of plantation: 7,000 vines per hectare

Average yields: 58 hectoliters per hectare

Elevage: Fermentation and 3–4 week maceration in temperature-controlled vats. Twelve to fifteen months aging in barrels that are renewed by 20–25% each year. Fining, light filtration upon bottling.

WINES PRODUCED

Château Lieujean: 280,000 bottles

Château Lagrave: 65,000–100,000 bottles

Plateau of maturity: Within 3–8 years of the vintage

LOUSTEAUNEUF (MÉDOC)

Classification: Cru Bourgeois

Location of vineyards: Valeyrac

Owner: Bruno Second

Address: 2, route de Lousteauneuf, 33340 Valeyrac

Telephone: 05 56 41 52 11; Telefax: 05 56 41 38 52

E-mail: chateau.lousteauneuf@wanadoo.fr

Website: www.chateau-lousteauneuf.com

Visits: By appointment Monday to Friday, 9 A.M.–noon and 2–5 P.M.

Contact: Bruno Second

VINEYARDS

Surface area: 55.6 acres

Grape varietals: 50% Cabernet Sauvignon, 36% Merlot, 10% Cabernet Franc, 4% Petit Verdot

Average age of vines: 25 years

Density of plantation: 5,300 vines per hectare

Average yields: 54 hectoliters per hectare

Elevage: One week cold maceration. Fermentation and maceration with pumpings-over and *pigéages.* Twelve months aging with 20% of yield in vats and the rest in barrels that are renewed by half each year. (The lots aged in vats complete their malolactics in barrel.) No fining, no filtration.

WINES PRODUCED

Château Lousteauneuf: 75,000 bottles

No second wine is produced.

Plateau of maturity: within 2–8 years of the vintage

DE MALLERET (HAUT-MÉDOC)

Classification: Cru Bourgeois

Location of vineyards: Le Pian-Médoc

Owner: Grands Vins de Gironde

Address: 33290 Le Pian-Médoc

Telephone: 05 56 35 05 36; Telefax: 05 56 35 05 38

Visits: By appointment only

Contact: Lionel Barès

VINEYARDS

Surface area: 123.5 acres

Grape varietals: 60% Cabernet Sauvignon, 30% Merlot, 8% Cabernet Franc, 2% Petit Verdot

Average age of vines: 35 years

Density of plantation: 8,000 vines per hectare

Average yields: 47 hectoliters per hectare

Elevage: Fermentation (28°C) and 28 day maceration in temperature-controlled stainless-steel vats. Twelve months aging in barrels that are renewed by a third at each vintage. Fining and filtration.

WINES PRODUCED

Château de Malleret: 130,000 bottles

Château Barthez: 150,000 bottles

Plateau of maturity: Within 2–8 years of the vintage

MALMAISON (MOULIS)

Classification: Cru Bourgeois

Location of vineyards: Moulis

Owner: Baroness Nadine de Rothschild

Address: 33480 Moulis-en-Médoc

Telephone: 05 56 58 38 00; Telefax: 05 56 58 26 46

Visits: By appointment and for professionals of the wine trade only.

Contact: Jean-Claude Boniface, Château Clarke, 33480 Listrac, Médoc.

Tel. 06 56 58 38 00, Fax 05 56 58 26 46

VINEYARDS

Surface area: 59.3 acres

Grape varietals: 80% Merlot, 20% Cabernet Sauvignon

Average age of vines: 22 years

Density of plantation: 6,600 vines per hectare

Average yields: 49 hectoliters per hectare

Elevage: Cold maceration. Fermentation and 21–25 day maceration in temperature-controlled stainless-steel vats with micro-oxygenation. Fifteen months aging in barrels with 20–30% new oak. Fining depends upon the vintage, light filtration upon bottling.

WINES PRODUCED

Château Malmaison: 100,000 bottles

Les Granges des Domaines Edmond de Rothschild: Variable (Haut-Médoc)

Plateau of maturity: Within 4–12 years of the vintage

LE MEYNIEU (HAUT-MÉDOC)

Classification: Cru Bourgeois

Location of vineyards: Vertheuil

Owner: SCEA des Domaines Pedro

Address: 33180 Vertheuil

Telephone: 05 56 73 32 10; Telefax: 05 56 41 98 89

E-mail: dompedro@aol.com

Visits: Monday to Friday, 9 A.M.–noon and 2–5 P.M. By appointment for groups.

Contact: Jacques Pedro or Frank Maroszak

VINEYARDS

Surface area: 46.9 acres

Grape varietals: 62% Cabernet Sauvignon, 30% Merlot, 8% Cabernet Franc

Average age of vines: 25 years

Density of plantation: 6,500 vines hectare

Average yields: 50–55 hectoliters per hectare

Elevage: Prolonged fermentation and maceration with frequent pumpings-over in temperature-controlled vats. Eighteen months aging in barrels with 30% new oak. Fining, no filtration.

WINES PRODUCED

Château Le Meynieu: 40,000–60,000 bottles

Château La Gravière: 40,000–60,000 bottles

Plateau of maturity: Within 3–10 years of the vintage

MOULIN DE LABORDE (LISTRAC)

Classification: Cru Bourgeois

Location of vineyards: Listrac

Owner: François Marret

Address: 33480 Listrac

Telephone: 05 56 58 03 83; Telefax: 05 56 58 06 30

Visits: Every day, 2–6 P.M.

Contact: Yann Ollivier

VINEYARDS

Surface area: 29.6 acres

Grape varietals: 50% Cabernet Sauvignon, 50% Merlot

Average age of vines: 25–30 years

Density of plantation: 6,700 vines per hectare

Average yields: 55 hectoliters per hectare

Elevage: Fermentations and macerations last four weeks in stainless-steel tanks equipped with a trickle cooling system. Pumpings-up are done twice a day. Two thirds of the yield is then aged in oak barrels for 6–8 months by rotation. Wines are fined and filtered.

WINES PRODUCED

Château Moulin de Laborde: 75,000 bottles

Plateau of maturity: Within 4–14 years of the vintage

NOAILLAC (MÉDOC)

Classification: Cru Bourgeois

Location of vineyards: Médoc

Owner: Marc Pagès family

Address: 33590 Jau-Dignac-Loirac

Telephone: 05 56 09 52 20; Telefax: 05 56 09 58 75

E-mail: noaillac@noaillac.com

Website: www.noaillac.com

Visits: Monday to Friday, 9 A.M.–noon and 1:30–4:30 P.M.

Contact: Xavier Pagès

VINEYARDS

Surface area: 113.6 acres

Grape varietals: 55% Merlot, 40% Cabernet Sauvignon, 5% Petit Verdot

Average age of vines: 20 years

Density of plantation: 5,500 vines per hectare

Average yields: 57 hectoliters per hectare

Elevage: Three to four week fermentation and maceration in stainless-steel and concrete tanks. Twelve months aging in vats for 40% of the yield and in barrels with 10% new oak for the rest. Fining and filtration.

WINES PRODUCED

Château Noaillac: 150,000 bottles

Moulin de Noaillac: 120,000 bottles

Plateau of maturity: Within 3–12 years of the vintage

RAMAFORT (MÉDOC)

Classification: Cru Bourgeois

Location of vineyards: Blaignan

Owner: Domaines CGR

Address: 33340 Blaignan

Mailing address: Les Domaines CGR, 40, rue Notre-Dame des Victoires, 75002 Paris

Telephone: 05 56 73 31 51 *or* 01 42 21 11 80; Telefax: 05 56 73 31 52 *or* 01 42 21 11 85

E-mail: gcharloux@domaines-cgr.com

Website: www.chateau-ramafort.com

Visits: Monday to Friday, 8:30 A.M.–12:30 P.M. and 1:30–5 P.M.

Contact: Annelis Bosq (Telephone: 05 56 73 31 51; Telefax: 05 56 73 31 52)

VINEYARDS

Surface area: 46.9 acres

Grape varietals: 50% Cabernet Sauvignon, 50% Merlot

Average age of vines: 28 years

Density of plantation: 7,500 vines per hectare

Average yields: 59 hectoliters per hectare

Elevage: Fermentation and maceration in temperature-controlled stainless-steel tanks. Twelve months aging in barrels that are renewed by half each year. Fining, filtration not systematic.

WINES PRODUCED

Château Ramafort: 110,000 bottles

Château Barbaran: Variable

Plateau of maturity: Within 3–6 years of the vintage

ROLLAN DE BY (MÉDOC)

Classification: Cru Bourgeois

Location of vineyards: Bégadan

Owner: Jean Guyon

Address: 7, route Rollan de By, 33340 Bégadan

Telephone: 05 56 41 58 59; Telefax: 05 56 41 37 82

E-mail: rollan-de-by@wanadoo.fr

Website: www.rollandeby.com

Visits: By appointment only Monday to Friday,
9 A.M.–noon and 2–5 P.M.

VINEYARDS

Surface area: 101.3 acres

Grape varietals: 70% Merlot, 20% Cabernet Sauvignon, 10% Petit Verdot

Average age of vines: 30 years

Density of plantation: 8,500 vines per hectare

Average yields: 45 hectoliters per hectare

Elevage: Cold maceration. Fermentation and three week maceration in temperature-controlled stainless-steel vats. Malolactics and 12 months aging on lees in new oak barrels. No fining, no filtration.

WINES PRODUCED

Château Rollan de By: 240,000 bottles

Fleur de By: 100,000 bottles

Plateau of maturity: Within 4–12 years of the vintage

ROSE SAINTE-CROIX (LISTRAC)

Classification: Cru Bourgeois

Location of vineyards: Listrac

Owner: Philippe Porcheron

Address: Route d'Avensan, 33480 Moulis-en-Médoc

Mailing address: 287, avenue de la Libération, 33110 Le Bouscat

Telephone: 05 56 42 69 50; Telefax: 05 56 42 69 88

E-mail: philippe.porcheron@wanadoo.fr

Visits: By appointment only

Contact: Philippe Porcheron

VINEYARDS

Surface area: 22.2 acres

Grape varietals: 56% Merlot, 44% Cabernet Sauvignon

Average age of vines: 22 years

Density of plantation: 6,600 vines per hectare

Average yields: 50 hectoliters per hectare

Elevage: Prolonged fermentation and 3–4 week maceration in temperature-controlled stainless-steel vats. Twelve months aging in barrels with 30% new oak. Fining, no filtration.

WINES PRODUCED

Château Rose Sainte-Croix: 40,000 bottles

Château Pontet Salanon: 15,000 bottles

Plateau of maturity: Within 5–14 years of the vintage

SAINTE-GEMME (HAUT-MÉDOC)

Classification: Cru Bourgeois

Location of vineyards: Cussac-Fort-Médoc

Owner: GFA des Domaines Bouteiller

Address: 33460 Cussac-Fort-Médoc

Telephone: 05 56 58 94 80; Telefax: 05 56 58 93 10

Visits: By appointment only

VINEYARDS

Surface area: 24.7 acres

Grape varietals: 50% Cabernet Sauvignon, 50% Merlot

Average age of vines: 15 years

Density of plantation: 6,800 vines per hectare

Average yields: 59 hectoliters per hectare

Elevage: Fermentations and macerations last 12 days in temperature-controlled concrete tanks. After malolactics in vats, wines are transferred to oak barrels (no new oak) for 12 months aging. They are fined and filtered.

WINES PRODUCED

Château de Sainte-Gemme: 60,000 bottles

No second wine is produced.

Plateau of maturity: Within 3–12 years of the vintage

TOUR BLANCHE (MÉDOC)

Classification: Cru Bourgeois

Location of vineyards: St.-Christoly-de-Médoc

Owner: Société des Vignobles d'Aquitaine

Address: 15, route du Breuil, 33340 St.-Christoly-de-Médoc

Telephone: 05 56 58 15 79; Telefax: 05 56 58 39 89

E-mail: hessel@moulin-a-vent.com

Visits: By appointment only

Contact: Dominique Hessel

VINEYARDS

Surface area: 96.3 acres

Grape varietals: 45% Merlot, 40% Cabernet Sauvignon, 10% Cabernet Franc, 5% Petit Verdot

Average age of vines: 30 years

Density of plantation: 5,555 vines hectare

Average yields: 56 hectoliters per hectare

Elevage: Fermentation and three week maceration in temperature-controlled stainless-steel tanks. Twenty to twenty-two months aging by rotation in vats and in barrels with 20% new oak. No fining, light filtration upon bottling.

WINES PRODUCED

Château La Tour Blanche: 180,000 bottles

Château Guiraud Peyrebrune: 100,000 bottles

Plateau of maturity: Within 2–10 years of the vintage

TOUR SERAN (MÉDOC)

Classification: Cru Bourgeois

Location of vineyards: Bégadan

Owner: Jean Guyon

Address: 7, route Rollan de By, 33340 Bégadan

Telephone: 05 56 41 58 59; Telefax: 05 56 41 37 82

E-mail: rollan-de-by@wanadoo.fr

Website: www.rollandeby.com

Visits: By appointment only Monday to Friday,
9 A.M.–noon and 2–5 P.M.

VINEYARDS

Surface area: 24.7 acres

Grape varietals: 80% Merlot, 10% Cabernet Sauvignon, 10% Petit Verdot

Average age of vines: 30 years

Density of plantation: 10,000 vines per hectare

Average yields: 35 hectoliters per hectare

Elevage: Fermentation and maceration in temperature-controlled tanks. Malolactics and 12 months aging in new oak barrels. No fining, no filtration.

WINES PRODUCED

Château Tour Seran: Production not indicated

Plateau of maturity: Within 3–7 years of the vintage

THE RED AND WHITE WINES OF PESSAC-LÉOGNAN AND GRAVES

It was the wines of Graves that were the first Bordeaux wines to be made and exported. Barrels of Graves wine were shipped to England during the English reign over this region of France between 1152 and 1453. The region's most hallowed property, Haut-Brion, can trace its history back to the 1600s, long before any of the Médoc blue bloods were ever mentioned. Even the Americans, led by the multitalented Thomas Jefferson in 1785, seemed to think that the wines of Graves were among the best wines made in Bordeaux.

Times have changed, and no wine-producing region in Bordeaux has lost more ground, literally and figuratively, than the region of Graves.

Graves, which includes the appellation of Pessac-Léognan (created in 1987 for the most cherished *terroirs* of this sprawling area), gets its name from the gravelly soil, a vestige of Ice Age glaciers. Totally different from the other wine regions of Bordeaux, it begins in what most tourists would think is still the city of Bordeaux but is actually the congested southern suburbs known as Talence and Pessac, two high-rise, modern, heavily populated centers of middle-class Bordelais and University of Bordeaux students. The major vineyards in this area, Haut-Brion, La Mission Haut-Brion, Pape Clément, and the microscopic treasure Les Carmes Haut-Brion, being the most renowned, happen to be the finest of the region, but since the last century they have had to fight off both urban sprawl and blight. A visit to these vineyards will offer a noisy contrast to the tranquil pastoral settings of the vineyards in the Médoc, Pomerol, and St.-Emilion. All the vineyards in this northern sector of Graves now carry the appellation of Pessac-Léognan. Unless you have a satellite navigational system on your vehicle, first-time visitors will have considerable trouble finding these vineyards among the urban/suburban sprawl.

Heading south from Talence and Pessac for the better part of 20 kilometers are the widely scattered vineyards of Pessac-Léognan. The region, once past the commercial suburb of Gradignan, does become pastoral and rural, with vineyards intermingled with pine forests and small farms. The two southern areas of Graves that produce the best wine are Léognan and Martillac, two small bucolic towns that seem much farther away from the bustling city of Bordeaux than they actually are. These wines too carry the appellation name of Pessac-Léognan.

The entire Graves region produces and is famous for both red and white wines. The top white wines of this region are rare and expensive and, in a few cases, capable of rivaling the finest white wines produced in France. They are produced from three grape varieties: Sauvignon Blanc, Semillon, and Muscadelle. However, the finest wines of Graves are the reds.

Graves's most famous estate, the American-owned Château Haut-Brion in the northern suburb of Pessac, was the first Bordeaux wine to receive international recognition. It was referred to in 1663 by the English author Samuel Pepys and between 1785 and 1789 by America's preeminent Francophile, Thomas Jefferson. The international acclaim for the distinctive wines of Haut-Brion was no doubt the reason why this property was the only non-Médoc to be included in the 1855 Classification of the Wines of the Gironde. Along with Haut-Brion, the other exceptional red wines produced in Graves are Haut-Brion's cross-street sibling, La Mission Haut-Brion, as well as the nearby estates of Pape Clément and Les Carmes Haut-Brion.

There are other fine Pessac-Léognan wines, most notably La Tour Haut-Brion in Talence, and Haut-Bailly, La Louvière, Smith Haut Lafitte, Domaine de Chevalier, and de Fieuzal near Léognan, but the overall level of quality winemaking, looked at from a consumer's perspective, is not as high as in such Médoc communes as St.-Julien, Pauillac, and St.-Estèphe, yet significant improvements were evident in the late 1990s.

The wines of Pessac-Léognan, like those of the Médoc, have their own quality classification. It, too, falsely serves as a quality guide to unsuspecting wine enthusiasts. The first classification occurred in 1953 and the most recent classification in 1959. The 1959 classification listed 13 châteaux producing red wine, with Haut-Brion appearing first and the remaining 12 listed alphabetically. For the white wine producers (often the same châteaux), there were nine châteaux listed in alphabetical order, with Haut-Brion's minuscule production of white wine excluded at the château's insistence.

The personality traits of the northern Graves are individualistic and singular and not difficult to decipher when tasted blind in a comparative tasting with Médocs. While top wines such as Haut-Brion and La Mission Haut-Brion differ considerably in style, they do share a rich, earthy, almost tobacco-scented (cigar box), roasted, scorched-earth character. With the exception of La Mission Haut-Brion, most of these red wines

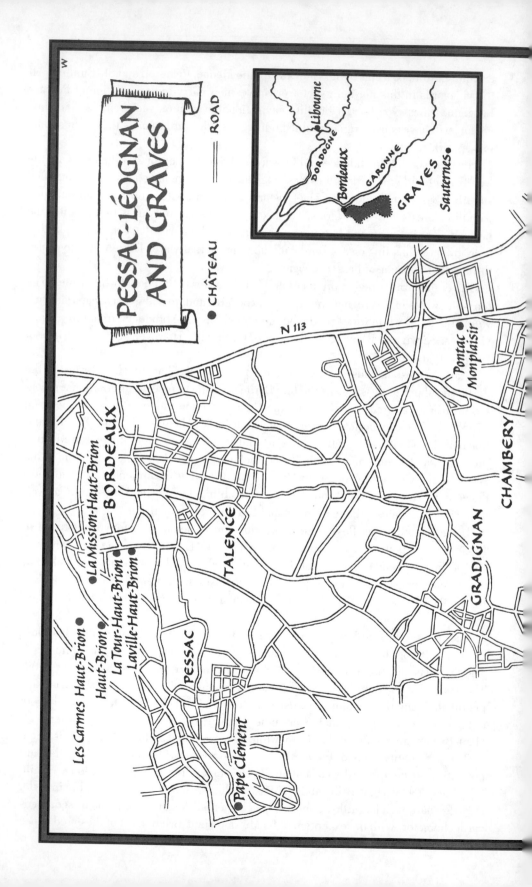

PESSAC-LÉOGNAN AND GRAVES

● CHÂTEAU
— ROAD

Libourne
DORDOGNE
Bordeaux
GARONNE
GRAVES
Sauternes ●

N 113

BORDEAUX
La Mission-Haut-Brion ●
Les Carmes Haut-Brion ●
Haut-Brion ●
La Tour-Haut-Brion ●
Laville-Haut-Brion ●

TALENCE

PESSAC

Pape Clément ●

GRADIGNAN

CHAMBERY

Pontac Momplaisir ●

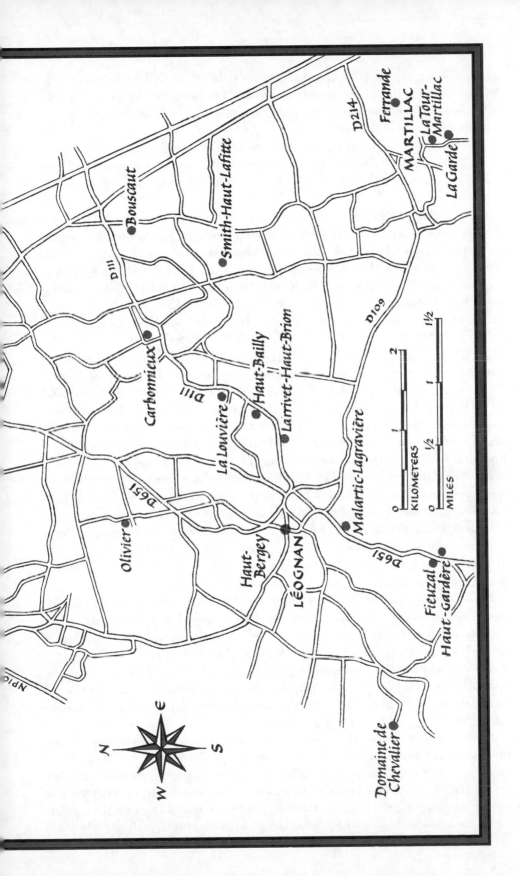

appear more fragrant, but lighter and more supple, than their Médoc counterparts. Yet the finest wines of this region almost always have a compelling fragrance. For my olfactory sense, there is no more provocative and profound bouquet in Bordeaux than that of a top vintage of Haut-Brion.

This particular characteristic reaches its most intense level with the Pessac vineyards of Haut-Brion, La Mission Haut-Brion, Pape Clément, Les Carmes Haut-Brion, and, to a lesser extent, Haut-Bailly, Domaine de Chevalier, Smith Haut Lafitte, and La Louvière.

Like two championship fighters staring down each other before a match, La Mission Haut-Brion and Haut-Brion face each other across Route N250. Prior to 1983, neither the proprietors nor the winemakers of each property ever had many kind things to say about the other: the La Mission winemaking team calling Haut-Brion's wines too light, overpriced, and overmanipulated; the Haut-Brion team accused La Mission of making overly big, alcoholic, savage, sometimes volatile wines that lacked finesse. This long-standing dispute came to an end in 1983 when Haut-Brion purchased La Mission, but the truth is that both properties produce profound, but different, wine.

La Mission Haut-Brion tends to be a bigger, richer, more deeply colored wine than Haut-Brion. It has also been one of Bordeaux's most successful wines in mediocre or poor vintages. The 1997, 1994, 1993, 1987, 1974, 1972, 1967, 1960, 1958, and 1957 are vivid proof of that fact. When mature, the wine has the classic Graves bouquet of tobacco and earthy, mineral scents. Haut-Brion can be noticeably lighter, a trend particularly evident during the period 1966–1976, but before and after this era Haut-Brion has been a prodigious wine and, to my taste, one of the most provocative and compelling of the first growths. In particular, vintages since the mid-1980s have been spectacular as well as consistent. While American-owned, Haut-Brion has long been managed by the same family. Since 1961, Jean-Bernard Delmas has made a succession of brilliant wines. For three decades prior to that, his father was in charge. Son Jean-Philippe now apprentices under the watchful eyes of his father and will be the Delmas that takes over in 2004. In my 25-plus years of interaction with the Who's Who of Bordeaux, there is no greater winemaker than Jean-Bernard Delmas.

Pape Clément, since 1986, comes closer in style to Haut-Brion than to La Mission Haut-Brion. Because of the high percentage of Merlot used in the blend and the thin, gravelly soil, Pape Clément does, in top vintages, have the roasted, mineral, tobacco-scented nose and a smooth, supple, even opulent, plummy fruitiness that recalls a top Pomerol. It is cunningly made to be delicious young, yet the best vintages can last for up to 20 years. In the late 1990s the proprietor became even more fanatical about quality and the results in 2001, 2000, and 1998 were sensational. Pape Clément is making considerable noise . . . or should I say music?

Once away from the annoyingly noisy, traffic-cluttered roads of Pessac and Talence, the Graves region takes on more charm. The suburbs of Bordeaux segue into pastures, farms, and small forests. This is the southern Graves, and the wines are less earthy, less smoky and tobacco-scented than the Graves from Pessac and Talence. They are also lighter. Léognan is the center for the best southern Graves. The tiny Domaine de Chevalier, a relatively obscure vineyard hidden by thick forests, performs splendidly well, making minuscule quantities of compelling white Graves and moderate quantities of the aforementioned smooth, very flavorful, rich, creamy, complex red wine, although several recent vintages have been distressingly woody.

Nearby is Haut-Bailly. Haut-Bailly produces a subtle yet fruity Graves wine that is usually ready to drink within 5–7 years of the vintage. Some of this château's wines can be long-lived, but this is one wine for which patience is not required. A measured, even restrained wine, the finest vintages possess an ethereal lightness about them that can be easily overlooked when tasted next to bigger, more dramatic wines. Nearby is de Fieuzal, which has made significant strides in quality since the 1980s. The white wine has been among the most splendid examples of the appellation since 1985, and the red wine has also taken on more depth, size, and complexity. At present, de Fieuzal may be the most undervalued wine of the entire appellation.

Two of the success stories of the 1990s include Smith Haut Lafitte and Malartic-Lagravière. An underachiever for decades, the beautiful estate of Smith Haut Lafitte was sold to the Cathiard family, who immediately turned this moribund producer into a bright, shining star of the appellation for both white and red wines. Now a luxury spa/hotel/restaurant (also owned by the Cathiards) sits adjacent to the vineyards of Smith Haut Lafitte, cleverly named Sources de Caudalie. Under a new owner, Malartic-Lagravière also soared in quality at the end of the 1990s. Two other estates that have exploded on the world stage and merit significant attention are Haut-Bergey and Larrivet-Haut-Brion. Both were perennial underachievers, yet changes in ownership, major investments, and new winemaking teams (the brilliant Libourne oenologist, Michel Rolland, oversees both estates) have propelled them into the upper hierarchy of quality. In 2003 both estates are among the stars of Pessac-Léognan for both red and white. And much to the chagrin of the reactionaries of Bordeaux, Haut-Bergey's owners have created the first *vin de garage* of the region, the sumptuous, super-concentrated Branon, first made in 2000.

There are, of course, numerous other wines, yet most of the other classified growths making red wine tend to produce light, rather one-dimensional wines that can be satisfying but will rarely offer much excitement. Carbonnieux is interesting and to my taste has the potential to be a higher-quality wine, if only the ownership would aspire to more lofty goals. Oddly enough, the white is consistently delicious, the red less so. Bouscaut remains the only classified growth that seems to need a wake-up call that would propel them out of the 19th century.

Pessac-Léognan and the larger area, Graves, are regions to investigate when Bordeaux has a mediocre or poor vintage. The drainage is excellent, and in years like 1994, 1993, 1987, 1974, 1964, and 1958, when many wines from the Médoc were diluted and disappointing, properties such as La Mission Haut-Brion, Domaine de Chevalier, and Haut-Brion produced excellent wines from healthy, relatively mature grapes. On the other hand, exceptionally hot, drought-like years that often result in superb wines in the northern Médoc, St.-Emilion, and Pomerol tend to severely stress the vineyards of Graves, causing a blockage in the grapes' maturity process. Most recently, particularly hot years such as 1990, 1989, and 1982 produced many superb wines, but these vintages were less consistent in Graves than elsewhere for this very reason. Recent outstanding vintages for Graves have been 2000, 1998, 1995, 1990, 1988 (better than 1990 and 1989 for some properties), 1987 (a sleeper year), 1985, 1983 (more consistent than 1982), 1978, 1971, 1970, 1964, and 1961.

There are numerous properties in Graves, many of them not even classified, that have been making significant qualitative progress and are, if anything, undervalued. Excellent producers such as La Louvière, Picque Caillou, La Garde, Clos Floridene, Haut-Gardère, and de France are names to take seriously.

GRAVES/PESSAC-LÉOGNAN
(An Insider's View—Red Wines)

Overall Appellation Potential: Average to Superb

The Most Potential for Aging: Branon, Domaine de Chevalier, Haut-Bailly, Haut-Bergey, Haut-Brion, La Mission Haut-Brion, Pape Clément, Smith Haut Lafitte

The Most Elegant: Bahans Haut-Brion (second wine of Haut-Brion), Les Carmes Haut-Brion, Haut-Bailly, Haut-Brion, Malartic-Lagravière, Pape Clément, Smith Haut Lafitte

The Most Concentrated: Branon, de Fieuzal, Haut-Bergey, Haut-Brion, La Louvière, La Mission Haut-Brion, Pape Clément, Smith Haut Lafitte

The Best Value: Chantegrive, Les Carmes Haut-Brion, Clos Floridene, La Garde, La Louvière, Rochemorin

The Most Exotic: Branon, Haut-Bergey

The Most Underrated: La Garde, La Louvière

The Most Difficult to Appreciate Young: Domaine de Chevalier

The Easiest to Appreciate Young: Les Carmes Haut-Brion, Chantegrive, Clos Floridene, La Garde, La Louvière

Up-and-Coming Estates: La Garde, Haut-Bergey, Larrivet-Haut-Brion, La Louvière, Malartic-Lagravière, Smith Haut Lafitte

Greatest Recent Vintages: 2000, 1998, 1995, 1994, 1990, 1988, 1983, 1979, 1978, 1975, 1964, 1961, 1959

GRAVES/PESSAC-LÉOGNAN
(An Insider's View—White Wines)

Overall Appellation Potential: Average to Superb

The Most Potential for Aging: Carbonnieux, Domaine de Chevalier, de Fieuzal, Haut-Brion, Laville Haut-Brion, Smith Haut Lafitte

The Most Elegant: Carbonnieux, Couhins-Lurton, La Garde, Haut-Brion, Latour-Martillac, Pape Clément, Smith Haut Lafitte

The Most Concentrated: de Fieuzal, Haut-Brion, Laville Haut-Brion, La Louvière, Smith Haut Lafitte

The Best Value: Chantegrive, La Garde, La Louvière, Magneau, Rahoul, Rochemorin, Roquetaillade, La Vieille-France, Vieux-Château-Gaubert

The Most Exotic: Clos Floridene, Latour-Martillac, La Vieille-France

The Most Difficult to Understand (when young): Domaine de Chevalier

The Most Underrated: Clos Floridene, La Garde, Magneau, Rochemorin, Smith Haut Lafitte, La Vieille-France

Up-and-Coming Estates: Haut-Bergey, Larrivet-Haut-Brion, La Louvière, Smith Haut Lafitte

Greatest Recent Vintages: 2001, 1998, 1997, 1995, 1994, 1989, 1985, 1983, 1978, 1975, 1966, 1962

PESSAC-LÉOGNAN—AN OVERVIEW

Location: On the left bank of the Garonne River, this subregion of Graves covers the northernmost sector, which is essentially 10 communes

Acres Under Vine: 2,964

Communes: Cadaujac, Canéjan, Graignan, Léognan, Martillac, Mérignac, Pessac, St.-Médard-d'Eyrans, Talence, Villenave-d'Ornon

Average Annual Production: 560,000 cases, of which 80% is red and 20% is white

Classified Growths: Total of 16 in Graves/Pessac-Léognan, all of which are located in the subregion of Pessac-Léognan; 6 are classified for both their red and white wines, 7 are classified for red wines, and 3 are classified for white wines

Principal Grape Varieties: Red—Cabernet Sauvignon and Merlot dominate, with Cabernet Franc playing a backup role; white—Sauvignon Blanc and Semillon, with a tiny quantity of Muscadelle

GRAVES—AN OVERVIEW

Location: A relatively large area located mostly to the south of the city of Bordeaux on the left bank of the Garonne River

Acres Under Vine: 7,657

Communes: Nearly 30 separate communes, the most prominent being Cerons, Illats, Landiras, Langon, Podensac, Portets, and Saucats

Average Annual Production: 1,950,000 cases, of which 70% is red and 30% is white

Classified Growths: Total of 16 in Graves/Pessac-Léognan, none of which are located in the subregion of Graves

Principal Grape Varieties: Red—Merlot and Cabernet Sauvignon; white—Semillon and Sauvignon Blanc, with small quantities of Muscadelle

A CONSUMER'S CLASSIFICATION OF THE RED AND WHITE
WINE–PRODUCING CHÂTEAUX OF GRAVES

OUTSTANDING

Domaine de Chevalier (white only), Haut-Brion (red and white), Laville Haut-Brion (white only), La Mission Haut-Brion, Pape Clément (red and white)

EXCELLENT

Branon (since 2000), Les Carmes Haut-Brion, Couhins-Lurton (white only), de Fieuzal (red and white), Haut-Bailly, Haut-Bergey (since 1998), Larrivet-Haut-Brion (red and white), La Louvière (red and white), Malartic-Lagravière, Smith Haut Lafitte (red and white since 1991)

VERY GOOD

Bahans Haut-Brion, Clos Floridene (white only), Domaine de Chevalier (red only), La Garde, Roquetaillade (white only), La Tour Haut-Brion

GOOD

Archambeau, Baret, Carbonnieux, Chantegrive, Cheret-Pitres, Cruzeau, Ferrande, Graville-Lacoste, Haut-Gardère, Olivier, Picque Caillou, Pontac Monplaisir, Rahoul, Rochemorin, La Tour-Martillac, La Vieille-France

OTHER NOTABLE GRAVES PROPERTIES

Bardins, Bouscaut, Boyrein, Brondelle, Cabannieux, Cantelys, Coucheroy, Courrèges Seguès du Château de Gaillat, La Fleur Jonquet, de France, Gaillat, Gazin Rocquencourt, Jean Gervais, Grand-Abord, Haut-Calens, Haut Lagrange, Haut-Nouchet, l'Hospital, Lafargue, Lamouroux, Landiras, Lespault, Magence, Mauves, Perin de Naudine, Pessan, Peyreblanque, Piron, St.-Jean des Graves, St.-Robert, Le Sartre, Seuil, Domaine de la Solitude, Thil Comte Clary, La Tour de Boyrin, Tourte, Le Tuquet, Villa Bel Air

BOUSCAUT

Classification: Classified growth (for reds and whites)

Owner: SA Château Bouscaut

Address: 33140 Cadaujac

Telephone: 05 57 83 12 20; Telefax: 05 57 83 12 21

Visits: By appointment only

Contact: Laurent Cogombles

VINEYARDS (RED)

Surface area: 123.5 acres

Grape varietals: 50% Merlot, 47% Cabernet Sauvignon, 3% Malbec

Average age of vines: 35 years

Density of plantation: 7,200 vines per hectare

Average yields: 48 hectoliters per hectare

Elevage: Twenty to thirty day fermentation in stainless-steel vats. Sixteen months aging in barrels with 50% new oak. Fining depending upon the vintage, filtration.

RED WINES PRODUCED

Château Bouscaut: 100,000 bottles

La Flamme de Bouscaut: 100,000 bottles

Plateau of maturity: Within 4–12 years of the vintage

VINEYARDS (WHITE)

Surface area: 14.8 acres

Grape varietals: 65% Semillon, 35% Sauvignon

Average age of vines: 30 years

Density of plantation: 7,200 vines per hectare

Average yields: 48 hectoliters per hectare

Elevage: Cold maceration for part of the yield. Fermentation and 11 months aging in barrels with 60% new oak. Fining depending upon the vintage, no filtration.

WHITE WINES PRODUCED

Château Bouscaut: 18,000 bottles

Lamothe Bouscaut: 18,000 bottles

Plateau of maturity: Within 2–6 years of the vintage

GENERAL APPRECIATION

Even though the 2001 and 2000 red Bouscaut (which are good as opposed to excellent) represent a marked improvement over their so-so predecessors, this consistent underperformer still has a long way to go if it wants to live up to its cru classé status. Despite reasonable prices, much better values are available from the Graves, especially among many of the well-run nonclassified growths like La Louvière or Rochemorin.

It was widely believed that after the American syndicate sold Bouscaut in 1979 to the well-known Bordeaux château owner Lucien Lurton, the quality at Bouscaut would improve. It has not. This property, among all of the classified growths of Graves, remains content to turn out unexciting white and red wines. The 18th-century château, with a lovely pool, was restored completely in the 1960s and is one of the most attractive in the region. Tasting the wines leaves the impression that there is a lack of a selection process. Some claim the high percentage of Merlot in the red wine (from young vines) has been detrimental to the wine's quality. I do not agree with that; I simply think Bouscaut produces too much wine without a severe enough selection to put the best under the château's name. Observers are hoping that the proprietor, Sophie Lurton (who was given the property by her father, Lucien Lurton, in 1992) will increase the level of quality. Both 2001 and 2000 represent a modest move in the right direction.

IMPORTANT VINTAGES (RED)

2001 This may be the finest Bouscaut I have ever tasted. It exhibits a deep ruby/purple
87–88 color as well as an earthy, tobacco-scented nose, medium body, excellent richness and purity, and more texture as well as depth than I have seen in these wines for more than 20 years. Anticipated maturity: 2005–2015.

2000 Finally, a reasonably good effort from this underachiever, Bouscaut's 2000 pos-
86 sesses a dark ruby/purple color in addition to aromas of spicy new oak, red and black currant fruit. While superficial, there is more to it than most previous vintages have contained. Medium bodied, with sweet tannin, and a nicely textured, moderately endowed finish, it will drink well until 2015. Last tasted, 1/03.

1999
82
Sweet ripe currants, cherries, and berries intermixed with minerals, smoke, and new oak compete in this soft, straightforward, pleasant offering. Drink it over the next 8–10 years. Last tasted, 3/02.

1998
75
Although the color is an attractive dark ruby, this light- to medium-bodied effort reveals considerable hollowness in the mid-palate. While some Pessac-Léognan aromas of scorched earth, red currant, and gravel emerge, there is little depth or length. Anticipated maturity: now–2012. Last tasted, 3/02.

1990
78
Deep in color, with an appealing smoky, oaky, ripe berry–scented nose, the 1990 Bouscaut possesses less substance and aging potential than the 1989 or 1988. Last tasted, 1/93.

1989
82
The 1989 Bouscaut is light, medium-bodied, and correct, but it has more alcohol, extremely high tannins that appear excessive for its straightforward, fruity personality, and a great deal of oak. If it fills out and develops a mid-palate (unlikely), this offering may merit a higher score. Anticipated maturity: now. Last tasted, 1/93.

IMPORTANT VINTAGES (WHITE)

2001
86
This is a crisp, elegant white, offering notes of grapefruits and minerals. It is light to medium-bodied, with fine fruit, a moderate bouquet, and the potential for 10–12 years of longevity. Last tasted, 1/03.

2000
84
Straightforward and correct, Bouscaut's unexciting 2000 white wine reveals notions of minerals, mint, and citrus. Drink this light-bodied, monolithic offering over the next 7–8 years. Last tasted, 1/03.

ANCIENT VINTAGES (RED)

In short, there is virtually nothing of interest from the 1980s and 1970s.

BRANON

Classification: None

Owner: Sylviane Garcin-Cathiard

Address: 33850 Léognan

Mailing address: c/o Château Haut-Bergey, 33850 Léognan

Telephone: 05 56 64 05 22; Telefax: 05 56 64 06 98

E-mail: haut.bergey@wanadoo.fr

Visits: By appointment only

Contact: Hélène Garcin-Lévêque

VINEYARDS (RED)

Surface area: 3.7 acres (in production)

Grape varietals: 50% Cabernet Sauvignon, 50% Merlot

Average age of vines: 35 years

Density of plantation: 7,140 vines per hectare

Average yields: 30 hectoliters per hectare

Elevage: Fermentation in temperature-controlled wooden vats of small capacity (50 hectoliters) with indigenous yeasts. Malolactics and 18 months aging in new oak barrels. No fining, no filtration.

RED WINES PRODUCED

Château Branon: 6,000 bottles

No second wine is produced.

Plateau of maturity: Within 15 years of the vintage

GENERAL APPRECIATION

A luxury cuvée from Haut-Bergey, Branon is fashioned under the supervision of Bordeaux's two most talented consultants, Jean-Luc Thunevin and Michel Rolland. It is a shocker in terms of its extraordinary richness as well as sense of place. Small quantities make it difficult to find, but the wine is worth a search of the marketplace. A must buy!

IMPORTANT VINTAGES

2001 The impressive, dense, purple-colored 2001 offers up notes of sweet tobacco, soil
90–93 overtones, blueberry and blackberry liqueur, smoky, toasty oak, and a hint of espresso. A sweet, rich attack, sensational concentration, medium body, ripe tannin, and profound depth suggest a blockbuster 2000 rather than 2001. Anticipated maturity: 2006–2018. Last tasted, 1/03.

2000 The debut vintage, 2000 is undoubtedly the real deal. Its opaque purple color is
96 followed by strikingly sweet, smoky, black currant, cocoa, scorched earth, and graphite aromas. Full-bodied, remarkably concentrated, pure, and multitextured, with a finish that lasts nearly a minute, this fabulous wine will be fascinating to follow. Anticipated maturity: 2009–2025. Last tasted, 1/03.

BROWN

Classification: None

Owner: Bernard Barthe

Address: 33850 Léognan

Telephone: 05 56 87 08 10; Telefax: 05 56 87 87 34

E-mail: chateau.brown@wanadoo.fr

Website: www.chateau-brown.com

Visits: By appointment only

Contact: Odile Lepetit or Catherine Gabrile

VINEYARDS (RED)

Surface area: 57 acres

Grape varietals: 65% Cabernet Sauvignon, 32% Merlot, 3% Petit Verdot

Average age of vines: 15 years

Density of plantation: 7,400 vines per hectare

Average yields: 45 hectoliters per hectare

Elevage: Fermentation and 21–27 day maceration in temperature-controlled stainless-steel vats. Eighteen months aging in barrels, with 33% new oak. Fining, no filtration.

RED WINES PRODUCED

Château Brown: 80,000 bottles

Le Colombier de Château Brown: 30,000 bottles

Plateau of maturity: Within 3–12 years of the vintage

VINEYARDS (WHITE)

Surface area: 12 acres

Grape varietals: 67% Sauvignon Blanc, 33% Semillon

Average yields: 45 hectoliters per hectare

Elevage: Fermentation and 8–10 months aging in barrels that are renewed by half for each vintage. Fining, no filtration.

WHITE WINES PRODUCED

Château Brown: 20,000 bottles

Le Colombier de Château Brown: 20,000 bottles

Plateau of maturity: 2–7 years

GENERAL APPRECIATION

An underrated estate that has come on strongly in the 21st century, Château Brown is producing some of the finest wines I have ever tasted.

This estate, named after an 18th-century English wine merchant by the name of John Louis Brown, was acquired by the Barthe family in 1994. Considerable investments have been made in the well-placed vineyards (not far from Léognan) as well as the winery. The entire vineyard is planted on a gravel-based ridge with an excellent exposure. This is a property to watch.

IMPORTANT VINTAGES (RED)

2001   A strong effort from this underrated estate, this deep ruby–colored 2001 reveals
88–90   big, sweet aromas of tobacco, cedar, fruitcake, and red currants. Medium bodied, with sweet tannin, excellent, possibly outstanding ripeness, and a long, pure, nicely textured finish, it will be at its finest between 2004 and 2012. Last tasted, 1/03.

2000   Undoubtedly the most impressive wine I have ever tasted from Brown, the dense
89   ruby/purple-colored 2000 offers up excellent aromas of cassis, red currants, cedar, and tobacco. Medium bodied, with super concentration as well as purity, power combined with elegance, and a moderately tannic finish. Anticipated maturity: 2005–2015. A sleeper of the vintage.

1999   A medium-weight Graves, this savory, perfumed 1999 offers spicy, earthy tobacco,
87   and sweet cherry/currant fruit in a medium-bodied, soft style. Enjoy it over the next 3–4 years. Last tasted, 3/02.

1998   Soft, scorched-earth, currant, cherry, and graphite-like flavors characterize this
87   spicy, sweet, medium-bodied, elegant, supple offering. A delicious, textbook Graves made in a medium-weight style, it will drink well for 3–4 years. Last tasted, 3/02.

IMPORTANT VINTAGES (WHITE)

2001
89
Citrus, fig, green bean, and smoky scents jump from the glass of this medium-bodied, nicely textured, ripe, concentrated dry white Graves made from 67% Sauvignon Blanc and 33% Semillon. It should drink well for 7–8 years. Last tasted, 1/03.

CARBONNIEUX

Classification: Classified growth (reds and whites)

Owner: Société Civile des Grandes Graves—Perrin family

Address: 33850 Léognan

Telephone: 05 57 96 56 20; Telefax: 05 56 96 59 19

E-mail: chateau-carbonnieux@wanadoo.fr

Website: www.carbonnieux.com

Visits: By appointment Monday to Friday, 8:30–11 A.M. and 2–5 P.M.

Contact: Béatrice Arnaud

VINEYARDS (RED)

Surface area: 111.2 acres

Grape varietals: 60% Cabernet Sauvignon, 30% Merlot, 7% Cabernet Franc, 2% Malbec, 1% Petit Verdot

Average age of vines: 40 years

Density of plantation: 7,200 vines per hectare

Average yields: 50 hectoliters per hectare

Elevage: Fermentation and 21 day maceration in temperature-controlled stainless-steel vats.

Eighteen months aging in barrels that are renewed by a third at each vintage. Fining and filtration.

RED WINES PRODUCED

Château Carbonnieux: 200,000 bottles

Château Tour Léognan: 40,000 bottles

Plateau of maturity: Within 7–10 years of the vintage

VINEYARDS (WHITE)

Surface area: 103.7 acres

Grape varietals: 60% Sauvignon Blanc, 38% Semillon, 2% Muscadelle

Average age of vines: 40 years

Density of plantation: 7,200 vines per hectare

Average yields: 50 hectoliters per hectare

Elevage: Fermentation and 10 months aging on lees in barrels that are renewed by a third at each vintage. Fining and filtration.

WHITE WINES PRODUCED

Château Carbonnieux: 200,000 bottles

Château Tour Léognan: 40,000 bottles

Plateau of maturity: Within 3–20 or more years of the vintage

GENERAL APPRECIATION

Very Burgundian, with a Volnay-like personality, the red Carbonnieux has much improved since 1985 and now lives up to its status. It can sometimes be perceived as somewhat light, but this is the mode of expression of this supple and tasty wine, which is graceful and elegant in a low-key manner. Consumers looking for potentially long-lived efforts should stay clear of it, but lovers of fruity and quintessentially elegant Graves will be satisfied in most vintages. Prices remain reasonable. As for the white wines, they have always been excellent, and in some vintages very long-lived.

Carbonnieux, one of the largest estates of Graves, had, until the mid-1980s, fit into the pattern of many of the winemaking estates of the Pessac-Léognan area—the white wines were frequently delicious, but the red wines innocuously light and bland. Since the mid-1980s that has changed for the better, with the white wine taking on even higher-quality aspirations and the red wine becoming tasty, elegant, supple, and well made.

The property is not only of historic significance, but is among the most scenic of the region. The history of the vineyards can be traced to the 13th century, but the modern era of Carbonnieux began in 1956 when Marc Perrin acquired the estate. His son, Anthony, now oversees the winemaking. In the mid-1980s Anthony Perrin hired the famed Denis Dubourdieu, to give the whites even more fragrance and concentration. Additionally, the reds have taken on greater depth and intensity.

Most vintages of Carbonnieux, both the red and white wines, should be drunk in their first 7–10 years. Some of the white wine vintages have a remarkable potential to last for up to two or three decades.

IMPORTANT VINTAGES (RED)

2001
87–88 An elegant, graceful effort (much like the proprietor), this deep ruby–colored 2001 reveals aromas of sweet black cherries intermixed with loamy soil scents. Medium-bodied, with supple tannin as well as a long, flowing finish, it is a classic effort of restraint and measured richness that should drink well young yet age nicely for 10–15 years. Last tasted, 1/03.

2000
89 Probably the finest Carbonnieux I have tasted in more than three decades, this deep ruby/purple–colored offering reveals complex aromas of black cherries, currants, tobacco, soy, and earth. Medium bodied with gorgeous purity, more glycerin and depth than usual, and subtle toasty oak in the background, this is a beautiful example of refinement and breeding. Anticipated maturity: 2006–2018. Last tasted, 1/03.

1999
86 This light-bodied, soft, round, picnic-styled claret reveals jammy cherry fruit mixed with herb-tinged tobacco notes. It is best consumed over the next 5–6 years. Last tasted, 3/02.

1998
87
Very Burgundian-like in its vivid black cherry/smoky nose, this medium-bodied, somewhat light but racy, tasty wine is graceful in a low-keyed manner. It will not make old bones, but it is well knit and charming. Enjoy it over the next 7–8 years. Last tasted, 3/02.

1997
81
This is a light-bodied, picnic-styled claret with evidence of dilution as well as soft cherry/raspberry fruit flavors reminiscent of a lighter-styled Burgundy. Drink it over the next 2–3 years. Last tasted, 1/02.

1996
86
This is a stylish, medium-bodied, dark ruby–colored wine with attractive cherry and raspberry fruit intermixed with toasty notes in both the aromatics and flavors. This elegant wine reveals a Volnay-like personality. It should drink well until 2008. Last tasted, 1/02.

1995
87
An attractive, sexy effort from Carbonnieux, this medium-bodied, deep ruby–colored wine reveals subtle aromas of smoky oak intertwined with tobacco, kirsch, and black currant fruit. In the mouth, elegance, balance, suppleness, finesse, and an overall allure characterize this round, lightly tannic, lush, and captivating claret. Anticipated maturity: now–2011. Last tasted, 3/01.

1994
79
Carbonnieux's 1994 displays a medium dark ruby color, a sweet, ripe nose of currants and cherries, spicy new oak, austere, lean flavors, and high tannin. There is a lack of complexity, fruit, and flesh in this dry, hard, woody wine. Anticipated maturity: now. Last tasted, 1/97.

IMPORTANT VINTAGES (WHITE)

2001
91
A gorgeous Carbonnieux, this is the finest dry white I have tasted in many years. A light straw color accompanies enticing aromas of figs, lemon zest, grapefruit, and honeysuckle. Medium bodied with good acidity, loads of fruit and depth, and a long, concentrated finish, it should evolve beautifully for 15+ years. Last tasted, 1/03.

2000
87
Although monolithic, this is a competent effort displaying notes of lemon zest and honey. Medium bodied with admirable fruit, but neither the depth nor complexity of the 2001, it should drink well for 10–12 years. Last tasted, 1/03.

ANCIENT VINTAGES (RED)

Most of the top vintages of the 1980s and 1990s were competent efforts, meriting scores between 85 and 87 points. Some of the great old vintages (1961, 91 points; last tasted 3/99; and 1959, 89 points; last tasted 1/03) remain brilliant wines. I hope recent vintages are capable of achieving this level of quality.

LES CARMES HAUT-BRION

Classification: None

Owner: Furt/Chantecaille families

Administrator: Didier Furt

Address: 197, avenue Jean Cordier, 33600 Pessac

Telephone: 05 56 51 49 43; Telefax: 05 56 93 10 71

E-mail: chateau@les-carmes-haut-brion.com

Website: www.les-carmes-haut-brion.com

Visits: By appointment only

Contact: Didier Furt

VINEYARDS (RED)

Surface area: 11.4 acres

Grape varietals: 50% Merlot, 40% Cabernet Franc, 10% Cabernet Sauvignon

Average age of vines: 35–40 years

Density of plantation: 10,000 vines per hectare

Average yields: 46 hectoliters per hectare

Elevage: Fifteen to twenty-one day fermentation and maceration in temperature-controlled stainless-steel vats. Malolactics and 18 months aging in barrels with 50% new oak. Fining and filtration depending upon the vintage.

RED WINES PRODUCED

Château Les Carmes Haut-Brion: 22,000 bottles

Le Clos des Carmes: 4,000 bottles

Plateau of maturity: Within 6–15 years of the vintage

GENERAL APPRECIATION

This tiny gem of an estate offers superb wines that are difficult to find because of the minuscule production. Recent vintages have consistently qualified as sleepers. In top vintages, the wines possess nearly as much complexity as the great Haut-Brion, but not the density of that renowned *terroir*. They owe their extraordinary finesse as well as explosive aromatics to their relatively high percentage of Cabernet Franc. This underrated effort undoubtedly merits more attention from shrewd consumers as it remains reasonably priced. It would also deserve upgrading to cru classé status.

In the early 1970s I had the good fortune to walk into a wine shop that was discounting magnums of the 1959 Les Carmes Haut-Brion. I knew nothing about the wine, but I took a chance and bought two magnums. Both proved to be spectacular, and every effort I made to find the wine thereafter was futile. Little did I know then that this tiny jewel of a vineyard, situated on a gravelly knoll in the Bordeaux suburb of Pessac, near the famed Haut-Brion and La Mission Haut-Brion, is the most obscure and least known top-quality red wine of Pessac-Léognan. A visit is highly recommended as this estate has the look of a medieval fairy-tale castle surrounded by beautiful grounds.

The vineyard is named for the group of friars, called Les Carmes, who owned this vineyard between 1584 and 1789. During the French Revolution, the religious order was divested of ownership.

Les Carmes Haut-Brion is a rich, full wine, no doubt because the Merlot vines benefit from the gravelly and clayey soil in which they are planted. A traditional approach to winemaking results in wines that are classic expressions of Graves, deeply colored, intense, and complex. Unfortunately, most of the wine from Les Carmes Haut-Brion is sold by Monsieur Chantecaille through his *négociant* business in Bordeaux to European markets. Since so little wine is made, the chances of finding any in America are remote.

This is a wine that comes closest to expressing the quality of Haut-Brion and La Mission Haut-Brion, not surprisingly, as the vineyards and *terroir* are essentially the same. This small, consistently top-notch performer in Pessac is worth searching out.

IMPORTANT VINTAGES

2001
87–89 Modeled along the lines of the 1999, but even more elegant, this dark ruby/purple–colored 2001 reveals aromas of sweet berry fruit, spice box, and smoke. It is light to medium bodied, soft, tasty, and potentially complex and nuanced. While it does not possess the size, volume, or aging potential of the 2000 or 1999, the 2001 is a beautifully made wine. Anticipated maturity: 2005–2012. Last tasted, 1/03.

2000
94 A quintessential model of both Graves and the elegance of high-class Bordeaux, the 2000 is probably the finest Les Carmes I have ever tasted. It ratchets up the level of concentration, opulence, and sumptuousness. Medium to full-bodied, layered, and lush, with extraordinary aromatic complexity (cigar tobacco, earth, coffee, black currants, and ripe plums/prunes), stunning purity, a seamless texture, and sweet tannin, it will provide thrilling drinking between 2005 and 2020. At present, it is tight and closed, but aeration brings out its perfume. A big-time sleeper of the vintage. Last tasted, 1/03.

1999
89 An elegant, soft, tobacco-infused, red currant and cherry-flavored effort, this dark ruby/purple–colored 1999 is sweet and expansive on the attack, sexy, complex, earthy, and long. Consume this medium-weight Graves during its first 6–10 years of life. It is an impressive 1999. Last tasted, 3/02.

1998
90 A stunning wine, as well as one of the sleepers of the vintage, this dense purple–colored 1998 offers up classic Graves aromas of tar, roasted meats, scorched earth, black currants, and barbecue spices. It is beautifully elegant, yet rich, concentrated, and deep, with medium to full body, laudable sweetness on the entry, and ripe tannin in the finish. A bottle kept open for 24 hours was significantly better than it was upon opening, suggesting this wine will have terrific longevity. Haut-Brion enthusiasts are advised to check out this beautifully made offering. Anticipated maturity: 2004–2020. Last tasted, 3/02.

1997
87 Hippie-incense-like smells jump from the glass of this complex, herb, tobacco, smoky, peppery, fragrant wine. Medium ruby–colored, with light to medium body, it is full of finesse, fruit, charm, and suppleness. This is a sexy offering to enjoy over the next 2–3 years. While there is neither great depth nor length, this example of Les Carmes Haut-Brion is beautifully complex and supple. Last tasted, 1/02.

1996
87 A medium ruby–colored, sexy, seductive Graves, with loads of tobacco-tinged, jammy cherry fruit intermixed with smoke and earth, this spicy, round, generous 1996 reveals no hard edges. It continues to be one of the most stylish, underrated wines from the Pessac-Léognan region. Although it will not be long-lived, this wine offers plenty of appeal for drinking over the next 5–6 years. Last tasted, 3/01.

1995
87 A classic example of Graves's smoky, tobacco-tinged, berry fruit, this is a medium-bodied, sweet, round, berry, complex, elegant, savory 1995 with no hard edges. Low acidity and a luscious, ripe Merlot component dominate the wine, giving it immediate appeal. This is a plump, delicious wine. Anticipated maturity: now–2006. Last tasted, 12/00.

ANCIENT VINTAGES (RED)

Nearly all the top vintages merit scores of 86–88, although occasionally this property hits the high points (the 1959, 92 points, last tasted 12/85; and 1945, 93 points, last tasted 12/95).

DE CHANTEGRIVE

Classification: None

Owner: Françoise and Henri Lévêque

Address: 33720 Podensac

Telephone: 05 56 27 17 38; Telefax: 05 56 27 29 42

E-mail: courrier@chateau-chantegrive.com

Website: www.chantegrive.com

Visits: Monday to Saturday 9 A.M.–noon and 2–5 P.M.

Contact: Hélène Lévêque

VINEYARDS (RED)

Surface area: 140.8 acres

Grape varietals: 50% Cabernet Sauvignon, 50% Merlot

Average age of vines: 25 years

Density of plantation: 6,600 vines per hectare

Average yields: 42 hectoliters per hectare

Elevage: Fermentation and maceration in temperature-controlled stainless-steel tanks of 100 hectoliter capacity with frequent pumpings-over. Malolactics and 14 months aging in barrels that are renewed by a third at each vintage. Fining, no filtration.

RED WINES PRODUCED

Château de Chantegrive: 150,000 bottles

Benjamin de Chantegrive: 120,000 bottles

Plateau of maturity: Within 3–10 years of the vintage

VINEYARDS (WHITE)

Surface area: 86.5 acres

Grape varietals: 50% Sauvignon Blanc, 50% Semillon

Average age of vines: 34 years

Density of plantation: 6,600 vines per hectare

Average yields: 35 hectoliters per hectare

Elevage: *Generic*—Fermentation and nine months aging in stainless-steel vats. No fining, filtration upon bottling. *Cuvée Caroline*—Skin maceration, fermentation, and nine months aging on lees in barrels (50% new oak) with weekly stirrings. No fining, light filtration upon bottling.

WHITE WINES PRODUCED

Château de Chantegrive: 70,000 bottles

Château de Chantegrive Cuvée Caroline: 65,000 bottles

Plateau of maturity: Within 2–4 years of the vintage (best vintages of Cuvée Caroline may hold 6–7 years)

GENERAL APPRECIATION

While rarely profound, the red Chantegrive is soundly made and represents a good value because of its reasonable price. In terms of quality, this wine is equivalent to a good Médoc Cru Bourgeois. The whites are excellent, especially the best vintages of Cuvée Caroline, which can rival the classified growths of Pessac-Léognan.

When I am eating in a Bordeaux restaurant, the red and white wines I often search out for value and quality are those made at the attractive Château de Chantegrive, located just north of the village of Podensac, adjacent to Route Nationale 113. While proprietor Henri Lévêque can trace his family's wine heritage back to 1753, he alone resurrected this property from obscure standing in 1962 to one that is now recognized for high-quality red and white wines that represent excellent quality/price rapport.

This is one cellar where everything from barrel cellar to fermentation rooms are temperature and humidity controlled. In the mid-1980s a luxury *cuvée* of Lévêque's white Graves, the Chantegrive Cuvée Caroline, was introduced. It is as good as some of the more renowned crus classés. Neither the white nor the red wine is meant to be long-lived, but rather to be drunk in the first 5–7 years of life. A strong argument can even be made for drinking the white wines before they reach the age of 5. Nevertheless, the wines are consistently well made, even in lighter-weight vintages, and are textbook examples of their appellation.

Frugal consumers looking for wines that satisfy both the palate and the purse should seek out this consistent overachiever in the southern Graves region.

IMPORTANT VINTAGES (RED)

2000
88
The excellent 2000 displays aromas of scorched earth, ripe black cherry and currant fruit, tobacco, and cigar smoke. Ripe, medium bodied, soft, and attractive, it will be drinkable young and until 2012. Last tasted, 1/03.

IMPORTANT VINTAGES (WHITE)

2001
89
Cuvée Caroline: A top-notch effort, the 2001 Cuvée Caroline exhibits well-integrated toasty notes intermixed with scents of honeysuckle, orange marmalade, smoky nuts, and citrus. Medium bodied, with delicious fruit as well as good underlying acidity, this beauty will drink well over the next 3–4 years. It is a fine value.

DOMAINE DE CHEVALIER

Classification: Classified growth (reds and whites)

Owner: Bernard family

Administrator: Olivier Bernard

Address: 102, chemin de Mignoy, 33850 Léognan

Telephone: 05 56 64 16 16; Telefax: 05 56 64 18 18

E-mail: domainedechevalier@domainedechevalier.com

Website: www.domainedechevalier.com

Visits: By appointment Monday to Friday 9 A.M.–noon and 2–5 P.M.

Contact: Oliver Bernard or Rémy Edange

VINEYARDS (RED)

Surface area: 74.1 acres

Grape varietals: 65% Cabernet Sauvignon, 30% Merlot, 2.5% Cabernet Franc, 2.5% Petit Verdot

Average age of vines: 30 years

Density of plantation: 10,000 vines per hectare

Average yields: 45–48 hectoliters per hectare

Elevage: Fermentation at temperatures below 30°C and three-week maceration in temperature-controlled stainless-steel and epoxy-lined vats of 100- and 150-hectoliter capacity. Eighteen to twenty-two months aging in barrels that are renewed by a third at each vintage. Fining and filtration.

RED WINES PRODUCED

Domaine de Chevalier: 80,000 bottles

L'Esprit de Chevalier: 90,000 bottles

Pessac-Léognan: 25,000 bottles

Plateau of maturity: Within 5–15 years of the vintage

VINEYARDS (WHITE)

Surface area: 11.1 acres

Grape varietals: 70% Sauvignon Blanc, 30% Semillon

Average age of vines: 30 years

Density of plantation: 10,000 vines per hectare

Average yields: 40 hectoliters per hectare

Elevage: Fermentation and 18 months aging on lees in barrels with 30% new oak. Fining and filtration.

WHITE WINES PRODUCED

Domaine de Chevalier: 12,000 bottles

L'Esprit de Chevalier: 10,000 bottles

Plateau of maturity: Within 10–35 years of the vintage

GENERAL APPRECIATION

As far as the reds are concerned, Domaine de Chevalier was a notorious underperformer during the early 1990s. Since then, the red wines have improved dramatically. The whites have always been top-notch, but the minuscule production makes them difficult to find. Domaine de Chevalier is expensive.

The tiny estate of Domaine de Chevalier, tucked away in the midst of a forest on the southwest outskirts of Léognan, is a true connoisseur's wine. The production is tiny and the wines are among the most highly sought of Pessac-Léognan, but most important, the quality can be impeccably high.

Domaine de Chevalier's fame was no doubt due to the aristocratic Claude Ricard, who inherited the property in 1942 but because of family squabbles had to sell the estate in 1983 to the large Bernard distilling company. Claude Ricard was retained to run the property but finally turned over the reins of Domaine de Chevalier to Olivier Bernard.

The red wines of Domaine de Chevalier do not resemble the intense, rich, earthy style of Graves, best exemplified by Haut-Brion and La Mission Haut-Brion. Until the 1990s, the Domaine de Chevalier wines possessed a subtle, mineral, earthy aspect but were much lighter in body and tended to be more Médoc-like in style than the Graves wines from Pessac and Talence. Since the new owners acquired the property, there has been an intentional effort to produce a bigger, more structured, and powerful wine. There are no problems with that, but excessive oakiness in the early 1990s often obliterated the wine's charm and finesse, the telltale personality traits of Domaine de Chevalier.

The white Domaine de Chevalier is the only wine I know of in the Bordeaux region that spends over a year and a half in new oak casks. The production is tiny, and the wine, while fabulous when drunk from cask, usually closes up after bottling, not to blossom for 10 or more years. Yet it has the distinction of actually taking longer to mature, and aging even more gracefully, than the superb red wine. It can easily last 25–35 years, clearly outliving the red wine in most vintages.

Anyone who visits the southern portion of Pessac-Léognan (the northern sector of Graves) will have a difficult time finding Domaine de Chevalier. I became impossibly lost on my first trip to the property in the late 1970s. The cream-colored château, surrounded on three sides by a pine forest, can be found by taking D109 east from Léognan in the direction of Cestas. Signs indicating the entrance to the vineyard of Domaine de Chevalier will guide the traveler to the château.

The soil of this relatively small vineyard has a gravel bed but also contains clay, iron, and considerable black sand. Two problems encountered here are that spring frosts and frequent hail can severely damage the crop. Inexplicably, no other major châteaux of the Bordeaux region suffer these two natural calamities as frequently as Domaine de Chevalier.

Domaine de Chevalier is an expensive wine, fetching prices similar to those of a Médoc second growth.

IMPORTANT VINTAGES (RED)

2001　This wine has taken on considerable weight during its upbringing in cask. A deep
88–90　ruby/purple color is accompanied by aromas of spicy tobacco, licorice, black currants, fruitcake, and minerals. Medium bodied and elegant, it is a model of finesse allied to considerable flavor authority. Anticipated maturity: 2006–2015. Last tasted, 1/03.

2000　The finest Domaine de Chevalier in over a decade, this opaque purple–colored
90　effort exhibits abundant character with its striking aromatic profile of burning coals, plums, currants, tobacco, and spice box. Some oak is present, but it is well

integrated in this rich, medium- to full-bodied, elegant, pure 2000. Anticipated maturity: 2008–2025. Last tasted, 1/03.

1999
88
A classic, finesse-styled Graves, the 1999 Domaine de Chevalier reveals scorched earth, tobacco, and red currant aromas along with rich, elegant, savory flavors, sweet tannin, and better integrated oak than previous vintages have exhibited. Enjoy this medium-bodied effort during its first 10–12 years of life. Last tasted, 3/02.

1998
87
This dark ruby–colored Domaine de Chevalier reveals aggressive spicy new oak in the nose, along with notions of tobacco, smoke, and black cherries. While medium bodied and stylish, it lacks the necessary depth to qualify as one of the stars of the vintage. Anticipated maturity: now–2015. Last tasted, 3/02.

1997
85
Medium light ruby–colored, with sweet, smoky, herb-tinged, toasty, cherry, and berry flavors, this is an attractive, light- to medium-bodied wine with soft tannin, low acidity, and little depth or finish. Drink it over the next 3–4 years. Last tasted, 1/02.

1996
88
The 1996 has turned out beautifully from the bottle. It is an exceptionally elegant wine, with well-integrated oak and tobacco-tinged, cherry and cassis fruit. It appears to be a return to the style of the 1970s and early 1980s. Lush, with excellent concentration, a beautiful texture, and a flattering, potentially complex aromatic profile, this medium-bodied wine should be at its finest between now and 2016. Last tasted, 3/01.

1995
80?
A shockingly high oak component obliterates any attempt at discerning the level of fruit that might be present. Yes, the wine is backward; yes, it is light bodied; yes, it hints at having some minerality, but where's the weight, ripeness, and fruit intensity? Anticipated maturity: 2007–2015. Last tasted, 3/00.

1990
89
This wine displays better integrated oak than my initial tasting note suggested. The color is a dark garnet with amber at the edge. A sweet nose of brown sugar, cherry and currant fruit, herbs, tobacco, and toast is followed by a medium-bodied, stylish wine with sweet tannin as well as excellent purity. This graceful, fully mature 1990 has hit its apogee. Anticipated maturity: now–2012. Last tasted, 1/03.

1989
89
A dark plum/garnet color is followed by a perfume of black fruits, smoke, herbs, Chinese black tea, and vanilla. Medium bodied with moderate tannin, the 1989 is less evolved than its younger sibling, the 1990. The finish reveals dry, astringent tannin. Anticipated maturity: 2004–2014. Last tasted, 1/03.

1988
90
Domaine de Chevalier produced one of the finest wines of this vintage in 1988. Dark ruby with an unevolved but generous bouquet of smoky new oak, cassis, and flowers, this fleshy, generously endowed, medium-bodied wine is the finest effort from this property since their 1983. Anticipated maturity: now–2008. Last tasted, 3/97.

1986
88
This wine has evolved less evenly than I'd hoped. The attractive nose of roasted earth, herbs, minerals, and red and black fruits is pleasant. In the mouth, the wine reveals unresolved, astringent tannin. Although short in the finish, it is a very good, possibly excellent Domaine de Chevalier that should continue to evolve and, I hope, fatten up over the next decade. Anticipated maturity: now–2012. Last tasted, 11/95.

1983
92
This beautiful, fully mature 1983 exhibits a dark garnet color in addition to gorgeous aromas of smoked herbs, earth, licorice, black fruits, and minerals. The elegant, complex perfume is followed by equally compelling, medium-bodied, expansive, savory flavors. It is a model of opulence, elegance, and finesse. Anticipated maturity: now–2006. Last tasted, 1/03.

1982 The 1982 Domaine de Chevalier continues to be one of the vintage's major disap-
71? pointments. In cask the wine exhibited more fruit, but from 375-milliliter and
750-milliliter bottles, it reveals glaring fruit and extraction deficiencies, a hard,
hollow personality with considerable astringent tannin, and too much weedy, underripe herbaceousness. Hail damaged part of the 1982 crop at Domaine de
Chevalier, and it appears the final wine has been tainted by those grapes. I have
received reports of good bottles, and Michael Broadbent has rated it 4 out of 5
stars, so perhaps I have just been unlucky. Last tasted, 9/95.

ANCIENT VINTAGES (RED)

The glorious 1978 (93 points; last tasted 1/03) is one of the vintage's superstars. Fully
mature, and unlikely to get any better, owners should not push their luck. The 1970 (90
points; last tasted 6/96) has always been one of my favorites, but I suspect it is now beginning to decline. Other top-flight vintages have been the 1964 (90 points; last tasted
11/89), 1959 (89 points; last tasted 3/88), and 1953 (92 points; last tasted 1/89). These
have been among the most sensational Domaine de Chevaliers in my experience. None
of them are blockbuster, powerful, massive efforts, but rather wines of extraordinary finesse, aromatic complexity, and balance.

IMPORTANT VINTAGES (WHITE)

2001 One of the great white Domaine de Chevaliers, the loaded 2001 tastes like liquid
95 stones intermixed with honeyed grapefruit, orange marmalade, and smoked herbs.
It boasts great intensity, a surprising amount of glycerin, and tremendous depth as
well as persistence on the palate. It will undoubtedly close down and go into a
backward stage, but it looks to be a legendary Domaine de Chevalier. Anticipated
maturity: 2010–2040. Last tasted, 1/03.

2000 One of the best dry whites of the vintage, the 2000 offers up notes of lanolin, cit-
90 rus, grapefruit, smoke, and minerals with notions of toasty wood in the background. This medium- to full-bodied, deep, concentrated, pure, intense effort is a
success for the vintage. It should hit its peak in 5–6 years and last for two decades.
Last tasted, 1/03.

1999 A zesty, herb-tinged, mineral-styled effort, the light straw–colored 1999 exhibits
87 closed flavors, good acidity, but little depth and follow-through on the palate. Bottled Domaine de Chevaliers are tricky to taste, but the 1999 does not appear to
have enough depth or intensity, particularly when compared to the 2001 and 2000.
Anticipated maturity: 2005–2015. Last tasted, 3/02.

1998 Tightly knit, with hints of green beans, melons, figs, and minerals, the 1998 is
88 showing better from bottle than it did early in life. Medium bodied with the fig,
melon, bell pepper, and grapefruit notes abundantly displayed in the flavors, it reveals a surprisingly long, refreshing finish. Anticipated maturity: 2007–2020.
Last tasted, 3/02.

1995 This is a solidly made, tightly knit, high-strung dry white wine with plenty of sul-
85 phur, wood, and acidity. The wine is slowly fleshing out, so it may ultimately deserve a higher rating, but the shrill levels of tart acid and pronounced oakiness
give cause for concern. Nevertheless, it is a medium-bodied, reasonably well-
made dry white Graves that should age effortlessly for two decades. Anticipated
maturity: 2005–2015. Last tasted, 3/97.

1994
91+
This could turn out to be the finest Domaine de Chevalier since the 1983 and 1985. Displaying less oak than normal, the big, honeyed, cherry, smoky, and melon scents in the nose are followed by a full-bodied, powerful, dense, highly concentrated wine that lingers on the palate for nearly 45 seconds. This should be one of the bigger, more concentrated and powerful Domaine de Chevaliers made in the last 20 years. Given the performance of past top vintages, expect this wine to close up for 10–15 years after bottling. It will age well for 25–30+ years. Last tasted, 3/97.

1990
88?
Although somewhat monolithic, the 1990 Domaine de Chevalier blanc is still a relatively young dry white. It displays a hint of lemon zest, orange blossom, figs, and melons. Medium bodied and austere, but reasonably long in the finish, it is hard to know in what direction it will go as it does not appear to possess the delineation of the great vintages. Anticipated maturity: now–2012. Last tasted, 6/02.

1989
87?
An intense oakiness remains noticeable in this 1989, which has never been as exciting as the estate's reputation would indicate. Notes of wet stones, cold steel, Provençal herbs, and underripe peach and melon characteristics are still dominated by wood. This medium-bodied effort is a bit short in the finish. Anticipated maturity: now–2010. Last tasted, 6/02.

1988
92
A great white from Domaine de Chevalier, the 1988 offers up sumptuous aromas of honeysuckle, minerals, white flowers, figs, and smoky wood. Rich and medium to full-bodied, with tremendous persistence on the palate, this youthful offering should have a tremendous upside over the next two decades. Anticipated maturity: now–2020. Last tasted, 6/02.

1987
88
1987 is a terribly underrated vintage for white Graves. This wine has more depth, ripeness, and complexity than either the 1989 or 1986, the two vintages that most casual observers would think to be superior. Pale straw in color with a more evolved, honeyed, herb-, mineral-, and orange-scented bouquet, this medium-bodied, surprisingly soft, forward Domaine de Chevalier has excellent depth, moderate acidity, and an oaky, alcoholic finish. Anticipated maturity: now. Last tasted, 11/90.

1986
85
Pale straw in color, with a decidedly oaky, ungenerous bouquet, the 1986 is steely, tightly knit, extremely austere, and difficult to appreciate or assess. If it develops more concentration and charm, it could merit a higher score, but my notes have been consistent since I first tasted it from barrel. Anticipated maturity: now. Last tasted, 3/90.

1985
93
Another terrific vintage for Domaine de Chevalier, this sumptuous, dry white retains a light straw color with a hint of green as well as a stunning, herbaceous bouquet of passion fruit, figs, honeyed grapefruit, and spice box. A wine of great delineation, purity, and depth, it is just hitting its apogee. Anticipated maturity: now–2015. Last tasted, 6/02.

1983
94
One of the all-time great Domaine de Chevalier blancs, the 1983 still looks like a 4–5-year-old wine. Its light to medium straw color is followed by glorious aromas of lanolin, marmalade, figs, minerals, and smoke. This intense, full-bodied, mouth-filling wine is gorgeously fresh yet explosively rich and persistent. It can be drunk now but promises to evolve for another 20 years. Last tasted, 6/02.

ANCIENT VINTAGES (WHITE)

Few Bordeaux producers of dry white wines have such an impeccable track record as Domaine de Chevalier. The fabulous 1971 (93 points; last tasted 8/00) remains extraordinarily young and vivacious. The 1970 (93 points; last tasted 12/90) undoubtedly is still going strong, as is the renowned 1962 (93 points; last tasted 3/87). The top vintages of this estate's white wines are almost immortal in terms of ageability. To reiterate, they consistently outlast the red wines by one to two decades.

COUHINS-LURTON

Classification: Classified growth (for whites only)

Owner: André Lurton

Address: 33850 Villenave d'Ornon

Mailing address: Vignobles André Lurton, Château Bonnet, 33420 Grézillac

Telephone: 05 57 25 58 58; Telefax: 05 57 74 98 59

E-mail: andrelurton@andrelurton.com

Website: www.andrelurton.com

No visits

VINEYARDS (WHITE)

Surface area: 14.8 acres

Grape varietals: 100% Sauvignon Blanc

Average age of vines: 15–18 years

Density of plantation: 6,500 vines per hectare

Average yields: 45 hectoliters per hectare

Elevage: After cold settling, 10 to 15 day fermentation (at 18–23°C) in barrels with 30–50% new oak. One year aging on lees with regular stirrings. Fining and filtration.

WHITE WINES PRODUCED

Château Couhins-Lurton: 20,000 bottles

Plateau of maturity: Within 3–15 years of the vintage

GENERAL APPRECIATION

Couhins-Lurton easily merits its cru classé status. It is also a fine value.

André Lurton, another member of the ubiquitous Lurton family, enthusiastically runs this small gem of a property. Made from 100% Sauvignon Blanc, fermented in new oak, and aged for nearly 10 months prior to bottling, this is a consistently superb white Graves of surprising complexity, richness, and length. I would not age it past 10–15 years, but that reflects my personal predilection for drinking these wines relatively young and fresh. The price of Couhins-Lurton has not yet caught up to the quality, and enthusiasts of white Graves should be seeking out this difficult to find but impeccably made wine.

IMPORTANT VINTAGES (WHITE)

2001 A beautiful, pure Sauvignon, the 2001 offers opulent notes of grapefruit, honey-
91 suckle, melons, and figs. It is a light- to medium-bodied, well-delineated, crisp offering with a long finish. Anticipated maturity: now–2015. Last tasted, 1/03.

1998 A powerful Couhins, the 1998 exhibits abundant quantities of herbs and smoke in
92 the background. With tart acidity as well as a creamy texture, it is well worth
searching out. Anticipated maturity: now–2012. Last tasted, 1/03.

ANCIENT VINTAGES

My experience with Couhins suggests it should be drunk relatively young, but my tasting notes for 1993 (90 points) and 1990 (91 points) were filled with enthusiasm when
last tasted in spring 2000.

DE FIEUZAL

Classification: Classified growth (for reds only)

Owner: Lochlann Quinn

Address: 124, avenue de Mont-de-Marsan, 33850 Léognan

Telephone: 05 56 64 77 86; Telefax: 05 56 64 18 88

E-mail: ch.fieuzal@terre-net.fr

Website: www.fieuzal.com

Visits: By appointment only

Contact: Brigitte Talon

VINEYARDS (RED)

Surface area: 93.9 acres

Grape varietals: 60% Cabernet Sauvignon, 30% Merlot, 8% Cabernet Franc, 2% Petit
Verdot

Average age of vines: 30 years

Density of plantation: 9,091 vines per hectare

Average yields: 40 hectoliters per hectare

Elevage: Cold maceration. Fermentation (at 27°C) in temperature-controlled vats.
Malolactics and 18–24 months aging in barrels that are renewed by a third every vintage.
Fining, no filtration.

RED WINES PRODUCED

Château de Fieuzal: 100,000 bottles

L'Abeille de Fieuzal: 60,000 bottles

Plateau of maturity: Within 5–25 years of the vintage

VINEYARDS (WHITE)

Surface area: 24.7 acres

Grape varietals: 50% Sauvignon Blanc, 50% Semillon

Average age of vines: 30 years

Density of plantation: 9,091 vines per hectare

Average yields: 40 hectoliters per hectare

Elevage: Direct pressing. Fermentation and 16–18 months aging on lees in barrels (50% new oak for Semillon and one-year-old barrels for Sauvignon Blanc). Fining, no filtration.

WHITE WINES PRODUCED

Château de Fieuzal: 40,000 bottles

L'Abeille de Fieuzal: 40,000 bottles

Plateau of maturity: Within 4–10 years of the vintage

GENERAL APPRECIATION

While they have always been good, the wines of this estate have improved considerably since the mid-1980s. In the best vintages, both the reds and whites can compete with the stars of the appellation. Despite their consistently high quality, the wines of de Fieuzal do not seem to enjoy the popularity of some of their peers (for example, Pape Clément). Because it is still underrated, de Fieuzal represents a very good buy, especially in the great vintages.

De Fieuzal has always been one of the more obscure Graves, which is surprising given the fact that it is a relatively old property and is well recognized by the inhabitants of the region. The cellars are located in the rolling countryside adjacent to D651 on the outskirts of Léognan in the direction of Saucats. De Fieuzal's obscurity appears to have ended abruptly during the mid-1980s, when the wines became noticeably richer and more complex. This is not to say that older vintages were not well made. Many of them were, but they certainly did not have the dazzling character that more recent years have possessed.

Much of the credit for de Fieuzal's rise in quality must go to the enthusiastic administrator, Gérard Gribelin, who took over the running of the property in 1974. In 1977 stainless-steel, temperature-controlled fermentation tanks were installed, and there has been an increasing tendency since the 1980s to prolong the maceration period and use more new oak. The breakthrough for the white wine of de Fieuzal came in 1985, when the property made the first of what was to be a series of stunning white Graves. Gribelin recognizes that his now retired technical director and winemaker, Monsieur DuPouy, contributed greatly to the restoration of de Fieuzal's reputation. DuPouy was, by any standard of measurement, a perfectionist and displayed remarkable talent and flexibility in supervising the winemaking at de Fieuzal. Amazingly, the high quality has not been accompanied by soaring prices, as de Fieuzal represents one of the best quality/price ratios in the entire Graves region.

IMPORTANT VINTAGES (RED)

2001   A successful effort, this deep ruby/purple–colored, medium-bodied, elegant 2001
87–89   exhibits notes of sweet tobacco, red as well as black currants, and spicy oak. With
fine density, sweet tannin, and good definition, it should be at its best between
2007 and 2018. Last tasted, 1/03.

2000
90+
This opaque ruby/purple–colored offering is one of the finest de Fieuzals produced over the last decade. Aromas of lead pencil, tobacco leaf, licorice, and crème de cassis are offered in an outstanding, medium- to full-bodied, concentrated style. There is tremendous purity as well as flavor dimension. Anticipated maturity: 2007–2022. Last tasted, 1/03.

1999
87
Olive, cedar, earth, charcoal, and smoky characteristics are present in this light- to medium-bodied, attractive, soft, well-made 1999. Captivating but not deep, it will provide pleasure over the next 3–4 years. Last tasted, 3/02.

1998
86
The medium dark ruby–colored 1998 de Fieuzal offers aromas of grilled herbs, tobacco smoke, and red currants. This austere, light- to medium-bodied effort lacks the concentration found in top de Fieuzals. Anticipated maturity: now–2015. Last tasted, 3/02.

1997
86
The dark ruby/purple–colored 1997 offers jammy black fruit aromas intermixed with lavish quantities of toasty new oak. The wine is low in acidity, without the volume and power of the 1996, but it is a well-made, forward effort. Anticipated maturity: now–2012. Last tasted, 1/99.

1996
88+
De Fieuzal's 1996 exhibits a saturated purple color in addition to an intense charcoal, smoky, mineral, and black fruit–scented nose. Highly extracted and rich, with a sweet, concentrated mid-palate and plenty of muscle and tannin in the moderately long finish, this backward yet promising Fieuzal should last for 15–16 years. Anticipated maturity: 2006–2020. Last tasted, 2/01.

1995
90
This quintessentially elegant wine reveals a deep ruby/purple color and an attractive smoky, black currant, mineral, and floral-scented nose. There are sweet, ripe, lush flavors, medium body, ripe tannin, and a velvety texture that borders on opulence. There is no heaviness to the wine. Moreover, not the tannin, acidity, nor alcohol are intrusive. This seamless, extremely well-made claret is a candidate for early drinking, yet it possesses excellent aging potential. Anticipated maturity: now–2020. Last tasted, 12/01.

1994
?
Before bottling, the 1994 de Fieuzal appeared to be as good as, if not better than, the 1993, but two bottles tasted after bottling exhibited moldy, wet cardboard–like noses that made judgment impossible. It is rare to get two corked bottles in a row. Last tasted, 1/97.

1990
88
This wine has improved immensely in the bottle, making my earlier notes look particularly stingy. The color is a healthy dark ruby/purple. Aromatically the wine has opened considerably, revealing plenty of cranberry, black cherry, and cassis fruit. There are also notes of lavish new oak, earth, and cedar in the moderately intense bouquet. Medium bodied, with sweet fruit, gobs of glycerin (a hallmark of many 1990s), and soft tannin, this wine has fleshed out considerably, with the tannin becoming better integrated. It is still a youthful, promising wine. Anticipated maturity: 2000–2012. Last tasted, 8/97.

1989
87
De Fieuzal's 1989 exhibits a deep ruby/purple color with some lightening at the edge. This lavishly oaked wine displays copious quantities of toasty new oak as well as earth/herb-tinged red and black currant fruit in its moderately intense bouquet. On the palate, the wine reveals medium body, low acidity, and elevated tannin in the finish. It is a more compact, leaner style of wine than its slightly sweeter, fleshier sibling, the 1990. Anticipated maturity: 1999–2010. Last tasted, 3/97.

1988
86
The 1988 de Fieuzal is an extracted, darkly colored wine with an excellent nose of sweet curranty fruit, medium body, and a compact, very tannic (nearly astringent) finish. The wine has closed up since its bottling and appears to need considerable time in the bottle. This wine appears to be made in a style that will never shed its tannin, and it may always have a certain astringency and austerity. It is capable of

lasting another two decades, but it will always remain an angular style of de Fieuzal. Anticipated maturity: now–2012. Last tasted, 1/97.

ANCIENT VINTAGES (RED)

I have good notes for the 1986 (87 points; last tasted 1/97), 1985 (87 points; last tasted 1/97), and 1970 (87 points; last tasted 1/97). However, vintages since the mid- to late-1990s are far superior to what was produced in the past.

IMPORTANT VINTAGES (WHITE)

2001
93   A tremendous effort from de Fieuzal, this exceptionally rich, dry white offers up aromas of honeysuckle, orange marmalade, roasted herbs, figs, and melons. Medium to full-bodied, exceptionally concentrated, with great definition and zestiness, this impressive effort should have 20–25 years of longevity. Anticipated maturity: 2007–2020. Last tasted, 1/03.

2000
86   This is a competent albeit monolithic, straightforward, foursquare effort without the nuances one expects. It exhibits plenty of oak, some melony fruit, but a short finish. Anticipated maturity: now–2010. Last tasted, 1/03.

ANCIENT VINTAGES (WHITE)

De Fieuzal produced an excellent 1996 (88 points; last tasted 1/03), 1995 (88 points; last tasted 3/97), and a brilliant 1994 (92 points; last tasted 3/97). Top efforts were produced in years such as 1993 and 1992, both of which were rated 90 when last tasted in 1/03. While I have not had them recently, the 1988 (92 points; last tasted 1/96) and 1985 (93 points; last tasted 7/97) were turnaround vintages for de Fieuzal's white wine program. It is unquestionably one of the top half-dozen dry white wines of Bordeaux, and it is worth a special effort to find and purchase.

LA GARDE

Classification: None

Owner: Dourthe Frères

Address: 1, chemin de la Tour, 33650 Martillac

Mailing address: 35, rue de Bordeaux, 33290 Parempuyre

Telephone: 05 56 35 53 00; Telefax: 05 56 35 53 29

E-mail: contact@cvbg.com

Visits: By appointment only

Contact: Marie-Hélène Inquimbert

VINEYARDS (RED)

Surface area: 124.9 acres

Grape varietals: 52% Cabernet Sauvignon, 48% Merlot

Average age of vines: 23 years

Density of plantation: 6,250 vines per hectare

Average yields: 42–43 hectoliters per hectare

Elevage: Cold maceration. Fermentation and maceration in temperature-controlled stainless-steel and wooden vats with pigeage. Part of yield undergoes malolactics in barrel. Twelve to eighteen months aging with 40–60% new oak.

RED WINES PRODUCED

Château La Garde: 160,000 bottles

La Terrasse de La Garde: 100,000 bottles

Plateau of maturity: Within 2–6 years of the vintage

VINEYARDS (WHITE)

Surface area: 4.5 acres

Grape varietals: 100% Sauvignon

Average age of vines: 10 years

Density of plantation: 6,000 vines per hectare

Average yields: 42–43 hectoliters per hectare

Elevage: Skin maceration. Fermentation and 12 months aging on fine lees in new oak barrels.

WHITE WINES PRODUCED

Château La Garde: 12,000 bottles

No second wine is produced.

Plateau of maturity: Within 2–4 years of the vintage

GENERAL APPRECIATION

This is a reliable estate, particularly since the large *négociant* Dourthe became the proprietor in 1990.

An impressive-looking estate sitting on gravel outcroppings south of the village of Martillac, this ancient property appears set to make an important rebound.

IMPORTANT VINTAGES (RED)

2001 An excellent, textbook Graves, this 2001 reveals sweet red currant, cherry,
87–89 smoked herb, and earth aromas. Its opaque ruby/purple color is accompanied by firm tannin, medium body, and excellent ripeness as well as depth. Anticipated maturity: 2006–2013. Last tasted, 1/03.

2000 Elegant, smoky, roasted herb, tobacco, and sweet red and black currant aromas
89 jump from the glass of this opaque ruby/purple–colored offering. Medium bodied and lush, with copious sweetness, low acidity, and ripe tannin, this is a sleeper of the vintage. Anticipated maturity: 2006–2017. Last tasted, 1/03.

1999 This textbook Graves offers notes of scorched earth, tobacco, and sweet red and
87 black currants in a savory, elegant, suave style. Soft tannin, low acidity, and delicious fruit suggest drinking over the next 5–6 years. Last tasted, 3/02.

1998 An excellent red currant, smoky, gravelly, red fruit–scented bouquet is accompa-
87 nied by a medium-bodied, plush, attractively fruity wine. The oak is restrained, and the acidity and tannin are well integrated in this supple effort. Enjoy it over the next 4–5 years. Last tasted, 3/02.

HAUT-BAILLY

Classification: Classified growth (for reds only)

Owner: Robert G. Wilmers

Address: 103, route de Cadaujac, 33850 Léognan

Telephone: 05 56 64 75 11; Telefax: 05 56 64 53 60

E-mail: mail@chateau-haut-bailly.com

Website: www.chateau-haut-bailly.com

Visits: By appointment only

Contact: Véronique Sanders

GRAND CRU CLASSE DE GRAVES

CHATEAU HAUT-BAILLY
PESSAC-LÉOGNAN
APPELLATION PESSAC-LEOGNAN CONTROLEE
1995
G.F.A. SANDERS, PROPRIETAIRE A LEOGNAN-GIRONDE
13% vol   MIS EN BOUTEILLE AU CHATEAU   750 ml
Produce of France

VINEYARDS (RED)

Surface area: 79 acres

Grape varietals: 65% Cabernet Sauvignon, 25% Merlot, 10% Cabernet Franc

Average age of vines: 35 years

Density of plantation: 35 vines per hectare

Average yields: 40–45 hectoliters per hectare

Elevage: Three-week fermentation and maceration in temperature-controlled vats. Fifteen months aging in barrels with 50–60% new oak. Fining, no filtration.

RED WINES PRODUCED

Château Haut-Bailly: 80,000–100,000 bottles

La Parde de Haut-Bailly: 40,000–60,000 bottles

Plateau of maturity: Within 5–20 years of the vintage

GENERAL APPRECIATION

Haut-Bailly encountered some difficulties in the 1990s but is back on track. From their marvelous *terroir*, they fashion one of the lightest, most elegant offerings from Pessac-Léognan. As I have learned (the hard way), Haut-Bailly often tastes light and innocuous when young, but 5–7 years later, it is often significantly better, due primarily to the abundant Cabernet Sauvignon in the blend. Qualitatively, Haut-Bailly compares with a Médoc third growth.

By Graves standards, Haut-Bailly is a relative newcomer. The history, however, is not uninteresting. A Monsieur Bellot des Minières, who was the second owner of Haut-Bailly in 1872, apparently believed that the wine was greatly improved by the addition of copious quantities of cognac, which was left in the barrels after they were rinsed with this spirit. Today one hears rumors of Burgundy producers who fortify weaker vintages with eau-de-vie or brandy, but Monsieur Bellot des Minières was proud of his wine's "extra" dimension.

The Sanders family became the proprietors in 1955. According to the family, Daniel Sanders—a wine enthusiast from Belgium—was so astounded by the 1945 Haut-Bailly that, after some investigation, he decided to buy the property. His son, Jean, who lives at the nearby estate of Château Courbon (which produces a pleasant, dry white

Graves), managed the property after his father's death. The property was sold to Robert G. Wilmers in July 1998.

Since the early 1960s Haut-Bailly has had an inconsistent track record for quality. The 1961 was fabulous, as was the delicious 1964, but it was not until 1979 that the quality began to bounce back after a prolonged period of mediocrity. The decision to relegate as much as 30% of the crop to a second wine, increase the percentage of new oak, and to harvest later in order to obtain riper grapes all resulted in increasingly better wines for Haut-Bailly during the 1980s.

When young, this is not the easiest wine to evaluate. I am not sure why, but it often comes across as a bit skinny and light yet seems to take on weight and depth in the bottle. When I asked Jean Sanders about this, he said he was not the least bit interested in making a wine to impress writers, particularly before it is bottled. He believes the extremely old age of his vineyard and his traditional winemaking style with absolutely no filtration result in a wine that requires some time to reveal all of its charm and character. Haut-Bailly will never have the size or power of its nearby neighbor de Fieuzal, but it does exhibit exceptional elegance in the top vintages.

IMPORTANT VINTAGES

2001 A restrained, graceful, subtle effort, the 2001 Haut-Bailly exhibits aromas and
87–89 flavors of black cherries, lead pencil, mushrooms, and earth. Medium bodied, delicate, and fresh, with lively acidity, light tannin, and a subtle, nuanced personality, it will be at its finest between 2005–2014. Last tasted, 1/03.

2000 The deep ruby–colored 2000 is one of the most impressive youthful Haut-Baillys
90 I have ever tasted. It reveals endearing notes of black cherries, raspberries, and currants mixed with tobacco smoke, soil overtones, and subtle wood. The acidity is low, the tannin is present, and the overall quality is pure and well balanced. This is a classic example of finesse and elegance. Anticipated maturity: 2007–2025. Last tasted, 1/03.

1999 Light to medium bodied, with sweet currant and smoke-infused flavors and some
88 oak in the background, but plenty of red fruits, vanilla, and dried herbs, this is a soft, well-balanced wine to drink now and over the next 12 years. Last tasted, 3/02.

1998 Typical of this estate, this restrained, polite, light- to medium-bodied offering re-
87 veals attractive smoke, berry, and currant aromas, little concentration, and a soft yet expanding finish. Offering charm, sweet tannin, and fine balance, it can be drunk through the end of the decade. Last tasted, 3/02.

1997 Light to medium bodied, with pleasant spicy tobacco and sweet black cherry/berry
86 fruit, this low-acid, delicate wine can be drunk now and over the next 4–5 years. Last tasted, 1/02.

1996 Haut-Bailly's 1996 displays less charm than usual, but it does offer moderately in-
87 tense red currant/cherry fruit combined with earth, smoke, and new oak. An elegant, medium-bodied wine with dry tannin in the finish, it will never be a heavyweight, but it possesses considerable personality and potential complexity. Anticipated maturity: now–2015. Last tasted, 1/02.

1995 A beauty, this deep ruby–colored wine offers a classic, smoky, cherry, red and
90 black currant–scented nose, sweet, lush, forward fruit, medium body, true delicacy and elegance (as opposed to thinness and dilution), perfect balance, and a lovely, long, supple, velvety-textured finish. This is a ballerina of a claret, with

beautiful aromatics, lovely flavors, and impeccable equilibrium. Anticipated maturity: now–2018. Last tasted, 11/97.

1994
88
One of the finest 1994s from the Pessac-Léognan appellation, Haut-Bailly's 1994 possesses a dark ruby color with purple hues. The sweet, black currant, earthy and mineral nose, and ripe, medium-bodied, fleshy flavors represent the quintessentially elegant style of red Graves. The wine is rich yet ethereal in the mouth. This charming wine exhibits no hard edges (no small achievement in the 1994 vintage), as well as beautifully integrated acidity and new oak. Anticipated maturity: now–2005. Last tasted, 1/97.

1990
92
The 1990 Haut-Bailly, which I have always preferred slightly to the 1989, was once again the stronger vintage. It displays a richer, more saturated dark ruby color, followed by a textbook bouquet of smoky tobacco, blackberry, and cassis. Ripe, supple-textured, and generous, with no hard edges, this is a stylish, well-crafted wine with all the component parts in balance. Drink this medium-bodied effort over the next 15 years. Last tasted, 11/96.

1989
89
The 1989 is a ripe, sweet, supple wine with a deep ruby color and an attractive nose of herbs, sweet berry fruit, and smoky tobacco. This soft, low-acid wine is ready to drink now and should continue to evolve gracefully, offering elegant, smooth-as-silk drinking for another 12+ years. Last tasted, 11/96.

1988
89
The 1988 is full and rich, with that profound, mineral, spicy, sweet oaky, curranty aroma, gentle yet full-bodied, creamy-textured flavors, and a long, smooth, marvelous finish. This wine may well turn out to be outstanding with another 3–4 years in the bottle. Anticipated maturity: now. Last tasted, 1/93.

1986
85
Considering the strong, tannic personality of the vintage, Haut-Bailly's 1986 is a soft wine that can be drunk at a very early age. The full-intensity bouquet of sweet, smoky oak and ripe, plummy fruit is very attractive. On the palate, this medium-bodied wine is long, rich in fruit, supple, and finishes surprisingly smoothly. Anticipated maturity: now–2005. Last tasted, 1/97.

1985
86
There is not a great deal of depth to this Haut-Bailly. Nevertheless, it offers charm, finesse, and a sweet blackberry/curranty fruitiness. Some of the new oak and smokiness that were present when the wine was young has dissipated to reveal a slight herbaceousness behind the new oak. The wine is medium-bodied, with soft tannin and some flesh on the attack that quickly narrows out to a lighter-style, supple yet unexciting wine. Anticipated maturity: now. Last tasted, 1/97.

1983
87
A typical Haut-Bailly, the 1983 is dark ruby in color, with a rich, voluptuous, ripe, black currant bouquet, and some attractive vanilla oaky aromas. On the palate, the wine is forward, with lush, silky, ripe, round tannins evident. Medium bodied, with a Pomerol-like, silky, fat texture, this wine is already fully mature. Anticipated maturity: now. Last tasted, 1/91.

ANCIENT VINTAGES (RED)

One of the sleeper vintages for Haut-Bailly, 1981 (89 points; last tasted 1/03) is clearly superior to the disappointing 1982. 1979 (88 points; last tasted 1/00) has always stood out as a pretty, elegantly styled example that showcases the telltale finesse and measured, restrained flavors of berry fruit, smoke, herbs, subtle oak, and minerals. It was still drinking beautifully when last tasted in January 2000. The 1982 was a major disappointment and continues to be an austere, washed-out wine with no intensity. Except for the 1970 (87 points; last tasted 10/88), the vintages of the 1970s were all disappointing. The 1964 (88 points; last tasted 3/90) and profound 1961 (93 points; last tasted 3/90) were top efforts, but I suspect they are both in decline. One of the most renowned Haut-Baillys is the 1928 (90 points), which was last tasted December 1995. At that time, it was in remarkable shape, and pristine bottles may be in far better shape than more recent vintages.

HAUT-BERGEY

Classification: None

Owner: Sylviane Garcin-Cathiard

Address: 69, cours Gambetta, 33850 Léognan

Mailing address: BP 49, 33850 Léognan

Telephone: 05 56 64 05 22; Telefax: 05 56 64 06 98

E-mail: haut-bergey@wanadoo.fr

Visits: By appointment only

Contact: Hélène Garcin-Lévêque

VINEYARDS (RED)

Surface area: 56.8 acres

Grape varietals: 60% Cabernet Sauvignon, 40% Merlot

Average age of vines: 30 years

Density of plantation: 6,500 vines per hectare

Average yields: 35 hectoliters per hectare

Elevage: Fermentation with indigenous yeasts and prolonged maceration in temperature-controlled stainless-steel vats. Sixteen to eighteen months aging in barrels with 50% new oak. Fining, no filtration.

RED WINES PRODUCED

Château Haut-Bergey: 55,000 bottles

L'Etoile de Bergey: 20,000 bottles

Plateau of maturity: Within 5–15 years for post-1998 vintages

VINEYARDS (WHITE)

Surface area: 4.9 acres

Grape varietals: 65% Sauvignon, 35% Semillon

Average age of vines: 30 years

Density of plantation: 6,500 vines per hectare

Average yields: 35 hectoliters per hectare

Elevage: Fermentation and aging on lees in barrels with 30% new oak. Fining, filtration not systematic.

WHITE WINES PRODUCED

Château Haut-Bergey: 5,000 bottles

L'Etoile de Bergey blanc: variable

Plateau of maturity: Within 3–10 years of the vintage

GENERAL APPRECIATION

This is one of the most amazing quality turnarounds I have ever seen. In less than five years, Haut-Bergey (red) has gone from an obscure, indifferent wine to one of the stars of Pessac-Léognan. Credit should be given to the Garcin-Cathiard family, who are also behind the succession of inspiring efforts from both Clos l'Église in Pomerol and Barde-Haut in St.-Emilion, and responsible for the *vin de garage* Branon that emerges from part of this vineyard.

Château Haut-Bergey is a beautiful estate dating back to the 16th century. However, it was not until it was acquired in the 1990s by the Garcin-Cathiard family (who also own the Pomerol estate of Clos l'Église) that it began to produce interesting wine. Not surprisingly, in Pomerol, the owners utilize the services of Michel Rolland, and for Haut-Bergey, they use both Michel Rolland and Jean-Luc Thunevin, two of the most highly respected wine consultants in Bordeaux, if not the world. This is akin to being tutored on foreign policy by Condoleezza Rice and Henry Kissinger.

IMPORTANT VINTAGES (RED)

2001 **90–92**
The 2001 Haut-Bergey's saturated ruby/purple–colored 2001 boasts intense aromas of melted road tar, licorice, tobacco, smoke, and copious black cherry/currant fruit. New oak also makes an appearance. With supple tannin, a rich, layered texture, medium to full body, and outstanding purity as well as length, this is a tremendous success, especially given the vintage conditions. Anticipated maturity: 2006–2016. Last tasted, 1/03.

2000 **94**
A stunning achievement from this unheralded vineyard, the saturated ruby/purple–colored 2000 displays a striking perfume of cigar smoke, scorched earth, roasted espresso, and black cherry/currant fruit. It possesses luxurious richness, medium to full body, sweet tannin, and a seamless, silky-textured finish that lasts for nearly 45 seconds. This brilliant achievement satisfies both the hedonistic and intellectual senses. Moreover, it is a good value, and surprisingly accessible in spite of its density. Anticipated maturity: 2005–2020. Last tasted, 1/03.

1999 **90**
A classic Graves, the 1999 Haut-Bergey is extraordinarily complex aromatically, light on its feet in the mouth, as well as a model of elegance and symmetry. The color is dark ruby, and the splendid nose reveals notes of cigar tobacco intermixed with plum, cherry, and currant fruit, grilled herbs, and roasted nuts. It is medium bodied, with sweet fruit on the attack, and an expansive Burgundian-like finish with light tannin and enough acidity to provide grip, freshness, and delineation. This terrific effort needs to be consumed during its first 7–8 years of life. Last tasted, 3/02.

1998 **87**
Elegant, spicy, tobacco, cranberry, and red cherry characteristics emerge from this finesse-styled, sweet, flavorful, medium-bodied wine. Already delicious as well as complex, it is best consumed over the next 5–6 years. Last tasted, 3/02.

ANCIENT VINTAGES (RED)

Vintages prior to 1998 are of little interest to quality-conscious wine buyers.

IMPORTANT VINTAGES (WHITE)

2001   The finest dry white yet produced by Haut-Bergey, this medium-bodied offering
90   reveals notes of honeysuckle, grapefruit, citrus, candle wax, figs, and spicy oak. Ripe, dense, well delineated, and concentrated, it will be at its peak from now through 2014. Last tasted, 1/03.

2000   Notes of freshly mown grass intermixed with citrus and lemon zest emerge from
87   this very good, richly fruity, but straightforward white Graves. Enjoy it over the next 7–8 years. Last tasted, 1/03.

HAUT-BRION

Classification: First classified growth in 1855

Owner: Domaine Clarence Dillon SA

Address: 135, avenue Jean Jaurès, 33600 Pessac

Mailing address: c/o Domaine Clarence Dillon, 33608 Pessac Cedex

Telephone: 05 56 00 29 30; Telefax: 05 56 98 75 14

E-mail: info@haut-brion.com or visites@haut-brion.com

Website: www.haut-brion.com

Visits: By appointment Monday to Thursday, 8:30–11:30 A.M. and 2–4:30 P.M.; Friday, 8:30–11:30 A.M.

Contact: Turid Hoel-Alcaras and Carla Kuhn

VINEYARDS (RED)

Surface area: 106.7 acres

Grape varietals: 45% Cabernet Sauvignon, 37% Merlot, 18% Cabernet Franc

Average age of vines: 36 years

Density of plantation: 8,000 vines per hectare

Average yields: 35–45 hectoliters per hectare

Elevage: Fermentation and maceration in temperature-controlled stainless-steel vats of 225-hectoliter capacity. Twenty-two months aging in new oak barrels. Fining, no filtration.

RED WINES PRODUCED

Château Haut-Brion: 132,000 bottles

Château Bahans Haut-Brion: 88,000 bottles

Plateau of maturity: Within 10–40 years of the vintage

VINEYARDS (WHITE)

Surface area: 6.7 acres

Grape varietals: 63% Semillon, 37% Sauvignon

Average age of vines: 36 years

Density of plantation: 8,000 vines per hectare

Average yields: 35 hectoliters per hectare

Elevage: Fermentation and 13–16 months aging in new oak barrels. No fining, no filtration.

WHITE WINES PRODUCED

Château Haut-Brion: 7,800 bottles

Les Plantiers du Haut-Brion: 5,000 bottles

Plateau of maturity: Within 5–30 years of the vintage

GENERAL APPRECIATION

A strong argument can be made that this great first growth is the world's most elegant and aromatically complex wine. Since the early 1980s, no first growth has been as consistent or as brilliant in quality as Haut-Brion.

Located in the bustling commercial suburb of Pessac, Haut-Brion is also the only first growth to be American owned. The Dillon family purchased Haut-Brion in 1935 in very poor condition and invested considerable sums of money in the vineyards and wine cellars. This lovely property is now one of the showpiece estates of Graves.

The winemaking at Haut-Brion is managed by the articulate and handsome Jean Delmas (one of the wine world's most gifted administrators), who fervently believes in a hot, short fermentation. As Bordeaux wines go, Haut-Brion is kept a long time (up to 30 months) in new oak barrels. Along with Château Margaux and Pavie, it is often the last château to bottle its wine.

The style of wine at Haut-Brion has changed over the years. The magnificently rich, earthy, almost sweet wines of the 1950s and early 1960s gave way in the period 1966–1974 to a lighter, leaner, easygoing, somewhat simplistic style of claret that lacked the richness and depth one expects from a first growth. Whether this was intentional or just a period in which Haut-Brion was in a bit of a slump remains a question in search of an answer. The staff at Haut-Brion is quick-tempered and sensitive about such a charge. Starting with the 1975 vintage, the wines have again taken on more of the customary earthy richness and concentration that existed during the 1966–1974 era. Haut-Brion today is undoubtedly making wine that merits its first-growth status. In fact, the wines from 1979 onward have consistently proven to be among the finest wines produced in the region, as well as a personal favorite.

Coincidence or not, the quality of Haut-Brion began to rebound from the 1966–1974 era in 1975 when the late Douglas Dillon's daughter, Joan, became president of the company. After the death of her first husband, Prince Charles of Luxembourg, she married the Duc de Mouchy in 1978. It was at this time that the quantity of the crop relegated to Bahans Haut-Brion was increased, a practice that has irrefutably improved the quality of Haut-Brion. Moreover, it appears she gave Jean Delmas carte blanche authority and total responsibility for running the estate. As almost everyone in Bordeaux will acknowledge, Delmas is widely regarded as one of the most talented and knowledgeable winemakers/administrators in France, if not the world. His extraordinary state-of-the-art research with clonal selections is unsurpassed in France. With the advent of the super-abundant crops during the decade of the 1980s, Delmas began, much like his counterpart in Pomerol, Christian Moueix of Château Pétrus, to crop-thin by cutting off grape bunches. This has no doubt accounted for the even greater concentration, as well as the extraordinary quality, of the 1989, which may be the most compelling Haut-Brion made since the 1959 and 1961, and a modern-day legend.

It is interesting to note that in blind tastings Haut-Brion often comes across as the most aromatic as well as most forward and lightest of all the first growths. In truth, the wine is deceptive, and not all that light, but just different, particularly when tasted alongside the more oaky, fleshy, and tannic wines of the Médoc as well as the softer, Merlot-dominated wines from the right bank. Despite the precociousness, it has the ability to gain weight as well as texture, and to age for 30 or more years in top vintages, giving it a broader window of drinkability than any other first growth. Aromatically, a great vintage of Haut-Brion has no peers.

Accompanying the increased level of quality in Haut-Brion since 1975 has been the increased quality of the second label, Bahans Haut-Brion. This is now one of the best second wines of Bordeaux, surpassed in certain vintages only by the renowned second wine of Château Latour, Les Forts de Latour.

The white wine made at Haut-Brion continues to be rated the finest of the Graves region. However, at the request of the proprietors it has never been classified because the production is so tiny. Nevertheless, under Jean Delmas, who has sought to make a white Graves with the opulent texture of a prodigious Montrachet, the white wine has gone from strength to strength. Recent vintages such as 2001, 1998, 1994, 1989, and 1985 have been astonishing wines of majestic richness and complexity.

On a personal note, I should also add that after more than 30 years of intensely tasting as many Bordeaux wines as I can, the only general change I have noticed in my taste has been a greater and greater affection for Haut-Brion. The smoky, mineral, cigar box, sweet black currant character of this wine has increasingly appealed to me as I have gotten older and, as Jean Delmas would undoubtedly state, wiser as well.

IMPORTANT VINTAGES (RED)

2001
92–94
Haut-Brion's 2001 represents only 50% of the production. A blend of 52% Merlot, 36% Cabernet Sauvignon, and 12% Cabernet Franc, it is more evolved and slightly lighter than its fleshier, fuller-bodied sibling, the 2000. A moderately intense perfume of iron, sweet and sour cherries, earth, smoke, black currants, plums, and licorice is followed by a medium-bodied wine with excellent purity, fine density, supple tannin, and a long, persistent finish. As Haut-Brion often does in its youth, the 2001 is putting on weight. Anticipated maturity: 2008–2025. Last tasted, 1/03.

2000
98+
It will always be tempting to compare the 2000 Haut-Brion with the perfect 2000 La Mission Haut-Brion. However, it is not as fat, unctuous, or flamboyant as La Mission, but like a great diplomat, it is a wine of intensity, authority, and measured

restraint. A supremely elegant offering, its dense ruby/purple color, and burgeoning perfume of scorched earth, liquid minerals, plums, black currants, cherries, lead pencil, and subtle spicy oak are followed by a delicate yet powerfully flavorful, multilayered, highly nuanced, and extraordinarily pure and seamless wine. There have been so many recent classics from Haut-Brion, it is absurd to suggest the 2000 is better than the 1998, 1995, or 1990, but it is certainly a prodigious wine of great persistence, length, and complexity. A blend of 51% Merlot, 42% Cabernet Sauvignon, and 7% Cabernet Franc, it should prove to be uncommonly long-lived, even by the standards of Haut-Brion. Anticipated maturity: 2012–2040. Last tasted, 1/03.

1999
93

Deep plum, currant, and mineral notes emerge from the concentrated, beautifully balanced, pure 1999 Haut-Brion. It seems to be cut from the same mold as years such as 1985 and 1979. A hint of graphite as well as minerals is obvious in the abundant fruit. Medium- to full-bodied, nuanced, subtle, deep, and provocatively elegant, it is made in a style that only Haut-Brion appears capable of achieving. The finish is extremely long, the tannins sweet, and the overall impression one of delicacy interwoven with power and ripeness. Anticipated maturity: 2007–2025. Last tasted, 1/03.

1998
96+

This is a prodigious Haut-Brion. It exhibits a dense ruby/purple color in addition to a tight, but incredibly promising nose of smoke, earth, minerals, lead pencil, black currants, cherries, and spice. This full-bodied wine unfolds slowly but convincingly on the palate, revealing a rich, multitiered, stunningly pure, symmetrical style with wonderful sweetness, ripe tannin, and a finish that lasts for nearly 45 seconds. It tastes like liquid nobility. There is really no other way of describing it. It is unquestionably the finest Haut-Brion since the fabulous 1989 and 1990, and the titanic 2000. However, patience is warranted as it is not as flashy and forward as those two vintages. Anticipated maturity: 2008–2035. Last tasted, 1/03.

1997
89

This light- to middle-weight Haut-Brion exhibits an evolved, sweet red and black currant nose with notions of scorched earth, minerals, and tobacco. Although not big, it exhibits fine ripeness, harmony, and elegance, velvety tannin, and sweet fruit presented in a charming, open-knit, evolved format. The wine may develop even more complexity, meriting a higher score. It is comparable to the fine Haut-Brions produced in such difficult rain-plagued vintages as 1993 and 1994. Anticipated maturity: now–2014. Last tasted, 11/02.

1996
95

Only 60% of the total production made it into the final blend, which consists of 50% Merlot, 39% Cabernet Sauvignon, and 11% Cabernet Franc. This wine has completely shut down since it was first bottled. Nevertheless, there is immense potential. This is a relatively structured, backward style of Haut-Brion, without the up-front succulence that some of the sweeter vintages such as 1989 and 1990 provide. The wine has a deep ruby color to the rim and a subtle but emerging nose of scorched earth, dried herbs, black currants, smoke, and a hint of fig. The wine is very concentrated, powerfully tannic, with medium body and outstanding equilibrium, but currently the wine seems to have settled into a very dormant state. Anticipated maturity: 2008–2035. Last tasted, 11/02.

1995
96

It is fun to go back and forth between the 1995 and 1996, two superb vintages for Haut-Brion. The 1995 seems to have sweeter tannin and a bit more fat and seamlessness when compared to the more structured and muscular 1996. Certainly 1995 was a vintage that the brilliant administrator Jean Delmas handled flawlessly. The result is a deep ruby/purple–colored wine with a tight but promising nose of burning wood embers intermixed with vanilla, spice box, earth, mineral, sweet cherry, black currant, plum-like fruit, medium to full body, a high level of ripe but sweet tannin, and a finish that goes on for a good 40–45 seconds. This wine is just beginning to emerge from a very closed state where it was unyielding and backward. Anticipated maturity: 2006–2035. Last tasted, 11/02.

1994
92
This is one of the surprise sleeper wines of the vintage that has more successes than many people suspect in spite of all the rain. The tremendous drainage enjoyed by the Haut-Brion vineyard worked in its favor during this wet September harvest. The color is deep plum/ruby with a bit of lightening at the edge. Notes of compost, truffle, earth, spice box, dried herbs, and licorice compete with sweet black cherry and currant fruit. The wine is medium bodied, with a relatively plump, chewy feel to it. It is certainly one of the top half-dozen or so wines of the vintage. The tannins are still there, but the wine seems far more accessible than the two bigger wines that Haut-Brion produced in 1995 and 1996. Anticipated maturity: 2004–2024. Last tasted, 11/02.

1993
90
Quite a surprise in a difficult vintage, a strict selection and the superb *terroir* of Haut-Brion triumphed over a very challenging year that produced many hard, relatively herbaceous wines. The color is a surprisingly saturated deep plum/ruby. Some sweet berry fruit intermixed with menthol, graphite, damp earth, and a hint of mushroom emerges in this medium-bodied, very elegant Haut-Brion that is still firmly structured but has sweet tannin and surprising length and ripeness. The wine will always represent a sleeper style. Anticipated maturity: 2004–2015. Last tasted, 11/02.

1992
89
This wine is an immensely successful effort for the vintage, with elegance, sweetness, and a medium plum/garnet color already beginning to show some lightening at the edge. It has developed quickly, although the wine has surprising fruit and personality for such a dreadful vintage. The wine shows good cedary, spice box, cigar, and tobacco notes intermixed with minerals, sweet plum, and cherry. The finish is a bit short and attenuated, but the aromatics, attack, and mid-palate are delicious. Anticipated maturity: now–2008. Last tasted, 11/02.

1991
89
This wine has turned out far better than I ever expected. It started off life relatively austere, closed, and tannic, and seemed a bit light, but the wine has put on weight (as so many vintages of Haut-Brion tend to do) and now shows a very complex nose of cigar tobacco intermixed with scorched earth, sweet cherry and black currant fruit, and some high-quality toast. The wine is medium bodied and a great example of finesse, elegance, and just brilliant winemaking in a vintage where the odds were stacked against even a great *terroir* such as Haut-Brion. Anticipated maturity: now–2007. Last tasted, 11/02.

1990
98
A profound Haut-Brion and one of the great Haut-Brions of the last 25 years, this wine got somewhat lost in the enormous shadow cast by the immortal 1989. It continues to go from strength to strength and is actually more evolved than the 1989, but is showing the classic Haut-Brion scorched earth, fragrant smoked herbs, tobacco, sweet currant, fig, and black currant nose. A very opulent/voluptuously textured wine with full body, great concentration, superb purity, low acidity, and very sweet, seamlessly integrated tannin, the wine is already showing great complexity and accessibility, and is extremely difficult to resist. Anticipated maturity: now–2020. Last tasted, 1/03.

1989
100
This continues to be one of the immortal wines and one of the greatest young Bordeaux wines of the last half century. Consistently prodigious and almost a sure bet to top the scoring card of any blind tasting of this vintage as well as other years, the 1989 Haut-Brion is a seamless, majestic classic and a tribute to this phenomenal *terroir* and its singular characteristics. The wine still has a very thick, viscous-looking ruby/purple color, a spectacular, young but awesome smorgasbord of aromas ranging from scorched earth, liquid minerals, graphite, blackberry and black currant jam to toast, licorice, and spice box. The levels of fruit, extract, and glyc-

erin in this viscous, full-bodied, low-acid wine are awe-inspiring. The brilliant symmetry of the wine, extraordinary purity, and seamlessness are the hallmarks of a modern-day legend. It is still in its pre-adolescent stage of development, and I would not expect it to hit its full plateau of maturity for another 3–5 years, but this should be an Haut-Brion that rivals the greatest ever made at this estate. Life is too short not to drink this wine as many times as possible! A modern-day clone of the 1959? Anticipated maturity: 2005–2030. Last tasted, 1/03.

1988 A more firmly structured Haut-Brion, built somewhat along the lines of the 1996,
92   this dark garnet-colored wine is showing notes of licorice, underbrush, compost, truffles, dried herbs, creosote, and sweet black cherries and currants. Medium bodied, rich, but still structured, this wine unfolds incrementally on the palate, showing superb density and a lot of complex Graves elements. It is just beginning to hit its plateau of full maturity. Anticipated maturity: now–2025. Last tasted, 11/02.

1987 This is an example of a light vintage that produced an immensely seductive, sup-
88   ple, delicious wine that seemed nearly fully mature when released in 1989 yet has continued to offer a fragrant, round, elegant, delicious style of wine that never hit the blockbuster high marks of the great vintages but is, oh, so satisfying and so typically Haut-Brion. Remarkably, the wine seems to defy aging, staying fragrant, sweet, round, relatively light, but delicious and so well balanced. I would have thought this wine would have long faded, but it continues to drink beautifully, with only some amber creeping in at the edge. Anticipated maturity: now–2006. An example of how perfectly balanced even lighter-styled wines can last longer than anyone expects. Last tasted, 11/02.

1986 This wine continues to be backward, but the bouquet is beginning to develop sec-
94   ondary nuances from roasted herbs and sweet cigar tobacco to compost, leathery notes, along with plenty of sweet cherry and black currant fruit. I had somewhat higher hopes for it a decade ago. The wine is still youthful, quite pure, medium to full-bodied, but somewhat elevated, austere tannins in the finish at age 16 are starting to make me think they will never become fully integrated. As always, making a judgment call on a wine destined to have a half century of life is sometimes difficult, given the varying stages it goes through, but I wonder if this wine will turn out to be as profound as I once predicted. Anticipated maturity: 2008–2030. Last tasted, 11/02.

1985 A gloriously seductive, classic Haut-Brion showing the most savory side of this
95   elegant, finesse-styled wine, the 1985 Haut-Brion has reached its plateau of full maturity. The color is a deep ruby/garnet with some lightening at the edge. A very complex nose of cedar, dried herbs, smoke, creosote, and black cherries, plums, and currants jumps from the glass. In the mouth, it is round, concentrated, medium to full-bodied, with a velvety texture and beautifully integrated alcohol, acidity, and tannin. A beauty! Anticipated maturity: now–2012. Last tasted, 11/02.

1983 A somewhat controversial Haut-Brion, this wine reached full maturity at a shock-
88?   ingly fast pace and seems now to be giving signs of cracking up. A very earthy, melted asphalt, creosote-like nose intermixed with compost, decaying autumnal vegetation, and herb-tinged fruit is actually more appealing than it might sound. In the mouth the wine is fleshy, medium bodied, relatively lush, but the garnet color is showing considerable amber, and the finish starts to dry out after the wine sits in the glass for just a mere five minutes. And of course, I have tasted this wine from pristinely stored bottles, so I suspect those that have been less than perfectly stored are probably already in serious decline. Anticipated maturity: now. Drink up. Last tasted, 11/02.

1982   As far as first-growth 1982s go, this wine is certainly not one of the profound ex-
94   amples of the vintage. Administrator Jean Delmas has always compared it to the
1959, and perhaps it will magically put on weight and length, and ultimately be
comparable to that perfect wine. However, this wine seems a far cry from the immortal 1989, and even such recent Haut-Brion greats as the 2000, 1998, 1996,
1995, and 1990. Nevertheless, it is still a relatively youthful wine, with a deep
ruby color that is just revealing a bit of pink at the edge. The wine shows sweet red
currant, plum, and sweet mineral notes, followed by a medium-bodied, very elegant style, with ripe tannin, beautiful fruit, and a 45-second length. Its youthfulness is not surprising, but the wine does not seem to have the weight, opulence,
and viscosity of the top 1982s. Anticipated maturity: now–2022. Last tasted,
11/02.

1979   One of the top three or four wines of the vintage, the 1979 Haut-Brion has put on
93   weight in its evolution in the bottle and, although fully mature, shows no signs of
decline. The color is a dark garnet with some amber at the edge. The wine shows a
very sweet nose of fruitcake intermixed with damp earth, tobacco, smoke, liquid
mineral, black currants, and a hint of creosote. Medium to full-bodied, with excellent power and lushness, this is an atypically rich, layered, authoritatively flavorful wine that seems almost out of character for the vintage. Anticipated maturity:
now–2015. Last tasted, 11/02.

1978   In decline, this wine seems to have become kinkier and weirder as it has devel-
86   oped over the last 5–6 years. The color is a dark plum, and the wine offers up a
very sweet nose of rotting vegetation, melted asphalt, and compost autumnal
leaves. The wine shows plenty of amber at the edge, and the finish seems to be losing fruit and showing more tannin and acidity. This wine seems to be in major decline. Anticipated maturity: Drink up. Last tasted, 11/02.

1975   A wine I completely misjudged early in its life, the 1975 has turned out to be a
94   great wine and one of the top dozen or so wines of the vintage. It actually comes
close to competing with the immortal 1975 La Mission Haut-Brion, one of the
most powerful, concentrated wines made in Bordeaux in the last 25 years. The
1975 Haut-Brion shows a dark plum/garnet color, a gorgeously sweet nose of
singed saddle leather, scorched earth, tobacco, herb, red as well as black currants,
plum, fig, and creosote. Very full-bodied, intense, with noticeable but sweet tannin, this layered wine is very opulent, rich, with striking aromatics. It is a fabulous
effort in a vintage that has lost considerable support from Bordeaux wine enthusiasts. This is one of the exceptions. Anticipated maturity: now–2025. Last tasted,
11/02.

ANCIENT VINTAGES (RED)

Between 1966 and 1974, Haut-Brion's track record is far less successful than one
would suspect based on what they achieved between 1975 and 2002. The 1970 (85
points; last tasted 6/96) has always been an understated, somewhat straightforward
wine with the telltale perfume but never a lot of complexity, depth, or intensity. The
same could be said for the 1966 (88 points; last tasted 12/00). This wine has consistently been a mid- to upper-80-point wine, showing earthy, tobacco, and herbal notes
in a light- to medium-bodied, relatively austere style. The wine is fully mature, but has
the structure and freshness to last another 5–10 years. Certainly the 1964 (90 points;
last tasted 10/88) has always performed in an outstanding but somewhat more rustic
style than one expects from Haut-Brion. The 1962 is an elegant beauty of finesse and

sweetness (90 points; last tasted 12/00). Of course, the two immortal wines are the 1961 (100 points; last tasted 1/01) and 1959 (100 points; last tasted 9/02). Both of these wines are extraordinary, with the 1961 seemingly at the end of its plateau of maturity, and the 1959 showing no signs of weakness and capable of lasting another 10–15 years. Both are extraordinary Haut-Brions that are pure perfection from pristine bottles, with the classic nose of cedar, tobacco, minerals, sweet red and black fruits, and an extremely full-bodied, opulent texture. The 1959 is a bit more viscous and probably has more in common with the 1989 than the 1961.

In January 1997, I had the exceptionally smoky, sweet, rich, impressively endowed 1957 Haut-Brion (90 points). The wine was fully mature, as evidenced by its dark garnet color with considerable rust. The wine was very aromatic, plump, and succulently textured, with fleshy flavors, plenty of glycerin, and sweet fruit. It is another example of an unheralded vintage producing a top-flight wine. A dark ruby–colored wine with noticeable amber/rust, the 1955 Haut-Brion (97 points; last tasted 1/03) offers a huge, fragrant bouquet of walnuts, tobacco, wet stones, and smoky, cassis-like fruit. Medium bodied, with extraordinary elegance and sweetness, this rich, concentrated wine exhibits no hard edges. Remarkably youthful, as well as concentrated and impeccably well balanced, it is capable of lasting for another 10–20 years. Haut-Brion's 1953 (95 points; last tasted 10/94) is best purchased today in magnums or larger-format bottles. Although it has been fully mature for decades, it has retained the hallmark, singed leather, tobacco leaf, superripe fragrance that makes Haut-Brion so distinctive. The wine is extremely soft, revealing considerable amber and rust at the edge, but it still possesses rich, creamy fruit and medium to full body. It does require drinking, so be very careful with regular-size bottles.

The 1949 Haut-Brion (91 points; tasted 12/95) revealed some of the textbook cigar, ashtray, tobacco-scented notes, as well as scents of roasted herbs and ripe fruit. The color was a medium garnet with considerable rust at the edge. Medium bodied, round, sweet, and soft, this wine is past its prime, although it remains exceptional. Drink it up. Neither Haut-Brion's 1948 nor 1947 have ever left me with a favorable impression. The 1948 (75 points; last tasted 3/97), from a private cold cellar in Bordeaux, was attenuated, muddled, and extremely disjointed and unimpressive. Several tastings of the 1947 (my birth year) have always been too alcoholic, with high levels of acidity and not enough fruit and flesh to cover the wine's imposing structural components. The 1945 (100 points; last tasted 10/94) Haut-Brion is profound. It demonstrates the essence of Haut-Brion's style. The color remains a healthy, opaque garnet with only slight amber at the edge. A huge, penetrating bouquet of sweet black fruits, smoked nuts, tobacco, and tar soars from the glass. The wine possesses extraordinary density and extraction of fruit, massive, full-bodied, unctuously textured flavors that reveal little tannin, and copious quantities of glycerin and alcohol. It is a fabulously rich, monumental example of a fully mature Haut-Brion that exhibits no signs of decline. Awesome! One of my more interesting tasting experiences was Haut-Brion's 1943 (89 points; last tasted 1/97). 1943 was believed to be the finest vintage of the World War II years. This wine, bottled after the war ended, exhibited a deep garnet color and a scorched earth/melted tar/aged beef-like aroma. The provocative aromatics were followed by a wine with copious quantities of sweet fruit, astringent tannin, and a dry, angular finish. Extremely complex, with most of the fruit remaining on the attack, this wine is just beginning to narrow out and become more austere and angular.

The 1937 vintage has a justifiable reputation for being hard, but one could see through the austere, still tannin-dominated 1937 Haut-Brion (89+? points; tasted 12/95) to admire the healthy, dark, dense color with only some amber at the edge. Minerals, tobacco, cedar, and coffee aromas were followed by a muscular, medium-bodied wine with plenty of power and fruit. But the vintage's telltale hard tannin was still present. This particular magnum of 1937 Haut-Brion would have lasted another 20–30+ years. I had mixed tasting notes on the 1928 (anywhere from 96–100 points; last tasted 8/02). At its best, it is the most concentrated, port-like wine I have ever tasted from Haut-Brion. Its huge, meaty, tar, caramel, and jammy black fruit character is unctuously textured. The wine oozes out of the glass and over the palate. In some tastings it has been overripe, yet healthy and intact, but nearly bizarre because of its exaggerated style. There is a timeless aspect to it. The 1926 vintage, one of the best years in the decade of the 1920s, has always been overlooked in favor of the 1929, 1928, and 1921. Reputed to be one of the great wines of the vintage, the 1926 Haut-Brion (97 points; last tasted 10/94) is unusual in its roasted, chocolaty, sweet, dense, thick style. It reveals an impressive deep color with some orange at the edge and a huge nose of tobacco, mint, chocolate, grilled nuts, and smoked duck. Full-bodied and powerful, with amazing thickness and unctuosity, but extremely tannic and rustic, this atypical Haut-Brion will last for another 20–30 years. The 1921 Haut-Brion (79 points; last tasted 12/95) possessed a dense, impressive color, extremely high tannin levels, and an old, sweaty, leathery, locker-room nose with vague coffee and chocolaty, roasted herb-like flavors. The astringent tannin gave the wine a coarse and disjointed personality.

IMPORTANT VINTAGES (WHITE)

2001
93+
This dense, full-bodied, concentrated, lively Haut-Brion blanc exhibits aromas of honeyed citrus, flowers, smoke, and melon. It should age marvelously for three decades. Anticipated maturity: 2005–2030. Last tasted, 1/03.

2000
90
An outstanding effort for the vintage, although shy when compared to the 2001 or evolved, complex 1999, the 2000 reveals a rich lanolin and honeyed melon bouquet with a hint of fig in the background. Made in a medium-bodied, straightforward style with loads of fruit, glycerin, and smoky wood, but not the nuances, persistence, and depth of the 2001 or 1999, it can be drunk now and over the next 12 years. Last tasted, 1/03.

1999
92
A beautiful Haut-Brion blanc, the 1999 has put on considerable weight. It reveals characteristics of dried herbs, olives, smoke, buttery citrus, grapefruit, and a hint of orange skin. The wine is medium bodied, with good acidity as well as a luscious flavor profile. Anticipated maturity: now–2020. Last tasted, 1/03.

1998
96
A prodigious example, the 1998 tastes like liquid minerals intermixed with honeyed grapefruit, lanolin, citrus, smoke, and passion fruit. Full-bodied, with good acidity, plenty of structure, and a tremendously long finish, it remains youthful and tight, but the upside is awesome. Anticipated maturity: 2007–2035. Last tasted, 1/03.

1997
96

This opulent, full-bodied, flashy, flamboyant, evolved Haut-Brion blanc exhibits a light gold color in addition to deep, concentrated, honeysuckle, lanolin, orange peel, and white peach aromas as well as flavors. This opulent, viscous 1997 can be drunk now and over the next 15–20 years. Last tasted, 1/03.

1996
92

In a vintage that produced a lot of high acid, emaciated dry whites, Haut-Brion's 1996 is the wine of the vintage. It displays exceptional concentration, tangy acidity, and gorgeously layered flavors of buttery citrus-like fruit, olives, and smoke. This medium-bodied, concentrated wine is quite backward. It will need a considerable amount of bottle age to shed some of its structure. Anticipated maturity: 2010–2025. Last tasted, 11/97.

1995
92

In this vintage, the Haut-Brion blanc contained less Semillon because Jean Delmas thought the drought had negatively impacted this varietal more than Sauvignon. Consequently, the 1995 is less grandiose in its proportions but still one of the two best dry white Graves of the vintage. The wine possesses a light gold color, and a citrusy, honeyed nose with subtle toasty oak. Medium bodied, with exquisite concentration and delineation, this beautifully pure wine can be expected to close down and not reemerge from its dormant stage for a decade. Anticipated maturity: 2007–2025. Last tasted, 11/97.

1994
98

This spectacular dry white Graves is a likely candidate to rival the 1989 produced at Haut-Brion. The harvest began at the end of August. The wine possesses the texture of a great Burgundy grand cru given its thick unctuousness. The superb nose of honeyed fruits and smoky oak is far more developed and ostentatious than its sister, the more subtle and backward Laville Haut-Brion. Awesomely rich, with a chewy texture and great purity and definition, this is a ravishingly intense, full-bodied, dry white wine that should age well for 30+ years. Last tasted, 7/97.

1993
94

Slightly superior to the sensational 1992 Haut-Brion blanc, the 1993 exhibits a flattering nose of oily, mineral-scented, ripe, honeyed fruit, full-bodied, super-concentrated flavors, admirable acidity, great vibrancy and delineation, and a rich, long, dry, refreshing finish. It is a rich Haut-Brion blanc with more aromatic complexity than the muscular and chewy 1992. These wines are almost ageless. Like its older sibling, the 1993 will age effortlessly for 20–30 years. Last tasted, 11/94.

1992
93

This is another blockbuster Haut-Brion blanc, with a big, ostentatious bouquet of sweet, honeyed fruit. Full-bodied, with layers of richness, this creamy-textured, fleshy wine is at present more evolved and dramatic than its sibling, the 1992 Laville. The wine possesses fine acidity and an explosively long, dry finish. This dazzling Haut-Brion blanc should drink well for 30+ years. Last tasted, 1/94.

1989
100

This is the most immense and large-scaled Haut-Brion blanc I have ever tasted. Jean Delmas, administrator of the Dillon properties, justifiably felt the 1989 fully replicated the fleshy, chewy texture of a great grand cru white Burgundy. Only 600 cases were made of this deep yellow/gold-colored, rich, alcoholic, sumptuous wine. It is amazingly full and long in the mouth, with a very distinctive mineral, honeyed character. The low acidity would seemingly suggest a shorter life than normal, but I am convinced this wine will last 25 or more years. It is a real show-stopper! Sweet, honeyed peach, caramel, and buttery aromas tumble from the glass of this prodigious effort. Anticipated maturity: now–2025. Last tasted, 1/03.

ANCIENT VINTAGES (WHITE)

This wine can last for four decades, but I have had little opportunity to taste older vintages. One of the most remarkable vintages I have tasted is the 1985 (98 points; last tasted 12/00).

BAHANS HAUT-BRION

IMPORTANT VINTAGES

2001
87–89
A fine second wine, the stylish 2001 Bahans Haut-Brion offers abundant quanti-ties of black currant fruit intermixed with spice and subtle earth notes. With medium body, outstanding pu-rity, and a sweet attack, it will drink well for a dozen or so years. Approximately 30% of the crop made it into this *cuvée*. Last tasted, 1/03.

2000
90
The dark ruby/purple–colored, deep, rich, medium-bodied 2000 Bahans Haut-Brion exhibits scents of graphite, black cherry liqueur, cassis, and minerals. This second wine has a lot in common with its bigger sibling, displaying impressive volume, depth, and complexity. Anticipated maturity: 2005–2016. Last tasted, 1/03.

1999
88
Somewhat closed aromatically when I tasted it, the black cherry, plum, and mineral-scented 1999 Bahans Haut-Brion has medium body, excellent purity, good texture, and firm tannin. Anticipated maturity: 2004–2015. Last tasted, 3/02.

1998
88
Readers looking for the taste of Haut-Brion for about one-third the price should check out the 1998 Bahans Haut-Brion. It possesses a scorched earth, mineral, smoky, red and black currant-scented bouquet, terrific complexity, purity and ele-gance, and a harmonious palate. The finish is slightly tannic. This is a serious ef-fort that should age well for 12+ years. Last tasted, 3/02.

1997
85
The 1997 Bahans Haut-Brion exhibits a dark ruby color, as well as a subtle min-eral, tobacco, earthy, black plum and currant-scented nose. Light tannin is pres-ent in the finish, but this is an up-front, hedonistic wine to drink during its first 7–8 years of life. Last tasted, 3/98.

1996
87
The 1996 Bahans Haut-Brion is an atypically powerful, rich, tobacco and black fruit–scented wine that is much less forward than normal, but rich, with a nose that is unmistakably Haut-Brion-like. It reveals roasted herbs, scorched earth, and sweet black fruits in both its aromas and flavors. This tannic, structured Bahans will be at its finest between now and 2012. Last tasted, 3/01.

1995
89
The 1995 Bahans Haut-Brion is an aromatic, round, complex, elegant wine that possesses all the characteristics of its bigger, richer sibling, but less depth and more immediate appeal. Very "Graves" with its smoky, roasted nose and sweet, smoke-infused black cherry and currant fruit, it should drink well for another 5–6 years. Last tasted, 11/97.

1994
88
An excellent wine that has managed to avoid the vintage's telltale toughness and occasional hollowness, this Bahans exhibits a dark ruby color, excellent, sweet, spicy, black currant, smoky aromas, surprisingly ripe, concentrated flavors, a vel-vety texture, and a delicious, easygoing finish. This top effort is superior to many more famous 1994 offerings. It should drink well for 3–4+ years. Last tasted, 1/97.

1990
88
The 1990 has put on weight since I first had it, although it is displaying some amber at the edge. The smoky, weedy tobacco, roasted herb, and black currant nose is followed by a fleshy, soft wine with well-integrated tannin and a jammy, low-acid finish. It should drink well for another 6–7 years. Last tasted, 11/96.

1989
90
I am amazed by just how delicious the 1989 Bahans Haut-Brion continues to be. Although it is approaching full maturity, it reveals no signs of amber. The 1989 is a textbook Graves in its sweet, black currant, tobacco, roasted-herb nose. Medium

to full-bodied, with succulent texture, rich, fleshy flavors, and low acidity, it is a pure, beautifully made wine. It should continue to drink well for 5–8 years. Last tasted, 11/96.

LARRIVET-HAUT-BRION

Classification: Grand Cru de Graves

Owner: Philippe Gervoson

Address: 84, route de Cadaujac, 33850 Léognan

Mailing address: BP 41, 33850 Léognan

Telephone: 05 56 64 75 51; Telefax: 05 56 64 53 47

Visits: By appointment Monday to Friday, 8:30–noon and 1:30–5 P.M.

Contact: Christine Gervoson or Jocelyne Duval

VINEYARDS (RED)

Surface area: 111.2 acres

Grape varietals: 50% Cabernet Sauvignon, 50% Merlot

Average age of vines: 20 years

Density of plantation: 7,692 vines per hectare

Average yields: 45 hectoliters per hectare

Elevage: Twenty-one to twenty-eight day fermentation and maceration. Eighteen months aging in barrels with 60–70% new oak. No fining, filtration.

RED WINES PRODUCED

Château Larrivet-Haut-Brion: 100,000 bottles

Domaine de Larrivet: 100,000 bottles

Plateau of maturity: Within 8–20 years of the vintage

VINEYARDS (WHITE)

Surface area: 22.2 acres

Grape varietals: 60% Sauvignon Blanc, 35% Semillon, 5% Muscadelle

Average age of vines: 15 years

Density of plantation: 7,692 vines per hectare

Average yields: 40 hectoliters per hectare

Elevage: Fermentation and 12 months aging on lees in new oak barrels. Fining and filtration.

WHITE WINES PRODUCED

Château Larrivet-Haut-Brion: 30,000 bottles

Domaine de Larrivet: 20,000 bottles

Plateau of maturity: Within 5–15 years of the vintage

GENERAL APPRECIATION

Larrivet-Haut-Brion's owners, Christine and Philippe Gervoson, have done considerable work restoring this beautiful estate to the list of serious Bordeaux wine producers. Like Malartic-Lagravière, Haut-Bergey, and Picque Caillou, this Pessac-Léognan property has demonstrated a renewed commitment to quality, and thus the wines have improved significantly after a long period of mediocrity. Post-1998, all vintages merit attention.

Larrivet-Haut-Brion is well known in European wine circles but until recently was rarely seen in America. The vineyard, located in the southern section of Graves near Léognan, is adjacent to that of the much more famous Haut-Bailly. This beautiful estate, with an attractive château sitting among trees in a shady, park-like atmosphere, has improved dramatically over the last five or so years. The famed Libourne oenologist, Michel Rolland, was brought in and has instituted a strict selection process as well as a later harvest, resulting in the finest wines I have ever tasted from Larrivet-Haut-Brion. This is a property with tremendous upside potential as the vineyards are a respectable age and are planted on pure gravelly soil.

IMPORTANT VINTAGES (RED)

2001
89–91
A stylish, gracious offering, the 2001 Larrivet-Haut-Brion offers sweet black cherry and currant fruit intermixed with tobacco, smoke, dried Provençal herbs, and a touch of new oak. There is great fruit on the attack, admirable sweetness, wonderful freshness and liveliness, medium body, and an undeniably elegant, pure style. Lighter than the 2000, but beautifully etched, it should be at its best between 2006 and 2015. Last tasted, 1/03.

2000
90
The deep ruby/purple–colored 2000's rich, complex perfume displays aromas of cocoa, black cherry liqueur, melted licorice, scorched earth, espresso, and new oak. The wine is rich, firm, tannic, concentrated, and full-bodied with admirable sweetness of fruit. It is a beautiful effort that should be drinkable between 2007 and 2020. Last tasted, 1/03.

1999
89+
Complex aromas of scorched earth, Provençal *garrigue* notes, and black cherries dominate this perfumed, sexy effort. Medium-bodied, with serious concentration, moderate tannin, and a long finish, this plum/garnet-colored wine will benefit from 1–2 more years of cellaring. Anticipated maturity: 2005–2015. Last tasted, 3/02.

1998
88
Classic scents of smoky tobacco, cigar box, scorched earth, black currants, and cherries are vividly displayed in this wine's intense aromas. In the mouth, it is medium bodied, spicy, soft, as well as expressive. This elegant beauty will keep until 2015. Last tasted, 3/02.

1997
86
Spicy, peppery, Provençal *garrigue*, smoky aromas, sweet fruit, attractive ripeness, low acidity, and fine concentration characterize this easygoing, dark ruby–colored wine. Consume it over the next 3–4 years. Last tasted, 3/01.

1996
87
I was seduced by the 1996 Larrivet-Haut-Brion. Although not a powerhouse, it is medium bodied, with expressive tobacco-tinged black currant fruit, a succulent, velvety texture, and smoky, expressive aromatics and flavors. This stylish, evolved 1996 can be drunk now and over the next 5–6 years. Last tasted, 3/01.

ANCIENT VINTAGES (RED)

Virtually everything produced before 1996 was rated between the low 70s and low 80s. The tasting notes were equally unimpressive. Undoubtedly the efforts of owners Christine and Philippe Gervoson as well as their winemaking staff have elevated Larrivet-Haut-Brion to one of the most exciting wines of Pessac-Léognan. They are now exploiting the full potential of this beautifully situated vineyard. Vintages from the 1980s, 1970s, and 1960s should be approached with considerable caution.

IMPORTANT VINTAGES (WHITE)

2001
90 A gorgeous perfume of smoked herbs, toast, honeyed melon, and citrus fruit jumps from the glass of this medium-bodied, elegant, tangy 2001. It possesses good acidity, excellent definition, and intense flavors. A beauty, it is the finest white Larrivet-Haut-Brion I have tasted. Anticipated maturity: now–2012. Last tasted, 1/03.

2000
87 Notes of melons are present in this citrusy, medium-bodied, pleasant but undistinguished effort. While it pales in comparison to the brilliant 2001, it is an easygoing white Graves to consume during its first 8–10 years of life. Last tasted, 1/03.

LATOUR-MARTILLAC

Classification: Classified growth (for reds and whites)

Owner: Kressmann family

Address: Chemin de la Tour, 33650 Martillac

Telephone: 05 57 97 71 11; Telefax: 05 57 97 71 17

E-mail: latour-martillac@latour-martillac.com

Website: www.latour-martillac.com

Visits: By appointment Monday to Friday,
10 A.M.–12:30 P.M. and 1–5 P.M.

Contact: Tristan Kressmann

VINEYARDS (RED)

Surface area: 74.1 acres

Grape varietals: 60% Cabernet Sauvignon, 35% Merlot, 5% Cabernet Franc, Malbec, Petit Verdot

Average age of vines: 35 years

Density of plantation: 7,500 vines per hectare

Average yields: 45 hectoliters per hectare

Elevage: Fermentation and maceration in temperature-controlled vats. Eighteen months aging in barrels with 50% new oak. Fining, no filtration.

RED WINES PRODUCED

Château Latour-Martillac: 120,000 bottles

Lagrave-Martillac: 30,000–40,000 bottles

Plateau of maturity: Within 5–18 years of the vintage

VINEYARDS (WHITE)

Surface area: 24.7 acres

Grape varietals: 55% Semillon, 40% Sauvignon Blanc, 5% Muscadelle

Average age of vines: 40 years

Density of plantation: 7,500 vines per hectare

Average yields: 48 hectoliters per hectare

Elevage: Fermentation and 15 months aging on lees with regular stirring in oak barrels with 50% new oak. Fining, no filtration.

WHITE WINES PRODUCED

Château Latour-Martillac: 30,000 bottles

Lagrave-Martillac: 15,000 bottles

Plateau of maturity: Within 5–15 years of the vintage

GENERAL APPRECIATION

While the whites of this estate have always been good, especially since the mid-1980s, the reds were too often innocuous and blatantly oaky. Things have changed over recent years (since Michel Rolland has been brought in as a consultant) and post-1998 vintages have shown a marked improvement over their predecessors. While soundly made, thereby meriting consumers' attention, the wines of Latour-Martillac are still somewhat of a work in progress.

By the standards of other Graves properties, Latour-Martillac is not an old estate, as the history of the vineyard traces only to the mid-19th century. However, it has been owned by one of Bordeaux's most famous families, the Kressmanns, since 1930, and is now managed by Tristan Kressmann.

IMPORTANT VINTAGES (RED)

2001
86–88
This well-made, attractive 2001 displays a bit too much new oak, but it exhibits lovely notes of black currant fruit intermixed with licorice, menthol, and spice box. Elegant, clean, and sweet, it should be drinkable early. Anticipated maturity: 2005–2014. Last tasted, 1/03.

2000
89
The finest Latour-Martillac I have ever tasted, this evolved, dense ruby/purple–colored 2000 offers a big, sweet, flamboyant bouquet of cedar, mulberries, black currants, and smoke. Medium to full-bodied, ripe, concentrated, and substantial, this impressive effort should be at its finest between 2005 and 2016. Last tasted, 1/03.

1999
86
This elegant 1999 reveals a heavy dosage of wood, but it also possesses briery currant fruit, medium weight, and fine purity. Drink it over the next 7–8 years. Last tasted, 1/02.

1998
87
A concentrated effort for this estate, the 1998 Latour-Martillac exhibits sweet, toasty, black currant fruit intertwined with tar and earth scents. With ripe tannin, medium body, and fine balance, this excellent wine should drink well between now and 2016. Last tasted, 1/02.

1997
86
The 1997 is a rich, sweet wine with color, extract, and length. It offers smoky, toasty oak in the nose, attractive black currant fruit, and notes of licorice. It should drink well for 7–8 years. Last tasted, 3/00.

1996
83
Latour-Martillac's 1996 is a medium-bodied, straightforward wine with good spice, moderate fruit, and a simple personality. There is some tannin, but the wine is light. Anticipated maturity: now–2008. Last tasted, 3/00.

1995   An olive, tobacco, smoky, red currant, and cherry-scented nose is followed by an
86   elegant, medium-bodied, soft, smoothly textured wine that can be drunk now or
over the next 5 years. Last tasted, 11/97.

IMPORTANT VINTAGES (WHITE)

2001   A strong effort, this honey, grapefruit, and citrus-filled white possesses medium
89   body, smoky oak, a touch of minerality, fine acidity, and a long finish. It should
drink well for 10–15 years. Last tasted, 1/03.

2000   Typical of this vintage (which produced great reds but average-quality whites), the
85   dull, monolithic 2000 Latour-Martillac reveals nice fruit on the attack, but it falls
off quickly in the mouth. Drink it over the next 7–8 years. Last tasted, 1/03.

ANCIENT VINTAGES (WHITE)

Latour-Martillac's whites have shown well in many vintages, including 1994 (90
points; last tasted 3/97), 1992 (90 points; last tasted 1/94), 1989 (89 points; last tasted
11/00), and a brilliant 1988 (90 points; last tasted 11/88).

LAVILLE HAUT-BRION

Classification: Classified growth (for whites)

Owner: Domaine Clarence Dillon SA

Address: 33400 Talence

Mailing address: c/o Domaine Clarence Dillon, Château
Haut-Brion, 33608 Pessac Cedex

Telephone: 05 56 00 29 30; Telefax: 05 56 98 75 14

E-mail: info@haut-brion.com

Website: www.laville-haut-brion.com

No visits

VINEYARDS (WHITE)

Surface area: 9.1 acres

Grape varietals: 70% Semillon, 27% Sauvignon, 3% Muscadelle

Average age of vines: 51 years

Density of plantation: 10,000 vines per hectare

Average yields: 35 hectoliters per hectare

Elevage: Fermentation and 13–16 months aging in new oak barrels. No fining, no
filtration.

WHITE WINES PRODUCED

Château Laville Haut-Brion: 10,200 bottles

No second wine is produced.

Plateau of maturity: Within 10–45 years of the vintage

GENERAL APPRECIATION

Laville Haut-Brion is one of the world's greatest dry white wines. It has an uncanny ability to improve for 30–40 years.

This tiny vineyard produces one of the most remarkably long-lived white wines of France. The soil is less gravelly and heavier than the vineyard of La Mission Haut-Brion. The production is tiny, adding to the rarity value of this white wine. Fermented and aged in new oak casks, Laville Haut-Brion takes on a waxy richness with aging. It is marvelous to taste from cask, but after bottling, it completely closes up, not to reopen in some instances for 5–10 years. Reputation and a consistent high level of quality ensure that it sells for a frighteningly high price. Perhaps that explains why 95% of the production is exported.

IMPORTANT VINTAGES (WHITE)

2001
91+
Citrusy, grapefruit, honeysuckle, and white peach characteristics dominate the 2001's waxy bouquet. Big, bold, reserved and tight, but full-bodied, structured, and intense, it should be forgotten for the next 5–6 years. Anticipated maturity: 2010–2025. Last tasted, 1/03.

2000
89
This stylish, medium-bodied example of Laville Haut-Brion exhibits notes of citrus, minerals, white corn, and melons. Ripe and precociously styled, it should be at its best in five years and last through 2015. Last tasted, 1/03.

1999
91
Aromas of apricots, peaches, honeysuckle, lanolin, and candle wax emerge from the glass of this smoky, medium- to full-bodied, fleshy 1999. Having put on considerable weight in the bottle, it is pure with good acidity, and it appears to be on a fast evolutionary track. Anticipated maturity: now–2017. Last tasted, 1/03.

1998
95
A profound Laville Haut-Brion, with a light yellow/green/gold color, the 1998 boasts a super bouquet of smoke, herbs, candle wax, passion fruit, honeysuckle, and white peaches. Full-bodied, with an unctuous texture yet zesty acidity for delineation as well as vibrancy, this majestic, multilayered, young, backward 1998 should age for many decades. Anticipated maturity: 2010–2030. Last tasted, 1/03.

1996
90
Laville's 1996 is one of the lighter-styled efforts from this estate in the 1990s. Nevertheless, it has managed to cram gorgeous levels of complexity and elegance into a citrusy, melony, richly fruity format. While it does not possess the weight and body of such blockbuster vintages as 1994, it is impressive. There is good acidity, and the wine comes across as clean, crisp, and stylish in an understated, restrained manner. This wine should drink well for 12–15+ years. Last tasted, 1/00.

1995
88
The 1995 Laville Haut-Brion lacks some of the complexity and intensity of the 1994 and other top years. The wine is tart, with ripe fig, melony, and waxy fruit in the nose and flavors. Light to medium-bodied, with high acidity and outstanding purity, this is a tasty, refreshing Laville to drink between 2000 and 2010. Last tasted, 11/97.

1994
94
This tightly knit, medium-bodied wine exhibits an intense, sweet nose of toast, minerals, honey, and spices. There is ripe fruit and intensity on the palate, but the overall impression is that of a backward, undeveloped wine. It has 20–25 years of aging potential. Last tasted, 3/97.

1993
90
While the 1993 Laville Haut-Brion should rival the 1992 after a few more years of cellaring, at present it is tight and lighter bodied than the fat, robust 1992. This stylish, backward yet finesse-styled Laville Haut-Brion exhibits aromas of spicy,

honeyed fruit and toasty new oak, crisp acidity, and a rich, firmly structured personality. Last tasted, 11/94.

1992
91
Laville's 1992 was the most backward, dry white Graves I tasted. It possesses a medium straw color, a tight but promising nose of sweet waxy fruit, long, rich, full-bodied flavors, adequate acidity, an opulent, chewy richness, and tremendous length. Although not as monumental as the 1989, this is a top-class Laville Haut-Brion that should drink well for 20–30 years. Last tasted, 1/94.

1989
96
This utterly mind-blowing effort from Laville Haut-Brion, with its decadent bouquet of honeyed, superripe melons, figs, and toasty new oak is a real turn-on. In the mouth, the wine is stunningly rich, concentrated, and intense, with a texture more akin to a grand cru white Burgundy than an austere white Graves. Acidity is low and the alcohol level is high, suggesting this wine will have to be drunk in its first 10–15 years. For pure power, as well as a sumptuous texture, this may well be the most dramatic Laville Haut-Brion ever produced. Production was tiny; only 900 cases were made. Anticipated maturity: now–2020. Last tasted, 12/02.

1988
87
While lacking the personality of the blockbuster 1989, the 1988 is a beautifully made, waxy, melon-scented wine with a touch of herbs and smoky oak. It has better acidity and a more delineated personality than the 1989, but not the latter vintage's flamboyant character. Nevertheless, this should turn out to be an extremely long-lived Laville, and while it may not hit the heights of hedonism that the 1989 will, it still offers plenty of flavor in a more polite and civilized fashion. Anticipated maturity: now–2010. Last tasted, 3/97.

1987
86
The 1987 turned out to be a very good vintage for the white wines of Graves. This is a lighter-weight Laville Haut-Brion, but its wonderfully precise herb, melon, and fig flavors are offered in a medium-bodied format with a great deal of charm and character. There is enough acidity to give the wine some lift and add focus to its medium-bodied flavors. Drink this charmer over the next decade. Anticipated maturity: now. Last tasted, 1/90.

1985
93
This is a sumptuous, rich, honeyed Laville Haut-Brion that should drink beautifully for the next two decades. It is among the more powerful and richer wines produced by the château, yet it has the requisite acid to give it balance and freshness. Not quite as superripe and alcoholic as the 1989, it is perhaps more typical of Laville Haut-Brion at its richest and fullest. Anticipated maturity: now–2008. Last tasted, 12/90.

ANCIENT VINTAGES

The 1983 Laville Haut-Brion (90 points; last tasted 12/02) is an elegant, classy, textbook Laville, whereas the 1982 (87 points, last tasted 4/00) is a chunky, foursquare, heavyweight Laville that lacks the finesse and elegance of the 1983. Older vintages I have tasted include a powerhouse, now fully mature 1976 (91 points, last tasted 6/99), a classic, long-lived, tightly knit, well-structured 1975 (90 points, last tasted 8/00), a glorious 1966 (92 points, last tasted 8/00) and a 1962 (88 points, last tasted 8/00). In 1990 I finally had a chance to taste the Laville Haut-Brion that Michael Broadbent dubbed spectacular, the 1945 "Crème de Tête." In a blind tasting against the regular cuvée of the 1945 Laville Haut-Brion, there was indeed a difference. The wines were stunning efforts that resembled old, powerful Sauternes more than white Graves. Both were massive, rich, honeyed wines that were quite dry, but because of their richness and fullness, they had overwhelming impact on the palate. The Crème de Tête clearly was richer and fuller. I rated it a 93.

LA LOUVIÈRE

Classification: Unclassified

Owner: André Lurton

Address: route de Cadaujac, 33850 Léognan

Mailing address: Vignobles André Lurton, Château Bonnet, 33420 Grézillac

Telephone: 05 57 25 58 58; Telefax: 05 57 74 98 59

E-mail: andrelurton@andrelurton.com

Website: www.andrelurton.com

Visits: By appointment Monday to Friday, 9 A.M.–5 P.M.

Contact: Véronique Bouffard

VINEYARDS (RED)

Surface area: 82.7 acres

Grape varietals: 64% Cabernet Sauvignon, 30% Merlot, 3% Cabernet Franc, 3% Petit Verdot

Average age of vines: 20–22 years

Density of plantation: 6,500–8,500 vines per hectare

Average yields: 45 hectoliters per hectare

Elevage: Three-week fermentation and maceration in temperature-controlled stainless-steel vats. Twelve months aging in barrels with 50–75% new oak and racking every three months. Fining and filtration.

RED WINES PRODUCED

Château La Louvière: 150,000 bottles

L de la Louvière: 80,000 bottles

Plateau of maturity: Within 3–15 years of the vintage

VINEYARDS (WHITE)

Surface area: 33.3 acres

Grape varietals: 85% Sauvignon Blanc, 15% Semillon

Average age of vines: 20–22 years

Density of plantation: 6,500–8,500 vines per hectare

Average yields: 45 hectoliters per hectare

Elevage: After cold settling, 10–15 day fermentation (at 18–23°C) in barrels with 30–50% new oak. One year aging on lees with regular stirrings. Fining and filtration.

WHITE WINES PRODUCED

Château La Louvière: 50,000 bottles

L de La Louvière: 30,000 bottles

Plateau of maturity: Within 2–8 years of the vintage

GENERAL APPRECIATION

As could be expected from an André Lurton estate, La Louvière offers one of the most consistently well-made wines of Pessac-Léognan, as well as one of the better values . . . in both red and white. It could easily compete with many a classified growth of the appellation.

While unclassified, La Louvière (which can trace its origins to 1200) is now making wines superior to many of the crus classés. In particular, recent vintages have been on a quality level with a Médoc fourth growth. The proprietor, André Lurton, acquired the property in 1965 and has thoroughly rejuvenated the estate, which has its vineyards impressively situated between Haut-Bailly and Carbonnieux.

The emphasis is on producing wines of immediate drinkability, but also wines that are concentrated, fresh, and pure. Lurton has achieved all of that. While it used to be true that the red wines could not match the brilliance of the whites, that has changed since the mid-1980s, as both wines are now excellent. Moreover, La Louvière remains notoriously undervalued, so consumers still have an opportunity to stock up on some delicious high-quality wines that compete with many of the most renowned Graves properties.

This is another château well worth visiting. The building is classified as one of France's historic monuments.

IMPORTANT VINTAGES (RED)

2001   La Louvière's 2001 offers a dense opaque ruby/purple color as well as a smoky,
88–89   earthy-scented perfume with plenty of black cherry and currant fruit. It is sweet on the attack, possesses a true mid-section, fine purity, and sweet tannin in the low-acid finish. Anticipated maturity: 2005–2016. Last tasted, 1/03.

2000   A top-notch effort, this opaque ruby/purple–colored 2000 exhibits plenty of
90   earthy, black currant, vanilla, graphite, licorice, and smoky cherry aromas as well as flavors. Medium bodied with sweet tannin, good acidity, and a long, concentrated finish, this is the finest La Louvière since the 1990. Anticipated maturity: 2005–2015. Last tasted, 1/03.

1999   Although La Louvière tends to be consistently well made, the 1999 is light, lean,
85   and underwhelming. The color is medium ruby, and the wine displays a lack of sweetness, texture, and richness. It will last for 4–5 years. Last tasted, 3/02.

1998   An excellent dark ruby/purple–colored effort, the 1998 offers a classic scorched-
88   earth, smoky, black cherry, and currant-scented bouquet. Medium bodied, with sweet tannin, well-integrated acidity, and excellent flavor as well as richness, it is a complex, textbook Graves. Anticipated maturity: now–2014. Last tasted, 3/02.

1996   La Louvière's dark ruby/purple–colored, ripe 1996 exhibits an excellent combi-
87   nation of sweet black currant fruit meshed with notes of Provençal olives, licorice, smoke, and toasty new oak. With medium to full body, excellent sweetness, and a layered, concentrated finish, this wine should be at its finest between now and 2015. Last tasted, 3/01.

1995   An exceptionally seductive, open-knit 1995, La Louvière's telltale tobacco,
87   smoky, leafy, herb-tinged red and black currant fruit jumps from the glass of this aromatic wine. Exhibiting excellent ripeness, a supple texture, medium body, and a delicious, roasted fruitiness, this textbook Graves can be drunk now or over the next 7–8 years. Last tasted, 12/01.

1994 88	One of the sleepers of the vintage, the deep ruby/purple color and smoky, black currant, herb-tinged nose of the 1994 are provocative. Rich, powerful, and dense, with moderate tannin, excellent to outstanding concentration, and admirable purity, this is an impressively endowed wine for drinking between now and 2012. Last tasted, 3/96.
1990 90	The 1990 exhibits a saturated purple/garnet color, an unevolved nose of black fruits, smoke, and grilled meats, full body, low acidity, and intense, concentrated fruit, all crammed into a layered, pure, sweet, fruity, ripe wine. Anticipated maturity: now–2010. Last tasted, 7/00.
1989 88	Fully mature, the soft, well-developed 1989 displays a dark ruby/garnet color, with some lightening at the edge. The wine offers a ripe, curranty nose intertwined with scents of new oak, herbs, olives, and tobacco. Medium bodied and smoothly textured, this lush wine should drink well for another 4–5 years. Last tasted, 7/00.
1988 89	Among the finest La Louvières I have tasted, the 1988 is a concentrated, well-balanced wine possessing a delectable roasted, cassis fruitiness that expands on the palate. Impressively concentrated, with an opulent texture and velvety tannins, this complete wine should provide delicious drinking over the next decade. Anticipated maturity: now. Last tasted, 1/93.

IMPORTANT VINTAGES (WHITE)

2001 90	A superb effort, an evolved, complex nose of buttery melons intermixed with figs, dried herbs, minerals, and smoke is followed by a fruit-driven, medium-bodied wine with loads of glycerin, excellent depth, fine purity, and a persistent finish. It should drink well for a decade. Last tasted, 1/03.
2000 87	A noteworthy effort in a challenging vintage for dry white wines, the 2000 La Louvière offers up scents of orange peel, smoke, dried herbs, and minerals. This medium-bodied, evolved example is best drunk over the next 5–6 years. Last tasted, 1/03.

MALARTIC-LAGRAVIÈRE ——————————

Classification: Classified growth (red and white)

Owner: Alfred-Alexandre Bonnie

Address: 43, avenue de Mont de Marsan, 33850 Léognan

Mailing address: BP 7, 33850 Léognan

Telephone: 05 56 64 75 08; Telefax: 05 56 64 99 66

E-mail: malartic-lagraviere@malartic-lagraviere.com

Website: www.malartic-lagraviere.com

Visits: By appointment only

Contact: Pascale Norton

VINEYARDS (RED)

Surface area: 91.4 acres

Grape varietals: 50% Merlot, 40% Cabernet Sauvignon, 10% Cabernet Franc

Average age of vines: 35 years

Density of plantation: 10,000 vines per hectare

Average yields: 25 hectoliters per hectare

Elevage: Three to five week fermentation and maceration in temperature-controlled stainless-steel vats. Fifteen to eighteen months aging in barrels with 40–80% new oak. Fining and filtration.

RED WINES PRODUCED

Château Malartic-Lagravière: 80,000 bottles

Le Sillage de Malartic: 80,000 bottles

Plateau of maturity: Within 5–15 years of the vintage

VINEYARDS (WHITE)

Surface area: 17.3 acres

Grape varietals: 80% Sauvignon Blanc, 20% Semillon

Average age of vines: 35 years

Density of plantation: 10,000 vines per hectare

Average yields: 25 hectoliters per hectare

Elevage: Fermentation and 8–12 months aging in barrels with 25% new oak. Fining and filtration.

WHITE WINES PRODUCED

Château Malartic-Lagravière: 60,000 bottles

Le Sillage de Malartic: 60,000 bottles

Plateau of maturity: Within 3–10 years of the vintage

GENERAL APPRECIATION

Under its present administration, Malartic-Lagravière has come to life. This once perennial underachiever has made an astonishing leap in quality since 1997, largely because of the efforts of new owners Alfred-Alexandre and Michèle Bonnie. Both reds and whites are now worthy of consumers' interest and also remain reasonably priced. Visitors to Bordeaux may desire to schedule a visit, if only to see the space-age technology in the *cuverie*.

One of the numerous estates in the southern Graves region of Léognan, Malartic-Lagravière's vineyard is a single parcel planted on the area's high gravel terraces. Historically, the production per hectare at this estate has been high as the former proprietor, Jacques Marly, held the minority point of view that young vines and high yields produced a better wine than low yields and old vines.

With the acquisition of the estate by the Bonnie family in 1997, there has been a dramatic shift in the quality of the wines. Significant investments in a new, state-of-the-art, high-tech winemaking facility, more new oak, and the introduction of a stricter selection for the second wine quickly changed Malartic-Lagravière from being a largely ignored underachiever to one of the most elegant and interesting wines of Pessac-Léognan. This is clearly one of the region's emerging stars. While the wines will never be blockbusters, both the reds and whites are models of elegance and definition. The higher quality began in 1997, and has been built on in each subsequent vintage. Moreover, prices have not yet caught up with the fascinating new offerings emerging from this estate.

IMPORTANT VINTAGES (RED)

2001
88–89 A sweet, soft, seductive effort, the 2001 Malartic-Lagravière is neither as concentrated as the 2000 nor as provocatively perfumed and charming as the 1999. Nevertheless, it is impressively made, particularly from a property that has enjoyed a complete renaissance in quality over the last four to five years. Sweet berry scents mix with leafy tobacco, smoke, and new oak in this dark ruby/purple–colored offering. Medium bodied, precise, pure, and seductive, it will drink well for 10–12 years. Last tasted, 1/03.

2000
90 The finest Malartic-Lagravière yet produced, the dense ruby/purple–colored 2000 displays sweet aromas of plums, currants, tobacco, and smoke as well as abundant power, concentration, extract, glycerin, and length. This elegant, expansive, juicy, layered, medium-bodied effort should prove long-lived. Anticipated maturity: 2006–2020. Last tasted, 1/03.

1999
90 A sleeper of the vintage, this sexy, open-knit, layered, dense ruby–colored 1999 is a light but delicious effort displaying super-sweet tobacco, black currant, and scorched-earth notes. Pure, with beautiful balance and pinpoint precision, it should be drunk during its first 10–12 years of life. This is a classic example of elegance and finesse that only Bordeaux can achieve. Last tasted, 3/02.

1998
89 The 1998 represents a breakthrough effort for this property. The color is a dense, dark ruby/purple, and the nose reveals stylish, sweet black currant fruit intermixed with earth, minerals, licorice, and spice box. The wine is medium bodied, with ripe tannin, no hard edges, and a beautifully knit, concentrated finish that lasts for more than 30 seconds. Anticipated maturity: now–2015. Last tasted, 3/02.

1997
88 Undoubtedly a sleeper of the vintage, this exceptionally charming, complex, elegant 1997 is neither big, weighty, nor powerful, yet it offers cedar, roasted herb, and sweet plum/cherry fruit in its aromas and flavors. The taster is seduced by the wine's silky, seamless texture, gorgeous aromatics, low acidity, and lovely levels of fruit. It will not make old bones, but who cares since it is so endearing? Enjoy it over the next 3–4 years. Last tasted, 12/01.

1996
76 The unsubstantial 1996 reveals a feeble light ruby color. It offers plenty of new oak and moderate cherry fruit in the nose, medium body, and a pleasant, straightforward, one-dimensional finish. The wine possesses tannin and structure, but not much extract or richness. Anticipated maturity: now–2010. Last tasted, 3/01.

ANCIENT VINTAGES (RED)

Virtually nothing between the mid-1970s and 1995 merited a score above the low 80s. Even such top vintages as 1995 (76 points; last tasted 11/97), 1990 (73 points; last tasted 1/93), 1989 (82 points; last tasted 1/93), 1988 (77 points; last tasted 1/93), and 1985 (84 points; last tasted 3/90) were largely disappointing offerings produced under the previous administration. However, that is all in the past, and not indicative of the wines that have emerged from this estate since 1997.

IMPORTANT VINTAGES (WHITE)

2001
90
Crisp pea pod, fig, mineral, and smoky notes emerge from this delineated, medium-bodied, elegant, flavorful dry white Graves. It should drink well for 10–12 years. Last tasted, 1/03.

2000
85
Muted grapefruit-like characteristics are present in this medium-bodied, foursquare 2000, which lacks the aromatic intensity and sparkle of its younger sibling. Drink it over the next 7–8 years. Last tasted, 1/03.

1999
86
Honeyed citrus, melons, freshly mown grass, and cold steel characteristics are found in this light- to medium-bodied, dry, refreshing 1999. Consume it over the next 7–8 years. Last tasted, 1/03.

1998
89
The first reassuringly top-flight white to emerge from this estate in many years, the 1998 exhibits aromas of honeyed grapefruit, citrus, smoke, peach skin, and toasty oak. Medium bodied, impressively concentrated, long, and pure, it should drink well for 10–12 more years. Last tasted, 1/03.

ANCIENT VINTAGES (WHITE)

Under the administration of Jacques Marley, old vintages of this 100% Sauvignon Blanc–based wine were often extremely high in acidity, tart, herbaceous, and uninteresting. It could last for many years, but the distinctive aromas of underripe green peas and other vegetables was decidedly unappealing.

LA MISSION HAUT-BRION

Classification: Classified growth (red wines)

Owner: Domaine Clarence Dillon SA

Address: 67, rue Peybouquey, 33400 Talence

Mailing address: c/o Domaine Clarence Dillon, Château Haut-Brion, 33608 Pessac Cedex

Telephone: 05 56 00 29 30; Telefax: 05 56 98 75 14

E-mail: info@haut-brion.com or visites@haut-brion.com

Website: www.mission.haut-brion.com

Visits: By appointment Monday to Thursday, 9–11:30 A.M. and 2–4:30 P.M.; Friday, 9 to 11:30 A.M.

Contact: Carla Kuhn

VINEYARDS (RED)

Surface area: 51.6 acres

Grape varietals: 45% Merlot, 48% Cabernet Sauvignon, 7% Cabernet Franc

Average age of vines: 21 years

Density of plantation: 10,000 vines per hectare

Average yields: 45 hectoliters per hectare

Elevage: Fermentation and maceration in temperature-controlled stainless-steel vats of 180-hectoliter capacity. Twenty months aging in new oak barrels. Fining, no filtration.

RED WINES PRODUCED

Château La Mission Haut-Brion: 72,000 bottles

La Chapelle de La Mission Haut-Brion: 36,000 bottles

Plateau of maturity: Within 8–50 years of the vintage

GENERAL APPRECIATION

The long-time cross-street rival of Haut-Brion has, since 1983, been under the same ownership/administration. Fears that the wine would change and become nothing more than the second wine of Haut-Brion have proven to be without merit. What is still evident is that La Mission Haut-Brion is a wine of first-growth quality, and its pricing policy reflects that. This is a great estate producing large-scaled, dense reds that represent the quintessential, full-bodied, scorched-earth Graves style. Moreover, the wines possess legendary aging potential. It is unquestionably one of the world's most singular and distinctive wines. In essence, life is too short not to drink La Mission Haut-Brion.

La Mission Haut-Brion in Talence produces one of the greatest wines in the entire Bordeaux region. This estate sits across the road (RN 250), confronting its long-time rival, Haut-Brion, and has a record of virtually unmatched brilliance that covers much of the 20th century.

This estate has a long history, having been founded by the congregation of the Mission in the 17th century. Much of the wine was made for important members of the church. One of France's most powerful historic figures, Richelieu (a La Mission devotée), was quoted as saying, "If God forbade drinking, would he have made such good wine?" As a result of the French Revolution, the estate was divested from the church and sold to a private buyer. The Woltner family acquired La Mission in 1919. It was they—particularly the late Frederic and his son Henri—who were responsible for the ascendancy of La Mission Haut-Brion's wine quality to a level that matched and frequently surpassed the first growths of the Médoc and neighboring Haut-Brion.

Woltner's genius was widely recognized in Bordeaux. He was known as a gifted taster and oenologist and pioneered the installation of easy-to-clean, metal, glass-lined fermentation tanks in 1926. Many observers attributed the dense, rich, powerful, fruity character of La Mission to these short, squat vats that, because of their shape, tended to increase the grape-skin-to-juice contact during the fermentation. These vats were replaced under the new administration with computer-controlled, state-of-the-art fermenters.

La Mission Haut-Brion's style of wine has always been that of intense richness, full body, great color and extract, and plenty of tannin. I have had the pleasure of tasting all of the best vintages of La Mission back to 1921, and it is a wine that can easily last 30–50 years in the bottle. It has always been a much richer and more powerful wine than that of its one-time archrival Haut-Brion. For this reason, as well as remarkable consistency in poor and mediocre vintages (along with Latour in Pauillac, it has had the finest record in Bordeaux for good wines in poor vintages), La Mission had become one of the most popular wines of Bordeaux.

Henri Woltner passed away in 1974, and until the sale of La Mission Haut-Brion to the present owners of Haut-Brion in 1983, La Mission was managed by Françoise and Francis Dewavrin-Woltner. Internal family bickering over the administration of this property ultimately led to the sale of La Mission and two sister properties, La Tour Haut-Brion and the white wine–producing estate of Laville Haut-Brion. The Woltners settled in Napa Valley, where they produce wine from the steep hillsides of Howell Mountain.

Since 1983 Jean Delmas has moved quickly to stamp his winemaking philosophy on the wines of this estate. After the property was sold in 1983, the winemaking staff was promptly dismissed and Delmas began to augment the percentage of new oak that had deteriorated due to the financial difficulties experienced by the Woltner regime. Now La Mission, like Haut-Brion, is aged in 100% new oak. In addition, the amount of Merlot has been increased to 45%, with the amounts of both the Cabernet Sauvignon and Cabernet Franc lowered.

The first vintages under Delmas were very good but lacked the power and extraordinary richness seen in La Mission in previous top years. They were technically correct wines but lacked a bit of soul and personality. With the installation of a state-of-the-art winemaking facility at the estate in time for the 1987 vintage, the quality of the wine quickly returned to that of its glory years. The wine is cleaner, and flaws such as elevated levels of volatile acidity as well as rustic tannin that appeared in certain older vintages of La Mission are unlikely ever to rear their unpleasant heads under the meticulous management of Jean Delmas. Nevertheless, after a transitional period between 1983 and 1986, La Mission Haut-Brion returned in the late 1980s to produce one of the very best wines of the vintage in 1987, a beauty in 1988, and a sumptuous, perfect 1989, the latter wine undoubtedly the finest La Mission of the decade. Vintages of the 1990s, while more vexing because of rainy Septembers, have all produced wines that are among the finest in Bordeaux. Of course, the 2000 is immortal, the 1998 nearly so.

It is unlikely that the newer style of La Mission will age as long as older vintages, but neither will it be as unapproachable and tannic in its youth. In the final analysis, La Mission Haut-Brion remains a wine of first-growth quality.

IMPORTANT VINTAGES

2001
91–94   While it is virtually impossible to duplicate the surreal wine made at La Mission-Haut-Brion in 2000, the 2001 La Mission is an elegant, vibrant, well-defined effort with sweet, concentrated rich fruit. A blend of 62% Merlot, 35% Cabernet Sauvignon, and 3% Cabernet Franc, it boasts a dense plum/purple color along with a sweet perfume of mineral-infused black currant fruit with a hint of tar in the background. Ripe, medium to full-bodied, with good texture, sweet tannin, and a long finish, it is stylistically similar to the 1999, but with more fruit density, concentration, and size. Anticipated maturity: 2006–2020. Last tasted, 1/03.

2000
100   A superstar of the vintage, the 2000 La Mission Haut-Brion is as profound as such recent superstars as 1989, 1982, and 1975. In time, one might have to return to the prodigious duo of 1961 and 1959 to find a La Mission with this much potential. While still tight from bottling, its inky purple color is accompanied by extrava-

gantly sweet aromas of blackberries, blueberries, toast, scorched earth, coffee, asphalt, graphite, and smoke. Super-intense and unctuously textured, with a sumptuous mid-palate and finish, this is an explosively rich, layered effort that possesses everything I could ever want from a *terroir* that has given me as much hedonistic and intellectual pleasure as any other wine in the world. It is an amazing achievement for administrator Jean-Bernard Delmas, his son, Jean-Philippe, and the entire winemaking team. The phenomenal aftertaste goes on for more than a minute. This wine will be less flamboyant and accessible than the 1989, but what upside potential it possesses! Anticipated maturity: 2011–2045. Last tasted, 1/03.

1999
91
Beautifully complex, with notes of cherry liqueur, plums, cigar smoke, fresh tobacco, and scorched earth, the deep, elegant, yet precise, medium- to full-bodied 1999 La Mission Haut-Brion is cut from the same mold as the 1985, 1983, 1971, and 1962. Not a heavyweight, it is gorgeously complex, supple, and both hedonistic and intellectual. Anticipated maturity: now–2018. Last tasted, 3/02.

1998
94
Complex aromas of scorched earth, minerals, black fruits, lead pencil, and subtle wood accompany this classic, full-bodied La Mission. It boasts superb purity, an expansive, concentrated mid-palate, and sweet tannin in the long, muscular yet refined finish. This superb wine, which requires 3–4 years of cellaring, gets my nod as the finest La Mission since the super duo produced in 1990 and 1989. Anticipated maturity: 2007–2030. Last tasted, 3/02.

1997
87
This dark ruby/plum–colored wine offers a big, spicy, tobacco leaf, and black fruit–scented nose, more structure and tannin than its famous sibling (Haut-Brion), good depth, medium body, and enough accessibility to be consumed now (although it will improve for 3–4 years and last for a decade or more). Last tasted, 3/02.

1996
90
A backward, somewhat austere, muscular style of La Mission Haut-Brion, the color is still a dense, opaque ruby/purple and the aromatics shut down but promising, offering up black fruit, a hint of chocolate, and some sweet oak. The wine is a brawny, muscular, full-bodied La Mission that is going to take some time to reach its apogee. I am not sure it will not always be a somewhat austere wine compared to the top vintages for La Mission. Anticipated maturity: 2008–2025. Last tasted, 9/02.

1995
94
Emerging from a very backward state, the 1995 La Mission has a dense ruby/purple color to the rim. Its nose of smoke, sweet charred earth intermixed with black currant and blueberry as well as mineral is beginning to gain intensity. In the mouth this structured, muscular, medium- to full-bodied wine has impressive levels of concentration, extract, and tannin. The wine is still very youthful, and not even an adolescent in terms of its development, but quite long in the mouth and extremely promising. Anticipated maturity: 2010–2030. Last tasted, 9/02.

1994
91
A superb La Mission from a difficult vintage, this wine shows classic scorched-earth notes intermixed with a hint of dried herbs, pepper, sweet tobacco, and smoky black currant and cherry fruit. It is medium to full-bodied, with loads of glycerin, surprising depth, and no evidence of dilution or vegetal tannins. Anticipated maturity: now–2015. Last tasted, 9/02.

1993
90
Another superb wine in an off year, the 1993 La Mission shows a deep plum/ruby color and a sweet nose of black fruits intermixed with charcoal and mineral. The wine is medium bodied, with ripe tannin and elegant, concentrated richness that persists on the palate. This wine is coming into full maturity and should last for at least 10–12 years. This is undoubtedly the sleeper of the vintage. Last tasted, 9/02.

1992 Soft, delicious, and fully mature, this is very fine wine and quite an accomplish-
88 ment in a dreadful vintage. The wine shows dark plum/ruby color with some amber
at the edge. The nose offers black fruits intermixed with a hint of herbs, mineral,
and mushroom. The wine is round, richly fruity, with some sweet tannin in the finish. Drink it over the next 5–6 years. Last tasted, 9/02.

1991 La Mission enjoyed considerable success in the 1991 vintage. This deep ruby–
87 colored wine boasts a fragrant, smoky, mineral, and berry-scented nose. Suave, elegant, and rich, with noticeable fatness to its harmonious flavors, good balance,
and a long, medium-bodied finish, the wine exhibits fine ripeness and a tasty, aromatic personality. This precocious La Mission should drink well for the next 6–10
years. Last tasted, 1/94.

1990 Like its more elegant and feminine sibling, Haut-Brion, the 1990 La Mission has
96 continued to build weight and richness and is now certainly one of the great La
Missions of the last 25 years. The wine has a deep ruby/purple/plum color and a
sweet nose of Provençal herbs intermixed with cedar, scorched earth, creosote,
and black currant as well as blackberry. Very full-bodied, even viscous, with low
acidity and layers of concentration, this is a spectacular La Mission Haut-Brion
that is already showing considerable complexity. Anticipated maturity: now–
2025. Last tasted, 1/03.

1989 This is a profound bottle of La Mission Haut-Brion with a deep ruby/purple color
100 and a gorgeous nose of espresso, tar, tobacco, mineral, and blackberry, blueberry,
and black currant fruit. The extraordinary smorgasbord of aromatics is matched by
a full-bodied, viscous, opulent style of wine with sweet, jammy fruit yet enough
tannin and acidity to provide uplift and definition. Still somewhat of an adolescent
in terms of its development, and far less evolved than its gorgeous sibling, the
1990, this is a prodigious, multidimensional wine that is a modern-day legend.
Anticipated maturity: 2004–2025. Last tasted, 1/03.

1988 A very concentrated, sweet, yet at the same time well-delineated 1988 that has a
90 dark plum/garnet color with some lightening at the edge, this rather muscular,
earthy wine shows notes of creosote, scorched earth, deep, sweet black cherries,
coffee, and a hint of chocolate. It is a chewy, dense wine that will never be the most
harmonious La Mission, but it is mouth-filling and substantial. Anticipated maturity: now–2014. Last tasted, 9/02.

1987 Delicious, but at the end of its plateau of maturity, the 1987 La Mission gave me
88 considerable pleasure in a lighter style that is a reference point for just how seductive, perfumed, and interesting an off-year vintage of Bordeaux can be. The
wine has always been supple, with plenty of smoky black fruits intermixed with a
whiff of herbs and tobacco. The wine has still retained that fragrance, but in the
mouth the finish is becoming increasingly attenuated. Nevertheless, I suspect
magnums and larger formats of this wine could provide drinking that could possibly even hit a 90-point score from a pristinely stored large format. Anticipated maturity: Drink up. Last tasted, 9/02.

1986 Dark plum/ruby with a dusty, earthy, cigar box–scented nose, this somewhat
89 austere, medium-bodied La Mission Haut-Brion shows plenty of tannin in a somewhat muscular style without the charm and seductiveness of the ripest years. Nevertheless, the aromatics are there, and the wine still tastes young, but I suspect
there will always be a certain austerity to La Mission Haut-Brion's 1986. Anticipated maturity: 2004–2016. Last tasted, 9/02.

1985 A complex, smoky, earthy nose, with a bit of camphor intermixed with jammy
91 black currants and melted road tar is followed by a medium-bodied, very soft, low-
acid wine that is loosely knit, very fleshy, and fully mature. Anticipated maturity:
now–2008. Last tasted, 9/02.

1983   Damp earth, truffles, compost, and mushrooms intermixed with licorice, sweet

88   currants, and black cherries jump from the glass of this fully mature, medium-bodied, very soft La Mission Haut-Brion. The wine shows considerable amber to its garnet color, and the tannins and acidity seem to poke their heads through as the wine sits in the glass. Anticipated maturity: Drink up. Last tasted, 9/02.

1982   The most powerful, concentrated, and enormously endowed La Mission-Haut-

100   Brion between 1975 and 2000, this wine still seems very backward and yet, oh, so promising. I have gone back and forth over its life, wondering whether it is a modern-day clone of the 1961 or 1959, but more and more I am leaning toward the 1959. The wine has a murky, opaque plum/garnet color with no lightening at the edge. With hours of aeration, the wine begins to reveal a prodigious perfume of black fruits, scorched earth, licorice, truffles, and some graphite as well as damp earth. Enormously concentrated, with extraordinary power and depth, this wine continues to remind me of a modern-day equivalent of the 1959. The interesting comparison, of course, is the 1989, and, for the future, probably the 2000. The 1989 has sweeter tannin, more finesse and elegance, but perhaps not the sheer power, muscle, and palate impact of this extraordinary wine. Both of them are pure perfection for my palate, but completely different in style. The 2000 has as much extract and power, but tastes slightly more refined. The 1982 still reveals plenty of tannin, which should guarantee it at least another three decades of longevity. This is clearly a 50-year wine. Anticipated maturity: 2007–2040. Last tasted, 1/03.

1981   Elegant and somewhat undersized by La Mission Haut-Brion standards, but still

90   a beauty and one of the best wines of the vintage, the 1981 still has a deep ruby/purple color and a nose of cassis intermixed with damp earth, mineral, smoke, and some wood. This medium-bodied, relatively elegant La Mission Haut-Brion is close to full maturity. Anticipated maturity: now–2012. Last tasted, 9/02.

1979   The last several bottles have had a more rustic character than I had thought ear-

89   lier. Some tannins and acidity have poked through what is otherwise a relatively deep, concentrated, very aromatic style of La Mission Haut-Brion. Elegant, with gorgeous notes of sweet earth intermixed with creosote, mineral, black currant, and cherry, the wine is smoky, rich, but a bit rough and astringent in the finish. Anticipated maturity: now–2008. Last tasted, 9/02.

1978   A consistently profound La Mission Haut-Brion and a strong candidate for the

95   wine of the vintage, this wine continues to evolve at a glacial pace. Among the most powerful, concentrated wines of the vintage, the 1978 La Mission Haut-Brion has a classic Graves nose of scorched earth, roasted coffee, tobacco, and smoky, sweet black currant and cherry fruit. It is very full-bodied, with supple tannins and sweet, concentrated, layered fruit offering up sumptuous flavors that seem almost atypical for the vintage. A great 1978, and a wine to look for at auction, as it is probably undervalued. Anticipated maturity: now–2015. Last tasted, 9/02.

1975   A wine that I have always considered virtually perfect, I have backed off slightly

99   simply because, at 27 years of age, it seems certain that the enormous tannins of this wine are never going to be totally assimilated. Nevertheless, this is a wine that is going to easily last at least 30 more years. It still has a 100-point bouquet of scorched earth, tobacco, black fruits, liquid minerals, roasted herbs, cedar, and licorice. Huge, massive, and full-bodied, with enormous concentration, this behemoth is one of the biggest, most concentrated and tannic wines made in Bordeaux. Perhaps it will ultimately absorb its tannin, but this is a modern-day clone of the 1945 La Mission Haut-Brion, and a wine that can be drunk now but promises to evolve effortlessly for at least three more decades. Anticipated maturity: now–2035. Last tasted, 9/02.

ANCIENT VINTAGES (RED)

La Mission Haut-Brion produced a good 1971 (87 points; last tasted 11/99) and a very irregular 1970 (largely because of high levels of volatile acidity and too many bottles that were defective and problematic). Among the vintages of the early and mid-1960s, the 1966 is excellent (89 points; last tasted 12/00), as are the 1964 (93 points; last tasted 2/02) and 1961 (100 points; last tasted 1/01). The argument will always be whether the 1961 or the 1959 (100 points; last tasted 1/03) is the greater vintage. The 1961 seems far more evolved and probably best drunk over the next 7–10 years, while the 1959 seems capable of lasting another 15–20 years. It is interesting to note that many 1959s, much like the 1982s, were maligned for lacking both acidity and aging potential. How does one explain the fact that many 1959s are less evolved, as well as richer, fresher, and more complete than many 1961s? For example, as great as the 1961 La Mission is, the equally perfect 1959 remains a less evolved and even richer, deeper-colored, more concentrated, and more powerful wine! It needs at least 3–5 more years of cellaring to reach its plateau of maturity. Spicy and super-concentrated, with a dense, plummy/purple color, this young, broodingly backward, formidably endowed wine should be at its best by the end of the century and drink well for the first 20–25 years of the next millennium. Even allowing for the greatness of Haut-Brion and Mouton Rothschild, the 1955 La Mission (100 points; last tasted 12/01) is the "wine of the vintage." It possesses a sweet, cedary, clove, smoke, and black raspberry nose and rich, full-bodied, remarkably harmonious flavors that ooze with ripe fruit, glycerin, and heady alcohol. The tannin has totally melted away, and the wine reveals considerable rust at the edge, so it is unlikely that the 1955 will improve with further cellaring. There is no indication of any fragility or decline, so this wine can be safely drunk for 10–15 more years. It is an amazing, complex, superbly well-balanced La Mission Haut-Brion! I have been told by a number of people who have followed the 1953 (93 points; last tasted 10/94) vintage from its youth that it drank exceptionally well in the late 1950s. Apparently it has lost none of its hedonistic, supple, explosive fruit. It will not get any better, so consumption is recommended. It offers a delicious smoky, berry fragrance, a silky, creamy texture, and a long, heady finish. The low acidity provides vibrance, and the tannins have melted away. Should you be fortunate enough to have the beauty cellared, drink it over the next several years. La Mission also made a decent 1951 (81 points) and a great 1952 (93 points). Neither of these wines has been tasted since 1991. The 1950 (95 points; last tasted 10/94) possesses a huge nose of freshly brewed coffee, hickory wood, cedar, and chocolate. Superrich and dense, with little evidence of its age (the color is still an opaque dark garnet), this full-bodied, concentrated wine is at its apogee. It should continue to drink well for another 15–20 years.

The 1949 (100 points; last tasted 1/00) exhibits an intense, singed nose of roasted herbs, smoky black currant fruit, and grilled-meat aromas. Enormously rich yet sweet, soft, fat, and opulent, the fully mature 1949 La Mission is awesomely intense and long. It is a magnificent bottle of wine from the most harmonious Bordeaux vintage of the century. The 1948 (93 points; last tasted 3/01) offers up a powerful, roasted, rich bouquet of tobacco, ripe curranty fruit, and smoky chestnuts. It reveals no amber or brown, concentrated, highly extracted fruit, full body, and plenty of alcohol and tannin in the finish. The wine is clearly at its plateau of maturity and shows no signs of losing its fruit. It should last for another 10–20 years. A huge, port-like bouquet of chocolaty, cedary, earthy, plummy fruit demonstrates the extraordinary ripeness that was achieved in the 1947 (95 points; last tasted 12/02) vintage. Very alcoholic, powerful and rich, but at the same time velvety and sweet, this wine was probably as close to a late-harvest La Mission Haut-Brion as one is likely to experience. It is an exceptional wine with great flavor dimension and length. The 1945 La Mission (92? points; last tasted 6/00) is certainly a great wine with fabulous concentration but also a leathery, tough, hard texture. It is very powerful, broodingly rich and opaque, but the tannin is extremely elevated, and one wonders what is going to fall away first, the fruit or the tannin? This wine still has the potential to last for another 20–25 years, and therein lies much of the mystique of this vintage.

The extraordinary 1929 (97 points; last tasted 10/94) vintage—which may well have been the vintage of the century, with a style that old-timers compare to modern-day 1982s or, more recently, the 1990s—produced wines that were wonderfully opulent and unctuous. Henri Woltner wrote that the 1929 La Mission drank fabulously well in 1933, yet he doubted its ability to age well. How wrong he was! Still deep garnet in color, with only a trace of amber at the edge, this wine exhibits a fabulously exotic, sensual bouquet filled with aromas of tobacco, black currants, cedar, and leather. On the palate it reveals high alcohol, as well as the remarkably sweet, rich, expansive, staggering concentration of fruit necessary to stand up to the alcohol. This is a velvety, lush, full-bodied wine that it is an incredible privilege to drink.

IMPORTANT VINTAGES (LA CHAPELLE DE LA MISSION)

2001
87–88 The 2001 La Chapelle de la Mission exhibits supple tannin, and sweet black currant fruit intermixed with roasted herb and gravel-like scents. This elegant, medium-bodied offering will be delicious upon release and should drink well for 5–6 years. Last tasted, 1/03.

2000
89 The 2000 La Chapelle de la Mission is surprisingly fat, juicy, and succulent, offering notes of roasted herbs, tobacco, black cherry and cassis fruit, scorched earth, and asphalt. This luscious second wine can be drunk now and over the next 12–15 years. Last tasted, 1/03.

1999
88 A wonderful second wine, the 1999 La Chapelle offers sweet tobacco and currants in a smoky, straightforward, luscious style. Enjoy it over the next 5–6 years. Last tasted, 3/02.

1998
89 Readers looking for a *petite* La Mission should check out the 1998 La Chapelle, a gorgeously complex, rich, Graves-styled wine with a smoky, tobacco, black currant, earthy-scented nose, fat, luscious, concentrated, seamless flavors, and beautifully integrated acidity and tannin. This fleshy, complex offering is already delicious, yet will last for 8 more years. Last tasted, 3/02.

OLIVIER

Classification: Classified growth (red and white)

Owner: Jean-Jacques de Bethmann

Address: 175, avenue de Bordeaux, 33850 Léognan

Telephone: 05 56 64 73 31 or 05 56 64 75 16;
Telefax: 05 56 64 54 23

E-mail: chateau-olivier@wanadoo.fr

Website: www.chateau-olivier.com

Visits: By appointment only

Contact: Marie-France Héron

VINEYARDS (RED)

Surface area: 108.7 acres

Grape varietals: 50% Merlot, 40% Cabernet Sauvignon, 10% Cabernet Franc

Average age of vines: 25 years

Density of plantation: 7,500 vines per hectare

Average yields: 45 hectoliters per hectare

Elevage: Fermentation and three to four week maceration in temperature-controlled stainless-steel vats.

Twelve months aging in barrels with 33% new oak. Fining, no filtration.

RED WINES PRODUCED

Château Olivier: 180,000 bottles

Seigneurie d'Olivier: 60,000 bottles

Plateau of maturity: Within 5–15 years of the vintage

VINEYARDS (WHITE)

Surface area: 19.7 acres

Grape varietals: 50% Sauvignon Blanc, 50% Semillon

Average age of vines: 35 years

Density of plantation: 7,500 vines per hectare

Average yields: 45 hectoliters per hectare

Elevage: Fermentation and nine months aging in barrels with 33% new oak. No fining, filtration.

WHITE WINES PRODUCED

Château Olivier: 42,000 bottles

Seigneurie d'Olivier: 3,000 bottles

Plateau of maturity: Within 2–12 years of the vintage

GENERAL APPRECIATION

The latest vintages from Olivier have been the finest tasted from this one-time underachiever. After years of uninspiring performances, Olivier has begun to fashion more elegant and stylish wines that are less richly fruity than many of their peers but undoubtedly much better than their predecessors.

A fairy-tale château with striking towers as well as a surrounding moat, this estate is one of the oldest in the entire Bordeaux region, tracing its history back to the 12th century. One of its most famous visitors in the 14th century was the Black Prince (son of King Edward III of England), the Bordeaux commander who led many of England's greatest knights in their battles against the French for control of Aquitaine. Since the end of World War II, a family of German origin, the de Bethmanns, have been the proprietors. It has not been a management that has resulted in profound wines. Until the mid-1990s, both the white and red wines vinified at Olivier were mediocre in quality and unusually simple, light, and innocuous for a cru classé with vineyards so well placed in the Léognan region. The entire vineyard is one parcel of beautifully situated vines with a full southerly exposure. Insiders in Bordeaux argue that the exclusivity the Bethmanns gave to the large *négociant* firm of Eschenauer often prevented the wine from being shown in comparative tastings, where its weaknesses would have been obvious. However, that exclusivity ended in the mid-1980s, and now the wine can easily be compared with that of its neighbors. Improvements have been made, and my tastings have convinced me that live-in proprietor Jean-Jacques de Bethmann is in the process of making a major effort to improve the quality of Olivier's wines. The selection process has been increasingly strict since the 1990s, and with the purchase of a concentrating machine (the reverse osmosis type) to be used in the 1998 vintage, readers can expect Olivier to become a far more interesting wine.

IMPORTANT VINTAGES (RED)

2001 Smoky, herbal notes intertwined with red currant and cherry fruit characterize this
85–86 medium-bodied, fresh, vibrant, light claret. It will require consumption during its first decade of life. Last tasted, 1/03.

2000 A sexy, lush effort, this deep ruby–colored, medium-bodied 2000 exhibits plenty
87 of grapy, black currant fruit, smoke, tobacco, and spice box aromas. Elegant, with excellent purity as well as low acidity and ripe tannin in the finish, it will drink well upon release and over the following decade. Along with the 1998, it is the finest Olivier in more than 25 years (hardly high praise). Last tasted, 1/03.

1999 Aromas of ripe currants, tar, smoke, strawberry jam, and tobacco emerge from this
86 medium-bodied, supple-textured, lush Graves. It should drink well for 7–8 years. Last tasted, 1/00.

1998 A dark plum/ruby color is accompanied by a sexy bouquet of cigar tobacco, red
88 and black currants, earth, and vanilla. This medium-bodied, seamless, lush, savory 1998 is difficult to resist. How long it will age is debatable, but it will certainly drink well for 10–15 years. Last tasted, 3/02.

1997 Deep ruby/purple–colored, with a straightforward, sweet, black cherry/berry
86 character complemented by tobacco leaf and toasty new oak, Olivier's medium-bodied, low-acid, fruit-driven 1997 should be consumed over the next 6–7 years. Last tasted, 3/01.

1996 The 1996 is a soft, medium-bodied wine with a moderate display of red and black
86 currants, adequate acidity, and sweet tannin. Although not a big wine, it is well constructed and harmonious. Anticipated maturity: now–2012. Last tasted, 3/01.

1995   Compact, lean, tannic, and more austere than the 1996, the 1995 is a light- to
84   medium-bodied, competent but uninspiring effort. Anticipated maturity: now–
        2008. Last tasted, 3/98.

1994   Light to medium ruby–colored, the 1994 exhibits a spicy, cherry, and currant-
85   scented nose with toasty oak in the background. This medium-bodied wine pos-
        sesses reasonably good fruit, spice, and some of the earthy, mineral, and tobacco
        characteristics that come from wines made in this sector of Graves. Last tasted,
        3/98.

ANCIENT VINTAGES (RED)

This estate had a deplorable record throughout the 1980s and 1970s, with most wines
meriting scores in the 70s.

IMPORTANT VINTAGES (WHITE)

2001   Crisp, green pea, herb, and grapefruit notes characterize this medium-bodied,
87   dry, refreshing but uninspiring white. Drink it over the next decade. Last tasted,
        1/03.

2000   Surprise, surprise! This is a noteworthy effort in a vintage that was far more suc-
88   cessful for red Bordeaux than dry whites. Aromas of honeyed grapefruit, melon,
        and smoke emerge from a tasty, medium-bodied, crisp, structured 2000. It is best
        drunk during its first decade of life. Last tasted, 1/03.

PAPE CLÉMENT ——————————————————————

Classification: Classified growth (reds only)

Owner: Bernard Magrez

Address: 216, avenue du Dr Nancel Penard, 33600
Pessac

Mailing address: BP 164, 33600 Pessac

Telephone: 05 57 26 38 38; Telefax: 05 57 26 38 39

E-mail: chateau@pape-clement.com

Website: www.pape-clement.com

Visits: By appointment only

Contact: Eric Larramona

VINEYARDS (RED)

Surface area: 74.1 acres

Grape varietals: 58% Cabernet Sauvignon, 42% Merlot

Average age of vines: 27 years

Density of plantation: 8,000 vines per hectare

Average yields: 39 hectoliters per hectare

Elevage: Three day cold maceration. Fermentation and 21–23 day maceration (26–29
days for Cabernet Sauvignon) in temperature-controlled wooden vats with manual
pigeages. Malolactics and 20 months aging in new oak barrels. No fining, filtration
depending upon the vintage.

RED WINES PRODUCED

Château Pape Clément: 95,000 bottles

Clémentin du Pape Clément: 45,000 bottles

Plateau of maturity: Within 5–20 years of the vintage

VINEYARDS (WHITE)

Surface area: 6.9 acres

Grape varietals: 45% Sauvignon Blanc, 45% Semillon, 10% Muscadelle

Average age of vines: 20 years

Density of plantation: 8,000 vines per hectare

Average yields: 37 hectoliters per hectare

Elevage: Fermentation and 11 months aging on lees with stirring in barrels with 70% new oak. Fining and filtration.

WHITE WINES PRODUCED

Château Pape Clément: 6,000 bottles

Clémentin du Pape Clément: 4,500 bottles

Plateau of maturity: Within 3–8 years of the vintage

GENERAL APPRECIATION

One of the quintessentially elegant, complex, and most distinctive wines of Bordeaux, Pape Clément has been in top form since the 1986 vintage and especially since its acquisition by Bernard Magrez, who is making every effort to push this estate into Bordeaux's highest echelon, as vintages since the late 1990s have demonstrated. A must buy for shrewd amateurs!

One of the oldest vineyards and châteaux in Bordeaux, Pape Clément is located in the suburban sprawl of Pessac, several miles from the famed Château Haut-Brion. Historically Pape Clément is among the most significant estates of the Bordeaux region. One of the original owners, Bertrand de Goth, purchased this country estate in 1299 and six years later became Pope Clément V. He was admired by the French for his bold decision to move the papacy to the sun-drenched, hallowed Provençal city of Avignon, where the historical period of the papacy became known as the Babylonian Captivity and the wine produced by Clément at his country estate outside Avignon became known as Châteauneuf du Pape. While Pope Clément V remained in Avignon, he turned over the vineyards of Pape Clément to the church, where they remained undisturbed until divested during the French Revolution.

The vineyard, which was totally destroyed by a ferocious hailstorm in 1937, was resurrected by Paul Montagne, a prominent agricultural engineer who purchased the estate in 1939. It is now controlled by Paul Montagne's heirs, and managed with great passion and energy by Bernard Magrez.

While no one doubted the quality of Pape Clément's wines in the early 1970s, 1960s, and 1950s, lack of attention to detail and little investment in winemaking equipment or barrels resulted in a significant deterioration of quality at Pape Clément after 1975. For the next decade the wines produced at the château were often musty, lacked freshness, and, in short, were poorly made. The succession of poor to mediocre results ended in 1985 subsequent to the hiring of the young, enthusiastic Bernard Pujol. Pujol was given total responsibility for resurrecting the quality of Pape Clément, and the result, first evidenced with a profound 1986, has been a succession of wines that now come close to rivaling the great Haut-Brion and La Mission Haut-Brion. Pujol left in the late 1990s, and Bernard Magrez hired the brilliant winemaking consultant Michel Rolland.

Pape Clément, which sits on extremely light, gravelly soil, produces a wine that at its best has a fascinating and compelling bouquet offering up gobs of black fruits intermingled with strong smells of tobacco and minerals. Because of the relatively high percentage of Merlot, it is a wine that can be drunk extremely young yet can age easily for several decades in the best vintages. In the last half of the decade of the 1980s, Pape Clément became one of the stars of Bordeaux, producing profound wines in 2001, 2000, 1998, 1996, 1990, 1988, and 1986.

The new commitment to quality has also been evidenced by an increase in the vineyard area for their rare white wines. Previously, the microscopic production, usually less than 100 cases, was reserved for exclusive use by the château. The property now produces nearly 600 cases. In short, this has become one of the superstar estates of Bordeaux.

IMPORTANT VINTAGES (RED)

2001 A brilliant achievement and one of the wines of the vintage, Pape Clément's re-
94–96 markable 2001 should surpass their fabulous 2000. A magnificent effort, it was produced from yields of 28.6 hectoliters per hectare, and the final blend (70% of the production) consisted of equal parts Cabernet Sauvignon and Merlot. The 2001 boasts an opaque purple color, amazing purity and presence on the palate, a sensational texture, and loads of graphite, lead pencil, plum, fig, black cherry, and currant fruit. Medium bodied, extraordinarily elegant as well as remarkably concentrated, pure, and suave, it is a tour de force in winemaking. Anticipated maturity: 2009–2028. Last tasted, 1/03.

2000 The profound 2000 (a blend of equal parts Cabernet Sauvignon and Merlot) has
95 put on weight. An opaque purple color is accompanied by stunning aromas of wood smoke, cocoa, black currant and cherry liqueur, coffee, scorched earth, and new oak. A wine of extraordinary concentration, elegance, and complexity, it is one of the finest Pape Cléments of the last three decades, but look out . . . the 2001 may be even better! Only 55% of the production made it into the final blend. Anticipated maturity: 2007–2025. Last tasted, 1/03.

1999 A blend of 54% Cabernet Sauvignon and 46% Merlot, the stunning 1999 Pape
91 Clément is showing magnificently from bottle. A fabulous bouquet of smoke, blueberries, raspberry cassis, and liquid minerals is followed by a medium- to full-bodied, layered, concentrated wine with no hard edges. As it sat in the glass, additional aromas of cedar wood, graphite, and cigar smoke emerged. This is a classic, sexy, knockout Pessac-Léognan with a surprisingly dense, rich style for a 1999. Anticipated maturity: now–2018. Last tasted, 3/02.

1998 A prodigious effort from Pape Clément, this wine is smoking. It boasts a dense
93 ruby/purple color in addition to a terrific nose of charcoal, blackberries, cassis, tobacco, minerals, and spice. This brilliantly focused, medium- to full-bodied 1998

already reveals a boatload of complexity as well as a remarkably long finish. A large-size effort for this estate, it exhibits a sweet mid-palate and ripe tannin. Anticipated maturity: now–2025. Bravo! Last tasted, 3/02.

1997
87
An attractive, complex wine, the 1997 Pape Clément exhibits a dark, saturated ruby color in addition to a gorgeous, smoky, herb, red currant, and cherry liqueur–scented bouquet, a silky texture, spicy oak, and a round, complex, low-acid, fleshy finish. As the wine sat in the glass, notes of hot bricks/scorched earth also emerged. This is a complex, supple, delicious wine to drink over the next 7–8 years. Last tasted, 1/02.

1996
94
A great wine that has put on considerable weight and continues to show more and more depth and complexity, the dark plum/ruby–colored 1996 Pape Clément has a gorgeous nose of barbecue spices intermixed with black currant, plum, coffee, and a hint of white chocolate. The wine is exceptionally rich, full-bodied, and a fabulous success, particularly in the Pessac-Léognan sector. The tannin is sweet and the wine has tremendous richness and length. Anticipated maturity: 2005–2020. Last tasted, 4/02.

1995
89
Deep ruby/purple, with a tight but promising nose of herb-tinged black currants, graphite, vanilla, and smoke, this medium-bodied wine is elegant, with very pure, concentrated fruit, moderate extract, and a long finish. The wine is reaching its adolescence and is certainly accessible, although far from full maturity. Anticipated maturity: 2006–2016. Last tasted, 4/02.

1994
86
A bit hard around the edges, this dark plum/garnet–colored wine shows notes of red currant, sweet tobacco, dried herbs, and coffee in a restrained, measured style, with some tannin in the finish. This wine may have a tendency to become increasingly attenuated with cellar age. Anticipated maturity: now–2012. Last tasted, 4/02.

1993
86
An unimpressive medium ruby color is followed by a textbook Graves nose of berries, tobacco, and spicy scents with that notion of scorched earth and hot rocks. This is a lighter wine than the great 1990, but within the style of the vintage, it is well balanced, exhibiting sweet, red currant, plummy fruit, undeniable elegance and finesse, and a soft, round finish. The wine is more pleasurable than the score indicates. Drink it over the next 7–8 years. Last tasted, 1/97.

1990
94
A superb wine that has reached full maturity rather quickly, the 1990 offers a gorgeous display of smoked herbs, barbecue spices, roasted meats, black currants, chocolate, and coffee. The wine is full-bodied, opulent, almost viscous, with chewy, thick, juicy flavors and far greater intensity and richness than I originally thought. Anticipated maturity: now–2018. Last tasted, 4/02.

1989
87
A bit tightly knit, with some noticeably high tannin, the restrained but emerging bouquet of smoke, mineral, graphite, and red currants shows a slight herbaceousness to it. In the mouth it is medium bodied, structured, and somewhat muscular, but lacking the charm, opulence, and overall depth of its more famous sibling, the 1990. Anticipated maturity: 2004–2015. Last tasted, 4/02.

1988
92
A gorgeous wine and one of the vintage's most successful efforts, Pape Clément's dark plum/purple–colored 1988 has a nose of roasted herbs, sweet tobacco smoke, red as well as black currants, and scorched earth. The wine still has a deep ruby color, with only a hint of lightening at the rim. The wine is medium to full-bodied, with sweet but high tannin and a lot of smoke, earth, and asphalt notes. This is a chewy, very complex, aromatic, and authoritatively flavorful wine that has reached its plateau of maturity. Anticipated maturity: now–2014. Last tasted, 4/02.

1986
91
Still young and vibrant, with a deep ruby/purple color and a sweet nose of black currants intermixed with earth and some vanilla, this medium-bodied wine is very graceful, stylish, and classic, with relatively high tannin, a cooler-climate flavor

profile, and long, moderately tannic finish. Still youthful and vigorous, this wine should evolve effortlessly for at least another 10–15 years. Anticipated maturity: now–2016. Last tasted, 4/02.

ANCIENT VINTAGES (RED)

Pape Clément really did not return to form until the mid-1980s, and vintages from the early 1980s and 1970s are problematic and sometimes disastrous. The 1982 is an appalling wine, and nearly matched in its moldy, mushroom characteristics by the 1981, 1979, 1978, and 1976. The only real strong effort from Pape Clément in the 1970s was the 1975, a very muscular, strong, tannic wine (87 points; last tasted 10/97). In the 1960s, 1961 is the triumph, but it is now in full decline (86? points; last tasted 1/01). This was a wine that could easily score in the low 90s, and I suspect well-kept magnums or larger formats would still be superb.

IMPORTANT VINTAGES (WHITE)

2001
91
A blend of 45% Sauvignon Blanc, 45% Semillon, and 10% Muscadelle, this elegant, medium-bodied white exhibits aromas of orange marmalade intertwined with honeyed citrus, candle wax, and subtle notes of smoky oak. It possesses excellent flavors, good underlying acidity, impressive delineation, and a long, concentrated, fresh, vibrant finish. Drink it over the next 10–12 years. Last tasted, 1/03.

2000
90
One of the finest efforts of this mediocre vintage for white Graves, this 2000 offers up fruit cocktail–like aromas intermixed with scents of passion fruit, orange peel, lemon zest, and vanilla. Medium bodied, with copious fruit, a fleshy mid-palate, and a dry, crisp, well-balanced finish, it will provide immense enjoyment over the next 7–8 years. Last tasted, 1/03.

PICQUE CAILLOU ——————————

Classification: None

Owner: Isabelle and Paulin Calvet

Address: avenue Pierre Mendès-France, 33700 Mérignac

Telephone: 05 57 47 37 98; Telefax: 05 57 97 99 37

E-mail: chatcaupiquecaillou@wanadoo.fr

Visits: By appointment only

Contact: Nicolas Leclair

VINEYARDS (RED)

Surface area: 46.9 acres

Grape varietals: 45% Cabernet Sauvignon, 45% Merlot, 10% Cabernet Franc

Average age of vines: 25 years

Density of plantation: 6,900–10,000 vines per hectare

Average yields: 45 hectoliters per hectare

Elevage: Fermentation and maceration in temperature-controlled (26–30°C) stainless-steel vats. Twelve to fourteen months aging in barrels with 30% new oak. No fining, no filtration.

RED WINES PRODUCED

Château Picque Caillou: 60,000–70,000 bottles

Château Chênevert: 30,000–40,000 bottles

Plateau of maturity: Within 2–12 years of the vintage

VINEYARDS (WHITE)

Surface area: 2.5 acres

Grape varietals: 60% Sauvignon Blanc, 40% Semillon

Average age of vines: 12 years

Density of plantation: 6,900–10,000 vines per hectare

Average yields: 45 hectoliters per hectare

Elevage: Fermentation in vats (20–22°C) and 8 months aging on lees in barrels with stirrings. No fining, no filtration.

WHITE WINES PRODUCED

Château Picque Caillou: 2,000 bottles

Château Chênevert: 2,000 bottles

Plateau of maturity: Within 2–10 years of the vintage

GENERAL APPRECIATION

Under the helmsmanship of Paulin Calvet, the wines of Picque Caillou have progressed considerably. Traditionally made, as opposed to some of their more flamboyant, modern-styled peers, they are, in both red and white, fruity, elegant, rather restrained in a low-key manner—in a word, they deliver the goods.

Picque Caillou is the last surviving vineyard of the commune of Mérignac, which is now better known as the location of Bordeaux's ever-expanding international airport. The light, gravelly, stony soil, plus the high percentage of Cabernet Sauvignon in the blend, produce an aromatic, fruity wine that can be undeniably seductive when drunk young. The soil is not unlike the terrain of the famous Pessac châteaux of Haut-Brion and Pape Clément, not surprising since they are neighbors. The quality of the wine-making is excellent.

IMPORTANT VINTAGES (RED)

2000 **88** This classy, complex Pessac-Léognan is as good as its 1998 counterpart. A sleeper of the vintage, notes of scorched earth, cranberry jam, black cherries, and spice are followed by a sweet, medium-bodied, impeccably balanced, restrained yet flavorful wine. Enjoy it over the next 4–5 years. Last tasted, 1/03.

1999 **85** The elegant, light-bodied 1999 Picque Caillou offers aromas of dark fruits, scorched earth, and a hint of ashtray. It is a superficial, pleasant effort to consume during its first 3–4 years of life. Last tasted, 3/02.

1998 **85** This elegant, medium-bodied 1998 is a classic Graves with its tobacco, smoke, tar, and earthiness. It offers good fruit, medium body, and a straightforward, pleasant style. Drink it over the next 2–3 years. Last tasted, 3/02.

ANCIENT VINTAGES (RED)

This property's track record in the early 1990s and 1980s was disappointing, but that has all changed over recent vintages.

SMITH HAUT LAFITTE

Classification: Classified growth (reds only)

Owner: Daniel and Florence Cathiard

Address: 33650 Martillac

Telephone: 05 57 83 11 22; Telefax: 05 57 83 11 21

E-mail: f.cathiard@smith-haut-lafitte.com

Website: www.smith-haut-lafitte.com

Visits: By appointment, every day of the week, 9 A.M.–12:30 P.M. and 2 P.M.–6:30 P.M. (except on Friday, 5:30 P.M.)

Contact: Virginie Bertot Fletcher

VINEYARDS (RED)

Surface area: 111.2 acres

Grape varietals: 55% Cabernet Sauvignon, 35% Merlot, 10% Cabernet Franc

Average age of vines: 30 years

Density of plantation: 7,500–10,000 vines per hectare

Average yields: 32 hectoliters per hectare

Elevage: Fermentation at 30°C and 24–32 day maceration in temperature-controlled wooden vats of 85-hectoliter capacity on average. Malolactics and 18–20 months aging on lees (with stirring) in barrels with 80% new oak. No fining, no filtration.

RED WINES PRODUCED

Château Smith Haut Lafitte: 100,000 bottles

Les Hauts de Smith: 45,000 bottles

Plateau of maturity: Within 5–25 years of the vintage

VINEYARDS (WHITE)

Surface area: 27.2 acres

Grape varietals: 90% Sauvignon Blanc, 5% Sauvignon Gris, 5% Semillon

Average age of vines: 30 years

Density of plantation: 7,500–10,000 vines per hectare

Average yields: 35 hectoliters per hectare

Elevage: Fermentation at 20°C and 12 months aging on lees with stirring in barrels with 50% new oak. Fining, no filtration.

WHITE WINES PRODUCED

Château Smith Haut Lafitte: 30,000 bottles

Les Hauts de Smith: 21,000 bottles

Plateau of maturity: Within 5–15 years of the vintage

GENERAL APPRECIATION

This once mediocre wine has dramatically improved under the dynamic ownership of Florence and Daniel Cathiard. Smith Haut Lafitte is now among the finest Pessac-Léognans.

For decades, while under the ownership of Bordeaux's Eschenauer family, Smith Haut Lafitte was a perennial underachiever. However, this magnificent estate was sold in 1991 to Florence and Daniel Cathiard. Admittedly they had the misfortune of having to deal with the rain-plagued vintages of 1995, 1994, 1993, 1992, and 1991, but through their extraordinary commitment to quality, a ruthless selection process, and a long-term vision for this estate, they produced better wines in the difficult vintages of the early 1990s than the previous owner was able to do in such exceptional years as 1990 and 1982. Today Smith Haut Lafitte is one of Bordeaux's shining success stories, reflecting what hard work and conscientious proprietors can achieve in a short period of time.

The style of both the white and red wines combines authoritative richness with considerable elegance, finesse, and complexity. The international marketplace is often fickle, and it seems to me the prices fetched by recent vintages of Smith Haut Lafitte are below what they ultimately will be once the quality of these wines becomes known by the wine world.

IMPORTANT VINTAGES (RED)

2001
91–93
The 2001 is another beauty from this property. The impressive, perfumed aromatics consisting of black raspberries, spring flowers, currants, graphite, and new oak are followed by an elegantly etched, medium-bodied, moderately weighty Graves with abundant quantities of sweet fruit. Although it does not possess the power and volume of the 2000, it is a complex, harmonious effort with excellent definition as well as delicacy. Proprietor Florence Cathiard believes it to be just as good as the 2000, and she may prove to be right. Certainly it is a wine of exceptional freshness, purity, and complexity. Anticipated maturity: 2006–2015. Last tasted, 1/03.

2000
94
The finest Smith Haut Lafitte I have ever tasted, the opaque purple–colored 2000 offers scents of tobacco, camphor, graphite, crème de cassis, and licorice. This full-bodied, concentrated effort possesses low acidity, a multilayered texture, and a persistent finish with considerable ripe, well-integrated tannin. It is an impressive tour de force for this estate. Kudos to the Cathiards. Anticipated maturity: 2008–2025. Last tasted, 1/03.

1999
90
This is a sizable wine for the vintage, although I do not believe it will have the longevity of the 1998 or 2000. A deep ruby/purple color is accompanied by sweet, asphalt-tinged, earthy, cassis fruit with toasty notes in the background. There are loads of fruit and charm as well as a creamy texture revealing hints of tobacco, currants, and wood smoke. Medium bodied and supple textured, it will provide ideal drinking over the next 12 years. Last tasted, 3/02.

1998
90
A beautiful wine of symmetry, finesse, and elegance, this deep ruby/purple–colored offering reveals classic aromas of black currants, new wood, and scorched earth. This pure, medium-bodied, restrained, measured, graceful 1998 offers impressive overall symmetry and well-integrated tannin. Anticipated maturity: now–2018. Last tasted, 3/02.

1997 Splendid aromatics of tobacco, ripe black currant fruit, minerals, and toasty oak
87   emerge from this dark ruby–colored effort. Quintessentially elegant, with sweet
      fruit on the attack, medium body, and no hard edges, this smoothly textured wine
      can be drunk now as well as over the next 7–8 years. Last tasted, 1/02.

1996 The 1996 Smith Haut Lafitte is the quintessentially elegant Bordeaux. With a
90   dark ruby/purple color, it displays a beautiful presentation of blackberry and cas-
      sis fruit nicely dosed with subtle new oak. On the attack, the wine is sweet and
      pure, with striking symmetry, and a compellingly balanced mid-palate and finish.
      Although not as big as some blockbusters from this vintage, it is extremely com-
      plex (both aromatically and flavor-wise), and impressive for its restraint. Antici-
      pated maturity: now–2016. Last tasted, 1/02.

1995 This wine's deep ruby/purple color is followed by scents of roasted herbs inter-
90   mixed with sweet black currant fruit, truffles, vanilla, and minerals. Lush, with
      ripe cassis fruit on the attack, outstanding balance, medium body, and layers of in-
      tensity, this is an elegant, graceful, smoothly textured, beautifully made Bordeaux.
      Anticipated maturity: now–2018. Last tasted, 1/00.

1994 Smith Haut Lafitte has managed to subdue the potential for astringent tannin in
88   this vintage, producing a surprisingly soft, supple, velvety-textured 1994. This
      wine possesses a healthy purple color, a smoky, spicy, black currant-scented nose,
      sweet, medium-bodied, well-endowed flavors, a youthfulness and grapiness that
      does not yet exhibit the complexity of the 1993, and a moderately tannic finish.
      The 1994 should keep another 10 years. Last tasted, 1/97.

1993 A deep ruby/purple color is impressive for a 1993 Pessac-Léognan. The wine ex-
87   hibits a textbook Graves nose of smoke, hot rocks, sweet currant and mulberry
      fruit, and a touch of roasted herbs. Elegant yet flavorful, this medium-bodied, con-
      centrated wine reveals a sweet ripeness and entry on the palate, light tannin, a
      beautiful dose of toasty new oak, and a suave, savory style. This wine defines what
      I mean when I say that French wines often possess intensity without significant
      weight. Drink this lovely offering over the next 6–7 years. Last tasted, 1/97.

1992 The 1992 is unquestionably a successful wine for this vintage. It exhibits elegant,
86   spicy, mineral and black cherry-scented notes in its smoky bouquet, medium
      body, fine ripeness and extraction, a velvety texture, and light tannin in the finish.
      Drink it over the next 7–8 years. Last tasted, 11/94.

ANCIENT VINTAGES (RED)

The wines produced prior to this estate's acquisition by the Cathiards are largely disappointing. The words "caveat emptor" would certainly be operative should consumers run into any vintages from the 1980s or 1970s.

IMPORTANT VINTAGES (WHITE)

2001 A fabulous, complex perfume reveals scents of herbs, licorice, white peaches,
92   honey, and citrus. This medium-bodied, gorgeously proportioned dry white
      Graves exhibits flavors of figs, lanolin, and white flowers. Beautifully textured,
      tremendously pure, and authoritatively flavored yet remarkably elegant, it can be
      drunk now and over the next 12–15 years. Last tasted, 1/03.

2000 A competent effort in a so-so vintage for dry whites from Pessac-Léognan, Smith
87   Haut Lafitte's 2000 exhibits notions of lemon zest, grapefruit, and minerals in its
      medium-bodied, earthy personality. Drink it over the next 5–8 years. Last tasted,
      1/03.

LA TOUR HAUT-BRION

Classification: Classified growth (reds only)

Owner: Domaine Clarence Dillon SA

Address: 33400 Talence

Mailing address: c/o Domaine Clarence Dillon, Château Haut-Brion, 33608 Pessac Cedex

Telephone: 05 56 00 29 30; Telefax: 05 56 98 75 14

E-mail: info@haut-brion.com

Website: www.la-tour-haut-brion.com

No visits

CHÂTEAU
LA TOUR HAUT-BRION
CRU CLASSÉ DE GRAVES
1996
DOMAINE CLARENCE DILLON S.A.
Propriétaire à Talence (Gironde) France

VINEYARDS (RED)

Surface area: 12.1 acres

Grape varietals: 42% Cabernet Sauvignon, 35% Cabernet Franc, 23% Merlot

Average age of vines: 23 years

Density of plantation: 10,000 vines per hectare

Average yields: 45 hectoliters per hectare

Elevage: Fermentation and maceration in temperature-controlled stainless-steel vats of 180-hectoliter capacity. Twenty months aging in oak barrels with 30% new oak. Fining, no filtration.

RED WINES PRODUCED

Château La Tour Haut-Brion: 30,000 bottles

No second wine is produced.

Plateau of maturity: Within 8–25 years of the vintage

GENERAL APPRECIATION

Prior to 1983, this was the second wine of La Mission Haut-Brion. The owners at that time, the Woltner family, tended to add more press wine in this offering than in La Mission, resulting in dense, tannic wines. For that reason, some of the ancient vintages have aged fabulously well, and are worth a search of auction houses. Since 1983, administrator Jean Delmas has produced wines with more supple tannin as well as finesse. Delmas instituted a lot of new plantings, and the vines are thus relatively young. Since the late 1990s, La Tour Haut-Brion has taken on more texture and richness as the vineyard matures.

La Tour Haut-Brion was, until 1983, owned by the Woltner family, also the proprietors of La Mission Haut-Brion. In 1983, these two properties, plus the white wine–producing Woltner property—Laville Haut-Brion—were sold to the American owners of Haut-Brion.

The wines of La Tour Haut-Brion up to 1983 were vinified at La Mission Haut-Brion and handled identically. After both wines were completely finished with the secondary (or malolactic) fermentation, a selection process commenced in which the most promising barrels were chosen for the wine of La Mission Haut-Brion, and the others reserved for La Tour Haut-Brion. In vintages such as 1982 and 1975, the difference in quality between these two wines was negligible. To give La Tour Haut-Brion a unique personality, the wine had more of the black/purple-colored, very tannic press wine added to it than La Mission Haut-Brion. The result was a wine with more size, tannin, color, and grip than even La Mission Haut-Brion. The addition of press wine caused most vintages of La Tour Haut-Brion to evolve slowly. In a few vintages—notably 1973 and 1976—the wine turned out better than those of the more famous sibling.

Since the Dillon family and Jean Delmas assumed control of the winemaking, the style of La Tour Haut-Brion has changed considerably. It is no longer the second wine of La Mission Haut-Brion. Delmas has chosen to make La Tour Haut-Brion in a more refined style from the property's own vineyards, which are now planted with relatively young vines. The result has been a less imposing, more supple wine that is significantly inferior not only to La Mission, but even to the second wine of Haut-Brion, Bahans Haut-Brion. For admirers of the old beefy, muscular, brawny style of La Tour Haut-Brion made before 1983, the new style must be a shock to their palates.

IMPORTANT VINTAGES (RED)

2001 This vibrant, dense ruby/purple–colored effort offers up aromas of creosote, herbs,
89–91 mocha, and vanilla. Made in an elegant, medium-bodied style, it exhibits more flesh and texture as some of the vineyard's young vine Merlot is making it into the blend. This forward 2001 will be at its best in 4–5 years, and should age well for 15+. Anticipated maturity: 2007–2015. Last tasted, 1/03.

2000 There are 2,500 cases of the 2000 La Tour Haut-Brion, the finest wine made under
92 the ownership of the Dillon family and their brilliant administrator, Jean Delmas. The vintage yielded fabulous raw materials, the vineyard is older, and more Merlot is making it into the blend, thus fattening up what was once a herbaceous, more Cabernet Sauvignon–dominated wine. The dense purple-colored 2000 boasts a gorgeously sweet perfume of plums, black currants, tobacco, and a hint of olives. Sweet, ripe, and medium to full-bodied, with terrific richness, purity, and copious tannin, this is the finest La Tour Haut-Brion since the 1982. Anticipated maturity: 2007–2020. P. S. The blend of 52% Merlot, 43% Cabernet Sauvignon, and 5% Cabernet Franc is completely different than the composition of the vineyard. Last tasted, 1/03.

1999 The 1999 has put on weight in the course of its élevage. A sexy, open-knit, deep
90 ruby–colored effort, it exhibits a smoky nose of melted asphalt, truffles, cassis, and tobacco, enticing sweetness on the attack, low acidity, and a smoky, ripe rich finish. Drink this captivating, complex Graves over the next 10–12 years. Last tasted, 3/02.

1998 My rating may be too conservative, as the 1998 is showing as well as any La Tour
89 Haut-Brion from the 1990s. A dense ruby/purple color is followed by sweet aromas of black currants intermixed with tobacco, cedar, and spice box. The wine is beautifully pure, rich, medium bodied, with sweet tannin and well-integrated acidity as well as wood. It should drink well after several years of aging and last for 15 years. Last tasted, 3/02.

1997 An elegant, harmonious, spicy, aromatic offering, without a great deal of body, the
86 1997 reveals sweet black currant and smoky tobacco-like flavors. Drink this soft wine over the next 3–4 years. Last tasted, 1/02.

1996 La Tour Haut-Brion's 1996 is an aromatic, surprisingly evolved wine for the vin-
87   tage with a dark plum color, and a pronounced, smoky, cassis, weedy, dried herb–
scented bouquet. A medium-bodied, classic, mid-weight Bordeaux, with plenty of
spice, sweet fruit, elegance and complexity, it is a blend of 50% Cabernet Franc
and 50% Cabernet Sauvignon. It should provide delicious drinking early, and last
for 5–6 years. Last tasted, 12/00.

1995 The 1995 offers a heady perfume of coffee beans, tobacco, spice, smoke, grilled
88   herbs, and sweet red and black fruits. It is long and round, with copious quantities
of red currants, as well as good underlying acid, which gives the wine definition,
and a spicy, lush, sweet finish with light but noticeable tannin. Anticipated maturity: now–2015. Last tasted, 12/00.

1994 A surprisingly supple-textured, fragrant, rich, medium-bodied wine has been pro-
87   duced in a vintage with a propensity to turn out stern, tannic, and occasionally hollow wines. La Tour Haut-Brion's 1994 possesses a deep ruby/purple color as well
as that telltale, textbook Graves, smoky, weedy, tobacco and sweet black fruit–
scented nose. This wine displays fine precision, a clean, crafted, pure winemaking
style, and a smooth finish with well-integrated tannin. It can be drunk now as well
as over the next 10–14 years. Last tasted, 12/00.

1990 Less concentrated than the 1989, the soft, fruity, earthy, fully mature, dark garnet–
86   colored 1990 exhibits the mineral, tobacco, roasted character one finds in wines
from the northern viticultural region of Graves. Plump and fleshy, it has reached
its zenith. Anticipated maturity: now–2005. Last tasted, 12/00.

1989 The 1989 La Tour Haut-Brion is excellent. Primarily a Cabernet Sauvignon–
88   based wine (85% Cabernet, 15% Merlot), it exhibits a bold bouquet of herbs,
smoke, and cassis, plenty of ripeness, medium to full body, and a big, alcoholic,
low-acid finish. Anticipated maturity: now–2006. Last tasted, 1/93.

1988 The 1988 La Tour Haut-Brion has the telltale aggressive, hard tannins so promi-
83   nent in this vintage, good body, and adequate persistence on the palate. Not
charming, but austere and forceful, it should be drunk up. Last tasted, 1/93.

1986 The 1986 has turned out to be a soft, supple, commercial wine that lacks depth, di-
82   mension, and complexity. Anticipated maturity: now. Last tasted, 11/90.

1985 The 1985 is good but a little short, a trifle too tannic for the amount of fruit present,
84   and lacking length and excitement. Anticipated maturity: now. Last tasted, 3/89.

1983 A potentially good La Tour Haut-Brion. However, it is lighter and more supple in
84   texture than previous vintages of this wine. The 1983 is a product of the different
approach to winemaking employed by the staff at Haut-Brion, who controlled the
vinification for the first time in this vintage. Good medium to dark ruby color,
spicy, soft, supple, and very approachable, this wine should mature fairly quickly.
Anticipated maturity: now—probably in decline. Last tasted, 3/89.

1982 A remarkable wine, and one of the great sleeper wines of the vintage, this 1982,
96   which has a formidable plum/purple color showing little evolution, offers up very
roasted, scorched-earth characteristics and notes that almost smell like burning
embers and barbecue spices. Some black fruits and truffle are also in the background. In the mouth, this behemoth is full-bodied, with a huge, highly extracted,
unctuous texture, ferocious tannins, and remarkable intensity. It is even bigger
and denser than the 1982 La Mission Haut-Brion, no doubt because this wine had
far more press wine added to the blend than La Mission. If there is a flaw, it might
be a tendency to be slightly rustic, but this is a Bordeaux on steroids. Anticipated
maturity: 2005–2030. Last tasted, 1/03.

1981 The 1981 La Tour Haut-Brion is a robust, aggressive, rather tannic wine, with
85   plenty of power and guts but lacking finesse. The color is impressively dark, and
the weight of fruit and body on the palate considerable, but this is not a wine for

Bordeaux enthusiasts who want immediate gratification. Anticipated maturity: now–2005. Last tasted, 3/88.

1979   Somewhat similar in style to the 1981, only less tannic, more open knit and fruity,
85   yet darkly colored, the 1979 La Tour Haut-Brion has a spicy bouquet and good weight, richness, medium to full body, and length on the palate. The bouquet is beginning to mature, revealing earthy, Graves, smoky, mineral scents. This is an attractively forward La Tour Haut-Brion that can be drunk now. Anticipated maturity: now. Last tasted, 10/84.

1978   A great wine, and another wine to look for at auction houses because no one would
95   expect this wine to be so profound. Deep plum/purple, with a fabulous nose of graphite, truffle, roasted meats, dried herbs, licorice, sweet black currant fruit, and smoke, this powerful, ruggedly constructed, chewy wine is very full-bodied, high in extract, and very intense, with some noticeable tannin in the finish. Anticipated maturity: now–2020. Last tasted, 11/02.

1975   A worthy challenger to the prodigious, sometimes perfect 1975 La Mission Haut-
96   Brion, La Tour Haut-Brion's 1975 still has a dense purple color, and an extraordinary nose of liquid minerals intermixed with smoky plum, fig, and currant notes as well as cedar, melted asphalt, creosote, and scorched earth. Huge in the mouth, with high tannin and mouth-staining levels of extract, this immense wine is close to full maturity, yet should last for at least two more decades. Anticipated maturity: now–2023. Last tasted, 11/02.

ANCIENT VINTAGES (RED)

The 1970 (88? points; last tasted 6/96) is a powerful, beefy, husky wine, but often reveals an excess of astringent tannin as well as noticeable volatile acidity. Also excellent, the 1966 (88 points; last tasted nearly two decades ago) may well remain in good shape. As for the 1961 (95 points; last tasted 3/79), this wine undoubtedly has plenty of life left in it based on my ancient tasting note. I would love to have come across more examples of old vintages of La Tour Haut-Brion, as those that I have tasted were extraordinary in quality. The 1947 (95 points; last tasted 1/03) was magnificently rich, with the last bottle tasted showing none of the volatile acidity that others had exhibited. It possessed huge quantities of fruit, as well as a chewy, even viscous texture. It is a great wine that should continue to drink well for another decade. The other two great vintages of La Tour Haut-Brion I have had an opportunity to taste include a massive, still backward, and frightfully young 1959. I last had this wine at a restaurant in Bordeaux in 1988, and it was still black/purple in color and at least a decade away from maturity. I rated it 92, but I am sure that when this wine has reached its apogee, it will merit a higher score. Lastly, the 1955 (94 points in 1990), while not having quite the blockbuster bouquet of its sibling—the 1955 La Mission—is still an enormously concentrated, chewy, old-style Graves that should continue to last for a minimum of two more decades. It is a shame that La Tour Haut-Brion is no longer made in this style, but shrewd buyers at auctions are well advised to seek out top vintages of old La Tour Haut-Brions that may show up from time to time.

OTHER GRAVES ESTATES

D'ARCHAMBEAU

Classification: None

Owner: Sarl Vignobles Famille Dubourdieu

Address: 33720 Illats

Telephone: 05 56 62 51 46; Telefax: 05 56 62 47 98

Visits: By appointment Monday to Saturday 10 A.M.–noon and 2–5 P.M.

Contact: Jean-Philippe and Corinne Dubourdieu (Telephone: 06 09 79 01 02)

VINEYARDS (RED)

Surface area: 44.5 acres

Grape varietals: 50% Cabernet Franc, 50% Merlot

Average age of vines: 20 years

Density of plantation: 5,500 vines per hectare

Average yields: 50 hectoliters per hectare

Elevage: Three-week fermentation and maceration in stainless-steel vats. Twelve months aging in vats for 50% of the yield and in barrels (with 20% new oak) for the rest. Fining, no filtration.

RED WINES PRODUCED

Château d'Archambeau: 120,000 bottles

Château Mourlet: 24,000 bottles

Plateau of maturity: Within 3–10 years of the vintage

VINEYARDS (WHITE)

Surface area: 22.2 acres

Grape varietals: 70% Sauvignon, 30% Semillon

Average age of vines: 20 years

Density of plantation: 5,500 vines per hectare

Average yields: 50 hectoliters per hectare

Elevage: Three-week fermentation and maceration in stainless-steel vats. Twelve months aging in vats for 50% of the yield and in barrels (with 20% new oak) for the rest. Fining, no filtration.

WHITE WINES PRODUCED

Château d'Archambeau: 120,000 bottles

Château Mourlet: 24,000 bottles

Plateau of maturity: Within 2–5 years of the vintage

The pride and joy of this small property in the commune of Cérons is the white wine, which comes from a gravelly, clay-like soil and is made under the auspices of the great white wine–making family of Dubourdieu. This means cold fermentation and the famed *macération pelliculaire* (prolonged skin contact with the fermenting juice). The results are wines that are remarkably fresh and fragrant, with a honeyed, creamy texture, and a long, vividly fruity, generous finish. Consumers should search out recent vintages of this white Graves for drinking in its first 5 years of life. Prices for d'Archambeau remain reasonable.

BARDINS

Classification: None

Owner: Bernardy de Sigoyer family

Address: 124, avenue de Toulouse, 33140 Cadaujac

Telephone: 05 56 30 75 85; Telefax: 05 56 30 04 99

E-mail: chateau-bardins@free.fr

Visits: By appointment only

Contact: Stella Puel

VINEYARDS (RED)

Surface area: 22.2 acres

Grape varietals: 30% Cabernet Franc, 30% Cabernet Sauvignon, 30% Merlot, 10% Petit Verdot and Malbec

Average age of vines: 27 years

Density of plantation: 6,500 vines per hectare

Average yields: 55 hectoliters per hectare

Elevage: Fermentation and four to five week maceration in temperature-controlled stainless-steel vats. Twelve months aging in barrels that are renewed by a quarter each year. Fining, light filtration upon bottling.

RED WINES PRODUCED

Château Bardins: 36,000 bottles

Château Bardey: 10,000 bottles

Plateau of maturity: Within 3–7 years of the vintage

VINEYARDS (WHITE)

Surface area: 1 acre

Grape varietals: Equal parts of Sauvignon, Semillon, Muscadelle

Average age of vines: 27 years

Density of plantation: 6,500 vines per hectare

Average yields: 55 hectoliters per hectare

Elevage: Fermentation (18–20°C) and nine months aging on lees in barrels with 20% new oak and twice weekly stirrings. Fining, no filtration.

WHITE WINES PRODUCED

Château Bardins: 1,500 bottles

Plateau of maturity: Within 2–4 years of the vintage

I have seen only a handful of vintages from this tiny property in the commune of Cadaujac, situated adjacent to the more renowned Château Bouscaut. The proprietor has settled on an interesting percentage of grapes, with the very high percentage of Cabernet Franc for the red wines giving them a soft, spicy, herbaceous scent, and an extraordinarily high percentage of Muscadelle for the white wines to make them richly fruity, soft, and ideal for drinking young.

BARET

Classification: None

Owner: Ballande family

Address: 43, avenue des Pyrénées, 33140 Villenave d'Ornon

Telephone: 05 56 87 87 71; Telefax: 05 56 87 87 71

Visits: By appointment only

Contact: Philippe Castéja

VINEYARDS (RED)

Surface area: 45.7 acres

Grape varietals: 55% Merlot, 40% Cabernet Sauvignon, 5% Cabernet Franc

Average age of vines: 20 years

Density of plantation: 8,000 vines per hectare

Average yields: 55 hectoliters per hectare

Elevage: Three-week fermentation and maceration in temperature-controlled stainless-steel vats. Twelve to eighteen months aging in barrels with 30% new oak. Fining, no filtration.

RED WINES PRODUCED

Château Baret: 115,000 bottles

Château de Camparian: 18,000 bottles

Plateau of maturity: Within 4–10 years of the vintage

VINEYARDS (WHITE)

Surface area: 4.9 acres

Grape varietals: 70% Sauvignon, 30% Semillon

Average age of vines: 20 years

Density of plantation: 8,000 vines per hectare

Average yields: 55 hectoliters per hectare

Elevage: Twenty-four hour cold maceration. Fermentation and eight months aging in barrels with 20% new oak. Fining, no filtration.

WHITE WINES PRODUCED

Château Baret: 18,000 bottles

Château de Camparian: variable

Plateau of maturity: Within 2–5 years of the vintage

GENERAL APPRECIATION

The Ballande family (also the proprietors of Prieuré-Lichine) are slowly improving the quality of the wines from this well-situated estate in Pessac-Léognan. Oenologist Denis Dubourdieu, who works marvels, especially with whites, has been brought in to assist, and perhaps that explains the qualitative upgrade. Prices remain reasonable.

BOIS-MARTIN

Classification: None

Owner: GFA du Château Le Sartre et Bois-Martin—Perrin family

Address: 33850 Léognan

Telephone: 05 57 96 56 20; Telefax: 05 56 96 59 19

E-mail: chateau.carbonnieux@wanadoo.fr

Website: www.carbonnieux.com

Visits: By appointment Monday to Friday, 8:30–11 A.M. and 2–5 P.M.

Contact: Eric Perrin

VINEYARDS (RED)

Surface area: 18.5 acres

Grape varietals: 65% Cabernet Sauvignon, 35% Merlot

Average age of vines: 15 years

Density of plantation: 7,200 vines per hectare

Average yields: 50 hectoliters per hectare

Elevage: Twenty-one day fermentation and maceration in temperature-controlled stainless-steel tanks. Fifteen to eighteen months aging in barrels with 25% new oak. Fining and filtration.

RED WINES PRODUCED

Château Bois-Martin: 50,000 bottles

No second wine is produced.

Plateau of maturity: Within 5–10 years of the vintage

BOYREIN

Classification: None

Owner: Médeville family

Address: 33410 Roaillan

Mailing address: c/o Jean Médeville et Fils, Château Fayau, 33410 Cadillac

Telephone: 05 57 98 08 08; Telefax: 05 56 62 18 22

E-mail: medeville-jeanetfils@wanadoo.fr

Visits: By appointment only

Contact: Jacques Médeville

VINEYARDS (RED)

Surface area: 19.8 acres

Grape varietals: 50% Merlot, 40% Cabernet Sauvignon, 10% Cabernet Franc

Average age of vines: 35 years

Density of plantation: 3,000–5,000 vines per hectare

Average yields: 42 hectoliters per hectare

Elevage: Fermentation and 15–25 day maceration in temperature-controlled concrete vats. Twenty-four months aging in vats. Fining, no filtration.

RED WINES PRODUCED

Château Boyrein: 60,000 bottles

No second wine is produced.

Plateau of maturity: Within 2–7 years of the vintage

VINEYARDS (WHITE)

Surface area: 9.9 acres

Grape varietals: 50% Sauvignon Blanc, 30% Muscadelle, 20% Semillon

Average age of vines: 15 years

Density of plantation: 3,000–5,000 vines per hectare

Average yields: 40 hectoliters per hectare

Elevage: Cold stabilization. Eight to ten day fermentation at low temperature. Six months aging on lees. Fining, no filtration.

WHITE WINES PRODUCED

Château Boyrein: 30,000 bottles

No second wine is produced.

Plateau of maturity: Within 2–8 years of the vintage

BRONDELLE

Classification: None

Owner: Vignobles Belloc-Rochet

Address: 33210 Langon

Telephone: 05 56 62 38 14; Telefax: 05 56 62 23 14

E-mail: chateau.brondelle@wanadoo.fr

Visits: Monday to Friday, 9 A.M.–12:30 P.M. and 2–6 P.M.

Contact: Jean-Noël Belloc

VINEYARDS (RED)

Surface area: 61.7 acres

Grape varietals: 57% Cabernet Sauvignon, 40% Merlot, 3% Petit Verdot

Average age of vines: 20 years

Density of plantation: 5,000–6,600 vines per hectare

Average yields: 55 hectoliters per hectare

Elevage: Fermentation (20–28°C) and three to five week maceration in temperature-controlled vats. Malolactics in barrel for part of yield. Twelve months aging in barrels with 80% new oak. Fining, no filtration.

RED WINES PRODUCED

Château Brondelle: 50,000 bottles

Château La Rose Sarron: 60,000 bottles

Plateau of maturity: Within 4–10 years of the vintage

VINEYARDS (WHITE)

Surface area: 37 acres

Grape varietals: 50% Semillon, 45% Sauvignon, 5% Muscadelle

Average age of vines: 20 years

Density of plantation: 5,000–6,600 vines per hectare

Average yields: 55 hectoliters per hectare

Elevage: Fermentation and 10 months aging in barrels with 60% new oak and regular stirrings. No fining, light filtration upon bottling.

WHITE WINES PRODUCED

Château Brondelle: 60,000 bottles

No second wine is produced.

Plateau of maturity: Within 5–7 years of the vintage

CABANNIEUX

Classification: None

Owner: Régine Dudignac-Barrière

Address: 44, route de Courneau, 33640 Portets

Telephone: 05 57 67 22 01; Telefax: 05 56 67 32 54

E-mail: dudignacbarriere@free.fr

Visits: By appointment Monday to Friday 9 A.M.–noon and 2–7 P.M.

Contact: Régine Dudignac-Barrière

VINEYARDS (RED)

Surface area: 32.1 acres

Grape varietals: 50% Merlot, 45% Cabernet Sauvignon, 5% Cabernet Franc

Average age of vines: 30 years

Density of plantation: 5,500 vines per hectare

Average yields: 50 hectoliters per hectare

Elevage: Fermentation and 21 day maceration in temperature-controlled tanks. Fifteen to eighteen months aging in barrels with 20% new oak. Fining and filtration.

RED WINES PRODUCED

Château Cabannieux: 90,000 bottles

Château de Curcier: 90,000 bottles

Plateau of maturity: Within 2–8 years of the vintage

VINEYARDS (WHITE)

Surface area: 17.3 acres

Grape varietals: 80% Semillon, 20% Sauvignon Blanc

Average age of vines: 25 years

Density of plantation: 5,500 vines per hectare

Average yields: 50 hectoliters per hectare

Elevage: Fermentation and eight months aging on lees in vats for part of the yield and in new oak barrels for the rest. Fining and filtration.

WHITE WINES PRODUCED

Château Cabannieux: 40,000 bottles

Château de Curcier: 40,000 bottles

Plateau of maturity: Within 2–4 years of the vintage

DU CAILLOU

Classification: None

Owner: Oudinot family

Address: route de Saint-Cricq, 33720 Cérons

Telephone: 05 56 27 17 60; Telefax: 05 56 27 00 31

Visits: By appointment only

Contact: Philippe Oudinot

VINEYARDS (RED)

Surface area: 9.9 acres

Grape varietals: 90% Merlot, 10% Cabernet Sauvignon

Average age of vines: 35 years

Density of plantation: 6,000 vines per hectare

Average yields: 55 hectoliters per hectare

Elevage: Three day cold maceration. Fermentation and 21–28 day maceration with frequent pigeages in temperature-controlled vats. Twelve months aging in one-year old barrels. Fining, no filtration.

RED WINES PRODUCED

Château du Caillou: 12,000 bottles

Plateau of maturity: Within 2–5 years of the vintage

VINEYARDS (WHITE)

Surface area: 15.7 acres

Grape varietals: 50% Semillon, 25% Sauvignon Blanc, 25% Sauvignon Gris

Average age of vines: 35 years

Density of plantation: 6,000 vines per hectare

Average yields: 55 hectoliters per hectare

Elevage: Fermentation and eight months aging on lees in stainless-steel vats (for the generic *cuvée*) or in new oak barrels (for the special *cuvée*). Fining and filtration.

WHITE WINES PRODUCED

Château du Caillou: 30,000 bottles

Château du Caillou Cuvée Saint-Cricq: 12,500 bottles

Plateau of maturity: Within 2–5 years of the vintage

CANTELYS

Classification: None

Owner: SARL D. Cathiard

Address: 33650 Martillac

Mailing address: c/o GFA Malice, 4, chemin de Bourrau, 33650 Martillac

Telephone: 05 57 83 11 22; Telefax: 05 57 83 11 21

E-mail: f.cathiard@smith-haut-lafitte.com

No visits

VINEYARDS (RED)

Surface area: 44.5 acres

Grape varietals: 60% Merlot, 35% Cabernet Sauvignon, 5% Cabernet Franc

Average age of vines: 30 years

Density of plantation: 7,500–10,000 vines per hectare

Average yields: 30 hectoliters per hectare

Elevage: Fermentation at 30°C and 24–32 day maceration in temperature-controlled wooden vats of 85-hectoliter capacity on average. Malolactics and 14 months aging on lees (with stirring) in barrels with 80% new oak. Fining if necessary, no filtration.

RED WINES PRODUCED

Château Cantelys: 60,000 bottles

No second wine is produced.

Plateau of maturity: Within 3–12 years of the vintage

VINEYARDS (WHITE)

Surface area: 24.7 acres

Grape varietals: 75% Sauvignon Blanc, 25% Semillon

Average age of vines: 30 years

Density of plantation: 7,500–10,000 vines per hectare

Average yields: 30 hectoliters per hectare

Elevage: Fermentation at 20°C and 10 months aging on lees with stirring in barrels with 50% new oak. Fining, no filtration.

WHITE WINES PRODUCED

Château Cantelys: 60,000 bottles

No second wine is produced.

Plateau of maturity: Within 2–5 years of the vintage

DE CARRELASSE

Classification: None

Owner: SCEA du Château de Gaillat

Address: 33210 Langon

Mailing address: c/o Château de Gaillat, 33210 Langon

Telephone: 05 56 63 50 77; Telefax: 05 56 62 20 96

Visits: By appointment only

Contact: Yves Bertrand and Hélène Bertrand-Coste

VINEYARDS (RED)

Surface area: 14.8 acres

Grape varietals: 50% Merlot, 40% Cabernet Sauvignon, 10% Cabernet Franc

Average age of vines: 30 years

Density of plantation: 5,000 vines per hectare

Average yields: 45–50 hectoliters per hectare

Elevage: Seven day cold maceration. Fermentation at 30–32°C and 21–35 day maceration in temperature-controlled vats. Twelve to eighteen months aging by rotation in barrels (10% new oak) for half the yield and in vats for the other half. Fining and filtration.

RED WINES PRODUCED

Château de Carrelasse: 35,000 bottles

No second wine is produced.

Plateau of maturity: Within 5–12 years of the vintage

CHERET-PITRES

Classification: None

Owner: Pascal and Caroline Dulugat

Address: 33640 Portets

Telephone: 05 56 67 27 76; Telefax: 05 56 67 27 76

Visits: By appointment only

Contact: Caroline or Pascal Dulugat

VINEYARDS (RED)

Surface area: 13.8 acres

Grape varietals: 60% Merlot, 40% Cabernet Franc

Average age of vines: 40 years

Density of plantation: 5,600 vines per hectare

Average yields: 60 hectoliters per hectare

Elevage: Fermentation and prolonged maceration in temperature-controlled vats. Twelve months aging with 60% of yield in barrels (40% new oak), the rest in vats, followed by six months further aging in vats. Fining and filtration.

RED WINES PRODUCED

Château Cheret-Pitres: 20,000 bottles

Château Cheret: 10,000 bottles

Plateau of maturity: Within 3–8 years of the vintage

I have frequently been satisfied by the smoky, tobacco, richly fruity character of the wines of Cheret-Pitres, and I have enthusiastic tasting notes of many vintages. It is not a well-known wine, but because of that it is often a super value. The vineyard is located in the commune of Portets, and no doubt the old vines and high percentage of Merlot give this wine its characteristic fatness and suppleness. No white wine is made at this property.

CHICANE

Classification: None

Owner: François Gauthier

Address: 1, route de Garonne, 33210 Toulenne

Telephone: 05 56 76 43 73; Telefax: 05 56 76 42 60

Visits: By appointment only

Contact: François Gauthier

VINEYARDS (RED)

Surface area: 13.3 acres

Grape varietals: 55% Cabernet Sauvignon, 35% Merlot, 10% Malbec

Average age of vines: 20 years

Density of plantation: 3,300–5,000 vines per hectare

Average yields: 45–50 hectoliters per hectare

Elevage: Fermentations last three weeks in temperature-controlled stainless-steel tanks. Wines are transferred to oak casks, which are renewed by one-quarter each vintage, for 12 months aging. They are fined and filtered.

RED WINES PRODUCED

Château Chicane: 28,000 bottles

No second wine is produced.

Plateau of maturity: Within 2–5 years of the vintage

CLOS FLORIDENE

Classification: None

Owner: Denis and Florence Dubourdieu

Address: 33210 Pujol-sur-Cirons

Mailing address: c/o Château Reynon, 33410 Beguey

Telephone: 05 56 62 96 51; Telefax: 05 56 62 14 89

E-mail: reynon@gofornet.com

Visits: By appointment only

Contact: Florence Dubourdieu

VINEYARDS (RED)

Surface area: 32.1 acres

Grape varietals: 80% Cabernet Sauvignon, 20% Merlot

Average age of vines: 25 years

Density of plantation: 5,550 vines per hectare

Average yields: 40 hectoliters per hectare

Elevage: Fermentation and three-week maceration in temperature-controlled stainless-steel vats. Twelve months aging in barrels with 35% new oak. Fining and filtration.

RED WINES PRODUCED

Clos Floridene: 25,000 bottles

Château Montalivet: variable

Plateau of maturity: Within 2–8 years of the vintage

VINEYARDS (WHITE)

Surface area: 12.4 acres

Grape varietals: 45% Sauvignon Blanc, 45% Semillon, 10% Muscadelle

Average age of vines: 25 years

Density of plantation: 7,150 vines per hectare

Average yields: 37 hectoliters per hectare

Elevage: Fermentation and 11 months aging on lees in barrels with 25% new oak. Fining and filtration.

WHITE WINES PRODUCED

Clos Floridene: 5,500 bottles

Château Montalivet: 5,000–10,000 bottles

Plateau of maturity: Within 2–5 years of the vintage

GENERAL APPRECIATION

This estate, somewhat of an insider's secret, produces fine red and white wines. The brilliant dry white wine is full of fruit as well as character. It would merit cru classé status if a new classification were implemented. The well-made red wine offerings are best drunk early in life.

This small domain is owned by the white wine–making guru of Bordeaux, Denis Dubourdieu. He has long been given credit, and justifiably so, for revolutionizing the making of white wine in the Bordeaux region with his technique called *macération pelliculaire*. This process permits a period of contact between the skins of the grapes and the juice at a relatively low temperature. This is done because of Dubourdieu's belief, now confirmed by other authorities, that it is the components in the grape's skin that give the wine its aromatic complexity and richness of fruit.

One taste of the wonderful wines he makes reveals that Clos Floridene is a superb white Graves, nearly matching the quality of such legends as Laville Haut-Brion, Haut-Brion-Blanc, and Domaine de Chevalier. The price remains a relative steal, although Dubourdieu's talents have been recognized throughout Europe and Great Britain; Clos Floridene has indeed been discovered. This is a terribly underestimated, excellent wine that deserves to be a classified growth in the Graves firmament. A modest quantity of good, smooth, red wine is made, but it doesn't share the dazzling qualities of the white wine.

CLOS MARSALETTE

Classification: None

Owner: Stephan von Neipperg, Francis Boutemy, and M. Sarpoulet

Address: route de Labrède, 33650 Martillac

Mailing address: c/o Château Haut Lagrange, 31, route de Labrède, 33850 Léognan or c/o

Château Canon-la-Gaffelière, 33330 St.-Emilion

Telephone: 05 56 64 09 93

E-mail: chateau.haut-lagrange@wanadoo.fr

Visits: By appointment only

Contact: Franci Boutemy

VINEYARDS (RED)

Surface area: 15.8 acres

Grape varietals: 55% Cabernet Sauvignon, 45% Merlot

Average age of vines: 10 years

Density of plantation: 7,700 vines per hectare

Average yields: 50 hectoliters per hectare

Elevage: Forty-eight hour maceration at room temperature. Fermentation and 20 day maceration in temperature-controlled concrete vats. After malolactics, 18 months aging by rotation in vats for 75% of the yield and in new oak barrels for the rest. Fining and filtration.

RED WINES PRODUCED

Clos Marsalette: 40,000 bottles

No second wine is produced.

Plateau of maturity: Within 3–10 years of the vintage

VINEYARDS (WHITE)

Surface area: 1.5 acres

Grape varietals: 50% Sauvignon, 50% Semillon

Average age of vines: 10 years

Density of plantation: 7,700 vines per hectare

Average yields: 40 hectoliters per hectare

Elevage: Whole cluster pressing, settling over one to three days, fermentation and eight months aging on lees in vats (for 90% of the yield) and in new oak barrels (for 10% of the yield) with twice weekly stirrings. No fining, filtration.

WHITE WINES PRODUCED

Clos Marsalette: 3,000 bottles

No second wine is produced.

Plateau of maturity: Within 2–5 years of the vintage

COSTE DE MONS

Classification: None

Owner: SCEA du Château de Gaillat

Address: 33210 Saint-Pierre de Mons

Mailing address: c/o Château de Gaillat, 33210 Langon

Telephone: 05 56 63 50 77; Telefax: 05 56 62 20 96

Visits: By appointment only

Contact: Yves Bertrand and Hélène Bertrand-Coste

VINEYARDS (RED)

Surface area: 4.9 acres

Grape varietals: 80% Cabernet Sauvignon, 10% Carmenère, 7% Merlot, 3% Cabernet Franc

Average age of vines: 45–50 years

Density of plantation: 8,000 vines per hectare

Average yields: 32 hectoliters per hectare

Elevage: Seven day cold maceration. Fermentation at high temperatures and five months maceration in temperature-controlled vats. Eighteen months aging in new oak barrels. Fining and filtration.

RED WINES PRODUCED

Château de Coste de Mons: 8,500 bottles

Plateau of maturity: Within 2–8 years of the vintage

COUCHÉROY

Classification: None

Location of vineyards: Martillac

Owner: André Lurton

Address: 33650 Martillac

Mailing address: SCEA Les Vignobles André Lurton, Château Bonnet, 33420 Grézillac

Telephone: 33 5 57 25 58 58; Telefax: 33 5 57 74 98 59

No visits

VINEYARDS (RED)

Average age of vines: 10–12 years

Blend: 50% Cabernet Sauvignon, 50% Merlot

Density of plantation: 6,500–8,500 vines per hectare

Elevage: 12–14 months in oak casks. Fermentations last about 21 days in temperature controlled stainless-steel tanks. Malolactics occur partly in tanks and partly in oak barrels. Wines are transferred for 12 months aging to oak barrels in November (25–30% new oak). The wines are fined and filtered.

RED WINES PRODUCED

Château Couchéroy: 80,000 bottles

No second wine is produced.

Plateau of maturity: Within 3–10 years of the vintage

VINEYARDS (WHITE)

Average age of vines: 10–12 years

Blend: 90% Sauvignon, 10% Semillon

Density of plantation: 6,500 to 8,500 vines per hectare

Elevage: 8 months in cask and vat. Fermentations occur partly in temperature controlled stainless-steel vats and partly in oak barrels. Wines remain on lees for approximately 10 months and are fined and filtered before bottling.

WHITE WINES PRODUCED

Château Couchéroy: 25,000 bottles

No second wine is produced.

Plateau of maturity: Within 2–8 years of the vintage

COURRÈGES SEGUÈS DU CHÂTEAU DE GAILLAT

Classification: None

Owner: Hélène Bertrand-Coste

Address: 33210 Saint-Pierre de Mons

Mailing address: c/o Château de Gaillat, 33210 Langon

Telephone: 05 56 63 50 77; Telefax: 05 56 62 20 96

Visits: By appointment only

Contact: Yves Bertrand and Hélène Bertrand-Coste

VINEYARDS (RED)

Surface area: 7.4 acres

Grape varietals: 70% Cabernet Sauvignon, 20% Merlot, 10% Malbec

Average age of vines: 30–50 years

Density of plantation: 7,200 vines per hectare

Average yields: 45 hectoliters per hectare

Elevage: Seven day cold maceration. Fermentation at high temperatures and five months maceration in temperature-controlled vats. Twelve to fifteen months aging in barrels (35% new oak). Fining, no filtration.

RED WINES PRODUCED

Courrèges Seguès du Château de Gaillat: 15,000 bottles

No second wine is produced.

Plateau of maturity: Within 2–8 years of the vintage

DE CRUZEAU

Classification: None

Owner: André Lurton

Address: 33650 Saint-Médard-d'Eyrans

Mailing address: Vignobles André Lurton, Château Bonnet, 33420 Grézillac

Telephone: 05 57 25 58 58; Telefax: 05 57 74 98 59

E-mail: andrelurton@andrelurton.com

Website: www.andrelurton.com

Visits: By appointment Monday to Friday, 9 A.M.–5 P.M.

Contact: Véronique Bouffard

VINEYARDS (RED)

Surface area: 165.5 acres

Grape varietals: 55% Cabernet Sauvignon, 43% Merlot, 2% Cabernet Franc

Average age of vines: 20–22 years

Density of plantation: 6,500–8,500 vines per hectare

Average yields: 50 hectoliters per hectare

Elevage: Three week fermentation and maceration in temperature-controlled stainless-steel vats. Twelve months aging in barrels with 25–30% new oak and racking every three months. Fining and filtration.

RED WINES PRODUCED

Château de Cruzeau: 150,000 bottles

No second wine produced.

Plateau of maturity: Within 5–8 years of the vintage

VINEYARDS (WHITE)

Surface area: 74.1 acres

Grape varietals: 100% Sauvignon Blanc

Average age of vines: 20–22 years

Density of plantation: 6,500–8,500 vines per hectare

Average yields: 50 hectoliters per hectare

Elevage: After cold settling, 10–15 day fermentation (at 18–23°C) in barrels with 30–50% new oak. Nine months aging on lees with regular stirrings. Fining and filtration.

WHITE WINES PRODUCED

Château de Cruzeau: 60,000 bottles

No second wine produced.

Plateau of maturity: Within 2–6 years of the vintage

GENERAL APPRECIATION

A shrewd choice for knowledgeable wine buyers, this estate fashions excellent white as well as red wine, no doubt because of the attention to detail lavished on the wines by proprietor André Lurton. The vineyards are situated on one of the Graves region's highest ridges, with a full southerly exposure. The soil is pure, deep, sandy gravel of the highest quality for top white and red wines.

André Lurton, who has created quite a viticultural empire for himself in the Graves region, purchased this property in 1973 and began extensive replanting in 1979. The new vineyard is young by Bordeaux standards, but the wine has already begun to show promising potential. Using machine harvesters for the red wine and producing a creamy textured, open-knit, richly fruity, smoky-scented red Graves have proven beneficial for attracting buyers looking for immediate gratification.

The white wine, made from grapes that are hand-harvested and vinified in stainless steel with no exposure to oak, has an almost California-like style, with a great deal of fruit. However, the wine must be drunk within its first several years of life.

Prices for the wines of Cruzeau are remarkably fair, and therein lies much of this wine's appeal.

FERRANDE

Classification: None

Owner: SCE du Château Ferrande

Address: 33640 Castres

Telephone: 05 56 67 05 86

Visits: By appointment only

VINEYARDS (RED)

Surface area: 84 acres

Grape varietals: 34% Merlot, 33% Cabernet Franc, 33% Cabernet Sauvignon

Average age of vines: 25 years

Density of plantation: 4,500–5,500 vines per hectare

Average yields: 50 hectoliters per hectare

RED WINES PRODUCED

Château Ferrande: 200,000 bottles

Château Guillon: 12,000 bottles

Plateau of maturity: Within 3–10 years of the vintage

VINEYARDS (WHITE)

Surface area: 22.2 acres

Grape varietals: 60% Semillon, 35% Sauvignon, 5% Muscadelle

Average age of vines: 25 years

Average yields: 45 hectoliters per hectare

WHITE WINES PRODUCED

Château Guillon: 54,000 bottles

No second wine is produced.

Plateau of maturity: Within 2–7 years of the vintage

This is a consistently reliable, if uninspiring, estate in the commune of Castres. The property has been under the ownership of the Delnaud family since 1954. I have found both the red and white wines of Ferrande to be among the most earthy of the Graves region. In tastings I have noticed that this characteristic can either be admired or disliked intensely.

The white wines have improved a great deal in the last decade and now have much more charm and fruit in evidence. The white wine has a tendency to be not only aggressively earthy, but also extremely austere and angular. The wines are priced fairly and age fairly well, particularly the reds.

LA FLEUR JONQUET

Classification: None

Owner: Laurence Lataste

Address: Le Puy de Choyne, Arbanats, 33640 Portets

Mailing address: 5, rue Amélie, 33200 Bordeaux

Telephone: 05 56 17 08 18; Telefax: 05 57 22 12 54

E-mail: l.lataste@en.france.com

Visits: By appointment Monday to Friday (except Wednesdays), 9 A.M.–noon and 2–6 P.M.

Contact: Laurence Lataste

VINEYARDS (RED)

Surface area: 14.8 acres

Grape varietals: 70% Merlot, 20% Cabernet Sauvignon, 10% Cabernet Franc

Average age of vines: 15 years

Density of plantation: 5,800 vines per hectare

Average yields: 58 hectoliters per hectare

Elevage: Fermentation and 21 day maceration in temperature-controlled concrete tanks. Eighteen months aging in barrels with 25% new oak. Fining and light filtration upon bottling.

RED WINES PRODUCED

Château La Fleur Jonquet: 22,000 bottles

J de Jonquet: 4,000 bottles

Plateau of maturity: Within 2–5 years of the vintage

VINEYARDS (WHITE)

Surface area: 2.5 acres

Grape varietals: 50% Sauvignon Blanc, 50% Semillon

Average age of vines: 15 years

Density of plantation: 5,800 vines per hectare

Average yields: 57 hectoliters per hectare

Elevage: Fermentation and 12 months aging on lees in barrels with 30% new oak and frequent stirrings. Fining and filtration.

WHITE WINES PRODUCED

Château La Fleur Jonquet: 5,000 bottles

J de Jonquet: 1,600 bottles

Plateau of maturity: Within 2–4 years of the vintage

DES FOUGÈRES—CLOS MONTESQUIEU

Classification: None

Owner: SCEA des Vignobles Montesquieu

Address: 33650 La Brède

Telephone: 05 56 78 45 45; Telefax: 05 56 20 25 07

E-mail: montesquieu@montesquieu.com

Visits: By appointment only

Contact: Hélène Guigné

VINEYARDS (RED)

Surface area: 12.4 acres

Grape varietals: 80% Merlot, 20% Cabernet Sauvignon

Average age of vines: 25 years

Density of plantation: 8,000 vines per hectare

Average yields: 35 hectoliters per hectare

Elevage: Fermentation and 28 day maceration in temperature-controlled stainless-steel tanks with manual pigeage. Malolactics and 18 months aging on lees with micro-oxygenation in barrels (35% new oak and 65% one-year-old barrels). Fining, no filtration.

RED WINES PRODUCED

Des Fougères—Clos Montesquieu: 36,000 bottles

GENERAL APPRECIATION

It is not too soon to offer some exciting news. This estate is supervised by Patrick Baseden, who is better known as the owner of the St.-Emilion estates of La Bienfaisance and Sanctus. Baseden brought in the hot-shot wine guru Stéphane Derénoncourt to begin making the wines in 2002. This obscure property could become a name to reckon with in the future. Stay tuned.

DE FRANCE

Classification: None

Owner: SA B. Thomassin

Address: 98, avenue de Mont de Marsan, 33850 Léognan

Telephone: 05 56 64 75 39; Telefax: 05 56 64 72 13

E-mail: chateau-de-france@chateau-de-france.com

Website: www.chateau-de-france.com

Visits: By appointment Monday to Friday, 9 A.M.–5 P.M.

Contact: Bernard Thomassin

VINEYARDS (RED)

Surface area: 76.6 acres

Grape varietals: 60% Cabernet Sauvignon, 40% Merlot

Average age of vines: 20 years

Density of plantation: 6,950 vines per hectare

Average yields: 52 hectoliters per hectare

Elevage: Fermentation and one month maceration in temperature-controlled stainless-steel vats. Fourteen months aging in barrels that are renewed by half at each vintage. Fining and filtration.

RED WINES PRODUCED

Château de France: 100,000 bottles

Château Coquillas: 60,000 bottles

Plateau of maturity: Within 4–10 years of the vintage

VINEYARDS (WHITE)

Surface area: 14.8 acres

Grape varietals: 70% Sauvignon Blanc, 30% Semillon

Average age of vines: 20 years

Density of plantation: 6,950 vines per hectare

Average yields: 52 hectoliters per hectare

Elevage: Fermentation and 10 months aging on lees in barrels with 50% new oak and 50% one-year-old barrels. Fining and filtration.

WHITE WINES PRODUCED

Château de France: 10,000 bottles

Château Coquillas: 4,000 bottles

Plateau of maturity: Within 2–5 years of the vintage

GENERAL APPRECIATION

De France is another Graves estate that has improved over the past years. Both the reds and whites of this estate are traditional-styled, soundly made wines that deliver the goods, and even more than that in the best vintages.

Virtually the entire vineyard of this property, which is a neighbor of the more-renowned Château de Fieuzal, has been replanted since 1971. The proprietor—an industrialist—has spared little expense in renovating the property and building a new winery with state-of-the-art stainless-steel fermentation tanks. The early results were not impressive, but in 1986 proprietor Thomassin began to do two things that have had a positive impact on the resulting wines. First, he decided to harvest as late as possible. Second, a severe selection of the finished wine was employed so that only the best vats were sold under the de France name.

DE GAILLAT

Classification: None

Owner: Hélène Bertrand-Coste

Address: 33210 Langon

Mailing address: c/o Château de Gaillat, 33210 Langon

Telephone: 05 56 63 50 77; Telefax: 05 56 62 20 96

Visits: By appointment only

Contact: Yves Bertrand and Hélène Bertrand-Coste

VINEYARDS (RED)

Surface area: 29.6 acres

Grape varietals: 65% Cabernet Sauvignon, 30% Merlot, 5% Malbec

Average age of vines: 30 years

Density of plantation: 6,600 vines per hectare

Average yields: 50 hectoliters per hectare

Elevage: Seven day cold maceration. Fermentation at 30–32°C with pumpings-over and pigeages and 21–35 day maceration in temperature-controlled vats. Twelve to eighteen months aging by rotation in barrels (10% new oak) for half the yield and in vats for the other half. Fining and filtration.

RED WINES PRODUCED

Château de Gaillat: 60,000 bottles

No second wine is produced.

Plateau of maturity: Within 2–5 years of the vintage

GAZIN ROCQUENCOURT

Classification: None

Owner: Michotte family

Address: 74, avenue de Cestas, 33850 Léognan

Telephone: 05 56 64 77 89; Telefax: 05 56 64 77 89

Visits: By appointment only

Contact: M. Fernandes

VINEYARDS (RED)

Surface area: 34.6 acres

Grape varietals: 67% Cabernet Sauvignon, 33% Merlot

Average age of vines: 18 years

Density of plantation: 6,500 vines per hectare

Average yields: 50 hectoliters per hectare

Elevage: Fermentation and 21 day maceration in temperature-controlled stainless-steel vats. Twelve months aging in barrels that are renewed by a third at each vintage. Fining and filtration.

RED WINES PRODUCED

Château Gazin Rocquencourt: 48,000 bottles

Château Gazin Michotte: 17,000 bottles

Plateau of maturity: Within 2–10 years of the vintage

DU GRAND ABORD

Classification: None

Owner: Vignobles M.C. Dugoua

Address: 56, route des Graves, 33640 Portets

Telephone: 05 56 67 22 79; Telefax: 05 56 67 22 23

Visits: By appointment only

Contact: Colette Dugoua

VINEYARDS (RED)

Surface area: 42 acres

Grape varietals: 90% Merlot, 10% Cabernet Sauvignon

Average age of vines: 40–50 years

Density of plantation: 5,000–5,500 vines per hectare

Average yields: 55 hectoliters per hectare

Elevage: Fermentation and 18 day maceration in temperature-controlled stainless-steel vats. Eighteen months aging with half the yield in vats and the other half in barrels that are renewed by half at each vintage. Fining and filtration.

RED WINES PRODUCED

Château du Grand Abord: 20,000 bottles

Château Bel Air/Château Lagarde: 80,000 bottles

Plateau of maturity: Within 2–5 years of the vintage

VINEYARDS (WHITE)

Surface area: 7.4 acres

Grape varietals: 80% Semillon, 20% Sauvignon

Average age of vines: 40–50 years

Density of plantation: 5,000–5,500 vines per hectare

Average yields: 55 hectoliters per hectare

Elevage: Fermentation and three to four months aging in stainless-steel tanks. Fining and filtration.

WHITE WINES PRODUCED

Château du Grand Abord: 7,000 bottles

No second wine is produced.

Plateau of maturity: Within 1–4 years of the vintage

DU GRAND BOS

Classification: None

Owner: André Vincent

Address: chemin de l'Hermitage, 33640 Castres

Telephone: 05 56 67 39 20; Telefax: 05 56 67 16 77

E-mail: chateau.du.grand.bos@free.fr

Visits: By appointment only

Contact: Philippe Fort (Telephone: 05 56 67 02 21; Telefax: 05 56 67 16 77)

VINEYARDS (RED)

Surface area: 31.4 acres

Grape varietals: 46.5% Cabernet Sauvignon, 44% Merlot, 6.5% Petit Verdot, 3% Cabernet Franc and Malbec

Average age of vines: 30 years

Density of plantation: 5,600 vines per hectare

Average yields: 46 hectoliters per hectare

Elevage: Cold maceration. Fermentation and prolonged maceration in temperature-controlled vats with frequent pumpings-over. Twelve to fifteen months aging in barrels with 33–50% new oak. Fining not systematic, no filtration.

RED WINES PRODUCED

Château du Grand Bos: 370,000 bottles

Château Plégat La Gravière: 20,000–25,000 bottles

Plateau of maturity: Within 2–5 years of the vintage

VINEYARDS (WHITE)

Surface area: 2.5 acres

Grape varietals: 60% Semillon, 30% Sauvignon Blanc, 10% Muscadelle

Average age of vines: 20–60 years

Density of plantation: 5,600 vines per hectare

Average yields: 25–30 hectoliters per hectare

Elevage: Fermentation and eight months aging on lees in new oak barrels with frequent stirrings. No fining, light filtration upon bottling.

WHITE WINES PRODUCED

Château du Grand Bos: 3,000 bottles

No second wine is produced.

Plateau of maturity: Within 1–4 years of the vintage

GRAVILLE-LACOSTE

Classification: None

Owner: Hervé Dubourdieu

Address: 33720 Pujols-sur-Ciron

Mailing address: c/o Château Roumieu-Lacoste, 33720 Barsac

Telephone: 05 56 27 16 29; Telefax: 05 56 27 02 65

E-mail: hervedubourdieu@aol.com

Visits: By appointment only

Contact: Hervé Dubourdieu

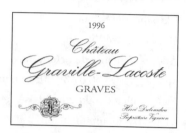

VINEYARDS (WHITE)

Surface area: 19.8 acres

Grape varietals: 70% Semillon, 20% Sauvignon, 10% Muscadelle

Average age of vines: 45 years

Density of plantation: 4,800 vines per hectare

Average yields: 49 hectoliters per hectare

Elevage: Cold stabilization at 2°C before fermentation. Fermentation and six months aging in stainless-steel vats. Fining, no filtration.

WHITE WINES PRODUCED

Château Graville-Lacoste: 52,000 bottles

No second wine is produced.

Plateau of maturity: Within 2–5 years of the vintage

GENERAL APPRECIATION

This excellent white wine, which consistently qualifies as a value pick, is a must buy. Consumers take note, as it is well worth many a grand cru classé of the appellation.

Note: The estate also produces a white Bordeaux: Château Ducasse: 30,000–60,000 bottles (depending upon the vintage).

DOMAINE DU HAURET LALANDE

Classification: None

Owner: Jean-Frédéric Lalande

Address: 33720 Illats

Mailing address: c/o Château Piada, 33720 Barsac

Telephone: 05 56 27 16 13; Telefax: 05 56 27 26 30

Visits: Monday to Friday, 9 A.M.–noon and 1:30–6 P.M.
By appointment on weekends.

Contact: Jean-Frédéric Lalande

VINEYARDS (RED)

Surface area: 6.2 acres

Grape varietals: 80% Cabernet Sauvignon, 20% Merlot

Average age of vines: 13 years

Density of plantation: 6,600 vines per hectare

Average yields: 58 hectoliters per hectare

Elevage: Fermentation and maceration in temperature-controlled stainless-steel vats. Thirteen months aging in three- to five-year-old barrels. Fining, no filtration.

RED WINES PRODUCED

Domaine du Hauret-Lalande: 13,000 bottles

No second wine is produced.

Plateau of maturity: Within 2–8 years of the vintage

VINEYARDS (WHITE)

Surface area: 7.4 acres

Grape varietals: 75% Semillon, 25% Sauvignon

Average age of vines: 36 years

Density of plantation: 5,500 vines per hectare

Average yields: 60 hectoliters per hectare

Elevage: Fermentation and five months aging in temperature-controlled stainless-steel vats. Fining, no filtration.

WHITE WINES PRODUCED

Domaine du Hauret Lalande: 9,000 bottles

No second wine is produced.

Plateau of maturity: Within 1–5 years of the vintage

HAUT-CALENS

Classification: None

Owner: EARL Vignobles Albert Yung

Address: 10, allée des Aulbnes, 33640 Beautiran

Telephone: 05 56 67 05 25; Telefax: 05 56 67 24 91

E-mail: vignobles.albertyung@wanadoo.fr

Visits: Monday to Friday, 9–11:30 A.M. and
2 P.M.–5:30 P.M.

Contact: Albert Yung

VINEYARDS (RED)

Surface area: 27.2 acres

Grape varietals: 50% Cabernet Sauvignon, 50% Merlot

Average age of vines: 20 years

Density of plantation: 5,000 vines per hectare

Average yields: 55 hectoliters per hectare

Elevage: Fermentation and 28 day maceration in temperature-controlled stainless-steel
vats with twice-daily pigeages during fermentation. Twenty-four months aging in vats.
Fining and filtration.

RED WINES PRODUCED

Château Haut-Calens: 30,000 bottles

Château de Pontac: 5,000 bottles

Plateau of maturity: Within 2–5 years of the vintage

HAUT-GARDÈRE

Classification: None

Owner: Loeclann Quinn

Address: 124, avenue de Mont de Marsan, 33850 Léognan

Telephone: 05 56 64 77 86; Telefax: 05 56 64 18 88

E-mail: ch.fieuzal@terre-net.fr

Website: www.fieuzal.com

Visits: By appointment only

Contact: Brigitte Talon

VINEYARDS (RED)

Surface area: 69.9 acres

Grape varietals: 70% Cabernet Sauvignon, 26% Merlot, 4% Cabernet Franc

Average age of vines: 30 years

Density of plantation: 10,000 vines per hectare

Average yields: 45 hectoliters per hectare

Elevage: Cold maceration. Fermentation (at 27°C) in temperature-controlled vats. Malolactics and 18–24 months aging in barrels that are renewed by a third every three months. Fining, no filtration.

RED WINES PRODUCED

Château Haut-Gardère: 35,000–40,000 bottles

No second wine is produced.

Plateau of maturity: Within 5–12 years of the vintage

VINEYARDS (WHITE)

Surface area: 14.1 acres

Grape varietals: 50% Sauvignon Blanc, 50% Semillon

Average age of vines: 30 years

Density of plantation: 10,000 vines per hectare

Average yields: 45 hectoliters per hectare

Elevage: Direct pressing. Fermentation and 16–18 months aging on lees in barrels (50% new oak for Semillon and one-year-old barrels for Sauvignon Blanc). Fining, no filtration.

WHITE WINES PRODUCED

Château Haut-Gardère: 15,000 bottles

No second wine is produced.

Plateau of maturity: Within 4–6 years of the vintage

Note: This estate belongs to de Fieuzal.

GENERAL APPRECIATION

This property is extremely well run. In spite of the youth of the vines, the last several vintages have produced generously rich, tobacco-scented, flavorful red wines and stylish white wines. The vineyard sits on a very fine outcropping of gravelly soil in the Léognan area. Prices are remarkably low, largely because word has not circulated about how good these wines can be. Before World War II Haut-Gardère had such a high reputation, it sold for the same price as Domaine de Chevalier, de Fieuzal, and Malartic-Lagravière.

HAUT LAGRANGE

Classification: None

Owner: Francis Boutemy

Address: 31, route de Loustalade, 33850 Léognan

Telephone: 05 56 64 09 93; Telefax: 05 56 64 10 08

E-mail: chateau.haut-lagrange@wanadoo.fr

Visits: By appointment only, Monday to Friday

Contact: Francis Boutemy

VINEYARDS (RED)

Surface area: 44.5 acres

Grape varietals: 55% Cabernet Sauvignon, 45% Merlot

Average age of vines: 10 years

Density of plantation: 7,700 vines per hectare

Average yields: 55 hectoliters per hectare

Elevage: Fermentation and 20 day maceration in temperature-controlled concrete tanks. Eighteen months aging, with 25% of yield in new oak barrels, the rest in vats. Fining and filtration.

RED WINES PRODUCED

Château Haut Lagrange: 130,000 bottles

No second wine is produced.

Plateau of maturity: Within 2–6 years of the vintage

VINEYARDS (WHITE)

Surface area: 4.2 acres

Grape varietals: 50% Semillon, 45% Sauvignon Blanc, 5% Sauvignon Gris

Average age of vines: 10 years

Density of plantation: 7,700 vines per hectare

Average yields: 50 hectoliters per hectare

Elevage: Fermentation in vats (90% of yield) and new oak (10% of yield) and eight months aging, with stirring of the lees for the wines in vats. No fining, filtration.

WHITE WINES PRODUCED

Château Haut Lagrange: 11,000 bottles

No second wine is produced.

Plateau of maturity: Within 2–4 years of the vintage

HAUT-NOUCHET

Classification: None

Owner: Louis Lurton

Address: 33650 Martillac

Telephone: 05 56 72 69 74; Telefax: 05 56 72 56 11

Visits: By appointment only

VINEYARDS (RED)

Surface area: 69.2 acres

Grape varietals: 72% Cabernet Sauvignon, 28% Merlot

Average age of vines: 10 years

Density of plantation: 6,600 vines per hectare

Average yields: 32 hectoliters per hectare

Elevage: Fermentations are rather long (three to four weeks) and occur in stainless-steel tanks. Wines are transferred to oak casks (renewed by a third at each vintage) and are aged for 16 months. They are fined but not filtered.

RED WINES PRODUCED

Château Haut-Nouchet: 78,000 bottles

Domaine du Milan: 42,000 bottles

Plateau of maturity: Within 2–5 years of the vintage

VINEYARDS (WHITE)

Surface area: 27.2 acres

Grape varietals: 72% Cabernet Sauvignon, 28% Merlot

Average age of vines: 13 years

Density of plantation: 6,600 vines per hectare

Average yields: 21 hectoliters per hectare

Elevage: Fermentations occur in barrels, renewed by a quarter at each vintage. Wines remain on lees for six to eight months with regular stirring. They are fined and filtered.

WHITE WINES PRODUCED

Château Haut-Nouchet: 30,000 bottles

Domaine du Milan: variable

Plateau of maturity: Within 2–4 years of the vintage

HAUT-VIGNEAU

Classification: None

Owner: GFA du Château Haut-Vigneau—Perrin family

Address: 33850 Léognan

Telephone: 05 57 96 56 20; Telefax: 05 56 96 59 19

E-mail: chateau.carbonnieux@wanadoo.fr

Website: www.carbonnieux.com

Visits: By appointment Monday to Friday, 8:30–11 A.M. and 2–5 P.M.

Contact: Eric Perrin

VINEYARDS (RED)

Surface area: 49.4 acres

Grape varietals: 70% Cabernet Sauvignon, 30% Merlot

Average age of vines: 15 years

Density of plantation: 7,200 vines per hectare

Average yields: 50 hectoliters per hectare

Elevage: Twenty-one day fermentation and maceration in temperature-controlled stainless-steel tanks. Fifteen to eighteen months aging in barrels with 20% new oak. Fining and filtration.

RED WINES PRODUCED

Château Haut-Vigneau: 120,000 bottles

No second wine is produced.

Plateau of maturity: Within 2–5 years of the vintage

DE L'HOSPITAL

Classification: None

Owner: Jean-Paul and Marie-Claude Lafragette

Address: Lieu-dit Darrouban, 33640 Portets

Mailing address: c/o Château Loudenne, 33340 Saint-Yzans-de-Médoc

Telephone: 05 56 67 54 73; Telefax: 05 56 67 09 93

Visits: By appointment only

Contact: Florence Lafragette (Telephone: 05 56 73 17 80; Telefax: 05 56 09 02 87; e-mail: chateau-loudenne@wanadoo.fr)

VINEYARDS (RED)

Surface area: 29.6 acres

Grape varietals: 85% Merlot, 15% Cabernet Sauvignon

Average age of vines: 25–50 years

Density of plantation: 5,500 vines per hectare

Average yields: 50–55 hectoliters per hectare

Elevage: Fermentation and 15–21 day maceration in temperature-controlled stainless-steel vats. Twelve months aging in barrels that are renewed by a third every vintage. Fining and filtration.

RED WINES PRODUCED

Château de l'Hospital: 65,000 bottles

Château Thibaut-Ducasse: 18,000 bottles

Plateau of maturity: Within 5–10 years of the vintage

VINEYARDS (WHITE)

Surface area: 7 acres

Grape varietals: 60% Sauvignon Blanc, 40% Semillon

Average age of vines: 30–50 years

Density of plantation: 5,500 vines per hectare

Average yields: 42 hectoliters per hectare

Elevage: Alcoholic fermentation in vats. Aging on lees in new oak barrels with regular stirrings. Fining, no filtration.

WHITE WINES PRODUCED

Château de l'Hospital: 10,000 bottles

Château Thibaut-Ducasse: 18,000 bottles

Plateau of maturity: Within 3–8 years of the vintage

GENERAL APPRECIATION

Lamentably, I have never been impressed with the wines from this property, whose château is classified as a historic monument under French law. The red wines tend to be stubbornly hard, austere, dusty, and not always the cleanest examples of winemaking. The minuscule quantity of white wine is flinty, smoky, sometimes overwhelmingly earthy and austere. They would seemingly benefit from a small quantity of Semillon to give the wines more fat, flesh, and charm. The wines of l'Hospital are seen in some marketplaces but are generally overpriced.

JEAN GERVAIS

Classification: None

Owner: SCEA Counilh et fils

Address: 51/53, route des Graves, 33640 Portets

Telephone: 05 56 67 18 61; Telefax: 05 56 67 32 43

Visits: Monday to Friday, 9 A.M. to noon and 1–6 P.M. By appointment on weekends.

Contact: Francois Counilh or Denis Counilh

VINEYARDS (RED)

Surface area: 69.2 acres

Grape varietals: 60% Merlot, 40% Cabernet Sauvignon

Average age of vines: 25 years

Density of plantation: 6,000 vines per hectare

Average yields: 50 hectoliters per hectare

Elevage: Fermentation and 12–18 day maceration in temperature-controlled stainless-steel rototanks with frequent pumpings-over. Eighteen months aging in epoxy-lined vats. Fining, no filtration.

RED WINES PRODUCED

Château Jean Gervais: 120,000 bottles

Château Tour de Cluchon: 40,000 bottles

Plateau of maturity: Within 2–5 years of the vintage

VINEYARDS (WHITE)

Surface area: 32.1 acres

Grape varietals: 90% Semillon, 5% Sauvignon Blanc, 5% Muscadelle

Average age of vines: 35 years

Density of plantation: 5,000 vines per hectare

Average yields: 58 hectoliters per hectare

Elevage: Fermentation and 9–12 months aging on lees in temperature-controlled stainless-steel rototanks. Fining and filtration.

WHITE WINES PRODUCED

Château Jean Gervais: 60,000 bottles

Château Tour de Cluchon: 20,000 bottles

Plateau of maturity: Within 1–4 years of the vintage

LAFARGUE

Classification: None

Owner: Jean-Marie Leymarie

Address: 5, impasse de Domy, 33650 Martillac

Telephone: 05 56 72 72 30; Telefax: 05 56 72 64 61

E-mail: chateau-lafargue@wanadoo.fr

Website: www.chateau-lafargue.com

Visits: By appointment Monday to Friday, 8 A.M. to noon and 2–6 P.M. (to 4 P.M. on Fridays)

Contact: Jean-Pierre Leymarie or Muriel Brunel

VINEYARDS (RED)

Surface area: 54.3 acres

Grape varietals: 40% Cabernet Sauvignon, 40% Merlot, 15% Cabernet Franc, 2.5% Malbec, 2.5% Petit Verdot

Average age of vines: 25 years

Density of plantation: 6,500 vines per hectare

Average yields: 52 hectoliters per hectare

Elevage: Four to five week fermentation and maceration in temperature-controlled stainless-steel vats with micro-oxygenation of lees. Twelve to fifteen months aging in barrels that are renewed by a third at each vintage. Fining, filtration not systematic.

RED WINES PRODUCED

Château Lafargue: 150,000 bottles

No second wine is produced.

Plateau of maturity: Within 2–4 years of the vintage

VINEYARDS (WHITE)

Surface area: 4.9 acres

Grape varietals: 70% Sauvignon Blanc, 30% Sauvignon Gris

Average age of vines: 25 years

Density of plantation: 6,500 vines per hectare

Average yields: 52 hectoliters per hectare

Elevage: Fermentation and aging on lees with stirring in oak barrels with 50% new oak. Fining and filtration.

WHITE WINES PRODUCED

Château Lafargue: 9,000 bottles

No second wine is produced.

Plateau of maturity: Within 2–6 years of the vintage

LAFONT MENAUT

Classification: None

Owner: Philibert Perrin

Address: 33850 Léognan

Telephone: 05 57 96 56 20; Telefax: 05 56 96 59 19

E-mail: chateau.carbonnieux@wanadoo.fr

Website: www.carbonnieux.com

Visits: By appointment Monday to Friday 8:30–11 A.M. and 2–5 P.M.

Contact: Philibert Perrin

VINEYARDS (RED)

Surface area: 29.6 acres

Grape varietals: 60% Cabernet Sauvignon, 40% Merlot

Average age of vines: 12 years

Density of plantation: 7,200 vines per hectare

Average yields: 50 hectoliters per hectare

Elevage: Twenty-one day fermentation and maceration in temperature-controlled stainless-steel tanks. Fifteen to eighteen months aging in barrels with 20–25% new oak. Fining and filtration.

RED WINES PRODUCED

Château Lafont Menaut: 70,000 bottles

No second wine is produced.

Plateau of maturity: Within 2–8 years of the vintage

VINEYARDS (WHITE)

Surface area: 7.4 acres

Grape varietals: 80% Sauvignon, 20% Semillon

Average age of vines: 12 years

Density of plantation: 7,200 vines per hectare

Average yields: 50 hectoliters per hectare

Elevage: After cold settling, fermentation and 10 months aging in barrels with 20% new oak. Fining and filtration.

WHITE WINES PRODUCED

Château Lafont Menaut: 20,000 bottles

No second wine is produced.

Plateau of maturity: Within 2–6 years of the vintage

LAMOUROUX

Classification: None

Owner: Olivier Lataste

Address: Grand Enclos du Château de Cérons, 33720 Cérons

Telephone: 05 56 27 01 53; Telefax: 05 56 27 08 86

Visits: By appointment only

Contact: Olivier Lataste

VINEYARDS (RED)

Surface area: 4.9 acres

Grape varietals: 50% Cabernet Sauvignon, 50% Merlot

Average age of vines: 20 years

Density of plantation: 6,000 vines per hectare

Average yields: 45 hectoliters per hectare

Elevage: Fermentations last 15–20 days depending upon the vintage. Wines are aged for 16 months in two- to three-year-old oak barrels. They are fined and filtered.

RED WINES PRODUCED

Château Lamouroux: 12,000 bottles

No second wine is produced.

Plateau of maturity: Within 3–12 years of the vintage

VINEYARDS (WHITE)

Surface area: 59.3 acres

Grape varietals: 60% Semillon, 40% Sauvignon

Average age of vines: 30 years

Density of plantation: 6,000 vines per hectare

Average yields: 40 hectoliters per hectare

Elevage: Fermentations occur in barrels renewed by a third at each vintage, and wines are bottled after 18 months. They are fined and filtered.

WHITE WINES PRODUCED

Grand Enclos du Château de Cérons: 12,000 bottles

Château Lamouroux: 60,000 bottles

Plateau of maturity: Within 2–10 years of the vintage

DE LANDIRAS

Classification: None

Owner: SCA Domaine La Grave

Address: 33720 Landiras

Telephone: 05 56 62 44 70; Telefax: 05 56 62 43 78

Visits: By appointment only

Contact: Peter Vinding-Diers

VINEYARDS (RED)

Surface area: 3.7 acres

Grape varietals: 67% Cabernet Sauvignon, 33% Merlot

Average age of vines: 30 years

Density of plantation: 5,000 vines per hectare

Average yields: 45 hectoliters per hectare

Elevage: Fermentations are rather short and occur in stainless-steel vats. Wines undergo malolactics in barrels. Percentage of new oak depends upon the vintage. Wines are fined but not filtered.

RED WINES PRODUCED

Château de Landiras: 2,400 bottles

La Colombe de Landiras: 3,600 bottles

Plateau of maturity: Within 3–10 years of the vintage

VINEYARDS (WHITE)

Surface area: 31.6 acres

Grape varietals: 80% Semillon, 20% Sauvignon Gris

Average age of vines: 7 years

Density of plantation: 9,100 vines per hectare

Average yields: 40 hectoliters per hectare

Elevage: Fermentations occur in casks, with indigenous yeasts. Wines are aged for six to nine months. They are not fined.

WHITE WINES PRODUCED

Château de Landiras: 24,000 bottles

La Colombe de Landiras: 36,000 bottles

Plateau of maturity: Within 2–8 years of the vintage

LESPAULT

Classification: None

Owner: SC du Château Lespault

Address: 33650 Martillac

Mailing address: c/o SCF Domaines Kressmann, Chemin Latour, 33650 Martillac

Telephone: 05 57 97 71 11; Telefax: 05 57 97 71 17

Visits: By appointment only

Contact: Tristan Kressmann

VINEYARDS (RED)

Surface area: 12.4 acres

Grape varietals: 75% Merlot, 20% Cabernet Sauvignon, 5% Malbec

Average age of vines: 40 years

Density of plantation: 7,200 vines per hectare

Average yields: 45 hectoliters per hectare

Elevage: Twenty-one to twenty-eight day fermentation and maceration in temperature-controlled stainless-steel vats. Sixteen months aging in barrels with 20% new oak. Fining and filtration.

RED WINES PRODUCED

Château Lespault: 30,000 bottles

No second wine is produced.

Plateau of maturity: Within 2–6 years of the vintage

VINEYARDS (WHITE)

Surface area: 2.5 acres

Grape varietals: 100% Sauvignon

Average age of vines: 35 years

Density of plantation: 7,200 vines per hectare

Average yields: 50 hectoliters per hectare

Elevage: Slow pressing. Fermentation and eight months aging on lees in oak barrels with 25% new oak. Fining and filtration.

WHITE WINES PRODUCED

Château Lespault: 5,000 bottles

No second wine is produced.

Plateau of maturity: Within 2–4 years of the vintage

MAGENCE

Classification: None

Owner: Guillot de Suduiraut d'Anthras family

Address: 33210 Saint-Pierre de Mons

Telephone: 05 56 63 07 05; Telefax: 05 56 63 41 42

E-mail: magence@magence.com

Website: www.magence.com

Visits: Preferably by appointment Monday to Friday, 9–11 A.M. and 2–5 P.M.

Contact: Comte Jacques d'Anthras

VINEYARDS (RED)

Surface area: 64.2 acres

Grape varietals: 44% Merlot, 43% Cabernet Sauvignon, 13% Cabernet Franc

Average age of vines: 28 years

Density of plantation: 3,500 and 5,500 vines per hectare

Average yields: 52 hectoliters per hectare

Elevage: Fermentation and 20–30 day maceration in temperature-controlled stainless-steel vats. Eighteen months aging in stainless-steel vats (for the generic *cuvée*) or in barrels that are renewed by half at each vintage for the special *cuvée*. Fining, filtration if necessary.

RED WINES PRODUCED

Château Magence (generic and oak-aged): 115,000 bottles

Château Brannens: 20,000 bottles

Plateau of maturity: Within 2–10 years of the vintage

VINEYARDS (WHITE)

Surface area: 27.2 acres

Grape varietals: 50% Sauvignon, 50% Semillon

Average age of vines: 28 years

Density of plantation: 3,500 and 5,500 vines per hectare

Average yields: 45 hectoliters per hectare

Elevage: Fermentation and eight months aging in stainless steel vats on fine lees.

WHITE WINES PRODUCED

Château Magence: 25,000 bottles

Plateau of maturity: Within 2–10 years of the vintage

DE MAUVES

Classification: None

Owner: Bernard Bouche

Address: 25, rue François Mauriac, 33720 Podensac

Mailing address: BP 60, 33720 Podensac

Telephone: 05 56 27 17 05; Telefax: 05 56 27 24 19

Visits: Preferably by appointment Monday to Friday, 8 A.M.–noon and 2–7 P.M.

Contact: Bernard, Dominique, or Michel Bouche

VINEYARDS (RED)

Surface area: 71.6 acres

Grape varietals: 70% Cabernet Sauvignon, 30% Merlot

Average age of vines: 20 years

Density of plantation: 5,000 vines per hectare

Average yields: 55 hectoliters per hectare

Elevage: Fermentation and 20–25 day maceration in temperature-controlled concrete and stainless-steel vats. Eighteen to twenty-four months aging in vats. Fining and filtration.

RED WINES PRODUCED

Château de Mauves: 100,000 bottles

No second wine is produced.

Plateau of maturity: Within 4–10 years of the vintage

VINEYARDS (WHITE)

Surface area: 2.5 acres

Grape varietals: 100% Semillon

Average age of vines: 20 years

Density of plantation: 5,000 vines per hectare

Average yields: 55 hectoliters per hectare

Elevage: Fermentation at low temperature and nine months aging in stainless-steel vats. Fining and filtration.

WHITE WINES PRODUCED

Château de Mauves: 6,000 bottles

No second wine is produced.

Plateau of maturity: Within 2–6 years of the vintage

DU MOURET

Classification: None

Owner: Médeville family

Address: 33410 Roaillan

Mailing address: c/o Jean Médeville et Fils, Château Fayau, 33410 Cadillac

Telephone: 05 57 98 08 08; Telefax: 05 56 62 18 22

E-mail: medeville-jeanetfils@wanadoo.fr

Visits: By appointment only

Contact: Jacques Médeville

VINEYARDS (RED)

Surface area: 22.2 acres

Grape varietals: 50% Cabernet Sauvignon, 45% Merlot, 5% Cabernet Franc

Average age of vines: 35 years

Density of plantation: 3,000–5,000 vines per hectare

Average yields: 45 hectoliters per hectare

Elevage: Fermentation and 15–20 day maceration in temperature-controlled concrete vats. Twenty-four months aging in vats. Fining, no filtration.

RED WINES PRODUCED

Château du Mouret: 60,000 bottles

No second wine is produced.

Plateau of maturity: Within 4–12 years of the vintage

VINEYARDS (WHITE)

Surface area: 9.9 acres

Grape varietals: 60% Sauvignon Blanc, 40% Semillon

Average age of vines: 15 years

Density of plantation: 3,000–5,000 vines per hectare

Average yields: 45–50 hectoliters per hectare

Elevage: Cold stabilization. Eight to ten day fermentation at low temperature. Six months aging on lees in vats. Fining, no filtration.

WHITE WINES PRODUCED

Château du Mouret: 3,000 bottles

No second wine is produced.

Plateau of maturity: Within 2–8 years of the vintage

LE PAPE

Classification: None

Owner: Patrick Monjanel

Address: 34, chemin Le Pape, 33850 Léognan

Telephone: 05 56 64 10 90; Telefax: 05 56 64 17 78

E-mail: pmontjanel@chateaulepape.com

Website: www.chateaulepape.com

Visits: By appointment only

Contact: Patrick Montjanel (Telephone: 06 07 66 01 60)

VINEYARDS (RED)

Surface area: 14.8 acres

Grape varietals: 70% Merlot, 30% Cabernet

Average age of vines: 35–40 years

Density of plantation: 5,000 vines per hectare

Average yields: 50 hectoliters per hectare

Elevage: Cold maceration, three- to four-week fermentation and maceration in temperature-controlled concrete tanks of small capacity. Twelve months aging in barrels with 50% new oak. No fining, no filtration.

RED WINES PRODUCED

Château Le Pape: 15,000 bottles

L'Emule du Pape: 15,000 bottles

Plateau of maturity: Within 2–6 years of the vintage

PÉRIN DE NAUDINE

Classification: None

Owner: Olivier Colas

Address: 8, impasse des Domaines, 33640 Castres-Gironde

Telephone: 05 56 67 06 65; Telefax: 05 56 67 59 68

E-mail: chateauperin@wanadoo.fr

Website: www.chateauperin.com

Visits: By appointment only

Contact: Frank Artaud

VINEYARDS (RED)

Surface area: 22.2 acres

Grape varietals: 66% Merlot, 23% Cabernet Sauvignon, 11% Cabernet Franc

Average age of vines: 20 years

Density of plantation: 5,700 vines per hectare

Average yields: 58 hectoliters per hectare

Elevage: Fermentation and three week maceration in temperature-controlled vats. Ten percent of yield undergoes malolactics in barrels. Twelve months aging in barrels with 33% new oak. Fining, no filtration.

RED WINES PRODUCED

Château Périn de Naudine: 50,000 bottles

Les Sphinx de Naudine: 10,000 bottles

Plateau of maturity: Within 4–8 years of the vintage

VINEYARDS (WHITE)

Surface area: 7.4 acres

Grape varietals: 80% Semillon, 20% Sauvignon Blanc

Average age of vines: 28 years

Density of plantation: 5,700 vines per hectare

Average yields: 58 hectoliters per hectare

Elevage: Fermentation and nine months aging on lees in barrels with 50% new oak. Fining, no filtration.

WHITE WINES PRODUCED

Château Périn de Naudine: 10,000 bottles

No second wine is produced.

Plateau of maturity: Within 2–4 years of the vintage

PESSAN

Classification: None

Owner: Paul-Henry de Bournazel

Address: 33640 Portets

Mailing address: c/o Château de Malle, 33210 Preignac

Telephone: 05 56 62 36 86; Telefax: 05 56 76 82 40

E-mail: chateaudemalle@wanadoo.fr

Website: www.chateau-de-malle.fr

Visits: By appointment only

VINEYARDS (RED)

Surface area: 17.3 acres

Grape varietals: 50% Cabernet Sauvignon, 50% Merlot

Average age of vines: 20 years

Density of plantation: 6,600 vines per hectare

Average yields: 55 hectoliters per hectare

Elevage: Fermentation and maceration with frequent pumpings-over in temperature-controlled vats. Twelve months aging in barrels with 50% new oak. Fining and filtration.

RED WINES PRODUCED

Château Pessan: 25,000 bottles

No second wine is produced.

Plateau of maturity: Within 4–6 years of the vintage

Note: This estate was bought recently by the Château de Malle. 2002 is the first vintage produced under the new ownership. It should be a property to watch as improvements appear to be coming.

PEYREBLANQUE

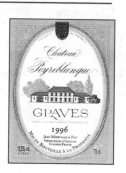

Classification: None

Owner: Médeville family

Address: 33410 Roaillan

Mailing address: c/o Jean Médeville et Fils, Château Fayau, 33410 Cadillac

Telephone: 05 57 98 08 08; Telefax: 05 56 62 18 22

E-mail: medeville-jeanetfils@wanadoo.fr

Visits: By appointment only

Contact: Jacques Médeville

VINEYARDS (RED)

Surface area: 17.3 acres

Grape varietals: 70% Cabernet Sauvignon, 30% Merlot

Average age of vines: 12 years

Density of plantation: 5,000 vines per hectare

Average yields: 50 hectoliters per hectare

Elevage: Fermentation and 19–25 day maceration in temperature-controlled concrete vats. Ten to fifteen months aging in barrels. Fining, no filtration.

RED WINES PRODUCED

Château Peyreblanque: 40,000 bottles

No second wine is produced.

Plateau of maturity: Within 2–5 years of the vintage

VINEYARDS (WHITE)

Surface area: 2.5 acres

Grape varietals: 80% Muscadelle, 20% Sauvignon Blanc

Average age of vines: 12 years

Density of plantation: 5,000 vines per hectare

Average yields: 52 hectoliters per hectare

Elevage: Five day cold stabilization. Fermentation at low temperature and 10 months aging on lees with weekly stirrings. Fining, no filtration.

WHITE WINES PRODUCED

Château Peyreblanque: 6,000 bottles

No second wine is produced.

Plateau of maturity: Within 2–5 years of the vintage

PIRON

Classification: None

Owner: Boyreau family

Administrator: Lionel Boyreau

Address: 33650 Saint-Morillon

Telephone: 05 56 20 25 61; Telefax: 05 56 78 48 36

Visits: By appointment only

Contact: Lionel Boyreau

VINEYARDS (RED)

Surface area: 19.8 acres

Grape varietals: 50% Cabernet Sauvignon, 50% Merlot

Average age of vines: 30 years

Density of plantation: 5,000 vines per hectare

Average yields: 50 hectoliters per hectare

Elevage: Fermentation and maceration in temperature-controlled stainless-steel vats. Twelve to eighteen months aging in barrels. Fining not systematic, filtration.

RED WINES PRODUCED

Château Piron: 25,000–30,000 bottles

Château Coureau: 25,000–30,000 bottles

Plateau of maturity: Within 2–6 years of the vintage

VINEYARDS (WHITE)

Surface area: 29.6 acres

Grape varietals: 50% Sauvignon Blanc, 50% Semillon

Average age of vines: 30 years

Density of plantation: 5,000 vines per hectare

Average yields: 50 hectoliters per hectare

Elevage: Fermentation and six months aging in vats for part of the yield and in barrels for the rest. No fining, filtration.

WHITE WINES PRODUCED

Château Piron: 25,000–30,000 bottles

Château Coureau: 25,000–30,000 bottles

Plateau of maturity: Within 2–6 years of the vintage

PONTAC MONPLAISIR ―――――――――――――――――

Classification: None

Owner: Jean Maufras

Address: 33140 Villenave d'Ornon

Telephone: 05 56 87 08 21; Telefax: 05 56 87 35 10

Visits: By appointment only

Contact: Alain Maufras (Telephone: 06 09 28 80 88)

VINEYARDS (RED)

Surface area: 39.5 acres

Grape varietals: 60% Merlot, 40% Cabernet Sauvignon

Average age of vines: 30 years

Density of plantation: 6,000 vines per hectare

Average yields: 58 hectoliters per hectare

Elevage: Fermentation in temperature-controlled stainless-steel and epoxy-lined stainless-steel tanks. Fourteen to sixteen months aging with 30% new oak. No fining, no filtration.

RED WINES PRODUCED

Château Pontac Monplaisir: 70,000 bottles

Château Limbourg: 8,000–10,000 bottles

Plateau of maturity: Within 4–6 years of the vintage

VINEYARDS (WHITE)

Surface area: 39.5 acres

Grape varietals: 55% Sauvignon Blanc, 45% Semillon

Average age of vines: 30 years

Density of plantation: 6,000 vines per hectare

Average yields: 58 hectoliters per hectare

Elevage: Fermentation and 10 months aging in barrels with 40% new oak. No fining, no filtration.

WHITE WINES PRODUCED

Château Pontac Monplaisir: 25,000 bottles

No second wine is produced.

Plateau of maturity: Within 2–4 years of the vintage

GENERAL APPRECIATION

The vineyard of Pontac Monplaisir sits on very sandy, light gravelly soil near Château Baret. The white wine from this estate is a textbook white Graves with a pronounced intense, herbaceous, mineral character, medium body, and gobs of fruit. Some people find it almost too herbaceously scented. It is not a wine to lay away in the cellar, but rather to be drunk in its first 2–3 years. The red wine is of less interest—soft, straightforward, relatively light, but tasty and correctly made.

POUMEY

Classification: None

Farmed by: Château Pape Clément

Address: rue du Professeur Bernard, 33190 Gradignan

Mailing address: c/o Château Pape Clément, 216, avenue du Dr Nancel Pénard, BP 164, 33600 Pessac Cedex

Telephone: 05 57 26 38 38; Telefax: 05 57 28 38 39

Visits: By appointment only

Contact: Eric Larramona

VINEYARDS (RED)

Surface area: 19.8 acres

Grape varietals: 60% Cabernet Sauvignon, 40% Merlot

Average age of vines: 20 years

Density of plantation: 7,500 vines per hectare

Average yields: 39 hectoliters per hectare

Elevage: Fermentation in temperature-controlled stainless-steel vats. Malolactics and 18–20 months aging in barrels with 75% new oak. No fining, filtration.

RED WINES PRODUCED

Château Poumey: 20,000 bottles

No second wine is produced.

Plateau of maturity: Within 5–12 years of the vintage

Note: In 2001, a special cuvée of 6,000 bottles was launched, called Sérénité de Poumey, an impressive, very rich wine made under the guidance of renowned oenologist Michel Rolland.

RAHOUL

Classification: None

Owner: Alain Thienot

Address: 4, route de Courneau, 33640 Portets

Telephone: 05 56 67 01 12; Telefax: 05 56 67 02 88

E-mail: château-rahoul@alain-thienot.fr

Visits: By appointment only

Contact: Nathalie Schwartz

VINEYARDS (RED)

Surface area: 96.3 acres

Grape varietals: 70% Merlot, 30% Cabernet Sauvignon

Average age of vines: 30 years

Density of plantation: 6,000 vines per hectare

Average yields: 48 hectoliters per hectare

Elevage: Fermentation and 20 day maceration in temperature-controlled stainless-steel vats. Twelve months aging in barrels that are renewed by a third at each vintage. Fining and filtration.

RED WINES PRODUCED

Château Rahoul: 90,000 bottles

La Garance: 70,000 bottles

Plateau of maturity: Within 5–14 years of the vintage

VINEYARDS (WHITE)

Surface area: 7.4 acres

Grape varietals: 70% Semillon, 30% Sauvignon Blanc

Average age of vines: 35 years

Density of plantation: 6,000 vines per hectare

Average yields: 30 hectoliters per hectare

Elevage: Fermentation and six months aging on lees in barrels that are renewed by half at each vintage. Fining and filtration.

WHITE WINES PRODUCED

Château Rahoul: 6,000 bottles

La Garance: 6,000 bottles

Plateau of maturity: Within 3–6 years of the vintage

GENERAL APPRECIATION

This property near the village of Portets is highly regarded in some circles, but to date I have found the wines almost overwhelmingly oaky, as well as slightly out of balance. The vineyard is still young, and perhaps when mature the concentration of fruit in the wines will be sufficient to stand up to the wood. Certainly those readers who prefer more oaky-styled wines would rate these wines more highly. In 1991 Rahoul was sold to Alain Thienot, a wealthy property owner from Champagne.

DE ROCHEMORIN

Classification: None

Owner: André Lurton

Address: 33850 Martillac

Mailing address: Vignobles André Lurton, Château Bonnet, 33420 Grézillac

Telephone: 05 57 25 58 58; Telefax: 05 57 74 98 59

E-mail: andrelurton@andrelurton.com

Website: www.andrelurton.com

Visits: By appointment Monday to Friday, 9 A.M.–5 P.M.

Contact: Véronique Bouffard

VINEYARDS (RED)

Surface area: 214.9 acres

Grape varietals: 60% Cabernet Sauvignon, 40% Merlot

Average age of vines: 15–18 years

Density of plantation: 6,500–8,500 vines per hectare

Average yields: 50 hectoliters per hectare

Elevage: Three week fermentation and maceration in temperature-controlled stainless-steel vats. Twelve months aging in barrels with 25–30% new oak and racking every three months. Fining and filtration.

RED WINES PRODUCED

Château de Rochemorin: 180,000 bottles

No second wine is produced.

Plateau of maturity: Within 3–8 years of the vintage

VINEYARDS (WHITE)

Surface area: 29.6 acres

Grape varietals: 90% Sauvignon Blanc, 10% Semillon

Average age of vines: 15–18 years

Density of plantation: 6,500–8,500 vines per hectare

Average yields: 50 hectoliters per hectare

Elevage: After cold settling, 10–15 day fermentation (at 18–23°C) in barrels with 30–50% new oak. Nine months aging on lees with regular stirrings. Fining and filtration.

WHITE WINES PRODUCED

Château de Rochemorin: 45,000 bottles

No second wine is produced.

Plateau of maturity: Within 2–5 years of the vintage

This is an up-and-coming estate in the commune of Martillac, one whose name is believed to have been taken from the Moorish expression for a fortified château. Many Graves observers feel the vineyard is one of the best placed of the appellation, sitting on high ground with superb drainage. The vineyard, however, remains relatively young, as André Lurton, the dynamic empire builder in the Léognan area of Graves and Entre-Deux-Mers, only acquired the property in 1973. Lurton has replanted the vineyard, which had become covered with large trees.

DE ROUILLAC

Classification: None

Owner: Marie-Claude and Jean-Paul Lafragette

Address: 33610 Canéjan

Mailing address: c/o Château Loudenne, 33340 Saint-Yzans-de-Médoc

Telephone: 05 56 89 41 68; Telefax: 05 56 89 41 68

E-mail: chateau-loudenne@wanadoo.fr

Visits: By appointment only

Contact: Florence Lafragette (Telephone: 05 56 73 17 80; Telefax: 05 56 09 02 87)

VINEYARDS (RED)

Surface area: 42 acres

Grape varietals: 60% Cabernet Sauvignon, 40% Merlot

Average age of vines: 30 years

Density of plantation: 6,500 and 10,000 vines per hectare

Average yields: 55 hectoliters per hectare

Elevage: Fermentation and 20–25 day maceration in temperature-controlled wooden vats with pigeages and pumpings-over. Malolactics and 14–16 months aging in barrels with 70% new oak and 30% one-year-old barrels. Fining and filtration not systematic.

RED WINES PRODUCED

Château Rouillac: 40,000 bottles

Moulin de Rouillac: variable

Plateau of maturity: Within 3–10 years of the vintage

SAINT-JEAN-DES-GRAVES

Classification: None

Owner: Jean-Gérard David

Address: 33210 Pujols-sur-Ciron

Mailing address: c/o Château Liot, 33720 Barsac

Telephone: 05 56 27 15 31; Telefax: 05 56 27 14 42

E-mail: chateau.liot@wanadoo.fr

Website: www.chateauliot.com

Visits: By appointment Monday to Friday, 9 A.M.–noon and 2–5 P.M.

Contact: Jean-Gérard David

VINEYARDS (RED)

Surface area: 29.6 acres

Grape varietals: 70% Merlot, 30% Cabernet Franc

Average age of vines: 20 years

Density of plantation: 5,500 vines per hectare

Average yields: 50 hectoliters per hectare

Elevage: Fermentation and 20–25 day maceration in vats. Eighteen months aging by rotation every six months in vats and in barrels. Fining and filtration.

RED WINES PRODUCED

Château Saint-Jean-des-Graves: 55,000 bottles

Château Pinsas: 35,000 bottles

Plateau of maturity: Within 2–7 years of the vintage

VINEYARDS (WHITE)

Surface area: 19.8 acres

Grape varietals: 70% Sauvignon Blanc, 30% Semillon

Average age of vines: 15 years

Density of plantation: 5,500 vines per hectare

Average yields: 50 hectoliters per hectare

Elevage: Skin maceration. Ten day fermentation and nine months aging on lees in vats. No fining, filtration.

WHITE WINES PRODUCED

Château Saint-Jean-des-Graves: 45,000 bottles

No second wine is produced.

Plateau of maturity: Within 2–6 years of the vintage

SAINT ROBERT

Classification: None

Owner: Foncier Vignobles

Address: 33210 Pujols-sur-Cirons

Telephone: 05 56 63 27 66; Telefax: 05 56 76 87 03

E-mail: bastor-lamontagne@dial.oleane.com

Visits: By appointment Monday to Friday,
8:30 A.M.–12:30 P.M. and 2–6 P.M.

Contact: Michel Garat

VINEYARDS (RED)

Surface area: 69.2 acres

Grape varietals: 55% Merlot, 25% Cabernet Sauvignon, 20% Cabernet Franc

Average age of vines: 22 years

Density of plantation: 7,000 vines per hectare

Average yields: 45 hectoliters per hectare

Elevage: Fermentation and three week maceration in temperature-controlled stainless-steel vats. Thirteen to fifteen months aging in 100% new oak for the *cuvée* Poncet-Deville and with 20% new oak for the generic wine. Fining and filtration.

RED WINES PRODUCED

Château Saint Robert: 120,000 bottles

Cuvée Poncet-Deville: 120,000 bottles

Plateau of maturity: Within 4–8 years of the vintage

VINEYARDS (WHITE)

Surface area: 14.8 acres

Grape varietals: 60% Sauvignon, 40% Semillon

Average age of vines: 12 years

Density of plantation: 7,000 vines per hectare

Average yields: 40 hectoliters per hectare

Elevage: Fermentation and eight months aging in barrels with 33% new oak. Fining and filtration.

WHITE WINES PRODUCED

Château Saint Robert: 32,000 bottles

No second wine is produced.

Plateau of maturity: Within 2–4 years of the vintage

LE SARTRE

Classification: None

Owner: GFA du Château Le Sartre et Bois Martin—Perrin family

Address: 33850 Léognan

Telephone: 05 57 96 56 20; Telefax: 05 56 96 59 19

E-mail: chateau.carbonnieux@wanadoo.fr

Website: www.carbonnieux.com

Visits: By appointment Monday to Friday, 8:30–11 A.M. and 2–5 P.M.

Contact: Eric Perrin

VINEYARDS (RED)

Surface area: 44.5 acres

Grape varietals: 65% Cabernet Sauvignon, 35% Merlot

Average age of vines: 20 years

Density of plantation: 7,200 vines per hectare

Average yields: 50 hectoliters per hectare

Elevage: Twenty-one day fermentation and maceration in temperature-controlled stainless-steel tanks. Fifteen to eighteen months aging in barrels with 20–25% new oak. Fining and filtration.

RED WINES PRODUCED

Château Le Sartre: 120,000 bottles

No second wine is produced.

Plateau of maturity: Within 2–8 years of the vintage

VINEYARDS (WHITE)

Surface area: 17.3 acres

Grape varietals: 70% Sauvignon, 30% Semillon

Average age of vines: 20 years

Density of plantation: 7,200 vines per hectare

Average yields: 50 hectoliters per hectare

Elevage: After cold settling, fermentation and 10 months aging in barrels with 20% new oak. Fining and filtration.

WHITE WINES PRODUCED

Château Le Sartre: 35,000 bottles

No second wine is produced.

Plateau of maturity: Within 2–5 years of the vintage

LA SÉRÉNITÉ DE POUMEY

Classification: None

Farmed by: Château Pape Clément (since 1995)

Address: rue du Professeur Bernard, 33190 Gradignan

Mailing address: c/o Château Pape Clément, 216, avenue du Dr Nancel Pénard, BP 164, 33600 Pessac Cedex

Telephone: 05 57 26 38 38; Telefax: 05 57 28 38 39

Visits: By appointment only

Contact: Eric Larramona

VINEYARDS (RED)

Surface area: 4.9 acres

Grape varietals: 55% Cabernet Sauvignon, 45% Merlot

Average age of vines: 20 years

Density of plantation: 7,500 vines per hectare

Average yields: 39 hectoliters per hectare

Elevage: Manual destemming. Fermentation in temperature-controlled stainless-steel vats with pigeages (four times daily until a density of 1,000 is attained, and then twice daily until the fermentation process ends). Malolactics and 18–20 months aging in barrels with 75% new oak. No fining, filtration.

RED WINES PRODUCED

Sérénité de Poumey: 6,000 bottles

No second wine is produced.

Plateau of maturity: Within 4–15 years of the vintage

GENERAL APPRECIATION

The luxury *cuvée* from Château Poumey, this 6,000-bottle offering is made by the renowned consultant Michel Rolland for proprietor Bernard Magrez. The debut vintage was 2001.

IMPORTANT VINTAGES

2001   A *vin de garage*, the 2001 La Sérénité de Poumey boasts super extract, ripeness,
90–92   and intensity as well as a multidimensional texture. Cropped at a mere 24 hecto-
liters per hectare, and picked very ripe, this well-balanced effort will be at its finest between 2005 and 2015. A revelation. Last tasted, 1/03.

DOMAINE DE LA SOLITUDE

Classification: None

Owner: Communauté Religieuse de la
Sainte-Famille (Convent)

Address: 33650 Martillac

Mailing address: Domaine de Chevalier,
33650 Martillac

Telephone: 05 56 72 74 74; Telefax: 05 56 72 52 00

Visits: By appointment only

Contact: Evelyne Brel

VINEYARDS (RED)

Surface area: 49.4 acres

Grape varietals: 40% Merlot, 30% Cabernet Franc, 25% Cabernet Sauvignon, 5% Malbec

Average age of vines: 30 years

Density of plantation: 5,500 vines per hectare

Average yields: 43 hectoliters per hectare

Elevage: Fermentations last three weeks in temperature-controlled vats—maximum
temperature 30°C. Wines are aged in oak casks (one, two, and three years old) for 15
months and are fined and filtered.

RED WINES PRODUCED

Domaine de la Solitude: 60,000 bottles

No second wine produced.

Plateau of maturity: Within 2–5 years of the vintage

VINEYARDS (WHITE)

Surface area: 12.4 acres

Grape varietals: 50% Sauvignon, 50% Semillon

Average age of vines: 30 years

Density of plantation: 5,500 vines per hectare

Average yields: 35 hectoliters per hectare

Elevage: Fermentations occur in oak barrels, 15% of which are new (the rest are between
one and five years old). Wines are kept on lees for 14 months and are bottled after fining
and filtration.

WHITE WINES PRODUCED

Domaine de la Solitude: 18,000 bottles

No second wine produced.

Plateau of maturity: Within 1–4 years of the vintage

LE THIL COMTE CLARY

Classification: None

Owner: GFA Le Thil—Jean de Laitre

Address: 33850 Léognan

Telephone: 05 56 30 01 02; Telefax: 05 56 30 04 32

E-mail: jean-de-laitre@chateau-le-thil.com

Website: www.chateau-le-thil.com

Visits: By appointment only

Contact: Jean de Laitre

VINEYARDS (RED)

Surface area: 21 acres

Grape varietals: 70% Merlot, 30% Cabernet Sauvignon

Average age of vines: 10 years

Density of plantation: 6,700 vines per hectare

Average yields: 55 hectoliters per hectare

Elevage: Fermentation (27–31°C) and four week maceration in temperature-controlled stainless-steel vats with pumpings-over. Malolactics at 20°C. Twelve months aging in barrels with 20% new oak. No fining, no filtration.

RED WINES PRODUCED

Château Le Thil Comte Clary: 40,000 bottles

Refets du Château Le Thil Comte Clary: 20,000 bottles

Plateau of maturity: Within 4–8 years of the vintage

VINEYARDS (WHITE)

Surface area: 7.6 acres

Grape varietals: 50% Sauvignon, 50% Semillon

Average age of vines: 10 years

Density of plantation: 6,700 vines per hectare

Average yields: 55 hectoliters per hectare

Elevage: Two day cold settling at 10°C. Fermentation and nine months aging on lees in new oak barrels, with regular stirring. Fining, light filtration.

WHITE WINES PRODUCED

Château Le Thil Comte Clary: 20,000 bottles

No second wine is produced.

Plateau of maturity: Within 2–6 years of the vintage

LA TOUR DE BOYRIN

Classification: None

Owner: Jacques Goua

Address: 41, cour du Maréchal-de-Lattre-de-Tassigny, 33210 Langon

Telephone and telefax: 05 56 63 18 62

Visits: By appointment only

Contact: Jacques Goua

VINEYARDS (RED)

Surface area: 29.6 acres

Grape varietals: 60% Cabernet Sauvignon, 35% Merlot, 5% Cabernet Franc

Average age of vines: 50 years

Density of plantation: 5,000 vines per hectare

Average yields: 57 hectoliters per hectare

Elevage: Fermentation, 21 day maceration and aging in vats. Fining and filtration.

RED WINES PRODUCED

Château Tour de Boyrin: 37,500 bottles

No second wine is produced.

Plateau of maturity: Within 2–8 years of the vintage

VINEYARDS (WHITE)

Surface area: 19.8 acres

Grape varietals: 70% Semillon, 20% Sauvignon, 10% Muscadelle

Average age of vines: 50 years

Density of plantation: 5,000 vines per hectare

Average yields: 57 hectoliters per hectare

Elevage: All of the wine is sold to the trade. No bottling is done at the château.

WHITE WINES PRODUCED

Sold in bulk to *négociants*.

DU TOURTE

Classification: None

Owner: Hubert Arnaud

Address: route de la Tourte, 33210 Toulenne

Mailing address: c/o Databail, 146, boulevard Voltaire, 92600 Asnières

Telephone: 01 46 88 40 08 or 06 60 68 40 08; Telefax: 01 46 88 01 45

E-mail: hubert.arnaud@cra.fr

Visits: Monday to Friday, 9 A.M. to 6 P.M.

Contact: Hubert Arnaud

VINEYARDS (RED)

Surface area: 14.8 acres

Grape varietals: 66% Merlot, 34% Cabernet Sauvignon

Average age of vines: 35 years

Density of plantation: 5,500 vines per hectare

Average yields: 40 hectoliters per hectare

Elevage: Fermentation and three week maceration in temperature-controlled stainless-steel vats. Sixteen months aging in barrels that are renewed by half at each vintage. Fining and filtration.

RED WINES PRODUCED

Château du Tourte: 25,000 bottles

Château Tourte des Graves: 5,000 bottles

Plateau of maturity: Within 2–6 years of the vintage

VINEYARDS (WHITE)

Surface area: 9.9 acres

Grape varietals: 80% Semillon, 20% Sauvignon Blanc

Average age of vines: 35 years

Density of plantation: 5,500 vines per hectare

Average yields: 40 hectoliters per hectare

Elevage: Fermentation and nine months aging on lees with weekly stirrings in barrels with 30% new oak. Fining and filtration.

WHITE WINES PRODUCED

Château du Tourte: 20,000 bottles

No second wine is produced.

Plateau of maturity: Within 2–6 years of the vintage

LE TUQUET

Classification: None

Owner: GFA Château Le Tuquet

Address: 33640 Beautiran

Telephone: 05 56 20 21 23; Telefax: 05 56 20 21 83

Visits: By appointment only

Contact: Paul Ragon

VINEYARDS (RED)

Surface area: 98.8 acres

Grape varietals: 50% Merlot, 40% Cabernet Sauvignon, 10% Cabernet Franc

Average age of vines: 25 years

Density of plantation: 5,000 vines per hectare

Average yields: 52 hectoliters per hectare

Elevage: Fermentation and 21–25 day maceration in temperature-controlled stainless-steel tanks. Twelve months aging in one- and two year-old barrels. Fining and filtration.

RED WINES PRODUCED

Château Le Tuquet: 90,000 bottles

Château de Bellefont/Château Couloumey-Le Tuquet: 120,000

Plateau of maturity: Within 2–5 years of the vintage

VINEYARDS (WHITE)

Surface area: 37 acres

Grape varietals: 80% Semillon, 20% Sauvignon Blanc

Average age of vines: 25 years

Density of plantation: 6,000 vines per hectare

Average yields: 52 hectoliters per hectare

Elevage: Fermentation at low temperature and aging in temperature-controlled stainless-steel tanks. Fining and filtration.

WHITE WINES PRODUCED

Château Le Tuquet: 60,000 bottles

Château de Bellefont/Château Couloumey-Le Tuquet: 40,000

Plateau of maturity: Within 1–5 years of the vintage

LA VIEILLE FRANCE

Classification: None

Owner: Michel Dugoua and sons

Address: 1, chemin du Malbec, 33640 Portets

Mailing address: BP 8, 33640 Portets

Telephone: 05 56 67 19 11; Telefax: 05 56 67 17 54

E-mail: courrier@chateau-la-vieille-france.fr

Website: www.château-la-vieille.fr

Visits: Monday to Friday, 9 A.M. to 7 P.M. By appointment on weekends.

Contact: François Dugoua

VINEYARDS (RED)

Surface area: 59.3 acres

Grape varietals: 70% Merlot Noir, 25% Cabernet Sauvignon, 5% Petit Verdot

Average age of vines: 35 years

Density of plantation: 5,500 vines per hectare

Average yields: 55 hectoliters per hectare

Elevage: Fermentation and 24 day maceration (32°C) in temperature-controlled concrete vats. Twelve to fourteen months aging in barrels that are renewed by a third at each vintage. Racking every six months. Fining and filtration.

RED WINES PRODUCED

Château La Vieille France: 30,000 bottles

Château Cadet La Vieille France: 65,000 bottles

Plateau of maturity: Within 2–8 years of the vintage

VINEYARDS (WHITE)

Surface area: 59.3 acres

Grape varietals: 75% Semillon, 20% Sauvignon Blanc, 5% Muscadelle

Average age of vines: 35 years

Density of plantation: 5,500 vines per hectare

Average yields: 55 hectoliters per hectare

Elevage: Skin maceration. Cold settling. Fermentation and 8–10 months aging in barrels with 60% new oak and regular stirrings. Fining and filtration.

WHITE WINES PRODUCED

Château La Vieille France: 10,000 bottles

Château Cadet La Vieille France: 20,000

Plateau of maturity: Within 2–6 years of the vintage

VILLA BEL-AIR

Classification: None

Owner: Cazes family

Address: 33650 Saint-Morillon

Telephone: 05 56 20 29 35; Telefax: 05 56 78 44 80

E-mail: infochato@villabelair.com

Website: www.villabelair.com

Visits: By appointment only

Contact: Guy Delestrac

VINEYARDS (RED)

Surface area: 79 acres

Grape varietals: 50% Cabernet Sauvignon, 40% Merlot, 10% Cabernet Franc

Average age of vines: 13 years

Density of plantation: 5,500 vines per hectare

Average yields: 50 hectoliters per hectare

Elevage: Fifteen to twenty-one day fermentation and maceration in temperature-controlled stainless-steel vats. Twelve months aging in barrels with no new oak. Fining and filtration.

RED WINES PRODUCED

Villa Bel-Air: 180,000 bottles

Tonnelle de Bel-Air: 20,000 bottles

Plateau of maturity: Within 2–6 years of the vintage

VINEYARDS (WHITE)

Surface area: 29.6 acres

Grape varietals: 42% Sauvignon Blanc, 42% Semillon, 16% Muscadelle

Average age of vines: 13 years

Density of plantation: 5,500 vines per hectare

Average yields: 50 hectoliters per hectare

Elevage: Cold settling. Fermentation and nine months aging on lees with regular stirrings in barrels with 15% new oak. Fining, filtration.

WHITE WINES PRODUCED

Villa Bel-Air: 60,000 bottles

Tonnelle de Bel-Air: 20,000 bottles

Plateau of maturity: Within 1–5 years of the vintage

GENERAL APPRECIATION

This estate is owned by Jean-Michel Cazes (the renowned proprietor of the Pauillac estate of Lynch Bages), and significant efforts have been made to improve the property and fashion high-quality wines. Recent vintages of both the reds and whites have demonstrated dramatic improvement. High quality combined with the fact that the world has not yet discovered Villa Bel-Air have kept prices low . . . at least as of 2003.

IMPORTANT VINTAGES (RED)

2001
88–91 A potential sleeper of the vintage, this deep ruby/purple–colored 2001 exhibits aromas of tobacco leaf, black currants, licorice, smoke, and earth offered in a sweet, expansive, elegant but fleshy style. It appears to be even better than the 2000. Anticipated maturity: 2004–2010. Last tasted, 1/03.

2000
88 A savory, complex perfume of tobacco, earth, smoke, dried herbs, and red as well as black currants jumps from the glass of this medium-bodied, elegant, soft, velvety-textured effort. Anticipated maturity: now–2010. Last tasted, 1/03.

1999
86 This light-bodied, attractive, tobacco, berry, and cherry-scented, well-made, elegant 1999 is best drunk over the next 3 years. Like most vintages, it is a blend of 50% Cabernet Sauvignon, 45% Merlot, and 5% Cabernet Franc. Last tasted, 3/02.

IMPORTANT VINTAGES (WHITE)

2001
90 A rich nose of orange skin intermixed with lemon zest, grapefruit, and honey is followed by a complex, medium-bodied wine revealing loads of fruit, subtle notes of wood, and a striking minerality. This beauty is a sleeper of the vintage. Drink it over the next 5–7 years. Last tasted, 1/03.

2000
87 Straightforward aromas of candle wax intermixed with figs, melons, and citrus are followed by a medium-bodied, monolithic, attractively fruity red to drink over the next 4–5 years. Last tasted, 1/03.

POMEROL

The smallest of the great red wine districts of Bordeaux, Pomerol produces some of the most expensive, exhilarating, and glamorous wines in the world. Yet Pomerol, whose wines are in such demand that they must be severely allocated, remains the only major appellation of Bordeaux never to have had its wines formally placed in a rigid hierarchy of quality. When members of the Bordeaux wine trade established the now famous and historic 1855 Classification of the Wines of Gironde, they completely ignored Pomerol and St.-Emilion, both some 18 miles east of Bordeaux on the right bank of the Gironde River. These areas had developed reputations for high-quality wine, but because travel across the Gironde to Libourne was difficult (bridges were not built until after 1820), St.-Emilion and Pomerol developed most of their trade with northern France, Belgium, and Holland. In contrast, the larger wine-producing estates in the Médoc worked through brokers in Bordeaux. In many cases, these firms, called *négociants,* were run by transplanted English, as well as Irish families that relied on existing contacts with the British wine trade. The 1855 classification was, in essence, a short list of well-known Médoc estates, plus the famous Haut-Brion in Graves. Why? Because these châteaux traditionally sold most of their production to Bordeaux brokers who then exported the wine to England. Since the brokers, who did little or no business with the châteaux of Pomerol and St.-Emilion until the late 1860s, were responsible for the 1855 classification, they were ignorant—or worse, self-serving—when they classified the top five dozen or so châteaux of the Bordeaux region.

Since 1855 the wines of St.-Emilion have been classified four times—first in 1954, with revisions in 1969, 1985, and 1997. The wines of Pomerol, however, have never been classified. This is surprising because they began to gain great popularity and notoriety in the late 1940s, after being highly touted by the well-known English wine buyer, the late Harry Waugh, who was then working for the respected house of Harvey's in Bristol. Their reputation has continued to soar to the point that many Pomerol wines are now in greater demand than some of the most celebrated Médocs and Graves.

While St.-Emilion covers an enormous area (with 13,434 acres under vine), Pomerol, its northern neighbor, is tiny, with only 1,939 acres of vineyards—less than the total acreage for the Médoc's smallest appellation, St.-Julien.

To understand the success of the wines of Pomerol, one must take into consideration the Merlot grape (the dominant varietal of the appellation), the changing drinking habits of consumers, and the influence of an empire built by Jean-Pierre Moueix and his two sons, Christian and Jean-François. First, there is the Merlot grape, which, according to the INAO (Institute National des Appellations d'Origine), accounts for 70–75% of the grapes planted in Pomerol. Cabernet Franc follows with 20–25% and the Cabernet Sauvignon with 5%. No other major appellation of Bordeaux has as much Merlot planted. Merlot-based wines are generally softer, more opulently and obviously fruity and lush, lower in apparent tannin, and higher in alcohol than wines based primarily on Cabernet Sauvignon.

Second, many modern-day consumers (and restaurants) seek wines that can be drunk at a younger age, so the wines of Pomerol have a ready-and-waiting audience. Most Pomerols tend to be ready to drink within 4–6 years of the vintage. Yet despite the early maturation of these Pomerols, the top wines retain their fruit and evolve extremely well, frequently lasting 15–25 years, with the legendary vintages sometimes lasting and improving for 40 or more years.

Third, no other wine region in France owes its success to a single individual more than Pomerol does to the late Jean-Pierre Moueix. This great man of taste and erudition passed away in 2003. In 1930, when he was in his early 20s, Jean-Pierre Moueix arrived in Libourne from France's Corrèze region, a desolate section of the Massif Central. He was regarded as an outcast by the aristocratic blue bloods who traded in Médoc wines on the famous riverfront street called the Quai des Chartrons. Moueix turned east to the viticultural areas the Bordeaux brokers considered an afterthought—Pomerol and St.-Emilion. His timing and luck were bad, however, for in the early 1930s the world was in the midst of a depression, not to fully emerge until after World War II. Yet, prior to the war, the young Moueix was smart enough to realize that the his-

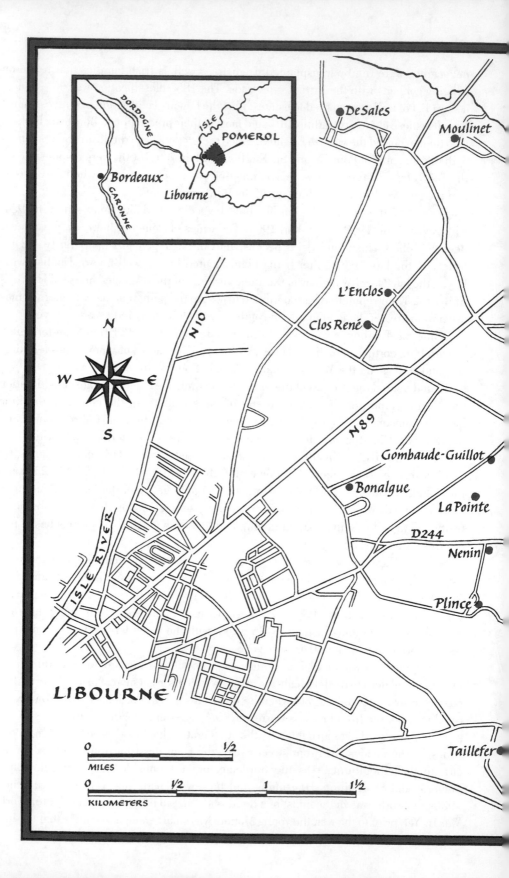

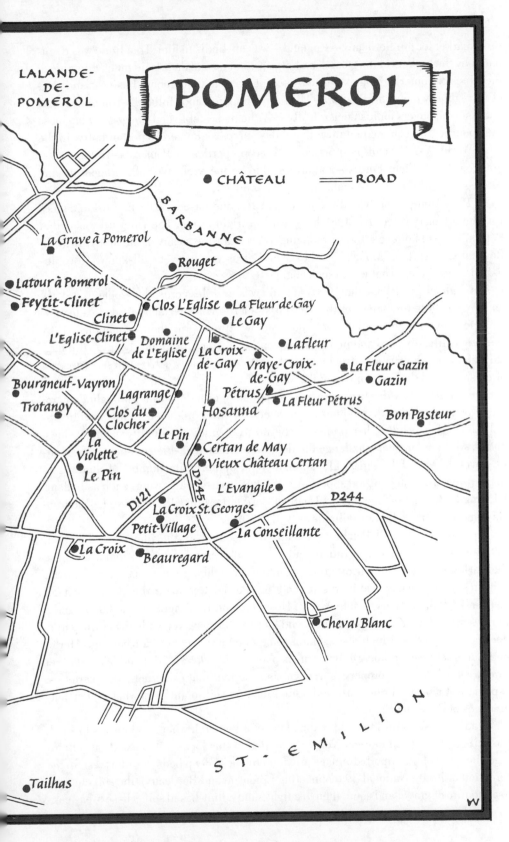

toric market for top Bordeaux—England—was off-limits to him. That trade was dominated by the brokers of the Quai des Chartrons, but no one there paid much attention to the wines of Pomerol. Moueix began by setting up a small merchant business and traveling regularly to northern Europe—Brittany, Belgium, and Holland—where he found enthusiastic buyers for his Pomerols. By 1937 he had established a *négociant* business in Libourne, the commercial town that today serves as Pomerol's port of entry. In the post–World War II years he purchased three properties in Pomerol—Trotanoy, Lagrange, and La Fleur Pétrus—and arranged to be the exclusive selling agent for any estate's wine where he was unable to buy the property.

In 1964 Moueix finally realized his dream and purchased a 50% interest in a vineyard he'd long coveted. By 2000, he was the outright owner. The vineyard was called Pétrus. Moueix believed it was producing as great a wine as any of the first growths in Bordeaux. In spite of Moueix's enthusiasm, Pétrus was not yet well-known in established wine circles. That would soon change.

Throughout the 1950s and 1960s Moueix was a tireless crusader (some would say an inexhaustible promoter) for the wines of Pomerol. His spectacular rise to a leadership position and accumulation of enormous wealth was, in short, accomplished by working extremely hard and producing exceptional wines, particularly at his two flagship châteaux, Pétrus and Trotanoy. In the 1960s and early 1970s, these two wines often surpassed the first growths of the Médoc.

The extraordinary rise to prominence of both Moueix and his wines brought Pomerol attention and prestige that did not go unnoticed by other producers in this bucolic appellation. As a result, other properties began to upgrade the quality of their wines. Today, while no one can challenge the domination that Jean-Pierre Moueix's firm enjoys over the sale of the wines of Pomerol, there is an increasing number of challengers to the previously uncontested superiority of Pétrus, particularly wines such as Lafleur, L'Evangile, L'Eglise-Clinet, Vieux Château Certan, Le Pin, Clos l'Église, La Fleur de Gay, and sometimes La Conseillante as well as Clinet.

The most celebrated Pomerol châteaux are located on the plateau of Pomerol. Pétrus sits on the highest elevation, and most of its acreage benefits from a soil base that is largely clay; the surrounding prestigious neighbors have much more gravel. Within shouting distance of Pétrus are La Fleur Pétrus, Certan de May, Vieux Château Certan, Le Pin, La Conseillante, Gazin, Hosanna, and L'Evangile. Immediately to the northwest are Lafleur, L'Eglise-Clinet, and La Fleur de Gay. Yet while these vineyards' deep, gravelly soils (which also contain some clay) are excellent for both the Merlot and Cabernet Franc grapes, only Pétrus is planted with 95% Merlot and 5% Cabernet Franc. Other Pomerol properties, recognizing the fact that Cabernet grape varieties, especially Cabernet Franc, are well suited for this soil, plant somewhat higher percentages of Cabernet Franc.

Heading west, toward the end of the plateau of Pomerol, where Trotanoy is located, the soils become even more gravelly. Properties in this locale often excel in wet vintages because of the superb drainage provided by these deep beds. Farther west, in the direction of Route National 89 (connecting Libourne and Bordeaux), the soil changes to a mixture of gravel and sand, then to a light sandy, flint-based soil. These areas cannot support the production of long-lived wine, but many soft, fruity, extremely pleasant and supple Pomerols are made in this sector. However, even the best of these wines will never have the strength, aging potential, or richness of the Pomerols from the gravel and gravel/clay/iron-based soils of the plateau.

For those familiar with the Médoc and Graves regions of Bordeaux, Pomerol—with its limited acreage and modest farmhouse "châteaux"—must come as a surprise. Pétrus itself is a remarkably humble building that truly stretches the definition of "château" to the limit. The appellation's largest estate, de Sales, is the only Pomerol property to have a building that could be said to resemble a Médoc château—and a modest one at that. The other three sizable vineyards of Pomerol are Nenin, Taillefer, and La Pointe. Not one of these three estates, however, could be accused of being in the top-league of quality, although Nenin's purchase by the late Michel Delon (of Léoville Las Cases) in 1997 was cause for excitement for Pomerol enthusiasts. Most of the best Pomerol vineyards encompass between 20 and 34 acres, but many are much smaller. For example, three current Pomerol superstars are true micro-estates. Lafleur, Clos l'Église, or L'Eglise-Clinet could sell their entire production within the Bordeaux city limits if they desired. None of these estates is larger than 15 acres.

What are the telltale characteristic traits of Pomerol wines? The dense ruby color, the intense berry fruit, plummy, sometimes truffle, mocha, and caramel-scented, ripe, fruity, often black cherry and raspberry-dominated bouquet, and a lush, voluptuous, almost unctuous texture—at least in the top vintages—are all hallmarks of a top Pomerol. Welcome to the glories of the Merlot grape.

As for the styles of wine produced in Pomerol, generally these are Bordeaux's most gentle, smooth, silky, lush, and richly fruity wines. However, that does not explain the diversity of styles that can be found; the individual producers do. At the top end, the overall quality of winemaking in Pomerol is extremely high, but once past the obvious stars, quality slips badly.

Pétrus is frequently claimed to be this appellation's greatest wine. Massively concentrated, rich, and long-lived in the 1940s, 1950s, 1960s, and early 1970s, Pétrus had few rivals for its concentrated, almost vintage Port-like style that characterized such legendary vintages as 1975, 1971, 1970, 1964, 1961, 1950, 1949, 1947, and 1945. Yet manager Christian Moueix (his brother, Jean-François, a significant *négociant* in Bordeaux, is the actual owner) and his ultraconservative oenologist, Jean-Claude Berrouet, began in the late 1970s to move Pétrus toward a more disciplined, polite, and elegant (some said Médocain) style. This new style of Pétrus rarely had the weight, unctuosity, and depth of the vintages that made this property famous. To my palate, only the 2000, 1998, 1990, and 1989 resemble, in a more elegant style, the marvels of the past. But lest anyone forget, the heavy clay soil that the vineyard of Pétrus still sits on results in a powerful, very tannic wine. Yet until the early 1980s Trotanoy was often indistinguishable from Pétrus in blind tastings and was clearly the most complete and demanded Pomerol (along with Lafleur) after Pétrus. Not surprisingly, Pétrus is made from 95% Merlot and Trotanoy 90%, and they are treated identically by the same Berrouet-led winemaking team.

Before 1976, the other Pomerol that had always rivaled, and in many vintages eclipsed, Pétrus, but is terribly obscure, is the tiny estate of Lafleur. Interestingly, Lafleur's vineyard sits adjacent to that of Pétrus on the plateau, and it, too, has extremely old vines that render small quantities of very concentrated, exotically flavored, highly structured grape juice, but Cabernet Franc gives Lafleur a totally different character than Pétrus.

If Pétrus, Trotanoy, and Lafleur have traditionally made Pomerol's richest, deepest colored, most massive wines, L'Evangile, La Conseillante, Petit Village, La Fleur-Pétrus, and L'Eglise-Clinet produce this appellation's most graceful, smooth, elegant, Burgundian-like wine. Prior to 1976, none of these properties could lay claim to making as massive or as rich a wine as Pétrus, Trotanoy, or Lafleur, but today Pomerol enthusiasts are likely to find some of these wines bigger and more concentrated than Pétrus, particularly L'Eglise-Clinet, L'Evangile, and in 1989 and 1990, Clinet.

L'Evangile and La Conseillante justifiably have two of Pomerol's finest reputations but have been irregular performers. La Conseillante was a notorious underachiever during much of the 1960s and 1970s but came on strong in the 1980s, making some of the greatest wines in its famed history. The 2000, 1998, 1990, 1989, 1985, 1983, 1982, and 1981 are decadently hedonistic beauties. L'Evangile has also been inconsistent. But when it makes superb wines, they rival the best of the appellation. L'Evangile made spectacular wines in 2000, 1998, 1995, 1990, 1985, 1982, 1975, 1961, 1950, and 1947. Given the fact that L'Evangile was acquired by the Rothschild family (of Lafite Rothschild), this property finally has the financial resources to challenge Pétrus, both in quality and price; the sumptuous 1995 and dreamy 1990 were starting points. Both the 2000 and 1998 should provide persuasive evidence that L'Evangile is worthy of Pétrus and Lafleur.

La Fleur-Pétrus has the right name for fame, yet it rarely seems to produce wines at a level its name suggests it could. With the acquisition of a parcel of old vines from Le Gay in the mid-1990s, this has changed. Historically, it is a very good rather than superb Pomerol, velvety, quick to mature, yet elegant and graceful. The 2000 and 1998 are glory bound.

Petit Village lacked the meticulous care and concern that comes from a committed proprietor. This potentially great vineyard began to make top-flight wines in the late 1970s under the guidance of Bruno Prats. Prats then sold the property, and Petit-Village improved in quality, with superb vintages in 1990, 1988, 1985, and 1982. More recently the wine has been very good but less consistent than I would have expected. At the time of writing, a proposed sale of this estate to St.-Emilion's wunderkind, Gerard Perse, was suspended indefinitely.

Since the release of their great 1985, L'Eglise-Clinet has been a rising superstar of the appellation. Historically, L'Eglise-Clinet has had plenty to boast about. The 1959, 1957, 1950, 1949, 1948, 1947, 1945, 1929, and 1921 are amazingly rich wines that have stood the test of time. Yet an undistinguished period in the 1960s and 1970s caused many to forget this splendid estate. Possessed with some of Pomerol's oldest vines, this traditionally run property produces an explosively fruity, densely colored Pomerol that always seems to taste like the essence of black fruits and minerals. Significantly, it is one of the few tiny Pomerol estates to employ a second wine for vats considered not rich enough for the grand vin.

One style of Pomerol might be compared to the "Médoc" wines. Two Pomerol estates, Vieux Château Certan and Clos l'Église, do indeed make wine with a high percentage of Cabernet Sauvignon and Cabernet Franc (rather than Merlot), and their wines often have more Médoc-like characteristics than other Pomerols. Vieux Château Certan has the greater reputation of the two, and in the 19th century and first half of the 20th century it was considered among the greatest Pomerols. The 1950, 1948, and 1947 are legendary. However, this property's wines passed through an uninspired period in the 1960s and 1970s that resulted in a decline in their reputation. That has been reversed since the 1982 vintage. The 2000, 1998, and 1990 are profound wines. Clos l'Église, a major disappointment under the management of Christian Moueix and his overly cautious oenologist, Jean-Claude Berrouet, was sold in 1997 to the Garcin-Cathiard family. In just one vintage, 1998, the new proprietors, backed by Bordeaux's most talented oenologist and taster, Michel Rolland, took a moribund estate and produced a compelling wine. That success was followed by additional triumphs in 2001, 2000, and 1999, making the failures of the Moueix era even more difficult to comprehend.

Another school of Pomerols produces wines that are light and supple and that offer immediate drinking. These wines rarely last more than a decade, but they do provide considerable value in an appellation whose wines are fetching higher and higher prices. Most of these Pomerols are located in the western part of the area on light, sandy soils. None of them has great a reputation, but several of these estates, particularly L'Enclos, Clos René, and de Sales, make complete wines that satisfy the palate, the purse, and the impatient.

There are numerous other Pomerols, and perhaps the greatest story of the 1980s was the emergence of such estates as Certan de May, Clinet, La Fleur de Gay, and Le Pin.

La Fleur de Gay was inaugurated in the 1982 vintage by Dr. Alain Raynaud, the proprietor of the well-known Pomerol château La Croix de Gay. It is very unusual in Bordeaux to see a proprietor take a parcel of his very best vines (in this case a plot of 100% Merlot located near Pétrus and Lafleur) and make a separate wine from it. La Fleur de Gay, aged in 100% new oak casks, is a wine of astonishing richness and exotic superripeness. One sip of the 2000, 1998, 1990, 1989, or 1988 will make anyone a believer. Ironically, the debut vintage, 1982, was a disappointment.

Clinet was another perennial underachiever until 1985, when the son-in-law of the proprietor, the late Jean-Michel Arcaute, assumed management of the property. In a remarkably short time, Clinet shed a cloak of mediocrity and started to produce wines that are among the most complex and profoundly concentrated of the appellation. This quickly became one of the titans of Pomerol, capable of challenging the very best. For example, virtually perfect expressions of wine were produced in 1990 and 1989. After Arcaute drowned in a tragic boat accident, Clinet was sold. The new proprietor is, however, serious about quality.

The other superstar to emerge during the decade of the 1980s is the micro-estate of

Le Pin. This wine, made from a tiny vineyard that is nearly 100% Merlot, is perhaps the most extraordinarily perfumed, hedonistic, kinky wine in Bordeaux. The proprietor, Jacques Thienpont, decided to make a wine in the image of Pétrus but even more exotic. The only question concerning Le Pin is how well it will age. Undeniably, it has become a cult wine for international billionaires willing to pay the astronomical prices this wine fetches at auction, and it is often cited as the catalyst for the "garage wine" movement in neighboring St.-Emilion. Moreover, the wine has aged better than its critics have acknowledged. None of the early vintages have fallen apart as predicted by provincial wine writers who seemingly live only to protect the status quo.

Other top-flight Pomerols include Latour à Pomerol, which has made some legendary wines (1961, 1959, 1950, and 1947), but has done little to distinguish itself since; and Le Bon Pasteur, an estate run by two of the world's most gifted oenologists, the husband and wife team of Dany and Michel Rolland. Two properties to watch are Nenin and Hosanna. Huge investments have been made at Nenin by the late Michel Delon and his son Jean Hubert. The early returns, particularly the powerful 1998 and 2000, look very promising. Hosanna represents the best part of the now defunct Certan-Giraud estate and is a micro-cuvée of 1,500 cases. The first vintage, 1999, was followed by even more impressive wines in 2001 and 2000. A potentially brilliant wine, Hosanna is the property of Christian Moueix, and Hosanna may be a much more accurate expression of his philosophy of wine than the wine he is most associated with Pétrus.

All things considered, Pomerol has fewer underachievers today than it did a decade ago. Nevertheless, there is no question that some of the larger properties, such as Taillefer and La Pointe, could make better wines. In addition, some of the lesser estates in the Jean-Pierre Moueix portfolio too often produce indifferent wines. It is a shame, since they are large vineyards by Pomerol standards and could provide a good introduction to the rich, fleshy, hedonistic wines of this appellation.

POMEROL
(An Insider's View)

Overall Appellation Potential: Average to Superb

The Most Potential for Aging: Clinet, Clos l'Église, La Conseillante, L'Eglise-Clinet, L'Evangile, La Fleur de Gay, La Fleur-Pétrus, Le Gay, Gazin, Lafleur, Pétrus, Trotanoy

The Most Elegant: Clos l'Église, La Conseillante, Gazin, Château La Grave, Hosanna, Lafleur, Latour à Pomerol, Pétrus, Vieux Château Certan

The Most Concentrated: Clinet, L'Eglise-Clinet, L'Evangile, Gazin, Hosanna, Lafleur, Pétrus, Trotanoy

The Best Value: Le Bon Pasteur, Bonalgue, L'Enclos, Château La Grave, La Loubière, de Sales

The Most Exotic: Hosanna, Le Moulin, Le Pin

The Most Difficult to Understand (when young): Clinet, Lafleur, Pétrus, Vieux Château Certan

The Most Underrated: None

The Easiest to Appreciate Young: Le Bon Pasteur, La Conseillante, Le Moulin, Petit Village, Le Pin, de Sales

Up-and-Coming Estates: Bourgneuf Vayron, La Clémence, L'Evangile, La Fleur-Pétrus, Hosanna, Nenin

Greatest Recent Vintages: 2000, 1998, 1995, 1990, 1989, 1982, 1975, 1970, 1964, 1961, 1950, 1949, 1948, 1947, 1945

POMEROL—AN OVERVIEW

Location: On the right bank of the Dordogne, Pomerol is banded on the south by the railroad line between Libourne and Bergerac, as well as Libourne, and on the north by the tributary named Barbanne.

Acres Under Vine: 1,939

Communes: Pomerol

Average Annual Production: 368,000 cases

Classified Growths: None; the wines of Pomerol have never been classified.

Principal Grape Varieties: Merlot dominates, followed by small plantations of Cabernet Franc and even less of Cabernet Sauvignon.

Principal Soil Type: Gravel with clay and iron dominates those vineyards on the plateau of Pomerol. Gravel with increasing amounts of sand is found in those vineyards that border Lalande-de-Pomerol.

A CONSUMER'S CLASSIFICATION OF THE CHÂTEAUX OF POMEROL

OUTSTANDING

Clos l'Église, La Conseillante, L'Eglise-Clinet, L'Evangile, La Fleur de Gay, Hosanna, Lafleur, Pétrus, Le Pin, Trotanoy
Vieux Château Certan

EXCELLENT

Le Bon Pasteur, Certan de May, Clinet, La Croix du Casse, La Fleur-Pétrus, Gazin, Latour à Pomerol, Nenin (since 1998), Petit Village

VERY GOOD

Beauregard, Bourgueneuf, La Croix de Gay, Domaine de L'Eglise, L'Enclos, Le Gay, Gombaude Guillot, La Grave à Pomerol (formerly La Grave-Trigant-de-Boisset)

GOOD

Bellegrave, Bonalgue, Clos du Clocher, Clos René, La Croix, Feytit-Clinet (since 2001), Haut-Maillet, Rouget, de Sales, La Violette, Vraye-Croix-de-Gay

OTHER NOTABLE POMEROL PROPERTIES

Beau Soleil, Beauchêne, La Cabanne, Le Caillou, Cantelauze, Le Carillon, Clos du Pèlerin, La Commanderie, Croix Taillefer, La Croix Toulifaut, Ferrande, Feytit-Clinet, La Ganne, Guillot, Guillot Clauzel, Grand Moulinet, Grange-Neuve, Haut Cloquet,

Haut Ferrand, Lafleur-Gazin, Lafleur du Roy, Lagrange, La Loubière, Mazeyres, Montviel, Moulinet, Nouvelle Église, La Patache, Plince, Plincette, La Pointe, Pont-Cloquet, Prieurs de la Commanderie, La Renaissance, Reve d'Or, La Rose Figeac, Saint-Pierre, Tailhas, Taillefer, Thibeaud-Maillet, Valois, Vieux Maillet, Vieux Château Ferron

BEAUREGARD

Owner: Foncier Vignobles

Address: 33500 Pomerol

Telephone: 05 57 51 13 36; Telefax: 05 57 25 09 55

E-mail: pomerol@chateau-beauregard.com

Website: www.chateau-beauregard.com

Visits: Monday to Friday 9 A.M.–noon and 2–5 P.M.

Contact: Vincent Priou

VINEYARDS

Surface area: 43.2 acres

Grape varietals: 70% Merlot, 30% Cabernet Franc

Average age of vines: 30 years

Density of plantation: 6,000 vines per hectare

Average yields: 43 hectoliters per hectare

Elevage: Three to five week fermentation and maceration in temperature-controlled stainless steel vats. A proportion of the wine undergoes malolactics (at 20° C) in barrel. Sixteen to 22 months aging in barrel with 60–80% new oak. Fining with egg whites if necessary, no filtration.

WINES PRODUCED

Château Beauregard: 60,000 bottles

Le Benjamin de Beauregard: 30,000 bottles

Plateau of maturity: Within 5–12 years of the vintage

GENERAL APPRECIATION

Never one of the biggest or most concentrated Pomerols, Beauregard is good as opposed to great. Soundly made with a low-key profile, it is reliable, typical of its appellation in terms of roundness, fruitiness, and early accessibility. However, because of its relative lightness, it is a candidate for near-term consumption rather than for long-term aging. Beauregard is one of the most realistically priced Pomerols.

As one leaves the tiny village of Catusseau, the vineyards of Beauregard are situated on the southern perimeter of the plateau of Pomerol. This is one of the few properties in the appellation that actually has a building grand enough to be called a château. The vineyard has significant potential. Most Pomerol observers consider the deep, gravelly soil to be ideal for producing high-quality wine. Until the mid-1980s, most of the vintages produced quick-to-age, rustic wines. Since, Beauregard has been making finer wine, with better color and more ripeness and concentration. Moreover, greater attention is also being paid to sanitary conditions in the cellar. The Clauzel family sold the property in 1991 to Crédit Foncier de France, and the progression in quality has continued under administrator Michel Garat and his oenologist, Vincent Priou.

IMPORTANT VINTAGES

2001
86–87
A low-acid, deep ruby–colored effort, the 2001 Beauregard does not offer much complexity, but it possesses abundant fruit in its medium-bodied, forward personality. Although straightforward and lacking substance, it is a savory, round, sensual Pomerol for drinking during its first 10–11 years of life. Last tasted, 1/03.

2000
89+
This up-and-coming Pomerol estate has fashioned a potentially outstanding 2000 revealing the vintage's wonderful sweetness as well as a dense purple color, an opulent texture, a layered, concentrated mid-palate, and moderate tannin in the impressively deep, structured finish. It will require a few years of bottle age. Anticipated maturity: 2005–2016. Last tasted, 1/03.

1999
88
An excellent wine for the vintage, this consumer-friendly Pomerol exhibits a deep ruby color along with a sweet nose of cola, mocha, cherry jam, and new oak. The wine is dense and round with an excellent texture, a big succulent mid-palate, and a long, lightly tannic finish. It should be accessible very soon. Anticipated maturity: now–2014. Last tasted, 3/02.

1998
88
The deep ruby/purple–colored 1998 Beauregard exhibits a perfume of smoke, black cherry cough syrup, chocolate, and smoky wood. Thick, tannic, and medium to full-bodied, it will keep for 12 years. Last tasted, 3/02.

1997
87
Another sexy, open-knit, elegant, sweet, round, short-lived, but pleasurable Pomerol, the 1997 Beauregard offers abundant grilled herbs, toasty oak, and black cherry fruit aromas and flavors. Medium bodied and supple, it is ideal for drinking over the next 3–4 years. Last tasted, 3/01.

1996
87
Beauregard's deep ruby–colored 1996 reveals a sweet, jammy cherry–scented nose with noticeable strawberry notes. The wine is medium bodied, soft, elegant, and moderately weighty with hints of toasty new oak. It should drink well for 2–4 years. Last tasted, 1/01.

1995
87
An excellent wine, this 1995 offers an alluring deep ruby color with a smoky, vanilla, berry, chocolaty-scented nose. Medium bodied and ripe with sweet fruit, moderate tannin, and low acidity, this is a fine example of Beauregard. Anticipated maturity: now–2010. Last tasted, 11/97.

BELLEGRAVE

Owner: Jean-Marie Bouldy

Address: "René," 33500 Pomerol

Telephone: 05 57 51 20 47; Telefax: 05 57 51 23 14

Visits: By appointment only

Contact: Jean-Marie or Pascale Bouldy

VINEYARDS

Surface area: 20.3 acres

Grape varietals: 75% Merlot, 25% Cabernet Franc

Average age of vines: 35 years

Density of plantation: 6,000 vines per hectare

Average yields: 45 hectoliters per hectare

Elevage: Three to four-week fermentation and maceration in temperature-controlled stainless-steel vats. Fourteen to eighteen months aging in barrels with 30–40% new oak. Fining and filtration only if necessary.

WINES PRODUCED

Château Bellegrave: 35,000–40,000 bottles

Château des Jacobins: 8,000–14,000 bottles

Plateau of maturity: Within 3–8 years of the vintage

GENERAL APPRECIATION

While this estate does not benefit from the finest *terroirs* of the appellation, year in and year out it manages to produce wines that range from good to very good in the best vintages. Bellegrave is generally straightforward, lacking in finesse and complexity (is that due to the sandy soils it emerges from?), but it delivers sufficient fruit and roundness. Because of its lightness and sometimes lack of concentration, it is not meant for long-term aging.

The Bellegrave vineyard, located west of RN 89, on light, sandy, gravelly soil, produces soft, easy to drink, and easy to understand wines that must be consumed in their youth. It would appear that the proprietor, Jean-Marie Bouldy, has a sensible view of what he is able to achieve in one of the less promising soil types of Pomerol. The results are cleanly made, fresh, fruity wines with mass appeal.

IMPORTANT VINTAGES

2001 Dark ruby with an attractive bouquet of sweet berry fruit, caramel, as well as a
86   touch of vanilla, this medium-bodied, moderately tannic, vibrant, low-keyed, re-
      strained Pomerol is cleanly made and deliciously fruity. Anticipated maturity:
      2005–2012. Last tasted, 1/03.

2000 An excellent, beefy Pomerol, this dark ruby/purple–colored wine has depth,
88   medium to full body, a layered palate feel, and some tannin to shed. A substantial
      wine for this estate, it should age well. Anticipated maturity: 2007–2015. Last
      tasted, 1/03.

1998 Surprisingly soft and open-knit, without the power and tannin often present in this
86   vintage, this dark ruby–colored 1998 displays round, fruity flavors (primarily
      spice and cherries) and good weight, but not the overall charm found in the 1997.
      It will require consumption during its first 7–8 years of life. Last tasted, 3/01.

LE BON PASTEUR

Owner: SCEA Rolland

Address: "Maillet," 33500 Pomerol

Telephone: 05 57 51 23 05; Telefax: 05 57 51 66 08

Visits: By appointment only

Contact: Dany Rolland

VINEYARDS

Surface area: 16.4 acres

Grape varietals: 80% Merlot, 20% Cabernet Franc

Average age of vines: 30 years

Density of plantation: 6,000 vines per hectare

Average yields: 37 hectoliters per hectare

Elevage: Twenty-five to thirty-five day maceration and fermentation in small temperature-controlled tanks of 70 hectoliter capacity. Wines undergo malolactics in barrel. Fifteen to twenty months aging in 100% new oak. No fining, no filtration.

WINES PRODUCED

Château Le Bon Pasteur: 30,000 bottles

No second wine is produced.

Plateau of maturity: Within 5–20 years of the vintage

GENERAL APPRECIATION

Le Bon Pasteur is the property of Michel Rolland, the world-famous oenologist from Libourne. The style of the wines produced is unfairly controversial, but I suspect this has more to do with the man behind the estate than with the intrinsic quality of the wines. I consider Le Bon Pasteur one of the finest Pomerols. Irrespective of vintage conditions, it is always seductive (presumably because of its low acidity—a trait criticized by its detractors) and characterized by a round, rich, generous, and ripe fruit (cynical tongues argue this *sur-maturité* ruins the *terroir* character) and a close-to-perfect equilibrium. A must buy.

Le Bon Pasteur is the property of two of Bordeaux's most gifted oenologists, Dany and Michel Rolland, who have a laboratory in Catusseau. Additionally, Michel boasts a list of clients that reads like a Who's Who of Pomerol, St.-Emilion, and the other major appellations of Bordeaux. His fame is such that he has been retained as the consultant for many of the world's leading wineries, from Ornellaia in Italy to Casa Lapostolle in Chile, to the renowned Napa Valley treasures of Harlan Estate and Bryant Family Vineyard.

Michel Rolland's success, as well as the formation of an association of Pomerol estates called the Circle of Prestige of Pomerol, has given rise to two prevailing schools of thought about harvest dates and winemaking philosophies. One school—represented by the firm of Jean-Pierre Moueix and its two leading spokespeople, Christian Moueix and their cautious oenologist, Jean-Claude Berrouet—believes that the Merlot grape should not be picked too late. Their argument is that early harvesting is essential to preserve the wine's stability and acidity. Furthermore, Moueix and Berrouet believe in shorter maceration periods to give the wines more elegance. At times, Berrouet seems almost fearful of too much flavor or hedonistic qualities in wine.

In contrast, Michel Rolland and his colleagues believe in harvesting as late as possible in order to obtain fruit that has an element of *sur-maturité* (overripeness). Rolland also believes in extended macerations to produce wines of profound color, richness, and aging potential. There is no doubt that Rolland's philosophy has caught the fancy of some of France's leading writers, particularly the outspoken Parisian Michel Bettane, probably Europe's finest taster and wine critic. He is a solid defender of Rolland, who he believes possesses the philosophy necessary to produce extraordinary wines. Interestingly, three of Rolland's clients, Clos l'Église, Clinet, and La Fleur de Gay, are now turning out wines that can compete with Pétrus.

Coincidentally or not, Rolland's philosophy is winning more converts. Most of the hot shot gurus of winemaking in Bordeaux are true believers of Rolland. This includes Gerard Perse, Jean-Luc Thunevin, Stéphane Derénoncourt, Hubert de Boüard and Alain Raynáud.

The Le Bon Pasteur vineyard is not one of the best situated in Pomerol. The 16.4 acres are spread out in northeast Pomerol, near the village of Maillet. There are essentially two soil types, one gravel based and the other clay based, as well as lighter, deep gravel beds. Because of the extremely old vines, late picking, long maceration, and the use of 100% new oak, Rolland gets as much out of his vineyard as is possible. He made extraordinary wines in vintages such as 2001, 2000, 1998, 1995, 1990, 1989, 1988, and 1982. If the truth be known, the 1982, which remains celestial, validates Rolland's philosophy.

IMPORTANT VINTAGES

2001 A strong effort, Le Bon Pasteur's 2001 is nearly as fine as the sensational 2000.
91–93 An opaque ruby/purple color accompanies subtle notes of charcoal, mocha, and black cherry liqueur intermixed with plums and blackberries. This ripe, impressively textured, low-acid, vibrant, well-defined Pomerol displays more uplift and freshness than the 2000, but less weight, mass, and power. A beautiful, elegant effort from this well-known overachiever, it will be at its finest between 2005–2016. Last tasted, 1/03.

2000 Undeniably the finest Le Bon Pasteur since both the 1998 and 1982, the 2000 ex-
94 hibits notes of roasted herbs, crème de cassis, cherry liqueur, new oak, and mocha. Powerful and intense, with moderately high tannin, a layered mid-palate, beautiful sweetness, and well-integrated wood, this low-acid, large-scaled effort is a brilliant wine from a *terroir* that can only produce wines of such quality because of the talents and efforts of the proprietors. Anticipated maturity: 2006–2017. Last tasted, 1/03.

1999 A superb effort for the vintage, Le Bon Pasteur has produced a dense, ruby/
90+ purple-colored wine with an intriguing perfume of espresso, sweet vanilla, and black cherry jam. Powerful and concentrated for a 1999, this medium- to full-bodied, moderately tannic Pomerol is atypically structured with plenty of grip, length, and intensity. Anticipated maturity: 2005–2016. Last tasted, 3/02.

1998 Undoubtedly one of the finest Le Bon Pasteurs (along with the 2000, 1990, and
92   1982), the dense purple–colored 1998 boasts a beautifully rich, complex perfume
      of blackberries, plums, lead pencil, cherries, mocha, and caramel. Powerful and
      rich, with a multilayered texture and an opulent, viscous finish revealing enough
      sweet tannin for definition, this is a terrific, full-bodied, seamless effort. Antici-
      pated maturity: now–2016. Last tasted, 3/02.

1997 Readers looking for a delicious chocolate, smoky, cherry, black currant, and
88   plum-scented and flavored wine will admire the fleshy, open-knit, medium-bodied
      1997 Le Bon Pasteur. Seamless and smooth, with surprisingly fine concentration,
      it is reminiscent of a 1987, but with more muscle and richness. Drink it over the
      next 5–6 years. Last tasted, 1/01.

1996 Le Bon Pasteur's 1996 reveals dry, slightly gritty tannin in the finish, which kept
88   my score more conservative. It exhibits spicy new oak, medium body, abundant
      smoky, black cherry, and mocha-tinged fruit, good weight, excellent purity, and a
      firm, structured, muscular finish. This wine should evolve nicely for 7–8 years.
      Last tasted, 3/00.

1995 This wine offers a dark plum color and high-quality aromatics consisting of toast,
90   lead pencil, mocha, smoke, and black cherry and currant fruit. In the mouth, this
      is a sweet, medium-bodied, round, spicy, succulently textured Le Bon Pasteur
      with a plump, fleshy finish that lasts at least 25 seconds. Anticipated maturity:
      now–2015. Last tasted, 10/02.

1994 A telltale Merlot/Pomerol nose of mocha, chocolate, tobacco, and sweet black
89   cherry/plummy fruit is followed by a medium-bodied wine with moderate tannin,
      excellent purity, outstanding richness, and a sweet finish. Anticipated maturity:
      now–2012. Last tasted, 1/97.

1990 For current drinking, this is one of my favorite Le Bon Pasteurs. It has put on
92   weight in the bottle and now exhibits a dark plum/garnet color with a bit of light-
      ening at the edge. The huge, almost intoxicating nose of fruitcake and sweet,
      jammy, red and black fruits intermixed with mocha and caramel soars from the
      glass. In the mouth notes of espresso are joined with a concoction of fruit that is
      full-bodied, loaded with glycerin, and very succulent, fleshy, and hedonistic. It is
      a wine of considerable pleasure, yet it seems to be becoming delineated and com-
      plex as it ages. Anticipated maturity: now–2010. Last tasted, 6/02.

1989 This wine has reached full maturity very quickly. The wine shows some amber at
89   the edge, with a sweet nose of roasted coffee intermixed with caramel, mocha,
      black cherry, and tobacco. The wine is medium bodied and beautifully sweet and
      fleshy on the attack, but then narrows out ever so slightly in the mouth. There re-
      mains some tannin to be resolved. Anticipated maturity: now–2014. Last tasted,
      12/02.

1988 A very powerful Le Bon Pasteur with more obvious tannin than most vintages, this
89   nicely structured, still surprisingly youthful wine shows notes of cigar smoke in-
      termixed with mocha, caramel, coffee, earth, truffle, and black cherry. The wine is
      still relatively dense and garnet in color, with no lightening at the edge. Medium
      bodied with firm tannin in a more structured and muscular style than most Le Bon
      Pasteurs, this wine can be drunk now but promises to age easily for at least another
      decade. Anticipated maturity: now–2018. Last tasted, 6/02.

1986 Close to full maturity, this effort is more sinewy and austere than most Le Bon
87   Pasteurs, but has a complex nose of cola, herbs, coffee, and sweet kirsch. The wine
      is medium bodied, slightly edgy, with some dry tannins noticeable in the finish. I
      expect this wine will not get any better, although it certainly has the structure to
      last for at least another decade. Anticipated maturity: now–2010. Last tasted,
      6/02.

1985
86 Starting to show some cracks around the edges, this Le Bon Pasteur has considerable amber at the edge of its dark ruby/garnet color. The wine has an herbaceous nose intermixed with cedar wood, sweet plums, prunes, and cherries. The wine is medium bodied, and shows some elements of dilution in the finish, which is a bit thin and attenuated. Drink it up. Last tasted, 6/02.

1983
85? In decline, this wine is showing notes of ashtray, dried earth, smoke, and damp earth. Mushroomy notes have also become apparent, and the wine seems to be losing its fruit at a relatively accelerated pace. This medium-bodied, somewhat attenuated wine is showing increasing evidence of desiccation. It needs to be drunk up. Last tasted, 6/02.

1982
94 Consistently one of the most magnificent 1982s in the vintage that brought Le Bon Pasteur and Michel Rolland to the world stage, this wine, last tasted at a blind tasting in October 2002, was spectacular and was the group favorite over some of the top wines of the vintage. I had the wine on seven occasions in 2002, since it was the 20th anniversary of the vintage and there were many, many 1982 tastings. I thought the wine had hit its peak, and I still believe that, but the wine continues to amaze me with its vibrancy and freshness. The color is a dark garnet with some amber creeping in at the edge. The nose is simply spectacular, an ice-cream fountain smorgasbord of roasted nuts, chocolate, mocha, toffee, and sweet black cherries, plums, and currants intermixed with spice box and cedar. It is very full-bodied, expansive, opulent, and lush, yet light on its feet. This wine is a spectacular confirmation of the winemaking philosophy of Michel Rolland and his wife, Dany. Out of magnum and larger formats, I am sure this wine can go on for another 15 or more years, but I still would not tempt fate—I am assuming that every time I have had it, it has been from pristinely stored bottles. Anticipated maturity: now–2010. Last tasted, 10/02.

BONALGUE

Owner: Pierre Bourotte

Address: Rue de Bonalgue, 33500 Libourne

Mailing address: Pierre Bourotte SA, BP 79, 6é, quai du Priourat, 33502 Libourne

Telephone: 05 57 51 62 17; Telefax: 05 57 51 28 28

E-mail: jeanbaptiste.audy@wanadoo.fr

Visits: By appointment only

Contact: Pierre Bourotte

VINEYARDS

Surface area: 16 acres

Grape varietals: 85% Merlot, 15% Cabernet Franc

Average age of vines: 25 years

Density of plantation: 6,000 vines per hectare

Average yields: 48 hectoliters per hectare

Elevage: Four-week fermentation and maceration in temperature-controlled stainless-steel vats. Fifteen to sixteen months aging in barrels with 50–60% new oak. Fining and filtration.

WINES PRODUCED

Château Bonalgue: 28,000–30,000 bottles

Château Burgrave: 9,000 bottles

Plateau of maturity: Within 4–10 years of the vintage

GENERAL APPRECIATION

Bonalgue is always good and soundly made. Made in a lighter style, it offers sweet fruit and presents an elegant character that makes up for its lack of complexity. In view of its reasonable pricing, it qualifies as one of the best bargains in Pomerol.

Bonalgue remains a relatively obscure Pomerol, but the quality is consistently sound and, in top vintages, very good. The vineyard, situated on a mixture of gravelly and sandy soil just at the entrance of Libourne, behind the racetrack on RN 89, turns out deeply colored, chunky, fleshy wines that lack complexity, but not character, fruit, or mouth-filling pleasure. Proprietor Pierre Bourotte is one of Pomerol's consummate gentlemen; he is also the owner of Clos du Clocher.

IMPORTANT VINTAGES

2001 Another excellent effort from this perennial reasonably priced overachiever, the
87–89 plump, fat, juicy 2001 Bonalgue exhibits a saturated ruby/purple color as well as sweet mocha and black cherry liqueur-like aromas, a layered attack, and sweet tannin in the finish. This luscious sleeper of the vintage will drink well during its first 10–12 years of life. Last tasted, 1/03.

2000 The 2000 may be the finest wine this estate has produced. Its dense purple color is
89 accompanied by aromas of figs, blackberries, and cherries, low acidity, a voluptuous texture, and excellent concentration. There are no hard edges in this seamless, bigger than usual Bonalgue. Anticipated maturity: now–2014. Last tasted, 1/03.

1999 A very good effort, the deep ruby/purple–colored 1999 Bonalgue offers mocha-
87 infused, sweet black cherry fruit, low acidity, excellent texture, and a plump, fleshy finish. It is expressive as well as hedonistic. Anticipated maturity: now–2009. Last tasted, 1/03.

1998 Deep ruby/purple–colored, with a ripe nose of black cherries, earth, underbrush,
87 smoke, and mocha, the 1998 is dense, chewy, and succulent, with oodles of fruit as well as glycerin. A fleshy, up-front character will provide appeal over the next eight years. Last tasted, 3/02.

1997 A jammy, prune, raisiny, sweet cherry–scented bouquet jumps from the glass of
86 this medium ruby–colored wine. Attractive, soft, and diffuse, this medium-bodied effort requires consumption sooner than later. Last tasted, 1/01.

1996 The 1996 is a well-made wine. It offers up a sweet nose of plum fruit intertwined
86 with cherries. Sweet fruit, good fat, and a touch of oak give the wine a plump, savory mouth-feel. This is a charming, bistro-styled red with more depth and ripeness than many wines costing twice as much. Drink it over the next 3–4 years. Last tasted, 3/01.

1995 A dark ruby–colored wine with sweet, spicy, berry fruit and a roasted peanut–
86 scented nose, the 1995 Bonalgue is soft, round, and velvety textured, with low acidity and moderate weight. It is an attractive wine for near-term drinking. Anticipated maturity: now. Last tasted, 12/00.

BOURGNEUF VAYRON

Owner: Xavier Vayron

Address: 1, le Bourg Neuf, 33500 Pomerol

Telephone: 05 57 51 42 03; Telefax: 05 57 25 01 40

E-mail: chateaubourgneufvayron@wanadoo.fr

Visits: By appointment

Contact: Xavier or Dominique Vayron

VINEYARDS

Surface area: 22.2 acres

Grape varietals: 90% Merlot, 10% Cabernet Franc

Average age of vines: 40 years

Density of plantation: 6,000 vines per hectare

Average yields: 38–40 hectoliters per hectare

Elevage: Three to four week fermentation and maceration in temperature-controlled concrete vats with daily pumpings-over. Fifteen months aging in barrels with 40% new oak. Fining, filtration depending upon the vintage.

WINES PRODUCED

Château Bourgneuf Vayron: 48,000 bottles

Plateau of maturity: Within 5–15 years of the vintage

GENERAL APPRECIATION

The quality level at this estate has improved immensely since the mid-1990s. While Bourgneuf Vayron produced average efforts in the past (vintages prior to 1994 need to be considered with caution), it has come forward with a new style of vinification and now offers wines that are concentrated, rich, and generous, but also reveal a ruggedness and coarseness that the proprietors have not been able to tame.

Given the well-situated position of Bourgneuf Vayron's vineyard in the center of the appellation on the plateau just to the west of Trotanoy, it has always puzzled me why higher-quality wines do not emerge from this estate. The ruggedly impressive wines that have emerged since 1995 do seem to suggest better things. The production yields are reasonable and, when talking to the proprietors, it is clear that they pay a great deal of respect to a traditional vinification. This estate has been in the Vayron family since 1821. A property that is clearly on the rise, Bourgneuf Vayron merits more and more consumer interest.

IMPORTANT VINTAGES

2001
87–89 Although less rustic than previous efforts, the 2001 Bourgneuf Vayron is a well-endowed, rich Pomerol displaying an impenetrable ruby/purple color as well as huge fruit and body. The 2001 has it more elegance and charm than usual without sacrificing its blockbuster mouthful of Claret style. Anticipated maturity: 2008–2018. Last tasted, 1/03.

2000
89+
This wine lacks refinement, but for readers seeking an exuberant, rustic, muscular, robust, concentrated Claret, there is a lot to enjoy in it. The 2000 Bourgneuf Vayron has put on weight, but it still possesses brutally high tannin. However, the muscle, extract, and bigness are impressive in a powerful, unrefined manner. Cellaring may bring more sophistication and elegance, but for now, this is a dark and gothic wine. Anticipated maturity: 2007–2020? Last tasted, 1/03.

1999
87?
Dark ruby–colored with notes of scorched earth intermixed with Provençal herbs, plums, and chocolate, this medium-bodied wine is spicy and dense, with astringent tannin in the finish. If the tannin becomes better integrated without a loss of fruit, it will merit its excellent rating and last for 12+ years. Last tasted, 3/02.

1998
89+?
A dense, saturated ruby/purple color is followed by aromas of green peppercorns, plums, roasted meat, leather, tobacco, and black fruits. The wine is chunky, full-bodied, concentrated, and chewy, with tough tannin in the finish. If the green pepper component becomes better integrated and the tannin melts away, this 1998 will merit an outstanding rating, but patience will be required. Is this a wine for those with 19th century tastes? Anticipated maturity: 2006–2020. Last tasted, 3/02.

1997
87?
A strong, albeit rustic effort, this opaque dark ruby/purple–colored 1997 reveals herbaceous black cherry, earthy, licorice aromas, a tannic, medium- to full-bodied, chewy constitution, and less charm than most 1997s, but more weight, intensity, and volume. Let's hope the tannin will become better integrated. Anticipated maturity: now. Last tasted, 3/00.

1996
87+?
The 1996 has turned out well, although it is somewhat monolithic. The color is saturated ruby/plum. The wine has an earthy, black cherry, licorice, and dried herb–scented nose, medium to full body, and muscular, concentrated flavors with moderately high tannin. It is a mouth-filling, robust Pomerol to drink between now and 2012. Last tasted, 12/01.

1995
89
A sleeper of the vintage, Bourgneuf Vayron's 1995 has an opaque purple color. The wine offers a closed but promising nose of black cherries, raspberries, and coffee-tinged fruit. Packed and stacked, as they say in the vernacular, this medium- to full-bodied, powerful, mouth-filling Pomerol is big, bold, and boisterous. This excellent, decadently rich wine will be at its apogee until 2014. Last tasted, 3/00

LA CABANNE

Owner: Estager family

Address: route de La Cabanne, 33500 Pomerol

Mailing address: SCEA des Vignobles J.-P. Estager, 33–41, rue de Montaudon, 33500 Libourne

Telephone: 05 57 51 04 09; Telefax: 05 57 25 13 38

E-mail: estager@estager.com

Website: www.estager.com

Visits: By appointment only

Contact: Mrs. Estager

VINEYARDS

Surface area: 24.7 acres

Grape varietals: 94% Merlot, 6% Cabernet Franc

Average age of vines: 25 years

Density of plantation: 5,000 vines per hectare

Average yields: 48 hectoliters per hectare

Elevage: Cold maceration, three to four week fermentation, and maceration in temperature-controlled stainless-steel vats. After completion of malolactics, 14–18 months aging with 60% new oak. Fining, filtration depending upon the vintage.

WINES PRODUCED

Château La Cabanne: 54,000 bottles

Domaine de Compostelle: variable

Plateau of maturity: Within 5–12 years of the vintage

GENERAL APPRECIATION

In theory, the wines of La Cabanne seem to be soundly made, but in practice they often turn out to be disappointedly thin, overly tannic, and oaked, without the generosity of fruit found in the best Pomerols or from a Merlot-based wine. Despite these traits, this wine has its followers.

La Cabanne is run by the Estager family. In addition to owning Château La Cabanne, they also own property in Montagne-St.-Emilion (Château La Papeterie) and lease another estate in Pomerol (Château Haut-Maillet). La Cabanne, whose sizable production is distributed internationally, represents a solidly made, plump Pomerol that offers rustic aromas of dusty, cedary, plummy fruit, followed by a generous yet often coarse texture that can lack finesse and be overcharged with tannin and undercharged with fruit. Nevertheless, if never dazzling, it is a reliably made wine that can stand the test of time. The vineyard is highly morseled, but the château itself is situated in the heart of Pomerol, not far from the famed Château Trotanoy.

IMPORTANT VINTAGES

None of my tasting notes have ever scored the wines above 85–86, and therefore I have not included them in this book. For those who think I have been too conservative, they may want to take a look at La Cabanne's 2000, 1998, 1990, and 1989.

CERTAN MARZELLE

Owner: Ets Jean-Pierre Moueix

Address: 33500 Pomerol

Mailing address: c/o SA Ets Jean-Pierre Moueix, BP 129, 54, quai du Priourat, 33502 Libourne

Telephone: 05 57 51 78 96; Telefax: 05 57 51 79 79

Visits: By appointment and exclusively for professionals of the wine trade dealing with the firm

Contact: Frédéric Lospied

VINEYARDS

Surface area: 8 acres

Grape varietals: 100% Merlot

Average age of vines: 20 years

Density of plantation: 6,250 vines per hectare

Average yields: 38 hectoliters per hectare

Elevage: Twenty day fermentation and maceration in temperature-controlled concrete tanks. Eighteen months aging in barrels with 30% new oak. Fining, no filtration.

WINES PRODUCED

Château Certan Marzelle: 12,000 bottles

Plateau of maturity: Within 5–10 years of the vintage

GENERAL APPRECIATION

Judging by its short history, this estate belonging to the Libourne-based firm of JP Moueix has only two vintages to evaluate. It is vinified by the same technical team that cares for such stars as Pétrus, Hosanna, and Trotanoy, and the vineyard is well placed in Pomerol.

A new wine launched by Christian Moueix, Certan Marzelle comes from a parcel of the original Certan-Giraud vineyard. The finest section of that vineyard was renamed Hosanna, another parcel was sold to Nenin, and the third parcel was resurrected to create this 100% Merlot offering. Sadly, there are only 1,000 cases of this effort, which may be Christian Moueix's answer to the famed Le Pin.

IMPORTANT VINTAGES

2001 A crisp, cool-climate style of Pomerol, the dark ruby–colored 2001 has cherry and
87–89 red currant fruit interwoven with underbrush and herb notes. Medium bodied with good tannin and a well-delineated personality, this restrained yet supple as well as meaty Pomerol will need to be drunk early on. Anticipated maturity: 2004–2012. Last tasted, 1/03.

2000 The debut vintage for this 100% Merlot *cuvée* is strikingly precocious and sexy.
90 This, lush, soft, supple, disarming wine exhibits a deep ruby/purple color followed by a sweet, expressive flavors of cocoa, cherry liquor and a fleshy, full-bodied texture. This is a total hedonistic turn-on. Anticipated maturity: now–2014. Last tasted, 1/03.

CERTAN DE MAY

Owner: Odette Barrau-Badar

Address: 33500 Pomerol

Telephone: 05 57 51 41 53; Telefax: 05 57 51 88 51

Visits: By appointment only

Contact: Jean-Luc Barrau

POMEROL
Château Certan
De May de Certan
APPELLATION POMEROL CONTROLEE
== 1990 ==
Mme BARREAU-BADAR
PROPRIÉTAIRE A POMEROL (GIRONDE) FRANCE
PRODUCE OF FRANCE

VINEYARDS

Surface area: 12.3 acres

Grape varietals: 70% Merlot, 25% Cabernet Franc, 5% Cabernet Sauvignon

Average age of vines: 25 years

Density of plantation: 5,500 vines per hectare

Average yields: 40 hectoliters per hectare

Elevage: Four to five week fermentation and maceration in temperature-controlled stainless-steel tanks with frequent pumpings-over. Fourteen to sixteen months aging in barrels with 70% new oak. Fining, no details regarding filtration.

WINES PRODUCED

Château Certan de May: 24,000 bottles

Plateau of maturity: Within 6–20 years of the vintage

GENERAL APPRECIATION

This estate, which benefits from a remarkable situation, is extremely famous for its older vintages, especially those of the 1940s and 1950s. It also did well in the 1980s. After a slump in the 1990s, it now seems to be rebounding.

This tiny gem of a vineyard has become a star in the Pomerol firmament. Certan de May's vineyard is superbly located on the highest ground of Pomerol, right between Vieux Château Certan and Pétrus. For years the wine was made by another château, but since 1974 the present proprietors, Madame Odette Barrau-Badar and her son, Jean-Luc, have been responsible for every detail. The result has been a series of remarkably rich, concentrated Pomerols that make Certan de May one of this appellation's most interesting wines. That said, in the 1990s, Certan de May, for unknown reasons, became increasingly herbaceous and less concentrated.

There are a number of reasons why Certan de May has emerged as one of Pomerol's most promising wines since 1976. In 1976 the old wooden fermentation vats were replaced with stainless-steel. Additionally, the increasing responsibilities given to Jean-Luc Barrau have resulted in several decisions that no doubt account for the higher quality of Certan de May. This estate believes in harvesting as late as possible. Also, the extremely long maceration—nearly one month—insures that the wines are super-extracted, opaque black/purple–colored, and loaded with tannin for a long evolution. The use of 70% new oak casks seems to result in the perfect marriage between new oak and the ripe, concentrated fruit obtained by Certan de May.

However, this is not a Pomerol that can be drunk young. Most top vintages since the mid-1970s have needed at least 7–10 years of bottle age before they have exhibited a great deal of development. Sadly, the estate's increasingly irregular performance over the last 10–15 years must be considered.

IMPORTANT VINTAGES

2001
87–88
The 2001 is reminiscent of the 1988 Certan de May, but without as much stuffing, depth, and body. A deep ruby/purple color is followed by Médoc-like aromas of cedar, spice box, and black currant fruit. Medium bodied, with a low-acid, herbaceous character and ripe tannin, this elegant Pomerol will be at its peak between 2005–2014. Last tasted, 1/03.

2000
91
Aromas of sweet kirsch intermixed with blackberries, underbrush, and plums jump from the glass of this opaque ruby/purple–colored 2000. Full-bodied, moderately tannic, dense, and structured, this is the finest Certan de May produced during recent years. Curiously, it does not reveal the firm, tough tannin found in many top Pomerols. Anticipated maturity: 2005–2018. Last tasted, 1/03.

1999
87
This is a sexy, lightweight Certan de May with notes of tobacco, herbs, balsam wood, cherries, and other assorted black fruits. Although light, it is flavorful, accessible, round, and best drunk over the next 8–10 years. Last tasted, 3/02.

1998
86?
Essentially, this is a medium ruby/garnet–colored, lean effort lacking concentration. It reveals notes of herbs, saddle leather, spice box, red currants, and cherries, but readers used to the superb Certan de Mays from 2000, 1995, 1988, 1985, 1982, 1981, and 1979 will find it disappointing. Anticipated maturity: now–2010. Last tasted, 10/02.

1997
86
Toasty oak and soil/earth-like overtones compete for the taster's attention in this tannic, medium-bodied effort. With herb-tinged black cherry fruit and a spicy personality, this 1997 can be drunk over the next 2–3 years. Last tasted, 12/01.

1996
87?
This wine reveals an intensely aromatic, cedary, dried herb, and black cherry–scented nose, but its abrasive tannin level is troublesome. Although well made, it displays a gritty texture, medium body, and an angular, rustic character to the tannin. Anticipated maturity: 2004–2015. Last tasted, 2/01.

1995
90+
An impressive Certan de May, the 1995 exhibits a dense ruby/purple color and a moderately intense nose of black olives, cedar, raspberries, and cherry fruit intermixed with toasty new oak. In the mouth, the new oak is noticeable, as is an elevated level of tannin. Notwithstanding the aggressive vanilla flavors and powerful tannin, this wine has outstanding depth and a layered, concentrated style with considerable muscle and power. It is a big, backward, formidably endowed Certan de May that may turn out, along with the 2000, to be the finest wine made at this estate since the 1988, but patience is most definitely required. Anticipated maturity: 2006–2020. Last tasted, 11/01.

1994
87
Dark ruby/purple–colored with Certan de May's telltale roasted peanut, herbal, black cherry, curranty-scented nose, this wine is reminiscent of the fleshy, open-knit 1983. There is moderate tannin, but the wine is surprisingly forward, soft, and texturally appealing. However, readers must be willing to tolerate a strong herbaceousness to enjoy this 1994. Anticipated maturity: now–2009. Last tasted, 12/00.

1990
88
This proved to be a very quick-evolving vintage for Certan de May. Somewhat loosely knit from its early days, the wine now has a dark garnet color with considerable amber at the edge, and its aromatics suggest an open-air Provençal market with the addition of crème de cassis. The wine is expansive, low in acidity, and

very good, but hardly has inspirational levels of concentration or depth. The tannins are, as the French say, *fondu* (meaning melted), and the wine is not likely to get any better. It is such a renowned vintage, one would have hoped for greater concentration and intensity. Anticipated maturity: now–2008. Last tasted, 4/02.

1989

89

It has always been interesting to compare this vintage with the 1990. As the wines have aged, the 1989 has shown more and more dry tannin and structure, but like the 1990, essentially it lacks the great concentration one expects of a top property in a potentially superb vintage. An herbaceous nose intermixed with hints of tapenade, cedar, new oak, spice box, and red and black fruits is certainly complex and inviting. In the mouth, this medium-bodied wine seems close to full maturity except for the rather dry, astringent, tannic finish. I do not think this wine is going to flesh out or deepen in richness, so I would suggest drinking over the next 10–12 years. The color is still quite dark, but there is plenty of amber at the edge. Again, the sweetness of red fruit, predominantly cherries, intermixed with cedar, fruitcake, and a distinctive herbaceousness make for an attractive although somewhat Provençal aromatic profile. The wine is medium bodied with plenty of sweetness up front, but then somewhat attenuated in the finish with the dry tannin kicking in. Anticipated maturity: now–2010. Last tasted, 4/02.

1988

92

For a vintage that has significantly less acclaim than 1990 or 1989, Certan de May produced a far better, more concentrated and complete wine in 1988 than in the two subsequent years. Still a dense garnet/ruby/purple with no amber at all, the aromatics offer up notes of truffle, licorice, compost, cedar, black currant, and cherry. The wine is very concentrated, powerful, muscular, and still youthful, with good underlying acidity, firm tannin, and a full-bodied, concentrated feel. The wine has a firmness but not any astringency. This is certainly one of the vintage's most successful wines. Anticipated maturity: 2004–2016. Last tasted, 10/02.

1986

89

Excellent, nearly outstanding, the 1986 Certan de May has a dark garnet color with some lightening at the edge. A nose of smoked herbs, damp earth, truffle, licorice, hickory barbecue spices, and sweet cherries and currants is very complex. In the mouth, this medium-bodied wine is close to full maturity, but still retains more austerity than I like to see. The tannins are there and will probably never be completely integrated, but the complex aromatics and almost Médoc-like performance of this wine are impressive. The wine can be approached now, but still needs another several years to reach full maturity. Anticipated maturity: 2005–2015. Last tasted, 3/02.

1985

92

Fully mature, this hussy of a wine offers up very complex notes of new saddle leather, smoked herbs, black currants and cherries, sweet licorice, melted asphalt, and a hint of truffle. Fleshy, succulent, and delicious but fully mature, this dark garnet–colored wine has medium body, wonderful sweetness, and a very vigorous, long, fleshy finish. A silky-textured, delicious wine, it needs to be drunk over the next 5–7 years. Anticipated maturity: now–2010. Last tasted, 4/02.

1983

85?

Cracking up and losing its fruit at an accelerated pace, this medium garnet–colored wine shows notes of mint, tarragon, licorice, and sweet cherries, with rather annoying, damp, mushroomy, earthy characteristics in the background. In the mouth, the wine is disjointed, medium bodied, and showing some sweet fruit but an increasingly attenuated/desiccated finish. Drink it up. Last tasted, 10/02.

1982

92+?

I think most of the 1982s have not only lived up to the potential I predicted for them long ago, but they actually over achieved in terms of their youthfulness, completeness, and potential for extended longevity. There are a handful of exceptions. One of the most perplexing wines to taste continues to be Certan de May. I have had bottles that I would rate in the mid- to upper 90s and others that have barely hit 90 points. Of course, the most accurate tastings I tend to rely on come from my cellar, where I know the wine has been pristinely stored since it arrived in the United States. On that basis, this is a wine that is very dense, muscular, powerful, and rich, and just turning the corner in terms of maturity. It has been one of the most backward right bank wines of the vintage, and it seems to still have a considerable upside to it. The dense, murky garnet color with no lightening at the edge offers up a very complex nose of truffles, smoked meats, licorice, black currant, plum, and a hint of prune. In the mouth, it is full-bodied, extremely muscular, with high levels of tannin, a very firm underpinning of acidity, and a dense, very chewy mid-section and finish. The wine still seems to have plenty of tannin to shed, but at age 21, I would have expected more evolution and sweetness. This is undoubtedly an impressively endowed, full-throttle effort in 1982, but will the wine become as seamless and compelling as so many other top 1982s have? Anticipated maturity: 2005–2020+. Last tasted, 10/02.

1981
89
Still dense ruby with some purple nuances, this large-boned Certan de May seems almost atypical for the vintage, which produced such elegant, lighter weight wines. Notes of licorice, dried herbs, red and black fruits, and spice are presently followed by a medium-bodied, relatively vigorous palate with a lot of depth and intensity. Drink it over the next 10 years. Anticipated maturity: now–2013. Last tasted, 5/02.

1979
90
A brilliant wine from this generally unappreciated vintage, Certan de May's 1979 remains relatively youthful in its appearance (a dense, saturated, dark plum/ruby with only a bit of lightening at the rim). The wine has a sweet nose of truffle, barbecue spice, earth, and black cherry/currant fruit. Medium to full-bodied, with good acidity, moderate tannin, and a surprisingly long, layered finish, it is a very strong, vigorous, muscular wine that has many years ahead of it. Last tasted, 5/02.

ANCIENT VINTAGES

Since the last edition of this book, I have not seen any extremely old vintages of Certan de May. As I indicated in the last edition, the 1945 (96 points; last tasted 10/94) was a spectacular wine that still had 20 years of life left in it.

LA CLÉMENCE

Owner: Anne-Marie Dauriac

Address: 33500 Pomerol

Mailing address: c/o SC Dauriac, Château Destieux, 33330 St.-Emilion

Telephone: 05 57 40 25 05 *or* 05 57 24 77 44; Telefax: 05 57 40 37 42

Visits: By appointment only

Contact: Anne-Marie Dauriac (05 57 40 10 23)

VINEYARDS

Surface area: 7.4 acres

Grape varietals: 85% Merlot, 15% Cabernet Franc

Average age of vines: 45 years

Density of plantation: 6,000 vines per hectare

Average yields: 20 hectoliters per hectare

Elevage: Fermentation and maceration in temperature-controlled wooden vats. Wines undergo malolactics and are aged 18–20 months in new oak barrels. No fining, no filtration.

WINES PRODUCED

Château La Clémence: 7,000 bottles

Plateau of maturity: Within 5–18 years of the vintage

GENERAL APPRECIATION

This newly created garage operation is ambitious. It is too soon to predict whether the wines will live up to expectations. However, knowing the superb work proprietors Christian and Anne-Marie Dauriac have accomplished at Destieux, their St.-Emilion property, one can assume no effort will be spared to propel La Clémence to the top echelon of Pomerols. For the time being, the debut is encouraging, but prices are steep.

Produced from a vineyard planted with old-vine Merlot and Cabernet Franc (yields are a meager 20 hectoliters per hectare), La Clémence receives the full garage wine treatment. The 2000 is the first vintage that Christian Dauriac (Destieux's proprietor) has released.

IMPORTANT VINTAGES

2001
88–90　I tasted the 2001 La Clémence on three separate occasions. On two of them, I thought the wood was overdone and the wine slightly disjointed. However, there is no doubting the exciting levels of concentration, thickness, and richness. There is considerable substance, a layered, opulent mid-palate, exceptional purity as well as length, and loads of blackberry and cherry fruit, but the wood is aggressive and obtrusive. My instincts suggest lees aging will lessen the noticeable new oak. As it fills out and gains more harmony, this 2001 should merit a score in the low 90s. Anticipated maturity: 2005–2016. Last tasted, 1/03.

2000
91　The full-bodied, super-extracted 2000 La Clémence boasts a deep opaque purple color as well as a gorgeous perfume of sweet blackberry and cherry fruit intertwined with vanilla and spice. While long, concentrated, and powerful, it has not lost its sense of place or purpose. Anticipated maturity: 2005–2018. Last tasted, 1/03.

CLINET

Owner: Jean-Louis Laborde

Address: route de Feytit, 33500 Pomerol

Mailing address: 3, rue Fénelon, 33000 Bordeaux

Telephone: 05 56 79 12 12; Telefax: 05 56 79 01 11

E-mail: contact@wines.uponatime.com

Website: www.wines.uponatime.com

Visits: By appointment only

Contact: Eric Herguido

VINEYARDS

Surface area: 22.2 acres

Grape varietals: 85% Merlot, 10% Cabernet Franc, 5% Cabernet Franc

Average age of vines: 40 years

Density of plantation: 6,600 vines per hectare

Average yields: 35 hectoliters per hectare

Elevage: Thirty to forty day fermentation and maceration in temperature-controlled wooden vats of small capacity. Eighteen to twenty-four months aging in 100% new oak barrels. No fining, no filtration.

WINES PRODUCED

Château Clinet: 28,000 bottles

Fleur de Clinet: 12,000 bottles

Plateau of maturity: Within 7–18 years of the vintage

GENERAL APPRECIATION

Over recent years, Clinet has never attained the quality of the nearly perfect 1990 and 1989, but it continues to produce one of the finest Pomerols. The wine is generally difficult to understand and approach in its youth (it is extremely closed and tannic in infancy), but it reveals itself beautifully after some 5–8 years aging, when it shows nicely melted tannins and fully reveals the sheer generosity and roundness that characterize the best Pomerols.

One of the appealing arguments often offered for the quality of a wine is the notion of *terroir*, that magical sense of a vineyard's soil giving a wine a particular character. However, Clinet, which does indeed possess a magnificent *terroir* at the summit of the plateau of Pomerol (not more than one-half mile from such superstars as Lafleur and Pétrus and immediately adjacent to L'Eglise-Clinet), is an example where a dedicated man proved that the human commitment to quality can have greater influence than just relying on the vineyard's soil to turn out high-quality wine.

I am speaking of the late Jean-Michel Arcaute, who married the daughter of the proprietor, George Audy. In 1986 Arcaute assumed control of Clinet and in less than four years he took this perennial underachiever to the very top of the Pomerol hierarchy. How did he do it? First, the famed oenologist Michel Rolland was given full responsibility regarding picking dates and style of vinification and *élevage*. This meant that Clinet would be harvested as late as possible. In fact, since 1987 the vineyards of Clinet have been among the last harvested in Pomerol. Moreover, the use of mechanical harvesters, utilized first with the 1982 vintage, was discontinued. The results have been a 1987 that is probably not only the wine of the appellation, but may well be one of the two best wines produced in the vintage (the other being Mouton Rothschild), a glorious 1988, and compellingly great wines in 1990 and 1989. Arcaute believed in macerating Clinet for up to a month. He also reduced the onetime high percentage of Cabernet Sauvignon to just less than 15%. To the surprise of everyone in Bordeaux, the property was sold to Jean-Louis Laborde, who has quietly been rebuilding Clinet's reputation and the pinnacle of quality it attained in 1990 and 1989.

IMPORTANT VINTAGES

2001
88–90
While it would be a mistake to compare the 2001 with the great Clinets of 1990 and 1989, it is a strong effort from Jean-Louis Laborde. It possesses a dense ruby/purple color along with copious quantities of toasty new oak, blackberries, plums, figs, and cherries. The wine builds incrementally in the mouth, revealing excellent glycerin, a nicely layered mid-section, and medium body. Although it remains un-evolved and backward, there is a lot going on. Anticipated maturity: 2008–2020. Last tasted, 1/03.

2000
92
Tasted four times from bottle (two were corked), this wine is somewhat mono-lithic, but there is a lot going on, hence the high score. Its youthful disjointedness is certainly a thing of the past, as the wine now exhibits a saturated ruby/purple color and a pure nose of Asian spices intermixed with smoky black currant, rasp-berry, and blueberry notes with some wood in the background. The wine is full-bodied, pure, sweet, and dense, with a multilayered texture. There is plenty of tannin in the finish, but it is largely concealed by impressive quantities of extract and fruit. Certainly this is the finest Clinet made under the relatively new admin-istration of Jean-Louis Laborde. Anticipated maturity: 2008–2020+. Last tasted, 1/03.

1999
88
Clinet's 1999 is surprisingly accessible in the attack, but there is some firm tannin in the finish. The wine is medium bodied with notes of licorice, blackberry/cherry/currant fruit, some sweet but slightly rustic tannin, and an excellent, broad mouth-feel. The wine is well made but falls short of being exceptional. Antici-pated maturity: 2005–2015. Last tasted, 3/02.

1998
90?
Clinet often goes through a reduced, awkward stage following bottling. The 1998 reveals a dense, thick-looking purple color, as well as a closed bouquet. With coaxing, notes of damp earth, spicy new oak, truffles, blackberry, and plum fruit emerge. Dense with jagged tannin, considerable power, and a roasted, chocolaty character, this wine has not yet meshed together. Still monolithic yet less dis-jointed, Clinet's 1998 is a powerful and muscular wine that will ultimately deserve an outstanding score. However, patience will be required. Anticipated maturity: 2008–2020. Last tasted, 3/02.

1997
89
The 1997 Clinet has turned out well. Its exotic nose of truffles, vanilla, plum liqueur, black fruits, and Asian spices leads to a plump, fat wine with notes of cof-fee, coconut cream, and blackberries. Surprisingly dense and revealing more tan-nin than most 1997s, it should drink well for 8–9 years. Although a top success, it is one of the less pleasurable 1997s for current consumption. Anticipated matu-rity: now–2012+. Last tasted, 11/01.

1996
91+?
Much like its neighbor of L'Evangile, the 1996 Clinet is somewhat controversial. This is a backward, muscular, highly extracted wine with a boatload of tannin, thus the question mark. The saturated plum/purple color is followed by an aggres-sively oaky nose with scents of roasted coffee, blackberries, and prunes. It is somewhat of a freak for a 1996 Pomerol given its richness, intensity, and overripe style. Medium bodied and powerful, but extremely closed and in need of 2–3 years of cellaring, it will be interesting to follow this wine's evolution to determine if the tannin fully integrates itself into the wine's concentrated style. If not, it will have a slight rusticity to its tannin and structure. Anticipated maturity: 2007–2020. Last tasted, 12/01.

1995
95
Another provocative wine made in a backward *vin de garde* style, the 1995 Clinet represents the essence of Pomerol. The blackberry, cassis-like fruit of this wine is awesome. The color is saturated black/purple, and the wine is extremely full-bodied and powerful with layers of glycerin-imbued fruit, massive richness,

plenty of licorice, blackberry, and cassis flavors, and a thick, unctuous texture. This is a dense, impressive offering from the late Jean-Michel Arcaute. This wine should continue to improve for another 10–25 years. Anticipated maturity: 2006–2025. Last tasted, 12/01.

1994
90
Inky purple/garnet-colored, with an outrageously intense nose of black truffles, licorice, cedar, and black fruits, this phenomenally extracted wine borders on being too concentrated for its own good. This massive, huge wine possesses 20–25 years of potential longevity. The fruit's remarkable intensity and purity, as well as the liqueur-like richness and unctuosity, are something to experience. This is an exceptionally dense, massively endowed, controversial style of Pomerol that will reward those with patience. The tannins are strong, but so is the extract level. Anticipated maturity: 2004–2025. Last tasted, 12/01.

1990
96
More evolved than its world-famous sibling, the 1989, the 1990 continues to gain weight and stature every time I taste it. In a blind tasting, it is not easy to pick the difference between the younger, less evolved 1989 and the blockbuster 1990. The color is just starting to lighten a bit, but is still a saturated purple. Notes of smoke, chocolate, espresso, mocha, and blackberry and cassis jump from the glass of this full-bodied, splendidly aromatic, and prodigiously concentrated wine. It is compelling stuff. Anticipated maturity: now–2017. Last tasted, 9/02.

1989
100
One of the great modern day Bordeaux, the 1989 Clinet still has a saturated purple color and a sweet nose of crème de cassis intermixed with incense, licorice, smoke, and mineral. As the wine sits in the glass, more blueberry and blackberry notes emerge, intermixed with some toasty oak, earth, and spice. This spectacularly concentrated, full-bodied, multidimensional wine is the stuff of dreams. Anticipated maturity: 2005–2025. Last tasted, 10/02.

1988
92
The first topflight wine made under the late Jean-Michel Arcaute, the 1988 continues to evolve splendidly. Notes of espresso coffee, sweet blackberry, and cherry fruit intermixed with plum and currant jump from the glass of this medium- to full-bodied, very concentrated 1988. This is another wine from this vintage that has evolved beautifully and is somewhat of a sleeper pick, as the vintage remains, at least for a wine such as Clinet, underrated. Anticipated maturity: now–2012. Last tasted, 10/02.

1987
90
Approaching full maturity, this is one of the great sleepers of the vintage and a wine to search out on restaurant wine lists and at auction. Phenomenally concentrated for the vintage, Clinet's 1987 still has a dense plum/garnet/purple color and a gorgeously sweet nose of cedar, truffles, caramel, violets, black currants, and licorice. Surprisingly full-bodied, powerful, and concentrated, the 1987 Clinet seems somewhat magical in terms of the quality this vintage produced elsewhere. A brilliant effort. Anticipated maturity: now–2007. Last tasted, 10/02.

1986
88?
With relatively high tannin, there is a certain dryness and astringency in the finish of this dark plum/garnet–colored wine. Nevertheless, what precedes it remains impressive. The wine exhibits a big, spicy nose, with still some lingering oak intermixed with licorice, floral, and blueberry fruit. Medium bodied, with excellent depth but hard tannin, this wine seems typical of so many 1986s—still youthful and promising, but always in danger that the tannins will overtake the fruit. Anticipated maturity: now–2012. Last tasted, 9/02

1985
88
The first vintage in the turnaround in quality of Clinet, the 1985 has a smoky, earthy nose intermixed with black cherry, currant, plum, and a hint of prune. Fully mature on the palate, with sweet tannin, excellent ripeness, and broad, fleshy, almost herbaceous flavors, this low-acid, very ripe style of Clinet needs to be drunk up. Anticipated maturity: now. Last tasted, 6/02.

ANCIENT VINTAGES

Clinet's performance in the early 1980s (even including the great 1982 vintage), 1970s and 1960s was abysmal. One dirty, thin, unattractive wine after another was produced, making their efforts from 1985 onward even more impressive. The only persuasively great wine I tasted was a magnum of 1947 Clinet (96 points; last tasted 12/95). I suppose from a pristinely kept bottle, this wine would still be magnificent.

CLOS DU CLOCHER

Owner: Pierre Bourotte (Audy family)

Address: Catusseau, 33500 Pomerol

Mailing address: SC Clos du Clocher, Ets J.-B. Audy, BP 79, 33502 Libourne Cedex

Telephone: 05 57 51 62 17; Telefax: 05 57 51 28 28

E-mail: jeanbaptiste.audy@wanadoo.fr

Visits: By appointment only

Contact: Pierre Bourotte

VINEYARDS

Surface area: 14.8 acres

Grape varietals: 80% Merlot, 20% Cabernet Franc

Average age of vines: 25 years

Density of plantation: 6,000 vines per hectare

Average yields: 46 hectoliters per hectare

Elevage: Four week fermentation and maceration in temperature-controlled cement tanks. Wines undergo malolactics in barrels. Eighteen months aging in barrels with 60% new oak. Fining and filtration.

WINES PRODUCED

Clos du Clocher: 21,000–22,000 bottles

Château Monregard La Croix: 12,000 bottles

Plateau of maturity: Within 5–12 years of the vintage

GENERAL APPRECIATION

Very close in style to its stablemate Bonalgue, Clos du Clocher reveals a pleasant roundness and offers a rich fruitiness and medium-bodied style that makes up for its lack of elegance and finesse. In the best vintages, Clos du Clocher merits serious attention.

A terribly under publicized property (with a fabulous *terroir*) situated just south of the large church that dominates the landscape of Pomerol's vineyards, Clos du Clocher's 2,000-case production rarely makes its way outside Europe. The savvy Belgians remain enthusiastic buyers of this wine. The vineyard, planted with 80% Merlot and 20% Cabernet Franc, produces a generously flavored, full-bodied wine that lacks some polish and finesse but is quite attractive. Clos du Clocher consistently produces very Burgundian-styled wines with a silky, supple texture that offer considerable charm and fruit.

All things considered, this is a slightly underrated Pomerol that in top vintages can produce excellent wines. Prices, however, have never been inexpensive because the tiny production is gobbled up by the enthusiastic fans of Clos du Clocher. My instincts suggest that Pierre Bourotte, capably assisted by Ludovic David, will push this property into a higher echelon of quality.

IMPORTANT VINTAGES

2001
88–90 An impressive effort from this well-situated Pomerol estate, the 2001 Clos du Clocher offers notes of blueberries, black cherry liqueur, and cassis in its sweet, concentrated, thick personality. Additional complexity should emerge with further aging. Medium to full-bodied, nicely textured, low in acidity, and loaded with fat and glycerin, it will be drinkable between 2004–2016. Bravo! Last tasted, 1/03.

2000
90 One of the strongest efforts from this estate in many years, the 2000 Clos du Clocher exhibits a style reminiscent of some 1975 Pomerols . . . powerful tannin, dense concentration, and plenty of body as well as potential. A sweet, soft, surprisingly seductive effort, hedonistic and fleshy, with copious quantities of mocha and blackberry/cherry fruit in addition to a hint of caramel and coffee, this full, rich, supple wine is a candidate for two decades of aging. Anticipated maturity: 2007–2020. Last tasted, 1/03.

1999
87 This dense, opaque purple–colored Pomerol displays surprisingly tough tannin for the vintage, but there is plenty of depth to this nearly rustic effort. It possesses admirable texture, size, and concentration, but it will require patience. Anticipated maturity: 2006–2014. Last tasted, 3/02.

1998
88 A serious, structured, moderately tannic effort, the dense ruby/purple–colored 1998 offers aromas and flavors of black raspberries, cherries, plums, Asian spices, earth, and new oak. It possesses a fat, succulent mid-palate as well as excellent sweetness from glycerin and ripeness, and it will be at its apogee until 2015. Last tasted, 3/02.

1997
86? A somewhat overripe style of wine that is medium bodied and fully mature, with low acidity and some tasty fig, plum, and cherry fruit intermixed with hints of tea and tomato skin, this wine needs to be drunk up. Last tasted, 12/01.

1996
86 Fully mature, this mid-weight Pomerol has a medium ruby color with some amber at the edge, notes of balsam wood intermixed with dried herbs, sweet black cherry jam, and a hint of mocha. The wine has dropped most of its tannins and should be drunk over the next 2–3 years. Last tasted, 12/01.

1995
87 This wine still has some noticeable tannin, but shows more weight and richness in a more backward style than the 1996. The aromatics suggest full maturity, with notes of cola, espresso, caramel, and sweet black cherry and plum fruit. In the mouth it is medium bodied with good ripeness and moderate concentration, and it has some light tannins in the finish. Anticipated maturity: now–2007. Last tasted, 12/01.

ANCIENT VINTAGES

Since most of the vintages of Clos du Clocher need to be drunk relatively early, the best vintages that I have tasted, and I assume all of them are now either fully mature or just beginning to decline, are 1990 (87 points; last tasted 1/93), 1989 (88 points; last tasted 1/93), and 1982 (87 points; last tasted 10/02).

CLOS L'ÉGLISE

Owner: Sylviane Garcin-Cathiard

Address: 33500 Pomerol

Mailing address: c/o Château Haut-Bergey, BP 49, 33850 Léognan

Telephone: 05 56 64 05 22; Telefax: 05 56 64 06 98

E-mail: haut.bergey@wanadoo.fr

Visits: By appointment only

Contact: Hélène Garcin-Lévêque

VINEYARDS

Surface area: 14.8 acres

Grape varietals: 60% Merlot, 40% Cabernet Franc

Average age of vines: 33 years

Density of plantation: 7,100 vines per hectare

Average yields: 31 hectoliters per hectare

Elevage: Fermentation and prolonged maceration in temperature-controlled wooden vats of 60-hectoliter capacity with *pigéages*. Running off by gravity. Wines undergo malolactics in barrels. Eighteen months aging in 100% new oak. No fining, no filtration.

WINES PRODUCED

Clos l'Église: 15,000 bottles

Esprit de l'Eglise: 10,000 bottles

Plateau of maturity: Within 5–15 years of the vintage

GENERAL APPRECIATION

While Clos l'Église was a mediocre performer until the mid-1990s, it has rebounded beautifully afer its acquisition in 1997 by the Garcin-Cathiard family. This wine, which now stands as one of the most opulent of its appellation, is a benchmark Pomerol that can easily compete with, if not surpass, many of the stars of the right bank, including the likes of Le Pin and Pétrus.

The vineyard of Clos l'Église, one of the numerous châteaux in Pomerol with the word *église* in its name (because so many of the vineyards abut the large church that sits amongst the vines), is well situated on the plateau adjacent to that of Château Clinet. The entire vineyard is planted on a slope of clay and gravel with a westerly exposure. Until 1997 I had tasted some good vintages from Clos l'Église (1964 is a favorite); the relatively high percentage of Cabernet Sauvignon and Cabernet Franc formerly used in the blend tended to give the wine a Médoc-like austerity. In fact, it is this lack of richness and opulence in top vintages that causes it to come across as anorexic. In years where the Cabernet does not fully ripen, Clos l'Église can be herbaceous to the point of being vegetal. Under the new owners, the Cabernet Sauvignon has been ripped out in favor of Merlot and Cabernet Franc.

In 1997, the new proprietors hired Michel Rolland to make the wine, and the result has been a succession of brilliant wines from Clos l'Église. This transformation from ugly duckling to beautiful superstar makes the indifferent efforts of the last 30 years under the Moueix management difficult to comprehend.

IMPORTANT VINTAGES

2001
92–94 The 2001 Clos l'Église is a candidate for the wine of the vintage. An opaque purple color is followed by gorgeous aromas of mocha, plums, figs, black cherry liqueur, and espresso. Deep, multilayered, and textured, with extraordinary purity and palate presence, this is a stunningly rich, well-proportioned, extremely long (the finish lasts 30–35 seconds) 2001 to consume between 2007–2017. Bravo! Last tasted, 1/03.

2000
96 I am not sure the 2000 will ultimately surpass the 1998 (a staggeringly great effort), but it appears equivalent in quality. It possesses great intensity and massive concentration, yet is extremely light and delicate. The opaque purple color is followed by a prodigious wine displaying surreal levels of extract and richness as well as a phenomenally complex bouquet of blueberry liqueur, mocha, camphor, cigar smoke, new saddle leather, plums, and roasted nuts. Amazingly pure, textured, and voluptuous, with moderately high tannin in the finish, this knockout 2000 will be at its finest between 2010–2030. Last tasted, 1/03.

1999
93 A tremendous success for the vintage, the 1999 Clos l'Église is performing well from bottle. A stunningly complex nose of vanilla, espresso, plums, figs, charcoal, and black cherry liqueur jumps from the glass of this flamboyantly scented wine. In the mouth, it is all sex appeal, with silky, voluptuous flavors, sweet tannin, low acidity, and ripe, concentrated flavors. Drink it over the next 10–14 years; it might last even longer given its brilliant balance. Last tasted, 3/02.

1998
96 A classic Pomerol, the 1998 boasts a superb, complex bouquet of mocha fudge, vanilla, black cherries, roasted coffee, smoke, and berries. The dazzlingly explosive aromatic display is followed by a creamy-textured, medium- to full-bodied, beautifully layered wine with no hard edges. A supple texture leads to a finish with notes of caramel and spice that lingers for more than 40 seconds. This is a gorgeous, complex Pomerol. Anticipated maturity: now–2018. Last tasted, 10/02.

1997
90 One of the few stars of this soft, consumer-friendly vintage, Clos l'Église has fashioned a dark ruby/purple–colored, sexy wine with ostentatious aromas of mocha, fudge, coffee, and sweet berry fruit intermixed with toasty new oak. Medium to full-bodied and opulently textured, with low acidity, abundant glycerin, and lovely fruit, this is a triumph for the vintage. Drink this gorgeous Pomerol over the next 10 years. Last tasted, 6/02.

1990
87 The 1990 is the best wine in years from this estate. It exhibits an excellent bouquet of cassis, spicy new oak, and subtle herbs. In the mouth, it is medium bodied with an attractive ripeness, elegance, and a fleshy, surprisingly rich, long finish. Drink it over the next 7–10 years. Last tasted, 1/93.

1989
76 The 1989 is light, intensely herbaceous, and short on the palate. Anticipated maturity: now. Last tasted, 1/93.

1988
72 The disappointing 1988, which is similar to the 1989 but with less alcohol and body, should be drunk up. Anticipated maturity: Probably in decline. Last tasted, 1/93.

1986
81
Because of the vintage, the 1986 demonstrates more class and richness than the watery, lightweight 1985. Perhaps the late-picked Cabernet Sauvignon has given the wine more depth, but it still comes up short in comparison with other Pomerols. There is an attractive oakiness, but overall this is a lightweight wine that could use more flesh and muscle. Anticipated maturity: now. Last tasted, 3/90.

1985
78
I found the 1985 to be light, medium bodied, and elegant, but a little short on substance and length. Anticipated maturity: now. Last tasted, 3/90.

1982
65
Until the new owners got serious about quality, Clos l'Église was one of my least favorite Pomerols. The 1982 Clos l'Église has never exhibited much extract, intensity, or the trademark characteristics of the vintage—sweet, expansive, ripe fruit and an opulent, chewy texture. The wine offers light-bodied, vegetal, tea-like aromas presented in a spicy, diluted format. It is in full decline. Last tasted, 10/02.

CLOS RENÉ

Owner: Garde-Lasserre families

Administrator: Jean-Marie Garde

Address: 33500 Pomerol

Telephone: 05 57 51 10 41; Telefax: 05 57 51 16 28

Visits: By appointment only

Contact: Jean-Marie Garde

VINEYARDS

Surface area: 29.6 acres

Grape varietals: 70% Merlot, 20% Cabernet Franc, 10% Malbec

Average age of vines: 35 years

Density of plantation: 5,500 vines per hectare

Average yields: 45 hectoliters per hectare

Elevage: Three week fermentation and maceration in temperature-controlled concrete vats. Sixteen months aging in barrels that are renewed by 25% at each vintage. Fining, no filtration.

WINES PRODUCED

Clos René, 70,000 bottles

No second wine is produced.

Plateau of maturity: Within 5–15 years of the vintage

GENERAL APPRECIATION

Though Clos René has improved since the mid-1980s, it remains a lighter styled, open-knit, supple, and accessible Pomerol. The wine is good to very good, but rarely great. Prices are reasonable.

Clos René sits well to the west of the major châteaux of Pomerol, in an area that is just south of the appellation of Lalande-de-Pomerol. The wines made in this area tend to be open-knit in style, quite fruity, supple, and easy to drink. While the style of Clos René is no exception to this rule, I have noticed a perceptible change to a wine that is a bit bigger framed, darker colored, and a little more substantial and concentrated. Perhaps the counseling of Michel Rolland, the highly respected Libourne oenologist and proprietor of Le Bon Pasteur, has made the difference. Whatever the reason, there is no doubt that some vintages of the 1980s and 1990s have produced the best wines from Clos René in recent memory. Because it is not one of the best-known Pomerols, Clos René remains reasonably priced.

IMPORTANT VINTAGES

2001 This dark ruby–colored, medium-weight 2001 is deficient in substance/stuffing. It
86–87? offers a sweet bouquet of ripe berry fruit intermixed with herbs, wood, and underbrush. Although well made, it is superficial. Drink it over the next decade. Last tasted, 1/03.

2000 A potential sleeper of the vintage, this opaque ruby/purple–colored Pomerol ex-
88+ hibits black fruits, coffee, and praline characteristics with hints of sweet oak. Fleshy, with excellent richness and more structure than usual, it will be at its best between 2006–2017. Last tasted, 1/03.

1999 This is an open-knit, attractive, superficial but delicious Pomerol revealing notes
87 of mocha, dried herbs, black cherries, currants, and caramels. Round and medium bodied, it will provide delicious drinking now and over the next 7–8 years. Last tasted, 3/02.

1998 Soft, round, and medium bodied, the 1998 possesses copious quantities of black
86 cherry fruit, toasty new oak, low acidity, and an up-front, savory style. Drink it over the next 4–5 years. Last tasted, 3/02.

ANCIENT VINTAGES

Relatively straightforward wines meriting scores in the low to mid-80s have been the rule for Clos René in any good vintage of the 1990s, 1980s, and 1970s. The 1985 and 1982, probably in decline by now, were certainly wines that I rated better than that. The finest Clos René I have ever tasted was the 1947 (95 points; last tasted 10/94). It had a viscosity that was typical of most of the great Pomerols of that vintage. Any readers lucky enough to run across a well-stored bottle of this vintage will have a treasure to look forward to.

LA CONSEILLANTE

Owner: Nicolas family
Address: 33500 Pomerol
Telephone: 05 57 51 15 32; Telefax: 05 57 51 42 39
E-mail: chateau.la.conseillante@wanadoo.fr
Visits: By appointment only
Contact: Arnaud de Lamy

VINEYARDS

Surface area: 19.6 acres

Grape varietals: 80% Merlot, 20% Cabernet Franc

Average age of vines: 40+ years

Density of plantation: 5,500 vines per hectare

Average yields: 45 hectoliters per hectare

Elevage: Thirty day fermentation and maceration in temperature-controlled stainless-steel vats. After completion of malolactics, 18 months aging in new oak barrels. Fining, no filtration.

WINES PRODUCED

Château La Conseillante: 65,000 bottles

No second wine is produced.

Plateau of maturity: Within 5–20 years of the vintage

GENERAL APPRECIATION

One of the most characteristic Pomerols, La Conseillante is close in style to a grand cru Burgundy. This wine, which benefits from a sumptuous *terroir* that is not always fully exploited, can sometimes be exceptional. While some vintages lack concentration and structure, when La Conseillante hits the bull's-eye, it remains unequaled in terms of aromatic power and elegance. It remains an expensive Pomerol.

A very highly regarded Pomerol estate, La Conseillante produces some of this appellation's most elegant, lush, and delicious wines. On the negative side, many of the vintages during the 1970s had a tendency to turn out diluted, and they matured at an overly rapid rate. This was especially noticeable between 1971 and 1980. La Conseillante, owned by the Nicolas family, has been brilliant in most vintages of the 1980s, with the 1990, 1989, 1985, 1982, and 1981 among the finest wines produced in all of Bordeaux. The 1990s were again more erratic, giving further credibility to the estate's inconsistent track record. The vineyard is superbly situated in eastern Pomerol next to L'Evangile, Petit Village, and Vieux Château Certan, right on the boundary of the St.-Emilion/Pomerol appellations. In fact, the deep, gravelly soils intermixed with clay and iron deposits in this area are common not only to La Conseillante and neighbor, L'Evangile, but also to the two great St.-Emilion estates across the road, Figeac and Cheval Blanc.

La Conseillante is a meticulously made wine. It is vinified in stainless-steel tanks and aged in oak barrels of which 100% are new each year. The wine is not as powerful in style as Pétrus, Trotanoy, Lafleur, or Certan de May, but it is always more supple and ready to drink sooner. Because La Conseillante never seems to show as well early on as it does after several years in the bottle, I have consistently underrated it, only to find myself revising my ratings upward. Perhaps it is the elevated percentage of Cabernet Franc (20%) that makes the wine look lighter in its infancy than it ultimately turns out to be. Recent vintages have, as a general rule, reached full maturity within 6–8 years. Being highly prized, as well as occasionally profound, La Conseillante is an expensive wine, normally selling at a price well above most Médoc second growths.

IMPORTANT VINTAGES

2001
88–91?
Sample variation is the reason for the question mark. At best, this 2001 is an exceptionally elegant combination of black raspberries, cherries, smoke, and toasty oak. However, one sample tasted was short in the mouth, and although very good, hardly exceptional. Nevertheless, it is a wine of finesse, nobility, and elegance. While it does not possess the weight, power, or concentration of the marvelous 2000, the 2001 is a successful effort that can be drunk young or cellared for 12–15 years. Last tasted, 1/03.

2000
96
The prodigious 2000 is one of the great wines of the vintage. Undoubtedly the finest La Conseillante since the 1990 and 1989, it is more structured, concentrated, powerful, and denser than either of those wines. An opaque purple color is followed by a tight but immensely promising nose of black raspberry liqueur intermixed with blueberries, cassis, licorice, and toasty new oak. There is stunning concentration and purity, high tannin for this estate, full body, and that layered, sweet mid-section that only comes from low yields and/or great vintages. Anticipated maturity: 2008–2030. Last tasted, 10/02.

1999
89
A beautifully complex, evolved, seductive style of La Conseillante, the dark ruby–colored 1999 exhibits sweet black raspberry and cherry liqueur notes intermixed with cedar, toasty oak, licorice, new saddle leather, and dried herbs. The wine is medium bodied with no hard edges, extremely pure, and almost sweet (from ripe fruit, not sugar). A lush, delicious La Conseillante, it merits its reputation as a "Burgundy from Bordeaux." Anticipated maturity: now–2012. Last tasted, 3/02.

1998
90
An evolved dark plum/garnet color is followed by captivating, sexy, raspberry, soy, Asian spice, kirsch, and toasty vanilla aromas. While not a blockbuster, this opulently textured, medium-bodied effort is a model of elegance, harmony, finesse, and complexity. Why can't Burgundy grand crus be this balanced and seductive? This wine's low acidity as well as wonderfully ripe fruit invite immediate consumption; it should last for 10–12 years. Last tasted, 3/02.

1997
88
Dark ruby–colored, with lavish, high-quality toasty new oak intermixed with black raspberry fruit, this open-knit, medium-bodied, complex wine changes quickly in the glass, revealing smoky, mocha-infused notes. Although not massive, it is sexy, charming, and fruity—in short, a typical La Conseillante. Consume it over the next eight years. Last tasted, 1/02.

1996
88
La Conseillante has turned out an open-knit, seductive wine in the generally tough-textured, tannic year of 1996. The color is a deep ruby. The wine possesses medium body and a sweet, open-knit nose of black raspberries intermixed with toast, licorice, and smoke. Soft, round, and charming, this *terroir's* raspberry fruit is well displayed. This 1996 should keep nicely for 8–10 years. Anticipated maturity: now–2014. Last tasted, 4/02.

1995
89
It is tempting to give this wine an outstanding score because of its seductiveness. However, I do not think it possesses quite the level of extract and concentration to merit an exceptional rating. Nevertheless, it is an extremely pleasing style of Claret. The deep ruby color is followed by an open-knit, black cherry, raspberry, and smoky, roasted herb-scented nose. There is round, lush, ripe fruit, medium body, exceptional elegance and purity, and a soft, velvety-textured finish. Think of it as liquid charm and silk. Anticipated maturity: now–2014. Last tasted, 3/01.

1994
87
Aromatics merit a higher score in this dark ruby/garnet wine, which has a big, spicy, herbal, cedary nose with hints of pepper, sweet raspberries, and black cherries. The wine is medium bodied but slightly austere in the finish, no doubt because the tannins in the 1994 never achieved full phenolic maturity. Nevertheless,

there is a lot to like in the wine, and with the right food, this wine will probably drink better than my conservative score suggests. Anticipated maturity: now–2010. Last tasted, 4/02.

1990 One of the all-time great La Conseillantes, this wine, which to me has similarities

98 to a grand cru Burgundy from the likes of Henri Jayer, still has a deep ruby/purple color and an exotic, even flamboyant bouquet of vanilla, kirsch, raspberries, licorice, and Asian spice. Full-bodied, very opulent, with low acidity, yet consistently a velvety-textured mouthful, this endearing, very seductive wine clearly demonstrated why Pomerols are often called the "Burgundies of Bordeaux." The wine still seems surprisingly youthful despite its accessibility, and it should continue to develop for up to another 10–15 years. Anticipated maturity: now–2018. Last tasted, 12/02.

1989 Somewhat similar to the 1990, but slightly more structured, with more noticeable

96 tannin and a meatier style, this is still a very perfumed, exotic, expansive, sensationally concentrated wine that should age effortlessly for another 10–15 years. In that sense, it might actually outlast the 1990, but what a pair these two wines make. The wine has a dark garnet/ruby color and fabulous aromatics of black raspberries, kirsch, licorice, and copious amounts of toasted new oak. Relatively full-bodied for a La Conseillante, with great purity and sweet tannin, but noticeable structure and muscle, this is a relatively large-scaled La Conseillante that has always been one of the top wines of the vintage. Anticipated maturity: now–2020. Last tasted, 12/02.

1988 This wine has actually turned out better than I initially thought. It suffers in com-

87 parison to the 1990 and 1989, but the color is a dark garnet and the wine offers up notes of cigar smoke, loamy, earthy scents, a hint of truffle, and some sweet cherry fruit that is interwoven with a streak of herbaceousness. The wine is a medium-bodied, mid-weight La Conseillante with a slightly rugged finish. Anticipated maturity: now–2004. Last tasted, 4/02.

1987 A surprisingly delicious, expansive, always fruity and charming wine, this seduc-

87 tive, mid-weight La Conseillante has been delicious from early in its life, yet shows no signs of decline—somewhat surprising for this vintage. The wine is medium bodied, not a blockbuster by any means, but impeccably well balanced. Drink it up. Last tasted, 4/02.

1986 A somewhat disjointed La Conseillante showing considerable amber at the edge,

87? this fragrant wine still offers a compelling nose of sweet cherries, toasty oak, tobacco, cigar smoke, and cedar. The wine is medium bodied, very sweet and ripe on the attack, but then becomes slightly tannic and clipped in the finish. Anticipated maturity: now–2006. Last tasted, 4/02.

1985 Consistently one of the glorious wines of the vintage and far better than its more

94 renowned stablemate Pétrus, La Conseillante's 1985, which has been fully mature since the late 1980s continues to hold at its magical plateau of maturity. The ostentatious aromatics of smoked herbs, sweet raspberry, and cherry fruit intermixed with licorice, Asian spice, and truffle soar from the glass. On the palate, the wine is beautifully concentrated and silky-textured. It is not a blockbuster, but more of an elegant, medium-bodied style, with delicious fruit, impeccable balance, and fabulous purity and staying power in the mouth. This is what great Bordeaux is all about! Anticipated maturity: now–2007. Last tasted, 4/02.

1983 This wine is approaching the end of its useful life. The wine still has La Conseil-

86? lante's aromatic fireworks (cedar, cigar smoke, Provençal herbs, pepper, licorice, and some decaying vegetation). However, considerable amber is at the edge of the wine; the wine exhibits low acidity and some rather nasty tannins in the finish, and it fades very quickly in the glass. It has been fully mature since the late 1980s and, unless it is coming from large-format bottles, needs to be drunk up immediately. Anticipated maturity: now. Last tasted, 4/02.

1982

96

My problem with this wine is that I suspect the case I bought as futures was somehow slightly damaged in shipment, as none of the bottles from my own collection were ever as good as those tasted elsewhere. Tasted four times in 2002, all from other cellars, the wine was absolutely brilliant. This is a candidate that tasted so delicious young, I would have never expected it to be so magnificent 20 years later. Nevertheless, it is an example of how balance and concentration, in spite of extremely low acidity and sweet tannin, can fool even experienced tasters. The wine has not fully matured in more than a decade, and shows no signs of decline. There is considerable amber to the color, but the aromatics are spectacular. Notes of Christmas fruitcake intermixed with jammy black currants, sweet kirsch, toasty oak, licorice, and truffle are stunningly intense and persistent. In the mouth, this is all silk, with a voluptuous texture, almost unctuous thickness to the concentrated fruit, and a long, lush, heady finish. It is a slightly deeper wine than either the 1990 or 1989, but at the same time slightly heavier, no doubt because of the elevated alcohol and glycerin. Nevertheless, this is prodigious stuff. Anticipated maturity: now–2012. Last tasted, 10/02.

ANCIENT VINTAGES

The late 1970s were a period of considerable mediocrity, as were most of the 1970s, except for the 1975 (89 points; last tasted 9/02) and 1970 (93 points; last tasted 6/96). The 1970 is probably beginning to decline, while the 1975, with all of its tannic muscle, is probably capable of lasting another 5–10 years. Otherwise, the two vintages that many Pomerols did exquisitely well in, 1964 and 1961, are both good rather than superb efforts.

The truly museum pieces among La Conseillante's portfolio (none of these have been retasted since the last edition of this book) are La Conseillante's 1959 (95 points; last tasted 10/94), 1949 (97 points; last tasted 5/95), and 1947 (92 points; last tasted 12/95). These wines were fully mature when I had them, so unless they come from cold cellars where the wine has been impeccably stored for most of its life, I suspect these wines are largely over the hill.

LA CROIX

Owner: Joseph Janoueix family

Address: Catusseau, 33500 Pomerol

Mailing address: 37, rue Pline Parmentier, BP 192, 33506 Libourne Cedex

Telephone: 05 57 51 41 86; Telefax: 05 57 51 53 16

E-mail: info@j-janoueix-bordeaux.com

Website: www.j-janoueix-bordeaux.com

Visits: By appointment Monday to Friday, 8 A.M.–noon and 2–6 P.M. (5 P.M. on Fridays)

Contact: Ets Janoueix

VINEYARDS

Surface area: 24.7 acres

Grape varietals: 60% Merlot, 20% Cabernet Franc, 20% Cabernet Sauvignon

Average age of vines: 45 years

Density of plantation: 6,000 vines per hectare

Average yields: 45 hectoliters per hectare

Elevage: Twenty-five to twenty-seven day fermentation and maceration in temperature-controlled vats. Malolactics and 12–14 months aging in barrels with 80% new oak. Fining, no filtration.

WINES PRODUCED

Château La Croix: 42,000 bottles

Château Gabachot: 18,000 bottles

Plateau of maturity: Within 10–14 years of the vintage

GENERAL APPRECIATION

These are reliable, somewhat rustic, wines that rarely disappoint but are never inspiring.

La Croix, located on the outskirts of Libourne just off route D24, has a soil composition of gravel and sand. No wine made in this area ranks in the top dozen or so estates of Pomerol. Nevertheless, La Croix is a reputable property, producing big, dark-colored, tannic, full-bodied wines that can be criticized only for their lack of refinement and finesse. The best examples offer a mouth-filling, plump, rustic, simple pleasure that repays 6–12 years of cellaring. I have noticed in some vintages that a musty quality does intrude, suggesting that the cellar's sanitary conditions could be improved. Fortunately, this happens infrequently. The château never receives a great deal of press, and given the fact that La Croix can turn out wines that are representative of the appellation, it remains a somewhat undervalued estate.

IMPORTANT VINTAGES

In the 25 years I have been tasting the wines of La Croix, nothing of significant interest has ever emerged. Certainly the wines were capable of hitting mid-80 point scores, but other than the occasional wine that I rated higher (the 1990, for example), this has been an underperforming estate in Pomerol.

LA CROIX DU CASSE ────────────────────────

Owner: Societié Civile

Address: 33500 Pomerol

Mailing address: c/o Château Jonqueyres, 33750 Saint-Germain du Puch

Telephone: 05 57 34 51 66; Telefax: 05 56 30 11 45

E-mail: delphine.moussay-derouet@gamaudy.com

No visits

VINEYARDS

Surface area: 22.2 acres

Grape varietals: 70% Merlot, 30% Cabernet Franc

Average age of vines: 35 years

Density of plantation: 6,000 vines per hectare

Average yields: 48 hectoliters per hectare

Elevage: Fermentations and macerations can last up to six weeks in temperature-controlled stainless-steel vats. Completion of malolactics and 24 months aging in new oak barrels. No fining, no filtration.

WINES PRODUCED

Château La Croix du Casse: 48,000 bottles

Domaine du Casse: 7,200 bottles

Plateau of maturity: Within 4–10 years of the vintage

GENERAL APPRECIATION

A consistently good Pomerol since the late 1980s, La Croix du Casse is generally closed and tannic in its youth. In most cases, the fruit is so generous that this trait is not a problem. However, in certain vintages the tannins are rugged and coarse, so much so that the wine's evolution may be compromised. While it is a soundly made wine, La Croix du Casse does not enjoy the reputation of its more famous siblings of the appellation.

The late Jean-Michel Arcaute, the manager who took Château Clinet from mediocrity to superstardom, passed away in a tragic drowning accident in 2001. His untimely death has left a void at this estate. Located south of the village of Catusseau, on a terrace of sandy and gravel-based soils, this tiny Pomerol estate is not as renowned or as well placed as many other Pomerols, but the quality can be a positive surprise. The entire vineyard had to be replanted following the catastrophic freeze of 1956.

IMPORTANT VINTAGES

2001
88–90   A sexy, opulent, flamboyantly styled Pomerol, this deep ruby/purple–colored 2001 exhibits medium to full body, low acidity, and a sumptuous style. Never pretending to be elegant, it offers loads of flesh, superripe fruit, and a juicy, succulent style. Enjoy it over the next 10–12 years. Last tasted, 1/03.

2000
88+?   This wine displays some of the problems encountered in certain 2000s. Highly extracted, but extremely dry, austere tannins are ferocious as well as unrelenting. The wine exhibits impressive color saturation and plenty of black fruit, earthy, and spicy new oak characteristics, but the tannin level really is bothersome. Certainly this 2000 is concentrated, pure, and well made, but in the war between fruit and tannin, history usually favors the tannin. Anticipated maturity: 2008–2018? Last tasted, 1/03.

1999
89   A potential sleeper, the opaque ruby/purple–colored 1999 displays superripe (*sur-maturité* as the French say) flavors of jammy black fruits intermixed with minerals, smoke, spice box, and new oak. Layered, with low acidity as well as a thick, expansive texture, this topflight Pomerol should evolve more quickly than the 1998, yet age well. Anticipated maturity: now–2015. Last tasted, 1/03.

1998
90
An outstanding effort, as well as one of the sleepers of the vintage, this dense ruby/purple–colored 1998 exhibits ripe, jammy notes of blackberries and cherries intermixed with licorice, smoke, and new wood. Full-bodied, with terrific fruit extraction, considerable muscle, and moderate tannin levels, it is not a wine to gulp down over the near-term. Anticipated maturity: 2005–2016. Last tasted, 3/02.

1997
88
A sleeper of the vintage, this wine exhibits a dark plum color in addition to open-knit aromas of black cherries, plums, cedar, herbs, coffee, and vanilla. Round, delicious, and easy to understand and consume, this sexy, medium-bodied 1997 should drink well for 3–4 years. Last tasted, 3/01.

1996
88
An impressive Pomerol, the 1996 possesses a saturated plum/purple color and a pure nose of spicy, sweet oak, minerals, black fruits, and prunes. The wine is surprisingly open-knit for a 1996, with an expansive, medium- to full-bodied, succulent texture. There is tannin in the finish, but it is nearly obscured by the wine's glycerin, fruit extraction, and ripeness. Drink this attractive, silky Pomerol now and over the next 7–8 years. Last tasted, 3/01.

1995
90
An outstanding wine, this dense ruby/purple–colored 1995 offers a knockout nose of blackberries, cassis, minerals, and spicy new oak. Medium to full-bodied, with plenty of toasty-like flavors and abundantly sweet fruit imbued with glycerin and tannin, this wine possesses a long mid-palate, as well as a finish that builds in the mouth. It is an impressively built, pure, rich Pomerol that merits considerable attention. Anticipated maturity: now–2015. Last tasted, 12/01.

LA CROIX DE GAY

Owner: Raynaud and Lebreton families

Address: 33500 Pomerol

Telephone: 05 57 51 19 05; Telefax: 05 57 74 15 62

E-mail: contact@chateau-lacroixdegay.com

Website: www.chateau-lacroixdegay.com

Visits: Preferably by appointment Monday to Thursday and Saturday, 9 A.M.–1 P.M. and 2–5 P.M.; Friday, 2–5 P.M.

Contact: Chantal Lebreton

VINEYARDS

Surface area: 24.7 acres

Grape varietals: 90% Merlot, 5% Cabernet Franc, 5% Cabernet Sauvignon

Average age of vines: 30 years

Density of plantation: 5,000 vines per hectare

Average yields: 35 hectoliters per hectare

Elevage: Four week fermentation and maceration in temperature-controlled concrete tanks. Fifty percent of the yield undergoes malolactics in barrel. Eighteen months aging with 50% new oak and 50% one-year-old barrels.

WINES PRODUCED

Château La Croix de Gay: 40,000–45,000 bottles

No second wine is produced.

Plateau of maturity: Within 5–17 years of the vintage

GENERAL APPRECIATION

La Croix de Gay is very good but never exceptional, probably because the finest parcels are culled out to produce their special *cuvée*, La Fleur de Gay. After a slump in the 1970s, the estate beautifully rebounded in the 1980s, producing very good wines. However, all in all, La Croix de Gay is a good to very good Pomerol that is worthy of interest, provided the prices are reasonable.

La Croix de Gay, one of the greatest discoveries of Englishman Harry Waugh in the late 1940s proved to be an inconsistent, even inadequate, performer in the 1970s and early 1980s. However, the proprietor, the handsome Dr. Raynaud, has increasingly up-graded the quality and now produces one of the most attractive and easy to drink Pomerols. In 1982 Dr. Raynaud launched his luxury *cuvée* of La Croix de Gay—called La Fleur de Gay—from a parcel of very old vines of Merlot planted between Pétrus and Lafleur. This luxury *cuvée* of old vines (profiled separately, see page 667) is very rare in Bordeaux, but it is one of the most magnificent wines of the appellation, rivaling the finest Pomerols in complexity and intensity. Some skeptics have argued that Dr. Raynaud's decision to make a special *cuvée* robs the primary wine, La Croix de Gay, of its best source of richness and backbone. But despite the addition of a luxury *cuvée*, one cannot ignore the fact that La Croix de Gay has improved immensely. His sister, Chantal Lebreton, assumed control of the estate in the mid-1990s.

The vineyards of La Croix de Gay sit at the very northern section of Pomerol's plateau, immediately behind a cemetery and the tiny road called D245 that traverses the appellation. The soil in this area is gravel intermixed with sand.

IMPORTANT VINTAGES

2001
87–88
A strong effort from this property, the 2001 was produced from low yields of 35 hectoliters per hectare. A blend of 90% Merlot, equal parts Cabernet Sauvignon and Cabernet Franc, this dark ruby/purple–colored Pomerol offers sweet cherry fruit along with subtle wood and earth notes. Medium bodied and pure, with vibrant fruit and a nicely textured, medium-bodied finish, this finesse-styled wine possesses excellent sweetness as well as palate presence. Drink it over the next 10–12 years. Last tasted, 1/03.

2000
89+
Starting in 2000, Cabernet Sauvignon was eliminated from the final blend, resulting in a more interesting wine. Deep, textured, rich, and concentrated, it should drink well for 15 years. Black fruits, earth, toast, and mocha characterize this medium-bodied, impressively endowed yet elegant Pomerol. Anticipated maturity: 2005–2016. Last tasted, 1/03.

1999
88
This elegant, delicate, well-balanced, dark ruby–colored 1999 is made from a blend of 90% Merlot and 10% Cabernet Franc. While light, it reveals exceptional purity, sweet, round, strawberry, black cherry, and currant fruit intermixed with subtle wood and an enticing texture. Drink it over the next 8–10 years. Last tasted, 3/02.

1998
87
Moderately intense aromas of sweet black cherry fruit intermixed with minerals, smoke, and spice box are followed by a well-balanced, harmonious wine with excellent richness, sweetness (from glycerin), and a spicy, soft finish. Drink it over the next eight years. Last tasted, 3/02.

1996
85
While some tannin still exists, this dark plum/garnet–colored wine is showing considerable amber at the edge and has been one of the vintage's fastest maturing wines. A rather seductive nose of tobacco, Provençal herbs, licorice, cherries, and

loamy soil notes is followed by a medium-bodied wine with low acidity in a somewhat loosely knit, unconcentrated style. Drink it up. Last tasted, 12/01.

1995   Fully mature, this dark plum–colored wine has taken on considerable amber at a
87   relatively accelerated pace. The wine exhibits a sweet nose of tar, roasted herbs,
       black cherry, and plum fruit with a hint of prune. The wine is medium bodied with
       some subtle oak thrown in the flavor mix, which mirrors the aromatics. Soft, round,
       with some slightly firm tannins still noticeable in the finish, this wine needs to be
       drunk up over the next 6–7 years. Anticipated maturity: now–2007. Last tasted,
       3/02.

1994   A surprisingly good effort in a more stern, tannic, masculine vintage, the color is
87   deep plum/garnet and the wine has notes of underbrush, compost, smoke, vanilla,
       and herb-tinged cherries. Rather firmly structured, with some stiff rigid tannin
       still to dissipate, this wine is medium bodied, relatively powerful for a Croix de
       Gay, with more muscle and power than most vintages. Anticipated maturity:
       now–2010. Last tasted, 3/02.

ANCIENT VINTAGES

This is not a wine, except in the very greatest vintages, to push past 10–15 years of cellaring. My top notes are from 1989 (87 points; last tasted 3/97), 1982 (rated 92; last
tasted 3/97), 1964 (90 points; last tasted, 3/90), and 1947 (92 points; last tasted
10/99). To date, the 1964 and 1947 look to be the finest wines made at La Croix de Gay,
but for readers looking for a soft, very agreeable, accessible style of Pomerol, this wine
certainly has merit.

LA CROIX ST.-GEORGES

Owner: Joseph Janoueix family

Administrator: Jean-Philippe Janoueix

Address: 33500 Pomerol

Mailing address: 83, cours des Girondins, 33500 Libourne

Telephone: 05 57 25 91 19; Telefax: 05 57 48 00 04

Visits: By appointment only

Contact: Jean-Philippe Janoueix

VINEYARDS

Surface area: 11.1 acres

Grape varietals: 100% Merlot

Average age of vines: 35 years

Density of plantation: 6,500 vines per hectare

Average yields: 35 hectoliters per hectare

Elevage: Four to six week fermentation and maceration in temperature-controlled open-
top wooden fermenters of 60 hectoliter capacity, with manual *pigéage*. Malolactics and 18
months aging in normal barrels for half the yield and in cigar-shaped barrels for the other
half. No fining or filtration.

WINES PRODUCED

Château La Croix St.-Georges: 15,000 bottles

Le Prieuré: 5,000–7,000 bottles

Plateau of maturity: Within 5–20 years of the vintage

GENERAL APPRECIATION

Jean-Philippe Janoueix's aim is to propel La Croix St.-Georges amongst the first five best Pomerols.

This 11.1 acre vineyard owned by the Janoueix family (of De Chambrun fame) and situated among some of the stars of Pomerol (i.e., Vieux Château Certan) burst on the scene with a blockbuster 1999, which has been followed by an equally impressive 2000 and 2001. This super-*cuvée* of 100% Merlot is another garage wine that receives all the fashionable winemaking treatments that are now the rage in Pomerol and St.-Emilion (i.e., fermentation in open-top wood *cuves*, punching down of the must, malolactic in barrel, extensive lees contact, and bottling without fining or filtration). Sadly, the quantities produced are small and the wine is nearly impossible to find.

IMPORTANT VINTAGES

2001
89–91+
The impressive 2001 is produced from yields of 39 hectoliters per hectare. It sports a dense purple color as well as a sweet, expansive perfume of black cherry liqueur, blackberries, licorice, and toasty oak, full body, and layers of glycerin as well as sweet tannin. If the 2001 behaves like the 2000 (which gained weight and texture with aging), it will merit a score in the low 90s. Anticipated maturity: 2005–2017. Last tasted, 1/03.

2000
95
The 2000 has put on considerable weight. I would never have guessed it would become this rich, concentrated, or compelling. An incredibly sweet perfume of blackberry liqueur, kirsch, cassis, new saddle leather, truffles, toasty oak, and smoke soars from the glass of this full-bodied, massively concentrated effort with an extraordinary finish. Anticipated maturity: 2007–2020+. Last tasted, 1/03.

1999
93
The 1999 La Croix St.-Georges is even better than I anticipated. It is an amazingly opaque purple–colored wine with extraordinary fat and richness, concentrated, jammy blackberry and cherry fruit, and liqueur-like intensity. Multilayered, extremely generous, and sumptuous on the palate, with a remarkable finish, it is a star of the vintage. Wow! Anticipated maturity: 2004–2020. Last tasted, 3/02.

DOMAINE DE L'EGLISE

Owner: Indivision Castéja

Address: 33500 Pomerol

Mailing address: 86, cours Balguerie Stuttenberg, 33082 Bordeaux

Telephone: 05 56 00 00 70; Telefax: 05 57 87 48 61

E-mail: domaine.boriemanoux@dial.oleane.com

Visits: By appointment only

Contact: Mrs. Marquasuzaa (05 56 00 00 97)

VINEYARDS

Surface area: 17.3 acres

Grape varietals: 95% Merlot, 5% Cabernet Franc

Average age of vines: 40 years

Density of plantation: 7,200 vines per hectare

Average yields: 38 hectoliters per hectare

Elevage: Three to five week fermentation and maceration in temperature-controlled stainless-steel tanks. Sixteen to eighteen months aging in barrels with 60% new oak. Fining, no filtration.

WINES PRODUCED

Domaine de L'Eglise: 30,000 bottles

Plateau of maturity: Within 4–12 years of the vintage

GENERAL APPRECIATION

Long an uninspiring Pomerol (be cautious when dealing with vintages prior to 1990), Domaine de L'Eglise has improved significantly since the 1990s. While it is not one of the most opulent and richest wines of the appellation, it is unquestionably seductive, exhibiting a pleasant, soft fruitiness and some elegance. I believe this wine could be significantly better if the potential of its *terroir* were fully exploited. Proprietor Philippe Castéja continues to make improvements at this property (especially noticeable since 1995).

This beautifully situated vineyard is adjacent to the cemetery of Pomerol on the high plateau and has a gravelly soil intermixed with some sand. The château and vineyard are believed to be the oldest of Pomerol. The property was run as a winemaking estate by the Hospitaliers de Saint-Jean de Jerusalem who managed a hospital known as Domaine Porte Rouge in Pomerol for lepers long before the French Revolution. As with many church-run properties, the revolution resulted in divestiture and placement in private hands, where it has remained. It was acquired by the *négociant* firm of Borie-Manoux in 1973.

Solid and reliable wines were made in the 1970s and early 1980s but since the late 1980s the quality has increased. Domaine de L'Eglise was particularly damaged during the 1956 freeze, and the vineyard was totally replanted. The lighter, more commercial style of wines produced in the 1970s and 1980s as well as the 1990s gave way in the late 1980s to a richer, more profound and compelling product.

IMPORTANT VINTAGES

2001   Even though it revealed an impressively saturated black/ruby/purple color, this
87–88+? wine lacked acidity and came across as monolithic, although there is plenty of
depth, ripeness, and richness. In the past, wines such as this have tended to become more delineated and reveal more grip after some extra barrel aging. If that happens, this Pomerol will easily merit a score in the high 80s. There is plenty going on in this pure, concentrated effort. Anticipated maturity: 2006–2015. Last tasted, 1/03.

2000
89+
This should turn out to be the finest wine from Domaine de L'Eglise in many years. It possesses the brutal tannin found in top Pomerols from the plateau sector, but also an opaque purple color, high levels of extract, medium to full body, and superb purity. It is a rich, impressive *vin de garde* to drink between 2008–2020. Last tasted, 1/03.

1999
88
Deep ruby/purple–colored and medium to full-bodied, with notes of new oak and chocolate-covered truffles, this toasty, low-acid, plump, approachable wine should be drunk over the next 10 years. Last tasted, 3/02.

1998
87
A soft, plump, forward, deep ruby–colored Pomerol, the 1998 offers abundant quantities of toffee, black cherry, mocha, chocolaty, and toasty new oak aromas as well as flavors. Drink this medium-bodied, user-friendly wine over the next eight years. Last tasted, 3/02.

1997
85
Intriguing roasted coffee, berry, chocolate, and toast aromas emerge from this medium dark–ruby colored wine. Round, plump, and succulent, with moderately good concentration, this is a cleanly made, competent Pomerol to drink over the next two years. Last tasted, 3/01.

1995
87
An impressive saturated black/purple color is followed by a wine with excellent black cherry and cassis fruit, medium body, fine purity, and surprising opulence and unctuosity. Anticipated maturity: now–2016. Last tasted, 11/97.

1994
84
Dark ruby–colored, with attractive, jammy, cherry, earth, and spicy scents, this mid-weight, ripe 1994 displays no hard edges or vegetal notes, but lacks stuffing and length. It should drink well for 2–3 years. Last tasted, 3/99.

ANCIENT VINTAGES

The best vintage I have tasted over the last 25 years was the 1989 (89 points; last tasted 3/98). The wine is still showing considerable power, richness, and a far denser color and more extracted flavors than most other vintages. A hint of prune was the only negative in an otherwise impressive performance. The wine exhibits a nose of sweet black cherries, plums, and earth. It reached maturity relatively quickly and needs to be drunk over the next 6–7 years.

L'EGLISE-CLINET

Owner: GFA du Château L'Eglise-Clinet

Address: 33500 Pomerol

Telephone: 05 57 25 90 00; Telefax: 05 57 25 21 96

E-mail: eglise@denis-durantou.com

Website: www.eglise-clinet.com

Visits: By appointment only

Contact: Denis Durantou

VINEYARDS

Surface area: 14.8 acres

Grape varietals: 85% Merlot, 15% Cabernet Franc

Average age of vines: 45 years

Density of plantation: 6,500 vines per hectare

Average yields: 35 hectoliters per hectare

Elevage: Fifteen to twenty-one day fermentation and maceration in small temperature-controlled stainless-steel tanks of 30 to 50 hectoliter capacity. Fifteen to eighteen months aging with 40–70% new oak. Fining, no filtration.

WINES PRODUCED

Château L'Eglise-Clinet: 12,000–15,000 bottles

La Petite L'Eglise: 15,000–20,000 bottles

Plateau of maturity: Within 10–30 years of the vintage

GENERAL APPRECIATION

While it is one of the least known wines of the appellation because of its tiny production, L'Eglise-Clinet has always ranked among the finest Pomerols and is generally richly fruity, generous, and fat. In terms of quality, it is on par with today's new stars such as Clos l'Église, L'Evangile, or La Conseillante. L'Eglise-Clinet is still very much of an insider's secret, but it has a fiercely loyal following, so latching on to a few bottles of this beauty is difficult. Its quality and rarity account for the high price it fetches—but the wine is worth it. A must buy.

One of the least known Pomerol estates, L'Eglise-Clinet often produces a typically fat, succulent, juicy, richly fruity style of Pomerol. The wine is well/known and admirably and traditionally made, but because of the tiny production, it is rarely tasted. The vineyard is well situated on the plateau of Pomerol behind the church where the soils are deep gravel beds intermingled with sand, clay, and iron.

L'Eglise-Clinet is one of the few Pomerol vineyards not replanted after the 1956 killing freeze (nor was there any vine damage in the frosts of 1985 and 1987), and consequently it has very old vines, a few of which exceed 100 years in age.

Until 1983, Pierre Lasserre, the owner of the bigger and better-known Pomerol property of Clos René, farmed this vineyard under the *métayage* system (a type of vineyard rental agreement) and turned out a wine that was rich, well balanced, supple, firm, and always well vinified. Since then, the winery has been run by the young, extremely dedicated Denis Durantou, who is trying to take this tiny vineyard to the very top of the unofficial Pomerol hierarchy. The secret here is not only Durantou's remarkable commitment to quality, but vines that average 40–45 years in age, plus the fact that in abundant and/or difficult vintages one-fourth of the crop is relegated to the second wine called La Petite L'Eglise. One cannot applaud the efforts of Denis Durantou enough.

The price for a bottle of L'Eglise-Clinet is high, as connoisseurs recognize that this is one of the top dozen wines of the appellation.

IMPORTANT VINTAGES

2001
91–93 An outstanding effort that sells for less than half the price of the 2000, the 2001's deep saturated ruby/purple color is followed by aromas of caramel and pure black cherries intermixed with hints of plums, currants, truffles, and well-integrated tasty oak. The wine is medium to full-bodied, with tremendous purity, impressive

concentration, and undeniable elegance and classicism. One will rarely go wrong buying any wine made by proprietor Denis Durantou, a true purist. Anticipated maturity: 2008–2020. Last tasted, 1/03.

2000
96
Truly spectacular, this could be another of the great classics proprietor Durantou has produced over recent years. For now, it is hard to believe it could rival or eclipse the fabulous 1998 or, for that matter, the 1995, but the 2000 has gone from strength to strength in its evolution. From bottle, it is dazzling. The saturated ruby/purple color offers up pure fruit notes of mulberries, figs, and cassis intermixed with hints of licorice and toasty oak. Revealing great palate presence, tremendous texture, sweet tannin, relatively low acidity, and a finish that exceeds 60 seconds, I assume this wine will close down, not to reopen for nearly a decade. This is a profound example form a proprietor who has never subscribed to the new, progressive/razzle-dazzle techniques being employed by some of the cutting edge producers. Here it is low yields, ripe fruit, and non-interventionalistic winemaking at its purist. Anticipated maturity: 2010–2035+. Last tasted, 1/03.

1999
92
The 1999 L'Eglise-Clinet has evolved beautifully. One of the stars of the vintage, it is an extraordinary expression of elegance married to power. An opaque purple color is followed by aromas of black raspberries, currants, licorice, graphite, truffles, and earth. Sweet and expansive, it is a model of purity, symmetry, and balance. Moderate tannin suggests some more cellaring is required. Anticipated maturity: 2005–2025. Last tasted, 3/02.

1998
94+
This effort should turn out to be one of the longest-lived Pomerols of the vintage. It is backward and has closed down since bottling, but make no mistake about it . . . this is a dazzling, serious *vin de garde.* An opaque purple color is followed by a restrained but promising bouquet of sweet black raspberries intermixed with vanilla, caramel, and minerals. The wine is full-bodied, powerfully tannic, beautifully textured, and crammed with extract (an assortment of black fruits). While it is bursting at the seams, purchasers will need to wait a minimum of 3–4 years. Anticipated maturity: 2008–2035. Last tasted, 3/02.

1997
91
One of the vintage's most concentrated, seductive, and ageworthy offerings, this dark ruby/purple–colored 1997 possesses gorgeous symmetry, abundant quantities of seductive black raspberry and cherry fruit, full body, a fat, chewy mid-palate, and roasted blackberries, coffee, and toasty oak in the finish. A superb effort for the vintage, it can be drunk now (because of its low acidity and sweet tannin) or cellared for 12+ years. Bravo! Last tasted, 3/02.

1996
93
One of the few profound Pomerols in 1996, L'Eglise-Clinet turned out an uncommonly rich, concentrated wine that is performing well from bottle, even though it is displaying a tightly knit structure. The dark ruby/purple color is followed by notes of charcoal, jammy cassis, raspberries, and a touch of *sur-maturité.* Spicy oak emerges as the wine sits in the glass. It is fat, concentrated, and medium to full-bodied, with a layered, multidimensional, highly nuanced personality. This muscular Pomerol will be at its apogee until 2020. Last tasted, 3/01.

1995
96
One of the vintage's most awesome wines, L'Eglise-Clinet's 1995 has been fabulous from both cask and bottle. The color is opaque purple. The wine is closed aromatically, but it does offer a concoction of black raspberries, kirsch, smoke, cherries, and truffles. Full-bodied and rich with high tannin, but profound levels of fruit and richness, this dense, exceptionally well-delineated, layered, multidimensional L'Eglise-Clinet only hints at its ultimate potential. This looks to be a legend in the making. I could not get over the extraordinary texture of this wine in the mouth. Intensity and richness without heaviness—a tour de force in winemaking! Anticipated maturity: 2010–2030. Last tasted, 9/02.

1994
89

The dense plum-colored 1994 offers a tight but promising nose of ripe cherries, mulberries, and currants, along with a vague notion of black truffles as well as soil scent. Medium to full-bodied, with pure fruit, a layered impression, and stubborn tannin in the muscular finish, this wine is not charming but is a large, rich wine. If it has a defect, it is the high tannin and lack of sweetness in the finish, a common trait of the 1994s. Anticipated maturity: 2007–2020. Last tasted, 11/02.

1990
92

Seemingly close to its plateau of maturity, yet at the same time still relatively youthful and fresh, the dark plum/purple–colored 1990 is beginning to have a hint of amber at the edge. A sweet nose of cola, black cherry jam, smoke, malt chocolate, and earth is followed by a full-bodied, opulently textured wine with very little acidity, still noticeable tannin, a very chewy mid-section, and a sweet, layered finish. A very impressive wine that continues to go from strength to strength. Anticipated maturity: now–2023. Last tasted, 5/02.

1989
89

Somewhat inconsistent in all of my tastings, this wine has far more evolved color than the 1990, showing considerable amber at the edge. The moderately intense nose of brown sugar, malt chocolate, cedar, mulberries, and cherries is followed by a medium-bodied wine that seems to be fully mature. Its texture is a bit gritty, with some tannins poking their heads through, and the wine is not as sweet and opulent as its sibling, the 1990. Nevertheless, this is an excellent bottle. It just seems short of magic, missing the extra layers of flavor and length that merit its lofty reputation. Anticipated maturity: now–2016. Last tasted, 5/02.

1988
87

Seemingly fully mature, this wine exhibits some amber at the edge of its dark garnet color. The nose exhibits dark fruit, earth, and underbrush, with hints of smoke, plum, cherry, and Provençal herbs. It is medium bodied yet firmly tannic. It is certainly going to last for at least another 8–10 years, but I am not sure it has the relative charm or succulence of the top vintages. Anticipated maturity: now–2017. Last tasted, 5/02.

1986
90

This wine has become a bit more attenuated with cellaring, and yet while it tastes young and capable of lasting another two decades, I am not quite as enthusiastic about it as I once was. Nevertheless, it is an outstanding effort and certainly one of Pomerol's top performers in this vintage that favored the Médoc. Still deep, dense ruby with some purple, the aromatics require coaxing from the glass. Notes of cedar, sweet plum, Christmas fruitcake, and black cherries and berries finally emerge with a hint of licorice and mushroom. The wine has excellent concentration, a medium- to full-bodied, layered mid-section, and moderately high tannins in the finish. It was the relatively dry, hard tannins in the finish that lowered my score over previous tastings. Anticipated maturity: 2006–2020. Last tasted, 5/02.

1985
95

A superstar of the vintage, the last time I tasted this was next to a rather pathetic performance of a very herbal, green, emaciated Pétrus (one of the great deceptions of the vintage). This wine still has a very saturated opaque ruby/purple color that is far less evolved than almost any other 1985. The wine has sweet cranberry, black cherry, and blackberry fruit notes intermixed with mineral, cold steel, and a hint of cedar. Rich, full-bodied, with fabulous purity, a very well-delineated feel in the mouth, enormous richness, and a long finish that goes on for nearly 45 seconds, the wine seems to grow incrementally in the glass with increasing amounts of air, and is certainly a 1985 that has evolved at a snail's pace compared to most wines of this vintage. Anticipated maturity: now–2023. Last tasted, 5/02.

1983
86?

Beginning to show some cracks around the edges and considerable amber, this wine has notes of wet soil, mushroom, and black cherries in a decidedly earthy, herbal concoction. The wine has medium to full body, low acidity, but very dry tannins in the finish that are starting to give the wine a somewhat desiccated feeling, a sign that an imminent crack-up of the wine is not far off. Anticipated maturity: now. Last tasted, 5/02.

1982 This is a somewhat old-styled wine that has put on significant weight since its
90? early days in cask and bottle. Its rugged level of tannin is the reason for the question mark, but there is no doubt this wine has tremendous depth underlined with tannin, and seems richer and fuller-bodied than I ever remembered young. The wine still has a sort of opaque, murky ruby/garnet color, a big sweet nose of mushrooms, licorice, damp earth, spice box, and figs. In the mouth it is chunky and substantial, but the aggressive tannins and somewhat coarse finish make one wonder if it is still just a very young wine that needs more time or something rather uncivilized. It certainly seems worth the gamble if it can be purchased at a reasonable price. Anticipated maturity: now–2020? Last tasted, 11/02.

ANCIENT VINTAGES

L'Eglise-Clinet, like most châteaux, has an erratic record, but the peaks seem to confirm what a great *terroir* this property possesses. Some of my favorite vintages are as follows: 1975 (92? points; last tasted 11/02) is a hugely concentrated, still very young wine that is somewhat similar, with its astringent tannin, to the 1982. It is a massive wine, still youthful, but also shows immense potential along with the possibility that it still needs another 8–10 years. No question this wine will evolve through the first three decades of the 21st century, but will it ever attain perfect harmony? Fully mature and now starting to fade, the 1971 (92 points; last tasted 12/95) is certainly one of the three best Pomerols of the vintage (Trotanoy and Pétrus being the other two). Anyone who owns it should not push their luck any further. The 1961 (92 points; last tasted 9/95) was a fabulous example of that vintage, showing a huge nose of soy sauce, grilled meats, mocha chocolate, and black cherry fruit, with full body and opulent texture. Even better was the 1959 L'Eglise-Clinet (96 points; last tasted 10/95) with an absolutely amazing nose of kirsch intermixed with Asian spices, Häagen-Dazs Jamocha Chocolate Chip ice cream, and caramel. It is unctuously textured, very viscous, and certainly one of the most concentrated and layered examples from L'Eglise-Clinet in the last 40 years.

Several masterpieces should be noted. The 1950 (95 points; last tasted 9/95), from a great vintage in Pomerol, was phenomenal. The virtually perfect 1949 (99 points; last tasted 9/95) is another masterpiece, and the 1947 (100 points; last tasted 9/95), 1945 (98 points; last tasted 9/95), and 1921 (100 points; last tasted 9/95) are all extraordinary wines that were tasted from pristinely stored bottles and, in several cases, magnums. They are the kind of wines that would certainly give L'Eglise-Clinet the ability to argue that when it hits all cylinders, it is every bit as profound a Pomerol as Pétrus.

L'ENCLOS

Owner: GFA du Château L'Enclos

Address: lieu-dit L'Enclos, 20, rue du Grand Moulinet, 33500 Pomerol

Telephone: 05 57 51 04 62; Telefax: 05 57 51 43 15

E-mail: chateaulenclos@wanadoo.fr

Website: www.chateau-lenclos.com

Visits: By appointment Monday to Friday

Contact: Hugues Weydert

VINEYARDS

Surface area: 23.3 acres

Grape varietals: 82% Merlo, 17% Cabernet Franc, 1% Pressac

Average age of vines: 31 years

Density of plantation: 6,000 vines per hectare

Average yields: 45 hectoliters per hectare

Elevage: Three to four week fermentation (28–32°C) and maceration (22–24°C) in temperature-controlled stainless-steel vats with 2–4 daily pumpings-over. Twelve to fourteen months aging in barrels with 40% new oak. Fining, light filtration upon bottling.

WINES PRODUCED

Château L'Enclos: 52,000 bottles

No second wine is produced.

Plateau of maturity: Within 3–15 years of the vintage

GENERAL APPRECIATION

This discrete, low-key estate produces elegant wines that fully reveal themselves after 4–5 years of age. In the best vintages, L'Enclos can be very good to excellent. Over recent years, it has not performed to the level it had attained in the 1980s, but I hope this is temporary, as L'Enclos represents a good buy.

Located on sandy, gravelly, and flinty soil in the most western portion of the Pomerol appellation, L'Enclos is an unheralded property that can produce fine wine. The finest vintages offer consistently smooth, velvety, rich, supple, nicely concentrated, pure blackberry fruitiness and overall harmony. In most vintages L'Enclos only needs 3–4 years of bottle age to reveal the opulent, rich, silky fruitiness, yet the wines hold up well in the bottle.

IMPORTANT VINTAGES

2001 A soft, creamy-textured wine with sweet caramel-infused berry and cherry fruit,
86 this medium-bodied Pomerol needs to be drunk over the next 5–10 years. Anticipated maturity: now–2011. Last tasted, 1/03.

2000 The 2000 is light and lacking in both density and concentration. Notes of caramel,
85   mocha, and cherries are present in this medium-bodied, soft Pomerol. It requires
      consumption during its first 5–6 years of life. Last tasted, 1/03.

ANCIENT VINTAGES

L'Enclos's performance in the 1990s was mediocre, with most of my scores ranging from the low to high 70s, with the 1995 vintage rated 86 points (last tasted 3/99). The only other exception was the delicious 1990 (88 points; last tasted 11/01). In the 1980s, the track record was erratic but more consistent, with the 1989 rated 87 (last tasted 3/96) and the 1982 rated 88 (last tasted 11/02). Of the two stars of the vintage, only the 1982 seems capable of lasting another 5–10 years, and certainly gets my nod as the best L'Enclos of the last 25 years. Another vintage to keep an eye out for, although I expect it is in decline now is the 1975 (89 points; last tasted 1/85). The vintage certainly has stood the test of time but remains very controversial.

L'EVANGILE

Owner: Domaines Barons de Rothschild (Lafite)

Address: 33500 Pomerol

Telephone: 05 57 55 45 55; Telefax: 05 57 55 45 56

E-mail: evangile@wanadoo.fr

Website: www.lafite.com

Visits: By appointment only

Contact: Jean-Paul Vazart

VINEYARDS

Surface area: 34.6 acres

Grape varietals: 75% Merlot, 25% Cabernet Franc

Average age of vines: 40 years

Density of plantation: 6,000 vines per hectare

Average yields: 40 hectoliters per hectare

Elevage: Twenty-five to thirty day fermentation and maceration in temperature-controlled stainless-steel and concrete tanks. After completion of malolactics in vats, 18 months aging in barrels with 80% new oak. Fining and filtration if necessary.

WINES PRODUCED

Château L'Evangile: 3,500–4,000 cases

Blason de L'Evangile: 1,000–1,500 cases

Plateau of maturity: Within 6–30 years of the vintage

GENERAL APPRECIATION

While L'Evangile has always been a star of its appellation, it managed to improve over recent years under the ownership of the Rothschilds (of Lafite) and qualitatively rivals

Pétrus and Lafleur. This exceptional wine magnificently translates its *terroir* through its sumptuous richness and opulence. Always distinctive, it is one of the longer lived Pomerols. The only criticism I would express concerns the fining and filtration, which in certain vintages has robbed the wine of that extra-richness. Unfortunately, prices have followed the curve of quality—but the wine is worth it.

Anyone who has tasted the 2001, 2000, 1998, 1995, 1990, 1989, 1985, 1982, 1975, 1961, 1950, and 1947 L'Evangile knows full well that this property can make wines of majestic richness and compelling character. Bordered on the north by the Who's Who of vineyards, La Conseillante, Vieux Château Certan, and Pétrus, and on the south by the great St.-Emilion Cheval Blanc, the 34.6-acre vineyard is brilliantly situated on deep, gravelly soil mixed with both clay and sand. With these advantages, I believe that L'Evangile (never a model of consistency) can produce wines that rival Pétrus, Lafleur, and Cheval Blanc.

That is now happening. In 1990 the Rothschild family (of Lafite Rothschild) purchased a controlling interest. In 2000 they became 100% owners along with Albert Frère (a wealthy Belgian who also has an interest in Cheval Blanc). They are fully aware of the unlimited potential of this estate, and L'Evangile may soon be challenging Pétrus and Lafleur in both quality and, lamentably, price.

Certainly the late Louis Ducasse must have realized the distinctiveness of his vineyard because he often browbeat visiting wine critics with his observation that L'Evangile was as good as, and even more complex than, neighboring Pétrus. The remarkable Madame Ducasse died several years ago while in her mid-90s and still running L'Evangile on a day-to-day basis. I remember having lunch with this amazing woman in the early 1990s, where she poured the 1964, 1961, and 1947 from her personal cellar. At the end of a sumptuous lunch of gigantic portions of truffles, *ris de veau*, and *filet de boeuf*, I remarked that the only person who had eaten everything, and who had finished each glass of glorious wine even more quickly than the guests, was Madame Ducasse!

Now that L'Evangile is completely under Rothschild ownership, I fully anticipate this property will challenge Pétrus as well as Cheval Blanc year in and year out. It is a magical vineyard, as evidenced by the great wines that have been produced in years where there was no selection and a somewhat seat-of-the-pants vinification and upbringing of the wine. That will all change under the perfectionist regime of the Rothschilds. This is a Pomerol with a great track record already that looks poised to attain even greater heights . . . and prices.

IMPORTANT VINTAGES

2001   A rich, saturated ruby/purple color is accompanied by sweet, perfumed notes of
90–93 mocha, black raspberries, and cassis. As the wine is swirled, licorice aromas also emerge. A blend of 79% Merlot and 21% Cabernet Franc, this deep ruby/purple–colored 2001 reveals a fine texture as well as a seductive personality. Its low acidity and sweet tannin ensure that it will be enjoyable young, yet it possesses the depth and concentration to evolve for 15–18 years. Anticipated maturity: 2004–2017. Last tasted, 1/03.

2000 My handwritten notes on the 2000 began with the words "awesome stuff." An inky
96+   purple color is accompanied by scents of violets, blueberries, blackberries, cassis,
graphite, and truffles. Aromatically, it is the finest young L'Evangile I have ever
smelled. Splendidly rich and full-bodied, with great intensity, exquisite purity, astonishing harmony, and a blockbuster finish that lasts nearly a minute, this is a
potential legend in the making. Like its neighbor, La Conseillante, L'Evangile is
now revealing more grip and tannin, making my initial comments that this was "a
clone of the spectacular 1975" look increasingly accurate. Patience will be required, but, wow, this is a prodigious effort. Anticipated maturity: 2010–2035.
Last tasted, 1/03.

1999 A blend of 75% Merlot and 25% Cabernet Franc, the dark purple–colored 1999
89   L'Evangile reveals an unexpected touch of herbaceousness, which cost it a point or
two in the ultimate rating. Nevertheless, the striking, evolved, hedonistic perfume
of melted licorice intermixed with black raspberries, minerals, and truffles is an
intellectual turn-on. A beautiful, medium- to full-bodied L'Evangile with a sweet
attack and mid-palate, it may merit a higher score, depending on its evolution. Anticipated maturity: 2004–2015. Last tasted, 3/02.

1998 A blend of 80% Merlot and 20% Cabernet Franc aged in 45% new oak, this ter-
95+   rific, dense ruby/purple–colored L'Evangile is stuffed with concentrated blackberry and raspberry fruit. There is also an acacia-like floral character that gives
the wine even more complexity. Notes of toffee, licorice, and truffles add to the
aromatic fireworks. The wine is full-bodied, with superb purity as well as moderate tannin in the finish. A worthy rival to the 2000, the 1998 should be the finest
L'Evangile since the superb 1995 and 1990. Anticipated maturity: 2009–2035.
Last tasted, 4/02.

1997 A pure, truffle and black raspberry–scented nose with oak in the background de-
89   fines the classic style of L'Evangile. Nearly outstanding, this sexy, ripe, medium-
bodied wine offers gorgeous levels of fruit—not a great deal of density, length, or
tannin, but plenty of near-term appeal. Many consumers will score this offering
higher on the pleasure meter than the rating above might suggest, as it is very seductive. Anticipated maturity: now–2012. Last tasted, 3/02.

1996 Much like its neighbor, Clinet, the 1996 L'Evangile is a controversial wine. The
90?   wine gives the impression of being overextracted in its dark ruby/purple color and
notes of prunes, raisins, Chinese black tea, blackberries, and cherry liqueur. It is
rich and powerful, as well as tannic and disjointed, but medium to full-bodied,
with excellent richness and a long, overripe finish. It may take a few more years to
round into shape, but this could turn out to be an outstanding wine. Anticipated
maturity: 2005–2016. Last tasted, 3/02.

1995 This wine is closed, backward, and marginally less impressive than I thought from
92   cask. It is still an outstanding L'Evangile that may prove to be longer lived than the
sumptuous 1990, but perhaps not as opulently styled. It remains one of the year's top
efforts. The dense ruby/purple color is accompanied by aromas of minerals, black
raspberries, earth, and spice. The bottled wine seems toned down (too much fining
and filtration?) compared with the pre-bottling samples, which had multiple layers
of flesh and flavor dimension. High tannin in the finish and plenty of sweet fruit on
the palate suggest this wine will turn out to be extra special. Could it have been even
better if the filters had been junked in favor of a natural bottling? I think so, yet that
being said, the wine's ferocious tannin level cannot conceal its outstanding ripeness,
purity, and depth. Anticipated maturity: 2007–2020. Last tasted, 10/02.

1994 One of the vintage's most notable successes, L'Evangile's 1994 has a dense plum/
90   ruby color, a sweet nose of licorice, black raspberry, and currant with a hint of
roasted herbs and damp soil. Medium to full-bodied and very opulent, it has con-

siderable richness in the front end and mid-section. Like most of the best 1994s, the one defect is the lack of sweetness and the relatively dry, tannic finish. Nevertheless, this is top-notch stuff from a vintage that provides many good surprises, although the style of the wines tends to be relatively firm, muscular, and structured. Anticipated maturity: now–2020. Last tasted, 10/02.

1990
96
A fabulous example of L'Evangile at its best. Dense ruby/purple with some amber at the edge, this wine has a gorgeous nose of black truffles intermixed with caramel, malt chocolate, sweet black raspberries, and blackberries. The wine is full-bodied with loads of glycerine giving it a very opulent, almost viscous feel on the palate. It still tastes youthful, but has always been accessible throughout its entire life. The wine does have plenty of tannin, but most of it is concealed by the wealth of fruit extract and the wine's viscosity. It is a sensational L'Evangile that is just beginning to develop the secondary nuances of adolescence. Anticipated maturity: now–2024. Last tasted, 11/02.

1989
89
Fully mature and not likely to improve, although certainly capable of lasting another 10–15 years, the dark plum/garnet–colored 1989 L'Evangile (considerable amber exists at the edge) offers a nose of toffee, caramel, malt chocolate, sweet black cherry, and currant fruit. The wine has low acidity and plump, fleshy, forward appeal. With sweet tannin and a ripe, moderately endowed, long finish, it has nowhere near the weight, aging potential, or volume of the 1990, but it is still a top-class effort. Anticipated maturity: now–2015. Last tasted, 11/02.

1988
87
Dark plum/garnet with some lightening at the edge, this wine has that telltale characteristic of the vintage—licorice, underbrush, and compost intermixed with plum, blackberry, and currant fruit. The wine shows sweetness on the attack but then becomes a bit desiccated and medium bodied, with some dry, hard tannins in the finish. It is fully mature, but not likely to become any more graceful. Anticipated maturity: now–2010. Last tasted, 3/01.

1986
87?
Very herbaceous notes intermixed with loamy soil scents and a shortage of sweet fruit make for a very differently styled L'Evangile. The wine is somewhat awkward and clumsy, with some hard edges and high tannins desiccating the finish. My best instincts suggest that it needs to be drunk up before it loses more fruit and charm. Anticipated maturity: now. Last tasted, 3/02.

1985
95
A beautiful L'Evangile and one of the vintage's top successes, the color still retains a very dense ruby/purple with only a bit of lightening at the edge. A classic nose of liquid intermixed with black raspberries, blackberries, licorice, and a hint of truffle jumps from the glass of this medium- to full-bodied, very concentrated, well-balanced, sweet, authoritatively powerful yet at the same time elegant wine. It has reached full maturity, where it should rest for some time to come. Anticipated maturity: now–2017. Last tasted, 11/02.

1983
88
Losing some of its luster, this wine reached maturity very quickly and now seems to be turning the corner in a slow downward spiral. The wine has a dark plum color with considerable amber at the edge. The exotic nose of dried herbs, camphor, Asian spice, licorice, and black fruits is followed by a soft, round, medium-bodied wine that is beginning to show some hardness to the tannin and a rather dry, scratchy finish. It needs to be drunk up, but still remains a very tasty, elegant style of L'Evangile. Anticipated maturity: now–2007. Last tasted, 11/02.

1982
98
A spectacular wine that seems to have put on weight every time I go back to it, this old-style wine (meaning reminiscent of some of the late 1940s vintages), has an opaque, murky plum/purple color with only a bit of lightening at the edge. The nose offers up notes of new saddle leather intermixed with very jammy notes of blackberry liqueur, licorice, smoke, beef blood, and truffles; it is a total turn-on. Very opulent, viscous, and intense, with full body, great richness, and loads of

glycerin this wine seems set for at least another 15–20 years of evolution. A remarkable effort and, to my taste, the greatest L'Evangile made after 1975 and 1961. Anticipated maturity: now–2025. Last tasted, 12/02.

ANCIENT VINTAGES

In the 1970s, the undeniable success was the 1975 (98 points; last tasted 8/02). It is a fabulous wine, fully mature, with more evolved aromas than the 1982 but not terribly dissimilar from that forceful, very powerful, highly extracted wine. It seems capable of lasting at least another 15–20 years, and it is one of the great classics of this controversial vintage. Other vintages of the 1970s have proven to be relatively disappointing, as have most of the vintage of the 1960s, with ratings from the low 70s to mid-80s on my score card. Pristine bottles of the 1961, however, proved the exception (99 points; last tasted 3/94). This is a wine where 66% of the blend came from three-year-old vines. This is a wine of extraordinary Port-like richness and even more viscosity and concentration than the 1982. Another great wine is the 1947 (rated 100 when tasted 3/97 and rated 97 when tasted 12/95). Another ancient vintage to look for is the 1950 (90 points; last tasted 3/00). It is fully mature and faded quickly in the glass, but the first 20 minutes were gorgeous.

FEYTIT-CLINET

Owner: Chasseuil family

Address: 33500 Pomerol

Telephone: 05 57 25 51 27 *or* 06 85 52 33 18;
Telefax: 05 57 25 93 97

Visits: By appointment only

Contact: Jérémy Chasseuil

VINEYARDS

Surface area: 17.3 acres

Grape varietals: 90% Merlot, 10% Cabernet Franc

Average age of vines: 25 years

Density of plantation: 6,900 vines per hectare

Average yields: 40 hectoliters per hectare

Elevage: Four to five week fermentation and maceration in temperature-controlled concrete vats. Wines undergo malolactics in barrels. Sixteen to eighteen months aging in barrels with 70% new oak. No fining, no filtration.

WINES PRODUCED

Château Feytit-Clinet: 20,000–25,000 bottles

(name not yet defined): 8,000 bottles

Plateau of maturity: Within 5–12 years of the vintage

GENERAL APPRECIATION

Long in the throes of mediocrity, Feytit-Clinet has spectacularly improved during the last 3–4 years, with vintages from 1998 onward being close to excellent. Obviously, there is still room for improvement, but the quality level is far higher than it used to be. The good news is that the renaissance of Feytit-Clinet is still much of an insider's secret, so shrewd consumers should be on the lookout for the coming vintages, especially as prices remain reasonable.

This 17.3-acre vineyard planted with 90% Merlot and 10% Cabernet Franc is situated near Trotanoy and Latour à Pomerol. For a long time one of Pomerol's underachievers, it has immensely improved over the last three or four vintages. The estate, which had been farmed for a number of years by the Libourne-based firm of Jean-Pierre Moueix, is now managed by its owners, the Chasseuil family. Yields were reduced significantly, and a second wine was introduced. Quality has improved dramatically since Feytit-Clinet escaped Moueix control, making one wonder what was going on during their period of occupancy of this vineyard.

IMPORTANT VINTAGES

2001
88–90
The 2001 Feytit-Clinet is the finest wine I have tasted from this estate. Production was 2,000 cases from yields of 40 hectoliters per hectare. An impressive ruby/purple color is followed by sweet aromas of black fruits and licorice (or is it truffles?). With admirable texture, low acidity, excellent to outstanding ripeness, as well as concentration and medium to full body, it will be at its apogee between 2005–2015. Last tasted, 1/03.

2000
87
A solid as well as substantial wine, this dark ruby, medium-bodied Pomerol offers a bouquet of melted licorice, black cherries, and earth. Good power, ripe tannin, and a chunky, somewhat monolithic style suggest aging/cellaring is warranted. Anticipated maturity: 2007–2014. Last tasted, 1/03.

1998
88+
Dark purple–colored with a deep, intense, extracted feel, the 1998 is a moderately closed, yet promising, medium- to full-bodied wine with excellent richness and earthy, licorice, and black cherry/cranberry-like fruit flavors. There is plenty of glycerin, moderately high tannin, and a mouth-filling personality to this large-scaled effort. Anticipated maturity: now–2016. Last tasted, 3/02.

ANCIENT VINTAGES

If truth be told, there is virtually nothing of interest I have ever tasted in the 1970s, 1980s, and early 1990s from Feytit-Clinet that I would want to own in my cellar or would want anyone reading this book to purchase. Several vintages, like the 1990, were pleasant but, by and large, this was a diluted, thin, often herbaceous wine that turned out uninspiring year in and year out.

LA FLEUR DE GAY

Owner: Raynaud and Lebreton families

Address: 33500 Pomerol

Telephone: 05 57 51 19 05; Telefax: 05 57 74 15 62

E-mail: contact@chateau-lafleurdegay.com

Website: www.chateau-lafleurdegay.com

Visits: Preferably by appointment Monday to Thursday and
Saturday, 9 A.M.–1 P.M. and 2–5 P.M.; Friday, 2–5 P.M.

Contact: Chantal Lebreton

VINEYARDS

Surface area: 7.4 acres

Grape varietals: 100% Merlot

Average age of vines: 45 years

Density of plantation: 5,000 vines per hectare

Average yields: 20 hectoliters per hectare

Elevage: Cold maceration, three to four week fermentation and maceration in
temperature-controlled concrete tanks. Wines undergo malolactics and are aged in 100%
new oak for 18 months. No fining, no filtration.

WINES PRODUCED

Château La Fleur de Gay: 6,000–9,000 bottles

Plateau of maturity: Within 5–20 years of the vintage

GENERAL APPRECIATION

This wine, the special *cuvée* from La Croix de Gay, can be one of the most exciting
Pomerols in the best vintages, as evidenced by the 1990 and 1989. After a difficult period
at the beginning of the 1990s, the estate seems to have rebounded beautifully and has
come back to its former quality level. Among the top-notch Pomerols, La Fleur de Gay
remains a reasonably good buy. However, limited availability makes it difficult to find.

La Fleur de Gay, the luxury *cuvée* of La Croix de Gay, was launched by Dr. Alain Raynaud in 1982 (see page 651). The wine comes from a small parcel of very old vines
situated between Pétrus and Vieux-Château-Certain that is part of Dr. Raynaud's
better-known estate called La Croix de Gay. Aged in 100% new oak, it is a wine that is
characterized by a compelling opulence and sweetness, as well as exceptional purity of
fruit. Michel Rolland oversees the vinification and upbringing of this luxuriously flavored, intense, full-bodied wine. Vintages to date give every indication of possessing
10–20 years of aging potential. The secret . . . low yields and a ripe harvest. The 7.4
acre, 100% Merlot vineyard situated in the heart of the Pomerol plateau keeps yields
of approximately 25 hectoliters per hectare. Malolactic fermentation takes place in
barrel, and the wine is bottled without fining or filtration.

IMPORTANT VINTAGES

2001
88–90
This estate has followed their sensational 2000 with a 2001 that is potentially outstanding. An opaque purple color and sweet perfume of licorice, blueberries, and crème de cassis, along with hints of violets and truffles are followed by a pure, deep, medium- to full-bodied Pomerol revealing excellent freshness as well as definition. It is an impeccably made, classy, potentially long-lived effort. Anticipated maturity: 2006–2017. Last tasted, 1/03.

2000
94
This is the strongest effort from this estate since the wonderful duo of 1990 and 1989. The blockbuster 2000 rivals the great 1989. Opaque purple–colored with an extraordinarily intense nose of concentrated blackberries, minerals, and toast, it builds incrementally on the palate, but never becomes heavy or ponderous. It is a wine of exceptional delineation, purity, and length with a wealth of fruit that easily hides the high tannin. Anticipated maturity: 2004–2018. Last tasted, 1/03.

1999
90
Only 7,000 bottles were produced of the 1999 La Fleur de Gay. This wine exhibits a deep ruby/purple color, serious concentration, and a lovely perfume of black fruits mixed with minerals, toast, and cherries. Nicely textured and pure, with wonderful sweetness, harmony, and ripe tannin, it will be at its best between now and 2016. Last tasted, 3/02.

1998
90
This elegant, dark ruby/purple–colored 1998 exhibits aromas of lead pencil, blackberries, black raspberries, licorice, and vanilla. Deep, rich, and full-bodied, with excellent ripeness, beautiful symmetry as well as harmony, and moderate tannin in the finish, it will be at its best between now and 2016. Last tasted, 3/02.

1997
87
An evolved medium ruby color offers cranberry, dried herb, cherry, and subtle spicy oak aromas. Medium bodied and supple textured, the wine exhibits a certain sexiness, but little depth or density. This pretty, elegant, precocious Pomerol reveals some fat, but is best drunk over the next 2–3 years. Last tasted, 3/02.

1996
85
A very disappointing effort from La Fleur de Gay, this somewhat emaciated style of winemaking has resulted in a medium to dark ruby/garnet–colored wine with obvious sweet new oak dominating the rather herbaceous, red currant–infused aromatics. In the mouth, the wine is austere and somewhat hollow, with astringent tannin in the finish. Those who think this wine is going to soften and flesh out are entirely too optimistic. Anticipated maturity: now–2010. Last tasted, 12/01.

1995
88+?
Very closed and seemingly excessively tannic, this wine has a dense ruby/purple color, a tight, promising nose of minerals, vanilla, black fruit, and a hint of blueberry. In the mouth some herbs come forth, as do ferocious tannins. The wine has impressive credentials up front and on the initial attack, but then seems to become excessively dry, astringent, and harsh. Perhaps it is going through an unflattering stage of development, but I am losing some optimism from my early enthusiasm for this vintage of La Fleur de Gay. Anticipated maturity: 2007–2015. Last tasted, 4/02.

1994
89
Surprise, surprise, this wine may actually be turning out better than the more heralded vintages of 1996 and 1995. Dark ruby/garnet with notes of olive, licorice, black currant, and smoky oak, this medium-bodied wine has some firm, even hard tannin in the finish, but there is good depth and intensity. I am not sure it will ever shed all the tannin, but the wine is a very elegant, medium-bodied, stylish example. Anticipated maturity: now–2014. Last tasted, 9/02.

1990
94
A sensational wine that has developed exceptionally well, this dense, saturated, garnet/purple-colored wine has a super nose of smoke, camphor, mineral, black currant, and blueberry. The oak seems to take a backseat to the wealth of fruit and mineral notes. In the mouth it is full-bodied, with high but ripe tannin, wonderful sweetness, extract, high levels of glycerin, and relatively low acidity. It is a wine of

great character, richness, and complexity, as well as having multiple dimensions. Anticipated maturity: now–2015. Last tasted, 11/02.

1989   Possibly the finest La Fleur de Gay made, this rich, very large-scaled, tannic wine
95   has a compelling nose of cassis, licorice, white flowers, minerals, and other sorts of black fruits along with some subtle new oak. Full-bodied, with great delineation, purity, and dazzling concentration and intensity, this is a fabulous example of a La Fleur de Gay and it is a wine that seems capable of lasting at least another two decades. Anticipated maturity: now–2020. Last tasted, 12/02.

1988   A terrific example for the vintage and the first of a remarkable trilogy for La Fleur-
92   de-Gay, the dark garnet–colored 1988 has notes of melted licorice intermixed with espresso, sweet red and black fruits, mineral, and spice. The wine's exuberant fragrance is followed by a very delineated, moderately tannic, medium- to full-bodied wine with superb concentration, sweet but noticeable tannin, and outstanding depth. A beautiful wine to drink over the next 10–15 years. Anticipated maturity: now–2015. Last tasted, 11/02.

1986   Becoming increasingly austere and a bit dried out, this wine showed a lot of prom-
88   ise early on. It is still very good, but the tannins seem sharper and more aggressive. The wine has a deep ruby color with some amber at the edge. Sweet new oak still dominates the nose and, along with some ripe black currant and cherry fruit, the wine shows an earthiness and a hint of herbaceousness, something that has emerged over the last few years. Anticipated maturity: now–2010. Last tasted, 12/02.

1985   Fully mature, this sweet, open-knit wine is medium bodied, with floral notes inter-
89   mixed with blackberry, cherry, toast, and earth. The wine is low in acidity and delicious, as it has been for some time. Anticipated maturity: now–2007. Last tasted, 3/02.

ANCIENT VINTAGES

The debut vintage for La Fleur de Gay, 1982, was a disappointment, and when last tasted (3/02; 75 points) it was in decline and completely diffuse and unattractive. The 1983 (rated 87?; last tasted 3/02) is also starting to crack up and needs to be drunk now. Herbaceous notes mixed with compost, Chinese black tea, and red currant fruit notes are still there, but the tannins have become more noticeable, giving the wine a desiccated feel in the mouth.

LA FLEUR-PÉTRUS

Owner: SC Château La Fleur-Pétrus

Address: 33500 Pomerol

Mailing address: c/o Ets Jean-Pierre Moueix, BP 129, 54, quai du Priourat, 33502 Libourne Cedex

Telephone: 05 57 51 78 96; Telefax: 05 57 51 79 79

Visits: By appointment and exclusively for professionals of the wine trade dealing with the firm

Contact: Frédéric Lospied

VINEYARDS

Surface area: 33.2 acres

Grape varietals: 85% Merlot, 15% Cabernet Franc

Average age of vines: 35 years

Density of plantation: 6,250 vines per hectare

Average yields: 39 hectoliters per hectare

Elevage: Twenty to twenty-four day fermentation and maceration in temperature-controlled concrete vats. Twenty months aging in barrels that are renewed by a third at each vintage. Fining, no filtration.

WINES PRODUCED

Château La Fleur-Pétrus: 50,000 bottles

Plateau of maturity: Within 5–15 years of the vintage

GENERAL APPRECIATION

While this wine has always enjoyed a fine reputation, its performance from the end of the 1960s through the mid-1990s was not exceptional. However, in 1995 the wines began to improve.

Located on the eastern side of the plateau of Pomerol between Lafleur and Pétrus (hence the name) where so many of the best estates are found, La Fleur-Pétrus should be one of the most exquisite Pomerols. The famous firm of Jean-Pierre Moueix purchased the estate in 1952, and the vineyard was entirely replanted after 1956, when it was virtually destroyed by the apocalyptic winter freeze. The wine at La Fleur-Pétrus is lighter in weight and texture than other Mouiex Pomerols, such as Pétrus, Trotanoy, and Latour à Pomerol, but connoisseurs prize it for elegance and a supple, smooth, silky texture. It usually matures quickly and can be drunk as soon as five or six years after the vintage. Recent vintages have produced very fine wines, but I cannot help thinking that the quality could and should be higher. This appears to be happening. Readers should recognize that Christian Moueix is trying to push this estate's quality level to greater heights. To this end, he has acquired the finest section of old vines from Château Le Gay, and has instituted a more rigorous selection in both the vineyard and cellars. The winery itself has also been renovated. Some of La Fleur-Pétrus's finest wines have been produced only since 1998.

IMPORTANT VINTAGES

2001 The dark ruby/purple colored 2001 has added weight and richness. Deep, dense,
88–91 muscular, and rich, this traditionally vinified wine is not meant to be flattering young. A wine of excellent purity, it possesses noticeably sweet black cherry, and currant fruit intermixed with subtle wood and damp foresty aromas. Medium bodied, elegant, well delineated, and more powerful than I thought, it will be drinkable between 2010–2022. Last tasted, 1/03.

2000 A revelation in my bottle tastings was the fabulous performance of La Fleur-
95 Pétrus's 2000. This is a wine of great concentration with a fabulous dense purple color, powerful, long, highly extracted flavors, and copious sweet tannin in the finish. Unlike many 2000 Pomerols, the tannin is well integrated and sweet, but it shares its neighbor's large size as well as impressive concentration and power. If it continues to perform in this manner, it will eclipse the great 1998. However, it will not be as accessible young. A modern-day bigger and better 1975? Anticipated maturity: 2007–2025. Last tasted, 1/03.

1999 Performing well, with more power and depth after bottling than before, this wine
89   exhibits a dense ruby color as well as a sweet nose of pure black cherry jam intermixed with hints of raspberry, new wood, and earth. Surprisingly powerful for a
1999, with admirable ripeness, sweet tannin, and low acidity, it will be at its peak
between 2004 and 2015. Last tasted, 3/02.

1998 Along with the 2000, this is the finest La Fleur-Pétrus I have tasted. This dense
95   ruby/purple–colored wine exhibits aromas and flavors of Chinese black tea, raspberries, kirsch and flowers. Elegant, yet crammed with concentrated fruit, it is
symmetrical, harmonious, and long, with tremendous persistence on the palate.
While not a blockbuster/heavyweight, it is a wine of finesse and richness that admirably balances power with elegance. A great success! Anticipated maturity:
now–2020. Last tasted, 3/02.

1997 This 1997 is sexy, opulently textured, full-flavored, with low acidity as well as de-
87   licious, up-front appeal. Lavish cherry fruit intermixed with mocha, dried herbs,
spice box, and toasty oak are present in this medium- to full-bodied, fruit-driven
wine. Already evolved, complex, and tasty, it will age well for 7–8 years. Last
tasted, 3/02.

1996 The 1996 boasts an impressively saturated ruby/purple color, as well as a pure,
89   sweet nose of cherries, plum liqueur, spicy oak, and floral scents. The wine possesses excellent depth, medium body, superb purity, and an overall elegant personality offering a combination of power and finesse. Anticipated maturity:
now–2015. Last tasted, 3/01.

1995 A saturated dark purple color suggests a wine of considerable depth and concen-
91+   tration. The nose offers up gorgeous aromas of sweet kirsch intermixed with black
raspberry, mineral, and smoky notes. Full-bodied, with superb richness and purity, loads of tannin, and a layered, multidimensional personality, this terrific La
Fleur-Pétrus is one of the three finest wines I have tasted at this property in the 20
years I have been visiting Bordeaux. It is a splendid effort! Anticipated maturity:
2007–2025. Last tasted, 10/02.

1994 The attractive kirsch, cherry, toasty nose is followed by a medium-bodied, re-
88   strained, pure, measured wine. The 1994 offers an impressively saturated color,
as well as an inner core of sweet, concentrated fruit and moderate tannin in the
finish. All the richness, extract, and balance are present in this impressively
endowed wine that should be drunk between now and 2018. Last tasted,
10/02.

1990 Fully mature, with a very complex nose of roasted coffee, mocha, cedar, and
88   Provençal herbs, all backed up by some sweet cherry fruit, this medium-bodied,
relatively elegant, soft, very accessible wine is already showing considerable
amber to its garnet color. The finish also begins to fall off a bit, but the complexity
and delicious attack make for a very satisfying drink. Anticipated maturity: now–
2006. Last tasted, 3/02.

1989 In the ongoing competition between the 1990 and 1989 vintages, in the case of La
91   Fleur-Pétrus, the 1989 comes out a clear winner. The dense plum/garnet color offers up notes of underbrush, dried herbs, caramel, sweet cedar, and jammy black
cherries intermixed with some balsam wood. In the mouth the wine is deep, very
pure, ripe, with moderate tannins still to be shed. A very impressive, gorgeous La
Fleur-Pétrus that is the best wine made during a somewhat indifferent period for
this property. Anticipated maturity: 2004–2015. Last tasted, 3/02.

1988 Very vegetal on the nose and becoming more cedary as the wine sits in the glass,
83?   the flavors are dusty, with gritty tannin and almost desiccated red currant fruit
notes. The wine seems to be drying out and in decline. Anticipated maturity:
Drink up. Last tasted, 3/02.

1986   A very simple, one-dimensional La Fleur-Pétrus that is holding on to life but
84?   showing very little depth or concentration. The nose is somewhat muted, but does
offer up some dusty, earthy, loamy soil scents intermixed with the smell of underripe tomatoes and Provençal herbs. In the mouth, the wine is attenuated, compact,
medium bodied, and lacking concentration. Anticipated maturity: now–2010.
Last tasted, 3/02.

1985   This wine merits attention largely because of the very complex aromatics that con-
86   sist of menthol, tomato skin, cedar, smoke, sweet cherries, and plums. In the
mouth, the attack is impressive, medium bodied, elegant, soft, and pure, and the
finish is all velvet, but there is not much intensity or follow-through. The wine is
also fully mature, as evidenced by the considerable amber creeping at the color's
rim. Anticipated maturity: Drink up. Last tasted, 3/02.

1983   Drying out, becoming desiccated, with the herbaceous element taking over what
78   little fruit is left, this wine was fully mature 5–8 years after the vintage and is now
in complete decline. Anticipated maturity: Drink up. Last tasted, 3/02.

1982   Very inconsistent in more than a dozen tastings, this wine has never fully lived up
89   to the expectations I had for it prior to bottling. This was a period when Christian
Moueix and his conservative oenologist Jean-Claude Berrouet were, in my opinion, doing entirely too much fining and filtration, often killing much of the texture
and flavor in too many wines that tasted great out of cask. Obviously things
changed, but we still have great vintages like this that are perplexing and not what
they should be. The wine still shows a nice plum, mulberry, herbaceous, coffee-
scented nose with some cedar and spice box. In the mouth, it is medium bodied
with surprising acidity and moderate tannin. The finish is a bit short. After tasting
through much of a case, and never seeing the wine live up to my expectations, I am
convinced now this wine is in decline, somewhat unusual for a well-stored 1982.
Anticipated maturity: Drink up. Last tasted, 11/02.

ANCIENT VINTAGES

A bevy of mediocrities exist except for the 1975 (90 points; last tasted 3/02), 1971 (90
points; last tasted 12/01), 1970 (88 points; last tasted 3/02), and the fabulous 1961 (92
points; last tasted 12/95). Of those vintages, the only one I would still gamble with
would be the 1975, as it seemed to have the extract and tannic structure to continue to
drink well through 2015 or so.

Among the museum pieces in the La Fleur-Pétrus portfolio, the 1952 (91 points,
last tasted 3/89), 1950 (95 points; last tasted 3/89), and 1947 (90 points; last tasted
12/95) are wines I have not tasted since the last edition of this book, but I assume they
are largely in decline, although well-stored bottles of the 1950 and 1947 would certainly be worth the gamble and would probably be less expensive than other great
wines from those two vintages.

FRANC-MAILLET

Owner: Gérard Arpin

Address: Maillet, 33500 Pomerol

Telephone: 09 09 73 69 47; Telefax: 05 57 51 96 75

E-mail: vignobles-g-arpin@hotmail.com

Visits: By appointment only

Contact: Gaël Arpin

VINEYARDS

Surface area: 12.6 acres

Grape varietals: 80% Merlot, 20% Cabernet Franc

Average age of vines: 25 years

Density of plantation: 5,500 vines per hectare

Average yields: 48 hectoliters per hectare

Elevage: Thirty day fermentation and maceration in temperature-controlled epoxy-lined metal vats. Fourteen months aging in barrels with 80% of yield in barrel (50% new oak) and 20% of yield (Cabernet Franc) in concrete vats. Light fining with egg whites.

WINES PRODUCED

Château Franc-Maillet: 32,000 bottles

Plateau of maturity: Within 5–20 years of the vintage

GENERAL APPRECIATION

Although less concentrated and less rich than the special *cuvée* Jean-Baptiste, Château Franc-Maillet is soundly made. This wine, which is accessible at an earlier age than its sibling, represents a very good buy, especially for a Pomerol of this level. Prices will probably rise as consumers become aware of the quality of this gem.

Readers take note: This property has been fashioning fine wines over recent vintages. The *"bête-noire"* and *"garagiste extraordinaire"* of St.-Emilion, Jean-Luc Thunevin is responsible for the *Cuvée* Jean-Baptiste and his magical touch has produced an impressive wine.

IMPORTANT VINTAGES

2001 The 2001 Franc-Maillet offers a deep ruby/purple color as well as a sweet perfume
88–90 of plums, figs, black cherries, minerals, and subtle wood presented in a medium-bodied, ripe, low-acid, fleshy style. Anticipated maturity: 2004–2012. Last tasted, 1/03.

2001 *Cuvée* Jean-Baptiste: The saturated blue/purple–colored 2001 Franc-Maillet
92 *Cuvée* Jean-Baptiste is followed by abundant quantities of blackberries, cherries, and oak, medium to full body, considerable glycerin, an unctuous texture, and a 30-second finish. This impressive 2001 Pomerol appears to be one of the finest efforts of the appellation. Anticipated maturity: 2005–2015. Last tasted, 1/03.

| 2000 89 | Surprisingly, the 2000 Franc-Maillet is not performing as well as the excellent 1999 (atypical for this vintage). It possesses more muscle and tannin, a saturated color, and notes of licorice, black fruits, mineral, and new oak. Anticipated maturity: 2005–2014. Last tasted, 1/03. |

| 2000 92 | *Cuvée* Jean-Baptiste: The 2000 *Cuvée* Jean-Baptiste has added considerable weight during its *élevage*and is now significantly better than it was in its prime. An inky black color is followed by a superb bouquet of jammy black fruits intermixed with wet stones and flowers (acacia?). Fat yet structured, with sensational concentration as well as superb length, it will be drinkable between 2005–2020. Last tasted, 1/03. |

| 1999 88 | Dark ruby/purple colored with notes of plum, black cherries, currants, and berries, the medium-bodied, pure, well-structured 1999 Franc-Maillet is atypically tannic for a 1999. It should drink well for 10–12 years. Last tasted, 3/02. |

| 1999 90 | *Cuvée* Jean-Baptiste: Beautiful aromas of melted licorice intermixed with crème de cassis, black raspberries, and new oak cascade from the glass of the full-bodied, opaque purple–colored 1999 Franc-Maillet *Cuvée* Jean-Baptiste. Pure and ripe, with low acidity yet high tannin, it is a surprisingly muscular 1999. Anticipated maturity: 2004–2020. Last tasted, 3/02. |

| 1998 87 | *Cuvée* Jean-Baptiste: A good effort, this 1998 offers sweet, berry, mocha fruit intermixed with coffee andcaramel. Medium bodied, ripe, supple, and moderately weighty, its low acidity and plump fruit suggest it should be drunk over the next 3–4 years. Last tasted, 3/02. |

LE GAY

Owner: Catherine Péré-Vergé

Address: 33500 Pomerol

Telephone: 05 57 84 67 99; Telefax: 05 57 74 96 51

Visits: By appointment only

Contact: François Boyé

VINEYARDS

Surface area: 19.8 acres

Grape varietals: 50% Cabernet Franc, 50% Merlot

Average age of vines: 20 years and 5 years

Density of plantation: 5,900 vines per hectare

Average yields: 40 hectoliters per hectare

Elevage: Twenty-one day fermentation and maceration in temperature-controlled concrete vats. Aged for 18 to 20 months in barrels (60–80% new oak). Fining and filtration.

WINES PRODUCED

Château Le Gay: 24,000 bottles

No second wine is produced.

Plateau of maturity: Within 10–25 years of the vintage

GENERAL APPRECIATION

A very inconsistent estate that has a tendency to "hit or miss" with alarming frequency. At best, these are muscular, large-scaled, brawny wines of considerable power and mass. The acquisition of this estate in 2003 by Catherine Péré-Vergé and the hiring of Michel Rolland should result in dramatically increased quality.

Le Gay has been a vineyard of enormous potential, with old vines and minuscule yields of 15–20 hectoliters per hectare, but historically it has been inconsistent. Great raw materials from the vineyard are often translated into mediocre wine as a result of old and sometimes dirty barrels. Until 1982 the ancient barrels that housed the wine at Le Gay had to share space with flocks of chickens and ducks. Several years ago, a section of Le Gay vineyard (a parcel of old-vine Merlot) was sold to La Fleur-Pétrus in an effort to propel that property to a higher quality level. Not surprisingly, the vintages of Le Gay following this sale were disappointing (i.e., the 1996). However, over recent years, the estate seems to be coming back to form, but it no longer fashions marvels like the wines it produced in the 1940s and 1950s. The 1950, 1948, 1947, and 1945 Le Gays that I once tasted from magnum all remain superlative wines, with the 1950, 1947, and 1945 flirting with perfection. Shrewd Pomerol enthusiasts should search out the ancient vintages of Le Gay, as some are splendid. For example, the 1947 (rated 98 in 3/98) and the 1950 (rated 94 in 4/98) are two compelling examples of Le Gay.

The style of winemaking at Le Gay has resulted in powerful, rich, tannic, sometimes massive and impenetrable wines. In some years Le Gay can turn out to be coarse and overbearing, whereas in other vintages the power of Le Gay is in harmony and well balanced against ripe fruit, firm acidity, and tannin. Le Gay is almost always the least flattering Pomerol to taste at a young age, often needing 8–10 years of cellaring to shed its cloak of tannin. For those who prefer their Claret soft and easy to drink, Le Gay is an intimidating sort of wine. I await the result of the new administration; their first vintage will be 2003.

IMPORTANT VINTAGES

2001 A strong effort from this estate, the medium-bodied, dense ruby/purple–colored
88–90 2001 displays aromas of damp earth, animal fur, and sweet black cherry and plum-like fruit. Sweet on the attack, ripe, with moderate tannin and medium body, it will be at its peak between 2007–2016. Last tasted, 1/03.

2000 The finest Le Gay produced in years, the 2000 still reveals old-style, rugged tan-
90 nin (as do many 2000 Pomerols) and there is a hint of awkwardness, but I was super-impressed with its opaque purple color, sweet black cherry nose, and outstanding ripeness, purity, and structure. Notes of truffle and saddle leather can be discerned, but fruit dominates, and the glycerin and extract have married well with the moderately high tannin. It is a wine for those with 19th-century tastes. Anticipated maturity: 2007–2020. Last tasted, 1/03.

1999 Plum, earth, and black cherry scents intermix with licorice and soil overtones in
87 the 1999 Le Gay. The wine is medium bodied with surprisingly soft tannin for Le Gay, and also with more ripeness and length than I recall tasting over the last several years. It should drink well for a dozen or more years. Last tasted, 1/03.

1998 Along with the 2001 and 2000, this is one of the finest Le Gays of the last decade.
89 This dark plum/purple–colored 1998 exhibits an earthy, truffle, smoke, iron, graphite, black cherry, and plum-scented bouquet. It is less rustic, with sweeter tannin than normal, fleshier, riper, more concentrated fruit, medium to full body, and a long, spicy finish. Anticipated maturity: 2004–2016. Last tasted, 3/02.

1996
74
There is no mid-palate in the dark ruby–colored, hollow, tannic 1996, nor does it exhibit much depth, charm, or fat. Anticipated maturity: now–2008. Last tasted, 3/02.

1995
82
Lacking the depth, flesh, fruit, and charm that one expects in most Pomerols, this dark ruby–colored wine exhibits an excess of tannin, body, and structure for the amount of fruit it possesses. It will not provide near-term consumption given its severe personality. Anticipated maturity: 2005–2015. Last tasted, 3/02.

1994
86
This wine is medium bodied, with a deep ruby/purple color and some spicy oak, minerals, and black fruits in the nose. It is a beefy, muscular, tannic wine, with sufficient fruit to balance out its structure. Drink it over the next 3–4 years. Last tasted, 3/02.

1990
88
This wine is made in a very rough and tumble style, although it still has an attractive upside, given its dense garnet, murky ruby color, a big sweet nose of cow pasture droppings, roasted meats, dried herbs, earth, and smoky, licorice-infused black fruits. The high level of tannin and relatively tough texture all suggest a style of wine for those with 19th-century taste. Nevertheless, like so many vintages of Le Gay, there is plenty of depth and richness underlying all the tannin, but it is hard to believe this wine will ever come into complete harmony. However, one still admires it, even in a somewhat masochistic way. Anticipated maturity: 2005–2018+? Last tasted, 11/02.

1989
92
This wine seems to get better and better and is certainly the only great Le Gay of recent years. This dark ruby/purple–colored wine has a nose of blueberries, minerals, and white flowers. The wine shows plenty of sweetness, real opulence, and high tannins, but sweeter, more civilized tannins than most Le Gays tend to possess. It is a very muscular, full-bodied style of wine that should age effortlessly for another 15–20 years. Anticipated maturity: now–2020. Last tasted, 11/02.

1988
87
Notes of wet dog/animal fur intermixed with damp earth, licorice, mushroom, and even a hint of truffle compete with some sweet, dusty cherries in this medium-bodied, slightly stern and tannic wine. Anticipated maturity: now–2012. Last tasted, 3/02.

1986
87
Another vintage for those who have primarily 19th-century taste, this beefy, rather coarse wine still has a dark garnet color with some lightening at the edge. The wine has a dusty, earthy nose with hints of truffle, licorice, mushroom, and meat. The wine is dense and ruggedly constructed, with medium body and some high tannin in the finish. Again, it is impressive from a structural standpoint, but the tannins will probably be too much for most modern-day palates. Anticipated maturity: 2004–2016. Last tasted, 11/02.

1985
87
This wine has come along better than I suspected, which always gives hope for Le Gay purchasers, given how muddled, tannic, and backward these wines can be. Deep ruby/garnet with some slight amber, this wine has a smoky, earthy nose with notes of wet stone, truffle, black cherries, and stewed vegetables and herbs. Again, meatiness seems to permeate the flavors, as if someone has squeezed blood into the fermentation vats. The wine still has some tannins to lose, although it will probably never drop all of it. There is fine depth and an excellent finish. Anticipated maturity: now–2012. Last tasted, 11/02.

1982
90
A wine that can compete with the 1989 for high quality, this dark ruby/garnet colored wine shows some amber at the edge. A big, sweet, pungent, earthy, jammy nose of black fruits intermixed with mushrooms, earth, and tree bark jumps from the glass of this full-bodied, dense, rather powerful wine. Bottle variation has been a problem, as I have noted before, because of a distinct mustiness in some bottles, but the last two bottles I have tasted have been healthy tastings, with sweet, jammy black cherry fruit, a hint of licorice, earth, and some mushrooms. The finish is still

austere, but there is plenty of sweet fruit underlying all the tannin. Anticipated maturity: 2004–2018. Last tasted, 3/02.

ANCIENT VINTAGES

The fabulous 1975 (92 points; last tasted 11/02) is just beginning to hit its stride after 27 years of sleep. The wine is very rich, has a dense color, and notes of liquid minerality infused with black fruits and truffle. Other top vintages such as 1966, 1962, and 1961 have been very disappointing. However, two ancient vintages that are pure perfection include the 1950 and 1947. Both wines (last tasted 12/01 from magnum) were 100-point efforts, opulent, viscous, with extraordinary sweetness of fruit and a level of concentration and freshness that was hard to believe. The corks were original, and the wines had not been moved from their Belgian cellars, where they had been kept for nearly 50 years. Obviously, this might be a wine that needs 25–30 years of cellaring before it comes into its own.

GAZIN

Owner: Bailliencourt dit Courcol family

Address: 33500 Pomerol

Telephone: 05 57 51 07 05; Telefax: 05 57 51 69 96

E-mail: contact@gazin.com

Website: www.gazin.com

Visits: By appointment only Monday to Friday, 9 A.M.–7 P.M.

Contact: Nicolas de Bailliencourt dit Courcol

VINEYARDS

Surface area: 59.9 acres

Grape varietals: 90% Merlot, 7% Cabernet Sauvignon, 3% Cabernet Franc

Average age of vines: 35 years

Density of plantation: 5,500–6,000 vines per hectare

Average yields: 42 hectoliters per hectare

Elevage: Eighteen to twenty-eight day fermentation and maceration in temperature-controlled concrete tanks of small capacity. Wines undergo malolactics in barrel and frequent stirring of the lees. Eighteen months aging in barrels with 50–60% new oak. Fining and filtration only if necessary.

WINES PRODUCED

Château Gazin: 25,000 bottles

L'Hospitalet de Gazin: 32,000 bottles

Plateau of maturity: Within 5–20 years of the vintage

GENERAL APPRECIATION

Gazin is a reliable growth, producing excellent wines on a regular basis. Moreover, availability is large and prices remain within limits. That being said, this estate has had a tendency to use too much new oak for the wine's upbringing. Certain vintages do present pronounced woody aromas that I believe will never be fully meshed. This is the only reservation I have about this otherwise fruity, rich, relatively large-scaled Pomerol.

Most commentators on Bordeaux have generally held Gazin in high regard, no doubt because the vineyard is ideally situated behind Pétrus as well as adjacent to L'Evangile. In fact, Gazin sold 12.5 acres of its vineyard to Pétrus in 1969. Even then, Gazin is still one of the largest Pomerol estates, totaling nearly 60 acres. The track record for Gazin was mediocre throughout the 1960s and 1970s. Yet since the late 1980s Gazin has rebounded impressively, producing a succession of topflight wines.

Strangely enough Gazin has always been an expensive wine. A historic reputation and the strategic placement on the Pomerol plateau with excellent clay/gravel soils have served Gazin well. The optimistic signs that began in 1989 and 1988 mark a new period of higher-quality wines from Gazin and should be greeted enthusiastically by consumers wanting a tasty, plump, succulent Pomerol.

IMPORTANT VINTAGES

2001 Gazin's proprietor thinks 2001 is more successful than 2000, and he might be cor-
90–91+ rect. An impressive, extracted, tannic, powerful effort, this inky purple–colored Pomerol was produced from a vineyard adjacent to Pétrus. Deep and muscular, with good delineation, abundant quantities of smoky, black cherry fruit, excellent purity, and admirable definition, it will require patience. Anticipated maturity: 2008–2018. Last tasted, 1/03.

2000 This is a sweet, very ripe, rich, rather dense Gazin. While the ruby/purple–colored
90 2000 is not a blockbuster in the mold of the 1998, nor as charming as the evolved 1999, it possesses excellent fruit, medium to full body, plenty of toasty oak, and notes of dried herbs, saddle leather, and cassis with a hint of licorice. Anticipated maturity: 2008–2020. Last tasted, 1/03.

1999 An excellent sweet nose of lavish toasty oak intertwined with plums, black cher-
89 ries, and currants dominates the olfactory senses. In the mouth, this wine is elegant, lush, flavorful, and savory, with medium body and no hard edges. Drink it over the next 10–12 years. Last tasted, 3/02.

1998 A dense ruby/purple color is followed by aromas of charred wood, coffee, black-
91 berry and cherry fruit, and new saddle leather. Full-bodied, dense, chewy, and intense, this muscular as well as backward *vin de garde* requires 2–3 years cellaring. Anticipated maturity: 2005–2020. Last tasted, 3/02.

1997 A dark plum color is accompanied by an exotic nose of roasted espresso beans,
87? sweet cherry jam, and lavish toasty oak. Soft, round, and medium bodied, with attractive fruit, this wine pushes the oak to its limit, but there is no doubting its luscious fruit and seductive, open-knit style. Drink it over the next 4–5 years. Last tasted, 3/01.

1996 The 1996 is an atypically tannic, serious Gazin with a dense ruby/purple color and
89 lavish quantities of toasty new oak in the nose intermixed with licorice, black cherries, and mocha/coffee notes. The wine displays excellent concentration, but is backward, with medium to full body and moderately high tannin. Give it another 2–3 years of cellaring as it will be potentially long-lived. It is unquestionably an impressive effort for a 1996 Pomerol. Anticipated maturity: 2005–2018. Last tasted, 3/02.

1995   While this deep ruby/purple–colored Pomerol hints at some of its exotic grilled
90+   herb and meat-like character, the reluctant nose primarily reveals new oak,
       smoke, spice, and background jammy fruit. On the palate, the wine is deep,
       medium to full-bodied, refined, and, except for some noticeably hard tannin in the
       finish, relatively seamless. This expansively flavored effort offers plenty of spice,
       new oak, fruit, and depth. Anticipated maturity: now–2018. Last tasted, 3/02.

1994   This opaque ruby/purple–colored, lavishly oaked wine displays a huge, cedary,
89   cassis, smoky, roasted meat–scented nose, unctuously textured, chewy, thick fla-
       vors, and considerable power and richness in the muscular, moderately tannic fin-
       ish. This big, impressively structured Pomerol will require patience. Anticipated
       maturity: now–2018. Last tasted, 1/97.

1990   Perhaps the best Gazin I have ever tasted, this full-bodied, opulent wine has a
93   dark murky plum/purple color with some amber at the edge. The huge, lavishly
       oaked nose also shows plenty of sweet black cherries, malt chocolate, cedar, tape-
       nade, and licorice. Very full-bodied, viscous, and rich, with a sweet entry and
       large-scaled, dense, and chewy mid-section and finish, this is among the most
       concentrated and complete Gazins of my tasting experience. Anticipated matu-
       rity: now–2016. Last tasted, 12/01.

1989   Fully mature, this wine offers up notes of dried Provençal herbs intermixed with
88   toffee, caramel, cedar, sweet black cherries, and candied licorice. The wine is
       medium to full-bodied, with low acidity, ripe tannin, and a soft, silky finish. It is
       far less voluminous and intense than the 1990, and also more evolved. Antici-
       pated maturity: now–2010. Last tasted, 12/02.

1988   Becoming increasingly herbaceous as it has aged, with notes of licorice inter-
87   mixed with cedar wood, red cherries, and smoke, this medium-bodied, soft wine
       has been fully mature for a number of years and is not likely to improve. Its low
       acidity and plump, forward character have always made it an attractive wine, but
       owners of it will be pushing their luck to hold it any longer. Anticipated maturity:
       Drink up. Last tasted, 12/01.

ANCIENT VINTAGES

Gazin had a deplorable record in the 1980s, including even the great vintage of 1982.
The 1970s were even worse, as were most of the 1960s. The only top note that I have on
my tasting score card is the 1961 (93 points; last tasted 12/95).

LA GRAVE À POMEROL ————————————————

**(known as La Grave-Trigant-de-Boisset
prior to 1992)**

Owner: Ets Jean-Pierre Moueix

Address: 33500 Pomerol

Mailing address: c/o SA Ets Jean-Pierre Moueix, 54,
quai du Priourat, BP 129, 33502 Libourne Cedex

Telephone: 05 57 51 78 96; Telefax: 05 57 51 79 79

Visits: By appointment and exclusively for professionals
of the wine trade dealing with the firm.

Contact: Frédéric Lospied

VINEYARDS

Surface area: 21.5 acres

Grape varietals: 85% Merlot, 15% Cabernet Franc

Average age of vines: 30 years

Density of plantation: 6,250 vines per hectare

Average yields: 42 hectoliters per hectare

Elevage: Eighteen day fermentation and maceration in temperature-controlled concrete vats. Twenty months aging in barrels with 25% new oak. Fining and filtration.

WINES PRODUCED

Château La Grave à Pomerol: 30,000 bottles

Domaine Trigant-de-Boisset (since 2000): variable

Plateau of maturity: Within 5–15 years of the vintage

GENERAL APPRECIATION

This is one of Pomerol's most elegant, fruity and stylish wines. It is never very dense or powerful, but always seductive and impeccably made.

La Grave à Pomerol is another of the relatively obscure Pomerol estates that are now making better and better wine. Since 1971 the château has been owned by the meticulous and introspective Christian Moueix, who directs the business affairs of his firm in Libourne.

La Grave à Pomerol is located just to the east of Route Nationale 89 in the direction of France's truffle capital, Périgueux. It is adjacent to the border of Lalande-de-Pomerol and situated on unusually gravelly, sandy soil, which results in wines that are a little lighter and less powerful than those from the Pomerol plateau. Perhaps it is because this property is owned by Christian Moueix that La Grave à Pomerol always displays a Pétrus-like personality, although it is a lighter, less concentrated and voluminous effort.

All the vintages from 1980 on have been successful, and the 1998, 1990, and 1982 are classics. Normally La Grave is a wine to drink after 5–6 years of bottle age, although in some vintages it can be cellared for 12–15 years. While not one of the most expensive Pomerols, neither is it one of the bargains of this appellation. However, given the increasing quality exhibited by this wine in recent vintages, this is a property to take more and more seriously.

IMPORTANT VINTAGES

2001
87–88 A refined, elegant Pomerol, this 2001 offers up aromas of spicy wood intermixed with pure black cherry fruit. Medium bodied, soft, fresh, and vibrant, it will drink well for 7–8 years. Last tasted, 1/03.

2000
88 Atypically powerful, the concentrated, medium- to full-bodied 2000 displays more tannin and structure than usual as well as abundant concentration and sweet black cherry fruit. The dark ruby-colored 2000 should prove to be uncommonly long-lived by the standards of this estate. Anticipated maturity: 2006–2017. Last tasted, 1/03.

1999
87
Notes of sweet almonds, black cherries, and subtle herbs are found in this 1999's moderately intense, perfumed bouquet. Medium bodied, with elegance and finesse, it will be drinkable between now and 2008. Last tasted, 3/02.

1998
90
Is this a "petit Pétrus?" While it does not have the weight, power, or volume of Pétrus, the 1998 displays character similar to that of its more majestic sibling. The finest La Grave à Pomerol I have ever tasted, it boasts a deep ruby color as well as a gorgeously elegant, sweet, graceful perfume of jammy blackberries and cherries intermixed with toasty oak and mocha. Refined and sweet with a savory mid-palate, medium body, ripe fruit, and admirable succulence as well as graceful-ness, its tannin is beautifully integrated, and the wine is hedonistic and complex. A sleeper of the vintage! Drink it over the next 12 years. Last tasted, 3/02.

1997
86
A sexy, open-knit wine, this 1997 reveals toffee/caramel notes intermixed with herb-infused cherry fruit, vanilla, and toasty oak. Medium bodied, moderately intense, sweet, harmonious, jammy, and velvety-textured, this delicious offering can be consumed over the next 2–3 years. Last tasted, 3/01.

1996
86
A well-made, smoky, coffee, and cherry-scented wine, the 1996 La Grave à Pomerol exhibits good concentration, nicely integrated acidity and tannin, and a round, attractive softness that makes it an ideal candidate for consuming in its youth. Anticipated maturity: now–2007. Last tasted, 3/98.

1995
88
This lovely, charming 1995 reveals a deep ruby color and plenty of sweet cherry fruit intertwined with high quality, spicy new oak. Medium bodied, with excellent concentration and a nicely layered, sexy personality, this is a textbook mid-weight Pomerol for drinking over the next 5–6 years. Last tasted, 3/01.

ANCIENT VINTAGES

As mentioned, one of the few classics in the last 15 years prior to 1995 was the 1990 (90 points; last tasted 1/01). This wine is fully mature but delicious, and it does have a somewhat Pétrus-like character, although far lighter than its bigger brother. I would opt for drinking it over the next 3–4 years. The 1989 (87 points; last tasted 4/00) is also very good, but the other surprising wine from La Grave à Pomerol that has stood the test of time is the 1982 (87 points; last tasted 11/02). This wine was fully mature 5–6 years after the vintage, but continues to hold on to life without drying out, something that great vintages have a tendency to do. Still, for anyone who owns a few bottles, it is best drunk up sooner rather than later.

HOSANNA

(previously known as Certan-Giraud)

Owner: Ets Jean-Pierre Moueix

Address: 33500 Pomerol

Mailing address: c/o SA Ets Jean-Pierre Moueix, BP 129, 54, quai du Priourat, 33502 Libourne

Telephone: 05 57 51 78 96; Telefax: 05 57 51 79 79

Visits: By appointment and exclusively for professionals of the wine trade dealing with the firm.

Contact: Frédéric Lospied

VINEYARDS

Surface area: 24.6 acres

Grape varietals: 71% Merlot, 29% Cabernet Franc

Average age of vines: 40 years

Density of plantation: 7,000 vines per hectare

Average yields: 35 hectoliters per hectare

Elevage: Twenty day fermentation and maceration in temperature-controlled concrete tanks. Eighteen months aging in barrels with 50% new oak. Fining, no filtration.

WINES PRODUCED

Château Hosanna: 18,000 bottles

Plateau of maturity: Within 5–15 years of the vintage

GENERAL APPRECIATION

While this estate has a reputation for irregular quality when known as Certan-Giraud, it offers one of the finest Pomerols since its acquisition by the Jean-Pierre Moueix firm of Libourne. In the capable hands of talented Christian Moueix, who apparently spares no effort to push the envelope of quality as high as possible, Hosanna is meant to compete with the trendy new-style Pomerols like Clos l'Église. The wine produced is all at once generous, rich, structured, with a little touch of *sur-maturité* (a trait common to many topflight Pomerols). The results to date have been splendid.

This property, planted with 71% Merlot and 29% Cabernet Franc, well situated on the plateau of Pomerol, was acquired in 1998 by the Jean-Pierre Moueix firm, and it is now one of their stars. The vineyard, planted with 35- to 40-year-old vines, is sandwiched between such superstars as Pétrus, Lafleur, Vieux Château Certan, and the balance of the former Certan-Giraud vineyard, now called Certan Marzelle. In the past, the wine has been good, but there was little selection and yields were simply too high to produce superb wine. That has obviously changed (dramatically) with the 1999 vintage, when the name of Certan-Giraud was changed to Hosanna.

The wine is now an extraordinarily elegant Pomerol made from blend of 80% Merlot and the rest Cabernet Franc. Based on the first three vintages, Hosanna comes closest in aroma, taste, and texture to a hypothetical blend of Cheval Blanc and L'Evangile, both only about one mile away.

IMPORTANT VINTAGES
HOSANNA

2001 A blend of 80% Merlot and 20% Cabernet Franc, the 2001 possesses an undeni-
91–93 able character that mirrors the personality of its nearby neighbor, Cheval Blanc. A complex perfume of blueberries, licorice, and black currants is both intense and captivating. Sweet, ripe, and layered on the attack with a serious mid-palate and stunning depth, the old vines give this Pomerol a delicious, deep, textured feel in the mouth. Hosanna is a topflight success in 2001. Anticipated maturity: 2005–2016. Last tasted, 1/03.

2000
96

Produced from 70% Merlot and 30% Cabernet Franc, this offering has evolved spectacularly well. Its deep saturated ruby/purple color is followed by aromas of incense, minerals, blackberries, and cassis with hints of licorice, truffles, and new oak. A seamless, seductive Pomerol displaying both power and charm, it is totally different than its predecessors made under the Certan-Giraud administration. This brilliant effort should age graciously for two decades. This is a ravishing wine of exceptional symmetry. Anticipated maturity: 2005–2020. Last tasted, 1/03.

1999
90

A star of the vintage, this sexy, lush, complex, perfumed Pomerol exhibits a saturated ruby/purple color as well as a knockout nose of black fruits intermixed with menthol, saddle leather, licorice, and minerals. It is fleshy, silky, and voluptuous in its elegant, feminine style. Anticipated maturity: now–2016. Last tasted, 3/02.

CERTAN-GIRAUD

1996
84

I noticed some sample variation with this wine, but in the majority of tastings, it was a dense, low-acid, fat, ripe Pomerol with a touch of prunes, jammy black cherries, smoke, and dried herbs in its smoky, ripe, flamboyant nose. Plump, succulent, medium- to full-bodied flavors are forward for the vintage, but appealing and delicious. Anticipated maturity: now–2007. Last tasted, 3/98.

1995
87

The 1995 has turned out to be a very good Pomerol with sweet, jammy flavors that border on overripeness. The wine displays a deep ruby color with a flamboyant nose of smoke and black fruits. There is noticeable glycerin on the palate, medium to full body, low acidity, and plenty of power, intensity, and richness in this big, fleshy, mouth-filling, savory, hedonistic Pomerol. Anticipated maturity: now–2009. Last tasted, 11/97.

ANCIENT VINTAGES

In the early 1990s or 1980s, the only vintage of merit was the 1982, which was still going strong when last tasted (88 points; last tasted 10/02).

LAFLEUR

Owner: Jacques Guinaudeau and family

Address: 33500 Pomerol

Mailing address: Château Grand Village—33240 Mouillac

Telephone: 05 57 84 44 03; Telefax: 05 57 84 83 31

Visits: By appointment only

Contact: Sylvie and Jacques Guinaudeau

VINEYARDS

Surface area: 11.1 acres

Grape varietals: 50% Cabernet Franc, 50% Merlot

Average age of vines: More than 30 years

Density of plantation: 5,900 vines per hectare

Average yields: 38 hectoliters per hectare

Elevage: Fermentations and macerations last 15–21 days depending upon the vintage. Wines are transferred directly into oak barrels for malolactics, where they remain for 18–20 months in cask (one-third to one-half new oak). Wines are fined with fresh egg whites but not systematically filtered.

WINES PRODUCED

Château Lafleur: 12,000 bottles

Les Pensées de Lafleur: 3,000 bottles

Plateau of maturity: Within 8–40 years of the vintage

GENERAL APPRECIATION

Along with Pétrus, it is a titan of Pomerol as well as one of Bordeaux's most prodigious wines. It is rarer than Pétrus and often just as expensive.

I have always had a personal attachment to this tiny Pomerol vineyard. In the mid-1970s, when I first started tasting the wines of Lafleur, I could find nothing written about them. Yet in my small tasting group we frequently found the wine to be every bit as compelling as Pétrus. I made my first visit to Lafleur in 1978, speaking very little French, and found the two elderly proprietors, now deceased, sisters Thérèse and Marie Robin, decrepit, but even then both were utterly charming. The Lafleur château was, and remains today, more of a barn than a winery. Despite the advanced age of these two spinsters, they would ride their bikes out to Le Gay, the official reception center for both Lafleur and Le Gay, on my visits in the late 1970s. They were no doubt amused by my size, referring to me as Monsieur Le Taureau (Bull). I probably did look a bit oversized walking in the tiny *chai*, where the barrels, as well as a bevy of ducks, chickens, and rabbits, were housed. It always amazed me how wines of such great extraction and utterly mind-blowing character could be produced in such filthy conditions.

Today Lafleur is both owned and managed by the niece and nephew, Sylvie and Jacques Guinaudeau. They took responsibility starting with the 1985 vintage and purchased it in 2002. One of their first decisions was to refuse to bottle any 1987 Lafleur. At the same time they introduced a second wine, Les Pensées de Lafleur. This is rather remarkable given the tiny production of this micro-estate. The cellars remain the same, but they are now devoid of ducks, chickens, and rabbits, as well as the dung they left behind. Additionally, Lafleur now benefits from at least 50% or more new oak casks for each vintage.

Is the wine any better? Certainly Lafleur remains one of the few wines of Pomerol that is consistently capable of challenging, and in some cases surpassing, Pétrus. Even the late Jean-Pierre Moueix once admitted this to me, and I have been fortunate to have had Lafleur and Pétrus side by side enough times to know the former is a wine every bit as extraordinary as Pétrus. In many vintages, from an aromatic point of view, it is more complex than Pétrus, no doubt because of the old vine Cabernet Franc the vineyard possesses.

Much of the greatness of Lafleur lies in the soil, which is a deep, gravelly bed enriched with iron and some sand but also characterized by extremely important deposits of phosphorus and potassium. Over the years the yields have been tiny, reflecting the motto of the Robin sisters' father: "Quality surpasses quantity."

Old vintages of Lafleur are legendary, but the history of the property has not been without mixed results. The 1971 and 1970 should have been better, and more recently, the 1981 is flawed by the presence of fecal aromas. However, the wine is now being looked over by an oenologist, and even though the old vines (there was no replanting at Lafleur after the freeze of 1956) are having to be grubbed up, the average age is still impressive. Since 1982 (the 1982 and 1983 were made by Christian Moueix and his ultra-conservative oenologist Jean-Claude Berrouet) Lafleur has become less exotic and perhaps more influenced by modern-day ocnologists and their obsession with wines that fall within certain technical parameters. Nevertheless, Lafleur, measured by the highest standards of Bordeaux, while now made within proper technical parameters, still remains one of the most distinctive, most exotic, and greatest wines—not only from Pomerol, but in the world.

IMPORTANT VINTAGES

2001
93–95+ A Merlot-dominated *cuvée* with full body, a dense, murky, ruby/purple color, sweet cola and black cherry fruit, kirsch, and an unctuous texture, Lafleur's 2001 has a long finish with surprisingly supple tannin. This appears to be a provocative, outstanding Lafleur as well as slightly more precocious and accessible. Anticipated maturity: 2007–2020. Last tasted, 1/03.

2000
100 An awesome effort, the 2000 Lafleur continues to add more weight in the bottle. Truly prodigious, it has a skyscraper-like feel in the mouth, huge extract, massive body, a saturated purple color, and a finish that lasts well over one minute. Its flavors, and aromas to a certain extent, represent the essence of black truffle juice infused with kirsch, raspberries, and liquified minerals. At my first *en-primeur* tasting, it reminded me of the great 1975. I still tend to think that, but my instincts suggest the 2000 is more meticulously vinified with a cleaner upbringing. A boatload of tannin is evident, thus anyone older than sixty years of age might want to reconsider buying it. Sadly, there are only 1,000 cases of this awesome Lafleur. Anticipated maturity: 2012–2040+. Last tasted, 1/03.

1999
93 A brilliant success, the 1999 is one of the stars of the vintage. Lafleur's 1999 is atypically powerful and concentrated, with an inky, saturated purple color followed by a sensational nose of black cherry jam intermixed with liquid minerals, raspberries, and licorice. Super-concentrated, extraordinarily pure, with moderately high tannin, this dense, powerful, impressively endowed wine should turn out to be a classic for Lafleur. Anticipated maturity: 2010–2025. Last tasted, 3/02.

1998
94 This wine was incredibly tannic and backward from cask, but out of bottle it has shrugged off the excess tannin and seems to be developing far better than I thought it would. The color is dense/ruby purple, and the wine shows notes of sweet kirsch and blackberry liqueur, with a liquid minerality and a hint of violets. The wine is full-bodied, quite tannic, very dense and backward, but gorgeously concentrated, pure, and intense. This looks to be a classic Lafleur meant for significant long-term aging. Anticipated maturity: 2015–2040+. Last tasted, 11/02.

1997
88? The dark ruby–colored 1997 is impossibly tannic with a tough texture and lean constitution. Paradoxically, the wine has weight, ripeness, and richness, but its dry, astringent finish is reminiscent of a 1998 Médoc. This wine's development is

questionable, but I have serious reservations about its ratio of tannin to fruit. It may turn out to be excellent, but patience will be required. Anticipated maturity: 2006–2015. Last tasted, 3/01.

1996 Another Lafleur that has come on in bottle, in contrast to the pre-bottling tastings
92+   where the wine was painfully backward and austere; I still tend to think it represents a modern-day clone of the gorgeous 1966. It is not the most intense and expansive Lafleur, but it has a saturated ruby/purple color, a sweet nose of minerals, black raspberries, blackberries, and almost steely mineral liquidity to it. A powerful wine with Médoc-like tannin and structure, the wine is still very closed but much more promising and less of a gamble than I thought early on. Nevertheless, this is a wine for patient connoisseurs. Anticipated maturity: 2012–2030+. Last tasted, 12/02.

1995 Another amazingly backward, tannic Lafleur that has an opaque ruby/purple color
93+   and a tight but promising nose of blackberry liqueur intermixed with blueberries, raspberries, and minerals, this wine is full-bodied, has searingly dry, astringent tannins, but a layered, very large-scaled, weighty feel in the mouth. The wine is very young and formidable, but oh so prodigious. I cannot see this wine being ready to drink for at least two decades, and it may actually need more time than the 1998. Anticipated maturity: 2020–2050. Last tasted, 11/02.

1994 Still backward, but one of the great successes of the vintage, the 1994 still has a
91   deep ruby/purple color, notes of plums, a hint of prunes, earth, truffle, and mineral. As the wine sits in the glass, some of the steely mineral Lafleur character emerges. This remains an excruciatingly tannic, backward, medium- to full-bodied wine that needs plenty of cellaring. I am not so sure the tannins will always mesh, given the fact that this wine does not quite have the concentration that some of the other top vintages of Lafleur possess. Anticipated maturity: 2010–2025. Last tasted, 12/02.

1990 Still developing but becoming more formed, this wine shows fabulous extract, a
96   dense purple color, and a sweet nose of kirsch that is almost similar to the famed Château Rayas of Châteauneuf-du-Pape. This wine is full-bodied, somewhat exotic, but still very youthful and not yet in its adolescence. The viscous texture, profound richness in the mouth, and extraordinary purity all suggest a potential legend in the making. The wine still needs considerable cellaring. Anticipated maturity: 2008–2040. Last tasted, 8/02.

1989 The 1989 Lafleur, tasted side by side with the 1990 on two occasions in 2002,
95   plays it closer to the vest. The wine needs far more coaxing to produce the licorice, black cherry liqueur, earth, and truffle notes from the nose. In the mouth, the wine is full-bodied, tannic, backward, and very tightly knit, with mouth-searing levels of tannin and extremely high extract. The tannins are firmer, the fruit seemingly less sweet, but still extremely ripe, and the evolutionary process is far slower in the 1989 than the 1990. Anticipated maturity: 2012–2045. Last tasted, 8/02.

1988 Consistently one of the strongest candidates for the wine of the vintage, Lafleur's
93   1988 has a dark plum/ruby color and a gorgeous nose of white flowers intermixed with kirsch and raspberries. The wine is full-bodied, sweet, round, and beautifully pure, with moderate tannin, medium to full body, and great elegance and complexity. This wine has come around faster than I would have thought. Anticipated maturity: now–2025. Last tasted, 8/02.

1986 Dark dense ruby/purple, with very little evolution to the color, Lafleur's 1986
92+? seems frozen in time, a structured, tannic, backward monster that still needs considerable cellaring. No matter how much airing I have given this wine, it does not ever seem to emerge from its cloak of tannin and structure. The fruit seems sweet,

and the wine has Lafleur's telltale notes of kirsch intermixed with raspberries, minerals, flowers, and truffles. The wine is medium bodied, weighty in the mouth, but so, so tannic and backward. Will it ever blossom? Anticipated maturity: 2008–2035. Last tasted, 8/02.

1985   This is one of the greatest wines of the vintage, possibly the slowest to mature wine
94   of the vintage and potentially its longest lived. Tasted next to Pétrus twice in 2002, the 1985 Lafleur seemed like it came from a different vintage. It was not herbal like the Pétrus, far denser, the color more saturated, and it had more body, volume, and intensity. In fact, the Pétrus looked like an emanciated, herbaceous, thin cousin to Lafleur. This wine is very special, with notes of figs, plums, minerals, violets, black raspberries, and licorice. Still a dense saturated ruby/purple with full body, great purity, and fabulous fruit, this is an immense vintage for Lafleur, and it certainly ranks as one of the greatest wines this small micro-estate has ever produced. Anticipated maturity: 2008–2030. Last tasted, 8/02.

1983   Fully mature, yet still in far better condition than most 1983 Pomerols, Lafleur's
92   1983 has a medium ruby color with considerable pink at the edge. A very exotic, almost kinky nose of Asian spice, licorice, truffle, and jammy kirsch is followed by a medium- to full-bodied, plum, fleshy wine with sweet tannin and low acidity in a very evolved style. Certainly among the very good vintages of Lafleur over the last 20 years, this is the most evolved and drinkable. Anticipated maturity: now–2015. Last tasted, 8/02.

1982   Tasted five times in 2002, once in 2003, this wine, on each occasion, stood out as
100   a colossal effort even in this great vintage. The wine still has a very dense, murky ruby/purple color, a nearly overripe nose of black cherry liqueur intermixed with raspberries, minerals, smoke, and some cold steel as well as white flowers that soar from the glass with tremendous force and staying power. Very thick, with a viscous texture reminiscent of some of the late 1940's vintages of Pomerol, high extract, and huge, opulent flavors, this wine hits the palate with a cascade of glycerin, fruit, and extract. Almost over the top, but surprisingly well delineated for its massive size, this is an extraordinary, concentrated, fabulously compelling wine that should prove to be immortal. The wine has never tasted better in its entire life than in recent tastings done in 2002, yet it still seems relatively young. Anticipated maturity: now–2025. Last tasted, 1/03.

1979   Along with Haut-Brion, this is one of the two candidates for the wine of the vin-
98+   tage. The wine is approaching full maturity, yet still seems so atypical for a 1979, a phenomenally concentrated, thick, massively endowed wine with huge levels of extract, tannin, and power. The wine still has some dusty tannins and a huge nose of sweet black truffles intermixed with blackberries, plums, figs, and minerals. Very powerful, as well as enormously endowed, this is a remarkable effort in this vintage. I am still not sure if the tannins will ever resolve themselves, but this wine, which is just approaching full maturity, should go on for at least another 25 years or more. Anticipated maturity: now–2030. Last tasted, 11/02.

1978   More and more, the 1978 Lafleur is looking like one of the two or three finest wines
93   of the vintage, along with La Mission Haut-Brion and Latour. This dark plum/ garnet–colored wine exhibits a knockout nose of black cherry fruit intermixed with licorice, minerals, cedar, and spice. Medium to full-bodied, with powerful tannin remaining, this highly extracted wine is atypical for the 1978 vintage. It is a weighty, broad-shouldered, muscular, virile 1978 that is just beginning to reveal secondary nuances and complexity. I have always thought this wine could develop along the lines of the 1966, and I am more convinced than ever that it is the 1970s clone of that vintage. Anticipated maturity: now. Last tasted, 11/97.

1975　At one time a perfect wine, my three-digit score has dropped simply because I am
98　not sure the huge tannins this wine possesses will ever fully melt away. Nevertheless, it is still one of the greatest wines I have ever tasted for its tremendous singu-
larity and intensity. The color is still a murky plum/purple that shows a bit of
amber at the edge. The nose is strikingly intense, with an almost liquid minerality
intermixed with fig, truffle, spice, plum, and black cherry as well as blueberry. In
the mouth the wine is massive, with searing levels of tannins, but monumental levels of extract and concentration. I would not be surprised if some of the great
1928s or 1945s tasted like this in their first 20 years of life. This wine is still very
backward, yet with decanting of 6–10 hours (the normal operative procedure when
opening this wine), the wine is prodigious. A 50- to 75-year wine? Anticipated maturity: 2005–2050. Last tasted, 8/02.

ANCIENT VINTAGES

Lafleur's track record in the early 1970s was relatively disappointing, with a light,
herbal, thin 1971 and an extremely irregular 1970 that, from the best bottles, could
merit an upper-80-point score but nothing better. The three great vintages of the 1960s
were the 1966 (96 points; last tasted 12/99), 1962 (91 points; last tasted 12/96), and
1961 (98 points; last tasted 12/95). The 1961 Lafleur was actually appallingly bad out
of several bottles, but from well-kept bottles, or those from selected barrels, as I am
sure the wine was bottled barrel by barrel, the wine is prodigious.

The 1959 (rated 88 in 12/87) is a ruggedly built, muscular, tough-textured wine that
is impressive for its size and weight. But much like the 1964 and 1970, it lacks charm
and finesse. It should continue to age well for another 10–15 years. I have always preferred the 1955 (rated 92 in 12/87). It possesses that exotic, mineral, black fruit character so typical of Lafleur, massive weight, an unctuous texture, and plenty of hard
tannin still left in the finish.

Perhaps the greatest-kept secret in all of Bordeaux is how spectacular the 1950 vintage was in Pomerol. The 1950 Lafleur (100 points; last tasted 10/94) could easily pass
for a 1947 or 1945 wine given its extraordinary level of concentration. The color remains black/purple, and the bouquet offers aromas of cedar, spices, and black fruits.
The wine is unbelievably concentrated, massively full and rich, with sweet tannin in
the finish. With a viscous, chewy texture, this pure wine could easily last for another
15–20 years. The 1949 Lafleur (96+ points; last tasted 10/94) offers a saturated pur-
ple/garnet color followed by a reluctant nose that, with coaxing, reveals intense, pure,
cherry, jammy aromas intermingled with scents of minerals and licorice. Sensationally
concentrated, with layers of thick, rich fruit and high tannin, this sweet, remarkably
youthful wine is still not fully mature! It will last for another 20–30 years. There were
many 1947s bottled in Belgium. I have had the 1947 Lafleur Belgian bottling, which
ranges from very good to occasionally outstanding. As good as it is, the château bottling, from which this tasting note emanates, can leave you speechless. This is an extraordinarily profound wine that surpasses Pétrus and Cheval Blanc in this vintage,
even though they can all be perfect wines. The 1947 Lafleur (100 points; last tasted
10/94) is more developed and forward than the 1949 and 1945. It reveals a thick, Port-
like color with slight amber at the edge. The nose offers a smorgasbord of aromas, rang-

ing from caramel to jammy black raspberries and cherries, honeyed nuts, chocolate, and truffles. The wine's unctuousness and viscosity are unequaled in any other dry wine I have tasted. There is neither volatile acidity nor residual sugar present, something that many of the greatest 1947s possess. This wine's richness and freshness are unbelievable. The finish, which lasts more than a minute, coats the mouth with layers of concentrated fruit. There have been many great Lafleurs, but the 1947 is the quintessential expression of this tiny yet marvelous vineyard that was ignored by wine critics for most of the 20th century. To date, it is the only wine that has ever brought me to tears! Similar to the 1947 Lafleur in aromatic complexity and flavor, richness, and textural thickness, the 1945 (100 points; last tasted 10/94) is blacker in color, less evolved, and possesses a more classic structural profile than the Port-like 1947. The 1945 tastes young, yet astonishingly unctuous, rich, and powerful. It will easily last for another 40–50 years. Will the 1975 turn out to be this memorable?

LAFLEUR-GAZIN

Owner: Nicole Delfour-Borderie

Farmer: Ets Jean-Pierre Moueix

Address: 33500 Pomerol

Mailing address: c/o SA Ets Jean-Pierre Moueix, BP 129, 54, quai du Priourat, 33502 Libourne

Telephone: 05 57 51 78 96; Telefax: 05 57 51 79 79

Visits: By appointment and exclusively for professionals of the wine trade dealing with the firm.

Contact: Frédéric Lospied

VINEYARDS

Surface area: 21 acres

Grape varietals: 80% Merlot, 20% Cabernet Franc

Average age of vines: 30 years

Density of plantation: 6,000 vines per hectare

Average yields: 45 hectoliters per hectare

Elevage: Eighteen day fermentation and maceration in temperature-controlled concrete tanks. Twenty months aging in barrels with 25% new oak. Fining, no filtration.

WINES PRODUCED

Château Lafleur-Gazin: 36,000 bottles

Plateau of maturity: Within 5–12 years of the vintage

GENERAL APPRECIATION

I am surprised that this estate, which benefits from a superb situation, does not produce better wines. Lafleur-Gazin is generally pleasant, supple, and fruity, but consistently lacking in stuffing and complexity.

Lafleur-Gazin is situated between the two estates of Gazin and Lafleur. The wine is produced by the firm of Jean-Pierre Moueix, which farms this property under a lease arrangement. The wine is supple, round, and straightforward in style. Given the vineyard's location, it remains perplexing that the wines are so simple and light.

IMPORTANT VINTAGES

2001
87–88 The medium-bodied 2001 exhibits notes of prunes, plums, black cherries, and damp earth, good ripeness, spice, and moderate tannin in the finish. Anticipated maturity: 2004–2012. Last tasted, 1/03.

2000
87 A sweet, superficial, but attractive effort, the 2000 Lafleur-Gazin reveals chalky tannin in the finish. A dark ruby/purple color is accompanied by ripe plum, prune, and berry fruit, medium body, and plenty of structure as well as tough tannin. Anticipated maturity: now–2014. Last tasted, 1/03.

1999
86 Plums, figs, sweet cherries, and underbrush emerge from this soft, supple, garnet-colored wine. Round, cleanly made, and medium bodied with unobtrusive tannin and acidity, it will drink well for 8–9 years. Last tasted, 3/02.

1998
89 One of the sleepers of the vintage, this is the finest Lafleur-Gazin I have tasted in many years. The wine is deep ruby/plum/purple–colored with a sweet, sexy bouquet of overripe black cherries, kirsch, smoke, and spice box. The seductive, fat, concentrated palate is open-knit and loaded with fruit, glycerin, and character. The acidity is low, the tannin ripe, and the finish succulent as well as velvety. Drink it over the next 12 years. Last tasted, 3/02.

ANCIENT VINTAGES

Virtually nothing in the 1990s and 1980s elicited excitement, not even the 1982. A château to avoid when buying old vintages, and many young ones as well.

LAGRANGE

Owner: Ets Jean-Pierre Moueix

Address: 33500 Pomerol

Mailing address: c/o SA Ets Jean-Pierre Moueix, BP 129, 54, quai du Priourat, 33502 Libourne

Telephone: 05 57 51 78 96; Telefax: 05 57 51 79 79

Visits: By appointment and exclusively for professionals of the wine trade dealing with the firm.

Contact: Frédéric Lospied

VINEYARDS

Surface area: 11.6 acres

Grape varietals: 95% Merlot, 5% Cabernet Franc

Average age of vines: 30 years

Density of plantation: 6,250 vines per hectare

Average yields: 42 hectoliters per hectare

Elevage: Twenty day fermentation and maceration in temperature-controlled concrete tanks. Twenty months aging in barrels with 25% new oak. Fining, no filtration.

WINES PRODUCED

Château Lagrange: 24,000 bottles

Plateau of maturity: Within 5–12 years of the vintage

GENERAL APPRECIATION

Lagrange is not one of the best Pomerols. Generally robust, powerful, and tannic, it lacks finesse and complexity and is difficult to approach in its youth, which is unusual for a Merlot-based wine. I am surprised that this growth does not fare better in the hands of Christian Moueix and his team.

One rarely sees the wine of Lagrange. It is well situated near the plateau of Pomerol, but the vineyard has been recently replanted significantly, with the composition being changed to 95% Merlot and 5% Cabernet Franc. The wine tends to be a rather brawny, densely colored Pomerol, with significant power and tannins but not much complexity. Older vintages such as 1978, 1975, and 1970 have all proven to be stubbornly big, brooding, coarse wines that have been slow to develop. This is not a style of wine that I find attractive.

IMPORTANT VINTAGES

2000   A clone of the 1975, this dense plum/garnet–colored 2000 exhibits aromas of
87?   black fruits, truffles, licorice, and underbrush. However, the finish is all gritty tannin, raising the question of whether it will age gracefully. The wine has gained texture and fat during its *élevage*, so there is some hope for future harmony. Anticipated maturity: 2006–2020? Last tasted, 1/03.

1999   Notes of prunes, fig, underbrush, and sweet cherry fruit emerge from this medium-
86   bodied, soft Pomerol. The finish is tannic and austere. Consume it during its first decade of life. Last tasted, 3/02.

1998   A dense ruby/purple color and sweet blackberry and cherry fruit can be found in
86   this medium- to full-bodied, nicely concentrated wine. With power, moderate tannin, and good intensity, it should age well. Anticipated maturity: 2005–2015. Last tasted, 3/02.

ANCIENT VINTAGES

Another property that has a mediocre track record. The only wines I ever found with some merit might include the 1995 (86 points; last tasted 11/97), 1990 (86 points; last tasted 1/93), and 1982 (85 points; last tasted 9/02).

LATOUR À POMEROL

Owner: Foyer de Charité de Châteauneuf de Galaure

Farmer: Ets Jean-Pierre Moueix

Address: 33500 Pomerol

Mailing address: c/o SA Ets Jean-Pierre Moueix, BP 129, 54, quai du Priourat, 33502 Libourne

Telephone: 05 57 51 78 96; Telefax: 05 57 51 79 79

Visits: By appointment and exclusively for professionals of the wine trade dealing with the firm.

Contact: Frédéric Lospied

VINEYARDS

Surface area: 19.5 acres

Grape varietals: 90% Merlot, 10% Cabernet Franc

Average age of vines: 35 years

Density of plantation: 6,500 vines per hectare

Average yields: 40 hectoliters per hectare

Elevage: Twenty day fermentation and maceration in temperature-controlled concrete tanks. Twenty months aging in barrels that are renewed by a third at each vintage. Fining, no filtration.

WINES PRODUCED

Château Latour à Pomerol: 25,000–30,000 bottles

Plateau of maturity: Within 6–20 years of the vintage

GENERAL APPRECIATION

In the 1940s, 1950s, and 1960s, Latour à Pomerol was one of the most sumptuous Bordeaux. It then went through a difficult period, and during the following 30 years produced good wines (as opposed to great), with the exception of the superb 1982. In recent years, it has improved and now ranks amongst the top 20 or so Pomerols. In style, it is much closer now to Trotanoy or La Fleur-Pétrus than to Pétrus, to which it used to be compared during its glory days.

Latour à Pomerol produces splendidly dark-colored wines that usually represent a powerful, opulent, fleshy style of Pomerol. The vineyard is made up of two parcels. One is located near the church of Pomerol on a deep, gravelly bed. The second, the smaller parcel, is located farther west near RN 89 on sandier, lighter soil. The second parcel is closest to the vineyard owned by Christian Moueix called La Grave.

Latour à Pomerol can be majestic and, historically, was one of the two or three greatest wines of the appellation in certain vintages. The 1970, 1961, 1959, 1950, 1948, and 1947 offer persuasive evidence that this estate can rival the greatest wines of Bordeaux; except for the 1982, nothing in the last 30+ years even remotely recalls those legends. While some observers have claimed that Latour à Pomerol comes closest in weight and structure to Pétrus, that would not appear to be the case. This is a wine that, while rich and full, tends to have more in common with other Moueix-controlled properties such as Trotanoy than Pétrus.

Latour à Pomerol is usually about one-fifth the price of Pétrus and about one-half the price of Trotanoy and Lafleur. For a limited-production Pomerol of such high quality, it remains a relative bargain.

IMPORTANT VINTAGES

2001 This impeccably made blend of 85% Merlot and 15% Cabernet Franc exhibits an
88–90 impressive dark ruby/purple color as well as a sweet, pure nose of black fruits intermixed with iron, dried herbs, and smoke. Layered, elegant, and well delineated, with fresh, vibrant fruit typical of the finest 2001s, it will be at its finest between 2005–2016. Last tasted, 1/03.

2000 The 2000 has added weight as well as texture during its *élevage*. A saturated ruby
91+ color is followed by aromas of black cherries, caramel, truffles, and sweet earth. Textured and medium to full-bodied, with moderately high tannin (typical of Pomerol's finest 2000s), it will require patience. Anticipated maturity: 2007–2019. Last tasted, 1/03.

1999 This is an excellent, forward, complex Pomerol with creamy opulence on the mid-
88 palate and a complex nose of cedar, licorice, plum, black cherries, and a hint of herbaceousness. The sweet, fleshy, sexy, seductive style will be popular with many tasters. Drink it over the next 12 years. Last tasted, 3/02.

1998 A beautiful effort, the 1998 is, along with the 2000, one of the finest wines pro-
90 duced at this estate in the last 30 years. However, it is unlikely to turn out better than the 1982 or 1970. Revealing characteristics of vanilla, leather, highly extracted black cherry fruit, and caramel, this deep, rich, full-bodied, powerful, layered, sweetly tannic 1998 is not as profound as I originally thought, but it is still an outstanding wine. Anticipated maturity: 2006–2020. Last tasted, 3/02.

1997 This type of wine will please many consumers, so readers should give it a try. A
88 dark ruby color is followed by a deep, rich, excellent display of roasted nuts, jammy berry fruit, dried herbs, and tomato skins. It is seductive, lush, and medium to full-bodied, with impressive levels of glycerin, fruit, and intensity. Low acidity and a forward style suggest it is best consumed over the next 3–4 years, although it will undoubtedly last longer. Last tasted, 1/01.

1996 This wine reveals a saturated dark ruby color and excellent blackberry and cherry
88 aromas intermixed with toast, roasted nuts, and vanilla. Medium bodied with admirable concentration, moderate levels of spicy oak, and sweet tannin, this dense wine has been delicious since its prime and should hold until 2014. Last tasted, 3/01.

1995 This might have a chance of hitting a magical outstanding score, as the wine still
89+ seems to be holding back much of its potential. A deep ruby/purple with a distinctive, very singular nose of wet steel, licorice, spice box, Provençal herbs, and roasted black fruits, as the wine hits the palate, there is generosity, ripeness, and purity, with sweet black fruits intermixed with cedar, earth, and some subtle herbs. Medium to full body and excellent richness are the hallmarks, but the wine's tannic structure and level of astringency have kept my scores conservative. In any event, I am still waiting for this wine to emerge from behind its cloak of tannin, which is formidable. This could be a top effort for Latour à Pomerol if everything comes together. Anticipated maturity: 2007–2020. Last tasted, 1/02.

1994   Weediness and a slight shortness in the finish are the only flaws in an otherwise
87   relatively good effort from Latour à Pomerol. The color is a deep, dark garnet with
        some amber at the edge. A big, spicy, sweet nose of black fruits, tobacco, espresso,
        and stewed roasted vegetables is followed by a relatively fat, ripe, medium-bodied
        wine with low acidity and some sweet tannins in the finish. Drink it over the next
        5–7 years. Last tasted, 1/02.

1990   I expected far greater things of this wine from cask. From bottle, the wine seems to
87   have aged at a very accelerated pace, and it is now showing considerable amber at
        the edge of its garnet color. The wine shows a very complex nose of cedar, spice
        box, mocha, caramel, and sweet red and black currant fruit. The initial generosity
        and sweet fruit seems to dry out in the finish, with some hints of fig, dusty, loamy
        soil, and old wood. For the vintage and the vineyard, a disappointment. Antici-
        pated maturity: now–2007. Last tasted, 1/02.

1989   A very pleasant, medium-bodied, fleshy Pomerol. A fully mature nose of smoke,
87   roasted vegetables, dried herbs, sweet currants, and caramel, with medium to full
        body on the attack, but some drying (even desiccating) tannins in the finish make
        for a very good but somewhat uninspiring effort from Latour à Pomerol. Antici-
        pated maturity: now–2012. Last tasted, 1/02.

1988   Licorice, Chinese black tea, dried herbs, and some plum and fig-like fruit as
87   well as freshly ground pepper emerge from the complex aromatics of the dark
        garnet–colored 1988 Latour à Pomerol. In the mouth the wine shows good concen-
        tration and some sweetness, but a somewhat chunky, monolithic style with
        scratchy tannins in the finish. Drink it over the next 6–10 years. Last tasted, 1/02.

1985   Sexier in its life, but again far less impressive from bottle than cask, the 1985
87   Latour à Pomerol shows considerable amber at the edge. Some sweet mulberry,
        cranberry, and cherry fruit is intermixed with fruitcake, cedar, and black tea
        notes. The wine is medium bodied and very elegant, with soft tannin in a modest
        finish. Drink it up. Anticipated maturity: now–2007. Last tasted, 1/02.

1983   At one time a very delicious example, I made the mistake of holding on to the last
88   bottles far too long. The wine has hit full maturity and now seems to be in decline.
        The color is a dark garnet with considerable amber at the edge. The nose shows
        some stewed notes of plums, prunes, caramel, chocolate, and vegetables. The wine
        still has some sweetness and plump fruit on the attack, but then narrows out and
        becomes a bit attenuated in the finish. It is starting to crack up and needs to be
        drunk up. Anticipated maturity: now. Last tasted, 12/00.

1982   Fully mature and not likely to get any better, the 1982 has a medium garnet color
93   with considerable amber at the edge. The wine shows a stunning nose of sweet
        caramel intermixed with jammy kirsch, spice box, vanilla, Asian spice, and
        licorice. Once past the fragrant, exuberant aromatics, the wine exhibits a medium-
        to full-bodied, plump, very opulent texture with sweet, concentrated fruit, low
        acidity, and very ripe tannin that is now seamlessly integrated in the wine's per-
        sonality. P.S.: The problem I had with half my case of wine being corked, four out
        of five bottles opened, has not reappeared in subsequent tastings . . . thankfully.
        Anticipated maturity: now–2012. Last tasted, 11/02.

ANCIENT VINTAGES

Nothing in the 1970s was particularly interesting except for the fabulous 1970 (93
points; last tasted 6/96). This wine is fully mature yet is holding on to most of its character. Of course, few châteaux in Bordeaux have the kind of track record Latour à
Pomerol produced in the late 1940s. One hundred point scores are certainly rare, but

the 1961 (100 points; last tasted 12/96), 1959 (98 points; last tasted 12/00), 1950 (98 points; last tasted 3/97), 1948 (96 points; last tasted 3/96), and 1947 (100 points; last tasted 3/97) are legendary wines that make what's going on today at Latour à Pomerol a mystery. All of these wines have extraordinary freshness and remarkable intensity, amazing color saturation, and voluminous, mouth-filling, highly concentrated styles, but all in balance. From well-kept bottles, drinking any of these vintages of Latour à Pomerol is one of the great wine drinking experiences of a lifetime.

LE MOULIN

Owner: SCEA Le Moulin de Pomerol

Administrator: Michel Querre

Address: Moulin de Lavaud, La Patache, 33500 Pomerol

Mailing address: SCEA Le Moulin de Pomerol, BP 51, 33330 St.-Emilion

Telephone: 05 57 55 51 60; Telefax: 05 57 55 51 61

Visits: By appointment only

Contact: Michel Querre

VINEYARDS

Surface area: 5.9 acres

Grape varietals: 80% Merlot, 20% Cabernet Franc

Average age of vines: 35 years

Density of plantation: 5,400 vines per hectare

Average yields: 32 hectoliters per hectare

Elevage: Three to four week fermentation and maceration (with the skins) in temperature-controlled wooden vats of small capacity (20 and 25 hectoliters). Fifteen to twenty months aging in new oak barrels. Fining and filtration depend upon the vintage.

WINES PRODUCED

Château Le Moulin: 6,000 bottles

Le Petit Moulin: 1,000–2,000 bottles

Plateau of maturity: Within 4–15 years of the vintage

GENERAL APPRECIATION

Beginning with 1998, Le Moulin has considerably changed its winemaking style. This up-and-coming, small estate, which appears to prefer an exotic style of Pomerol, produces a Le Pin look-alike, made in a similar style, with extravagant, toasty new oak and ripe Merlot fruit. The wine generally offers flamboyant notes of caramel, mocha, and jammy berry/cherry fruit. The debut vintage, 1998, was a sensational effort, and the 1999, while not as outstanding, was savory and delicious. The superb 2000, which should rival the 1998, was followed by a compelling 2001. Wines produced prior to 1997 are of good quality, but not exceptional.

IMPORTANT VINTAGES

2001
90–92
Produced from ripe fruit, the 2001 Le Moulin exhibits obvious new oak in the ostentatious nose of jammy black fruits, incense, and smoke. Dense and medium to full-bodied, with low acidity and loads of glycerin, it is a sensual, hedonistic effort to enjoy during its first 10–14 years of life. Last tasted, 1/03.

2000
92
Its flamboyant bouquet of roasted coffee, cherry liqueur, chocolate, and toasty oak is accompanied by a full-bodied, deep, luxuriously rich, powerful wine with more structure than the 1998, but similar length, concentration, and intensity. This is Pomerol at its most extravagant. Anticipated maturity: now–2016. Last tasted, 1/03.

1999
89
An up-front, lush, exotic Pomerol with black raspberry liqueur and cassis notes presented in a sweet, soft, hedonistic style, the 1999 Le Moulin does not possess the concentration of the 1998 or 2000, but what's there is savory and undeniably interesting and delicious. Drink it over the next 10 years. Last tasted, 3/02.

1998
90
A hedonistic, exotic, creamy-textured effort, the 1998 exhibits gorgeous espresso, plum, raspberry, and cherry liqueur aromas as well as flavors. Medium to full-bodied and lush, it is best consumed over the next 10 years. Last tasted, 3/02.

1997
86
A solid effort for the vintage, the 1997 Le Moulin possesses cherry/raspberry fruit, medium body, fine ripeness, no herbaceousness or sharpness, but a pinched finish. Its personality invites consumption over the next 1–2 years. Last tasted, 3/01.

NENIN

Owner: SCA Château Nenin (Delon family)

Address: Catusseau, 33500 Libourne

Telephone: 05 57 51 00 01; Telefax: 05 57 51 47 77 (estate)

Telephone: 05 56 73 25 26; Telefax: 05 56 59 18 33 (offices)

E-mail: leoville-las-cases@wanadoo.fr

Visits: By appointment only

Contact: Secretary's office

VINEYARDS

Surface area: 61.8 acres

Grape varietals: 75% Cabernet Franc, 25% Merlot

Average age of vines: 28 years

Density of plantation: 6,250 vines per hectare

Average yields: 45 hectoliters per hectare

Elevage: Eighteen to twenty day fermentation and maceration in temperature-controlled stainless-steel vats. Eighteen months aging in barrels with 30% new oak and 70% one-year-old barrels. Fining, no filtration.

WINES PRODUCED

Château Nenin: Variable

Fugue de Nenin: Variable

Plateau of maturity: Within 5–20 years of the vintage

GENERAL APPRECIATION

Long in the throes of mediocrity, Nenin has been resurrected under the ownership of the Delon family (of Las-Cases fame) and is quickly gaining ground as well as respect. Judging by what the Delons have accomplished with Léoville Las Cases in St.-Julien, I would not be surprised if Nenin were to improve further during the coming years. Since 1998, the estate has produced wines that are rich and generous. Nenin is expensive.

This is a historic estate of Pomerol, owned by the Despujol family between 1847 and 1997, when the property was sold to Michel and Jean-Hubert Delon, the proprietors of Léoville Las Cases. Obviously great things have been anticipated. Nenin has a loyal following of wine enthusiasts, but I have never been able to figure out why. I was certainly taken by a bottle of their 1947 I tasted in 1983 and an excellent 1975, but aside from those splendid wines I have always found Nenin to be good but unfortunately somewhat coarse and rustic.

Traditionally Nenin tends to be a firm, hard, chewy wine. Since 1976 the property has not performed well, turning out wines that have lacked intensity, character, and complexity. Were the yields too high? Did the decision to employ a mechanical harvester starting in 1982 negatively affect quality?

Now that this property has been acquired by the Delon family (proprietors of Léoville Las Cases) and Jean-Hubert Delon, has been put in charge, Nenin is quickly surging to the forefront of Pomerols.

IMPORTANT VINTAGES

2001 Made from low yields of 29 hectoliters per hectare, this blend of 70% Merlot and
88–90 30% Cabernet Franc is monolithic yet delineated in style. High tannin, considerable structure, a large size, and deep black fruit make for a sizable mouthful of wine. At present, it lacks charm and suppleness. It is a firmly styled Pomerol that should be at its finest between 2007–2020. Last tasted, 1/03.

2000 This is the finest Nenin to yet emerge under the Delon ownership. A blend of 65%
93 Merlot and 35% Cabernet Franc (high for Pomerol), the opaque purple–colored 2000 Nenin displays an unevolved but classic nose of sweet, jammy black fruits (primarily cherries and currants), licorice, underbrush, and subtle wood. Full-bodied with copious amounts of 1975-ish tannin and a long, structured, well-delineated finish, it will require significant patience. Anticipated maturity: 2009–2025. Last tasted, 1/03.

1999 Nenin has fashioned a 1999 with elegance, structure, and outstanding purity. A
88 dark ruby color is followed by a medium-weight Pomerol offering aromas and flavors of black fruits mixed with dried herbs, minerals, and oak. Anticipated maturity: 2006–2018. Last tasted, 3/02.

1998 The finest Nenin in many decades, the dense ruby/purple–colored 1998 exhibits
90 aromas of coffee, melted caramel, vanilla, plums, and black cherry jam. It is full-bodied with an unctuous texture, superb purity, and a silky, seamless finish. There is abundant tannin submerged beneath the wine's fatness and richness. Anticipated maturity: 2004–2025. Last tasted, 3/02.

1997 The Delons did not have control over the vineyard and entire vinification for this
87 vintage, but they instituted a strict selection, resulting in an attractive, elegant, richly fruity wine with copious quantities of cherries and black currants presented in a lush, supple style. It should drink well for six years. Last tasted, 3/01.

ANCIENT VINTAGES

Prior to the acquisition of Nenin by the Delon family, the success record of this property in the 1980s and early 1990s was nonexistent. The wines were often mediocre, with even the 1982 a mid-70-point wine. The only wine that comes up on my scoring sheet as having merit is the 1975 (88 points; last tasted 3/01). That wine is probably still in good shape and no doubt inexpensive, given the reputation for mediocrity that ensued for the following 20 years.

PETIT VILLAGE

Owner: AXA Millésimes

Administrator: Christian Seely

Address: 33500 Pomerol

Telephone: 05 57 51 21 08; Telefax: 05 57 51 87 31

E-mail: infochato@petitvillage.com

Website: www.petit-village.com

Visits: By appointment only

Contact: Madame Malou Le Sommer, Chateau and Associes 33250 Pauillac

VINEYARDS

Surface area: 27.2 acres

Grape varietals: 65% Merlot, 18% Cabernet Sauvignon, 17% Cabernet Franc

Average age of vines: 35 years

Density of plantation: 5,600 vines per hectare

Average yields: 50 hectoliters per hectare

Elevage: Eighteen to thirty-five day fermentation and maceration in temperature-controlled stainless-steel vats. Completion of malolactics in barrel. Fifteen to eighteen months aging with 75% new oak and 25% one-year-old barrels. Fining, no filtration.

WINES PRODUCED

Château Petit Village: 42,000 bottles

Le Jardin de Petit Village: 15,600 bottles

Plateau of maturity: Within 5–12 years of the vintage

GENERAL APPRECIATION

While this estate has done well since 1982, its performance between 1991 and 1997 has been perplexing. Given the potential of the vineyard, Petit Village can do better. Its wines seem to lack the fruitiness, suppleness, and generosity they have exhibited in the past, but the most recent efforts have been reassuring.

Petit Village is a Pomerol estate on the move. In 1971, when Bruno Prats, also the dynamic owner of the famous Médoc estate of Cos d'Estournel, took over responsibility for the making of the wine, the quality increased dramatically. Petit Village had the benefit of significant capital investment, the care of a dedicated owner, and the state-of-the-art technology necessary for producing wine. The result was a succession of wines that ranged in quality from good to exceptional. In 1989, Prats sold Petit Village to an insurance conglomerate that installed Jean-Michel Cazes and his brilliant wine-making team, led by Daniel Llose, from Lynch-Bages as administrators. With the retirement of Cazes, Christian Seeley took over as manager. In 2002, a pending sale of Petit Village to St. Emilion's Gerard Perse fell through.

The style of Petit Village emphasizes the toasty, smoky character of new oak barrels, a fat, supple, black currant fruitiness, and impeccably clean winemaking and handling. Recent vintages have the ability to age for 10–15 years, although they are fully ready to drink by age five or six. Older vintages (prior to 1982) have generally proven to be a disappointment, so wine enthusiasts are well advised to restrict their purchases to vintages since 1978.

It can be argued strongly that Petit Village has joined the top hierarchy of Pomerol estates and now ranks as one of the top 20 wines of the appellation. Certainly the vineyard is superbly situated. Bordered by Vieux Château Certan and Certan de May on the north, La Conseillante on the east, and Beauregard on the south, the vineyard has plenty of gravel as well as an iron-rich subsoil intermixed with deposits of clay. The high percentage of Merlot insures a rich, voluptuous wine in years when the Merlot reaches full maturity and yields are reasonable. Petit Village is a Pomerol to buy, as the price has not kept pace with its rejuvenated quality level.

IMPORTANT VINTAGES

2001
88–90 The opaque ruby/purple–colored 2001 is a low-acid, monolithic effort that tends toward flatness. However, the ripeness, juicy texture, and thick, lovely, black cherry and plum-like fruit are impressive. It needs to add more definition and complexity to merit a 90-point score, but it will certainly be in the upper 80s. Anticipated maturity: 2006–2015. Last tasted, 1/03.

2000
89 The 200 is surple and surprisingly evolved. A medium-bodied, very savory wine, it exhibits a dense purple color along with a monolithic, deep, chewy personality offering notes of chocolate, black fruits, new oak, and earth. Anticipated maturity: 2007–2017. Last tasted, 1/03.

1999
88 This dark ruby–colored, evolved, lush, sexy Pomerol offers aromas of licorice, dried herbs, asphalt, and sweet currant/cherry fruit. While it does not have a great deal of weight or persistence on the palate, it is up-front, mainstream, appealing, and accessible. Enjoy it over the next decade. Last tasted, 3/02.

1998
89+ A strong candidate for an outstanding rating, this dark ruby/purple–colored wine offers a sweet nose of plums, prunes, blackberries, chocolate, and mocha. Soft on the entry, revealing notes of smoke, licorice, and coffee, this fleshy, multilayered effort finishes with abundant glycerin, tannin, and extract. Anticipated maturity: now–2016. Last tasted, 3/02.

1996
86 Somewhat disjointed but pleasing in an open-knit, very straightforward style, this medium-bodied, dark garnet–colored wine has notes of grilled meats, smoked herbs, and sweet cherries and currants. The wine is fruity, lush, and best drunk over the next 5–6 years. Last tasted, 6/02.

1995
85
Soft, easygoing, straightforward, but a bit simple, this fully mature wine has notes of tapenade intermixed with smoke, tobacco, licorice, and sweet cherries and currants. It was a relatively seductive wine when first released, but it has aged quickly and needs to be drunk up. Last tasted, 6/02.

1990
90
A very strong effort from Petit Village and made before a very noticeable decline in the quality of wines over the subsequent seven years, the fully mature 1990 has plenty of amber at the edge, a dark garnet color, a sweet nose of melted licorice, espresso, dried herbs, and black cherries and currants. The wine is fleshy, silky-textured, and very easy to drink and understand. Anticipated maturity: now–2010. Last tasted, 3/01.

1989
88
Asian spice, black tea, chocolate, espresso, plum, figs, as well as copious quantities of sweet oak jump from the glass of this fully mature, expansive, ripe, medium-bodied wine. The acidity is low, the tannin is sweet, and the fruit is in full form. It needs to be drunk over the next 3–5 years. Anticipated maturity: now. Last tasted, 11/01.

1988
92
An outstanding success for the vintage, Petit Village's dark plum–colored 1988 has more structure and muscle than most vintages of this château. A complex nose of melted licorice, new saddle leather, soy, black cherries, black currants, and some hints of bacon fat emerge along with toasty new oak that makes for quite a lavish aromatic display. In the mouth the wine has more muscle, extract, and tannin than usual. It is rich, medium to full-bodied, very sweet, and expansive. Anticipated maturity: now–2007. Catch the magic before it disappears. Last tasted, 10/02.

1986
85?
The tannins seem to be becoming more noticeable as the wine loses fruit at a relatively accelerated pace. The result is a somewhat disjointed effort from Petit Village, with the dark garnet color already exhibiting plenty of pink and amber at the edge. The wine's nose is a bit herbaceous and earthy, with hints of mushroom. In the mouth, the wine shows moderate concentration but is beginning to crack up, with the tannins taking over. This should be drunk up. Last tasted, 8/02.

1985
87
This wine was fully mature within a decade of the vintage and now seems to be slowly in decline. The one-time opulent, rather explosively aromatic wine is now showing some dry tannins in the finish. The fruit seems to have mellowed out and no longer has the sweetness and exuberance it once possessed. Anticipated maturity: Drink up. Last tasted, 3/02.

1982
93
I began drinking this wine on a regular basis in the mid-1980s, as I could not resist its dramatic, ostentatious display of roasted herbs, mocha, black cherries, and smoky new oak scents and flavors. The wine has consistently been opulent, thick, juicy, and jammy. What's interesting is how much delineation and class the 1982 Petit Village has begun to develop, although I do not see any reason for further aging. The wine displays a dark garnet color with considerable amber at the edge. Its knockout nose is followed by corpulent, fat, ripe flavors exhibiting oodles of jammy fruit. Extremely low in acidity, this lush, chunky wine offers a gorgeous mouthful of thick, fleshy Merlot. If wine were a candy, Petit Village would taste like a hypothetical blend of a Milky Way and Reese's Peanut Butter Cup. I have been saying this should be drunk up since 1990, but the wine continues to hold together. Last tasted, 11/02.

PÉTRUS

Owner: SC Château Pétrus

Address: 33500 Pomerol

Mailing address: c/o SA Ets Jean-Pierre Moueix, BP 129, 54, quai du Priourat, 33502 Libourne

Telephone: 05 57 51 78 96; Telefax: 05 57 51 79 79

Visits: By appointment and exclusively for professionals of the wine trade dealing with the firm.

Contact: Frédéric Lospied

VINEYARDS

Surface area: 28.2 acres

Grape varietals: 95% Merlot, 5% Cabernet Franc

Average age of vines: 35 years

Density of plantation: 6,500 vines per hectare

Average yields: 36 hectoliters per hectare

Elevage: Twenty to twenty-four day fermentation and maceration in temperature-controlled concrete tanks. Twenty months aging in 100% new oak barrels. Fining, no filtration.

WINES PRODUCED

Pétrus: 25,000–30,000 bottles

Plateau of maturity: Within 10–30 years of the vintage

GENERAL APPRECIATION

Pétrus benefits from an outstanding situation on the plateau of Pomerol. It is one of the most famous red wines in the world, which explains the stratospheric prices it fetches, especially at auction. While this growth was unrivaled for decades (despite its irregular performance in the 1970s and 1980s), in recent years it has had to face increasing competition from many other Pomerols that have improved significantly. In terms of reputation and speculative value, Pétrus remains the king. But in terms of sheer quality, wines such as Lafleur, L'Evangile, Clos l'Église, Le Pin, and several other estates produce equal, sometimes better wines. However, Pétrus represents more than the best Pomerol can offer; it symbolizes a myth more than a wine.

The most celebrated wine of Pomerol, Pétrus has, during the last four decades, become one of Bordeaux's most renowned as well as expensive red wines. Situated on a buttonhole of black clay in the middle of Pomerol's plateau, the tiny 28.4-acre vineyard renders wines that are treated as well and as carefully as any wines produced on earth. After administrator Christian Moueix (his brother Jean-François is the actual owner) makes his selection, most vintages of Pétrus turn out to be 100% pure Merlot.

There have been a tremendous number of legendary Pétrus vintages, which no doubt has propelled prices into the stratosphere. The 2000, 1998, 1990, 1989, 1975,

1971, 1970, 1964, 1961, 1950, 1948, 1947, 1945, 1929, and 1921 are among the most monumental wines I have ever tasted. Yet as Pétrus has become deified by much of the world's wine press, one must ask, particularly in view of this property's track record from 1976 on, "Is Pétrus as great today as it once was?" There is no doubt that Pétrus slumped in vintages such as 1988, 1986, 1983, 1981, 1979, 1978, and 1976, but since 1989 Pétrus has been in top form, producing a succession of brilliant wines.

IMPORTANT VINTAGES

2001 There are slightly less than 2,400 cases of the 2001 Pétrus. Although revealing
91–93+ more acidity than is normally found in a young Pétrus, it possesses the telltale power, mass, and concentrated essence produced by this vineyard. The color is a healthy dark ruby/purple. The wine is full-bodied, with cherry and mulberry fruit as well as nicely integrated toasty new oak. It is still young, unevolved, and surprisingly tannic. Anticipated maturity: 2008–2020+. Last tasted, 1/03.

2000 The 2000 Pétrus has turned out to be magically endowed and has gained layers of
100 flavor and power since its early days in cask. Reminiscent of dry vintage Port, its inky black/ruby/purple color is followed by a stunning perfume of concentrated black fruits, great ripeness, huge, tannic structure, immense body, and a majestic 60-second finish. Although it may not possess the seamlessness or surreal qualities of the 1998, the 2000 is equally prodigious, just a bit more macho and backward in orientation. There are 2,300 cases of this great Pétrus. Anticipated maturity: 2013–2050. Last tasted, 1/03.

1999 This wine is turning out much in the style of such wonderful Pétrus vintages as
94 1967 and 1971. Although not as compelling as either the 1998 or 2000, it displays beautiful intensity and finesse in a more evolved style than one normally expects from this estate. The wine has a dense, nearly opaque ruby/purple color, sweet black cherry, mulberry, truffle-infused fruit, full body, low acidity, admirable purity, and sweet tannin. Only 2,400 cases were produced. It should be ready to drink in 3–4 years, and it will last for two decades. Anticipated maturity: 2007–2030. Last tasted, 1/03.

1998 Christian Moueix feels the 1998 is even better than his 1989 or 1990, and he ulti-
100 mately may be proven right. However, it will be 5–6 years or more before it can be known which of these profound efforts might turn out to be the most compelling. The 1998 Pétrus is unquestionably a fabulous effort boasting a dense plum/purple color as well as an extraordinary nose of black fruits intermixed with caramel, mocha, and vanilla. Exceptionally pure, super-concentrated, and extremely full-bodied, with admirable underlying acidity as well as sweet tannin, it reveals a superb mid-palate in addition to the luxurious richness for which this great property is known. The finish lasts for 40–45 seconds. Patience will definitely be required. Production was 2,400 cases, about 1,600 cases less than normal. Anticipated maturity: 2010–2040. Last tasted, 11/02.

1997 The backward 1997 (2,300 cases produced) needs another 2–3 years of cellaring.
91 The dense plum/ruby/purple color is accompanied by a closed bouquet of mocha, dried tomato skin, and black fruits. In the mouth, it is one of the most muscular 1997s, exhibiting outstanding concentration, length, intensity, and depth, copious tannin, and a fine mouth-feel. Consider the 1997 Pétrus a modern-day version of their superb 1967. Anticipated maturity: 2006–2025. Last tasted, 5/02.

1996　The 1996 Pétrus is a big, monolithic, foursquare wine with an impressively
92　opaque purple color and sweet berry fruit intermixed with earth, toast, and coffee
scents. Full-bodied and muscular, with high levels of tannin and a backward style,
this wine (less than 50% of the production was bottled as Pétrus) will require patience. It is a mammoth example, but without the sweetness of the 1997 or the
pure, exceptional richness and layers of the multidimensional 1995. Anticipated
maturity: 2010–2035. Last tasted, 12/01.

1995　Unquestionably one of the vintage's superstars, the 1995 Pétrus is taking on a per-
95+　sonality similar to the extraordinarily backward, muscular 1975. This is not a
Pétrus that could be approached in its youth (i.e., the perfect duo of 1989 and
1990). The wine exhibits an opaque ruby/purple color followed by a knockout
nose of toast, jammy black fruits, and roasted coffee. On the palate, it possesses
teeth-staining extract levels, massive body, and rich, sweet black fruits buttressed
by powerful, noticeable tannin. A formidably endowed wine with layers of extract,
this is a huge, tannic, monstrous-size Pétrus that will last for 50+ years. Anticipated maturity: 2012–2050. Last tasted, 7/02.

1994　Opaque purple/black in color, with a sweet vanilla, toasty, jammy cherry, and cas-
92　sis nose, this full-bodied, densely packed wine reveals layers of flavor and an
inner core of sweetness with huge quantities of glycerin and depth. A tannic, classic style of Pétrus, with immense body, great purity, and a backward finish, this
wine will be at its apogee between 2006 and 2035. Last tasted, 7/02.

1993　A candidate for the most concentrated wine of the vintage, this 1993 exhibits a
90+　saturated purple/plum color and a sweet nose of black fruits, Asian spices, and
vanilla. Huge and formidably rich, this powerful, dense, super-pure wine is a
tour de force in winemaking. For a vintage not known for wines of this immense
richness and length, this brawny, splendidly endowed Pétrus possesses low acidity and high tannin, suggesting that 8–10 years of cellaring are required. This
should be a 30-year wine, as well as the vintage's longest-lived effort. Last tasted,
7/02.

1992　The 1992 Pétrus is clearly one of the two candidates for the wine of the vintage.
90　The normal production of 4,500 cases was severely reduced to only 2,600 cases,
resulting in an atypically concentrated, powerful, rich wine with a dark, saturated
ruby/purple color and a tight but promising nose of sweet black cherry fruit,
vanilla, caramel, and herb-tinged mocha notes. Concentrated and powerful, with
superb density of fruit and richness as well as wonderful sweetness to its tannin,
this is a brilliant effort for the vintage. The wine requires 1–3 more years of cellaring and should keep for 10–15 years.

Interestingly, the Pétrus vineyard, along with that of its sibling Trotanoy, was
covered with black plastic in early September 1992 to trap most of the rain rather
than allowing it to saturate the vineyard's soil and dilute the grapes. It was a strat-
egy that obviously paid off. Interestingly, this technique was declared illegal by
French appellation authorities in the late 1990s when utilized by several of
Moueix's rivals, Michel Rolland and Jean-Luc Thunevin. Last tasted, 10/02.

1990　This is a spectacular Pétrus, made much in the style of the 1970 or a more modern-
100　day version of the 1947. This wine still has a very dense, ruby/purple color with no
lightening at the rim. With considerable aeration the wine offers up spectacular
aromas of caramel, sweet vanilla, and black cherry and blackberry liqueur with a
hint of tobacco and cedar. The wine is massively big, viscous, and full-bodied,
with low acidity but magnificent richness and an almost seamless personality.
The wine remains youthful and not even in its adolescence, but it has a certain accessibility, even though so much is yet to come. This is a compellingly great
Pétrus, slightly sweeter and more opulent than the 1998, and perhaps on a quicker

evolutionary track than the 1998 or 1989. Anticipated maturity: 2007–2040. Last tasted, 8/02.

1989
100
This wine is more tightly knit and more tannic, but every bit the blockbuster concentrated effort that its younger sibling, the 1990, is. It seems to need more coaxing from the glass, but the color is virtually identical—a dense ruby/purple with no lightening at the edge. In the mouth the wine cuts a broad swath, with spectacular intensity, richness, massive concentration, and high levels of tannin, yet the wine is fabulously well delineated and, like its sibling, has a finish that goes on for nearly a minute. It does not seem to be quite as evolved as the 1990, and my instincts suggest there is a bit more tannin, but both are as prodigious as Pétrus can be. Anticipated maturity: 2010–2040. Last tasted, 8/02.

1988
91?
This wine has become increasingly herbaceous with the tannins pushing through the fruit. It is also becoming more aggressive. The wine started off life impressively deep ruby/purple, but is now showing some amber at the edge. It is a medium-bodied, rather elegant style of Pétrus with a distinctive cedary, almost celery component intermixed with a hint of caramel, sweet mulberry, and black cherry fruit. It has aged far less evenly than I would have thought and is probably best drunk over the next 8–10 years. Last tasted, 11/02.

1986
86
This is another wine made during the period when Christian Moueix and his conservative oenologist, Jean Claude Berrouet, were obviously harvesting very early and also, to my mind, doing entirely too much fining and filtration before the wine got in bottle. My cask tasting notes were significantly higher on all the vintages in the early to mid-1980s, but as most of the wines have aged in the bottle, they have become increasingly weedy and herbaceous, with Médoc-like austerity and excessive tannins for the meager fruit. The 1986 is showing medium ruby/garnet color with considerable amber at the edge. The indifferent bouquet offers up notes of roasted vegetables, Japanese green tea, some smoke, a hint of sweet cherry, and some loamy, earthy, almost mushroomy notes in the background. The wine is austere on the palate, with high tannin and moderate fruit. For Pétrus, this is a major disappointment and continues to decline in quality. Anticipated maturity: now–2010. Last tasted, 11/02.

1985
88
This is a wine that I bought at a high price, and every bottle I have tasted from a six-bottle allocation has been increasingly disappointing. The wine still has its admirers, particularly Michael Broadbent, who continues to find it virtually perfect. Either we have different palates or we are tasting different wine, but this wine now has a medium ruby color with considerable amber at the edge. The nose smells like fresh vegetable market, with spice box, celery seed, and fennel all there, along with a hint of tobacco and Provençal herbs. There is sweet cherry fruit, but the weediness dominates everything. In the mouth, the wine is light, medium bodied, and fading. This is a wine to taste with the label clearly in front of you, to think of other Pétrus vintages as opposed to what is in the 1985. Caveat emptor. Anticipated maturity: now–2010. Last tasted, 11/02.

1983
86?
Weedy, herbaceous, vegetal notes intermixed with notes of tea, earthy cherries, and a hint of licorice are all present in the aromas and the attack. In the mouth the wine is medium bodied and beginning to show some very hard, astringent tannin in the finish, which has become increasingly attenuated over the last several years. This wine needs to be drunk up. Another disappointing Pétrus. Anticipated maturity: now. Last tasted, 11/02.

1982
90–98
I have gone through a complete case of this wine, stored perfectly, and this has been a perplexingly irregular wine to taste. Some bottles are spectacular, sweet, rich, full-bodied, and opulent, but even those have a distinctive herbaceousness to the nose, which offers up notes of chocolate, cedar, black cherry jam, and cur-

rants. It is full-bodied, tannic, and, from the best bottles, very concentrated and rich. Other bottles seem somewhat vegetal and roasted, with sweetness but not the prodigious qualities of other bottles. It is hard to know what is really going on. The wine seems to be close to full maturity, but should hold where well stored for at least another two decades. As a postscript, from cask, this wine is still to this day one of the most memorable wines I have ever tasted and certainly a perfect wine. From my perspective, though, it has never lived up to that after bottling, which I suspect involved entirely too much fining and filtration, something not being done since the late 1980s at Pétrus. Anticipated maturity: now–2023. Last tasted, 11/02.

1981 I remember how thrilling the 1981 Pétrus was from cask, but it has never per-
86 formed as well from bottle. I have continued to downgrade it. In this tasting, the wine exhibited an understated, light, washed-out personality, with vegetal cherry/coffee-flavored fruit in the nose intermingled with scents of spicy oak. Tart, lean, and austere, this is a Médoc-tasting wine without any of the Pétrus sweetness, chewiness, or unctuosity. This must be one of the most overrated wines of the past two decades. As there was virtually no sediment in this 16-year-old wine, I wonder if it was excessively fined and/or filtered? Anticipated maturity: now–2015. Last tasted, 12/95.

1979 I remember how stunning the 1979 Pétrus was from cask, but it has never lived up
86 to its early potential. Even from an Imperial, the 1979 Pétrus is a lean, compact, tannic, hard, austere wine lacking the richness and charm of the vintage's top Pomerols. The color was a healthy medium ruby. While the wine does not possess the vegetal overtones of the 1978, it leaves a great deal to be desired. Anticipated maturity: now–2010. Last tasted, 12/95.

1978 I have never been a fan of the 1978 Pétrus, but even I was ready to give it the ben-
83 efit of the doubt and be seduced when it was served out of an Imperial. The wine revealed a medium ruby color, followed by an herbal, underripe tomato, vegetal nose, medium body, and average flavor concentration and length. It is neither distinguished nor Pomerol-like. Anticipated maturity: now–2006. Last tasted, 12/95.

1975 One of the most rustic and powerful Pétruses of the last 25 years, this wine still has
98+ a murky garnet/plum/purple color, a gorgeous nose of overripe black cherries, mocha, caramel, chocolate, and a hint of iron and blood. Full-bodied and super-concentrated, with massive tannin and extract, this behemoth Pétrus can be enjoyed, but it still seems another 5–10 years away from maturity. It is certainly a 50–70 year wine, with exquisite concentration and intensity, but seemingly the rough edges will no doubt be less appealing to those looking for pure seamlessness. Perhaps that will emerge with bottle age. Anticipated maturity: 2005–2040. Last tasted, 11/02.

1971 This wine has been seemingly fully mature since the mid- to late 1970s. It is a se-
95 ductive, opulent vintage for Pétrus. The color is now a dark garnet with considerable amber at the rim. The incredible nose of Christmas fruitcake intermixed with mocha, jammy kirsch, and black currants is followed by a silky textured, full-bodied, very opulent wine that is still totally intact. The tannins have totally dissipated, and the wine is an unctuous, seductive Pétrus that is certainly one of the most delicious and compelling vintages. A sensational wine and probably the wine of the vintage. Anticipated maturity: now–2011. Last tasted, 11/02.

1970 This dark garnet–colored wine shows considerable amber at the edge. I have al-
99 ways had a tendency to taste this side by side with the 1971, and it has been fascinating how the 1971 was fully mature at a much younger age yet continued to hold on to life without losing any of its seductive fruit and intensity. The 1970 started off life more tannic, backward, and massive but needing considerable time, and it

has now hit full stride. It is a profound Pétrus, and certainly one of the great Pétruses of the last half century. The wine has a huge nose of cedar, caramel, vanilla, tobacco, fruitcake, and licorice-infused black cherry jam. It is unctuously textured and very full-bodied, with extraordinary sweetness and glycerin and a layered, viscous finish. This wine should continue to drink well for at least another 20 years. Anticipated maturity: now–2025. Last tasted, 11/02.

1967
91
In all fairness, the last bottle in the vertical tasting I had of Pétrus came from a pristinely stored magnum that I owned, so perhaps a regular bottle of this wine might be fading a bit. Nevertheless, this has always been the best wine of the vintage and a gorgeous example of Pétrus. The wine shows considerable amber to its garnet color and has a sweet nose of coffee beans intermixed with cedar, herbs, black cherries, and roasted nuts. The wine is sweet, elegant, medium to full-bodied, and totally savory and seamless. It is a gorgeous wine and one of the great sleeper vintages for Pétrus. Anticipated maturity: Drink up. Last tasted, 11/02.

1966
90
A very Médoc-like Pétrus and somewhat in the style of the wines made during most of the 1980s, this dark plum/garnet–colored wine shows plenty of amber at the edge and a sweet nose of melted caramel, licorice, roasted herbs, and sweet curranty and cherry fruit. The wine is medium-bodied and slightly austere, but very complex and elegant. The wine has been fully mature since the early 1990s. Anticipated maturity: now–2010. Last tasted, 1/02.

1964
99
A mammoth Pétrus of stupendous extraction and power, this wine seems to be aging at a glacial pace. I suppose the 1975 is somewhat similar in style, with high levels of tannin and equally impressive levels of richness. This wine has a dark, murky garnet color with some orange and rust at the edge. The flamboyant aromatics soar from the glass, offering up roasted herbs, espresso coffee, mocha, caramel, and plenty of jammy red and black fruits. A huge, viscous, spectacularly concentrated wine that is almost over the top in a style that even wine administrator Christian Moueix would probably find too big and intense for his more delicately styled taste. Nevertheless, lucky owners of this Pétrus have decades of thrills still ahead of them. This is spectacular stuff! Anticipated maturity: now–2030. Last tasted, 11/02.

1962
91
The fully mature 1962 is reminiscent of a Médoc, with its minty, chocolaty, herbal, cedary nose, medium-bodied, well-proportioned flavors, and structured personality. The wine still possesses a healthy dark ruby color with only slight amber at the edge. Although not that powerful or opulent, it is an outstanding example of Pétrus made in a more graceful, elegant manner. Tasted blind I would never have picked it out as a Pomerol. Last tasted, 12/95.

1961
100
The fully mature 1961 Pétrus possesses a Port-like richness (reminiscent of the 1947 Pétrus and 1947 Cheval Blanc). The color reveals considerable amber and garnet, but the wine is crammed with viscous, thick, overripe black cherry, mocha-tinged fruit flavors. Extremely full-bodied, with huge amounts of glycerin and alcohol, this unctuously textured, thick wine makes for an awesome mouthful. Imagine a Reese's Peanut Butter Cup laced with layers of coffee and cherries and encased in a shell of Valrhona chocolate! This is vinous immortality. Anticipated maturity: now–2010. Last tasted, 6/98.

ANCIENT VINTAGES

Much of the legendary/mythical status of Pétrus is based on what they did in 1950, 1947, 1945, 1929, and 1921. The 1959 (rated 93 in 12/95) was unctuous, sweet, gloriously fruity, thick, and jammy, with gobs of glycerin, full body, and a viscous, long, heady finish. Fully mature, but revealing considerable intensity and life, this is a wine that will drink well for another 10–15 years. It was the extraordinary 1950 Pétrus (99 points; last tasted 6/98) along with the 1950 Lafleur, first served to me years ago by the late Jean-Pierre Moueix, that made me realize how spectacular this vintage must have been in Pomerol. The wine is still a young, mammothly constituted Pétrus that is less evolved than more recent knockout vintages such as 1961. Massive and rich, with spectacular color saturation and the sweet, unctuous texture Pétrus obtains in ripe years, the 1950 will last for another 20–30 years.

While variable, the 1949 (95 points; last tasted 10/94) has always been a huge, thick, chewy, immense wine without the unctuosity and Port-like quality of the 1950 or 1947. The first time I tasted it a decade ago it seemed to be chunky and one-dimensional but enormously rich. Since then the wine has begun to display the huge, exotic, fleshiness of Pétrus, as well as marvelously pure, plum, black cherry, mocha, and coffee-flavored fruit. It is developing well and remains remarkably youthful for a 45-year-old wine. The 1948 (95 points; last tasted 11/97) is another one of those vintages that was largely ignored by the press. Shrewd consumers would be smart to take a look at well-stored bottles of 1948s that might appear in the marketplace. In the past I have reported on some of the other great 1948s, such as Vieux Château Certan, La Mission Haut-Brion, and Cheval Blanc, but the 1948 Pétrus has fooled me completely in blind tastings. The nose of cedar, leather, herbs, and cassis suggested to me that this was a first-growth Pauillac. The color is still dense, with only a moderate orange hue at the edge. The wine is rich, more austere and lineal than usual, but full-bodied with considerable flavor and a spicy, moderately tannic finish. It has peaked but is clearly capable of lasting another 10–15 years. A word of caution: Some bottles possess excessive (even for this epoch) volatile acidity. The 1947 Pétrus (100 points; last tasted 6/98) is the most decadent wine of the century. While not as Port-like as the 1947 Cheval Blanc, it is a massive, unctuously textured, viscous wine with amazing power, richness, and sweet fruit. The nose explodes from the glass, offering jammy fruit, smoke, and buttery caramel scents. The wine's viscosity is reminiscent of 10 W-40 motor oil. It is so sweet, thick, and rich, one suspects a spoon could stand upright in it. The wine is loaded with dream-like quantities of fruit as well as high alcohol, but there is no noticeable tannin. While drinkable now, given its amazing fruit extract and high levels of glycerin and alcohol, it is capable of lasting two more decades. While the 1947 Pétrus is a big, juicy, succulent, fruity wine, the 1945 (98+ points; last tasted 10/94) remains a backward, tannic colossus needing another 5–10 years of cellaring. The color reveals more purple hues than the 1947, and the nose offers aromas of black fruits, licorice, truffles, and smoked meat. Massively constituted, with formidably high tannin and extract levels, this sleeping giant may evolve into another perfect example of Pétrus.

The 1929 Pétrus displays a deep ruby/garnet color with some amber/orange at the edge. A huge, thick wine with extraordinary aromas of coffee, mocha, black cherries, herbs, and cedar, this unctuously textured, thick, tannic, massively concentrated wine was remarkably intact. It could have easily been mistaken for a 30–35-year-old wine. When I drank it in September 1995, the 1921 Pétrus (100 points) was, to state it mildly, out of this universe! The opaque color displayed considerable amber at the edge, but the blockbuster nose of black raspberries, freshly brewed coffee, and mocha/toffee-like candy was followed by one of the sweetest, most opulent, thick, juicy wines I have ever tasted. Extraordinarily rich and opulent, with interesting cedar notes to the succulent flavors, this huge, unbelievably concentrated wine could have been mistaken for the 1950 or 1947. In December 1996, I tasted what was believed to be a magnum of the 1900 Pétrus found in a private cellar in St.-Emilion. It was excellent rather than exceptional (I rated it 89), still revealing evidence of sweet cherry and blackberry fruit.

Note: Potential purchasers of Pétrus should be aware of the numerous examples of fraudulent bottles that exist in the marketplace. The most sought after vintages—1990, 1989, 1982, 1970, 1961, and 1947—are the most usual suspects. Provenance of any bottle purchased must be guaranteed. The Moueix family has recognized the problem and began utilizing an engraved bottle in the late 1990s.

LE PIN

Owner: Jacques Thienpont

Address: 33500 Pomerol

Mailing address: Hof te Cattebeke, Bossenaarstraat 14, 9680 Etikhove, Belgique

Telephone and Telefax: 05 57 51 33 99 (France)

Telephone: 32 55 31 17 59; Telefax: 32 55 31 09 66 (Belgium)

E-mail: wine@thienpont-etikhove.be

Visits: By appointment only

Contact: Jacques or Fiona Thienpont

VINEYARDS

Surface area: 5 acres

Grape varietals: 92% Merlot, 8% Cabernet Franc

Average age of vines: 28 years

Density of plantation: 6,000 vines per hectare

Average yields: 34 hectoliters per hectare

Elevage: Ten to fifteen day fermentation and maceration in temperature-controlled stainless-steel vats. Wines undergo malolactics and are aged 15–18 months in 100% new oak. Fining, no filtration.

WINES PRODUCED

Château Le Pin: 7,000 bottles

No second wine is produced.

Plateau of maturity: Within 8–25 years of the vintage

GENERAL APPRECIATION

The most exotic and flamboyant of Pomerols, Le Pin is the forerunner of the garage wine movement that is more associated with St.-Emilion than Pomerol. It has its followers, and the craving for this particular style of wine combined with the limited availability have contributed to make Le Pin one of the most expensive wines of Bordeaux. Le Pin remains unequaled in terms of seduction, charm, and the sheer pleasure of drinking.

Another Thienpont, this time Jacques, produces this exotic, ripe Pomerol. The original garage wine (500–600 cases are produced from this tiny, postage stamp–size vineyard sandwiched between Vieux Château Certan, Le Croix St.-Georges, and Gombaude Guillot), Le Pin can begin life a bit over the top, with high levels of oak and an excessive exoticism, but it puts on weight and richness with aging. The greatest vintages to date (there have been many) are 2000, 1998, 1990, 1989, and 1982. Other years, such as 1999, 1995, and 1985 are not far off. This tiny vineyard was acquired by the Thienpont family in 1979. By his own admission, Jacques Thienpont is trying to make a wine of great richness and majesty.

Much of the gaudy character of Le Pin is probably explained by the fact that it was one of the first Bordeaux estates to actually conduct the malolactic fermentation of the wine in new oak casks, a technique widely utilized today in neighboring St.-Emilion. This is a labor-intensive procedure and can only be done by estates that have relatively small productions, where the wine can be monitored constantly. However, I believe it is this technique that gives Le Pin its huge, smoky, and exotically scented bouquet. Whatever the secret, no doubt the iron-enriched, gravelly soil on this part of the Pomerol plateau has helped to create a cult following for the microscopic quantities of Le Pin.

Le Pin is still criticized, largely on the grounds that the wine may not fare well with extended cellaring. This may have been a legitimate concern 10 years ago, but none of the early vintages of Le Pin (the first vintage was 1979) have gone off the deep end. In fact, the wine has tended to firm up in the bottle and put on weight. It has even shown greater delineation and richness after 10–15 years than it did when young. Hence, the doom and gloom kindergarten critics who tend to evaluate the price of the wine more than the wine itself have been wrong. The early vintages, which are now about 20 years of age, have held up magnificently. Thus it seems to me that Le Pin is a wine that certainly has the potential to last, in the great years, 25–30+ years.

IMPORTANT VINTAGES

2001
91–94
Yields were 32 hectoliters per hectare in 2001. Le Pin is the leading candidate for the sexiest, kinkiest, most exotic wine of the vintage. Aromas and flavors of overripe black fruits intermixed with coconut, vanilla, toast, and espresso beans nearly overwhelm the taster. In the mouth, it is fleshy and succulent, with low acidity, ripe tannin, and a pure, sensual personality. Anticipated maturity: 2005–2020. Last tasted, 1/03.

2000
98+
An explosive, virtually perfect example of Le Pin, the dense purple–colored 2000 boasts luxurious levels of extract and richness. This intense, unctuously textured Pomerol bursting with black fruits is thick enough to drink with a spoon. It reveals abundant tannin and definition for such a young Le Pin, typical of many of the blockbuster, but backward and tannic 2000 Pomerols. It is a great wine for the multimillionaires who are able to latch on to a few bottles. Anticipated maturity: 2005–2025. Last tasted, 1/03.

1999
93
This is an example of a wine that has gained considerable weight since I first tasted it. Exotic and sexy, with a cunning display of superripe mocha and toast-infused, jammy black cherry fruit, low acidity, and a savory personality, it appears ready to drink, but will undoubtedly take on more delineation and structure as it ages in the bottle. A luxuriously rich, decadent, 100% Merlot, it will be at its finest between 2004–2015. Last tasted, 3/02.

1998
95
A beautifully made, dark ruby/garnet/plum–colored wine, the full-bodied 1998 Le Pin offers an exotic bouquet of coconut, kirsch, and jammy blackberries, all flamboyantly dosed with smoky new oak. It is dense, rich, and plush, with a good tannic framework. At one time, Le Pin was the most exotic wine from Bordeaux's right bank, but there is now considerable competition from all the new St.-Emilion upstarts. While this remains an outstanding, often compelling Pomerol, many far less expensive, equally prodigious alternatives have emerged. Anticipated maturity: now–2018. Last tasted, 9/02.

1997
86?
While not the strongest effort from this small estate, Le Pin's 1997 reveals an excessive amount of oak for the concentration of fruit. However, even richer vintages have tended to reveal abundant oak early in life, only to have it absorbed as the wine ages. The 1997 possesses sweet currant and cherry fruit, abundant toasty oak, and a seductive style, but the oak is elevated. The wine will probably not last long enough for the wood to become fully integrated. Or am I wrong about that? Anticipated maturity: now–2008. Last tasted, 3/02.

1996
92
Like many 1996 Pomerols, there is a certain austerity to the tannins, and the wines are not as generous and voluminous as they would be from a great right bank–vintage like 1998 or 2000. Nevertheless, this is a top-notch example, more structured than usual, but it still has the exotic notes of melted chocolate, roasted espresso, a hint of coconut, and a plethora of jammy black fruits. Relatively supple, even for the vintage, this flamboyant, medium-bodied wine shows superb ripeness, purity, and overall balance with a bit of dry tannin in the finish. Anticipated maturity: 2004–2020. Last tasted, 5/02.

1995
94
Some of the hard tannins this wine possessed early in life have sloughed off to reveal a wine that has a stunning nose of roasted herbs, caramel, smoke, and barbecue notes along with fruitcake, blackberry and black cherry jam, and a bit of white chocolate entering the smorgasbord of scents. Full-bodied with low acidity but moderately high tannin, it is still a tightly knit, very concentrated wine that is surprisingly structured and backward for Le Pin. It is also a bit more massive than most vintages. Anticipated maturity: 2008–2025. Last tasted, 5/02.

1994
91
A beautiful 1994, and certainly one of the best wines of the vintage, this medium-bodied Le Pin shows notes of sweet oak intermixed with espresso bean, vanilla, black cherry, licorice, and white chocolate. The wine is medium-bodied and has moderately high tannin, but a luscious, sweet, succulent attack before the tannins begin to kick in. It is hard to peg the actual plateau of maturity for this wine, which seems evolved and complex aromatically but then still has plenty of tannin to shed. Anticipated maturity: 2004–2016. Last tasted, 5/02.

1990
99
For my taste one of the two finest Le Pins made to date, the 1990 is just starting to hit its adolescent stage and develop secondary nuances. Still a very deep ruby/purple with just a bit of pink at the rim, its explosive aromatics consist of Asian spice, kirsch, fig, blackberry, cherry, and smoky, toasty oak. In the mouth there are layers of concentration, glorious ripeness, copious glycerin, and a seamlessness that has to be tasted to be believed. This a voluptuously textured, full-bodied, remarkable wine that should still have a tremendous upside to it. Anticipated maturity: now–2022. Last tasted, 12/01.

1989

96

A slightly firmer, more structured wine than the 1990, with similarly low-acid but more noticeable tannin, the color remains a very healthy saturated ruby/purple. The nose needs more coaxing and offers up notes of coconut, roasted herbs and *jus de viande*, along with plenty of black currant and sweet cherry fruit with nicely integrated toasty oak. The wine has similarly high levels of glycerin to the 1990, but less accessibility and more structure and possibly power. This is a remarkable wine, and certainly one of the great vintages for Le Pin. Anticipated maturity: 2005–2022. Last tasted, 12/01.

1988

92

This wine has developed nicely in the bottle. The color is a deep ruby with purple nuances. The aggressive oakiness has melted away to reveal plenty of toast and sweet, rich, black cherries, black currants, and a touch of prunes. Chocolaty and rich, this medium- to full-bodied, super-concentrated Le Pin possesses more structure and tannin than is noticeable in many vintages. It is still a beautifully plump, hedonistic wine. Anticipated maturity: now–2010. Last tasted, 11/97.

1986

90

One of the more structured examples of Le Pin and still surprisingly youthful for a wine that critics say needs to be drunk in its first 5–10 years, this dark garnet–colored wine has notes of licorice, loamy soil scents, sweet black cherries, and currants along with some truffle and vanilla. The wine is medium bodied with a certain firmness and delineation, and less of the charm, glycerin, and opulence that the ripe, more generous vintages provide. The finish is long and almost Médoc-like. Anticipated maturity: now–2015. Last tasted, 12/01.

1985

94

A sexy tart of a wine, this open-knit, expensive, fleshy wine offers up sumptuous notes of smoked herbs, melted caramel, espresso, jammy black currant and cherry fruit, and plenty of licorice. Very sweet, round, and luscious in the mouth with an unctuous texture, no obvious tannins, and a silky-textured, lush finish, this fully mature Le Pin should continue to drink well for 5–10 more years. Anticipated maturity: now–2012. Last tasted, 12/01.

1983

94

This wine seems to have been better several years ago. It still is a great bottle of wine, but may just be beginning to slip in terms of intensity and complexity. Dark garnet with some orange/amber at the rim, its sweet ripe nose of Provençal herbs intermixed with licorice, tree bark, truffle, and blackberry and cherry jam is followed by a medium-bodied, very lush, flavorful wine that is kinky, exotic, and just sumptuous. It needs to be drunk up, however. Anticipated maturity: now–2009. Last tasted, 12/01.

1982

100

A wine that has gained stature and weight in the bottle, the 1982 now seems to have hit its magical stride, where hopefully it will stay for another 5+ years. The color is a dense ruby/garnet with some amber at the edge. The soaring aromatics consist of melted caramel, espresso, Asian spice, and sweet, almost overripe prune, black currant, and fig. In the mouth it is layered, lavishly concentrated, very full-bodied, and sweet (from ripe fruit, not sugar). The wine seems very low in acidity, but the tannins remain, although they are very ripe and integrated. This is a decadent, extravagantly rich style of wine that is nearly over the top. Anticipated maturity: now–2012. Last tasted, 11/02.

ANCIENT VINTAGES

I have not tasted the 1981, 1980, or 1979, (the 1979 being the debut vintage for Le Pin) since the last edition of this book, but I suspect they are sound wines if well stored.

Note: Le Pin is another luxury wine that has become the darling of criminals specializing in the production of phony bottles. In particular, the 1982 is a favorite of counterfeiters.

LA POINTE

Owner: d'Arfeuille family

Address: 33500 Pomerol

Telephone: 05 57 51 02 11; Telefax: 05 57 51 42 33

E-mail: chateau.lapointe@wanadoo.fr

Website: www.chateaulapointe.com

Visits: By appointment only

Contact: Stéphane d'Arfeuille

VINEYARDS

Surface area: 54.3 acres

Grape varietals: 75% Merlot, 25% Cabernet Franc

Average age of vines: 35 years

Density of plantation: 5,500 vines per hectare

Average yields: 47 hectoliters per hectare

Elevage: Four to five week fermentation and maceration in temperature-controlled concrete vats. Fifteen to eighteen months aging in barrels with 35% new oak. Fining and filtration.

WINES PRODUCED

Château La Pointe: 130,000 bottles

La Pointe Riffat: 20,000 bottles

Plateau of maturity: Within 3–10 years of the vintage

GENERAL APPRECIATION

This is a solidly made Pomerol that has improved in quality since the late 1990s.

La Pointe has been an irregular performer. The wines can be round, fruity, simple, and generous, as in 1970, but far too frequently they are boringly light and unsubstantial. Older vintages, such as 1979, 1978, 1976, and 1975, were all uncommonly deficient in the rich, chewy, supple, zesty fruit that one finds so typical of a good Pomerol. The large production insures that the wine is widely promoted. The owners have increased the percentage of Merlot significantly since the early 1970s. All things considered, this once mediocre Pomerol has shown improvement during recent vintages.

IMPORTANT VINTAGES

2001 A noteworthy effort from La Pointe, the 2001 exhibits a deep ruby/purple color,
87–88 sweet fruit, medium body, fine purity, and sweet tannin. Very good, it will drink well young. Anticipated maturity: 2005–2014. Last tasted, 1/03.

2000 This is an elegant, soft, medium-bodied, straightforward wine with abundant
88 black cherry fruit intermixed with earth, oak, and spice. Although slightly compressed, it is well made, medium-bodied and clean. Drink it over the next decade. Last tasted, 1/03.

1999
87
The 1999 La Pointe's deep ruby/purple color is accompanied by an excellent, multilayered personality, a chewy texture, abundant quantities of plum, cherry, cola, and mocha flavors, excellent concentration, sweet tannin, and low acidity. Anticipated maturity: now–2012. Last tasted, 3/02.

1998
84
Soft, fruity, and diffuse, this elegant, lightweight effort is pleasant, but lacks substance as well as follow-through on the palate. Drink it over the next 1–2 years. Last tasted, 3/02.

ROUGET

Owner: Labruyère family

Address: 33500 Pomerol

Telephone: 05 57 51 05 85; Telefax: 05 57 51 05 85

Visits: By appointment only

Contact: Mr. Ribeiro

VINEYARDS

Surface area: 43.4 acres

Grape varietals: 85% Merlot, 15% Cabernet Franc

Average age of vines: 28 years

Density of plantation: 6,000 vines per hectare

Average yields: 35 hectoliters per hectare

Elevage: Fermentations occur in temperature-controlled stainless-steel vats. Wines are aged in oak barrels and renewed by a third at each vintage for approximately 15 months. (Starting in 1977, malolactics occur in new oak barrels.)

WINES PRODUCED

Château Rouget: 29,000 bottles

Vieux Château des Templiers: 29,000 bottles

Plateau of maturity: Within 5–15 years of the vintage

GENERAL APPRECIATION

While Rouget enjoyed a fine reputation in the 1940s, it was a less than stellar performer until the mid 1980s. Since its acquisition by the Labruyère family, its wines have improved considerably and, though they retain their characteristic rusticity, they now show more concentration, stuffing, and suppleness than in the past. Recent vintages have been very good.

Historically, Rouget is one of Pomerol's most illustrious estates. In one of the early editions of Cocks et Féret's *Bordeaux et ses Vins,* the vineyard was ranked fourth among all the Pomerols. At present, their reputation has been surpassed by numerous properties, but there is no question that Rouget can be a rich and interesting wine. For example, both the 1947 and 1945 vintages were dazzling wines that were both still drinking superbly in the late 1980s. Until recently François-Jean Brochet ran this old yet beautiful estate that sits in the northernmost part of the Pomerol appellation on very sandy soil, with a lovely view of the Barbanne River visible through the trees. The wine was traditionally made by Brochet, who also maintained an immense stock of old vintages. Brochet's sale of the property to the Lambruyère family has resulted in much-needed improvements.

The style of Rouget is one that makes no concessions to consumers who want to drink their wine young. It is a darkly colored, rich, full-bodied, often very tannic wine that usually is in need of a minimum of 8–10 years of cellaring. It is sometimes too coarse and rustic, but almost always a delicious, rich, ripe, spicy wine. Recent vintages of the late 1990s have tasted more supple. The vintages of the late 1960s, 1970s, 1980s, and early 1990s are of little merit. After two decades of mediocrity, this property rebounded beautifully over the last few vintages and is now producing impressive wines. The price is beginning to escalate accordingly as more Bordeaux wine traders and consumers catch on.

IMPORTANT VINTAGES

2001
88–90 The noteworthy 2001 is, along with the 2000, one of the biggest, richest Rougets I have tasted. Its deep ruby/purple color is accompanied by a sweet perfume of balsam wood, plums, and black cherry liqueur presented in a nicely extracted, well-balanced style. Medium to full-bodied, with low acidity and abundant thickness as well as flavor, it should drink well young and last for 10–13 years. Last tasted, 1/03.

2000
90 The most complete, complex, and powerful Rouget since 1964 and 1961, the dense plum/ruby–colored 2000 boasts a knockout nose of smoked herbs, jammy fruit with a liqueur-like intensity, terrific purity, and admirable sweetness on the attack and mid-palate. It has become richer and more textured over the last year, but unlike many 2000 Pomerols, it does not possess the hard tannin that recalls the 1975 vintage. Anticipated maturity: 2006–2020. Last tasted, 1/03.

1999
89 An excellent, textbook Pomerol with notes of roasted coffee, mocha, cola, and black cherry liqueur, this lush, sexy, tasty, medium-bodied 1999 is low in acidity with plenty of ripe tannin. It is ideal for drinking over the next decade. Last tasted, 3/02.

1998
89 Dark ruby/purple–colored, with a ripe nose of chocolate, black fruits, brandy-macerated cherries, figs, and prunes, this medium- to full-bodied, plush Rouget reveals a chewy, concentrated texture as well as a ripe, fat finish. With a bit more definition and complexity, it would have merited an outstanding score. Anticipated maturity: now–2015. Last tasted, 3/02.

DE SALES

Owner: GFA du Château de Sales

Address: 33500 Libourne

Telephone: 05 57 51 04 92; Telefax: 05 57 25 23 91

Visits: By appointment only

Contact: Bruno de Lambert

VINEYARDS

Surface area: 117.3 acres

Grape varietals: 70% Merlot, 15% Cabernet Sauvignon, 15% Cabernet Franc

Average age of vines: 30 years

Density of plantation: 5,600 vines per hectare

Average yields: 49 hectoliters per hectare

Elevage: Eighteen to twenty-four day fermentation and maceration in temperature-controlled concrete vats (max 30°C). After completion of malolactics, 18 months aging, wines in barrels (renewed by a third at each vintage) for half the time and in vats for the other (rotation at the time of racking off, every three months). Fining, light filtration upon bottling.

WINES PRODUCED

Château de Sales: 150,000 bottles

Château Chantalouette: 60,000 bottles

Plateau of maturity: Within 3–10 years of the vintage

GENERAL APPRECIATION

After a difficult period in the 1980s and until the mid 1990s, de Sales is back on track, which is good news for consumers. The estate offers one of the most pleasant and most reasonably priced Pomerols.

De Sales is the largest vineyard in Pomerol and boasts the appellation's only grand château. The property is located in the northwestern corner of Pomerol with a vineyard planted primarily on sandy soil intermixed with gravel. The owners and managers are the de Lambert family. The wines are increasingly among the most enjoyable of the Pomerols. They are prized for their sheer, supple, glossy, round, generous, ripe fruitiness, and lush, silky personalities. De Sales has had an irregular track record in the 1980s and 1990s but the recent vintages have been particularly strong. It is never a powerful, aggressive, oaky, or big wine, and it always offers immediate drinkability. In spite of a precocious style, it has a cunning ability to age well for 10–12 years.

While consistently good, de Sales will never be a great Pomerol, but its price remains modest, making it a good value.

IMPORTANT VINTAGES

2001 The 2001 is a savory, ripe, medium-bodied offering with plenty of flesh and
87–88 up-front charm. It possesses a saturated deep ruby color, copious quantities of black cherry fruit, medium body, and a soft, succulent finish. Consume this hedonistic, totally charming, mid-weight Pomerol during its first 8–10 years of life. Last tasted, 1/03.

2000 The finest de Sales since the 1982 (probably better), the deep ruby/purple–
89 colored 2000 boasts sweet aromas of soil, kirsch, raspberries, and currants. Layered and opulent, with sweet tannin and medium to full body, it is atypically large-scaled for a wine from this estate. Bravo! Anticipated maturity: 2005–2015. Last tasted, 1/03.

1999 Readers seeking a Burgundian-style wine with gobs of black cherry fruit, expan-
88 sive, savory texture, sexy aromatics, and loads of glycerin and fruit should check out this medium-bodied, lush Pomerol. It should be drunk over the next decade. Last tasted, 3/02.

1998
88
Together with the 2000, this is one of the finest de Sales produced since the early 1980s. The medium ruby/garnet–colored 1998 is forward and soft, revealing notions of white chocolate, mocha, and kirsch. Made in a seductive, luscious style, it possesses sweet tannin, a supple mid-palate as well as finish, and excellent concentration. Purchasers will have no need to defer their gratification. Anticipated maturity: now–2010. Last tasted, 3/02.

ANCIENT VINTAGES

This is a wine that normally needs to be drunk in the first 10–12 years of life. Older vintages are generally of little importance. Those that may still be drinking well if stored properly include the 1995 (87 points; last tasted 3/99), 1990 (89 points; last tasted 11/99), and 1982 (87 points; last tasted 11/02).

TROTANOY

Owner: SC Château Trotanoy

Address: 33500 Pomerol

Mailing address: c/o SA Ets Jean-Pierre Moueix, BP 129, 54, quai du Priourat, 33502 Libourne

Telephone: 05 57 51 78 96; Telefax: 05 57 51 79 79

Visits: By appointment and exclusively for professionals of the wine trade dealing with the firm.

Contact: Frédéric Lospied

APPELLATION POMEROL CONTRÔLÉE

CHÂTEAU TROTANOY
POMEROL
1996

SOCIÉTÉ CIVILE DU CHATEAU TROTANOY
PROPRIÉTAIRE A POMEROL · GIRONDE · FRANCE
MIS EN BOUTEILLES A LA PROPRIÉTÉ PAR JEAN-PIERRE MOUEIX VITICULTEUR A LIBOURNE
Alc. 13,5% Vol.   75 cl

VINEYARDS

Surface area: 17.8 acres

Grape varietals: 90% Merlot, 10% Cabernet Franc

Average age of vines: 35 years

Density of plantation: 6,200 vines per hectare

Average yields: 39 hectoliters per hectare

Elevage: Twenty day fermentation and maceration in temperature-controlled concrete tanks. Twenty months aging in barrels with 40% new oak. Fining, no filtration.

WINES PRODUCED

Château Trotanoy: 30,000 bottles

No second wine is produced.

Plateau of maturity: Within 7–25 years of the vintage

GENERAL APPRECIATION

Trotanoy was excellent before the 1970s, then went through a difficult period in the 1980s and the beginning of the 1990s, producing much lighter wines than in the past. However, it rebounded beautifully in 1995 and since then has offered an uninterrupted string of fine vintages. The vineyard benefits from an exceptional situation, and when Trotanoy hits the bull's-eye, it can easily rival its stablemate Pétrus. In terms of quality, in the late 1990s this wine is on par with such stars of the appellation as L'Eglise-Clinet, L'Evangile, and La Conseillante.

Trotanoy has historically been one of the great wines of Pomerol and all of Bordeaux. Since 1976, Trotanoy has been the quality equivalent of a second growth. In vintages prior to 1976, Trotanoy was often as profound as a first growth.

Since 1953, Trotanoy has been owned by the firm of Jean-Pierre Moueix. The château is unmarked (it is the residence of Jean-Jacques Moueix). The vineyards of this modest estate, which lie a kilometer to the west of Pétrus between the church of Pomerol and the village of Catusseau, are situated on soil of clay and gravel. The wine is vinified and handled in exactly the same way as Pétrus, except only 40% new oak barrels are used each year.

Until the late 1970s, Trotanoy was an opulently rich, intense, full-bodied wine that usually needed a full decade of cellaring to reach its zenith. In some vintages the power, intensity, and concentration came remarkably close to matching that of Pétrus. It had an enviable track record of producing good, sometimes brilliant, wines in poor Bordeaux vintages. The 1974, 1972, and 1967 were three examples of vintages where Trotanoy was among the best two or three wines of the entire Bordeaux region.

In the late 1970s the style became lighter, although Trotanoy appeared to return to full form with the extraordinarily opulent, rich, decadent 1982. Until 1995 there was a succession of good, rather than thrilling, wines. There is no question that there has been some major replanting of the micro-size vineyard of Trotanoy and that the production from these younger vines was blended in. Whatever the case might be, Trotanoy no longer seems to be one of the top three or four wines of Pomerol, and it was surpassed in the 1980s (with the exception of the 1982 vintage) by such châteaux as Clinet, L'Eglise-Clinet, Vieux Château Certan, Le Pin, Lafleur, La Fleur de Gay, L'Evangile, La Conseillante, and even Le Bon Pasteur in specific vintages. Given the competitiveness and talent of Christian Moueix and his staff, this situation appears to be changing. Recent vintages have all been strong, including a beautiful 1995 and sensational 1998, as well as 2000.

Trotanoy is an expensive wine because it is highly regarded by connoisseurs the world over. Yet it rarely sells for more than half the price of Pétrus—a fact worth remembering since it does (in certain vintages) have more than just a casual resemblance to the great Pétrus itself.

IMPORTANT VINTAGES

2001 With considerable harmony, elegance, and medium weight, the 2001 Trotanoy
89–92 might evolve along the lines of the 1979 or the incredible 1967. It possesses a deep plum/ruby/purple color as well as a sweet nose of earth, truffles, black cherries, and currants, medium-bodied flavors, and impeccable purity. Tannin is present, but is not overdone. This wine has put on considerable weight and is not far off the mark of the 2000. Anticipated maturity: 2006–2016. Last tasted, 1/03.

2000 The 2000 Trotanoy may be nearly as profound as the prodigious 1998. A dense
92+ murky ruby/purple color is followed by sensational aromas of black fruits, cherries, figs, plums, truffles, and earth. Extremely full-bodied and deep, with huge flavor extraction, sweet but noticeable tannin, and a 50-second finish, this compelling Trotanoy signals a return to form for this great *terroir*, which, during the 1950s, 1960s, and early 1970s, often rivaled Pétrus. Anticipated maturity: 2009–2030. Last tasted, 1/03.

1999

89

Delicious, elegant aromas and flavors of earth, mocha, cherries, and tobacco characterize this middle weight, dark ruby–colored 1999. It offers low acidity, sweet fruit, and an appealing combination of accessibility and balanced elegance. Drink it over the next 10–12 years. Last tasted, 3/02.

1998

96+

The finest Trotanoy since the 1961, this structured, formidably endowed, deep ruby/purple–colored, full-bodied, superrich wine exhibits notes of toffee, truffles, and abundant blackberry, cherry, and currant fruit. It cuts a large swath across the palate and possesses copious but sweet tannin as well as a chewy, muscular mid-palate and finish. This is a compelling effort from one of the great vineyards of Pomerol. Anticipated maturity: 2006–2035. Last tasted, 11/02.

1997

89+?

The 1997 is an atypically structured, rich, powerful wine for the vintage, with hard tannin in the finish. It is ripe and medium bodied, with surprising depth as well as copious quantities of plum, cherry, currant, truffle, herb, and earth aromas and flavors. Could this be a modern-day version of the underrated 1967? It should age for 12+ years. Last tasted, 3/02.

1996

88

Dark ruby with surprising pink at the rim, the 1996 Trotanoy seems very tightly knit, with dusty tannins and hints of sweet-and-sour cherry fruit, finishing to a somewhat liquid minerality and spicy note. The wine has plenty of muscle, very high levels of tannin, but a somewhat unimpressive mid-palate. Whether it fleshes out remains to be seen, but I am somewhat doubtful. This wine seems to be increasingly less impressive. Anticipated maturity: 2008–2016. Last tasted, 2/02.

1995

93

Certainly the best Trotanoy between 1998 and 1982, the 1995 has a deep saturated ruby color that is dark to the rim. Relatively shut down when tasted in 2002 on several occasions, the wine, with coaxing, does offer some notes of earth, raspberry, black cherries, and a hint of licorice. Medium to full-bodied, powerful, and backward, it is an impressively constituted Trotanoy that is relatively large-scaled, but the huge level of tannin also means it might be a modern-day version of the 1970. Time will tell. Anticipated maturity: 2010–2025. Last tasted, 2/02.

1994

88

Beginning to show some evolution, the dark plum/garnet–colored 1994 Trotanoy has a certain herbaceousness and an interesting beef bouillon smell intermixed with some sweet cherries and earth. On the palate, it is a medium-bodied wine with sweet fruit, good brightness, but some relatively hard and slightly astringent tannins in the finish. That latter characteristic may become worrisome if they do not melt away. Anticipated maturity: 2004–2016. Last tasted, 2/02.

1990

90

Very evolved and far more mature than its bigger sibling (the 1990 Pétrus), this dark plum–colored wine is already showing some amber at the edge. It is forward and sweet, with sweet-and-sour cherry fruit intermixed with a hint of herbs, licorice, fig, and earth. The wine is medium bodied with sweet fruit, low acidity, and a very nicely layered finish. All things considered, it is a very elegant, understated Trotanoy that is outstanding, but well behind the best Pomerols of the vintage. Anticipated maturity: now–2012. Last tasted, 2/02.

1989

88

A very delicate, elegant wine that has reached full maturity, again the notes of baked herbs, even tapenade, are intermixed with sweet-and-sour cherries. Medium bodied, soft, and easy to drink, this rather lightweight Trotanoy needs to be consumed over the next decade. Last tasted, 2/02.

1988

86

An unexciting, somewhat indifferent style of wine, the medium garnet color offers up a nose of mushrooms, earth, and licorice, with some ripe cherry fruit. In the mouth there is not much concentration, and some dry astringent tannins are in the finish. It is not going to get any better, but it is certainly capable of lasting for up to a decade. Anticipated maturity: now–2010. Last tasted, 2/02.

1986 Another rather hollow, commercial style of wine that shows vegetal aromas along
85   with herbal tea, licorice, and some faded candied cherry notes. The color is an
      evolved medium ruby with plenty of amber. The wine's finish is short, medium-
      bodied, with evidence of dilution. Anticipated maturity: Drink it up. Last tasted,
      2/02.

1985 Made during a disappointing era for Trotanoy when the wines lacked concentra-
85   tion and often tasted vegetal, this wine is fully mature with notes of tapenade in-
      termixed with *herbes de Provence,* cherry jam, and even a hint of strawberry and
      red currant. Some acidity and tannin continue to assert themselves in the wine's
      finish, suggesting this wine has seen better days and needs to be drunk up. Antic-
      ipated maturity: now. Last tasted, 2/02.

1982 Fully mature, gorgeously fragrant, with a knockout nose of sweet herbs intermixed
92   with toast, jammy strawberry, and black cherry fruit as well as mocha and cedar,
      this dense garnet–colored wine is medium to full-bodied, expansive, and lush,
      with low acidity and a long, concentrated finish with considerable glycerin. It is
      not going to improve, but certainly this wine will hold for at least another 10–15
      years. Last tasted, 12/02.

ANCIENT VINTAGES

Trotanoy's 1975 (94 points; last tasted 11/02) is stunning and was drunk on three different occasions in 2002. The 1971 is another great wine (93 points; last tasted 7/97),
but it has been fully mature for nearly 20 years, so I would not push its evolution any
further. A wine that seems to have fallen in stature is the 1970, rated as high as 96+ in
8/96, but recent bottles, both from magnums (rated 92 and 94), seemed alarmingly
high in tannin while youthful. The color is still a dark ruby/purple with little lightening
at the edge. The wine is sweet on the attack with plenty of berry fruit, earth, meat, and
leather, but the tannins seem increasingly astringent. I have always felt this wine could
last through 2030 and don't doubt that it will, but I wonder about its overall balance
and the dry astringency of the tannins. Among other ancient vintages, the 1967 (which
hasn't been tasted in many a year) was a stunning wine and one of the top two or three
wines of the vintage. The 1964 was also great and probably still delicious, but I have
not tasted it in over a decade. The 1961 could be immortal. I rated it 100 when last
tasted 1/01 from a magnum. The wine was opulent, viscous, rich—just an extraordinary glass of wine, and, for my tastes, the finest Trotanoy I have ever had. From pristine
bottles this wine is prodigious and can easily last another 20 years.

VIEUX CHÂTEAU CERTAN

Owner: Thienpont family

Address: 33500 Pomerol

Telephone: 05 57 51 17 33; Telefax: 05 57 25 35 08

E-mail: info@vieuxchateaucertan.com

Website: www.vieuxchateaucertan.com

Visits: By appointment only Monday to Friday, 10
A.M.–noon and 2–6 P.M.

Contact: Alexandre Thienpont

VINEYARDS

Surface area: 34.6 acres

Grape varietals: 60% Merlot, 30% Cabernet Franc, 10% Cabernet Sauvignon

Average age of vines: 35 years

Density of plantation: 5,800 vines per hectare

Average yields: 40 hectoliters per hectare

Elevage: Thirty day fermentation and maceration in wooden vats. The Merlots undergo malolactics in barrel. Eighteen to twenty-two months aging in new oak. Fining, no filtration.

WINES PRODUCED

Vieux Château Certan: 40,000 bottles

La Gravette de Certan: 20,000 bottles

Plateau of maturity: Within 5–25 years of the vintage

GENERAL APPRECIATION

Vieux Château Certan was once considered the most elegant and finesse-styled Pomerol, but it was surpassed by Pétrus in the post–World War II period. However, the vineyard benefits from an exceptional situation and the potential of its *terroir* has been fully exploited over recent years. While the wines have retained their Médoc-like elegance and aromas, they possess more stuffing and structure.

One of the most famous names in Pomerol is the pride and joy of the Thienpont family, the owners of Vieux Château Certan. In the 19th century, as well as the early part of the 20th century, Vieux Château Certan was considered to have produced the finest wine of Pomerol. However, following World War II, this distinction was surpassed by Pétrus. The two wines could not be more different. Vieux Château Certan bases its style and complexity on a high percentage of Cabernet Franc, whereas Pétrus is nearly 100% Merlot. The vineyard, located in the heart of the plateau, is surrounded by much of the reigning aristocracy of the appellation—Lafleur, Certan de May, La Conseillante, L'Evangile, Petit Village, and Pétrus—and has a gravelly soil with a subsoil of iron-enriched clay. The wine that emerges from the vineyard never has the strength of a Pétrus, or other Merlot-dominated wines of the plateau, but it often has a perfume and elegance that recalls a top wine from the Médoc.

A visit to the *chai* of Vieux Château Certan reveals a healthy respect for tradition. For most of the post–World War II era, Vieux Château Certan was made by Léon Thienpont, but since his death in 1985 the property has been managed by his son, Alexandre, who apprenticed as the *régisseur* at the St.-Emilion château of La Gaffe-lière. When the young, shy Thienpont took over the estate, old-timers scoffed at his lack of experience, but he asserted himself immediately, introducing crop-thinning techniques and malolactic in barrel for the Merlot.

Because of its historic reputation for excellence, Vieux Château Certan is an expensive wine.

IMPORTANT VINTAGES

2001
91–94
A blend of 80% Merlot and 20% Cabernet Franc, the dense opaque purple–colored 2001 offers phenomenally sweet aromas of black cherry liqueur intermixed with charcoal, vanilla, new saddle leather, and a hint of fruitcake. It is full-bodied and opulently textured, with low acidity, ripe tannin, and a remarkably layered, unctuous texture that has more in common with the 2000 than 2001. Alexandre Thienpont feels the unusual blend, with all the old-vine Merlot (from vineyards planted in 1932, 1942, and 1959), has given the wine a profound depth and unctuosity that even the 2000 does not possess. This is a splendid achievement! Anticipated maturity: 2008–2025. Last tasted, 1/03.

2000
94+
The 2000, a blend of 70% Merlot, 20% Cabernet Franc, and 10% Cabernet Sauvignon, appears to be a more elegant version of the powerful, dense, concentrated 1998. Its saturated ruby/purple color is followed by an exceptional bouquet of blackberries, cassis, spice box, licorice, and minerals. Deep and full-bodied, with great intensity, tremendous purity, low acidity, and high tannin, this is another majestic Vieux Château Certan that will require patience. Anticipated maturity: 2010–2030. Last tasted, 1/03.

1999
91
Three thousand cases of the 1999 were made from a blend of 85% Merlot, 10% Cabernet Franc, and 5% Cabernet Sauvignon. It seemed to reveal an element of dilution during its *élevage*, but as always, the truth is in the bottle, and presently there is no evidence of lightness or liquidity. Deep ruby/purple–colored, with a striking perfume of black cherries, truffles, cedar, and vanilla, this layered, opulently textured wine displays extraordinary purity, elegance, and finesse. A classic Bordeaux with superb palate presence, it builds incrementally on the palate. The finish is long, with plenty of sweet tannin. Very impressive! Anticipated maturity: 2006–2018. Last tasted, 3/02.

1998
94+
Undoubtedly the finest offering from this estate since 1990, the 1998 has closed down since bottling, but there is no doubting its fabulous potential. The color is a dense purple. The wine reveals high tannin, huge body, and classy black fruits intermixed with minerals, spice box, cedar, and tobacco. A long, persistent, tannic finish gives this majestic effort a closed but formidable personality. Patience will be required. Anticipated maturity: 2008–2030. Last tasted, 1/03.

1997
85
Tobacco, cedar, herbs, cherry, and plum notes are light in intensity, but elegant and pleasant. Although it lacks depth, the wine possesses medium body, sweet tannin, and weediness. Drink it over the next 2–3 years. Last tasted, 3/01.

1996
87
This wine exhibits a dark plum color and a complex nose of roasted herbs, Asian spices, earth, and sweet black cherry fruit. A refined Claret, with excellent concentration, a sweet mid-palate, and moderate tannin in the finish, it is a finesse-styled Pomerol. Anticipated maturity: now–2016. Last tasted, 1/02.

1995
88?
Frightful bottle variation left me perplexed about just where this wine fits in Bordeaux's qualitative hierarchy. I tasted the wine three times since bottling, all within a 14-day period. Twice the wine was extremely closed and firm, with an evolved plum/garnet color, high levels of tannin, sweet black currant, prune, and olive-tinged fruit, and astringent tannin in the medium-bodied finish. Those two bottles suggested the wine was in need of at least 5–7 more years of cellaring, and would keep for two decades. The third bottle was atypically evolved, with a similar color, but it was far more open-knit, displaying Provençal herbs, black cherry, and cassis fruit in a medium-bodied, jammy, lush style. I expect marginal bottle variation, but while the quality was relatively the same in all three bottles, the forward, open-knit example left me puzzled. Anticipated maturity: 2007–2020. Last tasted, 11/97.

1994 The 1994 is performing well, with no harsh tannin or vegetal characteristics.
88   It displays a deep ruby color and a sweet nose of jammy cherry and Asian
      spice scents with a touch of smoke. Dense, rich, medium-bodied flavors ex-
      hibit excellent concentration and fine purity. The wine possesses low acidity
      and plenty of flesh, so it should drink well between now and 2010. Last tasted,
      1/97.

1990 This wine continues to put on weight and is looking stronger and stronger every
93   time I go back to it. The color is still a very deep ruby with some purple nuances.
      The wine seems young and just approaching adolescence, but still has the
      vintage's hallmark superripeness and low acidity. The wine exhibits a sweet, al-
      most menthol-infused black currant nose, with a hint of licorice, truffle, and un-
      derbrush. It is full-bodied and relatively muscular for a Vieux Château Certan,
      with sweet tannin and a long, very authoritative finish. This is a brilliant wine that
      balances elegance with authoritative flavor. Anticipated maturity: 2005–2025.
      Last tasted, 1/02.

1989 The last two tastings have been better than early tastings, suggesting I underrated
87   the wine. It is still somewhat austere, with a rather evolved dark garnet color al-
      ready revealing some amber. The wine shows some sweet plums and currants, with
      some dusty earth overtones and a hint of dried herbs. The wine is medium bodied,
      sweet on the front end, but a bit astringent at the rear. The wine could probably
      benefit from several more years of cellaring. Anticipated maturity: 2004–2016.
      Last tasted, 1/02.

1988 One of my favorite wines from this château, as well as from a vintage that remains
91   somewhat underrated. Sweet black fruits intermixed with earth, charcoal, licorice,
      and compost jump from the glass of this medium-bodied, deep, beautifully ex-
      tracted Pomerol that has a real Médoc structure to it. The wine is sweet, relatively
      evolved, and just beginning to enter its plateau of full maturity. Anticipated matu-
      rity: now–2015. Last tasted, 1/02.

1986 Certain austerity and Médoc-like firmness have always fooled me with this wine in
91   blind tastings. The color remains a very healthy deep ruby, and the nose of black
      currants, cherries, spice box, cedar, and mineral clearly seems more Médoc-like
      than Pomerol. In the mouth, its firm tannin is still present. The wine has a certain
      youthful vibrancy because of good acidity and outstanding purity. It is a young,
      still somewhat unformed, but very promising wine on the way up. Anticipated ma-
      turity: 2004–2016. Last tasted, 1/02.

1985 Somewhat herbal, even vegetal, the sweet perfume also includes notes of olive,
88   tobacco, and roasted, jammy strawberry and black cherry fruit. Quite seductive,
      medium bodied, and soft as well as fully mature, this savory wine needs to be
      drunk up. Anticipated maturity: now–2008. Last tasted, 1/02.

1983 Beginning to break apart, this very herbal, even minty Vieux Château Cer-
86?   tan shows a dark plum color, hints of prunes, raisins, and old saddle leather
      intermixed with a hint of mushroom. The wine seems to be in total free fall,
      but there is still some merit to it. Anticipated maturity: Drink up. Last tasted,
      1/02.

1982 Bottle variation, for reasons that escape me, have plagued all my tastings of this
90   wine. It has hit full maturity and is certainly not one of the most profound Vieux
      Château Certans, but nevertheless a very seductive, delicious, round, and savory
      wine that offers notes of open wood fire intermixed with roasted herbs, dried sweet
      cherry fruit, and an intriguing peppery, almost tapenade sort of nose that suggests
      Provence more than Bordeaux. In the mouth it is lush, succulent, and medium
      bodied, with outstanding concentration, low acidity, and sweet tannin. The wine
      may turn out to fool everybody and last another two decades, but it seems to me

that, to maximize its pleasures, it should be consumed over the next decade. Anticipated maturity: now–2010. Last tasted, 11/02.

ANCIENT VINTAGES

In the 1970s Vieux Château Certan's performance was shaky, with only the 1975 (90 points; last tasted 12/88) being a wine of considerable merit. In the 1960s everyone has long acknowledged the brilliance of the 1964 (90 points; last tasted 6/00). The 1961 has never been an exciting wine. Among the other vintages, Vieux Château Certan's fame could not have been greater than during the period between 1945 and 1950. The 1952 Vieux Château Certan (94 points; last tasted 10/94) is in extraordinary condition. The wine, a sleeper, was sweet and cedary, with a huge, almost hickory, roasted, smoky nose that was reminiscent of a top Graves. Full-bodied, with glorious concentration and richness, this wine still possesses plenty of tannin and youthfulness. It will easily keep for another 10–20 years. The 1950 (99 points; last tasted 12/02) is a remarkably rich, still youthful wine from this fabulous vintage in Pomerol. The color remains an amazing garnet/purple, and the nose offers sensationally ripe, chocolaty, cassis aromas intertwined with herbs, licorice, Asian spices, and coffee. Extremely full bodied with Port-like viscosity similar to the 1947, this blockbuster wine must be one of the least-known profound wines of the century.

The 1948 Vieux Château Certan (98 points; last tasted 7/02) is another profoundly great wine from the forgotten vintage of the 1940s. I have tasted this wine four times in the last year, and it was exceptional in each tasting. The opaque dark purple/garnet color is followed by a huge, exotic nose of caramel, sweet cassis, soy sauce, walnuts, and coffee. Thick, chewy, fabulously concentrated flavors with low acidity and high tannin coat the palate. There is amazing glycerin and an elevated alcohol level to this super-concentrated wine. Although fully mature, it exhibits no signs of decline and will easily last for 15–20 more years. Remarkable! A dazzling wine, which I have tasted a number of times over the years, the 1947 Vieux Château Certan (99 points; last tasted 1/01) is typical of so many 1947 Pomerols. Its thick, viscous, Port-like style and texture are the hallmarks of this vintage. More advanced than the 1948, it reveals a smoky, meaty, truffle, and black currant–scented nose, as well as massive, chewy flavors loaded with glycerin, extract, and alcohol. It exhibits more amber at the edge than the 1948, but, wow, what a mouthful of wine! Like many 1947 Pomerols, its unctuosity and thickness make me wonder if a spoon would stand up in the glass without any support. Drink it over the next 10–12 years. Tasted twice and rated highly each time, the 1945 (98 points; last tasted 1/01) is an exceptional winemaking effort in what can be a frightfully tannic vintage. It exhibits a dark, murky, plum color, with little garnet at the edge. It also possesses a huge nose of smoked meats, black raspberries, plums, licorice, and tar. Dense, chewy, and powerful, with gobs of tannin and amazing fruit extraction, this full-throttle wine must be at its plateau of maturity, yet I see no reason it cannot last for two more decades.

Dark garnet, with noticeable rust/amber at the edge, the spicy, peppery, herbaceous, sweet, caramel- and black fruit–scented 1928 Vieux Château Certan (96 points; last tasted 10/94) possesses huge, chewy flavors, copious quantities of tannin, full body, and a rustic, astringent finish. Still in superb condition, it is capable of lasting 10–20 more years.

OTHER POMEROL ESTATES

BEAU SOLEIL

Owner: Anne-Marie Audy-Arcaute

Address: 33500 Pomerol

Mailing address: c/o Château Jonqueyres, 33750 Saint-Germain du Puch

Telephone: 05 57 34 51 66; Telefax: 05 56 30 11 45

E-mail: delphine.mousset-derouet@gamaudy.com

No visits

VINEYARDS

Surface area: 7.4 acres

Grape varietals: 95% Merlot, 5% Cabernet Sauvignon

Average age of vines: 35 years

Density of plantation: 6,600 vines per hectare

Average yields: 48 hectoliters per hectare

Elevage: Two to three week fermentation and maceration in temperature-controlled stainless-steel vats of small capacity. Twenty-four months aging in new oak. No fining, no filtration.

WINES PRODUCED

Château Beau Soleil: 22,000 bottles

No second wine is produced.

Plateau of maturity: Within 5–15 years of the vintage

GENERAL APPRECIATION

Beau Soleil is a soundly made Pomerol. Generally rich and fruity, it is less well-known than its sibling, La Croix du Casse, but it is nearly as good while selling for a lower price.

IMPORTANT VINTAGES

2000 Opaque purple–colored with notes of blackberries, mocha, and licorice, this is a
88   strong, powerful effort with moderate tannin, medium to full body, and good sweetness as well as purity. The 2000 Beau Soleil was the last vintage produced by Jean-Michel Arcaute before his tragic, premature death in 2001. Anticipated maturity: 2006–2016. Last tasted, 1/03.

1999 Excellent sweet fruit is nicely complemented by toasty oak, licorice, and ripe
87   black cherry scents. Soft, round, and consumer-friendly, with low-acid and sweet tannin, this appealing wine should be drunk over the next 7–8 years. Last tasted, 3/02.

1998 This dark ruby–colored offering reveals mocha, caramel, jammy black plums,
87 cherries, and smoke characteristics, a soft, up-front, medium- to full-bodied personality, and an open-knit, creamy texture. Drink this sexy 1998 over the next 10
years. Last tasted, 3/02.

BEAUCHÊNE

Owner: Leymarie family

Address: 15, impasse du Vélodrome, 33500 Libourne

Mailing address: Charles Leymarie et Fils, 90–92, avenue Foch, 33500 Libourne

Telephone: 05 57 51 07 83; Telefax: 05 57 51 99 94

Visits: By appointment only

Contact: Gregory Leymarie

VINEYARDS

Surface area: 24 acres

Grape varietals: 65% Merlot, 30% Cabernet Franc, 5% Cabernet Sauvignon

Average age of vines: 40 years

Density of plantation: 5,500 vines per hectare

Average yields: 44 hectoliters per hectare

Elevage: Fifteen to thirty day fermentation and maceration in temperature-controlled concrete vats. The grand vin undergoes malolactics in barrel. Eighteen months aging in new oak. Fining and light filtration.

WINES PRODUCED

Château Beauchêne: 12,000 bottles

Clos Mazeyres: 43,000 bottles

Plateau of maturity: Within 3–15 years of the vintage

BOURGUENEUF

Owner: Meyer family

Address: Vignobles Meyer, 7, chemin de la Cabanne, 33500 Pomerol

Telephone: 05 57 51 16 73; Telefax: 05 57 25 16 89

Visits: By appointment only

Contact: Jean-Michel Meyer

VINEYARDS

Surface area: 12.4 acres

Grape varietals: 70% Merlot, 15% Cabernet Franc, 15% Cabernet Sauvignon

Average age of vines: 40 years

Density of plantation: 6,000 vines per hectare

Average yields: 50 hectoliters per hectare

Elevage: Three to four week fermentation and maceration in temperature-controlled stainless-steel and concrete vats. Twelve to sixteen months aging in barrels with 50% new oak. Fining and filtration.

WINES PRODUCED

Château de Bourgueneuf: 20,000 bottles

Clos Grangeneuve: 5,000 bottles

Plateau of maturity: Within 5–20 years of the vintage (since 1994)

LE CAILLOU

Owner: GFA Giraud-Bélivier

Address: 33500 Pomerol

Mailing address: c/o SARL André Giraud, 33500 Pomerol

Telephone: 05 57 51 06 10; Telefax: 05 57 51 74 95

E-mail: giraud-belivier@wanadoo.fr

Visits: By appointment only weekdays except Wednesdays, 9 A.M.–noon and 2–6 P.M.

Contact: André Giraud

VINEYARDS

Surface area: 17.3 acres

Grape varietals: 75% Merlot, 25% Cabernet Franc

Average age of vines: 25 years

Density of plantation: 5,500 vines per hectare

Average yields: 48 hectoliters per hectare

Elevage: Three to four week fermentation and maceration in concrete tanks. Twelve months aging, by rotation every three months (time of racking), with two-thirds of yield in oak barrels and the rest in concrete vats. Fining, no filtration.

WINES PRODUCED

Château Le Caillou: 39,000 bottles

La Fleur Lacombe: Variable

Plateau of maturity: Within 5–15 years of the vintage

CANTELAUZE

Owner: Jean-Noël Boidron

Address: 6, place Joffre, 33500 Libourne

Telephone: 05 57 51 64 88; Telefax: 05 57 51 56 30

Visits: Monday to Friday, 8–11 A.M. and 2–5 P.M.

Contact: Emmanuel Boidron

VINEYARDS

Surface area: 2.2 acres

Grape varietals: 90% Merlot, 10% Cabernet Franc

Average age of vines: 20 years

Density of plantation: 5,865 vines per hectare

Average yields: 38 hectoliters per hectare

Elevage: Three to four week fermentation and maceration in temperature-controlled stainless-steel vats without addition of yeast. Eighteen months aging in 100% new oak. Fining, no filtration.

WINES PRODUCED

Château Cantelauze: 4,000 bottles

No second wine is produced.

Plateau of maturity: Within 4–12 years of the vintage

LE CARILLON

Owner: Louis Grelot

Address: 33500 Pomerol

Telephone: 05 57 84 56 61

Visits: By appointment only

Contact: Louis Grelot

VINEYARDS

Surface area: 2.47 acres

Grape varietals: 100% Merlot

Average age of vines: 8 years

Density of plantation: 5,500 vines per hectare

Average yields: 35 hectoliters per hectare

Elevage: Twenty-one day fermentation in wooden vats. Wines are transferred after malolactics to oak barrels (25% of which are new) for 18 months aging and sometimes more. Fining, no filtration.

WINES PRODUCED

Château Le Carillon: 4,700 bottles

No second wine is produced.

Plateau of maturity: Within 3–10 years of the vintage

CLOS DU PÈLERIN

Owner: Norbert and Josette Egreteau

Address: 3, chemin de Sales, 33500 Pomerol

Telephone: 05 57 74 03 66; Telefax: 05 57 25 06 17

Visits: By appointment only

Contact: Norbert and Josette Egreteau

VINEYARDS

Surface area: 8.6 acres

Grape varietals: 80% Merlot, 10% Cabernet Franc, 10% Cabernet Sauvignon

Average age of vines: 25 years

Density of plantation: 6,000 vines per hectare

Average yields: 50 hectoliters per hectare

Elevage: Twelve months aging in vats followed by 12 months in barrels that are renewed by a third every year. Fining, no filtration.

WINES PRODUCED

Clos du Pèlerin: 12,000 bottles

Plateau of maturity: Within 5–12 years of the vintage

LA COMMANDERIE

Owner: Marie-Hélène Dé

Address: Catusseau, 33500 Pomerol

Mailing address: 4, chemin de la Commanderie, 33500 Pomerol

Telephone: 05 57 51 79 03; Telefax: 05 57 25 31 91

Visits: By appointment only

Contact: Marie-Hélène Dé or Mr. Lamothe (05 57 51 75 94)

VINEYARDS

Surface area: 14.2 acres

Grape varietals: 80% Merlot, 20% Cabernet Franc

Average age of vines: 50 years

Density of plantation: 6,000 vines per hectare

Average yields: 40–45 hectoliters per hectare

Elevage: Two to three week fermentation and maceration in stainless-steel vats. Eighteen months aging in vats and in barrels, with 33–50% new oak. Light fining and filtration.

WINES PRODUCED

Château La Commanderie: 20,000 bottles

Château Haut-Manoir: 10,000 bottles

LA COMMANDERIE DE MAZEYRES

Owner: Clément Fayat

Address: 22 bis, avenue Georges Pompidou, 33500 Libourne

Mailing address: c/o Château La Dominique, 33330 St.-Emilion

Telephone: 05 57 51 31 36; Telefax: 05 57 51 63 04

E-mail: info@vignobles.fayat-group.com

Visits: By appointment Monday to Friday, 9 A.M.–noon and 2–6 P.M.

Contact: Cyril Forget

VINEYARDS

Surface area: 24.7 acres

Grape varietals: 55% Merlot, 45% Cabernet Franc

Average age of vines: 40 years

Density of plantation: 6,000 vines per hectare

Average yields: 40 hectoliters per hectare

Elevage: Thirty day fermentation and maceration in temperature-controlled wooden vats of 70 hectoliter capacity at rather high temperatures and with three to four daily pumpings-over or punching-downs, depending upon the vats. Wines undergo malolactics and are aged 18–22 months in 100% new oak barrels. No fining, no filtration.

WINES PRODUCED

Château La Commanderie de Mazeyres: 12,000 bottles

Château La Closerie de Mazeyres: 25,000–30,000 bottles

LA CROIX TAILLEFER

Owner: SARL La Croix Taillefer

Address: Catusseau, 33500 Pomerol

Mailing address: BP 4, 33500 Pomerol

Telephone and Telefax: 05 57 25 08 65

Visits: By appointment only

Contact: Romain Rivière

VINEYARDS

Surface area: 10.9 acres

Grape varietals: 100% Merlot

Average age of vines: 35 years

Density of plantation: 6,000 vines per hectare

Average yields: 48 hectoliters per hectare

Elevage: Cold maceration, three to four week fermentation and maceration in temperature-controlled stainless-steel tanks. A small part of the yield undergoes malolactics in barrel. Eighteen months aging in new oak. Fining and filtration.

WINES PRODUCED

Château La Croix Taillefer: 22,000 bottles

Château La Loubière: 5,000 bottles

Plateau of maturity: Within 3–10 years of the vintage

LA CROIX TOULIFAUT

Owner: Joseph Janoueix family

Address: Catusseau, 33500 Pomerol

Mailing address: 37, rue Pline Parmentier, BP 192, 33506 Libourne Cedex

Telephone: 05 57 51 41 86; Telefax: 05 57 51 53 16

E-mail: info@j-janoueix-bordeaux.com

Website: www.j-janoueix-bordeaux.com

Visits: By appointment Monday to Friday, 8 A.M.–noon and 2–6 P.M. (5 P.M. on Fridays)

Contact: Ets Janoueix

VINEYARDS

Surface area: 4 acres

Grape varietals: 85% Merlot, 15% Cabernet Franc

Average age of vines: 45 years

Density of plantation: 6,000 vines per hectare

Average yields: 45 hectoliters per hectare

Elevage: Twenty-five to twenty-seven day fermentation and maceration in temperature-controlled vats. Malolactics and 12–14 months aging in barrels with 80% new oak. Fining, no filtration.

WINES PRODUCED

Château La Croix Toulifaut: 7,200 bottles

No second wine is produced.

Plateau of maturity: Within 5–12 years of the vintage

FERRAND

Owner: Henry Gasparoux et fils

Address: lieu-dit Ferrand, 15, chemin de la Commanderie, 33500 Libourne

Telephone: 05 57 51 21 67; Telefax: 05 57 25 01 41

Visits: By appointment only Monday to Friday, 1:30–5 P.M.

Contact: Mrs. Petit

VINEYARDS

Surface area: 29.6 acres

Grape varietals: 50% Cabernet Franc, 50% Merlot

Average age of vines: 34 years

Density of plantation: 5,500 vines per hectare

Average yields: 50 hectoliters per hectare

Elevage: Fermentation and maceration in temperature-controlled stainless-steel vats. Twelve to eighteen months aging in barrels that are renewed by a third at each vintage. Fining and filtration.

WINES PRODUCED

Château Ferrand: 80,000 bottles

No second wine is produced.

FEYTIT-GUILLOT

Owner: Irène Lureau/Mrs. Rivière

Address: 34, route de Catusseau, 33500 Pomerol

Telephone: 05 57 51 46 58; Telefax: 05 56 63 19 37

E-mail: feytit-guillot@wanadoo.fr

Visits: By appointment only

Contact: Mrs. Lureau or Mrs. Rivière

VINEYARDS

Surface area: 3.2 acres

Grape varietals: 80% Merlot, 15% Cabernet Franc, 5% Malbec

Average age of vines: 30 years

Density of plantation: 6,000 vines per hectare

Average yields: 50 hectoliters per hectare

Elevage: Fermentation and maceration in concrete tanks. After seven months, wines are aged 12–14 months in barrels that are renewed by a quarter at each vintage. Fining, light filtration upon bottling.

WINES PRODUCED

Château Feytit-Guillot: 2,000 bottles

The rest of the production is sold to the Jean-Pierre Moueix firm.

Plateau of maturity: Within 3–10 years of the vintage

LA FLEUR DE PLINCE

Owner: Pierre and Sylvie Choukroun
Address: Chemin de Plince, 33500 Pomerol
Mailing address: Grand Moulinet, 33500 Pomerol
Telephone: 05 57 74 15 26; Telefax: 05 57 74 15 27
E-mail: gvbpe@wanadoo.fr
Visits: By appointment only
Contact: Pierre Choukroun

VINEYARDS

Surface area: 6.9 acres

Grape varietals: 90% Merlot, 10% Cabernet Franc

Average age of vines: 45 years

Density of plantation: 6,600 vines per hectare

Average yields: 45 hectoliters per hectare

Elevage: Three week fermentation and maceration in stainless-steel vats. Wines undergo malolactics and 14–16 months aging in barrels, with 80% new oak.

WINES PRODUCED

Château La Fleur du Roy: 1,600 bottles

No second wine is produced.

LA GANNE

Owner: Paule et Michel Dubois
Address: 224, avenue Foch, 33500 Libourne
Telephone: 05 57 51 18 24; Telefax: 05 57 51 62 20
E-mail: laganne@aol.com
Visits: By appointment only, Monday to Saturday
Contact: Paule Dubois

VINEYARDS

Surface area: 8.6 acres

Grape varietals: 80% Merlot, 20% Cabernet Franc

Average age of vines: 30 years

Density of plantation: 6,000 vines per hectare

Average yields: 38 hectoliters per hectare

Elevage: Five week fermentation and maceration in temperature-controlled tanks. Twelve months aging with 33% new oak. Fining, no filtration.

WINES PRODUCED

Château La Ganne: 15,000 bottles

Vieux Château Brun: 3,000–4,000 bottles

Plateau of maturity: Within 3–10 years of the vintage

GOMBAUDE GUILLOT

Owner: Claire Laval

Address: 3, Les Grandes Vignes-33500 Pomerol

Telephone: 05 57 51 17 40; Telefax: 05 57 51 16 89

Visits: By appointment only

Contact: Claire Laval

VINEYARDS

Surface area: 17.3 acres

Grape varietals: 65% Merlot, 30% Cabernet Franc, 5% Malbec

Average age of vines: 35 years

Density of plantation: 6,000 vines per hectare

Average yields: 43 hectoliters per hectare

Elevage: Twenty-one to twenty-eight day fermentation in temperature-controlled concrete vats. Twelve to fourteen months aging in barrel (50% new oak). Fining, no filtration.

WINES PRODUCED

Château Gombaude Guillot: 25,000–30,000 bottles

Cadet de Gombaude: 6,000 bottles

Plateau of maturity: Within 5–15 years of the vintage

This has become an intriguing property to follow. I remember tasting the wine in the early 1980s and being unimpressed with the range of vintages I saw from the 1970s, but a vertical tasting back through 1982 left me with the conclusion that in certain years Gombaude Guillot can produce a Pomerol of stunning quality.

The vineyard is comprised of three parcels made up of totally different types of soil. The only parcel from the plateau consists of a heavier soil, dominated by clay and gravel with a great deal of iron in it. A second parcel is primarily sandy soil intermixed with some gravel, and a third parcel consists largely of gravel.

The old vines and relatively low yields that are 30% below many of the more prestigious names often result in strikingly rich, concentrated wines. Interestingly, in 1985, Gombaude Guillot launched a Cuvée Speciale from a selection of wine that represented some of the best lots from their vineyards and aged it in 100% new oak. It was such an enormously successful wine that the château repeated this experiment in 1988 and 1989.

This is not a consistent wine, but when Gombaude Guillot does everything right, it merits attention. The recent vintages, 2001 and 2000, were disappointing.

GRAND MOULINET

Owner: Jean-Pierre Fourreau

Address: 33500 Néac

Telephone: 05 57 51 28 68; Telefax: 05 57 51 91 79

Visits: Every day of the week, 8 A.M.–noon and 2–6 P.M.

Contact: Jean-Pierre or Patrick Fourreau

VINEYARDS

Surface area: 7.4 acres

Grape varietals: 90% Merlot, 5% Cabernet Franc, 5% Cabernet Sauvignon

Average age of vines: 25 years

Density of plantation: 5,500 vines per hectare

Average yields: 51 hectoliters per hectare

Elevage: Five week fermentation and maceration in temperature-controlled tanks. Twelve months aging in 100% new oak barrels. Fining and filtration if necessary.

WINES PRODUCED

Château Grand Moulinet: 20,000 bottles

Plateau of maturity: Within 3–10 years of the vintage

No second wine is produced.

GRANGE-NEUVE

Owner: SGE Gros et Fils

Address: Grange-Neuve, 33500 Pomerol

Telephone: 05 57 51 23 03; Telefax: 05 57 25 36 14

Visits: By appointment only

Contact: Jean-Marie Gros

VINEYARDS

Surface area: 17.3 acres

Grape varietals: 100% Merlot

Average age of vines: 40 years

Density of plantation: 6,700 vines per hectare

Average yields: 45 hectoliters per hectare

Elevage: Fermentations last about a month, with numerous pumpings-over. Wines are transferred to oak casks, which are renewed by a third at each vintage in December (clarification occurs naturally with cold temperatures), and then they are aged for 12–18 months, depending on the vintage. They are fined with egg whites and are bottled after a light filtration.

WINES PRODUCED

Château Grange-Neuve: 30,000 bottles

La Fleur des Ormes: 12,000–13,000 bottles

Plateau of maturity: Within 3–10 years of the vintage

GUILLOT

Owner: GFA Lucquot Frères

Address: 22, rue des Grands Champs, 33500 Pomerol

Mailing address: 152, avenue de l'Epinette, 33500 Libourne

Telephone: 05 57 51 18 95; Telefax: 05 57 25 10 59

Visits: By appointment only, on working days

Contact: Jean-Paul Luquot

VINEYARDS

Surface area: 11.6 acres

Grape varietals: 70% Merlot, 30% Cabernet Franc

Average age of vines: 30 years

Density of plantation: 5,900 vines per hectare

Average yields: 48 hectoliters per hectare

Elevage: Four week fermentation and maceration in temperature-controlled concrete tanks. Fifteen months aging in barrels with 40% new oak. Fining, no filtration.

WINES PRODUCED

Château Guillot: 27,000 bottles

No second wine is produced.

Plateau of maturity: Within 3–10 years of the vintage

GUILLOT CLAUZEL

Owner: Mrs. Paul Clauzel

Address: 33500 Pomerol

Telephone: 05 57 51 14 09; Telefax: 05 57 51 57 66

Visits: By appointment only

Contact: Mrs. Paul Clauzel

VINEYARDS

Surface area: 4.2 acres

Grape varietals: 60% Merlot, 40% Cabernet Franc

Average age of vines: 50 and 25 years

Density of plantation: 7,000 vines per hectare

Average yields: 30–35 hectoliters per hectare

Elevage: Fermentations last between 20 and 35 days, depending on the vintage (1992: three weeks; 1995: five weeks) and occur at temperatures of 28–32°C. There are three pumpings-over daily, and malolactics occur in barrels. Wines are brought up in oak barrels, 50–60% of which are new (the rest are one vintage old), for 12–15 months. They are sometimes fined (depending on the vintage), but not filtered.

WINES PRODUCED

Château Guillot Clauzel: 4,200–4,800 bottles

Château Graves Guillot: 3,000–3,600 bottles

Plateau of maturity: Within 3–10 years of the vintage

HAUT CLOQUET

Owner: François de Lavaux

Address: 33500 Pomerol

Mailing address: Établissements Horeau-Beylot, BP125, 33501 Libourne Cedex

Telephone: 05 57 51 06 07; Telefax: 05 57 51 59 61

Visits: By appointment only

Contact: François de Lavaux

VINEYARDS

Surface area: 7.4 acres

Grape varietals: 50% Merlot, 30% Cabernet Sauvignon, 20% Cabernet Franc

Average age of vines: 15–20 years

Density of plantation: 5,500 vines per hectare

Average yields: 40–45 hectoliters per hectare

Elevage: Fermentations and macerations last 18–23 days in temperature-controlled stainless-steel and concrete tanks. Malolactics usually occur in tanks (sometimes a very small percentage of the yield completes this process in oak barrels). Wines are aged for 8–12 months by rotation in oak barrels, 10–15% of which are new (60% of the yield), and concrete tanks (40% of the yield). They are fined and filtered.

WINES PRODUCED

Château Haut Cloquet: 18,000 bottles

No second wine is produced.

Plateau of maturity: Within 3–10 years of the vintage

HAUT FERRAND

Owner: Henry Gasparoux and Sons

Address: Ferrand, 15, chemin de la Commanderie, 33500 Libourne

Telephone: 05 57 51 21 67; Telefax: 05 57 25 01 41

Visits: By appointment Monday to Friday, 1:30–5 P.M.

Contact: Chantal Petit

VINEYARDS

Surface area: 11.1 acres

Grape varietals: 70% Merlot, 30% Cabernet Franc

Average age of vines: 29 years

Density of plantation: 5,500 vines per hectare

Average yields: 46 hectoliters per hectare

Elevage: Fermentation and maceration in temperature-controlled stainless-steel vats. Fifteen to eighteen months aging in oak barrels that are renewed by a third at each vintage. Fining and filtration.

WINES PRODUCED

Château Haut Ferrand: 20,000 bottles

No second wine is produced.

Plateau of maturity: Within 3–10 years of the vintage

HAUT-MAILLET

Owner: Estager family

Address: 33500 Pomerol

Mailing address: c/o SCEA Vignobles JP Estager, 33-41, rue de Montaudon, 33500 Libourne

Telephone: 05 57 51 04 09; Telefax: 05 57 25 13 38

E-mail: estager@estager.com

Website: www.estager.com

Visits: By appointment only

Contact: Mrs. Estager

VINEYARDS

Surface area: 12.4 acres

Grape varietals: 80% Merlot, 20% Cabernet Franc

Average age of vines: 23 years

Density of plantation: 5,000 vines per hectare

Average yields: 49 hectoliters per hectare

Elevage: Cold maceration, 3–4 week fermentation and maceration in temperature-controlled stainless-steel tanks. After completion of malolactics in vats, 15–18 months aging in barrels with 40% new oak. Fining, filtration if necessary.

WINES PRODUCED

Château Haut-Maillet: 29,000 bottles

No second wine is produced.

Plateau of maturity: Within 4–10 years of the vintage

LAFLEUR DU ROY

Owner: Yvon Dubost

Address: 13, chemin de Jean Lande, 33500 Pomerol

Telephone: 05 57 51 74 57; Telefax: 05 57 25 99 95

Visits: By appointment only Monday to Friday, 9 A.M.–noon and 2–6 P.M.

Contact: Laurent Dubost

VINEYARDS

Surface area: 7.9 acres

Grape varietals: 85% Merlot, 10% Cabernet Franc, 5% Cabernet Sauvignon

Average age of vines: 40 years

Density of plantation: 5,500 vines per hectare

Average yields: 48 hectoliters per hectare

Elevage: Twenty to twenty-five day fermentation and maceration in temperature-controlled stainless-steel vats at temperatures not exceeding 30°C and with three daily pumpings-over. Fifteen months aging in barrels with 25–30% new oak. Fining with egg whites, no filtration.

WINES PRODUCED

Château Lafleur du Roy: 21,000 bottles

No second wine is produced.

Plateau of maturity: Within 4–10 years of the vintage

MAZEYRES

Owner: Caisse de Retraite de la Société Générale

Address: 56, avenue Georges Pompidou, 33500 Libourne

Telephone: 05 57 51 00 48; Telefax: 05 57 25 22 56

E-mail: mazeyres@wanadoo.fr

Website: www.mazeyres.com

Visits: By appointment only

Contact: Alain Moueix or Etienne Charrier

VINEYARDS

Surface area: 54.3 acres

Grape varietals: 80% Merlot, 20% Cabernet Franc

Average age of vines: 35+ years

Density of plantation: 6,270 vines per hectare

Average yields: 49 hectoliters per hectare

Elevage: Cold maceration, 3–4 week fermentation and maceration in temperature-controlled stainless-steel tanks of 50–123 hectoliter capacity. Wines undergo malolactics and are aged in barrels with 45% new oak. Light fining with egg whites, no filtration.

WINES PRODUCED

Château Mazeyres: 70,000 bottles

Le Seuil de Mazeyres: 44,000 bottles

Plateau of maturity: Within 3–8 years of the vintage

MONTVIEL

Owner: Catherine Péré-Vergé

Address: Le Grand Moulinet, 33500 Pomerol

Mailing address: 15, rue Henri Dupuis,
62 500 Saint-Omer

Telephone and Telefax: 03 21 93 21 03

E-mail: pvp.montviel@libertysurf.fr

Visits: By appointment only

Contact: Catherine Péré-Vergé

VINEYARDS

Surface area: 19.4 acres

Grape varietals: 75% Merlot, 25% Cabernet Franc

Average age of vines: 30 years

Density of plantation: 6,000 vines per hectare

Average yields: 45 hectoliters per hectare

Elevage: Four week fermentation and maceration. Aging in barrels with 50% new oak.

WINES PRODUCED

Château Montviel: 25,000 bottles

Château La Rose Montviel: 20,000 bottles

Plateau of maturity: Within 5–12 years of the vintage

MOULINET

Owner: GFA du Domaine Moulinet

Address: 33500 Pomerol

Mailing address: Château Fonplégade, 33330 St.-Emilion

Telephone: 05 57 74 43 11; Telefax: 05 57 74 44 67

No visits

VINEYARDS

Surface area: 44.5 acres

Grape varietals: 60% Merlot, 30% Cabernet Sauvignon,
10% Cabernet Franc

Average age of vines: 25 years

Density of plantation: 5,400 vines per hectare

Average yields: 48 hectoliters per hectare

Elevage: Twenty-one day fermentation and maceration in temperature-controlled
stainless-steel and concrete vats. Twelve to fifteen months aging in barrels that are
renewed by a third at each vintage. No fining, no filtration.

WINES PRODUCED

Château Moulinet: 60,000 bottles

Clos Sainte-Anne: 55,000 bottles

Plateau of maturity: Within 3–15 years of the vintage

GENERAL APPRECIATION

The wines of this underperformer have generally been plain and uninteresting. However,
things should improve as the management of the estate has been handed over to the
Libourne-based firm of Jean-Pierre Moueix. The first vintages produced under Christian
Moueix's control are considerably better than what has emerged from here over the past
years, but there is still much room for improvement.

One of Pomerol's largest estates, Moulinet is located in the northwest section of the
Pomerol appellation near the large estate of de Sales. The soil in this area renders
lighter-style Pomerols, and Moulinet is certainly one of the lightest. Unusually light in
color and faintly perfumed, the owners make Moulinet in a very commercial style.
Starting with the 2000 vintage, Christian Moueix has assumed control over the viticulture and winemaking at this estate, which has had an undistinguished history.

MOULINET-LASSERRE

Owner: Jean-Marie Garde

Address: 33500 Pomerol

Telephone: 05 57 51 10 41; Telefax: 05 57 51 16 28

Visits: By appointment only

Contact: Jean-Marie Garde

VINEYARDS

Surface area: 12.4 acres

Grape varietals: 70% Merlot, 20% Cabernet Franc, 10% Malbec

Average age of vines: 35 years

Density of plantation: 5,500 vines per hectare

Average yields: 45 hectoliters per hectare

Elevage: Fermentation and maceration in temperature-controlled concrete tanks. Sixteen months aging in oak barrels that are renewed by a quarter at each vintage. Fining, no filtration.

WINES PRODUCED

Château Moulinet-Lasserre: 25,000 bottles

No second wine is produced.

LA PATACHE

Owner: SARL de La Diligence

Address: La Patache, 33500 Pomerol

Mailing address: BP 78, 33330 St.-Emilion

Telephone: 05 57 55 38 03; Telefax: 05 57 55 38 01

Visits: By appointment Monday to Friday, 9 A.M.–noon and 2–6 P.M.

Contact: Philippe Lauret

VINEYARDS

Surface area: 7.7 acres

Grape varietals: 70% Merlot, 30% Cabernet Franc

Average age of vines: 20 years

Density of plantation: 6,000 vines per hectare

Average yields: 48 hectoliters per hectare

Elevage: Five week fermentation and maceration in temperature-controlled stainless-steel vats. Ten months aging with 50% new oak and 50% one-year-old barrels. Fining, no filtration.

WINES PRODUCED

Château La Patache: 20,000 bottles

No second wine is produced.

Plateau of maturity: Within 3–10 years of the vintage

PLINCE

Owner: SCEV Moreau

Address: 33500 Libourne

Telephone: 05 57 51 68 77; Telefax: 05 57 51 43 39

Visits: Preferably by appointment Monday to Friday, 9 A.M.–noon and 2–5 P.M.

Contact: Michel Moreau

VINEYARDS

Surface area: 21.4 acres

Grape varietals: 72% Merlot, 23% Cabernet Franc, 5% Cabernet Sauvignon

Average age of vines: 23 years

Density of plantation: 6,000 vines per hectare

Average yields: 50 hectoliters per hectare

Elevage: Three to four week fermentation in temperature-controlled concrete tanks. Wines undergo malolactics in barrel. Fifteen months aging in barrels that are renewed by a third at each vintage. Fining, no filtration.

WINES PRODUCED

Château Plince: 40,000 bottles

Pavillon Plince: 8,000 bottles

Plateau of maturity: Within 5–10 years of the vintage

GENERAL APPRECIATION

Plince is a pleasant Pomerol, rich and structured, but lacking in finesse and elegance, as well as in the concentration and generosity typical of the best wines of the appellation. In the top vintages, this wine is good but never great, even if the potential of its *terroir* is fully exploited. Plince is not one of the most expensive Pomerols, but then I do not believe its quality would allow an increase in prices.

Plince is a solid Pomerol, fairly rich, hefty, spicy, deep, and rarely complex, but usually very satisfying. The Moreau family owns this property, but the commercialization is controlled by the Libourne firm of Jean-Pierre Moueix.

I have found Plince to be a consistently sound, well-made wine. Though it may never have the potential to be great, it seems to make the best of its situation. It is a well-vinified wine in a big, chunky style that seems capable of aging for 8–10 years.

PLINCETTE

Owner: Estager family

Address: 33500 Pomerol

Mailing address: c/o SCEA des Vignobles JP estager, 33–41, rue de Montaudon, 33500 Libourne

Telephone: 05 57 51 04 09; Telefax: 05 57 25 13 38

E-mail: estager@estager.com

Website: www.estager.com

Visits: By appointment only

Contact: Mrs. Estager

VINEYARDS

Surface area: 3.7 acres

Grape varietals: 83% Merlot, 17% Cabernet Franc

Average age of vines: 32 years

Density of plantation: 5,000 vines per hectare

Average yields: 50 hectoliters per hectare

Elevage: Cold maceration, 3–4 week fermentation and maceration in temperature-controlled vats. After completion of malolactics, 15–18 months aging in barrels with 25% new oak. Fining, filtration if necessary.

WINES PRODUCED

Château Plincette: 10,000 bottles
No second wine is produced.
Plateau of maturity: Within 3–10 years of the vintage

PONT-CLOQUET

Owner: Stéphanie Rousseau

Address: 1, Petit Sorillon, 33230 Abzac

Telephone: 05 57 49 06 10; Telefax: 05 57 49 38 96

Website: www.vignoblesrousseau.com

Visits: By appointment only.

Contact: Stéphanie Rousseau

VINEYARDS

Surface area: 1.3 acres

Grape varietals: 90% Merlot, 10% Cabernet Sauvignon

Average age of vines: 40 years

Density of plantation: 6,000 vines per hectare

Average yields: 26 hectoliters per hectare

Elevage: Three to four week fermentation. Wines undergo malolactics in barrel. Twelve months aging in 100% new oak. No fining, no filtration.

WINES PRODUCED

Château Pont-Cloquet: 3,500 bottles

No second wine is produced.

Plateau of maturity: Within 3–10 years of the vintage

PRIEURS DE LA COMMANDERIE

Owner: Clément Fayat

Address: 33500 Pomerol

Mailing address: Château La Dominique, 33330 St.-Emilion

Telephone: 05 57 51 31 36; Telefax: 05 57 51 63 04

E-mail: info@vignobles.fayat-group.com

No visits

VINEYARDS

Surface area: 8.6 acres

Grape varietals: 75% Merlot, 15% Cabernet Franc, 10% Cabernet Sauvignon

Average age of vines: 40 years

Density of plantation: 6,000 vines per hectare

Average yields: 40 hectoliters per hectare

Elevage: Twenty-five to thirty day fermentation and maceration in small temperature-controlled stainless-steel vats with 3–4 daily pumpings over. Eighteen months aging in barrels that are renewed by a third at each vintage. Fining and filtration.

WINES PRODUCED

Château Prieurs de la Commanderie: 12,500 bottles

No second wine is produced.

Plateau of maturity: Within 3–10 years of the vintage

LA PROVIDENCE

Owner: Indivision Dupuy

Address: 7-8, route de Tropchaud, 33500 Pomerol

Mailing address: c/o Jean-Claude Dupuy, 120, route de St.-Emilion, 33500 Pomerol

Telephone: 06 07 56 75 73; Telefax: 05 57 51 25 44

Visits: By appointment

Contact: Jean-Claude Dupuy

VINEYARDS

Surface area: 6.5 acres

Grape varietals: 100% Merlot

Average age of vines: 20 years

Density of plantation: 5,800 vines per hectare

Average yields: 35 hectoliters per hectare

Elevage: Eighteen to twenty-five day fermentation and maceration in temperature-controlled stainless-steel vats. Fourteen months aging in oak barrels with 50% new oak. No fining, filtration.

WINES PRODUCED

Château La Providence: 20,000 bottles

Les Chemins de la Providence: 4,000 bottles

RATOUIN

Owner: GFA Famille Ratouin

Address: Village de René, 33500 Pomerol

Telephone: 05 57 51 19 58; Telefax: 05 57 51 47 92

Visits: Preferably by appointment

Contact: Jean-François Beney

VINEYARDS

Surface area: 7.9 acres

Grape varietals: 80% Merlot, 20% Cabernet Franc

Average age of vines: 40 years

Density of plantation: 6,000 vines per hectare

Average yields: 50 hectoliters per hectare

Elevage: Three week fermentation and maceration in temperature-controlled stainless-steel vats. Twelve months aging in barrels that are renewed by a quarter each year. Fining, filtration if necessary.

WINES PRODUCED

Château Ratouin: 16,000 bottles

No second wine is produced.

Plateau of maturity: Within 4–10 years of the vintage

DOMAINE DU REMPART

Owner: Paulette Estager

Address: 33500 Pomerol

Mailing address: c/o Vignobles J.-M. Estager, 55, rue des 4 Frères Robert, 33500 Libourne

Telephone: 05 57 51 06 97; Telefax: 05 57 25 90 01

E-mail: vignoblesestager@aol.com

Visits: By appointment only

Contact: Mme. Paganelli-Estager

VINEYARDS

Surface area: 5.4 acres

Grape varietals: 80% Merlot, 20% Cabernet Franc

Average age of vines: 30 years

Density of plantation: 5,500 vines per hectare

Average yields: 46 hectoliters per hectare

Elevage: Twenty-eight day fermentation and maceration in temperature-controlled stainless-steel and concrete vats (28–30°C). Eighteen months aging in French and American oak barrels that are renewed by a third at each vintage. Fining and filtration.

WINES PRODUCED

Domaine du Rempart: 12,300 bottles

No second wine is produced.

Plateau of maturity: Within 3–10 years of the vintage

LA RENAISSANCE

Owner: François de Lavaux

Address: 33500 Pomerol

Mailing address: Établissements Horeau-Beylot, BP125, 33501 Libourne

Telephone: 05 57 51 06 07; Telefax: 05 57 51 59 61

Visits: By appointment only

Contact: François de Lavaux

VINEYARDS

Surface area: 7.4 acres

Grape varietals: 85% Merlot, 15% Cabernet Sauvignon

Average age of vines: 15–25 years

Density of plantation: 5,500 vines per hectare

Average yields: 40 hectoliters per hectare

Elevage: Fermentation and maceration last 18–23 days in temperature-controlled stainless-steel and concrete tanks. Malolactics usually occur in tanks (sometimes a very small percentage of the yield completes this process in oak barrels), and wines are aged for 8–12 months by rotation in oak barrels, 10–15% of which are new (60% of the yield), and concrete tanks (40% of the yield). They are fined and filtered.

WINES PRODUCED

Château La Renaissance: 30,000 bottles

No second wine is produced.

Plateau of maturity: Within 3–10 years of the vintage

RÊVE D'OR

Owner: Maurice Vigier

Address: Cloquet, 33500 Pomerol

Telephone: 05 57 51 11 92; Telefax: 05 57 51 87 70

Visits: By appointment only

Contact: Maurice Vigier

VINEYARDS

Surface area: 17.3 acres

Grape varietals: 80% Merlot, 20% Cabernet Sauvignon

Average age of vines: 40 years

Density of plantation: 5,500 vines per hectare

Average yields: 45 hectoliters per hectare

Elevage: Fermentation and maceration last 3–4 weeks in temperature-controlled stainless-steel tanks. Wines are transferred to oak barrels, 30% of which are new, for 18 months aging. They are fined but not filtered.

WINES PRODUCED

Château Rêve d'Or: 18,000 bottles

Château du Mayne: 18,000 bottles

Plateau of maturity: Within 3–10 years of the vintage

LA ROSE FIGEAC

Owner: GFA Despagne-Rapin

Address: 33500 Pomerol

Mailing address: Maison-Blanche, 33570 Montagne

Telephone: 05 57 74 62 18; Telefax: 05 57 74 58 98

Visits: By appointment only

Contact: Gérard Despagne

VINEYARDS

Surface area: 13.6 acres (2.5 acres in the very northern part of Pomerol and 11.1 acres in the extreme south of the appellation)

Grape varietals: 85% Merlot, 15% Cabernet Franc

Average age of vines: 40 years

Density of plantation: 5,350 vines per hectare

Average yields: 50 hectoliters per hectare

Elevage: Fermentations last 15–20 days in epoxy-lined vats. Wines are then transferred for 12–15 months aging in new oak barrels. They are fined and filtered.

WINES PRODUCED

Château La Rose Figeac: 15,000 bottles

Château Hautes Graves Beaulieu: 3,000–4,000 bottles

Plateau of maturity: Within 3–10 years of the vintage

ST.-PIERRE

Owner: De Lavaux family

Address: 33500 Pomerol

Mailing address: Établissements Horeau-Beylot, BP125, 33501 Libourne

Telephone: 05 57 51 06 07; Telefax: 05 57 51 59 61

Visits: By appointment only

Contact: Mme. Dubreuil-Lureau

VINEYARDS

Surface area: 7.4 acres

Grape varietals: 65% Merlot, 20% Cabernet Franc, 15% Cabernet Sauvignon

Average age of vines: 35 years

Density of plantation: 5,500 vines per hectare

Average yields: 30–40 hectoliters per hectare

Elevage: Fermentations and macerations last 18–23 days in temperature-controlled stainless-steel and concrete tanks. Malolactics usually occur in tanks. Wines are aged for 8–12 months by rotation in concrete tanks for 40% of the yield and in oak barrels (10–15% of which are new) for the rest. They are fined and filtered.

WINES PRODUCED

Château St.-Pierre: 15,000–18,000 bottles

No second wine is produced.

Plateau of maturity: Within 3–10 years of the vintage

TAILHAS

Owner: SC Château du Tailhas

Address: route de Saint-Emilion, 33500 Pomerol

Telephone: 05 57 51 26 02; Telefax: 05 57 25 17 70

Visits: By appointment only

Contact: Anne-Marie Sublett

VINEYARDS

Surface area: 27.2 acres

Grape varietals: 80% Merlot, 10% Cabernet Franc, 10% Cabernet Sauvignon

Average age of vines: 35 years

Density of plantation: 5,500 vines per hectare

Average yields: 40 hectoliters per hectare

Elevage: Cold maceration, three week fermentation and maceration in temperature-controlled concrete tanks. Wines undergo malolactics in barrel. Twelve months aging, half in barrels (50% new oak) and half in concrete tanks. Fining and filtration.

WINES PRODUCED

Château Tailhas: 40,000 bottles

La Garenne: 20,000 bottles

Plateau of maturity: Within 3–10 years of the vintage

TAILLEFER

Owner: Heirs of Bernard Moueix

Address: 33500 Libourne

Mailing address: BP 9, 33501 Libourne Cedex

Telephone: 05 57 25 50 45; Telefax: 05 57 25 50 45

Visits: By appointment only

Contact: Catherine Moueix

VINEYARDS

Surface area: 28.4 acres

Grape varietals: 75% Merlot, 25% Cabernet Sauvignon

Average age of vines: 30 years

Density of plantation: 6,000 vines per hectare

Average yields: 45 hectoliters per hectare

Elevage: Three to four week fermentation and maceration in temperature-controlled concrete tanks. Fifteen months aging in barrels with 33% new oak. Fining and filtration.

WINES PRODUCED

Château Taillefer: 48,000 bottles

Château Fontmarty: 21,000 bottles

Plateau of maturity: Within 3–10 years of the vintage

THIBEAUD-MAILLET

Owner: Roger and Andrée Duroux

Address: 33500 Pomerol

Telephone: 05 57 51 82 68; Telefax: 05 57 51 58 43

Visits: By appointment

Contact: Roger and Andrée Duroux

VINEYARDS

Surface area: 3 acres

Grape varietals: 90% Merlot, 10% Cabernet Franc

Average age of vines: 25 years

Density of plantation: 5,000 vines per hectare

Average yields: 45–50 hectoliters per hectare

Elevage: Three to four week fermentation and maceration in temperature-controlled vats. Twelve to fourteen months aging with 50% new oak and 50% one-year-old barrels. Fining, filtration if necessary.

WINES PRODUCED

Château Thibeaud-Maillet: 6,000 bottles

Plateau of maturity: Within 3–10 years of the vintage

TOUR ROBERT

Owner: Dominique Leymarie

Address: 11 chemin de Grangeneuve, 33500 Libourne

Mailing address: c/o Dominique Leymarie, BP 132, 90, avenue Foch, 33502 Libourne Cedex

Telephone: 05 57 51 97 83; Telefax: 05 57 51 99 94

E-mail: leymarie@ch-leymarie.com

Visits: By appointment only

Contact: Dominique Leymarie

VINEYARDS

Surface area: 11.7 acres

Grape varietals: 75% Merlot, 20% Cabernet Franc, 5% Cabernet Sauvignon

Average age of vines: 35 years

Density of plantation: 6,500 vines per hectare

Average yields: 41 hectoliters per hectare

Elevage: Thirty-plus day fermentation and maceration in temperature-controlled concrete vats. Part of the yield undergoes malolactics in barrel. Sixteen to eighteen months aging in barrels with 67% new oak. No fining, light filtration upon bottling.

WINES PRODUCED

Château Tour Robert: 7,000 bottles

Château Robert: 18,000 bottles

Plateau of maturity: Within 3–10 years of the vintage

VALOIS

Owner: Frédéric Leydet

Address: Rouilledirat, 33500 Libourne

Telephone: 05 57 51 19 77; Telefax: 05 57 51 00 62

E-mail: frederic.leydet@wanadoo.fr

Visits: Monday to Friday, 9 A.M.–6 P.M.
By appointment on Sundays.

Contact: Frédéric Leydet (Mobile: 06 08 93 10 03)

VINEYARDS

Surface area: 18.9 acres

Grape varietals: 77% Merlot, 19% Cabernet Franc, 4% Cabernet Sauvignon

Average age of vines: 30 years

Density of plantation: 5,800 vines per hectare

Average yields: 50–53 hectoliters per hectare

Elevage: Four to six week fermentation and maceration at 28–32°C with frequent pumpings-over. Eleven to fifteen months aging in barrels with 50% new oak. Fining and filtration.

WINES PRODUCED

Château de Valois: 30,000–35,000 bottles

Château La Croix Saint-Vincent: 15,000–20,000 bottles

Plateau of maturity: Within 3–10 years of the vintage

CLOS DE LA VIEILLE ÉGLISE

Owner: Jean-Louis Trocard

Address: 33500 Pomerol

Mailing address: BP 3, 33570 Les Artigues-de-Lussac

Telephone: 05 57 55 57 90; Telefax: 05 57 55 57 98

E-mail: trocard@wanadoo.fr

Website: www.trocard.com

Visits: Monday to Friday, 8 A.M.–noon and 2–5:30 P.M. By appointment on weekends.

Contact: Benoît Trocard

VINEYARDS

Surface area: 3.7 acres

Grape varietals: 90% Merlot, 10% Cabernet Sauvignon

Average age of vines: 40 years

Density of plantation: 6,500 vines per hectare

Average yields: 45 hectoliters per hectare

Elevage: Three week maceration and fermentation. Eighteen months aging in new oak. Fining and filtration.

WINES PRODUCED

Clos de la Vieille Église: 6,500 bottles

No second wine is produced.

VIEUX CHÂTEAU FERRON

Owner: EARL Vignobles Garzaro

Address: 36, route de Montagne, 33500 Libourne

Mailing address: Château Le Prieur, Les vins Garzaro, 33750 Baron

Telephone: 05 56 30 16 16; Telefax: 05 56 30 12 63

E-mail: garzaro@vingarzaro.com

Website: www.vingarzaro.com

Visits: By appointment only

Contact: Elie Garzaro

VINEYARDS

Surface area: 9.9 acres

Grape varietals: 90% Merlot, 5% Cabernet Franc, 5% Petit Verdot

Average age of vines: 30–40 years

Density of plantation: 7,200 vines per hectare

Average yields: 47 hectoliters per hectare

Elevage: Three week fermentation and maceration in temperature-controlled vats. Twelve to eighteen months aging in 100% new oak barrels. Fining with egg whites, no filtration.

WINES PRODUCED

Château Vieux Ferron: 10,000 bottles

Clos des Amandiers: 15,000 bottles

Plateau of maturity: Within 3–10 years of the vintage

VIEUX MAILLET

Owner: Isabelle Motte

Address: 8, route de Maillet, 33500 Pomerol

Telephone: 05 57 51 04 67; Telefax: 05 57 51 04 67

E-mail: chateau.vieux.maillet@wanadoo.fr

Visits: By appointment only

Contact: Isabelle Motte

VINEYARDS

Surface area: 6.5 acres

Grape varietals: 80% Merlot, 20% Cabernet Franc

Average age of vines: 35 years

Density of plantation: 5,600 vines per hectare

Average yields: 40 hectoliters per hectare

Elevage: Three to four week fermentation and maceration in temperature-controlled concrete vats. Wines undergo malolactics in barrel. Twelve to fourteen months aging with 80% new oak, frequent stirring of the lees and two rackings. Fining, no filtration.

WINES PRODUCED

Château Vieux Maillet: 12,000 bottles

No second wine is produced.

Plateau of maturity: Within 3–10 years of the vintage

LA VIOLETTE

Owner: SCI Vignobles Servant-Dumas

Address: Catusseau, 33500 Pomerol

Mailing address: 1, Moulin Rouge, 33141 Villegouge

Telephone: 05 57 55 54 60; Telefax: 05 57 55 54 64

E-mail: servant-dumas@wanadoo.fr

Visits: By appointment only

Contact: Jean-Pierre Dumas

VINEYARDS

Surface area: 11.1 acres

Grape varietals: 80% Merlot, 20% Cabernet Sauvignon

Average age of vines: 25 years

Density of plantation: 6,000 vines per hectare

Average yields: 40 hectoliters per hectare

Elevage: Ten months aging in barrels and vats. Fining and filtration.

WINES PRODUCED

Château La Violette: 22,000 bottles

No second wine is produced.

Plateau of maturity: Within 5–15 years of the vintage

VRAY CROIX DE GAY

Owner: Olivier Guichard

Address: 33500 Pomerol

Mailing address: c/o SCE Baronne Guichard, Château Siaurac, 33500 Néac

Telephone: 05 57 51 64 58; Telefax: 05 57 51 41 56

Visits: By appointment only

Contact: Yannick Reyrel

VINEYARDS

Surface area: 9.1 acres

Grape varietals: 85% Merlot, 15% Cabernet Franc

Average age of vines: 35 years

Density of plantation: 6,000 vines per hectare

Average yields: 45 hectoliters per hectare

Elevage: Three to four week fermentation and maceration in temperature-controlled stainless-steel tanks. Fourteen to eighteen months aging in barrels with 30% new oak. Fining and filtration.

WINES PRODUCED

Château Vray Croix de Gay: 15,000 bottles

No second wine is produced.

Plateau of maturity: Within 5–15 years of the vintage

ST.-EMILION

St.-Emilion is Bordeaux's most aesthetically pleasing tourist attraction. Some will even argue that the walled, medieval village of St.-Emilion, perched on several hills amid a sea of vines, is France's most beautiful wine town. It is also the epicenter of a Bordeaux revolution, the so-called "garage wine movement" that will be discussed later. This is the largest serious red wine appellation of Bordeaux, encompassing more than 13,434 acres.

The wine community of St.-Emilion is a very closely knit fraternity that maintains a fierce belief that their wines are the best in Bordeaux. They have always felt slighted because the region was entirely omitted from the 1855 Classification of the Wines of Gironde.

St.-Emilion is only a forty-minute drive east from Bordeaux. Pomerol sits to the north, and the obscure satellite appellations of Montagne, Lussac, Puisseguin, and St.-Georges St.-Emilion, as well as the Côtes de Francs and the increasingly fashionable Côtes de Castillon, border it on the east and south. The top vineyards are centered in distinctive and geographically different parts of St.-Emilion. Historically, St.-Emilion's finest wines have tended to emerge from vineyards planted on the limestone plateau, the limestone hillsides (the so-called *côtes*), and the gravel terraces adjacent to Pomerol. Yet the decade of the 1990s has established that historically obscure and lowly regarded *terroirs*, if managed by perfectionist proprietors who practice extreme viticulture, can produce exceptionally fine wines. These are the controversial "garage wines."

The vineyards called "*côtes* St.-Emilions" cover the limestone hillsides that surround much of the walled town of St.-Emilion. There are even a few vineyards located within St.-Emilion. Most of St.-Emilion's best known wines—Ausone, both Beauséjours, Belair, Canon, Magdelaine, L'Arrosée, and Pavie—are located along these hillsides. Of the official 13 premier grand cru properties of St.-Emilion (the most recent classification took place in 1996), 10 have at least part of their vineyards on these limestone hillsides. The wines from the *côtes* vineyards are all unique and distinctive, but they share a firm, restrained, more austere character in their youth. However, with proper aging, as a general rule the youthful toughness gives way to wines of richness, power, and complexity.

Certainly Ausone, with its impressive wine cellars carved out of the rocky hillside and its steep vineyard filled with very old, gnarled vines, is the most famous wine of the St.-Emilion *côtes*. This property was considered capable of making one of Bordeaux's best wines in the 19th century, but much of the 20th-century wine of Ausone was surprisingly undistinguished. Ausone tends to be different from the other *côtes* St.-

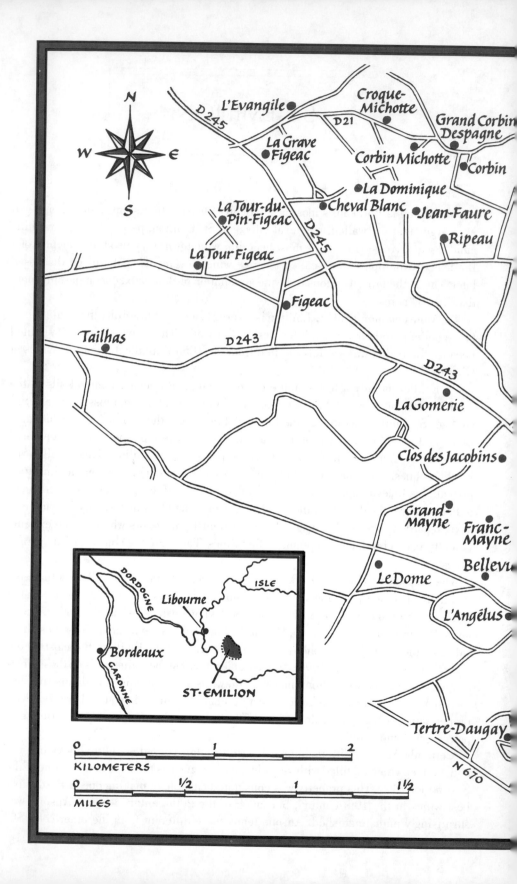

N
W E
S

D 245
L'Evangile
Croque-
Michotte
D 21
Grand Corbin
Despagne
La Grave
Figeac
Corbin Michotte
Corbin
La Dominique
La Tour-du-
Pin-Figeac
Cheval Blanc
Jean-Faure
D 245
Ripeau
La Tour Figeac

Figeac

Tailhas
D 243

D 243

La Gomerie

Clos des Jacobins

Grand-
Mayne
Franc-
Mayne

Bellevu

Le Dome

L'Angélus

DORDOGNE
ISLE
Libourne

Bordeaux

GARONNE

ST·EMILION

Tertre-Daugay

N 670

0   1   2
KILOMETERS

0   ½   1   1½
MILES

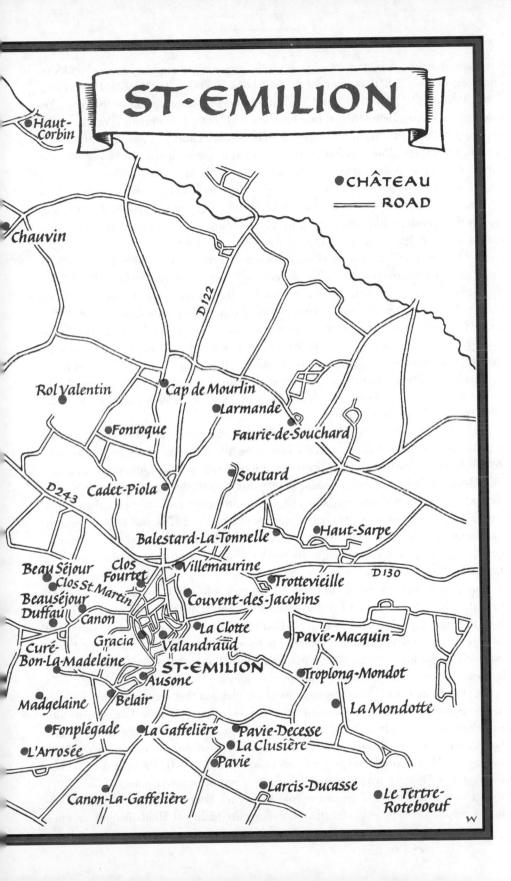

ST·EMILION

● CHÂTEAU
═══ ROAD

Haut-Corbin

Chauvin

Rol Valentin

Cap de Mourlin

Larmande

Fonroque

Faurie-de-Souchard

D 122

Soutard

D 243 Cadet-Piola

Balestard-La-Tonnelle

Haut-Sarpe

Beau Séjour

Clos Fourtet

Villemaurine

D 130

Clos St. Martin

Trottevieille

Beauséjour Duffau

Canon

Couvent-des-Jacobins

La Clotte

Gracia

Valandraud

Pavie-Macquin

Curé-Bon-La-Madeleine

ST·EMILION

Ausone

Troplong-Mondot

Madgelaine

Belair

La Mondotte

Fonplégade

La Gaffelière

Pavie-Decesse

L'Arrosée

La Clusière

Pavie

Canon-La-Gaffelière

Larcis-Ducasse

Le Tertre-Roteboeuf

W

Emilions. Tougher, more tannic, with an exotic, sweet bouquet, it has more of a Médoc austerity on the palate than many of its neighbors. In 2001, 2000, 1999, 1998, 1996, 1995, 1990, 1989, 1988, 1983, and 1982 the château produced magnificent wines. Yet internal bickering between the two families that shared ownership, Vauthier and Dubois-Challon, led to legal friction, with Alain Vauthier and his family buying out the interest of Madame Dubois-Challon. This has led to some significant changes in the winemaking philosophy, particularly evident with all vintages since 1995.

The only other *côtes* vineyards capable of achieving the complexity and sheer class of Ausone are Canon and Magdelaine. Much of Canon's vineyard, like that of Ausone, sits on the limestone hillside. Canon, which has always had an excellent reputation, soared to new heights under the leadership of Eric Fournier, who took over management of Canon in 1972. Canon has since become one of the most powerful and richest wines made from the *côtes* St.-Emilions. Yet this property slumped badly in the 1990s. A contamination in the barrel cellar resulted in far too many musty-tasting bottles. This problem, plus the increasing irregularity of Canon, led to its sale in 1996 to the firm of Chanel (also the proprietors of Rauzan-Ségla in Margaux) and the installation of a new team of administrators, led by the highly talented John Kolasa. They immediately renovated the entire aging cellars of Canon. I fully expect this estate to return to form under the new administration. However, despite the excellent aging potential, it is a wine that matures more quickly than Ausone (which can remain backward and impenetrable for 30 or more years).

Magdelaine could be a worthy challenger to Ausone, but it's not. The vineyard, like those of Ausone and Canon, sits on the limestone hillside to the south of St.-Emilion. However, whereas Ausone and Canon use approximately 50% Cabernet Franc and 50% Merlot in their formula for making great wine, Magdelaine uses up to 90% Merlot. For that reason, Magdelaine tends to be a fleshier, rounder, creamier wine than either Ausone or Canon. However, its general quality during the 1970s and 1980s was only good rather than inspirational. In the mid-1990s Magdelaine produced more complete wines, suggesting quality was being pushed to a higher level. Nevertheless, this is a surprisingly light wine that seems to reflect the tastes of its oenologist, Jean-Claude Berrouet, more than its *terroir*. Vintages in the very late 1990s, in addition to 2000, suggested that administrator Christian Moueix was intent on taking the quality higher.

Of the other top *côtes* vineyards in St.-Emilion, L'Arrosée, not a premier grand cru but a grand cru classé, can make splendid but very traditional wine. L'Arrosée's wine lasts well, and it has a richness and highly aromatic bouquet that lead some to call it the most Burgundy-like St.-Emilion of the *côtes* section.

For years, Pavie and Pavie Decesse, its sister château that sits farther up the hillside, were both owned by one of the friendliest and kindest men in St.-Emilion, the late Jean-Paul Valette. Pavie is the premier grand cru classé, Pavie Decesse the grand cru classé, and both have always been good, yet lighter, more elegant, easygoing styles of St.-Emilion. Valette produced several very good wines in 1990, 1986, and 1982, but quality was extremely irregular and too many disappointments emerged. In 1997, Pavie Decesse as well as Pavie were sold to Gérard Perse, the super-driven, high-quality proprietor responsible for the renaissance in quality at Monbousquet, another

St.-Emilion estate. Millions were invested in the cellars and the vineyards, and a draconian selection process was implemented to cull out anything less than perfect. The results were dramatic . . . and immediate. The 2001, 2000, 1999, and 1998 Pavies were monumental, clearly the greatest wines ever made at this splendidly situated vineyard.

Pavie Decesse was equally brilliant in these vintages. Perse also purchased St.-Emilion's only first-class hotel/restaurant, Plaisance, and turned it into a luxurious residence and eatery for rich tourists. His insatiable appetite for top vineyards, local landmarks, and an arrogant pricing policy (Pavie and Pavie Decesse prices skyrocketed—and frankly, they are worth every Euro) offended many of the Bordelais, who have used all of their sycophantic friends in the wine press to launch an assault on Perse. Perse's pricing policy is worthy of serious debate, but the quality of his wines is undeniably great. Those who have slammed the wines, not the prices, have behaved shamefully and played into the hands of the *ancien régime* of Bordelais, who would prefer the clock turned back to the 1800s.

Belair, the immediate neighbor of Ausone, rarely produces memorable wines. Lighter, more delicate, and earlier to mature than Ausone, Belair, when on form, can be a classy, stylish, medium-weight St.-Emilion that has the potential to reach modest heights, as it did in 1983 and 1989; but more often than not this is a rather dull, uninspiring wine that seems most suitable for arch-traditionalists who prefer their red wines to be austere, spartan, and reminiscent of the 19th century.

Of the other famous *côtes* vineyards of St.-Emilion, a number of poor performers have just recently begun to turn things around and produce better and better wine. The Beauséjour estate of Duffau-Lagarrosse and Clos Fourtet have both improved dramatically in quality since the late 1980s. Clos Fourtet's style of wine is the more commercial of the two, having abandoned its hard, tannic, stern, and unyielding style of *côtes* St.-Emilion in favor of a modern, supple, fruity, very easy to like and drink wine. Not so for Beauséjour, which has improved in quality but continues to emphasize the classic *côtes* style of St.-Emilion: tannic, firm, reasonably well colored, and ageworthy. Of note is the fact that this estate turned in a superlative effort in 1990, a true blockbuster and one of the most profound young red wines I have ever tasted.

The other Beauséjour estate on the western slopes of St.-Emilion is owned by the Bécot family (Beau Séjour Bécot). While its demotion from a premier grand cru to grand cru in the 1985 classification of St.-Emilion wines didn't surprise me, I was impressed by the way the Bécots immediately began to fashion richer and more complex wines following their declassification. They were rewarded in 1996 by being promoted back to premier grand cru classé. In addition, they have begun to produce a 100% Merlot, old vine *cuvée* called La Gomerie. The first vintages have been luxuriantly rich and intense in the style of Pomerol's mini-treasure, Le Pin.

Three other *côtes* St.-Emilion estates have the potential to produce some of the region's most profound wines, but until recently have rarely done so. The premier grands cru classés, La Gaffelière, Trotte Vieille, and Angélus, have superb vineyard expositions and the soil necessary to make wonderful wine.

La Gaffelière has always been a perplexing wine and one of the perennial underachievers among the premier grands cru classés of St.-Emilion. The location of the vineyard is superb, and in tasting through the wines from the 1960s and 1970s, one is struck by how wonderful the 1961 and 1970 are. But it was not until 1982 that the quality began to improve. Since the early 1980s, La Gaffelière has returned to form. While this will never be a blockbuster St.-Emilion, it is perhaps, along with Figeac, the most quintessentially elegant and finesse-styled St.-Emilion of all the premier grands cru classés.

Trotte Vieille used to be another disappointing property, and it remains distressingly irregular, but under the leadership of Philippe Castéja there has been progress since the late 1980s. Angélus was a grand cru classé until the recent 1996 reclassification, when it was justifiably promoted. This property, which went through a dreadfully mediocre period during the 1960s and 1970s, began to make good wines in the mid-1980s. Since 1988, it has made remarkably intense, rich, even outstanding wines that are among the most textured and complete wines of, not only St.-Emilion, but of all Bordeaux. This estate, more than any other in Bordeaux, symbolizes what exceptional things can take place when an inspired person, in this case Hubert de Boüard, embarrassed by the shoddy wines of his predecessors, embarks on a program of producing a wine with no compromises. Angélus has been magnificent in the recent vintages of 2000, 1998, 1995, 1990, and 1989. More noteworthy, Angélus has been superb in difficult years; 1994, 1993, and 1992 are three salient examples.

These are not the only up-and-coming estates that are either situated on the limestone plateau or the hillside sections of St.-Emilion. One of the newest superstars of St.-Emilion is Canon-la-Gaffelière, which actually is one of the châteaux often referred to as being located on the *pieds de côtes,* meaning that its vineyard is situated at the foot of the hillsides. This property made profound wines in the late 1980s and continues to be one of the stars of St.-Emilion.

Another property to watch carefully is Troplong Mondot. The exciting quality of Troplong Mondot has begun to be noticed outside St.-Emilion. The wine, produced by one of the leading ladies of Bordeaux, Christine Valette, has all of the earmarks for becoming one of the great classics of St.-Emilion. This undervalued wine has been especially brilliant during the late 1980s and 1990s and in my mind, it should have been promoted to a premier grand cru classé in 1996.

Another Pavie worth considering seriously is Pavie Macquin. This property, much like Angélus, Troplong Mondot, Canon-la-Gaffelière, and Trotte Vieille, produced wines of mediocre quality during the decade of the 1970s and into the early 1980s. However, Pavie Macquin finished the 1980s with superb wines in 1990, 1989, and 1988, and it has continued to build on this success with fascinating efforts in 1998 and 2000. It appears this is another up-and-coming star of the appellation. This organically farmed vineyard (a rarity in Bordeaux) is beautifully located on the plateau above the limestone hillside referred to as the Côte Pavie. One can taste the essence of low-yielding old vines in Pavie Macquin.

Le Tertre-Rôteboeuf is a tiny gem of a château located on the hillside section of St.-Emilion near its more famous neighbor, Larcis Ducasse. Le Tertre-Rôteboeuf has made monumental wines since the mid-1980s under the compulsive/obsessive eyes and hands of proprietor François Mitjavile. This property is the single greatest discovery I have ever made in the Bordeaux region. No compromises are made in producing the wine, and the result is the only St.-Emilion that can truly be called the Pétrus of St.-Emilion—it is that rich and compelling. Le Tertre-Rôteboeuf should have been promoted to a premier grand cru classé in the 1996 classification, but too many influential people are jealous of this estate's star status.

Another section where St.-Emilion's best wines can be found is called the *graves terraces,* often referred to as *graves et sablés anciens* (or stones and ancient sand). Only 4 kilometers from the town of St.-Emilion and immediately to the northeast of Libourne, the area derives its name from the soil, a gravelly bed intermixed with some clay and sand. The top properties, Cheval Blanc, Figeac, La Dominique, Corbin, and Corbin Michotte, produce a lush, more velvety, voluptuous wine that has the reputation of maturing more quickly than the St.-Emilions on the village hillside. In the top vintages these wines have excellent aging potential. These properties sit right on the southeastern border of Pomerol and often exhibit the same lush, supple fruitiness as the two closest Pomerol estates of L'Evangile and La Conseillante.

Many Bordeaux wine enthusiasts would argue that there is no greater St.-Emilion than Cheval Blanc. Even with the renaissance at Ausone, Cheval Blanc remains the quintessential St.-Emilion, opulent, decadently rich, exotic, surprisingly easy to drink at age 8 or 10, but capable of lasting 30 or more years in superb vintages such as 2000, 1998, 1990 and 1982, Cheval Blanc and Figeac are the only two premier grands cru from the *graves* section of St.-Emilion. An objective analysis of the top estates of this sector would reveal that La Dominique merits serious consideration for inclusion.

Cheval Blanc's vineyard is situated on deep gravelly soil with certain parts clay and sand as well as iron. Perhaps the most unique aspect of this wine is that nowhere else in Bordeaux does the Cabernet Franc grape produce such intoxicatingly perfumed and luxuriously rich, compelling wines. Cheval Blanc can be almost overpoweringly rich, deep, and fruity in vintages such as 2001, 2000, 1999, 1998, 1995, 1990, 1985, 1983, 1982, 1964, 1961, 1953, 1949, 1948, 1947, 1929, and 1921, and this fact, no doubt, explains why much of this wine is drunk before it ever achieves maturity. Figeac, the immediate neighbor of Cheval Blanc, is often compared to Cheval Blanc; however, Figeac is a different style of wine. With a high percentage of Cabernet Sauvignon for a St.-Emilion and much sandier soil than Cheval Blanc, Figeac tends to be a more herbaceous-scented, lighter wine. However, Figeac's great vintages produce complex fruity, soft, charming, concentrated wines that can be drunk when they are only 4–5 years old. Lamentably, only a handful of recent vintages—2000, 1998, 1990, 1982, 1975, 1970, and 1964—have exhibited the stuffing to suggest they can stand the test of time. Figeac has an extraordinary *terroir* and when it hits the bull's-eye it is a wine of singular complexity and character, but, sadly, that occurs infrequently.

La Dominique, an impressive wine and up-and-coming estate, sits just to the north of Cheval Blanc. La Dominique produces excellent wine with lush richness, a deep fruitiness, plenty of body, and aging potential of 10–20 years. It is a wine that might merit elevation to a premier grand cru classé. In some vintages—2000, 1998, 1995,

1990, 1989, 1982, 1971, 1970, and 1955—this property has produced wine rivaling the best in St.-Emilion.

It would be an oversimplification to think that the only fine wines of St.-Emilion come from the *graves* plateau and the hillsides or limestone plateau sectors of this appellation. There are other portions of St.-Emilion that have slightly different soils, and several properties in these sections of the appellation are capable of producing excellent wines.

On the sand-covered slopes, often called the plains of St.-Emilion, properties like Larmande produce excellent wine. The plateau that fans out to the east of St.-Emilion has predominantly clay and sand soil with a limestone base. Soutard is the outstanding estate in this area. Two other perennial overachievers are La Clotte and Balestard-La-Tonnelle; both are capable of producing excellent wines.

Last, one property that is not in any of the above mentioned geographic areas of St.-Emilion, but makes excellent wine, is Clos des Jacobins, a property located a kilometer northwest of St.-Emilion.

St.-Emilion developed its own classification of wine quality in 1954. On paper, this system should be the best of all the Bordeaux wine classifications. The classification is based on reputation, soil analysis, and tasting. Unlike the 1855 classification, which has been infinitely rigid and inflexible (except for the elevation of Mouton Rothschild in 1973), the St.-Emilion classification is supposed to be revised every 10 years, so that in theory top vineyards can be promoted and poorly run vineyards demoted. However, the first major revision in 1969 changed very little. The 1969 classification established a four-tiered hierarchy. The hierarchy that was in effect until 1985 established twelve premier grands crus classés at the top level, of which two were given recognition as the best. These were called premier grands cru classés "A," and the remaining 10 were labeled premier grands cru classés "B." The second rung of this ladder of quality was the grand crus classés, of which there were 72. The third level of quality was for wines entitled to the status grand cru. The bottom level of St.-Emilion's quality hierarchy was for the wines that were entitled only to the appellation St.-Emilion. In the 1996 reclassification there were no demotions from the premier grands cru level, yet two estates, Angélus and Beau Séjour Bécot, were promoted—justifiably, in my view.

St.-Emilion has, for the last decade, been the most exciting appellation of Bordeaux. A hotbed of radical viticulture and experimental vinifications, it has spawned what is known the world over as the "garage wine movement." Le Pin, the microscopic estate in Pomerol, was the original catalyst for the garage wine movement. But the trend that began in St.-Emilion (which continues to spread elsewhere in Bordeaux—like the plague, say its critics) is a movement toward small vinifications of selected vineyard parcels usually comprised of a high percentage of Merlot. French wine writer Nicholas Baby named them "vins de garage," as the production of most estates was so small (less than 500 cases) that it could be kept in a garage.

The early performances of the following wines has placed them among the most ravishing, exotic, concentrated, compelling wines being made in St.-Emilion. Only time will reveal how well they evolve and whether they justify their lofty, sometimes ridiculous prices. Certainly there is no disagreement with the fact that these wines are the result of perfectionist proprietors pushing the envelope of quality as far as it can go.

The usual formula for these wines incorporates all or some of the following:

1. Radical viticulture (extensive crop thinning and leaf-pulling for additional sun exposure) all designed to produce tiny yields and ripe fruit.
2. Open top small oak fermenters (à la Burgundy).
3. Pre-fermentation cold soaks (to increase phenolic ripeness as well as perfume, à la Burgundy).
4. Malolactic in barrel (à la Burgundy) and, since 2001, alcoholic and malolactic fermentations in small barrels.
5. Minimal racking and little exposure to oxidation; sometimes the use of a technique called micro-bullage (employed to add oxygen to the lees), the objective being to keep the fruit as pure and fresh as possible.
6. An upbringing (the French word is *élevage*) in cask (mostly new) on the wine's lees (to build more texture and fat).
7. Eschewing any fining or filtering (to preserve bouquet, flavor, texture, depth, and *terroir* characteristics).

Overall, all the techniques that I mention are, on paper, aimed at the objective of preserving fruit, nuances, and the character of the varietal, vintage, and vineyard. In theory, they should enhance a wine's so-called *terroir* characteristics. Will these techniques make a garage wine superior to Haut-Brion or Cheval Blanc? I don't think so, but they can result in interesting, sometimes compelling, yet different wines that are still very Bordelais.

In 1991, Château de Valandraud became the first notable St.-Emilion vin de garage to assemble several different vineyard parcels. (Le Pin's first vintage preceded this by 12 years.) Its proprietor, the highly talented Jean-Luc Thunevin, quickly made the wine a collector's dream, as it often sold for absurdly high prices, higher than even Cheval Blanc or Ausone. Of course, this was very unsettling to the ruling elite/status quo of St.-Emilion as well as the aristocracy in the Médoc. Some Bordeaux Neanderthals still refer to Thunevin as *tue-le-vin* (kill the wine).

Some garage wines are clearly the products of greedy marketers that "talk the talk," but anyone with a palate will realize after tasting that they don't "walk the walk." Moreover, as long as the prices for these limited production wines stay high, consumers can expect more and more phony pretenders to emerge. Some of the finest "vins de garage" from St.-Emilion include, in no particular order, Bellevue-Mondotte (St.-Emilion), Ferrand Lartigue (St.-Emilion), Gracia (St.-Emilion), Magrez-Fombrauge (St.-Emilion), Péby Faugères (St.-Emilion), Croix-de-Labrie (St.-Emilion), Clos Dubreuil (St.-Emilion), Rol Valentin (St.-Emilion), La Gomerie (St.-Emilion), Lynsolence (St.-Emilion), L'Hermitage (St.-Emilion), La Mondotte (St.-Emilion), La Confession (St.-Emilion), Clos de Sarpe (St.-Emilion), Lusseau (St.-Emilion), and Bellevue (St.-Emilion). Interestingly, the total production of *all* these wines is less than one major Médoc château such as Gruaud Larose.

Although few quality garage wines actually exist, the hysterical reaction (much of it critical) has resulted in a shrill and chilling wall of irrational criticism. This criticism has come mostly from the Médoc aristocracy as well as reactionaries in Pomerol and St.-Emilion, allied to supportive writers, most notably England's Jancis Robinson, who appears for reasons that escape me, to be on a personal crusade against these wines.

Think it over. Does anyone find fault with a young, energetic person who is committed to making world-class wine from an unheralded *terroir*? I know most of the people associated with the aforementioned wines. They are fanatical in the vineyard and cellar (or garage), and they are wine lovers first and foremost. They represent what is joyous about wine . . . its diversity and creative energy. Sadly, there remain strong reactionary voices that would silence diversity and discourage creativity. Do their opponents want to return to the Bordeaux of 30 or 40 years ago when less than one-third of the most renowned estates made wine proportional to their pedigree? When dilution was praised as elegance? When dirty, unclean aromas were justified as part of the *terroir* character? When disappointingly emaciated, austere, and excessive tannic wines from classified growths were labeled "classic" by a subservient wine press? The finest of the garagists have shaken up the status quo/establishment. I think there is room for these wines alongside the authentic classics of each appellation. Why can't others recognize that all wines don't have to taste the same or be made according to some strict time-honored formula? What are these critics so afraid of?

One of the well-traveled criticisms of these wines is that they are made from special "designer lots," culled out from an existing batch of wine that is decidedly inferior. Of the garage wines I mentioned earlier, only two are carved out of existing vineyards. Those are Péby and Magrez. At least for the 2000 vintage, the other non-garage wines made by these properties, particularly Faugères and Fombrauge, are also brilliant, although completely different from the two wines above.

Obviously skimming of the crème de la crème can have a deleterious effect on the regular *cuvée,* but keep in mind that Bordeaux's most serious estates, in fact almost every top classified growth, have been eliminating at least 30–70% of their production from their grand vin since the mid-1980s. The most draconian selections are at Léoville Las Cases and Lafite Rothschild where usually no more than 35% of the crop makes it into the top wine. The other first growths, with the exception of Mouton-Rothschild, tend to put 45–50% in the top wine, even in an exceptional vintage like 2000. This has been going on since the humongous crops of the mid-1980s (1985, 1986, etc.). Interestingly, it is often the case that the lots chosen for the grand vin emanate from the same parcels, seemingly regardless of vintage conditions.

This is not the same as a California "reserve" wine, where a selection made in the cellar is deemed richer and better than the other stuff and then is sold at a far higher price. If you think about it, consumers are actually getting a "reserve" or special *cuvée* from the top Bordeaux châteaux; they just don't call it that. The overall objective of the Bordelais is to put the very best wine out under the first label, use the second label for the next best, and then sell off in bulk anything that remains. Even many smaller properties in Graves, St.-Emilion, and Pomerol are making strict selections (Cheval Blanc has been eliminating close to 50% of its crop in recent years, and the microscopic Ausone has been declassifying 20–30% of its production into a second wine, or selling it in bulk). All of this is aimed at improving quality. It's one of the main reasons why the quality of modern-day Bordeaux is so much better than it was 30–40 years ago.

Another tiresome and totally untrue criticism is that all the garage wines taste the same. When I was profiled in November 2001, by the brilliant *Atlantic Monthly* writer, William Langewiesche, he brought up the criticisms by Jancis Robinson and other writers of my support for the finest garage wines. I suggested to Langewiesche (who is not a wine lover by any means) that when he was next in Bordeaux he should do a tasting of many of the garage wines and see for himself if the wines all taste the same, were too oaky and alcoholic, and as Jancis Robinson alleges, represented "caricature wine-making." He did that tasting and referred to it in his article. Now he's no professional, but even as an amateur he felt there were extraordinary differences between the wines and he actually liked most of them, which is in keeping with how anyone without an agenda tends to approach the garage wines.

The final attack on garage wines, and the most sinister, is the charge made by Jancis Robinson (parroting the same lines I have heard again and again in Bordeaux) that these wines "fail to express their place of origin." In winedom, this is akin to being accused of guilt by the Spanish Inquisition. No one can possibly challenge this, although every *terroirist* I have invited to a blind tasting to prove to me the "transparency of *terroir*" has always refused. Robinson cites as examples Boüard at Angélus and Neipperg at Canon-la-Gaffelière in toning back or exercising more restraint when making their 2001s and "repudiating" the style for their past vintages. This is totally contrary to my discussions with both Boüard and Neipperg. What she does not mention is that they both realized they didn't have the raw materials in 2001 to make a blockbuster 2000 or a super-duper 1998. What they did was what all intelligent wine-makers do—they let the vintage conditions dictate the style. The 2001s produced lighter, less concentrated wines than 2000, and less concentrated and powerful wines than the right bank 1998s. Dollars to doughnuts says that if Angélus and Canon-la-Gaffelière have the raw materials in a new vintage to produce another 2000, 1998, 1990, or 1989, they won't hesitate. I smell the proverbial straw man creation in all of these arguments.

Garage wine critics also state that these wines are "much higher in alcohol" than other Bordeaux wines. Forty years ago Emile Peynaud was pushing many of his Bordeaux clients to pick later and riper. The results are grapes higher in sugar, lower in acidity, and when vinified dry, higher in alcohol. His philosophy has been carried on by others, most notably Michel Rolland. A look at the technical analyses of modern-day Bordeaux classics (Haut-Brion, La Mission Haut-Brion, Pétrus, Lafleur, Vieux Château Certan, Lafite Rothschild, Latour, Mouton Rothschild, Château Margaux, Montrose, Lynch-Bages) will reflect that over the last 15–20 years the fruit is riper, the acidity is lower, and the alcohol levels are higher than 30 or 40 years ago. These are great wines, but they are not garage wines, nor are they made like garage wines.

Lastly, the garage wines I have mentioned could not be more different from one another, as anyone who sits down and takes the time to taste them will observe. Magrez Fombrauge has no similarity to La Gomerie or La Mondotte, Péby Faugères is totally different from Gracia, and so on and so on. To reiterate the basic question: Why is there so much fear of so little wine that most consumers don't care about and will probably never find in the marketplace? Why have so many writers come to the defense of the Bordeaux wine establishment? I would argue that there is room for all styles of wine, both in Bordeaux and in the world.

Given the extraordinary success of these limited-production wines to date, there is no reason to doubt that more imitators will be emerging from St.-Emilion, giving consumers plenty of wines to get excited about, assuming they can afford and find them. But remember, just because it is a so-called garage wine does not guarantee quality.

St.-Emilion produces wines that have enormous crowd appeal. Fleshy, quick maturing, round, and generous, they are easy to like, easy to drink, and easy to understand. While the premier grands crus classés and their detested competitors, the garage wines, are expensive, many of the grands crus classés are significantly undervalued and can represent excellent bargains.

Since quality of the soils, the winemaking, and the combination of grape varietals planted in the vineyards are so diverse in St.-Emilion, it is exceedingly difficult to generalize about vintages in this vast appellation. Certainly the great vintages for St.-Emilion have been 2000, 1998, 1990, and 1982 (probably the four best vintages for this region in the post–World War II era). The other top vintages have been 2001, 1999, 1995, 1989, 1986, 1983, 1970, 1964, and, of course, 1961. The key to any excellent or great vintage for St.-Emilion is the healthy flowering and ripening to full maturity of the Merlot and Cabernet Franc grapes, the two most important grapes for this region.

Since this area has an enormous number of wine-producing estates, I have emphasized in my tastings and in this chapter the premier grands crus classés, grand crus classés, and the highest quality garage wines. It may be arbitrary, even capricious, but given the sheer number of St.-Emilions that merit coverage from the aforementioned categories, I have generally disregarded the generic St.-Emilion, except where their level of quality merits interest. Some of these wines can, in fact, be good, but they never have the consistency of the top estates.

ST.-EMILION
(An Insider's View)

Overall Appellation Potential: Average to Superb

The Most Potential for Aging: Angélus, L'Arrosée, Ausone, Beau Séjour Bécot, Beauséjour-Duffau, Canon-la-Gaffelière, Cheval Blanc, Clos St.-Martin, La Dominique, La Mondotte, Pavie (since 1998), Pavie Decesse (since 1997), Pavie Macquin, Péby Faugères, Troplong Mondot

The Most Elegant: Ausone, Chauvin, Clos St.-Martin, Figeac, La Gaffelière, Moulin St.-Georges, Laplagnotte-Bellevue, Quinault, Trottvieille

The Most Concentrated: Angélus, L'Arrosée, Ausone, Beauséjour-Duffau, Bellevue-Mondotte, Canon-la-Gaffelière, Cheval Blanc, Clos St.-Martin, Destieux, La Dominique, Magrez Fombrauge, Monbousquet, La Mondotte, Moulin St.-Georges, Pavie (since 1998), Pavie Decesse (since 1997), Pavie Macquin, Péby Faugères, Troplong Mondot, Valandraud

The Best Value: Corbin, Corbin Michotte, Daugay, La Fleur, La Fleur de Jaugue, La Grave Figeac, Haut-Brisson, Pipeau, Rolland-Maillet, Yon-Figeac

The Most Exotic: Cheval Blanc, La Couspaude, Ferrand Lartigue, La Gomerie, Lusseau, Magrez-Fombrauge, La Mondotte, Quinault, Le Tertre-Rôteboeuf, Valandraud

The Most Difficult to Understand When Young: Ausone, Canon, Fonroque, Larcis Ducasse

The Most Underrated: Clos des Jacobins, Clos de l'Oratoire, Larmande, La Tour-Figeac, Monbousquet, Moulin St.-Georges, Pavie Macquin

The Easiest to Appreciate Young: Barde-Haut, La Clotte, La Couspaude, Dassault, Faugères, Fombrauge, Pipeau, Le Tertre-Rôteboeuf

Up-and-Coming Estates: Barde-Haut, Bellefont-Belcier, Chauvin, Clos Fourtet, Clos de l'Oratoire, Clos St.-Martin, Daugay, Destieux, Faugères, La Fleur de Jaugue, Fombrauge, Grand Mayne, Grand Pontet, Les Grandes Murailles, Lusseau, Monbousquet, Pavie, Pavie Decesse, Pavie Macquin, Quinault, Rol Valentin

Greatest Recent Vintages: 2001, 2000, 1998, 1995, 1990, 1983, 1982, 1964, 1961

ST.-EMILION—AN OVERVIEW

Location: This area, part of the right bank viticultural region of Bordeaux southeast of Pomerol, is approximately 20 miles from downtown Bordeaux.

Acres Under Vine: 13,434

Communes: St.-Emilion, St.-Hippolyte, St.-Christophe des Bardes, St.-Laurent des Combs, St.-Pey d'Arnens, St.-Sulpice de Faleyrens, Vignonnet, St.-Etienne de Lisse

Average Annual Production: 2,800,000 cases

Classified Growths: Total of 68; 2 premier grands crus classés A, 11 premier grands crus classés B, and 55 grands crus classés

Principal Grape Varieties: Merlot, Cabernet Franc, while microscopic quantities of Malbec and Cabernet Sauvignon exist.

Principal Soil Types: Great diversity is the rule of thumb. On the southern hillsides of the town of St.-Emilion are the limestone outcrops. In the direction of Pomerol, clay, sand, and gravel dominate the vineyards.

A CONSUMER'S CLASSIFICATION OF THE CHÂTEAUX OF ST.-EMILION

OUTSTANDING

Angélus, Ausone, Canon-la-Gaffelière, Cheval Blanc, Clos St.-Martin, La Gomerie, Magrez-Fombrauge, La Mondotte, Pavie (since 1998), Pavie Decesse (since 1998), Péby Faugères, Le Tertre-Rôteboeuf, Troplong Mondot, Valandraud

EXCELLENT

L'Arrosée, Barde-Haut, Beau Séjour Bécot, Beauséjour, Bellevue, Bellevue-Mondotte, Clos Dubreuil, Clos de l'Oratoire, Clos de Sarpe, La Couspaude,

Croix de Labrie, La Dominique, Ferrand Lartigue, Figeac, Gracia, Grand Mayne,
Larmande, Monbousquet (since 1994), Moulin St.-Georges, Pavie Macquin,
Quinault, Rol Valentin, Soutard

VERY GOOD

Balestard La Tonnelle, Bellefont-Belcier, Cadet-Piola, Canon, Chauvin, Clos Fourtet,
Clos des Jacobins, La Clotte, La Confession, Corbin Michotte, Faugères, Fombrauge,
La Gaffelière, Grand Corbin-Despagne, Grand Pontet, Laplagnotte-Bellevue, Pierre
de Lune, Lusseau, Magdelaine, Saint-Domingue, Yon-Figeac

GOOD

Berliquet, Cap de Mourlin, Chante Alouette Cormeil, Clos La Madeleine, Corbin,
Couvent des Jacobins, Croque Michotte, Curé-Bon, Dassault, Daugay, Destieux,
Faurie de Souchard, Château de Ferrand, Fleur Cardinale, La Fleur-Pourret,
Fonplégade, Fonroque, Franc-Mayne, Godeau, Haut-Brisson, Haut-Corbin,
Haut-Sarpe, Jean Faure, Le Jurat, Larcis Ducasse, Laroze, Mauvezin,
Petit-Faurie-de-Soutard, Ripeau, Rocher Bellevue Figeac, Rolland-Maillet,
Saint-Georges-Côte-Pavie, Tertre Daugay, La Tour-Figeac, La Tour du Guetteur,
La Tour-du-Pin-Figeac, Trotte Vieille

OTHER NOTABLE ST.-EMILION PROPERTIES

Belair, Bernateau, La Bienfaisance, Jacques Blanc, La Bonnelle, Bouquey, Cadet-
Bon, Cantenac, Capet-Guiller, Le Castelot, du Cauze, Cheval Noir, Clos Labarde,
Clos Larcis, Clos Trimoulet, La Commanderie, Cormeil-Figeac, Côtes de Rol,
La Couronne, Coutet, La Croix-Figeac, La Croix de Jaugue, Cruzeau, La Fleur,
Fonrazade, Galius, La Grâce Dieu, La Grâce Dieu Les Menuts, La Grâce Dieu des
Prieurés, Grand Corbin, Grand Corbin Manuel, La Grave Figeac, Guadet-St. Julien,
Haut Mazerat, Haut-Quercus, Lafleur Vachon, Laniote, Laroque, Leydet-Figeac,
Leydet-Valentin, Magnan La Gaffelière, Martinet, Matras, Monlot Capet, Moulin
Bellegrave, Moulin du Cadet, du Paradis, de Pasquette, Patris, Pavillon-Cadet,
Petit Figeac, Domaine de Peyrelongue, Pindefleurs, Pontet-Fumet, Le Prieuré,
Prieuré-Lescours, Puy-Blanquet, Puy-Razac, Quercy, Rocher, La Rose-Pourret,
Roylland, St.-Lô, Sansonnet, La Serre, Tauzinat L'Hermitage, Tour Baladoz,
La Tour-du-Pin-Figeac, Trimoulet, Val d'Or, Vieux-Château-Carré, Vieux Sarpe,
Villemaurine, Jean Voisin

ANGÉLUS

Classification: Premier Grand Cru Classé B

Owner: De Boüard de Laforest and sons

Address: 33330 St.-Emilion

Telephone: 05 57 24 71 39; Telefax: 05 57 24 68 56

E-mail: chateau-angelus@chateau-angelus.com

Website: www.chateau-angelus.com

Visits: By appointment only

Contact: Emmanuelle d'Aligny

VINEYARDS

Surface area: 57.8 acres

Grape varietals: 50% Merlot, 47% Cabernet Franc, 3% Cabernet Sauvignon

Average age of vines: 30 years

Density of plantation: 7,000–8,000 vines per hectare

Average yields: 32 hectoliters per hectare

Elevage: Three to five week fermentation and maceration in double-walled stainless-steel and concrete vats of small capacity. Malolactics and 18–24 months aging in new oak barrels. No fining, no filtration.

WINES PRODUCED

Château Angélus: 70,000 bottles

Le Carillon de l'Angélus: 15,000–20,000 bottles

Plateau of maturity: Within 4–25 years of the vintage

GENERAL APPRECIATION

Hubert de Boüard has had enormous influence on the higher overall quality level of many St.-Emilions. Under his helmsmanship, Angélus has been the first mediocre estate to resurrect its image and be the catalyst for the qualitative revolution in its appellation, pushing other wineries to achieve more. The property began turning things around in the mid-1980s, producing their first top-notch effort in 1988. Since then, there has not been a hiccup, even in such difficult rain-soaked vintages as 1992 and 1993, or hail-plagued vintages like 1999. Angélus was elevated to premier grand cru status in the 1996 St.-Emilion reclassification, and this promotion is undoubtedly well deserved. A topflight wine and a must buy for true St.-Emilion lovers.

Angélus has always been a St.-Emilion with great popular appeal. With a large production, much of it exported, a lovely label, and a charming, supple style of wine, Angélus has been able to build a strong following among enthusiasts of the wines of St.-Emilion. Angélus is located in the Mazerat Valley, with vineyards planted on calcareous clay loam and clay/sandy soil on the lower slopes. The entire vineyard enjoys a perfect southern exposure.

In the 1960s and 1970s Angélus produced a wine that started life with a charming fruity intensity, then proceeded to disintegrate in a matter of a few short years. This all changed in the 1980s. The well-known Bordeaux oenologist Michel Rolland was brought in to provide consultation, and he insisted that the property age the wine in 100% oak casks. Previously, the wine had been aged in vats and saw no oak aging at all. Fermenting (malolactics) the wine in small oak casks (much like the Pomerol Le Pin) tends to add an extraordinary amount of complexity and intensity to the wine. This can only be done by small estates or by those committed to spending huge sums of money on labor, because it is a time-consuming, back-breaking process.

The results have been stunning. No doubt the young proprietor, Hubert de Boüard de Laforest, is also making a much stricter selection of only the best lots for the final wine. Angélus was denied elevation to premier grand cru status in the 1985 classification of the wines of St.-Emilion, but it did receive that promotion in 1996.

The style of the "new" Angélus is one that still emphasizes early drinkability, with intense, rich, supple, fat fruitiness. However, the wine is now much deeper colored and more concentrated, and it has more supportive tannins to help it age better. Certainly the finest wines of the last three or four decades are the profound 2000, 1998, 1996, 1995, 1994, 1990, 1989, and 1988. Older vintages, prior to 1986, must be approached with extreme caution, as many of these wines have fallen completely apart.

IMPORTANT VINTAGES

2001
90–93
This should turn out to be an outstanding Angélus. Its opaque purple color is accompanied by aromas of blackberries, cassis, smoke, espresso, and new wood. Medium bodied, dense, ripe, and moderately structured, the 2001 displays the purity typically found in this estate's wines. While less massive and intense than such vintages as 2000, 1998, 1995, 1990, and 1989, it will provide enjoyment between 2007–2018. Last tasted, 1/03.

2000
96
An outrageously ripe, concentrated, dense effort, the 2000 offers up aromas of blackberry liqueur and vintage port. As the wine sits in the glass, graphite, wet stones, smoke, barbecue spices, and olives also make an appearance. It unfolds on the palate in layers, is full-bodied, big, and rich yet incredibly poised, well balanced, and pure. Quite backward, this is one of the greatest Angélus made to date. Bravo! Anticipated maturity: 2009–2030. Last tasted, 1/03.

1999
88
Forced to harvest early due to hail, Angélus, surprisingly, has turned out a very good 1999 offering scents of blackberries, licorice, tapenade, and figs. It lacks the length possessed by the great Angélus vintages such as 2000, 1998, 1990, and 1989, but it is ripe, pure, and moderately tannic. Drink it over the next 10–12 years. Last tasted, 3/02.

1998
95+
A dazzling effort, the 1998 boasts an opaque purple color in addition to an exceptional bouquet of smoke, licorice, plums, black raspberries, and blackberries. As the wine sits in the glass, coffee and chocolate also emerge. Full-bodied, flamboyant, well delineated, and beautifully balanced as well as layered, with well-integrated tannin in the powerful, rich finish, this 1998 requires cellaring. Anticipated maturity: 2008–2025. Last tasted, 12/02.

1997
89
The saturated, deep ruby/purple–colored 1997 is a big, rich, smoky St.-Emilion exhibiting this estate's telltale characteristics of Provençal olives, black cherry liqueur, prunes, and toasty new oak. The biggest of St.-Emilion's premier grand cru classés, it is soft, supple, and ideal for consuming over the next 7–8 years. Last tasted, 11/02.

1996
91+
A massive, powerful Angélus, this wine exhibits a saturated black/ruby/purple color as well as an impressively endowed nose of dried herbs, roasted meats, new saddle leather, plum liqueur, and cassis. In the mouth, olive notes make an impression. This sweet, full-bodied, exceptionally concentrated wine is atypically backward and ferociously tannic. It was revealing more sweetness and forwardness immediately prior to bottling, but I would now recommend at least 3–4 years of cellaring. Anticipated maturity: 2007–2025. Last tasted, 1/02.

1995
95
A superb effort in this vintage, Angélus's opaque purple–colored 1995 is a massive, powerful, rich offering with plenty of ripe, sweet tannin. The wine's aromatics include scents of Provençal olives, jammy black cherries, blackberries, truffles, and toast. A very full-bodied wine, it is layered, thick, and pure. This is the most concentrated of the 1995 St.-Emilion premier grand crus. Anticipated maturity: 2005–2025. Last tasted, 11/02.

1994
92
Another inky, purple/black-colored wine, the 1994 offers up heavenly scents of smoked meats, barbeque spices, hickory wood, and plenty of cassis and kirsch. The fruit's phenomenal purity and denseness, as well as its overall balance, is admirable in view of the massive, muscular personality of this huge, full-bodied wine oozing with extract. It is a tour de force in winemaking. Anticipated maturity: now–2020. Last tasted, 11/02.

1993
91
One of the four or five most concentrated wines of the vintage, this opaque, black/purple-colored 1993 offers an intensely fragrant nose of smoke, olives, chocolate, black fruits, hickory, and sweet, spicy oak. Amazingly rich and full-bodied, with massive extract, it is almost unbelievable that this wine could have been produced in a vintage such as 1993. Anticipated maturity: now–2015. Last tasted, 3/02.

1992
88
What a surprise in an incredibly difficult year! Angélus has turned out a fully mature wine that needs to be drunk up over the next 3–4 years, but notes of olive, black cherry, and currant are present, along with some leafy, fern-like, forest smells. The wine is medium-bodied, soft, and one of the undeniable successes for this miserable vintage. Anticipated maturity: now–2007. Last tasted, 4/02.

1991
87
One of the few successful wines of the vintage in St.-Emilion, the 1991 reveals a complex bouquet of chocolate, coffee, toasty new oak, herbs, and jammy red fruits. Lusciously ripe fruit is presented in a medium-bodied, sweet, round format that offers immediate gratification. It should drink well for another 5–6 years. Given how difficult the 1991 vintage was, this effort is noteworthy. Anticipated maturity: now–2007. Last tasted, 3/00.

1990
96
This is a softer, fleshier, even more flamboyant version of the 1989. The acid seemed lower and the alcohol and glycerin levels slightly higher, but this dense, ruby/purple-colored wine showing a bit of pink at the edge is developing beautifully, and it is an example of a wine that is incredibly satisfying both hedonistically and intellectually. Very full-bodied, splendidly rich, pure, with intense notes of creosote, smoke, blackberry and cassis, this provocative wine should drink well for at least another 10–15 years. How fascinating it always is to do a blind tasting between this vintage and the 1989. Anticipated maturity: now–2015. Last tasted, 1/03.

1989
96
A great Angélus and one of the two or three best vintages made under the talented young Hubert de Boüard, this wine still has a youthful, saturated ruby/purple color and a sweet nose of melted licorice intermixed with crème de cassis, tapenade, cedar, spice box, and vanilla. Very full-bodied, opulent, and rich, it is one of the 1989s that justifies the lofty reputation of this vintage. Extremely thick, this wine can be drunk now or cellared for at least another 10–15 years. Anticipated maturity: now–2015. Last tasted, 4/02.

1988 Still a dark garnet/purple color that shows some lightening at the edge, this wine
91 appears to be approaching a post-adolescent stage. A nose of earth, licorice, underbrush, and black fruits is followed by a medium-bodied wine with a lot of structure, muscle, tannin, and depth. Tannin is still present, but the wine is showing
very complex aromatics and good sweetness on the attack. Very drinkable, yet capable of holding for at least another decade. Anticipated maturity: now–2012.
Last tasted, 4/02.

1986 Fully mature, the garnet-colored 1986 has a broad, expansive, forward bouquet of
88 ripe plums, spicy, smoky new oak, compost, and tapenade. On the palate, this mature wine displays richness, length, and ripeness. It is unlikely to improve. Anticipated maturity: now. Last tasted, 12/02.

1985 The 1985 is a seductively smooth, supple, broadly flavored wine with aromas and
87 flavors of berry fruit and herbs. Full-bodied, concentrated, but forward and delicious, this is a luscious wine. Anticipated maturity: now. Last tasted, 3/90.

1982 Readers should remember that in 1982 there was no selection process, and a com-
77 pletely different winemaking style and philosophy were in place. The 1982, soft
and ripe after bottling, has deteriorated quickly. It reveals considerable amber, orange, and rust colors and is diffuse and flabby. While it still reveals some sweet,
jammy fruit, the wine exhibits an old, mushroomy, earthy note. It is clearly in decline and should be drunk immediately. Last tasted, 9/95.

ANCIENT VINTAGES

Prior to 1985, Angélus was largely a mediocre wine that required consumption within
5–7 years of the vintage. Nothing from the 1960s or 1970s has ever left me with a favorable impression.

L'ARROSÉE

Classification: Grand Cru Classé

Owner: EARL Famille Caille (Administrator Jean-
Philippe Caille)

Address: 33330 St.-Emilion

Telephone: 05 57 24 69 44; Telefax: 05 57 24 66 46

E-mail: chateau.larrosee@wanadoo.fr

Visits: No visits

VINEYARDS

Surface area: 23 acres

Grape varietals: 60% Merlot, 20% Cabernet Franc, 20% Cabernet Sauvignon

Average age of vines: 30 years

Density of plantation: 5,500 vines per hectare

Average yields: 35–40 hectoliters per hectare

Elevage: Three to four week fermentation and maceration in temperature-controlled
concrete tanks. Part of yield undergoes malolactics in barrels. Twelve to eighteen months
aging in new oak barrels. Fining, no filtration.

WINES PRODUCED

Château L'Arrosée: 30,000 bottles

No second wine is produced.

Plateau of maturity: Within 5–15 years of the vintage

GENERAL APPRECIATION

Such a traditional style is somewhat passé in St.-Emilion. At its best, L'Arrosée is a very Burgundy-like wine of telltale silkiness, with expansive black cherry and raspberry perfume intertwined with loads of high-quality, smoky new oak. I have always felt it could easily pass for a wine made by Burgundy's great genius, Henri Jayer. However, during the last 10 years this estate, once a great favorite of mine, has had some difficulty in trying to keep pace with its once usual level of excellence. Though good, the recent vintages of L'Arrosée are no longer as promising as they used to be. It is not that they are eclipsed by the more flamboyant St.-Emilions emerging from the modern school of vinification. The estate's sale in 2002 will no doubt result in much needed changes.

One of the least known and publicized wines of St.-Emilion, L'Arrosée, which sits on the slopes or *côtes* of St.-Emilion, is destined to become more famous as the high quality of its wine becomes better known.

The estate was purchased by the Rodhain family in 1911, and managed from 1956 until its sale in 2002 by François Rodhain. Until the mid-1960s, the production was, unfortunately, sold off in bulk to the local St.-Emilion cooperative for more than three decades because the property had no winemaking facilities. Since then the entire production has been made and bottled at the château.

The style of L'Arrosée's wine is unique. Fleshy, yet firm and powerful, fragrant, as well as rich and full, it is a wine with plenty of character, and it has a style that seems at times to recall a southern Médoc property such as La Lagune. At other times—for example in 1990, 1989, 1986, and 1985—the wine resembles a rich, lusty Burgundy. In fact, the 1985 continues to remind me of a Henri Jayer Richebourg! The renowned Dutch author Hubrecht Duijker called L'Arrosée the "finest wine of the appellation."

IMPORTANT VINTAGES

2001
87–88   A strong effort, this Burgundian-styled St.-Emilion is not a big, powerful wine, but it seduces the taster with its understated elegance, finesse, and purity. It possesses a sweet floral and red and black fruit–scented perfume, good texture, and a medium-bodied, restrained, authoritatively flavored style. If French model Carole Bouquet were a wine, this might be it. Anticipated maturity: 2007–2015. Last tasted, 1/03.

2000
89   The deep ruby/purple–colored 2000 is revealing more of a mid-palate and depth than previously. Sweet vanilla and black cherry jam aromas are followed by a wine of outstanding purity, attractive texture, moderate tannin, and a distinctive, traditional St.-Emilion style. There are also hints of mint and underbrush in this medium-bodied, elegantly wrought wine. Anticipated maturity: 2007–2018. Last tasted, 1/03.

1999
86   Although lacking substance, this elegant, light- to medium-bodied, medium ruby–colored 1999 exhibits sweet oak in its Burgundian-like bouquet of flowers and cherries. There is also a bit of dilution. Drink it over the next 6–7 years. Last tasted, 11/02.

1998 Scents of overripe red cherries, along with a boatload of toasty new oak are present
86   in this delicate, lacy, medium-bodied St.-Emilion. A 90-point nose is followed by
      82-point flavors, hence the score. This 1998 should drink well for 8–10 years, but
      it does not attain the quality level of many of its St.-Emilion peers. Last tasted,
      3/02.

1997 A wine of finesse and elegance, this tasty, soft, medium-bodied effort exhibits light
86   tannin, ripe cherry fruit, and an expressive bouquet consisting of damp soil, red
      fruit, and flower scents. Consume it over the next 2–3 years. Last tasted, 3/02.

1996 A tightly knit, closed wine, the 1996 L'Arrosée has not yet begun to put on weight
87+? or reveal its true character. It possesses a medium dark ruby color and muted aro-
      matics that, with airing, offer notes of dusty minerals mixed with black cherries
      and raspberries. Subtle high-quality toasty oak makes an appearance along with
      black raspberry and cherry fruit. This is a firmly knit, sinewy, austere, elegant
      wine. Anticipated maturity: 2004–2016. Last tasted, 3/02.

1995 With a medium dark ruby color and a complex, kirsch, toasty smoky, deliciously
90   complex and fruity nose, this fragrant wine offers a wealth of raspberry, currant,
      and cherry-like fruit. It is not a blockbuster, but rather an elegant, multidimen-
      sional, round, velvety-textured wine with a lushness and sweetness of fruit that
      makes it irresistible. This is one of the more seductive wines of the vintage. Antic-
      ipated maturity: now–2012. Last tasted, 3/02.

1994 A deep ruby color and reluctant aromatics suggest a wine in a dormant state. On
87   the palate, the wine offers little charm, but it does possess dense, medium-bodied,
      concentrated, but closed and tannic flavors. The wine should evolve well, although
      the tough tannin could prove troublesome. The 1994 L'Arrosée should last for 10
      more years. Anticipated maturity: 2005–2014. Last tasted, 3/01.

1990 An intense perfume of flowers, red and black fruits, minerals, and earth jumps
90   from the glass of this medium-bodied, very elegant, yet beautifully etched St.-
      Emilion. The wine has a dark ruby color with some amber at the edge. Sweet,
      round, and seemingly fully mature, this seductive, elegant wine shows tremendous
      perfume as well as the ability to caress the palate, but don't push its aging ability
      too far. Anticipated maturity: now–2010. Last tasted, 12/01.

1989 The 1989 exhibits a dark ruby color with slight lightening at the edge, as well as
88   plenty of earthy, black cherry fruit nicely touched by sweet, toasty oak. It exhib-
      ited more richness, glycerin, intensity, and precision than it has in previous tast-
      ings. Anticipated maturity: now–2007. Last tasted, 11/96.

1988 Dark garnet with a pink rim, the 1988 is medium bodied, spicy, and fruity, with
83   good depth but not much length. Moreover, the wine lacks complexity and inten-
      sity. Anticipated maturity: now. Last tasted, 11/00.

1986 For L'Arrosée, this vintage has taken an atypically long time to round into shape. It
92   has always possessed considerable power as well as a muscular, concentrated
      style and hefty tannin. Beginning to shed its tannin, it reveals an intriguing dusty
      herb, black cherry, kirsch, and mineral nose, with subtle vanilla from new oak in
      the background. There are medium-bodied, concentrated flavors with some firm
      tannin, but by and large this is a very accessible wine. It remains youthful, with
      only a hint of amber at the edge of its deep ruby/purple color. This will undoubt-
      edly be one of L'Arrosée's longest-lived wines since their 1961. Anticipated matu-
      rity: now–2015. Last tasted, 2/02.

1985 A gorgeous wine when young, but beginning to slip a bit as it approaches its 16th
88   birthday, this wine showed wonderfully floral notes of framboise, violets, and cher-
      ries in its youth, but is beginning to lose some of the sweetness and fatness it had
      early on, showing a more structured, drying finish. Still a beautiful wine aromati-

cally, but a bit attenuated in the finish, this wine needs to be drunk up. Anticipated maturity: now. Last tasted, 12/01.

1983   Fully mature for some time, although lighter than the 1982, this wine is an elegant
89   L'Arrosée with notes of dried herbs, mineral, sweet cherries, and an almost floral
       note. Again, it comes close to an almost Burgundian style, with medium body, a
       nice, expansive texture, and a bit of dryness beginning to creep into the finish.
       Drink it over the next 4–5 years. Anticipated maturity: now–2006. Last tasted,
       12/01.

1982   One of the great L'Arrosées of the last 30 years, this wine continues to age beauti-
92   fully even though it has been delicious almost from its inception. Considerable
       amber is poking its head through the dark garnet color. The nose of sweet cherry,
       cola, earth, almost black cherry liqueur, and some smoke jumps from the glass of
       this medium-bodied, opulent, fleshy wine that shows beautiful integration of acid-
       ity and tannin. Anticipated maturity: now–2010. Last tasted, 12/01.

ANCIENT VINTAGES

The two great classics for me have been the 1964 (90 points; last tasted 12/02) and
1961 (92 points; last tasted 1/03). Both wines remain vigorous, impressively deep and
persistent.

AUSONE

Classification: Premier Grand Cru Classé A

Owner: Micheline, Catherine, and Alain Vauthier

Address: 33330 St.-Emilion

Telephone: 05 57 24 68 88; Telefax: 05 57 74 47 39

E-mail: château.ausone@wanadoo.fr

Website: www.château.ausone.com

No visits

VINEYARDS

Surface area: 17.3 acres

Grape varietals: 50% Merlot, 50% Cabernet Franc

Average age of vines: 50–55 years

Density of plantation: 6,000–7,800 vines per hectare

Average yields: 35 hectoliters per hectare

Elevage: Twenty-one to twenty-eight day fermentation and maceration in temperature-
controlled wooden vats. Malolactics and 19–23 months aging in new oak barrels with
rackings every three months. Light fining, no filtration.

WINES PRODUCED

Château Ausone: 20,000–23,000 bottles

Chapelle d'Ausone: 7,000 bottles

Plateau of maturity: Within 5–100 years of the vintage, as from 1994

GENERAL APPRECIATION

Since the mid-1990s, Alain Vauthier has been in sole control of this famous property, strategically situated on the limestone hillsides of the village of St.-Emilion, and continues to build on the quality of Ausone. Under his inspired ownership, this estate regularly produces benchmark efforts designed to last 50–100 years. No expense is spared to make the best possible wine (for example, reduced yields, mature fruit, malolactic fermentation in small barrels as opposed to tank), and the results are even more expressive of this extraordinary *terroir*, yet richer and more intriguing aromatically than their elders. Following this radical change in orientation, many have suggested that Ausone had lost its soul. These are the reactionary voices (obedient parrots) of the old guard in St.-Emilion who prefer to turn back the clock a half century, when this property was producing far too many dried out, fruitless, hollow wines, marked by musty aromas. Given Alain Vauthier's commitment to excellence, Ausone is finally living up to its mythical status. Prices are high, but then the production is extremely small—the smallest of the so-called "Big Eight" of Bordeaux.

If the first-time visitor to Bordeaux had just one château and vineyard to visit, it should be the tiny Ausone property, perched on one of the hillsides outside the medieval walls of St.-Emilion. Ausone has a spectacular location, made all the more startling because of its tiny vineyard of very old vines and the extensive limestone caves that house the property's wine cellar. Ausone is named after the Roman poet Ausonius, who lived from A.D. 320–395. He was also known to have had a vineyard in the area (closer apparently to Bordeaux than to St.-Emilion), and while there are Roman ruins at Ausone, it is highly doubtful that Ausonius himself had anything to do with this estate.

Despite the great historical significance of Ausone and the fact that it has one of the most privileged locations for making wine in all of Bordeaux, the record of wine quality was mediocre—even poor—during the 1960s and 1970s.

The minuscule production of Ausone makes it almost impossible to find commercially. Even more rare than the famous Pomerol estate of Pétrus, yet considerably less expensive, Ausone has a style that is totally different from St.-Emilion's other famous estate, Cheval Blanc.

In spite of what appeared to be a cordial relationship between the two families that owned Ausone, Dubois-Chaillon and Vauthier, internal bickering and constant friction on the philosophy of winemaking resulted in the Vauthier family buying out Madame Dubois-Chaillon in the mid-1990s. Wine-maker Pascal Delbeck was replaced by Alain Vauthier, who receives oenological consultation from Libourne's Michel Rolland. While partisans of the Dubois-Chaillon/Delbeck team complain that Ausone is being made in a more forward, commercial style, this is nothing more than the whining of those who have an ax to grind. The most significant changes made under Vauthier/Rolland have been slightly later harvests if weather conditions permit, malolactic fermentation in barrel rather than tank, and a stricter selection with the introduction of a second wine. The initial efforts under the new regime were spectacular wines, with all of Ausone's elegance, finesse, and extraordinary mineral-based personality, as well as greater concentration and intensity. In fact, the development of these Ausones during their *élevage* in barrel and bottle has been brilliant, and the wines have lost none of their "typicity," as the Dubois-Chaillon/Delbeck whiners have opined. I expect Ausone to be more consistent and to reach even higher peaks of quality under the inspired leadership of Alain Vauthier.

IMPORTANT VINTAGES

2001
94–96 Another profound effort from perfectionist proprietor Alain Vauthier, the 2001 does not display the breadth of flavor or pure magic of the 2000, but it is already a candidate for the vintage's longest-lived wine. Its striking blue/purple color is accompanied by a classic bouquet of liquified minerals, blackberries, black currants, and flowers. It is sweet, ripe, structured, tannic, and impressively endowed, with a finish that lasts more than 30 seconds. Although the tannin is noticeable, so is the fruit purity, freshness, and delineation. This gorgeous Ausone is for connoisseurs only. Anticipated maturity: 2012–2050. Last tasted, 1/03.

2000
100 The 2000 is the greatest Ausone I have ever tasted, aside from 100+-year-old examples I tasted in Munich with the famous collector, Hardy Rodenstock. A saturated black/purple color is followed by sensational aromas of ink, cherries, blackberries, blueberries, and that wet stones/liquid minerality characteristic. The wine has phenomenal presence on the palate as well as astonishing richness and purity. Despite its extract, power, and richness, it is remarkably light, with a surreal delicacy and purity. It is a tour de force, in winemaking and a great expression of this magical *terroir*. It should prove to be legendary, but sadly, anyone over the age of 50 will probably not live to see it come close to maturity. Anticipated maturity: 2020–2075. P.S.: Even if you have to drink it young, everyone owes it to themselves to taste this prodigious effort. Last tasted, 1/03.

2000
90 Chapelle d'Ausone: The tightly structured, mineral-infused 2000 Chapelle d'Ausone exhibits outstanding concentration as well as depth in addition to floral, blackberry, and blueberry aromas and flavors. Deep and rich, it is better than many Ausones produced in the 1970s, 1960s, and 1950s . . . believe it or not! Anticipated maturity: 2008–2025. Last tasted, 1/03.

1999
95 Is the 1999 Ausone the wine of the vintage? Dense purple color, a compelling bouquet of licorice, minerals, black and blueberry liqueur, extraordinary delineation, high tannin, superb extract, and phenomenal richness all are the stuff of a legend. It seems impossible that this wine emerged from a vintage like 1999. Proprietor Alain Vauthier produced only 20,000 bottles because he eliminated one-fourth of the tiny crop. The result is out-and-out fabulous, but the wine needs 10–12 years of cellaring. Anticipated maturity: 2015–2050. Last tasted, 12/02.

1999
90 Chapelle d'Ausone: About 6,000 bottles of the 1999 Chapelle d'Ausone were made from the same blend as the grand vin (50% Cabernet Franc, 50% Merlot). It is a serious second wine, offering notes of blueberries, minerals, and flowers (violets). This dense purple–colored, deep, rich, outstanding effort will be drinkable between 2007–2020. Last tasted, 12/02.

1998
94+ A dense opaque purple color offers up restrained, but pure aromas of liquid minerals, blackberries, black raspberries, and flowers. Medium to full-bodied, with high tannin but a long, super-pure, symmetrical mouth-feel, this dazzling, extremely complex Ausone requires 6–7 years of cellaring. Anticipated maturity: 2010–2050. Last tasted, 3/02.

1997
91 One of the finest wines of the vintage, this dark purple–colored effort reveals black raspberry, blackberry, mineral, and floral aromas in its complex, multidimensional bouquet. In the mouth, it is medium bodied, with sweet, ripe fruit, firm tannin, good acidity for the vintage, and a long, impressively endowed, moderately tannic finish. Moreover, it will be one of the vintage's longest-lived wines. Anticipated maturity: 2007–2020. Last tasted, 3/01.

1996

93+

The color of the 1996 is a dense ruby/black/purple. Reluctant aromas of blue-berries, blackberries, minerals, flowers, truffles, and subtle new oak eventually emerge. Elegant on the attack, with sweet ripeness and a delicate, concentrated richness, the hallmark of this wine is subtlety rather than flamboyance. A sweet mid-palate sets it apart from many of the uninspiring Ausones of the 1980s and 1970s. The wine is stylish and presently understated, with tremendous aging po-tential. Anticipated maturity: 2008–2040. Last tasted, 3/01.

1995

93

Ausone's extraordinary minerality is present in the 1995, yet there are more aro-matics, a richer, more multidimensional palate impression, and a fuller texture—all with the *terroir* brilliantly expressed. The wine boasts a dense ruby/purple color and an emerging but tightly knit nose of spring flowers, minerals, earth, and black fruits. Rich, with an opulent texture and surprising sexiness for a young vin-tage of Ausone, the medium-bodied 1995 displays exquisite balance between its acid, tannin, alcohol, and fruit. Although it is not yet seamless, all the elements are present for an extraordinary evolution in the bottle. This wine will age at a gla-cial pace for 30–40 years. Anticipated maturity: 2010–2045. Last tasted, 3/01.

1994

86?

Medium to deep ruby–colored, with a noticeably vanilla, stony minerality, this austere, medium-bodied wine possesses good ripeness and depth of fruit, but it still comes across as undersized and unimpressive. Give it 1–2 years to see if there is any substance behind the abrasive tannin. Anticipated maturity: 2005–2018. Last tasted, 3/00.

1993

85?

The understated style of the 1993 Ausone offers mineral, lead pencil scents with some red currant fruit in the restrained, backward bouquet. Austere and medium bodied, this tannic, attenuated, lean wine will undoubtedly dry out long before the tannin melts away. It is a lightweight wine that is best drunk over the next 12 years—in spite of its astringency. Last tasted, 1/97.

1992

80?

Ausone's firmly structured, tannic 1992 reluctantly reveals a nose of dusty, flowery red fruits, wood, and minerals. Light bodied and shallow, with cherry fruit flavors intermingled with the taste of herbs, this wine appears to lack a finish, depth, and intensity. Too tannic and sinewy to enjoy over the near-term, Ausone's 1992 is a likely candidate to dry out before its tannins ever melt away. Last tasted, 11/94.

1990

92+

The 1990 is not a charming, precocious wine. It is closed, but the color is a dense, dark ruby with no amber or orange at the edge. The fruit is sweeter, and the wine is more muscular, richer, and broader in the mouth, without losing Ausone's telltale minerality, spice, and curranty fruit. There is a good inner core of sweet fruit in this medium- to full-bodied wine that needs another 15–20 years of cellaring. Can the 1990 possibly rival the 1983 or 1982? Perhaps . . . but don't bet on it. Antici-pated maturity: 2008–2030. Last tasted, 11/96.

1989

87?

Notes of melted caramel, coffee, fruitcake, and ripe currants are moderately in-tense in this relatively ripe year for Ausone. Nevertheless, in the mouth there is still high tannin, a somewhat attenuated finish with medium body and average quantities of red and black currant fruits. Drink it over the next 10–15 years. Last tasted, 11/02.

1988

80?

Dark ruby with some pink at the edge, the 1988 Ausone exhibits notes of licorice, fennel seed, cinnamon, mineral, and red and black currants. In the mouth, the wine is light to medium bodied and relatively disappointing. Again, a narrowness and hardness make for a wine that just simply doesn't deliver. The emperor's new clothes . . . again and again. Anticipated maturity: now–2020. Last tasted, 11/02.

1987

87

This is a successful vintage for Ausone, which produced a wine with nearly 13% natural alcohol. Surprisingly ripe, with the exotic, mineral-scented character so typical of this property, the 1987 Ausone is a medium-bodied, ripe, richly fruity, classy wine that should drink beautifully for another 12–20 years. If it continues to firm up and gain weight in the bottle, it may turn out to be as good as their wonderful 1976, as well as have 20 or more years of aging potential. A sleeper! Anticipated maturity: now–2015. Last tasted, 5/02.

1986
74

Another major disappointment, this emaciated, thin wine shows high levels of minerals, structure, and muscle, but no charm, fruit, or succulence. It will last for another 50 years, but will it ever provide any enjoyment? Anticipated maturity: now–2040. Last tasted, 12/99.

1985
75

A major disappointment, this wine continues to dry out, showing light body, high tannin, a weedy, red currant fruitiness, and a pinched, abrasive finish. It has gotten worse as it has aged in the bottle. Anticipated maturity: now. Last tasted, 11/99.

1983
91

A very successful vintage for Ausone, this wine seems to be close to full maturity, but knowing the history of this château, it is not unforeseen that it can last another 50 or more years. The wine shows a dark garnet color with considerable amber at the edge. Sweet notes of fruitcake, spice box, underbrush, licorice, and jammy red and black fruits tumble from the glass. The wine is medium bodied, round, nearly opulent by the standards of this château, with a spicy, somewhat pinched finish. Anticipated maturity: now–2025+. Last tasted, 1/03.

1982
90?

Amber at the edge is evident in this dark garnet–colored wine. Sweet notes of weedy tobacco intermixed with red currant jam, spice box, and cedar jump from the glass of this relatively perfumed vintage for Ausone. The attack is sweet, with surprising glycerin and ripeness, but then the finish narrows out with plenty of tannin, hardness, and structure. The wine seems to have come out of its dormant stage, but where it's going is anyone's guess. Anticipated maturity: 2008–2030. Last tasted, 12/02.

1981
82

This medium ruby wine remains closed but exhibits adequate ripeness of fruit. However, the hard tannins are cause for concern. A medium-weight wine, the 1981 Ausone has good concentration, but will, I believe, always be an austere, tough-textured, charmless wine. It still needs 10 years to soften and develop. Anticipated maturity: now–2010. Last tasted, 1/90.

1979
89?

A still youthful dark ruby with a pink rim, this wine shows notes of wet earth, red currants, mushroom, and spice box. The wine is medium bodied, has a sort of liquid minerality, good sweet fruit on the attack, but then a relatively dry, astringent, harsh finish. This is typical of so many vintages of this wine that are difficult for anyone with a modern-day taste for fruit to appreciate. Anticipated maturity: 2008–2025. Last tasted, 11/02.

1978
85?

Dark garnet, with notes of herbs, licorice, and fennel in an almost steely, very structured style, this medium-bodied wine lacks the flesh and intensity to stand up to the muscle and structure. Anticipated maturity: now–2015. Last tasted, 12/00.

1976
92

Considerable amber at the edge is evident in this dark garnet–colored wine. With a big nose of sweet maple syrup intermixed with foresty notes, plum, fig, and currants, it is sweeter and riper than its more famous sibling, the 1975. In the mouth, the wine shows some hard edges and angularity, which is so typical of Ausone, but there is a lot of character and a concentrated, medium-bodied mid-palate. The finish is paradoxically both sweet and sour, with ripeness and glycerin, but at the same time, high tannin. Seemingly at a plateau of maturity, this wine could easily hang at this level for decades. Anticipated maturity: now–2020. Last tasted, 1/02.

1975
88?

Considerable amber is creeping in at the edge of this wine, which shows notes of cinnamon, earth, red fruits, dried herbs, and mushroomy, forest floor notes. The wine is medium bodied, still somewhat tannic, and very complex aromatically. The wine is not showing signs of drying out, but this is hardly a hedonistic style of wine for those looking for more fruit-driven efforts. Anticipated maturity: now–2020. Last tasted, 1/02.

1971

78

Light to medium ruby, with a rust-colored edge, this pleasant yet insubstantial wine has a light perfume of spicy oak as well as scents of minerals and decaying leafy vegetation. Not terribly concentrated, but adequately fruity in a savory, satisfying manner, the 1971 is a nice wine for drinking immediately. A magnum drunk at the château in 1988 merited a more enthusiastic review (86 points), but it was far from profound. Anticipated maturity: now—probably in decline Last tasted, 3/88.

1970

69

The 1970 Ausone is very light, with a bouquet that suggests old, faded flowers and dusty fruit. Brown at the edges and beginning to dry out, this medium-bodied wine is the poorest of the "Big Eight" of Bordeaux in this excellent vintage. Very disappointing. Anticipated maturity: now—probably in decline. Last tasted, 1/87.

1967

65

A diluted, insipid bouquet is followed by a wine with bland, washed-out flavors and significant browning to the color. Although not a complete failure, it is extremely disappointing. Anticipated maturity: now—probably in decline. Last tasted, 9/83.

1966

78

Tasted twice from well-stored bottles in Bordeaux, this wine reveals an amber/rust overtone to its medium garnet color. At first the nose offers attractive faded fruit, old leather, and dried herb-like aromas. In the mouth, the wine possesses sweetness on the attack that fades quickly to reveal astringency, harshness, and a medium-bodied, hollow personality. Anticipated maturity: now—it is clearly in decline. Last tasted, 3/97.

1961

88

A ripe, Port-like nose of dried fruits, herbs, old tea, and minerals made for an intriguing set of aromatics. In the mouth, the wine reveals more sweetness and fat than one expects from Ausone, but an underlying pruny quality suggested the fruit was more than merely overripe. Hard tannin, acidity, and earthiness were noticeable in the background, but overall this was a good to excellent wine, with its positive attributes outweighing the more troublesome ones. Anticipated maturity: now–2008 Last lasted, 3/97.

ANCIENT VINTAGES

The kindest thing that can be said about many of the older vintages of Ausone, particularly those in the post–World War II era, is that they have survived. It is hard to find a vintage of Ausone from the 1940s or 1950s that is not at least drinkable. In spite of the fact that Ausone often has longevity, the question remains as to how much pleasure these wines ultimately provide. Top vintages such as 1959, 1955, 1952, 1947, and 1945, while still alive, all represent the austere, undernourished, and somewhat charmless style of Ausone. Why more richness and depth were not forthcoming escapes me, but there is no denying the high level of dry, astringent tannins in so many of these wines. My favorite older vintage of Ausone is the 1955, but even that wine is far from meriting an outstanding rating.

Tasted in September 1995, Ausone's 1949 (86 points) revealed a medium garnet color with considerable rust at the edge. Some attractive mineral and black fruit aromas emerge from what is otherwise an austere, lean, light- to medium-bodied, high-acid wine—a textbook Ausone.

The 1874 Ausone (96 points) made me think that the reason I have never fully appreciated and understood Ausone is that I have never had the opportunity to wait 121 years for an Ausone to reach full maturity! When drunk in September 1995, the wine still possessed a sweet, tomato, herb, mineral, and black fruit bouquet, medium body, glycerin-dominated, chewy, fat flavors, and a gorgeously long, heady, mineral-dominated, sweet finish. This wine may drink well for another 30–40 years.

The first comment in my notes on the 1929 (96 points; last tasted 9/94) was "cedar city." Although lightly colored, with a rusty tint to the entire wine, the 1929 Ausone exhibits a fabulous bouquet of spices, cedar, and sweet, jammy fruit. It displays wonderful ripeness, as well as the telltale austerity and dry finish that often characterize Ausone. The wine remains rich, medium bodied, and intact, but I would not gamble on holding it any longer. However, it possesses more fruit, richness, and complexity than the shallow color suggests. The 1921 Ausone (92 points; last tasted 9/95) was elegant and less viscous but still remarkably rich and fragrant. It also revealed more tannin, as well as Ausone's trademark, Médoc-like style. Complex yet sweet aromas of berry fruit intertwined with minerals, dried flowers, and spices were followed by a medium- to full-bodied, concentrated, fully mature, well-balanced wine. As the wine sat in the glass, it quickly began to lose its fruit.

My notes indicate that the 1900 Ausone (94 points; last tasted 9/94) had a 90-point nose and 99-point flavors. Most Ausones are big on bouquet but short on flavor. It is unbelievable that a 94-year-old wine could have this much richness and flavor. The huge nose of roasted cloves, coffee, and honeyed red fruits is followed by a wine with super-sweetness, big, jammy, alcoholic, ripe flavors, and remarkable length with elevated alcohol. The light color is akin to a rusty-colored white Zinfandel. The extreme sweetness makes me think the fermentation halted and the wine has some residual sugar. This stunning wine remains fresh as well as lively, a bottle such as this could last for another 15–30 years!

BALESTARD LA TONNELLE

Classification: Grand Cru Classé

Owner: Jacques Capdemourlin

Address: 33330 St.-Emilion

Mailing address: c/o SCEA Capdemourlin, Château Roudier, 33570 Montagne-St.-Emilion

Telephone: 05 57 74 62 06; Telefax: 05 57 74 59 34

E-mail: info@vignoblescapdemourlin.com

Website: www.vignoblescapdemourlin.com

Visits: By appointment only

Contact: Thierry Capdemourlin

VINEYARDS

Surface area: 26.2 acres

Grape varietals: 70% Merlot, 25% Cabernet Franc, 5% Cabernet Sauvignon

Average age of vines: 33 years

Density of plantation: 5,600 vines per hectare

Average yields: 41 hectoliters per hectare

Elevage: Twenty-one to twenty-eight day fermentation and maceration in temperature-controlled epoxy-lined concrete tanks. Fifteen to eighteen months aging in barrels with 50% new oak. Fining and filtration.

WINES PRODUCED

Château Balestard La Tonnelle: 60,000 bottles

No second wine is produced.

Plateau of maturity: Within 5–15 years of the vintage

GENERAL APPRECIATION

Always soundly made in the old-fashioned traditional St.-Emilion style, Balestard La Tonnelle has not yielded to more progressive vinifications that are in fashion throughout the appellation.

I have always regarded Balestard La Tonnelle as a downsized Lynch-Bages of St.-Emilion. This property, owned by the Capdemourlin family, produces a densely colored, big, deep, rich, and chewy style of wine. It can sometimes be too big and alcoholic for its own good, but this is an immensely enjoyable style of St.-Emilion that can normally be drunk after 5 or 6 years of bottle age, yet also evolve gracefully for 10 or more years.

The property takes its name from the writings of the 15th-century poet François Villon, who wrote about "drinking this divine nectar which carries the name of Balestard." The vineyard, enclosed by tall cypress (look for the windmill that sits on the knoll), is located on a limestone plateau adjacent to Château Soutard, to the east of the town of St.-Emilion. Balestard has been relatively successful since 1970.

IMPORTANT VINTAGES

2001
86–88
Dark plum/ruby, with a sweet nose of chocolate and black currant fruit, this medium-bodied, fleshy wine shows good density, low acidity, and ripe tannin. It should drink well for 5–8 years. Last tasted, 1/03.

2000
87
A very attractive, hedonistically styled wine, with a deep plum/garnet color and a sweet nose of compost, black cherry liqueur, cassis, and underbrush, this wine is a typical Balestard La Tonnelle, made in a corpulent, fleshy style with low acidity and some noticeable tannin. Drink it over the next 10–12 years. Last tasted, 1/03.

1999
86
Low acidity gives the dark ruby/purple–colored 1999 an up-front appeal. It possesses copious quantities of attractive cassis and cherry fruit, medium body, and an alluring, fleshy style. Give it 1–2 years to shed its rugged tannin, and enjoy it over the next 5–6 years. Last tasted, 3/02.

1998
86
A medium-bodied, spicy, earthy effort, the 1998 exhibits notions of cured olives, ripe cherries, cassis, and spice box. Although not complex, it is a solid, muscular wine that will provide a mouthful of tasty St.-Emilion. Anticipated maturity: now–2010. Last tasted, 3/02.

1997
78
This wine reveals tannin in addition to a compressed, one-dimensional personality, without enough sweetness, glycerin, or fruit to stand up to the wine's structure. Anticipated maturity: now. Last tasted, 3/01.

1996 The 1996 exhibits an evolved ruby/garnet color, a spicy, earthy, dried herb–
83 scented nose, medium body, and a nearly mature personality with sweet cherry
    fruit in the finish. Anticipated maturity: now–2006. Last tasted, 3/00.
1995 The 1995 reveals the low acidity and jammy ripeness of the vintage, as well as
85–86? medium to full body, but it is somewhat clumsy. The wine does possess plenty of
    guts and tannin. Anticipated maturity: now–2009. Last tasted, 12/02.

ANCIENT VINTAGES

The 1990 (87 points; last tasted 11/00) and 1982 (90 points; last tasted 12/01) were the two finest older vintages of Balestard La Tonnelle. Both, I would assume, are still drinking well, especially the 1982, which is the thickest, richest Balestard La Tonnelle I have ever tasted.

BARDE-HAUT

Classification: Grand Cru

Owner: Sylviane Garcin-Cathiard

Address: 33330 Saint-Christophe-des-Bardes

Mailing address: c/o Château Haut-Bergey, BP 49, 33850 Léognan

Telephone: 05 56 64 05 22; Telefax: 05 56 64 06 98

E-mail: haut.bergey@wanadoo.fr

Visits: By appointment only

Contact: Hélène Garcin-Lévêque

VINEYARDS

Surface area: 42 acres

Grape varietals: 80% Merlot, 20% Cabernet Franc

Average age of vines: 33 years

Density of plantation: 6,500 vines per hectare

Average yields: 30 hectoliters per hectare

Elevage: Prolonged fermentation (with indigenous yeasts) and maceration in temperature-controlled concrete vats of 50 hectoliter capacity with frequent *pigéages*. Malolactics and 18 months aging in new oak barrels. No fining, no filtration.

WINES PRODUCED

Château Barde-Haut: 40,000 bottles

Le Vallon de Barde-Haut: 25,000 bottles

Plateau of maturity: Within 5–20 years of the vintage

GENERAL APPRECIATION

In the capable hands of Dominique Philipe, Barde-Haut became a serious wine in St.-Emilion. Now under the helmsmanship of the Garcin-Cathiard family, the estate has confirmed over recent vintages that it will remain one of the most prominent wines of the appellation. Vinified in the rich, opulent style common to the "avant garde" modern-styled St.-Emilions, it still represents a fairly good buy.

Located in the commune of Saint-Christophe-des-Bardes, this beautifully situated hillside estate is planted in pure clay and limestone soils. With great exposure, there is no problem getting full phenolic ripeness, something that has certainly been emphasized over recent vintages and particularly by the new owners, the Garcin-Cathiard family, who have done so much to resurrect other estates, particularly Clos l'Église in Pomerol. This is an underpriced, up-and-coming estate that merits considerable attention.

IMPORTANT VINTAGES

2001
88–90 Well below the quality of the brilliant 2000, 1999, 1998, and 1997, Barde-Haut's 2001 is an elegant, restrained effort displaying sweet cherry and black currant fruit on the attack, medium body, and an attractive, very good finish. The wine is not too far off the pace of the 2000. Anticipated maturity: now–2012. Last tasted, 1/03.

2000
90 I am not sure the 2000 will turn out better than the 1998, but it has even more depth than that beautiful wine. Fat, with loads of fruit, glycerin, and length, this saturated dark ruby/purple–colored St.-Emilion reveals plenty of sweet new oak intermixed with blackberry and crème de cassis aromas. Lusty and rich, with low acidity, yet high tannin, this wine has a 25–30-second finish. It will be at its finest between 2008–2018. Last tasted, 1/03.

1999
89+ Possibly outstanding, the 1999 Barde-Haut is elegant, complex, savory, and hedonistic. A dark ruby/purple color is followed by copious quantities of black fruits intermixed with toasty oak and licorice. It is sweet and expansive, with low acidity, medium body, and a lush finish. Seductive stuff! Drink it over the next eight years. Last tasted, 3/02.

1998
90 A deep ruby/purple color is accompanied by pure, sweet aromas of blackberry and blueberry jam revealing nicely integrated oak. This wine exhibits medium to full body, a fat, concentrated mid-palate with structure as well as definition, admirable length and richness, low acidity, and abundant fruit and extract. Anticipated maturity: now–2018. Last tasted, 3/02.

1997
90 From the first tasting, this wine has possessed all of the earmarks of one of the vintage's stars, as well as a sleeper of the vintage. A saturated blue/purple color is followed by sumptuous aromas of blackberry/blueberry jam. This medium-bodied St.-Emilion offers rich, multilayered flavors, in an elegant yet authoritatively rich style. Some tannin needs to be resolved, but there is gorgeous purity, a sweet mid-palate, and fine length in this stunning offering. One of the vintage's richest, most well-balanced efforts, it can be drunk now and over the next 10 years. Last tasted, 3/02.

BEAU-SÉJOUR BÉCOT

Classification: Premier Grand Cru Classé B

Owner: Gérard and Dominique Bécot

Address: 33330 St.-Emilion

Telephone: 05 57 74 46 87; Telefax: 05 57 24 66 88

E-mail: contact@beausejour-becot.com

Website: www.beausejour-becot.com

Visits: By appointment only

Contact: Gérard or Dominique Bécot

VINEYARDS

Surface area: 40.8 acres

Grape varietals: 70% Merlot, 24% Cabernet Franc, 6% Cabernet Sauvignon

Average age of vines: 35 years

Density of plantation: 6,600 vines per hectare

Average yields: 37 hectoliters per hectare

Elevage: Twenty-eight to thirty day fermentation and maceration in temperature-controlled stainless-steel vats. Malolactics and 18 months aging in new oak barrels. No fining, no filtration.

WINES PRODUCED

Château Beau-Séjour Bécot: 70,000 bottles

Tournelle de Beau-Séjour Bécot: 10,000–12,000 bottles

Plateau of maturity: Within 5–14 years of the vintage

GENERAL APPRECIATION

Since Beau-Séjour Bécot regained its premier grand cru classé status in the 1996 St.-Emilion classification (it was declassified in 1986), the wine has been impressive (especially since the mid-1980s). This wine's ostentatious, nearly over-the-top style will have its detractors, but if wine is a beverage of pleasure, Beau-Séjour Bécot delivers the goods.

The quality of Beau-Séjour Bécot has improved significantly since the mid-1980s. Ironically, Beau-Séjour Bécot was demoted in the 1985 classification of the wines of St.-Emilion, only to be promoted back to premier grand cru classé in the 1996 classification. The vineyard, which is well situated on a limestone plateau, produces wines that are rich and full-bodied as well as supple and fleshy. No doubt the decisions to harvest very ripe fruit, utilize plent of new oak, and bottle the wines naturally contribute to the wine's chewy texture and rich, hedonistic appeal. The château's consulting oenologist is the well-known Michel Rolland of Libourne.

IMPORTANT VINTAGES

2001
89–91
While the 2001 Beau-Séjour Bécot does not possess the immense volume and power of the 2000, it is a fine effort. The dense purple color is accompanied by aromas of candied black currants and cherries, sweet toasty oak, licorice, and spice box. Medium bodied, with outstanding purity, adequate acidity, good uplift, and a fine finish, this wine will be drinkable between 2006–2015. Last tasted, 1/03.

2000
93
Is this the greatest Beau-Séjour Bécot ever produced? The 2000 has put on weight during its *élevage* and appears to be a spectacular effort in this vintage. The wood is now better integrated, and the fruit, glycerin, and overall dimensions are noteworthy. The color is an opaque purple. The bouquet smells of ink, jammy blackberries and currants, wet stones, and licorice. Super-pure and fabulously extracted, with high tannin, full body, and awesome richness and length, this blockbuster effort will be at its finest between 2008–2025. Last tasted, 1/03.

1999
86
From a hail-damaged vineyard that was forced to harvest early, this is a lean, small-scaled, but attractive 1999 offering herb-tinged black cherry and currant fruit. Drink it over the next 6–7 years. Last tasted, 3/02.

1998
91
As most recent vintages have, the 1998 exhibits flamboyant, obvious new oak, but unlike other years, there is more concentration, power, and depth behind the vanilla toasty notes. Full-bodied, dense, and chewy, with copious peppery, herb-tinged, red currant, black currant, and blackberry fruit, this is a lush, generously endowed offering with a lightly tannic finish. Anticipated maturity: now–2016. Last tasted, 3/02.

1997
89
One of the stars of the vintage, this sexy St.-Emilion offers a big, smoky, toasty new oak–scented nose with jammy strawberry and cherry fruit. Low acidity gives the wine a plump, fleshy feel. Medium to full-bodied, gorgeously pure, and attractive, it can be enjoyed over the next 5–6 years. Last tasted, 3/01.

1996
89
The lavishly oaked, hedonistically styled 1996 exhibits a dark plum/purple color. The nose offers up sweet jammy fruit (primarily black currants and cherries) intermixed with toasty new oak. Medium bodied, with excellent, nearly outstanding richness, a nicely layered mid-palate, and sweet tannin in the long finish, it should last for 10+ years. Anticipated maturity: now–2013. Last tasted, 4/02.

1995
89
Beau-Séjour Bécot's sexy 1995 offers a dark plum color, followed by a sweet, vanilla, spicy, black cherry, and curranty nose that jumps from the glass. In the mouth, this is a supple, round, hedonistically styled Claret with copious quantities of palate-pleasing plushness, no hard edges, and an impressively endowed, rich finish. Some tannin is present, but it is well integrated. Anticipated maturity: now–2014. Last tasted, 4/02.

1994
86
Dark ruby, with the Bécots' lavishly oaked, toasty nose in addition to licorice and herbs, this medium-bodied wine reveals fine structure. While it is good and long-lived, it lacks charm and precociousness. Anticipated maturity: now–2012. Last tasted, 3/00.

1990
89
Fully mature, the 1990 has a dark ruby/plum/garnet color, a spicy, oaky, vanilla, herbaceous, and black cherry–scented nose, medium to full body, sweet tannin, and a surprisingly long, structured finish, with impressive glycerin as well as fruit. Anticipated maturity: now–2007. Last tasted, 11/01.

1989
87
Tasted side by side with the 1990, it is interesting how much more tannic the 1989 seems to be. Colored a dark plum with some lightening at the edge, the nose shows notes of compost, melted licorice, oak, and black cherry fruit. The overt oakiness noticeable in its youth has become far more subtle and less aggressive. In the mouth the wine starts off large-scaled, fleshy, and fat, but then some relatively astringent tannins kick in for the finish. This has been a perplexing wine to follow,

since it was seemingly softer and more opulent in its youth and now seems to be taking on a more structured, tannic personality as the baby fat falls away. In any event, the wine seems to be close to full maturity, but capable of lasting for another decade. Anticipated maturity: now–2013. Last tasted, 11/01.

1988   This wine has turned out better than I initially thought. The wine has reached full
87   maturity, with notes of licorice, dried herbs, and sweet red and black currants intermixed with some toast and earth. The aggressive tannins of its youth have melted away, yet the fruit has held. The wine is medium bodied, quite classic in its proportions, and dense. It is somewhat monolithic compared to more recent vintages, but it is a nice chunky, muscular style of St.-Emilion. Anticipated maturity: now–2009. Last tasted, 11/01.

1986   A bit angular and disjointed, with some relatively lean tannins pushing through
87   the wine's personality, this wine shows complex smoke, herb, black currant, loamy earth, and spice box notes in the attractive aromatics. In the mouth the attack starts well, but there is a certain attenuated, tannic feel in the finish. This wine might be just beginning to dry out, with the tannins becoming the dominant characteristic. Anticipated maturity: now–2005. Last tasted, 11/01.

1983   Fully mature and beginning to fade, the 1985 shows a garnet color with consider-
86   able amber at the edge. Notes of herbs, sweet currants, and spice box are there in this medium-bodied, low-acid, plump wine. As it sits in the glass, the wine fades badly. Anticipated maturity: Drink now. Last tasted, 11/01.

ANCIENT VINTAGES

Little of interest was produced in the early 1980s and 1970s, with my notes from the last edition of this book scoring all of the top vintages of the 1960s and 1970s between the low 60s and mid-70s . . . the wine actually was that mediocre. Of course, that has all changed, as this is now one of the most successful and consistent wines of St.-Emilion, clearly meriting its premier grand cru classé status.

BEAUSÉJOUR

Classification: Premier Grand Cru Classé B

Owner: Heirs Duffau-Lagarrosse

Address: 33330 St.-Emilion

Telephone: 05 57 24 71 61; Telefax: 05 57 74 48 40

Visits: By appointment only

Contact: Jean-Michel Dubos

VINEYARDS

Surface area: 16.8 acres

Grape varietals: 70% Merlot, 20% Cabernet Franc, 10% Cabernet Sauvignon

Average age of vines: 35–40 years

Density of plantation: 6,600 vines per hectare

Average yields: 35 hectoliters per hectare

Elevage: Prolonged fermentation and maceration (25–30 days) in temperature-controlled concrete vats. Twelve to sixteen months aging in barrels that are renewed by half at each vintage. Fining, no filtration.

WINES PRODUCED

Château Beauséjour: 25,000–30,000 bottles

Croix de Beauséjour: Variable

Plateau of maturity: Within 10–30 years of the vintage

GENERAL APPRECIATION

There is no question that Beauséjour remains one of the most complex, ethereal wines of St.-Emilion. The 1990 is immortal.

There are two Beauséjour estates in St.-Emilion. Both are located on the *côtes* of St.-Emilion. Both are among the crème de la crème of St.-Emilion's hierarchy—that of premier grands cru. However, the two wines could not be more different. First of all, Beau-Séjour Bécot relies on unbridled jammy fruit intertwined with tons of toasty new oak for much of its appeal. In contrast, Beauséjour, while also a dense, powerful wine, is much more reserved, austere, and more mineral-dominated. In short, Beauséjour leans more in the direction of Ausone.

Beauséjour is run by Jean-Michel Dubos. He has improved the quality significantly since the mid-1980s and has also introduced a second wine for lesser *cuvées*. As the tasting notes indicate, the 1990 Beauséjour is one of the most profound young red wines I have ever had the pleasure to taste. It is one of the legends of the 20th century.

The vineyard, adjacent to the tiny church of Saint-Martin, has been owned by the same family since the original vineyard was divided in 1869, resulting in the two St.-Emilion Beauséjours. It is planted in a mixture of calcareous clay and limestone soil. Dubos's decisions to harvest later and make a stricter selection have undoubtedly contributed to the wine's greater richness and stature over recent years. However, this is not a wine for those who are unable to defer their gratification, as Beauséjour normally requires a decade of cellaring before it begins to soften.

IMPORTANT VINTAGES

2001
90–91
A success for the vintage, this tiny vineyard kept yields to 31 hectoliters per hectare. The 2001 blend of 70% Merlot, 20% Cabernet Franc, and 10% Cabernet Sauvignon exhibits the telltale floral/blueberry liqueur characteristic found in great vintages of Beauséjour (particularly the 1990). The dense, rich, medium- to full-bodied 2001 reveals elevated but ripe tannin, exceptional purity, and admirable harmony. This wine "speaks" of *terroir,* and the vineyard is one of the greatest in St.-Emilion. Anticipated maturity: 2007–2020. Last tasted, 1/03.

2000
92
The most complete Beauséjour since the mythical 1990, the black/purple-colored 2000 exhibits a Port-like bouquet of blackberry liqueur, minerals, blueberries, camphor, and melted asphalt. Its spectacular texture and ripeness are reminiscent of the perfect 1990, but this effort is not as rich or super-concentrated as that wine. Nevertheless, the 2000 should merit significant interest. Pure, complex, and reasonably priced, it will be at its apogee between 2009–2025+. Last tasted, 1/03.

1999
86?
I enjoyed this wine in its prime, but it appears to have suffered at bottling as it now reveals astringent tannin, an austere, clipped personality, and an emaciated, hard style. There are hints of intriguing black fruits, but also too much tannin for the wine's weight. Last tasted, 3/02.

1998
89
This dark ruby/purple–colored, mid-weight, restrained, graceful effort reveals aromas and flavors of minerals, blueberries, and flowers, not dissimilar from some of Burgundy's grand cru Vosne-Romanées. Nicely textured, soft, with adequate tannin to frame its medium-bodied style, it is approachable, yet should age nicely for 10–12 years. Last tasted, 3/02.

1997
85
This 1997 has turned out to be significantly lighter than expected. Smoky new oak, minerals, and a plum/cherry fruit concoction provide a pretty, elegant, lighter-styled St.-Emilion exhibiting moderate tannin in the finish. There is good complexity, but little density or depth. Anticipated maturity: now–2008. Last tasted, 3/02.

1996
87?
The 1996 Beauséjour is dark ruby–colored, with the telltale attractive black raspberry, pronounced mineral characteristics this small vineyard produces. It was lighter and more angular than in cask tastings, with dry, astringent tannin in the moderately long finish. This wine is very good, but it is not outstanding as I had expected. Moreover, the 1996 Beauséjour will have a tendency to dry out given the way the tannin is behaving. Anticipated maturity: 2005–2015. Last tasted, 3/01.

1995
88+?
Exhibiting a saturated dark purple color and a sweet kirsch, black cherry, mineral, and truffle-like character not dissimilar from the old-vine intensity found in the great Pomerol, Lafleur, this wine remains very closed on the palate, with excruciatingly high tannin. Some earth, minerals, and black fruits emerge only after extended airing. In the mouth, the wine was completely shut down. Anticipated maturity: 2007–2022. Last tasted, 3/01.

1994
87?
This has been a perplexing wine to evaluate. The color is a murky, dark garnet/plum. The nose exhibits a sweet, old-vine essence of cherries and minerals, with some spice and earth in the background. Dense, as well as ferociously tannic and traditionally styled, the 1994 Beauséjour may dry out if the fruit fades more quickly than the tannin. It is not a wine for those seeking immediate gratification to buy. Anticipated maturity: 2004–2016. Last tasted, 1/97.

1990
100
One of the great modern-day legends in Bordeaux, this is a wine that may, in time, be considered among informed connoisseurs the way 1961 Latour à Pomerol is often looked at, a rarity from a property that seems to have produced the equivalent of a one-hit wonder. It is still dense purple, with an extraordinary nose of liquified minerals infused with licorice, violets, blackberry, blueberry, and currant. The wine is opulent, full-bodied, and seamless, with an extraordinary integration of acidity, tannin, and wood. Spectacularly complex, rich, and full with a finish that goes on for 45+ seconds, this is an incredible achievement that is hard to believe in view of what this property seems to produce routinely. Nevertheless, I have had this wine a good two dozen or more times, and it just never fails to provide compelling drinking. Anticipated maturity: 2007–2030+. Last tasted, 1/03.

1989
88
Dark ruby/garnet with some lightening at the edge, this wine shows notes of licorice, smoke, earth, plum, and black currants in a medium-bodied, soft, very evolved style. It is fully mature and best drunk over the next decade. Last tasted, 4/02.

1988
87
The 1988 has excellent depth and fullness, with a spicy, earthy, rich bouquet filled with aromas of licorice, plums, spices, new oak, and subtle herbs. Exceptionally concentrated, with sound acidity and moderate alcohol, this is a beautifully made, complex wine. Anticipated maturity: now–2012. Last tasted, 1/93.

1986　From both cask and bottle, the 1986 has never seemed to be anything more than a
83　　lightweight, shallowly constructed, one-dimensional wine, with a lot of wood and
　　　　tannin in the finish. Some fruit and charm has developed, but this is not one of the
　　　　leaders in 1986. Anticipated maturity: now–2012. Last tasted, 3/89.

1985　The 1985 did not exhibit as much depth as I would have expected. It is lightweight
84　　and medium bodied, with a good spicy fruitiness, soft texture, and pleasant length.
　　　　However, for its class, it is an uninspiring effort. Anticipated maturity: now–2005.
　　　　Last tasted, 3/89.

1983　This has turned out to be a good example of Beauséjour. Medium dark ruby/garnet,
86　　with considerable amber at the edge, the wine offers up a moderately intense bou-
　　　　quet of black fruits, smoke, licorice, and minerals. In the mouth, the wine is
　　　　medium bodied and has some firm tannins to shed, but there appears to be very
　　　　good extract. Fully mature, it should be drunk up. Anticipated maturity: now. Last
　　　　tasted, 5/00.

1982　The 1982 Beauséjour surprised me with its youthfulness and tannic ferocity.
89+?　There is excellent, possibly outstanding concentration behind the wine's tough
　　　　veneer. Still possessing a healthy dark ruby/purple color with only a hint of garnet
　　　　and lightening at the edge, the wine's nose offers provocative aromas of overripe
　　　　black fruits, minerals, and leather. Full-bodied and rich, but tannic and atypically
　　　　austere for a 1982, this is a difficult wine to fully grasp. Will the fruit continue to
　　　　hold with the tannin softening, thus meriting an even higher rating, or will the wine
　　　　remain forbiddingly tannic and backward without ever fully developing? I would
　　　　gamble on it becoming at least excellent, perhaps outstanding—it is just a ques-
　　　　tion of patience. Anticipated maturity: 2006–2020. Last tasted, 9/95.

ANCIENT VINTAGES

My notes on some of the more prominent vintages of the 1970s and 1960s have been
littered with mediocre to poor tasting notes. This is another example of a property that
has been making far better wines during the last two decades than it did previously.

BELAIR

Classification: Premier Grand Cru Classé B

Owner: Heirs of Hélyette Dubois-Challon

Address: 33330 St.-Emilion

Telephone: 05 57 24 70 94; Telefax: 05 57 24 67 11

Visits: By appointment only

Contact: Mme. Delbeck

VINEYARDS

Surface area: 30.9 acres

Grape varietals: 60% Merlot, 40% Cabernet Franc

Average age of vines: 30 years

Density of plantation: 6,600 vines per hectare

Average yields: 39 hectoliters per hectare

Elevage: Fermentations are stimulated with indigenous yeasts obtained by a biodynamic culture of part of the vineyards. Wines are aged 18–26 months in oak barrels, half of which are new (this varies according to the vintage). They are racked regularly, fined with fresh egg whites, and remain unfiltered. All transfers of the grapes and wine are done by gravity.

WINES PRODUCED

Château Belair: 50,000 bottles

No second wine is produced.

Plateau of maturity: Within 5–15 years of the vintage

GENERAL APPRECIATION

This has never been an exciting wine. Today Belair is the most disappointing of the premier grands cru classés. Consistently light and austere, yet elegant, delicately fruity, as well as structured, this is a classic, old-style St.-Emilion.

Belair had a great reputation in the 19th century, and its history can be traced back as far as the 14th. The late Bernard Ginestet, a leading French writer on the wines of Bordeaux, boldly calls Belair, "the Lafite Rothschild among the hillsides of St.-Emilion." Is that overstating the case? The tiny vineyard of Belair is owned by the Dubois-Challon family, who were the former co-proprietors of Ausone, Belair's next-door neighbor. The level of wine quality at Belair has little in common with Ausone. The same team that made Ausone (until the change in ownership in the mid-1990s), Pascal Delbeck is responsible for Belair, and as the tasting notes that follow demonstrate, it remains a tight, austere, reserved, and restrained style of wine. While part of the vineyard lies on the hillside, another part is squarely on the plateau. Could Belair be further improved? To Delbeck's credit, his rigid faithfulness to traditional winemaking is to be admired, but this wine seems lost in the modern world.

IMPORTANT VINTAGES

2000 Probably the best Belair of the last 10 or so years, this dark ruby effort has a tight
87   but promising nose of loamy soil scents intermixed with crushed stone, red currants, and sweet and sour cherries. The wine is medium bodied, relatively high in tannin, with an austere, somewhat attenuated finish. Anticipated maturity: 2007–2020. Last tasted, 1/03.

1999 This is a relatively light to medium bodied wine, with a medium ruby color already
84   showing some pink at the rim. Notes of earth, wood, compost, and cherry as well as currant fruit gradually emerge from this tightly knit, somewhat low-key, restrained, and austerely styled wine. Very much an old style/traditional interpretation of Bordeaux, the 1999 Belair should hit its prime by 2005 and, in large part, be consumed within 5–10 years thereafter. Last tasted, 1/03.

1998 Excruciatingly tannic, this dark plum–colored wine has notes of earth, mineral,
78   and a vague hint of cherries. Some dried herbs also make an appearance. In the mouth the wine is shallow, tannic, and, for my palate, unappealing. The tannins seem entirely disproportionately high for the amount of concentration and extract. No doubt its creator, Pascal Delbeck, would suggest that I had confused thinness with the purity of expression of Belair's *terroir.* Anticipated maturity: 2005–2013. Last tasted, 1/03.

1997   The 1997 Belair is atypically soft, forward, and appealing. A dark ruby color is fol-
85   lowed by aromas of sweet, mineral-infused, black cherry fruit, medium body, and
light tannin in the round, attractive finish. This wine should keep for 6–7 years.
Last tasted, 3/00.

1996   Tasted on three separate occasions, this wine did not perform nearly as well as it
83?   had in its prime. An angular, light-bodied, mineral-scented wine came across as
austere and spartan, lacking fruit, glycerin, and flesh. Perhaps I caught it in an
awkward stage? Anticipated maturity: now–2012. Last tasted, 3/98.

1995   This is a low-key Claret with red and black currants competing with distinctive
85   wet stone and mineral-like components. New oak is present in this medium-
bodied, hard, austere, yet extraordinarily subtle and restrained St.-Emilion. It
may be too polite for its own good. Anticipated maturity: now–2015. Last tasted,
11/97.

1994   This medium dark ruby–colored wine exhibits sweet, red currant and cherry fruit,
85   low-acid, light body, some of Belair's telltale earthiness, a spicy, tannic personality, and a compact finish. Anticipated maturity: now–2007. Last tasted, 1/97.

1993   Medium garnet–colored, with a musty, old barrel aroma, this wine is dominated by
76   a powdered stone character, green, vegetal fruit flavors, and a lean, light-bodied
palate. Last tasted, 1/97.

1992   The light, washed-out color and weak, muted nose is followed by a wine lacking
74?   fruit, depth, and grip. There is little finish in this shallow, diluted wine. Three
notes revealed similar results. Anticipated maturity: now–probably in decline.
Last tasted, 11/94.

1990   There is sweet, nearly overripe fruit, plenty of mineral/stony scents, and evidence
89   of new oak underlying this medium-weight wine's backward personality. The aromas of overripe cherries and prunes are attractive. Anticipated maturity:
now–2010. Last tasted, 1/93.

1989   The 1989 exhibits a huge, smoky, roasted, exotic bouquet of plums and Asian
88   spices. The wine exhibits surprisingly crisp acidity and plentiful but soft tannins.
The formidable level of alcohol and sensationally extracted, multidimensional
fruit flavors make this a brilliant effort. Anticipated maturity: now–2010. Last
tasted, 1/93.

1988   The 1988 is a good rather than exceptional effort. Given the vintage, no one should
85   be surprised that it is a leaner, more austere wine. But it does have a good inner
core of currantly fruit, fine tannins, and a general sense of elegance and grace. Anticipated maturity: now–2010. Last tasted, 4/91.

ANCIENT VINTAGES

This is not a wine that I purchase, hence my experiences are generally limited to one or
two tastings where I have been invited to see a horizontal of a particular vintage. The
1980s are dotted with largely mediocre wines, except for a beautiful 1983 (88 points;
last tasted 2/89) and 1982 (88 points; last tasted 12/96). In the 1970s the 1979 was
pleasant, but most of the other vintages were typically Belair-like in their austerity,
high tannins, and earthy, mineral-dominated personalities, with an absence of charm
and fruit.

BELLEFONT-BELCIER

Classification: Grand Cru

Owner: SC Bellefont-Belcier

Address: 33330 St.-Laurent-des-Combes

Telephone: 05 57 24 72 16; Telefax: 05 57 74 45 06

E-mail: bellefontbelcier@aol.com

Visits: By appointment only

Contact: Mark Dworkin

VINEYARDS

Surface area: 31.7 acres

Grape varietals: 60% Merlot, 30% Cabernet Franc, 10% Cabernet Sauvignon

Average age of vines: 30 years

Density of plantation: 5,500 vines per hectare

Average yields: 36 hectoliters per hectare

Elevage: Four to five week fermentation and maceration in temperature-controlled, concrete, epoxy-lined vats. Malolactics and 16–18 months aging in new oak barrels. Fining, no filtration.

WINES PRODUCED

Château Bellefont-Belcier: 52,000 bottles

Marquis de Bellefort: 12,000 bottles

Plateau of maturity: Within 5–15 years of the vintage for post-1998 wines; within 3–8 years of the vintage for older wines

GENERAL APPRECIATION

Bellefont-Belcier has improved recently under the helmsmanship of new owners.

This vineyard, well situated in the commune of St.-Laurent-des-Combes, not far from the outstanding *terroirs* of Le Tertre-Rôteboeuf and Larcis Ducasse, began to produce more interesting wine in the mid-1990s. The wine has historically been straightforward, soft, and easy to drink, lacking distinction and coming across as monolithic. However, the property began to harvest later, picking riper fruit, and has been more selective in what is being bottled under the château's name.

IMPORTANT VINTAGES

2001   Dark plum, this herbaceous, sweet currant tasting wine has a dark ruby color,
86–88   medium body, very good fruit, but a somewhat compact finish. Anticipated maturity: 2005–2013. Last tasted, 1/03.

2000   Sweet, jammy black cherry fruit is accompanied by notes of cedar, licorice, and
90   spice box in this dense ruby/purple–colored offering. Medium to full-bodied, with a sweet attack as well as excellent concentration and symmetry, it will be drinkable between 2006–2016. Last tasted, 1/03.

1999 After multiple tastings from barrel, I thought this wine was going to be an upper-
87? 80, possibly 90-point wine. I have only seen it twice from bottle. The wine reveals
elegant, sweet cherry fruit, licorice, dried herb, and leather aromas. It is medium
bodied, well made, and spicy, but lacking depth, texture, and completeness. Drink
it over the next eight years. Last tasted, 3/02.

1998 A very good effort from Bellefont-Belcier, the 1998 reveals abundant quantities of
87 spice box, smoky new oak, cedar, black cherries, leather, and herbs, presented in
a medium-bodied, fleshy style with sweet tannin as well as good definition. Anticipated maturity: now–2010. Last tasted, 3/02.

1997 The 1997 has turned out far better than expected from barrel tastings. Open-knit,
84 easy to taste and understand, it possesses adequate acidity, some tannin, and a
medium-bodied, spicy, cherry-scented nose, adequate flavor concentration, and a
touch of toasty new oak. Lightweight yet pleasant, it can be enjoyed over the next
2–3 years. Last tasted, 3/01.

1996 The excellent 1996 is a potential sleeper of the vintage. The wine offers a dark
87 ruby color and sweet black cherry fruit intermixed with smoke, dried herbs, and
toast. This round, generous, medium- to full-bodied wine is already delicious;
enjoy it over the next 4–5 years. Last tasted, 3/01.

1995 The dark ruby/plum–colored 1995 is somewhat of a sleeper, exhibiting a dense
88 color and rich, jammy black fruits intermingled with scents of herb, licorice, and
toast. Thick, chewy flavors reveal fine extraction and glycerin. This is a soft, low-
acid, opulent wine. Anticipated maturity: now–2009. Last tasted, 11/01.

ANCIENT VINTAGES

Very little of merit was produced in the early 1990s and decade of the 1980s.

BELLEVUE

Classification: Grand Cru Classé

Owner: Pradel de Lavaud and Coninck families

Administrator: Nicolas Thienpont

Address: 33330 St.-Emilion

Telephone: 05 57 51 76 17; Telefax: 05 57 51 59 61

Visits: By appointment only

Contact: Nicolas Thienpont (Telephone: 05 57 24 74 23)

VINEYARDS

Surface area: 15.4 acres

Grape varietals: 80% Merlot, 20% Cabernet Franc

Average age of vines: 40 years

Density of plantation: 7,500 vines per hectare

Average yields: 30 hectoliters per hectare

Elevage: Four to six week fermentation and maceration in temperature-controlled
concrete vats with micro-oxygenation. Malolactics and 18 months aging in barrels with
60% new oak. No fining, no filtration.

WINES PRODUCED

Château Bellevue: 18,000 bottles

Plateau of maturity: Too soon to predict, but the 2000 should evolve for 15–20 years.

GENERAL APPRECIATION

Given the superb location of this vineyard and the talented team behind the winemaking, Bellevue will merit significant interest.

This is a classic newcomer to the exciting appellation of St.-Emilion. Made from a 15-acre, south and southeast-facing vineyard planted on limestone, with such highly prized neighbors as Beau-Séjour Bécot, Beauséjour-Duffau, and Angélus, Bellevue is the result of the combined talents of Nicolas Thienpont (Pavie Macquin) and Stéphane Derénoncourt, one of the superstar wine consultants of Pomerol and St.-Emilion.

IMPORTANT VINTAGES

2001 The 2001 Bellevue is a slightly lighter rendition of the prodigious debut vintage of
90–92 2000. It exhibits a deep ruby/purple color and sweet, pure, black cherry and berry fruit intermixed with minerals, smoke, and licorice. The attack is ripe and concentrated, the palate medium to full-bodied, with impressive purity as well as texture. An impressive successor to the 2000. Anticipated maturity: 2006–2015. Last tasted, 1/03.

2000 A blend of 80% Merlot and 20% Cabernet Franc from low yields of 30 hectoliters
95 per hectare, this wine boasts an opaque inky purple color as well as a glorious perfume of blackberries and blueberries underlaid with a striking minerality, full body, high tannin, abundant glycerin, concentration, muscle, and a 40-second finish. Will it shut down? I kept a bottle open for eight days without any oxidation. A tour de force! Anticipated maturity: 2005–2020. Last tasted, 1/03.

ANCIENT VINTAGES

Prior to 2000, I had never seen a bottle of Bellevue. Apparently the wine was undistinguished, yet the quality of the *terroir* was recognized as exciting for more than a century, with a reference in 1867 to Bellevue winning a gold medal at a wine fair in Paris.

BELLISLE MONDOTTE

Classification: Grand Cru

Owner: GFA Héritirs Escure

Address: 33330 St.-Laurent-des-Combes

Mailing address: 103, Grand Pey, 33330 Saint-Sulpice-de-Faleyrens

Telephone: 05 57 74 41 17 or 05 57 51 20 47; Telefax: 05 57 51 23 14

Visits: By appointment only Monday to Friday, 9 A.M.–noon and 2–5 P.M.

Contact: Jean-Marie Bouldy

VINEYARDS

Surface area: 11.1 acres

Grape varietals: 80% Merlot, 20% Cabernet Franc

Average age of vines: 30 years

Density of plantation: 5,500 vines per hectare

Average yields: 40 hectoliters per hectare

Elevage: Twenty-one to thirty day fermentation in temperature-controlled concrete vats. Eighteen months aging in barrels that are renewed by half at each vintage. No fining, filtration.

WINES PRODUCED

Château Bellisle Mondotte: 20,000 bottles

No second wine is produced.

Plateau of maturity: Within 5–15 years of the vintage

GENERAL APPRECIATION

A newcomer to the St.-Emilion ranks of high-quality wines, this estate is well situated near La Mondotte and Le Tertre-Rôteboeuf. The 1999 was the qualitative breakthrough.

IMPORTANT VINTAGES

2001
88–91
From an estate on the upswing, the 2001 has a dense ruby color and sweet blackberry and cassis flavors wrapped in a toasty, full-bodied style. Both elegant and powerful, the 2001 may come close to rivaling the 2000. Anticipated maturity: 2005–2016. Last tasted, 1/03.

2000
90+
The impressive 2000 is undoubtedly a sleeper of the vintage. It offers an opaque purple color along with copious quantities of sweet crème de cassis notes intermixed with coffee, smoke, earth, and mocha. Full-bodied and intense, with low acidity, a layered texture, sweet tannin, and a 35-second finish, it will drink beautifully between 2005–2017. Last tasted, 1/03.

1999
88
Excellent sweet mulberry, blackberry, and flowery notes with subtle oak in the background jump from the glass of this medium- to full-bodied, lusty, plump, dark ruby–colored St.-Emilion. Although it is big on flavor and fruit, it lacks complexity. Consume it over the next eight years. Last tasted, 3/02.

1998
82
Oaky and somewhat superficial, the dark ruby–colored 1998 has high tannin and a medium-bodied personality. More recent vintages are much more impressive. Anticipated maturity: 2005–2010. Last tasted, 3/02.

1997
85
This is a soundly made, richly fruity wine with good glycerin, low acidity, and fine purity of fruit. It is a candidate for another 1–2 years of drinkability. Anticipated maturity: now–2005. Last tasted, 3/02.

BERLIQUET

Classification: Grand Cru Classé
Owner: Vicomte Patrick de Lasquen
Administrators: Patrick and Jerôme de Lesquen
Address: 33330 St.-Emilion
Telephone: 05 57 24 70 48; Telefax: 05 57 24 70 24
Visits: By appointment only
Contact: Patrick de Lesquen or Patrick Valette
(consulting oenologist)

VINEYARDS

Surface area: 22.2 acres

Grape varietals: 70% Merlot, 25% Cabernet Franc, 5% Cabernet Sauvignon

Average age of vines: 38 years

Density of plantation: 5,500 vines per hectare

Average yields: 35 hectoliters per hectare

Elevage: Twenty to thirty day fermentation and maceration in temperature-controlled stainless-steel tanks of small capacity that allow the separate vinification of the different parcels and grape varieties. Malolactics and 14–16 months aging in new oak barrels. No fining, no filtration.

WINES PRODUCED

Château Berliquet: 28,000 bottles

Ailes de Berliquet: 5,000–7,000 bottles

Plateau of maturity: Within 3–14 years of the vintage

GENERAL APPRECIATION

The once insipid wines of Berliquet have improved since Patrick de Lesquen has taken charge of the estate, with Patrick Valette supervising the vinifications. It is slowly but surely climbing the echelons of the St.-Emilion qualitative hierarchy.

This is a beautifully situated property with splendid underground caves and a superb exposition just outside the village of St.-Emilion. In fact, one could not ask for a better position on the limestone plateau of St.-Emilion, adjoining Canon, Magdelaine, and Tertre Daugay. In 1985 Berliquet became the only château to be promoted to a grand cru classé. Its fame, however, must have been far greater in the 18th century: In 1794 a well-known Libourne courtier wrote about the excellent quality of a wine in St.-Emilion called Berliquet.

Berliquet was content to stay in the background, as all of its wine, until the 1978 vintage, which was made and produced by the huge cooperative in St.-Emilion. Until 1997 the staff at the cooperative supervised the production of Berliquet. In 1997 Patrick Valette was hired to oversee the winemaking, and the results since have been laudatory.

IMPORTANT VINTAGES

2001
87–89
Attractive sweet black cherry and currant fruit intermixed with foresty under brush, spice, and wood notes are present in Berliquet's moderately intense aromatics. The attack is sweet, but the wine quickly closes down, revealing medium body, ripe tannin, and a moderately long finish. Given the way this St.-Emilion has aged in barrel, more flesh, mid-palate, and texture should emerge. Anticipated maturity: 2006–2016. Last tasted, 1/03.

2000
90
The 2000, the finest Berliquet yet produced, exhibits an impressive saturated ruby/purple color as well as jammy cherry and cassis aromas, medium to full body, sweet tannin, a multitiered mid-palate, and a long finish. An elegant wine, it is a sleeper of the vintage. Anticipated maturity: 2006–2020. Last tasted, 1/03.

1999
88
Excellent sweet-and-sour cherry notes intermix with spicy new oak and leather in this medium-bodied, richly fruity, deep ruby/purple–colored 1999. Long, ripe, and attractive, it will drink well between now and 2013. Last tasted, 3/02.

1998
89
Along with the 2000, the 1998 is one of the finest Berliquets I have tasted to date. This dark ruby/purple–colored offering exhibits dense, saturated, flavorful black cherry notes intermixed with licorice, spice box, tobacco, and earth. Full-bodied, ripe, and concentrated, with moderate tannin and a closed but impressively built personality, this wine needs several years to resolve all of its tannin. Anticipated maturity: 2004–2016. Last tasted, 3/02.

1997
88
An excellent example of the vintage, the 1997 Berliquet exhibits abundant amounts of sweet black currant fruit, along with cedar, spice box, and toasty aromas. Medium to full-bodied, thick, and rich, with moderate tannin, fine sweetness, an open-knit texture, and admirable length, it will be at its best between now and 2012. Last tasted, 3/01.

1996
78
This is an angular, tough-textured, tannic wine with insufficient fruit to balance out the wine's muscle and structure. It is likely to dry out over its 10–15 year evolution. Last tasted, 11/97.

1995
75
Medium deep ruby–colored, with an earthy, tarry, spicy nose that dominates the wine's meager fruit, this wine is compressed and pinched, with an angular austerity and a lean, tannic, astringent finish. I do not see this wine ever coming around. Anticipated maturity: now–2010 Last tasted, 11/97.

1990
86
A soft, savory, herb- and cherry-scented wine with attractive earth and spice in the background, this medium-bodied, lush, fully mature St.-Emilion offers a plump feel on the palate. It should drink well for 5–6 years. Anticipated maturity: now–2003. Last tasted, 11/97.

1989
79
Fully mature, this garnet-colored wine has a spicy, earthy, berry-scented bouquet, with a distinctive herbaceous overtone. Medium bodied, with good acidity, tannin, and grip, it lacks the concentration and depth of the best wines of 1989. Still, it possesses some moderately astringent tannins. Anticipated maturity: now–2008. Last tasted, 12/02.

CADET-PIOLA

Classification: Grand Cru Classé

Owner: GFA Jabiol

Address: 33330 St.-Emilion

Mailing address: BP 24, 33330 St.-Emilion

Telephone: 05 57 74 47 69; Telefax: 05 57 24 68 28

E-mail: infos@chateaucadetpiola.com

Website: www.chateaucadetpiola.com

Visits: Monday to Friday, 9 A.M.–noon and 2–5 P.M.

Contact: Amélie Jabiol

VINEYARDS

Surface area: 17.3 acres

Grape varietals: 51% Merlot, 28% Cabernet Sauvignon, 18% Cabernet Franc, 3% Malbec

Average age of vines: 35 years

Density of plantation: 5,500 vines per hectare

Average yields: 34 hectoliters per hectare

Elevage: Twenty-one to twenty-five day fermentation and maceration in temperature-controlled concrete tanks. Fifteen to eighteen months aging in barrels with 40% new oak. Fining, no filtration.

WINES PRODUCED

Château Cadet-Piola: 32,000 bottles

Chevaliers de Malte: Production variable and not systematic at each vintage

Plateau of maturity: Within 6–15 years of the vintage

GENERAL APPRECIATION

A classical, unpretentious St.-Emilion, Cadet-Piola is consistently soundly made.

It must be the small production of Cadet-Piola that has kept this wine's quality relatively secret for so long a time. Cadet-Piola, which is neither a *côtes* St.-Emilion nor a *graves* St.-Emilion, is just one-half kilometer north of the town. The château—with a splendid view overlooking St.-Emilion—is located on a rocky outcropping with a clay and limestone base; it is used only for making wine and not as a residence. The proprietors claim the microclimate is warmer than elsewhere in the appellation.

The owners, the Jabiol family (who are also the proprietors of the St.-Emilion estate of Faurie de Souchard), are conservative wine-makers who produce a black/ruby-colored, rich and intense, full-bodied wine that over the last decade has outperformed many of the more famous and more expensive premier grands crus. Cadet-Piola is a solid value, and hopefully consumer demand will result in more of this estate's wine being imported to America.

IMPORTANT VINTAGES

2001
86–87
Seemingly less astringently tannic and rustic, the 2001 Cadet-Piola has a deep ruby color and a sweet nose of licorice, earth, and red as well as black currants. The wine shows sweetness on the attack, a soft underbelly, and good ripeness as well as medium body. It should drink well for 8–10 years. Last tasted, 1/03.

2000
86
Excellent currant, earthy, herb-tinged leather and black cherry fruit emerge from this medium-bodied, fleshy, yet somewhat rustic effort. Possessing sweeter tannin than generally found in Cadet-Piola, it should drink well for a decade. Last tasted, 1/03.

1996
83
Herbaceous notes intermixed with compost and a striking vegetal character make for a wine that seems to lack ripeness. In the mouth it is medium-bodied, with hard tannin and a somewhat attenuated, charmless finish. Anticipated maturity: now–2007. Last tasted, 3/01.

1995
85
Dark ruby, but relatively closed, aromatically this chunky, medium-bodied wine is muscular, dense, but tough and tannic. It is a typical Cadet-Piola, meant for evolving over a 10–15 year period. Anticipated maturity: 2005–2012. Last tasted, 3/01.

1990
87
This wine is just beginning to come around after a long closed period where it was forbiddingly backward and nearly impenetrable. The still saturated, dense ruby/purple color is showing only a bit of lightening at the edge. The nose offers up notes of melted licorice, dried herbs, black currants, and mineral. In the mouth it is medium bodied and relatively expansive for this particular estate, with some nice sweetness from glycerin and rich fruit. The wine is medium bodied and still slightly tannic, but it is hitting its plateau of full maturity. Anticipated maturity: now–2010. Last tasted, 11/01.

1989
87
A very successful effort for Cadet-Piola, the 1989 has a saturated plum/ruby color and an earthy, sweet berry and cherry nose with some licorice and mineral. The wine is medium bodied, spicy, and close to full drinkability. Anticipated maturity: 2004–2012. Last tasted, 12/99.

1988
86
The 1988 Cadet-Piola possesses excruciatingly high tannin levels, but the big, rich, black cherry flavors intertwined with new oak, scents of chocolate, and Provençal herbs gives me some basis for saying that the wine has the requisite depth to stand up to the tannin. A medium- to full-bodied wine, it should age well for up to two decades. Anticipated maturity: now–2010. Last tasted, 1/93.

1986
85?
The 1986 is an exceptionally backward, tannic, black-colored St.-Emilion. In fact, I was a bit worried about the level of tannin, except for the gobs of rich, long, chewy fruit one can easily sense when tasting. The only question that remains is, when will enough of the excruciatingly high tannin content fall away to make this wine round and seductive? Will the fruit hold? Anticipated maturity: now–2010. Last tasted, 11/90.

ANCIENT VINTAGES

Consistently, I have had very good success with Cadet-Piola's 1982 (88 points; last tasted 12/02). The wine is a bit chunky but very concentrated, with notes of black fruits, herbs, mineral, and creosote. I am not sure it will ever resolve all its tannin, but the wine is muscular, fleshy, and quite full-bodied. I would still opt for drinking over the next 5–7 years.

CANON

Classification: Premier Grand Cru Classé B

Owner: SC Château Canon

Administrator: John Kolasa

Address: 33330 St.-Emilion

Mailing address: BP 22-33330 St.-Emilion

Telephone: 05 57 55 23 45; Telefax: 05 57 24 68 00

E-mail: chateau-canon@wanadoo.fr

Visits: By appointment only Monday to Friday,
9 A.M.–noon and 2–5 P.M.

Contact: Béatrice Amadieu

VINEYARDS

Surface area: 35.8 acres in production (53.1 acres in all)

Grape varietals: 75% Merlot, 25% Cabernet Franc

Average age of vines: 35 years

Density of plantation: 5,500 and 6,500 vines per hectare

Average yields: 30–35 hectoliters per hectare

Elevage: Prolonged fermentation and 18 to 23 day maceration in temperature-controlled oak vats. Eighteen to twenty months aging in barrels, with 60% new oak, with one racking every three months. Fining, no filtration.

WINES PRODUCED

Château Canon: 30,000 bottles

Clos Canon: 30,000 bottles

Plateau of maturity: Within 5–15 years of the vintage for vintages of the 1990s

GENERAL APPRECIATION

This estate had to overcome the problems of the early 1990s (i.e., tainted wines with musty aromas and flavors), but I remain convinced it will rebound given the investments made by the new owners and the considerable job done by the management team. Recent vintages have hardly been inspirational.

One of the *côtes* St.-Emilions, Canon has a splendid location on the southwestern slopes of the town of St.-Emilion, where its vineyard is sandwiched between premier grands cru classés vineyards such as Belair, Magdelaine, Clos Fourtet, and Beauséjour. This vineyard, which lies partly on the hillside and partly on the plateau, has several different soil types, ranging from limestone and clay to sandy soils on a limestone base.

Canon, the property of the Fournier family since 1919, was sold in the mid-1990s to the firm of Chanel. The name, however, comes from the 18th-century owner, Jacques Kanon. A very traditional, long, hot fermentation in oak vats suggests that the property pays little heed to consumers who want to drink supple Bordeaux wines. This is a tannic, powerful wine, built to last and last. It is marked by a pronounced oakiness that can, in lighter vintages, obliterate the fruit. This overzealous, yet expensive use of new oak (a minimum of 60% is used in every vintage) is my only criticism of Canon. I adore this wine in vintages such as 1989, 1985, and 1982. In the 1980s, under the leadership of Eric Fournier and his brilliant *maître de chai*, Paul Cazenove, Canon has attained a quality that has often equaled, sometimes even surpassed, that of the St.-Emilion super-growths Cheval Blanc and Ausone, but a miserable record of performances following the excellent 1990 led to a lack of confidence in Canon. This was further exacerbated by a contamination in the aging cellars that caused many of the wines produced between 1992 and 1996 to smell and taste excessively musty. The new proprietors immediately renovated the old *chai*, thankfully eliminating the cause of the off-putting smells.

At its best, Canon is a splendidly rich, deep, and concentrated wine, muscular and full-bodied and, when mature, richly fruity, cedary, and often magnificent. It remains a mystery why this wine is not better known, because Canon has certainly been one of the top three or four St.-Emilions during the decade of the 1980s. While it has not regained its reputation, the new ownership has lofty ambitions, and the future looks encouraging.

IMPORTANT VINTAGES

2001
89–91 A closed, firm, mineral-laden effort, this medium-bodied, concentrated, backward St.-Emilion possesses a dense ruby/purple color as well as a sweet nose of black fruits and liquified stone aromas. It has excellent texture and considerable persistence. This may ultimately turn out to be as good as the 2000. Anticipated maturity: 2008–2020. Last tasted, 1/03.

2000
89 Canon's 2000 has put on additional weight during its *élevage*. The tannin is sweeter and the mid-palate is more expansive . . . all positive signs. Long in the mouth and muted aromatically, it reveals notes of strawberry jam intermixed with black cherries, minerals, oak, and herbs. An attractive, medium-bodied effort with outstanding ripeness, length, and balance, it is not a blockbuster, but it is intense, well delineated, and very pure. Anticipated maturity: 2008–2020. Last tasted, 1/03.

1999
87 Revealing deeper, richer fruit than during its *élevage*, this is an elegant, structured, mineral, coffee, and red fruit–scented and flavored 1999. Drying tannin in the finish may become worrisome after a decade of aging. Nevertheless, there is plenty of up-front, sweet fruit, good spice, and the undeniable liquid minerality so much a part of this vineyard's *terroir*. Anticipated maturity: now–2013. Last tasted, 3/02.

1998
88 Made in an elegant, restrained, subtle but interesting style, the dark ruby–colored 1998 Canon offers a sweet nose of crushed stones intertwined with flowers, red and black fruits, and moderate tannin. An attractive, charming, mid-weight effort, it will be at its finest before 2015. Last tasted, 3/02.

1997
82 This is a pleasant, delicate, medium ruby–colored wine with emaciated, underwhelming dried herb and sweet cherry fruit notes. Drink this medium-bodied effort over the next 2–3 years. Last tasted, 3/01.

1996
80 The 1996 Canon is a lean, austere, delicate wine with a dark ruby color and medium body, but little intensity or length. Angular and compressed, it is likely to dry out over the next 4–5 years. Anticipated maturity: now–2015. Last tasted, 3/01.

1995 I could not find any redeeming qualities in this sinewy, thin, austere, high-acid,
74 ferociously tannic wine. As hard as I tried, I could not see any positive side to the
manner in which this wine is going to develop. Anticipated maturity: now–2008.
Last tasted, 11/97.

1990 For the vintage and for the potential of this vineyard, Canon's 1990 is very good
87 but underperforms. The color is a dark plum/ruby with some pink at the rim. A
sweet nose of cherry/raspberry fruit intermixed with some earth, cocoa, and wood
notes is followed by a medium-bodied effort that shows moderately tight tannin,
some nice sweetness up front, but a slightly narrow, rather austere finish. The wine
is close to maturity but needs more time. Anticipated maturity: 2005–2016. Last
tasted, 10/02.

1989 A beautiful wine, and probably the last great Canon until the new administration
91 gets its act completely together, this wine still has a deep ruby/garnet color, with
some lightening at the edge. A knockout nose of sweet black fruits (primarily currants) intermixed with a bit of cherry, vanilla, and an almost roasted note is enticing and persistent. Full-bodied, moderately tannic, with excellent extraction,
flavor, expansiveness, and texture, this is a pure, impressively endowed Canon.
Anticipated maturity: now–2015. Last tasted, 10/02.

1988 This is a rather clipped, austere style of Canon, but the color remains a nicely sat-
87 urated ruby/garnet. The wine shows a distinct earthy, compost-like character
along with plum and currant fruit. Slightly austere, with moderate tannin, this is a
rather classic, mineral-laden style of Canon that should continue to age well for
another decade. Anticipated maturity: now–2012. Last tasted, 10/02.

1986 This wine is still bound up by its high tannin content. It reveals a dark garnet/ruby
89 color with no amber at the edge. The nose primarily offers minerals, earth, and
smoke, with black plum and cassis fruit in the background. On the attack, the
wine is rich, medium bodied, and elegant, with lofty tannin in the finish. Although
approachable, it remains youthful and vibrant. Anticipated maturity: now–2015.
Last tasted, 12/97.

1985 Just approaching full maturity, this St.-Emilion offers a delicious combination of
89 aromatics and flavors, including kirsch, cherries, minerals, and smoky oak, as
well as a soft, medium-bodied, lush, mellow, and nicely textured palate. This
charming, rich, stylish wine is now at its plateau of maturity. Anticipated maturity:
now–2007. Last tasted, 12/97.

1983 The 1983 Canon has reached full maturity. The wine's dark garnet/ruby color
88 reveals some rust/amber at the edge. The nose is forthcoming, with scents of
leather, earth, spice, sweet plums, and fruitcake. In the mouth, the wine possesses
good richness, heady alcoholic clout, low acidity, and rustic tannin in the finish.
This wine has matured quickly, but should hold (if stored in a cool cellar) for another 10–12 years. Last tasted, 12/97.

1982 A consistently spectacular 1982, this wine provided sumptuous drinking for the
94 first 5–6 years after bottling. Since the late 1980s the wine has become more structured without losing any of its power, fat, or concentration. It is capable of lasting
at least another decade, although I will not quibble with any readers who can no
longer defer their gratification. The dense color reveals no amber. Young, primary
aromas of black fruits, toasty oak, crushed stones, and flowers dominate the wine's
moderately intense nose. Thick, rich, full-bodied, and multidimensional, this is
unquestionably the most concentrated Canon I have ever tasted. This large-
scaled, superrich, sweet wine is one of the rare Canons that possesses more depth
of fruit than tannin. Drink it over the next 10–15 years. Anticipated maturity:
now–2018. Last tasted, 12/02.

ANCIENT VINTAGES

Canon had a very unimpressive decade in the 1970s, with most wines scoring between the upper 60s and mid-80s. In the 1960s, two excellent but hardly inspiring efforts, the 1964 (88 points; last tasted 4/91) and the 1961 (88 points; last tasted 11/95), are the stars. Due to the fact that the 1959 (95 points; last tasted 10/94) was undoubtedly made from relatively young vines (the 1956 freeze caused a significant loss of vines at Canon), this bottle performed spectacularly. The sweet, chocolaty, jammy, black cherry–scented nose and opaque garnet color revealed few signs of age. The wine exhibited an underlying herbaceous quality (young vines?), but its superb richness and chewy, viscous, thick flavors were sensational. There is enough richness and tannin for the wine to evolve for another 15–20 years. It is a magnificent example of Canon!

CANON-LA-GAFFELIÈRE

Classification: Grand Cru Classé

Owner: Comtes von Neipperg

Address: 33330 St.-Emilion

Mailing address: SCEV Vignobles Comtes de Neipperg, BP 34, 33330 St.-Emilion

Telephone: 05 57 24 71 33; Telefax: 05 57 24 67 95

E-mail: vignobles.von.neipperg@wanadoo.fr

Website: www.neipperg.com

Visits: By appointment only Monday to Friday, 9 A.M.–noon and 2–5 P.M.

Contact: Dominique Duluc

VINEYARDS

Surface area: 48.2 acres

Grape varietals: 55% Merlot, 40% Cabernet Franc, 5% Cabernet Sauvignon

Average age of vines: 40 years

Density of plantation: 5,500 vines per hectare

Average yields: 35–40 hectoliters per hectare

Elevage: Eighteen to twenty-six day fermentation and maceration in temperature-controlled wooden vats, with *pigéages*. Malolactics in barrel for 90–100% of yield. Fourteen to eighteen months aging on less in new oak barrels. No fining, no filtration.

WINES PRODUCED

Château Canon-la-Gaffelière: 50,000–60,000 bottles

Côte Migon la Gaffelière: 4,000–20,000 bottles (depending upon the vintage)

Plateau of maturity: Within 5–20 years of the vintage

GENERAL APPRECIATION

This is another superb St.-Emilion estate run with considerable passion, vision, and commitment to quality by Stephan von Neipperg. Since 1988, this has been one of St.-

Emilion's star performers, thanks to the tremendous efforts of its owner. No expense is spared to make the best possible wines, and Canon-la-Gaffelière benefits from its proprietor's uncompromising aim for excellence. One of the shining stars of St.-Emilion, if not of Bordeaux, Canon-la-Gaffelière has been an example for many. This sumptuous wine is still reasonably priced in view of its quality.

Another of the *côtes* St.-Emilions, Canon-la-Gaffelière vineyards are on flat, sandy soil at the foot of the hills. For more than two decades, Canon-la-Gaffelière was widely promoted, offering light, bland, mediocre wines at surprisingly high prices. That has changed dramatically since the young, brilliant Stephan von Neipperg assumed responsibility in 1983. In fact, few wines in Bordeaux have exhibited greater improvement than Canon-la-Gaffelière.

Changes that have led to the recent successes at this property include late harvesting to insure maximum maturity of the grapes, the introduction of a second wine for weaker vats, malolactic in barrel, micro-oxygenation, tiny yields, aging on its lees, and bottling after 14–16 months in 100% new oak with neither fining nor filtration. The results of all these changes are some of the most opulent and flattering wines of St.-Emilion. This is clearly one of the stars of the appellation, as vintages since the late 1980s so admirably attest.

IMPORTANT VINTAGES

2001 A brilliant effort for the vintage, this saturated purple-colored 2001 exhibits a
91–93 sweet nose of roasted nuts, blackberries, crème de cassis, licorice, smoke, and graphite. Medium to full-bodied, layered, and well textured, with sweet tannin, low acidity, and a 35-second finish, this impressive, precocious St.-Emilion should drink well young and evolve for 14–15 years. Last tasted, 1/03.

2000 Formidable notes of roasted espresso, melted chocolate, crème de cassis, toasty
95 new oak, and Asian spices jump from the glass of this sensationally perfumed, flamboyant 2000. It is enormously concentrated and pure, with low acidity and exquisite balance. Remarkably, in spite of its large size, viscosity, and opulence, it is fresh and delineated. Potentially the finest Canon-la-Gaffelière made to date, this classic will drink well between 2006–2022. Last tasted, 1/03.

1999 A strong effort for this vintage, Canon-la-Gaffelière's opaque purple–colored 1999
92 displays a sweet nose of toast, smoke, meats, graphite, blackberry, and cassis. Full-bodied, deep, powerful, and rich, with sweet tannin and low acidity, this is a blockbuster effort for a delicate vintage such as 1999. Anticipated maturity: now–2016. Last tasted, 12/02.

1998 This saturated purple-colored 1998 offers sumptuous aromas of prunes, blueber-
93 ries, overripe black cherries, chocolate, coffee, and spicy new oak. Full-bodied, opulent, and expressive, this flamboyant/ostentatious effort is crammed with glycerin and extract. The tannin is sweet in this accessible, multilayered 1998. Anticipated maturity: 2004–2022. Last tasted, 12/02.

1997 One of the most exotic, thick, rich wines of the vintage (as well as one of its few
90 stars), this 1997 reveals a dense plum/purple color in addition to sumptuous aromatics of vanilla, licorice, Asian spices, roasted coffee, and jammy black cherry and berry fruit. Medium to full-bodied, with silky tannin and low acidity, this thick, seamless, exotic St.-Emilion should drink well for 10–12 years. It is one of the vintage's most impressive efforts. Last tasted, 3/02.

1996　This is one of St.-Emilion's most impressively constituted and expressive wines.
90　From its saturated purple color to its soaring aromatics (toast, jammy black fruits, chocolate, roasted coffee, and smoke), this full-bodied, meaty, chewy, powerful wine is loaded with extract and sweet tannin for the vintage, and it possesses a layered, multidimensional finish. It should continue to improve for 4–5 years and drink well for 12–15 years. Anticipated maturity: 2007–2020. Last tasted, 3/02.

1995　A massive wine, with a cigar box, chocolaty, thick, black currant, and cherry-
91+　scented nose, this full-bodied wine is crammed with layers of fruit, extract, glycerin, and alcohol. Spicy yet rich with high tannin, the 1995 Canon-la-Gaffelière still needs some cellaring. The finish is long and rich, and the tannin sweet rather than astringent. Anticipated maturity: 2004–2020. Last tasted, 3/02.

1994　A dense purple color is accompanied by strikingly pure aromas of Provençal
90　olives, jammy cassis, and smoky toasty notes. Ripe and fat, this medium- to full-bodied, moderately tannic, muscular yet elegant wine should keep for 10–12 years. It is an impressive, well-balanced 1994. Last tasted, 1/97.

1993　This 1993's saturated dark purple color is among the most impressive of the vin-
87　tage. Aromatically the wine offers copious amounts of dark, earthy, plummy, licorice, smoke-tinged, rich fruit, a sweet, surprisingly ripe, glycerin-imbued entry, and medium to full body. With low-acid, and the fruit and texture concealing the wine's light tannin, this appealing, attractive effort should drink well for another 5–7 years. Moreover, it is a reasonable value from what is largely a forgotten vintage. Last tasted, 1/97.

1990　One of the brilliant wines from Canon-la-Gaffelière, the 1990 still has a dense
93　ruby/purple color. The flamboyant aromatics offer up sweet toasty notes intermixed with fruitcake, cedar, crème de cassis, and roasted Provençal herbs . . . an olfactory overload for sure. Full-bodied, with a tremendous opulence, and even an unctuosity, this thick, juicy, very succulent, low-acid Canon-la-Gaffelière hides some elevated tannins because of the incredible wealth of glycerin and fruit. A terrific wine that is just hitting its plateau of drinkability. Anticipated maturity: now–2013. Last tasted, 10/02.

1989　Fully mature, with considerable amber to its dark garnet color, this exotic, some-
90　what over-the-top style of wine shows lavishly wooded notes intermixed with tapenade, Asian spice, and sweet currant and plum-like fruit. Medium to full-bodied, very supple, without quite the level of concentrated and layered texture of the 1990, this is a wine to drink now and over the next 7–8 years. Last tasted, 10/02.

1988　A very strong effort and the first of a marvelous trilogy of wines from Canon-la-
90　Gaffelière, this dark plum/ruby–colored wine has a terrifically perfumed nose of smoked meats, jammy cherries and black currants, toast, roasted Provençal herbs, coffee, and a hint of chocolate. The wine is full-bodied, very rich and concentrated, with a bit more density and structure than the 1989. It is a wine that should continue to age beautifully even though it has hit its plateau of drinkability. Anticipated maturity: now–2008. Last tasted, 10/02.

1986　Showing considerable amber at the edge, this fully mature wine offers up notes of
87　sandalwood intermixed with cedar, fruitcake, black currants, and spice box. The wine is medium bodied, showing a bit of dry tannin in the finish, suggesting this wine's baby fat has completely fallen away and the wine needs consumption. Anticipated maturity: now–2006. Last tasted, 10/02.

ANCIENT VINTAGES

Canon-la-Gaffelière's record prior to 1985 is notoriously undistinguished ... and that's being diplomatic. Even top vintages like 1982 were thin and very vegetal, and have fallen apart.

CAP DE MOURLIN

Classification: Grand Cru Classé

Owner: GFA Capdemourlin

Address: 33330 St.-Emilion

Mailing address: SCEA Capdemourlin, Château Roudier, 33570 Montagne-St.-Emilion

Telephone: 05 57 74 62 06; Telefax: 05 57 74 59 34

E-mail: info@vignoblescapdemourlin.com

Website: www.vignoblescapdemourlin.com

Visits: By appointment only

Contact: Thierry Capdemourlin

VINEYARDS

Surface area: 34.6 acres

Grape varietals: 65% Merlot, 25% Cabernet Franc, 10% Cabernet Sauvignon

Average age of vines: 34 years

Density of plantation: 5,500 vines per hectare

Average yields: 37 hectoliters per hectare

Elevage: Twenty-one to twenty-eight day fermentation and maceration in temperature-controlled stainless-steel vats. Twelve to eighteen months aging in barrels with 50% new oak. Fining and filtration.

WINES PRODUCED

Château Cap de Mourlin: 70,000 bottles

No second wine is produced.

Plateau of maturity: Within 4–10 years of the vintage

GENERAL APPRECIATION

Resembling in style, though in a lower-keyed manner, its stablemate Balestard La Tonnelle, Cap de Mourlin is equivalent in quality to an average Médoc Cru Bourgeois.

The Capdemourlin family have been property owners in St.-Emilion for more than five centuries. They also own the well-known St.-Emilion Grand Cru Classé, Balestard La Tonnelle, as well as Petit-Faurie-de-Soutard and the excellent Montagne St.-Emilion, Château Roudier. Until 1983 there were two grand cru St.-Emilions with the name Cap de Mourlin, one owned by Jean Capdemourlin and one by Jacques Capdemourlin. These two estates have been united since 1983, and the confusion consumers have encountered in the past between these two different wines has ceased to exist.

Cap de Mourlin produces typically robust, rich, full-bodied St.-Emilions with a great deal of fruit and muscle. They sometimes fall short with respect to finesse, but they are consistently mouth-filling, satisfying wines. The vineyard is located on the flat, sandy, rocky soil of what is often called the *pieds de côtes*.

IMPORTANT VINTAGES

2001 This is a rather dense, chocolaty style of wine, with black fruits and earth pre-
86–87 sented in a medium-bodied, chunky style that typifies most wines from this château. Anticipated maturity: 2005–2012. Last tasted, 1/03.

2000 A very good effort by Cap de Mourlin, this dark plum/purple–colored wine has
87 notes of espresso, cocoa, black cherries, and underbrush in a medium-to full-bodied, moderately tannic, monolithic, but satisfying style. Anticipated maturity: 2005–2014. Last tasted, 1/03.

1999 A relatively light, straightforward, competent effort from Cap de Mourlin, this
84 medium ruby–colored 1999 shows sweet-and-sour cherry fruit intermixed with some herbaceous notes and earth. This is a wine to drink over the next 5–6 years. Anticipated maturity: now–2008. Last tasted, 3/02.

1998 Notes of herbs, red currants, mushrooms, and earth emerge from this medium-
84 bodied, attractive, but low-key wine. Some tannin in the finish needs resolution. The wine is best consumed in the near-term. Anticipated maturity: now–2008. Last tasted, 3/02.

ANCIENT VINTAGES

The best vintages of Cap de Mourlin for me have always been the 1990 (87 points; last tasted 1/93) and 1982 (87 points; last tasted 10/99).

DU CAUZE

Classification: Grand Cru

Owner: Bruno Laporte

Address: 33330 St.-Emilion

Telephone: 05 57 74 62 47; Telefax: 05 57 74 59 12

Visits: By appointment only

Contact: François Lladères (Telephone: 05 57 64 45 21)

VINEYARDS

Surface area: 49.4 acres

Grape varietals: 90% Merlot, 10% Cabernet Sauvignon

Average age of vines: 45 years

Density of plantation: 5,500 vines per hectare

Average yields: 40 hectoliters per hectare

Elevage: Twenty day fermentation and maceration. Eighteen months aging in barrels that are renewed by a third at each vintage. Fining, no filtration.

WINES PRODUCED

Château du Cauze: 100,000 bottles

No second wine is produced.

GENERAL APPRECIATION

This well-situated hillside vineyard produces bargain-priced wines . . . readers take note. du Cauze is making better and better wines from a blend of 90% Merlot and 10% Cabernet Franc, with partial malolactic in barrel.

IMPORTANT VINTAGES

2001 This well-made 2001 exhibits a deep purple color in addition to a sweet nose of
87–89 black cherry and black currant liqueur intermixed with licorice, vanilla, and espresso. Deep and medium to full-bodied, with nicely integrated acidity and ripe tannin, it will drink well for 10–12 years. Last tasted, 1/03.

2000 The deep ruby/purple–colored 2000 is an elegant, delicious, sexy, open-knit effort
88 displaying abundant quantities of currant and black cherry fruit, moderate tannin, and an excellent finish. Unlike most vintages, it will require 1–2 years of cellaring; it will keep for 12 years. It is a sleeper of the vintage. Anticipated maturity: 2005–2012. Last tasted, 1/03.

1999 Elegant, herb-tinged black cherry fruit is followed by a medium-bodied, soft,
86 lighter-styled wine that will provide competent drinking over the next 3–4 years. Last tasted, 3/02.

1998 Dark plum, with an attractive nose of red and black currants, leafy underbrush
87 notes, and some spice box, this medium-bodied, nicely structured, relatively deep wine shows good fruit, balance, and overall harmony. It is just approaching its plateau of drinkability. Anticipated maturity: now–2010.

CHAUVIN

Classification: Grand Cru Classé

Owner: Marie-France Février and Béatrice Ondet

Address: 33330 St.-Emilion

Mailing address: 1, Les Cabannes Nord, BP 67, 33330 St.-Emilion

Telephone: 05 57 24 76 25; Telefax: 05 57 74 41 34

E-mail: chateauchauvingc@aol.com

Website: www.chateauchauvin.com

Visits: By appointment only Monday to Friday, 9:30 A.M.–noon and 2–4:30 P.M.

Contact: Marie-France Février or Béatrice Ondet

VINEYARDS

Surface area: 37 acres

Grape varietals: 80% Merlot, 15% Cabernet Franc, 5% Cabernet Sauvignon

Average age of vines: 30 years

Density of plantation: 5,500 vines per hectare

Average yields: 35–38 hectoliters per hectare

Elevage: Prolonged fermentation and maceration in temperature-controlled stainless-steel vats. Malolactics in barrel. Eighteen months aging in barrels with 40–50% new oak and regular stirring of the lees. No fining, filtration.

WINES PRODUCED

Château Chauvin: 50,000 bottles

Borderie de Chauvin: 15,000 bottles

Plateau of maturity: Within 3–15 years of the vintage

GENERAL APPRECIATION

This impeccably made wine has quietly improved over the years and now counts among the excellent "new wave" St.-Emilions. Never showy or spectacular, it is charming and seductive in its own way, and clearly merits consumers' consideration since it is still reasonably priced.

This property, a neighbor of Cheval Blanc, has made remarkable progress in the last several vintages, particularly the 2000 and 1998. The decision to harvest later, as well as to institute a stricter selection with a second wine, has resulted in major improvements to the quality of the wines at this estate. And yes, the omnipresent Michel Rolland is the oenologist in charge. Chauvin may be an emerging star in St.-Emilion.

IMPORTANT VINTAGES

2001
88–90
Except for some elevated tannin, everything is well balanced in this dense ruby/purple–colored St.-Emilion. Aromas of sweet licorice, melted tar, and black cherry/currant fruit rise from this full- to medium-bodied, pure, rich, vibrant 2001. Anticipated maturity: 2007–2020. Last tasted, 1/03.

2000
92
One of the finest Chauvins ever made, this opaque purple–colored effort boasts a vividly pure nose of graphite, crème de cassis, and wet stones backed up by subtle, high-quality, spicy, new oak. Multilayered, full-bodied, dense, concentrated, and pure, with sweet tannin and superb length, this future classic will be at its best between 2006–2018. Last tasted, 1/03.

1999
89
An impressive effort, the 1999 Chauvin offers aromas of cassis and cherry liqueur admirably displayed in a lush, opulent, medium- to full-bodied, surprisingly deep format. Fleshy and pure, with moderate levels of smoky wood, low acidity, and nicely integrated tannin, this seductive St.-Emilion will drink well for 8–10 years. Last tasted, 3/02.

1998
89+
A deep, saturated ruby/purple color is followed by aromas of blackberry and cherry fruit intertwined with licorice, spice box, underbrush, and cedar. This thick, full-bodied, concentrated tasting 1998 exhibits sweet tannin as well as excellent purity. Low acidity in addition to gorgeous up-front fruit suggest early drinkability. Anticipated maturity: now–2015. Last tasted, 3/02.

1998
91
Vieux Château Chauvin: The only vintage for which the proprietor produced a luxury *cuvée*, this is a specialwine. A blockbuster effort, this garage wine is produced from a parcel carved out of the better known Chauvin estate. The opaque, thick, black/purple-colored 1998 boasts viscous, concentrated flavors of licorice, chocolate, blackberries, and currants. Full-bodied and voluptuous, with moderately high tannin, this massive wine will require another 1–2 years of cellaring de-

spite its hedonistic display of aromas and flavors. Anticipated maturity: 2004–2022. Last tasted, 3/02.

1997   The 1997 Chauvin is a seductive, silky-textured effort with a dark ruby/purple
88   color as well as abundant fat, juicy, jammy black cherry/currant fruit and toasty oak. A supple, low-acid wine with good depth and no hard edges, it should be consumed over the next 3–4 years. Last tasted, 3/01.

1996   The 1996 exhibits a dark ruby color, as well as an excellent bouquet of toast inter-
88   mixed with jammy cherry fruit. There is good glycerin, medium body, an overall sense of elegance, fine equilibrium, and a tasty, richly fruity finish. Some tannin is present, but this is a stylish, finesse-driven wine that should drink nicely for 7–8 years. Last tasted, 3/01.

1995   Chauvin's 1995 is not dissimilar from the 1994. Deep ruby/purple–colored, with a
87   sweet, nearly overripe, jammy nose of black fruits, oak, and spice, this lush, attractively textured, plump St.-Emilion will need to be drunk over the next 5–6 years because of its extremely low acidity. Last tasted, 11/97.

1994   The purple-colored 1994 Chauvin displays super-jammy black cherries and
87   abundant sweet, toasty oak. Opulent, medium- to full-bodied flavors are low in acidity, but moderately tannic. Anticipated maturity: now–2009. Last tasted, 3/96.

1990   The explosively rich, fruity, unctuous 1990 exhibits plenty of velvety, smooth tan-
88   nins, excellent concentration, and medium to full body. This admirably endowed, opulent, hedonistic Chauvin has reached full maturity. Anticipated maturity: now–2008. Last tasted, 11/98.

ANCIENT VINTAGES

My only experience with older vintages of Chauvin is the 1988 and 1989, both competent but uninspiring wines.

CHEVAL BLANC

Classification: Premier Grand Cru Classé A

Owner: Bernard Arnault and Albert Frère

Administrator: Pierre Lurton

Address: 33330 St.-Emilion

Telephone: 05 57 55 55 55; Telefax: 05 57 55 55 50

E-mail: contact@chateau-chevalblanc.com

Website: www.chateau-chevalblanc.com

Visits: By appointment only

Contact: Cécile Supéry

VINEYARDS

Surface area: 91.4 acres

Grape varietals: 58% Cabernet Franc, 42% Merlot

Average age of vines: 45 years

Density of plantation: 8,000 vines per hectare

Average yields: 35 hectoliters per hectare

Elevage: Twenty-one to twenty-eight day fermentation and maceration in temperature-controlled stainless-steel and concrete vats. After malolactics, 18 months aging in new oak barrels with rackings every three months. Fining with egg whites, no filtration.

WINES PRODUCED

Château Cheval Blanc: 100,000 bottles

Petit Cheval: 40,000 bottles

Plateau of maturity: Within 5–30 years of the vintage

GENERAL APPRECIATION

Since its acquisition by Bernard Arnault and Albert Frère, who spare no effort to cull out the best of this unique *terroir,* Cheval Blanc, more than ever before, is Bordeaux's most exotic and individualistic wine. A wine of majestic composure, it is never showy, never extreme; on the contrary, all its component parts (fruit, fat, silky texture, velvety tannins, unending finish, dazzling aromas) exhibit impeccable equilibrium. Although approachable in its youth, Cheval Blanc's unusually high percentage of Cabernet Franc produces wines that show better in bottle than in cask.

Cheval Blanc is undoubtedly one of Bordeaux's most profound wines. For most of the last 50 or so years, it has sat alone at the top of St.-Emilion's hierarchy, representing the finest wine this appellation can produce. Since the renaissance began at Ausone, in addition to the revolution in quality led by St.-Emilion's garagists, Cheval Blanc has had to share the limelight. Cheval Blanc is a remarkably distinctive wine. Sitting right on the Pomerol border, in the St.-Emilion *graves* sector, with only a ditch separating its vineyards from those of L'Evangile and La Conseillante, for years it has been accused of making a wine that is as much a Pomerol as it is a St.-Emilion.

Among the "Big Eight" of Bordeaux, Cheval Blanc probably has the broadest window of drinkability. It is usually delicious when first bottled, yet it has the ability in the top years to gain weight and last. None of the Médoc first growths, or Pétrus in Pomerol, can claim to have such flexibility. Only Haut-Brion comes closest to matching Cheval Blanc's early drinkability and precociousness, as well as the stuffing and overall balance and intensity to age for 20–30 years. For me, Cheval Blanc is Cheval Blanc—it is like no other St.-Emilion or Pomerol I have ever tasted. The distinctive choice of grape varieties used at Cheval Blanc, equal parts Cabernet Franc and Merlot, is highly unusual. No other major château uses this much Cabernet Franc. Yet curiously, this grape reaches its zenith in Cheval Blanc's gravelly, sandy, and clay soil that is underpinned by a bed of iron rock, producing an extremely rich, ripe, intense, viscous wine.

The style of wine produced at Cheval Blanc has no doubt contributed to its immense popularity. Dark ruby in color, in the very good vintages it is an opulently rich and fruity wine, full-bodied, voluptuous, and lush, and deceptively easy to drink when young. The bouquet is especially distinctive. At its best, Cheval Blanc is an even more fragrant wine than Médoc first growths such as Château Margaux. Scents of minerals, menthol, exotic spices, tobacco, and intense, superripe, black fruits can overwhelm the taster. Many tasters, fooled by its cunning show of precocious charm, falsely assume that it will not age well. In the big, rich vintages, Cheval Blanc evolves exceptionally well, although one suspects that far too much of this wine is consumed long before its real majesty begins to emerge.

As the tasting notes demonstrate, Cheval Blanc can produce a decadently exotic wine of unbelievable depth and richness. However, in some vintages, it has been one of the most disappointing wines of the "Big Eight" châteaux of Bordeaux. Cheval Blanc was not a strong performer during the decades of the 1960s and 1970s. However, with the increasing attention to quality and detail provided by former administrator Jacques Hébrard, the quality of this wine during the 1980s became more consistent. His successor, Pierre Lurton, has pushed the quality and consistency of Cheval Blanc to even greater heights. The consecutive vintages of 2000, 1999, and 1998 were the finest Cheval Blanc since the splendid trilogy of 1949, 1948, and 1947.

Cheval Blanc, along with Haut-Brion, remains one of the two least expensive members of Bordeaux's "Big Eight."

IMPORTANT VINTAGES

2001
92–94
Fifty percent of the crop made it into the 2001 Cheval Blanc, which includes an unusually high percentage of Merlot (60%, along with 40% Cabernet Franc). As administrator Pierre Lurton told me, it was a year where the vines had to be extensively pruned, so yields were kept low. The Cabernet Franc vineyards produced 32 hectoliters per hectare, and the Merlot vineyards, 39 hectoliters per hectare. The cool September weather resulted in a late harvest for this estate. The 2001 has a lot in common with the 1999 and 1988. Its opaque ruby/purple color is accompanied by a sweet bouquet of menthol, ripe black currant, plum, and cherry fruit, and an intriguing mineral characteristic. The wine is medium bodied, with wonderful sweetness and purity, good definition, a layered texture, and sweet tannin in the finish. It will not make anyone forget the prodigious 2000 or the increasingly impressive 1998, but it is a fruit-driven, dense effort with abundant quantities of vibrant acidity. Anticipated maturity: 2010–2030. Last tasted, 1/03.

2001
87–89
Petit Cheval: The second wine, the medium-bodied 2001 Petit Cheval (15,000 bottles), was made from 57% Cabernet Franc and 43% Merlot. It does not possess the weight of its bigger sibling, but there is admirable perfume, good vibrancy to the cool climate characteristics, and excellent definition. Drink it over the next 7–8 years. Last tasted, 1/03.

2000
100
Among the young Chevals of the last 25 years, this is the most Port-like I have ever tasted. It represents the essence of this noble vineyard. A blend of 53% Merlot and 47% Cabernet Franc, it boasts a saturated purple color along with a reticent but striking bouquet of blackberries, blueberries, truffles, and mocha. Beginning to close down, aeration reveals scents of licorice, menthol, and saddle leather. Opulent and full-bodied, with a diaphanous quality (each layer peels away to reveal even more nuances), low acidity, sweet tannin, and a 60-second finish, it is unquestionably as profound as the 1990 and 1982. It is the most compelling Cheval Blanc since the mythical 1947 and 1949, but patience is required. Potentially, this is a perfect wine. Anticipated maturity: 2010–2030+. Last tasted, 1/03.

2000 Petit Cheval: For those not lucky or rich enough to purchase the 2000 Cheval
90   Blanc, there is an alternative . . . the 2000 Petit Cheval. This offering has often
     been an afterthought, but the 2000 possesses some of its bigger sibling's character.
     A blend of equal parts Merlot and Cabernet Franc (40% of the production made it
     into this wine), it does not have the mass or depth of the Cheval, but this excep-
     tional effort offers sweet, concentrated, plush flavors, wonderful opulence, and
     lovely density. This beauty will be drinkable upon release, and will last for 12–15
     years. Believe it or not, the 2000 Petit Cheval is better than some vintages of
     Cheval Blanc have been over the last two decades. Anticipated maturity: 2005–
     2012. Last tasted, 1/03.

1999 A blend of 59% Merlot and 41% Cabernet Franc, the complex, explosively fra-
93   grant 1999 Cheval Blanc is already showing well, which is a good sign for a wine
     that traditionally is reserved early in life, but puts on weight and richness in the
     bottle. Stylistically, this wine is probably cut from the same mold as vintages such
     as 1985, 1966, and 1962. The color is a dense ruby with purple nuances. Once
     past the blockbuster bouquet of menthol, leather, black fruits, licorice, and
     mocha, the wine reveals medium body, extraordinary elegance, purity, and sweet,
     harmonious flavors with no hard edges. A seamless beauty of finesse, charm, and
     concentration, 1999 has produced an exciting Cheval Blanc to drink relatively
     young. Anticipated maturity: 2006–2022. Last tasted, 1/03.

1998 I seriously underestimated this wine, as I have often tended to do with Cheval
96+ Blanc. A potentially immortal example that has gained significant weight since it
     has been bottled, this blend of 55% Cabernet Franc and 45% Merlot has a satu-
     rated purple color and a glorious nose of menthol, plums, mulberries, new saddle
     leather, cocoa, and vanilla. Remarkably fuller bodied than I ever remembered it
     young, with an amazingly seamless texture and tremendous concentration and ex-
     tract, this full-bodied yet gorgeously pure and elegant wine is impeccably bal-
     anced and certainly one of the all-time great Cheval Blancs. If it continues to
     improve as much as it has over the last three years since bottling, this wine will
     certainly rival the 2000, 1990, and 1982. Anticipated maturity: 2009–2030. Last
     tasted, 1/03.

1997 A seductive, fragrant style of Cheval Blanc, with moderate density and weight,
88   this immediately appealing 1997 exhibits an exotic nose of coconut, plums, cherry
     liqueur, and sweet, toasty oak. The wine's alluring personality is accompanied by
     fine suppleness, low acidity, medium body, and current drinkability. Consume it
     over the next 5–6 years. Last tasted, 11/02.

1996 The elegant, moderately weighted 1996 Cheval Blanc reveals a deep garnet/plum,
90   evolved color. Quintessentially elegant, with a complex nose of black fruits, co-
     conut, smoke, and toast, this medium-bodied wine exhibits sweet fruit on the at-
     tack, substantial complexity, and a lush, velvety-textured finish. It is very soft and
     evolved for a 1996. Anticipated maturity: now–2015. Last tasted, 3/02.

1995 A pretty, attractive Cheval Blanc, the 1995 contains a higher than usual percent-
92   age of Merlot in the final blend (50% Cabernet Franc, 50% Merlot). This wine has
     not developed as much fat or weight as its younger sibling, the 1996, but it appears
     to be an outstanding Cheval Blanc with an enthralling smoky, black currant, cof-
     fee, and exotic bouquet. Complex, rich, medium- to full-bodied flavors are well
     endowed and pure, with surprisingly firm tannin in the finish. Unlike the sweeter,
     riper 1996, the 1995 may be more structured and potentially longer lived. Antici-
     pated maturity: now–2020. Last tasted, 12/02.

1994 Dark ruby/purple-colored, with a complex, spicy bouquet of tobacco, vanilla,
88+? black currant, mineral, and floral scents, the 1994 is a bigger, more structured
     wine than the 1993, its older sibling, but is it better? The wine finishes with

mouth-searing tannin, which detracts from the otherwise impressive aromatics and sweet, medium-bodied, lush attack. As I have written many times in the past, Cheval Blanc has a tendency to fatten up, put on weight, and expand both aromatically and texturally with age, so perhaps this wine will move in that direction. If it does, my rating will appear unduly conservative. But if the tannin continues to taste astringent and the fruit begins to fade, then I will have overrated it. Anticipated maturity: now–2017. Last tasted, 1/97.

1993
86
Dark ruby with a purple hue, this appealing style of Cheval Blanc offers the telltale nose of sweet black fruits, coconut, vanilla, and a touch of menthol. The wine is medium bodied, elegant, purely made, and, while it lacks volume and richness in the mouth, it is soft, delicious, and typical of this property's wines. This tasty, charming 1993 should drink well for 7–8 years. Last tasted, 1/97.

1992
77
A light-bodied, shallow wine for this great estate, the 1992 Cheval Blanc displays a vanilla-dominated nose with berry, jammy, herb, and coffee notes. There is not much depth, body, or length. Drink it over the next 4–5 years, as the hard tannin in the finish suggests that this wine will dry out quickly. Anticipated maturity: now. Last tasted, 11/94.

1990
100
This wine has overtaken its closest rival, the 1982. Dense ruby purple with only a bit of lightening at the edge, the explosive nose of black fruits and cassis intermixed with coffee, menthol, and leather is followed by an opulent, splendidly concentrated wine that is sheer nectar. With no hard edges, gorgeously integrated glycerin, tannin, acidity, and alcohol are all present in this seamless classic. The wine has been gorgeous since youth, but is now revealing more aromatic and flavor nuances into the game. This is spectacular stuff! Anticipated maturity: now–2015. Last tasted, 12/02.

1989
89
Somewhat of a disappointment in a sometimes great yet variable vintage, the color a dark ruby with amber at the edge, this wine shows sweet plum, fig, and currant notes, along with some herbs and earth. In the mouth, it is surprisingly lightweight for a wine from a superior year, medium bodied, relatively lush, but an essentially one-dimensional wine with a spicy, surprisingly short finish. Drink it over the next 10–15 years. Last tasted, 12/02.

1988
88
A very healthy dark ruby color with only a slight lightening at the edge, this wine shows sweet earth notes intermixed with ripe berry fruit, cassis, licorice, and leather. The wine is spicy and medium bodied, with a moderately tannic finish that is not likely to fully age out. Anticipated maturity: now–2014. Last tasted, 12/02.

1987
85
The 1987 Cheval Blanc is a successful wine for the vintage. The spicy, herbaceous, sweet nose is followed by a precocious, round, fat, fruity wine without much grip or structure. It does possess delicious, weedy, currant fruit buttressed by gobs of sweet, smoky oak. It is a seductive wine. Anticipated maturity: now. Last tasted, 3/90.

1986
89?
Another wine that seems to have some youthful characteristics, a high level of tannin and a lack of succulence and substance may ultimately prove this wine to be somewhat out of balance. The wine shows plum, fig, cherry, earthy, mineral notes and medium body, but the elevated tannins in the finish are distracting. Nevertheless, the wine has a youthfulness and vigor that make it far less evolved than its more seductive older siblings, the 1983 and 1985. Anticipated maturity: now–2011. Last tasted, 12/02.

1985
92
A rather seductive style of Cheval Blanc that has been delicious from its youth, this wine continues to develop beautifully. Although it seems to have attained full maturity, the wine shows plenty of sweet plum, mocha, coffee, and black currant fruit intermixed with some menthol, chocolate, and cola. The wine is lush,

medium to full-bodied, very soft, and ideal for drinking now and over the next 5–7 years. Last tasted, 11/02.

1983
93
A glorious wine, and one of the candidates for the wine of the vintage, Cheval Blanc's 1983 shows far more evolved color than its older sibling, the 1982. With explosive aromatic notes of sweet jammy plum, black currant, smoke, coffee, and Asian spice, opulent, medium to full-bodied, and lush, this is a gorgeous, very sexy, seductive style of Cheval Blanc that has been consistently delicious from the time it was bottled. It shows no signs of decline despite some increasing amber in the color. The tannins are still sweet, the fruit very present, and the wine totally intact. Anticipated maturity: now–2010. Last tasted, 1/03.

1982
96
This was consistently a perfect wine early in its life, but it seems to be going through a stage where the tannins are more present, and the extraordinarily exotic opulence the wine had young, while still present, is not now as dominant a characteristic. Nevertheless, there is plenty to admire in this full-bodied, very lush Cheval Blanc that has reached full maturity. Sweet notes of red and black fruits intermixed with licorice, spice box, and incense jump from the glass. On the palate, the wine is full-bodied, layered, and very rich. It seems to develop interesting nuances the more it sits in the glass, and then suddenly takes a dive. A very fascinating Cheval Blanc, and certainly the greatest Cheval Blanc after the 1964 and before the 1990. Anticipated maturity: now–2016. Last tasted, 1/03.

1981
89
This somewhat charming, lightweight Cheval Blanc is fully mature but elegant, with sweet red and black currant fruit intermixed with mineral, licorice, and a hint of herbs. Spicy, medium bodied, and very pleasant, this wine's harmony gives it considerable appeal. Drink up. Last tasted, 11/02.

1980
80
The 1980 Cheval Blanc is a relative success for this mediocre vintage. Medium ruby, with a moderately intense bouquet of herbal, cedary, fruity scents, this wine has medium body, adequate concentration, and a supple, soft finish. It may be in decline. Anticipated maturity: now. Last tasted, 10/90.

1979
86
A healthy dark garnet color is followed by a rather lean, one-dimensional Cheval Blanc with notes of red and black fruits, mineral, and earth, but compactly built and monolithic. It will age nicely for another 10–12 years, but there is not a whole lot of positive evolution to be expected. Drink up. Last tasted, 12/02.

1978
87
The 1978 is a rather green, herbal style of Cheval Blanc with a dark garnet color, some cedar and spice box, but medium bodied and tough-textured, with an absence of charm, fruit, and glycerin. Drink it up. Last tasted, 12/02.

1976
82
In this vintage marked by extreme drought, heat, and hope-crushing rains at harvest time, Cheval Blanc has produced an open-knit, superripe, roasted style of wine that is now fully mature. It has put on weight, and while there is some browning at the edge, the 1976 Cheval Blanc has a full-blown bouquet of ripe fruit, minerals, nuts, and toasty oak. On the palate, the wine is opulent, even fat, with generous, savory, fleshy, plummy, fruity flavors. Low in acidity and very soft, the 1976 Cheval Blanc has been drinkable since its release, yet it continues to expand and develop. I initially underestimated this wine. Anticipated maturity: now. Last tasted, 10/90.

1975
88
This wine is very complex aromatically, but if the bouquet deserves a 90-point score, the flavors are marginally disappointing. A big nose of spice box, cedar, black fruits, mineral, and an almost espresso-like note is followed by a somewhat tannic, medium-bodied wine with astringent tannin and a tough finish. It is showing considerable amber at the edge and probably needs to be drunk up. It is certainly in no danger of falling apart, but I suspect it will become more and more desiccated as the wine ages. Last tasted, 12/02.

1971 — Somewhat of a disappointment, the 1971, while very good, has in the last several
84 years begun to brown badly. Nevertheless, the wine still has plenty of sweet fruit, a burned, roasted character to its bouquet, and medium body. The 1971 is a pleasant, lowbrow Cheval Blanc that should be drunk over the next 2–3 years. Anticipated maturity: now. Last tasted, 10/90.

1970 — Consistently a disappointment, this herbaceous, lightweight Cheval Blanc shows
83 considerable amber to its color and has notes of earth, ashtray, spice box, and some currant fruit. In the mouth, it is rather narrowly constructed and already in decline. Anticipated maturity: now–2008. Last tasted, 11/02.

1966 — A good, rather than great, effort from Cheval Blanc, the 1966 is now fully mature.
85 Medium ruby with an amber edge, this is a restrained version of Cheval Blanc, with a stylish, reserved bouquet of mineral scents, black currants, and spicy oak. On the palate, the wine is medium bodied, moderately fleshy, but not as voluptuous or concentrated as one expects Cheval Blanc to be in this highly regarded vintage. Anticipated maturity: now. Last tasted, 10/90.

1964 — A blockbuster Cheval Blanc and probably the greatest Cheval Blanc made during
96 the 1960s and 1970s, this wine still has a dense, murky garnet color and knockout aromatics of coffee, black fruit, and spice box. The wine is opulent and fleshy with enormous glycerin and power. It is still very muscular, also with slightly robust tannins to shed, but this wine seems almost immortal in terms of longevity. My best guess is that, from pristinely stored bottles, this wine is still in late adolescence and not yet at its peak of maturity. Anticipated maturity: now–2025. Last tasted, 12/02.

1962 — Once somewhat of a sleeper wine from this underrated vintage, the 1962 Cheval
88 Blanc has held on to life longer than many, but is now in decline. The color shows considerable amber, and the wine seems a bit loose-knit and disjointed on the palate. Nevertheless, it has complex notes of herbs, earth, licorice, truffle, and some sweet fruits that linger. In the mouth, there is a hint of desiccation, leather, and hard tannin poking its head through in the finish. Anticipated maturity: now–2010. Last tasted, 12/02.

1961 — Well-kept bottles of this wine have been fully mature for 20–25 years but show no
91 signs of decline, one of the magical aspects of great vintages of profound Bordeaux wines. Showing considerable amber to the garnet color, this wine shows an exotic nose of licorice, sweet, jammy red and black fruits, spice box, and cedar. In the mouth, the wine is medium-bodied, lush, and fleshy, with plenty of glycerin and a very soft, tactile impression. The wine should be drunk up unless readers have access to pristinely stored, larger-format bottles such as magnums, double magnums, etc. Anticipated maturity: now. Last tasted, 12/02.

ANCIENT VINTAGES

In the 1950s, the greatest vintage is the 1953 (95 points; last tasted 3/96). I am sure this wine has been fully mature for at least 15–20 years. Nevertheless, it has held its magic for that considerable period and is still the most fragrant and, from an aromatic perspective, the most compelling Cheval Blanc I have ever tasted. Perhaps the 1982 will turn out to be this profoundly perfumed. It is not a blockbuster, but is incredibly seductive and so soft and silky. Another vintage of note during the 1950s is the 1959 (92 points; last tasted 2/95), a denser, more structured wine than the 1961, although I am not sure it will ever hit the heights the 1961 has already achieved. However, it certainly appears to have the stuffing and muscle to outlive the 1961. The 1955 (90 points;

last tasted 3/95) is a tougher-textured, fuller-bodied, less seductive style of Cheval Blanc. Nevertheless, it is immensely impressive, rich, and capable of another 5–10 years of evolution. It has been nearly a decade since I tasted it, but I loved the smooth as silk 1950, another top example from that underestimated vintage.

I have rated the 1949 Cheval Blanc as high as 100, but more consistently in the mid- to upper 90s. At a tasting in December 1995, I rated it 96 points. It is one of the great Cheval Blancs—not as Port-like and syrupy as the 1947, but more classically rendered. But do not take that to mean this is a wimpish wine. It is an unbelievably rich, sweet, expansive, full-bodied style of Cheval Blanc, with enormous quantities of glycerin, fruit, alcohol, and extract. Although it has been drinkable for decades, it continues to offer that exotic Asian spice, cedar, and huge, sweet, fruit-scented nose. Unctuously textured, thick, rich, vibrant, pure, and compelling, it should drink well for another 10–20 years. The 1948 (96 points; last tasted 3/01) is the most backward Cheval Blanc among vintages of the 1940s. The wine retains an opaque plum/licorice-like color. A huge, earthy, soy, cedar, roasted herb nose is followed by a wine of immense power, body, intensity, and structure. It will easily last for another 20+ years. Having a 1947 Cheval Blanc (100 points; last tasted 1/03) served out of an impeccably stored magnum four times during the last three years made me once again realize what a great job I have. The only recent Bordeaux vintages that come even remotely close to the richness, texture, and viscosity of so many of these right bank 1947s are the 1982 and 1990. What can I say about this mammoth wine that is more like Port than dry red table wine? The 1947 Cheval Blanc exhibits such a thick texture, it could double as motor oil. The huge nose of fruitcake, chocolate, leather, coffee, and Asian spices is mind-boggling. The unctuous texture and richness of sweet fruit are amazing. Consider the fact that this wine is, technically, appallingly deficient in acidity and excessively high in alcohol. Moreover, its volatile acidity levels would be considered intolerable by modern-day oenologists. Yet how can they explain that after 55 years the wine is still remarkably fresh, phenomenally concentrated, and profoundly complex? It has to make you wonder about the direction of modern-day winemaking. Except for one dismal, murky, troubled, volatile double magnum, this wine has been either perfect or nearly perfect every time I have had it. But beware, there are numerous fraudulent bottles in the marketplace, particularly magnums, of 1947 Cheval Blanc.

The wine that has always enjoyed the greatest reputation of the vintage is Cheval Blanc's 1921. I had tasted this wine twice before and had been disappointed with both bottles, but at a tasting in December 1995, the wine was unreal. I rated it 98 points. It offered an opaque color with considerable amber at the edge, followed by remarkably fresh, sweet, jammy aromas of black fruits, Asian spices, coffee, herbs, and chocolate. Thick, unctuously textured, with oodles of fruit, this huge, massive, full-bodied wine must have possessed 14% alcohol. It could easily have been mistaken for the 1947 or 1949.

CLOS BADON THUNEVIN

Classification: Grand Cru

Owner: Ets Thunevin

Address: 33330 St.-Emilion

Mailing address: c/o Ets Thunevin, 6 rue Guadet, 33330 St.-Emilion

Telephone: 05 57 55 09 13; Telefax: 05 57 55 09 12

E-mail: thunevin@thunevin.com

Website: www.thunevin.com

No visits

VINEYARDS

Surface area: 16 acres

Grape varietals: 70% Merlot, 30% Cabernet Franc

Average age of vines: 30 years

Density of plantation: 5,500 vines per hectare

Average yields: 35 hectoliters per hectare

Elevage: Prolonged fermentation and maceration. Malolactics and 18–20 months aging in new oak barrels. No fining, no filtration.

WINES PRODUCED

Clos Badon Thunevin: 15,000 bottles

No second wine is produced.

Plateau of maturity: Within 4–9 years of the vintage

GENERAL APPRECIATION

This wine by Jean-Luc Thunevin is fine in a lower-keyed manner than its more prestigious stablemate Valandraud. I have always wondered why Clos Badon, though very good, was not better than it actually is since it seemingly benefits from the same vinification as Valandraud.

IMPORTANT VINTAGES

2001 Very spicy, deep ruby/purple–colored, with notes of espresso, chocolate, and
87–88 black fruits, this medium-bodied wine shows good texture, elegance, and impressive purity. The low acidity and ripe tannins suggest drinking over the next 10 years. Last tasted, 1/03.

2000 This wine has benefited from Jean-Luc Thunevin's *élevage*, which includes con-
89 siderable lees contact, micro-oxygenation, and little or no racking. More enticing than it appeared in its prime, a deep purple color is accompanied by copious quantities of jammy blackberry and cherry fruit intermixed with smoky espresso and sweet leather aromas. Impressively pure and textured, with medium to full body, low acidity, ripe tannin, and a thick, glycerin-imbued finish, it will be at its apogee between now–2015. This is a sleeper of the vintage. Last tasted, 1/03.

1999 This is a sexy, ripe, low-acid, modern-style St.-Emilion offering notes of savory,
88   lush, concentrated black fruits, smoke, leather, and coffee. Sweet on the attack
     (from ripeness, not sugar), this pure wine should be drunk over the next eight
     years. Last tasted, 3/02.

1998 A sexy, ripe, opulently styled effort, the 1998 offers abundant quantities of choco-
90   late, coffee, fruitcake, and berry aromas and flavors. This lush, expansive, juicy,
     full-bodied wine will not make "old bones," but will provide impressive drinking
     over the next 4–5 years. It is a sleeper of the vintage. Last tasted, 3/02.

CLOS DUBREUIL

Classification: None

Owner: Marc Poyeton

Address: 11, Jean Guillot, 33330 Saint-Christophe-des-Bardes

Telephone: 05 57 74 48 60; Telefax: 05 57 24 63 06

Visits: By appointment only

Contact: Marc Poyeton

VINEYARDS

Surface area: 3.7 acres

Grape varietals: 95% Merlot, 5% Cabernet Franc

Average age of vines: 25 years

Density of plantation: 6,500 vines per hectare

Average yields: 30 hectoliters per hectare

Elevage: Fermentation and four-week maceration in temperature-controlled vats.
Malolactics and 18 months aging in new oak barrels. Fining and filtration depending upon
the vintage.

WINES PRODUCED

Clos Dubreuil: 6,000–7,000 bottles

No second wine is produced.

Plateau of maturity: Within 5–15 years of the vintage

GENERAL APPRECIATION

Readers lucky enough to find any of the 400-case production of this garage wine should
not pass it up. While less spectacular than some of its peers like Croix de Labrie, Clos
Dubreuil is always excellent, consistently meriting 90+ ratings since the 1997 vintage. A
must buy for amateurs of micro-cuvées.

This garage wine is made by Louis Mitjavile, the son of François (Le Tertre-
Rôteboeuf's proprietor). Readers lucky enough to find any of the 400-case production
should not pass it up.

IMPORTANT VINTAGES

2001
87–88 A medium-bodied, very elegant effort, this dark ruby–colored wine shows sweet, chocolaty, black cherry fruit intermixed with some espresso and smoky notes. It is medium bodied and savory, but best drunk during its first decade of life. Last tasted, 1/03.

2000
91 A superb example from this small estate, the dense purple–colored 2000 exhibits pure crème de cassis characteristics intermixed with hints of blueberries, acacia flowers, and smoky, toasty oak. Full-bodied, sumptuously textured, and rich yet structured and delineated with a long finish, it will be drinkable between 2006–2020. Last tasted, 1/03.

1999
90 This is a dense ruby/purple–colored, sensuous offering with gorgeously sweet black currant and jammy cherry fruit, medium to full body, a lush, layered texture, low acidity, and a plump, hedonistic finish. The wood, acidity, and tannin are beautifully integrated. Drink it over the next 10 years. Last tasted, 3/02.

1998
92 A spectacular offering, this massive, full-bodied 1998 boasts huge, concentrated, chocolaty, cedary, coffee, blackberry, and cherry aromas as well as flavors. This low-acid, multidimensional effort possesses oodles of glycerin, extract, and richness. It is a fabulously exotic, full-flavored, mouth-staining wine to drink over the next 12 years. Last tasted, 3/02.

1997
89 One of the stars of the vintage, this creamy-textured 1997 exhibits a sweet, cedary, chocolate, and fruitcake-scented nose. Additionally, copious quantities of black raspberries and cherries emerge with airing. Ripe and sensual, with low acidity, this gorgeous, user-friendly wine will have huge appeal. Drink it over the next three years. Last tasted, 3/01.

CLOS FOURTET

Classification: Premier Grand Cru Classé B

Owner: Philippe Cuvelier

Address: 33330 St.-Emilion

Telephone: 05 57 24 70 90; Telefax: 05 57 74 46 52

Visits: By appointment only

Contact: Tony Ballu

VINEYARDS

Surface area: 44.5 acres

Grape varietals: 80% Merlot, 15% Cabernet Sauvignon, 5% Cabernet Franc

Average age of vines: 25 years

Density of plantation: 6,600 vines per hectare

Average yields: 38 hectoliters per hectare

Elevage: Fifteen day fermentation and 30 day maceration in temperature-controlled, double-lined, open, flat top, stainless-steel vats of 50 and 70 hectoliter capacity (allowing the separate vinification of the different parcels), with *pigéages* done manually. Eighteen months aging in barrels with 80% new oak. Fining if necessary, no filtration.

WINES PRODUCED

Château Clos Fourtet: 55,000 bottles

Closerie de Fourtet: 25,000 bottles

Plateau of maturity: Within 3–15 years of the vintage

GENERAL APPRECIATION

Under the helmsmanship of the ubiquitous Lurton family, Clos Fourtet has improved during the 1980s and the 1990s. A reborn classic, Clos Fourtet was sold to Paris businessman Philippe Cuvelier, who has continued to improve the quality of this estate.

This property is on the *côtes* of St.-Emilion, almost at the entrance to St.-Emilion opposite the Place de l'Eglise and Hôtel Plaisance. Until recently the most interesting thing about Clos Fourtet was the vast underground wine cellars, among the finest in the Bordeaux region. This winery, like a number of highly respected yet overrated St.-Emilion premier grands cru classés, had been making wine during the last two decades that was good, but not up to the standards of its classification. The wines had been plagued by a bland, dull, chunky, dry, astringent fruitiness and had a curious habit of getting older without getting better. In short, they did not develop well in the bottle. That has all changed for the better, as first the Lurton family and now Philippe Cuvelier have made serious attempts to upgrade the quality of this wine, as evidenced by most vintages since 1989.

IMPORTANT VINTAGES

2001 Clos Fourtet's internationally styled 2001 exhibits a creamy, deep, medium- to
89–91 full-bodied style with abundant quantities of toasty new oak, jammy black cherries, blackberries, licorice, and a hint of chocolate. Rich, sweet, and ripe, with pure flavors, low acidity, and well-integrated tannin, it will provide ideal drinking during its first 12–16 years of life. Anticipated maturity: 2005–2017. Last tasted, 1/03.

2000 A saturated dark plum/purple color characterizes this substantial, full-bodied
90+ effort. This impressive, dense wine displays plenty of power as well as notes of charcoal, blackberry jam, licorice, and toasty new oak. With good size, firm tannin, outstanding ripeness, and overall richness, this exceptional offering is the finest Clos Fourtet produced in many years. It will also be very long-lived. Anticipated maturity: 2010–2022. Last tasted, 1/03.

1999 Although I had higher hopes for this wine from cask, it has turned out to be an ex-
88 cellent St.-Emilion, offering sweet black cherry, cola, smoke, plum, and mulberry characteristics. Medium bodied, plump, and fat, with low acidity and an up-front, flattering style, it should drink well for 10 years. Last tasted, 3/02.

1998 A strong effort from Clos Fourtet, the dark ruby/purple–colored 1998 offers pure
90 blackberry and cherry aromas with subtle wood and licorice in the background. Medium bodied, exceptionally pure, with low acidity as well as silky tannin, this sexy offering is already ideal for drinking. Anticipated maturity: 2004–2016. Last tasted, 3/02.

1997 This easygoing, delicious, creamy-textured 1997 exhibits abundant toasty new
87 oak along with jammy black fruits. There is not much grip or tannin in this supple, richly fruity, charming, tasty St.-Emilion. Enjoy it over the next 4–5 years. Last tasted, 3/01.

1996 On one of the three occasions I tasted the 1996 Clos Fourtet from bottle I rated it
89   outstanding (90 points). The color is a saturated dark ruby. The nose offers up
      sweet black raspberry and blackberry fruit intermixed with toasty oak and floral
      scents. It is fleshy, surprisingly expansive, and forward for a 1996, with low acid-
      ity and a long, multilayered, fruit-driven finish. The tannin is ripe and thus the
      fruit comes forward and the wine is seductive and charming. This 1996 possesses
      the weight, richness, and extract to last for 15–18 years, but it should be drinkable
      early. I would not be surprised for readers to feel my score is too conservative
      based on how well this wine is showing. Anticipated maturity: now–2018. Last
      tasted, 3/01.

1995 A fine effort from Clos Fourtet, the 1995 exhibits a medium dark plum color, fol-
88   lowed by sweet black cherry and kirsch fruit intertwined with minerals and toasty
      oak. Tightly wound on the palate with medium body, excellent delineation and pu-
      rity, and a spicy finish with plenty of grip, this example has closed down consider-
      ably since bottling, but it does possess excellent sweetness and depth. However,
      the tannin remains elevated, so this 1995 will require patience. Anticipated matu-
      rity: 2004–2018. Last tasted, 1/00.

1994 An impressive saturated purple color indicates a wine of strength and power. In
87   the mouth, it exhibits the vintage's high tannin level, but the tannins are balanced
      by layers of ripe cassis fruit, attractive smoky elements, and fine glycerin and
      length. This is a forceful, impressively constituted, potentially outstanding Clos
      Fourtet. Anticipated maturity: now–2018. Last tasted, 1/97.

1990 Fully mature and probably the best Clos Fourtet made during a rather undistin
90   guished period, this dark plum/garnet–colored wine has an enticing nose of
      melted licorice, Provençal herbs, smoked meats, and sweet cherry and black cur-
      rant fruit. Medium to full-bodied, with a luscious, succulent texture, excellent
      concentration, and sweet tannins, this hedonistic yet intellectually satisfying wine
      is a treat to drink. Anticipated maturity: now–2010. Last tasted, 1/03.

1989 The 1989 is an alcoholic, exuberantly styled, easy to drink wine, but its lack of
86   grip, definition, and tannin may give some concern. Anticipated maturity: now–
      2004. Last tasted, 1/93.

1988 The 1988 has not fared well in comparative tastings. The fruit has faded and the
79   tannins have become hard, lean, and noticeably aggressive. In fact, I would argue
      that the 1988 is overburdened with tannins to the detriment of its concentration
      and fruit. Caveat emptor. Anticipated maturity: now–2008. Last tasted, 4/91.

1986 The 1986 is one-dimensional and lacks grip and depth. Anticipated maturity:
78   now. Last tasted, 3/90.

1985 The 1985 Clos Fourtet is the lightest of all the premier grand cru classé wines.
84   Medium ruby, with a supple, monolithic, fruity taste, and soft tannins, it has an
      easy, agreeable finish. Anticipated maturity: now. Last tasted, 3/90.

1983 This is a one-dimensional, soft, light-bodied wine with hardly any tannin, as well
78   as a short finish. It is one of the disappointments of the 1983 St.-Emilion vintage.
      Anticipated maturity: now. Last tasted, 3/89.

1982 This St.-Emilion estate, long in the throes of mediocrity, produced a satisfying
84   wine in 1982. Medium ruby, with an attractive bouquet of vanilla oakiness and
      ripe, herb-scented, berry fruit, this medium-bodied wine has a forward, preco-
      cious, rich, supple fruitiness that caresses the palate. It is fully mature. Antici-
      pated maturity: now. Last tasted, 3/89.

ANCIENT VINTAGES

Much like most of the 1980s, the decade of the 1970s was one of extraordinarily disappointing wines for Clos Fourtet. I have no tasting notes for anything earlier than 1970.

CLOS DES JACOBINS

Classification: Grand Cru Classé

Owner: Gérard Frydman

Address: Lieu-dit La Gomerie, 33330 St.-Emilion

Telephone: 05 57 24 70 14; Telefax: 05 57 24 68 08

Visits: By appointment only

Contact: Hubert de Boüard

VINEYARDS

Surface area: 21 acres

Grape varietals: 70% Merlot, 30% Cabernet Franc

Average age of vines: 35 years

Density of plantation: 7,500 vines per hectare

Average yields: 40 hectoliters per hectare

Elevage: Three to four week fermentation and maceration in temperature-controlled wooden vats (since 2002) with frequent *pigéage* and pumpings-over. Eighteen months aging in new oak barrels. No fining, filtration.

WINES PRODUCED

Clos des Jacobins: 20,000 bottles

Prieur des Jacobins: Up to 10,000 bottles (depending upon the vintage)

Plateau of maturity: Within 3–15 years of the vintage

GENERAL APPRECIATION

These are reliable, pleasant, yet somewhat chunky wines. A new philosophy of vinification debuted in 2001, aimed at giving the wines more personality.

The large *négociant* firm of Cordier owned this lovely ivy-covered château located just outside the gates of St.-Emilion until recently, when it was sold. Clos des Jacobins, despite reasonably good wines, receives little publicity. This may be about to change since, starting in 2001, Hubert de Boüard (of Angélus fame) has been brought in to make the wine. It has been consistent over the last decade, producing a wine that is deeply colored, rich, round, creamy, and plummy, often with an opulence of ripe fruit. There is an absence of astringent, aggressive tannins, making Clos des Jacobins a wine that requires consumption within its first 10–12 years.

IMPORTANT VINTAGES

2001   The debut vintage for the new vinification and winemaking consultant Hubert de
87–88   Boüard, this wine has a deep ruby/purple color, a sweet nose of black currants, cherries, smoke, and earth. Medium bodied, with supple tannins, a silky texture, and excellent depth, this is a very encouraging first effort under the new administration. Anticipated maturity: 2005–2012. Last tasted, 1/03.

OTHER VINTAGES

Vintages of the 1990s were very disappointing from Clos des Jacobins, rather sad in view of some of the top-notch successes of the 1980s, particularly the 1982 and 1983. However, with the new owner and winemaking team, this property looks set to do some far better work.

CLOS DE L'ORATOIRE

Classification: Grand Cru Classé

Owner: Comtes de Neipperg

Address: 33330 St.-Emilion

Mailing address: c/o SC du Château Peyraud, BP 34, 33330 St.-Emilion

Telephone: 05 57 24 71 33; Telefax: 05 57 24 67 95

E-mail: vignobles.von.neipperg@wanadoo.fr

Website: www.neipperg.com

Visits: By appointment only Monday to Friday, 9 A.M.–noon and 2–7 P.M.

Contact: Dominique Duluc

VINEYARDS

Surface area: 25.5 acres

Grape varietals: 90% Merlot, 5% Cabernet Franc, 5% Cabernet Sauvignon

Average age of vines: 30 years

Density of plantation: 5,500 vines per hectare

Average yields: 35–40 hectoliters per hectare

Elevage: Eighteen to twenty-six day fermentation and maceration in temperature-controlled wooden vats, with *pigéages*. Malolactics in barrel on fine lees for 90–100% of the yield. Fourteen to eighteen months aging in new oak barrels. No fining, no filtration.

WINES PRODUCED

Clos de l'Oratoire: 40,000 bottles

No second wine is produced.

Plateau of maturity: Within 5–15 years of the vintage

GENERAL APPRECIATION

Of Stephan von Neipperg's three St.-Emilion estates, Clos de l'Oratoire is the least known, probably because it is not yet as superlative as its two more prestigious stablemates. The talented power behind this operation has invested as much time and skill in it as in Canon-la-Gaffelière and La Mondotte, producing an exquisite wine that is all at once rich, charming, and loaded with up-front fruit.

Readers should note that proprietor Stephan von Neipperg (also the proprietor of Canon-la-Gaffelière and La Mondotte) has pushed this wine's quality into St.-Emilion's top echelon. The vineyard is located in the northeastern sector of St.-Emilion on gravelly/sandy soils. As most consumers know, Bordeaux can be frightfully expensive, but Clos de l'Oratoire remains fairly priced for its quality. This is an estate to search out, as prices and fame will certainly come quickly.

IMPORTANT VINTAGES

2001
89–92 The deep blue/purple–colored 2001 offers sweet aromas of blackberries, raspberries, incense, licorice, and toasty oak. Sweet and medium-bodied, with an intense attack, it displays moderately high tannin in the finish. If it continues to flesh out and the tannin sweetens, it will be outstanding. Anticipated maturity: 2005–2015. Last tasted, 1/03.

2000
94 Undoubtedly the finest effort this property has yet produced, the black-colored 2000 offers up sexy notes of espresso, chocolate, Asian spices, black cherry liqueur, and blackberries. A blend of 68% Cabernet Sauvignon, 25% Merlot, and the rest Cabernet Franc and Petit Verdot, this full-bodied Claret has expanded, with the tannin becoming sweeter and better integrated. It is a very impressive effort! Anticipated maturity: 2006–2020. Last tasted, 1/03.

1999
91 One of the stars of the vintage, this opaque purple–colored St.-Emilion exhibits aromas of new saddle leather, damp earth, blackberries, incense, cassis, and toast. An intriguing tapenade note emerges with airing. Full-bodied, with sweet tannin, low acidity, and impressive concentration, it can be enjoyed now and over the next 10–12 years. Last tasted, 3/02.

1998
92 An opaque blue/purple color is accompanied by a sensational bouquet of melted fudge, plums, Asian spices, blackberries, and prunes. Smoky, barbecue-like spices also emerge with airing. Full-bodied, super-extracted, rich, pure, and mouth-saturating, this large-scaled effort can be consumed with pleasure, but it will age for two decades. Anticipated maturity: now–2020. Last tasted, 3/02.

1997
89 One of the stars of the vintage, this opaque ruby/purple–colored wine offers copious quantities of jammy black cherries and lavish, smoky new oak. Fat, fleshy, and rich, with sweet tannin, medium to full body, and gorgeous concentration and fruit, it can be drunk now and will last for 10+ years. Last tasted, 3/01.

1996
90 The 1996 is even better out of bottle than it was from cask. The wine boasts an opaque plum/purple color. Intense aromas of Asian spices, espresso, roasted meats, and sweet, exotic cedar and blackberry fruit soar from the glass of this exotic, ostentatiously styled St.-Emilion. It is medium to full-bodied, with moderate tannin, a sweet mid-palate (always a good sign), and a dense, concentrated, long, powerful finish. This muscular, impressively endowed offering should drink well before 2017. Last tasted, 3/01.

1995
89 An impressive, possibly outstanding wine, the 1995 Clos de l'Oratoire is a sleeper of the vintage. This dense ruby/purple–colored offering possesses attractive, meaty, sweet cherry fruit in the nose, intertwined with smoky, toasty oak. Medium to full-bodied, spicy, and layered on the palate, the wine reveals fine delineation, grip, and tannin in the long, heady, impressively endowed finish. Some bottle age is warranted. Anticipated maturity: now–2015. Last tasted, 12/00.

1994   The 1994 is a dense, ripe, chewy, medium- to full-bodied St.-Emilion with plenty
87   of pure black cherry fruit intermingled with scents of Provençal herbs, olives, and
       toasty oak. This low-acid, ripe Claret is ideal for drinking over the next 3–4 years.
       Last tasted, 3/96.

1990   Fully mature, this is the first in a succession of impressive wines to emerge from
90   this estate. Dark plum/ruby with some pink at the edge, the intoxicatingly heady
       nose of sweet, toasty oak, jammy black currants and cherries, licorice, fruitcake,
       and spice box soars from the glass. Medium to full-bodied, opulent, with gor-
       geously pure fruit, a nicely layered texture, and a long finish, this wine is just hit-
       ting its apogee. Anticipated maturity: now–2012. Last tasted, 1/03.

CLOS ST.-MARTIN

Classification: Grand Cru Classé

Owner: SA Les Grandes Murailles, Reiffers family

Address: 33330 St.-Emilion

Mailing address: Château Côte de Baleau,
33330 St.-Emilion

Telephone: 05 57 24 71 09; Telefax: 05 57 24 69 72

E-mail: lesgrandesmurailles@wanadoo.fr

Website: www.grandes-murailles.com

Visits: By appointment only

Contact: Sophie Fourcade

VINEYARDS

Surface area: 3.3 acres

Grape varietals: 70% Merlot, 20% Cabernet Franc, 10% Cabernet Sauvignon

Average age of vines: 35 years

Density of plantation: 5,500 vines per hectare

Average yields: 32–35 hectoliters per hectare

Elevage: Cold maceration. Twenty-five day fermentation and maceration in temperature-
controlled stainless-steel vats. Malolactics and 18–20 months aging in new oak barrels.
No fining, filtration if necessary.

WINES PRODUCED

Clos St.-Martin: 5,600 bottles

No second wine is produced.

Plateau of maturity: Within 5–12 years of the vintage

GENERAL APPRECIATION

The talented Sophie Fourcade has quietly taken this once practically unknown estate to
the top echelon of the New Wave St.-Emilion hierarchy, with the valuable assistance of
winemaking guru Michel Rolland. Together with the other Reiffers-owned St.-Emilion
estates (Grandes Murailles and Côte de Baleau), Clos St.-Martin represents one of the
best buys of the appellation.

Colleagues of mine in France—in particular, Dominique Renard from the *négociant* Bordeaux Millesimes—have long extolled the quality of the wines from this tiny St.-Emilion estate (the smallest grand cru classé of the appellation) located on clay and limestone soil behind the church of St. Martin, hence the name. Production is very tiny. The first great vintage I tasted was the 1990. Surrounded by premier grands crus, Clos St.-Martin has a full southerly exposure. This is a splendid jewel in St.-Emilion.

IMPORTANT VINTAGES

2001 The complex 2001 Clos St.-Martin offers up a concoction of black fruits inter-
89–91 mixed with liquified minerals. The showy aromatics are followed by a structured, medium-bodied St.-Emilion with impressive purity, texture, and length. Antici-pated maturity: 2009–2017. Last tasted, 1/03.

2000 Unlike the hail-damaged 1999, the gorgeous 2000 is a profound wine, even better
96 than the great 1998. Its saturated opaque blue/purple color is followed by a knock-out nose of blueberries, blackberries, and minerals, with subtle oak notes well hidden by the wealth of fruit. Medium to full-bodied and rich, with high tannin but fabulous symmetry as well as overall presence, it will require patience. This is magnificent juice! Anticipated maturity: 2010–2030. Last tasted, 1/03.

1999 Clos St.-Martin's 1999 effort was hail-damaged. Sweet cherry and black currant
86 fruit intermixed with wet stones characterize the attractive aromatics of this medium-bodied wine. It falls off in the mouth, revealing a short, slightly pinched/compressed finish. Drink it sooner rather than later . . . over the next eight years. Last tasted, 3/02.

1998 A classic *vin de garde*, the dense dark ruby/purple–colored 1998 reveals subtle
91 notes of minerals, black raspberries, cherries, and smoky oak. Medium to full-bodied, extremely well delineated, and moderately tannic, it requires 1–2 years of cellaring. Unlike many 1998 St.-Emilions, patience will be a virtue. Anticipated maturity: 2006–2020. Last tasted, 3/02.

1997 Burgundian-styled, with abundant black cherry aromas and flavors, this medium-
86 bodied 1997 exhibits notions of dried herbs, earth, and spice. Pure, with an un-derlying minerality, it can be drunk now and over the next 4–5 years. Last tasted, 3/01.

1995 Although the pleasant 1995 exhibits a deep ruby color and berry scents in the
81 nose, it is soft and diluted. It should be drunk over the next 1–2 years. Last tasted, 11/97.

1994 The medium ruby-colored 1994 Clos St.-Martin is a light-bodied, straightforward
81 wine, without much concentration or complexity. Drink it over the next 1–2 years. Last tasted, 3/96.

1990 This wine has reached full maturity, but has at least another 10–15 years of life left
90 to it. Dense plum/ruby, with a sweet nose of blackberry and blueberry liqueur in-termixed with a crushed stone/floral component, medium to full body, plenty of succulence, loads of glycerin, and a long, layered, concentrated finish, this is a beauty. Anticipated maturity: now–2015. Last tasted, 12/01.

1989 The one aspect of this wine that keeps my score from going any higher is the angu-
87 lar nature of the tannins, which seem to be not totally integrated and rather ele-vated. Other than that, the wine exhibits a dark plum/ruby color and a sweet nose of blackberry and cherry fruit intermixed with mineral, underbrush, and earth. The wine is medium to full-bodied, quite sweet and expansive on the palate, and very pure and long. Anticipated maturity: now–2010. Last tasted, 11/00.

CLOS DE SARPE

Classification: Grand Cru

Owner: Jean-Guy Beyney

Address: 33330 Saint-Christophe-des-Bardes

Mailing address: c/o SCA Beynet, 33330
Saint-Christophe-des-Bardes

Telephone: 05 57 24 72 39; Telefax: 05 57 74 47 54

E-mail: chateau@clos-de-sarpe.com

Website: www.clos-de-sarpe.com

Visits: By appointment only

Contact: Jean-Guy Beyney

VINEYARDS

Surface area: 9.1 acres

Grape varietals: 85% Merlot, 15% Cabernet Franc

Average age of vines: 10–25 years for one-third of the vineyard; 50–80 years for the rest

Density of plantation: 5,500 vines per hectare

Average yields: 25 hectoliters per hectare

Elevage: Eight to ten day cold maceration. Four to five week fermentation and maceration with *pigéages,* pumpings-over, and micro-oxygenation. Malolactics and 16–18 months aging on lees in new oak barrels. No fining, no filtration.

WINES PRODUCED

Clos de Sarpe: 12,000 bottles

Charles de Sarpe: 5,000 bottles

GENERAL APPRECIATION

There are approximately 1,000 cases of this stunning St.-Emilion, which has emerged since 1998 as one of the biggest, richest, fullest-bodied wines of the appellation. The wine is produced from a 10-acre vineyard (biodynamically farmed) that is planted with extremely old vines on a south-facing, limestone hillside. The blend of 85% Merlot and 15% Cabernet Franc is aged in 100% new French oak. Clos de Sarpe can border on being rustic, but there is so much power, depth, and concentrated fruit that serious Bordeaux consumers need to give it a try.

IMPORTANT VINTAGES

2001
89–91+
A backward, muscular St.-Emilion, the 2001 Clos de Sarpe (85% Merlot and 15% Cabernet Franc from small yields of 23 hectoliters per hectare) is powerful, full-bodied, rustic, intense, and tannic. Patience will be required as it is being aged in 100% new French oak and will be bottled with no fining or filtration. A beefy, larger than life effort, it will be drinkable between 2008–2025. Last tasted, 1/03.

2000
95+
A blockbuster effort made for readers with 19th-century tastes, this wine is intensely concentrated, with abundant yet sweet tannin. Its dense purple color is accompanied by a big, chewy bouquet of black fruits intermixed with minerals, smoke, and licorice. While immense on the palate, with high tannin, it has become

more civilized after bottling. However, patience is definitely a prerequisite for this monster St.-Emilion. A fascinating wine. Anticipated maturity: 2010–2035. Last tasted, 1/03.

1999 The 1999 may not compare to the other-worldly 2000 or powerful 1998, but it is a
90 rich, deep ruby/purple-colored effort offering gorgeous aromas of black raspberries, licorice, earth, and toast. Highly extracted, rich, and full-bodied, with moderately high tannin, it is a behemoth for the vintage. Anticipated maturity: 2007–2018. Last tasted, 3/02.

1998 The 1998 is a structured, closed, but enormously concentrated, rich, full-bodied
90+? effort that should turn out to be a sleeper of the vintage. My only reservation is the high tannin level, which seems ripe and reasonably well integrated. There are dazzling levels of black fruits intermixed with mineral, crushed stone, licorice, and vanilla characteristics. Anticipated maturity: 2005–2015. Last tasted, 3/02.

LA CLOTTE

Classification: Grand Cru Classé

Owner: Chailleau family

Address: 33330 St.-Emilion

Telephone: 05 57 24 66 85; Telefax: 05 57 24 79 67

E-mail: chateau-la-clotte@wanadoo.fr

Visits: By appointment only

Contact: Nelly Moulierac

VINEYARDS

Surface area: 9.9 acres

Grape varietals: 80% Merlot, 15% Cabernet Franc, 5% Cabernet Sauvignon

Average age of vines: 40 years

Density of plantation: 6,500 vines per hectare

Average yields: 36 hectoliters per hectare

Elevage: Twenty-five to thirty day fermentation (32°C) and maceration in temperature-controlled vats, with eight daily pumpings-over. Malolactics and 16 months aging in barrels with 50% new oak. Upbringing on lees with stirring during the first 12 months. No fining, filtration.

WINES PRODUCED

Château La Clotte: 15,000 bottles

No second wine is produced.

Plateau of maturity: Within 3–8 years of the vintage

GENERAL APPRECIATION

A small up-and-coming estate, La Clotte is quietly making its way toward the higher echelons of the St.-Emilion hierarchy with the valuable assistance of guru Stéphane Derénoncourt.

The tiny vineyard of La Clotte is owned by the Chailleau family, who are probably better known as the owners of the immensely popular restaurant snuggled in a back alley of St.-Emilion, Logis de la Cadène. I have often enjoyed this wine and have found it very typical of a plump, fleshy, well-made St.-Emilion. Drinkable when released, it holds its fruit and develops for 10–12 years. The vineyard is well situated on the edge of the limestone plateau, just outside the ancient town walls of St.-Emilion.

IMPORTANT VINTAGES

2001
87–88
While lighter than the superb 2000, without the volume or power of the former vintage, the 2001 La Clotte is an attractive offering with supple tannin and sweet black cherry fruit intermixed with herbs and cedar. Medium bodied and fleshy, it is best drunk during its first 8–15 years of life. Last tasted, 1/03.

2000
91
Unquestionably the finest La Clotte I have ever tasted, the 2000 La Clotte reveals an opaque ruby/purple color along with sweet aromas of liquid minerals, anise, plum, cassis, and smoke. Deep, rich, full-bodied, opulent, and moderately tannic, it will be at its peak between 2005–2016. Sexy stuff! Last tasted, 1/03.

1999
87
Readers looking for an up-front, fruit-driven St.-Emilion with notes of saddle leather, dried Provençal herbs, and copious cherry/black currant fruit should check out this expansive, open-knit, succulent 1999. The acid is low, the tannin ripe, and the fruit delicious. Enjoy it over the next 5–6 years. Last tasted, 3/02.

1998
89
A seductive, dark ruby/plum–colored effort, the 1998 exhibits a viscous texture, rich, spicy, berry fruit, and abundant quantities of plums as well as cherries. Medium to full-bodied, it is best drunk over the next 6–7 years. Last tasted, 3/02.

ANCIENT VINTAGES

Until the late 1990s La Clotte was under an exclusive contract with the Libourne firm of Jean-Pierre Moueix, who managed the vineyard and in return received three-fourths of the crop for selling on an exclusive basis throughout the world. The vintages made by Moueix were always good, plump, fleshy, well-made St.-Emilions, but certainly the level of concentration and intensity in this wine has been dramatically increased now that the contract with Moueix has expired. Nevertheless, most of the older vintages were wines to drink during their first 8–10 years of life. The highest rating I ever gave any vintage in the 1980s or 1990s under the Moueix administration was the 1990 (89 points; last tasted 1/93).

LA CLUSIÈRE

Classification: Grand Cru Classé
Owner: Gérard and Chantal Perse
Address: 33330 St.-Emilion
Mailing address: c/o SCA Château Pavie, 33330 St.-Emilion
Telephone: 05 57 55 43 43; Telefax: 05 57 24 63 99
E-mail: vignobles.perse@wanadoo.fr
Website: www.chateaupavie.com
No visits

VINEYARDS

Surface area: 6.2 acres

Grape varietals: 100% Merlot

Average age of vines: 55 years

Density of plantation: 5,500 vines per hectare

Average yields: 15 hectoliters per hectare

Elevage: Four to five week fermentation and maceration in temperature-controlled wooden vats. Eighteen to twenty-two months aging in new oak barrels. No fining, no filtration.

WINES PRODUCED

Château La Clusière: 5,000 bottles

No second wine is produced.

Plateau of maturity: Within 6–15 years of the vintage

GENERAL APPRECIATION

La Clusière was another moribund St.-Emilion estate that was brought to fame by the energetic Gérard Perse, also the power behind Pavie, Pavie Decesse, and Monbousquet. After having produced five or six topflight vintages at this estate, the owner has decided to incorporate the production from this tiny vineyard into Pavie as of 2002.

On the high ridge above the vineyards of Pavie is the microscopic vineyard and *cuverie* of La Clusière. Prior to Gérard Perse's acquisition in 1997, the wine that emerged from this vineyard tended to be surprisingly tough textured, with hard tannins and an ungenerous personality. One would suspect that moderate cellaring would soften the wine, but that has not been my experience.

Under Perse, the wines of this 6.2-acre vineyard of extremely old vines (55 years), located next to Pavie, have been produced from 100% Merlot, cropped at incredibly low yields. It sees malolactic in barrel, aging on its lees for 24 months, and bottling with neither fining nor filtration. La Clusière is meant to be Perse's answer to Pomerol's Le Pin. However, 2001 is the last vintage for La Clusière as this tiny vineyard was incorporated into Pavie in 2002.

IMPORTANT VINTAGES

2001
93–95
Cropped at astronomically low yields of 15 hectoliters per hectare, the 2001 La Clusière, which rivals the amazing 2000, is a blockbuster powerhouse with an extraordinary velvety texture, remarkable sweet blackberry and cherry fruit, and density as well as extract that make it one of the two or three most concentrated and layered wines of the vintage. It should develop more quickly than either Pavie or Pavie Decesse, two of the other St.-Emilions owned by Chantal and Gérard Perse. A wine of enviable purity, La Clusière is one of the vintage's few superstars. Anticipated maturity: 2008–2022. Last tasted, 1/03.

2000
100
The 2000 is undoubtedly the finest La Clusière ever produced. A magnificent effort possessing off-the-chart extract levels as well as a remarkably intense palate impression, it tastes like the undistilled essence of a particular vineyard and wine type. The color is opaque purple. The bouquet reveals dense blackberry, plum, and cassis aromas infused with minerals, licorice, and graphite. Full-bodied, mas-

sively endowed, and concentrated with high tannin, this is a tour de force in wine-making. Anticipated maturity: 2008–2035. Last tasted, 1/03.

1999 The dense purple–colored 1999 La Clusière boasts a gloriously sweet, perfumed
93   bouquet of minerals, new oak, and plum liqueur intermixed with cherries and as-sorted black fruits. Medium to full-bodied, elegant, and flamboyant, with a chewy texture and well-integrated acidity, tannin, and wood, it should be at its finest be-tween now and 2020. Last tasted, 3/02.

1998 The 1998 possesses an opaque purple color as well as a firm but promising bou-
90+   quet of black fruits, crushed stones, and smoky new oak. There is plenty of depth and purity, as well as a well-delineated style in this backward, tannic, muscular effort. One of the finest La Clusières yet produced, it still requires 1–2 more years of cellaring. Anticipated maturity: 2005–2020. Last tasted, 3/02.

ANCIENT VINTAGES

All of the wines produced under the previous administration (the proprietor was the late Jean-Paul Valette) were disappointing, and they rarely scored above 80 points, with the exception of the 1990 (89 points; last tasted 1/93). Nevertheless, the handful of vintages produced by Gérard Perse have nothing in common with anything produced previously.

CORBIN

Classification: Grand Cru Classé

Owner: Blanchard-Cruse family

Address: 33330 St.-Emilion

Telephone: 05 57 25 20 30; Telefax: 05 57 25 22 00

E-mail: chateau.corbin@wanadoo.fr

Visits: By appointment only

VINEYARDS

Surface area: 31.4 acres

Grape varietals: 80% Merlot, 20% Cabernet Franc

Average age of vines: 30 years

Density of plantation: 6,060 vines per hectare

Average yields: 45 hectoliters per hectare

Elevage: Four week fermentation and maceration in temperature-controlled concrete tanks. Fifteen to eighteen months aging in barrels with 43% new oak. No fining, filtration.

WINES PRODUCED

Château Corbin: 60,000 bottles

Maximin: 20,000 bottles

Plateau of maturity: Within 3–10 years of the vintage

GENERAL APPRECIATION

The wines of Château Corbin are generally well made, charming, and fruity, but they rarely exhibit great depth or richness. They are delicious for quaffing and the reasonable pricing is admirable. The change in ownership in 1996 has had a positive effect on quality.

Corbin is clearly a property capable of making rich, deeply fruity, luscious wines. My first experience with this wine was at a dinner party where the 1970 was served blind. It was an immensely enjoyable, round, full-bodied, concentrated, delicious wine with plenty of fruit. Since then I have made it a point to follow this estate closely. In the great vintages—for instance, 2000, 1990, 1989, 1982, and 1970—this wine has merit. The problem has been inconsistency.

Corbin's vineyard, once owned by England's Black Prince, straddles the Pomerol border on the *graves* plateau. Bordeaux's famed Professor Enjalbert argues that Corbin's vineyard is situated on a similar band of soil that underpins the vineyards of Cheval Blanc. The style of wine produced at Corbin reaches heights in hot, sunny, drought years when the wine is dark in color, fat, ripe, full-bodied, and admirably concentrated. Unfortunately, Corbin is a moderately expensive wine, as it has long been popular in the Benelux countries and Great Britain.

IMPORTANT VINTAGES

2001 Not terribly dissimilar from the fleshy and succulent 2000, this vintage provided
87–88 slightly less mass and brighter acids, but the overall style is classic Corbin—soft, fruity, charming, and seductive. Anticipated maturity: 2004–2011. Last tasted, 1/03.

2000 Typical for this estate, the deep ruby/purple–colored 2000 is a fruit-driven effort
88 offering notes of plums, cherries, saddle leather, tobacco, and earth. It possesses medium body, excellent depth, moderate tannin, and a velvety texture. Anticipated maturity: 2004–2012. Last tasted, 1/03.

1999 Soft, straightforward, and fruity, with notes of herbs, cherries, and currants, this
85 wine has plenty of suppleness but not much depth. Anticipated maturity: now–2009. Last tasted, 3/02.

1998 A fine effort from this reliable St.-Emilion, Corbin's 1998 is a fat, fleshy, dense,
88 richly fruity offering with aromas and flavors of black cherries, spice box, earth, and licorice. There is good glycerin, a chewy entry and mid-palate, ripe tannin, and a soft, succulent finish. A very promising effort from the new owners. Anticipated maturity: now–2012. Last tasted, 3/02.

1997 A solidly made, plump, fruity St.-Emilion, with good depth, medium body, and
85 robust spice and black cherry fruit, this soft wine requires consumption now. Last tasted, 3/01.

1996 This wine possesses too much tannin for its uninspiring concentration of fruit. The
80? medium ruby color is accompanied by a wine with cherry, herb, and earth aromas. But the dusty tannin and other rustic characteristics of this wine do not bode well for future development. It should keep for a decade, but there is not enough flesh or fruit to cover the wine's framework. Anticipated maturity: now–2006. Last tasted, 3/99.

1995 The 1995 exhibits a saturated color as well as sweet fruit, low acidity, and good
86 ripeness. It comes across as a forward, easygoing style of St.-Emilion for drinking now. Last tasted, 3/99.

1990 This wine has reached full maturity at an accelerated pace. Notwithstanding that,
87 it is a delicious, plump Corbin with a dark garnet color already revealing moderate quantities of rust and orange at its rim. It offers an attractive fruitcake, spice, and

jammy-scented nose, followed by lush, soft, medium-bodied flavors with good levels of glycerin, flesh, and fat. The 1990 is similar to the 1989. It needs to be drunk up. Anticipated maturity: now. Last tasted, 11/97.

1989 — The 1989 has extremely low acidity and soft tannins, but the overall impression is
87 — one of power, an opulent, even unctuous texture, and precocious drinkability. Assuming you like this big, overripe, Australian style of wine and intend to drink it within its first decade of life, this wine will undoubtedly provide an enticing level of exhilaration. Anticipated maturity: now. Last tasted, 3/95.

CORBIN MICHOTTE

Classification: Grand Cru Classé

Owner: Jean-Noël Boidron

Address: 33330 St.-Emilion

Telephone: 05 57 51 64 88; Telefax: 05 57 51 56 30

Visits: By appointment Monday to Friday,
8 A.M.–noon and 2–5 P.M.

Contact: Emmanuel Boidron

VINEYARDS

Surface area: 17.3 acres

Grape varietals: 65% Merlot, 30% Cabernet Franc, 5% Cabernet Sauvignon

Average age of vines: 35 years

Density of plantation: 5,865 vines per hectare

Average yields: 40 hectoliters per hectare

Elevage: Prolonged fermentation and maceration in temperature-controlled vats, with no addition of yeasts. Twenty-four months aging in barrels with 70% new oak. Fining, no filtration.

WINES PRODUCED

Château Corbin Michotte: 37,000 bottles

Château Les Abeilles: 3,000 bottles (produced only in the less prestigious vintages)

Plateau of maturity: Within 3–12 years of the vintage

GENERAL APPRECIATION

Corbin Michotte seems always to aim for ripeness and a seductive, forward, fruity style with no hard edges. Most vintages are fruit-driven, succulent, juicy, and easygoing. This is a wine to buy by the case for its obvious hedonistic qualities.

Corbin Michotte is one of five châteaux that sit along the Pomerol border with "Corbin" in their name. One single parcel (rare in Bordeaux), it has the potential to be one of the best of the area. It is a small estate with relatively old vines that are planted on a sandy, loam soil intermixed with fine gravel, and what the French call *crasse de fer*, meaning a ferruginous iron-rich subsoil. The vineyard is also laden with minerals, which the proprietor claims gives the wine's bouquet its extra dimension. Much of Corbin Michotte is sold directly to clients in Europe and Switzerland, which remain the strongest market for this property. Vintages I have tasted have reminded me more of a Pomerol than a St.-Emilion. They have been deeply colored wines, with a very pronounced black fruit, plummy character, and a luscious, opulent texture.

IMPORTANT VINTAGES

2000 A totally delicious *vin de plaisir,* this medium-bodied, perfumed wine has no hard
88 edges, a plum, cherry, currant-based nose and flavors, and seamless integration of tannin and acidity. This is a sexy fleshpot of a wine to drink over the next 7–8 years. Anticipated maturity: now–2011. Last tasted, 1/03.

1998 This fruit-driven, succulent, juicy, easygoing St.-Emilion offers an intriguing nose
87 of dried herbs, seaweed, and black cherries. Soft, medium bodied, and velvety textured, it is a candidate for early consumption—over the next 4–5 years. Last tasted, 3/02.

1997 The 1997 is a jammy-styled wine with elements of *sur-maturité* and good fat,
86 cherry/berry fruit intermixed with smoke, earth, and spice scents. It is a medium-bodied, potentially excellent wine for the vintage with low acidity and a seductive, hedonistic appeal. Drink it over the next 2–3 years. Last tasted, 3/01.

1996 The 1996 follows in the style of most Corbin Michottes, even though the vintage
86 had a tendency to produce tannic, hard wines. However, Corbin Michotte always seems to aim for ripeness and a seductive, forward fruity style with no hard edges. The dark ruby–colored 1996 is round and soft, with plenty of herb-tinged berry fruit intermixed with smoke and earth. Ripe and medium bodied, it is ideal for drinking over the next 3–4 years. Last tasted, 3/01.

1995 A hedonistic effort from Corbin Michotte, the 1995 reveals a deep ruby color, a
89 jammy plum, cherry, and spice box nose, and medium-bodied, lush, low-acid, juicy, opulently textured, fruity flavors. This is an exuberantly fruity, tasty St.-Emilion that, on a pure scale of pleasure, merits even higher marks. Anticipated maturity: now–2008. Last tasted, 3/01.

1994 An undeniable success for the vintage, the 1994 exhibits a dense ruby/purple
88 color and a wonderfully expressive nose of jammy black currants, minerals, and flowers. Ripe, highly fruited, and medium to full-bodied with layers of flavor, it needs to be drunk up. Anticipated maturity: now. Last tasted, 3/01.

CÔTE DE BALEAU

Classification: Grand Cru

Owner: GFA Les Grandes Murailles—Reiffers family

Address: 33330 St.-Emilion

Telephone: 05 57 24 71 09; Telefax: 05 57 24 69 72

E-mail: lesgrandesmurailles@wanadoo.fr

Website: www.grandes-murailles.com

Visits: By appointment only

Contact: Sophie Fourcade

VINEYARDS

Surface area: 19.8 acres

Grape varietals: 70% Merlot, 20% Cabernet Franc, 10% Cabernet Sauvignon

Average age of vines: 35 years

Density of plantation: 5,500–6,300 vines per hectare

Average yields: 40 hectoliters per hectare

Elevage: Cold maceration. Twenty to twenty-five day fermentation and maceration in temperature-controlled stainless-steel vats. Malolactics and 18–20 months aging with 70% new oak and 30% one-year-old barrels. No fining, filtration if necessary.

WINES PRODUCED

Château Côte de Baleau: 42,000 bottles

No second wine is produced.

Plateau of maturity: Within 5–15 years of the vintage

GENERAL APPRECIATION

Another gem of a property belonging to the Reiffers family, Côte de Baleau's modest production is unquestionably very good. Over recent vintages, Sophie Fourcade's impeccable management of the estate, as well as Michel Rolland's valuable advice, have made this wine an emerging star of the appellation. I can only recommend this superb effort, which seems to have fared wonderfully well, irrespective of vintage conditions, since the mid-1990s.

IMPORTANT VINTAGES

2001   A powerful offering, Côte de Baleau's 2001 exhibits a deep blue/purple color as
88–89+   well as sweet black raspberry and blueberry fruit infused with minerals and earth. Deep, ripe, layered, and rich, it will be at its finest between 2006–2015. Last tasted, 1/03.

2000   This potentially outstanding, deep purple–colored 2000 exhibits sweet cherry,
90   plum, and currant aromas and flavors with subtle mineral and wood notes, excellent texture, medium to full body, and ripe tannin. The overall impression is a well-delineated, impeccably elegant wine with class and grace. Anticipated maturity: 2006–2018. Last tasted, 1/03.

1999   The 1999 is short in the mouth, suggesting the vineyard may have suffered hail
87?   damage. It exhibits aromas of sweet plum and cherry fruit, medium body, light tannin, and an abrupt finish. What is there is impressive, but I recommend consuming this wine over the next 5–6 years. Anticipated maturity: now–2009. Last tasted, 3/02.

1998   A serious, tight-fisted St.-Emilion, this dense ruby/purple–colored effort reveals
90   impressive thickness as well as notes of minerals, flowers, cherries, and spice box that are reminiscent of the aromas found in such hillside St.-Emilions as Canon and Ausone. Well delineated and elegant with a terrific mid-palate and finish, it requires 1–2 years of cellaring. It has turned out to be outstanding as the flesh emerges and the tannin becomes sweeter and better integrated. Anticipated maturity: 2007–2020. Last tasted, 1/03.

LA COUSPAUDE

Classification: Grand Cru Classé

Owner: SCE Vignobles Aubert

Address: 33330 St.-Emilion

Mailing address: BP 40, 33330 St.-Emilion

Telephone: 05 57 40 15 76; Telefax: 05 57 40 10 14

E-mail: vignobles.aubert@wanadoo.fr

Website: www.la-couspaude.com

Visits: By appointment only

Contact: Jean-Claude Aubert

VINEYARDS

Surface area: 18 acres

Grape varietals: 70% Merlot, 30% Cabernet Franc

Average age of vines: 30 years

Density of plantation: 6,500 vines per hectare

Average yields: 38 hectoliters per hectare

Elevage: Twenty-five to forty day fermentation and maceration in small, temperature-controlled, flat, cone-shaped wooden vats. Malolactics and 16–24 months aging in new oak barrels. No fining, no filtration.

WINES PRODUCED

Château La Couspaude: 24,000–30,000 bottles

Junior de la Couspaude: 12,000 bottles

Plateau of maturity: Within 5–15 years of the vintage

GENERAL APPRECIATION

Another garage operation, La Couspaude has always been a flashy, fleshpot sort of wine that goes right to the hedonistic senses. The French call this a *vin gourmand,* meaning a sensual, hedonistic offering designed to provide enormous pleasure. It is made in a modern style with plenty of creamy new oak (it is aged in 100% new French oak, and part of the yield is used to receive the so-called "200%" new oak treatment), and while some former vintages were slightly overoaked, more recent years exhibit better integrated wood. Today the gorgeous purity of fruit for this opulently textured, layered, fleshy effort is easily appreciated. While low-acid and luxuriant, La Couspaude must not be underestimated in terms of aging capacity.

This small, walled vineyard owned by the Aubert family has recently received significant attention because of its exotic, ripe, rich, sexy style. The wine's breakthrough came in 1995, but all the vintages have been made in a flamboyant, generously endowed style. While critics have complained that the wine is excessively oaky (and I would agree that oak is a prominent component of the wine), I believe the oak will be absorbed during the wine's evolution because of the richness and concentration possessed. I predict the wines from this small estate will become increasingly expensive once the international marketplace recognizes the quality.

IMPORTANT VINTAGES

2001 Proprietor Jean-Claude Aubert is doing a far better job of integrating the wood
89–91 than he has accomplished in the past, as evidenced by this 2001. Medium to full-bodied, with excellent depth of ripe black cherry and berry fruit, this is an opulently textured, layered, low-acid, fleshy effort. Atypical for the vintage, it is pure, perfumed, and already drinkable. Anticipated maturity: now–2012. Last tasted, 1/03.

2000 The terrific, fat, sweet, opulent, multilayered 2000 boasts a dense ruby/purple
92 color along with copious quantities of black cherry liqueur, espresso, mineral, toasty oak, and roasted nut characteristics. Layered, voluptuous, and pure, this full-throttle effort should be drinkable in 2–3 years and last for 16+. A full-bodied wine, it is very sexy stuff. Anticipated maturity: 2005–2016. Last tasted, 1/03.

1999 This is an attractive, elegant wine with obvious spicy new oak, sweet black cherry
87 liqueur notes, and a short finish. While lighter than usual, it is a savory, modern-styled St.-Emilion for drinking now and over the next 4–5 years. Last tasted, 3/02.

1998 Along with the 2000, the finest La Couspaude to date, the 1998 displays flamboy-
92 ant notes of toasty new oak as well as an exotic personality. Unctuous, thick, full-bodied, seamless flavors redolent with plums, cherry liqueur, and vanilla cascade over the palate. Low acidity and plush, concentrated, jammy fruit add to the impressive, hedonistic qualities of this explosively rich wine. Anticipated maturity: now–2015. Last tasted, 11/02.

1997 The 1997 is an exotic, rich, thick, jammy wine with abundant black cherry aromas
88 mixed with scents of roasted coffee, smoke, and toasty new oak. With low acidity and a delicious, medium-bodied, ostentatious personality, this seductive offering can be drunk now as well as over the next 6–7 years. Last tasted, 3/02.

1996 La Couspaude's 1996 has turned out well. This is a richly fruity, sexy, medium-
88 bodied, surprisingly soft and fragrant 1996. Its open-knit aromatics, consisting of toast, cherry liqueur, smoke, and black currants, are followed by a luscious, soft, lightly tannic wine. It is destined to be drunk during its first 10–12 years of life. Last tasted, 3/01.

1995 The first outstanding wine from this estate, the 1995 La Couspaude exhibits a ripe,
90 jammy kirsch, black currant, and licorice-scented nose with plenty of smoky, toasty notes. Full-bodied, with low acidity and a flamboyant personality, this wine will unquestionably cause heads to turn. Traditionalists may argue that it is too obvious and sexy, but this is a fun wine to taste, and no one can argue that it does not provide pleasure . . . and isn't that the ultimate objective of drinking this stuff? Moreover, it will age well and become even more civilized with cellaring. Anticipated maturity: now–2015. Last tasted, 11/97.

1994 The 1994 has put on more weight. The wine reveals a deep ruby/purple color and
88 a big, toasty, smoky nose filled with the scents of Provençal herbs and jammy black cherries. Dense, rich, and fat, this well-endowed, oaky wine should drink well for 7–8 years. Last tasted, 3/96.

COUVENT DES JACOBINS

Classification: Grand Cru Classé

Owner: Alain and Rose-Noëlle Borde

Address: SCEV Joinaud Borde, Rue Guadet, 33330 St.-Emilion

Telephone: 05 57 24 70 66; Telefax: 05 57 24 62 51

Visits: By appointment only

Contact: Alain Borde

VINEYARDS

Surface area: 26.4 acres

Grape varietals: 75% Merlot, 25% Cabernet Franc

Average age of vines: 40–45 years

Density of plantation: 7,000 vines per hectare

Average yields: 35–40 hectoliters per hectare

Elevage: Cold maceration. Twenty-five to thirty-five day fermentation and maceration in temperature-controlled vats. Malolactics in barrel for 20–30% of yield. Twelve to fifteen months aging on lees in barrels with 60–65% new oak and 30–35% one-year-old barrels, with frequent stirrings. Fining, no filtration.

WINES PRODUCED

Couvent des Jacobins: 35,000–40,000 bottles

Menut des Jacobins: 5,000 bottles

Plateau of maturity: Within 4–14 years of the vintage

GENERAL APPRECIATION

A reliable wine that could be improved with a stricter selection.

Couvent des Jacobins, named after the 13th-century Dominican monastery that was built on this site, is meticulously run by the Joinaud-Borde family, who have owned the property since 1902.

The vineyards are immediately situated adjacent to the town of St.-Emilion, on a sandy, clay soil of the *côtes* that produces darkly colored, rich, fairly alcoholic wines of some substance. The quality of Couvent des Jacobins is reliable rather than exciting.

Couvent des Jacobins, located immediately to the left-hand side of the main entrance to the town, has one of the most remarkable underground cellars of the region. It is a showpiece property that would make for an interesting visit even if the wines were not so distinguished.

IMPORTANT VINTAGES

2001　A strong performance by this estate, the 2001 Couvent des Jacobins exhibits a sat-
87–88　urated ruby/purple color along with scents of dried herbs, licorice, black fruits, and earth. Medium bodied, with good acidity, ripe tannin, and a moderately long

finish, this fruit-filled St.-Emilion will be at its finest between 2005–2013. Last tasted, 1/03.

2000 A deep ruby/purple color is accompanied by sweet aromas of earth-infused herbs
88   and black cherries. This lush offering will provide straightforward, plump, fruity enjoyment over the next 12 years. Last tasted, 1/03.

1999 A medium dark plum color is followed by aromas of broccoli, cherries, earth, and
85   a hint of Provençal herbs. The wine offers a fleshy attack, but narrows in the mouth and finishes abruptly. The tannin is light and the acidity adequate. Drink this 1999 over the next 4–5 years. Last tasted, 3/02.

1998 This is a medium-bodied, straightforward effort offering up scents of earth, ripe
86   black cherries, dried Provençal herbs, and new wood. A lean, austere finish kept my score low. Anticipated maturity: now–2012. Last tasted, 3/02.

CROIX DE LABRIE

Classification: Grand Cru

Owner: Michel et Ghislaine Puzio-Lesage

Address: 33330 St.-Emilion

Telephone: 05 57 24 64 60

No visits

VINEYARDS

Surface area: 3.7 acres

Grape varietals: 100% Merlot

Average age of vines: 40 years

Density of plantation: 4,500 vines per hectare

Average yields: 30 hectoliters per hectare

Elevage: Fermentation and maceration for 15–20 days in stainless-steel vats. Malolactics and aging for 16–22 months in new oak. Fining and filtration if necessary.

WINES PRODUCED

Château Croix de Labrie: 2,500 bottles

Petit Labrie: 1,000 bottles

Plateau of maturity: Within 4–15 years of the vintage

GENERAL APPRECIATION

The production of this handcrafted garage wine, which has been consistently impressive, is so small that the barrels in which it is aged are housed in the proprietor's living room, hence the name *vin de salon*. One of St.-Emilion's most dazzling garage wines since its debut vintage, it is made with the consultation of Jean-Luc Thunevin (of Valandraud fame). An extraordinarily pure expression of fruit and *terroir*, this is terrific stuff!

IMPORTANT VINTAGES

2001   The 2001 Croix de Labrie reveals body, density, and richness that are atypical for
88–91 this vintage. Its saturated purple color is followed by sweet, pure, blackberry and currant fruit intermixed with minerals, coffee, and vanilla. Layered and ripe, if it

continues to flesh out, it will merit an outstanding rating. Anticipated maturity: 2006–2015. Last tasted, 1/03.

2000   This is a sensational effort, but sadly, there are only 9,000 bottles of the big, block-
95   buster 2000. It boasts superb purity along with the essence of cassis and black cherry liqueur-like fruit intermixed with graphite, chocolate, espresso, and new oak notes. Sweet, layered, and luxuriously rich, with a wealth of fruit and glycerin, this stunningly full-bodied St.-Emilion should be drinkable young, yet age nicely for 15+ years. Anticipated maturity: 2006–2020. Last tasted, 1/03.

1999   The 1999 Croix de Labrie (only 3,000 bottles produced) offers sweet, Port-like
93   blackberry, cherry, and strawberry fruit, terrific texture, a savory, lush, explosive mid-palate, low acidity, and a ripe finish revealing notions of toasty oak and chocolate. It is an exuberant, full-bodied, lavishly rich effort to enjoy now and over the next 6–7 years. Last tasted, 3/02.

1998   An opaque purple color is accompanied by aromas of roasted meat, black fruits,
93   spicy oak, and coffee. The wine displays supple tannin, explosive richness, immense body, and beautifully integrated acidity as well as tannin. What a shame there are not more than 5,000 cases of this blockbuster effort. Anticipated maturity: now–2014. Last tasted, 3/02.

DASSAULT

Classification: Grand Cru

Owner: SARL Château Dassault

Address: 33330 St.-Emilion

Telephone: 05 57 55 10 00; Telefax: 05 57 55 10 01

E-mail: lbv@chateaudassault.com

Website: www.chateaudassault.com

Visits: By appointment only

Contact: Laurence Brun

VINEYARDS

Surface area: 66.7 acres

Grape varietals: 69% Merlot, 23% Cabernet Franc, 8% Cabernet Sauvignon

Average age of vines: 35 years

Density of plantation: 5,500 vines per hectare

Average yields: 39 hectoliters per hectare

Elevage: Three week fermentation and maceration. Malolactics and 16–18 months aging in barrels with 90–100% new oak. No fining, filtration.

WINES PRODUCED

Château Dassault: 70,000 bottles

Le «D» de Dassault: 45,000 bottles

Plateau of maturity: Within 3–10 years of the vintage

GENERAL APPRECIATION

Despite the considerable human and financial investments, Dassault has never managed to take off. Even allowing for a distressing period when it had to deal with tainted and musty aromas that marred its wines, Dassault produces wines that are sound but uninspiring, but several recent vintages have been encouraging.

Dassault—one of the loveliest châteaux in St.-Emilion, with particularly impressive grounds—consistently produces smooth-textured, fruity, supple, straightforward wines that are meant to be drunk in their youth. They are very cleanly made and perhaps somewhat commercial in orientation, but there is no denying their attractive, uncomplicated style. The only caveat here is that aging rarely results in a better wine. As long as one is prepared to drink this wine at a relatively early age, it is unlikely that Dassault will be disappointing. The perfect restaurant St.-Emilion?

In the early and mid-1990s, there was clearly a problem with too many musty bottles of Dassault. That problem has been completely alleviated, as evidenced by recent vintages.

IMPORTANT VINTAGES

2001 A very attractive, open-knit, deep ruby–colored wine, Dassault's 2001 has sweet
85–87 currant, plum, and cassis flavors, medium body, and more density and structure than usual. Anticipated maturity: 2005–2013. Last tasted, 1/03.

2000 This is a fruity, consumer-friendly St.-Emilion meant to be consumed during its
88 first decade of life. The sexy, low-acid 2000 reveals ripe black cherry fruit intermixed with notes of Provençal herbs, spice box, and new oak. It is round, expansive, fleshy, and cleanly made, with more tannin and persistence on the palate than previous vintages. Anticipated maturity: 2004–2014. Last tasted, 1/03.

1999 Soft, seductive, and tasty, with plenty of currant and plum fruit, this ripe, low-acid,
87 ruby-colored Dassault should be drunk over the next four years. Last tasted, 3/02.

1998 A dark ruby color is accompanied by a sweet bouquet of blueberry and black cur-
87 rant fruit. This medium-bodied, low-acid, fleshy, richly fruity, smooth 1998 will provide delicious drinking over the next 6–7 years. Last tasted, 3/02.

DAUGAY

Classification: Grand Cru

Owner: Christian de Boüard de Laforest

Address: 33330 St.-Emilion

Telephone: 05 57 24 78 12

No visits

VINEYARDS

Surface area: 13.8 acres

Grape varietals: 50% Merlot, 48% Cabernet Franc, 2% Cabernet Sauvignon

Average age of vines: 40 years

Density of plantation: 6,666 vines per hectare

Average yields: 50 hectoliters per hectare

Elevage: Eighteen to twenty-one day fermentation and maceration in temperature-controlled stainless-steel vats. Eighteen months aging in vats. Fining, no filtration.

WINES PRODUCED

Château Daugay: 37,000 bottles

No second wine is produced.

Plateau of maturity: Within 3–12 years of the vintage

GENERAL APPRECIATION

Daugay marches to its own beat and is an unpretentious, straightforward, pleasant wine, superior to many more ambitious wines, overoaked and excessively tannic through exaggerated extraction. Bordeaux needs to produce more of this kind of affordable *vin de plaisir!*

This small estate is owned by the brother of Hubert de Boüard of Château Angélus. In fact, until 1984, this vineyard was part of Angélus. The wine is a very good St.-Emilion that is somewhat undervalued given modern-day pricing.

IMPORTANT VINTAGES

2001 Possibly superior to the 2000, the dark ruby/purple–colored 2001 has a sweet
87–88 nose of plums, currants, and dusty earth. Medium bodied, supple textured, and fruity, this wine is an ideal candidate for drinking over the next 7–8 years. Last tasted, 1/03.

2000 The excellent, deep ruby/purple–colored 2000 exhibits aromas of melted licorice,
87 black currants, cherries, and a hint of Provençal herbs. The tannin is sweet, the acidity low, and the wine plush as well as nicely textured. Anticipated maturity: now–2012. Last tasted, 1/03.

1999 Sweet herb–tinged, cherry fruit with a hint of tobacco is followed by a medium-
86 bodied, elegant, ripe, attractive wine with no hard edges. Drink it over the next five years. Last tasted, 3/02.

1998 A delicious value in St.-Emilion, this deep ruby–colored 1998 reveals copious
87 quantities of ripe, jammy black cherry fruit, smoke, and minerals. Medium to full-bodied and plump, it is ideal for drinking over the next 5–6 years. Last tasted, 3/02.

DESTIEUX

Classification: Grand Cru

Owner: GFA Destieux—Dauriac family

Address: Saint-Hippolyte, 33330 St.-Emilion

Mailing address: SC Dauriac, Château Destieux, 33330 St.-Emilion

Telephone: 05 57 24 77 44; Telefax: 05 57 40 37 42

Visits: By appointment only

Contact: Christian Dauriac

VINEYARDS

Surface area: 19.8 acres

Grape varietals: 66% Merlot, 34% Cabernet Sauvignon

Average age of vines: 45 years

Density of plantation: 5,000 vines per hectare

Average yields: 33 hectoliters per hectare

Elevage: Fermentation (30–32°C) and 10-day maceration (fairly hot temperatures) in temperature-controlled wooden vats (eight in all—one per hectare) with *pigéage* by foot. Malolactics and 18–20 months aging in new oak barrels. No fining, no filtration.

WINES PRODUCED

Château Destieux: 30,000 bottles

No second wine is produced.

Plateau of maturity: Within 5–15 years of the vintage

GENERAL APPRECIATION

A solid, chunky, and rustic St.-Emilion, Destieux has much improved over recent years, and the latest vintages tend to be less stern and tannic than their predecessors. While the wines produced lately are unquestionably richer than their elders, their tannins, while better integrated than before, still remain a cause for concern. In fact, the short track record of the "improved" Destieux makes it difficult to judge the ability of these wines to age. However, the stuffing is there, and for amateurs of powerful, tannic, and old-styled St.-Emilions offered at realistic prices, Destieux delivers.

Located in the satellite commune of St.-Hippolyte on clay and limestone soils, in a particularly torrid St.-Emilion microclimate, Destieux makes an especially attractive, plummy, fleshy, tough-textured wine, with good concentration and plenty of alcohol.

    The force behind the recent string of successes is both the owner, M. Dauriac, and his talented consulting oenologist, Michel Rolland. The wines of Destieux are among the deepest colored and most powerful and dense of the appellation. If bulk and muscle were criteria for greatness, Destieux would be near the top.

IMPORTANT VINTAGES

2001   This may be proprietor Christian Dauriac's finest wine to date. Opaque purple, it
88–90   possesses aromas of sweet black fruits, licorice, truffles, and toasty oak. Atypically full-bodied and powerful, with plenty of extract, sweet tannin, and a muscular finish, it will require patience. Anticipated maturity: 2007–2018. Last tasted, 1/03.

2000   Along with the 2001, the 2000 Destieux is one of the finest efforts I have tasted
89+   from this property. The inky purple–colored 2000 boasts copious quantities of underbrush, truffle, blackberry, and cassis characteristics, along with high tannin, but a sweet mid-palate as well as more depth in the mid-section than exhibited in past vintages. It is a sleeper of the vintage. Anticipated maturity: 2007–2018. Last tasted, 1/03.

1999   Typically tannic, dense, and chewy, with an absence of charm but plenty of fruit,
87   size, and body, this 1999 will be at its best between 2004 and 2015. Last tasted, 3/02.

1998
87
Dense ruby/purple–colored, with earthy, licorice, beefy, blackberry, plum, and subtle underbrush aromas, this powerful, moderately tannic, rich, chewy, robust, full-bodied wine needs cellaring. Anticipated maturity: 2005–2015. Last tasted, 3/02.

1997
86
An earthy, muscular, aggressive style of St.-Emilion, the dark ruby–colored 1997 Destieux exhibits fine depth, rustic tannin, and a robust personality. Displaying power over finesse, it should drink well for 5–6 years. Last tasted, 1/02.

1996
86
The dark ruby/purple–colored 1996 displays sweet blackberry and cherry fruit, medium body, aggressive tannin, and a savory character. It will keep for a decade or more. Anticipated maturity: now–2012. Last tasted, 3/01.

LA DOMINIQUE

Classification: Grand Cru Classé

Owner: Clément Fayat

Address: 33330 St.-Emilion

Telephone: 05 57 51 31 36; Telefax: 05 57 51 63 04

E-mail: info@vignobles.fayat.group.com

Visits: By appointment Monday to Friday,
9 A.M.–noon and 2–6 P.M.

Contact: Cyril Forget

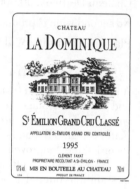

VINEYARDS

Surface area: 55.6 acres (45.7 acres for the Grand Cru Classé)

Grape varietals: 80% Merlot, 15% Cabernet Franc, 5% Cabernet Sauvignon

Average age of vines: 30 years

Density of plantation: 5,700 vines per hectare

Average yields: 32–38 hectoliters per hectare

Elevage: Cold maceration. Thirty to thirty-five day fermentation (29–32°C) and maceration in temperature-controlled vats of small capacity, which allow for separate vinification of the different parcels. Three to four daily pumpings-over. Malolactics in barrel for half of the yield. Eighteen to twenty-two months aging in barrels with 50% new oak. Fining and light filtration.

WINES PRODUCED

Château La Dominique: 55,000 bottles

Saint-Paul de Dominique: 10,000–25,000 bottles

Plateau of maturity: Within 5–20 years of the vintage

GENERAL APPRECIATION

La Dominique was one of the first St.-Emilions to adopt the modern-style vinification, producing very ripe, jammy, and low-acid wines of luxurious richness. It is not as fashionable as many garage operations, but it remains very much an insiders' secret, the sort of wine shrewd buyers squirrel away one vintage after the other because of its highly interesting quality–price ratio. To this day, La Dominique's track record under the ownership of Clément Fayat is topflight. Somewhat reminiscent of a hybrid blend of Cheval Blanc and La Conseillante (two of its neighbors), but available at a much lower price, it is a must buy.

This superbly situated estate, located near the border of Pomerol close to Cheval Blanc, has a soil base composed of limestone gravel and sandy clay. An intensive system of drain tiles installed in the mid-19th century has greatly enhanced this property's ability to produce fine wines in wet years. The truly great wines made at La Dominique—2000, 1998, 1995, 1990, 1989, 1982, and 1971—should easily have qualified La Dominique for elevation to a premier grand cru classé in the 1996 St.-Emilion classification. Sadly, that was not the case. The property continues to lack the glamour and reputation of many of the other premier grands cru classés, a fact that can be put to advantage by consumers looking for fairly priced St.-Emilions.

Proprietor Fayat, who purchased La Dominique in 1969 and who has invested significantly in the vineyards (totally destroyed by the 1956 frost) and winery, utilizes the services of the highly respected Libourne oenologist Michel Rolland to oversee the vinification and *élevage* of La Dominique. The resulting wine is richly colored, intense, superripe, opulent, and full-bodied. It benefits immensely from the 50% new oak barrels utilized each vintage. The decision to make a second wine for less successful vats and young vines has increased the quality even further.

La Dominique's wines continue to be undervalued.

IMPORTANT VINTAGES

2001
87–88?
Tasted five separate times, the 2001 La Dominique appears simple, straightforward, and unevolved. Nevertheless, it exhibits a saturated ruby/plum/purple color, medium body, and pleasing herb-tinged, leathery, black cherry, and cassis aromatics with hints of licorice and toasty oak in the background. It is more impressive up-front than it is in the mouth or finish. After some cask aging, it should take on more mid-palate, texture, weight, and length. Anticipated maturity: 2005–2014. Last tasted, 1/03.

2000
91
Even better than the superb 1998, the dense purple-colored 2000 La Dominique is the estate's finest wine since the wonderful duo of 1989 and 1990. It exhibits copious quantities of sexy, jammy blackberry and cassis fruit intertwined with licorice, cigar smoke, and spice box characteristics with a hint of herbs. Full-bodied and opulent, with low acidity but high tannin, this substantial, voluptuously textured, impressive St.-Emilion will be drinkable until 2017. Last tasted, 1/03.

1999
88
A sexy, evolved, lush La Dominique, the 1999 is filled with notes of ripe cherries, melted licorice, tobacco smoke, and herbs. While delicious, this medium-bodied, attractively fleshy, succulently styled St.-Emilion is not going to make old bones, as it does not possess the concentration of either the 1998 or 2000. Enjoy it over the next 5–6 years. Last tasted, 3/02.

1998
90
The 1998 is a soft, fat, voluptuously textured, opulent effort with a dense ruby/purple color and gorgeous aromas of olives, black cherry jam, blackberries, chocolate, and espresso. This full-bodied wine is hedonistic, flashy, and nearly decadent in its display of luxurious fruit, high glycerin, and spice. Anticipated maturity: now–2015. Last tasted, 3/02.

1997　La Dominique's 1997 is a savory offering for drinking over the next 3–4 years. This
86　wine offers abundant quantities of sweet, toasty oak as well as jammy black cherries and raspberries in its moderately intense aromatics. Medium body, low acidity, and admirable flesh and fruit result in a delightful St.-Emilion. Last tasted,
3/01.

1996　This smoky, lavishly oaked wine reveals an impressive dark ruby/purple color.
88　The nose offers up plenty of toast along with black cherries, raspberries, and dried
herbs and smoke. The wine provides sweet fruit on the attack, low acidity, medium
body, and a nicely textured finish with fat/glycerin in evidence. Prior to bottling, I
noted some astringency and awkward tannin, but neither were noticeable on the
three separate occasions I had the wine out of bottle. Anticipated maturity: now–
2012. Last tasted, 3/01.

1995　While 1995 is a tannic vintage for La Dominique, there is also sweeter fruit as well
89　as more ripeness and intensity (at least at present) in the wine's moderately intense nose of vanilla and blackberry and raspberry fruit. In the mouth, there is
good sweetness, medium to full body, moderate tannin, and a layered, rich, classic
tasting profile. Anticipated maturity: now–2016. Last tasted, 10/00.

1994　The 1994 La Dominique reveals some of the vintage's telltale astringent tannin
87?　and toughness, but it is loaded with creamy, ripe, black raspberry and currant
fruit. My instincts suggest a balance between fruit and tannin has been struck. The
wine is dense, dark ruby/purple–colored, with a sweet-smelling, oaky, earthy,
smoky, black currant–scented nose. This medium to full-bodied, ripe 1994 possesses admirable concentration, moderately high tannin, and excellent purity. Anticipated maturity: now–2016. Last tasted, 1/97.

1990　A wine of gorgeous ripeness, lavish fruit, and huge perfume, this succulent, full-
93　bodied, very fleshy, chewy wine has always been one of my favorite vintages of
La Dominique. Delicious from birth, the wine has never closed down or gone
into an ungrateful, stern stage. The wine is dark plum/ruby with some pink at
the rim. Once past the sweet nose of jammy cherry/cassis fruit intermixed with
notes of Provençal herbs, earth, and licorice, this full-bodied, low-acid, voluptuously textured wine is all pleasure. Anticipated maturity: now–2012. Last tasted,
11/02.

1989　It is a toss-up as to whether the 1990 or 1989 is the better vintage for La Do-
93　minique. The 1989 might have a bit more structure and definition, but still shares
many of the same characteristics that make the 1990 so special. The opaque
ruby/purple color is showing a bit of pink at the rim, but the lavishly exotic nose of
blackberries, crème de cassis, vanilla, licorice, coffee, and toast soars from the
glass. The very viscous, thick, juicy flavors are succulent, full-bodied, and very
sweet and expansive. This exuberant yet slightly more structured vintage than the
1990 seems to have only great things ahead of it, but why defer your gratification?
Anticipated maturity: now–2012. Last tasted, 11/02.

1988　A rather traditionally styled vintage of medium-bodied wine with plenty of tannin,
87　La Dominique's 1988 has reached full maturity. The wine shows notes of dried
herbs, licorice, and spice box along with plums and vanilla. The wine is medium
bodied and shows good sweetness on the attack, but it begins to narrow out ever so
slightly in the finish. Anticipated maturity: now. Last tasted, 11/02.

1986　The 1986 has a deep ruby/garnet color and a spicy bouquet of toasty new oak, rich,
88　plummy fruit, and minerals. This is followed by a wine that is full-bodied and intense, with impressive extract and tremendous power and persistence in its finish.
It does not have the opulence or precocious appeal of vintages such as 1990, 1989,
or 1982, yet it has reached full maturity. It is a firmer, structured, more Médoc-
styled La Dominique. Anticipated maturity: now–2005. Last tasted, 11/95.

1985
74
One of the most perplexing vintages for La Dominique, the 1985 continues to show a very vegetal character that is beginning to dissipate somewhat. The wine is loosely knit and dark garnet–colored with considerable amber at the edge. This wine seems to be in decline already. Anticipated maturity: Drink up now. Last tasted, 11/02.

1983
87
This wine needs to be consumed over the near-term. The color is a dark garnet, with considerable amber and orange at the edge. The wine possesses an enticing, expressive, herb, jammy fruit, earth, and vanilla nose. Some rustic tannin is noticeable on the palate, but this fleshy, soft, low-acid wine is fully mature, so readers should capture its intensity of fruit before it begins to fade, revealing more tannin, acidity, and alcohol. Anticipated maturity: now. Last tasted, 6/96.

1982
91
This is a rather muscular, full-throttle La Dominique that has aged longer and better than I ever suspected when it was young. Always low in acidity, with tremendous concentration but also high tannins, this wine still has a dark plum/ruby color with only a slight lightening at the edge. A nose of loamy soil scents intermixed with melted licorice, smoke, Provençal herbs, sweet black currants, plums, and a hint of prunes is enticing as well as intense. In the mouth this wine is full-bodied, chunky, and muscular, with more rustic tannins than either the 1989 or 1990. It has hit its plateau of maturity, but there is no danger of rushing to consume it. Anticipated maturity: now–2012. Last tasted, 12/02.

ANCIENT VINTAGES

Much of the 1970s were largely disappointing for La Dominique, as they were for most châteaux in Bordeaux. However, two exceptions were the brilliant 1971 (90 points; last tasted 1/90) and 1970 (88 points; last tasted 1/91). Both of these were wines that could score in the low 90s in their prime, but I have not had them for much more than a decade, and I suspect they are in serious decline, unless they are from magnums or larger formats.

FAUGÈRES

Classification: Grand Cru

Owner: Corinne Guisez

Address: 33330 Saint-Etienne-de-Lisse

Telephone: 05 57 40 34 99; Telefax: 05 57 40 36 14

E-mail: faugeres@chateau-faugeres.com

Website: www.chateau-faugeres.com

Visits: By appointment only Monday to Friday,
9 A.M.–noon and 1–4:30 P.M.

Contact: Valérie Grenier

VINEYARDS

Surface area: 54.3 acres

Grape varietals: 80% Merlot, 15% Cabernet Franc, 5% Cabernet Sauvignon

Average age of vines: 35 years

Density of plantation: 6,600 vines per hectare

Average yields: 38 hectoliters per hectare

Elevage: Cold maceration. Three to four week fermentation and maceration in temperature-controlled, flat, cone-shaped, stainless-steel vats. Malolactics in barrel for half of the yield. Fourteen months aging in barrels that are renewed by half at each vintage. No fining, filtration.

WINES PRODUCED

Château Faugères: 100,000 bottles

No second wine is produced.

Plateau of maturity: Within 5–15 years of the vintage

GENERAL APPRECIATION

Corinne Guisez's patience, talent, and tenacity have propelled Faugères to among the best wines of its appellation. A real New Wave St.-Emilion, this wine is all at once rich, up-front, jammy, ripe, and fruity, with plenty of appeal. Accessible in its youth because of its low acidity and ripe fruit, it also presents the necessary stuffing that enables it to age 10–15 years. A good buy indeed, it also represents a worthy introduction to Péby Faugères, the luxury *cuvée* produced by Corinne Guisez.

IMPORTANT VINTAGES

2001 Another top wine from this impeccably run estate, the dark purple–colored 2001
88–90 has a sweet aroma of crushed raspberries, currants, and smoke. Medium bodied, very pure, with excellent concentration and density, this wine admirably balances power and elegance. A very fine effort for the vintage. Anticipated maturity: 2005–2014. Last tasted, 1/03.

2000 Faugères has turned out an opaque black/purple–colored 2000 displaying aromas
91 of ink, blackberry liqueur, licorice, and toasty oak. Seamless, rich, and full-bodied, with even more weight and length than it revealed in its prime, it is a reasonably priced, serious wine that merits attention from consumers. Anticipated maturity: 2006–2018. Last tasted, 1/03.

1999 Pure, sweet fruit marks this medium-bodied, attractive, well-balanced St.-
88 Emilion. It offers abundant quantities of black cherry and currant fruit infused with toasty wood and mineral nuances. With sweet tannin and adequate acidity, it can be consumed now and over the next eight years. Last tasted, 3/02.

1998 A wine of beautiful purity, symmetry, and grace, this complex, dark purple–
90 colored 1998 reveals abundant quantities of black fruits infused with notions of new oak and graphite, medium to full body, sweet tannin, admirable elegance, and beautiful richness. Anticipated maturity: now–2015. Last tasted, 3/02.

1997 This impeccably run St.-Emilion estate has fashioned a fine 1997, exhibiting a
87 dark plum/ruby color, copious quantities of spicy oak, earth, black cherry, and berry fruit aromas and flavors, dry tannin, good ripeness, moderate oak, and a medium-bodied, structured finish. This is one 1997 that should drink nicely for 5–6 years. Last tasted, 3/01.

1996 The dense ruby/purple–colored 1996 offers aromas of toasty new oak, black fruits,
87 and spice. Rich and medium to full-bodied, with moderate tannin, this sleeper of the vintage will be at its best between now and 2012. Last tasted, 3/01.

1995 Dark ruby/purple–colored with a smoky, sexy nose of black cherry fruit, licorice,
87 vanilla, and spice, this medium-bodied, elegant yet flavorful, mouth-filling St.-Emilion possesses excellent depth and fine overall balance. The long finish ex-

hibits some tannin, but overall this is an accessible, up-front Claret to consume over the next 4–5 years. Last tasted, 11/97.

FERRAND LARTIGUE

Classification: Grand Cru

Owner: Pierre and Michelle Ferrand

Address: Route de Lartigue, 33330 St.-Emilion

Telephone: 05 57 74 46 19; Telefax: 05 57 74 46 19

E-mail: vincent.rapin@libertsurf.fr

Website: www.ferrand-lartigue.com

Visits: By appointment only

Contact: Vincent Rapin (Telephone: 06 15 42 39 12)

VINEYARDS

Surface area: 14.3 acres

Grape varietals: 80% Merlot, 15% Cabernet Franc, 5% Cabernet Sauvignon

Average age of vines: 40 years

Density of plantation: 5,500 vines per hectare

Average yields: 38 hectoliters per hectare

Elevage: Three week fermentation and maceration in temperature-controlled vats. Eighteen months aging in new oak barrels. Fining, no filtration.

WINES PRODUCED

Château Ferrand Lartigue: 23,000 bottles

FL de Ferrand Lartigue: 8,000 bottles

Plateau of maturity: Within 3–15 years of the vintage

GENERAL APPRECIATION

Ferrand Lartigue is one of the savory New Wave St.-Emilions that are worthy of consumers' interest.

IMPORTANT VINTAGES

2001
89–91 An impressive performance, Ferrand Lartigue's 2001 exhibits a dense ruby/purple color as well as a sweet, intense bouquet of cherry liqueur, new saddle leather, and toasty oak. Medium bodied, exceptionally pure, and nicely textured with sweet tannin in the persuasive finish, it will be at its apogee between 2005–2014. Last tasted, 1/03.

2000
91 The 2000 Ferrand Lartigue has added weight, expansiveness, and structure as well as tannin during its *élevage*, suggesting 1–2 years of cellaring is warranted. Cassis, licorice, tobacco smoke, and sweet fruit provide an expressive, medium- to full-bodied personality. Long, pure, and impressively built, it will be drinkable between 2005–2015. Last tasted, 1/03.

1999
89
This is a modern-styled St.-Emilion with copious quantities of smoky, toasty oak, ripe, fleshy, earthy, black cherry, and cassis characteristics, and plenty of toast notes. The wine exhibits excellent ripeness, purity, and more flesh and length than it did in cask. Drink it over the next eight years. Last tasted, 3/02.

1998
90
Ferrand Lartigue's 1998 exhibits a dark ruby/purple color as well as a tight but promising, internationally styled bouquet of new oak, black fruits, and saddle leather. The wine is medium to full-bodied, with excellent purity and clean, rich, concentrated flavors. Critics might argue that it is too "international," but it is an outstanding effort. Anticipated maturity: now–2015. Last tasted, 3/02.

1997
88
A sleeper of the vintage, the 1997 Ferrand Lartigue reveals more tannin and grip/structure than many of its St.-Emilion peers, but there is plenty of vanilla-infused, ripe black cherry and currant fruit, medium body, and a long, spicy finish. It should age well for 3–4 years. Last tasted, 3/01.

1996
90
The 1996 is superior to many wines with higher pedigrees. The dense purple–colored 1996 reveals lavish toasty new oak in the nose intermixed with framboise, kirsch, and black currant fruit. In the mouth, it displays a sweet mid-palate, gorgeous purity, moderate tannin, and a round, impressively long finish. This wine is accessible, but it will be atypically long-lived for a wine from this estate. Anticipated maturity: now–2013. Last tasted, 3/00.

1995
89
A sexy, open-knit wine, the 1995 Ferrand Lartigue exhibits a dark ruby/purple color, a jammy, candied fruit and toasty-scented nose, ripe, velvety-textured, complex, generous black cherry and cassis flavors, and low acidity. This medium-bodied, already delicious wine is ideal for drinking now and over the next 4–5 years. A sleeper of the vintage. Last tasted, 3/00.

1994
88
A powerful, medium- to full-bodied wine with a deep ruby/purple color and more noticeable size and weight, the fragrant (red and black fruits, smoke, and toast) 1994 is a smoothly textured, silky St.-Emilion for drinking during its first decade of life. This is a very sexy wine. Last tasted, 1/97.

FIGEAC

Classification: Premier Grand Cru Classé B

Owner: Thierry Manoncourt

Address: 33330 Saint-Emilion

Telephone: 05 57 24 72 26; Telefax: 05 57 74 45 74

E-mail: chateau-figeac@chateau-figeac.com

Website: www.chateau-figeac.com

Visits: By appointment Monday to Friday,
9 A.M.–11:30 P.M. and 2–5 P.M.

Contact: Mrs. Albino

VINEYARDS

Surface area: 98.8 acres

Grape varietals: 35% Cabernet Franc, 35% Cabernet Sauvignon, 30% Merlot

Average age of vines: 45 years

Density of plantation: 5,800 vines per hectare

Average yields: 45–50 hectoliters per hectare

Elevage: Twenty-one to twenty-five day fermentation and maceration in temperature-controlled wooden vats. Malolactics in vat or in barrels depending upon the vintage. Eighteen months aging in new oak barrels. Fining, no filtration.

WINES PRODUCED

Château-Figeac: 120,000 bottles

La Grange-Neuve de Figeac: Variable

Plateau of maturity: Within 3–15 years of the vintage

GENERAL APPRECIATION

The proprietors of this estate think I am unduly tough on their wines, but I am a huge fan of Figeac. When it is exceptional, as it certainly was in 2000, 1998, 1990, 1982, and 1964, one can understand why some tasters believe it is as complex as Cheval Blanc. In those cases, I purchase and drink it with great pleasure. However, too many vintages have lacked concentration and evolved too quickly, which explains the criticism. While always a wine of finesse, Figeac can sometimes underwhelm tasters because of a sense of dilution. It must also be stressed that the high percentage of Cabernet Sauvignon in the blend often accounts for its slightly vegetal character, especially in the years when this varietal does not achieve full maturity. However, over recent years, Figeac appears to have been living up to the responsibilities of its splendid *terroir*.

This moderately large property of just more than 98 acres sits on the gravel plateau diagonally across the road from Cheval Blanc. (It once was even larger, including land holdings that are now part of Cheval Blanc.) Many observers have long felt Figeac produced St.-Emilion's second-best wine. Its proprietor, Thierry Manoncourt, believes it to be the finest wine of the appellation and unashamedly shares these feelings with all visitors. The fact that the wine from what is now Cheval Blanc's vineyard used to be sold as Vin de Figeac only seems to strengthen his case. With the qualitative revolution in St.-Emilion and proliferation of high-quality wines from unheralded estates, in addition to the heightened consumer awareness of the excellence of other St.-Emilions, Figeac has had to contend with increased competition.

The aristocratic-looking and amiable Thierry Manoncourt makes Figeac in a very popular style. In top vintages the wine is much closer in style and quality to its fabulously expensive neighbor Cheval Blanc than the price difference would seemingly suggest. Usually ruby colored, richly fruity, with a distinctive perfume of menthol, herbs, cedar, and black fruits, the precociously supple and charming Figeac tends to show well young and mature quickly, despite the fact that it has the highest percentage of tannic and astringent Cabernet Sauvignon used in any major St.-Emilion. Most recent vintages (even those admirably concentrated) have tended to be fully ready for imbibing by the time they were five or six years old. Only the finest years of Figeac have had the ability to last well in the bottle for 15 or more years. This shortcoming has not gone unnoticed.

Figeac's critics claim the wine could be profound, perhaps the greatest wine of the appellation, if the vineyard were harvested later, the maceration period extended beyond its surprisingly short period, and a more severe selection made for the second wine. One of Libourne's most talented oenologists once told me that if he were making the wine, Figeac would be superior to Cheval Blanc.

Figeac has had a good record in off vintages. I often have difficulty judging Figeac when it is less than one year old. At this infant stage the wine frequently tastes thin, stalky, and overtly vegetal, only to fill out and put on weight in its second year in the cask. Perhaps the high percentages of Cabernet Sauvignon and Cabernet Franc from the vineyard's gravel-based soil account for this peculiar characteristic. In all fairness, I have had a similar problem in underestimating Cheval Blanc . . . and for similar reasons.

Figeac is generally priced at the high level of the best Médoc second growths, but the price seems fair and realistic given the quality of wines produced.

Visitors to St.-Emilion would be remiss in not making an appointment to visit Monsieur Manoncourt at his château. Be prepared for a beautiful country estate with enormous, tastefully done underground cellars—and a proprietor who fervently believes that Figeac should be spoken of not in the same breath as Cheval Blanc and Ausone, but before them!

IMPORTANT VINTAGES

2001
88–91 It is no surprise that in its second year, when tasting this wine immediately prior to bottling, it exhibited far more weight, texture, and depth of fruit than it did previously. Deep ruby/plum, with a sweet nose of black raspberries, blackberries, plum, and licorice, this medium-bodied, very elegant Figeac exhibits good sweetness, plenty of precocious complexity, and a ripe, long, nicely textured finish. As I predicted, it has developed more weight and texture, as so often this wine does. Anticipated maturity: 2006–2018. Last tasted, 1/03.

2000
93 A profound effort, the surprisingly full-bodied 2000 Figeac will rival 1990 and 1982. Its opaque purple color is accompanied by a terrific bouquet of camphor, graphite, black currants, licorice, and smoked herbs. With well-balanced, powerful tannin, concentration, and pinpoint precision, finesse, and purity, this expressive as well as textured effort will drink well between 2004–2018. When Figeac hits on all cylinders, one can understand why some tasters believe it is as complex as Cheval Blanc. Last tasted, 1/03.

1999
89 Complex aromas of figs, ripe plums, sweet cedar, tobacco, and new wood jump from the glass of this Burgundy-like St.-Emilion. It is medium-bodied, lush, and elegant rather than powerful, with supple tannin and a distinctive personality. Although it will not make old bones, it will offer graceful, well-balanced drinking over the next 10 years. Last tasted, 3/02.

1998
90 As befitting a wine with considerable Cabernet Sauvignon and Cabernet Franc in the blend, this is a stylish, mid-weight effort with an opulent, complex bouquet of licorice, Asian spices, tobacco, and fruitcake. Obvious black currants, smoke, vanilla, and new saddle leather are prominent in the wine's beautifully knit flavors. This opulent, rich, concentrated, layered, pure, complex 1998 reveals low acidity as well as ripe tannin, suggesting it will be impossible to resist young. Anticipated maturity: now–2016. Last tasted, 3/02.

1997
76 This wine, which was light but charming prior to bottling, appears to have lost what little flesh and allure it once possessed. Light ruby–colored, with insignificant body, a cedary, washed-out, vegetal nose, and a short finish, it is a thin, disappointing St.-Emilion. Drink it over the next 3–4 years. Last tasted, 3/01.

1996 Medium ruby–colored, with a mature nose of cedar, tobacco, fruitcake, and cherry
82   fruit, it is a light, medium-bodied wine with evidence of dilution. The finish is
      abrupt with light tannin. Drink it over the next 3–4 years. Last tasted, 3/02.

1995 Elegance, finesse, and a very forward style, particularly for this vintage, make this
90   a delicious wine to celebrate the 50th anniversary of the proprietors, the Manon-
      courts. The wine is medium bodied with distinctive weedy, tobacco, and red as
      well as black currant notes, along with cherry, vanilla, and cedar. It is soft, for-
      ward, and seemingly fully mature, but the cunning thing about Figeac is that it can
      last longer than it seems to suggest when young. This is Bordeaux at its most ele-
      gant. Anticipated maturity: now–2012. Last tasted, 12/02.

1994 The 1994's medium dark ruby color is followed by green pepper, olive, and black
84?   currant scents. The herbaceousness may develop a more cedary character with
      further cellaring. Although too tannic, the wine is medium bodied, with ripe, sweet
      fruit, good purity, and a mid-weight feel in the mouth. Readers who have a fond-
      ness for austere wines will be more enchanted with this offering than I was. Antic-
      ipated maturity: now–2010. Last tasted, 1/97.

1990 This is a fabulous Figeac with a deep ruby/garnet color and some lightening at the
92   edge. A sweet nose of licorice, cedar, black currants, cherries, and minerals is fol-
      lowed by a relatively fleshy Figeac with medium body and wonderful sweetness, in
      a very expansive, elegant style, with nothing out of place. The wine is fully mature
      and capable of lasting for at least another 10–15 years. Anticipated maturity:
      now–2016. Last tasted, 12/02.

1989 Consistently good but hardly special, the 1989 Figeac shows considerable amber
86   at the edge, medium body, and a distinctive weedy, vegetal character with notes of
      vanilla, red and black currant, and smoke. The wine finishes short, but the aro-
      matics and attack are very pleasant. There is just not much underneath this wine's
      superficial style. Anticipated maturity: now–2007. Last tasted, 12/02.

1988 Figeac's 1988 offers a moderate ruby color, high tannins, and a tart, lean, austere,
83   overtly herbaceous character. The wine is light, with a surprisingly short finish.
      Anticipated maturity: now. Last tasted, 1/93.

1986 Fully mature, this somewhat disjointed, austere Figeac shows plenty of amber at
86   the edge and a nose of creosote, ashtray, and tobacco notes along with some herbs
      and sweet currant fruit. The wine is elegant, but lacking substance, flesh, and tex-
      ture. Anticipated maturity: now. Last tasted, 12/02.

1985 Fully mature for a number of years, this wine continues to hold on to life, although
87   aging it any longer is probably fruitless (pardon the pun) unless it is from magnum
      or larger format. The wine shows a very stylish, cedary tobacco, spicy currant
      nose, with hints of licorice and new oak. Some sweet currant fruit is present, but
      the wine fades on the palate as well as in the glass. Drink up. Last tasted, 12/02.

1983 Herbal licorice, new wood, vanilla, cedar, and a hint of spice box are all in the
85   nose, but in the mouth this wine is cracking up, losing its fruit and becoming in-
      creasingly desiccated/austere. The tannin kicks in, and the fruit seems to be fad-
      ing quickly. This was once a delicious but never outstanding example that needed
      to be drunk up four or five years ago. Last tasted, 12/02.

1982 A gorgeous wine that rivals the 2000, 1995, and 1990 as the best of the great
92   Figeacs of the past 25 years, this exceptionally perfumed, complex wine shows
      ravishing notes of Asian spice, Provençal herbs, and sweet red and black currants,
      along with hints of coffee, cedar, and spice box. Very round and delicious, with no
      tannin showing but plenty of sweet fruit, glycerin, and ripeness, this is a beauty
      that needs to be drunk up in the next decade. Anticipated maturity: now–2012.
      Last tasted, 12/02.

ANCIENT VINTAGES

The 1970s were not kind to Figeac, with a competent effort in 1976 (86 points; last tasted 6/83), a very good 1975 (87 points; last tasted 12/95), and a brilliant 1970 (90 points; last tasted 1/91). In the 1960s the profound 1964 (94 points; last tasted 10/94) and 1961 (94? points; last tasted 7/97) were the stars and certainly are justifiably heralded as two of the château's finest wines. The 1959 (rated 91; last tasted 1990) has not been retasted since the last edition of this book, but I suspect well-stored bottles would still be impressive. It was a powerful, rich, roasted Figeac that typified the torrid weather conditions of the 1959 growing season. The 1955 (95 points; last tasted 10/94) is one of those brilliant, unknown great wines of the century that no doubt appears from time to time at auction and is undoubtedly sold for a song given the fact that it has received so little press. From a château that tends to produce quickly maturing wines, this offering is more backward than the fully mature 1964 and even richer than the 1982 and 1990 (at least as they appear today). The 1955 offers an extraordinary fragrance of ripe plums, cassis, mint, herbs, smoke, and spices. Dense and concentrated for a Figeac, with some tannin yet to melt away, this wine is a candidate for a half century of aging. Purchasing the 1953 (93 points; last tasted 10/94) can be a risky business if the bottle has not been stored impeccably. At its best, this wine exhibits a huge nose of smoky, earthy, herbal, mineral, fruity, and menthol scents, soft, velvety, medium-bodied flavors, no noticeable tannin, and heady alcohol in the finish. It has been fully mature for at least two decades, so it is unlikely to get any better. The 1950 (88 points; last tasted 12/96) is another fine wine from this underrated vintage, which produced some very fine St.-Emilions and splendid Pomerols. The wine revealed a garnet color, with considerable orange/amber at the edge. The nose offered up intense smoky barbecue spice, cedar, and dried fruit aromas, which were followed by a medium-bodied, soft, round, supple-textured wine that had obviously been fully mature for a decade or more.

The splendid 1949 (94 points; last tasted 1/96) is one of the greatest Figeacs I have ever tasted. This wine possessed a cigar box/fruitcake aromatic profile, gorgeously rich, seamless flavors that flowed across the palate with no heaviness, yet extraordinary sweetness of fruit and plenty of glycerin. It is a glorious Figeac that I would love to encounter in large formats such as magnums! The 1947 (70 points; last tasted 11/96) revealed an old, dried fruit, vegetal nose that was in keeping with its amber, rusty, ancient-looking color. In the mouth, there was some dusty tannin, spiky alcohol, and an absence of any real flesh or fruit. It was disappointing for a wine from my birth year.

FLEUR CARDINALE

Classification: Grand Cru

Owner: Dominique and Florance Decoster

Address: 33330 Saint-Etienne-de-Lisse

Telephone: 05 57 40 14 05; Telefax: 05 57 40 28 62

E-mail: fleurcardinale@terre.net.fr

Website: www.chateau-fleurcardinale.com

Visits: By appointment only

Contact: Robert Avargues

VINEYARDS

Surface area: 42 acres

Grape varietals: 70% Merlot, 15% Cabernet Franc, 15% Cabernet Sauvignon

Average age of vines: 40 years

Density of plantation: 5,000 vines per hectare

Average yields: 39 hectoliters per hectare

Elevage: Four to six week fermentation and maceration in temperature-controlled stainless-steel vats. Sixteen to eighteen months aging in new oak barrels. Fining and filtration not systematic.

WINES PRODUCED

Château Fleur Cardinale: 45,000 bottles

Château Bois Cardinale: 5,000 bottles

Plateau of maturity: Within 5–8 years of the vintage, for vintages prior to 2001

GENERAL APPRECIATION

This is an estate to watch, as its new owner Dominique Decoster hired the consulting genius Jean-Luc Thunevin when he took over the estate in 2001. His first effort, with the valuable assistance of St.-Emilion's bad boy, was a success, at once richer, deeper, and more charming than its predecessors.

Fleur Cardinale is made in a very satisfying, round, generous style that offers immediate satisfaction. The wine is rarely complex, but rather solid and robust. The vineyard, located in the commune of St.-Etienne de Lisse, is not well placed, but with a serious owner and the excellent counsel of the famed consultant/guru Jean-Luc Thunevin, the quality of Fleur Cardinale will certainly increase.

IMPORTANT VINTAGES

2001 The 2001 is a deeper, richer effort than usual. It boasts a dense ruby/purple color
87–88 along with ripe berry fruit intermixed with smoke, spice, and espresso characteristics. This medium-bodied, supple-textured St.-Emilion will provide delicious drinking during its first 6–8 years of life. Last tasted, 1/03.

2000 The dark ruby/purple–colored 2000 exhibits sweet, concentrated fruit, medium
87   body, admirable texture, and a fine finish. Enjoy it over the next 5–6 years. Last
      tasted, 1/03.

1999 The 1999 Fleur Cardinale is a light, fruity, straightforward St.-Emilion to drink
85   over the next three years. Last tasted, 3/02.

LA FLEUR DE JAUGUE

Classification: Grand Cru

Owner: Georges Bigaud

Address: 150, avenue du Général de Gaulle, 33500 Libourne

Telephone: 05 57 51 51 29; Telefax: 05 57 51 29 70

Visits: By appointment Monday to Thursday,
9 A.M.–noon and 3–6 P.M.

Contact: Georges Bigaud

VINEYARDS

Surface area: 13.1 acres

Grape varietals: 70% Merlot, 30% Cabernet Franc

Average age of vines: 30 years

Density of plantation: 6,800 vines per hectare

Average yields: 50 hectoliters per hectare

Elevage: Three to four week fermentation and maceration in temperature-controlled vats.
Twelve to fourteen months aging in barrels that are renewed by a third at each vintage.
Fining, no filtration.

WINES PRODUCED

Château La Fleur de Jaugue: 20,000 bottles

La Croix de Jaugue: 9,000 bottles

Plateau of maturity: Within 3–10 years of the vintage

GENERAL APPRECIATION

The small production from this impeccably run vineyard deserves more attention,
even though there is not a lot of it. Shrewd bargain hunters realize this is a top-notch
value/qualitative pick from Bordeaux. It is a delicious wine capable of lasting a decade
or more. A perennial best value entry, this consistently well-made St.-Emilion still sells
for a song.

IMPORTANT VINTAGES

2001   This wine is another very tasty, impeccably made example from this underrated
87–88 producer that seems to do everything right regardless of vintage conditions. Deep
       garnet/ruby, with a sweet nose of melted licorice interwoven with black cherry jam,
       this medium-bodied wine is plump, fleshy, and quite hedonistic. Low acidity, ripe
       tannins, and a seamless finish make for quite an enticing Bordeaux to drink during
       its first decade of life. Anticipated maturity: now–2011. Last tasted, 1/03.

2000
90
Unquestionably a sleeper of the vintage, this dense ruby/purple–colored effort reveals medium body, moderate tannin, good structure, and outstanding purity as well as concentration. Redolent with flavors of plum, cherry, and raspberry, with the telltale licorice note, this wine is not as fruit-forward as many of the estate's efforts, yet readers will not have to wait long for the pleasure to begin. Anticipated maturity: 2004–2014. Last tasted, 1/03.

1999
87
The 1999 La Fleur de Jaugue is a fruity, soft, dark ruby–colored effort with excellent purity, plenty of tobacco-tinged black currant and cherry fruit, and notions of licorice, earth, and spicy oak. Round and delicious, but less impressive than I anticipated, it is ideal for drinking over the next seven or so years. Last tasted, 3/02.

1998
90
Another sleeper of the vintage, the bouquet of this concentrated, powerful yet elegant 1998 is reminiscent of an overripe Griottes Chambertin. Blackberry, earth, mineral, and jammy cherry aromas jump from the glass. Deep, fleshy, and full-bodied, with supple tannin, low acidity, and a sexy, hedonistic style, this succulent St.-Emilion will be drinkable early. Anticipated maturity: now–2012. Last tasted, 3/02.

1997
87
A sleeper of the vintage, this excellent wine reveals copious quantities of herb-tinged, black cherry fruit, smoke, and earthy aromas. Nicely concentrated, low in acidity, with superb fruit, and overall harmony, this is a serious effort from a relatively maligned vintage. Sweet, with neither vegetal characteristics nor sharpness, it can be drunk over the next 2–3 years. Last tasted, 3/01.

1996
87
The very fine 1996 is deep ruby–colored, with plenty of sweet cherry and plum-like fruit intermixed with dried herbs, smoke, and a touch of earth and new oak. Fleshy, with excellent texture and ripe fruit, it is a tasty St.-Emilion to enjoy over the next 2–3 years. Last tasted, 1/01.

1995
89
Unquestionably a sleeper of the vintage, this delicious, dark plum/purple–colored offering reveals flashy, jammy red and black fruits (primarily cherries and cassis) in the nose, sweet vanilla, medium to full body, excellent, nearly outstanding ripeness and depth, and a low-acid, sumptuous, opulent personality. This is a delicious, plump, juicy St.-Emilion to consume over the next 5–6 years. Last tasted, 1/01.

FOMBRAUGE

Classification: Grand Cru

Owner: Bernard Magrez

Address: 33330 Saint-Christophe-des-Bardes

Telephone: 05 57 24 77 12; Telefax: 05 57 24 66 95

E-mail: chateau@fombrauge.com

Website: www.fombrauge.com

Visits: By appointment only

Contact: Ugo Arguti

VINEYARDS

Surface area: 128.4 acres

Grape varietals: 70% Merlot, 20% Cabernet Franc, 10% Cabernet Sauvignon

Average age of vines: 30 years

Density of plantation: 5,600 vines per hectare

Average yields: 45 hectoliters per hectare

Elevage: Cold maceration at 12°C. Four to five week fermentation and maceration (whole cluster) in temperature-controlled wooden vats of small capacity allowing for separate vinification of the different parcels of vine, with four daily *pigéages*. Malolactics and 16–18 months aging on fine lees with regular stirring in new oak barrels. Fining, no filtration.

WINES PRODUCED

Château Fombrauge: 160,000 bottles

Le Cadran de Fombrauge: 110,000 bottles

Plateau of maturity: Within 5–20 years of the vintage, for post-1999 vintages

GENERAL APPRECIATION

The largest vineyard in St.-Emilion, Fombrauge has been reinvigorated by the dynamic leadership of Bernard Magrez (the owner of Pape-Clément, La Tour Carnet, and other properties) and his hot-shot wine consultant, Michel Rolland. The result is one of the up-and-coming wines of the appellation, which is still available for a reasonable price. Readers looking for delicious, well-made St.-Emilions should check it out. Vintages prior to 1999 should be approached with caution.

IMPORTANT VINTAGES

2001   The 2001 nearly rivals the brilliant 2000. Cropped at a mere 36 hectoliters per
89–91   hectare, this blend of 70% Merlot and 30% Cabernet Franc offers a saturated ruby/purple color as well as a gorgeous bouquet of jammy blackberry and cherry fruit intermixed with vanilla, coffee, and smoke aromas. Dense, chewy, and opulent, it is a sleeper of the vintage. Low acidity and a ripe, flamboyant style should ensure considerable appeal. Anticipated maturity: 2005–2015. Last tasted, 1/03.

2000   A revelation, this stunning wine (also reasonably priced) has turned out to be even
90   better than I thought. Opaque purple–colored, with gorgeous ripeness and richness, a big, sweet mid-palate, and a seamless finish revealing loads of fruit, chocolate, glycerin, and ripe tannin, this opulently styled 2000 will have few detractors. It is hard not to be totally seduced by this effort. Bravo! Anticipated maturity: now–2015. Last tasted, 1/03.

1999   A deep ruby/purple color accompanies sexy, jammy, black cherry, strawberry, and
88   currant fruit intermixed with smoke and new wood. In the mouth, this wine is low in acidity, plump, succulent, and altogether a hedonistic turn-on. Drink it over the next 3–4 years. Last tasted, 3/02.

1998   Soft, ripe berry fruit presented in a straightforward, medium-bodied style is at-
86   tractive in a low-keyed, restrained way. Anticipated maturity: now–2007. Last tasted, 3/02.

FONPLÉGADE

Classification: Grand Cru Classé

Owner: Marie-José and Nathalie Moueix

Address: 33330 St.-Emilion

Mailing address: BP 45, 33330 St.-Emilion

Telephone: 05 57 74 43 11; Telefax: 05 57 74 44 67

E-mail: domaines-armand-moueix@wanadoo.fr

Website: www.domaines-armand-moueix.com

Visits: October to May: Monday to Friday, 10 A.M.–5 P.M.
June to September: Wednesday to Sunday and public holidays,
11 A.M.–6 P.M. Groups are requested to make an appointment.

Contact: Stephany Rosa (stephany.rosa@wanadoo.fr)

VINEYARDS

Surface area: 44.5 acres

Grape varietals: 60% Merlot, 35% Cabernet Franc, 5% Cabernet Sauvignon

Average age of vines: 35 years

Density of plantation: 5,600 and 6,500 vines per hectare

Average yields: 45 hectoliters per hectare

Elevage: Four to five week fermentation and maceration in temperature controlled
stainless-steel and concrete vats, with wattling at the end of the process. After completion
of malolactics in vats, 12–15 months aging in barrels with 50% new oak. Light fining, no
filtration.

WINES PRODUCED

Château Fonplégade: 60,000 bottles

Château Côtes Trois Moulins: 30,000 bottles

Plateau of maturity: Within 4–12 years of the vintage

GENERAL APPRECIATION

Until recently, the wines of Fonplégade were hardly inspirational. However, the estate
seems to have made a turnaround as of 2000, and it seems the quality is going to
increase—that should not be difficult since there was much room for improvement.

One of the oldest vineyards of St.-Emilion (Romans farmed and planted these hillsides), Fonplégade merits greater renown than it has received. The vineyard is beautifully situated on the southerly slopes of St.-Emilion, not far from the famous estate of
Magdelaine. The château, built in the late 19th century by the proprietor—a *négociant*
by the name of Boisard—is one of the more attractive of the appellation. Since 1953
the property has been owned by the Armand Moueix family.

Christian Moueix has recently taken over the viticulture and winemaking at this estate, which, despite its privileged *terroir,* has underperformed for many years. The style
of wine produced at Fonplégade seems to have changed with the 2000.

IMPORTANT VINTAGES

2001
86–88 This wine seems to be in the process of putting on some weight and texture. Dark ruby/purple, with a sweet nose of black cherries, currants, plums, earth, and licorice, the wine is medium bodied with a nice plush entry on the palate, adequate acidity, and moderately ripe tannin in the finish. It does not appear to have the volume, depth, and power of the 2000, but there are good things going on. Anticipated maturity: 2005–2013. Last tasted, 1/03.

2000
89+ The 2000 is the finest Fonplégade in nearly two decades. Thankfully, there are 4,000 cases of this structured, deep, concentrated wine, with high levels of tannin, but equally impressive levels of extract and richness. Medium to full-bodied, with plum, black currant, and cherry fruit intermixed with mineral and earth, this pure, rich St.-Emilion is an admirable achievement. It is a blend of 70% Merlot, 25% Cabernet Franc, and 5% Cabernet Sauvignon. Anticipated maturity: 2005–2018. Last tasted, 1/03.

OTHER VINTAGES

The record during the 1990s forgetting the excellent 1990 (88 points; last tasted 7/97), was mediocre, with one lackluster wine after another. Of course, that was under a different winemaking team than the two most recent vintages. In the 1980s the record was even more lamentable than the 1990s. Fortunately, this is all past history that is easily forgotten in view of the efforts now being expended on resurrecting this well-placed estate.

FONROQUE

Classification: Grand Cru Classé

Owner: GFA du Château Fonroque

Address: 33330 St.-Emilion

Mailing address: 56, avenue Georges Pompidou, 33500 Libourne

Telephone: 05 57 24 60 02; Telefax: 05 57 24 74 59

E-mail: alain.moueix@wanadoo.fr

Visits: By appointment only

Contact: Alain Moueix (Telephone: 05 57 51 00 48; Telefax: 05 57 25 22 56)

VINEYARDS

Surface area: 43.5 acres

Grape varietals: 85% Merlot, 15% Cabernet Franc

Average age of vines: 35+ years

Density of plantation: 6,270 vines per hectare

Average yields: 38–40 hectoliters per hectare, as of 2001

Elevage: Cold maceration. Three to four week fermentation and maceration in temperature-controlled concrete vats. Malolactics in barrel for the whole yield. Sixteen to eighteen months aging in barrels with 70% new oak. Rackings done from one barrel to another, without pumping. Fining, no filtration.

WINES PRODUCED

Château Fonroque: 65,000 bottles

Château Cartier: 25,000 bottles

Plateau of maturity: Within 4–12 years of the vintage

GENERAL APPRECIATION

The wines of Fonroque have done little to distinguish themselves from most other commercial, straightforward St.-Emilions. Formerly under the control of Jean-Pierre Moueix, the estate is now run by Alain Moueix, who is also the managing director of Mazeyres in Pomerol. The present management is intent on culling more from this *terroir.*

Fonroque is situated in an isolated location north and west of St.-Emilion. In style it tends to be of the robust, rich, tannic, medium-bodied school of St.-Emilions. It can take aging quite well and in good vintages actually needs cellaring of at least 2–3 years before being consumed.

IMPORTANT VINTAGES

2001   This looks to be a very promising effort, and possibly better than the 2000. The
87–88   color is a dark plum/ruby, and the wine offers up dusty, earthy notes interwoven with plum, currant, and a hint of prune. Some licorice and new oak also make an appearance. The wine is medium bodied and ripe, without the rusticity and emaciated feel many previous vintages have exhibited. Anticipated maturity: 2005–2015. Last tasted, 1/03.

2000   Spicy aromas of new saddle leather, cherry and currant fruit, as well as liquid min-
86   erals compete for the taster's attention. This ripe, medium-bodied offering displays more depth than many recent vintages, but earth and tannin dominate the finish. Over time, the battle between the fruit and tannin will undoubtedly favor the latter. Anticipated maturity: now–2009. Last tasted, 1/03.

OTHER VINTAGES

Except for the 1990 (88 points; last tasted 1/93), the 1980s were a period of mediocrity for Fonroque. The same could be said for the 1970s and the 1960s, as this property has languished in spite of an excellent exposition on the west face of what is called the "cadet slope" of St.-Emilion, giving it full exposure to the sun and protection from spring frost. Certainly the more recent vintages show an improvement, which hopefully will continue throughout the 21st century.

FRANC-MAYNE

Classification: Grand Cru Classé

Owner: Georgy Foureroy and partners

Address: La Gomerie, 33330 St.-Emilion

Telephone: 05 57 24 69 62; Telefax: 05 57 24 68 25

E-mail: contacts@chateau-francmayne.com

Website: www.chateau-francmayne.com

Visits: By appointment only March to November,
9 A.M.–5 P.M. Closed December to February.

Contact: Catherine Montant

VINEYARDS

Surface area: 17.3 acres

Grape varietals: 90% Merlot, 10% Cabernet Franc

Average age of vines: 35 years

Density of plantation: 5,900 vines per hectare

Average yields: 40 hectoliters per hectare

Elevage: Three to five day cold maceration. Three to six week fermentation and maceration in temperature-controlled vats. Malolactics in barrel. Sixteen to twenty months aging in barrels with 70–90% new oak. No fining, filtration.

WINES PRODUCED

Château Franc-Mayne: 35,000–37,000 bottles

Les Cèdres de Franc-Mayne: 12,000–15,000 bottles

Plateau of maturity: Within 3–9 years of the vintage

GENERAL APPRECIATION

Though the wines of Franc-Mayne have improved over recent years, they still remain outside the group of top St.-Emilions. Neither entirely classical nor New Wave, they are accessible and commercially styled wines.

The huge insurance company AXA acquired Franc-Mayne in 1987. They very wisely hired the proprietor of Lynch-Bages, Jean-Michel Cazes, and his talented wine-maker, Daniel Llose, to oversee the renovation of the estate and the making of the wine. In 1996 the property was sold to the Fourcoy family from Belgium.

Franc-Mayne is by far the best known of the St.-Emilion châteaux with the word "Franc" in their name; there are 17 others, although none produces wines of the quality level of Franc-Mayne. The vineyard is located in the northwest section of the St.-Emilion appellation, on the same hillside that runs into the appellation called the Côtes de Francs.

This has never been one of my favorite St.-Emilions, although improvements were made under the Cazes management and are expected to continue under the new administration. This is a wine that requires consumption within the first 7–10 years of life.

IMPORTANT VINTAGES

2001
86–88
Elegant, medium bodied, yet somehow uninspiring, this dark ruby/purple colored wine shows notes of menthol, red and black currants, licorice, and vanilla. It is well made and clean, but somewhat monolithic. Anticipated maturity: 2005–2014. Last tasted, 1/03.

2000
88
An elegant as well as concentrated 2000, this dense ruby/purple–colored wine reveals sweet, jammy red and black fruit, underbrush, and spicy new wood aromas. Deep, chiseled, and well delineated, with good acidity, sweetness from glycerin, and moderately high tannin, this looks to be one of the best Franc-Maynes ever made. It is a sleeper of the vintage. Anticipated maturity: 2006–2018. Last tasted, 1/03.

1999
87
The deep purple–colored 1999 is an impressive effort from Franc-Mayne. It possesses sweet tannin, a luscious, concentrated, multilayered mid-palate, and abundant quantities of black fruits intermixed with smoke, licorice, and earth. Dense, opulent, and full-bodied, with admirable sweetness, it can be drunk now and over the next 15 years. Last tasted, 3/02.

1998
88
A very good effort, this medium-bodied 1998 reveals plenty of toasty new oak along with jammy black cherry and cassis fruit, excellent purity, medium to full body, sweet tannin, and fine overall symmetry. It will be at its prime between now and 2015. Last tasted, 3/02.

1997
76
Dark ruby–colored, with an earthy, herbaceous, black cherry–scented bouquet, this lean, medium-bodied 1997 lacks depth and length. Drink it over the next 4–5 years. Last tasted, 3/01.

1996
84
While the 1996 possesses a touch of herbs, the wine exhibits medium body and attractive ripe red and black currant fruit presented in a slightly minty, forward, lush style. This wine should last another 4–5 years. Last tasted, 11/97.

ANCIENT VINTAGES

Two vintages worth looking at from Franc-Mayne include the 1989 (87 points; last tasted 1/93) and the 1990 (89 points; last tasted 1/93). The latter wine is the highest in-the-bottle review I have ever given Franc-Mayne, and it is a wine that should still be drinking well in 2003.

LA GAFFELIÈRE

Classification: Premier Grand Cru Classé B

Owner: Léo de Malet-Roquefort

Address: 33330 St.-Emilion

Telephone: 05 57 24 72 15; Telefax: 05 57 24 69 06.

E-mail: chateau-la-gaffeliere@chateau-la-gaffeliere.com

Website: www.chateau-la-gaffeliere.com

Visits: By appointment only Monday to Friday, 8 A.M.–noon and 2–6 P.M.

Contact: Jean-Marc Galieri

VINEYARDS

Surface area: 54.3 acres

Grape varietals: 65% Merlot, 30% Cabernet Franc, 5% Cabernet Sauvignon

Average age of vines: 40+ years

Density of plantation: 5,800 vines per hectare

Average yields: 40 hectoliters per hectare

Elevage: Five to six week fermentation and maceration in temperature-controlled stainless-steel vats with micro-oxygenation of lees. Twelve to fifteen months aging in new oak barrels. Fining, light filtration.

WINES PRODUCED

Château La Gaffelière: 85,000 bottles

Clos La Gaffelière: 5,000 bottles

Plateau of maturity: Within 5–15 years of the vintage

GENERAL APPRECIATION

Forget about the vintages prior to the 1970s. From the mid-1980s onward, La Gaffelière has improved slowly but steadily and justifies its classification. Exhibiting a style of its own, it will surprise tasters used to the New Wave flamboyant St.-Emilions, but it is seductive in its own way, with its delicately fruity style, its sensual lightness and elegance, as well as its nicely perfumed aromas. Do not expect La Gaffelière to be enormously endowed or long-lived (it is equivalent in quality to a Médoc third growth), but it remains an interesting buy among St.-Emilion first growths.

The impressive four-story château and cellars of La Gaffelière sit opposite each other just outside the walls of St.-Emilion. Historically, this has been one of the most distinguished properties in Bordeaux because the de Malet-Roquefort family has owned the property for more than four centuries. The current proprietor, Comte Léo de Malet-Roquefort, is both an experienced rider and hunter—not surprising, given that members of his family, descendants of the Normans, were honored by William the Conqueror for their heroism and fighting skills at the battle of Hastings.

La Gaffelière, however, has been a perplexing wine to evaluate. The wine was well made during the 1960s, and the 1970 was impressive. However, after 1970 it took 12 years for another top-notch vintage of La Gaffelière to emerge from the cellars. I am not sure why this happened because the vineyard is well situated on limestone/clay soils, and on every one of my visits I have been impressed by the cleanliness of the winemaking facilities and the dedication of the count and his staff. Nevertheless, there were far too few wines to get excited about prior to the mid-1980s. Since then La Gaffelière has been making wines befitting its status as one of St.-Emilion's elite premier grands cru classés.

The style aimed for at this estate is one of elegance and tenderness. This will never be a large-scaled, tannic monster of a wine, but when the wine is at its best, it will have a degree of finesse generally unmatched by other St.-Emilions.

Comte de Malet-Roquefort is also the proprietor of the St.-Emilion property Tertre Daugay.

IMPORTANT VINTAGES

2001
88–91
A rich effort for this estate, which is known for their elegant, finesse-styled wines, the deep ruby/purple–colored 2001 offers sweet, floral, berry aromas with restrained new oak notes. With loads of fruit and freshness, decent acidity, and light tannin, this pure, nicely delineated, moderately weighty St.-Emilion will be at its peak between 2006–2015. Last tasted, 1/03.

2000
90
Sweet aromas of mocha, black cherries, cassis, and subtle toasty oak emerge from this dense purple-colored 2000. Although light in the mouth, it possesses wonderful expansive richness, a deep mid-section, and sweet tannin in the persistent finish. It is not a wine that knocks you out with a blast of fruit and wood, but rather one that impresses for its nobility/subtlety. Anticipated maturity: 2007–2019. Last tasted, 1/03.

1999
89
Typical for this property, the 1999 is an elegant, finesse-styled, medium-bodied effort revealing lovely strawberry and currant fruit with a hint of sour cherries, a judicious touch of oak, medium body, and excellent purity. It creeps up on the taster in subtle increments. I always laugh when critics of Michel Rolland, the great international oenologist who has done so much to improve wine quality throughout the world, say that his wines all taste the same. Do these ignorant observers realize he is the consultant for this stylish, restrained St.-Emilion? Anticipated maturity: now–2015. Last tasted, 3/02.

1998
89
Elegant and soft, with admirable restraint and subtlety, yet surprising richness and seductiveness, the 1998 offers pure notes of strawberries and black cherries gently infused with high-quality toasty oak. Round, medium bodied, and well balanced, it can be drunk now and over the next 12 years. Last tasted, 3/02.

1997
85
This wine has turned out to be lighter than I initially thought. Nevertheless, it is a pleasant cranberry and cherry scented and flavored effort with considerable finesse, medium body, and undeniable elegance. Drink it over the next five years. Last tasted, 3/01.

1996
87
This is a quintessentially elegant wine, with charm, sweet fruit, and a velvety texture. Tannin in the finish suggests it will last longer than expected. The color is a deep ruby, and the nose offers up sweet black cherries intermixed with a peppery, mineral character, subtle new oak, and well-integrated acidity and tannin. The finish is long and pure. Anticipated maturity: now–2012. Last tasted, 10/00.

1995
87
This dark ruby–colored wine offers spicy, smoky oak and soft, ripe, cherry, and red currant flavors presented in a compressed but alluring, medium-bodied, finesse-filled format. Some tannin is present, but the overall impression is one of pretty fruit and a dry, crisp finish. Anticipated maturity: now–2010. Last tasted, 10/00.

1990
90
The dark garnet–colored 1990 offers up abundant aromas of sweet new oak, ripe berry fruit, and floral scents. In the mouth, this stylish, medium-weight, beautifully proportioned wine has excellent concentration, decent acidity, soft tannins, and a considerable sense of elegance and richness. Along with the 2000, it is the finest La Gaffelière since the 1970 and 1947. Anticipated maturity: now–2008. Last tasted, 11/00.

1989
89
The 1989 displays an enthralling bouquet of black cherries, spring flowers, minerals, and toasty new oak. Medium to full-bodied, it possesses good acidity for the vintage, soft tannins, and a long, velvety, rich finish. This is a stylish yet authoritative La Gaffelière. Anticipated maturity: now–2010. Last tasted, 1/93.

1986
87
The 1986 La Gaffelière has the potential to be one of the property's best wines. It is a rich, elegantly rendered wine with a bouquet of spicy new oak, cedar, and black currants. Medium to full-bodied, with wonderful focus and grip, this stylish,

graceful wine should drink well for the next three years. Anticipated maturity: now–2006. Last tasted, 3/91.

1985
86
The 1985 has a full-intensity, spicy, herbaceous, richly fruity bouquet, medium body, soft tannins, and a supple finish. Anticipated maturity: now. Last tasted, 3/91.

1982
88
The 1982 is one of the few successful wines made during a disappointing period for La Gaffelière. It displays the subtle, elegant style this estate favors, as well as an attractive, graceful bouquet of sweet, toasty oak intermingled with ripe black cherries. Medium bodied and silky smooth with plenty of spice, this low-acid wine has no hard edges. It should be drunk up. Last tasted, 9/95.

ANCIENT VINTAGES

The two finest vintages I have seen of La Gaffelière included a deliciously elegant, round, very perfumed 1953 (rated 89, last tasted 1988) and a rich, fat, surprisingly intense, full-bodied 1947 (rated 88; drunk when I celebrated my 40th birthday in 1987).

LA GOMERIE

Classification: Grand Cru

Owner: Gérard and Dominique Bécot

Address: 33330 St.-Emilion

Telephone: 05 57 74 46 87; Telefax: 05 57 24 66 88

E-mail: contact@beausejour-becot.com

Website: www.beausejour-becot.com

Visits: By appointment only

Contact: Gérard or Dominique Bécot

VINEYARDS

Surface area: 6.2 acres

Grape varietals: 100% Merlot

Average age of vines: 40 years

Density of plantation: 6,600 vines per hectare

Average yields: 35 hectoliters per hectare

Elevage: Twenty-eight to thirty day fermentation and maceration in temperature-controlled wooden vats with *pigéages* done by foot. Malolactics and 18 months aging in new oak barrels. No fining, no filtration.

WINES PRODUCED

Château La Gomerie: 10,000 bottles

Mademoiselle de La Gomerie: 2,000–3,000 bottles

Plateau of maturity: Within 2–15 years of the vintage

GENERAL APPRECIATION

A Le Pin look-alike, La Gomerie is a micro-vinification *cuvée*, one of the new breed, handcrafted reds that have become so fashionable in St.-Emilion. Like most garage wines, it is made from extremely ripe fruit and low yields, with malolactic fermentation in barrel and 100% new oak for the *élevage*. Another fine success of the talented Bécot brothers, La Gomerie is a worthy addition to St.-Emilion's portfolio of high-class garage wines.

This wine is made by Gérard Bécot, the proprietor of Beau-Séjour Bécot. It is a micro-vinification/minuscule estate producing wine made from 100% Merlot, fermented and aged in 100% new oak. Not surprisingly, wines such as this garner enthusiastic accolades from the wine press. The difficulty of finding the wine and its high price aside, this is an impressive, rich, creamy-textured, blockbuster Merlot that will seduce anybody who tries it. It seems to me that Monsieur Bécot is trying—successfully, I might add—to produce a luxury-priced wine similar to Pomerol's Le Pin. To date, only a few vintages have been produced, but this is an impressive wine. How well will it age? Time will tell.

IMPORTANT VINTAGES

2001
91–94 This wine has filled out beautifully, and while it will never quite hit the heights that the compelling 2000 does, this is an exceptional wine, with plenty of exotic opulence, a deep ruby/purple color, and the telltale notes of espresso, toast, chocolate, and copious quantities of jammy black cherry and cassis fruit. The wine is medium to full-bodied, soft, lush, and a total hedonistic as well as intellectual turn-on. Anticipated maturity: 2005–2015. Last tasted, 1/03.

2000
96 A prodigious effort, the dense purple–colored 2000 La Gomerie boasts spectacufort aromas of roasted coffee, sweet, jammy black cherry and currant fruit, more tannin than normal, but a sumptuous, thick, expansive, juicy mid-section as well as finish. This terrific offering is made in a modern, cultish style aimed at unabashed hedonists. Anticipated maturity: 2004–2016. Last tasted, 1/03.

1999
86 The 1999 vintage suffered from hail damage, resulting in a foursquare, monolithic, lighter wine without this cru's typical nuances and depth. Deep ruby–colored with aromas of new oak and black cherries, this medium-bodied 1999 should be consumed over the next 6–7 years. Last tasted, 3/02.

1998
94 A spectacular effort, this blockbuster, in-your-face St.-Emilion boasts a saturated purple color as well as a gorgeous bouquet of framboise liqueur, blackberries, and smoky oak, an unctuous texture, full body, and a seamless finish with low acidity and ripe tannin. This 1998 scores high on both pleasure and cerebral meters. Anticipated maturity: now–2014. Last tasted, 12/02.

1997
89 This wine may deserve an outstanding rating, yet the lavish oak and international style are controversial. Nevertheless, it is a hedonistic, dark ruby/purple–colored, exotic, ostentatious 1997 with superb fruit and concentration. Enjoy it over the next 5–6 years. Last tasted, 1/02.

1996
92 The spectacular 1996 La Gomerie exhibits a dark ruby color and explosive aromatics of toast, roasted nuts, kirsch, and assorted black fruits. It is full-bodied with sweet tannin and a ripe, intensely concentrated finish with high levels of glycerin and extract. This flamboyant, full-bodied wine should be at its finest between now and 2018. Last tasted, 3/00.

1995
93 The debut vintage for La Gomerie, the 1995 is showing fabulously well. The color is dense ruby/purple, and the nose offers up exotic aromas of Asian spices, soy, coffee, and ripe berry/cherry fruit. This full-bodied, thick, unctuously textured wine is marvelously concentrated, with plenty of sweet, well-integrated tannin. The acidity is low, which only adds to the voluptuous personality of this strikingly rich, head-turning effort. Anticipated maturity: now–2012. Last tasted, 12/00.

GRACIA

Classification: None

Owner: Michel Gracia

Address: Saint-Christophe-des-Bardes, 33330 St.-Emilion

Telephone: 05 57 24 77 98; Telefax: 05 57 74 46 72

Visits: By appointment only

Contact: Michel Gracia

VINEYARDS

Surface area: 4.4 acres

Grape varietals: 79% Merlot, 16% Cabernet Franc, 5% Cabernet Sauvignon

Average age of vines: 27 years

Density of plantation: 5,000 vines per hectare

Average yields: 22 hectoliters per hectare

Elevage: Following a seven-day cold maceration, fermentations and macerations last approximately 30 days in concrete tanks. Wines undergo malolactics in new oak barrels and are aged 18–24 months. The wine is aged on its lees. Michel Gracia does not filter or fine.

WINES PRODUCED

Château Gracia: 4,000 bottles

No second wine is produced.

Plateau of maturity: Within 2–15 years of the vintage

GENERAL APPRECIATION

Since its debut vintage in 1997, Gracia has been one of the finest garage wines in St.-Emilion. Obviously, prices are high in view of the very small production, but in Gracia's case, only quality matters.

IMPORTANT VINTAGES

2001
90–92 Another top-notch effort from this garage operation, the 2001 Gracia, cropped at a meager 19 hectoliters per hectare, is a blend of 80% Merlot, 15% Cabernet Franc, and 5% Cabernet Sauvignon. The 2001 is soft, with a tendency toward diffuseness, but there is no doubting the ripe, sweet, lush black cherry fruit nicely wrapped in smoky, toasty new oak. Fleshy and seductive, it is best consumed during its first 10–12 years of life. Last tasted, 1/03.

2000
93 The 2000 (90% Merlot, 10% Cabernet Franc) is Gracia's greatest effort to date. Its opaque purple color is followed by gorgeous aromas of black fruits, minerals, smoky oak, and flowers. Layered and full-bodied, with sensational concentration and beautifully integrated acidity, wood, and tannin, this is a blockbuster yet incredibly harmonious wine to drink between 2004–2018. Last tasted, 1/03.

1999
91 Made from a blend of 90% Merlot and 10% Cabernet Franc, the dense, gorgeously perfumed 1999 boasts notes of jammy cherries infused with licorice, smoke, and minerals. With layers of concentration, low acidity, and tremendous purity as well

as length, it is nearly as glorious as the 1998 and 2000. Anticipated maturity: now–2020. Last tasted, 3/02.

1998
92
A spectacular effort, the 1998 exhibits an opaque purple color as well as a gorgeous bouquet of overripe black cherries intermixed with blackberries, blueberries, licorice, and smoky oak. Full-bodied, low in acidity, opulent, fleshy, and undeniably disarming, it offers layers of fruit in addition to sweet tannin in the finish. Anticipated maturity: now–2016. Last tasted, 3/02.

1997
89
This wine may deserve an outstanding rating since it is powerfully extracted, rich, full-bodied, and concentrated, with abundant quantities of smoky oak intertwined with liqueur-like, intense black cherry and berry fruit. Low acidity, supple tannin, and a rich, long finish are authoritative and impressive. Drink it over the next eight years. Last tasted, 1/01.

GRAND CORBIN

Classification: Grand Cru

Owner: Société Familiale Alain Giraud

Address: 5, Grand-Corbin, 33330 St.-Emilion

Telephone: 05 57 24 70 62; Telefax: 05 57 64 47 18

E-mail: grand-corbin@wanadoo.fr

Website: www.grand-corbin.com

Visits: By appointment only

Contact: Philippe Giraud

VINEYARDS

Surface area: 38.2 acres

Grape varietals: 68% Merlot, 27% Cabernet Franc, 5% Cabernet Sauvignon

Average age of vines: 38 years

Density of plantation: 5,500 vines per hectare

Average yields: 48 hectoliters per hectare

Elevage: Three to four week fermentation and maceration in temperature-controlled concrete vats. After completion of malolactics in vats, 11–15 months aging in barrels that are renewed by a third at each vintage. Fining, no filtration.

WINES PRODUCED

Château Grand Corbin: 85,000 bottles

No second wine is produced.

Plateau of maturity: Within 2–10 years of the vintage

GENERAL APPRECIATION

As with most Giraud efforts, Grand Corbin is soundly made but lacks the extra-stuffing characteristic of wines emerging from more reduced yields. However, the wine is good and reasonably priced.

Grand Corbin, a well-situated property on the Pomerol/St.-Emilion border, consistently produces round, chunky, generally well-colored St.-Emilions that require drinking in their first decade. The Girauds, an ancient family originally from Pomerol, own Grand Corbin and, like their nearby neighbor Figeac, employ a relatively high percentage of Cabernet Franc in the blend. This works well when the Cabernet ripens fully, but in years that it does not, there is a tendency for Grand Corbin to come across as too herbaceous, even vegetal.

IMPORTANT VINTAGES

2001 Deep ruby–colored but monolithic, this medium-bodied wine shows good ripe-
85–86 ness, some herb-tinged black cherry and currant fruit, adequate acidity, and soft tannin. It is a wine to drink over the next 7–8 years. Last tasted, 1/03.

2000 This is a relatively sweet, forward style of 2000, with a deep ruby color, jammy
87 black currant, and herb-tinged cherry notes intermixed with some underbrush, earth, and spice. The wine is medium bodied, lightly tannic, and a 2000 to drink during its first 7–8 years of life. Last tasted, 1/03.

1999 A thin, herbaceous, medium-bodied wine that lacks substance, the acidity and
70? tannin are already overtaking what fruit is present. Anticipated maturity: now. Last tasted, 12/02.

1996 A solid performance for this estate, this opaque purple–colored wine offers a
86 spicy, toasty, jammy fruit nose, rich, nicely concentrated flavors, medium to full body, and plenty of power and length. Good acidity allied with the wine's concentration suggest this wine will age for 12–15+ years. It is one of the most structured Grand Corbins I have ever tasted. Last tasted, 3/97.

GRAND CORBIN-DESPAGNE

Classification: Grand Cru (declassified in 1996)

Owner: Despagne family

Address: 33330 St.-Emilion

Telephone: 05 57 51 08 38; Telefax: 05 57 51 29 18

E-mail: f.despagne@grand-corbin-despagne.com

Website: www.grand-corbin-despagne.com

Visits: By appointment only

Contact: François Despagne

VINEYARDS

Surface area: 65.5 acres

Grape varietals: 75% Merlot, 20% Cabernet Franc, 2% Malbec, 3% Cabernet Sauvignon

Average age of vines: 37 years

Density of plantation: 6,000 vines per hectare

Average yields: 40 hectoliters per hectare

Elevage: Cold maceration. Fermentation and 25 day maceration in temperature-controlled vats. Malolactics in barrel for greater part of yield. Fourteen to eighteen months aging in barrel with 60% new oak and 40% one-year-old barrels. Fining, no filtration.

WINES PRODUCED

Château Grand Corbin-Despagne: 90,000 bottles

Petit Corbin-Despagne: 20,000 bottles, as of 1998

Plateau of maturity: Within 5–12 years of the vintage

GENERAL APPRECIATION

Grand Corbin-Despagne is an up-and-coming St.-Emilion estate fashioning muscular, powerful wines requiring cellaring. The breakthrough vintage for this vineyard was 1998. Vintages prior to 1998 should be approached with caution.

IMPORTANT VINTAGES

2001 This wine has filled out nicely and is a potential sleeper of the vintage. A deep
87–89 blue/purple color is followed by a wine with plenty of black fruit, earth, licorice, and some background new oak. The wine has sweetness, medium body, and the telltale power and muscular tannins in the finish that characterize the style of this estate. Anticipated maturity: 2007–2014. Last tasted, 1/03.

2000 The black/purple-colored 2000 is a sleeper of the vintage. Revealing aromas of
90 plum, wood smoke, iron, blackberries, licorice, underbrush, and cassis, this full-bodied, layered, powerful, muscular St.-Emilion has some tannin to shed, but its finish reveals considerable persistence. It is a very strong, virile, broodingly impressive effort. Anticipated maturity: 2006–2018. Last tasted, 1/03.

1999 Notes of wet stones along with foresty underbrush characteristics add complexity
88 to the deep black currant/cherry fruit. A hint of fennel is also noticeable. The wine is ripe and dense for a 1999, with light to moderate tannin and low acidity. Anticipated maturity: now–2013. Last tasted, 3/02.

1998 With a dense ruby/purple color, this closed yet promising, large-scaled, muscular
88+ 1998 offers earthy, black currant, and cherry aromas intertwined with scents of minerals and smoke. Powerful, dense, thick, and tannic, it is an uncompromising *vin de garde* requiring 2–3 years of cellaring. Anticipated maturity: 2006–2016. Last tasted, 3/02.

GRAND MAYNE

Classification: Grand Cru Classé

Owner: SCEV J.-P. Nony

Address: 33330 St.-Emilion

Telephone: 05 57 74 42 50; Telefax: 05 57 74 41 89

E-mail: grand-mayne@grand-mayne.com

Website: www.grand-mayne.com

Visits: By appointment only Monday to Friday, 9:30 A.M.–noon and 2–7 P.M.

Contact: Marie-Françoise Nony or Jean-Antoine Nony

VINEYARDS

Surface area: 42 acres

Grape varietals: 75% Merlot, 15% Cabernet Franc, 10% Cabernet Sauvignon

Average age of vines: 35 years

Density of plantation: 6,000 vines per hectare

Average yields: 35 hectoliters per hectare

Elevage: Thirty day fermentation and maceration in temperature-controlled stainless-steel and wooden vats of small capacity, which enable separate vinification of the different parcels. Malolactics and 14–20 months aging in barrels with 70% new oak. No fining, filtration only if necessary.

WINES PRODUCED

Château Grand Mayne: 60,000 bottles

Les Plantes du Mayne: 15,000 bottles

Plateau of maturity: Within 5–20 years of the vintage

GENERAL APPRECIATION

The late Jean-Pierre Nony did a terrific job at this estate, producing a string of superb wines of incredible richness. Fairly priced, Grand Mayne is a top choice for consumers looking for majestically flavored, long-lived St.-Emilions.

One of the most renowned authorities on the soils of Pomerol and St.-Emilion, the professor Enjalbert made it clear in his lectures and books that Grand Mayne possesses one of the most privileged sites in St.-Emilion. This ancient site (the history here can be traced to the 1600s) sits at an exceptionally high altitude—55 meters above sea level. The altitude and soil base, consisting primarily of clay and limestone intermixed with iron deposits, make this vineyard potentially one of the best of the entire appellation. Aesthetically, the magnificent vanilla ice cream–colored château has been totally renovated and is a striking sight to behold on a bright, blue-skied day.

The wines have gone from one strength to another during the 1980s, with the brilliant Libourne oenologist Michel Rolland asserting his winemaking philosophy. The results are some of the most opulent and richest wines now being made in St.-Emilion. This is a wine that can be exceptionally full-bodied, with gobs of glycerin because of the superb vineyard soil and great exposition the vineyard enjoys.

Grand Mayne is one of the up-and-coming stars of the appellation, yet prices have remained reasonable, a fact that should be put to good use by wine consumers. If my enthusiasm for Grand Mayne seems excessive, consider the fact that the late Baron Philippe de Rothschild, after tasting the 1955 Grand Mayne at a restaurant in Belgium, immediately placed an order for several cases, offering to replace the Grand Mayne with a similar number of bottles of the 1955 Mouton Rothschild!

IMPORTANT VINTAGES

2001 Showing far better right before bottling, the dense ruby/purple–colored Grand
88–90 Mayne shows the telltale blueberry/blackberry fruit intermixed with some creamy vanilla and new oak, a sweet entry on the palate, medium to full body, moderate tannin, and good vibrancy and delineation. Anticipated maturity: 2006–2015. Last tasted, 1/03.

2000
92

It will be hard for the opaque ruby/purple–colored 2000 to surpass the spectacular 1998, but it appears that more and more Grand Mayne is becoming the Lynch-Bages of St.-Emilion. The corpulent, fleshy, hedonistic 2000 is loaded with concentrated black fruits as well as impeccable purity and balance. Large-scaled and delicious, it is an attention-getter, but not overdone. The oak is beautifully integrated, the acidity low, and the tannin sizable but ripe. Another blockbuster effort, it will be at its finest between 2005–2018. Last tasted, 1/03.

1999
90

Grand Mayne has fashioned a superb 1999, with terrific concentration and a hedonistic, sexy style. This dense, purple-colored offering displays glorious levels of sweet blackberry and currant, fruit, a succulent, lush texture, full body, low acidity, and beautifully integrated wood and tannin. It offers a substantial mouthful of sumptuous St.-Emilion. Anticipated maturity: now–2013. Last tasted, 12/02.

1998
93

The finest Grand Mayne to date, this is a wine of majestic weight, richness, and volume. The most concentrated and powerful Grand Mayne yet produced, its saturated purple color is accompanied by a phenomenal nose of licorice, smoke, graphite, and blackberry/cassis aromas (reminiscent of dry vintage Port). This huge, massive effort is low in acidity and highly extracted, with an unctuous texture, gobs of glycerin, and a multidimensional, chewy, long finish. A dazzling wine, it is undoubtedly a sleeper of the vintage. Anticipated maturity: now–2020. Last tasted, 1/03.

1997
87

The telltale dark ruby color, pronounced minerality, and pure black raspberry fruit are the hallmarks of most Grand Mayne vintages. The 1997 possesses some tannin, but the overall impression is of an elegant, medium-bodied, slightly lighter than usual wine with sweet fruit, and the potential to drink well for 5–6 years. Last tasted, 3/02.

1996
88

The 1996 Grand Mayne exhibits a dense purple color and an attractive nose of white flowers, sweet blackberries, cherries, minerals, and toast. It is medium to full-bodied, with excellent depth, an elegant personality, and a clean, mineral-like finish with moderate tannin. New oak is noticeable in the flavors. Anticipated maturity: now–2014. Last tasted, 3/01.

1995
90

An unqualified sleeper of the vintage, the opaque purple–colored 1995 Grand Mayne displays a sweet, creamy, black raspberry–scented nose with subtle notes of smoky, toasty oak. Both powerful and elegant, this wine, still somewhat firm and closed, exhibits layers of richness, nicely integrated acidity and tannin, and an impressive full-bodied, long finish. Anticipated maturity: 2005–2015. Last tasted, 1/02.

1994
?

All tastings of this wine have revealed a musty, cardboard component. Three different tastings of this wine following bottling support the fact that something has flawed the wine's aromatics. Whether or not this mustiness will dissipate with cellaring remains to be seen. All of this is lamentable given the terrific efforts that the overachieving proprietors, the Nonys, have produced at Grand Mayne. Last tasted, 1/97.

1990
90

The 1990 offers an impressively saturated color, exhibiting a touch of amber and a black cherry, mineral, smoky component, with a dash of roasted herbs. Spicy, rich, long, and massive in the mouth, it is full-bodied, sweet, jammy, and capable of lasting for another 8–10 years. Last tasted, 5/01.

1989
92

A superb, still youthful 1989, this Grand Mayne will still benefit from several years of cellaring. It exhibits an opaque purple color (slight pink at the rim), a sweet, black raspberry, mineral, and toasty oak nose, dense, medium- to full-bodied flavors that possess terrific purity and harmony, and a spicy, long, sweet,

tannic finish. This is a beautifully made, harmoniously extracted wine. Anticipated maturity: 2004–2015. Last tasted, 1/03.

1988   The 1988 Grand Mayne is a big, alcoholic, obvious wine displaying an intense,
87   vanilla-scented, black plum–like fruitiness and fleshy, chewy flavors. Anticipated
       maturity: now–2003. Last tasted, 1/93.

GRAND-PONTET

Classification: Grand Cru Classé

Owner: Pourquet-Bécot family

Address: 33330 St.-Emilion

Telephone: 05 57 74 46 88 *or* 06 10 28 00 55;
Telefax: 05 57 74 45 31

E-mail: chateau.grand.pontet@wanadoo.fr

Visits: By appointment only Monday to Friday,
9 A.M.–noon and 2–6 P.M.

Contact: Sylvie Pourquet or Pascal Lucin

VINEYARDS

Surface area: 34.6 acres

Grape varietals: 75% Merlot, 15% Cabernet Franc, 10% Cabernet Sauvignon

Average age of vines: 35 years

Density of plantation: 5,500 vines per hectare

Average yields: 36 hectoliters per hectare

Elevage: Eight day fermentation and 30 day maceration in electronically temperature-
controlled stainless-steel tanks. Twelve to eighteen months aging in barrels with 90% new
oak, depending upon the vintage. No fining, filtration.

WINES PRODUCED

Château Grand-Pontet: 50,000 bottles

Dauphin de Grand-Pontet: 7,000–10,000 bottles

Plateau of maturity: Within 5–15 years of the vintage

GENERAL APPRECIATION

This excellent wine has merited its grand cru classé status since 1988. It has continued to
improve, benefiting from the winemaking skills of the Bécot brothers (whose farming
contract with this estate has recently been terminated). I am encouraged that the new
management will continue the impeccable track record of the previous administrator.

Grand-Pontet, owned and run by the sister of Gérard and Dominique Bécot (Beau-
Séjour and La Gomerie), is situated next to the more renowned property of the Bécot
family, Château Beau-Séjour. The vineyard sits in the highly regarded western limestone plateau of St.-Emilion. For years many of St.-Emilion's cognoscenti have suggested that this is a property that, with improvements and a more strict selection, could

emerge as a potential candidate for elevation to premier grand cru classé status. Improvements have indeed been made, and vintages since 1988 have been impressive.

While it is not unlikely that this property might merit elevation to premier grand cru classé status in the next classification of St.-Emilion, recent vintages have been brilliant.

IMPORTANT VINTAGES

2001 The 2001 is nearly as good as the 2000 Grand-Pontet. Produced from 75% Merlot
90–92 and 25% Cabernet Franc, and with modest yields of 33 hectoliters per hectare, the seamless 2001 exhibits a saturated ruby/purple color as well as sweet aromas of licorice, black fruits, smoke, and espresso. Ripe, lush, and hedonistic, with layers of glycerin and fruit and a long, velvety finish, this is a St.-Emilion to enjoy over the next 10–12 years. Last tasted, 1/03.

2000 Quality has exploded in 2000, offering an extra dimension in both aroma and
92 flavor. A blend of 75% Merlot, 15% Cabernet Franc, and 10% Cabernet Sauvignon produced from modest yields of 30 hectoliters per hectare, this opaque purple–colored, fat, ripe, exotic, flamboyant effort is a St.-Emilion fruit-bomb made in a modern style. With loads of character, glycerin, fruit, and concentration, this full-bodied, "stacked and packed" wine will be adored by consumers! Anticipated maturity: now–2015. Last tasted, 1/03.

1999 Straddled between the brilliant 2000 and 1998, the 1999 comes across as a
85 straightforward, rather easygoing wine that lacks the substance, concentration, and overall depth of its younger and older siblings. Nevertheless, there is some sweet black cherry fruit intermixed with vanilla, herbs, and licorice. This medium-bodied wine should be drunk over the next 5–7 years. Last tasted, 12/02.

1998 A superb effort, the 1998 has a saturated black/purple color and offers a knockout
90 nose of nearly overripe blackberry fruit, kirsch, licorice, smoke, and toasty new oak. Full-bodied, powerful, and rich, with impressive equilibrium, this concentrated, rich, deep wine will last for 12–15 years. Impressive! Last tasted, 3/02.

1997 Grand-Pontet's delicious 1997 exhibits the vintage's finest characteristics—
87 fleshy, succulent, low-acid, plump, spice, and cherry fruit nicely infused with toasty new oak. This lush, hedonistic effort should continue to drink well for 4–5 years. Last tasted, 2/00.

1996 The 1996 is a flamboyant, dark ruby/purple–colored wine with a soaring bouquet
89 of plum liqueur, toasty new oak, black cherries, smoke, and dried herbs. In the mouth, evidence of *sur-maturité* jamminess and richness emerge from this medium-bodied, rich, spicy, impressively endowed wine. There is tannin in the medium- to full-bodied finish. Anticipated maturity: now–2010. Last tasted, 12/00.

1995 Dark ruby/purple–colored with a forward, evolved nose of spice, black cherries,
88 and toast, this supple, round, generous, medium- to full-bodied wine possesses low acidity and some tannin in the finish. There is good delineation to this plump, succulently styled wine that can be drunk now as well as over the next 2–3 years. Last tasted, 11/97.

1990 Lusciously fruity, with tons of sweet, smoky new oak, the 1990 fairly oozes unctu-
89 ous flavors from the glass. The wine has copious quantities of fruit, a silky, full-bodied feel, and an opulent, splendidly long finish. For drinking over the next 6–10 years, it will provide considerable pleasure. This is a sleeper of the vintage! Last tasted, 11/95.

LES GRANDES MURAILLES

Classification: Grand Cru Classé

Owner: SA Les Grandes Murailles

Address: 33330 St.-Emilion

Telephone: 05 57 24 71 09; Telefax: 05 57 74 72 69

E-mail: lesgrandesmurailles@wanadoo.fr

Website: www.grandes-murailles.com

Visits: By appointment only

Contact: Sophie Fourcade

VINEYARDS

Surface area: 4 acres (in production)

Grape varietals: 95% Merlot, 5% Cabernet Franc

Average age of vines: 35 years

Density of plantation: 5,700 vines per hectare

Average yields: 35 hectoliters per hectare

Elevage: Cold maceration. Twenty-five day fermentation and maceration in temperature-controlled stainless-steel tanks. Malolactics and 18–20 months aging in new oak barrels. No fining, filtration depends upon the vintage.

WINES PRODUCED

Château Les Grandes Murailles: 7,000–7,500 bottles

Plateau of maturity: Within 5–15 years of the vintage

GENERAL APPRECIATION

Another Reiffers owned property, Les Grandes Murailles has followed the same qualitative trend as its two stablemates, Côte de Baleau and Clos St.-Martin. A wine to follow closely as of 1997, especially since the production is quite small.

IMPORTANT VINTAGES

2001 **89–91** The dense purple–colored 2001 exhibits aromas of blueberry liqueur, acacia flowers, minerals, and subtle wood. Sweet, opulent, medium to full-bodied, pure, and harmonious, it should be stunning young, yet age impeccably for 12–15 years. Last tasted, 1/03.

2000 **93** Opaque purple–colored, the 2000 is even more impressive from bottle than barrel: A sleeper of the vintage, this expansive and dense wine exhibits impressive extract levels, beautifully pure blueberry, blackberry, and cherry characteristics with a liquid minerality, as well as suave, well-integrated, toasty, espresso notes. Sweet tannin, medium to full body, and a long finish make for a sumptuous example of St.-Emilion. It should be accessible early. Glorious stuff! Anticipated maturity: 2005–2016. Last tasted, 1/03.

1999 **87** Although performing well, particularly for a property that was forced to harvest early because of hail damage, the 1999 Grandes Murailles does not possess the flavor dimension exhibited prior to bottling. It is a medium-bodied, richly fruity effort without the depth, length, and overall complexity of the 1998 or 2000. Drink it over the next 3–4 years as it will probably not improve. Last tasted, 3/02.

1998   A sleeper of the vintage, as well as one of the finest Grandes Murailles I have ever
90   tasted, this deep, saturated ruby/purple–colored 1998 offers up blueberry, plum,
   raspberry, and black cherry fruit intertwined with toast and minerals. Supple,
   complex, and medium to full-bodied, with a boatload of fruit and richness, there
   are no hard edges in this seamless, classic St.-Emilion. Anticipated maturity:
   now–2016. Last tasted, 3/02.

1997   The dark plum–colored 1997 displays considerable density as well as a sweet,
87   open-knit, cherry/blueberry jam, mineral, and a spicy, smoky oak–scented bouquet. The wine is medium bodied, silky-textured, with low acidity and a spicy,
   richly fruity, nicely layered finish. Moderate tannin suggests it may improve beyond a decade, but I would opt to drink it over the near-term. Anticipated maturity: now–2009. Last tasted, 3/01.

HAUT-VILLET

Classification: Grand Cru

Owner: GFA du Château Haut-Villet

Address: 33330 Saint-Etienne-de-Lisse

Mailing address: BP 17, 33330 St.-Emilion

Telephone: 05 57 47 97 60; Telefax: 05 57 47 92 94

E-mail: haut.villet@free.fr

Visits: By appointment only Monday to Saturday,
10 A.M.–noon and 2–6 P.M.

Contact: Eric Lenormand

VINEYARDS

Surface area: 18.5 acres

Grape varietals: 70% Merlot, 30% Cabernet Franc

Average age of vines: 45 years

Density of plantation: 5,500–6,400 vines per hectare

Average yields: 40 hectoliters per hectare

Elevage: Prolonged fermentation and maceration in temperature-controlled stainless-
steel vats with pumpings-over, manual *pigéages,* and micro-oxygenation. Fifteen months
aging in barrels with 40% new oak for Haut-Villet and Moulin de Villet. Fining and
filtration are not systematic. Eighteen to twenty months aging in barrels with 80% new oak
for the Cuvée Pomone, which is not fined or filtered.

WINES PRODUCED

Château Haut-Villet: 31,000 bottles

Château Moulin de Villet: 9,000 bottles

Château Haut-Villet Cuvée Pomone: 5,500 bottles

Plateau of maturity: Within 5–12 years of the vintage

GENERAL APPRECIATION

These are muscular, concentrated, full-bodied, aggressive St.-Emilions, the Cuvée Pomone
being Haut-Villet's luxury garage *cuvée.* It is extremely massive, with heavy, sometimes

excessive new oak, and a tannic, powerful style that suggests two decades of cellaring are possible. It is a far bigger wine than the regular *cuvée*, but I sometimes doubt it can age gracefully. Despite my reservations, there is no question both wines, and especially the Cuvée Pomone, are worth a gamble given their impressive extract level. In fact, I often have difficulty assessing these wines, largely because I have never tasted a mature Haut-Villet, so I do not know if they are capable of absorbing all their tannin and wood.

IMPORTANT VINTAGES

2000
87
The deep, rich, medium-bodied 2000 Haut-Villet possesses sweet earthy black fruit characteristics intermixed with oak, licorice, and vitamin-like notes. It reveals the vintage's hallmark high ripeness allied with moderate tannin. Anticipated maturity: 2005–2014. Last tasted, 1/03.

2000
90
Cuvée Pomone: A sleeper of the vintage, the opaque purple–colored, modern-styled 2000 Haut-Villet Cuvée Pomone offers a blast of new oak along with jammy cassis, licorice, spice box, and mineral-scented aromas. It is full-bodied and heady, with noticeable glycerin concealing moderately high levels of tannin. The tannin has mellowed considerably in the course of its *élevage* . . . a positive sign. This is an internationally styled garage wine that is showing impressive credentials from bottle. Anticipated maturity: 2006–2020. Last tasted, 1/03.

1999
86
The medium-bodied, elegant, dark ruby–colored 1999 Haut-Villet possesses attractive aromas of kirsch, dried herbs, and soil undertones. It is best drunk over the next eight years. Last tasted, 3/02.

1999
88
Cuvée Pomone: Exhibiting a more saturated ruby color than the standard *cuvée*, the 1999 Haut-Villet Cuvée Pomone is a sweet, modern-styled St.-Emilion with noticeable vanilla and toasty new oak notes, copious quantities of cherry and cassis fruit, outstanding ripeness, and a big, chewy personality. Long and fleshy, it will provide ideal drinking over the next 10 years. Last tasted, 3/02.

1998
87
A serious, deep ruby/purple–colored effort, the regular *cuvée* reveals tannin levels similar to the more oaky, luxury *cuvée*, as well as excellent concentration, a firm *vin de garde* style, and a spicy, long finish. Anticipated maturity: 2005–2016. Last tasted, 3/02.

1998
89+?
Cuvée Pomone: A saturated ruby/purple color is followed by flamboyant aromas of toasty, smoky new oak as well as jammy blackberries and cherries. The wine is thick, powerful, tannic, full-bodied, and in need of 3–4 years of cellaring. If the tannin becomes fully integrated, this offering will merit an outstanding score. Anticipated maturity: 2007–2020. Last tasted, 3/02.

L'HERMITAGE

Classification: Grand Cru

Owner: GFA de Matras

Address: 33330 St.-Emilion

Telephone: 05 57 51 52 39; Telefax: 05 57 51 70 19

Visits: By appointment only

Contact: Jérôme Gaboriaud (Telephone: 05 57 48 11 00)

VINEYARDS

Surface area: 7.4 acres

Grape varietals: 70% Merlot, 30% Cabernet Franc

Average age of vines: 45 years

Density of plantation: 6,500 vines per hectare

Average yields: 32 hectoliters per hectare

Elevage: Fifteen day cold maceration at 5°C. Fermentation and maceration in temperature-controlled stainless-steel vats. Malolactics and 18–20 months aging in new oak barrels. Fining, no filtration.

WINES PRODUCED

Château L'Hermitage: 10,000–12,000 bottles

No second wine is produced.

Plateau of maturity: Within 3–15 years of the vintage

GENERAL APPRECIATION

Since its debut vintage in 1997, L'Hermitage has become part of the controversial "garage wine" movement. The latest efforts were very good, if not excellent, and as such merit recommendation.

The small quantities of L'Hermitage emerge from a 45-year-old vineyard sandwiched between Beauséjour-Duffau and Angélus. L'Hermitage undergoes long pre-fermentation cold maceration and is aged in 100% new French wood. Virtually every radical New Wave technique designed to enhance color, fruit, *terroir*, texture, and longevity is employed at L'Hermitage.

IMPORTANT VINTAGES

2001 / 91–94 — This may be the finest L'Hermitage yet produced, even better than the 2000. The blend is 75% Merlot and 25% Cabernet Franc and the yield is 33 hectoliters per hectare. The inky/purple color is followed by scents of melted licorice, blackberries, cassis and complementary notes of toasty oak. A multidimensional texture, extraordinary fruit purity (a hallmark of many top 2001s), well-integrated tannin, and a long, lush finish are present in this medium-bodied, seamless effort. Anticipated maturity: 2006–2017. Last tasted, 1/03.

2000 / 91 — A wonderfully sweet bouquet of crème de cassis, melted licorice, mocha, and vanilla soars from the glass. The rich, pure, concentrated, opaque purple–colored 2000 displays all the hallmarks of this great vintage—power, concentration, depth, ripeness, and moderately high tannin. Dense and impressive, it will be drinkable between 2006–2018. Last tasted, 1/03.

1999 / 88 — Hail damage forced L'Hermitage's proprietors to harvest the Merlot and the Cabernet Franc two or three weeks before full maturity. Nevertheless, the 1999 has turned out amazingly well. This excellent, smooth, sweet, herb-tinged, blackberry and cherry-flavored wine displays a seductive, fleshy palate, good length (surprising for a hail-damaged St.-Emilion), and excellent ripeness. Drink it over the next six or so years. Last tasted, 3/02.

1998 / 89+ — Dense ruby/purple–colored, with blackberry, licorice, cherry, and toasty new oak aromas as well as flavors, this deep, medium- to full-bodied St.-Emilion is chewy, dense, concentrated, and well made. The finish is pure, concentrated, and moderately tannic. Anticipated maturity: now–2016. Last tasted, 3/02.

1997 A deep, saturated, ruby-colored effort, with copious quantities of sweet, jammy
88 cherry and black currant fruit complemented by high-quality toasty oak, this
medium-bodied 1997 displays excellent richness, a soft, velvety texture, light tannin, and low acidity. Drink it over the next 2–3 years. Last tasted, 3/01.

LANIOTE

Classification: Grand Cru Classé

Owner: Arnaud and Florence de la Filolie

Address: 33330 St.-Emilion

Telephone: 05 57 24 70 80; Telefax: 05 57 24 60 71

E-mail: laniote@wanadoo.fr

Visits: Monday to Friday, 9 A.M.–noon and 1:30–6 P.M.
Groups by appointment only.

Contact: Arnaud de la Filolie

VINEYARDS

Surface area: 12.4 acres

Grape varietals: 70% Merlot, 20% Cabernet Franc, 10% Cabernet Sauvignon

Average age of vines: 35 years

Density of plantation: 5,500 vines per hectare

Average yields: 47 hectoliters per hectare

Elevage: Fermentation and maceration in temperature-controlled tanks. Twelve months
aging in barrels with 40–45% new oak. Fining, no filtration.

WINES PRODUCED

Château Laniote: 30,000 bottles

La Chapelle de Laniote: Variable

Plateau of maturity: Within 3–12 years of the vintage

GENERAL APPRECIATION

When Laniote does well, Burgundy lovers may have a hard time distinguishing this
seductive and elegant effort from a Beaune premier cru. But this is not always the case as
this wine is not a regular performer, far too often producing wines that are overly tannic.
The price is reasonable.

An historic property in the same family for centuries, this ancient estate comes complete with chapel and extensive catacombs, making a visit mandatory. I have had very
limited experience with the wines from the tiny vineyard of Laniote. The property, located northwest of the town of St.-Emilion, sits on rich clay, limestone, and iron-
enriched soils.

IMPORTANT VINTAGES

2001 The dense 2001 is a significant improvement for Laniote. Although disjointed
86–88 and unevolved, it reveals high extract and tannin as well as plenty of deep, pure,
mineral-infused black cherry fruit. If everything comes together, it will be a good
effort. Anticipated maturity: 2006–2014? Last tasted, 1/03.

2000 The 2000 is a somewhat monolithic, foursquare, chunky wine, but it is corpulent
86 and dense, with plenty of rustic black cherry and currant fruit displayed in a
medium-bodied, slightly tannic style. Not a lot of complexity can be found, but the
wine certainly is substantial and mouth-filling. Anticipated maturity: 2005–2012.
Last tasted, 1/03.

1999 A very light but somewhat insipid effort with herb-tinged, dusty cherry fruit,
80 medium body, and a quickly evaporating finish, this wine needs to be drunk up.
Anticipated maturity: now. Last tasted, 3/02.

1998 A succulent, full-bodied, silky-textured, super-jammy, rich St.-Emilion, the 1998
88 Laniote offers copious quantities of black fruits intermingled with high-quality
oak as well as an attractive, spicy earthiness. Anticipated maturity: now–2014.
Last tasted, 3/02.

LAPLAGNOTTE-BELLEVUE

Classification: Grand Cru

Owner: Henry and Claude de Labarre

Address: 33330 Saint-Christophe-des-Bardes

Telephone: 05 57 24 78 67; Telefax: 05 57 24 63 62

Visits: By appointment only

Contact: Frank and Marguerite Glaunes

VINEYARDS

Surface area: 15 acres

Grape varietals: 70% Merlot, 15% Cabernet Franc,
15% Cabernet Sauvignon

Average age of vines: 30 years

Density of plantation: 6,000 vines per hectare

Average yields: 40–48 hectoliters per hectare

Elevage: Fermentation and maceration for 18–21 days in cement vats. Aged for 15–18
months in barrel (25–30% new oak). Fining with egg whites, very light filtration.

WINES PRODUCED

Château Laplagnotte-Bellevue: 30,000 bottles

Laplagnotte: 5,000 bottles (a prestige *cuvée*)

Plateau of maturity: Within 2–10 years of the vintage

GENERAL APPRECIATION

This estate is owned by Claude de Labarre, one of the former co-proprietors of Cheval
Blanc. The vineyard is planted with 70% Merlot, 15% Cabernet Franc, and 15%
Cabernet Sauvignon, and the wines are generally elegant, richly fruity, straightforward,

and tasty. As from 2000, Laplagnotte-Bellevue also offers a special *cuvée*, Laplagnotte, made in the manner of a garage wine.

IMPORTANT VINTAGES

2001
87–88
Laplagnotte-Bellevue: Showing quite well, this sweet, dark ruby/purple–colored wine has very pure mulberry and cherry fruit, with some subtle background wood and licorice. The wine is sweet, round, and quite delicious, and it should make a very tasty bottle of St.-Emilion to drink during its first decade of life. Anticipated maturity: 2004–2013. Last tasted, 1/03.

2001
87–90
Laplagnotte: Exhibiting more new oak than its sibling and certainly more extraction and power, think of the regular *cuvée* but add doses of steroids and you come up with a fuller, more expansive, fleshier, denser wine. Anticipated maturity: 2006–2015. Last tasted, 1/03.

2000
89
Laplagnotte-Bellevue: Showing far better out of bottle than it was from cask, the 2000 Laplagnotte-Bellevue exhibits a saturated dark ruby/purple color and a sexy, up-front nose of sweet jammy cassis and currant with some espresso, vanilla, and white flowers. The wine is opulent, medium to full-bodied, yet very elegant and pure. This is impressive and quite precocious. Anticipated maturity: 2004–2015. Last tasted, 1/03.

2000
90
Laplagnotte: A brilliant wine and, to date, the best that has been produced at the estate, this saturated dark ruby/purple–colored wine has a sweet nose of espresso, black currant, and kirsch intermixed with some licorice, tobacco leaf, and vanilla. The wine is full-bodied and opulent, with considerable richness hiding some moderately serious tannins. This is a sizeable yet elegant effort that adroitly marries finesse and power in a very pure style. Impressive! Anticipated maturity: 2007–2015. Last tasted, 1/03.

1999
88
Laplagnotte-Bellevue: This 1999's excellent, Burgundian-like, floral bouquet of black cherry fruit is so ripe it resembles kirsch. This medium-bodied, nicely layered, pure wine is seductive and delicious. Its sweet tannin and seamlessness suggest that consumption over the next six years is warranted. Last tasted, 3/02.

1997
86
Laplagnotte-Bellevue: The charming, open-knit, richly fruity 1997 is light to medium bodied and soft, with no hard edges. Drink it over the next 2–3 years. Last tasted, 3/02.

1996
86
A soft, richly fruity wine, the 1996 exhibits medium dark ruby color, an elegant, sweet nose of black cherry fruit intermixed with floral scents, earth, and spice, and dry tannin in the finish. This is an elegant, finesse-styled, fruit-driven wine for enjoying over the next 2–3 years. Last tasted, 1/00.

1995
86
A pretty wine, with sweet cherry fruit and vanilla in the nose, this ruby/purple-colored effort possesses good ripeness on the attack, soft tannin, low acidity, and a round, easygoing finish. Anticipated maturity: now–2006. Last tasted, 1/00.

LARCIS DUCASSE

Classification: Grand Cru Classé

Owner: Gratiot family

Administrator: Nicolas Thienpont

Address: 33330 St.-Emilion

Telephone: 05 57 24 70 84; Telefax: 05 57 24 64 00

Visits: By appointment only

Contact: Brigitte Seguin

VINEYARDS

Surface area: 26.9 acres

Grape varietals: 65% Merlot, 25% Cabernet Franc, 10% Cabernet Sauvignon

Average age of vines: 35 years

Density of plantation: 5,000 vines per hectare

Average yields: 40 hectoliters per hectare

Elevage: Three to four week fermentation and maceration in temperature-controlled concrete tanks. Twenty-four months aging in barrels with 30% new oak. Fining and filtration.

WINES PRODUCED

Château Larcis Ducasse: 50,000 bottles

No second wine is produced.

Plateau of maturity: Within 2–15 years of the vintage, for wines until 2001

GENERAL APPRECIATION

Though it benefits from an excellent *terroir,* Larcis Ducasse rarely lives up to its potential. They have been soundly made efforts, with no major faults. Starting in 2002, the owners hired the talented duo of Nicolas Thienpont and Stéphane Derenoncourt to produce the wines. A dramatic turnaround is surely guaranteed. This will be a property to watch closely.

Larcis Ducasse sits on the *côtes* of St.-Emilion, southeast of the town, with its vineyard abutting that of Pavie. The vines, planted on calcareous clay slopes, enjoy a full southerly exposure. This wine enjoys an excellent reputation, but until the early 1980s the quality was unimpressive, with too many wines consistently displaying a lean, austere, herbal taste along with excessive tannin.

IMPORTANT VINTAGES

2000   The 2000 is the finest Larcis Ducasse produced in many years. Full-bodied and
87   ripe, with intense black cherry fruit, admirable texture, and mid-palate, this elegant, moderately tannic wine is far superior to recent efforts. Anticipated maturity: 2007–2017. Last tasted, 1/03.

1999   An evolved pink edge to the ruby color raises questions concerning the longevity
82   of this medium-bodied, elegant, but essentially one-dimensional St. Emilion. It
       offers soft, herb-tinged cherry fruit, earth, old wood, and mushroom notes. Drink it
       over the next 3–4 years. Last tasted, 3/02.

1998   The 1998 exhibits a dark ruby color, a herbaceous, sweet, black cherry, mineral,
85   olive, cedar, and spice box–scented bouquet, medium body, light tannin, and a
       short finish. It is a wine to consume over the next 6–7 years. Last tasted, 3/02.

1997   The medium ruby–colored 1997 reveals sweet fruit in the aromatics, but little
84   else. Anticipated maturity: now–2009. Last tasted, 12/00.

1996   The medium ruby–colored 1996 displays an intriguing, herbaceously scented
81   black cherry nose with dusty, crushed seashell scents. A spicy, straightforward,
       monolithic, foursquare offering, it will drink well between now and 2008. Last
       tasted, 12/00.

LARMANDE

Classification: Grand Cru Classé

Owner: La Mondiale

Address: lieu-dit Larmande, 33330 St.-Emilion

Telephone: 05 57 24 71 41; Telefax: 05 57 74 42 80

E-mail: chateau-larmande@wanadoo.fr

Website: chateau-larmande@wanadoo.com

Visits: By appointment Monday to Friday,
8:30 A.M.–noon and 1:30–4:30 P.M.

Contact: Claire Chenard

VINEYARDS

Surface area: 61.8 acres

Grape varietals: 65% Merlot, 30% Cabernet Franc, 5% Cabernet Sauvignon

Average age of vines: 30 years

Density of plantation: 6,000 vines per hectare

Average yields: 36 hectoliters per hectare

Elevage: Fermentation and maceration in temperature-controlled stainless-steel vats.
Fifteen to eighteen months aging in barrels with 70% new oak. Fining, no filtration.

WINES PRODUCED

Château Larmande: 100,000 bottles

Le Cadet de Larmande: 20,000 bottles

Plateau of maturity: Within 4–15 years of the vintage

GENERAL APPRECIATION

Larmande routinely produces wines meriting scores in the upper 80s. In short, a reliable,
tasty wine that merits attention.

I remember when I first visited Larmande in the mid-1970s at the request of the late
Martin Bamford, one of Bordeaux's most knowledgeable observers. He had told me that

this would be one of the best wines made in St.-Emilion because of the commitment to quality evidenced by the Mèneret family (the former owners). Larmande, situated in the northern area of St.-Emilion, is named after the historic *lieux-dit* (place name) of the vineyard. It is one of the oldest vineyards in St.-Emilion, with a wine-producing history going back to the 13th century. For many years, the property was owned by the Mèneret-Capdemourlin family and run with great enthusiasm by Philippe and Dominique Mèneret. After establishing Larmande's reputation, they sold the property to La Mondiale in the nineties.

In the mid-1970s the entire *chai* was renovated with the introduction of temperature-controlled stainless-steel tanks. The percentage of new oak utilized was also increased to nearly 70% in top vintages.

The key to Larmande's quality is late harvesting, a strict selection (the production of a second wine was introduced during the 1980s), and relatively low yields. As a consequence, Larmande's track record since the mid-1970s has been impeccable. There are few premier grands cru classés that can boast such consistently fine wines.

IMPORTANT VINTAGES

2001 An impressive effort for the vintage, Larmande's 2001 (richer and deeper than the
89–91 2000) reveals surprisingly low acidity as well as a plump, easy to drink style. Nicely layered, smoky black currants and cherries are offered in a moderately weighty, pure, elegant format with a sweet attack, a well-textured mid-palate, and a good finish. As the wine sits in the glass, licorice, dried herbs, and abundant black fruits emerge. It should drink well for 10–15 years. Last tasted, 1/03.

2000 A deep ruby/purple–colored effort displaying notes of dried herbs, licorice, black
88 fruits, and toasty oak, the medium- to full-bodied 2000 is not complex, but it is well made and savory. It possesses low acidity as well as noticeable tannin. Anticipated maturity: 2004–2014. Last tasted, 1/03.

1999 This medium to dark ruby–colored 1999 exhibits elegant, sweet berry fruit inter-
86 mixed with saddle leather, dried herbs, and smoke, with medium body, soft tannin, and moderate depth. Drink it over the next five years. Last tasted, 3/02.

1998 This wine is initially tight, but with airing, aromas of licorice, spice box, berries,
87 herbs, and leather emerge. It is a medium- to full-bodied, well-made, attractive, well-structured effort. Anticipated maturity: now–2015. Last tasted, 3/02.

1997 Abundant, moderately intense aromas of toasty new oak intermingled with scents
86 of plum liqueur, licorice, and Provençal herbs are followed by a muscular, ripe wine with a distinctive cherry jam–like flavor profile. This solidly made, lightly tannic effort should be at its finest between now and 2008. Last tasted, 3/01.

1996 Larmande's 1996 is a big, toasty, rich, licorice, Asian spice, fruitcake, and smoky
88 black cherry–scented and flavored wine. It reveals medium body, good richness, moderate tannin, and a long, concentrated finish. Anticipated maturity: now– 2010. Last tasted, 12/01.

1995 The 1995 is cut from the same mold as the 1996, except the 1995 possesses more
88 accessible glycerin and fruit, as well as lower acidity. It offers a dense ruby/purple color and an intense herb, toasty, jammy blackberry and cassis-scented nose intertwined with woodfire-like aromas. The wine is soft, round, and medium to full-bodied, with a sexy combination of glycerin, fruit, sweet tannin, and heady alcohol. Anticipated maturity: now–2008. Last tasted, 12/01.

1994
86?

The plum/garnet-colored 1994 exhibits a dark ruby/purple color, a tight, oaky, subdued nose, and a sweet, impressive entry, but hard, bitter tannin distracts from an otherwise attractive, medium- to full-bodied, muscular effort. Atypically for Larmande, patience will be a valued asset. Anticipated maturity: now–2011. Last tasted, 12/01.

1990
88

The charming, personable 1990 Larmande displays fine color, excellent ripe plum and cassis fruit, full body, and considerable tannin in the finish. The telltale signs of the 1990 vintage—sweet tannins, plenty of succulent, chewy fruit, and exceptionally low acidity—are all present. Anticipated maturity: now–2005. Last tasted, 12/00.

1989
88

The dense plum/garnet–colored 1989 has more structure and tannin than the 1990. If you like wonderfully round, hedonistic, soft, alcoholic, luscious St.-Emilions, this superripe, heady, and voluptuously textured wine will offer many thrills. This wine has held up well. Anticipated maturity: now–2004. Last tasted, 12/00.

1988
90

One of the vintage's more hedonistic wines, Larmande's 1988 was delicious young yet continues to mature evenly and impressively. The wine remains a dark purple color, with only slight lightening at the edge. It offers an intense aromatic profile, with gobs of licorice, mineral, blackberry, and cherry fruit scents. Similar notes, in addition to a subtle tobacco weediness, can be detected on the palate of this full-bodied, rich, pure, spicy, smoky-styled wine. Anticipated maturity: now. Last tasted, 11/97.

LAROZE

Classification: Grand Cru Classé

Owner: Meslin family

Address: 33330 St.-Emilion

Telephone: 05 57 24 79 79; Telefax: 05 57 24 79 80

E-mail: ch.laroze@wanadoo.fr

Website: www.laroze.com

Visits: By appointment only

Contact: Guy Meslin

VINEYARDS

Surface area: 66.7 acres

Grape varietals: 68% Merlot, 26% Cabernet Franc, 6% Cabernet Sauvignon

Average age of vines: 20 years

Density of plantation: 6,000 vines per hectare

Average yields: 38 hectoliters per hectare

Elevage: Twelve to fourteen months aging in barrels that are renewed by half at each vintage. Fining, no filtration.

WINES PRODUCED

Château Laroze: 110,000 bottles

No second wine is produced.

Plateau of maturity: Within 4–8 years of the vintage

GENERAL APPRECIATION

Considering its price and the quality it has exhibited over the last five or six vintages, Laroze could well be one of the interesting values of its appellation.

While I have never considered the wines of Laroze to be that profound, there is something to be said for a style of wine that is fragrant, soft, fruity, and easy to drink. These are wines that require consumption within their first 4–8 years of life. If consumers keep that fact in mind, there is plenty of charm to be found with the wines of Laroze.

The vineyards do not possess one of St.-Emilion's better *terroirs,* being planted in light, sandy soil. The wines are vinified in a modern, up-to-date facility.

IMPORTANT VINTAGES

2001   A very sweet, fruit-driven, hedonistic wine that is all pleasure, this dark plum/
86–88   ruby–colored wine is quite tasty, expansive, and very pure. That is not going to silence its critics, who would say it is too obvious and not structured enough, but this wine delivers the goods in a fruit-forward style. Drink it over the next 7–8 years. Last tasted, 1/03.

2000   Dark ruby/purple, with very sexy, lush, jammy, black cherry fruit, as this wine sits
88   in the glass, notes of earth, dried Provençal herbs, and kirsch emerge, as if the wine was a hybrid between a southern Côtes du Rhône and a classic Bordeaux. There is some tannin in the finish, but this wine is all fruit, glycerin, and seductive appeal. Drink it over the next 7–8 years. Last tasted, 1/03.

1999   This soft, pleasant, light- to medium-bodied, one-dimensional St.-Emilion needs
84   to be consumed over the next 3–4 years. It offers moderate quantities of sweet-and-sour cherries intermixed with damp earth and mushroom characteristics. Last tasted, 3/02.

1998   The 1998 Laroze is a graceful, medium-bodied, richly fruity St.-Emilion that will
87   provide delicious drinking during its first decade of life. The color is a dark ruby, and the wine offers plenty of black cherry, kirsch, and spicy notes. Fleshy, medium bodied, and already delicious, it can be drunk now and over the next five years. Last tasted, 3/02.

LUCIA

(formerly Lucie)

Classification: Grand Cru

Owner: Michel Bartolussi

Address: 33330 St.-Emilion

Mailing address: 316 Grand Champ, 33330 Saint-Sulpice-de-Faleyrens

Telephone: 05 57 74 44 42 *or* 06 80 66 20 87; Telefax: 05 57 24 73 00

No visits

VINEYARDS

Surface area: 7.5 acres

Grape varietals: 90% Merlot, 10% Cabernet Franc

Average age of vines: 40–100 years

Density of plantation: 5,000 vines per hectare

Average yields: 30 hectoliters per hectare

Elevage: Three week fermentation and maceration. Fifteen to eighteen months aging in barrels with 60% new oak. Fining, no filtration.

WINES PRODUCED

Lucie: 10,000 bottles

No second wine is produced.

Plateau of maturity: Within 4–10 years of the vintage

GENERAL APPRECIATION

Here is another garage operation that started full-throttle in the mid-1990s only to show signs of fatigue just after leaving the starting blocks. Judging by the 2001 vintage, Lucia seems to be back on track. A new name (the wine was formerly called Lucie) and a new style of vinification (more substantial wines as opposed to the formerly charming but lighter and accessible efforts) are probably indicative of a new start. It remains to be seen whether the initial scenario will repeat itself or not. I reiterate, however, that the 2001 is unquestionably worthy of consumer interest.

If the 2001 is any indication, Lucia is a name to watch. The wine emerges from a small vineyard planted in 1901. The brilliant Stéphane Derenoncourt is the consultant. This is clearly another garage wine that looks serious about quality, something that could not be said prior to 2001.

IMPORTANT VINTAGES

2001　The 2001 is a dense, highly extracted, modern, garage-styled St.-Emilion offering
89–92　copious quantities of new oak, abundant glycerin, impressive jammy black cherry and currant fruit, medium to full body, and admirable purity. This is an extremely hedonistic wine of tremendous density. Anticipated maturity: 2004–2014. Last tasted, 1/03.

LUSSEAU

Classification: Grand Cru

Owner: Laurent Lusseau

Address: 287, Perey Nord, 33330 Saint-Sulpice-de-Faleyrens

Telephone: 05 57 74 46 54; Telefax: 05 57 74 46 09

Visits: By appointment only Monday to Friday, 8 A.M.–6 P.M.

Contact: Laurent Lusseau

VINEYARDS

Surface area: 1.2 acres

Grape varietals: 70% Merlot, 30% Cabernet Franc

Average age of vines: 46 years

Density of plantation: 5,400 vines per hectare

Average yields: 35 hectoliters per hectare

Elevage: Twenty-eight day fermentation and maceration in temperature-controlled stainless-steel vats. Eighteen months aging in new oak barrels. No fining, no filtration.

WINES PRODUCED

Château Lusseau: 2,500 bottles

No second wine is produced.

Plateau of maturity: Within 3–12 years of the vintage

GENERAL APPRECIATION

This micro-vinification by the cellar master of Pavie, Pavie Decesse, and Monbousquet is never great, but always excellent and reliable. Unfortunately, the quantities available are tiny and, as a consequence, the prices high.

IMPORTANT VINTAGES

2001
88–90
A blend of 80% Merlot and 20% Cabernet Franc, the silky, fat, fleshy 2001 is ideal for drinking during its first 5–8 years of life. This is a very sensual wine. Anticipated maturity: now–2011. Last tasted, 1/03.

2000
90
Dark plum/ruby–colored, the 2000 (a blend of 80% Merlot and 20% Cabernet Franc) is rich and dense, with a saturated ruby/purple color and a knockout nose of black cherry liqueur intertwined with cedar, smoke, earth, and toasty wood. Layered and pure, this lush, savory wine is medium to full-bodied as well as seamless. Anticipated maturity: now–2011. Last tasted, 1/03.

1999
89
A dark ruby color is accompanied by sweet aromas of roasted coffee, smoke, jammy black cherry fruit, and new wood. Medium to full-bodied and lush, with low acidity and sweet tannin, it will drink well for 3–4 years. Last tasted, 3/02.

1998
89
This is a very sexy wine, with a dark plum/garnet color and an evolved, exceptionally fragrant nose of licorice, cedar, incense, and sweet black cherries and currants. The wine is lush, round, generous, and medium to full-bodied, with no hard edges. In short, this is impossible to resist. Anticipated maturity: now–2008. Last tasted, 1/03.

LYNSOLENCE

Classification: Grand Cru

Owner: Denis Barraud

Address: 33330 Saint-Sulpice-de-Faleyrens

Telephone: 05 57 84 54 73; Telefax: 05 57 84 52 07

E-mail: denis.barraud@wanadoo.fr

Visits: By appointment only

Contact: Denis Barraud (Telephone: 06 08 32 26 04)

VINEYARDS

Surface area: 4.9 acres

Grape varietals: 100% Merlot

Average age of vines: 38 years

Density of plantation: 5,500 vines per hectare

Average yields: 28 hectoliters per hectare

Elevage: Seven day cold maceration at 10°C. Thirty-eight to forty day fermentation and maceration in temperature-controlled wooden vats with *pigéages,* pumpings-over and micro-oxygenation. Malolactics and 18 months aging on lees (no racking) in new oak barrels. Fining, no filtration.

WINES PRODUCED

Château Lynsolence: 7,500 bottles

No second wine is produced.

Plateau of maturity: Within 3–10 years of the vintage

GENERAL APPRECIATION

This garage wine, whose debut vintage was 1998, is as sexy and sensual as most of its peers. To date it has been excellent rather than superb.

IMPORTANT VINTAGES

2001
88–90 The 2001's opaque ruby/purple color is accompanied by sweet black fruits, decent acidity, ripe tannin, medium to full body, and a moderately long finish revealing impressive purity as well as integration of acid, tannin, and alcohol. The vineyard was cropped at 28 hectoliters per hectare in 2001. Anticipated maturity: 2005–2013. Last tasted, 1/03.

2000
90 With admirable size, intensity, and power, the dense ruby/purple–colored 2000 offers thick, chewy, black cherry, and currant fruit, medium to full body, low acidity, and layers of glycerin. It should be delicious young, but evolve for 12 years. The vineyard was cropped at a low 28 hectoliters per hectare. Last tasted, 1/03.

1999
87 Dark ruby/purple–colored, with an excellent nose of black and red fruits (cherries and raspberries), this deep, rich, low-acid, concentrated wine is foursquare, but it possesses plenty of depth, concentration, and texture. If it develops more complexity, the score should rise. Anticipated maturity: now–2010. Last tasted, 3/02.

1998
89 A dark ruby/purple color is followed by a jammy bouquet of black fruits and a medium- to full-bodied, straightforward, juicy, succulent, fleshy wine. There is good structure under all the fat and fruit, but it does not possess the complexity and nobility often found in these micro-*cuvées.* Drink it over the next eight years. Last tasted, 3/02.

MAGDELAINE

Classification: Premier Grand Cru Classé B

Owner: Ets Jean-Pierre Moueix

Address: 33330 St.-Emilion

Mailing address: c/o Ets Jean-Pierre Moueix, 54, quai du Priourat, BP 129, 33502 Libourne Cedex

Telephone: 05 57 51 78 96; Telefax: 05 57 51 79 79

Visits: By appointment and for professionals of the wine trade dealing with the house

Contact: Frédéric Lospied

VINEYARDS

Surface area: 27.2 acres

Grape varietals: 90% Merlot, 10% Cabernet Franc

Average age of vines: 34 years

Density of plantation: 6,000 vines per hectare

Average yields: 40 hectoliters per hectare

Elevage: Twenty to twenty-eight day fermentation and maceration in temperature-controlled stainless-steel vats. After malolactics, 18–20 months aging in barrels with 40% new oak. No fining, no filtration.

WINES PRODUCED

Château Magdelaine: 36,000 bottles

Château Saint-Brice: 12,000 bottles

Plateau of maturity: Within 6–15 years of the vintage, for post-1988 wines

GENERAL APPRECIATION

The style of Magdelaine, like that of L'Arrosée, is somewhat out of fashion in St.-Emilion. Amidst a growing number of garage wines and modern-styled efforts, Magdelaine clings to its traditional character, with understated, classy elegance and delicate mineral-scented fruit. It requires some cellaring to fully reveal itself. Never massive or powerful, it is a wine of finesse.

Magdelaine, one of the *côtes* St.-Emilions, with its vineyard beautifully situated on a limestone plateau overlooking the Dordogne Valley, has been one of the very best St.-Emilions since the early 1960s. Since 1952 the famous Libourne firm of Jean-Pierre Moueix has been the sole proprietor of this property. Magdelaine has the highest percentage of Merlot (90%) of any of the renowned châteaux located on the St.-Emilion limestone plateau.

Most experts have considered this property to have outstanding potential, yet in the late 1970s and much of the 1980s, the quality of Magdelaine was very good but rarely inspiring. However, from 1989 the quality has been more impressive, with added layers of fruit, flesh, and complexity.

Nevertheless, Magdelaine remains a very distinctive St.-Emilion, largely because of this high proportion of Merlot. One would assume that the wine is soft, fleshy, and forward. It is not. Because of the relatively long fermentation, early harvesting, and the use of a small percentage of stems, Magdelaine is an extremely tannic, slow to evolve wine. It normally requires 5–7 years after bottling to reveal its character.

Given the small production and its historic reputation, as well as its ownership by the Moueix firm, Magdelaine has always been an expensive wine, selling at prices comparable to a top Médoc second growth.

IMPORTANT VINTAGES

2001　Elegant and somewhat evolved for the vintage (only 60% of the production made it
87–89　into the top wine), this Magdelaine exhibits a deep ruby color and a sweet nose of
　　　　black cherries, mineral, spice box, and some earthy notes. In the mouth it is very

pure, nuanced, yet graceful and restrained. Anticipated maturity: 2005–2015. Last tasted, 1/03.

2000
92+
A worthy rival to the great 1998, the 2000 Magdelaine has a deep ruby/purple color and a very sweet nose of mulberries, black currants, and jammy cherry notes intermixed with mineral, licorice, and a hint of subtle toast. This wine is sweet, expansive, and dense, with the gorgeous fruit hiding some relatively elevated tannin. The finish is quite long, and the wine is in need of a good 4–5 years of cellaring. Anticipated maturity: 2008–2020. Last tasted, 1/03.

1999
88
A stylish, light- to medium-bodied effort, the dark ruby–colored 1999 Magdelaine possesses sweet, lush aromas and flavors redolent of cherries and currants. Subtle notions of earth, wood, and a touch of herbaceousness also emerge. Drink it over the next 10–12 years. Last tasted, 3/02.

1998
92
Undoubtedly the finest effort from Magdelaine in many years, the deep, saturated, ruby-colored 1998 offers up concentrated, jammy black cherry as well as subtle vanilla aromas. On the palate, it is full-bodied, opulent, and ripe, with outstanding concentration, purity, and moderate tannin in the finish. This Merlot-based St.-Emilion displays considerable intensity and structure. Anticipated maturity: 2005–2020. Last tasted, 12/02.

1997
87
This well-made, dark ruby–colored effort exhibits good body and a roasted herb/fruit characteristic intermixed with minerals, coffee, and strawberry/cherry fruit . . . hallmarks of this Merlot-based St.-Emilion. The wine's low acidity, medium body, and precociousness suggest it should be consumed over the next 3–4 years. Last tasted, 12/01.

1996
87
This somewhat evolved, weedy, tobacco-scented wine shows red currants along with some vanilla. In the mouth the wine is a bit angular but attractive on the front end, then somewhat dry in the finish. The wine has reached maturity quickly and should hold for another decade. Anticipated maturity: now–2012. Last tasted, 12/02.

1995
90
Firmly structured, tannic, but impressively concentrated, Magdelaine's 1995 has a deep ruby color and a sweet nose of vanilla, kirsch, plums, and flowers. It is a medium-bodied, very pretty wine that is feminine, seductive, and well balanced, although the tannins in the finish suggest it is not yet fully mature. Anticipated maturity: 2005–2012. Last tasted, 12/02.

1994
87
Slightly angular and bordering on austere, the sweet aromas of black cherries intermixed with herb, mineral, and a hint of asphalt are attractive. The wine is medium bodied and well balanced, with the tannin largely held in check by relatively good fruit and ripeness. The wine will never be great, but it is certainly an interesting effort that probably sells for a song. Anticipated maturity: now–2010. Last tasted, 12/02.

1990
90
A beautiful Magdelaine, with notes of sweet kirsch intermixed with hints of tobacco, herb, and other assorted berry fruit all wrapped together in a gracious, medium-bodied, lush style, with plenty of glycerin, concentration, and depth. This Magdelaine actually lives up to its famed *terroir*. It is neither too austere nor emaciated. Anticipated maturity: now–2008. Last tasted, 12/02.

1989
88
Showing a bit more stuffing than most vintages of Magdelaine, this wine is pure, sweet cherry cough syrup intermixed with a hint of plum and earth. The wine is medium bodied, very pure, with delicately etched flavors that never come across as overdone or too intense. Nevertheless, it is the type of wine that can easily get lost, given its subtlety and restraint. Anticipated maturity: now–2010, Last tasted, 11/02.

1988
87
Dark plum/garnet with a nose of sweet cherries intermixed with a hint of plum and vanilla, this stylish, very graceful, as well as medium-bodied wine is best drunk over the next 4–5 years. This is a Bordeaux for those searching for very restrained, delicately styled wines. Anticipated maturity: now–2008. Last tasted, 11/02.

1986
82
A pleasant, picnic-style wine with a light ruby color already showing, it also exhibits some pink/amber at the edge. The wine is light to medium-bodied and rather diluted, but the sweet cola/cherry fruit is intermixed with hints of mineral, earth, and spice box. The wine should be drunk up. Last tasted, 11/02.

1985
86
A somewhat insipid wine for such a great property, this rather dull, straightforward wine exhibits a medium ruby/garnet color with considerable amber at the edge. The nose offers an earthiness intermixed with dried herbs, vanilla, and some plum/cherry fruit. On the palate the wine is medium bodied but somewhat diluted. (Its defenders would call it elegant, I'm sure.) It is fully mature, with very little tannin or acidity. Drink up. Last tasted, 11/02.

1983
85
Brutally tannic, backward, and aggressive, the 1983 Magdelaine has excellent color, full body, and plenty of rich, ripe fruit and weight, but the ferocious tannins make it reminiscent of the 1975. Anticipated maturity: now–2010. Last tasted, 1/90.

1982
88
This wine has never lived up to my early prognostication. The color is medium ruby with considerable amber at the edge. Notes of sweet-and-sour cherry intermixed with caramel, herb, and an undertone of earthiness are pervasive in this medium-bodied, rather elegant wine, which ultimately lacks the substance and intensity one expects from the best wines of this vintage. It is fully mature yet capable of lasting up to another decade. Anticipated maturity: now–2012. Last tasted, 10/02.

ANCIENT VINTAGES

The 1970s were largely unimpressive for Magdelaine except for a relatively tannic but substantial 1975 (88 points; last tasted 10/96) and a nearly outstanding 1970 (89 points; last tasted 11/96). In the 1960s, the 1961 competes with the very best Magdelaines ever made (92 points; last tasted 3/97). This wine, where pristinely stored, is probably still a glorious example of classic St.-Emilion.

Bottle variation, as one might expect, is always a problem with the museum vintages. Many of the older vintages of Magdelaine were bottled in Belgium, as the practice of this property was to sell barrels of wine to their clients, who bottled them outside the château. While I have had uninspiring examples of the 1959, 1955, and 1953, the best bottles of these vintages were all impressive. The 1953 (rated as high as 88 points; last tasted 12/96), 1955 (87 points; last tasted 12/96), and 1959 (90 points; last tasted 11/96) have been impressive in their power and richness. The 1952, which I tasted only once, in 1991, was rated 88. It appeared to have the stuffing and structure to last another 10–15 years, but the providence and condition of the bottle are everything with respect to most vintages older than 20 years.

MAGREZ FOMBRAUGE

Classification: Grand Cru

Owner: Bernard Magrez

Address: 33330 Saint-Christophe-des-Bardes

Telephone: 05 57 24 77 12; Telefax: 05 57 24 66 95

E-mail: chateau@fombrauge.com

Website: www.fombrauge.com

Visits: By appointment only

Contact: Ugo Arguti

VINEYARDS

Surface area: 7.4 acres

Grape varietals: 80% Merlot, 20% Cabernet Franc

Average age of vines: 25 years

Density of plantation: 5,600 vines per hectare

Average yields: 35 hectoliters per hectare

Elevage: Cold maceration at 12°C. Four to five week fermentation and maceration (whole cluster) in temperature-controlled wooden vats of small capacity allowing for separate vinification of the different parcels of vine, with four daily *pigéages*. Malolactics and 24 months aging on fine lees with regular stirring in new oak barrels. Fining, no filtration.

WINES PRODUCED

Château Magrez Fombrauge: 6,000 bottles

No second wine is produced.

Plateau of maturity: Within 5–15 years of the vintage

GENERAL APPRECIATION

This sheer nectar of the vine is the result of the enthusiastic Bernard Magrez and his star wine consultant, the talented Michel Rolland. From its debut in 2000, Magrez Fombrauge has been sumptuous and obviously one of the superstars of St.-Emilion. This is a wine of exceptional opulence, richness, and luxuriance.

IMPORTANT VINTAGES

2001
92–94
Cropped at a mere 24 hectoliters per hectare, the 2001 does not possess the volume or mass of the 2000, but it is a remarkable expression of superripe Merlot that has had all the brilliance of winemaking guru Michel Rolland unleashed upon it. The color is a saturated black/purple. The bouquet offers up gorgeous scents of black cherry liqueur, mocha, and vanilla. Lush and opulent, with loads of glycerin and more freshness and definition than the more massive, voluminous 2000 possessed, it offers impressive length, low acidity, and a plush, gorgeous mouthful of ripe fruit. It will be fascinating to follow this St.-Emilion's evolution. Anticipated maturity: 2005–2019. Last tasted, 1/03.

2000
98
This is the debut vintage of this micro-*cuvée*. One of the vintage's superstars, this prodigious effort continues to put on weight and richness. An unctuously textured blockbuster, with a wealth of fruit and a sumptuous bouquet of spring flowers, espresso, blackberry liqueur, minerals, and toasty oak, it is full-bodied and seamless with extraordinary intensity, purity, and symmetry. As the wine sat in the glass, an intense note of graphite emerged, but the oak (it was aged and went through malolactic in 100% new oak) has totally disappeared! Where did it go? Sheer nectar of the vine! Anticipated maturity: 2006–2020. Last tasted, 1/03.

MILENS

Classification: Grand Cru

Owner: SARL Château Milens

Address: lieu-dit Le Sème, 33330 Saint-Hippolyte

Telephone: 05 57 55 24 47; Telefax: 05 57 55 24 44

E-mail: chateau.milens@wanadoo.fr

Visits: By appointment Monday to Friday, 8:30 A.M.–6 P.M.

Contact: Delphine Descat (Telephone: 05 57 55 24 45)

VINEYARDS

Surface area: 15.6 acres

Grape varietals: 71% Merlot, 29% Cabernet Franc

Average age of vines: 27 years

Density of plantation: 6,000 vines per hectare

Average yields: 41.5 hectoliters per hectare

Elevage: Fermentation and maceration in temperature-controlled stainless-steel and concrete tanks. Malolactics and 18 months aging in new oak barrels. Fining, light filtration upon bottling.

WINES PRODUCED

Château Milens: 20,000 bottles

Tour du Sème: 20,000 bottles

Plateau of maturity: Within 3–10 years of the vintage

GENERAL APPRECIATION

St.-Emilion's well-known revolutionary, Jean-Luc Thunevin, oversees the vinification of Milens, a wine that reveals his style of winemaking. Always a luscious low-acid effort, it is well worth checking out.

IMPORTANT VINTAGES

2001 87–88	The tasty, lush, elegantly styled 2001 displays a deep ruby/purple color in addition to a sweet perfume of black cherries, minerals, smoke, and earth. Round, fleshy, and medium bodied with ripe tannin, it will drink well for 8–10 years. Last tasted, 1/03.
2000 89	The blend is 71% Merlot and 29% Cabernet Franc. Yields are kept to a modest 31 hectoliters per hectare. The most impressive Milens to date, the opaque ruby/purple–colored 2000 exhibits deep, chewy, black cherry, and currant fruit intermixed with spicy new oak. Impressively textured, pure, and medium to full-bodied, with low acidity and moderate tannin, it will be at its finest between 2006–2018. Last tasted, 1/03.
1999 87	Excellent, sweet cranberry, strawberry, and black cherry fruit intermixed with smoke and earth are impressively pure and persistent. The 1999 Milens reveals fine denseness, sweet glycerin, a fleshy, expansive palate, and a straightforward, lightly tannic finish. Drink it over the next 6–7 years. Last tasted, 3/02.

1998
88

An attractive, lush, open-knit, expansive St.-Emilion, Milens's 1998 will please both the masses and connoisseurs. It possesses a dense ruby color, full body, and attractive black cherry fruit intermixed with smoke, earth, and spice box. A spicy, low-acid, corpulent finish adds to the hedonistic pleasure. Anticipated maturity: now–2008. Last tasted, 3/02.

MONBOUSQUET

Classification: Grand Cru

Owner: Gérard and Chantal Perse

Address: 42, route de St.-Emilion, 33330 Saint-Sulpice-de-Faleyrens

Telephone: 05 57 55 43 43; Telefax: 05 57 24 63 99

E-mail: vignobles.perse@wanadoo.fr

Website: chateaupavie.com

No visits

VINEYARDS

Surface area: 81.5 acres

Grape varietals: 60% Merlot, 30% Cabernet Franc, 10% Cabernet Sauvignon

Average age of vines: 40 years

Density of plantation: 5,500 vines per hectare

Average yields: 28–30 hectoliters per hectare

Elevage: Four to five week fermentation and maceration in temperature-controlled stainless-steel tanks. Eighteen to twenty-two months aging on fine lees in new oak barrels. No fining, no filtration.

WINES PRODUCED

Château Monbousquet: 80,000 bottles

Angélique de Monbousquet: 50,000 bottles

Plateau of maturity: Within 3–8 years of the vintage prior to 1993; within 5–20 years of the vintage from 1993 onward

GENERAL APPRECIATION

Those who remember the Monbousquets of the 1950s, 1960s, and 1970s as bland, insipid wines would be shocked at the quality and style of Monbousquet since 1994. Since the mid-1990s, it has been one of the stars of its appellation as well as one of Bordeaux's most exotic offerings. Under the helmsmanship of proprietor Gérard Perse, who fashions one of the appellation's most flamboyant and seductive Clarets, it asserts itself as a show-stopper in any tasting, blind or otherwise.

Monbousquet, a large estate, was the pride and joy of the Querre family, who produced a fruity, supple style of St.-Emilion that had broad commercial appeal and was always fairly priced. It was a wine to drink within its first 5–6 years of life, but simple and too frequently uninspiring.

In the early 1990s the Querre family sold Monbousquet to Gérard Perse, who had made a fortune in the supermarket business. Perse immediately renovated the cellars, hired Michel Rolland as a consulting oenologist, and began to produce what has become one of St.-Emilion's most concentrated and fascinating wines. Yields were cut to under two tons of fruit per acre. The first example of Perse's commitment to high-quality wine emerged from the difficult 1993 vintage, as Monbousquet's 1993 was one of the finest wines of the appellation. This property is now turning out exciting wines that will reward connoisseurs looking for multidimensional, complete St.-Emilions that will age for 15–20 years.

IMPORTANT VINTAGES

2001
92–94 Perse has gone over the top in terms of trying to get even more extraction from the 2001. It is an amazingly concentrated effort for the vintage. The 2001 offers smoky, superripe, jammy red and black fruits that are almost candied in their ripeness and sweetness. Infused with notes of espresso, smoke, charcoal, and toast, this is a rich, exotic, opulent, and pure effort. Nevertheless, it possesses plenty of tannin as well as more definition than most young vintages of Monbousquet. Anticipated maturity: 2007–2018. Last tasted, 1/03.

2000
95 A black beauty, the 2000 is truly great stuff! It represents the essence of this estate's style. Its saturated black/purple color is accompanied by extraordinary aromatics of sweet blackberries, chocolate, coffee, incense, new saddle leather, and vanilla. Remarkable intensity, lively acidity, and abundant tannin provide definition and grip. This is the most intense, muscular, and the "biggest" Monbousquet made to date, and that is saying something considering the 1998 and 1999! So be prepared, it is a remarkable wine. Anticipated maturity: 2005–2018. Last tasted, 1/03.

1999
94 A remarkable effort for the vintage, the dense ruby/purple–colored 1999 Monbousquet exhibits a Port-like bouquet of superripe black cherry and black currant fruit intermixed with scents of coffee, tobacco, and vanilla. Tipping the scales at a whopping 14% alcohol (extremely high for Bordeaux), this wine possesses an amazing texture, a mid-palate that you could get lost in, and a sensational 40–45 second finish. The exotic aromas, incredible texture, and abundant fruit are reminiscent of Pomerol's renowned micro-*cuvée*, Le Pin. The 1999 is even better from bottle than it was from cask. Anticipated maturity: 2005–2017. Last tasted, 1/03.

1998
94 Yields of 28–30 hectoliters per hectare are among the lowest in St.-Emilion, which no doubt accounts for the wine's explosive richness. The 1998 Monbousquet boasts a saturated plum/purple color in addition to an exotic bouquet of Asian spices, plum liqueur, prunes, and blackberries. Extremely full-bodied, unctuously textured, structured, and well defined, this spectacular achievement will drink well young, yet last for two decades. Anticipated maturity: now–2020. Last tasted, 1/03.

1997
90 One of the vintage's superstars, this dark plum/purple–colored 1997 offers flamboyant, explosive aromas of vanilla, cherry jam, licorice, and new oak. Deep, concentrated, rich, and surprisingly chewy (especially for a 1997), this full-bodied, gorgeously concentrated and proportioned St.-Emilion will be hard to resist young. The tannin has quickly fallen away in this ostentatious wine. Anticipated maturity: now–2010. Last tasted, 1/03.

1996
90 The 1996 Monbousquet is another outstanding effort, particularly for a vintage that favored the Médoc's late harvested Cabernet Sauvignon. The wine is more tannic than the 1995, but it exhibits an exotic nose of kirsch, cassis, roasted herbs,

espresso, and mocha. It possesses excellent texture, impressive depth and rich-ness, and sweet toasty oak. The saturated dark ruby/purple color suggests a dense wine. The finish is both long and well delineated, with moderate tannin. This beautifully etched Monbousquet will take several years longer to come around than the flamboyant, open-knit 1995. Anticipated maturity: now–2017. Last tasted, 1/03.

1995   Although similar to the 1996, the 1995 possesses more accessible fruit, and while
92   the tannin is elevated, it is buffered by lower acidity as well as more glycerin and fat. The 1995 offers an opaque purple color and a glorious nose of new oak, spice, and abundant black fruits. This full-bodied, super-extracted, multilayered wine just gets better and better, a characteristic I have noticed with all of the Gérard Perse wines in bottle. Approaching its plateau of drinkability, this blockbuster is a flashy head-turner. Anticipated maturity: now–2020. Last tasted, 1/03.

1994   Opaque purple/garnet with some pink at the rim, the promising nose of cherry jam,
90   black currants, smoked herbs, and grilled meats is followed by a chewy, medium-to full-bodied wine that exhibits the vintage's tough tannin. However, this 1994 possesses enough fruit, glycerin, and extract to counterbalance the wine's struc-ture. Anticipated maturity: now–2013. Last tasted, 11/02.

1993   One of the sleepers of the vintage, this lavishly oaked, dense purple–colored wine
89   reveals gobs of sweet black cherry and cassis fruit intertwined with aromas of smoke and new oak. Extracted and rich with no hard edges, this is a fat, glycerin-endowed, chewy, pure St.-Emilion that can be drunk young or cellared for 10–12 years. Last tasted, 1/97.

LA MONDOTTE

Classification: None

Owner: Comtes de Neipperg

Address: 33330 St.-Emilion

Mailing address: c/o SCEV des Comtes de Neipperg, BP 34, 33330 St.-Emilion

Telephone: 05 57 24 71 33; Telefax: 05 57 24 67 95

E-mail: vignobles.von.neipperg@wanadoo.fr

Website: www.neipperg.com

Visits: By appointment only Monday to Friday, 9 A.M.–noon and 2–7 P.M.

Contact: Dominique Duluc

VINEYARDS

Surface area: 11.1 acres

Grape varietals: 80% Merlot, 20% Cabernet Franc

Average age of vines: 37 years

Density of plantation: 5,500 vines per hectare

Average yields: 35–40 hectoliters per hectare

Elevage: Twenty-five to thirty day fermentation and maceration in temperature-controlled wooden vats, with *pigéages*. Malolactics in barrel on fine lees for 90–100% of the yield. Eighteen to twenty-four months aging in new oak barrels. No fining, no filtration.

WINES PRODUCED

La Mondotte: 10,000 bottles

No second wine is produced.

Plateau of maturity: Within 4–30 years of the vintage

GENERAL APPRECIATION

Stephan von Neipperg's talent is wonderfully reflected in this marvelous achievement. In no more than a couple of years, he managed to propel this garage operation to the top echelon of the appellation. No expense is spared to produce the best wine possible, and through a judicious marriage of tradition and the newest methods of vinification, Stephan von Neipperg routinely achieves brilliance. While superrich, powerful, massive, densely fruity, and ample, La Mondotte also manages impeccable equilibrium and harmony. Approachable in its youth, it is also capable of some 30 years of cellaring. This wine undoubtedly has its critics, especially among the old guard in Saint-Emilion and the most conservative Bordelais, but whatever may be said about it (too extracted, almost Port-like in style, etc.), there is no question that it stands as the ultimate garage wine, the most concentrated and richest being produced in Bordeaux. Frightfully expensive, yet worth every cent, it is a must buy for those wishing for one of the finest possible tasting experiences.

La Mondotte is one of the most concentrated young Bordeaux I have tasted. Whether it is trying to be the Pétrus or Le Pin of St.-Emilion is irrelevant, for this wine, made by the superbly talented Comte Stephan von Neipperg, proprietor of Canon-la-Gaffelière and Clos de l'Oratoire, and aided by hotshot guru/consultant Stéphane Derenoncourt, is a showcase offering that is already turning heads and leading to some uncalled-for jealousy. La Mondotte emerges from a 10+ acre parcel high on the limestone slopes above Pavie Decesse. A blend of 80% Merlot and 20% Cabernet Franc from vines averaging 37 years of age, the fruit is sorted before and after destemming, and the wine is given a long maceration with state-of-the-art winemaking treatments—micro-oxygenation of the lees, malolactic in new oak, and the highest quality barrels.

IMPORTANT VINTAGES

2001
92–95 Slightly restrained and elegant, this opaque purple–colored wine has a glorious, evolved bouquet of blackberry and cassis as well as coffee and toast. La Mondotte's 2001 is gorgeously pure, with more liveliness and definition than previous efforts have shown at a similar age. The pure mass of fruit concentration and the essence of the *terroir* character is obvious. It is a beautiful, medium-bodied, concentrated St.-Emilion that is among the finest wines of the vintage. The tannin is sweet, the acidity and wood are impressively integrated, and the finish is long (about 40 seconds). Anticipated maturity: 2005–2017. Last tasted, 1/03.

2000
98+ A candidate for perfection, the 2000 La Mondotte has a saturated, inky purple color to the rim and a tight but enormously promising nose of blackberry and cassis intermixed with cherry, vanilla, espresso, mocha, and a hint of acacia flower. The wine is enormously rich, with great intensity, fabulous purity, a layered texture, and a viscous, full-bodied finish that goes on for nearly one minute. This is another tour de force in winemaking from proprietor Stephan von Neipperg and winemaking consultant Stéphane Derenoncourt. Anticipated maturity: 2007–2030. Last tasted, 1/03.

1999   Along with the 1997, the 1999 is the most forward and accessible La Mondotte yet
94   produced. Its opaque purple color is followed by a glorious nose of candied black
fruits, graphite, licorice, and underbrush. Full-bodied and sumptuous, La Mondotte possesses amazing extract and richness for the vintage. Its high tannin is
hidden by a wealth of glycerin, fruit, and extract. Moreover, the finish lasts for
35–45 seconds. This is an amazing achievement in 1999. Anticipated maturity:
2005–2020. Last tasted, 3/02.

1998   An amazing tour de force in winemaking, this massive, opaque black/purple–
96+   colored offering boasts an extraordinarily pure nose of black fruits intermixed with
cedar, vanilla, fudge, and espresso. It is unctuously textured, with exhilarating
levels of blackberry/cassis fruit and extract, as well as multiple dimensions that
unfold on the palate. The 50-second finish reveals moderately high tannin. Despite its similarity to dry vintage Port, it is not a wine to drink early. It is a colossal
wine! Anticipated maturity: 2008–2030. Last tasted, 3/02.

1997   An amazing effort and unquestionably one of the wines of the vintage, La Mon-
94   dotte's 1997 boasts a saturated purple color as well as an explosive nose of blackberries, violets, minerals, and sweet toasty oak. Huge and massive, yet gorgeously
proportioned, it possesses an unctuous texture with no hard edges. More seductive
and easier to drink than the behemoth 1996, it should be consumed between now
and 2015. Last tasted, 1/03.

1996   An amazing wine, the 1996 La Mondotte is amazing for both its appellation and
97   the vintage, revealing a remarkable level of richness, profound concentration, and
integrated tannin. The thick purple color suggests a wine of extraordinary extract
and richness. This super-concentrated wine offers a spectacular nose of roasted
coffee, licorice, blueberries, and black currants intermixed with smoky new oak.
It possesses full body, a multidimensional, layered personality with extraordinary
depth of fruit, a seamless texture, amazing viscosity, and a long, 45-second finish.
The tannin is sweet and well integrated. A dry, vintage Port! This blockbuster
St.-Emilion should be at its best between 2006–2025. Last tasted, 1/03.

MONTLISSE

Classification: Grand Cru

Owner: GFA Dauriac

Address: 33330 Saint-Etienne-de-Lisse

Mailing address: SC Dauriac, Château Destieux,
33330 St.-Emilion

Telephone: 05 57 24 77 44; Telefax: 05 57 40 37 42

Visits: By appointment only

Contact: Christian Dauriac

VINEYARDS

Surface area: 17.3 acres

Grape varietals: 85% Merlot, 15% Cabernet Franc

Average age of vines: 35 years

Density of plantation: 5,000 vines per hectare

Average yields: 38 hectoliters per hectare

Elevage: Fermentation and maceration in temperature-controlled stainless-steel vats, the volume of which are adapted to each parcel of vines. Malolactics in barrel for 25% of yield. Twelve to fifteen months aging in new oak barrels. No fining, no filtration.

WINES PRODUCED

Château Montlisse: 35,000 bottles

No second wine is produced.

Plateau of maturity: Within 5–12 years of the vintage

GENERAL APPRECIATION

A fairly recent operation set up by Christian Dauriac, the proprietor of Destieux, Montlisse is more lightweight than its stablemate, more accessible, less rustic, and less ferociously tannic. A supple and fruity above average St.-Emilion, it is a very good bargain.

IMPORTANT VINTAGES

2001
87–88
The 2001 Montlisse exhibits a deep ruby/purple color as well as sweet aromas of chocolate, new oak, earth, blackberries, and cassis. This attractive, dense St.-Emilion has less volume and power than its 2000 sibling. Anticipated maturity: 2005–2015. Last tasted, 1/03.

2000
90
The impressive 2000 qualifies as a sleeper of the vintage. This dense plum/purple–colored offering displays excellent sweet mocha-infused blackberry and cherry liqueur notes with hints of truffles and caramel. Full-bodied, with sumptuous sweetness, low acidity, and ripe tannin, it will be drinkable between 2005–2020. Last tasted, 1/03.

1999
88
Notes of plums, prunes, figs, and jammy black cherries emerge from this rich, smoky, supple-textured wine. Strong on the front end but short in the finish, it is medium to full-bodied, with excellent purity and a lusty mouth-feel. Drink it over the next 10 years. Last tasted, 3/02.

MOULIN DU CADET

Classification: Grand Cru Classé

Owner: GFA Moulin du Cadet

Director: Isabelle Blois

Address: 33330 St.-Emilion

Mailing address: 92, cours Toumy, 33500 Libourne

Telephone: 05 57 25 37 45

E-mail: brd.blois@wanadoo.fr

Visits: By appointment only

Contact: Pierre Blois

VINEYARDS

Surface area: 11.4 acres

Grape varietals: 100% Merlot

Average age of vines: 35 years

Density of plantation: 6,000 vines per hectare

Average yields: 30,000 hectoliters per hectare

Elevage: Twenty to twenty-five day fermentation and maceration in temperature-controlled concrete vats. Twelve to eighteen months aging in barrels with 30% new oak. Fining, no filtration.

WINES PRODUCED

Château Moulin du Cadet: 30,000 bottles

No second wine is produced.

Plateau of maturity: Within 3–8 years of the vintage

GENERAL APPRECIATION

Moulin du Cadet, which has a regular track record for producing good but uninspiring efforts, was until recently under the control of the Jean-Pierre Moueix firm of Libourne. It is now run by Isabelle Blois, and I hope the new management will succeed in increasing the quality.

Moulin du Cadet is a micro-estate of 12 acres located on the plateau north of St.-Emilion. It tends to produce rather fragrant, lighter-styled wines that lack depth but display attractive bouquets.

MOULIN ST.-GEORGES

Classification: Grand Cru

Owner: Catherine and Alain Vauthier

Address: 33330 St.-Emilion

Telephone: 05 57 24 70 26; Telefax: 05 57 74 47 39

No visits

VINEYARDS

Surface area: 17.3 acres

Grape varietals: 60% Merlot, 34% Cabernet Franc, and 6% Cabernet Sauvignon

Average age of vines: 25 years

Density of plantation: 5,500 vines per hectare

Average yields: 45 hectoliters per hectare

Elevage: Twenty-one to twenty-eight day fermentation and maceration in temperature-controlled stainless-steel vats. Malolactics and 15–18 months aging in new oak barrels. Fining and filtration depending upon the vintage.

WINES PRODUCED

Château Moulin St.-Georges: 35,000 bottles

No second wine is produced.

Plateau of maturity: Within 3–15 years of the vintage

GENERAL APPRECIATION

This estate is owned by Alain Vauthier, a gentleman best known for having resurrected the quality of Ausone. Readers should think of Moulin St.-Georges as a more forward, earlier drinking, less expensive alternative to Ausone. The two vineyards are not far apart, and Moulin St.-Georges often possesses some of the characteristics of its more prestigious stablemate. This wine usually qualifies as one of the vintage's top sleepers. Reasonable prices make it one of the best buys in St.-Emilion.

IMPORTANT VINTAGES

2001   While the 2001 Moulin St.-Georges is good, it is well behind the quality of the
87–88   2000, 1999, and 1998. Its dark ruby color is followed by sweet, mineral-infused, black cherry, raspberry, and currant fruit, but without the persistence and body normally exhibited. It will require consumption during its first decade of life. Last tasted, 1/03.

2000   The finest Moulin St.-Georges ever produced, the exuberant, rich, textured 2000
91   boasts sumptuous aromas and flavors of crème de cassis and blueberry liqueur. The new oak is concealed by the wealth of fruit. While there is abundant tannin in the finish, it is both sweet and well integrated. This seamless beauty, which is not terribly dissimilar from the perfect 2000 Ausone, is a sleeper of the vintage. Anticipated maturity: 2004–2018. Last tasted, 1/03.

1999   Another sleeper of the vintage, this dense, ruby/purple–colored, elegant St.-
90   Emilion exhibits a sweet blackberry/blueberry nose with striking minerality and purity. The wine is medium bodied, long, rich, and structured. This 1999 will actually benefit from some more cellaring. Anticipated maturity: 2005–2016. Last tasted, 3/02.

1998   Elegant blackberry, licorice, and mineral notes jump from the glass of this
89   medium-weight, stylish, exceptionally pure offering. It reveals impressive levels of black fruits as well as nicely integrated acidity, tannin, and wood. With decanting, this 1998 can be drunk now, but it promises to age well for 10 years. Last tasted, 3/02.

1997   The 1997 exhibits a fruit-driven nose of raspberries and cherries, followed by
87   sweet jammy flavors, medium body, low acidity, and a soft, plump finish. It should drink well for 2–4 years. Last tasted, 11/02.

1996   This dark ruby/purple–colored 1996 offers a complex nose of plums and other
88   black fruits, steely mineral notes, and subtle new oak. A classic, elegant, rich, medium-bodied wine with outstanding purity, readers should think of it as the frugal buyer's Ausone. Anticipated maturity: now–2015. Last tasted, 11/02.

1995   A gorgeous wine, and another sleeper of the vintage, Moulin St.-Georges' 1995
90   exhibits a dense purple color and a sweet, black raspberry and currant nose intertwined with high-quality toasty oak and minerals. Deep, rich, impressively pure, ripe, elegant, and harmonious, this gorgeous, persuasive St.-Emilion has a bright future. Anticipated maturity: now–2016. Last tasted, 11/97.

PAVIE

Classification: Premier Grand Cru Classé B

Owner: Gérard and Chantal Perse

Address: 33330 St.-Emilion

Telephone: 05 57 55 43 43; Telefax: 05 57 24 63 99

E-mail: vignobles.perse@wanadoo.fr

Website: chateaupavie.com

Visits: By appointment and for professionals of the wine trade only, Monday to Friday, office hours

Contact: Delphine Rigau or Christine Fritegotto (by fax or e-mail only)

VINEYARDS

Surface area: 86.5 acres

Grape varietals: 60% Merlot, 30% Cabernet Franc, 10% Cabernet Sauvignon

Average age of vines: 43 years

Density of plantation: 5,500 vines per hectare

Average yields: 28–30 hectoliters per hectare

Elevage: Four to five week fermentation and maceration in temperature-controlled wooden tanks. Eighteen to twenty-two months aging on fine lees in new oak barrels. No fining, no filtration.

WINES PRODUCED

Château Pavie: 100,000 bottles

No second wine is produced.

Plateau of maturity: Within 7–35 years, for 1998 and subsequent vintages

GENERAL APPRECIATION

One of the most cherished *terroirs* of St.-Emilion, this estate has been run by Chantal and Gérard Perse since 1997. The Perses have made massive investments in both the vineyard and cellars and have spared no expense to produce the best possible wine (reduced yields, vinification in small open-top oak fermenters, malolactics in barrel, micro-oxygenation and aging on lees, bottling with neither fining nor filtration). The result is the essence of *terroir* as well as a wine of extraordinary finesse, richness, and potential complexity. Under this inspired leadership, Pavie is behaving more and more like the Lafite Rothschild of the right bank, and if wine is to be judged by what is in the bottle, Pavie has become a fabulous first-growth quality estate, offering extraordinary elegance married to prodigious levels of power. However, for whatever reason, over recent vintages Pavie does not seem to have enjoyed the commercial success its quality merits, probably because of the poor public image of the pre-Perse wines as well as the unjustifiable controversy surrounding Perse.

Pavie has the largest vineyard of all the St.-Emilion premier grands cru classés. With a production seven times the size of one of its neighbors, Ausone, and twice that of the adjacent vineyard, La Gaffelière, Pavie is widely known throughout the world.

The vineyard is superbly situated with a full southerly exposure just to the southeast of St.-Emilion (a five-minute drive) on the eastern section of the hillsides of the town. Therefore, it is one of the *côtes* St.-Emilions. Historically this vineyard, along with Ausone, was planted with vines by the Romans in the 4th century.

Until 1998, Pavie was owned and run by Jean-Paul Valette, who had been at Pavie since 1967 after giving up ranching in Chile. He was one of St.-Emilion's friendliest proprietors and his hospitality, combined with the fact that Pavie has some of the region's most interesting limestone caves for storing wine, makes this a must stop for tourists to the area.

Prior to the Perse acquisition, Pavie, despite the large production and popularity, had not been a top performer among the St.-Emilion first growths. In many vintages the wine was too light and feebly colored, with a tendency to brown and mature at an accelerated pace. Fortunately, this period of inconsistency is past history. However, this is not a St.-Emilion to drink young; most vintages, particularly in the 1980s and early 1990s, have been stubbornly hard at their outset, and a minimum of 7–10 years of bottle age is required for mellowing. The wine was particularly disappointing during the 1990s, and this undoubtedly played a role in Mr. Valette's decision to sell the estate. Perse's first vintage was 1998. The quality of what he has achieved in a mere five years is one of the most compelling stories of modern-day Bordeaux.

Pavie has become one of the most expensive premier grand cru classé St.-Emilions.

IMPORTANT VINTAGES

2001
94–96+ The wine of the vintage? It's too early to know for sure, but it certainly rivals the 1998 and 2000. The black/purple–colored 2001 (70% Merlot, 20% Cabernet Franc, and 10% Cabernet Sauvignon) boasts sensational aromatics of sweet, pure, macerated black fruits intermixed with smoke, licorice, iron, and toasty oak. It is medium to full-bodied and extraordinarily well delineated, with aggressive tannin and acidity, yet huge extract as well as layers of concentration. The *terroir*'s nobility screams through all the extract in this amazing effort. It will require at least a decade of cellaring. Anticipated maturity: 2012–2040. Last tasted, 1/03.

2000
100 I give Gérard Perse credit, as he has said time and time again, that 2000 was the greatest Pavie ever produced. People thought it was premature as well as arrogant, but tasted six times out of bottle, this extraordinary blend of 60% Merlot, 30% Cabernet Franc, and 10% Cabernet Sauvignon is undoubtedly one of the most monumental wines Bordeaux has ever produced. The color is an opaque purple, and the wine offers up notes of liquid minerals, blackberry, cherry, and cassis intermixed with spice box, cedar, and white flowers. On the palate, the wine exhibits a massive display of richness and extract, yet with pinpoint delineation and vibrancy. An immortal effort that has a finish well over a minute, this is the kind of phenomenal wine that all of Perse's critics were afraid he could produce—a no-compromise and ageless wonder that is the essence of one of the greatest *terroirs* of Bordeaux. Life is too short not to own and consume some of the 2000 Pavie. Anticipated maturity: 2012–2050. Last tasted, 1/03.

1999
95 A candidate for wine of the vintage, the 1999 Pavie boasts an opaque ruby/purple color in addition to gorgeous aromas of crushed minerals, smoke, licorice, cherry liqueur, and black currants. It is exceptionally pure and multilayered, with stunning texture and overall balance. The tannin level suggests 1–2 years of cellaring is warranted; it should age gracefully for 25+ years. Anticipated maturity: 2005–2030. Last tasted, 3/02.

1998 A 50-year wine, this opaque purple–colored offering exhibits a strong, precise
95+ nose of black fruits, liquid minerals, smoke, and graphite. Extremely full-bodied, yet brilliantly delineated, powerful, and awesomely concentrated, it boasts a fabulous mid-palate as well as a finish that lasts for nearly a minute. This *vin de garde* requires 2–3 years of cellaring. A tour de force in winemaking! Anticipated maturity: 2006–2045. Last tasted, 1/03.

1997 Perse did not make this wine, but he did insist upon a strict selection, resulting in
86 an elegant, medium-bodied, soft, cherry, and spicy-scented, pleasant, picnic-styled Bordeaux. It should drink well for another 2–3 years. Last tasted, 1/03.

1996 The dark ruby–colored 1996 Pavie exhibits a pinched, tart personality with mod-
84 erate quantities of red currant fruit in the nose, along with earth and spice. Although it exhibits good, clean winemaking, this understated, lean, angular wine does not possess much stuffing, flesh, or length. It should keep for 10 years. Anticipated maturity: now–2012. Last tasted, 3/98.

1995 Medium plum/ruby in color, with a distinctive peppery, leafy, spicy nose that has
78 vague hints of red cherry and currant fruit, this is a rigid, austere wine with an angular personality and severe tannin. There is some ripe fruit on the attack, but that is quickly dominated by the wine's structural components. This may turn out to be a pleasant wine, but my best guess is that it will dry out. Anticipated maturity: now–2010. Last tasted, 11/97.

1994 A very light-bodied Pavie showing considerable amber at the edge, the nonde-
72 script nose seems to lack fruit but does offer up some dusty, rustic, earthy notes intermixed with vegetables and herbs. Light to medium bodied, with shrill acidity and high tannin, this wine has nowhere to go but down. Anticipated maturity: now. Last tasted, 1/03.

1993 Dark ruby–colored, with an earthy, nondescript nose offering vague red fruit and
75 green pepper aromas, this sinewy, highly structured, hard, astringent wine will dry out long before the tannin fades. Anticipated maturity: now - probably in decline. Last tasted, 1/97.

1990 This is the most impressive Pavie between 1982 and 1998, and certainly the last
90 very noteworthy effort from the late proprietor Jean-Paul Valette. Dark ruby with some amber at the edge, the spicy, herb-tinged nose offers up notes of earth, black cherries, minerals, and spice box. Medium to full-bodied, meaty, and fleshy, with low acidity and moderate tannin, this wine seems to have approached its plateau of maturity. Anticipated maturity: now–2015. Last tasted, 1/03.

1989 Dark plum/garnet with an aroma comprised of underbrush, compost, mushroom,
88 fruitcake, sweet exotic cherries, and Asian spice, this medium-bodied, relatively hard and angular-styled Pavie is a lot younger than the 1990 and a candidate for two decades of cellaring. Anticipated maturity: 2005–2015. Last tasted, 1/03.

1988 The backward 1988 Pavie is a structured, tannic wine, balanced nicely by elegant,
86 ripe, tobacco and black cherry–scented fruit, good acidity, and a long, spicy, tannic finish. Anticipated maturity: now–2005. Last tasted, 1/93.

1986 Beginning to fade and show a more attenuated style than it did earlier, the 1986
87 Pavie has a garnet color with considerable amber at the edge. A nose of sweet stewed vegetables, dried Provençal herbs, sweet-and-sour cherries, and earth is followed by a medium-bodied wine, with the tannins beginning to take over the wine's personality. The wine was quite impressive young, but has not held up with cellaring. Anticipated maturity: now–2006. Last tasted, 1/03.

1985 The 1985 is firm, tannic, and unyielding, particularly for a wine from this vintage.
86 Deep in color, ripe, medium bodied, but needing time, this wine will provide graceful drinking if cellared. Anticipated maturity: now. Last tasted, 3/90.

1983 Now reaching full maturity, the 1983 Pavie has an attractive bouquet of rich rasp-

88 berry and plummy fruit intermingled with the scents of new oak and herbs. The color is still medium dark ruby, but some amber has crept in at the edge. On the palate, the wine is crammed with rich, opulent, expansive, red fruit flavors, but it has enough acidity and tannin to give it grip and focus. This is a surprisingly drinkable, exuberantly styled Pavie. Anticipated maturity: now–2005. Last tasted, 3/91.

1982
89 Pavie's 1982 is beginning to open and shed its tannin. The wine exhibits an impressive saturated garnet/ruby color, a textbook, Médoc-like nose of cedar, black currants, vanilla, and roasted herbs, medium body, excellent concentration, and moderate tannin still in evidence. This is an elegant, measured style of wine that can be drunk now, although it will not hit its plateau of maturity for another 2–4 years. Anticipated maturity: now–2012. Last tasted, 9/95.

ANCIENT VINTAGES

Most of the vintages of the 1970s were appallingly bad, as were those of the 1960s. The 1961 (90 points; last tasted 2/88) was certainly an impressive effort, but I suspect it is now in decline. The 1929 (93 points; last tasted 3/99) was opened at a tasting at Pavie by proprietor Gérard Perse to show that this was a vintage that he had targeted as what he wanted to produce with more recent years, but in a more progressive fashion.

PAVIE DECESSE

Classification: Grand Cru Classé

Owner: Gérard and Chantal Perse

Address: 33330 St.-Emilion

Mailing address: c/o Château Pavie, 33330 St.-Emilion

Telephone: 05 57 55 43 43; Telefax: 05 57 24 63 99

E-mail: vignobles.perse@wanadoo.fr

No visits

VINEYARDS

Surface area: 22.2 acres

Grape varietals: 90% Merlot, 10% Cabernet Franc

Average age of vines: 41 years

Density of plantation: 5,500 vines per hectare

Average yields: 28–30 hectoliters per hectare

Elevage: Four to five week fermentation and maceration in temperature-controlled wooden tanks. Eighteen to twenty-two months aging on fine lees in new oak barrels. No fining, no filtration.

WINES PRODUCED

Château Pavie Decesse: 30,000 bottles

No second wine is produced.

Plateau of maturity: Within 5–10 years of the vintage, for pre-1998 vintages; within 5–30 years of the vintage from then on

GENERAL APPRECIATION

This is another estate that has been resurrected under the inspired leadership of Gérard Perse, who has done so much at Monbousquet and Pavie.

Between 1971 and 1997, this small estate was owned by Jean-Paul Valette, the proprietor of the premier grand cru classé Pavie, which sits several hundred feet farther down the hill below Pavie Decesse. In 1997 Valette sold the estate to Gérard Perse, the ambitious young proprietor of Monbousquet. This is a *côtes* St.-Emilion, with a vineyard situated on chalky, clay, and limestone soils. The quality at this estate has followed that of its bigger, more famous sibling, Pavie. Consequently, after some mediocre wines in the 1970s, 1980s, and 1990s, the 1997, produced by the new owners, left me with the impression that great things can be expected from Pavie Decesse.

For visitors to the area, I highly recommend a visit not only to Pavie, but also to Pavie Decesse. It is reached by a long and winding road, farther up the hill from Pavie. The view of the vineyards from Pavie Decesse is breathtaking.

IMPORTANT VINTAGES

2001 Cropped at 30 hectoliters per hectare, the 2001 enjoyed a five-week maceration.
92–94+ An opaque purple–colored effort, it is more firm and mineral-dominated than Perse's Monbousquet or Pavie. Pavie Decesse reveals thick, rich flavors, high tannin, medium body, and a liquid minerality to the blackberry, cherry, and currant fruit. This backward St.-Emilion requires 7–10 years of cellaring. Anticipated maturity: 2010–2030. Last tasted, 1/03.

2000 In 2002, a big section of this vineyard will be incorporated into Pavie. The 2000
96 Pavie Decesse, made from 90% Merlot and 10% Cabernet Franc at yields of 30 hectoliters per hectare, enjoyed a five-week maceration and was aged in 100% new oak, with aging on its lees for the first six months. It was bottled unfined and unfiltered, as are all the Perse wines. This wine, for about one-half the price of Pavie, is well worth checking out. A brilliant effort, the wine has an opaque bluish/purple color and a gorgeous nose of sweet blueberries, blackberries, charcoal, and mineral. The wine is full-bodied, very rich, with striking purity, fabulous delineation, immense body and extract, and very sweet but high levels of tannin in the finish, which goes on for nearly one minute. This is undoubtedly the greatest Pavie Decesse ever produced and a modern-day legend in Bordeaux. Anticipated maturity: 2008–2030. Last tasted, 1/03.

1999 A strikingly delineated St.-Emilion with an opaque ruby/purple color and aromas
93 of black currants, blackberries, and wet steel/liquified minerals, this layered, rich, intense 1999 possesses superb fruit purity and medium to full body. This is one of the most concentrated and potentially longest-lived wines of the vintage. Anticipated maturity: 2007–2025. Last tasted, 3/02.

1998 Wet stones, minerals, vanilla, black cherries, and smoke aromas as well as flavors
91+ are present in this powerful, muscular, medium to full-bodied 1998. Crammed with fruit and built for the long haul, it is not as accessible as many of this vintage's offerings. Anticipated maturity: 2005–2025. Last tasted, 3/02.

1997 Dense ruby/purple–colored, with copious quantities of black raspberry and cherry
89 fruit intermixed with spicy oak, this deep, rich, medium- to full-bodied 1997 possesses sweet tannin, low acidity, excellent length, and admirable concentration. Already delicious, it promises to keep for 10 years or so . . . atypically long for a 1997. Last tasted, 3/02.

1996
77?
Gérard Perse had the unenviable task of trying to sell the 1996 Pavie Decesse, the last vintage made under the former regime. The wine is pleasant, but there is very little to it. Moreover, the dry tannin in the finish suggests that graceful aging will be almost impossible. The overall impression is one of leanness, high tannin, and not enough fruit or concentration. This wine has no place to go but down. Anticipated maturity: now–2007. Last tasted, 3/01.

1995
82?
I may have badly misled readers when I rated this wine (giving it an 86–88 score) after the *primeur* tasting. The bottled 1995 Pavie Decesse is extraordinarily austere, with elevated tannin levels, some sweet black currant, cranberry, and cherry fruit, but a hollow mid-palate, and a dry, sharp finish with noticeable astringent tannin. I liked this wine much better from three separate cask tastings, but two tastings from bottle have made me question my earlier reviews. Anticipated maturity: now–2010. Last tasted, 11/97.

1994
82?
The 1994's saturated dark purple color suggests good intensity, but this wine is dominated by its acid and bitter tannin. It is a big, structured, charmless wine in need of more glycerin, mid-palate, and depth. I suspect this will turn out to be an attenuated, compact wine. Anticipated maturity: now–2009. Last tasted, 1/97.

1990
90
The 1990 offers powerful aromas of sweet fruit, minerals, chocolate, and herbs that are followed by a low-acid wine with a huge, chewy texture, gobs of tannin, and plenty of extract and depth. This is an exceptionally powerful wine that should prove to be sensational. Anticipated maturity: now–2010. Last tasted, 1/93.

1989
88
The 1989 Pavie Decesse is a dense, tannic, full-bodied, rich, and, not surprisingly, backward wine for the vintage. It displays an herbaceous, mineral-scented, black cherry fruitiness, full body, and crisp acidity. Anticipated maturity: now–2010. Last tasted, 1/93.

1988
86
The 1988 Pavie Decesse has fine concentration, good length, an enticing bouquet of earthy, mineral, and exotic fruit, but tremendous tannin in the finish. Cellaring is most definitely needed. Anticipated maturity: now–2009. Last tasted, 1/93.

1986
89
An extremely impressive wine that is very tannic and powerful, the 1986 will require long-term cellaring. It is almost opaque in color and very reserved and backward in terms of development, but with the requisite patience to wait at least a decade, it should prove to be one of the sleepers of the vintage. Anticipated maturity: now–2010. Last tasted, 4/91.

1985
88
The 1985 Pavie Decesse has turned out to be even better than Pavie. Very deep in color, with an intense aroma of black currant fruit, toasty oak, and tar-like scents, this rich, long, very big, and structured wine has loads of fruit that is tightly bound in a full-bodied format. It should be a very long-lived 1985. Anticipated maturity: now–2005. Last tasted, 3/90.

PAVIE MACQUIN

Classification: Grand Cru Classé

Owner: Corre-Macquin family

Address: 33330 St.-Emilion

Telephone: 05 57 24 74 23; Telefax: 05 57 24 63 78

E-mail: pavie.macquin@wanadoo.fr

Visits: By appointment only

Contact: Nicolas Thienpont

VINEYARDS

Surface area: 37.5 acres

Grape varietals: 70% Merlot, 25% Cabernet Franc, 5% Cabernet Sauvignon

Average age of vines: 35 years

Density of plantation: 6,000 vines per hectare

Average yields: 35–40 hectoliters per hectare

Elevage: Four to five week fermentation and maceration. Aging in barrels with 60–80% new oak. No fining, no filtration.

WINES PRODUCED

Château Pavie Macquin: 55,000 bottles

Château Les Chênes de Macquin: 10,000 bottles

Plateau of maturity: Within 10–20 years of the vintage

GENERAL APPRECIATION

Biodynamically farmed Pavie Macquin has been producing brilliant wines for most of the last decade. Readers may want to think of it as the Lafleur of St.-Emilion. The old-vine intensity, back-strapping, super-concentrated, highly extracted style, with an abundance of fruit, body, and tannin, combine to produce a noteworthy candidate for extended cellaring. It is definitely not a wine for hedonists seeking immediate gratification. However, even if one does not have to be a gambler to purchase this effort, it must be pointed out that some vintages do present a level of aggressive tannin that makes forecasting fraught with peril.

Pavie Macquin takes its name from Albert Macquin, who was the leading specialist of his time in grafting European vines onto American root stocks, a practice that became essential after the phylloxera louse destroyed most of the vineyards of Bordeaux in the late 19th century. The vineyard is well situated on what is frequently referred to as the Côte Pavie, adjacent to the more renowned vineyards of Troplong Mondot and Pavie. The exposition is highly favorable, overlooking the Fongaban Valley and having its own very sunny and warm microclimate. The wines of Pavie Macquin, which were frequently disappointing in the 1970s and 1980s made a significant leap in quality with the 1990, 1989, 1988, and subsequent vintages, largely because the Corre family hired the brilliant Nicolas Thienpont (of Vieux Château Certan) to look after the estate and viticulture. Moreover, the hiring of the great Libourne oenologist Michel Rolland as well as Stéphane Derénoncourt to look after the vinification and *élevage* have completely turned around the fortunes of this well-placed St.-Emilion. This estate, organically farmed, has become one of the stars of St.-Emilion.

IMPORTANT VINTAGES

2001 After a relatively unimpressive, somewhat monolithic showing during its first year
89–91+ in cask, this wine has blossomed beautifully, and certainly looks like a candidate for an outstanding rating once bottled. A tighter, more elegant, less exuberant and forthcoming Pavie Macquin, this wine nevertheless is impressive, with a saturated blue/purple color and gorgeous but somewhat reticent aromas of sweet cherries interwoven with cassis, licorice, and mineral. Medium to full-bodied, very pure, with

high extract, moderately high tannin, and impressive richness, this is a wine that will require some patience. Anticipated maturity: 2010–2022. Last tasted, 1/03.

2000 A terrific wine of great density, concentration, and intensity, the opaque bluish/
95 purple 2000 Pavie Macquin needs considerable aeration, but with decanting the prodigious bouquet of graphite, camphor, blackberry, blueberry, mineral, coffee, and smoky oak finally makes an appearance. Very persuasive, expansive, full-bodied, and muscular, this enormously endowed, rich wine looks set for a very long life, at least three decades. A terrific effort that rivals the compelling 1998. Anticipated maturity: 2010–2025. Last tasted, 1/03.

1999 The dense plum/purple–colored 1999 offers up aromas of truffles, underbrush, es-
90 presso, black cherries, and roasted meats. Powerful and muscular with high extract and mouth-searing tannin, it is an atypically backward effort for the vintage. Patient connoisseurs who admire wines with this level of intensity will be handsomely repaid for their discipline. Anticipated maturity: 2007–2020. Last tasted, 3/02.

1998 Nearly exaggerated levels of intensity, extract, and richness are apparent in this
95 opaque blue/purple–colored wine. Sumptuous aromas of blueberries, blackberries, and cherries combine with smoke, licorice, vanilla, and truffles to create a compelling aromatic explosion. The wine is fabulously dense, full-bodied, and layered, with multiple dimensions, gorgeous purity, and superbly integrated acidity as well as tannin. One of the most concentrated wines of the vintage, it possesses immense potential, but patience is required. Anticipated maturity: 2006–2030. Last tasted, 3/02.

1997 Exhibiting a saturated black/purple color, the 1997, produced from old vines and
90 low yields, requires some more cellaring (atypical of the vintage). It boasts superb flavors of cassis, blackberries, minerals, licorice, and new oak. Intense, powerful, and backward, this is a classic, long-lived Bordeaux made in an uncompromising fashion. Although a blockbuster effort for the vintage, it is not as seductive as some of its peers. Anticipated maturity: 2006–2015. Last tasted, 12/01.

1996 The 1996 Pavie Macquin could be served next to the 1996 Lafleur. They appear to
89 be cut from the same old-vine, super-concentrated, yet backward, ferociously tannic style. It is an uncompromising wine with a *vieilles vignes* intensity, as well as an abrasively high tannin level. Some of the *terroir*'s telltale mineral and blueberry fruit comes through in the nose and flavors, but this medium-bodied, structured, muscular wine will require 6–8 years of cellaring. Anticipated maturity: 2010–2020. Last tasted, 12/01.

1995 Made in a style similar to the 1996, the 1995 reveals copious quantities of black
89 fruits, obvious old-vine intensity (note the minerals and deep mid-palate), but mouth-searing levels of tannin that will only be enjoyed by masochists. There are many good things about this wine, but the elevated tannin level is cause for concern. If the tannin melts away and the fruit holds, this will be an outstanding effort. Anticipated maturity: 2008–2025. Last tasted, 11/97.

1994 The dark ruby–colored 1994 reveals a Musigny-like nose of violets, black cher-
88? ries, and powdered stone. This tough-textured, tannic, muscular wine exudes personality and character. It may turn out to be an outstanding wine, but it has become dominated by its tannin and is less of a sure thing than I originally thought. While it possesses plenty of personality and richness, it is questionable as to whether this wine will evolve gracefully or eventually dry out. A tough call. Anticipated maturity: 2005–2020. Last tasted, 1/97.

1990 The 1990 Pavie Macquin is fat, sweet, and ripe, with its pronounced smoky oak
91 component intertwined with jammy black raspberry and curranty aromas and flavors. The wine's sweet fruit (from ripeness, not sugar) and concentrated, medium- to full-bodied, low-acid style suggests early maturity, but the wine is still

youthful and unevolved. While already delicious, this wine will benefit from another 2–3 years of cellaring. It will be at its peak between now and 2008. Last
tasted, 11/96.

1989 The 1989 continues to be one of the vintage's sleepers. The color remains a youth-
90   ful ruby/purple. The bouquet offers copious quantities of black raspberry and cassis fruit nicely touched by stony/mineral and floral scents. The spicy, vanilla component is subtle. This full-bodied, highly extracted, elegant wine should reach full
maturity in 2–3 years; it will last through the first 15 years of this century. Last
tasted, 11/96.

1988 The 1988 Pavie Macquin is an excellent wine. Deep in color, with a spicy, black
87   fruit–scented bouquet caressed gently by sweet vanilla oak, this medium-bodied,
concentrated, classy wine offers considerable generosity, as well as finesse and
length. It should be drunk over the next 8–10 years. Last tasted, 1/93.

PÉBY FAUGÈRES

Classification: Grand Cru

Owner: Corinne Guisez

Address: 33330 Saint-Etienne-de-Lisse

Telephone: 05 57 40 34 99; Telefax: 05 57 40 36 14

E-mail: faugeres@chateau-faugeres.com

Website: www.chateau-faugeres.com

Visits: By appointment Monday to Friday,
9 A.M.–noon and 1:30–5 P.M.

Contact: Valérie Grenier

VINEYARDS

Surface area: 19.8 acres

Grape varietals: 100% Merlot

Average age of vines: 40 years

Density of plantation: 5,000 vines per hectare

Average yields: 32 hectoliters per hectare

Elevage: Cold maceration. Four week fermentation and maceration in temperature-
controlled flat cone-shaped wooden vats. Malolactics and 16–18 months aging on lees
in new oak barrels. No fining, no filtration.

WINES PRODUCED

Château Péby Faugères: 20,000 bottles

No second wine is produced.

Plateau of maturity: Within 5–20 years of the vintage

GENERAL APPRECIATION

There is no question that this wine has proved stellar since its debut (1998). This micro-
cuvée is carved out of a parcel of the Faugères vineyard, with a full southerly exposure.
Since its debut vintage, Péby Faugères has fashioned prodigious wines from its tiny
hillside vineyard planted primarily with Merlot.

IMPORTANT VINTAGES

2001
91–93
A brilliant success for the vintage, the 2001 Péby Faugères exhibits a saturated black/ruby color as well as gorgeous aromatics of melted licorice infused with crème de cassis, blackberry liqueur, and a generous dosage of smoke and espresso. Dense, rich, medium to full-bodied, and layered, it is nearly a sumptuous as the 2000 and 1998. It is built along the lines of the gorgeously perfumed, accessible 1999. Anticipated maturity: now–2015. Last tasted, 1/03.

2000
96
A prodigious wine as well as one of the superstars of the vintage, the spectacular 2000 represents the essence of Bordeaux with an inky black/purple color, monumental richness, and massive concentration. A sumptuous bouquet of smoke, liquified minerals, cocoa, blackberries, blueberries, and vanilla is accompanied by a multiple-tiered wine with sweet tannin and dry vintage Port-like richness. With high tannin and extract as well as a whoppingly long finish, it will easily rival, possibly surpass, the other-worldly 1998. I kept a bottle open eight days without any evidence of oxidation. Anticipated maturity: 2006–2020. Last tasted, 1/03.

1999
94
An amazing wine for the vintage, this opaque, purple-colored 1999 boasts a gorgeous nose of blueberry liqueur intermixed with cedar, spice box, coffee, and cassis. Extremely supple textured, spicy, with an expansive, savory, full-bodied palate, no hard edges, and a finish that lasts for nearly 35 seconds, it will be at its finest between now and 2018. Another brilliant effort! Last tasted, 3/02.

1998
95
A terrific effort, and one of the stars of the vintage, the 1998 boasts an opaque, thick looking, black/purple color in addition to gorgeous aromatics consisting of blackberries, blueberries, smoke, minerals, and vanilla. Extremely full-bodied and rich, yet harmonious, with a seamless personality as well as beautifully integrated acidity and tannin, this blockbuster effort is one of the great surprises of the vintage. Anticipated maturity: now–2018+. Last tasted, 3/02.

PIPEAU

Classification: Grand Cru

Owner: Mestreguilhem family

Address: 33330 Saint-Laurent-des-Combes

Telephone: 05 57 24 72 95; Telefax: 05 57 24 71 25

E-mail: chateau.pipeau@wanadoo.fr

Website: www.chateaupipeau.com

Visits: Monday to Friday, 9 A.M.–noon and 2–6 P.M.

Contact: Dominique Lauret and Richard Mestreguilhem

VINEYARDS

Surface area: 86.5 acres

Grape varietals: 80% Merlot, 10% Cabernet Franc, 10% Cabernet Sauvignon

Average age of vines: 30 years

Density of plantation: 6,600 vines per hectare

Average yields: 51 hectoliters per hectare

Elevage: Eighteen to twenty-four day fermentation and maceration in temperature-controlled stainless-steel tanks. Twelve months aging in barrels with 50–60% new oak and racking every three months. Fining with egg whites, filtration only if necessary.

WINES PRODUCED

Château Pipeau: 180,000 bottles

No second wine is produced.

Plateau of maturity: Within 5–15 years of the vintage

GENERAL APPRECIATION

This wine, a fairly recent discovery, is one of the top values of St.-Emilion. Definitely unfaithful to its name ("pipeau" in French means reed-pipe or . . . hoax), it is a reliable, richly fruity, and charming wine that consumers should not hesitate to buy by the case. Though accessible in its youth (the 2000 is already drinking beautifully), it is capable of lasting 10 years.

IMPORTANT VINTAGES

2001
87–90 A delightful, juicy, very sexy combination of black fruits and licorice in a medium-bodied, lush, very pure style is the hallmark of Pipeau's interpretation of St.-Emilion. This appealing, fruit-driven gorgeously up-front style of wine is meant to be drunk now and over the next decade. Last tasted, 1/03.

2000
90 This is a more massive and structured wine out of bottle than I thought when I tasted it out of barrel, where it was undeniably a St.-Emilion fruit-bomb. The color is a deep ruby/purple, and the wine shows gorgeously sweet raspberry and cherry fruit, a bigger framework and more muscle than I would have thought from barrel, and loads of glycerin in the finish. This is a sumptuous, opaque ruby/purple–colored wine that is quite a beauty, but probably 6–12 months or even two years of bottle age will bring around more supple tannins and even more glorious enjoyment. This is certainly the best wine I have ever tasted from Pipeau, and it is probably capable of drinking well for 10–15 years. Last tasted, 1/03.

1999
89 This delicious, hedonistic, fruit-driven St.-Emilion exhibits medium to full body, soft tannin, low acidity, and a long, lush personality dominated by black cherry, raspberry, and currant fruit. Enjoy it over the next 5–6 years. Last tasted, 3/02.

1998
88 The dark ruby–purple colored 1998 offers lush, gorgeous, cherry and blackberry flavors revealing little evidence of oak. The wine is smoky, lush, unbelievably flattering to drink, and, as the French say, is a complete *vin de plaisir*. Because of its low acidity, this fruit-bomb should be drunk over the next 5–6 years. Last tasted, 3/02.

QUINAULT L'ENCLOS ───────────────

Classification: Grand Cru

Owner: Alain et Françoise Raynaud

Address: 30, boulevard de Quinault, 33500 Libourne

Telephone: 05 57 74 19 52; Telefax: 05 57 25 91 20

E-mail: raynaud@chateau-quinault.com

Website: www.chateau-quinault.com

Visits: By appointment only

Contact: Françoise Raynaud

VINEYARDS

Surface area: 49.4 acres

Grape varietals: 70% Merlot, 15% Cabernet Franc, 10% Cabernet Sauvignon, 5% Malbec

Average age of vines: 50 years

Density of plantation: 5,800 vines per hectare

Average yields: 38 hectoliters per hectare

Elevage: Ten day cold maceration at 7°C, followed by three day fermentation at 28°C and 10 day maceration in temperature-controlled concrete and wooden vats. Malolactics and 16 months aging in new oak barrels, including eight months upbringing on fine lees (no racking, barrels being rotated instead). Fining, no filtration.

WINES PRODUCED

Château Quinault l'Enclos: 60,000 bottles

La Fleur Quinault: 16,000 bottles

Plateau of maturity: Within 5–25 years of the vintage, as of 1997

GENERAL APPRECIATION

This emerging St.-Emilion superstar is run by Alain and Françoise Raynaud who, since their first vintage in 1997, have taken this estate to new heights. No effort is spared here to produce a great wine (double sorting of grapes, Burgundian-styled *pigéage*, reverse osmosis, micro-oxygenation, and lees stirring). Quinault is meticulously made with no compromises; beautifully pure and elegant, while extremely ripe and jammy, it is impeccably balanced and owes its special intensity to the old vines from which it emerges.

This walled vineyard (possessing some of the appellation's oldest vines) within the Libourne city limits is owned by Françoise and Alain Raynaud, the latter one of Bordeaux's most accomplished, enlightened, and talented consultants/proprietors. It tends to be a blend of 70% Merlot, 15% Cabernet Franc, 10% Cabernet Sauvignon, and, in 2001, small quantities of Malbec were included in the final assemblage. This wine sees lees aging, malolactic fermentation in barrel, and a new high-tech system that automatically rotates the barrels so the lees are constantly mixed in with the fruit. This is St.-Emilion at its most eloquent and pure expression.

IMPORTANT VINTAGES

2001　A brilliant success, this 2001 should rival Quinault's 2000. It exhibits a deep, sat-
92–94　urated purple color as well as a sweet bouquet of black raspberries intermixed with blueberries, black currants, minerals, spring flowers, and subtle, nicely integrated wood. The flamboyant aromatics are followed by an opulent, medium- to full-bodied, textured wine that should age effortlessly for 15+ years. Anticipated maturity: 2005–2017. Last tasted, 1/03.

2000　The powerful, multilayered 2000 should rival 1998 as the finest Quinault pro-
94　duced. It boasts an opaque purple color as well as glorious aromatics of crushed blackberries, blueberries, and black currants intermixed with violets, licorice, and subtle smoky oak. It cuts a broad swath across the palate with an expansive chewiness in addition to terrific concentration, purity, and overall equilibrium. In spite of that, it is remarkably light on its feet. Although it will probably close down,

it will still be drinkable within 2–3 years of bottling, and will evolve nicely for 15–18 years. Last tasted, 1/03.

1999
91
This elegant, exotic, lush, medium-bodied, Burgundian-styled St.-Emilion boasts great complexity along with an enticing perfume of blueberries, blackberries, and flowers. Although it does not possess a great deal of weight, it offers pure fruit, sweet tannin, and no hard edges. A textbook example of Bordeaux at its richest and most elegant, it will be delicious in a few years and evolve gracefully for 10–12 years. Last tasted, 3/02.

1998
94
An elegant as well as powerful effort, this dense ruby/purple–colored 1998 reveals notes of plums, black raspberries, vanilla, minerals, licorice, and spice. Exceptionally rich with an outstanding texture, this medium- to full-bodied wine possesses a distinctive, individualistic style, largely because of its floral, blueberry fruit flavors. Although accessible, it will age for two decades. Anticipated maturity: now–2020. Last tasted, 1/03.

1997
88
If the 1997 lacks density and length, it still reveals an unmistakable similarity to the famed Pomerol Lafleur. Kirsch, spice, and mineral notes are the hallmarks of this wine, which combines breed, power, and elegance. Supple tannin, a medium-bodied, plush texture, and fine purity characterize this delicious, complex, stylish St.-Emilion. Drink it now as well as over the next 8+ years. Last tasted, 11/02.

ROCHEBELLE

Classification: Grand Cru

Owner: Philippe Faniest

Address: 33330 St.-Emilion

Mailing address: BP 73, 33330 St.-Emilion

Telephone: 05 57 51 30 71; Telefax: 05 57 51 01 99

E-mail: chateau-rochebelle@grand-cru-st-emilion.com

Website: www.grand-cru-st-emilion.com

Visits: By appointment only

Contact: Philippe Faniest or Bétarice Frank

VINEYARDS

Surface area: 7.4 acres

Grape varietals: 85% Merlot, 15% Cabernet Franc

Average age of vines: 45 years

Density of plantation: 6,000 vines per hectare

Average yields: 42 hectoliters per hectare

Elevage: Three to four week fermentation and maceration in temperature-controlled concrete tanks. After malolactics, 15–18 months aging in new oak barrels. Fining, light filtration upon bottling.

WINES PRODUCED

Château Rochebelle: 15,000–18,000 bottles

No second wine is produced.

Plateau of maturity: Within 5–12 years of the vintage

GENERAL APPRECIATION

A soundly made, reasonably priced St.-Emilion (a rarity nowadays), Rochebelle's recent vintages have often qualified as a sleeper pick in my tastings. This is an estate shrewd buyers will monitor closely.

IMPORTANT VINTAGES

2001
85–88 This wine has filled out nicely during its upbringing in barrel. The color is a dark ruby/purple, and the wine is somewhat monolithic but loaded with fruit intermixed with some toasty oak, dried herbs, earth, and spice. The wine is medium bodied, with ripe tannin, crisp acidity for delineation, and a moderately long, medium-bodied finish. Anticipated maturity: 2005–2012. Last tasted, 1/03.

2000
89 In the limited experience I have had with Rochebelle, this looks to be the best wine they have yet produced, even better than the 1998. Deep ruby/purple–colored, with notes of blackberry, cassis, licorice, vanilla, and mineral, this medium- to full-bodied wine is thick, juicy, and relatively muscular, with impressive extract, ripe but noticeable tannin, and a structured, somewhat closed, firm finish. Some patience will be required. Anticipated maturity: 2007–2017. Last tasted, 1/03.

1999
87 An excellent, dark plum/purple color is followed by copious quantities of sweet fruit, medium body, and a savory, delicious, fruit-driven mid-palate as well as finish. Ripe tannin and unobtrusive acidity suggest consumption over the next eight years is warranted. Last tasted, 3/02.

1998
88 Potentially a sleeper of the vintage, this wine exhibits a dense ruby/purple color in addition to a spicy, blackberry and cherry-scented bouquet with noticeable new oak. Fat, dense, and full-bodied, with excellent purity and length, it will be a savory, fleshy, mouth-filling St.-Emilion with a few more years of bottle age. Anticipated maturity: 2004–2016. Last tasted, 3/02.

1997
87 The dark purple–colored 1997 reveals aromas of black raspberry jam and toasty new oak. Medium bodied and richly fruity, with excellent purity and low acidity, it should drink well during its first 10–12 years of life. Last tasted, 1/02.

1996
87 The impressive 1996 Rochebelle displays a deep, saturated, ruby/purple color, and a sweet nose of black currants, cherries, incense, and smoky oak. The wine possesses a sweet, fleshy texture, elements of *sur-maturité*, surprisingly low acidity for a 1996, and an expansive, nicely layered finish. If this wine were slightly more complex, it would have merited an even higher score. Anticipated maturity: now–2010. Last tasted, 1/02.

ROCHER BELLEVUE FIGEAC

Classification: Grand Cru

Owner: Pierre and Charlotte Dutruilh

Address: Bellevue, 33330 St.-Emilion

Mailing address: 14, rue d'Aviau, 33000 Bordeaux

Telephone and Telefax: 05 56 81 19 69

Visits: By appointment only

Contact: Jean Dutruilh (Telephone: 06 73 89 18 13)

VINEYARDS

Surface area: 17.3 acres

Grape varietals: 75% Merlot, 25% Cabernet Franc

Average age of vines: 34 years

Density of plantation: 6,000 vines per hectare

Average yields: 42 hectoliters per hectare

Elevage: Cold maceration. Twenty-one to thirty day fermentation and maceration in temperature-controlled vats. Malolactics and 15–20 months aging on lees in barrels with 70–100% new oak. No fining, no filtration.

WINES PRODUCED

Château Rocher Bellevue Figeac: 31,000 bottles

Pavillon de la Croix Figeac: 6,000 bottles

Plateau of maturity: Within 3–10 years of the vintage

GENERAL APPRECIATION

Rocher Bellevue Figeac is always a very good wine that is still proposed at extremely reasonable prices. Consumers searching for a fine, unpretentious, and richly fruity St.-Emilion should latch onto this wine and buy it by the case.

This vineyard, situated on the plateau near both Figeac and the border of Pomerol, is planted with an extremely high percentage of Merlot. The result is a juicy, almost succulently fruity, round wine that makes for delicious drinking early, and is best consumed by 7–8 years of age. I would be cautious about buying anything older. This is an estate on the rise with Marc Dworkin, formerly in charge at Larmande, making the wine.

IMPORTANT VINTAGES

2001
89–90
A sleeper of the vintage, this wine, which in this vintage is a blend of 80% Merlot, 18% Cabernet Franc, and 2% Cabernet Sauvignon, shows a dense ruby/purple color and a sweet nose of crushed black cherries, blackberries, licorice, and vanilla. The wine is medium bodied, with very soft tannin, a plush, fat texture, and a long, concentrated finish. It is certainly a wine to check out, as it is usually very low priced. Anticipated maturity: 2005–2014. Last tasted, 1/03.

2000
88
This is a very well-made wine, with a dense ruby/purple color and thick, very ripe flavors of black fruits intermixed with underbrush, licorice, and some smoky, toasty oak. Medium to full-bodied, with abundant but sweet tannin, along with the 1998 and 2001 this is one of the most impressive wines to emerge from this well-placed estate in many a year. Anticipated maturity: 2005–2015. Last tasted, 3/01.

1999
87
The dark plum/ruby–colored 1999 reveals medium body and plenty of juicy, concentrated fruit in its mainstream, easy to understand, and delicious personality. Consume it during its first decade of life. Last tasted, 3/02.

1998
88
A consumer-friendly effort with an attractive quality/price rapport, this dark plum–colored 1998 offers up cassis, kirsch, licorice, smoke, spice box, and leather aromas. The wine is medium to full-bodied, with excellent richness, supple tannin, and a velvety finish. Drink it over the next eight years. It is a sleeper of the vintage. Last tasted, 3/02.

ROL VALENTIN

Classification: Grand Cru

Owner: Eric Prissette

Address: 33330 St.-Emilion

Telephone: 05 57 74 43 51; Telefax: 05 57 74 45 13

E-mail: info@rolvalentin.com

Visits: By appointment only

Contact: Eric Prissette

VINEYARDS

Surface area: 11.4 acres

Grape varietals: 85% Merlot, 8% Cabernet Sauvignon, 7% Cabernet Franc

Average age of vines: 38 years

Density of plantation: 6,600 vines per hectare

Average yields: 30 hectoliters per hectare

Elevage: Fermentation and maceration in 11 temperature-controlled wooden vats of small capacity (10, 20, and 30 hectoliters) corresponding to the different parcels of vines. Frequent *pigéages*. Malolactics with micro-oxygenation and stirring of the lees, and 18–24 months aging in new oak barrels. No fining, filtration if necessary.

WINES PRODUCED

Château Rol Valentin: 12,000–15,000 bottles

No second wine is produced.

Plateau of maturity: Within 5–15 years of the vintage

GENERAL APPRECIATION

Rol Valentin was one of the first St.-Emilion estates to emulate Valandraud, adopting a progressively styled vinification. The first steps were promising and propelled the estate among the small number of St.-Emilions that have soared into Bordeaux's limelight.

Although proprietor Eric Prissette's first vintage was only 1995, Rol Valentin has quickly become one of the leading quasi-garage wines of St.-Emilion. The 11.4-acre vineyard, situated on two sectors (two-thirds on sandy soils not far from Cheval Blanc and La Dominique and one-third on clay and limestone just north of La Gomerie), is planted with 85% Merlot, 8% Cabernet Sauvignon, and 7% Cabernet Franc. Yields are routinely kept under 30 hectoliters per hectare, and all of the fashionable winemaking techniques are employed (i.e., malolactic in barrel, micro-oxygenation, the utilization of 100% new oak, and no fining with only a slight filtration). Eric Prissette's consultant is the wunderkind Stéphane Derénoncourt.

IMPORTANT VINTAGES

2001   The 2001 Rol Valentin was tasted on six separate occasions, with somewhat diver-
88–91   gent reviews. At its best, the 2001 is another luxuriously rich, layered, and
     nuanced wine with considerable ripeness and intensity. The dense ruby/purple–

colored 2001 exhibits pure blackberry, black currant, and berry-like flavors with high-quality, smoky, toasty oak (from Taransaud barrels). With good acidity, ripe tannin, and stunning length, it will be at its best between 2005 and 2016. However, some caution may be necessary, since at least three of the samples tasted were aggressively oaky and less impressively deep. Last tasted, 1/03.

2000 This is Eric Prissette's best vintage to date. The wine has developed beautifully in
93 cask, and out of bottle it is a gorgeously seductive, full-bodied, very heady, perfumed style of wine, with a dense purple color and a sweet nose of blackberries, cassis, licorice, coffee, and toast. Quite layered, deep, and chewy, with considerable body, noticeable structure, and a lot of muscle and delineation, this is a large-scaled Rol Valentin that should age effortlessly yet be approachable in 2–3 years. Anticipated maturity: 2006–2018. Last tasted, 1/03.

1999 Tasting better from bottle than it did out of barrel, this is an opulent, sexy, modern-
89 style St.-Emilion possessing deep, superripe black cherry and cassis fruit, smoke, and character in a medium-bodied, lush format. The finish is excellent, but with more length, it would have jumped to the magical 90-point category. Some tannin is noticeable, but this wine is capable of lasting 10 years. Last tasted, 3/02.

1998 A superb effort, the dark ruby/purple–colored 1998 offers gorgeous aromas of
90 flowers, blackberries, cherries, smoke, licorice, and spice box. It is deep, succulent, and medium to full-bodied, with decent acidity, superb purity, and a creamy texture. Tannin is present, but it is well integrated and balanced by the wine's depth. Anticipated maturity: now–2014. Last tasted, 3/02.

1997 From barrel, this wine exhibited the potential to be outstanding. Now that it has
88 been bottled, it is lighter without sufficient aromatic or flavor dimension to merit an outstanding score. Nevertheless, there remains plenty to admire. The wine possesses a deep ruby color in addition to a sweet plum/cherry, woodsy bouquet with copious quantities of toasty new oak. A spicy St.-Emilion, with low acidity, medium body, and excellent richness and glycerin, it should drink well for 4–5 years. Last tasted, 1/02.

1996 The 1996 boasts a dark ruby/purple color, as well as a sweet nose of black currants
90 intermixed with licorice, toasty new-barrel aromas, and smoked herbs. Medium bodied, rich, ripe, and hedonistically styled, it can be drunk now and until 2014. Last tasted, 3/00.

1995 The debut vintage for Rol Valentin, this wine has held up beautifully and exhibits
90 a youthful deep ruby/purple color as well as a sweet nose of black cherry, cassis, vanilla, and coffee. The wine is medium bodied with velvety tannin, lush, concentrated flavors, no hard edges, and an impressive finish. The wine has just reached its plateau of drinkability. Anticipated maturity: now–2013. Last tasted, 1/03.

SAINT-DOMINGUE

Classification: Grand Cru

Owner: Clément Fayat

Address: 33330 St.-Emilion

Mailing address: c/o Château La Dominique, 33330 St.-Emilion

Telephone: 05 57 51 31 36; Telefax: 05 57 51 63 04

E-mail: info@vignobles.fayat-group.com

Visits: By appointment Monday to Friday, 9 A.M.–noon and 2–6 P.M.

Contact: Cyril Forget

VINEYARDS

Surface area: 6.7 acres

Grape varietals: 100% Merlot

Average age of vines: 30 years

Density of plantation: 5,700 vines per hectare

Average yields: 25 hectoliters per hectare

Elevage: Cold maceration. Twenty-five to thirty day fermentation (29–32°C) and maceration in temperature-controlled stainless-steel vats allowing the separate vinification of the different parcels, with frequent pumpings-over. Malolactics and 18–22 months aging in new oak barrels. No fining, no filtration.

WINES PRODUCED

Saint-Domingue: 6,000 bottles

No second wine is produced.

Plateau of maturity: Within 3–12 years of the vintage

GENERAL APPRECIATION

A garage wine from Clément Fayat (of La Dominique fame), Saint-Domingue has often perplexed me—always ripe and jammy, it has a tendency to be too low-acid, soft, and flabby, lacking in freshness and structure. The last two vintages have shown dramatic improvement.

IMPORTANT VINTAGES

2001
89–91 Typically exotic, with a hint of overripe black currants, plums, and even a touch of prune, this dark ruby/purple–colored wine is layered, thick, juicy, and meant for drinking during its first 10–12 years of life. Of course the wood is elevated, but it seems as if, over the last couple of vintages, it has been better integrated into the jammy, chocolaty, very flamboyant style of this wine with more discretion. Anticipated maturity: now–2013. Last tasted, 1/03.

2000
92 Undoubtedly the best Saint-Domingue I have tasted, this wine tastes like proprietor Clément Fayat's La Dominique on steroids. It is opaque purple–colored with a glorious nose of crème de cassis, vanilla, chocolate, and espresso. Once past the ostentatious aromatics, this chewy, low-acid, plump, very full-bodied wine is dense, rich, with great intensity, purity, and plenty of power. This is obviously a modern-styled St.-Emilion, but a huge crowd-pleaser and a wine capable of lasting 12–15 more years, possibly longer. Anticipated maturity: 2006–2017. Last tasted, 1/03.

1999
88? This has turned out to be a strong, exotic effort offering opulent black fruits intermixed with a hint of mint, leather, and licorice. This sexy, lush, aggressively oaked wine is not for everybody, but it possesses considerable glycerin and fruit. Anticipated maturity: now–2012. Last tasted, 3/02.

1998
88 The 1998 Saint-Domingue is made in an exotic, over-the-top style with Port-like, ripe notes of prunes, blackberry jam, coffee, and toasty new oak. The flamboyant bouquet characteristics are also apparent in this medium- to full-bodied, oaky, low-acid, almost flabby wine. Although it will be controversial, it is undeniably delicious. Anticipated maturity: now–2010. Last tasted, 3/02.

SOUTARD

Classification: Grand Cru Classé

Owner: Des Ligneris family

Address: 33330 St.-Emilion

Telephone: 05 57 24 72 23; Telefax: 05 57 24 66 94

Visits: By appointment only

Contact: François de Ligneris

VINEYARDS

Surface area: 54.3 acres

Grape varietals: 65% Merlot, 35% Cabernet Franc

Average age of vines: 35 years

Density of plantation: 5,500 vines per hectare

Average yields: 48 hectoliters per hectare

Elevage: Fermentations and macerations are long (in 1997, 40–45 days) and take place at low temperatures. Sometimes malolactics are not completed by July, in which case there is no addition of sulfites to the wines. These are aged for one year in oak barrels (several sizes and different types of wood) that are renewed by a third each vintage. They remain on lees during the winter and are unfined and unfiltered upon bottling.

WINES PRODUCED

Château Soutard: 120,000 bottles

Clos de la Tonnelle: 10,000 bottles

Plateau of maturity: Within 10–27 years of the vintage

GENERAL APPRECIATION

This is a serious, traditionally made wine that usually repays one's patience. Top vintages often require long term cellaring.

This is one of the oldest St.-Emilion estates and has been owned by the same family since 1762. Situated in the northern part of the appellation, the vineyard is located on a soil base composed primarily of limestone.

Soutard is highly prized in the Benelux countries, but the wine has largely been ignored outside Europe. That is a shame, because this is one of the most traditionally made and longest-lived wines in St.-Emilion. Most vintages can last for 20–25+ years and are often unapproachable for a decade.

The property employs at least one-third new oak for aging the wine and often bottles it much later than other St.-Emilion châteaux. Soutard is usually an opaque dark ruby color (there is no fining or filtration) and possesses a powerful, tannic ferocity that can be off-putting when the wine is young. Nevertheless, this is one of St.-Emilion's best-kept secrets. For consumers looking for wines capable of lasting 20 or more years, Soutard should be seriously considered.

IMPORTANT VINTAGES

1999
87
For Soutard, this is a relatively approachable style of wine, with a dark garnet/ruby color and a spicy, earthy nose of tobacco leaf intermixed with loamy soil scents, black cherries, currants, and some background oak. Medium bodied, moderately tannic, but accessible, this wine looks to be ready to drink relatively early for a vintage of Soutard. Anticipated maturity: 2006–2015. Last tasted, 1/03.

1998
90
A powerful, tannic *vin de garde*, Soutard's 1998 has a dark garnet color to the rim and a tight but promising nose of sweet black cherries, currants, roasted herbs, and a hint of truffle. The wine is medium to full-bodied, moderately high in tannin, very structured, delineated, and made in the typically no-compromise, traditional style that this château favors. Anticipated maturity: 2007–2020. Last tasted, 1/03.

1995
89+
This wine has completely closed down after bottling. The color is still an impressively saturated ruby/purple. The nose, even with extended decanting, only reveals hints of sweet plums, cherries, black currants, and some oak and dried herbs. In the mouth, the wine is medium bodied, with hints of fruitcake, spice box, cedar, and more black fruits. The tannins kick in in the finish, and the wine completely shuts down. This is a wine for patient traditionalists. Anticipated maturity: 2008–2018. Last tasted, 1/03.

1990
90
This wine has turned out beautifully and, despite being totally closed early on, it is developing considerable richness and sweetness. The Merlot component dominates, as evidenced by the copious plum, currant, black cherry, and cedary fruit. The wine is medium to full-bodied and still shows some old-style, rather astringent tannin, but there is plenty of fat and flesh to cover them up. This wine is just hitting its plateau of drinkability. Anticipated maturity: 2004–2017. Last tasted, 1/03.

1989
91
One of my all-time favorite vintages from Soutard, this wine, which is quite dense, concentrated, muscular, and full-bodied, still has a dark garnet/plum/purple color and a nose of damp earth, liquid minerals, plum, and cassis intermixed with some licorice and cedar. The wine is full-bodied, powerful, and aging at a glacial pace. Quite pure and intense, but still not ready to drink, this is a wine for serious connoisseurs. Anticipated maturity: 2004–2020. Last tasted, 1/03.

1988
87
Backward, dense, concentrated, and unforthcoming, the powerful, herbaceous, vanilla, and black currant-scented 1988 Soutard has plenty of extract, although it is buried beneath considerable quantities of tannin. It is a worthy candidate for 20 or more years of cellaring. Anticipated maturity: now–2020. Last tasted, 1/93.

1986
86
Soutard remains one of the longest-lived wines in the appellation of St.-Emilion. There is no doubt that the proprietors intentionally pack this wine with gobs of extract and mouth-searing tannins, making it a sure bet to last 20 years. The 1986 is a very backward, unyielding wine with tremendous tannin levels, but also rich, highly extracted, concentrated fruit. Anticipated maturity: now–2015. Last tasted, 3/90.

1985
90
The 1985 Soutard is a sensationally rich, tannic, deep, multidimensional wine that balances muscle and grace. It is more supple than usual but is still capable of 20 or more years of longevity. Anticipated maturity: now–2010. Last tasted, 3/90.

1982
87
The 1982 is an old-style St.-Emilion made to last and last. It belongs with enthusiasts who have the patience to lay it away for a decade or more. The 1982 is typically huge, backward, almost abrasively tannic. However, this wine—which is now quite closed—has a broodingly dark color and excellent richness, ripeness, and weight on the palate. It will no doubt receive a higher score circa 2000, but it is brutally tannic now. Anticipated maturity: now–2025. Last tasted, 3/89.

ANCIENT VINTAGES

The best two vintages for those lucky enough to find any would be the 1964 (90 points; last tasted 3/90) and 1955 (88 points; last tasted 10/89).

TERTRE DAUGAY

Classification: Grand Cru Classé

Owner: Léo de Malet-Roquefort

Address: 33330 St.-Emilion

Telephone: 05 57 24 72 15; Telefax: 05 57 24 69 06

E-mail: chateau-tertre-daugay@chateau-tertre-daugay.com

Website: www.chateau-tertre-daugay.com

Visits: By appointment only Monday to Friday, 8 A.M.–noon and 2–6 P.M.

Contact: Léo de Malet-Roquefort or Claude Diligeard

VINEYARDS

Surface area: 39.5 acres

Grape varietals: 60% Merlot, 40% Cabernet Franc

Average age of vines: 22 years

Density of plantation: 5,800 vines per hectare

Average yields: 39 hectoliters per hectare

Elevage: Prolonged fermentation and maceration in temperature-controlled stainless-steel tanks with micro-oxygenation of lees. Twelve to fourteen months aging in barrels with 70% new oak. Fining, light filtration.

WINES PRODUCED

Château Tertre Daugay: 60,000 bottles

Château de Roquefort: 3,000–4,000 bottles

Plateau of maturity: Within 3–14 years of the vintage

GENERAL APPRECIATION

The wines of Tertre Daugay have much improved over the last 15 years and are now soundly made. Vinified in the traditional St.-Emilion style, they are comparable in quality to a good Médoc Cru Bourgeois.

This was a property that, because of sloppy winemaking and the lack of effective management, lost complete credibility during the 1960s and 1970s. In 1978 the proprietor of La Gaffelière, Comte Léo de Malet-Roquefort, purchased the property and has made significant improvements both to the vineyards and to the wine cellar. It has taken some time for the vineyard to rebound, but recent years have been more promising, particularly after such a prolonged period of mediocrity.

Historically, Tertre Daugay is one of the most ancient properties in St.-Emilion. It is located on the hillside near most of the premier grands cru classés. The actual name is derived from the Gascon term "Daugay," which means "look-out hill." The excellent exposure enjoyed by the vineyard of Tertre Daugay ensures maximum ripening of the grapes. The soil, a combination of clay and limestone with significant iron deposits in the subsoil, is claimed to give the wines great body and concentration.

IMPORTANT VINTAGES

2001 This appears to be a very attractive, elegant, strong effort from Tertre Daugay. The
86–88 wine shows deep, sweet, herb-tinged black cherry and currant fruit intermixed with some spice box and fruitcake. It is elegant, medium-bodied, sweet, and ideal for drinking during its first 7–8 years of life. Last tasted, 1/03.

2000 I had hoped for better things, but this wine has turned out somewhat monolithic
86 and clumsy, with a dark ruby color, medium body, and no real charm or complexity. Nevertheless, that may well emerge in the future. Anticipated maturity: 2006–2012. Last tasted, 1/03.

1999 A good effort from Tertre Daugay, the 1999 exhibits a dense ruby color as well as
86 a stylish perfume of ripe berry fruit, tobacco, cedar, and spicy wood. Medium to full-bodied and dense yet soft, this is a candidate for delicious drinking now and over the following eight years. Last tasted, 3/02.

1998 Dark ruby/garnet colored with an elegant berry nose displaying scents of cedar,
87 earth, and spice, this medium-bodied, nicely delineated 1998 is long, rich, and graceful. In an age of bold, flamboyant offerings, particularly from St.-Emilion, this wine's measured restraint and attractive ripeness as well as richness are to be applauded. Drink it over the next eight years. Last tasted, 3/02.

LE TERTRE RÔTEBOEUF

Classification: Grand Cru

Owner: François and Emilie Mitjavile

Address: SCEA F. et E. Mitjavile, 1, le Tertre, 33330 Saint-Laurent-des-Combes

Telephone: Not listed; Telefax: 05 57 74 42 11

Visits: By appointment only

Contact: François Mitjavile

VINEYARDS

Surface area: 14.7 acres

Grape varietals: 85% Merlot, 15% Cabernet Franc

Average age of vines: 40 years

Density of plantation: 6,000–7,000 vines per hectare

Average yields: 33 hectoliters per hectare

Elevage: Three to four week fermentation and maceration. Eighteen to twenty-two months aging in new oak barrels. Fining and filtration depending upon the vintage.

WINES PRODUCED

Château Tertre Rôteboeuf: 25,000 bottles

No second wine is produced.

Plateau of maturity: Within 3–15 years of the vintage

GENERAL APPRECIATION

Since this estate burst on to the scene in the mid-1980s, the talent and extraordinary winemaking skills of François Mitjavile have produced one of Bordeaux's most luxurious, sensual, and sexy wines. It is terribly tantalizing because of its sumptuous richness, and that unmistakable jammy texture and roast coffee aromas make it special. Contrary to what one might be tempted to think, Le Tertre Rôteboeuf does not belong to the so-called modern school of vinification prevailing in St.-Emilion. It has an inimitable style of its own and has not, up to now, been duplicated.

It is unfortunate, but, I suppose, given the commercial world in which we live, totally understandable that there are few people in the wine world like François Mitjavile. While many famous producers push yields to such preposterous levels that they risk destroying any concept of *terroir* of the vineyard, or even muting the character of a vintage, here is one man whose talent and obsession for producing the finest possible wines is refreshing.

Le Tertre Rôteboeuf's micro-sized vineyard now receives worldwide attention. It is no doubt justified, but one hopes nothing changes at this estate, which is run with single-minded determination by Monsieur Mitjavile. He makes no compromises. What Mitjavile has in mind is to make a wine from this splendidly situated vineyard that has the extract and intensity of wines such as Lafleur, Pétrus, and Certan de May in Pomerol. To do so, Mitjavile is one of the last to harvest, keeps his yields small, and utilizes considerable new oak to harness the power of his wine. There is no doubt that recent vintages have had dazzling levels of fruit and a flashy flamboyance that have drawn numerous rave reviews from the European wine press.

The steep, sheltered vineyard (near Larcis Ducasse) is named after the oxen that are necessary to cultivate the soil. When translated, the name means the "hill of the belching beef." Le Tertre Rôteboeuf is irrefutably one of Bordeaux's superstars.

IMPORTANT VINTAGES

2001 Dark ruby/purple, the 2001 has leafy, cool climate aromas of dried herbs, fresh
88–90 coffee, hints of chocolate, and copious black cherry fruit that characterize the moderately intense perfume. Neither as kinky nor as sexy as previous examples (because it lacks glycerin and fat), this is a surprisingly elegant, civilized, atypical, but excellent Le Tertre Rôteboeuf. If it develops more of a mid-palate and length, it will merit an outstanding score. Anticipated maturity: 2006–2014. Last tasted, 1/03.

2000 I know this sounds crazy, but when I tasted the 2000 Le Tertre Rôteboeuf from
96 bottle, the only thought that jumped into my head was a déjà vu of the 1990 Pétrus at age two! Undeniably the finest Le Tertre Rôteboeuf since the spectacular 1998, 1990, and 1989, the dense ruby/purple–colored 2000 exhibits a sweet nose of roasted espresso, mocha, chocolate, black cherry jam, cassis, licorice, new saddle leather, and toasty oak. This explosive, hedonistic concoction is followed by a full-

bodied wine with silky tannin, a sumptuous, sweet, lavishly rich mid-palate and texture, and a 45-second finish. It reveals more noticeable structure and grip than the 1998 or 1990 possessed at a similar age, but this is a majestic wine. Anticipated maturity: 2005–2025. Last tasted, 1/03.

1999   A hedonistic, head-turning crowd-pleaser, this dark ruby–colored, flamboyant
91   1999 boasts a knockout perfume of scorched earth, smoked herbs, jammy black cherry fruit, chocolate, and roasted coffee. Plump and fleshy, with low acidity, excellent purity, outstanding concentration, and no hard edges, this is a seamless, gorgeous Le Tertre Rôteboeuf to drink over the next 12 years. Last tasted, 3/02.

1998   A dramatic, flamboyant nose of roasted espresso intermixed with chocolate fudge,
94   blackberries, Asian spices, and kirsch jumps from the glass of this ostentatious effort. Full-bodied and layered, with an unctuous texture, gorgeous purity, and an undeniable hedonistic explosion of fruit and glycerin, this dense ruby/purple–colored wine can be drunk now or cellared for 15–18 years. Last tasted, 3/02.

1997   This is a delicious, soft wine with aromas and flavors of mocha, coffee, chocolate,
87   cedar, and jammy red and black fruits. Medium to full-bodied, with low acidity, little density, but excellent fruit and a soft underbelly, it requires consumption over the next 2–3 years. It is ideal for consumers and restaurants seeking immediate drinkability. Last tasted, 1/02.

1996   Slightly less impressive than I originally thought, the 1996 has a dark plum/garnet
89   color and a sweet nose of dusty plums, currants, and cherries intermixed with hints of coffee, chocolate, and underbrush. The wine is medium bodied, has good sweetness, a silky texture, yet some firm tannins to be resolved in the finish. The wine is delicious, forward, and certainly one of the more successful wines of the right bank in 1996. Anticipated maturity: now–2012. Last tasted, 12/02.

1995   A very powerful, concentrated Le Tertre Rôteboeuf, but completely closed at
94+   present, this wine has a deep ruby/purple color and a sweet nose of black cherry and plum jam intermixed with hints of vanilla, chocolate, and espresso roast. The wine is medium to full-bodied, quite tannic, powerful, and one of the more backward wines I have tasted at this estate. It requires much more cellaring than I originally thought. Anticipated maturity: 2005–2020. Last tasted, 12/02.

1994   A very successful effort in a difficult vintage, Le Tertre Rôteboeuf's 1994 shows a
90   dark plum/ruby color with no lightening at the edge. A nose of roasted herbs intermixed with black cherry, plum, fig, and currant also has a hint of chocolate and earth. Medium bodied, with ripe but noticeable tannin, excellent definition, and fine purity, this is a nice, weighty, rich, surprisingly strong effort from Le Tertre Rôteboeuf. Anticipated maturity: now–2014. Last tasted, 12/02.

1993   Fully mature and best drunk up over the next 3–4 years, Le Tertre Rôteboeuf's
88   1993 is one of the better wines in this difficult vintage. Medium bodied, with plum, earth, mushroom, and prune aromas, this is a well-endowed 1993 that still has a surprisingly deep plum/cherry color, sweet fruit on the attack, medium body, and excellent depth, ripeness, and overall balance. The wine probably sells for a song, given the lackluster reputation of the vintage. This is one of the cherries to be plucked from 1993. Anticipated maturity: now–2014. Last tasted, 12/02.

1990   An absolutely spectacular Le Tertre Rôteboeuf, probably the only other vintage
98   that will reach this level of quality is the 2000. The 1990 has a deep plum/ruby color with some lightening at the edge and an extraordinarily flamboyant nose of jammy black cherry and berry fruit infused with smoke, caramel, and coffee notes that soar from the glass. This is a very viscous, full-bodied, silky textured wine that has a to-die-for finish and enough glycerin and body to get lost. It is just entering its plateau of full maturity. A wow-wow wine! Anticipated maturity: now–2015. Last tasted, 12/02.

1989 Deep ruby/purple with slightly more intensity to its hue than the 1990, this full-
95 bodied wine still has a very roasted character intermixed with sweet chocolate
Raisinets-like flavors. Sweet, overripe cherries also make an appearance in this
thick, juicy, yet structured, rather powerful Le Tertre Rôteboeuf that is aging more
slowly than its more renowned sibling, the 1990. This is a classic wine that should
continue to repay cellaring. Anticipated maturity: 2005–2020. Last tasted, 2/03.

1988 A sleeper vintage for proprietor Mitjavile's beloved Le Tertre-Roteboeuf, the 1988
92 has a deep plum/garnet color and a gorgeous nose of earth, underbrush, cherry
cough syrup, licorice, and caramel. It is full-bodied, very pure, ripe, with loads of
concentration, yet good definition and structure. No, it is not as dense as the 1989
nor as flamboyant and flashy as the 1990, but this is a classic Le Tertre Rôteboeuf
that should continue to drink well for at least another 10–15 years. Anticipated
maturity: now–2015. Last tasted, 12/02.

1986 This wine has lost some of its fat, opulent fleshiness, with the tannins showing a bit
89 more toughness than several years ago. The wine is fully mature, not likely to get
better, and probably best drunk up over the next 5–6 years. The color is showing
some amber at the edge, and the wine still has beautiful ripeness, richness, and a
very sweet, vanilla-infused, black cherry and berry character. The wine is medium
bodied, but the finish is just a bit shorter than it was several years ago. Anticipated
maturity: now–2006. Last tasted, 12/02.

1985 Almost Burgundian in its display of red currants, black cherries, fig, herb, and
90 flowers, this medium-bodied, very juicy, beautifully knit wine is pure charm and
seduction. The acidity is low, the tannin ripe and unobtrusive, and the wine fully
mature. Drink it over the next 5–6 years. Last tasted, 12/02.

1982 This was the first vintage of Le Tertre Rôteboeuf I tasted, and that was before pro-
87 prietor François Mitjavile began to use new oak casks and make strict selections.
Certainly the raw materials were among the finest he has ever had, but the wine
could use more grip and structure, which would have occurred if new oak had
been employed. The wine offers plenty of pleasure, with considerable quantities of
nearly overripe cherry fruit intermingled with scents of caramel, herbs, and earth.
Soft, supple, and fat, this is a wine to drink over the next 3–4 years. Last tasted,
9/95.

LA TOUR FIGEAC

Classification: Grand Cru Classé

Owner: Rettenmaier family

Address: 33330 St.-Emilion

Mailing address: BP 007, 33330 St.-Emilion

Telephone: 05 57 51 77 62; Telefax: 05 57 25 36 92

E-mail: latourfigeac@aol.com

Website: www.latourfigeac.com

Visits: By appointment only

Contact: Otto Rettenmaier

VINEYARDS

Surface area: 36 acres

Grape varietals: 60% Merlot, 40% Cabernet Franc

Average age of vines: 30 years

Density of plantation: 6,000–7,000 vines per hectare

Average yields: 42 hectoliters per hectare

Elevage: Three to four week fermentation and maceration in stainless-steel and wooden vats with frequent *pigéages* and micro-oxygenation. Malolactics and 15 months aging on lees (with regular stirring and micro-oxygenation) in oak barrels with 60–70% new oak. Light fining and/or filtration, if any.

WINES PRODUCED

Château La Tour Figeac: 40,000 bottles

L'Esquisse de La Tour Figeac: 10,000 bottles

Plateau of maturity: Within 4–14 years of the vintage

GENERAL APPRECIATION

Since 1998, this has been an estate to follow . . . high-quality wines that still sell for a song. Consumers take notice!

This property, like so many St.-Emilion estates with the name Figeac, was once part of the huge domain of Figeac until it was partitioned in 1879. The vineyard, which is easy to spot because of the tower that sits in the middle of the vineyards (from which the château takes part of its name), is bordered on one side by Cheval Blanc and on the south by Figeac. To the west is the appellation of Pomerol.

The winemaking has been very good at La Tour-Figeac, although vintages in the mid- and late 1980s were off form. Since the property was acquired by the Rettenmaier family in 1994, quality has increased dramatically, as evidenced by the 2000 and 2001—the best wines ever made at this estate. Not surprisingly, Stéphane Derenoncourt was brought here several years ago.

IMPORTANT VINTAGES

2001
88–90 The 2001 exhibits an opaque purple color as well as excellent, sweet, pure blackberry and cassis aromas with hints of smoke and licorice. Textured, ripe, and medium to full-bodied, with an admirable mid-palate presence as well as length, it should be drinkable young, but last for 12 years. Last tasted, 1/03.

2000
91 An enormously appealing, sexy wine, the 2000 exhibits an opaque ruby/purple color along with serious levels of concentrated cranberry, black cherry, and black currant fruit mixed with smoked herbs, licorice, and minerals. Once past the gorgeous perfume, this medium- to full-bodied, ripe wine is textured, expansive, and a total hedonistic as well as intellectual turn-on! Anticipated maturity: now–2015. Last tasted, 1/03.

1999
86 A pleasant, straightforward effort with smoky, roasted herb and currant fruit, this medium-bodied St.-Emilion has good purity and sweet fruit, but only moderate depth and staying power. Drink it over the next 2–3 years. Last tasted, 3/01.

1998
90 This is the finest La Tour-Figeac between 1982 and 2000. Dark ruby/purple–colored with a sensational bouquet of smoke-infused blackberries, jammy cherries, and coffee, this thick, unctuously textured, rich, full-bodied, structured, moderately tannic wine is already gorgeous to drink. A sleeper of the vintage. Anticipated maturity: now–2015. Last tasted, 3/02.

1996   A dark plum/ruby color is accompanied by dusty, earthy, sweet cherry, currant,
85   smoke, and vanilla scents. A medium-bodied wine with moderate levels of tannin,
       admirable extract, and a linear personality, this 1996 possesses fine raw materials
       and good ripeness, but may turn out to be angular and austere given the elevated
       tannin level. Anticipated maturity: now–2012. Last tasted, 3/02.

1995   In contrast to the more spartan 1996, the 1995 is a sexy, deep ruby–colored wine
87   with gobs of herb-tinged, spicy, berry fruit in the nose and flavors. Medium bodied,
       soft, friendly, and juicy, this is an appealing style of St.-Emilion for consuming
       over the next 3–4 years. A sleeper. Last tasted, 3/01.

LA TOUR DU PIN FIGEAC

Classification: Grand Cru Classé

Owner: Jean-Michel Moueix

Address: 33330 St.-Emilion

Telephone: 05 57 51 52 58; Telefax: 05 57 51 52 87

Visits: By appointment only

Contact: Francis Lafon (Telephone: 05 57 25 53 54)

VINEYARDS

Surface area: 19.8 acres

Grape varietals: 70% Merlot, 30% Cabernet Franc

Average age of vines: 30 years

Density of plantation: 5,500 vines per hectare

Average yields: 50 hectoliters per hectare

Elevage: Fermentation and maceration for 14–21 days in stainless-steel vats. Aged for
12–15 months in oak barrels (renewed by a third at each vintage). Fined with egg whites,
filtered if necessary.

WINES PRODUCED

Château La Tour du Pin Figeac: 45,000 bottles

No second wine is produced.

Plateau of maturity: Within 3–12 years of the vintage

GENERAL APPRECIATION

This is a well-situated property that produces competent but largely uninspiring wines.

La Tour du Pin Figeac is situated on a sandy, clay, gravelly soil base on the Pomerol
border between Cheval Blanc and La Tour-Figeac.

The wine of La Tour du Pin Figeac is made in a straightforward, fleshy, fruity style,
with good body, and an aging potential of 6–12 years. Few vintages of this wine will improve beyond their 12th birthday.

IMPORTANT VINTAGES

1995
87
Another sexy, up-front, flattering wine, the 1995 La Tour du Pin Figeac is not complex, but it possesses low acidity, gobs of ripe fruit, and medium body presented in a delicious, soft, enchanting style. Drink it over the next 3–4 years. Last tasted, 11/97.

1994
87
Similar to the 1993, with more raspberry, kirsch-like fruit, this medium-bodied, luscious, fruity, soft, low-acid wine has managed to avoid this vintage's high tannin and astringency. Drink it over the next 2–3 years. Last tasted, 1/97.

1990
88
The seductive, impressive, black/ruby-colored 1990 is another exhilarating St.-Emilion. Densely colored, this wine's huge bouquet of jammy fruits (plums and raspberries), meaty, full-bodied texture, and lavish quantities of fruit all combine to make this an impressive effort. Anticipated maturity: now–2008. Last tasted, 11/01.

1989
87
The 1989 is a concentrated, powerful, full-bodied wine, with gobs of extract and a penetrating bouquet of black fruits, new oak, and subtle herbs. A powerhouse of a wine, it is well balanced, with decent acidity for the vintage and a super finish. Anticipated maturity: now. Last tasted, 11/01.

1988
86
The 1988 from this estate is a worthy competitor with the 1989, with excellent extract, more elegance but less power, and a rich, toasty, plummy bouquet intertwined with scents of licorice, toast, and spring flowers. Full-bodied and intense for a 1988, it should be at its best between now and 2004. Last tasted, 11/01.

TROPLONG MONDOT

Classification: Grand Cru Classé

Owner: Christine Valette

Address: 33330 St.-Emilion

Telephone: 05 57 55 32 05; Telefax: 05 57 55 32 07

E-mail: chateautroplongmondot@wanadoo.fr

Visits: By appointment only Monday to Friday,
8 A.M.–noon and 2–6 P.M.

VINEYARDS

Surface area: 69.2 acres

Grape varietals: 80% Merlot, 10% Cabernet Franc, 10% Cabernet Sauvignon

Average age of vines: 50 years

Density of plantation: 5,600 and 6,600 vines per hectare

Average yields: 35 hectoliters per hectare

Elevage: Four to five week fermentation and maceration in temperature-controlled stainless-steel tanks of small capacity. Malolactics and 12–24 months aging, depending upon the vintage, in new oak barrels. Fining and filtration are not systematic.

WINES PRODUCED

Château Troplong Mondot: 90,000 bottles

Mondot: 30,000 bottles

Plateau of maturity: Within 5–18 years of the vintage

GENERAL APPRECIATION

Judging by its regular track record irrespective of vintage conditions since the mid-1980s, Troplong Mondot should have been upgraded to first-growth status in the 1996 reclassification of St.-Emilions. A brilliantly made wine.

This lovely château, with a magnificent view overlooking the town and vineyards of St.-Emilion, sits on a slope facing the Côte de Pavie. There are numerous old vines. Since the mid-1980s, when Michel Rolland was brought in as the oenologist and Christine Valette began assuming more control, the quality of the vintages has soared. There is an extended maceration in stainless-steel vats and aging of the wine for at least 12–24 months in oak casks, of which 70% are new. The wine is fined but rarely filtered. Flexibility and the avoidance of inflexible rules are the operative factors at Troplong.

I should also note that the introduction of a secondary label has resulted in weaker vats being relegated to that wine, which has only served to strengthen the wine that appears under the label Troplong Mondot.

Most of them have passed away, but St.-Emilion and Pomerol have had their share of famous, even legendary, female proprietors. Madame Fournier at Château Canon, the Robin sisters at Le Gay and Lafleur, Madame Ducasse at L'Evangile, and Madame Loubat of Pétrus. Now the appellation boasts Christine Valette, whose extraordinary commitment to quality is especially evident in the great wines produced at Troplong Mondot.

IMPORTANT VINTAGES

2001 This opaque ruby/purple–colored St.-Emilion exhibits gorgeously pure black
90–92 fruits intertwined with licorice, minerals, violets, and toasty new oak. Extremely concentrated for the vintage, this medium-bodied, pure, perfumed Troplong Mondot has turned out brilliantly. The tannin, acidity, and wood are all handsomely integrated into what is undeniably one of the vintage's most successful wines. Anticipated maturity: 2008–2018. Last tasted, 1/03.

2000 The finest wine from Troplong Mondot since the staggeringly great 1990, the 2000
96 is a blockbuster effort in this great vintage. Its saturated purple color is followed by aromas of ink, crème de cassis, graphite, and toasty oak. Full-bodied and powerful with excellent balance, this is a wine of extraordinary richness and massiveness, yet surreal freshness as well as vibrancy. The finish lasts for more than 45 seconds and nearly conceals some hefty tannins. With fabulous definition, richness, and intensity, this is a compelling 2000. Anticipated maturity: 2009–2026. Last tasted, 1/03.

1999 Elegant vanilla, black cherry, and smoky notes emerge from this textured,
89 medium-bodied 1999. It has a dense ruby/purple color as well as an enormous, concentrated, finesse-styled personality. Not a blockbuster, it is a beautifully symmetrical, pure, ripe, well-balanced Troplong Mondot that will age gracefully for 14–15 years. Last tasted, 3/02.

1998 A fabulous effort and a sleeper of the vintage, which may turn out to be the finest
93 Troplong Mondot since the 1990, the black/purple-colored 1998 exhibits floral, blueberry, blackberry, licorice, vanilla, and truffle-like aromas (or is it charcoal/graphite?). Dense, full-bodied, and pure, yet extremely fresh and elegant, this beautifully focused wine will be at its finest between 2005 and 2025. Last tasted, 3/02.

1997   The gorgeously elegant, concentrated 1997 exhibits a dark ruby/purple color and
89   a beautifully knit, blackberry and cherry-scented nose with toasty oak in the background. Not a massive effort, it offers beautifully supple fruit flavors, an attractive
fragrance, a ripe, sweet mid-palate, and soft tannin. Drink this seductive, lush
Troplong Mondot over the next 5–6 years. Last tasted, 11/02.

1996   I am still not sure which direction this wine is ultimately going to take. Its dense
88+?   ruby/purple color with notes of licorice, toasty new oak, and black currant and
berry fruit are certainly promising. In the mouth it is medium bodied, but still the
tannin levels are very high and the tannin a bit sharp/astringent. The wine has lost
some of its austerity, but still needs to flesh out to merit a score close to 90. Patience is still a prerequisite here, but will it ever become totally harmonious? Anticipated maturity: 2006–2018. Last tasted, 11/02.

1995   Totally shut down and enclosed, with an impressively saturated purple/black color
92   and a promising but tightly strung nose of mineral, vanilla, espresso, black cherry,
and currant, this wine has beautiful purity, medium to full body, relatively high but
sweet tannin, and a long 30–35 second finish. The wine is very firm but impressive
as well as promising. Patience please! Anticipated maturity: 2007–2020. Last
tasted, 11/02.

1994   A beautiful wine, with notes of tapenade, licorice, spice box, black currants, and
90   toasty oak, this medium-bodied wine has shed a lot of its tannin and exhibits excellent
purity, a real sweetness on the attack, a bit of firmness on the back end, but impressive
concentration and length overall. Anticipated maturity: now–2016. Last tasted, 10/01

1993   This dark ruby–colored wine with a purple center exhibits a spicy, toasty, plum,
87+   black cherry, and cassis nose, and medium-bodied, tannic flavors, with good
sweetness, purity, and ripeness. The wine is a backward 1993 that will require 2–4
years of cellaring; it will keep for a dozen or more years. Anticipated maturity:
now–2012. Last tasted, 1/97.

1992   Troplong Mondot's 1992 blows away much of the other St.-Emilion competition
89   and embarrasses many of the premier grand cru classés. The wine boasts a saturated black/purple color and a huge, sweet, ripe nose of black currant fruit intermingled with scents of toasty new oak, herbs, and licorice. It is amazingly
concentrated for the vintage, with superb denseness and ripeness of fruit, moderate tannin, and a long, pure, beautifully proportioned finish. It will benefit from
2–3 years of cellaring and last for 15 years. Once it has more bottle age, it may
merit an outstanding score. Last tasted, 11/94.

1990   An absolutely awesome Troplong Mondot that flirts with perfection, this dense
99   purple–colored wine has a thrilling bouquet of crème de cassis, espresso roast,
licorice, white flowers, vanilla, and blackberries. Full-bodied, gorgeously concentrated, yet light on its feet, this extravagantly rich, luxuriously fruited wine is just
beginning to reach its plateau of maturity. A profound tour de force in winemaking! Anticipated maturity: now–2020. Last tasted, 1/03.

1989   A very youthful wine that probably will never hit the heights of the 1990 (but how
95+   many wines do?), this dense ruby/purple–colored wine has a very pure nose of
roasted espresso, black cherry jam, blackberry, mineral, and even a hint of blueberry. Some smoke and high-quality toasty new oak are there, but now that seems
to be fading into the background. Quite full-bodied, powerful, and concentrated,
yet at the same time elegant, this wine still seems very young and unevolved. Anticipated maturity: 2007–2025. Last tasted, 11/02.

1988   A beauty that has reached full maturity, this elegant wine has notes of tapenade,
90   plums, black cherries, vanilla, and smoke, followed by medium-bodied, sweet, expansive flavors that show beautifully integrated tannin and acidity. Anticipated
maturity: now–2010. Last tasted, 11/02.

1986   Starting to become a bit more attenuated in the finish, but still very pleasingly per-
87   fumed, with notes of dusty earth, herbs, black cherries, tobacco, and licorice, this
        medium-bodied wine is behaving more like a Médoc than a typical St.-Emilion.
        Anticipated maturity: now–2005. Last tasted, 11/02.

1985   Fully mature, this dark garnet–colored wine shows plenty of amber at the edge.
87   The nose exhibits moderately intense black currant intermixed with cedar, spice
        box, and some Provençal herb notes. The wine is soft, medium-bodied, and very
        seductive, but needs to be drunk up. Anticipated maturity: now–2005. Last tasted,
        11/02.

1982   This is a soft, simple, one-dimensional wine that was made before proprietor
79   Christine Valette began to take Troplong Mondot to the heights of the Bordeaux hi-
        erarchy. The soft, herbal, pleasant 1982 is beginning to lose some of its fruit, with
        the acidity, tannin, and alcohol starting to dominate. Drink it up. Last tasted, 9/95.

ANCIENT VINTAGES

This château made relatively deplorable wines throughout the 1960s, 1970s, and early
1980s. Even the 1982 (79 points; last tasted 9/95) is somewhat of a disappointment.
However, the resurrection of Troplong Mondot began under Christine Valette with the
1985 and hit full gear with the trilogy of 1988, 1989, and 1990.

TROTTE VIEILLE

Classification: Premier Grand Cru Classé B

Owner: Philippe Castéja

Address: 33330 St.-Emilion

Mailing address: c/o Domaines Borie-Manoux, 86,
cours Balguerie-Stuttenberg, 33082 Bordeaux Cedex

Telephone: 05 56 00 00 70; Telefax: 05 57 87 48 61

E-mail: domainesboriemanoux@dial.oleane.com

Visits: By appointment only Monday to Friday,
9 A.M.–noon and 2–5 P.M.

Contact: Borie-Manoux

VINEYARDS

Surface area: 24.7 acres

Grape varietals: 50% Merlot, 45% Cabernet Franc, 5% Cabernet Sauvignon

Average age of vines: 45 years

Density of plantation: 5,000 vines per hectare

Average yields: 30 hectoliters per hectare

Elevage: Twenty-one day fermentation and maceration in temperature-controlled
concrete vats. Malolactics and 12–18 months aging in barrels with 98% new oak.
Fining, no filtration.

WINES PRODUCED

Château Trotte Vieille: 30,000 bottles

La Vieille Dame de Trotte Vieille: Variable (first vintage 2000)

Plateau of maturity: Within 5–15 years of the vintage

GENERAL APPRECIATION

Under the helmsmanship of Philippe Castéja, this wine has improved steadily from 1995 onward. It now exhibits more flesh and stuffing, while showing a fine complexity that was indeed lacking in previous vintages. However, because it emerges from a pure limestone *terroir*, do not ever expect Trotte Vieille to resemble the luxuriously rich New Wave St.-Emilions. It is a wine of finesse and delicacy, showing a generous minerality.

One of the celebrated premier grands cru classés of St.-Emilion, Trotte Vieille is located east of St.-Emilion on a relatively isolated hill of primarily limestone soil. Since 1949 it has been the property of Borie-Manoux, the well-known firm of Bordeaux *négociants*. This firm also owns Batailley, the fifth-growth Pauillac, and Domaine de l'Eglise, an up-and-coming Pomerol, as well as a bevy of lesser-known Bordeaux châteaux. Somewhat of a rarity, Trotte Vieille is a single vineyard surrounded by stone walls.

Trotte Vieille is a wine with which I have had many disappointing experiences. Until the mid-1980s, the property produced wines that were among the most mediocre of St.-Emilion. Prior to 1985 Trotte Vieille too frequently lacked concentration and character and was often disturbingly light and dull; in some vintages it was also poorly vinified.

The dedication of Philippe Castéja is largely responsible for the remarkable turnaround in the quality of this estate's wines. The stricter selection process, the use of more new oak, and the decisions to harvest later and extend the maceration has resulted in a relatively profound wine that now appears capable of challenging the best of the appellation.

IMPORTANT VINTAGES

2001
88–91
Dense ruby, even inky purple–colored, this sweet, layered, dense wine looks to be every bit as good as the 2000, and probably finer. The proprietor's decision to pick later and to introduce a second label (starting with the 2000) has resulted in a more concentrated, impressively deep wine that should age handsomely. Anticipated maturity: 2008–2018. Last tasted, 1/03.

2000
89+
Somewhat closed and monolithic, this deep plum/ruby/purple–colored wine has notes of blackberry, chocolate, espresso, and vanilla in the tight but emerging aromatics. In the mouth it is medium bodied, elegant, very pure, but may not quite have the depth, sweetness, and overall volume of the 2001. Anticipated maturity: 2008–2019. Last tasted, 1/03.

1999
89
This well-made St.-Emilion offers up aromas of melted chocolate, toasty new oak, black cherries, licorice, and strawberries. Medium bodied, pure, well balanced, and finely etched, it possesses sweet tannin, adequate acidity, and a moderately long finish. One to two years of cellaring will be beneficial. Anticipated maturity: 2004–2016. Last tasted, 3/02.

1998 A wine of finesse and elegance, without the weight and power of some of the newer,
86   more fashionable St.-Emilions, Trotte Vieille's 1998 exhibits a dark ruby color as
      well as aromas of sweet blackberry and cherry fruit with smoky oak and mineral
      notes in the background. Round and elegant, it is a wine of finesse rather than
      power. Drink it over the next 10–12 years. Last tasted, 3/02.

1997 Abundant quantities of toasty oak give this wine an international style. In the
86   mouth, supple, sweet, plum/cherry fruit mixed with herbs, earth, and smoke are
      both user-friendly and delicious. While not big, dense, or ageworthy, it is a pleas-
      ant, ripe, fruity, well-balanced offering for drinking over the next 4–5 years. Last
      tasted, 1/02.

1996 The 1996 Trotte Vieille appears to be a step up for this St.-Emilion premier grand
87   cru. Soft and elegant, it possesses nicely integrated smoky new oak along with
      blackberry and cherry fruit. It is medium bodied, with excellent purity and a
      nicely textured, stylish finish. This will be a 1996 to enjoy at an early age. Antici-
      pated maturity: now–2012. Last tasted, 1/02.

1995 A very perplexing wine, the 1995 has a dark ruby color and rather closed, muted
87?   aromatics consisting of earth, wood, mushroom, and some vaguely sweet red cur-
      rant and plum-like fruit. In the mouth it is tannic and hard, with pronounced min-
      erality and an austere, very astringent finish. Perhaps I am giving the wine the
      benefit of the doubt, but this looks to be a wine that needs considerable bottle age.
      Anticipated maturity: 2008–2016. Last tasted, 3/01.

1994 Dark ruby–colored, with a gentle, cedary, herb-infused, cherry-scented bouquet,
85   this soft, medium-bodied wine gives conflicting signals with its low acidity and
      high tannin. The attack is soft, but then the tannin kicks in, resulting in an atten-
      uated, short finish. Anticipated maturity: now–2007. Last tasted, 1/97.

1990 The 1990 is at least very good. A backward, oaky, tannic wine in need of some bot-
88   tle age, this full-bodied St.-Emilion exhibits plenty of power and guts. Anticipated
      maturity: now–2005. Last tasted, 1/93.

1989 The 1989 is an immensely impressive wine, exhibiting an opaque black color and
90   a sensational bouquet of licorice, chocolate, and superripe plums. In the mouth,
      the wine displays immense size, enormous concentration, a tremendous level of
      tannins, and an intense, alcoholic, long, opulent finish. Given the size of this wine,
      the acidity seems sound, and the fact that it is now aged in 100% new oak suggests
      that the wine will have the proper marriage of toasty oak for balancing out its awe-
      somely concentrated fruit flavors. The 1989 could well turn out to be the finest
      Trotte Vieille made in the last three or four decades. Anticipated maturity: now–
      2015. Last tasted, 4/91.

ANCIENT VINTAGES

There is nothing to get excited about in the 1960s, 1970s, and most of the 1980s at
Trotte Vieille. Most of my scores run between the low 60s to mid-70s, with an occasional mid-80 point score for vintages like 1988, 1986, and 1985.

VALANDRAUD

Classification: Grand Cru

Owner: Ets Thunevin

Address: 33330 St.-Emilion

Mailing address: c/o Ets Thunevin, 6 rue Guadet, 33330 St.-Emilion

Telephone: 05 57 55 09 13; Telefax: 05 57 55 09 12

E-mail: thunevin@thunevin.com

Website: www.thunevin.com

No visits

VINEYARDS

Surface area: 11.1 acres

Grape varietals: 70% Merlot, 30% Cabernet Franc

Average age of vines: 30 years

Density of plantation: 6,000 vines per hectare

Average yields: 35 hectoliters per hectare

Elevage: Malolactics and 18–20 months aging in new oak barrels. No fining, no filtration.

WINES PRODUCED

Château de Valandraud: 11,000 bottles

Virginie de Valandraud: 10,000 bottles

Plateau of maturity: Within 5–25 years of the vintage

GENERAL APPRECIATION

The creation of Jean-Luc Thunevin, the de facto leader of the St.-Emilion vin de garage movement, Valandraud is unquestionably Bordeaux's finest success story to date. Never before has a Bordeaux—or any other wine for that matter—with so short a track record enjoyed such huge commercial success and such dizzyingly high prices. The craze for Valandraud is such that it fetches prices equal, if not superior, to those of the first growths.

The obsessive/compulsive, highly talented proprietor, Jean-Luc Thunevin, has the Cheshire cat's grin these days given the publicity and prices his unfined, unfiltered, superrich Valandraud is fetching. Along with his wife, Murielle, Thunevin has established a microscopic estate from selected parcels in St.-Emilion. Having had experience with running wine shops and restaurants in St.-Emilion, and also being involved in the wine trade, could not have hurt Thunevin in respect to his philosophy for producing great wine.

Obviously the jury is still out as to how well Valandraud ages, but the wine is enormously rich, concentrated, and beautifully well delineated. It has been extraordinary, even in such difficult vintages as 1994, 1993, and 1992. More than any other St.-Emilion property, Valandraud has become the micro-treasure sought by billionaire wine collectors throughout the world. While Thunevin has no shortage of critics (largely the jealous aristocracy of Bordeaux), his influence continues to expand. He is one of the most sought-after consultants, and his dedication and commitment to excellence, as well as his tremendous palate (infinitely helped by his equally talented wife), has resurrected many obscure wines in St.-Emilion and its satellites to prime-time players in the minds of quality-minded consumers.

Along with Michel Rolland, Thunevin has inspired an entirely new generation of young vignerons to produce higher and higher quality wines. For this, all of Bordeaux has benefited enormously.

IMPORTANT VINTAGES

2001
93–95+ Jean-Luc Thunevin and his wife Murielle think 2001 might be superior to 2000 for them. They may well be right, as this is certainly one of the most impressive wines of the vintage. Inky blue/purple in color, with an extraordinary nose of espresso roast, chocolate, ripe blackberries, and cassis, this is a full-bodied, very dense, concentrated wine that looks like it is going to be one of the great Valandrauds made since this wine burst onto the scene. In short, this is a very serious, impressive effort from one of Bordeaux's qualitative revolutionaries. Anticipated maturity: 2008–2020. Last tasted, 1/03. P.S.: Readers should also look for the kosher cuvée of Valandraud in 2001, which I rated 91–92, qualifying it as the finest kosher wine I have ever tasted!

2000
93 Jean-Luc Thunevin tends to be very humble when he talks about his 2000, as if there were something wrong with it. Well, it is a spectacular wine, and having tasted it three times from bottle, I am in love with it. Dense purple–colored, with a glorious nose of espresso, cocoa, chocolate, plum, black currant, and cherry, offering a true smorgasbord of heavenly delights, this medium- to full-bodied wine still shows some relatively firm tannin, but the low acidity, layered, multi-textured mouth-feel, and tremendous purity are hallmarks of the Thunevin wine-making style. However, this might be one Valandraud that actually needs 3–5 years of cellaring prior to drinking. Anticipated maturity: 2008–2019. Last tasted, 1/03.

1999
90 Sweet coffee, mocha, leather, and black cherry and currant flavors dominate the pure, well-delineated, opulently textured, hedonistic 1999 Valandraud. It possesses definition, length, and a singular personality. Anticipated maturity: now–2015. Last tasted, 3/02.

1998
93 A classic St.-Emilion, the 1998 exhibits a dark plum/purple color as well as an elegant nose of mocha, coffee, cherries, blackberries, and chocolate. It has turned out to be more finesse-styled and less exotic than past vintages. This medium- to full-bodied, beautifully concentrated wine reveals chocolate overtones in the aromas and flavors. With exceptional purity, balance, and length, it should turn out to be one of the most elegant Valandrauds yet produced. Anticipated maturity: now–2020. Last tasted, 3/02.

1997
89 This wine may deserve an outstanding rating. One of the finest 1997s, it exhibits a dense ruby/purple color in addition to moderately intense aromas of spice box, licorice, plums, cherries, and toasty oak. Lush, full-bodied, and round, with excellent fruit richness, low acidity, and sweet tannin, it can be drunk now as well as over the next seven years. Last tasted, 3/02.

1996
91 This 1996 has firmed up significantly since bottling. The viscous wine displays the telltale thickness of color (saturated dark ruby/plum/purple). The exotic bouquet is just beginning to form, offering up notes of iodine, roasted coffee, jammy black fruits, and toast. In the mouth, it is medium to full-bodied, with sweet tannin, ter-

rific texture, and outstanding purity and length. Anticipated maturity: now–2018. Last tasted, 1/02.

1995
95
This splendid Valandraud ranks with the finest wines proprietor Jean-Luc Thuncvin has produced. The wine exhibits an opaque purple color and a sensational nose of roasted herbs, black fruits (cherries, currants, and blackberries), and high-class toasty oak (the latter component is more of a nuance than a dominant characteristic). Very concentrated, with layers of fruit, glycerin, and extract, yet seamlessly constructed, this wine contains the stuff of greatness and appears to be the finest Valandraud yet produced. The finish lasts for more than 30 seconds. The wine's high tannin is barely noticeable because of the ripeness and richness of fruit. Anticipated maturity: now–2020. Last tasted, 3/02.

1994
92+
An opaque purple color and a closed set of aromatics (sweet black currant, woodsy, smoky aromas emerge with airing) are revealed in this blockbuster 1994. The wine possesses fabulous purity, great flavor intensity, a sweet inner core of fruit on the mid-palate, and a full-bodied, layered, viscous finish. It is unquestionably one of the finest wines of the vintage. Anticipated maturity: now–2020. Last tasted, 3/02.

1993
93
This is undoubtedly one of the most concentrated wines of the vintage. The color is an opaque purple, and the wine exhibits fabulously sweet, ripe, black cherry and cassis fruit nicely infused with subtle oak and a touch of minerals and truffles. Full-bodied, with exceptional density and no hard edges, the unbelievably concentrated 1993 Valandraud is a tour de force, in a vintage that does not seem capable of producing wines such as this. Give it another 3–4 years of cellaring, and drink it over the following 15–20. Last tasted, 1/97.

1992
88
This tiny estate, dedicated to becoming the "Le Pin of St.-Emilion," has turned out a strong effort in 1992. The Valandraud wines, all handcrafted and bottled unfiltered, will be difficult to find, but given what they have produced in 1992 and 1993, one can imagine what heights Valandraud might achieve in Bordeaux's next exceptional vintage. The 1992 reveals a saturated, opaque, dark ruby/purple color and a rich nose of sweet oak backed by gobs of jammy black currants and cherries. The wine possesses excellent richness, medium to full body, surprising opulence and chewiness (a rarity in the 1992 vintage), and a long, lusty, low-acid, concentrated finish. It should drink well for 7–10 years. Last tasted, 11/94.

VILLEMAURINE

Classification: Grand Cru Classé

Owner: Grands Vins Robert Giraud SA

Address: 23 Villamaurine Sud, 33330 St.-Emilion

Mailing address: Grands Vins Robert Giraud SA, Domaine de Loiseau, BP 31, 33240 Saint-André-de-Cubzac

Telephone: 05 57 43 01 44; Telefax: 05 57 43 08 75

E-mail: commercial@robertgiraud.com

Website: www.robertgiraud.com

Visits: By appointment

Contact: Jean-Luc Duwa (Telephone: 05 57 74 46 44; Telefax: 05 57 74 47 30)

VINEYARDS

Surface area: 17.2 acres

Grape varietals: 85% Merlot, 10% Cabernet Sauvignon, 5% Cabernet Franc

Average age of vines: 30 years

Density of plantation: 6,000 vines per hectare

Average yields: 45 hectoliters per hectare

Elevage: Three to four week fermentation and maceration in temperature-controlled stainless-steel tanks. Seventeen months aging in barrels with 50% new oak. Fining, no filtration.

WINES PRODUCED

Château Villemaurine: 40,000 bottles

No second wine is produced.

Plateau of maturity: Within 3–10 years of the vintage

GENERAL APPRECIATION

Year after year, this estate produces wines that are hard, stern, tannic, and relatively devoid of fruit and charm.

Villemaurine is one of St.-Emilion's most interesting vineyards. The property gets its name from an 8th-century army of invading Moors who supposedly set up camp on this site, which was called Ville Maure ("the City of Moors") by the French. In addition, Villemaurine has enormous underground cellars that merit considerable tourist interest. As for the wine, it is considerably less interesting. Despite increasing promotional efforts by the proprietor, Robert Giraud—also a major *négociant*—claiming that Villemaurine's quality is improving, I have found the wines to lack richness and concentration, to be rather diffuse, hard, and lean, and to have little character.

IMPORTANT VINTAGES

Nothing has ever been rated 85 points or higher, so there are no tasting notes to follow. Nevertheless, I have tasted every vintage from Villemaurine since 1982.

OTHER ST.-EMILION ESTATES

ANDRÉAS

Classification: Grand Cru

Owner: Vignobles Rocher Cap de Rive SA

Address: 33330 St.-Emilion

Mailing address: c/o Château Rocher-Bellevue, BP 89, 33350 Saint-Magne-de-Castillon

Telephone: 05 57 40 08 88; Telefax: 05 57 40 19 93

No visits

VINEYARDS

Surface area: 3.7 acres

Grape varietals: 100% Merlot

Average age of vines: 40 years

Density of plantation: 5,500 vines per hectare

Average yields: 30 hectoliters per hectare

Elevage: Prolonged fermentation and maceration in concrete vats. Aging in new oak barrels. No fining, no filtration.

WINES PRODUCED

Andréas: 4,500 bottles

No second wine is produced.

Plateau of maturity: Within 5–12 years of the vintage

GENERAL APPRECIATION

A wine produced under the consultation of Jean-Luc Thunevin (from 1998–2001), Andréas is a solidly made effort, but it does not quite attain the level of its peers that have followed the garage wine movement. However, it is fine for uncritical quaffing.

IMPORTANT VINTAGES

2001 A straightforward, elegant, earthy wine with medium body and good ripeness, but
86–87 not a lot of personality or complexity. It will merit drinking during its first 7–8 years of life. Last tasted, 1/03.

2000 Deep ruby/purple with a sweet black cherry/currant nose intermixed with spice,
87 chocolate, and loamy, earthy notes, a hint of espresso also makes an appearance in this medium-bodied, very jammy, modern-style St.-Emilion that is seamless and ideal for drinking over the next 7–8 years. Last tasted, 1/03.

1999 Somewhat austere, lean, and a bit sharp and underwhelming, this straightforward,
84 dark ruby–colored wine is competent but unexciting. Drink it over the next 5–6 years. Last tasted, 3/02.

1998 Abundant quantities of creamy oak, smoke, espresso, and black fruits emerge
86 from this dark ruby–colored, tannic 1998. It possesses power and guts, but appears slightly disjointed. Drink it over the next 3–4 years. Last tasted, 3/02.

L'ARCHANGE

Classification: Grand Cru

Owner: Jeanine and André Chatonnet

Address: 33330 St.-Emilion

Mailing address: 33500 Néac

Telephone: 05 57 51 31 31; Telefax: 05 57 25 08 93

Visits: By appointment Monday to Friday, 9 A.M.–noon and 2–6 P.M.

Contact: Pascal Chatonnet

VINEYARDS

Surface area: 2.8 acres

Grape varietals: 100% Merlot

Average age of vines: 20 years

Density of plantation: 5,500 vines per hectare

Average yields: 38 hectoliters per hectare

Elevage: Eighteen months aging in new oak barrels.

WINES PRODUCED

Château L'Archange: 5,400 bottles

No second wine is produced.

Plateau of maturity: Within 5–12 years of the vintage

GENERAL APPRECIATION

Produced by highly respected oenologist Pascal Chatonnet, L'Archange is a new entry into the St.-Emilion portfolio.

IMPORTANT VINTAGES

2001 **86–88**	A very elegant, potentially excellent wine, with good sweetness, medium body, and impressive purity, this mid-sized St.-Emilion shows notes of black raspberries, blueberries, and currants in a very floral, expressive bouquet. Anticipated maturity: 2005–2012. Last tasted, 1/03.
2000 **89**	This wine might turn out to be outstanding. It is the best wine proprietor Pascal Chatonnet has yet produced. A deep saturated purple color, with a sweet nose of black cherries and blackberries, it is sweet, rich, medium to full-bodied, with low acidity and plush, concentrated fruit flavors. The wine reveals some tannin, but it is largely obscured by the impressive ripeness and fleshy style. Anticipated maturity: 2005–2014. Last tasted, 1/03.

ARMENS

Classification: Grand Cru

Owner: Alexandre de Malet Roquefort

Address: 23, lieu-dit Bourret, 33330 Saint-Pey-d'Armens

Mailing address: BP 12, 33330 St.-Emilion

Telephone: 05 57 56 05 06; Telefax: 05 57 56 40 89

E-mail: info@chateau-armens.com

Website: www.chateau-armens.com

Visits: Monday to Friday, 10 A.M.–6 P.M.

Contact: Anne Chagneau

VINEYARDS

Surface area: 44.5 acres

Grape varietals: 65% Merlot, 25% Cabernet Sauvignon, 10% Cabernet Franc

Average age of vines: 35 years

Density of plantation: 5,500 vines per hectare

Average yields: 42 hectoliters per hectare

Elevage: Three to four week fermentation and maceration in temperature-controlled stainless-steel vats. Malolactics and 18 months aging in barrels with 80% new oak. Fining, no filtration.

WINES PRODUCED

Château d'Armens: 50,000 bottles

La Fleur du Château d' Armens: 50,000 bottles

Plateau of maturity: Within 3–10 years of the vintage

GENERAL APPRECIATION

A new wine by Alexandre de Malet, Armens appears close in style to its stablemate La Gaffelière. Though modern styled, it is not luxuriant, but soundly made and nicely fruity. A good value.

IMPORTANT VINTAGES

2001
87–88 This excellent St.-Emilion exhibits a dense ruby/purple color in addition to a sweet perfume of black fruits, earth, and toasty new oak. Medium bodied, with admirable concentration, honeyed fruit on the attack, and unobtrusive acidity as well as tannin, it is a well-made, pure effort to enjoy between 2004–2013. Last tasted, 1/03.

2000
88 The structured, muscular, backward 2000 offers notes of minerals, red cherries, earth, and wood. Medium bodied and well concentrated, it will be very good to excellent. Anticipated maturity: 2004–2016. Last tasted, 1/03.

AURELIUS

Classification: Grand Cru

Owner: Union des Producteurs de St.-Emilion

Address: Lieu-dit Haut-Gravet, 33300 St.-Emilion

Mailing address: BP 27, 33330 St.-Emilion

Telephone: 05 57 24 70 71; Telefax: 05 57 24 65 18

E-mail: contact@udpse.com

Website: uniondeproducteurs-saint-emilion.com

Visits: By appointment Monday to Saturday, 8 A.M.–noon and 2–6 P.M.

Contact: Reception desk

VINEYARDS

Surface area: 48.2 acres of selected vines

Grape varietals: 85% Merlot, 15% Cabernet Franc

Average age of vines: 30 years

Density of plantation: 5,500 vines per hectare

Average yields: 40 hectoliters per hectare

Elevage: Fermentation and maceration in temperature-controlled epoxy-lined concrete vats. Fourteen months aging in new oak barrels. Fining and filtration.

WINES PRODUCED

Aurelius: 60,000 bottles

GENERAL APPRECIATION

For a wine produced by a cooperative, Aurelius is well made and worthy of interest.

BÉARD

Classification: Grand Cru

Owner: Véronique Goudichaud and Corinne Dubos

Address: 33330 Saint-Laurent-des-Combes

Telephone: 05 57 24 72 96; Telefax: 05 57 24 61 88

Visits: By appointment only

VINEYARDS

Surface area: 19.8 acres

Grape varietals: 60% Merlot, 25% Cabernet Franc, 15% Cabernet Sauvignon

Average age of vines: 30 years

Density of plantation: 5,500 vines per hectare

Average yields: 50 hectoliters per hectare

Elevage: Fermentation and maceration for 15–21 days in concrete vats. Aged for 12–13 months, half the time in vats and the rest in oak barrels (one-third new oak). Fining and filtration.

WINES PRODUCED

Château Béard: 48,000 bottles

No second wine is produced.

Plateau of maturity: Within 3–8 years of the vintage

GENERAL APPRECIATION

Unfortunately, I have not had enough experience with Béard to form a strong opinion about their wines. However, the vintages I have tasted were competently made wines that had good, pure fruit, and a chunky, robust character. The domaine, which can trace its existence to 1858, is now run by the Goudichaud family. The vineyard is situated in the commune of Saint-Laurent-des-Combes, and the Goudichauds believe in hand harvesting, no herbicides, and a traditional vinification and *élevage*. While this estate is not in the top rung of St.-Emilions, it would appear to offer a reliable, reasonably priced alternative.

BELLEVUE MONDOTTE

Classification: Grand Cru

Owner: Gérard and Chantal Perse

Address: 33330 Saint-Laurent-des-Combes

Mailing address: c/o Château Pavie, 33330 St.-Emilion

Telephone: 05 57 55 43 43; Telefax: 05 57 24 63 99

E-mail: vignobles.perse@wanadoo.fr

Website: www.chateaupavie.com

No visits

VINEYARDS

Surface area: 4.9 acres

Grape varietals: 90% Merlot, 5% Cabernet Franc, 5% Cabernet Sauvignon

Average age of vines: 45 years

Density of plantation: 5,500 vines per hectare

Average yields: 15 hectoliters per hectare, as of 2001

Elevage: Four to five week fermentation and maceration in temperature-controlled stainless-steel tanks. Malolactics and 20–24 months aging in new oak barrels. No fining, no filtration.

WINES PRODUCED

Château Bellevue Mondotte: 4,000 bottles

No second wine is produced.

Plateau of maturity: Too soon to predict

GENERAL APPRECIATION

A new trophy wine produced by Gérard and Chantal Perse, the 2001 Bellevue Mondotte is extreme wine! This tiny *cuvée* will undoubtedly fetch an astronomical price given the cost of Perse's other St.-Emilions (Pavie, Pavie Decesse, and Monbousquet), but consumers who can afford it can rest assured that the quality will be there.

The 2001 Bellevue Mondotte emerges from a five-acre vineyard near Pavie Decesse and Pavie Macquin. The vines average 45 years in age, and the blend consists of 90% Merlot, 5% Cabernet Franc, and 5% Cabernet Sauvignon. This is extreme wine! Cropped at 15 hectoliters per hectare, given a seven-week maceration, and aged in 100% new oak, this tiny *cuvée* of 4,500 bottles will undoubtedly fetch an astronomical price given the cost of Perse's other St.-Emilions (Pavie, Pavie Decesse, La Clusière, and Monbousquet).

IMPORTANT VINTAGES

2001   There is no questioning the quality of the 2001 Bellevue Mondotte. Its dry, vintage
94–95+ Port-like, blackberry, licorice, and cassis aromas and flavors flow through the ol-
        factory senses and over the palate like an out of control Rabelesian smorgasbord.
        Extremely full-bodied, unctuously textured (unusual for this vintage), and im-

mensely long, it borders on being over the top and too heavy, but it is a thrilling tour de force in winemaking, if somewhat international in style. Nevertheless, there is not a more concentrated wine from the vintage. Let's see how it ages. Anticipated maturity: 2008–2018? Last tasted, 1/03.

BERGAT

Classification: Grand Cru Classé

Owner: Castéja family

Address: 33330 St.-Emilion

Mailing address: c/o Borie-Manoux, 86, cours Balguerie-Stuttenberg, 33082 Bordeaux

Telephone: 05 56 00 00 70; Telefax: 05 57 87 48 61

E-mail: domainesboriemanoux@dial.oleane.com

Visits: By appointment only

Contact: Borie-Manoux

VINEYARDS

Surface area: 8.4 acres

Grape varietals: 50% Merlot, 40% Cabernet Franc, 10% Cabernet Sauvignon

Average age of vines: 40 years

Density of plantation: 5,000 vines per hectare

Average yields: 36 hectoliters per hectare

Elevage: Twenty-one day fermentation and maceration in concrete vats. Twelve to eighteen months aging in barrels with 50% new oak. Fining, no filtration.

WINES PRODUCED

Château Bergat: 14,000 bottles

No second wine is produced.

Plateau of maturity: Within 3–10 years of the vintage

GENERAL APPRECIATION

The wines of Bergat, unlike their more prestigious stablemates of Trotte Vieille, have not improved much over the past years. Traditionally made, of average quality, they will do for uncritical quaffing.

BERNATEAU

Classification: Grand Cru

Owner: Régis Lavau

Address: 33330 Saint-Etienne-de-Lisse

Telephone: 05 57 40 18 19; Telefax: 05 57 40 27 31

Website: www.pageszoom.com/chateau.bernateau

Visits: By appointment only

Contact: Régis Lavau

VINEYARDS

Surface area: 34.6 acres

Grape varietals: 82% Merlot, 15% Cabernet Franc, 3% Cabernet Sauvignon

Average age of vines: 35+ years

Density of plantation: 5,500 vines per hectare

Average yields: 46 hectoliters per hectare

Elevage: Fermentation and maceration in temperature-controlled stainless-steel tanks. Sixteen months aging, with one-half of the yield in vats and the other half in barrels (50% new oak). Fining and filtration.

WINES PRODUCED

Château Bernateau: 85,000 bottles

No second wine is produced.

LA BIENFAISANCE

Classification: Grand Cru

Owner: SA Château La Bienfaisance

Administrator: Patrick Baseden

Address: 33330 Saint-Christophe-des-Bardes

Telephone: 05 57 24 65 83; Telefax: 05 57 24 78 26

E-mail: info@labienfaisance.com

Website: www.labienfaisance.com

Visits: By appointment only

Contact: Christine Peytour

VINEYARDS

Surface area: 28.4 acres

Grape varietals: 85% Merlot, 15% Cabernet Franc

Average age of vines: 28 years

Density of plantation: 5,500 vines per hectare

Average yields: 40 hectoliters per hectare

Elevage: Thirty day fermentation and maceration in temperature-controlled vats with four daily pumpings-over during the first four days of the process. After completion of malolactics in vats, 18 months aging in barrels on fine lees with 30% new oak. No rackings. Fining, no filtration.

WINES PRODUCED

Château La Bienfaisance: 35,000 bottles

Vieux Château Peymouton: 25,000 bottles

Plateau of maturity: Within 5–15 years of the vintage

GENERAL APPRECIATION

Even though this wine seems to benefit from a state-of-the-art vinification, most of the vintages have left me indifferent. However, bearing in mind that Sanctus, the special *cuvée* produced by the same owner, has improved spectacularly over the last two years (with the valuable advice of winemaking guru Stéphane Derénoncourt), I believe this estate will be worth watching.

LA BONNELLE

Classification: Grand Cru

Owner: Sulzer family

Address: La Bonnelle, 33330 Saint-Pey-d'Armens

Telephone: 05 57 47 15 12; Telefax: 05 57 47 16 83

Visits: By appointment only

Contact: Olivier Sulzer

VINEYARDS

Surface area: 31.4 acres

Grape varietals: 65% Merlot, 30% Cabernet Franc, 5% Cabernet Sauvignon

Average age of vines: 35 years

Density of plantation: 5,500 vines per hectare

Average yields: 55 hectoliters per hectare

Elevage: Twenty-five day fermentation and maceration in stainless-steel and concrete vats. Malolactics in barrel for 25% of the yield. Twelve months aging in barrels with 35% new oak. Fining in vats, no filtration.

WINES PRODUCED

Château La Bonnelle: 60,000 bottles

Château La Croix Bonnelle: 20,000 bottles

BOUQUEY

Classification: Grand Cru

Owner: Mahler-Besse SA

Address: 33330 Saint-Hippolyte

Mailing address: c/o Malher-Besse SA, 49, rue Camille Godard, 33000 Bordeaux

Telephone: 05 56 56 04 30; Telefax: 05 56 56 04 59

E-mail: contact@mahler-besse.com

Website: www.mahler-besse.com

Visits: By appointment only

Contact: Mahler-Besse SA (Telephone: 05 56 56 04 48)

VINEYARDS

Surface area: 12.4 acres

Grape varietals: 70% Merlot, 30% Cabernet Franc and Cabernet Sauvignon

Average age of vines: 20 years

Density of plantation: 6,600 vines per hectare

Average yields: 50 hectoliters per hectare

Elevage: Three to four week fermentation and maceration in temperature-controlled, cone-shaped, stainless-steel vats. Six months aging in barrels with 30% new oak. Fining, no filtration.

WINES PRODUCED

Château Bouquey: 6,000 bottles

No second wine is produced.

CADET-BON

Classification: Grand Cru Classé

Owner: SCEV du Château Cadet-Bon

Address: 1, Le Cadet, 33330 St.-Emilion

Telephone: 05 57 74 43 20; Telefax: 05 57 24 66 41

Visits: By appointment only Monday to Friday, 9 A.M.–5 P.M

Contact: Guy Richard

VINEYARDS

Surface area: 11.1 acres

Grape varietals: 70% Merlot, 30% Cabernet Franc

Average age of vines: 35 years

Density of plantation: 5,000 vines per hectare

Average yields: 45 hectoliters per hectare

Elevage: Fermentation and maceration in temperature-controlled stainless-steel tanks of small capacity so as to vinify separately the different parcels and grape varieties. Twelve months aging in barrels with 25% new oak. Fining, no filtration.

WINES PRODUCED

Château Cadet-Bon: 23,000 bottles

No second wine is produced.

Plateau of maturity: Within 5–10 years of the vintage

GENERAL APPRECIATION

Cadet-Bon stands as an "ugly duckling" amidst its peers, most of which have improved spectacularly over recent vintages.

CANTENAC

Classification: Grand Cru

Owner: Nicole Roskam-Brunot

Address: Cantenac, 33330 St.-Emilion

Telephone: 05 57 51 35 22; Telefax: 05 57 25 19 15

E-mail: roskam@club.internet.fr

Website: www.chateaucantenac.fr

Visits: Monday to Friday, 9 A.M.–noon and 2–6 P.M.

Contact: Nicole Roskam-Brunot

VINEYARDS

Surface area: 29.6 acres

Grape varietals: 80% Merlot, 15% Cabernet Franc, 5% Cabernet Sauvignon

Average age of vines: 30 years

Density of plantation: 6,600 vines per hectare

Average yields: 45 hectoliters per hectare

Elevage: Ten day fermentation and 20 day maceration in vats. Twelve months aging in vats (30% of yield) and in barrels (with 70% of yield). Fining, filtration depends upon the vintage.

WINES PRODUCED

Château Cantenac: 45,000 bottles

Château Cantenac "Sélection Madame": 15,000 bottles

Plateau of maturity: Within 5–8 years of the vintage

GENERAL APPRECIATION

Cantenac is a reasonably priced, good quality St.-Emilion, a commodity that is increasingly difficult to find. Consumers take note, as quality has increased over the last several years.

IMPORTANT VINTAGES

2001 A fruit-driven St.-Emilion made from 80% Merlot, 15% Cabernet Franc, and 5%
86–88 Cabernet Sauvignon, this 2001 reveals ripe cherry fruit, spicy oak, herbs, cedar, and earth. Medium bodied and round, it should be consumed during its first 7–9 years of life. Last tasted, 1/03.

CAPET-GUILLIER

Classification: Grand Cru

Owner: Bouzerand and Galinou families

Address: 33330 Saint-Hippolyte

Telephone: 05 57 24 70 21; Telefax: 05 57 24 68 96

Visits: Monday to Friday 9 A.M.–noon and 2–5 P.M.
By appointment on weekends.

Contact: Élisabeth Galinou

VINEYARDS

Surface area: 37 acres

Grape varietals: 60% Merlot, 25% Cabernet Franc, 15% Cabernet Sauvignon

Average age of vines: 35 years

Density of plantation: 5,500 vines per hectare

Average yields: 52 hectoliters per hectare

Elevage: Fermentation and maceration approximately three weeks in concrete vats. Wines are then aged 13 months in oak barrels (new and one vintage old).

WINES PRODUCED

Château Capet-Guillier: 64,000 bottles
Château Grands Sables Capet: 43,000 bottles

CARTEAU CÔTES DAUGAY

Classification: Grand Cru

Owner: SCEA des Vignobles Jacques Bertrand

Address: Carteau, 33330 St.-Emilion

Telephone: 05 57 24 73 94; Telefax: 05 57 24 69 07

Visits: By appointment only

Contact: Anne-Marie Bertrand

VINEYARDS

Surface area: 32.7 acres

Grape varietals: 70% Merlot, 20% Cabernet Franc, 10% Cabernet Sauvignon

Average age of vines: 20 years

Density of plantation: 5,600 vines per hectare

Average yields: 45 hectoliters per hectare

Elevage: Four to five week fermentation and maceration in temperature-controlled concrete and stainless-steel tanks. Malolactics in barrel for 50% of yield. Thirteen to fifteen months aging in barrels with 35% new oak.

WINES PRODUCED

Château Carteau Côtes Daugay: 75,000 bottles

Château Vieux Lescours: 20,000 bottles

LE CASTELOT

Classification: Grand Cru

Owner: Jean-François Janoueix

Address: 33330 Saint-Sulpice-de-Faleyrens

Mailing address: c/o Vignobles Joseph Janoueix, 37, rue Pline Parmentier, BP 192, 33506

Libourne Cedex

Telephone: 05 57 51 41 86; Telefax: 05 57 51 53 16

E-mail: info@janoueix-bordeaux.com

Website: www.j-janoueix-bordeaux.com

Visits: By appointment Monday to Friday, 8 A.M.–noon and 2–6 p.m. (closes at 5 P.M. on Fridays.)

Contact: Vignobles Joseph Janoueix

VINEYARDS

Surface area: 22.2 acres

Grape varietals: 70% Merlot, 20% Cabernet Franc, 10% Cabernet Sauvignon

Average age of vines: 45 years

Density of plantation: 6,000 and 10,000 vines per hectare

Average yields: 45 hectoliters per hectare

Elevage: Twenty-five to twenty-seven day fermentation and maceration in temperature-controlled epoxy-lined vats. Malolactics and 12–14 months aging in barrels with 50–60% new oak. Fining with egg whites, no filtration.

WINES PRODUCED

Château Le Castelot: 42,000 bottles

Château Haut-Castelot: 34,000 bottles

CHANTE ALOUETTE

Classification: Grand Cru

Owner: Guy and Marie-France d'Arfeuille

Address: 33330 St.-Emilion

Telephone: 05 57 24 71 81; Telefax: 05 57 24 74 82

Website: www.chateau-chante-alouette.com

Visits: By appointment only

Contact: Benoît d'Arfeuille

VINEYARDS

Surface area: 12.4 acres

Grape varietals: 70% Merlot, 30% Cabernet Franc

Average age of vines: 20 years

Density of plantation: 5,500 vines per hectare

Average yields: 50 hectoliters per hectare

Elevage: Fermentation and maceration in temperature-controlled concrete (90%) and stainless-steel (10%) tanks. Aging in vats (35%) and in barrels (with 35% new oak). No precision as to fining and filtration.

WINES PRODUCED

Château Chante Alouette: 29,000 bottles

No second wine is produced.

CHEVAL NOIR

Classification: Grand Cru

Owner: Mahler-Besse SA

Address: 33330 St.-Emilion

Mailing address: Mahler-Besse, 49, rue Camille Godard, 33000 Bordeaux

Telephone: 05 56 56 04 30; Telefax: 05 56 56 04 59

E-mail: contact@mahler-besse.com

Website: www.mahler-besse.com

Visits: On weekdays, except public holidays

Contact: Export Sales Department, Mahler-Besse SA (Telephone: 05 56 56 04 48)

VINEYARDS

Surface area: 12.4 acres

Grape varietals: 60% Merlot, 40% Cabernet Franc and Cabernet Sauvignon

Average age of vines: 30 years

Density of plantation: 6,000 vines per hectare

Average yields: 55 hectoliters per hectare

Elevage: Five day maceration and 22 day fermentation in small temperature-controlled, cone-shaped stainless-steel tanks. Twenty-four months aging in vats. Fining and filtration.

WINES PRODUCED

Cheval Noir: 30,000 bottles

No second wine is produced.

GENERAL APPRECIATION

This wine always surprises me by its tendency to be overly tannic. I reckon the proprietors are trying too hard to extract, while the quality of the raw material does not allow it. This is not a wine for shrewd St.-Emilion lovers.

CLOS LABARDE

Classification: Grand Cru

Owner: Jacques Bailly

Address: lieu-dit La Barde, 33330 St.-Emilion

Mailing address: Bergat, 33330 St.-Emilion

Telephone: 05 57 74 43 39: Telefax: 05 57 74 40 26

Visits: Monday to Friday, 11 A.M.–noon and 2–6 P.M.

Contact: Nicolas Bailly

VINEYARDS

Surface area: 11.3 acres

Grape varietals: 70% Merlot, 20% Cabernet Franc, 10% Cabernet Sauvignon

Average age of vines: 35 years

Density of plantation: 5,000 vines per hectare

Average yields: 48 hectoliters per hectare

Elevage: Twenty-two to thirty day fermentation and maceration in temperature-controlled, concrete, epoxy-lined tanks. Twenty-two months aging, with 75% of yield in vats and 25% in barrels (renewed by a third at each vintage), with a rotation at the time of the rackings. Fining, light filtration.

WINES PRODUCED

Clos Labarde: 30,000 bottles

No second wine is produced.

CLOS LARCIS

Classification: Grand Cru

Owner: Grands Vins Robert Giraud SA

Address: 23 Villamaurine Sud, 33330 St.-Emilion

Mailing address: Grands Vins Robert Giraud SA,
Domaine de Loiseau, BP 31, 33240 Saint-André-de-Cubzac

Telephone: 05 57 43 01 44; Telefax: 05 57 43 08 75

E-mail: commercial@robertgiraud.com

Website: www.robertgiraud.com

Visits: By appointment

Contact: Jean-Luc Duwa (Telephone: 05 57 74 46 44; Telefax: 05 57 74 47 30)

VINEYARDS

Surface area: 2.47 acres

Grape varietals: 100% Merlot

Average age of vines: 30 years

Density of plantation: 5,660 vines per hectare

Average yields: 45 hectoliters per hectare

Elevage: Three to four week fermentation and maceration in temperature-controlled
stainless-steel tanks. Fifteen months aging in barrels with 50% new oak. Fining, no
filtration.

WINES PRODUCED

Clos Larcis: 6,000 bottles

No second wine is produced.

CLOS LA MADELEINE

Classification: Grand Cru (declassified in 1996)

Owner: GFA du Clos de la Madeleine

Address: La Gaffelière Ouest, 33330 St.-Emilion

Mailing address: BP 78, 33330 St.-Emilion

Telephone: 05 57 55 38 03; Telefax: 05 57 55 38 01

Visits: Monday to Friday, 9 A.M.–6 P.M.
By appointment for other days and dates.

VINEYARDS

Surface area: 4.9 acres

Grape varietals: 60% Merlot, 40% Cabernet Franc

Average age of vines: 32 years

Density of plantation: 5,000 vines per hectare

Average yields: 30 hectoliters per hectare

Elevage: Five week fermentation and maceration. Aging in barrels that are renewed by half at each vintage. Fining, no filtration.

WINES PRODUCED

Clos La Madeleine: 8,000 bottles

No second wine is produced.

Plateau of maturity: Within 4–10 years of the vintage

CLOS ST.-EMILION PHILIPPE

Classification: Grand Cru

Owner: Jean-Claude Philippe

Address: Le Bosquet, 2, Beychet, 33330 St.-Emilion

Mailing address: 101, avenue Gallieni, 33500 Libourne

Telephone: 05 57 51 05 93; Telefax: 05 57 25 96 39

E-mail: sandrine.closphilippe@caramail.com

Visits: By appointment only

Contact: Sandrine Philippe
(Telephone: 06 88 08 14 03)

VINEYARDS

Surface area: 19.8 acres

Grape varietals: 70% Merlot, 30% Cabernet Franc

Average age of vines: 50 years

Density of plantation: 5,500 vines per hectare

Average yields: 45 hectoliters per hectare

Elevage: Seven day cold maceration at 8°C. Twenty-one to twenty-eight day fermentation and maceration in temperature-controlled stainless-steel vats with *pigéages*. Malolactics in barrel and upbringing on lees for the special *cuvée*. Fifteen to eighteen months aging in new oak barrels for both wines. Fining and filtration.

WINES PRODUCED

Château Clos St.-Emilion Philippe: 30,000 bottles

Château Clos St.-Emilion Philippe Cuvée 101: 6,300 bottles

Note: The special *cuvée* is a 100% Merlot wine culled out from a two-hectare parcel of old vines (100+ years) and from yields of 27 hectoliters per hectare.

CLOS ST.-JULIEN

Classification: Grand Cru

Owner: Jean-Jacques Nouvel

Address: 33330 Saint-Emilion

Mailing address: c/o SCEA Vignobles J.-J. Nouvel, Catherine Papon-Nouvel, BP 84, 33330 Saint-Emilion

Telephone: 05 57 24 72 44; Telefax: 05 57 24 74 84

Visits: By appointment only

VINEYARDS

Surface area: 3 acres

Grape varietals: 60% Cabernet Franc, 40% Merlot

Average age of vines: 80 years for the Merlot; 40 years for the Cabernet Franc

Density of plantation: 6,000 vines per hectare

Average yields: 30 hectoliters per hectare

Elevage: Prolonged fermentation and maceration without addition of yeasts. Malolactics and 12–18 months aging on lees in new oak barrels. No fining, no filtration.

WINES PRODUCED

Clos St.-Julien: 4,500 bottles

No second wine is produced.

This garage wine is located near Château Soutard on pure limestone. Yields are low and, based on the few vintages I have tasted, this is an impressive wine.

IMPORTANT VINTAGES

2001
88–90   Made from yields of 28 hectoliters per hectare, this is an impressive, structured 2001, with a deep ruby/purple color and a sweet nose of black fruits, graphite, licorice, and mineral. The wine is deep, chewy, powerful, and in need of cellaring. Anticipated maturity: 2007–2016. Last tasted, 1/03.

2000
90   A beauty, this tiny estate has produced a wine with a very pronounced nose of jammy black cherries intermixed with cassis and a liquid minerality. Some spice shows through, as does a hint of espresso and licorice. This dense, purple-colored wine shows great purity, sweetness, expansiveness, and mid-palate texture and persistence. Anticipated maturity: 2007–2020. A sleeper of the vintage. Last tasted, 1/03.

1999
89   Although this 1999 reveals plenty of new oak, there is a lot going on in the mouth. Offering attractive tobacco, herb, black cherry, and currant fruit, superb purity, medium body, and finesse, elegance, and sweetness (rather than power and size), it will drink well for 5–6 years. Last tasted, 3/02.

CLOS TRIMOULET

Classification: Grand Cru

Owner: Appolot and sons

Address: 33330 St.-Emilion

Telephone: 05 57 24 71 96; Telefax: 05 57 74 45 88

Visits: By appointment only

Contact: Guy Appolot

VINEYARDS

Surface area: 24.7 acres

Grape varietals: 80% Merlot, 10% Cabernet Franc, 10% Cabernet Sauvignon

Average age of vines: 45 years

Density of plantation: 5,500 vines per hectare

Average yields: 45 hectoliters per hectare

Elevage: Three to four week fermentation and maceration in temperature-controlled vats. Fourteen months aging in vats for 40% of the yield and in barrels for the rest with 20% new oak. Fining, no precisions regarding filtration.

WINES PRODUCED

Clos Trimoulet: 60,000 bottles

No second wine is produced.

LA COMMANDERIE

Classification: Grand Cru

Owner: Gérard Frydman

Address: Lieu-dit La Gomerie, 33330 St.-Emilion

Telephone: 05 57 24 70 14; Telefax: 05 57 24 68 08

Visits: By appointment only

Contact: Hubert de Boüard

VINEYARDS

Surface area: 14.8 acres

Grape varietals: 85% Merlot, 15% Cabernet Franc

Average age of vines: 30 years

Density of plantation: 6,500 vines per hectare

Average yields: 40 hectoliters per hectare

Elevage: Three to four week fermentation and maceration in temperature-controlled wooden vats (since 2002) with frequent *pigéage* and pumpings over. Eighteen months aging in new oak barrels. No fining, filtration.

WINES PRODUCED

Château La Commanderie: 20,000 bottles

Les Chemins de la Commanderie: Up to 10,000 bottles (depending upon the vintage)

LA CONFESSION

Classification: Grand Cru

Owner: Jean-Philippe Janoueix

Address: 183, route de St.-Emilion, 33500 Libourne

Mailing address: 83, cours des Girondins, 33500 Libourne

Telephone: 05 57 25 91 19; Telefax: 05 57 48 00 04

Visits: By appointment only

Contact: Jean-Philippe Janoueix

VINEYARDS

Surface area: 6.7 acres

Grape varietals: 50% Merlot, 45% Cabernet Franc, 5% Cabernet Sauvignon

Average age of vines: 39 years

Density of plantation: 6,500 vines per hectare

Average yields: 33 hectoliters per hectare

Elevage: Five to six week whole-cluster fermentation and maceration in temperature-controlled, wooden open-top vats allowing manual *pigéage*. Malolactics and 18–24 months aging in new oak barrels, half of which are cigar-shaped, the other half being traditional.

WINES PRODUCED

Château La Confession: 9,000 bottles

Château Barreau: 3,000 bottles

Plateau of maturity: Too soon to predict, but 5–18 years appears plausible.

GENERAL APPRECIATION

This new garage operation from Jean-Philippe Janoueix, the man behind the brilliant wines of De Chambrun (Lalande-de-Pomerol) as well as La Croix St.-Georges (Pomerol), benefits from all the fashionable winemaking techniques (fermentation in small, open-top Taransaud fermenters, punching down, malolactic in barrel, lees aging, no fining or filtration). The 2001, the debut vintage, was impressive and, judging by the consistently topflight track record of all the wines made by Jean-Philippe Janoueix, one can suppose La Confession will maintain high standards, and even improve, if ever that is possible.

IMPORTANT VINTAGES

2001
88–
90+?

The first vintage for Jean-Philippe Janoueix, this blend of 50% Merlot, 45% Cabernet Franc, and 5% Cabernet Sauvignon, which had a five-week maceration period with punching down as well as pumping-over, is an immensely impressive, full-throttle St.-Emilion with an inky ruby/purple color and an exceptionally sweet nose of roasted espresso intermixed with crème de cassis, blackberry, melted licorice, and a hint of chocolate. The wine is full-bodied, with a viscous texture, tremendous opulence, and a long, seamless finish that nearly hides some serious tannins. This is a brilliant first effort from the same gentleman that produces the top-notch wines of De Chambrun, Lalande-de-Pomerol, and La Croix St.-Georges (Pomerol). Last tasted, 1/03.

CORMEIL-FIGEAC

Classification: St.-Emilion Grand Cru

Production: 4,000 cases

Blend: 70% Merlot, 30% Cabernet Franc

Secondary label: None

Vineyard size: 25 acres

Proprietor: Moreaud family

Time spent in barrels: 18–22 months

Average age of vines: 25 years

Evaluation of present classification: The quality equivalent of a Médoc Cru Bourgeois

Plateau of maturity: Within 3–8 years of the vintage

This is a vineyard with potential, given the location adjacent to the famed Château Figeac. However, its soils are more sandy than those of Figeac, and one wonders what could be obtained if the selection were a bit stricter and the proprietor used more new oak casks. From time to time there is an underlying mustiness that is off-putting. Otherwise the wines are supple, fleshy, and generally well endowed.

CÔTES DE ROL

Classification: Grand Cru

Owner: Grands Vins Robert Giraud SA

Address: 23 Villamaurine Sud, 33330 St.-Emilion

Mailing address: Grands Vins Robert Giraud SA, Domaine de Loiseau, BP 31, 33240 Saint-André-de-Cubzac

Telephone: 05 57 43 01 44; Telefax: 05 57 43 08 75

E-mail: commercial@robertgiraud.com

Website: www.robertgiraud.com

Visits: By appointment

Contact: Jean-Luc Duwa (Telephone: 05 57 74 46 44; Telefax: 05 57 74 47 30)

VINEYARDS

Surface area: 7.4 acres

Grape varietals: 75% Merlot, 20% Cabernet Franc, 5% Cabernet Sauvignon

Average age of vines: 30 years

Density of plantation: 6,000 vines per hectare

Average yields: 50 hectoliters per hectare

Elevage: Fifteen to twenty day fermentation and maceration in temperature-controlled stainless-steel tanks. Fifteen months aging in barrels with 30% new oak. Fining, no filtration.

WINES PRODUCED

Château Côtes de Rol: 20,000 bottles

No second wine is produced.

GENERAL APPRECIATION

Another stern and overly tannic wine confirming that St.-Emilion is at once capable of the best . . . and the worse.

LA COURONNE

Classification: Grand Cru

Owner: Mahler-Besse S.A.

Address: 33330 Saint-Hippolyte

Mailing address: Mahler-Besse SA, 49, rue Camille Godard, 33000 Bordeaux

Telephone: 05 56 56 04 30; Telefax: 05 56 56 04 59

E-mail: export@mahler-besse.com

Visits: By appointment only

Contact: Export sales department of Malher-Besse SA

VINEYARDS

Surface area: 37 acres

Grape varietals: 60% Merlot, 40% Cabernet Sauvignon

Average age of vines: 20 years

Density of plantation: 6,000 vines per hectare

Average yields: 50 hectoliters per hectare

Elevage: Thirty day fermentation and maceration in temperature-controlled cone-shaped vats. Twelve months aging in barrels with 30% new oak. Fining, no filtration.

WINES PRODUCED

Château La Couronne: 60,000 bottles

No second wine is produced.

COUTET

Classification: Grand Cru

Owner: David-Beaulieu family

Address: 33330 St.-Emilion

Telephone: 05 57 74 43 21; Telefax: 05 57 74 40 78

E-mail: coutet@chateau-coutet.com

Website: www.chateau-coutet.com

Visits: By appointment only

Contact: Alain David-Beaulieu

VINEYARDS

Surface area: 32.1 acres

Grape varietals: 60% Merlot, 35% Cabernet Franc, 5% Malbec

Average age of vines: 32 years

Density of plantation: 6,000 vines per hectare

Average yields: 40 hectoliters per hectare

Elevage: Three to four week fermentation and maceration in temperature-controlled stainless-steel vats with frequent pumpings-over and micro-oxygenation of lees. Eighteen months aging in all, with 12 months in oak barrels that are renewed by a third every three months. Fining and filtration.

WINES PRODUCED

Château Coutet: 50,000 bottles

(Name not defined): 10,000 bottles

LA CROIX FIGEAC LAMARZELLE

Classification: Grand Cru

Owner: Pierre and Charlotte Dutruilh

Address: Croix de Figeac, 33330 St.-Emilion

Mailing address: 14, rue d'Aviau, 33000 Bordeaux

Telephone and Telefax: 05 56 81 19 69

Visits: By appointment only

Contact: Jean Dutruilh (Telephone: 06 73 89 18 13)

VINEYARDS

Surface area: 8.6 acres

Grape varietals: 80% Merlot, 20% Cabernet Franc

Average age of vines: 30 years

Density of plantation: 6,500 vines per hectare

Average yields: 42 hectoliters per hectare

Elevage: Cold maceration. Twenty-one to thirty day fermentation and maceration in temperature-controlled stainless-steel vats. Malolactics and 15–20 months aging on lees in barrels with 70–100% new oak. No fining, no filtration.

WINES PRODUCED

Château La Croix Figeac Lamarzelle: 15,000 bottles

No second wine is produced.

GENERAL APPRECIATION

A sister wine of Rocher-Bellevue-Figeac, this excellent effort is also worthy of consumers' interest as the quality is always *au rendez-vous* and prices remain reasonable.

LA CROIZILLE

Classification: Grand Cru

Owner: Jacques de Schepper

Address: 33330 Saint-Laurent-des-Combes

Mailing address: c/o Château Tour Baladoz, 33330 Saint-Laurent-des-Combes

Telephone: 05 57 88 94 17; Telefax: 05 57 88 39 14

Visits: By appointment Monday to Friday, 8 A.M.–noon and 2–5:30 P.M.

Contact: Jean-Michel Garcion

VINEYARDS

Surface area: 12.3 acres

Grape varietals: 70% Merlot, 30% Cabernet Sauvignon

Average age of vines: 30 years

Density of plantation: 6,600 vines per hectare

Average yields: 45 hectoliters per hectare

Elevage: Four to five week fermentation and maceration. Fifteen to eighteen months aging in new oak barrels. No fining, no filtration.

WINES PRODUCED

Château La Croizille: 5,000 bottles

Château La Croizille Cuvée Baladoz: 20,000 bottles

CROQUE MICHOTTE

Classification: Grand Cru

Owner: GFA Geoffrion

Address: 33330 St.-Emilion

Telephone: 05 57 51 13 64; Telefax: 05 57 51 07 8

E-mail: croque-michotte@monax.com

Visits: By appointment only

Contact: Robert or Pierre Carle

VINEYARDS

Surface area: 33.8 acres

Grape varietals: 70% Merlot, 30% Cabernet Franc

Average age of vines: 40 years

Density of plantation: 6,000 vines per hectare

Average yields: 35 hectoliters per hectare

Elevage: Cold maceration. Four to five week fermentation and maceration, with indigenous yeasts. Twenty-one months upbringing in all, including 12 months aging in barrels with 60–80% new oak. No fining, no filtration.

WINES PRODUCED

Château Croque Michotte: 42,000–50,000 bottles

Les Charmilles de la Croque Michotte: 9,000 bottles maximum

Plateau of maturity: Within 4–12 years of the vintage

The vineyard of Croque Michotte is well situated in the *graves* section of the St.-Emilion appellation, adjacent to the Pomerol border, close to the better-known estates of Cheval Blanc and La Dominique. The wine produced here is usually ready to drink within the first five or six years of a vintage, and it rarely improves beyond a decade. Nevertheless, especially among those who lack patience, this fleshy, sumptuous style of wine has many admirers.

CROS FIGEAC

Classification: Grand Cru

Owner: SCEA du Château Cros Figeac

Address: 33330 St.-Emilion

Mailing address: BP 51, 33330 St.-Emilion

Telephone: 05 57 55 51 60; Telefax: 05 57 55 51 61

No visits

VINEYARDS

Surface area: 5.9 acres

Grape varietals: 75% Merlot, 25% Cabernet Franc

Average age of vines: 40 years

Density of plantation: 5,500 vines per hectare

Average yields: 30 hectoliters per hectare

Elevage: Three to four week fermentation and maceration in temperature-controlled stainless-steel tanks. Malolactics and aging in oak barrels with 70% new oak. No fining, no filtration.

WINES PRODUCED

Château Cros Figeac: 6,000 bottles

Prélude de Cros Figeac: 3,600 bottles

IMPORTANT VINTAGES

2000
88 Possibly the finest Cros Figeac I have ever tasted, the dense purple–colored 2000 possesses copious quantities of black fruits intermixed with new saddle leather, dried herbs, and spice. Medium bodied and tasty, it will have 10–12 years of aging potential. It is a sleeper of the vintage. Last tasted, 1/03.

1999
87 A good effort, this dark ruby–colored St. Emilion displays nice flesh, medium body, soft acid, and relatively ripe tannin. There is plenty of cedary, black currant, and cherry fruit, but the wine needs to be drunk during the next five years. Last tasted, 3/02.

1998
87 This sexy, jammy St.-Emilion is meant to be consumed during its first 7–10 years of life. A dark plum/ruby color is followed by appealing aromas of sweet oak and chocolaty, herb-tinged, black currant fruit. The wine is fleshy, expansive, low in acidity, and supple. Last tasted, 3/02.

CRUZEAU

Classification: Grand Cru

Owner: GFL Lucquot Frères

Address: 152, avenue de l'Epinette, 33500 Libourne

Telephone: 05 57 51 18 95; Telefax: 05 57 25 10 59

Visits: By appointment only

Contact: Jean-Paul Luquot

VINEYARDS

Surface area: 10.9 acres

Grape varietals: 75% Merlot, 25% Cabernet Franc

Average age of vines: 35 years

Density of plantation: 5,900 vines per hectare

Average yields: 50 hectoliters per hectare

Elevage: Four week fermentation and maceration in temperature-controlled concrete vats. Twelve months aging in barrels. Fining, no filtration.

WINES PRODUCED

Château Cruzeau: 27,000 bottles

No second wine is produced.

CURÉ-BON*

Classification: Grand Cru Classé

Owner: SA Lorienne

Address: 9, rue Magdeleine, 33330 St.-Emilion

Mailing address: SA Lorienne, 1, Le Cadet, 33330 St.-Emilion

Telephone: 05 57 74 43 20; Telefax: 05 57 24 66 41

Visits: By appointment only

Contact: Marceline and Bernard Gans

1992

CHATEAU CURÉ-BON

SAINT-EMILION GRAND CRU CLASSÉ

APPELLATION SAINT-EMILION GRAND CRU CONTRÔLÉE
SOCIÉTÉ LORIENE, PROPRIÉTAIRE A SAINT-ÉMILION, GIRONDE

VINEYARDS

Surface area: 10.4 acres

Grape varietals: 84% Merlot, 15% Cabernet Franc, 1% Petit Verdot et Malbec

Average age of vines: 30 years

Density of plantation: 6,660 vines per hectare

Average yields: 48 hectoliters per hectare

Elevage: Alcoholic fermentations take place in stainless-steel vats, and malolactic fermentations occur partly in new oak barrels (about 40–60%). Wines are entirely aged in oak barrels that are renewed by 40% at each vintage. They are fined but remain unfiltered.

WINES PRODUCED

Château Curé-Bon: 18,000 bottles

No second wine is produced.

Plateau of maturity: Within 5–15 years of the vintage

This tiny estate has a splendid location on the *côtes* St.-Emilion, sandwiched between the famous vineyards of Canon, Belair, and Ausone. It is a wine with a very good reputation, but one that is rarely seen in export channels. My experience with Curé-Bon is very limited, but the wines I have seen have been surprisingly tannic and firmly structured St.-Emilions that can support considerable cellaring. Of course, as of 2003 the vineyard is part of the estate of Château Canon.

* This estate was bought by Château Canon and the production of the vines is now incorporated into Château Canon.

FAURIE DE SOUCHARD

Classification: Grand Cru Classé

Owner: GFA Jabiol-Sciard

Address: 33330 St.-Emilion

Telephone: 05 57 74 43 80; Telefax: 05 57 74 43 96

E-mail: fauriedesouchard@wanadoo.fr

Visits: Monday, Tuesday, and Thursday, 9 A.M.–4 P.M.

Contact: Françoise Sciard

VINEYARDS

Surface area: 27.2 acres

Grape varietals: 65% Merlot, 26% Cabernet Franc, 9% Cabernet Sauvignon

Average age of vines: 25 years

Density of plantation: 5,500 vines per hectare

Average yields: 45 hectoliters per hectare

Elevage: Three week fermentation and maceration in vats. After completion of malolactics, 18–20 months aging in barrels that are renewed by a third at each vintage. Fining, filtration not systematic.

WINES PRODUCED

Château Faurie de Souchard: 58,000 bottles

Souchard: 7,000 bottles (rarely produced)

Plateau of maturity: Within 5–12 years of the vintage

Faurie de Souchard, one of the oldest properties in St.-Emilion, has been owned by the Jabiol family since 1933. The vineyard, located on both a limestone plateau as well as chalky clay and sandy soil, tends to produce relatively full-bodied, tannic, intense wines that require some patience in the bottle. Unlike many St.-Emilions that are made to be drunk within their first 5–6 years, most vintages of Faurie de Souchard can last up to 10–15 years. If the wines are to be criticized at all, it is because their tannins often exceed the extraction levels of fruit.

IMPORTANT VINTAGES

2000 Deep ruby purple, with a relatively reticent but promising nose of graphite, wet
87–88 stone, and cherries as well as black currants, this wine is medium bodied, moderately high in tannin, with good acidity and structure. This is a traditionally made wine that will require some patience. Anticipated maturity: 2008–2014. Last tasted, 1/03.

1999 Dark ruby/purple–colored, with a spice box, mineral, and black fruit–scented
86 nose, the medium-weight 1999 reveals moderate tannin as well as low acidity. Anticipated maturity: now–2015. Last tasted, 3/02.

1998 A plum/ruby color is followed by soft, round, attractive, spice box, cherry, smoky,
87 earthy aromas. The medium-bodied wine is elegant and stylish, with a supple finish. Drink it over the next 5–6 years. Last tasted, 3/02.

LE FER

Classification: Grand Cru

Owner: Mahler-Besse SA

Address: 33330 St.-Emilion

Mailing address: c/o Mahler-Besse SA, 40, rue Camille Godard, 33000 Bordeaux

Telephone: 05 56 56 04 30; Telefax: 05 56 56 04 59

E-mail: contact@mahler-besse.com

Website: le-fer.com

Visits: By appointment only

Contact: Export sales department at Mahler-Besse SA

VINEYARDS

Surface area: 4.9 acres

Grape varietals: 100% Merlot

Average age of vines: 35 years

Density of plantation: 6,000 vines per hectare

Average yields: 25 hectoliters per hectare

Elevage: Malolactics and aging on lees with regular stirring in 100% new oak barrels. Fining, no filtration.

WINES PRODUCED

Le Fer: 6,000 bottles

No second wine is produced.

GENERAL APPRECIATION

If this special *cuvée* wants to be a garage wine, it badly misses its goal as it is generally too woody and too tannic (due to overextraction).

DE FERRAND

Classification: Grand Cru

Owner: Heirs to Baron Bich

Address: 33330 Saint-Hippolyte

Telephone: 05 57 74 47 11; Telefax: 05 57 24 69 08

E-mail: ch-ferrand@wanadoo.fr

Visits: By appointment only Monday to Friday, 9 A.M.–noon and 2–5 P.M.

Contact: Jean-Pierre Palatin

VINEYARDS

Surface area: 74.1 acres

Grape varietals: 70% Merlot, 30% Cabernet Franc and Cabernet Sauvignon

Average age of vines: 30 years

Density of plantation: 5,400 vines per hectare

Average yields: 48 hectoliters per hectare

Elevage: Prolonged fermentation and maceration. Six months aging in new oak barrels. Fining, no filtration.

WINES PRODUCED

Château de Ferrand: 160,000 bottles

Château des Grottes: 20,000 bottles

Plateau of maturity: Within 4–12 years of the vintage

The Baron Bich, celebrated for his Bic pens, purchased de Ferrand in 1978 and significantly increased the quality of the wine.

The vineyard itself is located in the commune of St.-Hippolyte on a plateau of limestone. The key to the success of many de Ferrand vintages has been an unusually late harvest and the use of a significant percentage of new oak, ranging from 50% to nearly 100%. De Ferrand makes wines with the potential for a moderately long evolution in the bottle.

LA FLEUR

Classification: Grand Cru

Owner: SARL Château Dassault

Address: 33330 St.-Emilion

Telephone: 05 57 51 78 86; Telefax: 05 57 51 79 79

Visits: By appointment and for professionals of the wine trade only

VINEYARDS

Surface area: 22.2 acres

Grape varietals: 90% Merlot, 10% Cabernet Franc

Average age of vines: 20 years

Density of plantation: 5,500–6,000 vines per hectare

Average yields: 50 hectoliters per hectare

Elevage: Fermentations last approximately 18 days in non-temperature-controlled concrete vats. Wines undergo malolactics in vats and are transferred to oak casks, 20% of which are new, for 18 months aging. They are racked every three months from barrel to barrel, fined, but remain unfiltered.

WINES PRODUCED

Château La Fleur: 24,000 bottles

No second wine is produced.

Plateau of maturity: Within 2–6 years of the vintage

GENERAL APPRECIATION

For a number of years, this estate has been under the helmsmanship of the ubiquitous Ets Jean-Pierre Moueix, whose magic does not seem to have operated as well here as in several of the other estates they manage, but they nevertheless produced an in-your-face, deliciously fruity, open-knit, seductive, value-priced St.-Emilion. The estate has been bought recently by Dassault, and it is too soon to know what changes will result from this change of ownership.

For years the wines never exhibited a great deal of character but were, rather, straightforward, soft, light, and easygoing. In the mid-1990s I detected more fruit and depth, thus much more charm and appeal. The wines are vinified and distributed by the firm of Jean-Pierre Moueix. As a general rule, most vintages of La Fleur should be drunk in the first 7–8 years after the vintage, as the wines rarely have exhibited the stuffing necessary for extended cellaring.

IMPORTANT VINTAGES

1999
85
Close in style to the 1998, but lighter, this medium-bodied, fruit-driven 1999 will provide disarming/captivating drinking. It will not be long-lived, but should evolve easily for 5–6 years. Last tasted, 3/01.

1998
89
A sleeper of the vintage, this offering has turned out to be the best La Fleur I have ever tasted. Deep ruby–colored, with an opulent, sexy nose of jammy black cherries and berries, its fresh, lively flavors reveal terrific fruit, a chewy texture, and good balance. This medium-bodied St.-Emilion fruit-bomb should drink well for 5–6 years. Last tasted, 3/02.

1997
87
A seductive, open-knit, soft fruit-bomb, the 1997 La Fleur possesses medium weight as well as copious quantities of glycerin and sweet, jammy cherry fruit. Although it lacks density and aging potential, it is an appealing St.-Emilion to consume over the next 3–4 years.

1996
86
The excellent 1996 La Fleur is a good choice for restaurants and consumers looking for a wine with immediate drinkability. The medium ruby–colored 1996 reveals a gorgeous nose of overripe cherries intermixed with framboise and currants. In the mouth, the wine is medium bodied, with a velvety texture, fine purity, and gobs of fruit. This satiny-textured Claret will continue to drink well for 2–3 years.

1995
87
This seductive, medium- to full-bodied, round, velvety-textured St.-Emilion is medium deep ruby–colored, with an evolved, lovely nose of jammy black cherries, strawberries, and spice. The supple palate is all finesse, fruit, and succulence. Drink this delicious 1995 La Fleur now and over the next 3–4 years. Last tasted, 11/97.

LA FLEUR MORANGE

Classification: Grand Cru

Owner: Véronique and Jean-François Julien

Address: Ferrachat, 33330 Saint-Pay-d'Armens

Telephone: 05 57 47 10 90; Telefax: 05 57 47 16 72

E-mail: julienjf@aol.com

Website: www.saint-emilion-vin-grand-cru.com

Visits: By appointment only

Contact: Jean-François Julien (Telephone: 06 62 40 37 86)

VINEYARDS

Surface area: 3.7 acres

Grape varietals: 70% Merlot, 15% Cabernet Franc, 15% Cabernet Sauvignon

Average age of vines: 90 years

Density of plantation: 5,500 vines per hectare

Average yields: 25 hectoliters per hectare

Elevage: Fermentation and maceration in temperature-controlled double-lined and flat cone-shaped stainless-steel vats of 50 hectoliter capacity. Malolactics and 20–21 months aging in new oak barrels. No fining, no filtration.

WINES PRODUCED

Château La Fleur Morange: 5,000 bottles

No second wine is produced.

Plateau of maturity: Within 3–14 years of the vintage

GENERAL APPRECIATION

La Fleur Morange is another excellent and recent garage operation that benefits from advice from the consulting oenologist Claude Gros, the force behind some of the Languedoc-Roussillon's finest wines (Clos des Truffières and Porte de la Ciel). The wine receives state-of-the-art treatments like most of its peers. Unfortunately, quantities available are, as for most garage wines, extremely small.

Another so-called "garage wine," the tiny production of this wine from a 90-year-old vineyard is usually cropped at a remarkably low 20 hectoliters per hectare. The sand, clay, and limestone subsoils tend to produce low yields, but the consulting oenologist, Claude Gros, goes even further with leaf-pulling and severe crop-thinning. The wine, which really only made a dramatic improvement in 2000 and 2001, enjoys all of the state-of-the-art techniques designed to enhance fruit and *terroir* characteristics. Fermented in 50-hectoliter, truncated stainless-steel tanks and then given both punching down and pumpings-over, this wine receives malolactic in 100% new oak (Taransaud and Darnajou only) and is bottled unfined and unfiltered. The blend has changed dramatically with the first two vintages.

IMPORTANT VINTAGES

2001 Made from 20 hectoliters per hectare and a blend of 70% Merlot and 30% Caber-
90–92+ net Franc, this dense, ruby/purple-colored wine is structured, tannic, muscular, but layered and very full-bodied, with a huge concentration of fruit. Extremely dense and pure, it is a very impressive, yet atypically muscular, structured wine for 2001. Anticipated maturity: 2007–2016. Last tasted, 1/03.

2000 Showing even better from bottle than it did from barrel, this opaque purple–
91+ colored wine offers up notes of black raspberry liqueur intermixed with graphite, licorice, smoke, and cassis. A very, full-bodied, powerful, concentrated wine that seems like a hybrid style between something artisanal and something very progressive, the sweet, expansive mid-palate leads to a very tannic, structured, muscular finish with tremendous persistence (about 45 seconds). Anticipated maturity: 2008–2020+. Last tasted, 1/03.

LA FLEUR POURRET

Classification: Grand Cru

Owner: AXA Millésimes

Address: 33330 St.-Emilion

Mailing address: Château Petit Village, 33500 Pomerol

Telephone: 05 57 51 21 08; Telefax: 05 57 51 87 31

No visits

VINEYARDS

Surface area: 7.4 acres

Grape varietals: 60% Merlot, 30% Cabernet Franc, 10% Cabernet Sauvignon

Average age of vines: 30 years

Density of plantation: 9,500 vines per hectare

Elevage: Fermentation and maceration for 25–30 days in temperature-controlled concrete vats. Aging for 15–18 months in one-year-old barrels. Fining with egg whites and filtration.

WINES PRODUCED

Château La Fleur Pourret: Variable

No second wine is produced.

Plateau of maturity: Within 3–10 years of the vintage

I have been immensely impressed on the rare occasions when I have been permitted to taste this wine produced just outside the walls of St.-Emilion. The gravelly soil in this area is reputed to produce richly fruity, deeply colored, fleshy wines of surprising distinction and flavor extraction.

FONRAZADE

Classification: Grand Cru

Owner: Fabienne Balotte

Address: 33330 St.-Emilion

Telephone: 05 57 24 71 58; Telefax: 05 57 74 40 87

E-mail: chateau-fonrazade@wanadoo.fr

Visits: Monday to Friday, 8 A.M.–noon and 2–6 P.M.

Contact: Fabienne Balotte

VINEYARDS

Surface area: 27.2 acres

Grape varietals: 75% Merlot, 25% Cabernet Sauvignon

Average age of vines: 35 years

Density of plantation: 5,500 vines per hectare

Average yields: 50 hectoliters per hectare

Elevage: Four to five week fermentation and maceration in temperature-controlled tanks. Sixteen to eighteen months aging in barrels with 35–40% new oak. Fining, no filtration.

WINES PRODUCED

Château Fonrazade: 70,000 bottles

No second wine is produced.

FRANC LA ROSE

Classification: Grand Cru

Owner: Jean-Louis Trocard

Address: La Rose, 33330 St.-Emilion

Mailing address: BP 3, 33570 Les Artigues de Lussac

Telephone: 05 57 55 57 90; Telefax: 05 57 55 57 98

E-mail: trocard@wanadoo.fr

Website: www.trocard.com

Visits: By appointment Monday to Friday,
8 A.M.–noon and 2–5:30 P.M.

Contact: Benoît Trocard

VINEYARDS

Surface area: 14.8 acres

Grape varietals: 85% Merlot, 15% Cabernet Franc

Average age of vines: 35 years

Density of plantation: 6,500 vines per hectare

Average yields: 45 hectoliters per hectare

Elevage: Three week fermentation and maceration. Eighteen months aging in barrels with 60% new oak. Fining and filtration.

WINES PRODUCED

Château Franc la Rose: 40,000 bottles

No second wine is produced.

GALIUS

Classification: Grand Cru

Owner: Union des Producteurs de St.-Emilion

Director: Patrick Foulon

Address: lieu-dit Haut-Gravet, 33330 St.-Emilion

Mailing address: BP 27, 33330 St.-Emilion

Telephone: 05 57 24 70 71; Telefax: 05 57 24 65 18

E-mail: udp-vins.saint-emilion@gofornet.com

Visits: By appointment only

Contact: Reception desk

VINEYARDS

Surface area: 29.6 acres

Grape varietals: 60% Merlot, 30% Cabernet Franc, 10% Cabernet Sauvignon

Average age of vines: 36 years

Density of plantation: 5,500 vines per hectare

Average yields: 47 hectoliters per hectare

Elevage: Fermentation and maceration in temperature-controlled, concrete, epoxy-lined vats. Ten months aging in barrels with 45% new oak. Fining and filtration.

WINES PRODUCED

Galius: 60,000 bottles

No second wine is produced.

GODEAU

Classification: Grand Cru

Owner: Grégoire Bonte

Address: 33330 Saint-Laurent des Combes

Telephone: 05 57 24 72 64; Telefax: 05 57 24 65 84

E-mail: chateau.godeau@free.fr

Visits: By appointment only

Contact: Grégoire Bonte

VINEYARDS

Surface area: 13.8 acres

Grape varietals: 75% Merlot, 15% Cabernet Sauvignon, 10% Cabernet Franc

Average age of vines: 30 years

Density of plantation: 6,500 vines per hectare

Average yields: 49 hectoliters per hectare

Elevage: Three to four week fermentation and maceration in temperature-controlled stainless-steel tanks. Twelve to sixteen months aging in barrels that are renewed by a third at each vintage. Fining, no filtration.

WINES PRODUCED

Château Godeau: 27,000 bottles

Château Godeau Ducarpe: 9,000 bottles

DOMAINE DES GOURDINS

Classification: Grand Cru

Owner: Estager family

Address: 33330 St.-Emilion

Mailing address: SCEA des Vignobles J.-P. Estager, 33–41, rue de Montaudon, 33500 Libourne

Telephone: 05 57 51 04 09; Telefax: 05 57 25 13 28

E-mail: estager@estager.com

Website: www.estager.com

Visits: By appointment only

Contact: Mrs. Estager

VINEYARDS

Surface area: 4.2 acres

Grape varietals: 70% Merlot, 30% Cabernet Franc

Average age of vines: 23 years

Density of plantation: 5,000 vines per hectare

Average yields: 52 hectoliters per hectare

Elevage: Cold maceration. Three to four week fermentation and maceration in temperature-controlled vats. After malolactics, 15–18 months aging in barrels with 35% new oak. Fining, filtration depending upon turbidity.

WINES PRODUCED

Domaine des Gourdins: 10,500 bottles

No second wine is produced.

LA GRÂCE DIEU

Classification: Grand Cru

Owner: SCEA Pauty

Address: 33330 St.-Emilion

Telephone: 05 57 24 71 10; Telefax: 05 57 24 67 24

No visits

VINEYARDS

Surface area: 30.6 acres

Grape varietals: 80% Merlot, 20% Cabernet Franc

Average age of vines: 25 years

Density of plantation: 6,000 vines per hectare

Average yields: 49 hectoliters per hectare

Elevage: Eight day fermentation (28°C), prolonged maceration and malolactics in temperature-controlled vats. Eighteen months aging in epoxy-lined concrete vats for half the yield and in oak barrels (with 75% new oak) for the other half. Fining, filtration depending upon the vintage.

WINES PRODUCED

Château La Grâce Dieu: 80,000 bottles

No second wine is produced.

LA GRÂCE DIEU LES MENUTS

Classification: Grand Cru

Owner: Odile Audier

Address: EARL Vignobles Pilotte-Audier, 33330 St.-Emilion

Telephone: 05 57 24 73 10; Telefax: 05 57 74 40 44

Visits: Monday to Friday, 8 A.M.–noon and 2–6 P.M.

Contact: Odile Audier

VINEYARDS

Surface area: 32.1 acres

Grape varietals: 60% Merlot, 30% Cabernet Franc, 10% Cabernet Sauvignon

Average age of vines: 40 years

Density of plantation: 5,500 vines per hectare

Average yields: 45 hectoliters per hectare

Elevage: Twenty to thirty day fermentation and maceration in temperature-controlled concrete vats. Aging in barrels that are renewed by half at each vintage. Fining, no filtration.

WINES PRODUCED

Château La Grâce Dieu Les Menuts: 70,000 bottles

No second wine is produced.

LA GRÂCE DIEU DES PRIEURS

Classification: Grand Cru

Owner: Alain Laubie

Address: Fontin, 33330 St.-Emilion

Telephone: 05 57 74 42 97; Telefax: 05 57 24 69 59

E-mail: gracedieuprieurs@voonoo.net

Visits: By appointment only

Contact: Alain Laubie

VINEYARDS

Surface area: 19.2 acres

Grape varietals: 90% Merlot, 10% Cabernet Franc

Average age of vines: 42 years

Density of plantation: 5,500 vines per hectare

Average yields: 45 hectoliters per hectare

Elevage: Eighteen to twenty-two months aging in barrels with 25–35% new oak. Fining, no filtration.

WINES PRODUCED

Château La Grâce Dieu des Prieurs: 38,000 bottles

No second wine is produced.

GRAND CORBIN MANUEL

Classification: Grand Cru

Owner: Pierre Manuel

Address: 33330 St.-Emilion

Telephone: 05 57 51 12 47

Visits: Preferably by appointment

Contact: Pierre Manuel

VINEYARDS

Surface area: 17.3 acres

Grape varietals: 55% Merlot, 25% Cabernet Sauvignon, 20% Cabernet Franc

Average age of vines: 32 years

Density of plantation: 6,000 vines per hectare

Average yields: 45 hectoliters per hectare

Elevage: Fermentation and maceration is rather long (3–4 weeks) and takes place in temperature-controlled vats. After malolactics, wines are aged two years by rotation (one year each) in oak barrels (50% new oak) and vats. They are both fined and filtered.

WINES PRODUCED

Château Grand Corbin Manuel: 42,000 bottles

Clos de la Grande Métairie: Variable

LA GRANGÈRE

Classification: Grand Cru

Owner: Pierre Durand and Nadia Devilder

Address: 3, Tauzinat Est, 33330 Saint-Christophe-des-Bardes

Mailing address: BP 56, 33330 Saint-Christophe-des-Bardes

Telephone: 05 57 74 43 07; Telefax: 05 57 24 60 84

E-mail: devilder.durand@free.fr

Website: www.lagrangere.com

Visits: By appointment only Monday to Friday, 8:30 A.M.–5 P.M.

Contact: Nadia Devilder-Durand (Telephone: 06 09 82 13 87)

VINEYARDS

Surface area: 16.9 acres

Grape varietals: 75% Merlot, 15% Cabernet Sauvignon, 10% Cabernet Franc

Average age of vines: 30 years

Density of plantation: 5,000 vines per hectare

Average yields: 40 hectoliters per hectare

Elevage: Three to four week fermentation and maceration in temperature-controlled epoxy-lined concrete tanks. Malolactics in barrel for 50% of the yield. Twelve to eighteen months aging in barrels with 50% new oak. Fining, filtration if necessary.

WINES PRODUCED

Château La Grangère: 20,000–25,000 bottles

L'Etrier de la Grangère: 10,000–15,000 bottles

Plateau of maturity: Within 5–12 years of the vintage

GENERAL APPRECIATION

La Grangère's debut vintage under the helmsmanship of Nadia and Pierre Durand was promising, but it is too soon to know how things will evolve as their fine 2000, which was my first encounter with this wine, was followed by a 2001 I found a little disappointing (although that may have been due to less favorable vintage conditions). However, if it is the 2000 vintage that is reflective of its potential, then this estate deserves to be followed closely.

IMPORTANT VINTAGES

2001 An elegant style of wine, with notes of sweet black currants and cherries, pre-
85–87 sented in a medium-bodied, straightforward style, this wine should be drinkable
when released and last for up to a decade. Last tasted, 1/03.

2000 This debut release, made with the assistance of the well-known Bordeaux oenolo-
89 gist Professor Denis Dubourdieu, exhibits very pure blackberry and cherry fruit
intermixed with some subtle wood and licorice. The wine has sweet tannin,
medium to full body, low acidity, and a long and nicely textured finish. It is a
sleeper of the vintage. Anticipated maturity: 2006–2015. Last tasted, 1/03.

LA GRAVE FIGEAC

Classification: Grand Cru

Owner: Sabine and Jean-Pierre Clauzel

Address: 1, Cheval Blanc Ouest, 33330 St.-Emilion

Telephone: 05 57 74 11 74; Telefax: 05 57 74 17 18

Website: www.chateau-la-grave-figeac.fr

Visits: Monday to Saturday, 9 A.M.–7 P.M.

Contact: Jean-Pierre Clauzel

VINEYARDS

Surface area: 15.7 acres

Grape varietals: 65% Merlot, 35% Cabernet Franc

Average age of vines: 40 years

Density of plantation: 6,000 vines per hectare

Average yields: 45 hectoliters per hectare

Elevage: Cold maceration. Three week fermentation and maceration in temperature-controlled concrete vats. Twelve to fifteen months aging in barrels that are renewed by a third at each vintage. Fining, filtration depends upon the vintage.

WINES PRODUCED

Château La Grave Figeac: 30,000 bottles

Château Pavillon Figeac: 8,000 bottles

This property proved to be quite a discovery when I first tasted the 1982 and 1983—both of which were still drinking beautifully in 1991. However, after 1983 the production soared and the wines became more loosely structured, lacking the concentration and character of the previous vintages. The vineyard is extremely well located on the Pomerol border near the great estates of Figeac and Cheval Blanc. In 1993 the property was sold to Jean-Pierre Clauzel, and I fully expect the quality to improve dramatically.

LES GRAVIÈRES

Classification: Grand Cru

Owner: Denis Barraud

Address: 33330 Saint-Sumpice-de-Faleyrens

Telephone: 05 57 84 54 73; Telefax: 05 57 84 52 07

E-mail: denis.barraud@wanadoo.fr

Visits: By appointment only

Contact: Denis Barraud (Telephone: 06 08 32 26 04)

VINEYARDS

Surface area: 7.4 acres

Grape varietals: 100% Merlot

Average age of vines: 30–35 years

Density of plantation: 5,500 vines per hectare

Average yields: 40 hectoliters per hectare

Elevage: Thirty-six day fermentation and maceration in temperature-controlled stainless-steel vats of 99 hectoliter capacity, with an eight-day micro-oxygenation. Malolactics and 15–18 months aging on less (no racking) in new oak barrels. Fining, no filtration.

WINES PRODUCED

Château Les Gravières: 16,000 bottles

No second wine is produced.

Plateau of maturity: Within 5–12 years of the vintage

GENERAL APPRECIATION

This is a wine I have only tasted in four vintages, but it seems that proprietor Denis Barraud gives the same attention to the wines of this estate as he does to those of Lynsolence. Consumers can expect Les Gravières to be of high quality.

From a tiny vineyard on extremely gravelly, sandy soils in St.-Sulpice, this is one of the few St.-Emilions made from 100% Merlot. The proprietor, who also owns another St.-Emilion estate, Lynsolence, and a very high-quality, generic Bordeaux called La Cour d'Argent, ferments in small steel tanks, believes in modest yields of 40 hectoliters per hectare, relatively long *cuvaison,* and some high techniques such as microbullage, with malolactic in barrel as well as the use of 100% new oak. Early vintages have all been impressive.

IMPORTANT VINTAGES

2001
89–91 A deep ruby/purple–colored wine that may actually turn out to be better than the 2000, this full-bodied wine is quite rich, sweet, and expansive, with great purity and loads of mocha-infused black cherry and plum-like flavors. The wine has soft tannin, nicely integrated wood as well as acidity, and a long, opulent finish. Anticipated maturity: 2005–2015. Last tasted, 1/03.

2000
89 A very soft, lush, sexy wine, with a dark ruby/purple color and a striking nose of melted licorice intermixed with cocoa, plum, and berry fruit, this medium-bodied wine is impossible to resist. It is pure seduction, but does not appear to be a vintage capable of lasting beyond 8–10 years, although it is impeccably balanced, and that accounts for a lot in the wine's longevity. Anticipated maturity: now–2012. Last tasted, 1/03.

1999
87 A lower acid, more seductive version of the 1998, with less definition and a more evolved style, the 1999 will drink well for 3–4 years. Last tasted, 1/03.

1998
88 The 1998 is an open-knit, sexy, dark ruby–colored wine with plenty of sweet spice, jammy black cherry fruit, cigar box, and vanilla in the aromatics as well as flavors. Displaying excellent texture, supple tannin, and low acidity, it will drink well for 6–7 years. Last tasted, 3/01.

GUADET-ST. JULIEN

Classification: St.-Emilion Grand Cru Classé

Owner: Robert Lignac

Address: 4, rue Guadet, 33330 St.-Emilion

Telephone: 5 57 24 63 50; Telefax: 33 5 57 24 63 50

Visits: By appointment Monday to Friday

Contact: Mrs. Lignac

VINEYARDS

Surface area: 14.8 acres

Grape varietals: 75% Merlot, 25% Cabernet Franc

Average age of vines: More than 35 years

Density of plantation: 5,200 vines per hectare

Average yields: 35 hectoliters per hectare, over the last five years

Elevage: Fermentations last 15–21 days. Wines are transferred to oak barrels, 40% of which are new, for 18–20 months aging. They are fined but remain unfiltered.

WINES PRODUCED

Château Guadet-St. Julien: 24,000 bottles

No second wine is produced.

Plateau of maturity: Within 3–9 years of the vintage

This property's vineyard is located north of the town of St.-Emilion on the limestone plateau, but the cellars and winemaking facility are in St.-Emilion. The style of wine produced is soft, round, somewhat monolithic, and straightforward, but pleasant and attractive in top vintages. Buyers are advised to drink the wine when it is young.

HAUT-BRISSON

Classification: Grand Cru

Owner: GFA du Château Haut-Brisson

Address: Brisson, 33330 Vignonet

Telephone: 05 57 84 69 57; Telefax: 05 57 74 93 11

E-mail: haut-brisson@wanadoo.fr

Visits: By appointment only

Contact: Mr. Moulinet or Mme. de la Faye

VINEYARDS

Surface area: 32.1 acres

Grape varietals: 70% Merlot, 20% Cabernet Sauvignon, 10% Cabernet Franc

Average age of vines: 25–30 years

Density of plantation: 6,000 vines per hectare

Average yields: 48 hectoliters per hectare

Elevage: Twenty to thirty day fermentation and maceration. Fifteen to eighteen months aging in new oak barrels. No fining, no filtration.

WINES PRODUCED

Château Haut-Brisson: 36,000 bottles

Château Haut-Brisson La Grave: 24,000 bottles

Plateau of maturity: Within 3–10 years of the vintage

GENERAL APPRECIATION

This attractively priced, pleasant, richly fruity St.-Emilion deserves greater attention from consumers seeking good values.

IMPORTANT VINTAGES

2001 The deep ruby/purple–colored 2001 Haut-Brisson displays sweet black cherry
87–88 and cassis fruit intertwined with notions of subtle oak, earth, and herbs. Well made, long, ripe, and savory, it will provide immense enjoyment during its first 7–8 years of life. Last tasted, 1/03.

2000 One of St.-Emilion's most attractive overperformers, Haut-Brisson is generally
88 available for a realistic price. The well-made 2000 offers a deep ruby/purple color as well as sweet black currant and cassis fruit intertwined with fennel and underbrush characteristics. With good ripeness, sweet tannin, and low acidity, it will drink well between now–2010. Last tasted, 1/03.

1999 An elegant, dark ruby–colored St.-Emilion with subtle wood and excellent black
87 cherry fruit intermixed with licorice and dried herbs, this soft wine needs to be drunk over the next 3–4 years. Last tasted, 3/00.

HAUT-CORBIN

Classification: Grand Cru Classé

Owner: SMABTP group

Address: 33330 St.-Emilion

Telephone: 05 57 51 95 54; Telefax: 05 57 51 90 93

Visits: By appointment Monday to Friday, 9–11:30 A.M. and 2–5 P.M.

No visits in August and at harvest time.

Contact: Dominique Teyssou

VINEYARDS

Surface area: 14.8 acres

Grape varietals: 65% Merlot, 25% Cabernet Sauvignon, 10% Cabernet Franc

Average age of vines: 40 years

Density of plantation: 5,500–6,000 vines per hectare

Average yields: 50 hectoliters per hectare

Elevage: Thirty to thirty day fermentation and maceration in temperature-controlled concrete tanks. Malolactics in barrel for 30% of the yield. Twelve months aging in barrels with 35% new oak. Fining, filtration if necessary.

WINES PRODUCED

Château Haut-Corbin: 39,000 bottles

No second wine is produced.

HAUT LA GRÂCE DIEU

Classification: Grand Cru

Owner: Saby family

Address: 33330 Saint-Laurent-des-Combes

Telephone: 05 57 24 73 03; Telefax: 05 57 24 67 77

E-mail: info@vignobles-saby.com

Website: www.vignobles-saby.com

Visits: By appointment only

Contact: Jean-Philippe Saby

VINEYARDS

Surface area: 6.2 acres

Grape varietals: 95% Merlot, 5% Cabernet Franc

Average age of vines: 45 years

Density of plantation: 5,500 vines per hectare

Average yields: 25 hectoliters per hectare

Elevage: Four to five week fermentation and maceration in temperature-controlled stainless-steel and concrete tanks with pumpings-over and *pigéages*. Fifteen months aging in new oak barrels. Fining, no filtration.

WINES PRODUCED

Château Haut La Grâce Dieu: 7,200 bottles

No second wine is produced.

HAUT GRAVET

Classification: Grand Cru

Owner: Alain Aubert

Address: 33330 Saint-Sulpice-de-Faleyrens

Mailing address: c/o Alain Aubert, 57 bis, avenue del'Europe, 333350 Saint-Magne-de-Castillon

Telephone: 05 57 40 04 30; Telefax: 05 57 56 07 10

E-mail: domaines.a.aubert@wanadoo.fr

No visits

VINEYARDS

Surface area: 23.5 acres

Grape varietals: 60% Merlot, 30% Cabernet Franc, 10% Cabernet Sauvignon

Average age of vines: 25 years

Density of plantation: 6,000 vines per hectare

Average yields: 45 hectoliters per hectare

Elevage: Fermentation and maceration in temperature-controlled stainless-steel tanks. Malolactics and 18 months aging in new oak barrels. No fining, no filtration.

WINES PRODUCED

Château Haut Gravet: 55,000 bottles

No second wine is produced.

Plateau of maturity: Within 6–15 years of the vintage

GENERAL APPRECIATION

This relatively new operation is a worthy addition to the portfolio of the Aubert family (of La Couspaude fame). A topflight wine since its debut vintage, Haut Gravet is also a fine value.

IMPORTANT VINTAGES

2001 Another serious effort from St.-Emilion's Aubert family, their impeccable 2000
88–90 has been followed by a serious, rich, extracted, intense, layered, medium-bodied 2001 displaying abundant quantities of black fruits intermixed with obvious toasty new oak. Anticipated maturity: 2005–2014. Last tasted, 1/03.

2000 The finest wine this estate has produced, the saturated purple–colored 2000 Haut-
90 Gravet offers a sweet nose of blackberry, cherry, and cassis fruit intermixed with smoke and toast. Full-bodied, opulent, rich, and concentrated, with superb purity as well as melted tannin, it will be at its best between 2006–2020. A sleeper of the vintage. Last tasted, 1/03.

HAUT MAZERAT

Classification: Grand Cru

Owner: Christian Gouteyron

Address: 4, Mazerat, 33330 St.-Emilion

Telephone: 05 57 24 71 16; Telefax: 05 57 24 67 28

Visits: By appointment Monday to Saturday, 8 A.M.–noon

Contact: Christian Gouteyron

VINEYARDS

Surface area: 14.8 acres

Grape varietals: 60% Merlot, 30% Cabernet Franc, 10% Cabernet Sauvignon

Average age of vines: 35 years

Density of plantation: 5,800 vines per hectare

Average yields: 45 hectoliters per hectare

Elevage: Three day cold maceration. Fermentation (30°C max.) and 14–21 day maceration (30°C) in vats. Eighteen months aging in vats (40% of yield) and barrels (60% of yield) with 50% new oak. Fining and filtration.

WINES PRODUCED

Château Haut Mazerat: 40,000 bottles

No second wine is produced.

HAUT-QUERCUS

Classification: Grand Cru

Owner: Union des Producteurs de St.-Emilion

Address: 33330 St.-Emilion

Mailing address: B.P.27, Haut-Gravet, 33330 St.-Emilion

Telephone: 5 57 24 70 71; Telefax: 33 5 57 24 65 18

Visits: Monday to Friday, 8:30 A.M.–noon and 2–6 P.M.

Contact: Patrick Foulon

VINEYARDS

Surface area: 11 acres

Grape varietals: 60% Merlot, 25% Cabernet Franc, 15% Cabernet Sauvignon

Average age of vines: 30–37 years

Density of plantation: 5,500 vines per hectare

Average yields: 50 hectoliters per hectare, over the last five years

Elevage: Alcoholic fermentations at 30°C and malolactic last 15–20 days in temperature-controlled concrete vats. Wines are then aged 11 months in oak barrels, which are renewed by one-third at each vintage. They are fined and filtered.

WINES PRODUCED

Haut-Quercus: 30,000 bottles

No second wine is produced.

HAUT-SARPE

Classification: Grand Cru Classé

Owner: Marie-Antoinette Janoueix and Jean-François Janoueix

Address: 33330 Saint-Christophe-des-Bardes

Mailing address: c/o Vignobles Joseph Janoueix, 37, rue Pline Parmentier, BP 192, 33506

Libourne Cedex

Telephone: 05 57 51 41 86; Telefax: 05 57 51 53 16

E-mail: info@janoueix-bordeaux.com

Website: www.j-janoueix-bordeaux.com

Visits: By appointment Monday to Friday, 8 A.M.–noon and 2–6 P.M. Fridays to 5 P.M.

Contact: Vignobles Joseph Janoueix

VINEYARDS

Surface area: 51.9 acres

Grape varietals: 70% Merlot, 30% Cabernet Franc

Average age of vines: 45 years

Density of plantation: 6,000 and 10,000 vines per hectare

Average yields: 45 hectoliters per hectare

Elevage: Twenty-five to twenty-seven day fermentation and maceration in temperature-controlled vats. Malolactics and 12–14 months aging in barrels with 80% new oak. Fining with egg whites, no filtration.

WINES PRODUCED

Château Haut-Sarpe: 66,000 bottles

Château Vieux Sarpe: 34,000 bottles

Plateau of maturity: Within 5–12 years of the vintage

Haut-Sarpe is a reliable St.-Emilion owned by the Libourne *négociant* firm of J. Janoueix. The château, which is one of the most beautiful of the region, sits to the northeast of St.-Emilion next to the highly regarded estate of Balestard La Tonnelle. The style of wine produced here is darkly colored, rustic, generously flavored, and usually firmly tannic. In good vintages the wine should be cellared for at least 5–6 years. It will keep for 12 or more.

JACQUES BLANC

Classification: Grand Cru

Owner: Vignobles Rocher Cap de Rive SA

Address: 33330 Saint-Etienne de Lisse

Telephone: 05 57 56 02 97; Telefax: 05 57 40 01 98

E-mail: chateau.jacquesblanc@wanadoo.fr

Visits: By appointment only Monday to Friday, 8 A.M.–6 P.M.

Contact: Monique Lamothe (Telephone: 06 07 68 67 62)

VINEYARDS

Surface area: 54.3 acres

Grape varietals: 70% Merlot, 30% Cabernet Franc

Average age of vines: 35 years

Density of plantation: 5,500 vines per hectare

Average yields: 48 hectoliters per hectare

Elevage: Ten day fermentation and 3–4 week maceration in vats. Twelve to fourteen months aging in barrels with 33% new oak. Fining and filtration depending upon the vintage.

WINES PRODUCED

Château Jacques Blanc Cuvée du Maître: 30,000–45,000 bottles

Château Jacques Blanc Cuvée Aliénor: 40,000 bottles

Plateau of maturity: Within 4–9 years of the vintage

GENERAL APPRECIATION

Consumers looking for a St.-Emilion emerging from a biodynamically farmed vineyard will have an interest in this otherwise average and uninspirational wine.

JEAN FAURE

Classification: Grand Cru

Owner: Michel Amart

Address: 33330 St.-Emilion

Telephone: 05 57 51 49 36; Telefax: 05 57 25 06 42

Visits: Every day, 8 A.M.–noon and 2–7 P.M.

Contact: Michel Amart

VINEYARDS

Surface area: 49.4 acres

Grape varietals: 60% Cabernet Franc, 30% Merlot, 10% Malbec

Average age of vines: 42 years

Density of plantation: 5,555 vines per hectare

Average yields: 49 hectoliters per hectare

Elevage: Traditional fermentation and maceration. Aging in barrels (25% new oak). Fining, no filtration.

WINES PRODUCED

Château Jean Faure: 100,000 bottles

No second wine is produced.

This is often a perplexing wine to evaluate given the extremely high percentage of Cabernet Franc used in the blend. However, the proprietor has long argued that the sandy soils of Jean Faure's vineyard, near both Cheval Blanc and Figeac, are perfect for this much Cabernet Franc.

JEAN VOISIN

Classification: Grand Cru

Owner: SCEA du Château Jean Voisin; Chassagnoux family

Address: 33330 St.-Emilion

Telephone: 05 57 24 70 40; Telefax: 05 57 24 79 57

Visits: By appointment

Contact: P. Chassagnoux

VINEYARDS

Surface area: 34.6 acres

Grape varietals: 70% Merlot, 30% Cabernet Franc

Average age of vines: 25 years

Density of plantation: 5,500 vines per hectare

Average yields: 45 hectoliters per hectare

Elevage: Fifteen to eighteen months aging in barrels that are renewed by half at each vintage. Fining and filtration depending upon the vintage.

WINES PRODUCED

Château Jean Voisin: 30,000 bottles

Château Jean Voisin Fagouet: 50,000 bottles

LE JURAT

Classification: Grand Cru

Owner: SMABTP group

Address: 33330 St.-Emilion

Telephone: 05 57 51 95 54; Telefax: 05 57 51 90 93

Visits: By appointment only Monday to Friday, 9:30–11:30 A.M. and 2–5 P.M.

Contact: Dominique Teyssou

VINEYARDS

Surface area: 18.7 acres

Grape varietals: 80% Merlot, 20% Cabernet Sauvignon

Average age of vines: 30 years

Density of plantation: 5,500–6,000 vines per hectare

Average yields: 51 hectoliters per hectare

Elevage: Twenty-eight to thirty-two day fermentation and maceration in temperature-controlled concrete tanks. After malolactics, 12 months aging in barrels that are renewed by a third at each vintage. Fining and filtration.

WINES PRODUCED

Château Le Jurat: 49,000 bottles

No second wine is produced.

Plateau of maturity: Within 3–10 years of the vintage

LAFLEUR VACHON

Classification: Grand Cru

Owner: Andrée, Raymond, and Nicole Tapon

Address: 33330 St.-Emilion

Mailing address: c/ Château des Moines, Mirande, 33570 Montagne-St.-Emilion

Telephone: 05 57 74 61 20 *or* 05 57 24 71 20; Telefax: 05 57 74 61 19

E-mail: vinstapon@aol.com

Visits: By appointment only

Contact: Nicole Tapon or Jean-Christophe Renaut

VINEYARDS

Surface area: 9.9 acres

Grape varietals: 70% Merlot, 20% Cabernet Franc, 5% Cabernet Sauvignon, 5% Malbec

Average age of vines: 35 years

Density of plantation: 6,500 vines per hectare

Average yields: 50 hectoliters per hectare

Elevage: Four to six week fermentation and maceration in temperature-controlled stainless-steel and wooden tanks, with indigenous yeasts. Eighteen months aging in barrels for the whole yield, without any new oak. No fining, no filtration.

WINES PRODUCED

Château Lafleur Vachon: 25,000 bottles

No second wine is produced.

LAFON LA TUILERIE

Classification: Grand Cru, as of 2000

Owner: Pierre Lafon

Address: 33330 Saint-Etienne-de-Lisse

Mailing address: c/o EARL Lafon, 33490 Saint-André-du-Bois

Telephone: 05 56 76 42 74; Telefax: 05 56 76 49 78

E-mail: pierre-lafon@wanadoo.fr

Visits: By appointment only

Contact: Pierre Lafon

VINEYARDS

Surface area: 6.2 acres

Grape varietals: 95% Merlot, 5% Cabernet Sauvignon

Average age of vines: 35 years

Density of plantation: 5,500–6,000 vines per hectare

Average yields: 47 hectoliters per hectare

Elevage: Four to five week fermentation and maceration in temperature-controlled vats. Eighteen months aging in barrels with 80% new oak. Fining, no filtration.

WINES PRODUCED

Château Lafon La Tuilerie: 12,000–14,000 bottles

No second wine is produced.

LAROQUE

Classification: Grand Cru Classé

Owner: SCA Famille Beaumartin

Address: 33330 St.-Emilion

Telephone: 05 57 24 77 28; Telefax: 05 57 24 63 65

Visits: Preferably by appointment

Contact: Bruno Sainson

VINEYARDS

Surface area: 143 acres, but only 67 acres produce Château Laroque

Grape varietals: 87% Merlot, 11% Cabernet Franc, 2% Cabernet Sauvignon

Average age of vines: 30 years

Density of plantation: 5,265 vines per hectare

Average yields: 44 hectoliters per hectare

Elevage: Alcoholic fermentations and macerations with skins last approximately four weeks in temperature-controlled concrete vats. Wines are then run off from the less. They are aged in oak barrels, which are renewed by a third or by half at each vintage, for 12 months and are blended in vats. They are bottled after 22 months, after both fining and filtration.

WINES PRODUCED

Château Laroque: 150,000 bottles

Château Peymouton: 100,000 bottles

Plateau of maturity: Within 3–8 years of the vintage

LEYDET-FIGEAC

Classification: Grand Cru

Owner: Bernard Leydet

Address: 33330 St.-Emilion

Mailing address: EARL des Vignobles Leydet, Rouilledirat, 33500 Libourne

Telephone: 05 57 51 19 77; Telefax: 05 57 51 00 62

E-mail: frederic.leydet@wanadoo.fr

Visits: By appointment only Monday to Friday, 9 A.M.–noon and 2–6 P.M.

Contact: Bernard Leydet (Telephone: 06 08 93 10 03)

VINEYARDS

Surface area: 9.5 acres

Grape varietals: 70% Merlot, 15% Cabernet Franc, 15% Cabernet Sauvignon

Average age of vines: 30 years

Density of plantation: 5,800 vines per hectare

Average yields: 50 hectoliters per hectare

Elevage: Four to six week fermentation (28–32°C) and maceration in temperature-controlled concrete tanks with pumpings-over. Twelve months aging in barrels that are renewed by a third at each vintage. Fining and filtration.

WINES PRODUCED

Château Leydet-Figeac: 24,000 bottles

No second wine is produced.

LEYDET-VALENTIN

Classification: Grand Cru

Owner: Bernard Leydet

Address: 33330 St.-Emilion

Mailing address: EARL des Vignobles Leydet, Rouilledirat, 33500 Libourne

Telephone: 05 57 51 19 77; Telefax: 05 57 51 00 62

E-mail: frederic.leydet@wanadoo.fr

Visits: By appointment only Monday to Friday, 9 A.M.–noon and 2–6 P.M.

Contact: Bernard Leydet

VINEYARDS

Surface area: 12.4 acres

Grape varietals: 66% Merlot, 34% Cabernet Franc

Average age of vines: 25 years

Density of plantation: 5,500 vines per hectare

Average yields: 52 hectoliters per hectare

Elevage: Seven to ten day fermentation and 4–6 week maceration in temperature-controlled concrete tanks. Eleven to fourteen months aging in barrels that are renewed by half at each vintage. Fining, no filtration.

WINES PRODUCED

Château Leydet-Valentin: 18,000 bottles

Château Saint-Valentin: 12,000 bottles

MAGNAN LA GAFFELIÈRE

Classification: Grand Cru

Owner: GFA du Clos de la Madeleine

Address: La Gaffelière Ouest, 33330 St.-Emilion

Mailing address: BP 78, 33330 St.-Emilion

Telephone: 05 57 55 38 03; Telefax: 05 57 55 38 01

Visits: Monday to Friday, 9 A.M.–6 P.M. By appointment for other days and dates.

VINEYARDS

Surface area: 20.6 acres

Grape varietals: 65% Merlot, 25% Cabernet Franc, 10% Cabernet Sauvignon

Average age of vines: 23 years

Density of plantation: 5,500 vines per hectare

Average yields: 48 hectoliters per hectare

Elevage: Five week fermentation and maceration. Aging in barrels that are renewed by half at each vintage. Fining, no filtration.

WINES PRODUCED

Château Magnan La Gaffelière: 53,000 bottles

MARQUEY

Classification: Grand Cru

Owner: SCEA Château Franc-Mayne, Georgy Fourcroy and partners

Address: Cantealouette, 33330 St.-Emilion

Mailing address: c/o Château Franc-Mayne, 33330 St.-Emilion

Telephone: 05 57 24 67 61; Telefax: 05 57 24 68 25

E-mail: contact@chateau-francmayne.com

Website: www.chateau-francmayne.com

No visits

VINEYARDS

Surface area: 7.2 acres

Grape varietals: 90% Merlot, 10% Cabernet Franc

Average age of vines: 25 years

Density of plantation: 5,500 vines per hectare

Average yields: 45 hectoliters per hectare

Elevage: Three to five day cold maceration. Three to five week fermentation and maceration. Aging in vats (10% of the yield) and in barrels (90% of the yield) with 50% new oak. No fining, filtration.

WINES PRODUCED

Château Marquey: 17,000 bottles

No second wine is produced.

MARTINET

Classification: Grand Cru

Owner: Lavaux family

Address: 33330 St.-Emilion

Mailing address: Établissements Horeau-Beylot, BP 125, 33501 Libourne Cedex

Telephone: 05 57 51 06 07; Telefax: 05 57 51 59 61

Visits: By appointment only

Contact: François de Lavaux

VINEYARDS

Surface area: 49.4 acres

Grape varietals: 65% Merlot, 35% Cabernet Franc and Cabernet Sauvignon

Average age of vines: 50 years

Density of plantation: 5,500 vines per hectare

Average yields: 40–45 hectoliters per hectare

Elevage: Fermentations and macerations last 18–23 days in temperature-controlled stainless-steel and concrete tanks. Malolactics usually occur in tanks (sometimes a very small percentage of the yield completes this process in oak barrels), and wines are aged for 8–12 months by rotation in oak barrels, 10–15% of which are new (60% of the yield), and concrete tanks (40% of the yield). They are fined and filtered upon bottling.

WINES PRODUCED

Château Martinet: 120,000 bottles

No second wine is produced.

MATRAS

Classification: Grand Cru Classé

Owner: GFA du Château Matras

Address: 33330 St.-Emilion

Telephone: 05 57 24 72 46; Telefax: 05 57 51 70 19

Visits: By appointment only

Contact: Véronique Gaboriaud

VINEYARDS

Surface area: 22.2 acres

Grape varietals: 60% Cabernet Franc, 40% Merlot

Average age of vines: 40 years or more

Density of plantation: 5,500 vines per hectare

Average yields: 45 hectoliters per hectare

Elevage: Fermentations and macerations last three weeks in temperature-controlled stainless-steel vats. Wines undergo malolactics in tanks and are then aged 18 months with 30% new oak. They are fined but remain unfiltered.

WINES PRODUCED

Château Matras: 32,000 bottles

L'Hermitage de Matras: 20,000 bottles

Plateau of maturity: Within 3–10 years of the vintage

MAUVEZIN

Classification: Grand Cru (declassified in 1996)

Owner: GFA Pierre Cassat and family

Address: 33330 St.-Emilion

Mailing address: Domaine de Peyrelongue, BP 44, 33330 St.-Emilion

Telephone: 05 57 24 72 36; Telefax: 05 57 74 48 54

Website: www.advintage.com/mauvezin

Visits: By appointment Monday to Saturday, 8 A.M.–noon and 2–6 P.M.

Contact: Olivier Cassat (Telephone: 06 71 11 75 92)

VINEYARDS

Surface area: 8.6 acres

Grape varietals: 70% Merlot, 30% Cabernet Franc

Average age of vines: 50 years

Density of plantation: 5,400 and 6,600 vines per hectare

Average yields: 42 hectoliters per hectare

Elevage: Prolonged fermentation and maceration in temperature-controlled stainless-steel vats. Malolactics in barrel for 50% of the yield. Twelve to eighteen months aging in barrels with 60% new oak, with micro-oxygenation of lees. Fining and filtration.

WINES PRODUCED

Château Mauvezin: 15,000 bottles

No second wine is produced.

Plateau of maturity: Within 3–10 years of the vintage

MONLOT CAPET

Classification: Grand Cru

Owner: Bernard Rivals

Address: Saint-Hippolyte, 33330 St.-Emilion

Telephone: 05 57 74 49 47; Telefax: 05 57 24 62 33

Visits: Monday to Friday, 9 A.M.–noon and 2–6 P.M.

Contact: Bernard Rivals

VINEYARDS

Surface area: 17.3 acres

Grape varietals: 70% Merlot, 25% Cabernet Franc, 5% Cabernet Sauvignon

Average age of vines: 30 years

Density of plantation: 5,000 vines per hectare

Average yields: 45 hectoliters per hectare

Elevage: Eighteen months aging in barrels with 50% new oak. Fining and filtration.

WINES PRODUCED

Château Monlot Capet: 45,000 bottles

No second wine is produced.

MONTLABERT

Classification: Grand Cru

Owner: SC du Château Montlabert

Address: Montlabert 3, 33330 St.-Emilion

Mailing address: c/o Château Franc-Mayne, 33330 St.-Emilion

Telephone: 05 57 24 62 61; Telefax: 05 57 24 68 25

Visits: By appointment only every day, 9 A.M.–7 P.M.
Estate closed from January to March.

Contact: Catherine Montant

VINEYARDS

Surface area: 23.5 acres (in production)

Grape varietals: 90% Merlot, 10% Cabernet Franc

Average age of vines: 20 years

Density of plantation: 5,900 vines per hectare

Average yields: 50 hectoliters per hectare

Elevage: Three to five week fermentation and maceration. Aging in barrels with 30% new oak. Fining and filtration.

WINES PRODUCED

Château Montlabert: 18,000 bottles

Château La Croix Montlabert: 45,000 bottles

LA MOULEYRE

Classification: Grand Cru

Owner: GFA de Sainte-Colombe

Address: 33330 St.-Emilion

Mailing address: 17, La Cale, 33330 Vignonet

Telephone: 05 57 84 53 16; Telefax: 05 57 74 93 47

E-mail: vignobles@vignobles-bardet.fr

Website: www.vignobles-bardet.fr

Visits: By appointment onlyContact: Philippe Bardet

VINEYARDS

Surface area: 14.8 acres

Grape varietals: 88% Merlot, 12% Cabernet Franc

Average age of vines: 17 years

Density of plantation: 6,000 and 8,300 vines per hectare

Average yields: 55–60 hectoliters per hectare

Elevage: Fermentation and maceration in temperature-controlled stainless-steel and concrete vats. Twenty to twenty-four months aging in barrels that are renewed by a third at each vintage. Fining and filtration.

WINES PRODUCED

Château La Mouleyre: 36,000 bottles

No second wine is produced.

MOULIN BELLEGRAVE

Classification: Grand Cru

Owner: Florian Perrier

Address: Vignonet, 33330 St.-Emilion

Telephone: 05 57 74 97 08; Telefax: 05 57 74 92 79

Visits: By appointment only

Contact: Florian Perrier

VINEYARDS

Surface area: 17.2 acres

Grape varietals: 60% Merlot, 20% Cabernet Franc, 20% Cabernet Sauvignon

Average age of vines: 30 years

Density of plantation: 5,000 vines per hectare

Average yields: 45 hectoliters per hectare

Elevage: Fermentations and macerations are conducted in temperature-controlled stainless-steel vats. Malolactics occur in tanks, after which the wines are transferred to oak barrels (20% new) for six months aging. They are fined and filtered.

WINES PRODUCED

Château Moulin Bellegrave: 40,000 bottles

Château des Graves: 25,000 bottles

DU PARADIS

Classification: Grand Cru

Owner: Raby-Saugeon S.A.

Address: Vignobles Raby-Saugeon, 33330 St.-Emilion

Telephone: 05 57 55 07 20; Telefax: 05 57 55 07 21

E-mail: chateau.du.paradis@wanadoo.fr

Website: www.château-du-paradis.fr

Visits: By appointment Monday to Friday,
9 A.M.–noon and 2–6 P.M.

Contact: Janine Raby-Saugeon

VINEYARDS

Surface area: 29.5 acres

Grape varietals: 75% Merlot, 20% Cabernet Franc, 5% Cabernet Sauvignon

Average age of vines: 35 years

Density of plantation: 5,500 vines per hectare

Average yields: 47 hectoliters per hectare

Elevage: Traditional fermentation and maceration in temperature-controlled vats. Eighteen months aging, including 14 months in barrel with 30% new oak. Fining with egg whites and filtration.

WINES PRODUCED

Château du Paradis: 55,000 bottles

Reflet du Paradis: 20,000–25,000 bottles

DOMAINE DE LA PART DES ANGES

Classification: Grand Cru

Owner: Catherine and Gregory Leymarie

Address: 33330 Saint-Sulpice-de-Faleyrens

Telephone: 05 57 74 49 06; Telefax: 05 57 51 99 94

E-mail: partdesanges@wanadoo.fr

No visits

VINEYARDS

Surface area: 0.3 acres

Grape varietals: 94% Cabernet Franc, 6% Merlot

Average age of vines: 55 years

Density of plantation: 6,600 vines per hectare

Average yields: 9.3 hectoliters per hectare

Elevage: 35+ day fermentation and maceration in temperature-controlled wooden open-top vat that is renewed at each vintage. Malolactics and 18–20 months aging in a new oak half-barrel. No fining, no filtration.

WINES PRODUCED

Domaine de la Part des Anges: 120 bottles

No second wine is produced.

PAS DE L'ANE

Classification: Grand Cru (since 2001)

Owner: A. Delaire, Y. Blanc, N. Baptiste, R. Perreira

Address: Lieu-dit Jean Guillot, 33330 Saint-Christophe des Bardes

Mailing address: c/o Château Branda, Roques, 33570 Puisseguin

Telephone: 05 57 74 62 55; Telefax: 05 57 74 57 33

E-mail: n.baptiste@wanadoo.fr

Visits: By appointment only

Contact: N. Baptiste (Telephone: 06 80 88 18 78)

VINEYARDS

Surface area: 14.1 acres

Grape varietals: 50% Cabernet Franc, 50% Merlot

Average age of vines: 30 years

Density of plantation: 5,500 vines per hectare

Average yields: 30 hectoliters per hectare

Elevage: Fermentation and maceration in temperature-controlled wooden and stainless-steel vats. Eighteen months aging in new oak barrels. No fining, no filtration.

WINES PRODUCED

Château Pas de L'Ane: 20,000 bottles

No second wine is produced.

DE PASQUETTE

Classification: Grand Cru

Owner: GFA Jabiol

Address: 33330 Saint-Sulpice-de-Faleyrens

Mailing address: c/o Château Cadet-Piola, BP 24, 33330 St.-Emilion

Telephone: 05 57 74 47 69; Telefax: 05 57 24 68 28

E-mail: infos@chateaucadetpiola.com

Website: www.chateaucadetpiola.com

Visits: Monday to Friday, 9 A.M.–noon and 2–5 P.M.

Contact: Amélie Jabiol

VINEYARDS

Surface area: 7.9 acres

Grape varietals: 80% Merlot, 10% Cabernet Franc, 10% Cabernet Sauvignon

Average age of vines: 37 years

Density of plantation: 5,500 vines per hectare

Average yields: 39 hectoliters per hectare

Elevage: Twenty-one day fermentation and maceration in temperature-controlled stainless-steel tanks. Fifteen months aging in barrels with 25% new oak. Fining, no filtration.

WINES PRODUCED

Château de Pasquette: 15,000 bottles

No second wine is produced.

PATRIS

Classification: Grand Cru

Owner: Michel Querre

Address: 33330 St.-Emilion

Mailing address: BP 51, 33330 St.-Emilion

Telephone: 05 57 55 51 60; Telefax: 05 57 55 51 61

Visits: By appointment Monday to Friday (except public holidays), 9 A.M.–noon and 2–6 P.M.

Contact: Michel Querre or Thierry Delon

VINEYARDS

Surface area: 21 acres

Grape varietals: 90% Merlot, 10% Cabernet Franc

Average age of vines: 40 years

Density of plantation: 5,500 vines per hectare

Average yields: 35 hectoliters per hectare

Elevage: Four to five week fermentation and maceration in temperature-controlled stainless-steel tanks. Malolactics and 16–18 months aging in new oak barrels. No fining, no filtration.

WINES PRODUCED

Château Patris: 24,000 bottles

Filius du Château Patris: 12,000 bottles

Plateau of maturity: Within 3–10 years of the vintage

GENERAL APPRECIATION

This is an estate consumers are advised to monitor closely since it belongs to Michel Querre, the proprietor of up-and-coming Le Moulin in Pomerol. If prices remain within reasonable limits, Patris could prove quite a good buy.

PAVILLON-CADET

Classification: Grand Cru

Production: 1,300 cases

Grape varietals: 60% Merlot, 40% Cabernet Franc

Secondary label: None

Surface area: 6.2 acres

Proprietor: Morvan-Leamas

Time spent in barrels: 14–22 months

Average age of vines: 25 years

Evaluation of present classification: The quality equivalent of a good Médoc Cru Bourgeois

Plateau of maturity: Within 5–14 years of the vintage

PETIT-FAURIE-DE-SOUTARD

Classification: Grand Cru Classé

Owner: Françoise Capdemourlin

Address: 33330 St.-Emilion

Mailing address: c/o SCEV Aberlen, 33330 St.-Emilion

Telephone: 05 57 74 62 06; Telefax: 05 57 74 59 34

E-mail: info@vignoblescapdemourlin.com

Website: www.vignoblescapdemourlin.com

Visits: By appointment only

Contact: Thierry Capdemourlin

VINEYARDS

Surface area: 19.8 acres

Grape varietals: 65% Merlot, 30% Cabernet Franc, 5% Cabernet Sauvignon

Average age of vines: 30 years

Density of plantation: 5,500 vines per hectare

Average yields: 44 hectoliters per hectare

Elevage: Three week fermentation and maceration in temperature-controlled stainless-steel vats. Fifteen to eighteen months aging in barrels with 50% new oak. No fining, filtration.

WINES PRODUCED

Château Petit-Faurie-de-Soutard: 42,000 bottles

No second wine is produced.

Plateau of maturity: Within 5–10 years of the vintage

GENERAL APPRECIATION

Another Capdemourlin estate, Petit-Faurie-de-Soutard is a well-made wine for better than casual drinking.

This is an underrated St.-Emilion property with a relatively small production. The administrator, the Capdemourlin family, often promotes the wines from Balestard La Tonnelle more than those from Petit-Faurie-de-Soutard. Nevertheless, this vineyard, once part of the famous Soutard domaine, is well situated on the limestone plateau. The wines tend to have a great deal of fat and richness of fruit, much like Balestard, but also perhaps more structure and grip because of higher tannin levels.

IMPORTANT VINTAGES

2000 The finest example I have seen of this wine, the opaque purple–colored 2000 ex-
87 hibits copious quantities of jammy black cherries intertwined with soil, wet stone, and new oak aromas. Medium to full-bodied and powerful, with low acidity and abundant concentration, this fine effort will be drinkable between 2004–2014. Last tasted, 1/03.

1999   Dark ruby–colored with aromas of weedy, black currant fruit offered in a pleasant,
86   balanced, attractive, fruity style, this 1999 St.-Emilion should be consumed over
the next five years. Last tasted, 3/02.

PETIT FIGEAC

Owner: Chateau Figeac

Address: 33330 St.-Emilion

Telephone: 05 57 24 72 26; Telefax: 05 57 74 45 74

Visits: By appointment only

Contact: Eric D'aramon

VINEYARDS

Surface area: 7.5 acres

Grape varietals: 60% Merlot, 30% Cabernet Franc,
10% Cabernet Sauvignon

Average age of vines: 35 years

Density of plantation: 5,500 vines per hectare

Average yields: 45 hectoliters per hectare, over the last five years

Elevage: 12–15 months in oak casks prior to bottling

WINES PRODUCED

Château Petit Figeac: 1,500 cases

No second wine is produced.

Plateau of maturity: within 3–10 years of the vintage

DOMAINE DE PEYRELONGUE

Classification: Grand Cru

Owner: GFA Pierre Cassat and sons

Address: 33330 St.-Emilion

Mailing address: BP 4, 33330 St.-Emilion

Telephone: 05 57 24 72 36; Telefax: 05 57 74 48 54

Website: www.advintage.com/mauvezin

Visits: By appointment Monday to Saturday,
8 A.M.–noon and 2–6 P.M.

Contact: Olivier Cassat (Telephone: 06 71 11 75 92)

VINEYARDS

Surface area: 18.5 acres

Grape varietals: 70% Merlot, 25% Cabernet Franc, 5% Cabernet Sauvignon

Average age of vines: 35 years

Density of plantation: 5,400 vines per hectare

Average yields: 48 hectoliters per hectare

Elevage: Three week fermentation and maceration in temperature-controlled stainless-steel and enamel-lined vats. Malolactics in barrel for 10% of the yield. Twelve months aging in stainless-steel tanks (25% of yield) and in barrels (75% of yield) with 20% new oak, rackings and micro-oxygenation of lees. Fining and filtration.

WINES PRODUCED

Domaine de Peyrelongue: 47,000 bottles

No second wine is produced.

PIERRE DE LUNE

Classification: Grand Cru

Owner: Tony and Véronique Ballu

Address: 1, Chatelet Sud, 33330 St.-Emilion

Telephone: 05 57 74 49 72; Telefax: 05 57 74 49 72

E-mail: veronique.ballu@wanadoo.com

Visits: By appointment Monday to Friday, 9 A.M.–5 P.M.

Contact: Véronique Ballu

VINEYARDS

Surface area: 2.3 acres

Grape varietals: 90% Merlot, 10% Cabernet Franc

Average age of vines: 20 years

Density of plantation: 6,600 vines per hectare

Average yields: 30 hectoliters per hectare

Elevage: Thirty day fermentation and maceration with manual *pigéage*. Eighteen months aging with 50% new oak. No fining, no filtration.

WINES PRODUCED

Château Pierre de Lune: 3,500 bottles

No second wine is produced.

Plateau of maturity: Within 10 years of the vintage

GENERAL APPRECIATION

This garage wine from the manager of Clos Fourtet, which generally qualifies as a sleeper pick, is all at once open-knit, expansive, ripe, chewy, and fruit-driven with copious levels of glycerin. Some vintages have proven a little too woody, but if you can find it, buy it!

IMPORTANT VINTAGES

2001 This dark purple–colored 2001 provides a layered, textural, sensual feel in the
88–90 mouth along with attractive levels of black currant and jammy cherry fruit intermixed with abundant new oak. Surprisingly low in acidity for a 2001, with a lot of

plumpness, it will drink well over the next decade. A totally hedonistic wine! Last tasted, 1/03

2000 A friendly, opulent effort, the dense purple–colored 2000 possesses loads of glyc-
90 erin, sweet black cherry and currant fruit, and well-integrated toasty new oak. With low acidity, ripe tannin, and good depth, this sexy wine will be drinkable between now and 2012. Last tasted, 1/03.

1999 Dense ruby/purple–colored, with considerable size for a 1999, this rich wine's
88 only problem might be its level of wood, which is aggressive and somewhat intrusive. Nevertheless, one has to admire the ripe blackberry and cassis fruit, low acidity, and excellent purity. If the wood becomes better integrated, it will merit a solid 89 point rating . . . at the minimum. Anticipated maturity: 2006–2015. Last tasted, 3/02.

PINDEFLEURS

Classification: Grand Cru

Address: 33330 St.-Emilion

Telephone: 5 57 24 72 04

Production: 3,500 cases

Blend: 55% Merlot, 45% Cabernet Franc

Secondary label: Clos Lescure

Vineyard size: 21.2 acres

Proprietor: Micheline Dior

Time spent in barrels: 18–22 months

Average age of vines: 22 years

Evaluation of present classification: Should be elevated to a grand cru classé; the quality equivalent of a very good Médoc Cru Bourgeois

Plateau of maturity: Within 3–14 years of the vintage

LA POINTE CHANTECAILLE

Classification: Grand Cru

Owner: Paulette Estager

Address: Chantecaille, 33330 St.-Emilion

Mailing address: c/o Vignobles J.-M. Estager, 55, rue des 4 frères Robert, 33500 Libourne

Telephone: 05 57 51 06 97; Telefax: 05 57 25 90 01

E-mail: vignoblesestager@aol.com

Visits: By appointment only

Contact: M.-F. Paganelli-Estager

VINEYARDS

Surface area: 2.8 acres

Grape varietals: 80% Merlot, 20% Cabernet Franc

Average age of vines: 30 years

Density of plantation: 5,500 vines per hectare

Average yields: 46 hectoliters per hectare

Elevage: Twenty-five day fermentation (30°C) and maceration in temperature-controlled stainless-steel and concrete vats. Twelve to eighteen months aging in barrels that are renewed by a third at each vintage. Fining and filtration.

WINES PRODUCED
Château La Pointe Chantecaille: 7,100 bottles

PONTET-FUMET

Classification: Grand Cru

Owner: Roger Bardet

Address: 33330 St.-Emilion

Mailing address: 17, La Cale, 333330 Vignonet

Telephone: 05 57 84 53 16; Telefax: 05 57 74 93 47

E-mail: vignobles@vignobles-bardet.fr

Website: www.vignobles-bardet.fr

Visits: By appointment only

Contact: Philippe Bardet

VINEYARDS
Surface area: 27.2 acres

Grape varietals: 72% Merlot, 21% Cabernet Franc, 7% Cabernet Sauvignon

Average age of vines: 25 years

Density of plantation: 6,000 and 8,333 vines per hectare

Average yields: 60 hectoliters per hectare

Elevage: Prolonged fermentation and maceration in temperature-controlled stainless-steel and concrete tanks. Twenty to twenty-four months aging in barrels that are renewed by a third at each vintage. Fining and filtration.

WINES PRODUCED
Château Pontet-Fumet: 75,000 bottles

No second wine is produced.

LE PRIEURÉ

Classification: Grand Cru Classé

Owner: Olivier Guichard

Address: 33330 St.-Emilion

Mailing address: c/o SCE Baronne Guichard, Château Siaurac, 33500 Néac

Telephone: 05 57 51 64 58; Telefax: 05 57 51 41 56

Visits: By appointment only

Contact: Yannick Reyrel

VINEYARDS

Surface area: 15.4 acres

Grape varietals: 85% Merlot, 15% Cabernet Franc

Average age of vines: 40 years

Density of plantation: 6,000 vines per hectare

Average yields: 45 hectoliters per hectare

Elevage: Three to four week fermentation and maceration in temperature-controlled concrete tanks. Fourteen months aging in barrels with 30% new oak. Fining and filtration.

WINES PRODUCED

Château Le Prieuré: 22,000 bottles

L'Olivier: Variable

PRIEURÉ-LESCOURS

Classification: Grand Cru

Owner: Ets Thunevin

Address: 33330 Saint-Sulpice-de-Faleyrens

Mailing address: c/o Ets Thunevin, 6, rue Guadet, 33330 St.-Emilion

Telephone: 05 57 55 09 13; Telefax: 05 57 55 09 12

E-mail: thunevin@thunevin.com

Website: www.thunevin.com

No visits

VINEYARDS

Surface area: 9.9 acres

Grape varietals: 70% Merlot, 30% Cabernet Franc

Average age of vines: 30 years

Density of plantation: 6,000 vines per hectare

Average yields: 40 hectoliters per hectare

Elevage: Traditional fermentation and maceration. Eighteen to twenty months aging in new oak barrels. No fining, no filtration.

WINES PRODUCED
Château Prieuré-Lescours: 21,000 bottles

GENERAL APPRECIATION
Though I have not tasted this wine since the property was brought by Jean-Luc Thunevin in 2002, I can imagine, judging by the terrific job he has done over the past years, that Prieuré-Lescours will undoubtedly be of high quality.

PUY-BLANQUET

Classification: Grand Cru

Owner: Roger Jacquet

Address: 33330 Saint-Étienne-de-Lisse

Telephone: 05 57 40 18 18; Telefax: 05 57 40 29 14

Visits: By appointment only

Contact: Pierre Meunier

VINEYARDS
Surface area: 56.8 acres

Grape varietals: 80% Merlot, 15% Cabernet Franc, 5% Cabernet Sauvignon

Average age of vines: 25 years

Density of plantation: 5,300 vines per hectare

Average yields: 50 hectoliters per hectare

Elevage: Fermentations and macerations last three weeks in concrete vats. Malolactics occur in vats. Twenty percent of the yield is aged 12 months in oak barrels, one-third of which are new; the remaining 80% of the wines are aged in concrete vats. The wines are fined and filtered.

WINES PRODUCED
Château Puy-Blanquet: 120,000 bottles

Château Laberne: 33,000 bottles

Plateau of maturity: Within 3–8 years of the vintage

PUY-RAZAC

Classification: Grand Cru

Owner: Thoilliez family

Address: 33330 St.-Emilion

Telephone: 05 57 24 73 32; Telefax: 05 57 24 75 99

E-mail: puy-razac@wanadoo.fr

Visits: By appointment only

Contact: Guy Thoillez

VINEYARDS

Surface area: 14.8 acres

Grape varietals: 57% Merlot, 43% Cabernet Franc

Average age of vines: 30 years

Density of plantation: 5,500 vines per hectare

Average yields: 50 hectoliters per hectare

Elevage: Three week fermentation and maceration in temperature-controlled concrete tanks of small capacity. Twenty-two months aging in vats and barrels (which are renewed by half at each vintage). Fining, no filtration.

WINES PRODUCED

Château Puy-Razac: 15,000 bottles

Château Les Aigrières: 25,000 bottles

QUERCY

Classification: Grand Cru

Owner: Apelbaum-Pidoux family

Address: 3, Grave, Vignonnet, 33330 St.-Emilion

Telephone: 05 57 84 56 07; Telefax: 05 57 84 54 82

E-mail: chateauquercy@wanadoo.fr

Visits: By appointment only

Contact: Stéphane Apelbaum

VINEYARDS

Surface area: 15.4 acres

Grape varietals: 80% Merlot, 20% Cabernet Franc

Average age of vines: 45 years

Density of plantation: 6,500 vines per hectare

Average yields: 35–38 hectoliters per hectare

Elevage: Fifteen to twenty day fermentation and 2–4 week maceration in temperature-controlled, cone-shaped wooden vats and concrete and stainless-steel tanks, with frequent *pigéages* and pumpings-over. Part of the yield undergoes malolactics in barrels. Fifteen to twenty-four months aging in barrels with micro-oxygenation and regular stirring of lees. No fining, no filtration.

WINES PRODUCED

Château Quercy: 18,000 bottles

Château Graves de Peyroubas: 4,000 bottles maximum

RABY-JEAN VOISIN

Classification: Grand Cru

Owner: Raby-Saugeon SA

Address: Vignobles Raby-Saugeon, 33330 St.-Emilion

Mailing address: BP 1,33330 St.-Emilion

Telephone: 05 57 55 07 20; Telefax: 05 57 55 07 21

E-mail: chateau.du.paradis@wanadoo.fr

Website: www.château-du-paradis.fr

No visits

VINEYARDS

Surface area: 23.5 acres

Grape varietals: 75% Merlot, 20% Cabernet Franc, 5% Cabernet Sauvignon

Average age of vines: 35 years

Density of plantation: 5,500 vines per hectare

Average yields: 47 hectoliters per hectare

Elevage: Traditional fermentation and maceration in temperature-controlled vats. Eighteen months aging, including 14 months in barrels with 30% new oak. Fining and filtration.

WINES PRODUCED

Château Raby-Jean Voisin: 55,000–60,000 bottles

No second wine is produced.

RIOU DE THAILLAS

Classification: Grand Cru

Owner: GFA Béchet

Address: 33330 St.-Emilion

Mailing address: Fougas, BP 51, 33710 Lansac

Telephone: 05 57 68 27 36; Telefax: 05 57 68 28 59

E-mail: m.bechet@wanadoo.fr

Website: vignoblesbechet.com

Visits: By appointment only

Contact: Michèle Béchet

VINEYARDS

Surface area: 6 acres

Grape varietals: 100% Merlot

Average age of vines: 30 years

Density of plantation: 5,400 vines per hectare

Average yields: 40–45 hectoliters per hectare

Elevage: Cold maceration. Fermentation and maceration in temperature-controlled wooden tanks of 50 hectoliter capacity with *pigéages*. After malolactics, 18 months aging on lees with stirring in new oak barrels. Fining, filtration depends upon the vintage.

WINES PRODUCED

Château Riou de Thaillas: 12,000 bottles

Plateau of maturity: Within 3–10 years of the vintage

GENERAL APPRECIATION

This small, quasi–garage wine always shows considerable depth, purity, and ripeness. Although it has not met my expectations in 2001, this is a property to watch given the fact that proprietor Jean-Yves Béchet also makes another of the top sleepers from the Right Bank, the Côtes de Bourg called Fougas-Maldorer.

IMPORTANT VINTAGES

2001 **86–87** Medium bodied, with a deep ruby color, this somewhat pinched wine from this small estate shows some sweet black cherry, smoky oak, and licorice, but little else. Drink it over the next 7–8 years. Last tasted, 3/01.

2000 **89** The finest effort yet from this estate, this deep ruby/purple–colored wine shows smoky, oaky notes intermixed with chocolate, black currant, spice box, and licorice. The wine is medium to full-bodied, with lush, concentrated fruit, excellent purity, and a long layered finish. Anticipated maturity: 2005–2014. Last tasted, 1/03.

1999 **87** This is a sexy, New World-ish, modern-styled St.-Emilion revealing copious quantities of new oak, jammy black cherry and cassis fruit, low acidity, and sweet tannin. It is a sure-fire antidote for hedonists looking for immediate gratification. Anticipated maturity: now–2009. Last tasted, 3/02.

1998 **87** Produced from a vineyard on the Pomerol border, this deep ruby/purple–colored 1998 displays a structured, well-delineated personality, with spicy oak, dried herbs, and red and black fruits. It is a very good to excellent wine to enjoy during its first decade of life. Last tasted, 3/01.

RIPEAU

Classification: Grand Cru Classé

Owner: Françoise de Wilde

Address: 33330 St.-Emilion

Telephone: 05 57 74 41 41; Telefax: 05 57 74 41 57

E-mail: chat.ripeau@wanadoo.fr

Visits: By appointment only Monday to Friday,
9 A.M.–5 P.M.

Contact: Françoise de Wilde

VINEYARDS

Surface area: 38.3 acres

Grape varietals: 60% Merlot, 30% Cabernet Franc, 10% Cabernet Sauvignon

Average age of vines: 35 years

Density of plantation: 6,000 vines per hectare

Average yields: 40 hectoliters per hectare

Elevage: Fermentation and maceration in temperature-controlled stainless-steel vats.
Twelve to fourteen months aging in barrels that are renewed by half at each vintage.
Fining and filtration.

WINES PRODUCED

Château Ripeau: 60,000 bottles

La Garenne de Ripeau: 8,000 bottles

Plateau of maturity: Within 3–10 years of the vintage

GENERAL APPRECIATION

This estate has much improved over recent years, especially since the wines have
benefited from the judicious advice of Alain Raynaud of Quinault fame. While not one of
the best St.-Emilions, Ripeau is of higher than average quality and as such is worthy of
consumers' interest. Do not mistake it for Pipeau, which is far better.

Ripeau is one of the older estates of St.-Emilion, taking its name from the parcel of land
on which the vineyard and château are situated. The soil is primarily sand intermixed
with some gravel. Ripeau's vineyard sits near Cheval Blanc and La Dominique, but is
not as well-placed as either. The new owners acquired the property in 1976, and major
renovations have taken place. This has always been a relatively chunky, fruity wine
that lacks consistency, but when it is good it can be counted on to drink well for at least
a decade.

IMPORTANT VINTAGES

2000
87
This is a commercial, mainstream, yet delicious St.-Emilion for enjoying during
its first 7–10 years of life. Surprisingly soft for a wine from this vintage, but savory
and rich with considerable volume and ripe, leather-tinged black cherry and currant fruit, this 2000 has soft tannin and up-front appeal. Last tasted, 1/03.

1999 This is a commercial, mainstream, yet delicious St.-Emilion for drinking during
87   its first 7–10 years of life. The dense ruby/garnet color reveals considerable evolu-
      tion. Plum, fig, herb, tobacco, and weedy black currant fruit are followed by a lush,
      round wine that should be drunk over the next 6–8 years. Last tasted, 3/01.
1998 A dark ruby/plum color accompanies a sweet nose of prunes and black fruits. This
85?   wine is somewhat of a paradox in that the entry on the palate is soft and jammy, but
      hard, harsh, rustic tannin takes over and the wine becomes compressed as well as
      attenuated. Anticipated maturity: now–2007. Last tasted, 3/01.

DU ROCHER

Classification: Grand Cru

Owner: GFA du Château du Rocher

Address: 33330 Saint-Etienne de Lisse

Mailing address: c/o SCEA Baron de Montfort,
Château du Rocher, 33330 Saint-Etienne-de-Lisse

Telephone: 05 57 40 18 20; Telefax: 05 57 40 37 26

Visits: By appointment only

Contact: Baron de Montfort

VINEYARDS

Surface area: 37 acres

Grape varietals: 70% Merlot, 20% Cabernet Sauvignon, 10% Cabernet Franc

Average age of vines: 30 years

Density of plantation: 5,500 vines per hectare

Average yields: 45 hectoliters per hectare

Elevage: Three week fermentation and maceration in temperature-controlled stainless-
steel and concrete vats. Eighteen months aging in barrels that are renewed by a third at
each vintage. Fining and filtration.

WINES PRODUCED

Château du Rocher: 85,000 bottles
No second wine is produced.

ROLLAND-MAILLET

Classification: Grand Cru

Owner: SCEA Rolland

Address: Corbin, 33330 St.-Emilion

Mailing address: SCEA Fermière des Domaines Rollan
Maillet, 33500 Pomerol

Telephone: 05 57 51 23 05; Telefax: 05 57 51 66 08

E-mail: rolland.labo@wanadoo.fr

Visits: By appointment only

Contact: Dany Rolland

VINEYARDS

Surface area: 8.3 acres

Grape varietals: 75% Merlot, 25% Cabernet Franc

Average age of vines: 30 years

Density of plantation: 6,000 vines per hectare

Average yields: 35 hectoliters per hectare

Elevage: Twenty-five to thirty day fermentation and maceration in temperature-controlled vats of small capacity that allow separate vinification of the different parcels. Eighteen months aging in one-year-old barrels and vats. Fining and filtration depending upon the vintage.

WINES PRODUCED

Château Rolland-Maillet: 20,000 bottles

No second wine is produced.

Plateau of maturity: Within 3–8 years of the vintage

GENERAL APPRECIATION

This estate belongs to the Rolland family and the vinifications are supervised by the talented Michel and Dany.

Bordeaux insiders often look for this well-made St.-Emilion owned and vinified by the famous Libourne oenologist Michel Rolland. It tends to be a chunky, robust, deeply concentrated, opaquely colored St.-Emilion that can age for up to a decade. What it lacks in finesse and elegance it often makes up for with pure power and robustness.

IMPORTANT VINTAGES

2001 Loads of fruit characterize this jammy, medium to full-bodied, very lush, supple
87–88 textured wine that is pure and tasty—not meant for long-term aging but for drinking during its first 7–8 years of life. Last tasted, 1/03.

2000 Probably the finest effort I have ever tasted from this estate, the 2000 has a deep
88 ruby/purple color and loads of jammy black cherry fruit infused with licorice and a hint of cocoa. The wine is well made, very pure, lush, and just a sensual, hedonistic turn-on. Drink it over the next 8–10 years. Last tasted, 1/03.

LA ROSE-POURRET

Classification: Grand Cru

Owner: Bernardette Warion

Address: 33330 St.-Emilion

Telephone: 05 57 24 71 13; Telefax: 05 57 74 43 93

E-mail: contact@la-rose-pourret.com

Website: www.la-rose-pourret.com

Visits: Monday to Friday, 9 A.M.–noon and 2–6 P.M.

Contact: Philippe Warion

VINEYARDS

Surface area: 19.8 acres

Grape varietals: 70% Merlot, 25% Cabernet Franc, 5% Cabernet Sauvignon

Average age of vines: 40 years

Density of plantation: 6,000 vines per hectare

Average yields: 45 hectoliters per hectare

Elevage: Three to four week fermentation and maceration in temperature-controlled concrete vats. Twelve to fifteen months aging in barrels with 40% new oak. Fining and filtration.

WINES PRODUCED

Château La Rose-Pourret: 42,000 bottles

Château Vieux Tertre: 5,000 bottles

ROYLLAND

Classification: Grand Cru

Owner: Christine and Pascal Oddo and Chantal Oddo-Vuitton

Address: 33330 St.-Emilion

Telephone: 05 57 24 68 27; Telefax: 05 57 24 65 25

Visits: By appointment Monday to Friday, 9 A.M.–noon and 3–6 P.M.

Contact: Chantal Oddo-Vuitton (Telephone: 06 16 95 75 70)

VINEYARDS

Surface area: 23.5 acres

Grape varietals: 90% Merlot, 10% Cabernet Franc

Average age of vines: 30–35 years

Density of plantation: 6,500 vines per hectare

Average yields: 45 hectoliters per hectare

Elevage: Three to five week fermentation and maceration in temperature-controlled 90-hectoliter stainless-steel and 75-hectoliter concrete tanks. Twelve to fourteen months aging in concrete vats (10% of yield) and in barrels (90% of yield) that are renewed by a third at each vintage. Fining, no filtration.

WINES PRODUCED

Château Roylland: 35,000–40,000 bottles

Château Rocheyron: 10,000–15,000 bottles

Plateau of maturity: Within 5–8 years of the vintage

ROZIER

Classification: Grand Cru

Owner: Saby family

Address: 33330 Saint-Laurent-des-Combes

Telephone: 05 57 24 73 03; Telefax: 05 57 24 67 77

E-mail: info@vignobles-saby.com

Website: www.vignobles-saby.com

Visits: By appointment only

Contact: Jean-Philippe Saby

VINEYARDS

Surface area: 54.3 acres

Grape varietals: 90% Merlot, 10% Cabernet Franc

Average age of vines: 45 years

Density of plantation: 5,500 vines per hectare

Average yields: 45 hectoliters per hectare

Elevage: Four week fermentation and maceration in temperature-controlled stainless-steel and concrete tanks with pumpings-over and *pigéages*. Twelve months aging in barrels that are renewed by half at each vintage. Fining, no filtration.

WINES PRODUCED

Château Rozier: 85,000 bottles

Château de Monturon: 45,000 bottles

SAINT GEORGES CÔTE PAVIE

Classification: Grand Cru Classé

Owner: Jacques and Marie-Gabrielle Masson

Address: 33330 St.-Emilion

Mailing address: BP 66, 33330 St.-Emilion

Telephone: 05 57 74 44 23

Visits: By appointment, September and October only

Contact: Jacques Masson

VINEYARDS

Surface area: 13.6 acres

Grape varietals: 80% Merlot, 20% Cabernet Franc

Average age of vines: 30 years

Density of plantation: 5,500 vines per hectare

Average yields: 48 hectoliters per hectare

Elevage: Fermentation and maceration in stainless-steel tanks. Eighteen months aging in barrels with 33% new oak. Fining and light filtration.

WINES PRODUCED

Château Saint Georges Côte Pavie: 25,000–30,000 bottles

Côte Madeleine: Variable

Plateau of maturity: Within 8–12 years of the vintage

This is another tiny St.-Emilion vineyard that is extremely well placed on the hillside known as the Côte de Pavie. In fact, the vineyards of Pavie sit on one side of this property, with those of La Gaffelière on the other.

The only vintages I have tasted, 1990, 1989, and 1988, were round, generously endowed, easy to like St.-Emilion that lacked complexity but offered copious amounts of straightforward, chunky, black fruit married nicely with the scent of new oak and herbaceous aromas. My best guess is that they will last for 8–12 or more years. This could be a property to take seriously.

SAINT-LÔ

Classification: Grand Cru

Owner: Vignobles Réunis SA

Address: 33330 Saint-Pey-d'Armens

Mailing address: Vignobles Réunis SA, 41,
avenue de la Libération, 33110 Le Bouscat

Telephone: 05 57 47 15 22; Telefax: 05 57 47 14 98

E-mail: accucil@saint-lo-group.com

Visits: Monday to Friday, 8 A.M.–noon and 1:30–5 P.M.

Contact: Jean-François Vergne

VINEYARDS

Surface area: 37 acres

Grape varietals: 85% Merlot, 15% Cabernet Franc

Average age of vines: 27 years

Density of plantation: 5,000 vines per hectare

Average yields: 45 hectoliters per hectare

Elevage: Sixteen to eighteen months aging in barrels with 50% new oak. Fining and filtration.

WINES PRODUCED

Château Saint-Lô: 80,000 bottles

No second wine is produced.

GENERAL APPRECIATION

All the vintages of Saint-Lô I have tasted were generally dominated by hard tannins.

SANCTUS

Classification: Grand Cru

Owner: SA Château La Bienfaisance

Administrator: Patrick Baseden

Address: 33330 Saint-Christophe-des-Bardes

Telephone: 05 57 24 65 83; Telefax: 05 57 24 78 26

E-mail: info@labienfaisance.com

Website: www.sanctus.tm.fr

Visits: By appointment only Monday to Friday,
8:30 A.M.–noon and 2–6 P.M.Contact: Christine Peytour

VINEYARDS

Surface area: 9.4 acres

Grape varietals: 74% Merlot, 26% Cabernet Franc

Average age of vines: 35 years

Density of plantation: 5,500 vines per hectare

Average yields: 32 hectoliters per hectare

Elevage: Thirty day fermentation and maceration in temperature-controlled vats, with indigenous yeasts and manual *pigéages*. Malolactics and 20 months aging on lees in new oak barrels, with micro-oxygenation and no rackings. Fining, no filtration.

WINES PRODUCED

Sanctus: 12,000 bottles

No second wine is produced.

Plateau of maturity: Within 5–15 years of the vintage, for the 2001 and 2000

GENERAL APPRECIATION

Since its debut in 1998, this estate was considered by others to be one of St.-Emilion's finest cult wines, but initially I was not impressed, finding the first two vintages blatantly woody. However, as of 2000, with the hiring of super-guru/consultant Stéphane Derénoncourt, the improvement has been spectacular. Though it is too soon to predict if this trend will continue, I would strongly advise consumers to closely monitor the evolution of Sanctus, which is likely to turn out to be an important player in its appellation.

IMPORTANT VINTAGES

2001 **90–92** It is obvious that hotshot winemaking consultant Stéphane Derenoncourt has had a profound impact on the quality of these wines. The 2001 exhibits a deep purple color and a sweet nose of blackberry liqueur intermixed with cassis, licorice, vanilla, and espresso. It is deep, full-bodied, heady, and certainly one of the best wines in the vintage from St.-Emilion. Anticipated maturity: 2007–2017. Last tasted, 1/03.

2000 **90+** An imposing wine with high tannin but also equally high extract and richness, the heady smorgasbord of aromas range from blackberries to cassis to cherries, vanilla, coffee, and licorice. The wine is deep, full-bodied, and powerful, with a lot of structure but also a lot of sweetness. I would not touch a bottle for at least another 5–6 years. Anticipated maturity: 2008–2018. Last tasted, 1/03.

1999 **78** The 1999 Sanctus is a disappointingly thin, austere, attenuated offering with hard tannin and little charm or depth. Anticipated maturity: 2005–2012. Last tasted, 3/02.

1998 **80?** New oak obliterates the character of this medium ruby–colored, modestly endowed effort. Drink it over the next 3–4 years. Last tasted, 3/02.

SANSONNET

Classification: Grand Cru

Owner: D'Aulan family

Address: 33330 St.-Emilion

Mailing address: c/o Sopalia, 8 rue Piper, 51100 Reims

Telephone: 05 57 24 76 29; Telefax: 05 57 24 76 29

E-mail: delphine.moussay-derouet@wineplanet.com

Visits: By appointment only

Contact: Delphine Moussay (Telephone: 05 57 34 51 66; Telefax: 05 57 30 11 45)

VINEYARDS

Surface area: 17.3 acres

Grape varietals: 80% Merlot, 10% Cabernet Franc, 10% Cabernet Sauvignon

Average age of vines: 38 years

Density of plantation: 5,500 vines per hectare

Average yields: 36 hectoliters per hectare

Elevage: Twenty-five to twenty-eight day fermentation and maceration in temperature-controlled stainless-steel vats. Malolactics and 20–24 months aging in new oak barrels. Fining, no filtration.

WINES PRODUCED

Château Sansonnet: 20,000 bottles

Château Lasalle: 10,000 bottles

Plateau of maturity: Within 5–15 years of the post-1998 vintages

GENERAL APPRECIATION

This estate was recently bought by the d'Aulan family from Reims and is emerging from the throes of mediocrity under the helmsmanship of young Patrick d'Aulan. The latter has benefited from the valuable assistance of the late Jean-Michel Arcaute (who resurrected Clinet) and winemaking-guru Michel Rolland. As of 1999, the wines have improved and, given the commitment to excellence of the new owner, I would not be surprised if Sansonnet quickly rises to the higher echelons of the St.-Emilion hierarchy.

IMPORTANT VINTAGES

2001 I had high hopes that this wine would turn out better, but to date it has not exhib-
85–86 ited a great deal of character from barrel. The wine exhibits sweet-and-sour cherry notes intermixed with vanilla and spice box. The wine is medium bodied but a bit dry and astringent in the finish. Drink it over the next 8–10 years. Last tasted, 1/03.

2000 Deep ruby/purple, with sweet black currant and cherry fruit offered in a medium-
88 to full-bodied, ripe style with moderate tannin and a long finish, this wine could turn out to be a sleeper of the vintage. Anticipated maturity: 2006–2016. Last tasted, 1/03.

1999 A medium-bodied, elegant effort, the 1999 Sansonnet offers aromas of currants,
86 tobacco, dried herbs, and soil. Enjoy it over the next 5–6 years. Last tasted, 3/02.

LA SERRE

Classification: Grand Cru Classé

Owner: Luc d'Arfeuille

Address: 33330 St.-Emilion

Telephone: 05 57 24 71 38; Telefax: 05 57 24 63 01

E-mail: darfeuille.luc@wanadoo.fr

Visits: By appointment only Monday to Friday,
10 A.M.–noon and 2–5 P.M.

Contact: Luc d'Arfeuille

VINEYARDS

Surface area: 17.3 acres

Grape varietals: 80% Merlot, 20% Cabernet Franc

Average age of vines: 35 years

Density of plantation: 6,000 vines per hectare

Average yields: 38–43 hectoliters per hectare

Elevage: Fermentation and maceration in temperature-controlled concrete tanks. Aging
in barrels that are renewed by half at each vintage. Fining, no filtration.

WINES PRODUCED

Château La Serre: 25,000 bottles

Les Menuts de La Serre: 5,000 bottles

TAUZINAT L'HERMITAGE

Classification: Grand Cru

Owner: Heirs to Bernard Moueix

Address: 33330 Saint-Christophe-des Bardes

Mailing address: c/o Château Taillefer, BP 9,
33501 Libourne Cedex

Telephone: 05 57 25 50 45; Telefax: 05 57 25 50 45

No visits

VINEYARDS

Surface area: 22.2 acres

Grape varietals: 80% Merlot, 15% Cabernet Franc, 5% Cabernet Sauvignon

Average age of vines: 30 years

Density of plantation: 6,000 vines per hectare

Average yields: 45 hectoliters per hectare

Elevage: Three to four week fermentation and maceration in temperature-controlled
concrete vats. Twelve months aging in barrels with 33% new oak. Fining and
filtration.

WINES PRODUCED

Château Tauzinat L'Hermitage: 38,000 bottles

Château Le Grand Treuil: 16,000 bottles

Plateau of maturity: Within 3–8 years of the vintage

TOUR BALADOZ

Classification: Grand Cru

Owner: Jacques de Schepper

Address: 33330 Saint-Laurent-des-Combes

Telephone: 05 57 88 94 17; Telefax: 05 57 88 39 14

E-mail: ch-baladoz@aol.com

Visits: By appointment Monday to Friday

Contact: Jean-Michel Garcion

VINEYARDS

Surface area: 22.2 acres

Grape varietals: 70% Merlot, 25% Cabernet Franc, 5% Cabernet Sauvignon

Average age of vines: 25 years

Density of plantation: 6,600 vines per hectare

Average yields: 50 hectoliters per hectare

Elevage: Four to five week fermentation and maceration in temperature-controlled vats. Twelve to eighteen months aging in barrels, with 60% new oak. Fining and filtration.

WINES PRODUCED

Château Tour Baladoz: 30,000 bottles

Le Dauphin de Baladoz: 20,000 bottles

LA TOUR DU PIN FIGEAC

Classification: Grand Cru Classé

Owner: GFA Giraud-Bélivier

Address: 33330 St.-Emilion

Mailing address: c/o SARL André Giraud, Château Le Caillou, 33500 Pomerol

Telephone: 05 57 51 06 10; Telefax: 05 57 51 74 95

E-mail: giraud.belivier@wanadoo.fr

Visits: By appointment Monday to Friday, 9 A.M.–noon and 2–6 P.M.

Contact: André Giraud

VINEYARDS

Surface area: 27.2 acres

Grape varietals: 75% Merlot, 25% Cabernet Franc

Average age of vines: 35 years

Density of plantation: 5,500 vines per hectare

Average yields: 48 hectoliters per hectare

Elevage: Three to four week fermentation and maceration in temperature-controlled concrete tanks. Twelve months aging by rotation (at the time of rackings) in vats (for one-third of the yield) and barrels (for the rest). Fining, no filtration.

WINES PRODUCED

Château La Tour du Pin Figeac: 66,000 bottles

La Tournelle du Pin Figeac: Variable

Plateau of maturity: Within 3–8 years of the vintage

TRIMOULET

Classification: Grand Cru

Owner: Michel Jean

Address: 33330 St.-Emilion

Mailing address: BP 60, 33330 St.-Emilion

Telephone: 05 57 24 70 56; Telefax: 05 57 74 41 69

E-mail: infos@chateau-trimoulet.com

Website: www.chateau-trimoulet.com

Visits: By appointment only

Contact: Michel Jean

VINEYARDS

Surface area: 43 acres

Grape varietals: 60% Merlot, 35% Cabernet Franc, 5% Cabernet Sauvignon

Average age of vines: 30 years

Density of plantation: 5,500 vines per hectare

Average yields: 45 hectoliters per hectare

Elevage: Four to five week fermentation and maceration in temperature-controlled vats. After malolactics, 12 months aging in oak barrels that are renewed by a third at each vintage. Fining and filtration.

WINES PRODUCED

Château Trioulet: 50,000 bottles

Emilius de Trimoulet: 45,000 bottles

DU VAL D'OR

Classification: Grand Cru

Owner: Anne-Marie and Roger Bardet

Address: 33330 Vignonet

Mailing address: 17, La Cale, 33330 Vignonet

Telephone: 05 57 84 53 16; Telefax: 05 57 74 93 47

E-mail: vignobles@vignobles-bardet.fr

Website: www.vignobles-bardet.fr

Visits: By appointment only

Contact: Philippe Bardet

VINEYARDS

Surface area: 29.6 acres

Grape varietals: 82% Merlot, 12% Cabernet Franc, 6% Cabernet Sauvignon

Average age of vines: 27 years

Density of plantation: 6,000 and 8,300 vines per hectare

Average yields: 60 hectoliters per hectare

Elevage: Prolonged fermentation and maceration in temperature-controlled stainless-steel and concrete vats. Twenty to twenty-four months aging in barrels that are renewed by a third at each vintage. Fining and filtration.

WINES PRODUCED

Château du Val d'Or: 76,000 bottles

No second wine is produced.

VIEUX CHÂTEAU L'ABBAYE

Classification: Grand Cru

Owner: F. Lladères

Address: 33330 Saint-Christophe-des-Bardes

Mailing address: BP 69, 33330
Saint-Christophe-des-Bardes

Telephone: 05 57 47 98 76 *or* 06 07 60 74 97;
Telefax: 05 57 47 93 03

Visits: By appointment only Monday to Saturday,
10 A.M.–noon and 2–6 P.M.

Contact: F. Lladères

VINEYARDS

Surface area: 4.3 acres

Grape varietals: 85% Merlot, 15% Cabernet Franc

Average age of vines: 45 years

Density of plantation: 5,800 vines per hectare

Average yields: 42 hectoliters per hectare

Elevage: Five week fermentation and maceration. Fifteen months aging in barrels that are renewed by half at each vintage. No fining, no filtration.

WINES PRODUCED
Vieux Château l'Abbaye: 10,000 bottles
No second wine is produced.

VIEUX-CHÂTEAU-CARRÉ

Classification: Grand Cru

Production: 1,500 cases

Blend: 60% Merlot, 20% Cabernet Franc, 20% Cabernet Sauvignon

Secondary label: None

Vineyard size: 7.5 acres

Proprietor: Yvon Dubost

Time spent in barrels: 14–20 months

Average age of vines: 20 years

Evaluation of present classification: The quality equivalent of a Médoc Cru Bourgeois

Plateau of maturity: Within 3–7 years of the vintage

VIEUX FORTIN

Classification: Grand Cru
Owner: Claude Sellan
Address: 33330 St.-Emilion
Telephone: 05 57 24 69 97; Telefax: 05 57 24 69 97
E-mail: vieuxfortin@hotmail.com
Visits: By appointment
Contact: Claude Sellan

VINEYARDS
Surface area: 13.2 acres

Grape varietals: 60% Merlot, 40% Cabernet Franc

Average age of vines: 35 years

Density of plantation: 4,500 vines per hectare

Average yields: 43 hectoliters per hectare

Elevage: Fermentation and prolonged maceration in temperature-controlled stainless-steel tanks. Eighteen to twenty-four months aging in new oak barrels. Fining, no filtration.

WINES PRODUCED

Château Vieux Fortin: 30,000 bottles

Sellan: Variable, generally 5,000–7,000 bottles

Plateau of maturity: Within 3–10 years of the vintage

VIEUX SARPE

Classification: Grand Cru

Owner: Jean and Françoise Janoueix

Address: 33330 St.-Emilion

Mailing address: Maison Janoueix, 37, rue Pline-Parmentie
BP 192, 33506 Libourne Cedex

Telephone: 05 57 51 41 86; Telefax: 05 57 51 53 16

Visits: By appointment only

Contact: Maison Janoueix

VINEYARDS

Surface area: 27 acres

Grape varietals: 70% Merlot, 20% Cabernet Franc, 10% Cabernet Sauvignon

Average age of vines: 40 years

Density of plantation: 6,000 vines per hectare

Average yields: 45 hectoliters per hectare

Elevage: Fermentations and macerations last 3–4 weeks in temperature-controlled
concrete and stainless-steel vats. After malolactics, wines are aged two years in oak
barrels, 30% of which are new. They are fined with egg whites and remain unfiltered.

WINES PRODUCED

Château Vieux Sarpe: 35,000 bottles

Château Haut-Badette: 27,000 bottles

YON-FIGEAC

Classification: Grand Cru Classé

Owner: Denis Londeix

Address: 3-5, Yon, 33330 St.-Emilion

Telephone: 05 57 42 66 66; Telefax: 05 57 64 36 20

Visits: By appointment only

Contact: Marie Fabre

VINEYARDS

Surface area: 61.7 acres

Grape varietals: 80% Merlot, 20% Cabernet Franc

Average age of vines: 25 years

Density of plantation: 5,500 vines per hectare

Average yields: 45 hectoliters per hectare

Elevage: Cold maceration lasts 4–5 days. Fermentations and macerations last about 3–4 weeks in temperature-controlled stainless-steel tanks. Malolactics occur partially in oak barrels. Wines are transferred to oak casks for 12–15 months aging (30–40% new oak is utilized). They are racked twice during the aging process and fined with fresh egg whites, but remain unfiltered.

WINES PRODUCED

Château Yon-Figeac: 105,000 bottles

Château Yon-Saint-Martin: 25,000 bottles

Plateau of maturity: Within 3–10 years of the vintage

GENERAL APPRECIATION

Yon-Figeac has started producing very serious wines lately, but it is not yet at the level of some of its peers like Pipeau, Rochebelle, or Rocher Bellevue Figeac. I suggest, however, that consumers keep an eye on this property, which made a remarkable turnaround two or three years ago, especially so that availability is assured, as it has a relatively large vineyard. This might ultimately turn out to be a fine value of the appellation.

Yon-Figeac is a beautifully turreted château, with vineyards located northwest of the town of St.-Emilion on shallow, sandy soil. The style of wine produced tends to be round and silky, with a great deal of red and black fruit character. It is not a wine that would seemingly last long, although I have had no experience with vintages older than seven years.

IMPORTANT VINTAGES

2001 A very sexy concoction of plum, raspberry, and currant fruit jumps from the glass
87–89 of this medium-bodied, soft, very stylish, seductive wine. There is something about the wines of this estate that are very distinctive in character, with floral blue and black fruit characteristics and no hard edges. It is certainly a wine for drinking during its first 7–10 years of life. Last tasted, 1/03.

2000 The finest Yon-Figeac I have ever tasted, this deep ruby/purple–colored wine
90 offers an aromatic display and flavors not terribly dissimilar from a top vintage of the famed L'Evangile. Sweet blackberry and wild mountain berry fruit is interwoven with hints of raisins, plums, and white flowers. Medium to full-bodied, somewhat tight at present, but loaded and nicely textured with very sweet fruit, this is undoubtedly a sleeper of the vintage. As the wine sits in the glass, more black raspberries seem to emerge with aeration. Anticipated maturity: 2006–2015. Last tasted, 1/03.

1999 An elegant, medium-bodied effort with notes of sweet cherries, plums, figs, and
87 dried herbs, this round, attractive, straightforward St.-Emilion needs to be drunk during its first 7–8 years of life. Last tasted, 1/03.

BARSAC AND SAUTERNES

The Barsac and Sauternes wine-producing regions are located a short 40-minute drive south from downtown Bordeaux. Labor intensive and expensive to produce, the sweet wines of Barsac and Sauternes have long had huge climatic and manpower problems to overcome almost every year. Additionally, for most of the last hundred years the producers have had to confront a dwindling demand for these luscious, sweet, sometimes decadently rich and exotic wines because of consumers' growing demand for drier wines. Given the fact that it is rare for a particular decade to produce more than three excellent vintages for these wines, the producers in this charming and rural viticultural region have become increasingly pessimistic that their time has passed. Château owners have changed at a number of properties, and more and more vineyards are also producing a dry white wine to help ease cash-flow problems.

Yet surprisingly, many growers continue. They know they make one of the most remarkable wines in the world, and they hope that Mother Nature, good luck, and an increasing consumer awareness of their products will result in accelerated demand and appreciation of these white wines, which until recently were France's most undervalued and underappreciated great wines.

Perhaps their persistence has finally paid off. The second half of the 1980s may well be viewed by future historians as the beginning of the renaissance for Barsac and Sauternes. There are many reasons for this turnaround in fortune. The fact that Mother Nature produced three superb, perhaps even legendary vintages—1990, 1989, and 1988—helped focus attention on the regions' producers and their wines.

Second, a number of estates that had been in the doldrums for a while began to turn out wine that merited significant interest. In particular, the resurrection of the French Ministry of Agriculture's famed Château La Tour Blanche, with profound wines in 1990, 1989, and 1988, served as a sign that even the French government was interested in vindicating the great reputation of this famous estate.

Another premier grand cru classé, Rabaud-Promis, also began to make top-flight wines; culminating in sensational efforts in 1990, 1989, and 1988. Furthermore, the acquisition of one of the flagship estates of the region, Château Rieussec, by the Domaines Rothschild in 1984 suggested that the great red winemaking empire of the Rothschilds would be expanded to include lavishly rich, sweet white wines. That promise has been fulfilled, first with compelling efforts in 1990, 1989, and 1988, fol-

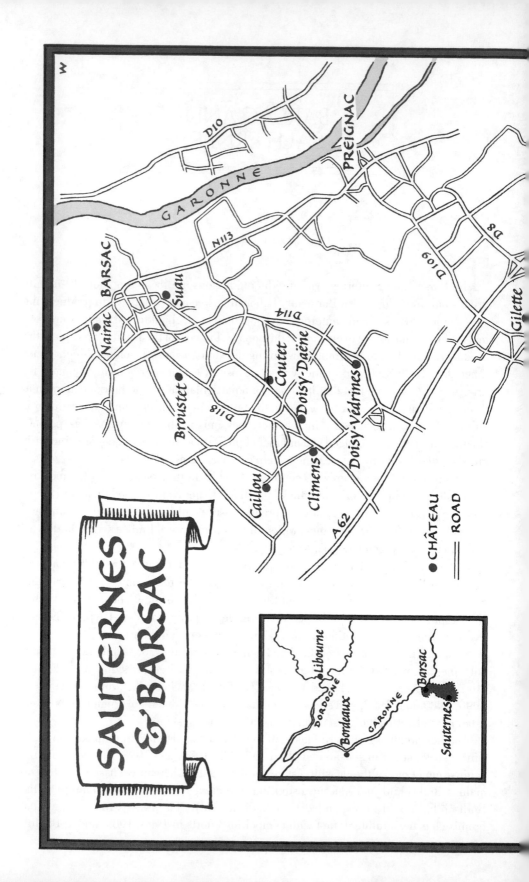

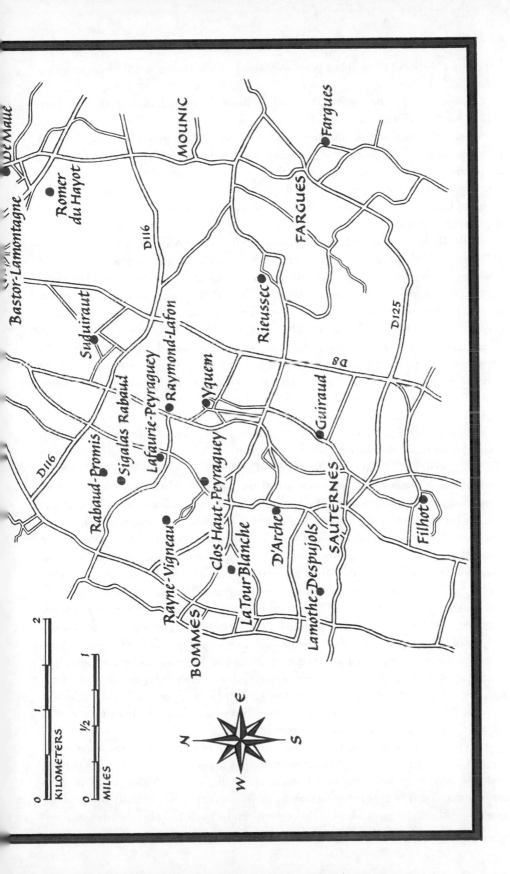

lowed by a series of triumphant years over the last few vintages, culminating with a colossal 2001.

At the same time, the continued revival of Château Guiraud, under Canadian ownership, went on with a succession of fine vintages.

All of this appeared to culminate with the 1990, 1989, and 1988 vintages, which were considered to be the greatest Sauternes vintages since 1937, until 2001 emerged, a truly monumental vintage. Futures of these vintages became difficult to find, and a renewed confidence emerged. After all the difficulties they had experienced, the sweet wines of Barsac and Sauternes appeared poised to become fashionable once again on the world's best tables.

While Mother Nature can be exceptionally kind to the region's producers (1986–1990 for example), the period between 1991 and 1995 produced few inspirational wines from this area. At the time of writing, my tastings of the 2001s revealed magnificent wines, clearly the finest since 1990, 1989, and 1988. Modern-day technology has helped producers combat nature with a radical new winemaking procedure called cryo-extraction. This technique could be employed in less successful vintages to freeze the grapes and transform many so-so wines into something much richer and more interesting. Whether or not this will gain favor with the top estates, and whether or not it produces weaknesses in the wines when they are 10–25 years old, cannot be measured until well into the 21st century. But there is no question that it has helped raise the current quality of many wines.

No one doubts that the winemakers of Barsac and Sauternes face the most forbidding odds for producing successful wines. The hopes and fears regarding the outcome of a vintage normally begin at the time most of the red wine–producing appellations to the north have commenced or even finished their harvests. During the latter half of September, Mother Nature begins to unfold the climatic conditions that will be important for the vintages of this region. The climate in Barsac and Sauternes is normally misty, mild, and humid at this time of year. The foggy, damp mornings (created by the Ciron River that runs through the heart of Sauternes) and sunny, dry afternoons encourage the growth of a mold called *Botrytis cinerea*. This mold—commonly called "noble rot"—attacks each ripe, mature grape individually, devouring the grape skin and causing the grape to die and become dehydrated. Of course, only grapes that are attacked by noble botrytis rot are selected. Botrytis causes a profound change particularly in the Semillon grape. It shrivels the skin, consumes up to 50% of the sugar content, forms glycerol, and decomposes the tartaric acids. The result is a grape capable of rendering only one-fourth of its volume of juice prior to the botrytis attack—an unctuous, concentrated, aromatic, sweet nectar. Curiously, the reaction causes a super-concentration of the grape's juice, which becomes considerably higher in sugar than normal. This happens without any loss of acidity.

This process is erratic and time-consuming. It can often take as long as one or two months for a significant portion of the white grapes to become infected by the botrytis mold. In some years very little botrytis develops, and the wines lack flavor dimension and complexity. When the noble rot does form, its growth can be painfully slow and uneven. Therefore, the great wines of this region can be made only by an arduous, time-consuming, labor-intensive process of sending teams of pickers into the vineyard to pick the afflicted grapes one at a time rather than bunch by bunch. The best estates have their pickers descend on the vineyard up to a half-dozen times over this period, which usually occurs throughout October and November, although some harvests have occurred in September. The famous Château d'Yquem often sends pickers through the vineyard ten separate times. As expensive and time-consuming as picking is, the most hazardous risk of all is the weather. Heavy rains, hailstorms, or frost—all common meteorological developments for Bordeaux in late fall—can instantly abort a promising vintage or turn it quickly into a disaster.

Since the conditions for making great wine are so different for Barsac and Sauternes, it is not surprising that what can be a great vintage for the red wines of Bordeaux can be challenging for the sweet white wines from this area. The years 2000, 1982, and 1961 are vintages in point. Undeniably profound years for the red wines, the sweet wines of Barsac and Sauternes had their problems. In contrast, 2001, 1988, 1980, 1967, and 1962 are five vintages for Barsac and Sauternes that most observers would consider very fine to superb. With the exception of 2001, 1988 and 1962, these vintages were less successful for most of the red wines of Bordeaux.

Like the red wines of the Médoc, the wines of Barsac and Sauternes were considered important enough to be classified into quality groupings in 1855. The hierarchy (see page 000) established Yquem as the best of the region, and it was called a "premier grand cru classé." Following Yquem were "premiers crus classés" (now 11 as a result of several vineyards' being partitioned), and 14 "deuxièmes crus classés" (now 12 because one has ceased to exist and two others have merged).

From a consumer's perspective, three unclassified Cru Bourgeois estates, Raymond-Lafon, de Fargues, and Gilette, also make exquisite wines that rival many of the classified growths except for Yquem. However, they were not included in the 1855 classification. Additionally, there are a number of first growths and second growths that simply cannot afford to make wine the traditional way—using numerous crews of pickers working sporadically over a four- to eight-week period. Several do not merit their current status and have been downgraded in my evaluations of the châteaux of these regions.

As for Château d'Yquem, it towers (both literally and figuratively) above the other estates here, producing a splendidly rich, distinctive, unique wine. In my opinion, it is Bordeaux's single most compelling wine. The official first growths of the Médoc have worthy challengers every year, often producing wine equally impressive, and the right bank trio of Cheval Blanc, Ausone, and Pétrus can in some vintages not only be matched, but surpassed by the brilliance of other estates in their respective appellations. Yquem, however, rarely has a challenger (except perhaps the elusive microscopic luxury *cuvée* of Coutet called Cuvée Madame). This is not because top Barsac and Sauternes properties such as Climens, Rieussec, or Suduiraut cannot produce superlative wine, but rather that Yquem produces a wine at such an extravagantly expensive level of quality that it is commercial madness for any other property even to attempt to emulate it.

When I wrote the first edition of *Bordeaux* in 1984, I was skeptical about the potential of all but a handful of the Barsac/Sauternes estates. Today the entire region has been transformed by the success of the 2001, 1990, 1989, 1988, and 1986 vintages and, for the most part, the estates are enjoying a degree of financial prosperity (perhaps even security) of which they would never have dreamed possible in the early 1980s. These wines, even with such revolutionary techniques as cryo-extraction, will always be among the most difficult in the world to produce, and a few bad vintages in a row or overreliance on new technology would no doubt dampen much of the appellation's enthusiasm, but for now, optimism reigns supreme in what once was one of the most distressingly sad regions of Bordeaux.

BARSAC AND SAUTERNES
(An Insider's View)

Overall Appellation Potential: Good to Superb

The Most Potential for Aging: Climens, Coutet Cuvée Madame, Gilette, Guiraud, Lafaurie-Peyraguey, Raymond-Lafon, Rieussec, Suduiraut, La Tour Blanche, Yquem

The Most Elegant: Climens, Coutet, Doisy-Daëne, Doisy-Védrines, Rieussec, La Tour Blanche

The Most Concentrated: D'Arche-Pugneau, Climens, Coutet Cuvée Madame, Lafaurie-Peyraguey, Raymond-Lafon, Rieussec, Suduiraut, Yquem

The Best Value: D'Arche-Pugneau, Bastor Lamontagne, Doisy-Daëne, Doisy-Védrines, Haut-Claverie, Les Justices, Rabaud-Promis, La Tour Blanche

The Most Exotic: D'Arche-Pugneau, Raymond-Lafon

The Most Difficult to Understand (when young): Until these wines are 4–6 years old, they rarely reveal much delineation or true personality

The Most Underrated: Rabaud-Promis, La Tour Blanche

The Most Difficult to Appreciate Young: All of them, at least until they are 4–6 years old

Up-and-Coming Estates: D'Arche-Pugneau, Rabaud-Promis, La Tour Blanche

Greatest Recent Vintages: 2001, 1990, 1989, 1988, 1986, 1983, 1976, 1975, 1967, 1962, 1959

BARSAC AND SAUTERNES—AN OVERVIEW

Location: Southeast of Bordeaux, about 26 miles from the center of the city

Acres Under Vine: 4,940; Sauternes—3,952; Barsac—998

Communes: Barsac, Bommes, Fargus, Preignac, and Sauternes

Average Annual Production: Sauternes—325,000 cases; Barsac—145,000 cases

Classified Growths: 26 classified growths and 1 premier cru supérieur—Château d'Yquem; 11 first growths, and 14 second growths

Principal Grape Varieties: Semillon and Sauvignon Blanc, with tiny quantities of Muscadelle

Principal Soil Type: Deep gravel beds over thick layers of limestone. In less desirable parts of the appellation, some sand and clay can be found.

A CONSUMER'S CLASSIFICATION OF THE CHÂTEAUX OF BARSAC AND SAUTERNES

OUTSTANDING
Climens, Coutet Cuvée Madame, Gilette, Rieussec, Suduiraut, Yquem*

EXCELLENT
D'Arche-Pugneau, Coutet, de Fargues, Guiraud, Lafaurie-Peyraguey, Raymond-Lafon, La Tour Blanche

VERY GOOD
Doisy Dubroca, Doisy-Védrines, Haut-Claverie, Rabaud-Promis, Sigalas Rabaud

GOOD
D'Arche, Bastor Lamontagne, Broustet, Clos Haut-Peyraguey, Doisy-Daëne, Filhot, Les Justices, Lamothe Guignard, Liot, de Malle, Nairac, de Rayne Vigneau, Romer du Hayot, Roumieu-Lacoste

OTHER NOTABLE PROPERTIES OF SAUTERNES AND BARSAC
Caillou, Lamothe, Lamourette, Piada, de Rolland, Saint-Marc, Suau

D'ARCHE

Classification: Second Growth in 1855

Owner: Société Themètre

Address: 33210 Sauternes

Telephone: 05 56 76 66 55; Telefax: 05 56 76 64 38

E-mail: chateau-arche@terrenet.fr

Website: www.chateaudarche.sauternes.com

Visits: Monday to Friday, 9 A.M.–12:30 P.M. and 1:30–4:30 P.M.

Contact: Sabine Cosson

VINEYARDS

Surface area: 66.7 acres

Grape varietals: 90% Semillon, 10% Sauvignon

Average age of vines: 45 years

Density of plantation: 7,000 vines per hectare

Average yields: 17 hectoliters per hectare

Elevage: Fermentation and 18–24 months aging in new oak barrels. Fining depending upon the vintage, filtration.

---

* Yquem, despite the existence of other outstanding estates, rarely has any competition and must be considered to be the only Bordeaux wine in a class by itself.

WINES PRODUCED

Château d'Arche: 35,000 bottles

Prieuré d'Arche: 15,000 bottles

Plateau of maturity: Within 5–15 years of the vintage

GENERAL APPRECIATION

A very reliable, reasonably priced wine that is impeccably well made.

Château d'Arche is another Sauternes that began producing better and better wine during the 1980s. Given the quality of the wines, their prices are among the most reasonable of the appellation. The style of wine produced at d'Arche offers very unctuous, rich fruit, no doubt because of the high percentage of Semillon, but also because of the late harvesting and the proprietor's serious commitment (there are normally 7–10 passes through the vineyard to pick only those grapes affected by botrytis).

IMPORTANT VINTAGES

2001
88–91 Honeysuckle, grapefruit, and citrus are present in this medium to full-bodied, very fresh, well-delineated wine. Relatively deep, concentrated, with good acidity, it should drink well for two decades. Anticipated maturity: now–2018. Last tasted, 3/01.

2000
87 Not a great deal of complexity, but plenty of glycerin, fat, and moderate sweetness characterize this somewhat monolithic wine that has some hints of pineapple and other tropical fruit. Drink it over the next decade. Last tasted, 1/03.

1997
87 This is an estate where the 1997 possesses more botrytis, complexity, potential ripeness, and longevity than the 1996. The 1997 d'Arche is an excellent, elegant, medium- to full-bodied Sauternes with noteworthy smoky, pineapple, and orange notes. Ripe and creamy-textured with moderate sweetness, this cleanly made wine should evolve nicely for 10–12+ years. Last tasted, 3/01.

1996
85 The lighter-styled, well-delineated, fruit-driven 1996 is simple and straightforward, with medium sweetness. Anticipated maturity: now–2010. Last tasted, 3/01.

1990
87? The 1990 d'Arche may be overripe and too alcoholic. It is quite powerful, but its lack of acidity may prove to be its undoing. If the wine pulls itself together, it will turn out to be a good to very good, muscular Sauternes that will offer big, thick, chewy fruit in a high alcohol, fiery format. Hopefully, it will evolve for another decade. Last tasted, 11/94.

1989
86 The 1989, which seemed heavy-handed and out of focus in both barrel and bottle, appears to have come together (a hopeful sign for the 1990), displaying straightforward, ripe, chewy, muscular fruit in a low-acid, moderately sweet style. It should drink well for 7–8 years. Last tasted, 11/94.

1988
88 This is a beautifully made, intense wine with a gorgeous nose of honeyed pineapple fruit. In the mouth, it is unctuous and full-bodied, with great sweetness and presence and a long, rich, nearly viscous finish. It is very forward for the vintage. Anticipated maturity: now. Last tasted, 4/91.

1986
88 This is another highly successful vintage for d'Arche. Not so rich or thick as the 1988, but more classy from an aromatic point of view, this full-bodied, concentrated wine exhibits telltale flavors of honeyed oranges and pineapples and even the smell of coconut. The finish is long and crisp, with a great deal of botrytis in evidence. Anticipated maturity: now–2006. Last tasted, 3/90.

ANCIENT VINTAGES

D'Arche made a very good 1983 and a less interesting 1982 and 1981. I also have notes on a surprisingly good 1969. I think it can be safely said that the efforts of the former proprietor, Pierre Perromat, who took over the running of the property in 1981, have resulted in far greater wines in the 1980s than in previous decades. That progression continues under the new owners.

BASTOR LAMONTAGNE

Classification: None

Owner: Foncier Vignobles

Address: 33210 Preignac

Telephone: 05 56 63 27 66; Telefax: 05 56 76 87 03

E-mail: bastor-lamontagne@dial.oleane.com

Website: www.atinternet.fr/bastor-lamontagne

Visits: By appointment Monday to Friday, 8 A.M.–noon and 2:30–6 P.M.

Contact: Michel Garat

VINEYARDS

Surface area: 138.3 acres

Grape varietals: 80% Semillon, 20% Sauvignon

Average age of vines: 37 years

Density of plantation: 7,000 vines per hectare

Average yields: 20 hectoliters per hectare

Elevage: Fermentation in barrels (80% of yield) and vats. Thirteen to eighteen months aging in barrels with 15% new oak. No fining, filtration.

WINES PRODUCED

Château Bastor Lamontagne: 60,000–70,000 bottles

Les Remparts de Bastor: 30,000–50,000 bottles

Plateau of maturity: Within 3–15 years of the vintage

GENERAL APPRECIATION

A very fruity style of wine that tends to be agreeable at a young age.

Bastor Lamontagne has always been a personal favorite of mine, particularly when I am looking for a reasonably priced Sauternes to buy as an alternative to some of the more glamorous (as well as more expensive) names. The property, located in Preignac, near the great estate of Suduiraut, has, to my knowledge, never made bad wines. Everything I have tasted from the mid-1970s onward has been made in an intelligent, ripe, rich, velvety style filled with opulent, pure fruit. These are not woody Sauternes since very little new oak (only 20%) is used. Rather they are luscious, amply endowed, sweet wines for drinking in their first 10–15 years of life.

As the following tasting notes attest, Bastor Lamontagne, while never outstanding, is consistently very fine. In fact, the great value is the realistic price and steady quality from vintage to vintage.

IMPORTANT VINTAGES

1997
87
Excellent tropical fruit (primarily pineapples) intermixed with scents of lanolin are attractive in this medium- to full-bodied, fresh, concentrated wine. Good underlying acidity nicely buttresses the wine's weighty feel in the mouth. An excellent lower-level Sauternes, it should drink well during its first two decades of life. Anticipated maturity: now–2020. Last tasted, 3/01.

1996
87
Compared to the 1997, the 1996 is made in a lighter style with less fat, as well as the telltale apricot/pineapple and lanolin characteristics of Semillon (which dominate the blend). Medium-bodied and refreshing, this mid-weight Sauternes is easily appreciated. Anticipated maturity: now–2012. Last tasted, 3/01.

1989
85
Very typical of the vintage, the 1989 Bastor Lamontagne is extremely low in acidity and ripe, with surprisingly evolved medium-gold color and a great deal of fruit and coarseness that I have rarely seen in other vintages of this wine. It will no doubt have to be drunk quite early. Anticipated maturity: now. Last tasted, 4/91.

1988
87
This is an excellent wine, with abundant quantities of botrytis, as evidenced by its honeyed pineapple-and-orange-scented nose. In the mouth, it is full, wonderfully pure, focused, and long, with moderate sweetness. This Sauternes could actually serve as a good apéritif as well as a dessert wine. Anticipated maturity: now. Last tasted, 4/91.

1986
86
Another excellent example of Bastor Lamontagne, the 1986 offers an enthralling nose of caramel, oranges, and spices intermixed with scents of flowers. Full-bodied and luscious, with a lot of alcohol and glycerin, as well as evidence of botrytis, this honeyed wine is already drinking beautifully. Anticipated maturity: now. Last tasted, 3/89.

1983
87
A voluptuous, luscious wine with oodles of ripe, botrytised pineapple fruit, medium- to full-bodied texture, and a long, rich, silky finish all combine to titillate the palate. This Bastor Lamontagne is precocious, but so tasty. Anticipated maturity: now. Last tasted, 3/88.

1982
85
Bastor Lamontagne made a shockingly good wine in 1982. It is a lovely, richly fruity, moderately sweet, well-balanced Sauternes with plenty of character. The wine is forward and ready. Anticipated maturity: now. Last tasted, 1/85.

BROUSTET

Classification: Second Growth in 1855

Owner: Didier Laulan

Address: 33720 Barsac

Telephone: 05 56 27 16 87; Telefax: 05 56 27 05 93

Visits: By appointment only

Contact: Didier Laulan

VINEYARDS

Surface area: 39.5 acres

Grape varietals: 63% Semillon, 25% Sauvignon, 12% Muscadelle

Average age of vines: 35 years

Density of plantation: 6,600 vines per hectare

Average yields: 15 hectoliters per hectare

Elevage: Twenty to twenty-five day fermentations in small temperature-controlled stainless-steel tanks of 25–50 hectoliter capacity. Wines are aged in oak barrels (20% new oak) for the first year and in stainless-steel vats for the second. They are fined and filtered.

WINES PRODUCED

Château Brouster: 20,000 bottles

6 Château de Séqur: 5–10,000 bottles

Plateau of maturity: Within 5–20 years of the vintage

GENERAL APPRECIATION

This is a solid but somewhat dull style of wine that ages well, but is rarely exciting.

Broustet is one of the rarely encountered and least-known Barsacs, largely because the production is so small. The property was in the Fournier family between 1885 and 1992, when it was sold to Didier Laulan.

Many improvements have been made at Broustet since the mid-1980s. While the wine is still fermented in stainless-steel tanks, the percentage of new oak barrels has been increased to 50%, and the château has introduced a second wine for weaker vats. They have also added a dry white wine to their portfolio.

IMPORTANT VINTAGES

1997
83
The diluted, light-bodied, undistinguished 1997 Broustet offers fruit-cocktail notes in the nose, light to moderate sweetness, medium body, and a clean finish. It should drink well young, and keep for eight more years. Anticipated maturity: now–2011. Last tasted, 3/01.

1996
84
This is another monolithic example, with more fruit, elegance, and potential complexity than the 1997. It is straightforward and foursquare, with some botrytis and honeyed orange and pineapple fruit. Drink it over the next 10–12 years. Last tasted, 3/01.

1989
86
The 1989 should be consumed in its first decade of life because it already offers a big, fat, plump, juicy mouthful of wine. Surprisingly elegant for a 1989, but still extremely alcoholic and not that complex, it is a sweeter wine than the 1988 but lacks the flavor dimension and character of the previous vintage. Anticipated maturity: now. Last tasted, 4/91.

1988
88
The 1988 has the advantage of having more acidity, additional complexity, and an uplifting bouquet of honeyed apricot/peach fruit, which, along with its vibrancy, gives its powerful, rich, intense flavors a sense of balance and focus. It is the best Broustet I have ever tasted. Anticipated maturity: now–2008. Last tasted, 4/91.

CAILLOU

Classification: Second Growth in 1855

Owner: Michel and Marie-Josée Pierre

Address: 33720 Barsac

Telephone: 05 56 27 16 38; Telefax: 05 56 27 09 60

E-mail: chateaucaillou@aol.com

Website: www.chateaucaillou.fr

Visits: By appointment only

Contact: Michel or Marie-Josée Pierre

VINEYARDS

Surface area: 32.1 acres

Grape varietals: 90% Semillon, 10% Sauvignon

Average age of vines: 35–40 years

Density of plantation: 6,600 vines per hectare

Average yields: 15 hectoliters per hectare

Elevage: Twenty-one to twenty-eight day fermentation in vats. Sixteen to twenty months aging in barrels with 33% new oak. Fining and filtration.

WINES PRODUCED

Château Caillou: 8,000–10,000 bottles

Les Erables du Caillou: 11,000–12,000 bottles

Plateau of maturity: Within 5–10 years of the vintage

GENERAL APPRECIATION

An elegant, fruity, reliable wine, Caillou is never a leader, but then again, it is never expensive.

This is a relatively obscure Barsac property located on route D118 to the east of Barsac. The vineyard's soil is limestone and clay. The château's twin towers dominate the modest two-and-a-half-story building and are easily seen from the road.

The reputation of Caillou's wines has been mixed, although many critics have claimed Caillou has been largely ignored as a competent producer of lighter-styled Barsacs. Fermentation takes place in temperature-controlled, stainless-steel tanks, after which the wine is filtered before it goes into small barrels, of which 20% are new each year. I have never been that impressed with the wines of Caillou, although a 1947 I tasted in 1987 was in good shape. Recently, there does appear to have been significant improvement, as the 1990, 1989, and 1988 all tasted more serious and complex than their predecessors.

IMPORTANT VINTAGES

1997 The 1997 Caillou possesses low acidity, an unctuous texture, plenty of honeyed
87 tropical fruit, medium to full body, and a cloying, fat, extremely sweet style. It needs to firm up and exhibit more focus. It will last for 10–12 years. Last tasted, 3/01.

1996 The 1996 is a foursquare, fruit-driven, clean, medium-bodied wine with a moder-
85   ately sweet finish. Anticipated maturity: now–2012. Last tasted, 3/01.

1990 Caillou tends to produce compact, richly fruity, moderately sweet wines that rarely
88   have the complexity found in the better Barsac/Sauterness estates. The 1990 dis-
      plays a honeyed, ripe cherry/apricot/orange-scented nose, surprisingly good acid-
      ity, and a medium to full-bodied, thick, chewy finish. About as impressive as
      Caillou can be, it will last for 10–15 years. Last tasted, 11/94.

1989 The 1989 is a fat, sweet, chunky wine without much complexity or delineation. I
84   liked previous examples more, but the wine's low acidity is causing it to taste more
      diffuse as it ages. Last tasted, 11/94.

1988 The 1988 is thick, ripe, and rich, with attractive honeyed pineapple-like fruit-
86   iness, medium to full body, and a more elegant personality than its two siblings. It
      should drink well for another decade. Last tasted, 11/94.

1986 This is an unexciting, even insipid wine that lacks depth and finishes with a short,
77   attenuated feel. It is hard to understand what went wrong in this excellent vintage.
      Anticipated maturity: now. Last tasted, 3/90.

1985 Light-intensity flavors of pineapples and oranges are attractive in a low-key way.
82   In the mouth, the wine is off dry, medium-bodied, and relatively light, with no ev-
      idence of botrytis. Anticipated maturity: now. Last tasted, 3/90.

CLIMENS

Classification: First Growth in 1855

Owner: Bérénice Lurton

Address: 33720 Barsac

Telephone: 05 56 27 15 33; Telefax: 05 56 27 21 04

E-mail: contact@chateau-climens.fr

Website: www.chateau-climens.fr

Visits: By appointment Monday to Friday, 9 A.M.–5 P.M.

Contact: Bérénice Lurton

VINEYARDS

Surface area: 76.6 acres

Grape varietals: 100% Semillon

Average age of vines: 35 years

Density of plantation: 6,300 vines per hectare

Average yields: 13 hectoliters per hectare

Elevage: Fermentation and 18–24 months aging in barrels with 30–50% new oak.
No fining, filtration.

WINES PRODUCED

Château Climens: 30,000 bottles

Cyprès de Climens: 15,000 bottles

Plateau of maturity: Within 7–25 years of the vintage

GENERAL APPRECIATION

One of France's monumental sweet wines, Climens is a personal favorite. It combines great nobility with laser-like flavor precision. A tour de force in winemaking.

The most famous estate of the Barsac/Sauternes region is, without question, Château d'Yquem, which makes the most concentrated and expensive sweet white wine in France. But the wine I find most companionable with food, and most complex and compelling to drink, is that of Château Climens in Barsac. Climens has been owned since 1971 by the Lurton family, who presides over a considerable empire of Bordeaux estates, including the famous Margaux properties of Châteaux Brane Cantenac, Durfort-Vivens, and Desmirail. All of these properties produce good wine, but none of them has quite the standing in its respective commune that Château Climens has in Barsac.

For much of the last two centuries, Climens has been considered one of the two leading estates in the commune of Barsac. The 72-acre vineyard and modest one-story château (the only physical distinctions are two slate-roofed towers at each end) is located just north of the tiny village of La Pinesse, sitting on the highest plateau of the Barsac region, a full 70 feet above sea level. Most observers claim that this elevation has contributed to the vineyard's excellent drainage, giving Climens a distinct advantage over lower-lying properties in wet years.

While the names of most châteaux here can be traced back to former owners, no one is quite sure how Climens acquired its name. For most of the 19th century the château was owned by the Lacoste family, who produced a wine they called Château Climenz-Lacoste. At that time the vineyard's 70 acres achieved an annual production of 6,000 cases, but the devastating effects of phylloxera in the late 19th century destroyed most of the vineyards in Bordeaux, including those of Climens. In 1871 Climens was sold to Alfred Ribet, the owner of another estate called Château Pexoto, which was subsequently absorbed into what is today known as Château Sigalas Rabaud.

In 1885 Ribet sold the property to Henri Gounouilhou, whose family managed Climens until the current proprietor, the dynamic Lucien Lurton, purchased it in 1971. It was Henri Gounouilhou, director of Bordeaux's most famous daily newspaper, *Sud-Ouest*, and his successors who raised not only the level of quality at Climens, but also the public's awareness of this great estate. The legendary vintages of 1947, 1937, and 1929 enabled Climens to surpass the reputation of its larger neighbor, Château Coutet, and rival even that of the great Château d'Yquem.

The Lurtons, Brigitte and Bérénice, have merely enhanced the extraordinary reputation of this outstanding property. Their only change has been the removal of the small quantities of Muscadelle planted in the gravel, red sand, and clay-like soil of the vineyard. The current plantings, which they believe produce the best wine from the *terroir* of Château Climens, are 100% Semillon. The Lurtons eschew Sauvignon in the blend because it has a tendency to lose its aroma after several years. The average age of the vines is maintained at an impressive 35 years, as the Lurtons believe in replanting only 3–4% of the vineyard per year. In addition, their yield of 16 hectoliters per hectare remains one of the smallest of all the estates in the Sauternes/Barsac region. (Today, when most major wine-producing estates are doubling the yields from their vineyards,

Climens commendably maintains an average annual production of only 3,333 cases, from a vineyard area 1.6 acres larger than it was in the mid-19th century.) No doubt this statistic alone accounts for the exceptional concentration and quality of the wine produced.

The wine is fermented in cask and aged for 12–18 months in 55-gallon barrels before being bottled. In most vintages, 33% new oak is used; this is believed to develop the proper marriage of honeyed pineapple-and-apricot-flavored fruit with the vanilla toastiness of new oak barrels.

What makes Climens so precious is that it produces the region's most compellingly elegant wine. There is no doubt that for sheer power, viscosity, and opulence, Climens will never rival Château d'Yquem, nor even Château Rieussec, Château Suduiraut, and the luxurious, rare Cuvée Madame of Château Coutet. However, if one measures the greatness of a wine by its extraordinary balance and finesse, Climens not only has no peers, it deserves the reputation as the most quintessentially graceful wine of the region. Many Sauternes can border on the cloying, but in the top vintages Climens seems to combine a rich, luscious, exotic character of honeyed pineapple fruit with a remarkable inner core of lemony acidity—giving the wine zestiness, precision to its flavors, and a profound, hauntingly pleasurable bouquet.

Consistently one of the most profound wines of Barsac/Sauternes, this wine, made from 100% Semillon, is one of the most ravishing examples of just how much elegance can be built into a powerful racehorse style of wine.

IMPORTANT VINTAGES

2001
96–99
I tasted this a few months prior to bottling. It looks to be one of the most remarkable Climens (and there have been many of those over the last 30 years) to be produced. The harvest started October 1, with tremendous levels of botrytis. The yields were an astonishingly low six hectoliters per hectare. The color is a light greenish gold and the nose flawless, with honeyed pineapple, citrus, lanolin, and floral notes. This wine, always 100% Semillon, aged usually 18 or so months in oak casks, has a finish that goes on for well over a minute. It is sweet, but the good acidity and tremendous extract should produce one of the most prodigious sweet wines in modern-day Bordeaux. Just monumental! Anticipated maturity: 2010–2045. Last tasted, 12/02.

2000
89+
The proprietors are extremely happy with what they were able to produce in 2000. Even though the vintage has a bad reputation, those producers who included only the early-picked grapes in their final blend have often turned out wines that are close to being exceptional. The yields for this were microscopic (four hectoliters per hectare) and the wine, although somewhat monolithic (I tasted it right after bottling), shows honeyed citrus, pineapple, a hint of pear, and a bit of butter and honeysuckle. The wine is medium bodied, elegant, with superb purity, always a hallmark of this great estate. Anticipated maturity: 2007–2020. Last tasted, 12/02.

1999
90
Medium-deep gold, this wine shows relatively high acidity, a somewhat monolithic character, but great purity, with the telltale honeysuckle, pineapple, and some tropical fruits, along with minerals, and a very subtle dosage of oak. Only 63% of the crop made it into this Climens, and the wine was produced from nine hectoliters per hectare in the vintage that took place between September 19 and Octo-

ber 18. This wine should be very long-lived, but obviously will never hit the highlights of the great vintages such as 2001, 1997, 1996, 1990, 1989, and 1988. Anticipated maturity: 2008–2025. Last tasted, 12/02.

1998
92
This is a very precocious and evolved style of Climens that should be immensely pleasing to all those looking for a moderately sweet Barsac to drink over the next 15–20 years. Made from 13 hectoliters per hectare (64% of the crop made it into this Climens), this 100% Semillon Barsac shows a medium-gold color with some green undertones. The wine has superb ripeness, unctuousness on the palate, with terrific intensity, decent acidity, and evolved honeysuckle, buttery, tropical fruit, and botrytised flavors. Anticipated maturity: now–2020. Last tasted, 12/02.

1997
93
A great classic from Climens, with the telltale nose of white flowers intermixed with buttered pineapple, citrus, honeysuckle, and vanilla, this medium- to full-bodied wine has great precision, purity, and stature. Anticipated maturity: now–2022. Last tasted, 11/02.

1996
90
A very delicate, finesse-styled Climens (made from 100% Semillon), this wine has pretty, almost steely citrus notes, with a hint of honeysuckle and buttery grapefruit. The wine shows good acidity and builds incrementally in the mouth. It is not a heavyweight, monster-size wine by any means, but it is pure elegance and pedigree. Anticipated maturity: now–2015. Last tasted, 11/02.

1995
87
A good but uninspiring example from Climens, the 1995 seems to lack the honeyed botrytis so evident in the top vintages. The color is pale greenish gold, and the wine has a straightforward nose of citrus and a hint of grapefruit. The wine is medium bodied, with good acidity, moderate weight, and moderate sweetness, but not much complexity or character. Anticipated maturity: now–2012. Last tasted, 11/02.

1994
86
Another mediocre effort, but certainly a good wine overall, just pale in comparison to the top vintages, the 1994 Climens has a light-gold color with a greenish hue to it. The wine has an herbal nose with some earthy background notes. The wine is medium bodied, has good acidity and some sweetness, but seems relatively monolithic and dull. Anticipated maturity: now–2013. Last tasted, 11/02.

1990
96
This vintage for Climens goes from strength to strength. The yields, which were a microscopic 10 hectoliters per hectare, have produced nearly 3,000 cases of a spectacular wine that has a medium-deep-gold color and a gorgeous nose of honeysuckle, vanilla, pineapple, acacia, crème brûlée, and roasted nuttiness. In the mouth, it is full-bodied, atypically powerful for a Climens (the residual sugar of 130 grams per liter is very high for this estate), and the massive finish goes on for well over a minute. In spite of such exceptional richness, there is good acidity, giving the wine uplift and definition. Anticipated maturity: now–2035. Last tasted, 11/02.

1989
94
This wine has continued to evolve, and although I still prefer its two closest siblings, the elegance of the 1988 and the power and mass of the 1990, this is a profound example of Climens. Produced from 11 hectoliters per hectare, this wine achieved 14.5% alcohol and has 123 grams per liter of residual sugar. The wine shows a deep medium-gold color, a glorious nose of crème brûlée intermixed with lanolin, candle wax, honeyed citrus, vanilla, and something that seems vaguely similar to passion fruit. Very full-bodied, quite sweet, with exceptional concentration, this looks to be a glorious Climens and has proved far better out of bottle than I thought from cask. Anticipated maturity: now–2025. Last tasted, 11/02.

1988
96
One of my all-time favorite Climens, but far less evolved than the 1990 or 1989, this is the quintessential elegant style of Barsac. Made from 12 hectoliters per hectare, with 14.4% sugar and 106 grams of residual sugar per liter, this wine has a very classy, delicate nose of tangerine skin, melted butter, overripe pineapples,

and subtle toasty oak. The wine is medium to full-bodied, does not quite have the mass and sweetness of either the 1990 or 1989, but there seem to be more nuances, and its lightness on its feet is impressive for a wine of such power and richness. This is a glorious Climens that still needs time in the bottle. Anticipated maturity: 2006–2025. Last tasted, 11/02.

1986   Another extraordinary Climens from a tiny crop (less than 1,000 cases) that
96   achieved 14.5% alcohol and residual sugar of 101 grams per liter, the 1986 Climens shows a deep-gold color and a crème brûlée nose with orange marmalade, pineapple liqueur, and tropical fruits, along with some coconut and vanilla in the nose. The wine is medium to full-bodied, with great concentration, very impressive levels of botrytis, and a long finish with hints of caramel and marmalade in an unctuous yet well-delineated style. Anticipated maturity: now–2020. Last tasted, 11/02.

1985   A very pale yellow/gold with a hint of green, this wine tastes like a late-harvested
85   white Graves as opposed to a Barsac. Notes of minerals and flowers emerge from this medium-bodied, straightforward, but very un-Climens-like effort, which exhibits medium body, some sweetness, but not a whole lot of complexity. Anticipated maturity: now. Last tasted, 11/02.

1983   A beautiful wine that continues to go from strength to strength, the honey, popcorn,
93   pineapple, and grapefruit notes are present, along with hints of candle wax and lanolin. The wine is full-bodied, very rich, with good acidity, considerable botrytis, and a full-bodied, expansive, intense mouthfeel. Another brilliant wine that seems to be closer to its plateau of maturity. Anticipated maturity: now–2016. Last tasted, 11/02.

1980   The 1980 is a wonderful vintage of Climens, which has produced an outstanding
90   Barsac. An exotic bouquet of tropical fruit, pineapples, and melons is really top class. On the palate, the wine is rich, yet never heavy or cloyingly sweet, with crisp, rich, medium-bodied, lush, velvety, ripe fruity flavors. This is a superb effort from Climens and one of the best sweet wines of the vintage. Anticipated maturity: now–2000. Last tasted, 12/90.

ANCIENT VINTAGES

Climens has a brilliant record, surpassed only by Yquem for consistency and the number of great wines that were produced. In the 1970s, the 1976 (90 points; last tasted 11/00), 1975 (91 points; last tasted 3/99), and 1971 (96 points; last tasted 8/02) are all great wines. Even the museum piece vintages can be stunning, including the 1962 (90 points; last tasted 3/97), 1949 (96 points; last tasted 1/01), 1947 (94 points; last tasted 11/90), 1937 (90 points; last tasted 11/88), and 1929 (92 points; last tasted 11/88). I suspect pristinely stored bottles of all these wines would still be in terrific condition.

CLOS HAUT-PEYRAGUEY

Classification: First Growth in 1855

Owner: GFA du Clos Haut-Peyraguey

Address: 33210 Bommes

Telephone: 05 56 76 61 53; Telefax: 05 56 76 69 65

E-mail: j.j.pauly@worldonline.fr

Visits: Every day of the week, by appointment for groups

Contact: Martine Langlais-Pauly

VINEYARDS

Surface area: 42 acres

Grape varietals: 90% Semillon, 10% Sauvignon

Average age of vines: 35 years

Density of plantation: 6,600 vines per hectare

Average yields: 16 hectoliters per hectare

Elevage: Fermentation in barrels with 50% new oak. Twenty-four months aging with 35% new oak. Fining, no filtration.

WINES PRODUCED

Château Clos Haut-Peyraguey: 24,000 bottles

Château Haut-Bommes: 12,000 bottles

Plateau of maturity: Within 5–12 years following the vintage

GENERAL APPRECIATION

This is an estate that is clearly improving in quality. Prices remain fair.

In the 1855 classification there was only one premier cru classé, Château Peyraguey, but in 1879 the property was divided. The smaller parcel became known as Clos Haut-Peyraguey. For much of the early 1980s, 1970s, and 1960s, the quality of the wines was indifferent. However, improvements have been made in the 1990s and late 1980s.

IMPORTANT VINTAGES

2001
90–92
One of the best examples from this estate in many a year, this superb wine has a light greenish-gold color and a gorgeous nose of honeyed fruit cocktail intermixed with caramel and vanilla. The wine is full-bodied, unctuously textured, with good acidity that gives definition and uplift. Anticipated maturity: 2006–2016. Last tasted, 1/03.

2000
86?
This wine's very evolved golden color is a bit worrisome. It is followed up by a very precocious nose of burnt caramel, toast, and some rather jammy fruit. The wine is dense, with the acidity and alcohol as well as wood not very integrated. It is a very controversial wine that seems disjointed/awkward. Anticipated maturity: 2005–2012. Last tasted, 1/03.

1997
87
While it was less concentrated than many of its peers, I enjoyed the 1997 Clos Haut-Peyraguey, a honeyed orange/citrusy–styled wine with elegance, medium body, and a fresh, lively personality. Exhibiting good botrytis and moderate sweetness, it should drink well for 8–10 years. Last tasted, 3/02.

1996
85
The 1996 is off dry, with apricot and fruit-cocktail scents and flavors, medium body, fine purity, unobtrusive oak, and a spicy, stylish finish. It will require consumption during its first 10–12 years of life, although I am sure it will live longer. Anticipated maturity: now–2016. Last tasted, 3/01.

1990
89
The 1990 is a rich, full-bodied, unctuously textured, and powerful wine. This dramatic, ostentatious, alcoholic Sauternes has 10 years of evolution ahead. Last tasted, 11/94.

1989
86
The 1989 suffers in comparison with the 1990 and 1988 vintages, largely because it is drier, with a waxy, Tokay-Pinot Gris–like personality. Although it shows well, it appears smaller scaled than the superrich 1990 and fragrant 1988. It will last for

two decades, but it does not have the same level of fruit extraction, so once it begins to dry out, it will be less interesting. Last tasted, 11/94.

1988   The finest bouquet and aromatics are found in the 1988, which exhibits a striking
89   nose of honeysuckle and sweet peaches, apricots, and pineapples. This medium-
        to full-bodied, elegant wine will last for 15 years. Last tasted, 11/94.

1986   While much lighter than most 1986s, this is still an attractive, and fruity, medium-
85   bodied wine with good length and balance and some evidence of botrytis in its
        peach/apricot flavors. Anticipated maturity: now. Last tasted, 3/89.

COUTET

Classification: First Growth in 1855

Owner: Château Coutet, SC, Philippe and Dominique Baly

Address: 33720 Barsac

Telephone: 05 56 27 15 46; Telefax: 05 56 27 02 20

E-mail: chateaucoutet@aol.com

Website: www.chateau-coutet.fr

Visits: By appointment only

Contact: Danièle Constantin

VINEYARDS

Surface area: 93.9 acres

Grape varietals: 75% Semillon, 23% Sauvignon, 2% Muscadelle

Average age of vines: 35 years

Density of plantation: 5,600 vines per hectare

Average yields: 13 hectoliters per hectare

Elevage: Fermentation and 16–18 months aging in new oak barrels. Fining and filtration.

WINES PRODUCED

Château Coutet: 30,000–50,000 bottles

Chartreuse de Coutet: 15,000–20,000 bottles

Plateau of maturity: Within 5–25 years of the vintage

COUTET CUVÉE MADAME

This special *cuvée* is produced only in great vintages. The grapes usually come from a
special parcel of 2–2.5 ha (35 years of age), and are picked one by one, when they are
considered extremely mature and of homogeneous concentration. They are usually picked
in one passage. Fermentations last three to six weeks in 100% new oak barrels, and wines
are aged 24 months. Wines are fined and filtered upon bottling. Quantities produced are
very small. (The blend is the same as for Château Coutet.)

GENERAL APPRECIATION

One of the classics of the region, Coutet is a model of elegance and balanced sweetness.

Coutet has always been one of the leading as well as one of the largest estates of Barsac.
Famous for an elegant, less sweet, and less powerful wine, Coutet is usually well made,

stylish, and probably a more flexible wine to serve with a variety of food dishes than many of the intense, super-concentrated, lavishly oaked wines that this region produces in abundance.

Coutet does produce a tiny amount of incredibly rich, unctuous wine that is rarely ever seen commercially but is worth mentioning because it is one of this region's two finest wines (the other, of course, being Yquem). In certain vintages Coutet produces a special *cuvée* called Cuvée Madame. Between 1997 and 1943 it was produced only in 1990, 1989, 1988, 1986, 1981, 1975, 1971, 1959, 1950, 1949, and 1943. Rumors were afloat that a 2001 would emerge. Approximately 1,200 bottles—or just four barrels—of this wine are made, and should you ever see any, do not hesitate to try it, because the Cuvée Madame of Coutet is pure nectar. The 1989, 1988, 1986, 1981, and 1971 vintages of Cuvée Madame, along with the 1921 Yquem, represent the greatest sweet wines from this region that I have ever tasted.

As for the regular *cuvée* of Coutet, the vintages produced immediately after Marcel Baly purchased the property in 1977 appeared light and indifferent, but since 1983 Coutet has been making top-notch wines nearly every vintage. In fact, this appears to be a property that is deadly serious about challenging Climens's historical role as the top estate in the Barsac region.

Coutet also produces a dry wine that is very fresh, attractively priced, and best drunk when it is 4–5 years old.

IMPORTANT VINTAGES

2001
91–94 One of the great Coutets I have tasted, with amazing definition, extraordinary vibrancy and force, and sweet, thick, juicy flavors of tropical fruits, peach, honeysuckle, and buttered popcorn, this glorious Barsac looks to be set for an incredibly long life. Anticipated maturity: 2007–2025. Last tasted, 1/03.

2000
87 Somewhat one-dimensional and simple, as are many 2000s, but with loads of fruit and moderate sweetness, this wine should be drunk over the next decade. Last tasted, 1/03.

1999
89 A big, lively, fruit-dominated wine, with hints of vanilla, mineral, pineapple, and peach, this medium-bodied wine shows good spice, zingy acidity, and plenty of structure. It is an elegant, understated, moderately sweet style that should evolve quickly. Anticipated maturity: now–2015. Last tasted, 1/03.

1998
90 This exquisite combination of elegance and finesse offers up notes of tropical fruits, particularly pineapple and some mandarin oranges, along with the telltale citrus and honeysuckle. It is medium to full-bodied, with good sweetness and terrific purity. Drink it over the next 10–15 years. Last tasted, 3/01.

1997
90 Another classic example of elegance allied to richness and intensity, Coutet's 1997 exhibits an expressive, floral, citrusy, honeyed nose, with notes of orange, Chinese black tea, pineapple, and spicy oak. It is all finesse, with honey, medium to full body, gorgeous delineation, and refreshing underlying acidity. It should drink well young. Anticipated maturity: now–2020. Last tasted, 3/01.

1996
88 A cooler, lighter-bodied wine than the 1997 with a greenish hue to its light-gold color, this ripe, medium-bodied Barsac reveals toasty notes along with fresh, citrusy tropical fruit, some sweetness, and a clean, pure finish. It is a good all-purpose Barsac to drink as an aperitif, with food, or after dinner with dessert. Anticipated maturity: now–2018. Last tasted, 3/00.

1990 The full-bodied 1990 is sweet, rich, and honeyed, but it lacks the clarity and com-
88   plexity of the 1989. Last tasted, 11/94.

1990 Cuvée Madame: Medium green/gold–colored, the 1990 is aging at a glacial pace.
98   It offers a profound bouquet of smoky, toasty new oak combined with honeyed
      peaches and apricots, as well as coconuts and a touch of crème brûlée. With ex-
      traordinarily rich, full-bodied, marvelously extracted personalities, as well as
      wonderful underlying acidity, it is a spectacular wine. Anticipated maturity:
      now–2035. Last tasted, 2/03.

1989 This was one of the few wines where the 1989 was the superior offering. The rich-
90   est, sweetest, and fattest, it offers a pure nose of pineapples, full body, and excel-
      lent concentration. Anticipated maturity: now–2015. Last tasted, 3/96.

1989 Cuvée Madame: Deep, bright gold in color, this blockbuster sweet wine offers up
95   aromas of coffee, custard, toastiness, honeyed tropical fruits, and a coconut note.
      Unctuously textured and oozing glycerin, extract, and richness, this full-bodied
      yet extraordinarily well-delineated wine offers the rare combination of power and
      complexity. It is an amazingly thick Cuvée Madame that suffers only in compari-
      son with its surrounding siblings. Anticipated maturity: now–2030. Last tasted,
      11/94.

1988 The lighter-bodied, drier 1988 is less weighty than the 1990 and 1989, with at-
89+   tractive, spicy, vanilla, citrus scents, medium body, and an earthy note that kept
      my score from going higher. Anticipated maturity: now–2018. Last tasted, 11/94.

1988 Cuvée Madame: Cut from the same mold as other Cuvée Madames, but perhaps
99   the ultimate example because the intense botrytis and unctuousness the wine pos-
      sesses is buttressed by slightly more acidity, giving the wine all the weight and
      massiveness of its two younger siblings, the 1990 and 1989, but with more focus
      and vibrancy. It is difficult for readers who have never tasted Cuvée Madame to
      imagine a wine of such honeyed richness, power, and flavor dimension not tasting
      heavy. The 1988 is still young, even more youthful than the 1990 and 1989, with
      good underlying acidity and luxuriantly rich layers of viscous, full-bodied flavors
      of crème brûlée, peaches, apricots, and pears. The finish lasts for over 40 seconds.
      This may turn out to be the most compelling of all the profound Cuvée Madames
      that have been made to date. Anticipated maturity: now–2035. Last tasted, 11/94.

1986 This is a fine example of Coutet, quite precocious, with an evolved bouquet of trop-
87   ical fruit, honey, and spring flowers. It is full-bodied and rich, with crisp acidity
      and plenty of evidence of botrytis in its apricot/peach-like flavors. The finish is
      heady and long, with just enough acidity for balance. Anticipated maturity:
      now–2005. Last tasted, 11/91.

1986 Cuvée Madame: This unbelievably decadent, unctuous wine has the type of ex-
96   tract (but without the overlay of heavy, toasty oak) that one normally finds only in
      a great vintage of Yquem. The wine is much less evolved than the regular *cuvée*
      of Coutet. At the moment, it is crammed with honeyed tropical fruit that comes
      across in a powerful format. This is an enormously rich, almost overwhelmingly
      intense Barsac that needs another decade to begin to reveal its subtleties and
      complexities. It is mind-blowing! Anticipated maturity: now–2020. Last tasted,
      3/97.

1985 The problem with so many 1985 Barsac/Sauternes is that they come across as
84   monolithic and one-dimensional, particularly when compared with years where
      there is a great deal more botrytis, such as 1988 and 1986. Nevertheless, for those
      readers who like to drink these wines as an apéritif, 1985 is the type of vintage
      where the wines can be drunk early in the meal. The 1985 is fresh, with plenty of
      fruit, but is lacking the complexity one normally associates with this château. An-
      ticipated maturity: now. Last tasted, 3/90.

1983   Not the biggest, most concentrated, or most luscious Coutet, this wine gets high
  87   marks because of undeniable elegance, breed, class, and a fresh, lively feel on the
        palate. The flavors reveal excellent ripeness, and the wine's refreshing crispness
        makes this an exceptionally enjoyable, non-cloying Barsac. Anticipated maturity:
        now–2005. Last tasted, 3/89.

1981   Surprisingly mature and ready to drink, the 1981 Coutet is an agreeable wine but
  78   lacks richness and complexity. What it does offer is straightforward, fruity,
        lemony, melon aromas and moderately sweet, somewhat short flavors. Drink up.
        Anticipated maturity: now. Last tasted, 6/84.

1981   Cuvée Madame: This is a medium-golden wine with a huge honeyed aroma filled
  96   with the scents of oranges, toast, coconuts, and other tropical fruits. Thick, unctu-
        ous flavors coat the palate. There is just enough acidity to provide lift and focus.
        This is a colossal wine. Anticipated maturity: now–2008. Last tasted, 12/90.

1971   Cuvée Madame: Wines such as this are almost impossible to describe effectively.
  98   Spectacular from the first time I tasted it in the mid-1970s, I have been fortunate
        enough to have had this wine three more times. Each bottle has been better than the
        last, suggesting that perhaps more magical things may emerge. There is an extraor-
        dinary fragrance of spring flowers, honeyed fruits, herbs, and vanilla, and a strong
        scent of crème brûlée. In the mouth, there is remarkable richness and super-
        acidity that give the wines clarity and lift. Gobs of botrytis are obvious, and the
        richness and extract levels are amazing. The color has changed little since I first
        tasted it. I would predict at least another 10–20 years of longevity. This is one wine
        to go out of your way to taste. Anticipated maturity: now–2005. Last tasted, 3/88.

DOISY DAËNE

Classification: Second Growth in 1855

Owners: Pierre and Denis Dubourdieu

Address: 33720 Barsac

Telephone: 05 56 27 15 84; Telefax: 05 56 27 18 99

Website: Under construction

Visits: By appointment only

Contact: Denis Dubourdieu (Telephone: 05 56 62 96 51;
Telefax: 05 56 62 14 89; E-mail: reynon@gofornet.com)

VINEYARDS

Surface area: 37 acres

Grape varietals: 80% Semillon, 20% Sauvignon

Average age of vines: 35 years

Density of plantation: 7,100 vines per hectare

Average yields: 18–20 hectoliters per hectare

Elevage: Fermentation and 18–24 months aging in barrels that are renewed by a third at
each vintage. Fining and filtration.

WINES PRODUCED

Château Doisy-Daëne: 36,000–40,000 bottles

No second wine is produced.

Plateau of maturity: Within 3–12 years following the vintage

Note: This estate also produces some 30,000 bottles of a 100% Sauvignon dry white Château Doisy-Daëne (fermentation and 10–15 months aging on lees in barrels that are renewed by quarter at each vintage). In some vintages, (2001, 1997, 1996, and 1990), the special *cuvée* l'Extravagance de Doisy-Daëne is produced. Availabilities are limited (4–5 barrels); hence, the wine is commercialized in 375 ml. bottles.

GENERAL APPRECIATION

This is a meticulously made wine with the emphasis on early drinkability as well as oodles of honey-drenched tropical fruit. In short, it is a wine certain to win a popularity contest.

One of the most ambitiously and innovatively run estates in Bordeaux, Doisy-Daëne produces a very fine Barsac that seems to be undervalued in the scheme of Barsac/Sauternes realities. While I would not rate it a premier cru classé, it is certainly one of the leaders among the deuxièmes crus classés. The proprietors of Doisy-Daëne, Pierre and Denis Dubourdieu, also produce one of the finest dry wines of the region, Doisy-Daëne Sec, a full and refreshing, vibrant, fruity, and—best of all—very inexpensive white wine. Pierre's son, Denis, a professor at the Institute of Oenology in Bordeaux, more than anyone else has totally revolutionized the making of white wine in the Bordeaux region with his classic *macération pelliculaire* (skin contact and very cool fermentation temperatures). The objective is to produce wines that retain their remarkable fruit and freshness and to reduce the amount of sulphur used in the winemaking process to negligible quantities.

Doisy-Daëne's sweet wine is surprisingly enjoyable when young, causing many tasters to think that it will not last. Although the style today is certainly different from when the 1959 and 1924 were made, I remember drinking both of those wines in 1984 when they were still fresh, lively, and full of fruit. Doisy-Daëne remains one of the more fairly priced sweet wines of the Barsac/Sauternes region. For those who want to drink their sweet wines on the younger side, this is a property of which to take note.

Note on l'Extravagance de Doisy-Daëne: This small cuvée of 50–125 cases has been made only in 2001 (100% Sauvignon Blanc), 1997 (100% Semillon), 1996 (100% Sauvignon), and 1990.

IMPORTANT VINTAGES

2001 A greenish light-gold color is followed by a richly fruity wine with loads of peach,
88–90+ pear, honey, and vanilla notes, an elegant, medium-bodied palate, good acidity, and plenty of botrytis. The wine is not one of the sweetest of the 2001s, but no doubt very flexible with food. Anticipated maturity: 2004–2015. Last tasted, 1/03.

2001 L'Extravagance de Doisy-Daëne: This is a huge, big, unctuous fruit bomb, but one
96 with botrytis, honeysuckle, and all the great things that make these wines so compelling. Is this wine significantly better than some of the other vintages of this limited 125-case *cuvée*? I am not sure, but this is a multidimensional, textured, massive wine with medium-gold color and great botrytis, yet, at the same time, good acidity. Anticipated maturity: 2010–2040. Last tasted, 1/03.

2000 Honeyed pineapple is the dominant aroma and flavor of this light gold–colored
88 wine. It shows good ripeness, plenty of fruit, and a somewhat unctuous texture. Anticipated maturity: now–2011. Last tasted, 1/03.

1999
89 This is a straightforward wine with a deep medium-gold color and ripe honeyed botrytis flavors, with some caramel and abundant exotic fruits such as pineapple and passion. The wine almost has a lychee nut characteristic as well. Drink it over the next 10–20 years. Last tasted, 12/02.

1998
90 Medium to full-bodied, with a moderately gold color showing some underlying green tints, this wine has good acidity, sweet attack, medium to full body, and a long, somewhat one-dimensional, but pure finish. It should drink well for 10–15 years. Last tasted, 12/02.

1997
89 The impressive 1997 regular bottling offers a moderately intense nose of coconuts intermixed with smoke, cherries, and honeyed lemons and pineapples. There is outstanding purity, gorgeous fruit, seemingly low acidity, and an excellent fat, fleshy finish. This wine may merit an outstanding score if it develops more complexity. Anticipated maturity: 2005–2015 Last tasted, 3/01.

1997
96 L'Extravagance de Doisy-Daëne: In total contrast to the 1996 L'Extravagance, which was 100% Sauvignon Blanc, the 1997 is 100% Semillon. It has a huge amount of residual sugar in a very sweet, unctuous/viscous style, with gobs of noble rot, plenty of buttered, honeyed fruits, still-reticent aromatics, but phenomenal intensity and mass on the palate. It does not quite seem to have the finesse of the 1996, but it is certainly a thicker, richer wine that hits all sensory receptors on the palate and in the olfactory senses. Anticipated maturity: now–2020. Last tasted, 11/02.

1996
86 The 1996 is a stylish, mineral-laden, moderately sweet wine with mid-weight, honeyed complexity, and a fresh, lively finish. Drink it over the next 8–10 years. Last tasted, 3/01.

1996
98 L'Extravagance de Doisy-Daëne: The 1996 has a light-gold color, an unctuous texture, and a gorgeous nose of caramel, buttered pineapple, coconut, and crème brûlée, followed by enormously concentrated, dense flavors that, in spite of their mass and richness, are not at all heavy given the surprising acidity. This wine should have 30 or more years of aging potential. Anticipated maturity: 2010–2035. Interestingly, the 1996 L'Extravagance is 100% botrytised Sauvignon Blanc. Last tasted, 11/02.

1990
91 The 1990 regular *cuvée* is revealing far more complexity and richness than it did in the past. It is a bold, opulent, exquisite example of Barsac, with more richness and intensity than I have encountered in previous vintages of Doisy-Daëne. Light- to medium-gold colored, with a honeyed, botrytised nose, huge amounts of alcohol and power, and a heady finish, the wine possesses just enough acidity to balance out its bold flavors and forcefulness. Drink it over the next 15+ years. Last tasted, 11/94.

1990
95 L'Extravagance de Doisy-Daëne: The 1990 possesses considerable botrytis, awesome extract levels and intensity, and, despite massive power, remarkable balance. Readers are unlikely to find any of this wine (bottled in a heavy 375 ml. bottle) outside Bordeaux. Its medium-gold color and extraordinary richness and power suggest it will age effortlessly for another 20+ years. Last tasted, 11/94.

1989
89 The 1989 exhibits plenty of honeyed ripe fruit, a more elegant personality, fine richness, chunkiness, and depth, full body, and low acidity. It does not reveal the botrytis found in the 1990 or 1988. Last tasted, 11/94.

1988
89 The 1988 is the lightest of these wines, with medium body and a fragrant pineapple, peach, and apple-scented nose, with a honeysuckle component that adds complexity. The wine is crisp, dry, and ideal for drinking now and over the next 10 years. Last tasted, 11/94.

1986
88 While less viscous and chewy than the 1983, this is still an admirably rich, husky, intense Barsac with vividly pure, well-focused fruit, full body, and a long, honeyed finish. Anticipated maturity: now–2005. Last tasted, 3/90.

1985   I could find no evidence of botrytis in this wine, which comes across as relatively
82   fat, uncomplex, and straightforward. Anticipated maturity: now. Last tasted, 3/90.

1983   Doisy-Daëne finished its harvest one month after Yquem and has possibly pro-
90   duced this property's finest wine in over two decades. A big, ripe bouquet of
pineapples, peaches, and spring flowers is very attractive. On the palate, the wine
is concentrated, full-bodied, and unctuous, without being too heavy or alcoholic.
Excellent acidity suggests a long, eventful evolution. Anticipated maturity: now–
2005. Last tasted, 3/90.

DOISY-VÉDRINES

Classification: Second Growth in 1855

Owner: Castéja family

Address: 33720 Barsac

Mailing address: 33720 Barsac

Telephone: 05 56 68 59 70; Telefax: 05 56 78 37 08

Visits: By appointment only

Contact: Olivier Castéja

VINEYARDS

Surface area: 66.7 acres

Grape varietals: 80% Semillon, 15% Sauvignon, 5% Muscadelle

Average age of vines: 30 years

Density of plantation: 6,500 vines per hectare

Average yields: 17 hectoliters per hectare

Elevage: Fermentation and 18 months aging in oak barrels with 60% new oak. Fining,
filtration if required.

WINES PRODUCED

Château Doisy-Védrines: 60,000 bottles

Generic Sauternes: 30,000 bottles

Plateau of maturity: Within 4–16 years of the vintage

GENERAL APPRECIATION

Always rich in fruit, but sometimes too blatantly obvious, Doisy-Védrines is normally a
good value.

This Barsac estate is well placed just to the southeast of the two most famous Barsacs,
Climens and Coutet. Unfortunately, the tiny production of sweet Doisy-Védrines pre-
vents many wine enthusiasts from ever discovering how good this wine can be. Most
wine drinkers are probably better acquainted with the dry white and red table wine
produced at this estate. It is called Chevalier de Védrines and is a delightful commercial wine that is equally good in either white or red. As for the sweet wine, Doisy-
Védrines is much fatter, richer, and more intense than the wine of next-door neighbor

Doisy-Daëne. Doisy-Védrines is a wine that is usually at its best 5–7 years after the vintage but will age considerably longer, particularly in the top vintages.

The estate is run by the well-known Castéja family that also controls the *négociant* firm Roger Joanne. Doisy-Védrines has been in the Castéja family since 1840. Castéja is one of the few Barsac producers who is quick to declassify any vintage they deem to be of unsatisfactory quality. For example, no wine was produced under the Doisy-Védrines label in 1974, 1968, 1965, 1964, or 1963.

IMPORTANT VINTAGES

2001
89–91 Light gold with a gorgeous nose of tropical fruit, caramel, spice, and honey, this wine is rich, intense, and full-bodied, with good acidity and loads of fruit and flesh. It is moderately sweet. Anticipated maturity: 2006–2016. Last tasted, 1/03.

2000
88 Honeyed apricots and white corn emerge from this light golden–colored wine. The wine has plenty of fruit and seems a bit simple compared to its younger sibling, the 2001. Anticipated maturity: now–2012. Last tasted, 1/03.

1999
87 This is a rather high-toned, crisp, medium-weight style of Sauternes with a pale straw/gold color and notes of underripe peaches and apricots intermixed with grapefruit and other citrus. The wine is medium bodied and moderately sweet, with very good acidity. Drink it over the next 10–12 years. Last tasted, 3/01.

1990
87 Although somewhat monolithically styled, there is no doubting the 1990's unctuously textured, thick, sweet style. The color is light-medium gold. The wine offers plenty of honeyed citrus fruit in addition to smoke and vanilla. Medium to full-bodied, with good acidity, some evidence of botrytis, and a plump, low-acid finish, this heavyweight, chunky wine should age nicely for 15–20 years. Anticipated maturity: now–2015. Last tasted, 3/97.

1989
88 Medium-gold colored, with botrytis, crème brûlée, and honeyed tropical fruits in the nose, this full-bodied, sweet wine possesses good acidity, layers of glycerin-imbued, plump, chewy, honeyed fruit, and plenty of spice and alcohol in the lusty finish. It is a luxuriously made, in-your-face style of sweet wine. Anticipated maturity: now–2012. Last tasted, 3/97.

1988
86 A youthful-tasting (the youngest when compared to the bigger, thicker 1990 and 1989 wine) the 1988 is made in a more elegant style, with smoky, crème brûlée, and honeyed citrus and pineapple notes in the aromatics and flavors, medium to full body, moderate sweetness, zesty acidity, and a fine finish. This promising, youthful wine possesses 20 more years of longevity. Anticipated maturity: now–2018. Last tasted, 3/97.

1986
90 Doisy-Védrines made a superb wine in 1986. It is powerful, complex, and nearly as mouth-filling as their great 1989. It does have crisper acidity and, for the moment, a more complex, floral, honeyed bouquet. There is no denying the unctuous, huge, tropical fruit flavors. Anticipated maturity: now–2005. Last tasted, 11/90.

DE FARGUES ——————————————————

Owner: Alexandre de Lur Saluces

Address: 33210 Fargues de Langon

Telephone: 05 57 98 04 20; Telefax: 05 57 98 04 21

E-mail: fargues@chateau-de-fargues.com

Website: www.chateau-de-fargues.com

Visits: By appointment Monday to Friday, 9 A.M. to noon and 2–5 P.M.

Contact: François Amirault

VINEYARDS

Surface area: 37 acres (34.6 in production)

Grape varietals: 80% Semillon, 20% Sauvignon

Average age of vines: 35 years

Density of plantation: 6,600 vines per hectare

Average yields: 12 hectoliters per hectare

Elevage: Fermentation and 36 months aging in new oak barrels. Fining, no filtration.

WINES PRODUCED

Château de Fargues: 15,000 bottles

No second wine is produced.

Plateau of maturity: Within 8 to 25 years of the vintage

Note: This estate also produces a dry white Bordeaux called Guilhem de Fargues in certain vintages (2000, 1999, 1996, 1994, and 1993). The production is around 3,600 bottles.

GENERAL APPRECIATION

The small production guarantees rarity. Additionally, shrewd consumers looking for a wine similar to Yquem at a fraction of the price keep most bottles of this wine from ever hitting a retailer's shelf.

In 1472, 300 years before the Lur Saluces family acquired the famous Château d'Yquem, they owned Château de Fargues. While de Fargues has never been classified, the quality of the wine produced is brilliant. Still owned by the Lur Saluces family, it receives virtually the identical winemaking care that Yquem does. In some vintages, de Fargues has often been the second-best wine produced in the Sauternes region, and when it is tasted blind, many tasters, including most experts, usually judge it to be Yquem. In all fairness, the wine lacks the aging potential of Yquem, but when young, the resemblance can be extraordinary.

Interestingly, the vineyard of de Fargues is located well to the east of Yquem's, and the harvest occurs on an average of 10 days later. Additionally, the yield is less than at Yquem, causing some to say that if Yquem's tiny yield per vine equals only one glass of wine, the yield of a vine at de Fargues must equal only two-thirds of a glass of wine.

De Fargues's similarity to Yquem is uncanny, and given the price charged for de Fargues—approximately one-third that paid for a bottle of Yquem—it is irrefutably a bargain. Unfortunately, the production of de Fargues is tiny, thereby reducing the opportunity for many wine enthusiasts to taste this wine (which some, by the way, jokingly call Yquem, Jr.).

IMPORTANT VINTAGES

1990   Medium-deep gold with a complex, perfumed bouquet of caramel, tea, pineapple,
93   and crème brûlée, this is an atypically powerful de Fargues with massive body as well as an unctuous finish. Anticipated maturity: 2005–2020. Last tasted, 12/02.

1988   Light-golden colored with a green hue, the 1988's smoky nose offers up scents of
91   tobacco, wood, honeysuckle, peaches, and orange skins. Medium to full-bodied
        and elegant, with moderate sweetness, good acidity, and loads of finesse, this is a
        restrained wine that builds incrementally in the mouth. Anticipated maturity:
        2004–2020. Last tasted, 12/02.

1986   The toasty, honeyed, rich bouquet is redolent of pineapples, coconut, crème
93   brûlée, and coffee. In the mouth, this fabulously rich, full-bodied wine offers
        plenty of the botrytised, pineapple, and other tropical fruit flavors, a lavish, unctu-
        ous texture, enough acidity to provide freshness and focus, and a heady, spicy,
        truly intoxicating finish. Anticipated maturity: now–2010. Last tasted, 3/90.

1985   This is a big, corpulent, chunky wine without much botrytis, but plenty of flesh
87   and a muscular, heady alcohol content. The wine drinks beautifully now because
        of the forward, lush fruit married with copious amounts of smoky, toasty new oak.
        The good acidity gives the wine freshness. While I am sure this wine will evolve
        nicely, I do not expect ever to encounter a great deal of complexity. Anticipated
        maturity: now. Last tasted, 3/90.

1983   While no match for the extraordinary wine produced at Yquem in this vintage, the
92   1983 de Fargues (aged three years in 100% new oak casks) is, nevertheless, a sen-
        sational example of a Sauternes with an amazing resemblance to Yquem. A big,
        buttery, caramel, smoky, crème brûlée, and honeyed pineapple nose is en-
        thralling. In the mouth, the wine is powerful, very sweet, rich, extremely full, and
        framed beautifully by toasty new oak. Quite full-bodied and intense, this large-
        scaled wine should have a great future. Anticipated maturity: now–2008. Last
        tasted, 3/90.

1981   This wine has improved significantly and actually tastes better than the 1981
90   Yquem—as hard as that may be to believe. Spectacularly rich, very sweet, and al-
        coholic, it has taken on a medium-gold color. There is plenty of evidence of botry-
        tis, but the low acidity and unctuous, thick, viscous feel on the palate suggest this
        is a wine probably best drunk over the next decade. Anticipated maturity: now.
        Last tasted, 3/90.

1980   A great vintage for de Fargues, the 1980 from this estate is very powerful, opulent,
91   and exotic. The bouquet of coconuts, apricots, grilled almonds, and spicy oak is
        sensational. In the mouth, the wine is decadently rich, full-bodied, and remark-
        ably similar in taste, texture, and viscosity to Yquem. Retasted twice in 1989 with
        equally enthusiastic notes. Anticipated maturity: now. Last tasted, 3/89.

1979   Less powerful and rich than normal, the 1979 de Fargues is light golden, with a
85   toasty, lemony, fruity, oaky bouquet, medium to full body, some botrytis, good acid-
        ity, and a clean, spicy, rich, alcoholic finish. Anticipated maturity: now. Last
        tasted, 3/86.

1976   A full-blown crème brûlée aroma intermingled with scents of caramel and apricots
90   is penetrating. Full-bodied, with viscous, sweet, ripe flavors of tropical fruit and
        smoked nuts, this big, robust, yet surprisingly mature wine remains fully mature but
        displays no signs of declining. Anticipated maturity: now–2005. Last tasted, 2/91.

1975   The 1975 is one of the finest de Fargues ever produced. It has the Yquem-like bou-
91   quet of coconuts, grilled nuts, ripe exotic fruit, and spicy oak. On the palate, the
        1975 is more tightly structured and less evolved than the 1976. It has a lighter
        golden color and more acidity, but every bit as much concentration and richness.
        Anticipated maturity: now–2010. Last tasted, 2/91.

1971   Incredibly rich, unctuous, fat, spicy, and chewy, this huge wine offers oodles of
90   coconut, apricot, and almond flavors, yet viscous fruitiness, huge body, and a
        head-spinning alcohol content. Fully mature, this is a big, old-style, intense
        Sauternes. Anticipated maturity: now. Last tasted, 12/80.

FILHOT

Classification: Second Growth in 1855

Owner: GFA Château Filhot—de Vaucelles family

Address: 33210 Sauternes

Telephone: 05 56 76 61 09; Telefax: 05 56 76 67 91

E-mail: filhot@filhot.com

Visits: By appointment only

Contact: Henri de Vaucelles, Gabriel de Vaucelles

VINEYARDS

Surface area: 153.1 acres

Grape varietals: 60% Semillon, 36% Sauvignon, 4% Muscadelle

Average age of vines: 37 years

Density of plantation: 6,000 vines per hectare

Average yields: 13–14 hectoliters per hectare

Elevage: Ten to thirty day fermentation in temperature-controlled stainless-steel vats. Twenty-four to thirty-six months aging by rotation in barrels (renewed by a third at each vintage) and in vats. No fining, light filtration upon bottling.

WINES PRODUCED

Château Filhot: up to 100,000 bottles

Château Sauternes and Château Pineau du Rey: up to 60,000 bottles

Plateau of maturity: Within 4–12 years of the vintage

GENERAL APPRECIATION

A lighter styled, very refreshing wine that rarely has the weight of the appellations blockbusters, but increasingly well made, and fairly priced.

Filhot, one of the most magnificent estates in the entire Sauternes region, possesses an 18th-century manor home beautifully situated among ancient trees that has the look of an Ivy League college campus. This property has the potential to produce extraordinary wines, particularly given this superb location just to the north of the village of Sauternes on gravelly hillside beds with a southwest orientation. However, it has been only since the mid-1980s that Filhot has begun to produce wines that merit its deuxième cru classé status.

Because of the relatively high percentage of Sauvignon and the utilization of only one-third new oak, Filhot tastes fruitier, more aromatic, and lighter than some of the larger-scaled Sauternes wines. That fact does not, however, account for the lack of consistency and the numerous indifferent and mediocre efforts that were turned out by Filhot during the early 1980s, 1970s, and 1960s. Yet quality clearly appeared to rebound in the late 1980s.

IMPORTANT VINTAGES

2001
88–89
Pineapple, citrus, sealing wax, and spice are in the aromatics and flavor of this finesse-styled, moderately sweet Sauternes/Barsac. The wine is elegant, with lively purity, medium body, and a reasonably long finish. Anticipated maturity: now–2012. Last tasted, 1/03.

2000
87
Light greenish-gold in color, this medium-bodied wine exhibits straightforward pear, pineapple, and peach flavors and a moderate sweetness. However, it is a bit simple and one-dimensional. Drink it over the next 7–8 years. Last tasted, 1/03.

1996
87
An elegant, medium-bodied wine with scents of quince, orange marmalade, and pineapple presented in a moderately endowed aromatic profile, this Sauternes displays moderate sweetness, excellent ripeness and purity, and a tasty, harmonious personality. Drink it over the next 10–12 years. Last tasted, 3/02.

1990
90
Filhot, which prefers to tank rather than barrel ferment its wines, produced a 1990 that is clearly the best wine I have tasted from this estate. It exhibits gorgeously ripe, honeyed tropical fruit, an intense, medium- to full-bodied personality, wonderful purity, fine acidity, plenty of botrytis, and a long, zesty finish. What makes this wine so appealing is its combination of richness, crisp acidity, liveliness, and zestiness. Anticipated maturity: now–2007. Last tasted, 11/94.

1989
86
The thick, very sweet, slightly heavy 1989 appears to be maturing at a fast pace. If drunk over the next 5–8 years it will provide an uncomplicated mouthful of sweet, candied fruit. Anticipated maturity: now. Last tasted, 11/94.

1988
88
The 1988 displayed a wonderfully pure, honeyed pineapple-scented nose, rich, medium- to full-bodied flavors, fine underlying acidity, an earthiness that added to the wine's complexity, and a clean, rich, crisp finish. Drinkable now, it should continue to evolve gracefully for 10–15 years. Last tasted, 11/94.

1986
87
The 1986 is the best Filhot in my memory. The light golden color is followed by a wine with a floral, pineapple, and tropical fruit bouquet, medium body, as well as lovely, elegant, and brilliantly pure, botrytised, lively flavors. Just medium sweet, this wine could be served as an apéritif wine. Anticipated maturity: now. Last tasted, 3/90.

GILETTE

Classification: Cru Bourgeois

Owner: Christian Médeville

Address: 33210 Preignac

Mailing address: BP 14, 33210 Preignac

Telephone: 05 56 76 28 44; Telefax: 05 56 76 28 43

E-mail: christian.medeville@wanadoo.fr

Visits: By appointment Monday to Thursday, 9 A.M.–noon and 2–5 P.M.; Friday, 9 A.M.–noon and 2–3 P.M.

Contact: Julie Gonet-Médeville

VINEYARDS

Surface area: 11.1 acres

Grape varietals: 90% Semillon, 9% Sauvignon, 1% Muscadelle

Average age of vines: 45 years

Density of plantation: 6,600 vines per hectare

Average yields: 9 hectoliters per hectare

Elevage: Fermentation and 15 months aging in temperature-controlled stainless-steel vats. No fining, filtration.

WINES PRODUCED

Château Gilette: 5,000 bottles

No second wine is produced.

Plateau of maturity: Within 20–40 years of the vintage

GENERAL APPRECIATION

An anomaly because of the practice of not releasing wine for 15–25 years, Gilette has a special place because of its high quality and remarkable longevity.

Gilette is one of the most unusually run properties in the Sauternes region. It is one of the finest-made wines in Sauternes despite the fact that Gilette was not classified. The vineyard, situated several miles north of Yquem, adjacent to route D109, is planted on sandy soil with a subsoil of rock and clay. However, what is bizarre and unbelievable in today's harsh world of commercial realities is that Gilette's proprietor, Christian Médeville, holds his sweet wines for over 20 years in concrete vats prior to bottling them. For example, he bottled the 1955 in 1984, 29 years after the vintage. The fact that his wines are excellent and have a honeyed maturity has caused some of France's leading restauranteurs (like Pierre Troisgros) to beat a path to his door to purchase his old vintages of Sauternes.

Gilette's late-released wines, called "Crème de Tête," are extremely well balanced, remarkably well-preserved wines, with plenty of viscous, fruity flavors and deep amber/golden colors. After being held in vats for decades, the wines often taste much younger when they are released than their vintage date would suggest. If my instincts are correct, most vintages of Gilette can benefit from another 15–25 years of cellaring after being released. The following are some of the vintages of Gilette that have been released for sale by M. Médeville over the last decade.

IMPORTANT VINTAGES

1979 Crème de Tête: A medium-gold color is followed by a buttery, earthy perfume
90   revealing hints of tropical fruits and crème brûlée. This medium-bodied 1979 displays surprising youthfulness (a characteristic of Gilette), good acidity, and a long, sweet finish. While not a blockbuster example, it is a noteworthy effort in what was a good rather than great vintage for Sauternes. Anticipated maturity: now–2012. Last tasted, 12/02.

1978 Crème de Tête: A terrific example from this vintage, Gilette's 1978 Crème de Tête
93   exhibits a deep gold color in addition to a sweet nose of honeysuckle intermixed with baked pears, pineapples, vanilla beans, and crème brûlée. Full-bodied and opulent, with tremendous levels of botrytis as well as extracted flavors, crisp acidity, and surprising power and intensity, it will be drinkable between now and 2012. Last tasted, 12/02.

1975 Crème de Tête: A stunning example of this vintage, Gilette's 1975, released in
93   1997, exhibits a deep-gold color, followed by a spicy vanilla-scented nose with
      loads of fresh, lively, honeyed citrus, buttery pineapple/pear–like fruit. The wine
      is probably sweeter than it tastes, but because of the good acidity, it comes across
      as an off-dry, dazzlingly rich, full-bodied, exceptionally fresh Sauternes with
      razor-sharp definition and a finish that lasts for more than 30 seconds. It is stun-
      ningly youthful, as well as complex and marvelous. Anticipated maturity:
      now–2010. Last tasted, 3/97.

1971 Crème de Tête: This is a more reserved, austere, restrained wine, with a tight but
88   attractive nose of loamy earth, roasted coffee, herbs, and sweet, honeyed fruit.
      Medium to full-bodied, with tightly wound flavors, good acidity, and moderate lev-
      els of botrytis, this is a less generous yet stylish, polite Gilette that should continue
      to age well for 15 or more years. Last tasted, 3/97.

1970 Crème de Tête: The 1970 has a deep, rich-golden color and a big, spicy bouquet of
88   buttery, apricot-scented fruit; it's full-bodied and amazingly fresh and youthful for
      its age, and will probably keep another 15–25 years. It lacks the complexity of the
      great vintages of Gilette but, nevertheless, is an impressively full, complex wine.
      Anticipated maturity: now-2005. Last tasted, 3/90.

1967 Crème de Tête: Everyone agrees that no greater wine was made in 1967 than
96   Château d'Yquem, but I would love to have the opportunity to taste Gilette's 1967
      Crème de Tête alongside Yquem. This fabulously rich wine has an awesomely in-
      tense bouquet of caramel and buttery hazelnuts, combined with intense aromas of
      honeyed fruit such as pineapples, oranges, and apricots. Decadently rich, with an
      unctuous, chewy texture, yet with enough acidity to provide great delineation and
      balance, this is a magnificent wine that has miraculously retained an amazing
      freshness for its 23 years of age. It should continue to evolve and improve for an-
      other 30, perhaps even 40, years. This is an outrageous thrill-a-sip Sauternes! An-
      ticipated maturity: now–2025. Last tasted, 3/90.

1962 Crème de Tête: The 1962 offers a very complex, honeyed nose filled with decadent
90   apricot and peach scents that can come from heavily botrytised fruit. Very full-
      bodied, with good acidity and opulent, rich crème brûlée flavors, this luscious,
      full-throttle Sauternes should continue to drink well for at least another 15–20
      years. Anticipated maturity: now–2015. Last tasted, 3/90.

1961 Crème de Tête: I have never tasted a great 1961 Sauternes, although I am sure this
87   region's wines benefited immensely from the great reputation of the reds in this
      vintage. However, the white wines were nowhere near the quality of either the
      1962s or 1959s. Most have turned out to be very good, relatively dry, old white
      wines with a great deal of alcohol but not much charm or fat. Gilette's 1961 is very
      fine, although significantly less rich and opulent than the 1962. It is almost dry. It
      could be the perfect partner with a rich dish that contained foie gras as one of the
      primary ingredients. Anticipated maturity: now–2001. Last tasted, 3/90.

1959 Crème de Tête: This is a decadent, honey pot of a wine. It is medium-deep golden,
94   with a huge bouquet of smoked nuts, coffee, mocha, coconut, and decadently
      jammy apricot and peach-like fruit. In the mouth, the wine has astonishing rich-
      ness, super-glycerin content, a great deal of body, and a long, alcoholic, smash-
      ingly intense, heady finish. Seemingly fully mature, yet still remarkably fresh and
      young, this wine can easily last for another 20 or more years. Anticipated maturity:
      now–2010. Last tasted, 3/90.

1955 Crème de Tête: Fully mature, but still astonishingly fresh and alive, the 1955
87   Gilette is deep golden in color, with a rich, honeyed bouquet, full body, and a ripe,
      long finish. It can probably last another 10–15 years. Anticipated maturity:
      now–2005. Last tasted, 11/90.

1953 Crème de Tête: Slightly less rich and fat than the 1955, the 1953 is spicy and oaky,
86 with a bouquet suggesting melted caramel and ripe pineapples. Full-bodied, still fresh and lively, this unctuous, rich wine is quite impressive. Anticipated maturity: now. Last tasted, 11/90.

1950 Quite fat and sweet, with excellent ripeness, full body, and a long, deep, velvety
89 finish, this wine is a revelation given its age. This is a big, heavyweight Sauternes that will last for 15–20 more years. Anticipated maturity: now–2005. Last tasted, 1/85.

GUIRAUD

Classification: First Growth in 1855

Owner: SA du Château Guiraud

Address: 33210 Sauternes

Mailing address: BP 1, 33210 Sauternes

Telephone: 05 56 76 61 01; Telefax: 05 56 76 67 52

E-mail: xplanty@club.internet.fr

Website: www.chateau.guiraud.fr

Visits: By appointment only

Contact: Noëlle Eymery or Mrs. Amirault

VINEYARDS

Surface area: 210 acres

Grape varietals: 65% Semillon, 35% Sauvignon

Average age of vines: 25 years

Density of plantation: 6,600 vines per hectare

Average yields: 12 hectoliters per hectare

Elevage: Fermentation and 30 months aging in new oak barrels. Fining and filtration.

WINES PRODUCED

Château Guiraud: 9,600 bottles

Le Dauphin du Château Guiraud: 30,000 bottles

Plateau of maturity: Within 5–20 years of the vintage

GENERAL APPRECIATION

This superb estate is on top of its game, thanks to the brilliant administrator, Xavier Planty. A delicious dry white wine called "G" is also made at Château Guiraud.

Guiraud is one of the largest estates of the Sauternes district, covering almost 300 acres, of which 210 are planted with vines. Curiously, the estate produces a red wine with the Bordeaux Supérieur appellation and a dry white wine called "G."

The sweet wine of Guiraud has undergone a metamorphosis. In 1981 an ambitious Canadian, Hamilton Narby, purchased the estate and made bold promises that Yquem-like techniques of individual grape picking, barrel fermentation, and long aging in new oak barrels would be employed at Guiraud. Consequently, Bordeaux wine enthusiasts, particularly the nectar lovers, have taken great interest in the goings-on at Guiraud in the hopes that his administrator, Xavier Planty, has the talent to bring Narby's dreams to fruition.

The most surprising thing about Guiraud is that the wine is so rich given the high percentage of Sauvignon Blanc (35%) used in the blend. No doubt the use of new oak, late picking, and numerous passes through the vineyard ensure that only the ripest Sauvignon Blanc is harvested. But I am still perplexed as to why this wine is so intense despite that Sauvignon Blanc. Vintages since 1983 have been especially strong, and Guiraud is often one of the top half-dozen wines now being made in the Barsac/Sauternes region.

IMPORTANT VINTAGES

2001 A gorgeous example of Guiraud, the honeysuckle, butterscotch, toasty new oak
91–94 aromas interplay with ripe tropical fruits and sautéed butter in a complex, full-throttle bouquet. Quite powerful, dense, full-bodied, beautifully delineated, with loads of botrytis, this is an impressive, backward yet tremendously promising wine. Anticipated maturity: 2008–2025. Last tasted, 1/03.

2000 A very sweet, medium-golden style, with caramelized pineapples intermixed with
89 some vanilla and crème caramel, this wine is full-bodied, with luscious fruit, but lacks complexity, which typifies so many of the 2000 Barsac/Sauternes. Anticipated maturity: now–2015. Last tasted, 1/03.

1999 A very vibrant style of wine from Guiraud, with less sweetness than usual, some
90 what monolithic, with relatively high acidity, 9,000 cases were produced of this medium gold–colored wine. It is quite tight, shows some botrytis, hints of coconut, pineapple, and crème brûlée, medium body, and a firm finish. Anticipated maturity: 2005–2018. Last tasted, 12/02.

1998 One of the vintage's most successful wines, the 1998 Guiraud (55% Semillon and
91 35% Sauvignon with a huge production of 12,000 cases) is very low in acidity, extremely intense, with loads of botrytis, noteworthy honeysuckle, jammy, pineapple and tropical fruit notes, along with some espresso and caramel. There is good freshness, but this is a Guiraud to drink during its first 15 or so years of life. Last tasted, 12/02.

1997 Medium gold, with a hint of green, this wine has somewhat foursquare notes of
90 honeyed, canned lychee nuts intermixed with orange marmalade, butter, and sautéed hazelnuts. The wine is full-bodied, thick, very fat, and seems destined to show more aromatics and delineation as it evolves in the bottle. The 1997 is a blend of 65% Semillon and 35% Sauvignon Blanc. Anticipated maturity: now–2020. Last tasted, 11/02.

1996 A very deep, evolved, golden color, this wine shows brandied tangerine and orange
90 blossom notes with hints of buttered white corn, caramel, crème brûlée, and roasted nuts. The wine is relatively complex, quite rich, and full-bodied, and it seems to be on a relatively quick evolutionary track. Anticipated maturity: now–2016. Last tasted, 11/02.

1990 In the past, I preferred the 1988 Guiraud, followed by the 1989, and, last, the
91 1990. In recent tastings the 1990 has taken first prize with its showy display of power, highly extracted, smoky, buttery, pineapple and orange-scented fruit, lavish quantities of toasty new oak, and unctuously thick, massive flavors and texture. This huge wine avoids being overbearing because of its adequate acidity. It should evolve well for 15–20 more years. Last tasted, 11/94.

1989
86
The 1989 is extremely disjointed. Although big and rich, it tastes like a glob of sugar, alcohol, and wood. This was a disappointing showing for the 1989. It should gain focus and return to the form predicted for it when it was in barrel. Last tasted, 11/94.

1988
89+
More tight and backward than I remembered it, the 1988 exhibits a stylish, spicy nose of ripe fruit, some botrytis, medium- to full-bodied flavors with well-integrated oak, an attractive, smoky, honeyed fruit character, and a lively finish. It is more shy and reticent than usual. It should last for 20–30 years. Last tasted, 5/98.

1986
92
Wealthy collectors will have a great deal of fun comparing the 1989, 1988, and 1986 as they evolve over the years. The 1986 was the finest Guiraud made up to that point, although I suspect the 1988 will last longer and have higher acidity and better overall balance. However, the 1986 is a super-concentrated, aromatic wine with gobs of botrytis and creamy, unctuous, peach, pineapple, and apricot flavors. There is plenty of new oak to frame the wine, although the overall acidity is less than in the 1988. The finish is exceptionally long and well balanced. This is a massive, concentrated wine that should easily develop over several decades. Anticipated maturity: now–2009. Last tasted, 3/90.

1985
85
Guiraud has turned out a well-made 1985, with a great deal of sweetness, plenty of ripeness, and obvious aromas of toasty, smoky new oak. There is no botrytis in evidence, and the wine exhibits less finesse and complexity than vintages such as 1986 and 1983. Nevertheless, this straightforward style of Sauternes will have its admirers, particularly among those who like to drink these wines as an apéritif. Anticipated maturity: now. Last tasted, 3/90.

1983
88
Light golden, with a ripe, intense bouquet of apricots and pineapples, as well as the vanilla scents from having been aged in cask, this full-bodied, lush, rich wine has excellent concentration, superb balance, and a zesty, long, alcoholic finish. Anticipated maturity: now–2005. Last tasted, 3/90.

LAFAURIE-PEYRAGUEY

Classification: First Growth in 1855

Owner: Groupe Suez

Address: Peyraguey, 33210 Bommes

Mailing address: 160, cours du Médoc, 33300 Bordeaux

Telephone: 05 57 19 57 77; Telefax: 05 56 95 53 01

Visits: By appointment only

Contact: Yannick Laporte (Telephone: 05 56 76 60 54; Telefax: 05 56 76 61 82)

VINEYARDS

Surface area: 101.3 acres

Grape varietals: 90% Semillon, 8% Sauvignon, 2% Muscadelle

Average age of vines: 40 years

Density of plantation: 6,666 vines per hectare

Average yields: 18 hectoliters per hectare

Elevage: Fermentation and 18–20 months aging in barrels that are renewed by a third each year. Fining and filtration.

WINES PRODUCED

Château Lafaurie-Peyraguey

La Chapelle de Lafaurie-Peyraguey

Plateau of maturity: Within 5–25 years of the vintage

GENERAL APPRECIATION

This is consistently one of the finest wines of Sauternes, always made in a full-throttle style.

Long in the doldrums, Lafaurie-Peyraguey has emerged in the 1980s as one of the great producers of decadently rich, complex, and compelling Sauternes wines. The decision to reduce the percentage of Sauvignon in the wine, to increase the amount of new oak, and to institute a stricter selection began to result in a string of highly successful Sauternes starting with 1981 and culminating with the great wines produced in 1990, 1989, 1988, 1986, and 1983.

The château, one of the most extraordinary in the Sauternes region, was built in the 13th century as a fortification overlooking the surrounding countryside. The property was acquired by the Cordiers in 1913. At present, based on the performance of Lafaurie-Peyraguey during the last decade, this is one of the top half-dozen Sauternes, combining an unctuous richness with great finesse and a profound fragrance of honeyed fruit.

In the late 1980s a dry white wine called Le Brut de Lafaurie was introduced. While I am not a great admirer of many of the relatively heavy, dry white wines made in the Sauternes region, this is the best I have tasted from the appellation. It is produced from 40% Sauvignon Blanc, 40% Semillon, and 20% Muscadelle and can be wonderfully delicious, perfumed, and surprisingly rich, yet totally dry and crisp.

IMPORTANT VINTAGES

2001
91–94 This is a stunning wine, with great acidity, plenty of noble rot, and notes of honeysuckle, caramel, peach, apricot, and caramelized figs as well as pears. Some sweet oak is there, but it is very subtle. This is a full-bodied, elegant, yet authoritatively flavorful wine that should last for decades. Anticipated maturity: 2007–2025. Last tasted, 1/03.

2000
90 This is one of the best examples I tasted from this vintage, which is not nearly as bad as many had predicted. Light golden in color, with a big, tactile impression on the palate, with notes of tropical fruit, caramel, orange marmalade, and buttered citrus, the wine is full-bodied, relatively evolved, and best drunk during its first 10–15 years of life. Last tasted, 1/03.

1998
90 This is a rather exotic, almost Alsatian Vendanges-Tardive–styled wine, with notes of lychee nuts and tropical fruits, but the new oak gives it away as a Sauternes. The wine is full-bodied, very generous, and honeyed, with significant quantities of botrytis. The underlying acidity is there to pull everything into focus in this rather flamboyant, viscous, thick Sauternes. Anticipated maturity: 2005–2020. Last tasted, 1/03.

1997 This 1997 displays gorgeous aromas of coconut, honeyed oranges, tangerines,
90   pineapples, mangoes, and other tropical fruits. The wine is medium to full-bodied
      and superrich, but not a blockbuster in the mold of such years as 1990 and 1988.
      It possesses low acidity (in flavor, but not in terms of analyses), and a long, 40-
      second finish. This superb 1997 exhibits considerable botrytis, as well as a thick,
      unctuously textured style. Anticipated maturity: now–2025. Last tasted, 1/03.

1996 Also outstanding, the 1996 offers aromas of Grand Marnier orange liqueur inter-
90   twined with toast, coconut, and other exotic fruits. It is dense and medium to full-
      bodied, with layers of fruit, more structure than the 1997, and a pure, viscous
      finish. Anticipated maturity: 2004–2025. Last tasted, 1/03.

1990 I remember how one-dimensional, diffuse, thick, and alcoholic this wine tasted
92   from cask and immediately after bottling, but it has progressed enormously. The
      1990 exhibits a deep golden corn-like color, followed by sensational aromatics
      (honeyed citrus, pineapple, and pear intertwined with smoke and crème
      brûlée–like notes). In the mouth, the wine is massive and full-bodied, with an unc-
      tuous texture and powerful, juicy flavors that possess mouth-staining extract, glyc-
      erin, and viscosity. This is a blockbuster-style, sweet Sauternes with at least 30
      years of longevity. Anticipated maturity: 2004–2030. Last tasted, 12/97.

1989 Sandwiched between two extraordinary vintages for Lafaurie-Peyraguey, the 1989
89   may turn out to be an outstanding wine with more aging potential. The problem is
      that I have always tasted it in a minivertical with two glorious examples of this
      château. The 1989 is an excellent, possibly outstanding, wine made in a more re-
      strained and less viscous style than the 1990 and 1988. The 1989 possesses a
      lively aromatic profile consisting of honeyed tropical fruits with a touch of a fresh
      Amontillado sherry added for complexity. Full-bodied, with good acidity, less evi-
      dence of botrytis than I would have expected, and excellent, possibly outstanding,
      extract, it reveals a more monolithic, oaky personality, but these wines often take
      8–10 years to reveal their true characters. There is good depth and richness in the
      finish, and the wine is long. Anticipated maturity: now–2025. Last tasted, 12/97.

1988 The massively rich, yet fresh, lively 1988 offers a compelling, flowery, honeyed
95   bouquet of vanilla custard, buttery orange/apricot scents, and smoky crème
      brûlée. The wine's zesty acidity brings everything into extraordinary clarity. With
      plenty of botrytis evident, this is a full-bodied, super-concentrated, fascinating,
      powerful yet elegant Sauternes that will age beautifully for 25–30 years. Antici-
      pated maturity: now–2030. Last tasted, 12/97.

1986 A wonderful bouquet of pineapples, smoky nuts, honeysuckle, and other flowers
92   soars from the glass. In the mouth, the wine is rich, with the essence of apricots,
      pineapples, and other tropical fruits. The acidity is crisp, giving the wine great
      definition and clarity. The finish is sweet, honeyed, and long. This beautifully
      made Sauternes is one of my favorites from the 1986 vintage. Anticipated matu-
      rity: now–2010. Last tasted, 11/96.

1985 Because of the lack of botrytis, the 1985 is a relatively straightforward, fruity, fat,
86   yet fresh-tasting Sauternes that would be ideal as an apéritif rather than a dessert
      wine. It will last for 10–15 years but is best drunk within the next decade. Antici-
      pated maturity: now. Last tasted, 3/91.

1983 The staff at Cordier have every right to be happy with this splendidly concen-
92   trated, complex, fully mature wine. Tremendous intensity, viscous, ripe, and lay-
      ered with honeyed, apricot-flavored fruit, this unctuous wine is not tiring or heavy
      to drink, but lively and effusively fruity. Anticipated maturity: now. Last tasted,
      3/91.

LAMOTHE DESPUJOLS

Classification: Second Growth in 1855

Owner: Guy Despujols

Address: 19, rue Principale, 33210 Sauternes

Telephone: 05 56 76 67 89; Telefax: 05 56 76 63 77

E-mail: guy.despujols@free.fr

Website: www.guy.despujols.free.fr

Visits: By appointment only

Contact: Guy Despujols

VINEYARDS

Surface area: 18.5 acres

Grape varietals: 85% Semillon, 10% Sauvignon, 5% Muscadelle

Average age of vines: 40 years

Density of plantation: 7,500 vines per hectare

Average yields: 18 hectoliters per hectare

Elevage: Fermentation in barrels. Twenty-six months aging (partly on lees) in barrels (with 75% new oak) for the Semillon and in vats (for the Sauvignon and Muscadelle). Fining and filtration.

WINES PRODUCED

Château Lamothe Despujols: 12,000 bottles

Les Tourelles de Lamothe: 3,000 bottles

Plateau of maturity: Within 3–12 years following the vintage

GENERAL APPRECIATION

This is an irregular performer.

Known in the 19th century as Lamothe-d'Assault, this property was partitioned, and there are now two Lamothe estates, both carrying the suffix of the current owner's family name. Lamothe Despujols tends to make relatively light wines, but they are worth tasting since there have been some surprises (as in 1986). With the high percentage of Muscadelle in the blend, the style is one of fragrance and soft, forward fruit. I thought there was a noticeable increase in quality in the late 1980s.

IMPORTANT VINTAGES

2001 The 2001 reveals a moldy/mushroomy note in its unexpressive aromatics. I at-
?   tempted to extrapolate what this wine might taste like without the mold, and it
      does appear to possess medium body, underlying minerality, and honeyed fruit,
      but it is straightforward and one-dimensional. Anticipated maturity: now–2012.
      Last tasted, 1/03.

1996 A lean, light-styled Sauternes with tropical fruit notes in its medium-bodied per-
86   sonality, this is a pleasant, straightforward, good wine for picnics, etc. Drink it
      over the next 8–10 years. Last tasted, 3/00.

1990 The 1990 reveals an oily personality, big, ripe, honeyed fruit flavors, low acidity,
88 plenty of intensity, and a full-bodied, chewy style that suggests it should be drunk over the next 10 years. Last tasted, 11/94.

1989 The 1989 is displaying far greater richness, intensity, and cleanliness than previ-
87 ous examples revealed. It exhibited good fatness, an unctuous texture, low acidity, and lovely rich, intense, tropical fruit. It should drink well for 7–8 years. Last tasted, 11/94.

1988 It is hard to understand what could have happened at Lamothe Despujols in such
72 a superb vintage as 1988. This wine is dull, muted, and lacking fruit, freshness, and character. It performed this way in three separate tastings. Anticipated maturity: now. Last tasted, 4/91.

1986 For as inconsistent and indifferent as Lamothe Despujols can be, the 1986 is ir-
88 refutably a sleeper of the vintage. A wonderful honeyed nose with a whiff of toasty oak is followed by an opulent, intense, rich, glycerin-filled, full-bodied, beauti-fully balanced Sauternes that should drink well for another 10–15 years. It is un-doubtedly the best example I have ever tasted from this property. Anticipated maturity: now–2005. Last tasted, 3/90.

1985 This big, fat, surprisingly rich and intense wine exhibits a great deal more weight
85 and character than many other properties in this vintage. There is very little evi-dence of botrytis, but there are gobs of fruit in a relatively straightforward, chunky style. Anticipated maturity: now. Last tasted, 3/90.

LAMOTHE GUIGNARD

Classification: Second Growth in 1855

Owners: Philippe and Jacques Guignard

Address: 33210 Sauternes

Telephone: 05 56 76 60 28; Telefax: 05 56 76 69 05

Visits: Monday to Friday, 8 A.M.–noon and 2–6 P.M.

Contact: Philippe and Jacques Guignard

VINEYARDS

Surface area: 79 acres

Grape varietals: 90% Semillon, 5% Sauvignon, 5% Muscadelle

Average age of vines: 40 years

Density of plantation: 6,600 vines per hectare

Average yields: 17 hectoliters per hectare

Elevage: Fermentation in small vats. Twelve to fifteen months aging in barrels with 20–25% new oak. Fining and filtration.

WINES PRODUCED

Château Lamothe Guignard: 30,000 bottles

L'Ouest de Lamothe Guignard: 5,000 bottles

Plateau of maturity: Within 5–15 years of the vintage

GENERAL APPRECIATION

An up-and-coming estate that merits a closer look.

The proprietors of Lamothe Guignard, Philippe and Jacques Guignard, purchased this property in 1981 and have set about in an aggressive manner to resurrect the image of Lamothe Guignard. This could be a property to keep a close eye on in the upcoming years, as the quality of the wines has been promising.

The vineyard is well located several miles to the south of Yquem, just off route D125. Sitting on a clay/gravel ridge, it overlooks the valley of the Ciron. Among the premiers crus classés, it is closest to Guiraud, La Tour Blanche, and Lafaurie-Peyraguey. The proprietors have increased the percentage of new oak and have begun making more passes through the vineyard to harvest only fully botrytised grapes. The results have been impressive and somewhat undervalued wines.

IMPORTANT VINTAGES

2001 Dense, full-bodied, very primary, but showing plenty of honeysuckle, candied cit-
89–91 rus, and orange marmalade notes, this wine looks to be an outstanding effort. Anticipated maturity: 2005–2015. Last tasted, 1/03.

2000 Deep golden, very fruity, somewhat simple, but lovely in a uncomplicated, lush
88 style, drink this wine over the next 10 years. Last tasted, 1/03.

1997 This wine reveals considerable botrytis, and a monolithic, fat, somewhat dis-
86 jointed personality. It does offer currant, coconut, and honeyed fruit, and medium to full body, but no focal point or potential complexity. It needs more time to reveal its true identity. Anticipated maturity: now–2015. Last tasted, 3/01.

1996 Less botrytis than the 1997 and a Sauvignon Blanc–dominated personality char-
87 acterize the melony, herb-tinged, honeyed nose of this medium-weight wine. Relying on elegance, purity, and finesse as opposed to power and blockbuster strength, this medium-bodied Sauternes should be drinkable young, yet keep for another 12 years. Last tasted, 3/01.

1990 The 1990 is a forceful, unctuous, thick, chewy Sauternes with plenty of heady al-
91 cohol, gobs of fruit, and an exuberant personality. It reveals greater aromatics, complexity, dimension, and delineation than it did several years ago. It should age well and evolve for 15–20 more years. Last tasted, 11/94.

1989 The 1989 also displays more personality and complexity. Although it possesses
91 very high alcohol (nearly 15%), it is a massive, highly extracted, extremely rich, impressively endowed wine that is oozing with honeyed, buttery, apricot, orange, pineapple, and lemony fruit. Noticeable acidity gives uplift and vibrance to this huge wine. Lamothe Guignard's 1989 has turned out to be a sleeper of the vintage and should be available at a reasonable price. It should last for 20+ years. Last tasted, 11/94.

1988 The backward, streamlined 1988 possesses a waxy, honeyed, Tokay-Pinot Gris–
89+ like fragrance and rich, full-bodied flavors that appear reticent and restrained because of the wine's good acidity. A shy example of this estate's wine, it is not nearly as ostentatious or muscular as the 1990 or 1989. It should last for 20–25 years. Last tasted, 11/94.

1986 The 1986 Lamothe Guignard has a lovely moderately intense, pineapple fruiti-
87 ness, rich, velvety flavors, plenty of botrytis, and a long, silky finish. While it will not be one of the longest-lived 1986s, it certainly is capable of providing immense satisfaction for another 5–7 years. Anticipated maturity: now. Last tasted, 3/90.

1985 Once again, the shortcomings of the 1985 Barsac/Sauternes vintage are obvious in
84   this straightforward, relatively fat, but uninteresting and monolithically styled
      Sauternes. It is sweet, rich, full, and heavy, but there is a lack of grip as well as
      complexity. Anticipated maturity: now. Last tasted, 3/90.

DE MALLE

Classification: Second Growth in 1855 Classification

Owner: Comtesse de Bournazel

Address: 33210 Preignac

Telephone: 05 56 62 36 86; Telefax: 05 56 76 82 40

E-mail: chateaudemalle@wanadoo.fr

Website: www.chateau-de-mall.fr

Visits: Cellars: By appointment only; Château and gardens:
April 1 to October 31 by appointment in the morning
and 2–6 P.M.

VINEYARDS

Surface area: 66.7 acres

Grape varietals: 70% Semillon, 27% Sauvignon, 3% Muscadelle

Average age of vines: 30–40 years

Density of plantation: 6,200 vines per hectare

Average yields: 20 hectoliters per hectare

Elevage: Direct pressing and 10 hour cold settling. Fermentation and 18 months aging in
barrels that are renewed by a third at each vintage. Fining and filtration.

WINES PRODUCED

Château de Malle: 50,000 bottles

Château de Sainte-Hélène: 25,000 bottles

Plateau of maturity: Within 5–15 years of the vintage

GENERAL APPRECIATION

In 2003, this is one of the most consistently excellent wines of the region.

This magnificent estate, with its extraordinary 17th-century château, was at one time
owned by a member of the Lur Saluces family (the proprietors of Yquem and de Fargues). However, that ownership ended in 1785. Since then the property has been in the
Bournazel family. De Malle is a vast estate, with over half its acreage in Graves. Those
readers who have tasted the excellent white Graves made by Château de Malle, the M.
de Malle, or their red wine, Château Cardaillan, know how serious those wines can be.
I also recommend that visitors to the Barsac/Sauternes region go out of their way to get
an appointment to visit Château de Malle, which was classified as a historic monument
by the French government in 1949.

Even if you have no interest in architecture, the wines are worth tasting; they are among the most elegant of the appellation. At times they can have a tendency to turn out light, but recent vintages (from the more restrained and refined school of Sauternes) have been extremely well made.

IMPORTANT VINTAGES

2001
90–94 A superb Sauternes, de Malle's moderately sweet wine has a light-gold color with some green tints. Honeyed citrus along with tropical fruits, peach, crème caramel, and smoked hazelnuts all jump from the glass of this layered, full-bodied, gorgeously pure and well-delineated wine. It is moderately sweet, but the good acidity and depth are impressive. Anticipated maturity: 2007–2020. Last tasted, 1/03.

2000
89 A very seductive nose of honeysuckle and pineapples follow through in the flavors of this medium- to full-bodied, very unctuously textured, chunky but fleshy and appealing wine. Drink it over the next 10–15 years. Last tasted, 1/03.

1999
87 Light gold in color, with a very spicy nose intermixed with some hints of apricot, white peach, and sweet corn, this wine is medium-bodied and fruit-driven, but somewhat short in the finish. Drink it over the next 7–10 years. Last tasted, 3/02.

1997
90 An exotic, flamboyant bouquet of orange marmalade, honeyed citrus, caramel, coconut, and toast soars from the glass of this well-bodied, potentially outstanding effort. In the mouth, it reveals an unctuous texture with tangy underlying acidity, medium to full body, and gobs of fruit. Anticipated maturity: 2004–2020. Last tasted, 3/01.

1996
87 This wine tastes high in acidity, with the Sauvignon Blanc more dominant (normally 75% of this wine is Semillon). It is medium bodied, slightly off dry as opposed to the sweeter, more viscous 1997, with evidence of pineapple and a clean, moderately long finish. Anticipated maturity: now–2016. Last tasted, 3/01.

1990
92 Château de Malle's 1990, the finest sweet wine the estate had made in decades, marks the resurrection of this château. Certainly it is an outstanding effort, and, given the reasonable price, it is a noteworthy purchase. The 1990 is full-bodied, with excellent sweetness, fine purity, and plenty of rich, honeyed fruit buttressed by noticeable new oak. It has not yet developed the complexity and aromatics displayed by the 1988, but the 1990 is clearly an outstanding effort for the vintage. Anticipated maturity: now–2022. Last tasted, 11/95.

1989
87 The 1989 appeared to be somewhat simple. It is medium to full-bodied, with ripe, rich fruit, enough acidity to provide uplift, and a fleshy finish. It should drink well for another decade. Last tasted, 11/94.

1988
91 The 1988 was "singing" at the top of its lungs in a recent tasting. Closer to maturity than the 1990, the 1988 offers a heavenly bouquet of cherries and coconuts as well as an ostentatious display of honeyed pineapples and toasty oak. Medium to full-bodied, with excellent purity, freshness, and ripeness, it is an ideal candidate for drinking or cellaring over the next 10–12 years. Last tasted, 11/94.

NAIRAC

Classification: Second Growth in 1855

Owner: Nicole Tari-Heeter

Address: 33720 Barsac

Telephone: 05 56 27 16 16; Telefax: 05 56 27 26 50

Visits: By appointment only

Contact: Nicolas Heeter

VINEYARDS

Surface area: 42 acres

Grape varietals: 90% Semillon, 6% Sauvignon, 4% Muscadelle

Average age of vines: 40 years

Density of plantation: 8,000 vines per hectare

Average yields: 7 hectoliters per hectare

Elevage: Fermentations last one to three months in oak barrels, and wines are aged two and a half years before bottling (30–100% new oak). They are fined and filtered.

WINES PRODUCED

Château Nairac: 10,000 bottles

No second wine produced.

Plateau of maturity: Within 5–15 years of the vintage

GENERAL APPRECIATION

Corpulent, well-oaked, big, and bold wines characterize the style of this property.

Nairac is one of the most meticulously and passionately operated Barsac estates. In 1971 the property was purchased by American-born Tom Heeter and Nicole Tari. Heeter apprenticed at the red wine–producing property Giscours, in the Margaux appellation, where he met his wife (they are now divorced), a member of the Tari winemaking family. During the 1980s the celebrated Emile Peynaud was brought in to provide oenological advice, and Nairac began to produce some of the best wines of Barsac.

Nairac is a relatively big-styled, oaky, ripe, concentrated wine for a Barsac, but it is rarely exciting. However, it represents a good value and should be sought out by consumers looking for a good Barsac at a reasonable price.

IMPORTANT VINTAGES

1999 88+ Deep medium gold–colored with a roasted/caramelized pineapple/apricot scent interwoven with oak, this medium-bodied wine possesses good sweetness, crisp acids, and an excellent finish. Anticipated maturity: 2007–2017. Last tasted, 1/02.

1998 86 Light gold in color, with muted aromatics, this crisp, tangy, tight, somewhat earthy as well as oaky wine offers excellent purity, but largely uninspiring flavors. Will it improve? Anticipated maturity: 2004–2013. Last tasted, 1/02.

1997 89 With 90% Semillon in the blend, in a year that favored this varietal, Nairac's 1997 is an impressively endowed, full-bodied, intensely sweet wine with layers of flavor, considerable glycerin, a chewy, cherry liqueur–like, honeyed, smoky new oak–scented bouquet, and a long, intense, thick finish. It exhibits plenty of botrytis, seemingly low acidity, and the potential for an outstanding rating. Anticipated maturity: 2005–2020. Last tasted, 1/02.

1990 87 Like many Nairacs, the 1990 is robust, solid, even corpulent, but it lacks great class as well as a focal point. Its medium deep-gold color is followed by aromas of burnt honey and apricots intermixed with vanilla beans and espresso. This sweet wine is fully mature. Anticipated maturity: now–2012. Last tasted, 1/02.

1989 When I first tasted the 1989 Nairac from cask, it appeared to be excessively oaky
87   as well as a bit too fat and alcoholic. However, it has evolved gracefully in the cask
      and now exhibits plenty of toasty vanilla-scented new oak, an opulently rich nose
      and texture, long, heady, unctuous flavors, and enough acidity for grip and focus.
      It will evolve quickly, as the color is already a deep-medium golden. Anticipated
      maturity: now. Last tasted, 4/91.

1986 This is one of the finest Nairacs I have ever tasted. It is an especially rich, power-
89   ful, concentrated wine with gobs of glycerin-injected pineapple fruit, full body,
      and a long, luscious, smooth finish. There is plenty of acidity and evidence of
      botrytis, so I would expect a relatively long evolution for this top-class wine. An-
      ticipated maturity: now–2010. Last tasted, 3/90.

1985 The 1985 lacks botrytis, a problem that is typical of most wines of the 1985 vin-
81   tage. Other than that, there is straightforward orange and pineapple fruit, heavily
      dosed with generous quantities of toasty new oak. Anticipated maturity: now. Last
      tasted, 3/89.

1983 Extremely aromatic, the 1983 Nairac has a flowery, tropical fruit–scented bou-
86   quet, big, rich, fruit salad–like flavors, full body, and a luscious, honeyed finish.
      Anticipated maturity: now. Last tasted, 3/90.

RABAUD-PROMIS

Classification: First Growth in 1855

Owner: GFA du Château Rabaud-Promis

Address: 33210 Bommes

Telephone: 05 56 76 67 38; Telefax: 05 56 76 63 10

Visits: By appointment only

Contact: Philippe Déjean

VINEYARDS

Surface area: 84 acres

Grape varietals: 80% Semillon, 18% Sauvignon, 2% Muscadelle

Average age of vines: 40 years

Density of plantation: 6,600 vines per hectare

Average yields: 14 hectoliters per hectare

Elevage: Three week fermentation and 12–14 months aging in barrels with 30% new oak.
Fining, light filtration upon bottling.

WINES PRODUCED

Château Rabaud-Promis: 36,000 bottles

Château Béquet or Domaine de l'Estrémade: 24,000 bottles

Plateau of maturity: Within 5–20 years following the vintage

GENERAL APPRECIATION

This is an example of a Sauternes estate that is making better and better wines.

Rabaud-Promis was once part of a huge ancient domain called Rabaud. In 1903
Rabaud was divided into Rabaud-Promis and the more well-known Sigalas Rabaud.

Curiously, the properties were reunited 26 years later, but then partitioned again in 1952.

Until 1986 Rabaud-Promis may have been the most disappointing wine among the premiers crus classés. However, no estate has made more progress in such a short period of time. Not only has a second wine been introduced, but the top wine now goes into small oak barrels, of which a healthy percentage is new each year. In the past, there was no selection, and the entire crop was matured in cement vats. Certainly the estate is beautifully situated on high ground at the junction of the Garonne and Ciron Rivers.

Shrewd connoisseurs of the sweet wines of Barsac/Sauternes should put such information to use, as it will probably take several years before the price catches up to the quality level now being exhibited. If the excellent examples of Rabaud-Promis that have emerged from the 2001, 1990, 1989, 1988, and 1986 vintages are typical of the new direction of this property, it will be one of the fuller-bodied, more luscious and intense Sauternes on the market.

IMPORTANT VINTAGES

2001 This is a big, sweet, honeyed style, with loads of fruit, not a great deal of complex-
90–92 ity, but there is a lot going on in this young but very promising wine. It is full-bodied and light gold–colored, with plenty of pineapple, honeysuckle, marmalade notes, and a hint of caramel. Anticipated maturity: 2007–2020.

1999 A rather restrained and measured style of Sauternes, with a light pale-gold color
85 with some green nuances, this wine shows high acidity, not a lot of botrytis, medium body, and moderate sweetness in a somewhat austerely styled Sauternes. Anticipated maturity: 2004–2014. Last tasted, 3/02.

1998 Light gold–colored with an earthy, herbal, compost-scented bouquet interwoven
86 with notes of cloves, gingerbread, and pineapple, this medium-bodied, moderately sweet wine has decent acidity, but a monolithic personality. Anticipated maturity: 2004–2014. Last tasted, 1/02.

1997 Sweet, plump, evolved, and tasty, the 1997 Rabaud-Promis exhibits a medium
87 deep-gold color, copious fruit, fat, and glycerin, yet it lacks focus and complexity. Nevertheless, there is a hefty, straightforward style that is superficially pleasing. Anticipated maturity: now–2014. Last tasted, 1/02.

1990 The 1990 reveals plenty of honeyed richness, a full-blown, heavyweight style, and
90 considerable spice. While there is a slight lack of acidity, it is a huge, full-bodied wine for drinking over the next 15 or so years. Last tasted, 11/94.

1989 The 1989 is rich and complex aromatically, as well as huge and massive. It ex-
92 hibits great delineation, with enough freshness and vibrancy to make a strong case for this estate's 1989. It should age well for 20–25 years. Last tasted, 11/94.

1988 The 1988 remains the most classic of the superb trilogy of 2000, 1989, and 1988.
93 It possesses great richness, sweetness, and unctuous texture, as well as higher acidity, plenty of botrytis, a wonderful, rich, honeyed pineapple, coconut, and orange-scented nose, gobs of rich fruit, and excellent delineation. Approachable now, it promises to age effortlessly for 25–30 years. Last tasted, 11/94.

1986 The 1986 marked the first in a succession of vintages manifesting the return of
89 Rabaud-Promis to its status as a premier cru classé. Full-bodied, with an intense bouquet of caramel, pineapples, and apricots, this wine has gobs of glycerin, adequate acidity for balance, and a full-bodied, oaky, rich finish. Its evolution should

continue to be graceful and long. Anticipated maturity: now–2010. Last tasted, 3/90.

1985 An attractive nose of flowers, pineapples, and coffee is followed by a straight-

83 forward, relatively powerful wine with a great deal of fruit, but it is lacking the complexity and focus that is essential for these large-scaled sweet wines. Antici- pated maturity: now. Last tasted, 3/90.

1983 This wine has turned out slightly better than I initially believed it would. It is fat,

84 round, and full-bodied, with gobs of fruit, but it comes across as a bit cloying and heavy-handed, without sufficient botrytis or acidity. It was made at a time when Rabaud-Promis was aging its wine in vats rather than small oak casks, which probably explains the wine's lack of delineation. Anticipated maturity: now. Last tasted, 3/90.

RAYMOND-LAFON

Classification: None

Owner: Meslier family

Address: 33210 Sauternes

Telephone: 05 56 63 21 02; Telefax: 05 56 63 19 58

Website: www.chateau-raymond-lafon.fr

Visits: By appointment only

Contact: Marie-Françoise Meslier

VINEYARDS

Surface area: 44.5 acres (39.5 in production)

Grape varietals: 80% Semillon, 20% Sauvignon

Average age of vines: 35 years

Density of plantation: 6,666 vines per hectare

Average yields: 10 hectoliters per hectare

Elevage: Fermentation and 36 months aging in new oak barrels. Fining, no filtration.

WINES PRODUCED

Château Raymond-Lafon: 20,000 bottles

Château Lafon-Laroze: variable

Plateau of maturity: Within 8–25 years following the vintage

GENERAL APPRECIATION

An impeccably run estate that produces top-flight wines, Raymond-Lafon has a connoisseur's following, but quantities are small.

Raymond-Lafon is a name to watch in the Sauternes district, particularly if one is look- ing for a wine that is close to the brilliance and majestic richness of Yquem for less than one-third the price.

This small estate abuts Yquem's vineyard and has had an excellent reputation. The 1921 Raymond-Lafon was considered even better than Yquem's wine in that great vintage. I have never tasted the 1921 Raymond-Lafon, but the single greatest Sauternes I have ever drunk was the Yquem of that vintage. However, the estate of Raymond-Lafon fell into neglect, and it was not until 1972 that Pierre Meslier, the manager of Yquem, purchased this vineyard and began to slowly rebuild this wine's once fabulous reputation.

With a tiny yield of nine hectoliters per hectare (even less than Yquem's), with the same grape blend and winemaking techniques employed as Yquem, and with the same ruthless selection procedure (normally 20–100% of a harvest is declassified), Raymond-Lafon has already produced a succession of splendid Sauternes, beginning with a great 1975 and just recently concluding with a monumental 1990.

Raymond-Lafon looks to be well on the road to becoming one of the great classic wines of Sauternes. Unfortunately, the wine is extremely difficult to find because of the tiny production and the fact that proprietor Pierre Meslier sells much of it to private clients in Europe. One must wonder why this vineyard, situated next to Yquem and surrounded by all the premiers crus classés of Sauternes, was overlooked in the 1855 classification.

IMPORTANT VINTAGES

2001
94–96 A fabulous wine, with big, thick, massive, unctuous flavors, redolent with notes of peach, apricot, crème caramel, and espresso, this opulent, thick, full-bodied wine is very powerful, concentrated, and rich. It should drink well young yet last up to three decades. Anticipated maturity: 2008–2030. Last tasted, 1/03.

1997
89 This light to medium gold–colored, fragrant, medium- to full-bodied, sweet wine is low in acidity, redolent with honeyed pineapple and pear notes intermixed with vanilla bean and crème brûlée. Luscious, rich, and evolved, it will drink well for 10–15 years. Anticipated maturity: now–2017. Last tasted, 11/02.

1996
90+ An outstanding wine, this light gold–colored, full-bodied wine exhibits honeysuckle, orange marmalade, and pineapple flavors intertwined with hints of vanilla and smoke. Rich, viscous, and deep, it is an impressive effort. Anticipated maturity: 2006–2022. Last tasted, 1/02.

1990
95 The 1990 may be the most complete and richest of recent Raymond-Lafons. It possesses a light to medium gold color, with massive, full-bodied, honeyed flavors. Last tasted, 3/96.

1989
91+ The 1989 exhibits aromas of honeyed pineapple/tropical fruit and toasty new oak, as well as an exotic, flashy perfume that is not as pronounced in either the 1990 or 1988. The 1989 exhibits less botrytis than the other two vintages. All three wines share opulent, full-bodied, exotic, lavishly rich personalities, moderate sweetness (the 1990 is the sweetest), and huge quantities of extract, glycerin, and alcohol in their finishes. The 1990 appears to be the richest. Anticipated maturity: now–2025. Last tasted, 3/96.

1988
92+ The 1988 offers the most refined aromatic profile and the tightest structure, and the 1989 tastes the most restrained. This wine can be drunk now, but purchasers are advised to wait until 2005 or so to enjoy over the following two decades. Anticipated maturity: now–2020. Last tasted, 11/94.

1987
84 Very light, with straightforward, fruity, slightly sweet flavors, this would make an attractive, but lowbrow apéritif wine. It does not have the requisite weight, sweetness, or complexity to stand by itself as a dessert wine. Anticipated maturity: now. Last tasted, 4/91.

1986
92

It is hard to believe this wine will eclipse the great 1983, but the differences in the two wines are negligible. I do not believe the 1986 makes quite the impact on the palate that the huge, massive 1983 does, but there is a great deal of botrytis and a profound, penetrating fragrance of sautéed pineapple, vanilla, toast, and honeyed peaches. In the mouth, the wine is more streamlined than the 1983, but lusciously rich and full-bodied, with very good acidity and a creamy, intense finish. It will be interesting to compare the 1986 and 1983 as they evolve. My guess is that the 1986 will age faster. Anticipated maturity: now–2012. Last tasted, 3/90.

1985
87

This is one of the best 1985s I have tasted from Sauternes. It is rich and full, and although there is a general absence of any botrytis, the quality of the fruit is impeccably high. There is plenty of citrusy, pear, peach, and apricot-scented fruit backed up by some vague notes of roasted almonds. This is a delicious 1985 that should evolve gracefully. Anticipated maturity: now. Last tasted, 3/90.

1983
93

This is a magnificent wine. Light golden, with a wonderfully pure tropical fruit aroma of ripe pineapples and melons, this decadently rich, full-bodied wine has layers of viscous, sweet fruit, an astonishing finish, and excellent balancing acidity. The wine remains stubbornly slow to evolve. Anticipated maturity: now–2020. Last tasted, 11/90.

DE RAYNE VIGNEAU

Classification: First Growth in 1855

Owner: SC du Château de Rayne Vigneau

Address: 33210 Bommes

Mailing address: Cordier—Mestrezat et Domaines, 109, rue Achard, BP 154, 33042 Bordeaux Cedex

Telephone: 05 56 11 29 00; Telefax: 05 56 11 29 41

E-mail: contact@cordier-wines.com

Visits: By appointment and for professionals of the wine trade only

VINEYARDS

Surface area: 207.5 acres

Grape varietals: 74% Semillon, 24% Sauvignon, 2% Muscadelle

Average age of vines: 30 years

Density of plantation: 6,000 vines per hectare

Average yields: 10–15 hectoliters per hectare

Elevage: Fermentation in barrels for part of the yield and in stainless-steel vats for the other. Eighteen to twenty-four months aging in barrels with 50% new oak. Fining and filtration.

WINES PRODUCED

Château de Rayne Vigneau: 36,000–100,000 bottles (depending upon the vintage)

Madame de Rayne: variable

Plateau of maturity: Within 5–20 years of the vintage

GENERAL APPRECIATION

This estate would appear to have unlimited potential. However, the wines, while good, are largely unexciting.

During the 19th century, the beautiful Château de Rayne Vigneau had a reputation second only to that of Yquem. Few estates in the region are as superbly located as de Rayne Vigneau. However, because of neglect and indifferent winemaking, the 20th century has not been kind to the reputation of de Rayne Vigneau. Quality has improved significantly since the early 1980s, but there are still too many uninspiring efforts.

This vineyard has a splendid situation on the high plateau of Bommes on gravely/sandy soils. The wine now spends nearly 24 months in oak barrels, of which 50% are new each year. In the past, the percentage of new oak utilized was minimal, and one always suspected there was a lack of strict selection.

IMPORTANT VINTAGES

2001
87–89
The very light greenish-gold color stands out as one of the palest of the 2001 Barsac/Sauternes wines. This wine is delicate, somewhat light, but shows some attractive honeysuckle and citrus notes. It is medium bodied, not terribly intense, but very pleasant in a low-key sort of manner. Anticipated maturity: now–2014. Last tasted, 1/03.

1999
86
Light gold, with straightforward notes of candied pineapple and spice box, this medium-bodied wine shows high acidity and a somewhat austere, emaciated style. Drink it over the next 5–10 years. Last tasted, 3/02.

1997
86
Both the 1997 and 1996 de Rayne Vigneau are uninspiring, mainstream, blatantly commercial examples of Sauternes. The 1997 exhibits a syrupy pineapple-scented nose, medium body, moderate sweetness, and a fruit-driven personality with little complexity. Anticipated maturity: now–2017. Last tasted, 1/02.

1996
87
More complex than the 1997, the 1996 reveals a honeyed melon and pineapple-scented nose, medium body, and fine purity and ripeness. Drink it over the next 10–12 years. Last tasted, 1/02.

1990
87
This sweet, thick, juicy Sauternes does not possess as much complexity as the top wines of the vintage. Perhaps more will emerge with aging, as the wine is more sugary, cloying, and plump than previous examples from this estate. The color is light golden. This honeyed, buttery de Rayne Vigneau does not reveal as much precision, definition, or evidence of botrytis as exists in the vintage's finest offerings. Nevertheless, there is plenty to enjoy in this straightforward, monolithic 1990. Anticipated maturity: now–2012. Last tasted, 3/97.

1989
89
The 1989's flowery, peach and honey nose and medium- to full-bodied, complex, finesse style is refreshing, yet has sweet, low acid. This commercially styled Sauternes is fully mature. Anticipated maturity: now–2006. Last tasted, 11/94.

1988
91
The 1988 is the best example I have tasted from this property. An intense, honeyed, pear, flower, and apricot fragrance is reminiscent of Muscat de Beaumes de Venise. In the mouth, there is exceptional richness, super focus because of fine acidity, a wonderful touch of toasty new oak, and an elegant, very positive, crisp finish. This is a beautifully made, authoritative tasting, and impeccably well-balanced Sauternes. Anticipated maturity: now–2009. Last tasted, 3/90.

RIEUSSEC

Classification: First Growth in 1855

Owner: Barons de Rothschild (Lafite)

Address: 33210 Fargues

Mailing address: Les Domaines Barons de Rothschild, 33, rue de la Baume, 75008 Paris

Telephone: 01 53 89 78 00; Telefax: 01 53 89 78 01

Website: www.lafite.com

Visits: By appointment only

Contact: Telefax: 05 57 98 14 10

VINEYARDS

Surface area: 185.3 acres

Grape varietals: 92% Semillon, 5% Sauvignon, 3% Muscadelle

Average age of vines: 25 years

Density of plantation: 7,500 vines per hectare

Average yields: 15 hectoliters per hectare

Elevage: Fermentation and 18–30 months aging in new oak barrels. Fining and filtration.

WINES PRODUCED

Château Rieussec: 60,000 bottles

Clos Labère: 60,000 bottles

Plateau of maturity: Within 6–25 years of the vintage

GENERAL APPRECIATION

Since its acquisition by Lafite Rothschild, Rieussec has become a legitimate superstar in the Sautemes.

As one approaches the heart of the Sauternes appellation, Château Rieussec and its prominent lookout tower can be spotted on one of the highest hillsides. The Rieussec vineyard, spread across the hillsides of Fargues and Sauternes overlooking the left bank of the Garonne, has the highest altitude after that of Yquem. Quite surprising for a Bordeaux property, the entire vineyard is one single unit, much of it bordering the hallowed Yquem.

Rieussec has always had an outstanding reputation, but after its acquisition by Albert Vuillier in 1971, the quality improved even more, largely because of the increase in new oak and more frequent passes through the vineyard to harvest only heavily botrytised grapes. In fact, some critics of Rieussec claimed that Vuillier's wines took on too deep a color as they aged (like the 1976, for example). Vuillier sold Rieussec to the Domaines Barons de Rothschild, who have spared no expense or permitted any compromising in the making of Rieussec. The results have been truly profound offerings that are now routinely among the top three or four wines of the appellation.

Wealthy collectors will no doubt argue for decades whether 2001, 1990, 1989, or 1988 produced the most profound Rieussec.

Rieussec's style, one of honeyed power and almost roasted richness, exhibits great precision as well as tremendous persistence. The wine is usually deeply colored and generally alcoholic, with excellent viscosity. Rieussec also produces a dry white wine called "R." Such wines help ease cash-flow problems considerably, and "R" is one of the most popular and best of the dry Sauternes.

IMPORTANT VINTAGES

2001 An absolutely monumental example of Sauternes, with extraordinary classicism,
95–98 great definition, and tremendous reserves of unctuously textured honeysuckle, peach, and other tropical fruits, this massive, full-bodied wine is long, layered, and compelling. The finish goes on for nearly 60 seconds. Anticipated maturity: 2006–2025. Last tasted, 1/03.

2000 The very deep golden, almost amber color reminds me of the 1983 in its youth.
91 Orange marmalade, crème brûlée, brown butter, and smoke all emerge from the relatively complex, very attractive, and full-bodied 2000. The wine has tremendous density, good acidity, and loads of fruit and botrytis. This is undoubtedly a candidate for the wine of the vintage in Sauternes. Anticipated maturity: 2005–2018. Last tasted, 1/03.

1999 Very good acidity characterizes this backward, somewhat tightly knit, but honeyed
91 wine, with notes of white flowers, peach, caramel, and relatively good botrytis. The wine is medium to full-bodied, not the most extravagant or flamboyant of Rieussecs because of its rather tightly knit personality, but long, layered, and impressive. However, patience is required. Anticipated maturity: 2006–2020. Last tasted, 1/03.

1998 A very strong effort from Rieussec, this wine shows medium deep-gold color and a
92 sweet nose of smoky, toasty oak, vanilla, coconut, honeysuckle, peach, and even some pineapple. It is very rich, very sweet, and in contrast with its younger sibling, the 1999, very forward and evolved. Drink it over the next 12–15 years. It is a candidate for the wine of the vintage. Last tasted, 1/03.

1997 A terrific example of Rieussec, this full-bodied, very sweet wine shows tremen-
93 dous botrytis and loads of honeysuckle, caramel, peach, and crème brûlée in a full-bodied, very flamboyant, opulent style. There is enough acidity to provide uplift and to balance out the relatively high level of sugar (120 grams per liter). Like most vintages, this is a blend of 90% Semillon, 7% Sauvignon, and 3% Muscadelle. Anticipated maturity: now–2025. Last tasted, 1/03.

1996 Deep gold with notes of new oak, smoke, caramel, crème brûlée, and honeysuckle,
92+ this relatively sweet yet structured wine seems to have closed down since I first tasted it after bottling. The wine is layered, very full, with a tremendous upside. However, patience will be required, as this looks to be a potentially very long-lived Rieussec. Anticipated maturity: 2008–2040. Last tasted, 1/03.

1995 For whatever reason, this wine has never impressed me. It lacks botrytis and
86 exhibits a somewhat straightforward, chunky style, with buttery, pineapple, and honeyed fruit, but no real complexity or nuances. Perhaps I am missing something, and a lot more will emerge with cellaring, but I am not convinced. Anticipated maturity: now–2018. Last tasted, 1/03.

1990 A spectacular wine with a relatively evolved gold color, the tremendous nose of
94 spice box intermixed with caramelized peaches, apricots, and honeysuckle soars from the glass. The wine is very full-bodied, thick, and juicy, with just enough

acidity to balance out the wine's power and intense sweetness. This is layered, very viscous stuff that seems to be drinkable already but no doubt will last for another 20–25 years. Anticipated maturity: now–2025. Last tasted, 1/03.

1989
93
What fun it is, as I did earlier this year, to taste the great trilogy of Rieussecs—1990, 1989, and 1988—together. This seems to be a synthesis in style between the more delicate, elegant, nuanced, almost restrained 1988 and the muscular, blockbuster 1990. This is no wimpish wine, however. The medium deep-gold color is not quite as intense as the 1990, but certainly darker than the 1988. The big, smoky, earthy nose offers up notes of crème brûlée, honeysuckle, ripe pineapples, and other tropical fruits. The wine is quite full-bodied, with low acidity, very sweet, and luxuriously rich, with a viscous texture and a huge, concentrated finish. This wine seems to continue to put on weight and become even more impressive, much like the 1990. Anticipated maturity: now–2025. Last tasted, 1/03.

1988
94
Perhaps it is the sheer delicacy of this wine that has always impressed me. It seems to take a backseat to the more flamboyant and powerful 1990 and 1989, but the nuances, the very polite yet authoritatively intense notes of coconut, orange marmalade, crème brûlée, honeysuckle, and some oak all seem to be beautifully integrated in both the aromas and flavors. The wine is full-bodied, not as sweet as either the 1990 or 1989, but extremely stylish, with good acidity and tremendous delineation and uplift. It is a brilliant Rieussec that should prove almost immortal. Anticipated maturity: now–2035. Last tasted, 1/03.

1986
90
This wine seems to have become less impressive as it has aged. Perhaps it has just shut down, but I always seemed to score it one to three points higher than I did recently. The wine has a deep medium-gold color, a sweet nose of honeysuckle, white corn, peach, and some toasty oak. The wine is medium to full-bodied, with a hint of marmalade, apricot, and roasted nuts. Good acidity gives the wine elegance and definition. However, the finish seems to be drying out and is noticeably shorter than it once was. Perhaps this wine is just going through an awkward stage. Anticipated maturity: now–2015. Last tasted, 1/03.

1985
86
This is a very good Sauternes for the vintage—rich, round, open knit, with a great deal of juicy, sweet, candied fruit—but the absence of botrytis results in a wine lacking in complexity, which comes across as plump and succulent, but not terribly interesting. Anticipated maturity: now. Last tasted, 11/90.

1983
92
Light golden with just the slightest tint of green, the 1983 Rieussec, from an excellent year for Sauternes, is certainly one of this property's greatest wines. Well structured, with excellent acidity and a deep, long, rich, full-bodied, viscous texture, this wine, despite the richness and power, is neither heavy nor cloying. It has gorgeous balance and a very long, lingering, spectacular finish. One of the great successes of the vintage. Anticipated maturity: now–2005. Last tasted, 3/88.

1982
82
A maligned vintage for the sweet white wines of Bordeaux, Rieussec has, through a very strict selection process, turned out a lovely, fruity, spicy, lighter-styled wine with medium body and delicate tropical fruit flavors. Anticipated maturity: now. Last tasted, 3/86.

ANCIENT VINTAGES

The 1976 (90 points; last tasted 1/01) is a controversial vintage for Rieussec. I still have a few bottles left in my cellar, and it is a huge wine, with over 15% alcohol, made from microscopic yields of 2.5 hectoliters per hectare. The color is very brown and deep, with a distinctive caramel flavor to the almost brown sugar and chocolaty fruit. There is some volatile acidity, but the wine is big, thick, juicy, and almost a hybrid cross between a Madeira and a Sauternes. Not everyone loves it, but I do. Anticipated maturity: now–2010. The 1975 (90 points; last tasted 1/01) shows good acidity, hints of caramel, and some notes of oxidation. The wine again comes across more like a hybrid between a Madeira and a Sauternes than what I consider a classic Sauternes, but the wine is impressive.

ROMER DU HAYOT

Classification: Second Growth in 1855

Owner: SCE Vignobles du Hayot

Address: 33720 Barsac

Telephone: 05 56 27 15 37; Telefax: 05 56 27 04 24

E-mail: vignoblesduhayot@ifrance.com

Visits: By appointment only

Contact: Fabienne du Hayot

VINEYARDS

Surface area: 37 acres

Grape varietals: 70% Semillon, 25% Sauvignon, 5% Muscadelle

Average age of vines: 35 years

Density of plantation: 6,500 vines per hectare

Average yields: 25 hectoliters per hectare

Elevage: Fermentation in temperature-controlled stainless-steel tanks. Eighteen months aging in barrels. Fining and filtration.

WINES PRODUCED

Château Romer du Hayot: 50,000 bottles

No second wine is produced.

Plateau of maturity: Within 3–15 years of the vintage

GENERAL APPRECIATION

This is an inexpensive, reliable wine that is well made but rarely exciting.

I have generally enjoyed the wines of Romer du Hayot, a small Sauternes estate located near the beautiful Château de Malle. The style of wine produced emphasizes a fresh fruity character, medium body, and moderate sweetness. The wine sees limited aging in barrels, so its exuberant fruitiness is not masked by spicy, oaky aromas and flavors.

While Romer du Hayot is a lighter-styled Sauternes, it has plenty of interest and generally ages well for 5–15 years. Fortunately, the price asked for the wines from this little-known property is reasonable.

IMPORTANT VINTAGES

1997 The 1997 possesses attractive pear liqueur, pineapple, and apricot fruit in its
87   moderate aromatics, plenty of botrytis, and a sweet, long, unctuously textured, thick finish. However, the wine comes across as disjointed and in need of delineation. It should keep and evolve for 12 or more years. Last tasted, 1/02.

1996 The 1996 is a classic, pure wine with well-integrated toasty oak, smoky, honeyed
89   pineapple, mineral and fruit cocktail–like notes, a firm underpinning of acidity, round, smoky richness, medium to full body, and outstanding purity. Anticipated maturity: now–2015. Last tasted, 1/02.

1990 The 1990 Romer du Hayot exhibits a moderately intense, pineapple-scented
86   nose, medium-bodied, ripe, sweet flavors, and a clean, fresh finish. It is an uncomplicated, easygoing wine for drinking over the next 7–8 years. Last tasted, 11/94.

1989 The 1989 revealed excessive sulphur in the nose, combined with a pronounced
85?   pungent, dirty earthiness in the mouth. Behind the annoying off components is a simple, medium-bodied, moderately sweet wine. Last tasted, 11/94.

SIGALAS RABAUD

Classification: First Growth in 1855

Owner: GFA Château Sigalas Rabaud

Address: Bommes, 33210 Langon

Mailing address: Domaines Cordier, 53, rue du Dehez, 33290 Blanquefort

Telephone: 05 56 95 53 00; Telefax: 05 56 95 53 01

Visits: By appointment only

Contact: Marie-Stéphane Malbec

VINEYARDS

Surface area: 34.6 acres

Grape varietals: 85% Semillon, 15% Sauvignon

Average age of vines: 45 years

Density of plantation: 6,660 vines per hectare

Average yields: 18 hectoliters per hectare

Elevage: Fermentations take place in barrels at low temperatures (18°C). Wines are aged 20 months minimum in oak barrels that are renewed by a third in each vintage, with regular racking every three months. They are fined and filtered.

WINES PRODUCED

Château Sigalas Rabaud: 30,000 bottles

Le Cadet de Sigalas: 8,000 bottles

Plateau of maturity: Within 5–25 years of the vintages

GENERAL APPRECIATION

With the spectacular 2001, perhaps this well-situated estate is finally going to exploit its vast potential.

This has always been a perplexing wine to evaluate. There is no question that the ideal positioning of the south-facing vineyard on the hillsides of Haut-Bommes, with gravelly clay soil, should produce exceptionally ripe grapes. However, when tasting the wines of Sigalas Rabaud, I have always sensed a certain laissez-faire attitude. Since the mid-1980s the wines have improved significantly.

IMPORTANT VINTAGES

2001 **91–93** Superb, and one of the best efforts from this property in many a year, the 2001 shows a light greenish-gold color and tremendous fruit intensity, with the smell of baked apple pie intermixed with crème brûlée, caramel, peach, honeysuckle, and a hint of vanilla. The wine is full-bodied, relatively sweet, with tremendous purity and definition. This is profound stuff! Anticipated maturity: 2006–2025. Last tasted, 1/03.

2000 **87** With a rather simple, straightforward nose of almond cookies intermixed with a hint of pineapple, the heady bouquet is followed by a medium-bodied wine with moderate sweetness but not a great deal of distinction or complexity. Drink it over the next decade. Last tasted, 1/03.

1999 **88** Light greenish-gold colors offer up notes of underripe apricot, a hint of peach, with some spice box, vanilla, and roasted nuts. The wine is quite sweet, very much in the style of Sigalas Rabaud, medium bodied, a bit cloying, but fleshy and reasonably succulent. Anticipated maturity: now–2014. Last tasted, 1/02.

1998 **88** Rich and honeyed, with obvious notes of caramel, honeysuckle, oranges, and peaches, this richly fruity 1998 is quite sweet, but it has good counter balancing acidity to give it focus and vibrancy. Anticipated maturity: 2005–2015. Last tasted, 1/03.

1997 **89+** An impressive effort from this estate, the honeyed, luscious, forward-styled 1997 exhibits low acidity and copious quantities of orange, pineapple, and mango-like fruit. In fact, the fruit almost hides the bouquet's other nuances. Full-bodied and rich, with a viscous texture, this lusty, unrestrained wine will be appreciated by tasters looking for immediate gratification. Anticipated maturity: now–2015. Last tasted, 1/03.

1996 **88** The 1996 Sigalas Rabaud is a cooler climate–styled wine than the 1997, with more quince, kiwi, and honeyed pineapple–like fruit. It is medium bodied, with less viscosity than its younger sibling, as well as zesty underlying acidity, and an austere yet clean, crisp, mineral-like finish. Drink it over the next 10–12 years. Last tasted, 1/03.

1990 **91** Moderate gold–colored, this is one of the finest wines produced at this château in a number of years. Sweet toast, toffee, and crème brûlée aromas are dominated by an explosion of honeyed citrus and tropical fruit. Full-bodied, sweet, unctuously textured, pure, and thick, with a Viognier-like overripe peach fruitiness in the flavors, this is a hefty, chewy, alcoholic Sauternes that should become more refined and subtle with extended cellaring. Anticipated maturity: now–2020. Last tasted, 3/97.

1989 **88** This is an evolved wine, with an advanced medium-gold color, a loosely knit personality, medium body, some bitterness in the finish, but ripe toffee/apricot fruit, low acidity, and earth and oak nuances. It is a muscular, forceful wine that is still slightly disjointed, although impressively large. The 1989 is not as rich or complete as either the 1990 or 1988. Anticipated maturity: now–2015. Last tasted, 3/97.

1988 **89** Typical of the vintage, the 1988 Sigalas Rabaud is a stylish, finesse-styled Sauternes, with a lovely roasted/sweet honeyed character with melon, tropical fruit, and vanilla scents. More restrained, and not as large, muscular, or sweet as either the 1990 or 1989, the 1988 is an elegant, complex, medium-weight wine that should drink well for 15 more years. Last tasted, 3/97.

1986 Sigalas Rabaud made a complex, elegant, botrytis-filled 1986. The honeyed, flow
90 ery, spicy aromas leap from the glass in this beautifully proportioned wine. In the mouth, there is fine acidity, some rich, honeyed, pear and pineapple-like fruit, and a soft, yet adequately delineated, long, alcoholic finish. Anticipated maturity: now. Last tasted, 11/90.

SUAU

Classification: Second Growth in 1855

Owner: Nicole Biarnes

Address: 33720 Barsac

Mailing address: c/o Château de Navarro, 33720 Illats

Telephone: 05 56 27 20 27; Telefax: 05 56 27 26 53

Visits: By appointment Monday to Saturday

Contact: Mr. or Mrs. Biarnes

VINEYARDS

Surface area: 19.8 acres

Grape varietals: 80% Semillon, 10% Muscadelle, 10% Sauvignon

Average age of vines: 35 years

Density of plantation: 6,000 vines per hectare

Average yields: 18–19 hectoliters per hectare

Elevage: Eighteen months aging in barrels that are renewed by a third at each vintage. Fining and filtration.

WINES PRODUCED

Château Suau: 19,000 bottles

No second wine is produced.

Plateau of maturity: 5–12 years

GENERAL APPRECIATION

This is a reasonably priced, pleasant, straightforward wine for uncritical quaffing.

The tiny estate of Suau tucked away on a back road of Barsac is largely unknown. Much of the production is sold directly to consumers. The quality is uninspiring. In general, this is a wine to consume within its first decade of life.

IMPORTANT VINTAGES

1997 My first impression of the 1997 Suau's aromas was reminiscent of apricots that had 87 been macerating in cognac. There is not much finesse in the nose, but in the mouth this medium- to full-bodied, somewhat clumsy wine is rustic, pure, rich, and substantial with plenty of botrytis. Perhaps it just needs more time to find its form. Anticipated maturity: now–2012. Last tasted, 1/02.

1996   In contrast with the 1997, the 1996 is a lighter-styled, well-made Barsac with cit-
85   rusy, white corn, apple, and white peach-like fruit. It is a moderately sweet, lightweight wine to enjoy over the next 7 years. Last tasted, 3/00.

1990   1990 is the most opulent, concentrated, and powerful Suau I have ever tasted. Big
89   and full-bodied, the wine now offers greater precision and complexity in its nose,
an improvement over its original monolithic personality. A fine example of Suau, it
should age well for 7–8 years. Last tasted, 11/94.

1989   The 1989 exhibits elegance combined with medium body, which is atypical for
87   this fat, heavyweight vintage. The wine possesses considerable finesse, a lovely
apricot/pineapple-like fruitiness, and a crisp, fresh personality. It is not a wine for
aging, but, rather, one for drinking over the next 5–7 years. Last tasted, 11/94.

SUDUIRAUT

Classification: First Growth in 1855

Owner: AXA Millésimes

Administrator: Christian Seely

Address: 33210 Preignac

Telephone: 05 56 63 61 90; Telefax: 05 56 63 61 93

E-mail: infochato@suduiraut.com

Website: www.chateausuduiraut.com

Visits: By appointment only

VINEYARDS

Surface area: 222.3 acres

Grape varietals: 90% Semillon, 10% Sauvignon

Average age of vines: 25 years

Density of plantation: 7,000 vines per hectare

Average yields: 17 hectoliters per hectare

Elevage: Two to three week fermentation and 18 months aging in barrels with 30% new
oak. Fining, no filtration.

WINES PRODUCED

Château Suduiraut: variable

Castelnau de Suduiraut: variable

Plateau of maturity: Within 8–30 years following the vintage

GENERAL APPRECIATION

Suduiraut is undeniably one of the great estates of Sauternes, and has been even more
consistent as well as brilliant since its acquisition by AXA.

Just down the road from Yquem, abutting Yquem's vineyards on the north, is the large,
beautiful estate of Suduiraut. Suduiraut can be one of the great wines of Sauternes. For
example, the 1990, 1989, 1988, 1982, 1976, 1967, and 1959 are staggering examples

of Suduiraut's potential. At its best, Suduiraut turns out very rich, luscious wines that in blind tastings can be confused with Yquem. However, I have always been perplexed by the shocking inconsistency in quality of the wines from this estate. In the first half of the 1970s, Suduiraut produced several wines well below acceptable standards, yet under the administration of AXA, the estate has fully exploited its immense potential.

When Suduiraut is good, it is very, very good. In great vintages, the wine needs a decade to be at its best, but will keep easily for 30 years. Richly colored, quite perfumed, and decadently rich, even massive in the top years, Suduiraut, while less consistent than properties like Climens and Rieussec, appears now to be back on track.

In 1989 and 1982 the château produced a sumptuous, super quality, rare, and expensive Crème de Tête—Cuvée Madame. This *cuvée*, much like the limited edition Cuvée Madame of Château Coutet, is capable of rivaling Yquem, but the production is minuscule—less than 1,000 cases.

IMPORTANT VINTAGES

2001
93–96 One of the truly remarkable wines made at this estate over the last 30 years, the 2001 has notes of white flowers intermixed with honeyed peach, tropical fruits (pineapples), and a sweet, very unctuous texture, yet tremendous freshness and definition because of good acidity. Everything is seamlessly pulled together in a relatively sweet, full-throttle, massively endowed wine that should become legendary. Anticipated maturity: 2008–2030. Last tasted, 1/03.

2000
89+ Notes of orange and apricot jam emerge from this very elegant, medium gold–colored wine. The wine shows good ripeness, medium to full body, plenty of sweetness, and more character and soul than most 2000 Sauternes. An excellent effort. Anticipated maturity: 2005–2020. Last tasted, 1/03.

1999
90 Notes of lanolin, candle wax, honeysuckle, and ripe tropical fruits cascade from the glass of this full-bodied wine, which shows good acidity, considerable botrytis, and a long, layered, powerful finish. This wine seems still somewhat closed in, but should have considerable aging potential. Anticipated maturity: 2007–2030. Last tasted, 12/02.

1998
89 Relatively sweet, this elegant, light to medium gold–colored wine with some green tints (a blend of 90% Semillon and 10% Sauvignon Blanc) shows elegant, fresh flavors, real pretty honeysuckle and butter notes intermixed with some pear, pineapple, and other fruit. It is very forward for a Suduiraut and should probably be drunk during its first two decades of life. Anticipated maturity: 2004–2018. Last tasted, 12/02.

1997
90 The 1997 Suduiraut reveals surprisingly crisp acidity for its weight, as well as excellent richness. An intense, weighty, moderately sweet feel in the mouth, with copious quantities of buttery, honeyed fruit, impressive power, and a corpulent style, characterize this well-delineated wine. It should develop more complexity, and may merit an outstanding score after bottling. Anticipated maturity: 2004–2025. Last tasted, 1/03.

1996
86 The 1996 is a greener, leaner, more tart style of Suduiraut, with spicy oak dominating its otherwise muted aromatics. For reasons that escape me, this wine does not have the fat and mass of top vintages. Anticipated maturity: now–2014. Last tasted, 12/00.

1990
94 This is a gorgeously rich, fat, concentrated wine with an intense, spicy nose of almost burnt peaches intermixed with brown butter, almond paste, and caramel. Extremely full-bodied, thick, and juicy, with almost marmalade-like sweetness,

this wine also seems to have hit its plateau of drinkability. Anticipated maturity: now–2020. Last tasted, 1/03.

1989
92
Very complex notes of roasted hazelnuts intermixed with brown butter, caramel, orange skin, and caramelized tropical fruits jump from the glass of this medium gold–colored wine. Very sweet, round, and delicious, it seems to be at its peak. Anticipated maturity: now–2016. Last tasted, 1/03.

1989
96
Cuvée Madame: This is an extraordinary Sauternes. Fabulously concentrated, with an unctuous texture and what must be nearly 14–15% natural alcohol, this mammoth size Sauternes should prove to be one of the monumental efforts of the vintage. For those who prefer power and finesse, the 1988 may take preference; for those who want pure brute strength and unbelievable size, the 1989 Cuvée Madame is without equal. Anticipated maturity: now–2025. Last tasted, 4/91.

1988
90+
Still very backward and tight, but weighty in the mouth, this vintage of Suduiraut has taken much longer to come around than I would have expected. Its light-gold color belies its 15 years of age. The wine shows hints of honeysuckle intermixed with citrus, earth, and oak. In the mouth it is tight, much less sweet than more recent vintages, with medium to full body, but a very tight-to-the-vest, defined-as-well-as-restrained style. Anticipated maturity: 2008–2020. Last tasted, 1/03.

1986
87
I would have expected Suduiraut to be outstanding in 1986, but it is not. It is very good, but this wine should have been a classic. Plump, rich, honeyed, pineapple, coconut, and buttery fruit flavors abound in this full-bodied, rich wine that falls just short of being profound. It is muscular and rich, but it is missing an element of complexity that I found in many other 1986s. Also, is it possible that the 1986 Suduiraut has less botrytis than the other top examples from this vintage? Anticipated maturity: now–2008. Last tasted, 3/90.

1985
79
Shockingly light, with straightforward, bland, even innocuous flavors, this fruity yet one-dimensional Suduiraut is disappointing given the reputation of the château. Anticipated maturity: now. Last tasted, 3/90.

1983
87
Medium golden in color, with a honeyed, rich, floral bouquet, this full-bodied wine is not as profound as the other 1983s. Sweet with fine honeyed flavors, this is an elegant, graceful Suduiraut with plenty of character. However, given the vintage, I had expected even more. Anticipated maturity: now. Last tasted, 3/90.

1982
90
Cuvée Madame: The 1982 vintage, while great for Bordeaux's red wines, is not special for the sweet wines. However, the 1982 Suduiraut Cuvée Madame is a smashing success. The *régisseur* thought this was the best wine made at the property since the great 1967 and 1959. Only the grapes harvested before the rains fell were used, and the result is a very concentrated, deep, luscious, honeyed wine, with great length, the buttery, viscous richness that Suduiraut is famous for, and superb balance. If it had just a trifle more botrytis character it would be perfect. Anticipated maturity: now–2010. Last tasted, 3/90.

ANCIENT VINTAGES

The 1976 (92 points; last tasted 3/90) is the finest Suduiraut of the 1970s. From the 1960s, the fabulous 1967 (93 points; last tasted 12/02) is fully mature. Ditto for the 1961 (92 points; last tasted 12/02). I have consistently rated the great 1959 between 92 and 94 on the occasions I have tasted it (most recently 12/89). Among the other vintages for which I have notes, I have given excellent ratings to the 1945 (90 points in 11/86) and the 1947 (93 points in 7/87). I have never seen a pre–World War II vintage, but the 1928 and 1899 are considered legendary years for this estate. The other years I have tasted, 1955 and 1949, left me unmoved.

LA TOUR BLANCHE

Classification: First Growth in 1855

Owner: Ministry of Agriculture

Address: 33210 Bommes

Telephone: 05 57 98 02 73; Telefax: 05 57 98 02 78

E-mail: tour-blanche@tour-blanche.com

Website: www.tour-blanche.com

Visits: Preferably by appointment Monday to Friday, 9 A.M. to noon and 2–5 P.M.

Contact: Corinne Reulet

VINEYARDS

Surface area: 91.4 acres

Grape varietals: 83% Semillon, 12% Sauvignon, 5% Muscadelle

Average age of vines: 26 years

Density of plantation: 6,200 vines per hectare

Average yields: 14 hectoliters per hectare

Elevage: Two to three week fermentation and 16–18 months aging in new oak barrels for the Semillon and in stainless-steel vats for Sauvignon and Muscadelle. Fining and filtration.

WINES PRODUCED

Château La Tour Blanche: 40,000 bottles

Les Charmilles de la Tour Blanche: 25,000 bottles

Plateau of maturity: Within 5–30 years following the vintage

GENERAL APPRECIATION

This estate has soared in quality since the late eighties, and is now one of the most consistent wines of the region.

La Tour Blanche was ranked in the top of its class right behind Yquem in the 1855 classification of the wines of the Sauternes region. Since 1910 the Ministry of Agriculture has run La Tour Blanche and until the mid-1980s seemed content to produce wines that at best could be called mediocre. That has changed significantly with the employment of 100% new oak beginning in 1988, followed by a complete fermentation of the 1989 in new oak barrels. The cellars are completely air-conditioned, and the yields have been reduced to a meager 14 hectoliters per hectare. All things considered, La Tour Blanche is now one of the superstars of the appellation. Fortunately, prices have not yet caught up with La Tour Blanche's new quality.

There are also small quantities of a second wine made from weaker vats, as well as two different dry Bordeaux blancs.

IMPORTANT VINTAGES

2001 With a rather remarkable, almost strawberry aroma intermixed with ripe peach
94–96 and pineapple, this beautifully balanced, full-bodied wine has great fruit presence, tremendous definition, large body, and, like so many 2001s, a remarkable
vibrancy and zestiness because of good acidity. This is probably the best example
from this estate since their sensational 1990. Anticipated maturity: 2007–2025+.
Last tasted, 1/03.

1999 This estate continues to come on stronger and stronger, seemingly regardless of
91 vintage conditions. Light gold with a nose of tangerines intermixed with apricots
and peach jam, with a hint of oak and acacia flower, this medium- to full-bodied,
very concentrated wine has excellent sweetness, noticeable botrytis, some sweet
oak, and enough acidity to frame everything up. It is not a blockbuster, but certainly very well made. Anticipated maturity: now–2018. Last tasted, 1/03.

1998 A brilliant effort from this resurrected property, the 1998 La Tour Blanche has
92 loads of sweet, concentrated honeysuckle, pineapple, and apricot-like fruit, great
harmony, good integrated acidity, subtle wood, and a full-bodied, very opulent,
flamboyant finish. This is a classic full-throttle Sauternes that can be drunk young
or aged for two decades. Anticipated maturity: now–2022. Last tasted, 1/03.

1997 The gorgeously perfumed and layered 1997 La Tour Blanche displays a medium-
90 gold color, as well as a honeyed, kinky nose of buttered roasted fruit, quince,
oranges, and minerals. Dense and full-bodied, with terrific fruit extraction, this
unctuously textured, sweet wine is one of the stars of the vintage. Anticipated maturity: now–2025. Last tasted, 1/02.

1996 The lighter-style 1996 possesses a light golden color, moderate sweetness, and a
89 flinty, citrusy, buttery nose with evidence of coconut, pears, oranges, and pineapples. In the mouth, it is medium bodied and stylish with considerable elegance.
Anticipated maturity: now–2015. Last tasted, 3/01.

1990 A sensational effort, fragrant notes of honeysuckle, orange marmalade, pineapple,
94 and lanolin jump from the glass of this full-bodied, very luxuriously sweet wine,
which has tremendous purity and definition. It is a very seductive style that has already reached full maturity. Anticipated maturity: now–2020. Last tasted, 1/03.

1989 Although loosely structured, the 1989 reveals plenty of intense, honeyed fruit in a
90 rich, authoritative, full-bodied format. A big, powerhouse, sweet, heavy wine with
a penetrating fragrance of honey and flowers, this generously endowed wine already drinks well but can easily last for 15–20 years. Last tasted, 11/94.

1988 The 1988 exhibits superb richness, plenty of botrytis, creamy, honeyed, tropical
92 fruit (pineapples galore), wonderfully integrated, toasty oak, crisp acidity, and a
rich, full-bodied, long finish. The wine is just beginning to evolve, and it is clearly
capable of lasting 25–35 years. Last tasted, 11/94.

1986 When I tasted this wine from cask I thought it would be better. But it has turned
82 out to be a relatively straightforward, compact, monolithic-styled Sauternes, with
good fruit but without the great underlying depth and evidence of botrytis one normally sees in this vintage. It should provide good but uninspired drinking for another decade or more. Anticipated maturity: now. Last tasted, 3/90.

1985 Normally the 1985 Sauternes are less impressive than the 1986s, but La Tour
84 Blanche's 1985 comes across as more concentrated, with greater intensity and
length than the 1986. Nevertheless, there is still a glaring lack of complexity and
botrytis. Anticipated maturity: now. Last tasted, 3/90.

ANCIENT VINTAGES

The finest older vintage of La Tour Blanche I have had the privilege of tasting was a very fine example of the 1975 (87 points in 1990). It was still youthful when tasted at age 15.

D'YQUEM

Classification: First Growth in 1855

Owner: SA du Château d'Yquem

Address: 33210 Sauternes

Telephone: 05 57 98 07 07; Telefax: 05 57 98 07 08

E-mail: v1@yquem.fr

Website: www.chateau-yquem.fr

Visits: By appointment and for professionals of the wine trade only

Contact: Valérie Lailheugue

VINEYARDS

Surface area: 308.8 acres (254.2 in production)

Grape varietals: 80% Semillon, 20% Sauvignon

Average age of vines: 30 years

Density of plantation: 6,500 vines per hectare

Average yields: 8 hectoliters per hectare

Elevage: Fermentation and 42 months aging in new oak barrels. Fining and filtration.

WINES PRODUCED

Château d'Yquem: 110,000 bottles

No second wine is produced.

Plateau of maturity: Within 10–100 years of the vintages

Note: This estate also produces a dry Bordeaux white called YGREC. It was made in the following vintages: 2000, 1996, 1994, 1998, 1985, 1980, 1979, 1978, 1977, 1973, 1972, 1971, 1969, 1968, 1966, 1965, 1964, 1962, 1960, 1959

D'Yquem was not produced in 1992, 1974, 1972, 1964, 1952, 1951, 1930, 1915, 1910

GENERAL APPRECIATION

A persuasive case can be made that Yquem is Bordeaux's single greatest wine.

Yquem, located in the heart of the Sauternes region, sits magnificently atop a small hill overlooking the surrounding vineyards of many of the premiers crus classés. Between 1785 and 1997 this estate was in the hands of just one family. Comte Alexandre de Lur Saluces is the most recent member of this family to have responsibility for managing this vast estate, having taken over for his uncle in 1968. In 1997 the estate was sold to the giant Moët-Hennessy conglomerate, but the sale was unsuccessfully contested by Comte de Lur Saluces, who has remained as administrator.

Yquem's greatness and uniqueness are certainly a result of a number of factors. First, it has a perfect location that is said to have its own microclimate. Second, the Lur Saluces family installed an elaborate drainage system with over 60 miles of pipes. Third, there is a fanatical obsession at Yquem to produce only the finest wines regardless of financial loss or trouble. It is this last factor that is the biggest reason why Yquem is so superior to its neighbors.

At Yquem they proudly boast that only one glass of wine per vine is produced. The grapes are picked at perfect maturity one by one by a group of 150 pickers who frequently spend six to eight weeks at Yquem and go through the vineyard a minimum of four separate times. In 1964 they canvassed the vineyard 13 separate times, only to have harvested grapes that were deemed unsuitable, leaving Yquem with no production whatsoever in that vintage. Few winemaking estates are willing or financially able to declassify the entire crop.

Yquem has unbelievable aging possibilities. Because it is so rich, opulent, and sweet, much is drunk before it ever reaches its tenth birthday. However, Yquem almost always needs 15–20 years to show best, and the great vintages will be fresh and decadently rich for as long as 50–75 or more years. The greatest Yquem I ever drank was the 1921. It was remarkably fresh and alive, with a luxuriousness and richness I shall never forget.

This passionate commitment to quality does not stop in the vineyard. The wine is aged for over three years in new oak casks, at a loss of 20% of the total crop volume due to evaporation. Even when the Comte de Lur Saluces deems the wine ready for bottling, a severe selection of only the best casks is made. In excellent years, such as 1980, 1976, and 1975, 20% of the barrels were eliminated. In difficult years, such as 1979, 60% of the wine was declassified, and in the troublesome vintage of 1978, 85% of the wine was declared unworthy of being sold as Yquem. To my knowledge, no other property has such a ruthless selection process. Yquem is never filtered for fear of removing some of the richness.

Yquem also produces a dry wine called "Y." It is a distinctive wine, with a bouquet not unlike that of Yquem, but oaky and dry to taste and usually very full-bodied and noticeably alcoholic. It is a powerful wine and, to my palate, best served with a rich food such as foie gras. Yquem, unlike other famous Bordeaux wines, is not sold *en primeur* or as a wine future. The wine is usually released four years after the vintage at a very high price, but given the labor involved, the risk, and the brutal selection process, it is one of the few luxury-priced wines that merits a stratospheric price tag.

IMPORTANT VINTAGES

1997
96
A sensational Yquem, and probably the best Yquem since the 1990, although I would not discount the 1996 finally turning out to be nearly this good, Yquem's 1997 shows a light-gold color and a gorgeous nose of caramel, honeysuckle, peach, apricot, and smoky wood. The wine is very full-bodied, unctuously textured, with good underlying acidity and loads of sweetness and glycerin. It looks

to be a very great vintage for Yquem. Anticipated maturity: 2005–2055. Last tasted, 1/03.

1996
95+
Compared with the rather flamboyant aromatics of the 1997, Yquem's 1996 plays it closer to the vest, although there is a lot below the surface; it just needs more coaxing. Light gold with a tight but promising nose of roasted hazelnuts intermixed with crème brûlée, vanilla beans, honey, orange marmalade, and peach, this medium- to full-bodied Yquem has loads of power but a sense of restraint and a more measured style. The acidity also seems to be holding the wine close to the vest. The weight is there, the texture impressive, and the purity, as always, impeccable. Patience will probably be a virtue with this vintage. Anticipated maturity: 2012–2060. Last tasted, 1/03.

1995
93
Hints of honeysuckle, orange marmalade, vanilla beans, and toasty oak are present in the moderately intense aromatics. In the mouth the wine is medium to full-bodied, with good acidity, a somewhat monolithic character at present, but a long, concentrated, relatively sweet finish, with good acidity. Anticipated maturity: 2007–2035. Last tasted, 12/02.

1994
90
Disjointed early in its life, this wine seems to be taking on more weight and focus. Medium gold, with a honeyed nose intermixed with toast, coconut, and a hint of pineapple as well as peaches, this medium-bodied Yquem is not one of the more ostentatious vintages, but exceptionally well made and certainly capable of lasting 30+ years. Anticipated maturity: 2008–2030. Last tasted, 12/02.

1991
88
This is a relatively low-key, somewhat foursquare Yquem, with a medium-gold color and a nose of burnt oak intermixed with some tropical fruit, vanilla, and a hint of sautéed peaches. The wine is medium bodied, moderately sweet, but lacks the glycerin, fat, and tremendous texture and plushness most top Yquems possess. The wine shows some acidity in the finish, but I am wondering where this wine is actually going to go from an evolutionary standpoint. Anticipated maturity: now–2025. Last tasted, 12/02.

1990
98+
A colossal Yquem from a blockbuster, very powerful, and very sweet vintage in the Barsac/Sauternes region, this medium gold–colored wine is evolving at a glacial pace, as is so common with this singular sweet wine. The nose has not moved much over the last 5–6 years, but there is plenty of coconut, tropical fruit, honeysuckle, and crème caramel notes that emerge. Very full-bodied, extremely viscous, yet with enough acidity to provide uplift and focus, this is an enormously constituted Yquem that should be one of the great vintages for this château, and one to last nearly 100 years. Like most vintages, it can be drunk in its infancy (that's where it is, even though it is 12 years old), but it will continue to develop even greater nuances. Anticipated maturity: now–2075. Last tasted, 12/02.

1989
98
What a remarkable trilogy of vintages for Château d'Yquem (I am speaking of the 1990, 1989, and 1988). This vintage leans more toward the 1990 than 1988 in style. It is a very unctuously textured, medium gold–colored Yquem that is oozing with honey-soaked oranges, pineapples, apricots, and peaches. This is a very powerful, rich, thick wine, with loads of glycerin, fabulous aromatics, and seemingly low acidity, but mind-boggling levels of depth and concentration, and a finish that goes on well over a minute. Like the 1990, it is a bit more flamboyant than its more restrained sibling, the 1988, and tends to be more impressive in terms of power and richness than the more nuanced 1988. A great, great Yquem! Anticipated maturity: now–2065. Last tasted, 12/02.

1988
99
This remarkable wine is much more backward, less flamboyant, and more gentlemanly than the 1990 or 1989. Its light-golden color is more youthful than its younger siblings, the bouquet powerful but restrained, with subtle yet intense notes of coconut, orange marmalade, crème brûlée, peach, and white corn emerg-

ing very gently but authoritatively. In the mouth it builds incrementally, as this is a wine of enormous richness, power, but far higher acidity than the 1990 or 1989. The wine is relatively light on its feet for such a powerful, highly extracted, and sensational effort. This is certainly one of the great Yquems, and probably more along the style of the 1975 than more recent vintages. Anticipated maturity: 2010–2070. Last tasted, 12/02.

1987
90
A sleeper vintage for Yquem, hardly one of the great Yquems, but well made, more medium bodied than full, with a relatively precocious/evolved personality, the 1987 Yquem shows notes of buttered hazelnuts, crème brûlée, smoke, and peach jam. It is medium bodied, moderately sweet, but showing evidence of approaching full maturity. Anticipated maturity: now–2020. Last tasted, 12/02.

1986
97
Starting to show some secondary nuances after nearly 16 years of age (this is just additional evidence of how slow this wine ages), the 1986 has a medium-gold color and a gorgeous nose of vanilla beans intermixed with sweet honey-drenched apricots, peaches, and hazelnuts. The wine is very opulent, full-bodied, with good underlying acidity and loads of botrytis. There is considerable sweetness and, again, a finish that goes on well past 60 seconds. This is a brilliant Yquem, somewhat less obviously complex and delineated when compared to the 1988, and less flamboyant than either the 1990 or 1989. Nevertheless, there is authority, power, richness, and immense upside potential. It is still a very young wine, just approaching its adolescence. Anticipated maturity: now–2050. Last tasted, 12/02.

1985
90?
A somewhat monolithic Yquem that has never developed, this wine has straightforward notes of tropical fruit and seems to lack the botrytis and honeysuckle that most of the great vintages possess. It is medium to full-bodied, with plenty of weight and sweetness but a certain monochromatic style. Am I being too severe? Anticipated maturity: now–2020. Last tasted, 3/02.

1984
87?
Under difficult vintage conditions, Yquem released a small quantity of wine that shows medium-gold color and an evolved bouquet of smoke and hazelnuts intermixed with caramel, butterscotch, peach, and new oak. The wine is medium to full-bodied and ripe, but again lacking the great complexity and definition of the best years. Anticipated maturity: now–2015. Last tasted, 3/02.

1983
98
A wine that is just hitting its adolescence, this spectacular Yquem is the great vintage of the early 1980s and the best Yquem since 1976 and before the trilogy of 1990, 1989, and 1988. The wine has a medium-gold color and an extraordinary nose of honey-dripped coconuts, pineapple, caramel, crème brûlée, orange marmalade, and no doubt a few other items. Unctuously textured and full-bodied, with massive richness and great sweetness, this is a seamless classic that will probably be immortal. My point score continues to go up, but the wine still is young, although I would call it just approaching its adolescence. Anticipated maturity: 2005–2075. Last tasted, 3/02.

1982
90
This is one of the few Yquems that is actually less impressive today than it was earlier in its life. Perhaps I caught it at a bad stage, or simply encountered one of the problems of tasting—that is, when a wine is surrounded by greater wines, the critic can sometimes be more severe than if the wine were tasted alone or with food. This is certainly an outstanding wine, but it is hardly a great Château d'Yquem. Notes of dried herbs intermixed with smoke and the telltale honey, pineapple, peach, and apricot are there. In the mouth it is somewhat monolithic, a bit thick and a little cloying, which is something Yquem rarely is. The sweetness is very obvious, and the wine seemingly lacks acidity and appears to be at a stage where it is a bit disjointed and awkward. In any event, it is still a brilliant wine, but not one of the great classic Yquems in my view. Anticipated maturity: now–2020. Last tasted, 3/02.

1981   Light to medium gold, with a straightforward nose of ripe tropical fruit, this full-
89   bodied Yquem lacks the honeysuckle and obvious botrytis-influenced flavors of
the great vintages. Nevertheless, it is large-scaled, deep, rich, sweet, but probably
best drunk over the next 10–15 years. Last tasted, 3/02.

1980   This is a sleeper vintage for Yquem. It exhibits superb honeysuckle intermixed
93   with loads of tropical fruit, plenty of botrytis, good acidity, and a staggeringly rich,
viscous palate with good freshness and vibrancy. This wine continues to evolve
very slowly, but remains a persuasive, authoritative, quite powerful Yquem that
can be drunk now or cellared for at least another 30–40 years. Anticipated maturity: now–2035. Last tasted, 3/02.

ANCIENT VINTAGES

It is remarkable tasting 25- to 50-year-old Yquems that are still relatively young in
their evolution. In the 1970s, two perfect Yquems, based on recent tastings, are very
different in style. The 1976 (100 points; last tasted 12/02) is an Yquem on a relatively
fast track for this property. It seems to be close to full maturity, and remains a very powerful, thick, viscous Yquem with notes of honeyed tropical fruits, spice box, crème
brûlée, smoke, and orange marmalade. The wine is viscous, rich, and an amazingly
great Yquem. Among the vintages of the last 30 years, this is perhaps the most complex
and ready to drink of the great years for Yquem. It should continue to evolve and last for
another 50 or more years. Another perfect Yquem, the 1975 (100 points; last tasted
12/02) could not be more different. Evolving at a snail's pace, this Yquem has always
reminded me of some of the legends of the 20th century, the 1937 and 1921, for example. The wine still has a relatively light-gold color, a restrained but fascinating bouquet
of smoke, honeyed peaches, pineapple, apricots, and hazelnuts intermixed with the
telltale orange marmalade, coconut, and crème brûlée notes. A wine of extraordinary
power but also remarkable finesse, it builds incrementally in the mouth, and just goes
on and on in the finish, with a persistence that I once timed to be almost two minutes. It
is a tour de force in winemaking and one of the all-time great Yquems. Believe it or not,
it still needs another 10–20 years to reach maturity. Anticipated maturity: 2015–2075.

The 1971 (91 points; last tasted 6/98) and 1970 (90? points; last tasted 12/02) are
both top-flight efforts, but hardly compelling examples of Yquem. A prodigious Yquem,
of course, is the 1967 (96 points; last tasted 6/98). Other vintages in the 1960s are less
impressive, although the 1962 (92 points; last tasted 3/02) can be outstanding. The
1961 (84 points; last tasted 4/82) is largely a disappointment.

There is no doubt that the two most profound and mature Yquems made in the 20th
century were the 1921 (rated 100 points on two separate occasions, most recently 9/96)
and the 1937 (rated between 96 and 99 points on three separate occasions in the late
1980s). After those two vintages, there are a number of superb Yquems that I have had
the good fortune to taste, but frankly, none have matched the 1937 and 1921. My favorites in order of preference are 1928 (97 points in 4/91), 1929 (97 points in 3/90),
1959 (between 94 and 96 points on three occasions in the late 1980s), and 1945 (91
points in 10/95). The 1945 is, by all responsible accounts, a magnificent wine. However, the bottle I tasted in October 1995 was brown and slightly maderized, although
well perfumed, but drying out. With any tasting of a wine over 20 years of age, it should

be remembered that "there are no great wines, only great bottles." Although I have only tasted the 1947 once (that is my birth year), I was surprised by how dry the wine tasted, without the fat and sweetness one finds in the great vintages of Yquem.

With respect to vintages from the 19th century, I had the good fortune to taste four 19th-century vintages at a tasting in October 1995. The 1825 Yquem (89 points) displayed a dark gold color and tasted nearly dry after having lost its fruit. It revealed high acidity in its crème brûlée-like flavors and finish. The very dry, earthy 1814 Yquem (67 points) possessed a dark-gold color and an unattractive mustiness that obliterated any fruit that may have remained intact. However, the 1811 Yquem (100 points), with its dark-gold color, awesomely intense, sweet nose, unctuous, thick, fabulous flavor extraction, pinpoint precision, and a finish that lasted a minute or more, is the kind of wine on which Yquem's reputation is based. It was liquified crème brûlée—an astonishing wine. Remember, this was the famous "year of the comet" vintage. (Incidentally, readers looking for a few good chuckles should rent the movie video *Year of the Comet*, a wine-dominated comedy that I highly recommend.) The 1847 Yquem (100 points) would have received more than 100 points if possible. The wine is massive, with a surprisingly youthful color, remarkable honeyed and botrytised flavors, staggering richness, and a finish that lasted 40+ seconds. The question that must be asked is whether the great modern-day Yquem vintages will last as long? I say yes, though I doubt any of my readers will live long enough to find out what the 1990, 1989, 1986, 1983, 1976 or 1975 will taste like at age 148!

OTHER BARSAC/SAUTERNES ESTATES

ANDOYSE DU HAYOT

Classification: None

Owner: SCE Vignobles du Hayot

Address: 33720 Barsac

Telephone: 05 56 27 15 37; Telefax: 05 56 27 04 24

E-mail: vignoblesduhayot@ifrance.com

Visits: By appointment

Contact: Fabienne du Hayot

VINEYARDS

Surface area: 49.4 acres

Grape varietals: 70% Semillon, 25% Sauvignon, 5% Muscadelle

Average age of vines: 35 years

Density of plantation: 6,500 vines per hectare

Average yields: 25 hectoliters per hectare

Elevage: Fermentation in temperature-controlled stainless-steel tanks. Eighteen months aging in barrels (with 33% new oak) for part of the yield and in vats for the other. Fining and filtration.

WINES PRODUCED

Château Andoyse du Hayot: 65,000 bottles

No second wine is produced.

Plateau of maturity: Within 3–10 years of the vintage

CANTEGRIL

Classification: None

Owner: Denis Dubourdieu and Jeanine Dubourdieu

Address: 33720 Barsac

Mailing address: c/o Château Doisy-Daëne, 33720 Barsac

Telephone: 05 56 27 15 84; Telefax: 05 56 27 18 99

E-mail: reynon@gofornet.com

Visits: By appointment only; Monday to Saturday

Contact: Denis Dubourdieu (Telephone: 05 56 62 96 51; Telefax: 05 56 62 14 89)

VINEYARDS

Surface area: 54.3 acres

Grape varietals: 75% Semillon, 25% Sauvignon

Average age of vines: 30 years

Density of plantation: 6,250 vines per hectare

Average yields: 20 hectoliters per hectare

Elevage: Slow pressings. Fermentation and 12 months aging in barrels with 20% new oak. Fining and filtration.

WINES PRODUCED

Château Cantegril: 40,000 bottles

No second wine is produced.

Plateau of maturity: Within 4–8 years of the vintage

CRU D'ARCHE-PUGNEAU

Owner: Jean-Francis Daney

Address: 24, Le Biton, Boutoc, 33210 Preignac

Telephone: 05 56 63 50 55; Telefax: 05 56 63 39 69

E-mail: francis.daney@free.fr

Website: www.arche.pugneau@free.fr

Visits: Monday to Friday, 8 A.M.–7 P.M.;
by appointment on weekends

Contact: Jean-Francis Daney

VINEYARDS

Surface area: 32.1 acres

Grape varietals: 75% Semillon, 20% Sauvignon, 5% Muscadelle

Average age of vines: 40 years

Density of plantation: 7,500 vines per hectare

Average yields: 16 hectoliters per hectare

Elevage: Eight day fermentation in barrels followed by 3–4 weeks in vats. Twenty-four months aging in barrels. Fining and filtration.

WINES PRODUCED

Cru d'Arche-Pugneau: 8,000 bottles

Peyraguey Le Rousset: 3,000 bottles

Plateau of maturity: Within 5–20 years of the vintage

This property is well-worth searching out, as the wines are exceptionally well made and clearly compete with the top classified growths of Barsac/Sauternes. I have had remarkable wines from Cru d'Arche-Pugneau, which I rated in the mid-90s, particularly vintages such as 1990, 1989, and 1988. Even the 1991 was an amazing wine. Readers should look for the limited *cuvée* called Cru d'Arche-Pugneau Trie Exceptionnelle, a wine that can approach Yquem and Coutet Cuvée Madame–like richness and intensity. This is a virtually unknown estate that makes terrific wines.

CRU BARRÉJATS

Classification: None

Owner: Mireille Daret and Philippe Andurand

Address: Clos de Gensac, Mareuil, 33210 Pujols-sur-Ciron

Telephone and telefax: 05 56 76 69 06

Visits: By appointment only

Contact: Mireille Daret

VINEYARDS

Surface area: 6.7 acres

Grape varietals: 85% Semillon, 10% Sauvignon, 5% Muscadelle

Average age of vines: 40 years

Density of plantation: 6,600 vines per hectare

Average yields: 16 hectoliters per hectare

Elevage: Fermentations take place in new oak barrels in which wines are aged for 18–36 months. Fining and filtration.

WINES PRODUCED

Cru Barréjats: 2,400–3,600 bottles

Accabailles de Barréjats: 1,200–3,000 bottles

Plateau of maturity: Within 3–8 years of the vintage

CRU PEYRAGUEY

Classification: None

Owner: GFA Musotte

Address: 10 Miselle, 33210 Preignac

Telephone: 05 56 44 43 48; Telefax: 05 56 44 43 48

Visits: By appointment only

VINEYARDS

Surface area: 20.3 acres

Grape varietals: 75% Semillon, 25% Sauvignon

Average age of vines: 20 years

Density of plantation: 6,600 vines per hectare

Average yields: 20 hectoliters per hectare

Elevage: Fermentation and 12 months aging in barrels with 25% new oak. Wines then sojourn in vats before bottling. No fining, filtration.

WINES PRODUCED

Château Cru Peyraguey: 10,000 bottles

No second wine is produced.

Plateau of maturity: Within 3–8 years of the vintage

DOISY DUBROCA

Classification: Second Growth in 1855

Owner: Louis Lurton

Address: 33720 Barsac

Mailing address: c/o Château Haut-Nouchet, 33650 Martillac

Telephone: 05 56 72 69 74; Telefax: 05 56 72 56 11

Website: www.louis-lurton.fr

No visits

VINEYARDS

Surface area: 8.1 acres

Grape varietals: 100% Semillon

Average age of vines: 20 years

Density of plantation: 6,600 vines per hectare

Average yields: 17 hectoliters per hectare

Elevage: Fermentation and 18 months aging in oak barrels (with 33% new oak) including six months *élevage* on fine lees. Fining and filtration.

WINES PRODUCED

Château Doisy Dubroca: 6,000 bottles

La Demoiselle de Doisy: 3,000 bottles

Plateau of maturity: Within 7–20 years of the vintage

Note: The vineyards of Château Doisy Dubroca are organically farmed and the wines produced are entitled to the Ecocert label.

GENERAL APPRECIATION

Although very difficult to find, this can be an undiscovered treasure of the region.

While I have tasted only a handful of recent vintages of Doisy Dubroca, this wine has an uncanny resemblance to the Barsac estate of Climens. In fact, for years the vinification and aging of the wines has been controlled by the same team that makes the wine at Climens.

As great as this wine has tasted in vintages such as 1989, 1988, and 1986, it has remained a fabulous value, largely because so little of it is made and most consumers know little about this château. It remains very much an insider's wine to buy.

DUDON

Classification: Cru Bourgeois

Owner: Evelyne and Michel Allien

Address: 1, Dudon, 33720 Barsac

Telephone: 05 56 27 29 38; Telefax: 05 56 27 29 38

E-mail: chateau.dudon.barsac@wanadoo.fr

Visits: Preferably by appointment

Contact: L. Bernard

VINEYARDS

Surface area: 29.1 acres

Grape varietals: 92% Semillon, 8% Sauvignon

Average age of vines: 28 years

Density of plantation: 6,600 vines per hectare

Average yields: 22 hectoliters per hectare

Elevage: Fermentation and 18 months aging in barrels with 25% new oak. Fining and filtration.

WINES PRODUCED

Château Dudon: 14,000 bottles

Château Gallien: 6,000 bottles

Plateau of maturity: Within 2–6 years of the vintage

GRAVAS

Classification: Cru Bourgeois

Owner: M. Bernard

Address: 33720 Barsac

Telephone: 05 56 27 06 91; Telefax: 05 56 27 29 83

Visits: Preferably by appointment, Monday to Friday,
9 A.M.–noon and 2–7 P.M.

Contact: M. Bernard

VINEYARDS

Surface area: 27.2 acres

Grape varietals: 80% Semillon, 10% Muscadelle, 10% Sauvignon

Average age of vines: 35 years

Density of plantation: 7,000 vines per hectare

Average yields: 23 hectoliters per hectare

Elevage: Four months fermentation in vats. Eighteen months aging by rotation in vats and
barrels. Fining and filtration.

WINES PRODUCED

Château Gravas: 20,000 bottles

Château Simon Carretey: 13,000 bottles

Plateau of maturity: Within 2–6 years of the vintage

GUITERONDE DU HAYOT

Classification: None

Owner: SCE Vignobles du Hayot

Address: 33720 Barsac

Telephone: 05 56 27 15 37; Telefax: 05 56 27 04 34

E-mail: vignoblesduhayot@ifrance.com

Visits: By appointment

Contact: Fabienne du Hayot

VINEYARDS

Surface area: 86.5 acres

Grape varietals: 60% Semillon, 30% Sauvignon, 10% Muscadelle

Average age of vines: 35 years

Density of plantation: 6,500 vines per hectare

Average yields: 25 hectoliters per hectare

Elevage: Fermentation in temperature-controlled stainless-steel tanks. Eighteen months
aging in barrels (with 33% new oak) for part of the yield and in vats for the other. Fining
and filtration.

WINES PRODUCED

Château Guiteronde du Hayot: 100,000 bottles

No second wine is produced.

Plateau of maturity: Within 3–10 years of the vintage

HAUT-BERGERON

Classification: None

Owner: Lamothe family

Address: 33210 Preignac

Telephone: 05 56 63 24 76; telefax: 05 56 63 23 31

E-mail: haut-bergeron@wanadoo.fr

Visits: By appointment Monday to Friday,
9 A.M.–noon and 2–7 P.M.

Contact: Hervé or Patrick Lamothe

VINEYARDS

Surface area: 63 acres

Grape varietals: 90% Semillon, 8% Sauvignon, 2% Muscadelle

Average age of vines: 55 years

Density of plantation: 7,500 vines per hectare

Average yields: 20 hectoliters per hectare

Elevage: Fermentation in temperature-controlled stainless-steel vats. Fourteen to twenty months aging in barrels with 50% new oak. Fining depending upon the vintage, light filtration upon bottling.

WINES PRODUCED

Château Haut-Bergeron: 31,000 bottles

Château Fontebride: 25,000 bottles

Plateau of maturity: Within 3–8 years of the vintage

HAUT-CLAVERIE

Classification: Cru Bourgeois

Owner: GFA du Domaine de Haut-Claverie

Address: Les Claveries, 33210 Fargues-de-Langon

Telephone: 05 56 63 43 09 or 06 81 28 90 02;
Telefax: 05 56 63 51 16

Visits: Preferably by appointment, every day
from 8 A.M. to 5 P.M.

Contact: Philippe Sendrey

VINEYARDS

Surface area: 32.1 acres

Grape varietals: 80% Semillon, 20% Sauvignon

Average age of vines: 35 years

Density of plantation: 5,800 vines per hectare

Average yields: 23 hectoliters per hectare

Elevage: Fermentation in stainless steel vats. Six to twelve months aging in barrels (no new oak) and 12–18 months aging in concrete vats. Fining and filtration.

WINES PRODUCED

Château Haut-Claverie: 17,000 bottles

No second wine is produced.

Plateau of maturity: Within 5 to 15 years of the vintage

Note: This estate also produces some 17,000–20,000 bottles of red Graves Château La Mourasse annually.

This obscure yet excellent property is located just south of the village of Fargues. The wine continues to sell at bargain basement prices. The secret here is not only an excellent microclimate, but late harvesting, several passes through the vineyard, and one of the most conscientious owners in the entire appellation.

DU HAUT-PICK

Classification: None

Owner: Foncier Vignobles

Address: Domaine de Lamontagne, 33210 Preignac

Telephone: 05 56 63 27 66; Telefax: 05 56 76 87 03

E-mail: bastor-lamontagne@dial.oleane.com

Website: www.atinternet.fr/bastor-lamontagne

No visits

VINEYARDS

Surface area: 22.2 acres

Grape varietals: 100% Semillon

Average age of vines: 35 years

Density of plantation: 7,000 vines per hectare

Average yields: 22 hectoliters per hectare

Elevage: Twenty-one day fermentation in vats. Twelve months aging by rotation in vats and in barrels (for 25% of the yield). No fining, filtration.

WINES PRODUCED

Château du Haut-Pick: 25,000 bottles

No second wine is produced.

Plateau of maturity: Within 5–10 years of the vintage

LES JUSTICES

Classification: Cru Bourgeois

Owner: Christian Médeville

Address: 33210 Preignac

Mailing address: BP 14, 33210 Preignac

Telephone: 05 56 76 28 44; Telefax: 05 56 76 28 43

E-mail: christian.medeville@wanadoo.fr

Visits: By appointment Monday to Thursday, 9 A.M.–noon
and 2–5 P.M.; Friday, 9 A.M. to noon and 2–3 P.M.

Contact: Julie Gonet-Médeville

VINEYARDS

Surface area: 21 acres

Grape varietals: 90% Semillon, 8% Sauvignon, 2% Muscadelle

Average age of vines: 35 years

Density of plantation: 6,600 vines per hectare

Average yields: 17 hectoliters per hectare

Elevage: Fermentation in temperature-controlled stainless-steel vats. Twelve to eighteen
months aging in barrels that are renewed by a third at each vintage. Fining and filtration.

WINES PRODUCED

Château Les Justices: 19,000 bottles

No second wine is produced.

Plateau of maturity: Within 5–14 years of the vintage

LAFON

Classification: None

Owner: Olivier Fauthoux

Address: 33210 Sauternes

Telephone: 05 56 63 30 82; Telefax: 05 56 63 30 82

Visits: By appointment only

Contact: Olivier Fauthoux

VINEYARDS

Surface area: 29.6 acres

Grape varietals: 95% Semillon, 5% Sauvignon

Average age of vines: 35 years

Density of plantation: 6,000 vines per hectare

Average yields: 22 hectoliters per hectare

Elevage: Fermentation in temperature-controlled stainless-steel vats. Ten months aging in one-year-old barrels. No fining, filtration.

WINES PRODUCED

Château Lafon: 5,000 bottles

No second wine is produced.

Plateau of maturity: Within 3–8 years of the vintage

LAMOURETTE

Classification: Cru Bourgeois

Owner: Anne-Marie Léglise

Address: 33210 Bommes

Telephone: 05 56 76 63 58; Telefax: 05 56 76 60 85

Visits: By appointment only

Contact: Anne-Marie Léglise

VINEYARDS

Surface area: 22.2 acres

Grape varietals: 90% Semillon, 5% Sauvignon, 5% Muscadelle

Average age of vines: 25 years

Density of plantation: 6,500 vines per hectare

Average yields: 25 hectoliters per hectare

Elevage: Twenty-one day fermentation in temperature-controlled stainless-steel vats. Wines are aged for 18 months in stainless-steel vats and in concrete vats. Fining and filtration.

WINES PRODUCED

Château Lamourette: 15,000 bottles

Château Cazenave: 7,000 bottles

Plateau of maturity: Within 3–8 years of the vintage

LIOT

Classification: None

Owner: Jean-Gérard David

Address: 33720 Barsac

Telephone: 05 56 27 15 31; Telefax: 05 56 27 14 42

E-mail: château.liot@wanadoo.fr

Website: www.chateauliot.com

Visits: By appointment Monday to Friday, 9 A.M.–noon and 2–5 P.M.

Contact: Jean-Gérard David

VINEYARDS

Surface area: 49.4 acres

Grape varietals: 85% Semillon, 10% Sauvignon, 5% Muscadelle

Average age of vines: 35 years

Density of plantation: 7,500 vines per hectare

Average yields: 22 hectoliters per hectare

Elevage: Twenty to twenty-five day fermentation in barrels and vats. Eighteen months aging by rotation in barrels (with 20% new oak) for 60% of the yield and in vats for the rest. Fining and filtration.

WINES PRODUCED

Château Liot: 37,000 bottles

Château du Levan: 16,000 bottles

Plateau of maturity: Within 2–8 years of the vintage

MAURAS

Classification: Cru Bourgeois

Owner: Société Vinicole de France

Address: 33210 Sauternes

Mailing address: Château Grava, 33350 Haux

Telephone: 05 56 67 23 89; Telefax: 05 56 67 08 38

Visits: By appointment only

Contact: Patrick Duale

VINEYARDS

Surface area: 37 acres

Grape varietals: 67% Semillon, 30% Sauvignon, 3% Muscadelle

Average age of vines: 25–30 years

Density of plantation: 6,000 vines per hectare

Average yields: 20–25 hectoliters per hectare

WINES PRODUCED

Château Mauras: 45,000 bottles

Clos du Ciron: 40,000 bottles

Plateau of maturity: Within 3–8 years of the vintage

DU MAYNE

Classification: None

Owner: Sanders family

Address: 33720 Barsac

Telephone: 05 56 27 16 07; Telefax: 05 56 27 16 02

Visits: Monday to Friday, during working hours

Contact: Jean Sanders (Telephone: 05 56 63 19 54)

VINEYARDS

Surface area: 19.8 acres

Grape varietals: 60% Semillon, 40% Sauvignon

Average age of vines: Over 30 years

Density of plantation: 7,800 vines per hectare

Average yields: 17 hectoliters per hectare

Elevage: Fermentations take place in vats, and wines are transferred to oak barrels, 20% of which are new, for 12 months aging. They are fined but remain unfiltered.

WINES PRODUCED

Château du Mayne: 19,000 bottles

No second wine is produced.

Plateau of maturity: Within 3–8 years of the vintage

MONT-JOYE

Classification: None

Owners: Frank and Marguerite Glaunès

Address: Quartier Miaille, 33720 Barsac

Mailing address: Domaine du Pas Saint-Georges, 33190 Casseuil

Telephone: 05 56 71 12 73; Telefax: 05 56 71 12 41

Visits: By appointment only

Contacts: Frank and Marguerite Glaunès

VINEYARDS

Surface area: 32.1 acres

Grape varietals: 75% Semillon, 15% Sauvignon, 10% Muscadelle

Average age of vines: 35 years

Density of plantation: 6,600 vines per hectare

Average yields: 20 hectoliters per hectare

Elevage: Regular *cuvée:* Fermentations take place partly in oak barrels and partly in lined vats. They are aged 24 months by rotation in vats and new oak barrels and are fined and filtered.

Cuvée spéciale: Fermentations last approximately 18 days in barrels, 30% of which are new, and wines are aged 20–24 months. They are fined and filtered.

WINES PRODUCED

Château Mont-Joye: 12,000 bottles

Château Jacques-le-Haut (*cuvée spéciale*): 5,000–10,000 bottles

Plateau of maturity: Within 4–10 years of the vintage

MONTEILS

Classification: Cru Bourgeois

Owner: Le Diascorn family

Address: 33210 Preignac

Telephone: 05 56 76 12 12;
Telefax: 05 56 76 28 63

E-mail: lediascornherve@wanadoo.fr

Website: www.chateau-monteils.com

Visits: By appointment only

Contact: Hervé Le Diascorn

VINEYARDS

Surface area: 27.2 acres (in production)

Grape varietals: 75% Semillon, 20% Sauvignon, 5% Muscadelle

Average age of vines: 25 years

Density of plantation: 5,500 vines per hectare

Average yields: 21–22 hectoliters per hectare

Elevage: Fermentation in small stainless-steel vats. Eighteen months aging in concrete epoxy-lined vats and in new oak barrels for the best lots. Fining and filtration.

WINES PRODUCED

Château Monteils: 30,000 bottles

No second wine is produced.

Plateau of maturity: Within 3–8 years of the vintage

DE MYRAT

Classification: Second Growth in 1855

Owner: Pontac family

Address: 33720 Barsac

Telephone: 05 56 27 09 06; Telefax: 05 56 27 11 75

Visits: By appointment, every day

Contact: Xavier de Pontac

VINEYARDS

Surface area: 54.3 acres

Grape varietals: 86% Semillon, 10% Sauvignon, 4% Muscadelle

Average age of vines: 15 years

Density of plantation: 7,000 vines per hectare

Average yields: 15 hectoliters per hectare

Elevage: Fermentation and 20–24 months aging in barrels with 30% new oak. Fining and filtration.

WINES PRODUCED

Château de Myrat: 25,000 bottles

No second wine is produced.

Plateau of maturity: Within 5–15 years of the vintage

PERNAUD

Classification: Cru Bourgeois

Owner: GFA Château Pernaud

Address: 33720 Barsac

Telephone: 05 56 27 26 52; Telefax: 05 56 27 32 08

Visits: By appointment only

Contact: Jean-Gabriel Jacolin

VINEYARDS

Surface area: 39.5 acres

Grape varietals: 85% Somalian, 10% Sauvignon, 5% Muscadelle

Average age of vines: 35–45 years

Density of plantation: 7,000 vines per hectare

Average yields: 25 hectoliters per hectare max.

Elevage: Fermentation (21°C max.) in temperature-controlled stainless-steel vats. Eighteen months aging in barrels with 5–10% new oak. No fining, filtration.

WINES PRODUCED

Château Pernaud: 30,000 bottles

Château Pey-Arnaud: variable

Plateau of maturity: Within 3–8 years of the vintage

PIADA

Classification: Cru Bourgeois

Owner: Jean-Frédéric Lalande

Address: 1, Château Piada, 33720 Barsac

Telephone: 05 56 27 16 13; Telefax: 05 56 27 26 30

Visits: Monday to Friday, 9 A.M.–noon and 1:30–6 P.M.;
by appointment on weekends

Contact: Jean-Frédéric Lalande

VINEYARDS

Surface area: 24.7 acres

Grape varietals: 95% Semillon, 3% Sauvignon, 2% Muscadelle

Average age of vines: 40 years

Density of plantation: 7,900 vines per hectare

Average yields: 23 hectoliters per hectare

Elevage: Fermentation and 12 months aging in barrels with 30% new oak. Fining, no filtration.

WINES PRODUCED

Château Piada: 12,000 bottles

Clos du Roy: 3,000 bottles

Plateau of maturity: Within 3–8 years of the vintage

DE ROLLAND

Classification: Cru Bourgeois

Owner: GFA Château de Rolland

Address: 33720 Barsac

Telephone: 05 56 27 15 02; Telefax: 05 56 27 28 58

E-mail: info@chateauderolland.com

Website: www.chateauderolland.com

Visits: Monday to Friday, 9 A.M.–noon and 1:30–5:30 P.M.;
by appointment on weekends and on public holidays

Contact: Lucie Faugère-Guignard

VINEYARDS

Surface area: 37 acres

Grape varietals: 80% Semillon, 15% Sauvignon, 5% Muscadelle

Average age of vines: 40 years

Density of plantation: 6,500 vines per hectare

Average yields: 22 hectoliters per hectare

Elevage: Fermentation in temperature-controlled stainless-steel vats. Twelve months aging in barrels with 10% new oak. Fining and filtration.

WINES PRODUCED

Château de Rolland: 40,000 bottles

ROÛMIEU-LACOSTE

Classification: Cru Bourgeois

Owner: Hervé Dubourdieu

Address: 33720 Barsac

Telephone: 05 56 27 16 29; Telefax: 05 56 27 02 65

E-mail: hervedubourdieu@aol.com

Visits: By appointment Monday to Saturday, 9 A.M. to 7 P.M.

Contact: Hervé or Sabine Dubourdieu

VINEYARDS

Surface area: 27.2 acres

Grape varietals: 90% Semillon, 10% Sauvignon

Average age of vines: 50 years

Density of plantation: 4,800 vines per hectare

Average yields: 18 hectoliters per hectare

Elevage: Fermentation in vats. Six months aging by rotation in vats and in new oak barrels. Fining, no filtration.

WINES PRODUCED

Château Roûmieu-Lacoste: 10,000–20,000 bottles

Plateau of maturity: Within 5 to 12 years of the vintage

Note: This estate also produces in the finest years some 5,000–10,000 bottles of a special *cuvée* called Sélection André Dubourdieu Château Roûmieu-Lacoste, which is fermented and aged 18 months in new oak barrels. This special *cuvée* is produced from the oldest vineyards of the estate.

The quality of the wines at Roumieu-Lacoste should not be surprising given the fact that this vineyard is adjacent to the famed Climens in Barsac. The old vines and im-peccable winemaking practices of the Dubourdieu family result in consistently high-quality wines. The style, as befitting a Barsac, is relatively light, but there is plenty of complexity, rich pineapple fruit, and just a touch of toasty new oak. This would appear to be a wine that is best consumed within 10–12 years of the vintage.

SAINT-AMAND

Classification: None

Owner: Anne-Mary Fachetti-Ricard

Address: 33210 Preignac

Telephone: 05 56 76 84 89; Telefax: 05 56 76 24 87

Visits: By appointment Monday to Thursday, 2:30–5:30 P.M.

Contact: Anne-Mary Fachetti-Ricard

VINEYARDS

Surface area: 49.4 acres

Grape varietals: 84% Semillon, 4% Sauvignon, 2% Muscadelle

Average age of vines: 40 years

Density of plantation: 6,400 vines per hectare

Average yields: 16 hectoliters per hectare

Elevage: Fermentation (24°C maximum) in temperature-controlled epoxy-lined concrete vats. Two to three years aging, with a small proportion of the yield in barrels. No fining, filtration.

WINES PRODUCED

Château Saint-Amand: 4,800 bottles

La Chartreuse: variable

Plateau of maturity: Within 3–8 years of the vintage

SAINT-MARC

Classification:

Owner: GFA André Laulan

Address: 33720 Barsac

Telephone: 05 56 27 16 87; Telefax: 05 56 27 05 93

E-mail: d.l.@wanadoo.fr

Visits: By appointment

Contact: Didier Laulan

VINEYARDS

Surface area: 34.6 acres

Grape varietals: 83% Semillon, 10% Sauvignon, 3% Muscadelle

Average age of vines: 35 years

Density of plantation: 6,600 vines per hectare

Average yields: 23–24 hectoliters per hectare

Elevage: Fermentation and 18 months aging in stainless-steel vats of small capacity. Fining and filtration.

WINES PRODUCED

Château Sant-Marc: 20,000 bottles

Château Bessan: 20,000 bottles

Plateau of maturity: Within 3–8 years of the vintage

SIMON

Classification: None

Owner: GFA Château Simon

Address: 33720 Barsac

Telephone: 05 56 27 15 35; Telefax: 05 56 27 24 79

E-mail: chateau.simon@worldonline.fr

Visits: Monday to Friday, 8 A.M.–noon and 1:30–6 P.M.

Contact: Jean-Hugues Dufour

VINEYARDS

Surface area: 42 acres

Grape varietals: 92% Semillon, 6% Sauvignon, 2% Muscadelle

Average age of vines: 40 years

Density of plantation: 6,600 vines per hectare

Average yields: 23 hectoliters per hectare

Elevage: Fermentation in temperature-controlled stainless-steel vats. Twelve months aging in barrels with 15% new oak. Fining and filtration.

WINES PRODUCED

Château Simon: 28,000 bottles

Château Piaut: 15,000 bottles

Plateau of maturity: Within 3–8 years of the vintage

THE SATELLITE APPELLATIONS OF BORDEAUX

There are very large quantities of wine produced in a bevy of other lesser-known appellations of Bordeaux. Most of these wines are widely commercialized in France, but have met with little success in America because of this country's obsession with luxury names and prestigious appellations. For the true connoisseur, the wines of Bordeaux's satellite appellations can in fact represent outstanding bargains, particularly in top vintages such as 2000, 1998, and 1990, where excellent climatic conditions and the improved use of modern technology by many of these estates resulted in a vast selection of fine wines at modest prices.

Each year, on my two trips to Bordeaux, I have spent considerable time tasting the wines from the satellite communes in an all-out effort to try to discover who's who in these obscure appellations. In this section, I have listed the top estates from the major satellite appellations of Bordeaux and I unhesitatingly recommend those wines rated as very good or excellent to Bordeaux wine enthusiasts looking for sensational values from this area.

The satellite appellations are listed in order of my opinion of their overall ability to produce high-quality wine. In short, this is the frugal consumer's guide to fine Bordeaux.

FRONSAC AND CANON-FRONSAC

In the 18th and 19th centuries the vineyards sprinkled over the hillsides and hollows of Fronsac and Canon-Fronsac—only several miles west of Libourne—were better known than the wines of Pomerol and sold for higher prices than the wines of St.-Emilion. But because access to Pomerol was easier and because most of the brokers had their offices in Libourne, the vineyards of Pomerol and St.-Emilion were exploited more than those of Fronsac and Canon-Fronsac. Consequently, this area fell into a long period of obscurity from which it has just recently begun to rebound.

While there is no village in all of Bordeaux that can match the scenic beauty of St.-Emilion, the tranquil landscape of Fronsac and Canon-Fronsac is among the region's most aesthetically pleasing. Both appellations are beautifully situated on rolling hills overlooking the Dordogne River and have a primarily clay/limestone-based soil run-

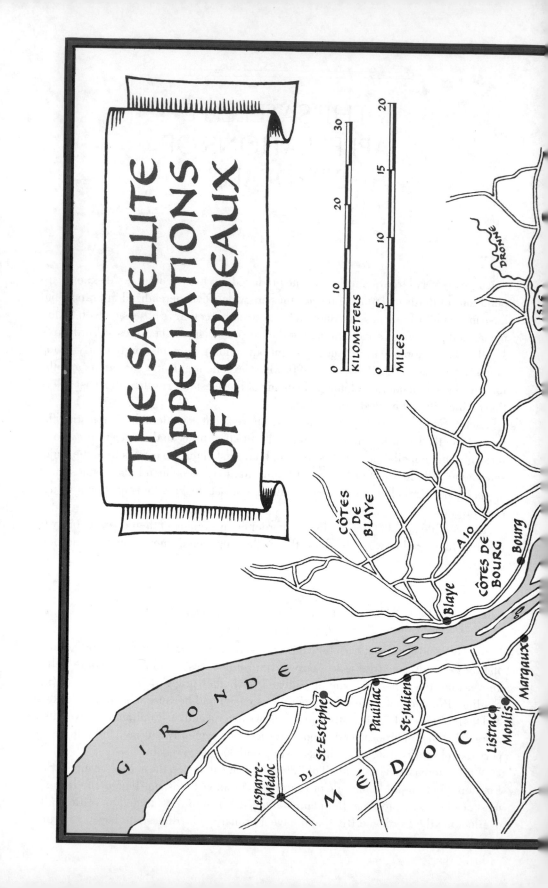

THE SATELLITE
APPELLATIONS
OF BORDEAUX

KILOMETERS
0   10   20   30

MILES
0   5   10   15   20

GIRONDE

CÔTES DE BLAYE

Blaye

Alo

CÔTES DE BOURG

Bourg

DRONNE

ISLE

Lesparre-Médoc

St-Estèphe

Pauillac

St-Julien

Listrac

Moulis

Margaux

MÉDOC

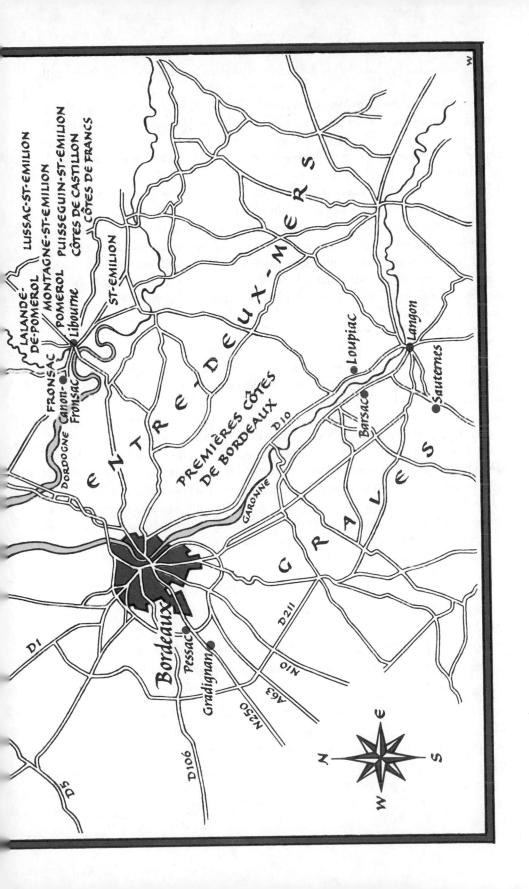

ning in veins that are shallow on the higher elevations and deeper on the lower hillsides.

The grapes of choice are Merlot (representing about 70% of the plantings), Cabernet Franc (15%), and Cabernet Sauvignon (15%). While Malbec still exists in a number of vineyards, its use has largely ceased. Largely ignored until the mid-1980s, the producers of Fronsac and Canon-Fronsac have begun to benefit from increasing interest in their wines. Once viewed as less expensive alternatives to Pomerol and the glamour wines of St.-Emilion, the best Fronsacs and Canon-Fronsacs are carving out their own identities and offering wines (particularly in top years such as 2000) that are rich, full, darkly colored, relatively large-scaled efforts with considerable aging potential. While less of a concern, the toughness and hardness, so much a problem with older-styled Fronsacs and Canon-Fronsacs, remains a perennial problem for many estates. Additionally, the fertile soils of many Fronsac vineyards, which can result in overproduction, are more carefully and conservatively managed. Oddly enough, far greater attention is paid to yields in these appellations than in many of the more famous Bordeaux winemaking regions.

I have been routinely tasting these wines at least twice a year, and I have visited most of the major estates in the region. There has been increasing quality in almost every vintage. The years 1989 and 1990 were the two best back-to-back vintages these appellations enjoyed until 2000. The classification that follows is based on the performance of these estates during the 1989–2001 period. All of the estates rated very good or excellent produced wines in top vintages that have the capacity to last for 10–12 years. I suspect many will last even longer. I remember a dinner at Château Dalem, where the proprietor of another Fronsac, Jean-Noel Hervé, brought a bottle of 1928 Moulin-Haut-Laroque. It was quite stunning at age 60. I am not suggesting these wines will routinely have that kind of aging potential, but they are wines with a great deal of firmness and richness that tend to possess a Médoc-like austerity and structure to them. Even though the vineyards are in close proximity to Pomerol, the wines seem, for the most part, very un-Pomerol-like.

FRONSAC—AN OVERVIEW

Location: On the right bank of Bordeaux's Dordogne River, 15 miles from Bordeaux's city center

Acres under vine: 2,062 (nearly three times the size of Canon-Fronsac)

Communes: Fronsac, La Rivière, Sailans, St.-Aignan, St.-Germain-La-Rivière

Average annual production: 550,000 cases

Classified growths: No classification exists for the châteaux of Fronsac

Principal grape varieties: Merlot dominates, followed by Cabernet Franc. Cabernet Sauvignon and Malbec have increasingly fallen out of favor.

Principal soil type: Clay and limestone, with some sandstone. Most of the Fronsac vineyards are on the lower ground

A CONSUMER'S CLASSIFICATION OF THE CHÂTEAUX OF FRONSAC

EXCELLENT
Aria de la Rivière, La Dauphine (since 2001), Fontenil, Haut-de-Carles, Moulin-Haut-Laroque, La Vieille-Cure, Villars

VERY GOOD
Dalem, La Rivière, Les Trois Croix

GOOD
Cardeneau, Clos du Roy, La Grave, Jeandeman, Meyney, Rouet

CANON-FRONSAC—AN OVERVIEW

Location: On the right bank of Bordeaux's Dordogne River, 15 miles from Bordeaux's city center

Acres under vine: 741

Communes: All of the châteaux are located within the communes of St.-Michel-de-Fronsac and Fronsac

Average annual production: 195,000 cases

Classified growths: None

Principal grape varieties: Merlot, followed by Cabernet Franc, Cabernet Sauvignon, and small quantities of Malbec

Principal soil type: Clay and limestone; most of the châteaux are on the upper slopes of this area's hills

A CONSUMER'S CLASSIFICATION OF THE CHÂTEAUX OF CANON-FRONSAC

VERY GOOD
Barrabaque, Canon, Canon-de-Brem, Cassagne-Haut-Canon-La-Truffière, La Croix-Canon, La Fleur-Cailleau, Grand-Renouil, Mazeris, Moulin-Pey-Labrie, Pavillon, Pez-Labrie

GOOD
Bodet, Mazeris-Bellevue, du Pavillon, Vrai-Canon-Bouché, Vray-Canon-Boyer

PROFILES—THE TOP CHÂTEAUX

Canon (Canon-Fronsac)

Proprietor: Mademoiselle Henriette Horeau
Vineyard size: 25 acres
Production: 4,000 cases
Plateau of maturity: Within 5–15 years of the vintage

Grape varieties:
Merlot—95%
Cabernet Franc—5%

Canon-de-Brem (Canon-Fronsac)

Proprietor: Syndicate (Jean Halley)
Vineyard size: 50 acres
Production: 8,000 cases
Plateau of maturity: Within 5–15 years of
the vintage

Grape varieties:
Merlot—66%
Cabernet Franc—34%

Cassagne-Haut-Canon-La-Truffière (Canon-Fronsac)

Proprietor: Dubois family
Vineyard size: 29.6 acres
Production: 4,500 cases, of which 2,000
cases of the luxury *cuvée* La Truffière is
produced
Plateau of maturity: Within 3–10 years of
the vintage

Grape varieties:
Merlot—70%
Cabernet Franc—20%
Cabernet Sauvignon—10%

Dalem (Fronsac)

Proprietor: Michel Rullier
Vineyard size: 29.6 acres
Production: 6,500 cases
Plateau of maturity: Within 4–12 years of
the vintage

Grape varieties:
Merlot—70%
Cabernet Franc—20%
Cabernet Sauvignon—10%

La Croix-Canon (Canon-Fronsac)

Proprietor: Syndicate
Vineyard size: 35 acres
Production: 4,800 cases
Plateau of maturity: Within 4–15 years of
the vintage

Grape varieties:
Merlot—75%
Cabernet Sauvignon—25%

La Dauphine (Fronsac)

Proprietor: Syndicate (Jean Halley)
Vineyard size: 25 acres
Production: 4,500 cases
Plateau of maturity: Within 4–10 years of
the vintage

Grape varieties:
Merlot—60%
Cabernet Franc—40%

Fontenil (Fronsac)

Proprietor: Michel Rolland
Vineyard size: 17.3 acres
Production: 3,500 cases
Plateau of maturity: Within 4–14 years of
the vintage

Grape varieties:
Merlot—85%
Cabernet Sauvignon—15%

Mazeris (Canon-Fronsac)

Proprietor: Christian de Cournuaud
Vineyard size: 35 acres
Production: 4,500 cases
Plateau of maturity: Within 5–15 years of
the vintage

Grape varieties:
Merlot—75%
Malbec—25%

Moulin-Haut-Laroque (Fronsac)

Proprietor: Jean-Noël Hervé
Vineyard size: 34.6 acres
Production: 6,000 cases
Plateau of maturity: Within 5–20 years of
the vintage

Grape varieties:
Merlot—65%
Cabernet Franc—20%
Cabernet Sauvignon—10%
Malbec—5%

Moulin-Pey-Labrie (Canon-Fronsac)

Proprietor: B. & G. Hubau
Vineyard size: 20 acres
Production: 4,000 cases
Plateau of maturity: Within 5–15 years of
the vintage

Grape varieties:
Merlot—75%
Cabernet Sauvignon—15%
Cabernet Franc—5%
Malbec—5%

Pez-Labrie (Canon-Fronsac)

Proprietor: Société Civile—Eric Vareille
Vineyard size: 14 acres
Production: 2,000 cases
Plateau of maturity: Within 4–12 years of
the vintage

Grape varieties:
Merlot—70%
Cabernet Sauvignon—20%
Cabernet Franc—10%

La Vieille-Cure (Fronsac)

Proprietor: S.N.C., an American syndicate;
contact—Colin C. Ferenbach
Vineyard size: 47 acres
Production: 8,000 cases
Plateau of maturity: Within 4–12 years of
the vintage

Grape varieties:
Merlot—80%
Cabernet Franc—15%
Cabernet Sauvignon—5%

LALANDE-DE-POMEROL

Lalande-de-Pomerol is a satellite commune of 2,717 acres of vineyards located just to
the north of Pomerol. It includes the two communes of Lalande-de-Pomerol and Néac.
The vineyards, which produce only red wine, are planted on relatively light, gravelly,
sandy soils in the northeastern sector with the meandering river, Barbanne, as the appellation's northern boundary. To the east and south, the soils become heavier with
more clay and gravel. The very top level of good Lalande-de-Pomerol is easily the
equivalent of a mid-level Pomerol, with certain wines, such as Belles-Graves, Grand-

Ormeau, Bertineau-St.-Vincent, Chambrun, Les Cruzelles, and La Fleur de Boüard, very good—even by Pomerol's standards.

Prices for these wines have risen, but the top efforts still represent reasonably good values for wines that are essentially dominated by their Merlot content.

LALANDE-DE-POMEROL—AN OVERVIEW

Location: 25 miles east of Bordeaux, adjacent to and north of Pomerol, 3 miles north-east of Libourne

Acres under vine: 1,384 acres

Communes: Lalande-de-Pomerol and Néac

Average annual production: 450,000–500,000 cases

Classified growths: none

Principal grape varieties: Merlot represents 80–90% of total plantings followed by Cabernet Franc

Principal soil type: diverse but largely fertile sand and gravel beds with adequate drainage

A CONSUMER'S CLASSIFICATION
OF THE CHÂTEAUX OF LALANDE-DE-POMEROL

OUTSTANDING
Chambrun, Les Cruzelles, La Fleur de Boüard, La Plus de la Fleur de Boüard

EXCELLENT
Belles-Graves, Grand-Ormeau, Jean de Gué—Cuvée Prestige, La Sergue

VERY GOOD
Bel-Air, Bertineau-St.-Vincent, du Chapelain, La Croix-St.-André, La Fleur-Saint-Georges, Haut-Chaigneau, Haut-Serget, Siaurac, Tournefeuille

GOOD
Des Annereaux, Clos des Templiers, Garraud, Haut-Chatain, Haut-Surget, Les Hauts-Conseillants, Laborde, Moncets

PROFILES—THE TOP CHÂTEAUX

Bel-Air

Proprietor: The Musset family
Vineyard size: 30 acres
Production: 5,000 cases
Plateau of maturity: Within 3–12 years of the vintage

Grape varieties:
Merlot—60%
Cabernet Franc—15%
Pressac—15%
Cabernet Sauvignon—10%

Belles-Graves

Proprietor: Madame Theallet
Vineyard size: 28.4 acres
Production: 5,500 cases
Plateau of maturity: Within 3–10 years of
    the vintage

Grape varieties:
Merlot—60%
Cabernet Franc—40%

Bertineau-St.-Vincent

Proprietor: Michel Rolland
Vineyard size: 10 acres
Production: 2,000 cases
Plateau of maturity: Within 3–10 years of
    the vintage

Grape varieties:
Merlot—80%
Cabernet Franc—20%

Chambrun

Proprietor: Jean-Philippe Janoueix
Vineyard size: 3.7 acres
Production: 800 cases
Plateau of maturity: Within 3–10 years of
    the vintage

Grape varieties:
Merlot—90%
Cabernet Franc—10%

Du Chapelain

Proprietor: Madame Xann Marc
Vineyard size: 2.5 acres
Production: 350 cases
Plateau of maturity: Within 5–10 years of
    the vintage

Grape varieties:
Merlot—90%
Cabernet Franc—10%

La Croix-St.-André

Proprietor: Francis Carayon
Vineyard size: 37 acres
Production: 6,500 cases
Plateau of maturity: Within 4–12 years of
    the vintage

Grape varieties:
Merlot—70%
Cabernet Franc—30%

Les Cruzelles

Proprietor: Denis Durantou
Vineyard size: 25 acres
Production: 2,000 cases
Plateau of maturity: Within 3–10 years of
    the vintage

Grape varieties:
Merlot—60%
Cabernet Franc—40%

La Fleur-Saint-Georges

Proprietor: AGF
Vineyard size: 42 acres
Production: 10,000 cases
Plateau of maturity: Within 3–8 years of
    the vintage

Grape varieties:
Merlot—70%
Cabernet Franc—30%

La Fleur de Boüard

Proprietor: Hubert de Boüard
La Fleur de Boüard—37.5 acres
La Plus de la Fleur de Boüard—4.75 acres
Production:
La Fleur de Boüard—5,000 cases
La Plus de la Fleur de Boüard—500 cases
Plateau of maturity: Within 3–15 years of
the vintage

Grape varieties:
La Fleur de Boüard: Merlot—85%
Cabernet Sauvignon—7%
Cabernet Franc—8%
La Plus de la Fleur de Boüard:
Merlot—100%

Grand-Ormeau

Proprietor: Jean-Claude Beton
Vineyard size: 28.4 acres
Production: 4,800 cases
Plateau of maturity: Within 4–10 years of
the vintage

Grape varieties:
Merlot—65%
Cabernet Franc—25%
Cabernet Sauvignon—10%

Jean de Gué—Cuvée Prestige

Proprietor: Aubert family
Vineyard size: 24.5 acres
Production: 3,000 cases
Plateau of maturity: Within 3–10 years of
the vintage

Grape varieties:
Merlot—75%
Cabernet Franc—20%
Cabernet Sauvignon—5%

Siaurac

Proprietor: Baronne Guichard
Vineyard size: 62 acres
Production: 7,500 cases
Plateau of maturity: Within 3–10 years of
the vintage

Grape varieties:
Merlot—75%
Cabernet Franc—25%

Tournefeuille

Proprietor: G.F.A. Sautarel
Vineyard size: 45 acres
Production: 6,500 cases
Plateau of maturity: Within 5–12 years of
the vintage

Grape varieties:
Merlot—70%
Cabernet Franc—15%
Cabernet Sauvignon—15%

CÔTES DE BOURG

The Côtes de Bourg, a surprisingly vast appellation of more than 9,600 acres (in vine),
is located on the right bank of the Gironde River, just a five-minute boat ride from the
more famous appellation of Margaux. The vineyards here are actually older than those
in the Médoc, as this attractively hilly area was once the center of the strategic forts
built during the Plantagenet period of France's history. The views from the hillside

vineyards adjacent to the river are magnificent. The local chamber of commerce, in an attempt to draw the public's attention to this area, has engaged in some incredible hyperbole, calling Bourg "the Switzerland of the Gironde." Forget the spin, they should instead stress the appeal of the best wines from the Côtes de Bourg (which are made in an uncomplicated, but fruity, round, appealing style) and the lovely port village of the area, the ancient hillside town of Bourg-Sur-Gironde.

The Bourg appellation, located north of Fronsac and south of the Côtes de Blaye, has variable soils. They are primarily limestone based, with different proportions of clay, gravel, and sand. The soils exhibit a far greater degree of fertility than in the Médoc, and consequently, the problem facing many producers is to keep their yields reasonable in order to obtain a degree of concentration in their wines. The dominant grape is Merlot, followed by Cabernet Franc, Cabernet Sauvignon, Malbec, and to a very small extent, Petit Verdot.

Most of the wines of the Côtes de Bourg are average to below average in quality, lack concentration (because of excessive yields), and often have tannins that are too green and high (because of the tendency to harvest too early). However, there are at least a dozen or so estates that consistently make good wines, and several whose wines can easily age for 10 or more years. This could be an increasingly important appellation in the future because the increased demand for wines from the prestigious appellations of Bordeaux has caused prices to soar. Most Côtes de Bourg wines are reasonably priced.

CÔTES DE BOURG—AN OVERVIEW

Location: 18 miles north of Bordeaux, on the right bank of the Dordogne River

Acres under vine: 9,600

Communes: Bayon, Bourg, Comps, Gauriac, Lansac, Mombrier, Prignac-et-Marcamps, St.-Ciers-de-Canesse, St.-Seurin-de-Bourg, St.-Trojan, Samonac, Tauriac, Teuillac, Villeneuve

Average annual production: 350,000 cases (of which approximately 1% is white wine)

Classified growths: There is no classification, but there are more than 300 estates and 4 cooperatives in the region

Principal grape varieties: Red wine—Merlot, followed by Cabernet Franc and Cabernet Sauvignon, with some Malbec; white wine—Sémillon, Sauvignon Blanc, and Muscadelle

Principal soil type: Everything from clay, limestone, sandstone, and pure gravel can be found in the Côtes de Bourg

A CONSUMER'S CLASSIFICATION OF THE CHÂTEAUX
OF THE CÔTES DE BOURG

OUTSTANDING
Fougas-Maldorer, Martinat-Epicurea, Roc des Cambes

EXCELLENT
Tayac—Cuvée Prestige

VERY GOOD
De Barbe, Brûlesécaille, Falfas, Guerry, Haut-Maco,
Mercier, Tayac—Cuvée Réservé

GOOD
Clos La Barette, La Grolet, Gros Moulin, Les Heaumes, Moulin des Graves,
Moulin Vieux, Nodoz, Rousselle, Rousset, Soulignac de Robert,
Tayac, La Tour-Séguy

PROFILES—THE TOP CHÂTEAUX

De Barbe

Proprietor: Savary de Beauregard
Vineyard size: 138 acres
Production: 35,000 cases
Plateau of maturity: Within 3–8 years of
the vintage

Grape varieties:
Merlot—70%
Cabernet Sauvignon—25%
Malbec—5%

Brûlesécaille

Proprietor: Jacques Rodet
Vineyard size: 50 acres
Production: 6,500 cases
Plateau of maturity: Within 3–8 years of
the vintage

Grape varieties:
Cabernet Franc—50%
Merlot—50%

Fougas-Maldorer

Proprietor: Jean-Yves Béchet
Vineyard size: 30 acres
Production: 3,500 cases
Plateau of maturity: Within 3–10 years of
the vintage

Grape varieties:
Merlot—75%
Cabernet Sauvignon—25%

Guerry

Proprietor: Bertrand de Rivoyre
Vineyard size: 54 acres
Production: 8,500 cases
Plateau of maturity: Within 4–12 years of
the vintage

Grape varieties:
Malbec—34%
Cabernet Sauvignon—33%
Merlot—33%

Haut-Maco

Proprietor: Mallet brothers
Vineyard size: 86 acres
Production: 12,000 cases
Plateau of maturity: Within 3–7 years of
the vintage

Grape varieties:
Cabernet Franc—70%
Merlot—30%

Martinat-Epicurea

Proprietor: S.C.E.V.
Vineyard size: 7.5 acres
Production: 500 cases
Plateau of maturity: Within 3–10 years of
　the vintage

Grape varieties:
Merlot—90%
Malbec—10%

Mercier

Proprietor: Philippe Chéty
Vineyard size: 74 acres
Production: 6,000 cases
Plateau of maturity: Within 3–10 years of
　the vintage

Grape varieties:
Merlot—55%
Cabernet Sauvignon—25%
Cabernet Franc—15%
Malbec—5%

Roc des Cambes

Proprietor: François Mitjavile
Vineyard size: 23 acres
Production: 3,000 cases
Plateau of maturity: Within 3–10 years of
　the vintage

Grape varieties:
Cabernet Sauvignon—75%
Merlot—20%
Cabernet Franc—5%

Tayac—Cuvée Prestige

Proprietor: Pierre Saturny
Vineyard size: 50 acres
Production: 1,000–2,000 cases
Plateau of maturity: Within 5–15 years of
　the vintage

Grape varieties:
Cabernet Sauvignon—80%
Merlot—20%

Note: This luxury *cuvée*, from very old vines, is only made in great years.

CÔTES DE BLAYE

There are a little more than 19,100 acres of vines in the Blaye region, located directly north of Bourg. The best vineyard areas are entitled to the appellation Premières Côtes de Blaye. While there are quantities of white wine produced in the Blaye region, most of the Premières Côtes de Blaye are dedicated to the production of red wine, which is very similar to the red wine of Bourg. At its best, it is forward, round, richly fruity, soft, and immensely satisfying in a low-key manner.

Blaye, like Bourg, is a much older wine-producing region than the more renowned Médoc. Its origins date back to Roman times when the area served as a defensive front line against invaders intent on attacking the city of Bordeaux. Today, the tourist route from Bourg to Blaye is one of the more charming in the Bordeaux region. In Blaye itself is a perfectly preserved 17th-century military fortress (the citadel) that is classified as a historical monument by the French government. Because of the growing population of sturgeon that make the nearby Gironde River their habitat, gourmets may be surprised to note that the French government permits limited sturgeon fishing and caviar preparation. Blaye is the center for this tiny industry.

Most of the Blaye vineyards sit on steeply sloping hills with a southerly exposure overlooking the Gironde. The soil tends to be dominated by limestone, with outbreaks of clay and, from time to time, gravel. It is a very fertile soil that must be cultivated conservatively if the yields are to be kept under control. The grape varieties are essentially the same as in Bourg, with Merlot dominating the blend, followed by Cabernet Franc, Cabernet Sauvignon, and Malbec. The best red wines from the Côtes de Blaye are extremely well made and richly fruity, and are best drunk within their first 5–6 years of life. There is an interesting group of white varietals planted in the appellation including Sémillon, Sauvignon Blanc, Muscadelle, Merlot Blanc, Folle Blanche, Colombard, Chenin Blanc, and Ugni Blanc.

CÔTES DE BLAYE—AN OVERVIEW

Location: On the right bank of the Gironde River, approximately 30 miles from Bordeaux's city center. The Côtes de Bourg lies to the south.

Acres under vine: 19,100 acres

Communes: There are more than 40 communes in this large appellation

Average annual production: 2,250,000 cases, of which 90% is red wine and 10% white

Classified growths: None, but there are 520 estates and 6 cooperatives boasting more than 500 members

Principal grape varieties: Red wine—Merlot dominates; white wine—Sauvignon and Sémillon, along with smaller quantities of Muscadelle and Colombard

Principal soil type: Clay intermixed with limestone, sand, and gravel

A CONSUMER'S CLASSIFICATION
OF THE CHÂTEAUX OF THE CÔTES DE BLAYE

OUTSTANDING
Passion du Prieuré-Malesan

EXCELLENT
Garreau, Garreau—Cuvée Armande, Gigault—Cuvée Viva, Les Grands Maréchaux, Prieuré-Malesan

VERY GOOD
Ségonzac, La Tonnelle

GOOD
Bellevue, La Bretonnière, Haut-Sociando, Les Jonqueyrès, Pérenne, Péyraud, Petits-Arnauds Péyraud, Roland La Garde

AVERAGE

Barbé, Chante Alouette-la-Roseraie, Clairac, Le Cone-Taillasson-de-Lagarcie, L'Escarde, La Grange, Loumede, Magveleine-Bouhou, Mayne-Boyer-Chaumet, Les Moines, Pardaillan, Peybonhomme, Peymelon, Ricaud, Sociando, Les Videaux

PROFILES—THE TOP CHÂTEAUX

Garreau

Proprietor: Société Civile
Vineyard size: 23.5 acres
Production: 3,700 cases
Plateau of maturity: Within 2–8 years of
 the vintage

Grape varieties:
Cabernet Sauvignon—75%
Merlot—25%

Gigault—Cuvée Viva

Proprietor: Christophe Reboul-Salze
Vineyard size: 35 acres
Production: 2,500 cases
Plateau of maturity: Within 2–10 years of
 the vintage

Grape varieties:
Merlot—85%
Cabernet Sauvignon—15%

Les Grands Maréchaux

Proprietor: Christophe Reboul-Salze
Vineyard size: 60 acres
Production: 5,000 cases
Plateau of maturity: Within 2–8 years of
 the vintage

Grape varieties:
Merlot—80%
Cabernet Franc—10%
Cabernet Sauvignon—10%

Haut-Bertinérie

Proprietor: Daniel Bantegnies
Vineyard size: 111 acres
Production: Red wine—26,000 cases;
 white wine—6,000 cases
Plateau of maturity: Red wine—Within
 3–10 years of the vintage; White wine—
 Within 1–2 years of the vintage

Grape varieties:
Cabernet Sauvignon—45%
Merlot—45%
Cabernet Franc—10%

Note: This is the only estate in the Blaye appellation producing an excellent white wine made from 95% Sauvignon Blanc, 2% Colombard, 2% Sémillon, and 1% Muscadelle.

Haut-Sociando

Proprietor: Louis Martinaud
Vineyard size: 35 acres
Production: 6,000 cases
Plateau of maturity: Within 2–3 years of
 the vintage

Grape varieties:
Merlot—65%
Cabernet Franc—35%

Les Jonqueyrès

Proprietor: Pascal Montaut
Vineyard size: 35 acres
Production: 5,000 cases
Plateau of maturity: Within 2–7 years of
   the vintage

Grape varieties:
Merlot—75%
Cabernet Franc—25%

Pérenne

Proprietor: A syndicate of Danish bankers
Vineyard size: 227 acres
Production: 32,000 cases
Plateau of maturity: Within 2–5 years of
   the vintage

Grape varieties:
Merlot—54%
Cabernet Franc—44%
Cabernet Sauvignon—1%
Malbec—1%

Péyraud

Proprietor: Rey family
Vineyard size: 25 acres
Production: 4,500 cases
Plateau of maturity: Within 3–6 years of
   the vintage

Grape varieties:
Merlot—50%
Cabernet Sauvignon—30%
Cabernet Franc—15%
Malbec—5%

Prieuré-Malesan

Proprietor: Bernard Magrez
Vineyard size: 175 acres, 5 acres for
   Passion du Prieuré-Malesan
Production: 500 cases
Plateau of maturity: Within 2–10 years of
   the vintage

Grape varieties:
Prieuré-Malesan:
Merlot—60%
Cabernet Sauvignon—33%
Cabernet Franc—6%
Malbec—1%
Passion du Prieuré-Malesan:
Merlot—80%
Cabernet Franc—20%

Ségonzac

Proprietor: Jacob Marmet
Vineyard size: 75 acres
Production: 19,000 cases
Plateau of maturity: Within 3–6 years of
   the vintage

Grape varieties:
Merlot—60%
Cabernet Sauvignon—20%
Cabernet Franc—10%
Malbec—10%

Note: There is also a very fine Cuvée Vieilles Vignes produced.

La Tonnelle

Proprietor: Eve Rouchi
Vineyard size: 25 acres
Production: 5,000 cases
Plateau of maturity: Within 2–5 years of
   the vintage

Grape varieties:
Merlot—75%
Cabernet Franc—25%

PUISSEGUIN-ST.-EMILION

Puisseguin-St.-Emilion, the easternmost of the satellite appellations, has been growing in size. The name is of Celtic origin, meaning "the hill with the powerful wine." More than one half of the appellation's production is dominated by the local cooperative under the label Roc de Puisseguin, but most of the estates that bottle their wines produce noteworthy wines that require drinking within 5–6 years of the vintage. They are considerably less expensive than most St.-Emilions.

Vintages in Puisseguin tend to follow those of the Libournais, with top years, such as 1998 and 2000, the best for bargain hunters in this appellation.

PUISSEGUIN-ST.-EMILION—AN OVERVIEW

Location: On the right bank of the Dordogne River, approximately 25 miles northeast of Bordeaux and 6 miles east of Libourne

Acres under vine: 2,445

Communes: Puisseguin

Average annual production: 575,000 cases

Classified growths: None, but there are 73 separate estates and one large cooperative

Principal grape varieties: Merlot dominates, followed by Cabernet Franc and small quantities of Cabernet Sauvignon

Principal soil type: Limestone and clay, with small amounts of sandstone

A CONSUMER'S CLASSIFICATION OF THE CHÂTEAUX OF PUISSEGUIN-ST.-EMILION

VERY GOOD
Branda, Guibot-La-Fourvieille

GOOD
Durand Laplagne, La Mauriannc, de Roques, Vieux-Château-Guibeau

AVERAGE
Beauséjour, Cassat, La Croix-de-Mouchet, Fayan, Gontet-Robin, de Mole, Moulin, Rigaud, Roc de Boissac, Soleil, Teyssier, La Tour Guillotin

PROFILES—THE TOP CHÂTEAUX

Branda

Proprietor: Société Civile
Vineyard size: 14.8 acres
Production: 2,500 cases
Plateau of maturity: Within 2–8 years of the vintage

Grape varieties:
Merlot—60%
Cabernet Sauvignon—30%
Cabernet Franc—10%

Durand Laplagne

Proprietor: The Consorts Bessou
Vineyard size: 32 acres
Production: 6,000 cases
Plateau of maturity: Within 3–7 years of
the vintage

Grape varieties:
Merlot—70%
Cabernet Franc—15%
Cabernet Sauvignon—15%

Guibot-La-Fourvieille

Proprietor: Société Civile
Vineyard size: 173 acres
Production: 20,000 cases
Plateau of maturity: Within 2–6 years of
the vintage

Grape varieties:
Merlot—70%
Cabernet Franc—15%
Cabernet Sauvignon—15%

De Roques

Proprietor: Société Civile
Vineyard size: 62 acres
Production: 12,000 cases
Plateau of maturity: Within 3–10 years of
the vintage

Grape varieties:
Merlot—60%
Cabernet Franc—40%

Vieux-Château-Guibeau

Proprietor: Société Civile
Vineyard size: 100 acres
Production: 25,000 cases
Plateau of maturity: Within 2–7 years of
the vintage

Grape varieties:
Merlot—66%
Cabernet Franc—17%
Cabernet Sauvignon—17%

LUSSAC-ST.-EMILION

Lussac, located in the northeastern portion of the viticultural region of St.-Emilion, encompasses more than 3,450 acres. More than one half of the vineyard area is controlled by the local cooperative, but there are a number of fine estates making smooth, delicious, round, fruity wine that must be consumed in the first 5–6 years of life.

The vineyards generally consist of limestone-dominated *terroirs,* with a handful on more sandy soils. As with the other satellite appellations in St.-Emilion, Lussac is a veritable treasure trove for bargains.

LUSSAC-ST.-EMILION—AN OVERVIEW

Location: 25 miles northeast of Bordeaux and six miles northeast of Libourne on the right bank of the Dordogne River

Acres under vine: 3,458

Communes: Lussac

Average annual production: 775,000 cases

Classified growths: None, although there are 215 estates and one cooperative with 80 members

Principal grape varieties: Merlot and Cabernet Franc

Principal soil type: Sand, clay, gravel, and clay/limestone dominate the diverse soil types of this appellation

A CONSUMER'S CLASSIFICATION OF THE CHÂTEAUX OF LUSSAC-ST.-EMILION

GOOD

Bel-Air, Bellevue, Cap de Merle, Carteyron, Courlat, Du Lyonnat, Mayne-Blanc, Villadière

PROFILES—THE TOP CHÂTEAUX

Bel-Air

Proprietor: Jean-Noel Roi
Vineyard size: 50 acres
Production: 10,000 cases
Plateau of maturity: Within 3–7 years of the vintage

Grape varieties:
Merlot—70%
Cabernet Franc—20%
Cabernet Sauvignon—10%

Bellevue

Proprietor: Charles Chatenoud
Vineyard size: 26 acres
Production: 4,000 cases
Plateau of maturity: Within 3–10 years of the vintage

Grape varieties:
Merlot—70%
Cabernet Franc—30%

Cap de Merle

Proprietor: Jacques Bessou
Vineyard size: 20 acres
Production: 3,000 cases
Plateau of maturity: Within 2–7 years of the vintage

Grape varieties:
Merlot—75%
Cabernet Franc—25%

Courlat

Proprietor: Pierre Bourotte
Vineyard size: 42 acres
Production: 8,000 cases
Plateau of maturity: Within 2–6 years of the vintage

Grape varieties:
Merlot—70%
Cabernet Franc—20%
Cabernet Sauvignon—10%

Du Lyonnat

Proprietor: Jean Milhade
Vineyard size: 111 acres
Production: 25,000 cases
Plateau of maturity: Within 5–12 years of
the vintage

Grape varieties:
Merlot—75%
Cabernet Franc—12.5%
Cabernet Sauvignon—12.5%

Mayne-Blanc

Proprietor: Jean Boncheau
Vineyard size: 37 acres
Production: 7,500 cases
Plateau of maturity: Within 2–6 years of
the vintage

Grape varieties:
Merlot—60%
Cabernet Sauvignon—30%
Cabernet Franc—10%

MONTAGNE-ST.-EMILION

Not far from the Graves sector of northern St.-Emilion and Pomerol is the satellite commune of Montagne-St.-Emilion. The hillside soils of this area consist of a clay/limestone blend, and the plateaus are primarily limestone-based soils intermixed with hard outbreaks of rock.

The best wines of Montagne almost always emerge from the hilly terrain along the southern border, in view of the splendid Barbanne River that runs through Lalande-de-Pomerol and Pomerol. Among all the satellite communes, some of the deepest, richest wines consistently come from Montagne. The top wines can represent excellent bargains since they are the qualitative equivalent of a good grand cru St.-Emilion.

MONTAGNE-ST.-EMILION—AN OVERVIEW

Location: 23 miles northeast of Bordeaux on the right bank of the Dordogne River

Acres under vine: 3,829

Communes: Montagne

Average annual production: 950,000 cases

Classified growths: None, but there are 220 estates and one cooperative with 30 members

Principal grape varieties: Merlot

Principal soil type: Limestone/clay

A CONSUMER'S CLASSIFICATION OF THE CHÂTEAUX OF MONTAGNE-ST.-EMILION

EXCELLENT
Faizeau-Vieilles Vignes, Roudier

VERY GOOD
Calon, Croix-Beauséjour, Maison Blanche, Tour-Musset, des Tours,
Vieux-Château-St.-André

PROFILES—THE TOP CHÂTEAUX

Calon

Proprietor: Jean-Noel Boidron
Vineyard size: 100 acres
Production: 14,000 cases
Plateau of maturity: Within 5–15 years of
　the vintage

Grape varieties:
Merlot—70%
Cabernet Franc—15%
Cabernet Sauvignon—15%

Croix-Beauséjour

Proprietor: Olivier Laporte
Vineyard size: 19 acres
Production: 3,500 cases
Plateau of maturity: Within 5–12 years of
　the vintage

Grape varieties:
Merlot—70%
Cabernet Franc—15%
Malbec—15%

Faizeau-Vielles Vignes

Proprietor: Chantel Lebreton and Alain
　Raynaud
Vineyard size: 25 acres
Production: 5,000 cases
Plateau of maturity: Within 2–8 years of
　the vintage

Grape varieties:
Merlot—85%
Cabernet Sauvignon—10%
Cabernet Franc—5%

Maison Blanche

Proprietor: Françoise and Gerard
　Despagne-Rapin
Vineyard size: 80 acres
Production: 15,000 cases
Plateau of maturity: Within 4–12 years of
　the vintage

Grape varieties:
Merlot—70%
Cabernet Franc—20%
Cabernet Sauvignon—10%

Roudier

Proprietor: Jacques Capdemourlin
Vineyard size: 75 acres
Production: 15,000 cases
Plateau of maturity: Within 5–12 years of
　the vintage

Grape varieties:
Merlot—60%
Cabernet Franc—25%
Cabernet Sauvignon—15%

Tour-Musset

Proprietor: Henri Guiter
Vineyard size: 62 acres
Production: 12,000 cases
Plateau of maturity: Within 2–7 years of
　the vintage

Grape varieties:
Cabernet Sauvignon—50%
Merlot—50%

Des Tours

Proprietor: G.F.A. Louis Yerles
Vineyard size: 175 acres
Production: 55,000 cases
Plateau of maturity: Within 2–5 years of
  the vintage

Grape varieties:
Cabernet Franc—34%
Merlot—34%
Malbec—32%

Vieux-Château-St.-André

Proprietor: Jean-Claude Berouet
Vineyard size: 15.8 acres
Production: 3,200 cases
Plateau of maturity: Within 3–12 years of
  the vintage

Grape varieties:
Merlot—75%
Cabernet Franc—25%

ST.-GEORGES ST.-EMILION

Beginning in 1972, the proprietors in the tiny commune of St.-Georges St.-Emilion were permitted to label their wines with the Montagne-St.-Emilion appellation. However, a number of them continued to seek their own identity with their appellation listed as St.-Georges St.-Emilion. There are several serious estates in St.-Georges, including Château St.-Georges and the much smaller Château Saint-André Corbin.

ST.-GEORGES ST.-EMILION—AN OVERVIEW

Location: 23 miles northeast of Bordeaux on the right bank of the Dordogne River

Acres under vine: 445

Communes: St.-Georges St.-Emilion is part of the Montagne commune

Average annual production: 95,000 cases

Classified growths: None, but there are 19 estates

Principal grape varieties: Merlot

Principal soil type: Clay/limestone

A CONSUMER'S CLASSIFICATION OF THE CHÂTEAUX OF ST.-GEORGES ST.-EMILION

VERY GOOD
Saint-André Corbin, St.-Georges

AVERAGE
Belair-Montaiguillon, Macquin-St. Georges, Tour-du-Pas-St. Georges

PROFILES—THE TOP CHÂTEAUX

Saint-André Corbin

Proprietor: GFA
Vineyard size: 42 acres
Production: 8,000 cases
Plateau of maturity: Within 4–12 years of
the vintage

Grape varieties:
Merlot—70%
Cabernet Franc—30%

St.-Georges

Proprietor: Georges Desbois
Vineyard size: 125 acres
Production: 25,000 cases
Plateau of maturity: Within 4–15 years of
the vintage

Grape varieties:
Merlot—60%
Cabernet Franc—20%
Cabernet Sauvignon—20%

CÔTES DE CASTILLON

Now the most fashionable of the satellite appellations, the Côtes de Castillon is a hotbed of activity as well as fertile hunting ground for a bevy of overachievers. Located east of Puisseguin-St.-Emilion, approximately 25 miles from Bordeaux, the appellation is named after the commune called Castillon-la-Bataille, which commemorates the Battle of Castillon. This 1453 battle marked the conclusion of the Hundred Years' War when the English commander, Talbot, died during the defeat of his army.

As one of the older winemaking regions in the area, viticultural practices can be traced to Roman times. The soils, which range from extremely fertile to gravelly to sandy, become mixed with more gravel and clay the farther up the hillsides they are. On the highest areas, the soils are limestone mixed with clay, marl, and sandstone. According to the syndicate, 65% of the area's production is controlled by the large Cooperative de Castillon. Appellation status was awarded in 1955 and there has been significantly more interest expressed in the wines as a lower-priced alternative to the wines of St.-Emilion.

Many of Bordeaux's cutting edge wine-makers have purchased properties in the Côtes de Castillon, and their stunning efforts are particularly evident beginning in the late 1990s, particularly the 2000 vintage. These Bordeaux movers and shakers, particularly Hubert de Boüard, Gérard Perse, Alain Raynaud, Jean-Michel Fernandez, Stéphane Derénoncourt, Corinne Guisez, and Stéphane Von Neipperg, are brilliant wine-makers with established reputations (largely in St.-Emilion) and are pushing the envelope of quality in Côtes de Castillon. For that reason, this appellation is currently one of Bordeaux's most exciting wine producing regions. It is only a matter of time before prices catch up with the flamboyant, concentrated, interesting wines being produced at Côtes de Castillon.

CÔTES DE CASTILLON—AN OVERVIEW

Location: On the right bank of the Dordogne River, 24 miles east of Bordeaux, bordered on the north by the appellation of Côtes de Francs, on the south by the Dordogne River, and on the west by St.-Emilion.

Acres under vine: 7,410

Communes: There are a total of eight communes, a bevy of which include the word "Castillon" as an appendage to the commune name. The principal communes include Belves-de-Castillon, Castillon-la-Bataille, Ste.-Colombe, St.-Jeanes-de-Castillon, St.-Magne-de-Castillon, Les Salles-de-Castillon, and St.-Philippe-d'Aiguille.

Average annual production: 1,650,000 cases

Classified growths: None, but there are 250 estates and one cooperative with more than 150 members

Principal grape varieties: Merlot, followed by Cabernet Franc

Principal soil type: Clay/limestone on the hillsides and more gravelly, sandy soil on the lower slopes

A CONSUMER'S CLASSIFICATION OF THE CHÂTEAUX OF THE CÔTES DE CASTILLON

OUTSTANDING
D'Aiguilhe, Clos des Lunelles

EXCELLENT
D'Aiguilhe-Querre, Brisson, Cap de Faugères, Clos l'Église, Clos Puy Arnaud, Domaine l'A, Joanin-Bécot, Laussac, Sainte-Colombe, Véyry, Vieux-Champs de Mars—Cuvée Johanna

VERY GOOD
De Belcier, Côte Montpezat, Dubois Grimon, Péyrou, Le Pin de Belcier, de Pitray, Puycarpin, La Roche Beaulieu Amarinum, La Terrasse

AVERAGE
Beynat, Blanzac, du Bois, Les Desmoiselles, Fontbaude, La Fourquerie, Haut-Tuquet, Lartigue, Maisières-Aubert, Moulin-Neuf, Moulin Rouge, Palanquey, Robin, Rocher-Bellevue, Roqueville, Tarreyro, Terasson

PROFILES—THE TOP CHÂTEAUX

Domaine l'A

Proprietor: Stéphane Derénoncourt
Vineyard size: 7.5 acres
Production: 500 cases
Plateau of maturity: Within 2–12 years of the vintage

Grape varieties:
Merlot—60%
Cabernet Franc—25%
Cabernet Sauvignon—15%

D'Aiguilhe

Proprietor: Comtes de Neipperg
Vineyard size: 103 acres
Production: 8,000 cases
Plateau of maturity: Within 3–13 years of
the vintage

Grape varieties:
Merlot—80%
Cabernet Franc—20%

D'Aiguilhe-Querre

Proprietor: Société Civile
Vineyard size: 3 acres
Production: 250 cases
Plateau of maturity: Within 2–10 years of
the vintage

Grape varieties:
Merlot—90%
Cabernet Franc—10%

Brisson

Proprietor: Pierre Valade
Vineyard size: 50 acres
Production: 5,000–6,000 cases
Plateau of maturity: Within 2–8 years of
the vintage

Grape varieties:
Merlot—75%
Cabernet Franc—20%
Cabernet Sauvignon—5%

Cap de Faugères

Proprietor: Corinne Guisez
Vineyard size: 64 acres
Production: 13,000 cases
Plateau of maturity: Within 2–8 years of
the vintage

Grape varieties:
Merlot—50%
Cabernet Franc—38%
Cabernet Sauvignon—12%

Clos l'Église

Proprietor: Gérard Perse and Dr. Alain
Raynaud
Vineyard size: 40 acres
Production: 5,000 cases
Plateau of maturity: Within 3–14 years of
the vintage

Grape varieties:
Merlot—70%
Cabernet Franc—15%
Cabernet Sauvignon—15%

Clos des Lunelles

Proprietor: Gérard and Chantal Perse
Vineyard size: 22.5 acres
Production: 1,650 cases
Plateau of maturity: Within 3–15 years of
the vintage

Grape varieties:
Merlot—80%
Cabernet Franc—10%
Cabernet Sauvignon—10%

Clos Puy Arnaud

Proprietor: Société Civile
Vineyard size: 18.5 acres
Production: 3,300 cases
Plateau of maturity: Within 2–10 years of
　the vintage

Grape varieties:
Merlot—70%
Cabernet Franc—20%
Cabernet Sauvignon—10%

Joanin-Bécot

Proprietor: Juliette Bécot
Vineyard size: 25 acres
Production: 2,500 cases
Plateau of maturity: Within 2–10 years of
　the vintage

Grape varieties:
Merlot—75%
Cabernet Franc—25%

Laussac

Proprietor: Dr. Alain Raynaud
Vineyard size: 29 acres
Production: 5,000 cases
Plateau of maturity: Within 2–10 years of
　the vintage

Grape varieties:
Merlot—70%
Cabernet Franc—30%

Véyry

Proprietor: Christian Véyry
Vineyard size: 5 acres
Production: 400 cases
Plateau of maturity: Within 2–8 years of
　the vintage

Grape varieties:
Merlot—80%
Cabernet Franc—20%

Vieux-Champs de Mars—Cuvée Johanna

Proprietor: Régis Moro
Vineyard size: 42 acres
Production: 9,500 cases
Plateau of maturity: Within 2–8 years of
　the vintage

Grape varieties:
Merlot—80%
Cabernet Franc—15%
Cabernet Sauvignon—5%

CÔTES DE FRANCS

The Côtes de Francs is one of the newer appellations in the environs of St.-Emilion. Although the area traces wine-producing origins to the 11th century, it received appellation status only in 1976. There are 1,480 acres of vines, of which 20% is planted in white wine varietals, such as Sémillon, Sauvignon Blanc, and Muscadelle.

　　The highest potential would appear to be for red wines, as the Côtes de Francs is a natural extension to the east of Puisseguin-St.-Emilion and Lussac-St.-Emilion. The soils are ideal, with the lower slopes and valley floors containing a lot of clay and the hillsides clay and limestone mixtures with outbreaks of marl and chalk. The grapes of choice are Cabernet Sauvignon, Cabernet Franc, Malbec, and Merlot. The Côtes de Francs does have the distinction of having one of Bordeaux's only east-facing vineyard areas.

CÔTES DE FRANCS—AN OVERVIEW

Location: Nearly 30 miles from Bordeaux's city center, on the right bank of the Dordogne River, Côtes de Francs is west of Puisseguin and Lussac

Acres under vine: 2,211

Communes: Francs, Saint-Cibard

Average annual production: 240,000 cases, of which 90% is red and 10% white

Classified growths: None, but there are 30 estates and one cooperative with 30 members

Principal grape varieties: Merlot

Principal soil type: Clay/limestone

A CONSUMER'S CLASSIFICATION OF THE CHÂTEAUX OF THE CÔTES DE FRANCS

VERY GOOD

Château de Francs, Marsau, La Prade, Puyguéraud, Puyguéraud—Cuvée Georges

GOOD

Les Charmes-Godard

PROFILES—THE TOP CHÂTEAUX

Château de Francs

Proprietor: Hébrard and Boüard families
Vineyard size: 67 acres
Production: 10,000 cases
Plateau of maturity: Within 3–8 years of the vintage

Grape varieties:
Merlot—60%
Cabernet Franc—40%

Marsau

Proprietor: Jean-Marie and Sylvie Chadronnier
Vineyard size: 24 acres
Production: 4,500 cases
Plateau of maturity: Within 2–8 years of the vintage

Grape varieties:
Merlot—85%
Cabernet Franc—15%

La Prade

Proprietor: Patrick Valette
Vineyard size: 11 acres
Production: 2,200 cases
Plateau of maturity: Within 2–6 years of
    the vintage

Grape varieties:
Merlot—80%
Cabernet Franc—10%
Cabernet Sauvignon—10%

Puyguéraud

Proprietor: Thienpont family
Vineyard size: 75 acres
Production: 15,000 cases
Plateau of maturity: Within 3–8 years of
    the vintage

Grape varieties:
Merlot—55%
Cabernet Franc—30%
Cabernet Sauvignon—15%

LOUPIAC AND STE.-CROIX-DU-MONT

With the wine prices of Barsac and Sauternes soaring, I predict a more important role for the producers of the sweet white wines of Loupiac and Ste.-Croix-du-Mont. These two appellations, 24 miles south of Bordeaux on the right bank of the Garonne, facing Barsac and Sauternes across the river, have an ideal southern exposure. These areas received appellation status in 1930, and many observers believe the excellent exposition of the top vineyards and the clay/limestone soil base is favorable for producing sweet wines, particularly in view of the fact that the morning mists—so essential for the formation of the noble rot, *Botrytis cinerea*—are a common occurrence in this area. Although the sweet wines are receiving increasing attention from wine lovers, dry white wines, as well as a moderate quantity of dry red wines, are also produced.

LOUPIAC—AN OVERVIEW

Location: On the right bank of the Garonne River, approximately 24 miles southeast of
    Bordeaux and only 6 miles from Langon

Acres under vine: 865

Communes: Loupiac

Average annual production: 115,000 cases

Classified growths: None, but there are 70 estates

Principal grape varieties: Sémillon, Sauvignon Blanc, and Muscadelle

Principal soil type: Clay/limestone and gravelly clay with sandstone

STE.-CROIX-DU-MONT—AN OVERVIEW

Location: 24 miles southeast of Bordeaux and 5 miles from Langon

Acres under vine: 1,087

Communes: Ste.-Croix-du-Mont

Average annual production: 175,000 cases

Classified growths: None, but there are 90 estates

Principal grape varieties: Sémillon, Sauvignon Blanc, and Muscadelle

Principal soil type: Clay/limestone dominates the region

A CONSUMER'S CLASSIFICATION OF THE CHÂTEAUX OF LOUPIAC AND STE.-CROIX-DU-MONT

VERY GOOD (SWEET WINES)

Bourdon-Loupiac, Clos Jean, Crabitan-Bell-Vue (Cuvée Speciale), du Cros, Domaine du Noble, Loubens, Loupiac-Gaudiet, La Rame, Ricaud

PROFILES—THE TOP CHÂTEAUX

Clos Jean

Proprietor: Lionel Bord
Vineyard size: 40 acres
Production: 10,800 cases
Plateau of maturity: Within 4–15 years of
the vintage for the sweet wine, and 1–3
years for the dry wine

Grape varieties:
Sémillon—80%
Sauvignon Blanc—20%

Note: This property also makes an excellent Graves-like dry white wine.

Crabitan-Bell-Vue (Cuvée Speciale)

Proprietor: GFA B. Solan and family
Vineyard size: 81 acres
Production: 15,000 cases
Plateau of maturity: Within 5–12 years of
the vintage

Grape varieties:
Sémillon—85%
Sauvignon Blanc—8%
Muscadelle—7%

Note: The production of the Cuvée Speciale is extremely limited.

Du Cros

Proprietor: Michel Boyer
Vineyard size: 106 acres
Production: 17,000 cases
Plateau of maturity: Within 3–10 years of
the vintage for the sweet wine, and 1–3
years for the dry wine

Grape varieties:
Sémillon—70%
Sauvignon Blanc—30%

Note: This property also makes one of the finest dry white wines of the region.

Domaine du Noble

Proprietor: Patrick Dejean
Vineyard size: 35 acres
Production: 4,400 cases
Plateau of maturity: Within 3–10 years of
  the vintage

Grape varieties:
Sémillon—85%
Sauvignon Blanc—15%

Loubens

Proprietor: Arnaud de Sece
Vineyard size: 50 acres
Production: 8,500 cases
Plateau of maturity: Within 5–10 years of
  the vintage

Grape varieties:
Sémillon—97%
Sauvignon Blanc—3%

Loupiac-Gaudiet

Proprietor: Marc Ducau
Vineyard size: 67 acres
Production: 7,500 cases
Plateau of maturity: Within 3–12 years of
  the vintage

Grape varieties:
Sémillon—80%
Sauvignon Blanc—20%

La Rame

Proprietor: Yves Armand
Vineyard size: 50 acres
Production: 4,000 cases
Plateau of maturity: Within 5–15 years of
  the vintage

Grape varieties:
Sémillon—75%
Sauvignon Blanc—25%

Note: A special *cuvée,* Réserve de Château, is even richer.

Ricaud

Proprietor: Alain Thienot
Vineyard size: 300 acres
Production: 2,000–2,500 cases
Plateau of maturity: Within 5–18 years of
  the vintage

Grape varieties:
Sémillon—80%
Sauvignon Blanc—15%
Muscadelle—5%

OTHER APPELLATIONS

While so much of the world of wine connoisseurship focuses on the great names and renowned appellations, there are a number of perennial overachievers operating in lowly regarded appellations.

Force of habit and an uncontrolled curiosity compel me to taste through the so-called *petits vins* of Bordeaux each time I visit. The following dry white and red wines represent the crème de la crème of my tastings from such appellations as Entre-Deux-Mers, Premières Côtes de Bordeaux, and generic Bordeaux. These wines are very fine, for the most part are humbly priced, and are made by highly motivated, sometimes compulsive/obsessive proprietors. I enthusiastically recommend that readers search them out. Even allowing for wide fluctuations in the value of the dollar vis-à-vis the euro, these wines rarely retail for more than $10 a bottle, yet frequently compete with wines selling for two to three times as much.

Note: Those marked with an asterisk are personal favorites.

RECOMMENDED PRODUCERS FROM THE APPELLATIONS OF ENTRE-DEUX-MERS, BORDEAUX, BORDEAUX SUPÉRIEUR, AND PREMIÈRES CÔTES DE BORDEAUX

WHITE WINES

Bauduc-Les Trois-Hectares (Bordeaux)
Bonnet (Entre-Deux-Mers)*
Bonnet—Cuvée Reservé (Entre-Deux-Mers)
Bourdicotte (Entre-Deux-Mers)
Carpia (Bordeaux)
Cayla (Bordeaux)
Cayla-Le Grand-Vent (Bordeaux)
La Closière (Bordeaux)*
Fondarzac (Entre-Deux-Mers)
Fongrave (Entre-Deux-Mers)
La Grande Clotte (Bordeaux)*
Launay (Entre-Deux-Mers)
Moulin-de-Launay (Entre-Deux-Mers)
Numero 1-Dourthe (Bordeaux)*
Château de Racaud (Cadillac)
Reignac (Bordeaux)*
Reynon-Vieilles Vignes (Bordeaux)*
Roquefort (Entre-Deux-Mers)
Thieuley (Bordeaux)*
Thieuley—Cuvée Francis Courselle (Bordeaux)
Toulet (Bordeaux)
La Tour Mirambeau (Entre-Deux-Mers)*
Turcaud (Entre-Deux-Mers)

RED WINES

Balestard (Bordeaux)*
Beaulieu Comtes de Tastes (Bordeaux Supérieur)*
Bois Pertuis (Bordeaux)*
Carsin (Premières Côtes de Bordeaux)
de Chastelet (Premières Côtes de Bordeaux)
Clos Chaumont (Premières Côtes de Bordeaux)*

La Cour d'Argent (Bordeaux Supérieur)
Courteillac (Bordeaux)*
La Croix de Roche (Bordeaux Supérieur)
Le Doyenné (Premières Côtes de Bordeaux)*
Epicure la Difference (Bordeaux)
L'Essence de Vignoble Dourthe (Bordeaux)*
Excellence de Bois Pertuis (Bordeaux)*
La Fleur Mongiron (Bordeaux)*
Fontenille (Bordeaux Supérieur)
Girolate (Bordeaux)*
La Grande-Chapelle (Bordeaux Supérieur)
Grand Mouëys (Premières Côtes de Bordeaux)
Grand Paris (Bordeaux Supérieur)*
Grée-Laroque (Bordeaux Supérieur)*
Haut-Nadeau (Bordeaux Supérieur)
Hostens-Picant (Ste.-Foy de Bordeaux)
Jonqueyrès (Bordeaux Supérieur)
La Joye (Bordeaux Supérieur)
La Maréchale (Bordeaux Supérieur)
Marjosse (Bordeaux)*
Parenchère (Bordeaux Supérieur)*
Parenchère—Cuvée Raphael Gazaniol (Premières Côtes de Bordeaux)*
Le Pin de Beau Soleil (Bordeaux Supérieur)*
Piras (Premières Côtes de Bordeaux)
Plaisance—Cuvée Aix (Premières Côtes de Bordeaux)
Plaisance—Cuvée Sortilège (Premières Côtes de Bordeaux)
Plaisance—Cuvée Tradition (Premières Côtes de Bordeaux)
de Plassan (Bordeaux)
Prieuré-Ste.-Anne (Premières Côtes de Bordeaux)
Rauzan Despagne—Cuvée Passion (Bordeaux Supérieur)*
Récougne (Bordeaux Supérieur)*
Reignac (Bordeaux Supérieur)*
Reynon (Premières Côtes de Bordeaux)*
Terres d'Agnes (Bordeaux Supérieur)
Thébot (Bordeaux)
Thieuley (Bordeaux)
Tire Pé-La Côte (Bordeaux)
Château de la Tour (Bordeaux Supérieur)
Tour de l'Espérance (Bordeaux Supérieur)
Tour de Mirambeau—Cuvée Passion (Bordeaux Supérieur)*
La Tuilerie de Puy (Bordeaux Supérieur)
Valmengaux (Bordeaux Supérieur)*

4: THE BORDEAUX WINE CLASSIFICATIONS

Bordeaux wines, in the minds of the wine trade and the wine consumer, are occasionally perceived by some as only as good as their official placement in one of the many classifications of wine quality. These classifications of wine quality have operated both for and against the consumer. Those few châteaux fortunate enough to "make the grade" have been guaranteed various degrees of celebrity status and respect. They have been able to set their price according to what their peers charge and have largely been the only châteaux to be written about by wine writers. As this book demonstrates, these top châteaux have not always produced wine becoming of their status in the official French wine hierarchy. As for the other châteaux, many have produced excellent wine for years, but because they were not considered of classified-growth quality in 1855, 1955, 1959, or 1995 (the dates at which the major classifications of wine quality occurred), they have received significantly less money for their wines and significantly less attention, particularly from writers. Yet it is the excellent wine produced from some of these lesser known châteaux that represents potential gustatory windfalls for the wine consumer.

THE 1855 CLASSIFICATION OF THE WINES OF GIRONDE

Of all the classifications of wine quality in Bordeaux, it is the 1855 Classification of the Wines of Gironde that is by far the most important. Among the thousands of châteaux in the Bordeaux region, 61 châteaux and winemaking estates in the Médoc and one in the Graves region were selected on the basis of their selling price and vineyard condition. Since 1855, only one change has occurred to the classification: In 1973, Château Mouton Rothschild was elevated to first-growth status. The 1855 classification, which established a five-tiered pyramid with originally four (now five as the result of the elevation of Mouton Rothschild) first growths, 15 second growths, 14 third growths, 10 fourth growths, and 18 fifth growths, while being a good general guide to the quality of some of the best Bordeaux wines, has numerous deficiencies that are chronicled in detail throughout this book. See page 1148: Bordeaux Wine: The Official Classification of 1855.

While the 1855 Classification of the Wines of Gironde dealt with red wine–producing estates, there was also a classification in 1855 of the estates in the Sauternes/Barsac region south of the city of Bordeaux that produces sweet, white wines. One estate, Château Yquem, was rated first, followed by 23 other châteaux divided equally into two groupings, "Premiers Crus" and "Deuxièmes Crus." See page 1149: Sauternes-Barsac: The Official Classification of 1855.

The other classifications of Bordeaux wine quality are much more modern-day creations, yet are no more accurate or reliable than the 1855 classification. In 1959, the wines of the Graves region immediately south of the city of Bordeaux were classified. Thirteen châteaux that produced red wine were given classified or "Cru Classé" status. Eight châteaux that produced white wine were classified. In 1955 the wines of St.-Emilion were classified into two categories, "Premiers Grands Crus Classés," or first great growths, and "Grands Crus Classés." This was followed by some corrections to the 1955 classification in 1959 and a revised classification in 1969. See page 1150: Graves: 1959 Official Classification. See also page 1151: St.-Emilion: 1995 Official Classification.

Pomerol, the smallest of the major Bordeaux wine districts, just northwest of St.-Emilion, has never had a classification of the wine quality of its châteaux. The lack of any categorization of Pomerol's wines has certainly not deterred quality. The most expensive and sought-after wine of all Bordeaux is Pétrus, and it is a Pomerol. In addition to Pétrus, there are at least another dozen châteaux in this district fetching prices for their wines that are equivalent to any one of the Médoc's famous second growths.

There is still another classification of Bordeaux wines that merits significant attention. It is the classification of the so-called Crus Bourgeois of the Médoc. Pejoratively called "petits châteaux" by many, these numerous small-, moderate- and large-size properties have never had the prestige or glory of the famous classified growths. Regardless of how high the quality of winemaking or how carefully the vineyards were managed and cared for, the Crus Bourgeois have been considered minor wines for years. In fact, many of them are, but there are increasing numbers of these châteaux that make wine on a very high level of excellence, comparable to at least a Médoc classified growth. Furthermore, they represent outstanding value and quality to knowledgeable wine consumers.

There were several unsuccessful attempts in the early half of the previous century to get an effective organization to promote the virtues of hundreds of the Médoc's lesser-known châteaux. A classification was accomplished in 1932 that listed 444 Cru Bourgeois châteaux, broken down into three categories. There are six "Crus Bourgeois Supérieurs Exceptionnels," 99 "Crus Bourgeois Supérieurs," and 339 "Crus Bourgeois."

Over the following decades many of these vineyards were absorbed by adjacent properties or went out of the winemaking business. In an effort to update this classification, new rankings were issued in 1966 by an organization of the Bourgeois châteaux called the Syndicat des Crus Bourgeois. The most recent result has been an updated list of 128 châteaux issued in 1978. Eighteen châteaux were given "Crus Grands Bourgeois Exceptionnels" status, 41 are entitled to the title "Crus Grands Bourgeois," and 68 are designated as "Crus Bourgeois." See page 1152: The Crus Bourgeois of the Médoc: The 1978 Syndicat's Classification.

The selection process utilized by the Syndicat left open a number of questions regarding the overall validity of the 1978 classification. First, only members of the Syndicat were entitled to recognition in the classification. For example, highly respected Cru Bourgeois châteaux such as de Pez in St.-Estèphe and Gloria in St.-Julien refused to join the Syndicat and are therefore excluded from its official rankings. In short, there is no question that while the current classification of the Crus Bourgeois is of some benefit, the exclusion of at least 10 well-known Crus Bourgeois producing top-quality wine merely on the grounds that they refused to become members of the Syndicat leaves a lot to be desired. In June 2003, a new revised classification of the Crus Bourgeois is to be announced.

While Bordeaux has an elaborate "ranking" system for its multitude of wine-producing châteaux, it is true that many of the châteaux clearly merit their placement, but many don't. In addition, there are quite a few châteaux that have not been officially recognized at all but make very fine wine year in and year out.

These historic classifications of wine quality were employed to both promote Bordeaux wines and establish well-delineated quality benchmarks. The classification system was based on the vineyard's soil base and reputation. However, owners and wine-makers change and, whereas others consistently make the best wine possible given the year's climatic conditions, some famous Bordeaux estates, because of negligence, incompetence, or just greed, produce mediocre and poor wine that hardly reflects its official pedigree.

The Bordeaux classifications are looked at in this book only from a consumer's or buyer's perspective. The quality of wine produced by a vineyard over the period 1961–2001 has been thoroughly examined. A qualitative rather than historical analysis of each major and many serious lesser known estates has been conducted, focusing on 1. the style and overall quality of the wine, 2. the wine's relative quality and record of quality over the period 1961–2001, and 3. its relative value.

The judgments, the commentaries, and the evaluations of the wines in this book are mine. They have been made on the basis of my extensive comparative tastings and numerous trips to Bordeaux since 1970. While no one will argue with the premise that the enjoyment of wine is strictly a personal and subjective matter, it is important to note that critical wine tasting at either the amateur or professional level without prejudice usually results in general agreement as to the greatest and worst wines. There are indeed quality benchmarks for Bordeaux wines, as there are for all the world's finest wines, and this book is intended to be a guide to those Bordeaux vineyards that establish the benchmarks for quality and value.

BORDEAUX WINE: THE OFFICIAL CLASSIFICATION OF 1855

FIRST GROWTHS

Château Lafite Rothschild (*Pauillac*)

Château Latour (*Pauillac*)

Château Margaux (*Margaux*)

Château Haut-Brion* (*Pessac, Graves*)

SECOND GROWTHS

Château Mouton Rothschild** (*Pauillac*)

Château Rausan-Ségla (*Margaux*)

Château Rauzan-Gassies (*Margaux*)

Château Léoville-Las Cases (*St.-Julien*)

Château Léoville Poyferré (*St.-Julien*)

Château Léoville Barton (*St.-Julien*)

Château Durfort-Vivens (*Margaux*)

Château Lascombes (*Margaux*)

Château Gruaud Larose (*St.-Julien*)

Château Brane Cantenac (*Cantenac-Margaux*)

Château Pichon-Longueville Baron (*Pauillac*)

Château Pichon-Lalande (*Pauillac*)

Château Ducru-Beaucaillou (*St.-Julien*)

Château Cos d'Estournel (*St.-Estèphe*)

Château Montrose (*St.-Estèphe*)

THIRD GROWTHS (*TROISIÈMES CRUS*)

Château Giscours (*Labarde-Margaux*)

Château Kirwan (*Cantenac-Margaux*)

Château d'Issan (*Cantenac-Margaux*)

Château Lagrange (*St.-Julien*)

* This wine, although a Graves, was universally recognized and classified as one of the four first growths.
** This wine was decreed a first growth in 1973.

Château Langoa Barton (*St.-Julien*)

Château Malescot St.-Exupéry (*Margaux*)

Château Cantenac Brown (*Cantenac-Margaux*)

Château Palmer (*Cantenac-Margaux*)

Château La Lagune (*Ludon-Haut-Médoc*)

Château Desmirail (*Margaux*)

Château Calon-Ségur (*St.-Estèphe*)

Château Ferriere (*Margaux*)

Château Marquis d'Alesme Becker (*Margaux*)

Château Boyd-Cantenac (*Cantenac-Margaux*)

FOURTH GROWTHS (QUATRIÈMES CRUS)

Château St.-Pierre (*St.-Julien*)

Château Branaire (*St.-Julien*)

Château Talbot (*St.-Julien*)

Château Duhart-Milon (*Pauillac*)

Château Pouget (*Cantenac-Margaux*)

Château La Tour Carnet (*St.-Laurent du Médoc*)

Château Lafon-Rochet (*St.-Estèphe*)

Château Beychevelle (*St.-Julien*)

Château Prieuré-Lichine (*Cantenac-Margaux*)

Château Marquis de Terme (*Margaux*)

FIFTH GROWTHS (CINQUIÈMES CRUS)

Château Pontet-Canet (*Pauillac*)

Château Batailley (*Pauillac*)

Château Grand-Puy-Lacoste (*Pauillac*)

Château Grand-Puy Ducasse (*Pauillac*)

Château Haut-Batailley (*Pauillac*)

Château Lynch-Bages (*Pauillac*)

Château Lynch-Moussas (*Pauillac*)

Château Dauzac (*Labarde-Margaux*)

Château Mouton-Baronne-Philippe (now D'Armhailac) (*Pauillac*)

Château du Tertre (*Arsac-Margaux*)

Château Haut-Bages Libéral (*Pauillac*)

Château Pedesclaux (*Pauillac*)

Château Belgrave (*St.-Laurent-Haut-Médoc*)

Château de Camensac (*St.-Laurent du Médoc*)

Château Cos Labory (*St.-Estèphe*)

Château Clerc Milon-Rothschild (*Pauillac*)

Château Croizet-Bages (*Pauillac*)

Château Cantemerle (*Macau-Haut-Médoc*)

SAUTERNES-BARSAC: THE OFFICIAL CLASSIFICATION OF 1855

FIRST GREAT GROWTH

Château d'Yquem

FIRST GROWTHS

Château Guiraud

Château La Tour Blanche

Château Lafaurie-Peyraguey

Château de Rayne-Vigneau

Château Sigalas-Rabaud

Château Rabaud-Promis

Clos Haut-Peyraguey

Château Coutet

Château Climens

Château Suduiraut

Château Rieussec

SECOND GROWTHS

Château d'Arche

Château Filhot

Château Lamothe

Château de Myrat

Château Doisy-Védrines

Château Doisy-Daëne

Château Suau

Château Broustet

Château Caillou

Château Nairac

Château de Malle

Château Romer

GRAVES: 1959 OFFICIAL CLASSIFICATION

CLASSIFIED RED WINES OF GRAVES

Château Haut-Brion (*Pessac*)

Château Bouscaut (*Cadaujac*)

Château Carbonnieux (*Léognan*)

Domaine de Chevalier (*Léognan*)

Château de Fieuzal (*Léognan*)

Château Haut-Bailly (*Léognan*)

Château La Mission Haut-Brion (*Pessac*)

Château La Tour Haut-Brion (*Talence*)

Château La Tour-Martillac (*Martillac*)

Château Malartic-Lagravière (*Léognan*)

Château Olivier (*Léognan*)

Château Pape-Clément (*Pessac*)

Château Smith Haut Lafitte (*Martillac*)

CLASSIFIED WHITE WINES OF GRAVES

Château Bouscaut (*Cadaujac*)

Château Carbonnieux (*Léognan*)

Domaine de Chevalier (*Léognan*)

Château Couhins (*Villenave-d'Ornon*)

Château La Tour-Martillac (*Martillac*)

Château Laville Haut-Brion (*Talence*)

Château Malartic-Lagravière (*Léognan*)

Château Olivier (*Léognan*)

ST.-EMILION: 1995 OFFICIAL CLASSIFICATION

FIRST GREAT GROWTHS (ST.-EMILION—PREMIERS GRANDS CRUS CLASSÉS)

Château Ausone

Château Cheval Blanc

Château Beau-Séjour Bécot

Château Angelus

Château Beauséjour

Château Belair

Château Canon

Château Figeac

Clos Fourtet

Château La Gaffelière

Château Magdelaine

Château Pavie

Château Trotte Vieille

GREAT GROWTHS (ST.-EMILION—GRANDS CRUS CLASSÈS)

Château L'Arrosée

Château Baleau

Château Balestard La Tonnelle

Château Bellevue

Château Bergat

Château Cadet-Bon

Château Cadet-Piola

Château Canon-La-Gaffelière

Château Cap de Mourlin

Château Chapelle Madeleine

Château Le Châtelet

Château Chauvin

Château Corbin Michotte

Château Coutet

Château Couvent-des-Jacobins

Château Croque Michotte

Château Curé-Bon

Château Dassault

Château Faurie-de-Souchard

Château Fonplégade

Château Fonroque

Château Franc-Mayne

Château Grand-Barrail-Lamarzelle-Figeac

Château Grand-Corbin

Château Grand Corbin-Despagne

Château Grand Mayne

Château Grand Pontet

Château Grandes Murailles

Château Guadet-St. Julien

Château Haut-Corbin

Clos des Jacobins

Château Jean-Faure

Château La Carte

Château La Clotte

Château La Clusière

Château La Couspaude

Château La Dominique

Clos La Madeleine

Château La Marzelle

Château La Tour-Figeac

Château La Tour-du-Pin-Figeac-Giraud-Bélivier

Château La Tour-du-Pin-Figeac

Château Laniote

Château Chapelle-de-la-Trinité

Château Larcis Ducasse

Château Larmande

Château Laroze

Château Lasserre

Château Le Couvent

Château Le Prieuré

Château Matras

Château Mauvezin

Château Moulin du Cadet

Château L'Oratoire

Château Pavie Decesse

Château Pavie Macquin

Château Pavillon-Cadet

Château Petit-Faurie-de-Soutard

Château Ripeau

Château St.-Georges-Côte Pavie

Clos St.-Martin

Château Sansonnet

Château Soutard

Château Tertre Daugay

Château Trimoulet

Château Trois-Moulins

Château Troplong Mondot

Château Villemaurine

Château Yon-Figeac

THE CRUS BOURGEOIS OF THE MÉDOC: THE 1978 SYNDICAT'S CLASSIFICATION

CRUS GRANDS BOURGEOIS EXCEPTIONNELS

d'Agassac (*Ludon*)

Andron Blanquet (*St.-Estèphe*)

Beau-Site (*St.-Estèphe*)

Capbern Gasqueton (*St.-Estèphe*)

Caronne-Ste.-Gemme (*St.-Laurent*)

Chasse-Spleen (*Moulis*)

Cissac (*Cissac*)

Citran (*Avensan*)

Le Crock (*St.-Estèphe*)

Dutruch-Grand Poujeaux (*Moulis*)

Fourcas Dupré (*Listrac*)

Fourcas Hosten (*Listrac*)

du Glana (*St.-Julien*)

Haut-Marbuzet (*St.-Estèphe*)

de Marbuzet (*St.-Estèphe*)

Meyney (*St.-Estèphe*)

Phélan Ségur (*St.-Estèphe*)

Poujeaux (*Moulis*)

CRUS GRANDS BOURGEOIS

Beaumont (*Cussac*)

Bel-Orme (*St.-Seurin-de-Cadourne*)

Brillette (*Moulis*)

La Cardonne (*Blaignan*)

Colombier-Monpelou (*Pauillac*)

Coufran (*St.-Seurin-de-Cadourne*)

Coutelin-Merville (*St.-Estèphe*)

Duplessis-Hauchecorne (*Moulis*)

La Fleur Milon (*Pauillac*)

Fontesteau (*St.-Sauveur*)

Greysac (*Bégadan*)

Hanteillan (*Cissac*)

Lafon (*Listrac*)

de Lamarque (*Lamarque*)

Lamothe-Cissac (*Cissac*)

Larose-Trintaudon (*St.-Laurent*)

Laujac (*Bégadan*)

Liversan (*St.-Sauveur*)

Loudenne (*St.-Yzans-de-Médoc*)

MacCarthy (*St.-Estèphe*)

de Malleret (*Le Pian*)

Martinens (*Margaux*)

Morin (*St.-Estèphe*)

Moulin à Vent (*Moulis*)

Le Meynieu (*Vertheuil*)

Les Ormes de Pez (*St.-Estèphe*)

Les Ormes Sorbet (*Couquèques*)

Patache d'Aux (*Bégadan*)

Paveil de Luze (*Soussans*)

Peyrabon (*St.-Sauveur*)

Pontoise Cabarrus (*St.-Seurin-de-Cadourne*)

Potensac (*Potensac*)

Reysson (*Vertheuil*)

Ségur (*Parempuyre*)

Sigognac (*St.-Yzans-de-Médoc*)

Sociando-Mallet (*St.-Seurin-de-Cadourne*)

du Taillan (*Le Taillan*)

La Tour de By (*Bégadan*)

La Tour du Haut-Moulin (*Cussac*)

Tronquoy-Lalande (*St.-Estèphe*)

Verdignan (*St.-Seurin-de-Cadourne*)

CRUS BOURGEOIS

Aney (*Cussac*)

Balac (*St.-Laurent*)

La Bécade (*Listrac*)

Bellerive (*Valeyrac*)

Bellerose (*Pauillac*)

Les Bertins (*Valeyrac*)

Bonneau (*St.-Seurin-de-Cadourne*)

Le Boscq (*St.-Christoly*)

du Breuilh (*Cissac*)

La Bridane (*St.-Julien*)

de By (*Bégadan*)

Cailloux de By (*Bégadan*)

Cap Léon Veyrin (*Listrac*)

Carcanieux (*Queyrac*)

Castera (*Cissac*)

Chambert (*St.-Estèphe*)

La Clare (*St.-Estèphe*)

Clarke (*Listrac*)

La Closerie (*Moulis*)

de Conques (*St.-Christoly*)

Duplessis Fabré (*Moulis*)

Fonpiqueyre (*St.-Sauveur*)

Fonréaud (*Listrac*)

Fort Vauban (*Cussac*)

La France (*Blaignan*)

Gallais-Bellevue (*Potensac*)

Grand Duroc Milon (*Pauillac*)

Grand-Moulin (*St.-Seurin-de-Cadourne*)

Haut-Bages Monpelou (*Pauillac*)

Haut-Canteloup (*Couquèques*)

Haut-Garin (*Bégadan*)

Haut Padarnac (*Pauillac*)

Houbanon (*Prignac*)

Hourton-Ducasse (*St.-Sauveur*)

De Labat (*St.-Laurent*)

Lamothe Bergeron (*Cussac*)

Le Landat (*Cissac*)

Landon (*Bégadan*)

Larivière (*Blaignan*)

Lartigue-de-Brochon (*St.-Seurin-de-Cadourne*)

Lasalle (*Potensac*)

Lavalière (*St.-Christoly*)

Lestage (*Listrac*)

Mac-Carthy-Moula (*St.-Estèphe*)

Monthil (*Bégadan*)

Moulin de la Roque (*Bégadan*)

Moulin Rouge (*Cussac*)

Panigon (*Civrac*)

Pibran (*Pauillac*)

Plantey de la Croix (*St.-Seurin-de-Cadourne*)

Pontet (*Blaignan*)

Ramage La Batisse (*St.-Sauveur*)

Romefort (*Cussac*)

La Roque de By (*Bégadan*)

de la Rose Maréchale (*St.-Seurin-de-Cadourne*)

St.-Bonnet (*St.-Christoly*)

Saint-Roch (*St.-Estèphe*)

Saransot (*Listrac*)

Soudars (*Avensac*)

Tayac (*Soussans*)

La Tour Blanche (*St.-Christoly*)

La Tour du Haut-Caussan (*Blaignan*)

La Tour du Mirail (*Cissac*)

La Tour St.-Bonnet (*St.-Christoly*)

La Tour St.-Joseph (*Cissac*)

des Tourelles (*Blaignan*)

Vernous (*Lesparre*)

Vieux-Robin (*Bégadan*)

WHO'S ON FIRST?

The 1855 Classification of the Wines of Gironde and the subsequent classifications of the wines of Graves and St.-Emilion created a rigid hierarchy that, to this day, dictates how much a consumer must spend for a bottle of classified-growth Bordeaux. Ironically, these historic classifications, which were created in an attempt to classify the quality of Bordeaux wine, are of little relevance in respect to determining the quality of wine produced by a specific château. At most, these classifications should be regarded by both the wine connoisseur and novice as informational items of historical significance only.

The following is my classification of the top 182 wines of Bordeaux, which I have divided into the same five-tiered hierarchy that was used in 1855. It is based on the performance of these châteaux from 1961–2001. More weight has been given to the direction the property is heading and the quality of wine produced from 1982–2001 than what the property may have done in the 1961–1981 period. This is done simply because today is the golden age of Bordeaux. Bordeaux is prosperous, and more properties are making better wine with better facilities and advice than ever before.

There are 182 properties in my classification. Since I have included the wines of all the major appellations of Bordeaux that were excluded (except for Haut Brion), particularly St.-Emilion, Pomerol, Graves, Fronsac, and Canon-Fronsac, the number of top classified growths is larger than the 61 that made the grade in 1855.

This classification is, of course, my own, but I can say that I have tasted all of these producers' wines from all of the significant vintages, not once, but numerous times. In addition, I have visited the great majority of these properties and have studied their placement in this classification intensely. Nothing I have stated is arbitrary, but it is a personal judgment based on years of tasting and years of visiting Bordeaux. Furthermore, I think I can say it was done with no bias. Some of the proprietors with whom I have had some very difficult times over the years are included as first growths. Some of the owners whom I personally like and respect have not done well. That is the risk, but in the end, I hope this consumer's look at the top estates in Bordeaux serves a constructive purpose for those properties who feel unfairly demoted, while I hope those that have won acclaim and recognition here will continue to do what it takes to make the best wine.

MY 2003 CLASSIFICATION OF THE TOP CHÂTEAUX OF BORDEAUX

FIRST-GROWTH QUALITY

Angelus (*St.-Emilion*)

Ausone (*St.-Emilion*)

Cheval Blanc (*St.-Emilion*)

Cos d'Estournel (*St.-Estèphe*)

Ducru-Beaucaillou (*St.-Julien*)

L'Eglise-Clinet (*Pomerol*)

L'Evangile (*Pomerol*)

Haut-Brion (*Graves*)

Lafite Rothschild (*Pauillac*)

Lafleur (*Pomerol*)

Latour (*Pauillac*)

Léoville-Las Cases (*St.-Julien*)

Margaux (*Margaux*)

La Mission Haut-Brion (*Graves*)

Montrose (*St.-Estèphe*)

Mouton Rothschild (*Pauillac*)

Palmer (*Margaux*)

Pavie (*St.-Emilion*)

Pétrus (*Pomerol*)

Le Pin (*Pomerol*)

SECOND-GROWTH QUALITY

Beauséjour-Duffau (*St.-Emilion*)

Bellevue (*St.-Emilion*)

Bellevue-Mondotte (*St.-Emilion*)

Calon-Ségur (*St.-Estèphe*)

Canon-La-Gaffelière (*St.-Emilion*)

Certan de May (*Pomerol*)

Clerc Milon (*Pauillac*)

Clinet (*Pomerol*)

Clos l'Église (*Pomerol*)

Clos St.-Martin (*St.-Emilion*)

La Conseillante (*Pomerol*)

Figeac (*St.-Emilion*)

La Fleur de Gay (*Pomerol*)

La Gomerie (*St.-Emilion*)

Grand-Puy-Lacoste (*Pauillac*)

Gruaud Larose (*St.-Julien*)

Hosanna (*Pomerol*)

Léoville Barton (*St.-Julien*)

Léoville Poyferré (*St.-Julien*)

Lynch-Bages (*Pauillac*)

Magrez-Fombrauge (*St.-Emilion*)

Malescot St.-Exupéry (*Margaux*)

Monbousquet (*St.-Emilion*)

La Mondotte (*St.-Emilion*)

Marojallia (*Margaux*)

Nenin (*Pomerol*)

Pape-Clément (*Graves*)

Pavie Decesse (*St.-Emilion*)

Pavie Macquin (*St.-Emilon*)

Péby Faugères (*St.-Emilion*)

Pichon-Longueville Baron (*Pauillac*)

Pichon-Longueville—Comtesse de Lalande (*Pauillac*)

Quinault-L'Enclos (*St.-Emilion*)

Rauzan-Ségla (*Margaux*)

Rol Valentin (*St.-Emilion*)

Smith-Haut-Lafite (*Pessac-Léognan*)

Le Tertre-Roteboeuf (*St.-Emilion*)

Troplong Mondot (*St.-Emilion*)

Trotanoy (*Pomerol*)

Valandraud (*St.-Emilion*)

Vieux-Château-Certain (*Pomerol*)

THIRD-GROWTH QUALITY

Beau-Séjour Bécot (*St.-Emilion*)

Bon Pasteur (*Pomerol*)

Branaire Ducru (*St.-Julien*)

Brane Cantenac (*Margaux*)

Les Carmes Haut-Brion (*Graves*)

Chauvin (*St.-Emilion*)

Domaine de Chevalier (*Graves*)

Clos des Lunelles (*Côtes de Castillon*)

Croix St.-Georges (*Pomerol*)

Duhart-Milon (*Pauillac*)

La Fleur-Pétrus (*Pomerol*)

La Gaffelière (*St.-Emilion*)

Gracia (*St.-Emilion*)

Grand Mayne (*St.-Emilion*)

Les Grandes Murailles (*St.-Emilion*)

Haut-Bailly (*Graves*)

Haut-Bergey (*Pessac-Léognan*)

L'Hermitage (*St.-Emilion*)

d'Issan (*Margaux*)

Kirwan (*Margaux*)

Lagrange (*St.-Julien*)

Larrivet-Haut-Brion (*Pessac-Léognan*)

Latour à Pomerol (*Pomerol*)

Magdelaine (*St.-Emilion*)

Pontet-Canet (*Pauillac*)

FOURTH-GROWTH QUALITY

D'Armailhac (*Pauillac*)

L'Arrosée (*St.-Emilion*)

Barde-Haut (*St.-Emilion*)

Chasse-Spleen (*Moulis*)

La Clémence (*Pomerol*)

La Couspaude (*St.-Emilion*)

La Dominique (*St.-Emilion*)

Ferrand-Lartigue (*St.-Emilion*)

de Fieuzal (*Graves*)

La Fleur de Boüard (*Lalande-de-Pomerol*)

Les Forts de Latour (*Pauillac*)

Gazin (*Pomerol*)

Giscours (*Margaux*)

Gloria (*St.-Julien*)

Lafon-Rochet (*St.-Estèphe*)

La Lagune (*Ludon*)

La Louvière (*Graves*)

St.-Domingue (*St.-Emilion*)

St.-Pierre (*St.-Julien*)

Sociando-Mallet (*Médoc*)

Soutard (*St.-Emilion*)

Talbot (*St.-Julien*)

FIFTH-GROWTH QUALITY

Domaine l'A (*Côtes de Castillon*)

D'Aiguilhe (*Côtes de Castillon*)

d'Angludet (*Margaux*)

Bahans Haut-Brion (*Graves*)

Balestard La Tonnelle (*St.-Emilion*)

Batailley (*Pauillac*)

Belair (*St.-Emilion*)

Berliquet (*St.-Emilion*)

Beychevelle (*St.-Julien*)

Cadet-Piola (*St.-Emilion*)

Canon (*St.-Emilion*)

Canon-de-Brem (*Canon-Fronsac*)

Cantemerle (*Macau*)

Cantenac Brown (*Margaux*)

Chambert-Marbuzet (*St.-Estèphe*)

De Chambrun (*Lalande-de-Pomerol*)

Charmail (*Médoc*)

Citran (*Médoc*)

Clos des Jacobins (*St.-Emilion*)

Clos la Madeleine (*St.-Emilion*)

Clos René (*Pomerol*)

Couvent-des-Jacobins (*St.-Emilion*)

La Croix du Casse (*Pomerol*)

La Croix de Gay (*Pomerol*)

Croque Michotte (*St.-Emilion*)

La Dauphine (*Fronsac*)

Destieux (*St.-Emilion*)

Durfort-Vivens (*Margaux*)

Domaine de l'Eglise (*Pomerol*)

Feytit-Clinet (*Pomerol*)

La Fleur de Jaugue (*St.-Emilion*)

Fombrauge (*St.-Emilion*)

Fontenil (*Fronsac*)

Fougas Maldorer (*Côtes de Bourg*)

Fontenil (*Fronsac*)

Le Gay (*Pomerol*)

Grand Pontet (*St.-Emilion*)

Grand-Puy Ducasse (*Pauillac*)

La Grave à Pomerol (*Pomerol*)

Jean de Gué—Cuvée Prestige (*Lalande-de-Pomerol*)

Haut-Bages Libéral (*Pauillac*)

Haut-Batailley (*Pauillac*)

Haut-Marbuzet (*St.-Estèphe*)

Labégorce Zédé (*Margaux*)

Lanessan (*Haut-Médoc*)

Langoa Barton (*St.-Julien*)

Larcis Ducasse (*St.-Emilion*)

Larmande (*St.-Emilion*)

Lascombes (*Margaux*)

Pierre de Lune (*St.-Emilion*)

Lynsolence (*St.-Emilion*)

Marquis de Terme (*Margaux*)

Maucaillou (*Moulis*)

Meyney (*St.-Estèphe*)

Moulin-Haut-Laroque (*Fronsac*)

Moulin-Pey-Labrie (*Canon-Fronsac*)

Les Ormes de Pez (*St.-Estèphe*)

Pavillon Rouge du Château Margaux
(*Margaux*)

Petit Village (*Pomerol*)

Potensac (*Médoc*)

Poujeaux (*Moulis*)

Prieuré-Lichine (*Margaux*)

Roc des Cambes (*Côtes de Bourg*)

Rouget (*Pomerol*)

de Sales (*Pomerol*)

Sanctus (*St.-Emilion*)

Siran (*Margaux*)

du Tertre (*Margaux*)

La Tour-Figeac (*St.-Emilion*)

La Tour Haut-Brion (*Graves*)

Tour Haut-Caussan (*Médoc*)

Tour du Haut-Moulin (*Haut-Médoc*)

Trotte Vieille (*St.-Emilion*)

La Vieille-Cure (*Fronsac*)

5: THE ELEMENTS FOR MAKING GREAT BORDEAUX WINE

Traditionalists often wax poetic about "the good ol' days" and that "they just don't make Bordeaux the way they used to." In fact, for Bordeaux wines, times have never been better, both climatically and financially. Moreover, the quality of winemaking in Bordeaux has never been higher. The greatest wines ever made in Bordeaux are those that are produced today. The most prominent factor about the best red and white wines of Bordeaux is their remarkable longevity. In great years, the aging potential of these wines is unequalled by any other table wines produced in the world. Even in lesser vintages, the wines often need a good 5–8 years to develop fully. The reasons? In order of importance: the grape varieties, the soil, the climate, and the methods of winemaking, which are discussed in the sections that follow.

BORDEAUX GRAPES FOR RED WINES

For red wines, three major grape varieties are planted and two minor varieties have largely fallen out of favor. The choice of grape varieties used for making Bordeaux has a profound influence on the style of wine that is ultimately produced. Hundreds of years of practice have allowed specific winemaking châteaux to select only the grape varieties that perform best in their soil.

If one were to give an average formula for a percentage of grapes planted at a majority of the Médoc châteaux for red wines in the Médoc, it would be 60–65% Cabernet Sauvignon, 10–15% Cabernet Franc, 0–15% Merlot (this varietal is falling out of favor), and 3–8% Petit Verdot. Each château has its own best formula for planting its vineyards; some prefer to use more Merlot, some more Cabernet Sauvignon or Cabernet Franc, and some more Petit Verdot. As a general rule, the very light, highly drained, gravelly soils tend to support Cabernet Sauvignon better than Merlot. For that reason, one finds very high percentages of Cabernet Sauvignon in the appellation of Margaux. In contrast, in the heavier, more clay-dominated soils of St.-Estèphe, Merlot tends to fare better. Consequently, a higher percentage of Merlot is found in St.-Estèphe. Of course, there are exceptions. In the Margaux appellation, Château Palmer uses a significant portion of Merlot in the final blend, as does Château Pichon-Longueville—Comtesse de Lalande in Pauillac. However, the two most important grapes for a highly successful vintage in the Médoc are Cabernet Sauvignon and Merlot. The Cabernet is more widely planted in the Médoc simply because it ripens well and flourishes in the gravelly, well-drained soil that exists in the top vineyards there. The Merlot is popular because, when blended with the tannic, tough, deeply colored Cabernet Sauvignon, it offers softness, flesh, and suppleness to balance out the sterner texture of the Cabernet Sauvignon.

If a château uses a high percentage of Cabernet Sauvignon in its blend, in all likelihood the wine will be densely colored, big, full-bodied, tannic, and very ageworthy. On the other hand, if a high percentage of Merlot is used in the blend, in most cases suppleness and precocious charm are the preferred personality traits.

In the Médoc, Cabernet Franc is also used in smaller percentages. Cabernet Franc lacks the color of Cabernet Sauvignon and Merlot, but does offer complex aromatic components (particularly aromas of mint, herbs, and spices) that the Bordelais call finesse. Yet it often has trouble reaching full phenolic maturity in the Médoc and is being replaced with Merlot. The Petit Verdot is planted in very small percentages despite the fact that it ripens very late and in most vintages rarely achieves full maturity. It is often used by those châteaux that employ a high percentage of Merlot because the Petit Verdot provides the hard tannic backbone that is otherwise absent as a result of a high concentration of Merlot.

Each of these four major red grape varieties ripens at a different time. The Merlot is always the first grape to blossom and to become fully mature. Cabernet Franc is second, followed by Cabernet Sauvignon and then Petit Verdot. Few wine consumers realize that spring frost and varying weather patterns at different times of the growing season can seriously affect some of these grape varieties, while sparing others. The production from the Merlot grape, because of its early flowering characteristic, is frequently curtailed by spring frost. In addition, Merlot is the grape most susceptible to rot from moist or damp weather conditions because its thin skin is not as tough and is less resistant to disease than that of the Cabernet Sauvignon or Petit Verdot.

This fact alone can be critical for the success of châteaux with extensive Merlot plantations. On more than one occasion, late-season rains have washed out the late-picking properties with vineyards dominated by Cabernet Sauvignon, while the vineyards of Merlot plantings have already been harvested under optimum conditions. When one asks why the Merlot-based wines, such as Pétrus and Trotanoy, were so successful in 1964 or 1967 compared to the disappointing Cabernet Sauvignon–based wines, such as Mouton Rothschild and Lafite Rothschild, the answer is that the Merlot crop was harvested in perfect weather conditions long before the Cabernet crop, which was drenched and diluted by late occurring torrential rains.

On the right bank of the Gironde River are the two principal appellations of St.-Emilion and Pomerol. Here, significantly higher percentages of the Merlot and Cabernet Franc grapes are planted. Much of the soil of these two appellations is not as well-drained and is frequently heavier because of a significant clay content. The Cabernet Sauvignon is not fond of such soils and accordingly smaller amounts of it are planted, unless the vineyard is situated on a particularly well-drained, gravelly soil base, as a few are in these appellations (for example, Figeac). The Merlot, however, takes well to this type of heavier soil and surprisingly so does the Cabernet Franc. There are many exceptions, but in St.-Emilion the standard formula for grape varieties is close to 70% Merlot and 30% Cabernet Franc with little Cabernet Sauvignon. In Pomerol, Merlot is clearly the key. Except for a handful of estates, such as Vieux Château Certan, little Cabernet Sauvignon is planted. The average vineyard's composition in Pomerol would be 70–100% Merlot, and the balance Cabernet Franc. Consequently, it is not surprising to find wines from these two regions maturing faster and being generally fruitier, more supple, and lusher than wines from the Médoc.

In the Graves region, the soil is extremely gravelly (as the name implies), thereby affording excellent drainage. As in the Médoc, the Cabernet Sauvignon is favored, but there is more Cabernet Franc and Merlot in Graves with wines that are usually lighter as a result. However, in rainy years, the Graves wines frequently turn out better than others simply because of the outstanding drainage the vineyards enjoy in this region. The 1994 vintage is a classic case in point.

The advantage of knowing the percentage of grape varieties planted at a particular château is that one can predict with some degree of certainty which areas may have performed better than others even before the critics begin issuing their tasting judgments. This can be done by knowing the climatic conditions leading up to and during the harvest and how the different grape varieties perform under such conditions.

Rarely does Bordeaux have a perfect vintage for all four red wine grape varieties. In

2000, 1990, 1989, 1985, and 1982, all the grape varieties ripened consistently. These years were profoundly influenced by the opulence and ripeness of the Merlot grape, and consequently, the wines are higher in alcohol and are fleshier and softer than in years that favor the Cabernet Sauvignon. Two classic examples of top Cabernet Sauvignon years are 1996 and 1986. In general, the Merlot overproduced and many wines that contain a large percentage of Merlot were fluid and lacking structure. Those Médocs with a high percentage of Cabernet Sauvignon produced superb wines that were very much influenced by the fully ripe Cabernet Sauvignon grapes that were harvested in early and mid-October under the influence of an "Indian summer."

CABERNET SAUVIGNON—A grape that is highly pigmented, very astringent, and tannic that provides the framework, strength, dark color, character, and longevity for the wines in a majority of the vineyards in the Médoc. It ripens late, is resistant to rot because of its thick skin, and has a pronounced black currant aroma that is sometimes intermingled with subtle herbaceous scents that take on the smell of cedarwood with aging. Virtually all Bordeaux châteaux blend Cabernet Sauvignon with other red grape varieties. In the Médoc, the average percentage of Cabernet Sauvignon in the blend ranges from 40–85%, in Graves 40–60%, in St.-Emilion 10–35%, and in Pomerol 0–20%.

MERLOT—Utilized by virtually every château in Bordeaux because of its ability to provide a round, generous, fleshy, supple, alcoholic wine, Merlot ripens, on the average, 1–2 weeks earlier than Cabernet Sauvignon. In the Médoc, this grape reaches its zenith in several châteaux that use high percentages of it (Palmer, Cos d'Estournel, and Pichon-Lalande), but its fame is in the wines it renders in Pomerol and St.-Emilion where it is used profusely. In the Médoc, the average percentage of Merlot in the blend ranges from 5–45%. In Graves, it ranges from 20–40%, in St.-Emilion 50–100%, and in Pomerol 35–100%. Merlot produces wines lower in acidity and tannin than Cabernet Sauvignon, and as a general rule, wines with a higher percentage of Merlot are drinkable sooner than wines with a higher percentage of Cabernet Sauvignon. In spite of this precociousness, the finest Merlot-based wines can age just as long as the Cabernet Sauvignons.

CABERNET FRANC—A relative of Cabernet Sauvignon that ripens slightly earlier, Cabernet Franc (called "Bouchet" in St.-Emilion and Pomerol) is used in small to modest proportions to add complexity and bouquet to a wine. Cabernet Franc has a pungent, often very spicy, minty, sometimes weedy, olive-like aroma. It does not have the fleshy, supple character of Merlot, nor the astringence, power, and color of Cabernet Sauvignon. It has increasingly grown out of favor in the Médoc. An average percentage of Cabernet Franc used in the blend in the Médoc is 0–20%, in Graves 5–35%, in St.-Emilion 0–66%, in Pomerol 5–30%.

PETIT VERDOT—A useful but generally difficult red grape because of its very late ripening characteristics, Petit Verdot provides intense color, mouth-gripping tannins, and high sugar—and thus high alcohol when it ripens fully, as it did in 2001, 2000, 1996, 1990, 1989, and 1982 in Bordeaux. When unripe, it provides a nasty, sharp, acidic character and tends to be eliminated from the final blend. In the Médoc, few châteaux (Palmer and Pichon-Lalande being the most notable exceptions) use more than 5% in the blend. In Graves, St.-Emilion, and Pomerol, Petit Verdot is virtually non-existent.

MALBEC—The least-utilized red grape (also called "Pressac" in St.-Emilion and Pomerol) of the major varietals, Malbec has fallen into disfavor, and in most vineyards it has now been replanted with Merlot. Its future in Bordeaux's best vineyards seems doubtful.

BORDEAUX GRAPES FOR WHITE WINES

Bordeaux produces both dry and sweet white wine. There are usually only three grape varieties used, Sauvignon Blanc and Sémillon for both dry and sweet wine, and Muscadelle, which is used sparingly for the sweet wines.

SAUVIGNON BLANC—Used for making both the dry white wines of Graves and the sweet white wines of the Sauternes-Barsac region, Sauvignon Blanc renders a very distinctive wine with a pungent, somewhat herbaceous aroma and crisp, austere flavors reminiscent of grapefruit and other citrus. Among the dry white Graves, a few châteaux employ 100% Sauvignon Blanc, but most blend it with Sémillon. Less Sauvignon Blanc is used in the winemaking blends in the Sauternes-Barsac region than in Graves.

SÉMILLON—Very susceptible to the famous noble rot called botrytis, which is essential to the production of excellent, sweet wines, Sémillon is used to provide a rich, creamy, intense texture as well as waxy, lanolin, honeyed flavors to both the dry wines of Graves and the rich, sweet wines of Sauternes-Barsac. Sémillon is quite fruity when young, and wines with a high percentage of Sémillon seem to accumulate weight and viscosity as they age. For these reasons, higher percentages of Sémillon are used in making the sweet wines of the Sauternes-Barsac region than in producing the white wines of Graves.

MUSCADELLE—The least planted of the white wine grapes in Bordeaux, Muscadelle is a very fragile grape that is quite susceptible to disease, but when healthy and mature, it produces a wine with an intense, flowery, perfumed character. It is used only in tiny proportions by châteaux in the Sauternes-Barsac region and sparingly by the white wine producers of Graves.

SOIL

It is not unusual to hear Bordeaux's best wine-makers say that the "wine is made in the vineyard," not the winery. This is the so-called "terroirist" point of view, in which 80–90% of the quality comes from the vineyard. They are correct, although a competent winery staff must be in place to translate these raw materials into topflight wines. It is interesting to compare the traditional attitude in California, where the primary considerations for making quality wine have been the region's climatic profile, the expertise of the wine-maker, and the availability of high technology to sculpture the wine. While a growing number of California wineries are beginning to pay greater attention to soil, few Bordelais will argue with the premise that the greatness of their wine is a result of the soil, or *terroir,* and not the wine-maker or vinification equipment.

MAKING SENSE OF TERROIR

"Knowing in part may make a fine tale, but wisdom comes from seeing the whole"
—AN ASIAN PROVERB

And so it is with the concept of *"terroir,"* that hazy, intellectually appealing notion that a plot of soil plays the determining factor in a wine's character. The French are the world's most obsessed people regarding the issue of *terroir.* And why not? Many of that country's most renowned vineyards are part of an elaborate hierarchy of quality based on their soil and exposition. And the French would have everyone believe that no one on planet Earth can equal the quality of their Pinot Noir, Chardonnay, Cabernet, Syrah, etc. because their privileged *terroir* is unequaled. One of France's most celebrated wine regions, Burgundy, is often cited as the best place to search for the fullest expression of *terroir.* Followers of *terroir* (the terroirists) argue that a particular piece of ground and its contribution to what is grown there give its product a character that is distinctive and apart from that same product grown on different soils and slopes. Burgundy, with its classifications of grand cru and premier cru vineyards, village vineyards, and generic viticultural areas, is the terroirists raison d'être.

Lamentably, *terroir* has become such a politically correct buzzword that in some circles it is an egregious error not to utter some profound comments about finding "a sense of somewhereness" when tasting a Vosne-Romanée-Les Malconsorts or a Latricières-Chambertin. Leading terroirists make a persuasive and often eloquent case about the necessity of finding, as they put it, "the true voice of the land" in order for a wine to be legitimized.

Yet like so many things about wine, especially tasting, there is no scientific basis for anything they propose. What they argue is what most owners of France's finest vineyards give lip service to—that for a wine to be authentic and noble it must speak of its *terroir.*

On the other side of this issue are the "realists" (or should I call them modernists?). They suggest that *terroir* is merely one of many factors that influence the style of a wine. The realists argue that a multitude of factors determine a wine's style, quality, and character. Soil, exposition, and microclimate (*terroir*) most certainly impart an influence, but so do the following:

1. Rootstock—Is it designed to produce prolific or small crop levels?
2. Yeasts—Does the wine-maker use the vineyard's wild yeasts or are commercial yeasts employed? Every yeast, wild or commercial, will give a wine a different set of aromatics, flavor, and texture.
3. Yields and vine age—High yields from perennial overcroppers result in diluted wine. Low yields, usually less than two tons per acre or 35–40 hectoliters per hectare, result in wines with much more concentration and personality. Additionally, young vines have a tendency to overproduce, whereas old vines produce small berries and less wine. Crop thinning is often employed with younger vineyards to increase the level of concentration.
4. Harvest philosophy—Is the fruit picked underripe to preserve more acidity, or fully ripe to emphasize the lushness and opulence of a given varietal?
5. Vinification techniques and equipment—There are an amazing number of techniques that can change the wine's aromas and flavors. Moreover, equipment choice (different presses, destemmers, etc.) can have a profound influence on the final wine.
6. *Élevage* (or the wine's upbringing)—Is the wine brought up in oak barrels, concrete vats, stainless-steel, or large oak vats (which the French call *foudres*)? What is the percentage of new oak? All of these elements exert a strong influence on the wine's character. Barrels from different coopers impart different flavors, something I have witnessed time and time again. Additionally, transferring wine (racking) from one container to another has an immense impact on a wine's bouquet and flavor. Is the wine allowed to remain in long contact with its lees (believed to give the wine more aromatic complexity and fullness)? Or is it racked frequently for fear of picking up an undesirable lees smell?
7. Fining and filtration—Even the most concentrated and profound wines that terroirists consider quintessential examples of the soil can be eviscerated and stripped of their personality and richness by excessive fining and filtering. Does the wine-maker treat the wine with kid gloves, or is the wine-maker a manufacturer/processor bent on sculpturing the wine?
8. Bottling date—Does the wine-maker bottle early to preserve as much fruit as possible, or does he bottle later to give the wine a more mellow, aged character? Undoubtedly, the philosophy of when to bottle can radically alter the character of a wine.
9. Cellar temperature and sanitary conditions—Some wine cellars are cold and others are warm. Different wines emerge from cold cellars (development is slower and

the wines are less prone to oxidation) than from warm cellars (the maturation of aromas and flavors is more rapid and the wines are quicker to oxidize). Additionally, are the wine cellars clean or dirty?

These are just a handful of factors that can have extraordinary impact on the style, quality, and personality of a wine. As the modernists claim, the choices that man himself makes, even when they are unquestionably in pursuit of the highest quality, can contribute far more to a wine's character than the vineyard's *terroir*.

Where do I stand on this issue? I do believe it is an important component in the production of fine wine. However, I would argue that the most persuasive examples of *terroir* do not arise in Bordeaux or Burgundy, but rather from Alsace. If one is going to argue *terroir*, the wine has to be made from exceptionally low yields, fermented with only the wild yeasts that inhabit the vineyard, brought up in a neutral medium, such as old barrels, cement tanks, or stainless-steel, given minimal cellar treatment, and bottled with little or no fining or filtration.

For example, if I were to take up the cause of the terroirists, I would use one of Alsace's greatest domaines, that of Leonard and Olivier Humbrecht, to make a modest case for *terroir*. The Humbrechts do everything to emphasize the differences in their vineyard holdings. Yet in a blind tasting, why is it so easy to identify the wines of Zind-Humbrecht? Certainly their Hengst-Riesling tastes different than their Riesling from Clos St.-Urbain. The question is, is one tasting the *terroir* or the wine-maker's signature? Zind-Humbrecht's wines, when matched against other Alsatian wines, are more powerful, richer, and more intense. Zind-Humbrecht's yields are lower and they do not filter the wine at bottling. Yet this is a case where the wines not only possess an identifiable wine-maker's signature, but also a distinctive vineyard character.

Lalou Bize-Leroy of the Domaine Leroy is often cited as France's (hence the world's) pre-eminent terroirist. She is a persuasive woman and talks a mighty game when it comes to how her vineyard parcels impart specific characteristics to her wines. But when Bize's wines are evaluated in blind tastings, the obvious conclusion is that she fashions more concentrated and ageworthy red burgundies than her peers. Once a taster is familiar with the style of her wines (there are subtle differences), Leroy's wines can be easily identified in a blind tasting because of their power, purity, richness, and exceptional intensity rather than by any particular *terroir* characteristic. The same can be said for many of Burgundy's finest producers. Anyone who is familiar with the style of the Domaine de la Romanée-Conti can usually pick their wine out of a blind tasting because of the singular style of its winemaking. Burgundy wine-maker Jacques Seysses, a producer who received a five-star rating in my book on Burgundy and someone I admire tremendously, runs up the *terroir* flag as fast as any Frenchman, saying, "man can destroy, not create." Seysses, who utilizes 100% new oak for all of his grand crus, produces wines of extraordinary finesse and elegance. However, when tasted, his wines are dominated by his own winemaking autograph and can be picked out, not because they emanate from vineyards such as Clos de la Roche, Clos St.-Denis, or Bonnes Mares, but because of his distinctive style.

Terroir, as used by many of its proponents, is often a convenient excuse for upholding the status quo. If one accepts the fact that *terroir* is everything and is essential to legitimize a wine, how should consumers evaluate the wines from Burgundy's most famous grand cru vineyard, Chambertin? This 32-acre vineyard boasts 23 different proprietors. But only a handful of them appear committed to producing an extraordinary wine. Everyone agrees this is a hallowed piece of ground, but I can think of only a few producers—Domaine Leroy, Domaine Ponsot, Domaine Rousseau, Domaine des Chézeaux (Ponsot makes the wine for Chézeaux)—that produce wines that merit the stratospheric reputation of this vineyard. Yet the Chambertins of three of these producers, Leroy, Ponsot, and Rousseau, are completely different in style. The Ponsot wine is the most elegant, supple, and round; Leroy's is the most tannic, backward, concentrated, and meaty; Rousseau's is the darkest-colored, most dominated by new oak, and most modern in style, taste, and texture. Among the other 18 or 20 producers (and I am not even thinking about the various *négociant* offerings) that Burgundy wine enthusiasts are likely to encounter on retailers' shelves range from mediocre to appallingly thin and insipid. What wine, may I ask, speaks for the soil of Chambertin? Is it the wine of Leroy, the wine of Ponsot, the wine of Rousseau?

Are terroirists kindergarten intellectuals who should be doing more tasting and less talking? Of course not. But they can be accused of naïvely swallowing the tallest tale in French winedom. On the other hand, the realists should recognize that no matter how intense and concentrated a wine can be from a modest vineyard, it will never have the sheer complexity and class of a Haut-Brion or Cheval Blanc.

In conclusion, think of *terroir* as you do salt, pepper, and garlic. In many dishes they can represent an invaluable component, imparting wonderful aromas and flavors. But if consumed alone, they are usually difficult to swallow. Moreover, all the hyperventilation about *terroir* obscures the most important issue of all—identifying and discovering those producers who make wines worth drinking and savoring!

In large measure, the Bordelais are less outspoken about *terroir* than their Burgundian counterparts. Yet *terroir* is used as a convenient excuse to defend their famous classifications of quality (in particular the 1855 hierarchy). It is also utilized by the Médoc aristocracy to diminish the accomplishments of many young St.-Emilion and Pomerol proprietors . . . "the other, more peasant side of the river (Gironde)," they claim in pejorative terms.

The famous Médoc area of Bordeaux is a triangular land mass, bordered on the west by the Atlantic Ocean, on the east by the wide Gironde River, and on the south by the city of Bordeaux. The top vineyards of the Médoc stretch out on the eastern half of this generally flat land on slightly elevated slopes facing the Gironde River. The soil is largely unfit for any type of agriculture other than grape growing. It is extremely gravelly and sandy, and the subsoil of the Médoc ranges from heavy clay soil (producing heavier, less fine wines) to lighter chalk and gravels (producing finer, lighter wines).

The very gravelly soil, which is the predominant geological characteristic of the Bordeaux vineyards, operates as an excellent drainage system, as well as being permeable enough for the vines' roots to penetrate deep into the subsoil for nutrients, water, and minerals.

In the Pessac-Léognan/Graves region south of the city of Bordeaux, the name of the region reflects the very rocky soil, which is even more deeply embedded with gravel than in the Médoc. This contributes to the unique flavor that some commentators have suggested is a mineral-like, earthy taste in the wines of this region. The regions of St.-Emilion and Pomerol are situated 20 miles to the east of the city of Bordeaux. St.-Emilion has various soil bases. Around the charming medieval city of St.-Emilion are the châteaux that are said to sit on the *côtes,* or hillsides. These hillsides were once the sides of a river valley, and the soil is primarily chalk, clay, and limestone. Some of the famous châteaux that sit on the *côtes* of St.-Emilion include Ausone, Canon, Pavie, and Belair.

Several miles to the northwest of St.-Emilion is the Graves section of St.-Emilion, a gravelly, sandy outcropping bordering the Pomerol appellation. The St.-Emilion châteaux located in this Graves area produce a different style of wine—more fleshy, more fruity, more accessible than the austere, tannic, and reserved wines produced from vineyards on the limestone, chalk, and clay hillsides of the town of St.-Emilion. Two of the best-known châteaux in this area of St.-Emilion are Cheval Blanc and Figeac. Of course, exceptions in style within each subregion exist, but in broad terms, there are two major types of St.-Emilion wines: a Graves style and a *côtes* style, and the style is a direct result of the soil base in which the vines are planted.

In Pomerol, which borders the Graves section of St.-Emilion, the soil composition is quite similar, yet variations exist. Pomerol's most famous estate—Pétrus—sits on an elevated plateau that has a unique, rather heavy clay soil unlike any other vineyard in Pomerol.

The subtle differences in soil composition and their effect on the style and personality of the wine are best exemplified by three examples of adjoining vineyards. On the border of the Médoc communes of Pauillac and St.-Julien, three highly respected properties—the first-growth Pauillac Latour, the second-growth St.-Julien Léoville-Las Cases, and the second-growth Pauillac Pichon-Longueville Baron—sit together with each one's vineyard contiguous to the other's. The yield from the vineyards, the percentage of each vine planted, the method of making the wine, the average age of the vines, the types of grape varieties, and finally, the time the wine spends aging in the cask are not dramatically different for all three châteaux. However, all three wines differ substantially in taste, style, texture, and evolution. This is because all three have totally different soil bases.

In Pomerol, one has only to compare the vineyard of that appellation's most famous wine, Pétrus—planted in heavy clay soil rich in iron—with the soil of its immediate neighbor, La Fleur Pétrus—which has little clay, but much more sand and gravel. Both wines could not, despite almost exactly the same vinifications by the same people, be more different.

Soil is undoubtedly a very important factor in the character and diverse style of Bordeaux wines. It is not, however, as the Bordelais would have one believe, the only element necessary to make a great wine. The importance of a hospitable climate, conservative viticultural practices whereby the use of fertilizers is kept to a minimum, aggressive pruning procedures, and of course, careful vinification and handling are all significant factors in the making of great wine. Even with the finest technology, a great winemaking team, and the best, well-drained, gravelly soil, great wine cannot be made without optimal climatic conditions that produce fully mature ripe grapes.

CLIMATE

The great vintages of Bordeaux have always been characterized by growing seasons that have been abnormally hot, dry, and sunny. The excellent to great vintages of Bordeaux, such as 2000, 1990, 1989, 1982, 1961, 1959, 1949, 1947, 1945, 1929, 1921, and 1900, have all shared several distinctive climatic characteristics—heat, sunshine, and drought-like conditions. Several prominent Bordeaux château proprietors, who have recently claimed that disastrous vintages such as 1968, 1965, and 1963 will never occur again because of vineyard treatment, advances in winemaking, and concentration machines, seem to forget that good wine cannot be made from unripe, vegetal-tasting grapes. Bordeaux, like any major viticultural area, must have plenty of sunshine, dry weather, and heat in order to produce excellent wine.

When the Bordeaux châteaux have to wait until October to harvest their grapes rather than September, it is usually a sign that the growing season has been abnormally cool and even worse, wet. A review of the finest vintages in Bordeaux reveals that the commencement date of the red wine harvest almost always occurs in September:

1870—September 10	1970—September 27
1893—August 18	1975—September 22
1899—September 24	1978—October 7
1900—September 24	1982—September 13
1921—September 15	1985—September 29
1929—September 23	1986—September 23
1945—September 13	1989—August 31
1947—September 15	1990—September 12
1949—September 27	1995—September 20
1953—September 28	1996—September 16
1959—September 20	2000—September 20
1961—September 22	

In comparison, here are the commencement dates of the harvests for some of Bordeaux's most notoriously bad vintages:

1951—October 9	1969—October 6
1954—October 10	1972—October 7
1956—October 14	1977—October 3
1957—October 4	1984—October 5
1963—October 7	1991—September 30
1965—October 2	1992—September 29
1968—September 20	1993—September 26

The pattern would appear to be obvious. Great years are characterized by plentiful amounts of sunshine, heat, and dry weather. Under such conditions the grapes ripen steadily and quickly and the harvests begin early. Poor years result from inadequate supplies of these precious natural commodities. The grapes never ripen fully and are picked in either an unripe or a rain-diluted condition.

There are few exceptions to the climatic patterns for excellent and poor vintages. For example, 1979 (picked October 3) was a late-harvest year that produced good wines. In recent years there has been a growing tendency by producers to attempt to obtain what they call *sur-maturité*. The old rule that governed the harvest in Bordeaux was the so-called 100-day rule, which dictated harvesting the grapes 100 days after the flowering. Now, in an effort to make wines full-bodied, richer, and lower in acidity, the 100-day custom has grown to 110 or even 120 days, Mother Nature permitting. This new trend in Bordeaux may well result in many more excellent October harvests, such as 1979, than in the past, when an October harvest often meant poorer quality. The great Cabernet Sauvignon vintages of 1986 and 1996 were the result of harvests that occurred during the first two weeks of October.

The climatic patterns leading to excellent vintages for red wines in Bordeaux do not apply to the production of the sweet white wines made in the Sauternes-Barsac region. Great vintages in this region require a combination of misty, humid mornings and dry, sunny afternoons. This daily pattern of climatic events enable the noble rot (botrytis) to begin to develop on the grapes. It is interesting that each grape succumbs to the botrytis infection on a different timetable. Some grapes quickly become totally infected, others not until weeks later. The key to forming the great, luscious, sweet wines in this area is an extended period of alternating humidity and dry heat that permits the botrytis infection to take place. During this period, the château must harvest the infected grapes by hand numerous times if the highest quality is to be achieved, for it is the botrytis infection that causes the remaining grape juice to be intensely concentrated and imparts to it the distinctive smell and flavor of a late-harvest, decadently rich, sweet wine. Of course, the harvest for the sweet wines of Sauternes-Barsac almost always takes place long after the red wine grapes have been picked and made into wine in the Médoc, Graves, St.-Emilion, and Pomerol. It also occurs when Bordeaux's weather becomes the most risky—late October and November.

A week or more of deluge can destroy the chances for a successful crop in Sauternes and Barsac. More often than not, the grape crop is damaged by late-season rains that wash the noble rot from the grapes and also cause other grapes to swell, thus diminishing their intensity. In the last 20 years, only 2001, 1996, 1990, 1989, 1988, 1986, 1983, 1976, 1975, and 1971 have been uniformly excellent growing seasons for the sweet wine producers of this region.

THE VINIFICATION AND *ÉLEVAGE* OF BORDEAUX WINES

The production of red wine begins when the freshly harvested grapes are crushed. The traditional practice unfolds as follows: 1. picking, 2. destemming and crushing, 3. pumping into fermentation tanks, 4. fermenting of grape sugar into alcohol, 5. macerating, or keeping the grape skins and pips in contact with the grape juice for additional extract and color, 6. racking, or transferring the wine to small 55-gallon barrels or large tanks for the secondary or malolactic fermentation to be completed, 7. putting the wine in oak barrels for aging, and 8. bottling the wine.

In Bordeaux, the average harvest takes three or more weeks to complete for the dry white and red wines. For the sweet wines, the harvest can take as long as two months to complete. The white wine grapes used for making the dry wines ripen earliest and are picked first. This is followed by the red grape Merlot, and then the other red grape varieties, Cabernet Franc, Cabernet Sauvignon, and lastly, Petit Verdot. The fact that the Merlot ripens earliest makes it an interesting sequence to monitor. In 1998, 1994, 1987, 1967, and 1964, the châteaux that had extensive plantings of Merlot, primarily those in St.-Emilion and Pomerol, harvested early and their vineyards produced much better wines than the châteaux in the Médoc that had to wait for their Cabernet to ripen and were caught by fall rains. In such a year when significant rains damage the overall crop quality, the early pickers, normally the right bank communes of St.-Emilion and Pomerol, will have completed most of their harvest. As the aforementioned vintages attest, they may have succeeded brilliantly whereas their counterparts in the Médoc had to deal with bloated, rain-swollen Cabernet Sauvignon grapes.

MAKING THE RED WINE IN THE TRADITIONAL STYLE

The most critical decision when it comes to making quality wine is the date of harvest. An error made at harvesting cannot be reversed, and a previous year's work can be largely undone. Grapes must be picked at the peak of maturity or the flavors will be marred by either too much acidity or herbaceousness. Assuming the grapes are harvested properly at full physiological ripeness, when the grapes arrive from the vineyards the top châteaux will go through a traditional and laborious method of hand sorting before they go to the destemmer-crusher machine. This process of sorting grapes and discarding those that are damaged, rotten, or underripe is essential to produce high-quality wine.

Most châteaux claim to get the best results by instructing their pickers to remove and discard damaged or unhealthy grape bunches in the vineyard. Certainly the need for careful picking of grapes exists every year, but in vintages where there has been extensive rot in the vineyards, pickers for the most reputable châteaux make a very severe selection—called a *triage*—in which the damaged berries are removed from each bunch at the time of picking.

The first decision the wine-maker must make is whether the grapes are to be partially destemmed or totally destemmed. Today the great majority of the châteaux destem completely. This policy is in keeping with Bordeaux's current passion to make rich, supple wines that can be drunk young but will age well. Several notable châteaux continue to throw a percentage of stems into the fermentation tank with the crushed grapes.

The opponents of adding the stems argue that they add a vegetal coarseness to a wine, soak up some of the color-giving material, and add too much tannin to the wine.

Once the grapes have been destemmed by an apparatus the French call a *fouloir égrappoir*, the partially crushed berries are pumped into tanks for the commencement of the fermentation.

For much of the 1980s, the trend in Bordeaux was to replace the large, old, oak and cement fermentation vats with stainless-steel, temperature-controlled tanks. They are easy to clean, and it is easy to control the temperature, an element that is especially important when the grapes are harvested in torridly hot conditions as in 1982. Despite the increasing number of properties that have converted to stainless-steel tanks, the traditional large oak *cuvées* and concrete *cuvées* can still be found. In the 1990s, with the advent of the so-called "garage wine" movement (see the introduction to St.-Emilion), it became increasingly fashionable at many small, right-bank estates, especially in St.-Emilion, to utilize the small, open top wood fermenters so common in Burgundy.

While stainless-steel may be easier to use, great vineyards managed by meticulous wine-makers have proven that great wine can be made in oak, cement, or steel fermentation tanks. Once the grapes have been put into the vat, the wild yeasts that inhabit the vineyard (and in many cases additional cultured yeasts) begin the process called fermentation—the conversion of the grape sugars into alcohol. At this critical point, the temperature of the fermenting juice must be monitored with extreme care, as how hot or how cold the fermentation is affects the resulting style of the wine.

Some of the breakthrough technology being utilized in Bordeaux today comes into play with grape must. Very expensive machines that perform procedures to remove water from swollen grapes via two primary methods—reverse osmosis and evaporation under a vacuum—are increasingly applied by many estates, particularly in years where Bordeaux has had too much rain. These techniques, which have been employed largely since the mid-1980s, do indeed concentrate the wines by removing water while leaving the extract of flavor and solids of the wine undisturbed. Leading Bordeaux oenologists and I have discussed at length the long-term effect reverse osmosis and evaporation by vacuum might have on the resulting wines. The results to date have been impressive, although wines made with these methods will need 10–20 years of cellaring before they can effectively be judged. Nevertheless, the early promise shown by these methods, such as removing water from the diluted must in rainy years, has been impressive, but I am sure that as with any technique, extremes in use will prove harmful to the finished wine.

Most Bordeaux wine-makers ferment a red wine at 25–30°C. Few châteaux allow the temperature to exceed 30°C. These properties allow the fermentation to go up to 32–33°C. The higher temperatures are aimed at extracting as much color and tannins as possible from the grape skins. The risk of a temperature in excess of 35°C is that acetic bacteria will grow and flourish. It is these acetic bacteria that cause a wine to take on a flawed, vinegary smell. An additional danger of fermentation temperatures in excess of 35°C is that the natural yeasts will be destroyed by the heat, and the fermentation will stop completely, causing what is referred to as a "stuck fermentation." As a general rule, the châteaux that ferment at high temperatures are normally aiming for high-extract, rich, and tannic wines. Those châteaux that ferment at cooler temperatures of 25°C or less usually are trying to achieve a lighter, fruitier, less tannic style of wine. However, for châteaux that ferment at high temperatures, constant vigilance is mandatory.

Fermentation tanks must be watched 24 hours a day, and if a dangerously high temperature is reached, the grape juice must be cooled immediately. With stainless-steel tanks, this can be done rather simply by running cool water over the outside of the tanks. For concrete and wooden tanks, the wine must be siphoned off and run through cooling tubes.

During the vinification, a cap or *chapeau* is formed as a result of the solid materials, grape skins, stems, and pips rising to the top of the fermentation tank. Wine-makers must be careful to keep the cap moist, even submerged in some cases, to encourage additional extractive material to be removed from the color- and tannin-giving skins. Additionally, the cap must be kept wet so as to prevent bacterial growth. The pumping of the fermented wine juice over the cap is called the *remontage* in French and "pumping over the cap" in English.

When the fermentation begins, the wine-maker must make another critical decision that will influence the style of the wine: to chaptalize or not. Chaptalization is the addition of sugar to increase the alcohol content. It is employed widely in Bordeaux because this region only occasionally has a vintage where perfect grape ripeness and maturity are obtained. In most years, the grapes do not have sufficient natural sugar content to produce wines with 12% alcohol. Therefore, the Bordeaux châteaux aim to increase the alcohol content by 1–2°C. Only in years such as 2000, 1990, 1989, 1982, and 1961 has little chaptalization been necessary because of the superb ripeness achieved by the grapes in those years.

After the total grape sugar (and added sugar if necessary) has been converted to alcohol, the primary or alcoholic fermentation is complete. It is at this stage that another important winemaking decision must be made: The wine-maker must decide how long to macerate the grape skins with the wine. The length of the maceration period has a direct bearing on whether the wine will be rich, well-colored, tannic, and long-lived, or supple, precocious, and ready to drink earlier. At most major Bordeaux châteaux the maceration period is 7–14 days, making the average total time the wine spends in contact with the skins about 21 days. This period is called the *cuvaison.* Today, some of the more avant garde wine producers are practicing extended macerations of 30–50 days.

Following the *cuvaison,* the infant wine is transferred off its lees, which are composed of the grape skins and pips and called the *marc,* into clean tanks or wood barrels. This free-run juice is called the *vin de goutte.* The skins are then pressed and the resulting press wine, or *vin de presse,* is a heavily pigmented, tannic, chewy, coarse wine that will, in many instances, be eventually blended back into the free-run wine juice. Some wine-makers, not wanting a firm, tannic wine, refuse to use any press wine in the blend. Others, who want to add a little muscle and firmness to their wines, will add 10–20%. Some wine-makers desirous of a robustly styled, intense wine will blend it all back in with the free-run *vin de goutte.* In most cases, the decision to utilize the press wine is conditioned on the type of wine the vintage produced. In a year such as 2000, 1996, 1986, or 1982, the addition of press wine would, in most cases, make the wine too tannic and robust. In light vintages such as 1973 and 1980, where the quality of the free-run juice lacks strength, firmness, and color, more of the highly pigmented, tannic press wine will be used.

The secondary fermentation, or malolactic fermentation, in which the tart malic acidity is converted into softer, creamier, lactic acidity, is a gentle step in the evolution of the young red wine. In some châteaux, the malolactic fermentation occurs simultaneously with the alcoholic fermentation, but at most properties the malolactic fermentation takes place over a period of months, usually October following the harvest through the end of January. In certain years, the malolactic fermentation may continue through spring and summer following the vintage, but this is rare in Bordeaux. Malolactic fermentation is especially critical for red wines because it adds roundness and character. One of the movements that began in the late 1980s and continued in the 1990s is that more and more top-quality châteaux did part or all of the malolactic fermentation in barrels as opposed to vats. This procedure, commonly employed in Burgundy, is relatively revolutionary in Bordeaux because the estates are so large and fermentations, both primary and malolactic, have traditionally occurred in vat. However, malolactic in barrel is believed to give the wines a creamier texture, as well as better integration of oak. Certainly those estates that have employed this procedure have produced very successful wines. To my thinking, malolactic in barrel does make the wine more flattering to taste when young, but at 18 months of age, whether malo took place in barrel or vat, the differences are negligible.

The use of new versus old oak barrels for wine aging has been hotly debated in winemaking circles. In Bordeaux, the famous first growths—Lafite Rothschild, Mouton Rothschild, Latour, Margaux, Haut-Brion, and the famous trio from the right-bank communes of St.-Emilion and Pomerol, Cheval Blanc, Ausone, and Pétrus—use 100%

new oak barrels for virtually every vintage. For the other well-run châteaux, 33–60% new oak barrels per vintage seems to produce a comfortable marriage of fruit, tannin, and oak. Unquestionably, the higher the percentage of new oak barrels used, the richer the wine must be so as not to be overwhelmed by the oaky, vanilla aromas and flavors. For example, many of the wines from the 1980 and 1973 vintages, which produced light yet fruity wines, were simply not big enough or rich enough to handle aging in the new oak barrels they received. New barrels impart a significant tannin content, as well as vanilla oakiness to a wine, and therefore, they must be used judiciously. In essence, it is no different than the use of salt, pepper, or garlic in a chef's preparation. Balance is everything.

One of the side effects of Bordeaux's modern-day prosperity from the success of recent vintages is the tremendous investment in new winery equipment, and, in particular, new barrels. Abuse of new oak can obliterate the fruit of a wine, and while the huge massive fruit and concentration of wines from vintages like 2000, 1990, or 1982 can easily handle exposure to ample amounts of new oak, my tastings of the more delicate, less intense and concentrated 1981s and 1997s has frequently left me wondering whether too much new oak cooperage was doing more harm than good. It seems that with many of the estates below the first-growth level now routinely using 50–75% new oak, there is a danger that too many Bordeaux wines are becoming excessively woody. While the use of new oak is recommended and avoids the potential sanitation problems posed by the usage of older barrels, the extremely high yields witnessed in Bordeaux since the mid-1980s and the lack of extract in many wines is not fully masked by the gobs of new oak aromas still found in some of these Bordeaux vintages. Fortunately, the better producers are increasingly cautious about overoaking their wines.

One of the remarkable aspects of a red Bordeaux wine is its long sojourn in small oak barrels. In most vintages, this period of aging will take from 12 months to as long as 24–30 months. This period of barrel aging has been shortened noticeably during the last several decades. Is the rush to get the wine in the bottle and to the marketplace becoming an obsession? Bordeaux wine-makers have tried to capture more fruit and freshness in their wines and reduce the risk of oxidation or overly woody, dry, tannic wines from too much exposure to wood. The great majority of Bordeaux châteaux now bottle their wine in late spring and early summer of the second year after the harvest. For example, even the blockbuster 2000 Bordeaux wines were bottled from May to July 2002. It is rare for a châteaux to bottle in late fall or the following winter, as was the practice 20 years ago. Several prominent châteaux that do bottle some vintages later than the others include Margaux and Calon-Ségur, both of which rarely bottle unless the wine has had at least 24 months in small oak casks.

The period of cask aging will be even shorter in vintages like 1997, 1993, 1992, 1981, 1979, or 1976 where the wines lack great concentration and depth of character, and it will be longer in years such as 2000, 1998, 1996, 1995, 1990, 1986, 1983, 1982, and 1975 where many wines are very full, rich, highly pigmented, and concentrated. The principle is simple: lighter, frailer wines can easily be overwhelmed by oak aging, whereas robust, virile, rich wines can take and need significantly more exposure to oak casks. However, there is no question that the practical and commercial realities of the

Bordeaux wine business now dictate that the wine will be bottled within two years of the harvest in all but the most unusual circumstances.

During the aging period in oak barrels, the new wine is racked up to four times the first year. Racking is an essential step necessary for clarifying the wine. This process involves transferring the clear wine off its deposit, or lees, that has precipitated to the bottom of the barrel. If racking is not done promptly and carefully, the wine will take on a smell of rotten eggs as a result of hydrogen sulfide emissions that come off the lees. The rackings are an intensely laborious process, but the French theory is that it is these lees, which float in the wines and eventually fall to the bottom of the barrel, that are the substance and material that give Bordeaux wines their remarkable aromatic and flavor complexity. In an effort to preserve fruit intensity, freshness, and purity as well as build fat and texture, in the late 1980s and 1990s the more progressive wine producers began to rack much less, preferring a much longer contact time for the wine to sit on its lees. A relatively new technique called micro-bullage, also became de rigueur at cutting-edge estates. This process involves little or no racking, but keeping the lees oxygenated by small tubes that aerate the lees.

One of the most significant technological developments of the 1970s and 1980s, which has now fallen from favor, is the filtration of the new wine prior to its placement in barrels. This process, employed widely in the New World, removes the solids from the wine and results in a clearer wine that needs to be racked significantly less—only one time the first year. The proponents of this process get a cleaner, purer wine that does not have to be handled as much, and therefore is less prone to oxidation. They can also get their wine into new oak barrels by the end of October, giving it a three- to four-month head start on its neighbors' wines when the critics arrive in April to do their tastings. Opponents of such a procedure argue that the process strips the wine of its solids and therefore deprives the wine of the important aromatic, flavor, and textural elements necessary for it to achieve complex aromas and flavors. The critics claim that it is only a labor-saving, cunning procedure designed to make the wine show well at an early stage. In 2003, the critics seem to have won the day as very few producers utilize such techniques.

While the red wine rests in barrels, all châteaux carry out another procedure designed to ensure that the wine is brilliant, clean, and free of hazy, suspended colloidal matter when bottled. It is called fining. Fining has traditionally been done with egg whites that function to attract and trap suspended solids in the barrel of wine. They then drop to the bottom of the barrel with the other solids that have been precipitated. Wines that are overly fined lose body, length, concentration, and character. Today, fining is often done immediately prior to bottling, in large tanks. Additionally, many châteaux have abandoned the traditional egg whites in favor of more efficacious substances like bentonite and gelatin. In Bordeaux, rarely is a wine fined more than twice for fear of removing too much flavor at the expense of absolute clarity. But there is no doubt that too many wines in Bordeaux are excessively fined and stripped of flavor and body. The trend in the 1980s and 1990s has been to curtail or totally eliminate the fining if possible.

In addition to the careful vinification and handling of the young red wine, one of the common characteristics at the best-run châteaux in Bordeaux is an extremely rigid selection process for determining which wine will be bottled under the château's name, and which wine will be bottled under a secondary label, or sold in bulk to a cooperative or broker in Bordeaux. The best châteaux make their first selection in the vineyard. For example, the wine from young vines (normally those 7–8 years old) is vinified separately from the wine from older vines. To even a neophyte taster, the difference between wine produced from 25-year-old vines and a wine from 5-year-old vines is remarkable. Young vines may produce a well-colored wine, but the wine rarely has the depth or rich, concentrated character of a wine from older vines. For that reason, the top châteaux never blend wine from the younger section of the vineyard in with the wine from the older vines.

There are a dwindling number of châteaux that refuse to discriminate between old and new vines, and the quality of their wines frequently suffers as a result. But in 2003, selection, often draconian in nature, is employed by all the top estates.

In addition to the selection process in the vineyard, the best châteaux also make a strict selection of the finished wine, normally in January or February following the vintage. At this time, the winemaking staff, together with the consulting oenologist and, in many cases, the owner, will taste all the different lots of wine produced in the vintage, and then decide which lots or *cuvées* will go into the château's wine, and which lots will be bottled under a secondary label or sold off in bulk. This procedure is also accompanied by the assemblage, wherein the best lots of wine are blended together, including the blending of the different red grape varieties, Merlot, Cabernet Sauvignon, Cabernet Franc, and Petit Verdot. It is no coincidence that the châteaux making the most severe selections frequently produce the best wines of Bordeaux. Virtually all châteaux make their assemblage in December or January following the vintage. The selection process for what goes in the château's grand vin has become increasingly brutal since the mid-1980s. In addition to the proliferation of second labels for the lots deemed lacking, there are now even third labels. Many of the finest Bordeaux châteaux will eliminate 35% to as much as 70% of the total harvest to produce something truly prodigious under the grand vin label. For example, the two most draconian selections take place at Lafite Rothschild and Léoville-Las Cases where it is not unusual for 65–70% of the total crop to be relegated to a second label or sold off in bulk. This has significantly increased the overall quality of Bordeaux's finest wines.

Unless something unusual occurs in the barrel (a dirty barrel that causes bacterial spoilage is the most common problem) during the aging process, called *élevage,* the wine will be transferred from the barrel to the fermentation tanks, given its last fining, and then bottled at the château.

The idea of exclusively bottling the wine at the château (it is designated on the label with the words "*mise en bouteille au château*") is a rather recent development. Until the late 1960s, many of the Bordeaux châteaux routinely sent barrels of their wine to brokers in Bordeaux and merchants in Belgium or England where the wine would be bottled. Such a practice was fraught with the potential not only for fraud, but for sloppy handling of the wine as a result of poor, unsanitary bottling facilities.

Now the châteaux all have modern bottling facilities, and all the classified growths, as well as the great majority of Crus Bourgeois, bottle their own wine. The bottling of the château's entire production in a given vintage can take from one month to almost three months at the largest properties. Yet one of the distinctive characteristics of Bordeaux wine is that each château's production for a given year is bottled within this time frame. This guarantees to the consumer that, given the same treatment and cellar storage, the wine should be relatively consistent from bottle to bottle. Moreover, most châteaux start and finish bottling within three weeks.

At the time of the bottling operation, the wine-maker has one last decision to make that will influence the style (and perhaps the quality) of the wine. The use of sophisticated micropore filter machines to remove any solids or other colloidal particles that may have escaped the various racking procedures and finings is the final step that can have serious consequences for the quality of the wine. Fortunately, most châteaux either continue to filter only by passing the wine through a coarse cellulose filter pad or eschew filtration completely. I don't know of any serious properties that sterile-filter their wines. Some châteaux believe that filtration is essential for a healthy, clean bottle of wine, whereas others claim that it is totally unnecessary and robs and strips the wine of body, flavor, and potential life.

Who is right? There is ample authority to support both sides in the filtration versus nonfiltration argument. Certainly, the fear on the part of retailers, restaurateurs, wholesalers, importers, and wine producers that wine consumers think that sediment in a wine is a sign of a flawed wine has tragically caused many châteaux to overreact and run their wines through very fine, tight filters that undoubtedly eviscerate the wine. Fortunately, the major châteaux have been content to do just a slight, coarse polishing filtration, aimed at removing large colloidal suspensions, or have simply refused to filter the wine at all, hoping the fickle consumer will learn one day that a sediment, or *dépôt* as the French say, is in reality one of the healthiest signs in an older bottle of Bordeaux.

Since filtration of wine is a relatively recent trend (it came of age in the mid-1970s) in oenology, only time in the bottle will tell whether filtration robs a wine of richness, complexity, and life as its opponents argue. For the record, if the wine is biologically stable and clear, as are most Bordeaux wines, excessive fining and filtration seems unnecessary. I have done enough blind tastings of filtered versus unfiltered *cuvées* to remain adamantly against the entire process. Anyone who says that filtration removes nothing from an otherwise stable wine is either a fool, a liar, or a paid publicist for the winery that vigorously filters.

Once the wine is bottled, the châteaux usually refuse to release the wine for shipment until it has rested for 2–4 months. The theory is that the bottling operation churns up the wine so much that it is shocked and requires at least several months to recover. My tastings of immediately bottled Bordeaux have often corroborated this fact.

MAKING THE WHITE WINE IN THE TRADITIONAL STYLE

The most important consideration when producing the dry white wines of Bordeaux is to retain an element of crispness and freshness in the wines. Otherwise they would taste stale or heavy. No one in Bordeaux has made more progress with white wine vinification than Denis Dubourdieu. It was Dubourdieu, the great white winemaking guru of Bordeaux, who pioneered the use of cold fermentation temperatures (15–17°C) and extended skin contact called *maceration péliculaire*. Because the skins impart the wine's aroma and flavor, this process extracts considerably more fragrance and flavor intensity. These techniques have resulted in a plethora of interesting, tasty, character-filled, dry white wines not only from the prestigious Graves region of Bordeaux, but also from such appellations as Premières Côtes de Bordeaux and Entre-Deux-Mers.

The style of the wine is also affected by whether it is vinified and/or aged in stainless-steel tanks or oak barrels. In either case, the wine-maker must be careful to guard against oxidation. This is easily done by treating the wine with sulphur dioxide, an antioxidant. Most of the high-class white wines, such as Domaine de Chevalier, Haut-Brion-Blanc, Laville Haut-Brion, and de Fieuzal, clarify the young, grapy white wine by a process known as *débourbage*. More commercially oriented producers use a centrifuge, or intensely filter the wine after the vinification to clarify it. The more traditional *débourbage*, in my opinion, produces a more complex and interesting wine.

Another of the most crucial decisions made regarding the ultimate style of white Bordeaux is whether or not the wine is allowed to go through a malolactic fermentation. Malolactic fermentation can be encouraged by heating the vats. While most burgundies are put through a malolactic fermentation, Bordeaux wines usually have their malolactic blocked by the addition of sulphur. The numerous low-acid vintages of the 1980s dictated that malolactic be eschewed.

If the wine is stable, most dry white wines of Bordeaux tend to be bottled within 3–6 months of the vintage in order to emphasize their freshness and crispness. Those white wines that are meant to be longer-lived and more ageworthy are often kept in new oak casks from one month to as long as 16–18 months (as in the case of the great white wine made at Domaine de Chevalier). All dry white Bordeaux wine is routinely fined and filtered at bottling. Yet producers of wines such as de Fieuzal, Laville Haut-Brion, Haut-Brion-Blanc, and Domaine de Chevalier process them as minimally as possible for fear of stripping the wines of their aromatic complexity and flavor dimension.

The production of the sweet white wines of Barsac and Sauternes is an even more labor-intensive and risky procedure. The best wines are almost always the result of numerous passes through the vineyard to select only those grapes that have been attacked by the noble rot, *Botrytis cinerea*. The yields from such selective harvesting (done grape by grape rather than bunch by bunch) are not permitted to exceed 25 hectoliters per hectare, which is well below two tons per acre. Compared to the 40–60 hectoliters per hectare that many of the neighboring red wine producers routinely obtain, the difficult economics of producing a Sauternes-Barsac wine are obvious. Once the Botrytized grapes are harvested, the grapes are crushed. The fermentation is allowed to continue until the sugar is converted into a 14–15% alcohol level in the wines. This still leaves unfermented sugar in the wine. The combination of the heady alcohol character with the sweetness of the wine, as well as the distinctive aromas and lavishly rich texture created in part by the botrytis, results in sweet wines that are among the most riveting in the world.

One of the interesting techniques developed in Sauternes-Barsac was the introduction in the late 1980s of a procedure called cryo-extraction. This controversial process involves chilling the incoming grapes in order to turn their water into ice particles before pressing, leaving the water behind and increasing the concentration of richness in the grape must. It has been practiced at such celebrated châteaux as Rayne-Vigneau, Rieussec, and Rabaud-Promis. A cryo-extraction machine even exists at Château Yquem. This procedure, while still in an experimental stage, has yielded impressive early results. Critics who claim that it is simply a labor-saving gimmick may be proven wrong. With cryo-extraction, the botrytis-affected grapes are processed without any potential for dilution because the frozen water is left behind, concentrating the extracted juice to just the essence of the grapes.

After the fermentation, the sweet white wines of the top estates are usually aged in cask, of which a significant percentage is new. At Yquem, the wine is always aged in 100% new oak for at least three years. At other top estates, such as Climens and Suduiraut, the percentage of new oak varies from 50–100%. There remain a handful of estates, most notably Gilette, that abhor new oak, yet also produce great wine.

At bottling, most of the sweet wines are fined and lightly filtered, although Yquem, along with neighboring de Fargues and Gilette, continue to bottle their wines after an assemblage without any filtration.

6: A USER'S GUIDE TO BORDEAUX

CELLARING

Bordeaux, like any fine wine, has to be stored properly if it is to be served in a healthy condition when mature. All wine enthusiasts know that subterranean wine cellars that are vibration free, dark, damp, and kept at a constant 55°F are considered perfect for wine. However, few of us have our own castle with such accommodations for our beloved wines. While such conditions are the ideal, Bordeaux wines will thrive and develop well in other environments as well. I have tasted many old Bordeaux wines from closet and basement cellars that reach 65°F in the summer, and the wines have been perfect. When cellaring Bordeaux, keep the following rules in mind and you are not likely to be disappointed by a wine that has gone prematurely over the hill.

RULE 1

Do try to guarantee that the wine is kept as cool as possible. The upper safe limit for long-term cellaring of 10 years or more is 65°F, but no higher. Wines kept at such temperatures will age a bit faster but they will not age badly. If you can somehow get the temperature down to 65°F or below, you will never have to worry about the condition of your wines. At 55°F—the ideal temperature—the wines actually evolve so slowly that your grandchildren will probably benefit from the wines more than you do. Constancy in temperature is highly prized and any changes in temperature should occur slowly. As for white wines, they are much more sensitive to less-than-ideal cellar temperatures. Therefore, while the dry white wines of Bordeaux should be kept at temperatures as close to 55°F as possible, the bigger, more alcoholic, sweet white wines of Barsac and Sauternes can age quite well at cellar temperatures up to 65°F.

RULE 2

Be sure the storage area is odor free, vibration free, and dark. A humidity level of 50–80% is ideal. Above 80% is fine for the wine, but the labels will become moldy and deteriorate. A humidity level below 50% can cause the corks to become drier than desired.

RULE 3

Bordeaux wines from vintages that produced powerful, rich, concentrated, full-bodied wines travel and age significantly better than wines from vintages that produced light-weight wines. For example, the oceanic voyage from Bordeaux can be traumatic for wines from vintages such as 1997, 1987, 1980, 1976, and 1971. The wines from these vintages—less concentrated, less tannic, and more fragile—often suffer considerably more from travel to the U.S. than big, rich, tannic, full-bodied wines such as 2000, 1998, 1996, 1995, 1990, 1989, 1988, 1986, 1985, 1983, 1982, 1978, 1975, and 1970. When you decide which Bordeaux wines to cellar, keep in mind that the fragile wines will develop much faster—even under ideal storage conditions.

RULE 4

When buying new vintages of Bordeaux to cellar, I personally recommend buying the wine as soon as it appears on the market, assuming of course you have tasted the wine and like it. The reason for this is that few American wine merchants, importers, wholesalers, or distributors care about how wine is stored. This attitude—that wine is just another spirit like whiskey or beer that can be left standing upright and exposed to dramatic extremes of temperature and damaging light—is fortunately changing as more knowledgeable wine people assume positions of control in major wine shops. However, far too many fine wines are damaged early in their life by terrible storage conditions, so the only way a wine enthusiast can prevent such tragedies from happening is to assume custody and control over the wine as early in its life as possible. This means acting promptly to secure your wines. My experience suggests that most Bordeaux arrive to our shores undamaged, but careless storage and shipping, particularly evident with the negligent attitude of many wholesalers, is where the damage occurs.

SERVING

There are no secrets concerning the formalities of serving Bordeaux. All one needs is a good corkscrew, a clean, odor-free decanter, and a sense of order as to how Bordeaux wines should be served and whether the wine should breathe.

Bordeaux wines do throw a sediment, particularly after they have attained 6–7 years of age. This mandates decantation—the procedure where the wine is poured into a clean decanter to separate the brilliant wine from the dusty particles that have precipitated to the bottom of the bottle. First, older bottles of Bordeaux should be removed carefully from storage so as not to disturb them and make the wine cloudy. Decanting can be an elaborate procedure, but all one needs is a clean, soap- and odor-free decanter and a steady hand. If you lack a steady hand, consider buying a decanting machine, which is a wonderful, albeit expensive, invention for making decanting fun and easy. Most important of all, be sure to rinse the decanter with unchlorinated well or mineral water regardless of how clean you think it is. A decanter or a wine glass left sitting in a china closet or cupboard acts as a wonderful trap for room and kitchen odors that are invisible, but rear their off-putting smell when the wine is poured into them. In addition, many glasses have an invisible soapy residue left inside from less-than-perfect dishwasher rinses. I can't begin to tell you how many dinner parties I have attended where the wonderful cedary, black currant bouquet of a 15- or 20-year-old Pauillac was flawed by the smell of dishwasher detergents or some stale kitchen smell that accumulated in the glass between uses.

Assuming that you have poured the wine into a clean decanter, you should also consider the optimal temperature at which the wine should be served, whether you should allow the wine to breathe, and, if you are serving several Bordeaux wines, the order of presentation.

The breathing or airing of a Bordeaux wine is rather controversial. Some connoisseurs adamantly claim that breathing is essential, while others claim it is simply all nonsense. Who is right? I have done numerous comparisons with wines to see if breathing works or doesn't. I still don't know the answers, if in fact they exist, but here are my observations. The act of decanting a Bordeaux wine is probably all the breathing most wines need. I have found that when serving young, muscular, rich, tannic vintages of Bordeaux, 20–90 minutes of breathing can sometimes result in a softer wine. However, the immediate gush of intense fruitiness that often spills forth when the wine is opened and decanted does subside a bit. So for the big, rich wines of Bordeaux, breathing is often a trade-off—you get some softening of the wine, but you also lose some of the wine's fruity aroma.

With lighter weight, less-tannic Bordeaux wines, I have found extended breathing to be detrimental to their enjoyment. Such wines are more fragile and often less endowed, and prolonged breathing tends to cause them to fade. With respect to older vintages of Bordeaux, 15–20 minutes of decantation is usually all that is necessary. With lightweight, older vintages and very, very old vintages, I recommend opening the wine, decanting it, and serving it immediately. Once an old wine begins to fade it can never be resuscitated.

There are many exceptions to such rules and I can easily think of 1945s, 1959s, 1961s, and more recently, 1982s that seemed at their peak 4–5 hours after decantation rather than the 20–25 minutes that I have suggested. However, it is always better to err on the side of needing more time to breathe and let the guest swirl and aerate the wine in the glass, than to wait too long and then serve a wine that, while magnificently scented when opened and decanted, has lapsed into a dumb comatose state by the time it is served. I have noticed that the more massive 2000s, 1996s, and 1982s have benefitted from 12–14 hours of airing, but that is probably because of their size and density.

The serving temperature of wine is another critical aspect of presenting Bordeaux. I am always surprised at how many times I am given a great Bordeaux wine that is too warm. Every wine book talks about serving fine red wines at room temperature. In America's overly warm and generously heated dining rooms, room temperature is often 70–75°F, a temperature that no fine red Bordeaux cares for. A Bordeaux served at such a temperature will often taste flat and flabby, and its bouquet will be diffuse and unfocused. The alcohol content will also seem higher than it should. The ideal temperature for red Bordeaux is 65–67°F, and for a white Bordeaux 55–60°F. If your best wines cannot be served at this temperature, then you are doing them a great injustice. If a red Bordeaux must be put in an ice bucket for ten minutes to lower its temperature, then do it. I have often requested on a hot summer day in Bordeaux or the Rhône Valley to have my Pomerol or Châteauneuf-du-Pape "iced" for ten minutes rather than drink it at a temperature of 80°F.

Lastly, the effective presentation of Bordeaux wines at a dinner party will necessitate a sense of order. The rules here are easy to follow: Lighter weight Bordeaux wines or wines from light vintages should always precede richer, fuller wines from great vintages. If such an order is not followed, the lighter, more delicate wines will taste pale after a rich, full-bodied wine has been served. For example, to serve a delicate 1999 Margaux like Issan after a 1982 Lafleur would be patently unfair to the Issan. Another guideline is to sequence the wines from youngest to oldest. This should not be blindly applied, but younger, more astringent wines should precede older, more mellow, mature wines.

BORDEAUX
WITH FOOD

The art of serving the right bottle of Bordeaux with a specific course or type of food has become one of the most overly legislated areas, all to the detriment of the enjoyment of both wine and food. Newspaper and magazine articles and even books are filled with precise rules that practically make it a sin not to choose the perfect wine for a particular meal. Thus, instead of enjoying their dinner party, most hosts and hostesses fret, usually needlessly, over choosing the wine. They would be better off to remember the wise advice from a noted French restaurateur, Henri Bérau, who stated it best: "The first conditions of a pleasant meal depend, essentially, upon the proper choice of guests."

The basics of the Bordeaux/food match up game are not difficult to master. These are the tried and true, allegedly cardinal principles, such as young wines before old, dry before sweet, white before red, red with meat, and white with fish. However, times have changed, and many of the old shibboleths have disappeared. Today one would not be surprised to hear that a certain variety of edible flower, nasturtiums for example, should be served with a flowery white Graves.

The question one should pose is, Does the food offer simple or complex flavors? Two of the favorite grapes of American wine drinkers are Merlot and Cabernet Sauvignon, both of which are able to produce majestic wines of exceptional complexity and depth of flavor. However, as food wines, they are remarkably one-dimensional. As complex and rewarding as they can be, they work well only with dishes that contain relatively simple flavors. Both marry beautifully with basic meat and potato dishes: filet mignon, lamb filets, steaks that are sautéed or grilled. Furthermore, as Cabernet Sauvignon- and Merlot-based wines get older and more complex they require increasingly simpler dishes to complement yet not overwhelm their complex flavors. This principle is applied almost across the board in restaurants and dining rooms in Bordeaux. The main courses chosen to show off red wines are usually a simple lamb or beef dish. Thus the principle is as follows: simple wines with complex dishes, complex wines with simple dishes. The late Richard Olney made this same observation in his classic treatise on food, *The French Menu Cookbook*.

Another question to be posed is, What is the style of wine produced in the vintage that you have chosen? Several of France's greatest chefs have told me they prefer off years of Bordeaux to great years and have instructed their sommeliers to buy the wines for the restaurant accordingly. Can this be true? From the chef's perspective, the food and not the wine should be the focal point of the meal. Many chefs feel that a great vintage of Bordeaux, with wines that are exceptionally rich, powerful, alcoholic, and concentrated, not only takes attention away from their cuisine, but makes matching a wine with the food much more troublesome. Thus, chefs prefer a 1999, 1997, 1994, or 1992 Bordeaux rather than a super-concentrated 2000, 1996, 1995, 1990, 1989, 1986, or

1982. Curiously, the richest vintages, while being marvelous wines, are not always the best years to choose when considering a food match up. Lighter weight yet tasty wines from unexceptional years can complement delicate and understated cuisine considerably better than the great vintages, which should be reserved for very simple food.

BUYING BORDEAUX WINE FUTURES: THE PITFALLS AND PLEASURES

The purchase of wine, already fraught with abundant pitfalls for consumers, becomes immensely more complex and risky when one enters the wine futures sweepstakes.

On the surface, buying wine futures is nothing more than investing money in a case or cases of wine at a predetermined "future price" long before the wine is bottled and shipped to this country. You invest your money in wine futures on the assumption that the wine will appreciate significantly in price between the time you purchase the future and the time the wine has been bottled and imported to America. Purchasing the right wine, from the right vintage, in the right international financial climate can represent significant savings. On the other hand, it can be quite disappointing to invest heavily in a wine future only to witness the wine's arrival, 12–18 months later, at a price equal to or below the future price and to discover the wine to be inferior in quality as well.

For years, future offerings have been largely limited to Bordeaux wines, although they are seen occasionally from other regions. In Bordeaux, during the spring following the harvest, the estates or châteaux offer a portion of their crops for sale. The first offering, or *première tranche*, usually provides a good indication of the trade's enthusiasm for the new wine, the prevailing market conditions, and the ultimate price the public will have to pay.

Those brokers and *négociants* who take an early position on a vintage frequently offer portions of their purchases to importers/wholesalers/retailers to make them available publicly as a "wine future." These offerings are usually made to the retail shopper during the first spring after the vintage. For example, the 2001 Bordeaux vintage was being offered for sale as a "wine future" in May 2002. Purchasing wine at this time is not without numerous risks. While 90% of the quality of the wine and the style of the vintage can be ascertained by professionals tasting the wine in its infancy, the increased interest in buying Bordeaux wine futures has led to a soaring number of journalists—some qualified, some not—to judge young Bordeaux wines. The results have been predictable. Many writers serve no purpose other than to hype the vintage as great and have written more glowing accounts of a vintage than the publicity firms doing promotion for the Bordeaux wine industry.

Consumers should read numerous points of view from trusted professionals and ask the following questions: 1. Is the professional taster experienced in tasting well as old Bordeaux vintages? 2. How much time does the taster actually sp ing Bordeaux during the year, visiting the properties, and studying the vintage. ᴏ. ᴅᴏᴇs the professional taster express his view in an independent, unbiased form, free of trade advertising? 4. Has the professional looked deeply at the weather conditions, harvesting conditions, grape variety ripening profiles, and soil types that respond differently depending on the weather scenario?

When wine futures are offered for sale there is generally a great deal of enthusiasm for the newest vintage from both the proprietors and the wine trade. The saying in France that "the greatest wines ever made are the ones that are available for sale" are the words many wine producers and merchants live by. The business of the wine trade is to sell wine, and consumers should be aware that they will no doubt be inundated with claims of "great wines from a great vintage at great prices." This line has been used time and time again for good vintages and, in essence, has undermined the credibility of many otherwise responsible retailers, as well as a number of journalists. In contrast, those writers who fail to admit or recognize greatness where warranted are no less inept and irresponsible.

In short, there are only four valid reasons to buy Bordeaux wine futures:

1. *Are you buying top-quality, preferably superb wine, from an excellent—or better yet, great—vintage?*

For 2001, the answer is no; for the 2000 vintage, the answer is yes. No vintage can be reviewed in black-and-white terms. Even in the greatest vintages there are disappointing appellations, as well as mediocre wines. At the same time, vintages that are merely good to very good can produce some superb wines. Knowing who the underachievers and overachievers are is paramount to making an intelligent buying decision. Look at the last 25 years. The only truly great vintages to emerge from Bordeaux, and only for the specific appellations listed, have been the following:

2001: Barsac/Sauternes
2000: All red wine appellations
1998: Pomerol, St.-Emilion, Pessac-Léognan/Graves
1996: St.-Julien, Pauillac, St.-Estèphe
1995: St.-Julien, Pauillac, St.-Estèphe, Graves, Pomerol, St.-Emilion
1990: St.-Julien, Pauillac, St.-Estèphe, Pomerol, St.-Emilion, Barsac/Sauternes
1989: Pomerol, Barsac/Sauternes
1988: Barsac/Sauternes
1986: St.-Julien, Pauillac, St.-Estèphe, Barsac/Sauternes
1982: St.-Julien, Pauillac, St.-Estèphe, Graves, Pomerol, St.-Emilion

Except for the top performers in a given vintage, there is no reason to buy wines as futures because prices generally will not appreciate in the period between the release of the future prices and when the wines are bottled. The exceptions are always the same—top wines and great vintages. If the financial climate is such that the wine will not be at least 25–30% more expensive when it arrives in the marketplace, then most purchasers are better off investing their money elsewhere. Keep in mind that even in 1990, a vintage that has soared in price over the last 13 years, the wines came out at a lower price than the 1989s. The 1990s did not begin to move up in price until the wines had been in the bottle for six months. The marketplace was saturated at the time the 1990s came out. The 1989s had received far too much hype as another "vintage of the century," and the big buyers had already spent their money on the 1989s and could not purchase the 1990s with any force. Once the wines were in the bottle and were tasted, prices for the 1990s began to soar in 1994 and 1995. That has continued as 1990 is unquestionably a great vintage.

Recent history of the 1975 and 1978 Bordeaux future offerings provides a revealing prospectus to "futures" buyers. Purchasers of 1975 futures did extremely well. When offered in 1977, the 1975 future prices included $140–160 per case for such illustrious wines as Lafite Rothschild and Latour, and $64–80 for second growths, including such proven thoroughbreds as Léoville-Las Cases, La Lagune, and Ducru-Beaucaillou. By the time these wines had arrived on the market in 1978, the vintage's outstanding and potentially classic quality was an accepted fact. The first growths were retailing for $325–375 per case; the lesser growths $112–150 per case. Buyers of 1975 futures have continued to prosper, as this vintage is now very scarce and its prices have continued to escalate to $900–1,200 a case for first growths and $350–550 for second through fifth growths. In 2003, the 1975 prices have come to a standstill because of doubts about how gracefully many of the wines are evolving. I would not be surprised to see some prices even drop—another pitfall that must always be considered when buying futures.

The 1978 Bordeaux futures, offered in 1980, present a different picture: 1978 was another good year, with wines similar in style but less intense than the excellent 1970 vintage. Opening prices for the 1978 Bordeaux were very high and were inflated because of a weak dollar abroad and an excessive demand for the finest French wines. Prices for first growths were offered at $429–499, prices for second through fifth growths at $165–230. Consumers who invested heavily in Bordeaux have purchased good wine, but when the wines arrived on the market in spring 1981, the retail prices for these wines were virtually the same as future price offerings. Thus consumers who purchased 1978 futures and invested their money to the tune of 100% of the case price could have easily obtained a better return by simply investing in any interest-bearing account. I predict the same is going to happen for 2001, a very good but hardly great vintage.

With respect to the vintages 1985, 1983, 1982, 1981, 1980, and 1979, the only year that has represented a great buy from a "futures" perspective is 1982. The 1980 was not offered to the consumer as a wine future because it was of mediocre quality. As for the 1979 and 1981, the enthusiast who purchased these wines on a future basis no doubt was able, within two years after putting his or her money up, to buy the wines when they arrived in America at approximately the same price. While this was not true for some of the highly rated 1981s, it was true for the 1979s. The 1982s have jumped in price at an unbelievable pace, outdistancing any vintage in the last 20 years. The first growths of 1982 were offered to consumers in late spring 1983 at prices of $350–450 for wines like Lafite Rothschild, Latour, Mouton Rothschild, Haut-Brion, and Cheval Blanc. By March 1985, the Cheval Blanc had jumped to $650–800, the Mouton to $800–1,000, and the rest to $700. In 2003, prices for first growths range from a low of $5,000 a case for Haut-Brion to $8,000–10,000 a case for any of the three Pauillac first growths. This is a significant price increase for wines so young, but it reflects the insatiable worldwide demand for a great vintage. Rare, limited-production wines, for instance the Pomerols, have also skyrocketed in price. Pétrus has clearly been the top performer in terms of escalating prices; it jumped from an April 1983 future price of $600 to a 2003 price of $25,000. This may be absurd, but it is an indication of the appreciation of great wines from great vintages. Other top 1982 Pomerols, such as Trotanoy, Certan de May, and L'Evangile, have quadrupled and quintupled in price. Trotanoy, originally available for $280, now sells (when you can find it) for at least $4,000. Certan de May has jumped from $180 to $2,500, as has L'Evangile.

The huge demand for 1982 Bordeaux futures and the tremendous publicity surrounding this vintage have led many to assume that subsequent years would similarly escalate in price. That has not happened, largely because Bordeaux has had too many high-quality, abundant vintages in the decade of the 1980s. The only exceptions have been the 1986 first growths that continue to accelerate because they are great, long-lived, so-called classic vintage wines.

2. Do the prices you must pay look good enough that you will ultimately save money by paying less for the wine as a future than for the wine when it is released in 2–3 years?

For 2001, the prices were much lower than 2000, and depending on the quality of 2002 and 2003, they will undoubtedly rise if these subsequent vintages are deemed less successful. Yet everything indicates very small price appreciation for 2001. The 2000 wines came out at historically high prices. However, it is both a great year and a millennium vintage. As expensive as they are, prices will only go higher and higher. Most 2000s were arriving to the marketplace in 2003 at prices 25–50% higher than their futures. Why? It is a very great vintage.

Many factors must be taken into consideration to make this determination. In certain years, Bordeaux may release wines at lower prices than it did the previous year (the most recent examples are 2001, 1990, and 1986).

After the buying frenzy for the millennium vintage, châteaux owners recognized the saturated marketplace in 2001 and dropped prices by 15–25%. Despite what is undoubtedly a good vintage, there was no reason to buy the wines as futures. At this writing, the bottled wines are coming on the marketplace at their release prices. This reinforces the lesson that consumers should only buy futures under the conditions I have stated. With respect to 2000, it was hard not to be astonished, appalled, and perplexed by the prices being fetched by some 2000 Bordeaux futures. Undoubtedly, this is one of the greatest vintages ever because of the consistency from top to bottom among the better estates. At the same time, when the 2000 Bordeaux wine futures came out in spring 2001, there was an almost irrational buying frenzy by consumers. What was inexcusable was the intentional manipulation of the marketplace by certain châteaux. This was accomplished by selling minuscule quantities of their wine in what is called the first *tranche* (release). Even in the second *tranche* the quantities were tiny, which created huge demand and the perception that there was no wine to be had by the throngs of potential Bordeaux buyers. By the time the third *tranche* came out, some châteaux were asking 50–100% more than they had for the first *tranche*, and only then were they willing to release adequate quantities. Remarkably, they were able to get the prices. This type of release program is disgusting. It was done in order to extract as high a price as possible from the market by creating the impression of a wine shortage. It also adds significantly to the market uncertainty and volatility. Yet anyone who bought the 2000 Bordeaux, even at these absurdly high prices, is probably sitting in a strong position, even considering what has happened since. The horrific terrorist attacks of September 11, 2001, plunged an already weakening U.S. economy into a major recession, which continues. The saturated marketplace and the reluctance of increasing numbers of serious wine consumers to pay top dollar for wines they feel are not worthy should have brought some common sense to the 2000 Bordeaux pricing. But guess what? The 2000 Bordeaux prices remain high. While they are not likely to appreciate significantly over the next few years given their already historically high levels for such infant wines, this is undeniably a great vintage that will continue to appreciate in value. For those who bought it, it is the equivalent of liquid gold in the cellar.

Some other things to consider: In 1991, when the 1990s were first priced, the American dollar was beginning to rebound but was still weak, not to mention the fact that our country was still mired in a recession. Other significant Bordeaux buying countries, such as England and France, had unsettled and troublesome financial problems as well. The Far East was not a principal player, and even Germany, which has always bought a lot of Bordeaux, was experiencing an economic downspin because of the financial ramifications of trying to revitalize the moribund economy of East Germany. In addition, there were two vintages of relatively high quality, 1989 and 1988, backed up in the marketplace. Hence the 1990s, as great as they were, did not increase in price until they had been in the bottle for almost a year. Those who purchased the 1990s as futures could have picked them up at the same price three years after the vintage. However, these cycles are short-lived. Look, for example, at the overheated buying frenzy for Bordeaux wine futures in the 1996 and 1995 vintages. In both cases, the wines came out at the highest future prices ever demanded, with some 1996s costing 100% more than their 1995 counterparts. Except for a few glitches in Asia, the international economic climate was buoyant, and the demand for luxury products, whether they be fine cars, wine, watches, etc., was insatiable. Consequently, Bordeaux had no problem selling everything of quality produced in 1996 and 1995 long before either vintage had been bottled. Prices for 1996s and 1995s soared, despite the fact that they came out at record high levels. Yet 6–8 years after the vintage, the top 1996s and 1995s have barely moved up or down in price. In 2003, the U.S. dollar dropped by 20% against the euro. This alone will impact prices of the 2002, 2001, and 2000 Bordeaux.

3. Do you want to be guaranteed to get top, hard-to-find wine from a producer with a great reputation who makes only small quantities of wine?

Even if the vintage is not irrefutably great or you cannot be assured that prices will increase, there are always a handful of small estates, particularly in Pomerol and St.-Emilion, that have worldwide followers that produce such limited quantities of wine that their wines warrant buying as futures if only to reserve a case from an estate whose wines have pleased you in the past. In Pomerol, limited-production wines such as Le Pin, Clinet, La Conseillante, L'Evangile, Le Fleur de Gay, Lafleur, and Bon Pasteur have produced many popular wines during the decades of the 1980s and 1990s, yet they are very hard to find in the marketplace. In St.-Emilion, some of the less-renowned, yet modestly sized estates such as Angelus, Clos St.-Martin, La Gomerie, Grand Mayne, La Mondotte, Pavie Macquin, Le Tertre-Roteboeuf, Troplong Mondot, and Valandraud, as well as all of the limited-production garage wines, produce wines that are not easy to find after bottling. Consequently, their admirers throughout the world frequently reserve and pay for these wines as futures. Limited-production wines from high-quality estates merit buying futures even in good to very good years.

4. Do you want to buy wine in half bottles, magnums, double magnums, jeroboams, or Imperials?

Frequently overlooked as one of the advantages of buying wine futures is the fact that you can request that your merchant have the wines bottled to your specifications. There is always a surcharge for such bottlings, but if you have children born in a certain year, or you want the luxury of buying half bottles (a size that makes sense for daily drinking), the only time to do this is when buying the wine as a future.

In summary, should you decide to enter the futures market, be sure you know the other risks involved. The merchant you deal with could go bankrupt and your unsecured sales slip would make you one of probably hundreds of unsecured creditors of the bankrupt wine merchant hoping for a few cents on your investment. Another risk is that the supplier the merchant deals with could go bankrupt or be fraudulent. You may get a refund from the wine merchant, but you will not get your wine. Therefore, be sure to deal only with a wine merchant who has a history of both selling wine futures and delivering them! And finally, buy wine futures only from a wine merchant who has received confirmed commitments as to the quantities of wine he or she will receive. Some merchants sell Bordeaux futures to consumers before they have received commitments from suppliers. Be sure to ask for proof of the merchant's allocations. If you do not, then the words "caveat emptor" could have special significance for you.

For many Bordeaux wine enthusiasts, buying wine futures of the right wine, in the right vintage, at the right time guarantees that they have liquid gems worth four or five times the price they paid for them. However, as history has proven, only a handful of vintages (2000, 1990, and 1982) over the last 25 years have appreciated so dramatically in their first two or three years as to justify buying the wines as futures.

7: A VISITOR'S GUIDE TO BORDEAUX

HOTELS AND RESTAURANTS

MÉDOC

Pauillac—**L'Hotel France et Angleterre** 3 Quai Albert Pichon (30 miles from downtown Bordeaux); Tel.—5.56.59.24.24; Fax—5.56.59.01.89

Twenty rooms for about $60 a person. Ask for a room in the annex, which is more quiet. The restaurant is surprisingly good with a competent wine list.

Pauillac—**Château Cordeillan Bages** (adjacent to Lynch-Bages on the south side of Pauillac next to D2); Tel.—5.56.59.24.24; Fax—5.56.59.01.89

The deluxe restaurant, hotel, and wine school of Jean Michel Cazes, the proprietor of Lynch-Bages. The excellent restaurant boasts a stupendous wine list and the hotel is quiet and spacious. It has already garnered two stars from the conservative Michelin Guide. This is the place to stay and eat when visiting châteaux in St.-Julien, Pauillac, and St.-Estèphe. Expect to pay $150–225 per night for lodging and approximately the same for dinner for two.

Margaux—**Relais de Margaux** (14 miles from downtown Bordeaux); Tel.—5.57.88.38.30; Fax—5.57.88.31.73

A luxury hotel with 28 rooms for $145–200 that has had ups and downs since opening in the mid-1980s. Rooms are splendid, the cooking overpriced, contrived, and inconsistent. The wine selection is good, but the mark-ups of 200–400% are appalling.

Margaux—**Pavillon de Margaux** (15 miles from downtown Bordeaux); Tel.—5.57.88. 77.54; Fax—5.57.88.77.73

Rooms are nice as well as affordable, between $75–100 a day. The charming restaurant turns out authentic regional cuisine that rarely hits the heights, but never disappoints.

Margaux—**Savoie;** Tel. and Fax—5.57.88.31.76

Rustic regional cooking can be found in abundance at this great value hotel inhabited more by local vignerons than tourists.

Arcins—**Lion d'Or** (in the village next to D2); Tel.—5.56.58.96.79

Jean-Paul Barbier's roadside restaurant in Arcins (several miles north of the village of Margaux) has become one of the hottest eating spots in the Médoc. Barbier, an enthusiastic chef of some talent, encourages clients to bring their own bottles to complement his rustic, country cooking. Portions are generous, the restaurant noisy, and if you bring a good bottle or you are with a well-known proprietor, chances are the gregarious Barbier will be at your side most of the night. Who can resist the idea of doing your own comparative tasting with such local specialties as shad in cream sauce and the famous lamb from Pauillac? This is a fun place with surprisingly good food, but if you are looking for a quiet, relaxing evening, Lion d'Or is not the place. Prices are moderate.

Gaillan-en-Médoc—**Château Layauga** (two miles from Lesparre); Tel.—5.56.41.26.83; Fax—5.56.41.19.52

This charming restaurant (there are also seven attached rooms) offers excellent cooking, featuring many wonderful fish courses, as well as local specialties such as the lamb of Pauillac and the famed *lamproie* Bordelais (eels cooked in their own blood). As reprehensible as that may sound, I find this dish superb and one of the few fish courses that works sensationally well with a big, rich bottle of red Bordeaux.

BORDEAUX

Hotel Burdigala, 115 Rue Georges Bonnac; Tel.—5.56.90.16.16; Fax—5.56.93.15.06

This is Bordeaux's only super-luxury hotel and the "in" spot for many business travelers. There are 68 rooms and 15 suites, an excellent restaurant, and the location in the center of the city, not far from the Place Gambetta, is ideal. Prices are $160–240 a night.

Hotel Normandie, 7 Cours du 30 Juillet; Tel.—5.56.52.16.80; Fax—5.56.51.68.91

Located several blocks from the opera and Maison du Vin in the center of the city, just off the Allées de Tourny, the Hotel Normandie has always been the top spot for visiting writers because of its ideal location (and cheap fares). The three leading Bordeaux wine shops are within a three-minute walk. The rooms are spacious but clearly not as modernly equipped as the newer hotels. There is a certain charm about the Hotel Normandie, but if you have a car, parking in this area is often troublesome. Rates ($50–120 a night) for one of the 100 rooms at the Normandie make it one of the best values in Bordeaux.

Hotel Sainte-Catherine, 27 Rue Parlement Ste.-Catherine; Tel.—5.56.81.95.12; Fax—5.56.44.50.51

Not as well known as many others, this lovely, moderately sized hotel with rooms that cost about $100 a night is located in the middle of the city. For those looking for privacy and anonymity, this discrete hotel is a good choice.

Mercure Château Chartrons, 81 Cours St.-Louis; Tel.—5.56.43.15.00; Fax—5.56.69.15.21

This large, modern hotel, situated just north of the city center, has easily accessible parking facilities as well as 144 rooms priced between $95–100.

Claret, 85 Parvis des Chartrons (located in the Cité Mondiale du Vin); Tel.—5.56.01.79.79; Fax—5.56.01.79.00

This hotel is exceptionally well located in downtown Bordeaux in the Cité Mondiale du Vin, which is a failed international showcase for wine producers. Room rates are $96–200.

Le Chapon Fin, 5 Rue Montesquieu; Tel.—5.56.79.10.10; Fax—5.56.79.09.10

One of the finest restaurants in Bordeaux, it always puzzled me as to why former Chef Garcia never received recognition from the Michelin Guide. Admittedly, I am unable to eat here anonymously and perhaps see better service than a stranger off the street. I have enjoyed extraordinary food from Garcia everywhere he has been. He was the force that resurrected the reputation of the Pessac restaurant/hotel La Reserve before he moved across from Bordeaux's train station and opened Clavel. Garcia has departed to reopen his bistro near the train station, but Le Chapon Fin remains a turn-of-the-century grotto-like restaurant just off the Place des Grands Hommes with superb ambiance, an excellent wine list, and outstanding cooking. Prices are high, but not unreasonable. Le Chapon Fin is closed on Sunday and Monday.

La Chamade, 20 Rue Piliers de Tutelle; Tel.—5.56.48.13.74; Fax—5.56.79.29.67

This basement restaurant in the old section of Bordeaux, just a few minutes' walk from the Place de la Bourse, consistently turns out fine cooking. It is one of my favorite places to eat on Sunday evening, when just about every other restaurant in the city has shut down. If you visit La Chamade, do not miss the superb first course called "Salade de Chamade." La Chamade's prices are moderately expensive.

Jean Ramet, 7 Place J. Jaurès; Tel.—5.56.44.12.51; Fax—5.56.52.19.80

Jean Ramet's tiny restaurant located just down the street from the Grand Theater, near the Gironde, and just past the Place J. Jaurès, should not be missed. The cooking merits two stars, but Ramet will never receive them because of the minuscule size of the restaurant, which seats only 27 people. Ramet and his wife run the restaurant with a staff of nine—one for every three clients. Ramet, who apprenticed under such great chefs as Pierre Troigros and Michel Guerard, is a wizard. I cannot recommend this moderately expensive restaurant enough. The Jean Ramet restaurant is closed Saturday and Sunday.

La Tupina, 6 Rue Porte de la Monnaire; Tel.—5.56.91.56.37; Fax—5.56.31.92.11

This moderately priced bistro in the old city is run by one of Bordeaux's great characters, Jean-Pierre Xiradakis. He is unquestionably a wine enthusiast, but his first love is his restaurant, which features the exuberant, intense flavors of southwestern France. Consequently, expect to eat rich, heavy, abundant quantities of food such as duck, foie gras, and roasted chicken, as well as the best pommes frites in Bordeaux. The wine list focuses on high-quality, little-known producers and there is also a selection of rare Armagnacs. The restaurant, which is difficult to find, is located near the Cathedral of Ste.-Croix, between the Rue Sauvageau and the riverside Quai de la Monnaie. This is President Chirac's favorite eatery when visiting Bordeaux.

Le Pavillon des Boulevards, 120 Rue Croix de Seguey; Tel.—5.56.81.51.02; Fax—5.56.51.14.58

This stylish, refined restaurant burst on the scene in the late 1980s and has become one of Bordeaux's hottest new restaurants. The cooking tends to reflect an Asian influence and those who have tired of *nouvelle* cuisine will find Pavillon des Boulevards a bit too precious. But the undeniable talent of Chef Franc is evident in every dish served. Prices are moderately expensive.

Le Père Ouvrard, 12 Rue du Maréchal-Joffre; Tel.—5.56.44.11.58

About as straightforward a bistro as I have ever been in, imagine approaching a restaurant with a plaque on the outside stating "Menu de Canard" and finding live ducks (clients can choose their victims) caged on the sidewalk outside the restaurant's entrance! This young couple (the Ouvards) is turning out marvelous renditions of traditional classics at this unassuming bistro.

Les Plaisirs d'Ausone, 10 Rue Ausone; Tel.—5.56.79.30.30; Fax—5.56.51.38.16

An elegant restaurant with elegant cuisine specializing in regional dishes, this top-class establishment was recently demoted by the Michelin Guide.

Gravelier, 114 Cours Verdun; Tel.—5.56.48.17.15; Fax—5.56.51.96.07

Probably the finest as well as the most authentic Bordelaise bistro, this well-located restaurant in the heart of town offers generous quantities of well-prepared food at low prices. Readers looking for a less pretentious dining experience, with some of the region's finest cooking, should not miss Gravelier.

THE SUBURBS OF BORDEAUX

Bordeaux Le Lac (10 minutes from the city center)

Hotel Sofitel Aquitania; Tel.—5.56.50.83.80; Fax—5.56.39.73.75

Hotel Novotel; Tel.—5.56.50.99.70; Fax—5.56.43.00.66

I have spent a considerable amount of my life at the Hotel Sofitel Aquitania and Hotel Novotel. Bordeaux Le Lac, an ambiance-free commercial center just north of Bordeaux, is an ideal lodging spot, particularly if you have a car. The hotels offer antiseptic rooms with hot running water, telephones, and fax machines that work. Sofitel Aquitania is more expensive, costing $100–125 a night, whereas the Novotel is about $90–100 a night. Both have similar rooms, although the Sofitel does offer mini-bars. Both have hassle-free parking, which I consider to be of considerable importance. They are also good choices, as the Médoc, Pomerol, and St.-Emilion are only 20 minutes away. If you like to gamble, an adjacent casino is a welcome relief from tasting and spitting.

Bouliac (a 20-minute drive from Bordeaux)

Le St.-James, Place C. Holstein; Tel.—5.57.97.06.00; Fax—5.56.20.92.58

One of the best restaurants in the Bordeaux region, this is the only Bordeaux restaurant to have garnered two stars in the Michelin Guide (and then lost one of them). For decades, the kitchen was the scene of the eccentric cooking of Chef Amat. I have had some remarkable courses, but having eaten there more than a dozen times during the last decade, I have also had disappointing courses, as well as listless, unenthusiastic service. Amat was booted out several years ago, yet I still find the restaurant overrated and too expensive, and I am still not used to the sommelier drinking at least three or four ounces of one's bottle of wine to "test it." A luxury hotel has opened nearby. Prices are extremely high. For infrequent visitors to Bordeaux, the best way to get to Bouliac is to take one of the bridges across the Garonne, immediately picking up D113 south. Within four or five miles, signs for Bouliac and Le St.-James restaurant should be visible on your left.

Martillac (a 10-minute drive from the city center)

Sources de Caudalie; Tel.—5.57.83.83.83; Fax—5.57.83.83.84
The new "in" spot for Bordeaux visitors, this luxury spa, hotel, and high-class restaurant was installed adjacent to the entrance of the well-known Pessac-Léognan estate, Château Smith Haut Lafitte. It is the only place in Bordeaux that caters to the every whim of millionaires, or wanna-be millionaires. The food is delicious. Additionally, you can get the "full monty" treatments for aches, pains, and obesity by taking *la cure* at this stunning location.

Langon (30 miles south of Bordeaux)

Claude Darroze, 95 Cours General Leclerc; Tel.—5.56.63.00.48; Fax.—5.56.63.41.15 (Chef Darroze)
Some of the finest meals I have eaten in France have been at the superb restaurant Claude Darroze, located in the center of Langon. Langon is a good place to stop if you are visiting the châteaux of Sauternes-Barsac. Of primary importance is the superb quality of Darroze's cooking, and there are also 16 rooms, reasonably priced at about $60–75 a night. Darroze's cooking emphasizes foie gras, truffles in season, and excellent lamb and fish. It is a rich, highly imaginative style of cooking that clearly merits the two stars it has earned from the Michelin Guide. The wine list is also super, as well as reasonably priced. Should you be an Armagnac lover, the finest Bas-Armagnacs from Darroze's brother, Francis Darroze, are available, going back to the beginning of the 20th century. Prices are a steal given the quality of these rare items. If you are driving from Bordeaux, the best way to get to Claude Darroze is to take the autoroute (A62), exit at Langon, and follow the signs for "Centre Ville." You cannot miss Darroze's restaurant/hotel once you are in the center of the city.

Langoiran (25 minutes from downtown Bordeaux)

Restaurant Saint-Martin (located directly on the Garonne River); Tel.—5.56.67.02.67
If you are looking for a tiny, charming restaurant/hotel in a historic village that few people other than the locals know about, consider eating and staying at the Restaurant Saint-Martin. Located on the Garonne, the food is country French, but imaginative, well prepared, and moderately priced. The wine list is excellent. To reach Langoiran, take autoroute A62, exit at La Brède, follow the signs and Route 113 to Portets, and then turn left, following the signs for Langoiran. This charming, quiet village is reached by a frightfully ancient bridge over the Garonne. Rooms are bargain priced at $45–60 a night.

Libourne (30 minutes from Bordeaux)

Hotel Loubat; Tel.—5.57.51.17.58

If you are forced to stay in town, this is one of several possibilities. A big advantage is the fact that the hotel's restaurant, Les Trois Toques, has some of the best cooking in the town of Libourne. It is not a place with refined cooking, but the chefs do an excellent job preparing local dishes. Not surprisingly, there is a reliable selection of Pomerols and St.-Emilions on the wine list.

Bistro Chanzy; Tel.—5.57.51.84.26; Fax—5.57.51.84.89

This respectable bistro offers traditional cooking in a menu that changes daily. Reservations are rarely needed, especially for lunch, at this reliable, inexpensive venue for hearty Bordelais cooking.

Chez Servais, 14 Place Decazes; Tel.—5.57.51.83.97

Except for the tediously slow service, this is a welcoming spot to eat in the heart of Libourne. Excellent cuisine, as well as a good wine list, make this a worthwhile rendezvous.

St.-Emilion (24 miles east of Bordeaux)

Hostellerie de Plaisance, Place Clocher; Tel.—5.57.55.07.55; Fax—5.57.74.41.11

This is the leading hotel in the fascinating walled town of St.-Emilion, which gets my vote as the most interesting and charming area in the entire Bordeaux region. This splendid establishment's owners (also the proprietors of Château Pavie, Pavie Decesse, and Monbousquet), Chantal and Gérard Perse, recently completed a multimillion-dollar renovation, turning this country hotel into a world-class destination. There are 16 rooms, ranging in price from $144–305. A talented chef was brought in to do the cooking, which is top-class, and in only one year the restaurant has garnered one star from the Michelin Guide. As one might expect, the wine list is spectacular. This has become *the* destination on Bordeaux's right bank.

Logis des Remparts, Rue Guadet; Tel.—5.57.24.70.43; Fax—5.57.24.70.43

There is no restaurant, but this is a fine hotel if you cannot get into the Hotel Plaisance. There are 15 rooms that range in price from $70–80.

Logis de la Cadène, Place Marché au Bois; Tel.—5.57.24.71.40

Run with great enthusiasm by the Chailleau family, this is my favorite restaurant in the city of St.-Emilion. Situated just down the hill from the Hotel Plaisance, Logis de la Cadène serves up copious quantities of robust bistro food. The wine list is interesting, but the real gems here are the numerous vintages of Château La Clotte, the Grand Cru Classé St.-Emilion that is owned by the restaurant owners. One of the better St.-Emilions, it is rarely seen in the export market because so much of the production is consumed on the premises of this eating establishment. Prices are moderate.

Château Grand Barrail; Tel.—5.57.55.37.00; Fax—5.57.55.37.49

This former wine-producing château is situated in the middle of St.-Emilion's vineyards, just on the outskirts of Libourne, on Route D-243. It is a luxury establishment, with 28 rooms priced between $220–450. For those with lots of discretionary income, who want to sleep in a château in the middle of a vineyard, this venue is hard to beat. The cooking is also topflight, offering creative, flavorful cuisine. The wine list reflects the riches of the region. This is another not-to-be-missed venue for visitors to Pomerol/St.-Emilion.

Bourg-Blaye—**Hotel La Citadelle;** Tel.—5.57.42.17.10; Fax—5.57.42.10.34

Monsieur Chaboz runs this superbly situated hotel with an unsurpassed view of the Gironde. The hotel is in the historic citadelle of Blaye. The restaurant serves up well-prepared, reasonably priced local specialties. The 21 rooms are a bargain (how many foreigners pass through Blaye?) at $50–60 a night. There is also a tennis court and a swimming pool.

Bourg-Charente—**Ribaudière;** Tel.—5.45.81.30.54; Fax—5.45.81.28.05

This is a restaurant for insiders. Located about 65 miles from Bordeaux (closer to the Cognac region than the Bordeaux region), it offers beautiful cooking that admirably reflects the region's specialties. Prices are a steal for food of this quality.

ROMANTIC AND HEDONISTIC EXCURSIONS

Brantome (about 60 miles northeast of Bordeaux)

Moulin de L'Abbaye; Tel.—5.53.05.80.22; Fax—5.53.05.75.27

Take plenty of money to this splendidly situated old mill located along the side of an easy-flowing river in the beautiful town of Brantome in the heart of the Dordogne. Brantome is a good two hours from Bordeaux, but it is a beautiful, scenic drive when you cross over the Garonne and take N89 through Libourne, past the vineyards of Pomerol and Lalande-de-Pomerol in the direction of Perigeux. Once in Perigeux, Brantome is only 15 minutes away. There are only nine rooms (costing about $152–229 a night) and three apartments in the gorgeous Moulin de L'Abbaye. The food is excellent, occasionally superb. My main objection is that the wine list is absurdly expensive.

Champagnac de Belair (two hours from Bordeaux)

Moulin du Roc; Tel.—5.53.02.86.00; Fax—5.53.54.21.31

Three miles northeast of Brantome, off D78, is the quaint village of Champagnac de Belair and another ancient mill that is built over a meandering river. This is the most romantic hotel and restaurant in the region. For those special occasions, or just for a sublime night away, ask for one of the four apartments in the Moulin du Roc. It will cost you close to $200 a night, but it is a magnificent setting and the charm and tranquility of this establishment, run with perfection by Madame Gardillou, is unsurpassed. The food is superb, though extremely expensive. Only the wine list leaves me less than excited because of its outrageously high prices. Nevertheless, even that can be overlooked when eating and sleeping in paradise.

Eugénie Les Bains (a two-hour drive south of Bordeaux)

Les Prés d'Eugénie; Tel.—5.58.05.06.07; Fax—5.58.51.13.59 (Chef Guérard)

If I had one last meal to eat, I would be hard pressed not to have it at this magnificent establishment located several hours south of Bordeaux. The nearest town is Mont-de-Marsan, which is approximately 18 miles to the north. Michel Guérard is an internationally famous chef, and his restaurant has long been one of the renowned three-star eating establishments in France. There are many three-star restaurants that I would downgrade to two stars, and there are others that are so superb one wonders why the Michelin Guide does not create a four-star category. The latter is the case at Les Prés d'Eugénie, where innovation, originality, and quality all come together with the formidable talents of Michel Guérard, who creates some of the most remarkable dishes my wife and I have ever eaten. Huge quantities of money are necessary to enjoy the food, but the 29-room hotel has surprisingly fair prices, averaging $275–300 a night. Should you want to splurge, there are seven apartments that cost $350–400 a night. If you have the time, money, and appetite, try to have at least two meals from this genius. Guérard also has a delicious regional bistro nearby (a five-minute walk) called Ferme aux Grives (Tel.—5.58.05.05.06; Fax—5.58.51.10.10)

OTHER DIVERSIONS

WINE SHOPS

Bordeaux—**L'Intendant,** 2 Allées de Tourny; Tel.—5.56.43.26.39; Fax—5.56.43.26.45
Buying Bordeaux either from the châteaux or in the city itself is usually far more expensive than buying the same wines in the United States. However, it is always interesting to see the wine selection in shops in another country. Bordeaux boasts L'Intendant, the most architecturally stunning wine shop I have ever seen. Furthermore, its selection of Bordeaux wines is exceptional. Located on the luxury shopping street, Allées de Tourny (just across from the Grand Theatre), it offers an extraordinary number of wines as well as many old vintages. Just visiting the shop is a must because of its fabulous design and spiral staircase. Within this four-floor tower are 15,000 bottles of Bordeaux. Bordeaux wine enthusiasts will require at least an hour to view the incredible selection. It is one of the greatest wine shops, not only in France, but in the world—exclusively for Bordeaux.

Bordeaux—**Badie,** 62 Allées de Tourny; Tel.—5.56.52.23.72; Fax—5.56.81.31.16
Badie, situated several blocks away from L'Intendant, has the same owners, although the selection is not as comprehensive. But it is still a fine shop that is renowned for its values and knowledgeable staff. Since 1880 it has been the *magasin des Bordelais.*

Bordeaux—**Badie Champagne;** Tel.—5.56.52.15.66; Fax—5.56.81.31.16
This shop has the largest selection of champagne in the world (about 450 different *cuvées*).

Bordeaux—**La Vinotheque,** 8 Cours du 30 Juillet; Tel.—5.56.52.32.05
La Vinotheque offers relatively high prices for decent wines, as well as a plethora of wine accessories, but it is overshadowed by L'Intendant, Badie, and Bordeaux Magnum.

Bordeaux—**Bordeaux Magnum,** 3 rue Godineau; Tel.—5.56.48.00.06
Bordeaux Magnum does not specialize so much in larger-format bottlings such as magnums, but in high-class Bordeaux wines.

BOOK SHOPS, ETC.

Bordeaux—**Librairie Mollat,** 15 Rue Vital-Carles; Tel.—5.56.56.40.40
One of the greatest book shops in France, the Librairie Mollat is located in the old city on one of the walking streets. Its collection of wine books is extraordinary, and just about anything you could ever want in terms of literature is available at Mollat. The collection of English books is limited.

Bordeaux—**Virgin Megastore,** Place Gambetta; Tel.—5.56.56.05.70
This high-tech, state-of-the-art shop is a must for those looking for that rare compact disc or wine book. The Bordelais, who are proud to have the second Virgin shop (the first is on the Champs Elysées in Paris), make this one of the most heavily trafficked spots in all of Bordeaux. The shop includes a small cafeteria that serves surprisingly good food and great coffee.

BEHAVING LIKE A BORDELAIS

There is a lot to do in Bordeaux, and if you want to blend in with the local populace, here are some not-to-be-missed walking tours and sites to see.

By the time this book is published in the fall of 2003, the high-tech monorail transportation system along Bordeaux's famous *Quai des Chartrons* will be finished. These majestic 18th-century stone buildings have recently been cleaned and refurbished under the dynamic leadership of former Prime Minister, and now Mayor of Bordeaux, Alain Juppé. Other spots to visit include the finest church in Bordeaux, the *Basilica de Saint-Michel*, which dominates the old city skyline from across the Garonne River. Most Bordelais can be found at one time or another walking in and around the shopping area known as the Place des Grands Hommes. This is where wealthy locals purchase their Feragamo, Kenzo, and other top-of-the-line goodies. Several local shops with historical reputations include *Bejottes*, 1 Place des Grands Hommes, which sells every kitchen item one can imagine, and *Baillardan Gallerie des Grands Hommes*, which makes the extraordinary miniature cakes called *caneles*, that are almost as famous as the region's wines.

Adjacent to the Place des Grands Hommes is the city's greatest walking tour. For visitors who proceed south on the Allées de Tourny, this glamourous walk passes the finest shops of the city. On the southern end is the Grand Theatre, a stunning neo-classical edifice that sits adjacent to the entrance into the labyrinth known as *Vieux Bordeaux*. Don't hesitate to enter this old quarter of tiny streets that seems centuries removed from the Allées de Tourny and the Quai des Chartrons.

The Bordelais adore their museums, all of which merit a visit.

Musée d'Art Contemporain, 7 Rue Ferrère (open Tuesday, and Thursday to Sunday, 11:00 A.M.–6:00 P.M., Wednesday 11:00 A.M.–8:00 P.M.). When I was last there, admission was approximately $6.

Musée des Beaux Arts, Jardin de la Mairie, 20 Cours d'Albret (open daily except Tuesday, 11:00 A.M.–6:00 P.M.). Admission: $4.50.

Art-en-Rêve Musée, 7 Rue Ferrère (open Tuesday, and Thursday to Sunday, 11:00 A.M.–6:00 P.M., Wednesday 11:00 A.M.–8:00 P.M.). Admission is free with a ticket to the Musée d'Art Contemporain.

Centre National Jean Moulin, Place Jean Moulin, 48 Rue Vital Carles (open Tuesday to Friday, 11:00 A.M.—6:00 P.M., Saturday and Sunday, 2:00–6:00 P.M.). Admission is free.

No visit to Bordeaux would be complete without a stop at one of France's great cheese purveyors, of which there are many. One of the finest is *Jean d'Alos*, 4 Rue Montesquieu. Monsieur d'Alos is legendary for his ability to select and ripen cheese. Known as an *affineur*, his historic shop is stuffed with extraordinary cheeses.

VISITING BORDEAUX CHÂTEAUX

When visiting Bordeaux, I recommend that someone in your party be able to speak a little French. Most of the big-name Bordeaux châteaux now employ someone who speaks English, but do not count on many châteaux other than first growths or super seconds to have anyone who speaks much English.

For getting the maximum out of your visit, you should write directly for an appointment or ask your local wine merchant to have an importer set up an appointment for you. If planning a program for visiting the Bordeaux châteaux, you should remember that four full visits a day are probably the maximum—unless you and your travel mates are true aficionados, four a day is probably too many. In deciding which châteaux to visit, you should always arrange visits at châteaux that are close to one another. For example, if you want to visit Château Margaux at 9:30 A.M., you should allow 45–60 minutes for a visit, as well as a 30- to 35-minute car drive from downtown Bordeaux. It is also advisable to schedule only one other visit that morning, preferably in the commune of Margaux. If you schedule an appointment in Pauillac or St.-Estèphe for 11:00 A.M., the 30- to 40-minute drive north from Margaux to either of these two appellations would probably make you late for your appointment. Remember, the French are far more respectful of appointment hours than most Americans tend to be, and it is an insult not to arrive on time. The following are several recommended itineraries that include visits to the most interesting properties and allow sufficient time to do so. You can expect to taste the two youngest vintages on your visit, but do not hesitate to ask to sample a recent vintage that has been bottled. Unless you are a Hollywood superstar, it is unlikely that anything older than 4–5 years will be opened. A visit generally involves a tour of the château, a tour of the cellars, and then a short tasting. Spitting the wine out is not only permissible, it is expected. Normally you spit in small buckets filled with sawdust. In some of the up-to-date tasting rooms that have been constructed at the châteaux, huge, state-of-the-art spittoons are available.

Must-visits in the Médoc are Mouton Rothschild with its splendid museum, Prieuré-Lichine, the home of the late Alexis Lichine and the only château open seven days a week, and of course, any property of which you have numerous vintages squirreled away in your cellar.

There are some important things to remember: Bordelais, as elsewhere in France, take a two-hour lunch between 12:00–2:00 P.M., which means you will not be able to see any properties during that time. Secondly, very few châteaux receive visitors during the harvest. During the decade of the 1980s the harvests tended to be relatively early because of the hot summers. In general, harvests can be expected to occur between mid-September and mid-October.

RECOMMENDED ITINERARIES

Itinerary I
(Margaux)
  8:45 A.M.—Leave Bordeaux
  9:30 A.M.—Château Giscours
10:30 A.M.—Château Margaux
  2:00 P.M.—Château Palmer
  3:30 P.M.—Prieuré-Lichine
  5:30 P.M.—D'Issan

Have lunch at the Lion d'Or in Arcins, a tiny village several miles north of Margaux.

Itinerary II
(Pauillac)
  8:15 A.M.—Leave Bordeaux
  9:30 A.M.—Château Latour
11:00 A.M.—Château Pichon-
    Longueville—Comtesse de Lalande
  2:00 P.M.—Château Lynch-Bages
  3:30 P.M.—Château Pichon-
    Longueville Baron
  5:00 P.M.—Château Mouton-
    Rothschild

Take your lunch at the restaurant Cordeillan-Bages, just south of the town of Pauillac and only five minutes from any of these châteaux.

Itinerary III
(St.-Julien)
  8:30 A.M.—Leave Bordeaux
  9:30 A.M.—Château Beychevelle
11:00 A.M.—Château Ducru-
    Beaucaillou
  2:00 P.M.—Château Talbot
  3:30 P.M.—Château Léoville-Las
    Cases

Lunch at Cordeillan-Bages.

Itinerary IV
(St.-Estèphe and Pauillac)
  8:15 A.M.—Leave Bordeaux
  9:30 A.M.—Château Lafite Rothschild
11:00 A.M.—Château Cos d'Estournel
  2:00 P.M.—Château Montrose
  3:30 P.M.—Château Calon-Ségur

It is preferable to stay at Cordeillan-Bages in Pauillac when visiting St.-Estèphe, St.-Julien, and Pauillac.

Itinerary V
(Graves)
  8:30 A.M.—Leave Bordeaux
  9:30 A.M.—Châteaux Haut-Brion and
  La Mission Haut-Brion
11:00 A.M.—Château Pape-Clément
  2:30 P.M.—Domaine de Chevalier
  4:00 P.M.—Haut-Bailly

*Have lunch at Sources de Caudalie in
Martillac, which can also be utilized as
your hotel if you want to save 20–35
minutes of travel time from Bordeaux.*

Itinerary VII
(St.-Emilion)
  8:30 A.M.—Leave Bordeaux
  9:30 A.M.—Château Cheval Blanc
11:00 A.M.—Château Canon
  2:00 P.M.—Château Ausone
  3:00 P.M.—Château Pavie

*Have lunch at either Plaisance (with its
magnificent views of St.-Emilion) or
Grand Barrail (two miles northwest of the
village). If you stay at a hotel in St.-
Emilion, the time to reach any St.-Emilion
or Pomerol estate is less than 10 minutes.*

Itinerary VI
(Sauternes-Barsac)
  8:30 A.M.—Leave Bordeaux
  9:30 A.M.—Château Yquem
11:00 A.M.—Château Suduiraut
  2:00 P.M.—Château Rieussec
  3:00 P.M.—Château Climens

*Have lunch at the great restaurant Claude
Darroze in Langon. If you decide to lodge
at Darroze's restaurant/hotel, travel time to
any of the Sauternes properties is less than
15 minutes.*

Itinerary VIII
(Pomerol)
  8:30 A.M.—Leave Bordeaux
  9:30 A.M.—Château Pétrus
11:00 A.M.—Vieux Château Certan
  2:00 P.M.—Château L'Evangile
  3:30 P.M.—Château La Conseillante

*Lunch in St.-Emilion at Plaisance or
Grand Barrail. If you stay in St.-Emilion,
travel time to Pétrus, or any of the Pomerol
estates, is less than 10 minutes.*

When arriving in Bordeaux, the Maison du Vin (1 Cours du 30 Juillet; Tel.—
5.56.52.82.82) in downtown central Bordeaux is a good place to pick up information on
Bordeaux wine regions in addition to some decent maps.

   To make an appointment, most châteaux can be contacted via their Internet site. If
you want to write directly to the châteaux to make an appointment, you can use a format
similar to the following letters, one in French and one in English. To address the letter,
just put the name of the château, its commune, and zip code. The major châteaux zip
codes are as follows:

for châteaux in St.-Estèphe	—33250 St.-Estèphe, France
for châteaux in Pauillac	—33250 Pauillac, France
for châteaux in St.-Julien	—St.-Julien-Beychevelle
	—33250 Pauillac, France
for châteaux in Margaux	—33460 Margaux, France
for châteaux in Graves (Pessac)	—33602 Pessac, France
for châteaux in Graves (Léognan)	—33850 Léognan, France
for châteaux in Sauternes	—33210 Langon, France
for châteaux in Barsac	—Barsac 33720 Podensac, France

for châteaux in St.-Emilion   —33330 St.-Emilion, France
for châteaux in Pomerol   —33500 Pomerol, France

These zip codes will cover a great majority of the châteaux, but some of the major properties are controlled by *négociants* or brokers, and it is better to write directly to the *négociant* to request an appointment at one of their châteaux. The following are the addresses for the top *négociants* that own some of the major Bordeaux châteaux.

RECOMMENDED FORM LETTER

(English version)

To: Château Margaux 33460 Margaux, France

Re: Visit

To Whom It May Concern:

I would like to visit Château Margaux on Monday, March 14, 2004, to see the winemaking facilities and receive a tour of the château. If possible, I would like to be able to taste several recent vintages of Château Margaux. If this is agreeable, I will arrive at the château at 9:30 A.M. on Monday, March 14.

I realize that you are busy, but I am an admirer of your wine and it would be a great pleasure to visit the property. I look forward to hearing from you.

Sincerely,

(French version)

Cher Monsieur ou Chère Madame,

Je suis un très grand admirateur de vos vins et je serais très reconnaissant si vous me permettriez de visiter Château XYZ.

lundi	mai
mardi	juin
mercredi	juillet
jeudi	aout
vendredi	septembre
janvier	octobre
fevrier	novembre
mars	décembre
avril	

Si possible, je voudrais bien aussi faire une dégustation des derniers 2 millésimes de votre vin.

Merci en avance, en attendant votre réponse et avec mes meilleurs sentiments.

Sincerement,

8: A GLOSSARY OF WINE TERMS

acetic—Wines, no matter how well made, contain quantities of acetic acid. If there is an excessive amount of acetic acid, the wine will have a vinegary smell.

acidic—Wines need natural acidity to taste fresh and lively, but an excess of acidity results in an acidic wine that is tart and sour.

acidity—The acidity level in a wine is critical to its enjoyment and livelihood. The natural acids that appear in wine are citric, tartaric, malic, and lactic. Wines from hot years tend to be lower in acidity, whereas wines from cool, rainy years tend to be high in acidity. Acidity in a wine preserves the wine's freshness and keeps the wine lively.

aftertaste—As the term suggests, the taste left in the mouth after one swallows is the aftertaste. This word is a synonym for length or finish. The longer the aftertaste lingers in the mouth (assuming it is a pleasant taste), the finer the quality of the wine.

aggressive—"Aggressive" is usually applied to wines that are either high in acidity or have harsh tannins, or both.

angular—Angular wines are wines that lack roundness, generosity, and depth. Wines from poor vintages or wines that are too acidic are often described as being angular.

aroma—"Aroma" is the smell of a young wine before it has had sufficient time to develop nuances of smell that are then called its bouquet. The word "aroma" is commonly used to mean the smell of a relatively young, unevolved wine.

astringent—Wines that are astringent are not necessarily bad or good wines. Astringent wines are harsh and coarse to taste, either because they are too young and tannic and just need time to develop or because they are not well made. The level of tannin in a wine contributes to its degree of astringence.

austere—Wines that are austere are generally not terribly pleasant wines to drink. An austere wine is a hard, rather dry wine that lacks richness and generosity. However, young, promising Bordeaux can often express itself as austere, and aging of such wine will reveal more generosity than its youthful austerity suggested.

balance—One of the most desired traits in a wine is good balance, where the concentration of fruit, level of tannin, and acidity are in total harmony. Well-balanced wines are symmetrical and tend to age gracefully.

barnyard—An unclean, farmyard, fecal aroma that is imparted to a wine because of unclean barrels or generally unsanitary winemaking facilities.

berrylike—As this descriptive term implies, wines, particularly Bordeaux wines that are young and not overly oaked, have an intense berry fruit character that can suggest blackberries, raspberries, black cherries, mulberries, or even strawberries and cranberries.

big—A big wine is a large-framed, full-bodied wine with an intense and concentrated feel on the palate. Bordeaux wines in general are not big wines in the same sense that Rhône wines are, but the top vintages of Bordeaux produce very rich, concentrated, deep wines.

black currant—A pronounced smell of the black currant fruit is commonly associated with red Bordeaux wines. It can vary in intensity from faint to very deep and rich.

body—"Body" is the weight and fullness of a wine that can be sensed as it crosses the palate. Full-bodied wines tend to have a lot of alcohol, concentration, and glycerine.

Botrytis cinerea—The fungus that attacks the grape skins under specific climatic conditions (usually interchanging periods of moisture and sunny weather). It causes the grape to become super-concentrated because it causes a natural dehydration. *Botrytis cinerea* is essential for the great sweet white wines of Barsac and Sauternes.

bouquet—As a wine's aroma becomes more developed from bottle aging, the aroma is transformed into a bouquet, which is hopefully more than just the smell of the grape.

brawny—A hefty, muscular, full-bodied wine with plenty of weight and flavor, although not always the most elegant or refined sort of wine.

briary—I usually think of California Zinfandel rather than Bordeaux when the term "briary" comes into play. Briary denotes that the wine is aggressive and rather spicy.

brilliant—"Brilliant" relates to the color of the wine. A brilliant wine is one that is clear, with no haze or cloudiness.

browning—As red wines age, their color changes from ruby/purple to dark ruby, to medium ruby, to ruby with an amber edge, to ruby with a brown edge. When a wine is browning it is usually fully mature and is not likely to get better.

cedar—Bordeaux reds often have a bouquet that suggests either faintly or overtly the smell of cedarwood. It is a complex aspect of the bouquet.

chewy—If a wine has a rather dense, viscous texture from a high glycerine content it is often referred to as being chewy. High extract wines from great vintages can often be chewy.

closed—The term "closed" is used to denote that the wine is not showing its potential, which remains locked in because it is too young. Young Bordeaux often close up about 12–18 months after bottling and, depending on the vintage and storage conditions, remain in such a state for anywhere from several years to more than a decade.

complex—One of the most subjective descriptive terms used, a "complex" wine is a wine that the taster never gets bored with and finds interesting to drink. Complex wines tend to have a variety of subtle scents and flavors that hold one's interest in the wine.

concentrated—Fine wines, whether they are light-, medium-, or full-bodied, should have concentrated flavors. "Concentrated" denotes that the wine has a depth and richness of fruit that gives it appeal and interest. Deep is a synonym of concentrated.

corked—A corked wine is a flawed wine that has taken on the smell of cork as a result of an unclean or faulty cork. It is perceptible in a bouquet that shows no fruit, only the smell of a musty cork or damp cardboard.

decadent—If you are an ice-cream and chocolate lover, you know the feeling of eating a huge sundae lavished with hot fudge, real whipped cream, and rich vanilla ice cream. If you are a wine enthusiast, a wine loaded with opulent, even unctuous layers of fruit, with a huge bouquet and a plump, luxurious texture can be said to be decadent.

deep—Essentially the same as concentrated, the word "deep" expresses the fact that the wine is rich, full of extract, and mouth-filling.

delicate—As this word implies, delicate wines are light, subtle, understated wines that are prized for their shyness rather than extroverted robust characters. White wines are usually more delicate than red wines.

diffuse—Wines that smell and taste unstructured and unfocused are said to be diffuse. Often when red wines are served at too warm a temperature, they become diffuse.

dumb—A dumb wine is also a closed wine, but the term "dumb" is used in a more pejorative sense. Closed wines may only need time to reveal their richness and intensity. Dumb wines may never become any better.

earthy—This term may be used in both a negative and a positive sense, however, I prefer to use "earthy" to denote a positive aroma of fresh, rich, clean soil. Earthy is a more intense smell than woodsy or truffle scents.

elegant—Although more white wines than red are described as being elegant, lighter-styled, graceful, well-balanced Bordeaux wines can be elegant.

exuberant—Like extroverted, somewhat hyper people, wines too can be gushing with fruit and seem nervous and intensely vigorous.

fat—When Bordeaux gets a very hot year for its crop and the wines attain a super sort of maturity, they are often quite rich and concentrated with low to average acidity. Often such wines are said to be fat, which is a prized commodity. If they become too fat, though, that is a flaw and they are then called flabby.

flabby—A wine that is too fat or obese is a flabby wine. Flabby wines lack structure and are heavy to taste.

fleshy—"Fleshy" is a synonym for chewy, meaty, or beefy. It denotes that the wine has a lot of body, alcohol, and extract, and usually a high glycerine content. Pomerols and St.-Emilions tend to be fleshier wines than Médocs.

floral—With the exception of some Sauternes, I rarely think of Bordeaux wines as having a floral or flowery aspect to their bouquets or aromas. However, wines like Riesling or Muscat do have a flowery component.

focused—Both a fine wine's bouquet and flavor should be focused. "Focused" simply means that the scents, aromas, and flavors are precise and clearly delineated. If they are not, the wine is like an out-of-focus picture: diffuse, hazy, and problematic.

forward—A wine is said to be forward when its charm and character are fully revealed. While it may not be fully mature yet, a forward wine is generally quite enjoyable and drinkable. "Forward" is the opposite of "backward."

fresh—Freshness in both young and old wines is a welcome and pleasing component. A wine is said to be fresh when it is lively and cleanly made. The opposite of fresh is stale.

fruity—A very good wine should have enough concentration of fruit so that it can be said to be fruity. Fortunately, the best Bordeaux wines will have more than just a fruity personality.

full-bodied—Wines rich in extract, alcohol, and glycerine are full-bodied wines.

green—Green wines are wines made from underripe grapes, and they lack richness and generosity as well as having a vegetal character. Green wines were often made in Bordeaux in poor vintages such as 1977 and 1972.

hard—Wines with abrasive, astringent tannins or high acidity are said to be hard. Young vintages of Bordeaux can be hard, but they should never be harsh.

harsh—If a wine is too hard it is said to be harsh. Harshness in a wine, young or old, is a flaw.

hedonistic—Certain styles of wine are meant to be inspected, and they are more introspective and intellectual wines. Others are designed to provide sheer delight, joy, and euphoria. Hedonistic wines can be criticized because in one sense they provide so much ecstasy they can be called obvious, but in essence, they are totally gratifying wines meant to fascinate and enthrall—pleasure at its best.

herbaceous—Many wines have a distinctive herbal smell that is generally said to be herbaceous. Specific herbal smells can be of thyme, lavender, rosemary, oregano, fennel, or basil.

hollow—A synonym for "shallow"; hollow wines are diluted and lack depth and concentration.

honeyed—A common personality trait of sweet Barsacs and Sauternes, a honeyed wine is one that has the smell and taste of bee honey.

hot—Rather than mean that the temperature of the wine is too warm to drink, "hot" denotes that the wine is too high in alcohol and therefore leaves a burning sensation in the back of the throat when swallowed. Wines with alcohol levels in excess of 14.5% are often hot.

jammy—When Bordeaux wines have a great intensity of fruit from excellent ripeness they can be jammy, which is a very concentrated, flavorful wine with superb extract. In great vintages such as 1982 and 1961, some of the wines are so concentrated that they are said to be jammy.

leafy—A leafy character in a wine is similar to a herbaceous character only in that it refers to the smell of leaves rather than herbs. A wine that is too leafy is a vegetal or green wine.

lean—Lean wines are slim, rather streamlined wines that lack generosity and fatness but can still be enjoyable and pleasant.

lively—A synonym for "fresh" or "exuberant," a "lively" wine is usually a young wine with good acidity and a thirst-quenching personality.

long—A very desirable trait in a fine Bordeaux is that it should be long in the mouth. Long (or length) relates to a wine's finish, meaning that after you swallow the wine, you sense its presence for a long time. (Thirty seconds to several minutes is great length.)

lush—Lush wines are velvety, soft, richly fruity wines that are both concentrated and fat. A lush wine can never be an astringent or hard wine.

massive—In great vintages where there is a high degree of ripeness and superb concentration, some wines can turn out to be so big, full-bodied, and rich that they are called massive. Great wines, such as the 1961 Latour and Pétrus and the 1982 Pétrus, are textbook examples of massive wines.

meaty—A chewy, fleshy wine is also said to be meaty.

mouth-filling—Big, rich, concentrated wines that are filled with fruit extract and are high in alcohol and glycerine are wines that tend to texturally fill the mouth. A mouth-filling wine is also a chewy, fleshy, fat wine.

nose—The general smell and aroma of a wine as sensed through one's nose and olfactory senses is often called the wine's nose.

oaky—Most top Bordeaux wines are aged from 12–30 months in small oak barrels. At the very best properties, a percentage of the oak barrels are new, and these barrels impart a toasty, vanilla flavor and smell to the wine. If the wine is not rich and concentrated, the barrels can overwhelm the wine, making it taste overly oaky. However, when the wine is rich and concentrated and the wine-maker has made a judicious use of new oak barrels, the results are a wonderful marriage of fruit and oak.

off—If a wine is not showing its true character or is flawed or spoiled in some way, it is said to be off.

overripe—An undesirable characteristic; grapes left too long on the vine become too ripe, lose their acidity, and produce wines that are heavy and imbalanced. This happens much more frequently in hot viticultural areas than in Bordeaux.

oxidized—If a wine has been excessively exposed to air during either its making or aging, the wine loses freshness and takes on a stale, old smell and taste. Such a wine is said to be oxidized.

peppery—A peppery quality to a wine is usually noticeable in many Rhône wines, which have an aroma of black pepper and a pungent flavor. It occasionally appears in some Bordeaux wines.

perfumed—This term is usually more applicable to fragrant, aromatic white wines than to red Bordeaux wines. However, some of the dry white wines and sweet white wines can have a strong, perfumed smell.

plummy—Rich, concentrated wines can often have the smell and taste of ripe plums. When they do, the term "plummy" is applicable.

ponderous—"Ponderous" is often used as a synonym for "massive," but in my usage a massive wine is simply a big, rich, very concentrated wine with balance, whereas a ponderous wine is a wine that has become heavy and tiring to drink.

precocious—Wines that mature quickly—as well as those wines that may last and evolve gracefully over a long period of time, but taste as if they are aging quickly because of their tastiness and soft, early charms—are said to be precocious.

pruney—Wines produced from grapes that are overripe take on the character of prunes. Pruney wines are flawed wines.

raisiny—Late-harvest wines that are meant to be drunk at the end of a meal can often be slightly raisiny, which in some Ports and sherries is desirable. However, in dry Bordeaux wines a raisiny quality is a major flaw.

rich—Wines high in extract, flavor, and intensity of fruit are described as being rich.

ripe—A wine is ripe when its grapes have reached the optimum level of maturity. Less than fully mature grapes produce wines that are underripe, and overly mature grapes produce wines that are overripe.

round—A very desirable character of wines, roundness occurs in fully mature Bordeaux that have lost their youthful, astringent tannins and also in young Bordeaux that are low in tannin and acidity and are meant to be consumed young.

savory—A general descriptive term denoting that the wine is round, flavorful, and interesting to drink.

shallow—A weak, feeble, watery, or diluted wine lacking concentration is said to be shallow.

sharp—An undesirable trait; sharp wines are bitter and unpleasant with hard, pointed edges.

silky—A synonym for "velvety" or "lush"; silky wines are soft, sometimes fat, but never hard or angular.

smoky—Some wines, either because of the soil or because of the barrels used to age the wine, have a distinctive smoky character. In Bordeaux, some of the Graves wines are occasionally smoky.

soft—A soft wine is one that is round and fruity, low in acidity, and has an absence of aggressive, hard tannins.

spicy—Wines often smell quite spicy with aromas of pepper, cinnamon, and other well-known spices. These pungent aromas are usually lumped together and called spicy. Scents and flavors of Oriental spices refer to wines that have aromas and/or flavors of soy sauce, ginger, hoisin sauce, and sesame oil.

stale—Dull, heavy wines that are oxidized or lack balancing acidity for freshness are called stale.

stalky—A synonym for "vegetal," but used more frequently to denote that the wine has probably had too much contact with the stems. The result is a green, vegetal, or stalky character to the wine.

supple—A supple wine is one that is soft, lush, velvety, and very attractively round and tasty. It is a highly desirable characteristic as it suggests that the wine is harmonious.

tannic—The tannins of a wine, which are extracted from the grape skins and stems, are, along with a wine's acidity and alcohol, its lifeline. Tannins give a wine firmness and some roughness when young, but gradually fall away and dissipate. A tannic wine is one that is young and unready to drink.

tart—Sharp, acidic, lean, unripe wines are called tart. In general, a red Bordeaux that is tart is not pleasurable.

thick—Rich, ripe, concentrated wines that are low in acidity are often said to be thick.

thin—A synonym for "shallow," a thin wine is an undesirable characteristic meaning that the wine is watery, lacking in body, and just diluted.

tightly knit—Young wines that have good acidity levels, good tannin levels, and are well made are called tightly knit, meaning they have yet to open up and develop.

toasty—A smell of grilled toast can often be found in wines because the barrels the wines are aged in are charred or toasted on the inside.

tobacco—Many red Graves wines have the scent of fresh burning tobacco. It is a distinctive and wonderful smell in wine.

unctuous—Rich, lush, intense wines with layers of concentrated, soft, velvety fruit are said to be unctuous. In particular, the sweet wines of Barsac and Sauternes are unctuous.

vegetal—An undesirable characteristic; wines that smell and taste vegetal are usually made from unripe grapes. In some wines a subtle vegetable garden smell is pleasant and adds complexity, but if it is the predominant characteristic, it is a major flaw.

velvety—A textural description and synonym for "lush" or "silky," a velvety wine is a rich, soft, smooth wine to taste. It is a very desirable characteristic.

viscous—Viscous wines tend to be relatively concentrated, fat, almost thick wines with a great density of fruit extract, plenty of glycerine, and high alcohol content. If they have balancing acidity, they can be tremendously flavorful and exciting wines. If they lack acidity, they are often flabby and heavy.

volatile—A volatile wine is one that smells of vinegar as a result of an excessive amount of present acetic bacteria. It is a seriously flawed wine.

woody—When a wine is overly oaky it is often said to be woody. Oakiness in a wine's bouquet and taste is good up to a point. Once past that point the wine is woody and its fruity qualities are masked by excessive oak aging.

INDEX

Page references in **boldface** refer to producer profiles.

GRAND VIN DE BORDEAUX

MIS EN BOUTEILLES AU CHATEAU

CHATEAU
LA BÉCASSE
PAUILLAC
APPELLATION PAUILLAC CONTROLÉE

1993

Roland FONTENEAU
VITICULTEUR
33250 PAUILLAC FRANCE

12.5%vol. 750ml
PRODUCE OF FRANCE

CHATEAU MOULINET
Pomerol
APPELLATION POMEROL CONTROLÉE
1994
12.5% vol. 75 cl
S.C.A. DU DOMAINE DE MOULINET, PROPRIÉTAIRE A POMEROL - GIRONDE - FRANCE

Réserve de la Propriété, bouteille N° 001807

Château Suau
1er CRU UN CLASSÉ EN 1855
BARSAC
APPELLATION BARSAC CONTROLÉE
1995
14% vol. 75 cl
MIS EN BOUTEILLES
AU CHATEAU
Roger BIARNÈS
PROPRIÉTAIRE A BARSAC (GIRONDE)
PRODUIT DE FRANCE

Château FILHOT
à SAUTERNES
APPELLATION SAUTERNES CONTROLÉE

M. de FILHOT, Conseiller au Parlement 1642-1728

MIS EN BOUTEILLE AU CHATEAU

S.C.E.A. GR. CHEVRY - 33210 SAUTERNES

CLOS RENÉ
POMEROL

APPELLATION POMEROL CONTROLÉE

1996

PIERRE LASSERRE
PROPRIÉTAIRE
à POMEROL (Gironde) - France

1994
CHATEAU GAZIN
POMEROL
APPELLATION POMEROL CONTROLÉE
Mis en bouteilles
au Château

S.C.E.A. CHATEAU GAZIN 33500 POMEROL
75 cl FRANCE

CHATEAU FEYTIT-CLINET
POMEROL
1996
Alc 13% vol 75 cl
MIS EN BOUTEILLES A LA PROPRIÉTÉ

Récolte 1996

CHATEAU BEAUCHENE
CHARLES LESPARRE & FILS

POMEROL
APPELLATION POMEROL CONTROLÉE
MIS EN BOUTEILLE AU CHATEAU

1997   1997

ÉLEVÉ EN FUTS DE CHÊNE

Domaine
du
Rempart
POMEROL
APPELLATION POMEROL CONTROLÉE

J.M. ESTAGER
PROPRIÉTAIRE A POMEROL - GIRONDE
PRODUIT DE FRANCE

63cl   75cl

MIS EN BOUTEILLE AU DOMAINE

MIS EN BOUTEILLE AU CHATEAU

GRAND CRU CLASSÉ en 1855
COS D'ESTOURNEL
SAINT-ESTÈPHE
APPELLATION SAINT-ESTÈPHE CONTROLÉE
1994
DOMAINES PRATS S.A. SAINT-ESTÈPHE FRANCE

PRODUCE OF FRANCE

CHATEAU PICHON LONGUEVILLE
COMTESSE DE LALANDE
1986
GRAND CRU CLASSÉ
PAUILLAC
12.5% vol. 75 cl
APPELLATION PAUILLAC CONTROLÉE

CHATEAU PICHON LONGUEVILLE COMTESSE DE LALANDE
SOCIÉTÉ CIVILE - PAUILLAC - GIRONDE

1996

CHATEAU
PEDESCLAUX
GRAND CRU CLASSÉ
PAUILLAC
APPELLATION PAUILLAC CONTROLÉE

12.5% vol.   1500 ml

Château Ratouin
1995
POMEROL
Appellation Pomerol Contrôlée

MIS EN BOUTEILLE AU CHATEAU

12.5% vol.   75cl

CHATEAU RAYMOND-LAFON
Appellation Sauternes Contrôlée
1994
Alc 13% vol.   FAMILLE MESLIER   750 ml
PROPRIÉTAIRE-SAUTERNES-FRANCE
MIS EN BOUTEILLE AU CHATEAU
SAUTERNES

CRU BOURGEOIS

Château
MAURAS
SAUTERNES
APPELLATION SAUTERNES CONTROLÉE
1996
SOCIÉTÉ VITICOLE DU TERRICE
EXPLOITANT A PREIGNAC (GIRONDE) FRANCE
MIS EN BOUTEILLE AU CHATEAU

Château La Pointe
1996

Pomerol
APPELLATION POMEROL CONTROLÉE
Mis en bouteille au Château
S.C. CHATEAU LA POINTE   FRANCE   d'ARFEUILLE
PROPRIÉTAIRES-VIGNERONS

12.5% vol.   75cl

Château Beauregard
POMEROL
APPELLATION POMEROL CONTROLÉE
1995
S.C.E.A. CHATEAU BEAUREGARD EXPLOITANT A POMEROL GIRONDE FRANCE
12% vol.   750ml
PRODUIT DE FRANCE

GRAND CRU CLASSÉ en 1855

CHATEAU
Haut-Batailley
PAUILLAC
1990
APPELLATION PAUILLAC CONTROLÉE
PRODUCE OF FRANCE
25% vol.   FRANÇOIS BORIE, PROPRIÉTAIRE A PAUILLAC - GIRONDE - FRANCE   750ml
MIS EN BOUTEILLE AU CHATEAU

CHATEAU BEYCHEVELLE
Grand vin 1988
SAINT-JULIEN
12.5%Vol   750ml
APPELLATION SAINT-JULIEN CONTROLÉE
SOCIÉTÉ CIVILE CHATEAU BEYCHEVELLE PROPRIÉTAIRE
A SAINT-JULIEN-BEYCHEVELLE (GIRONDE FRANCE)

CRU BOURGEOIS

CHATEAU
La Commanderie
SAINT-ESTÈPHE
APPELLATION SAINT-ESTÈPHE CONTROLÉE
1994
12.5% vol.   75cl
MIS EN BOUTEILLE AU CHATEAU

CHATEAU VIEUX MAILLET
POMEROL
APPELLATION POMEROL CONTROLÉE
1996
12.5% vol.   750 ml
MIS EN BOUTEILLE AU CHATEAU

GRAND VIN
CHATEAU
LYNCH★BAGES
GRAND CRU CLASSÉ
PAUILLAC
APPELLATION PAUILLAC CONTROLÉE
1990   12.5% VOL

GRAND VIN
CHATEAU BELLEGRAVE
1997
CRU BOURGEOIS
PAUILLAC
APPELLATION PAUILLAC CONTROLÉE
SC CHATEAU BELLEGRAVE
MIS EN BOUTEILLE AU CHATEAU   75 cl

1995
Château
Roûmieu-Lacoste
Haut-Barsac Sauternes

Henri Dubourdieu
Propriétaire Vigneron

COURRÈGES SÉGUES
GRAVES
APPELLATION GRAVES CONTROLÉE
MIS EN
BOUTEILLE
AU CHATEAU

1986

CHATEAU
GRAND-PONTET
SAINT-ÉMILION
GRAND CRU CLASSÉ
APPELLATION SAINT-ÉMILION GRAND CRU CLASSÉ CONTROLÉE
12.5% vol.   CHATEAU GRAND PONTET S.A.   750 ml
MIS EN BOUTEILLE AU CHATEAU